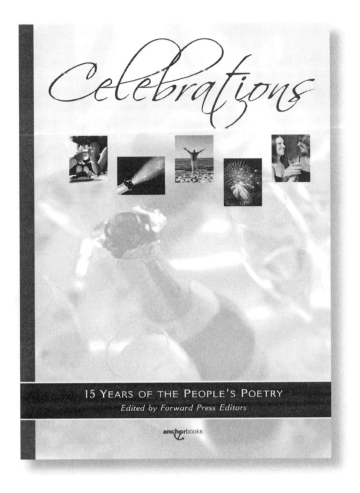

From humble beginnings with rich ideology
'Poetry by the people' the beacon of light
Aspiring to break down the doors of authority
On what the art should be, the 'wrong' and the 'right'

Flooded with creations, a sweeping away
Exposing us to the realms of thought
Weaving a beautiful, unrivalled, tapestry
With your visions, inspiring, timelessly caught.

Not all such plain sailing, some struggles we've faced
But bad times soon melt back to great
Defiantly onward, determined we head
Fighting fierce battles with fate

We arrive at this crystal year of *Celebrations*
An achievement we cannot deny
And our loyal patrons writing verse
Keep us reaching for the sky.

Forward Press Editors

First published in Great Britain in 2006 by
Anchor Books
Remus House
Coltsfoot Drive
Peterborough
PE2 9JX
Telephone: 01733 898102
www.forwardpress.co.uk

HB ISBN 1 84602 025 5

Celebrations – 15 Years Of The People's Poetry

It's been fifteen years since we at Forward Press threw open the very private doors of the publishing world, and like a breath of fresh air swept away the prejudices that were prevalent at the time. Embarking on a tireless crusade, whilst employing every last piece of expertise at our disposal; we have achieved what we had ultimately set out to accomplish, that was to bring poetry to the people - culminating with an invitation that would enable Joe Public to taste, for the first time, the unsurpassed pleasure to be gained from visualising creative formulations of their own in print for everyone to witness.

What could have been more fitting to celebrate this momentous anniversary; than to request the contributors, that made Anchor Books our most popular imprint, to submit poetry for inclusion in a unique and prestigious anthology, showcasing their poetic talent to its fullest potential?

So with that aspiration uppermost in our minds we did just that, and the unprecedented response that we received to our appeal, for examples of their favourite and finest poetry, quite literally bowled us over. Deluging us in work of the highest quality our poets outshone themselves in an admirable fashion.

As you can probably imagine the selection for the Celebrations anthology proved to be both a rewarding and arduous experience. Arduous due to the vast quality of entries involved (which needed to be narrowed down quite considerably), and rewarding because of the superior standard of poetry proffered.

That done and once the poetic content for this prestigious compilation was determined, the phenomenal task of hand picking the prize winner had to be addressed. Not an easy undertaking, I can assure you! However, after a lot of meticulous deliberation whilst drawing on years of professional judgement a first prize winner was finally decided upon by our expert team.

With regards to the identity of our winning poet, how could it be anyone other than Glenwyn Peter Evans? His ingenious manipulation of imagery, and the proficient way, in which he personifies the passage of time, blend perfectly to paint a spectacularly whimsical portrait of a life that has been lived to its uttermost extremity. A celebratory vision to be sure!

Crammed full of poetic versification that embrace a wide spectrum of topics and viewpoints penned by an equally sizeable cross-section of poets from all walks of life. A literary delight composed by our dedicated team of editors, and the piece de resistance, an imaginative contribution from the Forward Press founder Mr Ian Walton, a respected and published poet in his own right. Celebrations – 15 Years Of The People's Poetry, a beautifully crafted and intricately designed anthology, is bound to be cherished by all who read it and treasured for generations to come.

Heather Killingray & Sarah Marshall, Editors

PARLOUR GAMES

There is a look it's better to ignore:
a whisper in the eye, a sideward glance
designed to steal the heart and gently draw
those half breathed sighs that make the maybes dance.

There is a touch it's safer to deny:
an accidental brush against the skin,
an artful stroke that makes you wonder why
it leaves the smell of stranger, lingering.

There is a voice it's wiser not to hear:
a siren's breath that carries from the sea
the words unspoke, unsaid, that you most fear,
the cryptic code of lovers yet to be.

But if you should resist, you know the cost:
a lifetime's longing for a moment lost.

Ian Walton
Founder, Forward Press Ltd

Ian Walton was born in Leicester in 1951. He has travelled extensively and lived in many parts of Britain, from Devon to the Highlands of Scotland. His poetry has appeared in many magazines and has been broadcast by numerous radio stations. He currently works as a director for Forward Press Ltd.

A - Z of Poets

Name	No.	Name	No.	Name	No.	Name	No.
Bee Kenchington	500	Brenda Straw	503	Catherine Gregory	393	Clare Marie Zeidrah Keirrissia Marshall	575
Ben Henderson Smith	73	Brenda W Hughes	340	Catherine Haley	122	Clare M Ashton	645
Ben Lewis	500	Brian Bateman	305	Catherine Keepin	535	Clarence Gascoigne	626
Ber George Barter	361	Brian Beard	481	Catherine M Simpson	367	Cliff Holt	224
Bernadette O'Donoghue	585	Brian Christopher Wilkinson	207	Catherine Randle	486	Cliff Seaman	84
Bernard Brown	581	Brian Croft	220	Catherine Reay	603	Clive Cornwall	304
Bernie Morris	430	Brian Denton	117	Cathie Booth	270	Clive Goldsmith	195
Beryl Davidson	532	Brian Edwards	327	Cathy Mearman	231	Clive Robson	195
Beryl Elizabeth Moore	45	Brian Fisher	434	Catriona Thomson	564	Clive W Macdonald	620
Beryl Hall	152	Brian Ford	133	Caz Carty	656	C Matthews	31
Beryl Heathcote	203	Brian Henderson	210	C Boneham	222	C M Porter	506
Beryl Louise Penny	296	Brian Joseph Wood	426	C Bulley	611	C O Burnell	320
Beryl Manning	419	Brian M Wood	28	C Cannon	572	Colette McCormick	35
Beryl Mapperley	267	Brian Nolan	569	Cecilia Hill	295	Colette Thomson	169
Beryl M Malkin	191	Brian Norman	328	Cecilia Jane Skudder	453	Colin Farmer	554
Beryl O'Brien	136	Brian Porter	225	Cecil Lewis	145	Colin Farquhar	532
Beryl R Daintree	423	Brian R Russ	467	Celia Auld	325	Colin Horn	449
Beryl Sigournay	481	Brian Strand	21	Celia Saywell	102	Colin Metcalfe	573
Beryl Upshall	195	Brian Taylor	576	C Gaunt	626	Colin Ritton	94
Beryl Williams	265	Brian Travis	462	C Goldsmith	160	Colin Rouse	597
Bessie Martin	628	Brian Wells	545	C Growcott	246	Colin Winfield	364
Bessie Metcalfe	546	Bridie Sutton	96	Charles Boyett	549	Colleen Biggins	147
Beth Izatt Anderson	304	Bridie Taber Beeson	592	Charles Hardman	120	Colum Donnelly	52
Beth Stewart	37	Brigid Nicholson	288	Charles Peachey	355	Connie Garrard	211
Betty Brown	242	Brigitta D'Arcy-Hays	279	Charles Trail	194	Connie Lunn	402
Betty Farajallah	540	Bronwen Vizard	399	Charlie McInally	251	Constance Dewdney	163
Betty Gordon	512	Bruce Ripley	105	Charlotte A Penney	638	Constance Roper	258
Betty Greig	452	Bryce Forbes	481	Charlotte Meredith	209	Cora-E Barras	562
Betty Irwin-Burton	98	Bryn Bartlett	70	Charlotte Penfold (19)	139	Cora Woolcock	435
Betty Kirkham	617	Bryony Freeman	70	Cherry Hullock	130	Corinda Daw	51
Betty McIlroy	30	B Smedley	525	Cherry Thacker	456	Corin Jasmine Dienes	36
Betty M Dunne	379	B Smith	188	Chris Creedon	155	Corinne Kelly (8)	387
Betty Morton	256	B Spanswick	539	Chris Jackson	633	Corinne Lovell	428
Betty Nevell	156	B Strickson	212	Chris Silvester	270	Craig Stewart	351
Betty R Lloyd	487	B Thomas	145	Christa Todd	200	C R Slater	432
Beverley J Waldie	613	B W Ballard	83	Christian Ward	45	C S Hindshaw	30
Beverly Maiden	330	B Williams	23	Christina Harkness	124	C V Perkins	105
B Harrison	631	C A Keohane	261	Christina R Maggs	192	Cyn Jordan	336
B Haworth	242	Candida Lovell-Smith	570	Christine A Lee	308	Cynthia Scott	324
B Holland	396	Captain Valentine Daly	53	Christine A Walker	555	Cynthia Shum	80
Biddy Redgrove	81	Carl Fricker	329	Christine Clark	151	Cynthia Taylor	459
Bill Austin	77	Carl Nixon	138	Christine Collins	125	Daisie Cecil-Clarke	565
Bill Brittain	106	Carly Bareham	268	Christine Conway	623	Dale McFadden	101
Bill Burkitt	410	C Armstrong	543	Christine Cook	292	Dale Mullock	214
Bill Campbell	144	Carol A Alvis	148	Christine Corby	46	Damian Allen	451
Bill Chapman	603	Carol Ann Darling	237	Christine Frederick	393	Damien Plummer	221
Bill Dovey	369	Carol Anne Edwards	527	Christine Hardemon	122	D Andrews	518
Bill Jamieson	507	Carol Biddle	383	Christine Kitchen	153	Daniela M Davey	437
Bill Waugh	525	Carol Coney	124	Christine Lannen	613	Daniel P Callaghan	24
B J Davis	405	Carole Andrews	515	Christine Lemon	438	Dan Pugh	188
B Kerby	572	Carole Morris	74	Christine MacLeod	191	Daphne Foreman	93
Blanche Naughton	367	Carole Wale	154	Christine M Wilkinson	534	Daphne Fryer	244
B L Barnes	271	Carol Hudson	288	Christine Pointer	209	Daphne Hanson	95
B Morris	509	Caroline Baker	436	Christine Rank	370	Daphne Harman Young	525
Bob Lowe	298	Caroline Byron-Johnson	306	Christine Rowley	138	Daphne McFadyen	307
Bob Marsh	158	Caroline Dean	260	Christine Skeer	76	Daphne Richards	311
Bob Reynolds	440	Caroline E Ashton	372	Christine Stallion	183	Daphne Wilkinson	618
B Ratcliffe	287	Caroline Halliday	175	Christine Tracey	348	Daphne Young	316
B R Boyt	480	Caroline Helen Molton	562	Christine Wells	415	Darren Babbage	92
Brenda Artingstall	35	Caroline Lake	307	Christopher Bean	250	Dave Austin	62
Brenda Barber	457	Carol Irving	418	Christopher J Symonds	416	Dave Davis	123
Brenda Brownhill	465	Carol Paterson	628	Christopher Payne	420	Dave Smith	622
Brenda Casburn-Colvin	212	Carol Paxton	97	Christopher R Lawton	518	Dave White	472
Brenda Catherine Mentha	599	Carol Richardson	191	Christopher Rudd	290	David A Garside	71
Brenda Heath	231	Carol Subirats	490	Chris Webb	80	David Bilsborrow	457
Brenda Hill	119	Carol Turner	530	Chris Whooley	45	David Bridgewater	248
Brenda King	444	Carol Wilkins	597	Chrystal Collins	654	David Bromage	264
Brenda M Wylie	589	Carrie Ann Hammond	40	Cicely Heathers	475	David Chapman	103
Brenda Nicholson	173	Carrie Stuart	437	C J Hewish	400	David Daymond	220
Brenda Peel	132	Cassandra May Poultney	245	C Kelly	284	David Gasking	274
Brenda Pritchard	506	Cate Campbell	567	Claire-Lyse Sylvester	224	David Griffiths	346
Brenda Robinson	410	Catherine Atkinson	42	Claire Bartholomew	319	David G W Garde	462
Brenda Soderberg	487	Catherine Beagarie	543	Claire Woolmore	429	David Hall	425
Brenda Sohngen	572	Catherine Curtis	396	Clare L Pantling	314	David Horan	139

Name	No.	Name	No.	Name	No.	Name	No.
David Hulme	635	Diana Jones	596	Dorothy Jane Lewis	474	Eileen Barker	596
David J Hall	133	Diana Momber	477	Dorothy Margaret Smith	137	Eileen Carter	487
David Lees	181	Diana Morcom	530	Dorothy Marshall Bowen	99	Eileen Coates	361
David Light	281	Diana Richardson	75	Dorothy Mary Allchin	207	Eileen Combellack	75
David Lightfoot	513	Diane Alicia Spence-Crawford	580	Dorothy McGregor	62	Eileen Finlinson	61
David Lucas	235	Diane Burrow	321	Dorothy M Gillway	607	Eileen Hannah	476
David Martin	459	Diane Elizabeth Maltby	354	Dorothy M Kemp	503	Eileen Hope Hesselden	322
David Merrifield	644	Diane Harbottle	29	Dorothy M Mitchell	54	Eileen Kyte	186
David Morgan	377	Diane Haworth	382	Dorothy Moore	426	Eileen Martin	423
David O'Neill	75	Diane Howard	32	Dorothy M Parker	320	Eileen Mary Chamberlain	495
David Pike	213	Diane King	280	Dorothy Neil	573	Eileen M Child	422
David Radford	449	Diane Pointer	439	Dorothy Rowe	169	Eileen M Lodge	330
David Sewell Hawkins	21	Diane R Duff	413	Dorothy Steadman	94	Eileen M Wray	478
David Sheasby	61	Dick Porter	393	Dorothy Stirland	355	Eileen Shenton	613
David Shepherd	299	Dino	178	Dorothy Walker	608	Eileen Tracy	343
David Spanton	573	D J Dixe	307	Dorothy Wilbraham	543	Eileen W O'Brien	644
David Speed	113	D Kirk	404	Dorothy Woo	471	Eily Tatlow	443
David T Wicking	391	D Mason	312	Dory Phillips	510	Eirlys Howden	587
David Varley	225	D Morgan	42	Dot Ridings	158	Eithne McCrossan	157
David Wallace	398	D M Carne	320	Douglas Bishop	219	E J Clark	263
David Watkins	48	D M Pentlow	197	Douglas Bryan Kennett	217	E J Macdonald	608
David Wilson	190	Dolly Harmer	222	Douglas J Cleeves	596	E Joan Knight	286
David W Lankshear	438	Dominica Kelly	333	Dragana Mundzic	107	E Knapp	535
Davina Headland	427	Donald John Tye	45	D S Cromar	94	Elaine Beresford	123
Dawn Croft	408	Don Harris	508	D Seiglow	125	Elaine Day	443
Dawn Drickman	563	Don Hunt	159	D Squires	141	Elaine Donaldson	310
Dawn James	462	Don Okoko	608	D Townshend	300	Elaine Hunt	609
Dawn Madigan	477	Donoveen R Alcock	356	D Treadwell	609	Elaine McCulloch Smith	587
Dawn McClarren	316	Dora Beale	562	Duchess Newman	61	Elaine Priscilla Kilshaw	74
Dawn Rickatson	560	Dora Quinn	539	Dulcie Levene	429	Elaine Rowlands	534
Dayna Sherwin	464	Doreen Allenby	427	Dulcie Sharland	418	E L Blackburn	452
D Bainbridge	148	Doreen Brooks	451	Duncan Campbell	632	Eleanor Lloyd	68
D B Bowes	87	Doreen Cawley	113	Duncan MacFarlane	46	Elena Uteva	106
Deanna Dixon	269	Doreen Day	255	Duncan Robson	391	E L Hannam	629
Debbie Harris	178	Doreen E Hampshire	269	D Webster	587	Elinor Wilson	235
Debbie Hatchett	543	Doreen Fay	443	D W Fincham	327	Elise Henden	306
Debbie Nobbs	169	Doreen Fillary	445	Dylis M Letchford	48	Elizabeth Amy Johns	106
Deborah Hall	336	Doreen Hedison	478	E B	437	Elizabeth Ann Crompton	635
Declan Mullan	266	Doreen Jackson	550	E Bellis	561	Elizabeth Anne Gifford	603
Deena Howard	411	Doreen Kowalska	121	E B Evans	621	Elizabeth Ann Jameson	584
Deirdre Armes Smith	632	Doreen Lawrence	500	E Bevans	313	Elizabeth Atkinson	637
Deirdre Hill	407	Doreen McDonald Banks	146	E Blagrove	538	Elizabeth Banks (17)	162
Deirdre White	565	Doreen McGee-Osborne	453	E Bollington	253	Elizabeth Bennett	95
Denise Castellani	37	Doreen M Neu	260	E Brooks	134	Elizabeth Clarke	633
Denise Harmin	548	Doreen P Damsell	64	E Chapman	113	Elizabeth Hackman	222
Denise Jones	559	Doreen Quince	462	E C Inkpen	374	Elizabeth Hawkins	370
Denise Jones	611	Doreen Ranson	83	E Clarke	245	Elizabeth Hiddleston	382
Denise M Blunt	420	Doreen Reeves	220	E Crowhurst	331	Elizabeth Hunter	497
Denise Stock	116	Doreen Roberts	555	E D Bowen	46	Elizabeth Jenks	445
Denise Winder	563	Doreen Sylvester	423	Eddie Jepson	648	Elizabeth Jones	482
Denis O'Doherty	442	Doreen Tallack	624	Eddie Owers	394	Elizabeth Joyce Walker	351
Dennis A Calow	602	Doreen Wildrianne	526	Eddie Sykes	506	Elizabeth Latter	420
Dennis Marshall	26	Doris Donnell	446	Eddie Turner	177	Elizabeth Love	488
Dennis Overton	241	Doris E Pullen	255	Edith May Hughes	627	Elizabeth Mary Dowler	364
Dennis Parkes	48	Doris Hoole	60	Edith Stell	196	Elizabeth Mary Turner	338
Dennis R Beton	89	Doris Mary Miller	245	Edmund Saint George Mooney	216	Elizabeth McIntyre	531
Dennis W Turner	638	Doris Selina Moss	629	Edna Cosby	255	Elizabeth McNeil	431
Dereck Palmer	268	Doris Sproston	285	Edna D'Lima	70	Elizabeth Morris	484
Derek Rawcliffe	631	Doris Warren	129	Edna Holford	479	Elizabeth Morton	126
Deryck Southgate	489	Dorothy	641	Edna Parrington	516	Elizabeth M Rait	599
Desiree L Pearl Silsby	509	Dorothy-Ann Cluley	412	Edna Sarsfield	181	Elizabeth M Tumilty	363
Desmond Tarrant	531	Dorothy Baines	366	Edward Brookes	55	Elizabeth Rapley	448
Deva	651	Dorothy Beaumont	476	Edward Fursdon	261	Elizabeth Samson	623
D George	298	Dorothy Blakeman	290	Edward Hill	214	Elizabeth Taylor	652
D G Field	338	Dorothy Brookes	405	Edward Jackson Smyth	352	Elizabeth Williams	153
D Gilson	166	Dorothy Buyers	296	Edward McCartney	529	Elizabeth Zettl	612
D Hamey	420	Dorothy Chadwick	574	Edward Roberts	463	Ella Neal	590
D Hardwick	519	Dorothy Davis-Sellick	187	Edward Tanguy	410	Ellen Chaplin	483
D Haskett-Jones	362	Dorothy Edwards	155	Efrosyni Hobbs	499	Ellen Day	329
D Huff	234	Dorothy Fuller	324	E F Scott	473	Ellen M Lock	42
D H White	370	Dorothy Grey	397	E Gordon	586	Ellie Boardman	438
Diana Blench	36	Dorothy Haywood	207	E Gosney	132	Ellie Rose Guillory (10)	411
Diana Frewin	154	Dorothy Hill Bradshaw	168	E Hockley	156	Ellsie Russell	210
Diana H Adams	56	Dorothy Howard	549	E Hodson	397	Elsa Ivor	239

Name	No.	Name	No.	Name	No.	Name	No.
Elsie Balme	319	Fay Marshall	556	George A Tanner	460	Gordon West	475
Elsie Birch	639	F Baker	379	George Beckford	163	Gordon Wilson	240
Elsie Cooperwaite	408	F B Rylance	479	George Bryant	625	G Pash	541
Elsie Hamilton	263	Felicite Gill	475	George Camp	364	Grace Harding	252
Elsie J Sharman	227	Felicity Bentley-Taylor	498	George Carrick	58	Grace Maycock	170
Elsie Mather	378	Felix McCabe	139	George Coombs	172	Grace Wallace	547
Elsie Moore	202	Fergus Hilton	473	George D Conlon	537	Graeme Doherty	72
Elwyn Bull	87	F G Ward	152	George Holmes	24	Graeme Vine	234
Elwynne	276	F Ian Tiso	31	George Wright	82	Graham Bowers	39
E M Eagle	197	Finnan Boyle	57	Georgina Ivison	465	Grahame Garfield Evans	172
Emelia Wells	486	Fiona Carson	104	Georgina May Carey	100	Grahame Godsmark	502
Emelie Buckner	501	Fiona Gunn	161	Georgina Paraskeva	283	Graham Fairbrass	295
Emily M Dixon	214	Fiona Clark	112	Georgina Wilson	98	Graham John	99
Emily Thommes	458	F Jackson	142	Gerald Hampshire	358	Graham K A Walker	299
E M Lang	417	Flo Milburn Smith	618	Geraldine Frances Sanders	385	Graham Mitchell	441
Emma Bone	369	Flora Denning	279	Geraldine Taylor	386	Graham Peter Metson	88
Emma Eliott	287	Flora Hughes	265	Gerard Allardyce	243	Graham Watkins	144
Emma Francis	493	Florence Broomfield	159	Gerard Chamberlain	128	Graham Winterbourne	568
Emma Hardwick	229	Florence Davies	533	Gerard Kenny	167	Grant Meaby	500
Emma Jane Glenning	306	Florence May Scott	539	Gerasim	296	G R Bell	74
Emma Lockyer	398	F McConaghey	503	Germana Fry	485	Greta Craigie	523
Emma Louise Taylor	321	F M Perry	428	Gerry Boxall	611	Greta E Bray	65
Emma Morton	492	Frances Burrow	189	Gerry Dymock	96	Greta Elizabeth Beevers	102
Emma Towes-Phillips	143	Frances Maguire	368	Gertrude Schöen	305	Griselda Scott	418
Emma Whitehurst (18)	42	Frances M English	498	Gez	584	G Tapper	73
E Montgomery	140	Frances M Gorton	56	G F Hawkes	467	Gusty Cotterell	144
Ena Andrews	105	Frances M Searle	449	G F Snook	88	Guthrie Morrison	30
Ena Field	159	Frances Neale	388	G Halliwell	560	Guy Fletcher	248
Ena Page	203	Frances Phillips	548	G Hunter Smith	194	G V Lewis	520
Enid Gill	188	Frances Roberts	79	Gill D'Arcy	36	Gwen Collins	538
Enid Hewitt	646	Frances S Jaffray	521	Gillian A Brown	48	Gwenda Owen	442
Enid Thomas	37	Francis Allen	119	Gillian Elaine McKinley	65	Gwen Dunbar	338
E Peaford	184	Francis Hughes	141	Gillian Howarth	236	Gwen Ellis Hunt	219
E Phillis	271	Françoise de Pierpont	524	Gillian Robson	573	Gwen Haines	587
Erica Menzies	58	Frank A Zwolinski	253	Gillian S Gill	457	Gwen Liddy	259
Erica Roach	237	Frank Dean	474	Gillian Snaith	534	Gwennie Jones (Nen x)	187
Eric Chamberlin	251	Frank Dickinson	639	Gillian Thomas	138	Gwilym Beechey	127
Eric E Webb	93	Frank Hansford-Miller	539	Gillie Threadgold	539	Gwladys Mills	474
Eric Holt	283	Frank Harper	144	Gill Lawrence	322	Gwyneth E Scott	209
Ernest Barrett	256	Frank Howarth-Hynes	71	Gill Mainwaring	117	Gwyneth Pritchard	149
Ernest Errington Reid	509	Frankie Shepherd	126	Gill Pomfret	530	Hacene Rahmouni	385
Ernest Jones	238	Frank Tonner	199	Gilly Jones	431	Hal Takata	457
E Rose	587	Fran Merrett	428	Gina Bowman	349	Hannah Louise Lancaster (11)	625
Errol Johnson	137	Fraser Hicks	322	Giselle Harold	557	Hardeep Singh-Leader	75
E Saynor	19	Freda Bunce	476	G K (Bill) Baker	60	Harold Brawn	172
Eslyn Coke	429	Freda Grieve	106	Gladys Bartley	638	Harold Cotterill	482
Estelle James	641	Freda Symonds	445	Gladysemily	422	Harold Taylor	402
Esther Hawkins	376	Fred Brown	528	Glan Grey-Jones	334	Harriet Elizabeth Hobbs (13)	599
Esther Jones	47	Frederic Davies	189	Glenna Welsh	52	Harry Crompton-fils	50
Ethel Smith	568	Frederick Coles	610	Glennis Eccleston	69	Harry Ireland	121
E Thorpe	210	F Todd	580	Glenwyn Peter Evans	19	Harry Murtagh	78
Eunice Brown	164	Gabriela Alexander	634	Glenys Hannon	575	Harry Skinn	53
Eunice Doyle	598	Gabrielle Gascoigne	268	Glenys Moses	349	Hayley E Hanson	52
Eunice M Caines	552	Gael Nash	575	Gloria A Jackson	435	Hazel Blake	605
Eva A Perrin	410	Gail Cureton	477	Gloria B Rogers	230	Hazel Brydon	451
Eva Harper	142	Garry Bedford	48	Gloria D Hollister	195	Hazell Dennison	448
Eve Hughes	96	Garth Evans	458	Gloria Hargreaves	643	Hazel Mary Farrell	551
Eveline Nash Gaging	167	Gary Monaghan	355	Gloria McCrory	447	Hazel McNeil	480
Eveline Tucker	445	Gary S Morton	292	Gloria S Beeston	576	Hazel Michell	318
Evelyn A Evans	650	Gary T Pollard	103	Gloria Whitehouse	591	Hazel Russell	407
Evelyn D Alvis	295	G Ayling	590	G Louch	89	Hazel Wellings	227
Evelyn Golding	429	Gaynor Dexter	461	Glyn Davies	162	H D Hensman	142
Evelyn Hoy	82	G Baker	134	G Maynard	373	Heather Brackley	632
Evelyn Hughes	595	G B Moore	465	G Murphy	542	Heather Hill	546
Evelyn M Harding	259	G Bree	383	Godfrey Ackers	131	Heather Lynes	260
Evelyn Osman	198	G Burgess	130	Godfrey Dodds	417	Heather Overfield	419
Evelyn Westwood	311	G Drew	169	G O Parry	380	Heather Walker	527
Eve McGrath	318	G E Harrison	583	Gordon A Cameron	44	Helena Jaksic	151
Eve Turner	263	Gemma Edwards Gill	503	Gordon Barnett	60	Helen Barwood	505
E Walker	118	Gemma Musgrove	146	Gordon Finlay	395	Helen Dean	524
E Witt-Way	188	Gemma Steele	31	Gordon Paul Charkin (War Veteran)	196	Helen E Langstone	25
Fabian Montanaro	383	Geoffrey Lund	559	Gordon Reid Johns	600	Helen Johnson	215
Fae Turner	511	Geoff Von-Heizon	197	Gordon Starr	233	Helen Knott	559
Faith Honeysett	583	George Alexander	131	Gordon Vale	456	Helen Laurance	345

Name	No.	Name	No.	Name	No.	Name	No.
Helen Lock	222	Iris Brown	173	James S Cameron	354	Jean Bishop	496
Helen Marley	400	Iris Long	390	James Spoors	367	Jean Bradbury	382
Helen Perry	639	Iris McEvoy	655	James Stevenson	460	Jean Burrells	592
Helen Persse	427	Iris Morton	448	James Stirrat	525	Jean B Yates	364
Helen Saunders	591	Iris Owen	466	Jan Anderson	374	Jean Caldwell	214
Helen Steel	201	Iris Taylor	74	Jan Bevan	86	Jean Carroll	250
Helen Towner	269	Iris Woolford	456	Jan Caswell	205	Jean C Pease	132
Helen West	335	Iroulla A Kyriakou	523	Jane Bingeman	218	Jean Duckworth	452
Helga Dharmpaul	165	Irvine Hunt	353	Jane Clarke	304	Jean Dutfield	282
Helga Hopkinson	638	Isaac Smith	88	Jane Findlay	510	Jeanette Hursey	440
I Henry Disney	203	Isabel Cortan	571	Jane Finlayson	135	Jeanette Jackson	366
Henry Djuritschek	574	Isabel Kelly	591	Jane Oliver	369	Jeanette L Durk	204
Henry Harding Rogers	501	Isabella (Issy) Young	463	Janet Boulton	486	Jean Everest	497
Henry J Green	22	Isabella Anderson	404	Janet Bowen	626	Jean Ford	413
Herbert Wilson	409	Isabella Pownall	197	Janet Dowerman	223	Jean Greenall	104
Herdis Churchill	276	Isabella Shaw	119	Janet Cavill	163	Jean Humphris	283
H Gladding	413	Isobel Clanfield	201	Janet Collinson	529	Jean Lilian Bramhill	26
Hilary J Cairns	478	Isobel Scarlett	520	Janet Freeman	505	Jean Lloyd-Williams	72
Hilary Jill Robson	139	I Vale	391	Janet Greenwood	193	Jean Lowe	390
Hilary Jill Robson	272	Ivana Cullup	173	Janet Hannan	460	Jean Mackenzie	118
Hilary Mason	77	Ivan S Thomas	464	Janet Hewitt	242	Jean Martin-Doyle	110
Hilary Moore	223	Ivor Percival	234	Janet Hover	346	Jean McCoy	320
Hilary M Rose	73	Ivy E Baker	422	Janet Jannaway	288	Jean McPherson	134
Hilary Tozer	357	Ivy Gallagher	177	Janet Jones	217	Jean Medcalf	492
Hilary Vint	523	Ivy Griffiths	513	Janet Larkin	209	Jeannette Collett	479
Hilda Griffiths	262	J-C Chandenier	327	Janet Lawreniuk	592	Jeannette Kelly	409
H J Mazza	20	J A Alcock	226	Janet Llewellyn	72	Jeannette R D Jones	462
H John Griffin	638	Jack Blades	158	Janet M Pinto	578	Jeannie Hay	511
H Loseby	174	Jack Edwards	63	Janet Nella Ackroyd	519	Jeannie Price	435
H M Birch	311	Jack Georgion	167	Janet Petchey	329	Jeannine Anderson Hall	399
Howard Atkinson	24	Jack Holt	127	Janet P Wason	496	Jean Noble	643
Howard Gibbs	512	Jackie Allingham	461	Janet Robertson Jones	488	Jean P McGovern	383
H R Maybury	205	Jackie Barker-Smith	286	Janet Weatherhead	206	Jean Reynolds	414
Hywel Davies	256	Jackie Barlow	588	Janet Woods	533	Jean Roughton	536
Ian Benjamin	211	Jackie Davies	373	Jane Wade	567	Jean Skitrall	394
Ian Fisher	582	Jackie Gifford	91	Janey Wiggins	262	Jean Turner	44
Ian Hancock	496	Jackie Johnson	286	Jan Hall	422	Jean Wood	90
Ian McCrae	168	Jackie Phillips	384	Jan Hollinshead	581	Jefferson Faulkner	540
Ian McNamara	359	Jackie Richardson	232	Janice Gilbert	509	Jeffrey A Pickford	231
Ian Richardson	599	Jack John Georgion	216	Janice Honeybourne	282	Jemma Pinkerton	180
Ian R Woollcott	189	Jack Patterson	128	Janice Thorogood	590	Jenifer Ellen Austin	55
I Crumley	620	Jack Purdom	248	Janina Neale	544	Jeni Pierce	332
Ida Shewan	498	Jack Robinson	108	Janine Vallor	461	Jennie Hudson	404
Idris Woodfield	232	Jack Scrafton	224	Jan Ingram McCaffery	617	Jennie Rose Miles	491
I Dunwoodie	634	Jack Williamson	436	Jan Maissen	184	Jennifer Bell	421
I D Welch	266	Jacky Dale	522	Januarius	84	Jennifer Campbell	155
I Higginson	44	Jacqueline Abendstern	563	Jan Wickens	515	Jennifer Densham	???
I K Skinner	95	Jacqueline Appleby	232	Jan Yule	262	Jennifer D Wootton	73
Imelda Fitzsimons	308	Jacqueline Claire Davies	39	J Ashford	413	Jennifer Fox	570
Ina J Harrington	68	Jacqueline G Harris	63	Jasmine Grace Geddes	147	Jennifer K Cocks	608
Ines Newell	284	Jacqueline Gonzalez-Marina	370	Jason L Wolf	637	Jennifer Richards	552
I Obomhense	577	Jacquelyn Harby	522	Jay Leffew	451	Jennifer Smith	360
I R Cook	450	Jacqui Beddow	633	Jayne Poulter	484	Jennifer Stella Smeed	264
Irene Beckwith	492	Jacqui Dunne	283	Jayne Prime	409	Jennifer T Macleod	94
Irene Crawford	111	Jacquie Russell	215	Jay Smith	636	Jennifer Vine	365
Irene Foxcroft	417	Jacqui Haynes	547	Jay Whittam	452	Jennifer Vrahimis	459
Irene G Corbett	650	Jacqui Morgan	188	J Berry	445	Jennifer Wright	238
Irene Grahame	306	Jacqui Watson	276	J Bootle	431	Jenny Dukes	396
Irene Greenan	196	J A Finlayson	450	J Bowes	477	Jenny Johnson	227
Irene Hart	238	J A Godley	518	J Brown	320	Jenny Minor	394
Irene Kenny	531	Jalil Kasto	291	J C Fearnley	467	Jenny Pearce	561
Irene Lee	375	James Adams	567	J Coleridge	542	Jesamine Cook	106
Irene Lorch	452	James Ayrey	60	J Cox	267	Jessica Boak	208
Irene Low	557	James Baxter	221	J Cross	206	Jessica Jones	612
Irene McBurney	412	James Bellamy	57	J Curwen	624	Jessica Wright	279
Irene Millington	257	James Conboy	416	J Dawe	357	Jessie Bishop	337
Irene Morgans	406	James E Cragg	337	J D Mitchell	584	Jessie Edwards	613
Irene Morris	28	James Fraser	140	J Drummond	616	Jessie Moody	195
Irene Patricia Kelly	392	James McConalogue	430	Jean-Angela Smith	123	Jessie Morton	123
Irene Price	119	James Murray	649	Jean-Pamela Moore	561	J E Stangroom	457
Irene Ramsey	571	James O'Grady	567	Jean-Ruth	129	J Faith	384
Irene Reid	415	James Olley	235	Jean A Smith	446	J Feaviour	148
Irene Siviour	131	James P O'Keeffe	273	Jean Austin	41	J Ferguson	129
Iris A Davidson	397	James Rodger	380	Jean Bald	219	J Hickens	597

Name	No.	Name	No.	Name	No.	Name	No.
J H Newing	509	Joanne Powel	553	John Topham	160	J S Gillespie	216
J Howling Smith	384	Joanne Reader	326	John Tovey	350	J S Liberkowski	393
Jill Alcock	222	Joan Packwood	202	John Troughton	453	J S Lister	493
Jill Hudson	111	Joan Patrickson	399	John Waby	76	J Stillwell	252
Jillian Megram	102	Joan Peacock	25	John Wedge	390	J Stoles	131
Jillian Mounter	297	Joan Picton	444	John W Hewing	29	J Sweeney	302
Jill James	288	Joan Prentice	169	John Whittock	207	Judd Hulme	431
Jill Lesley Gilbert	103	Joan Smith	57	John Wilson Smith	639	Judith Aubrey	277
Jill M Ronald	536	Joan Thompson	79	John Young	515	Judith Garrett	546
Jill Willens	615	Joan Wright	363	Jo Lee	257	Judy McEwan	215
Jilly Tynan	293	Joan Zambelli	95	Jo Lewis	504	Judy Smith	83
Jim Crook	112	Jo Brookes	92	Jo Mackenzie	581	Julia Bush	517
Jim E Dolbear	656	Jodie McKane	520	Jonathan Gilbert	178	Julia Eva Yeardye	295
Jim Lucas	196	Joe Bayford	440	Jonathan Mills	571	Julia Holden	168
Jim Miller	230	Jo Ellis	593	Jo Robinson	179	Julia Keiser	546
Jimmy Sinclair (93)	619	Joe Oluwa	576	Josepha Blay	39	Julia Murphy	429
Jim Pritchard	214	Joe Solomon	578	Joseph Broadley	76	Julianne Clarke	336
Jim Rogers	508	Jo Gander	481	Josephine Giles	631	Julia Pegg	90
Jim Rogerson	33	John 'El' Wright	294	Josephine Thomas	482	Julia Perren	303
Jim Tan	278	John Aldred	281	Josephine Thompson	471	Julia Simpson	20
Jinty Wicks	537	John Alexander Harrison	360	Joseph Jezierski	65	Julie Brown	318
J J Clare	501	John Allison	312	Joseph Larkin	616	Julie Charsville	644
J Jones	58	John A Turner	289	Joseph McGarraghy	38	Julie Hinson	189
J Kattenburg	233	John Ball	104	Joseph Smedley	537	Julie Marie Laura Shearing	609
J Knott	528	John Beazley	278	Josh Brittain	59	Julie Smith	184
J Lanigan	128	John Bevan Stocks	80	Josh Morrall	300	Julie Smith	352
J Legg	177	John Birkett	569	Joshua Skelton	483	Juliet Borland	326
J Lovell	67	John Burton	640	Josie Davies	646	Juliet Fowler	428
J Mangan	135	John Campbell	590	Josie Hodges	417	Julya Bukowski	576
J Mary Kirkland	165	John Collard	262	Josie McClung (11)	126	June Barber	123
J McKinney	586	John Cook	132	Josie Pepper	420	June Benn	530
J M Cripsey	486	John Coombes	656	Josie Rawson	457	June Briggs	326
J M Davies	558	John Cowley	472	Josie Smith	551	June Coral Dye	233
J M Everingham	168	John C Traynor	580	Jo Stock	86	June Davies	347
J Millington	344	John D Burgoyne	594	Jo Taylor	216	June Dixon	637
J Milner	113	John Doherty	414	Joy Bartelt	581	June F Allum	95
J Nicoll	308	John D Savage	30	Joyce Alice Turner	118	June Jefferson	328
Jo Allen	596	John Edney	244	Joyce Atkinson	47	June Jobborn	491
Joan Baker	560	John Eldridge	471	Joyce Chadwick	485	June Johnson	641
Joan Beer	591	John Elias	455	Joyce Craufurd-Stuart	485	June Sedgebear	439
Joan Bourner	514	John E Lindsay	421	Joyce Dobson	433	June White	489
Joan Briggs	245	John Foster-Turner	313	Joyce Dunkley	72	June Witt	167
Joan Brocklehurst	386	John Gaze	25	Joyce Graham	438	June Worsell	137
Joan D Bailey	78	John Goulding	309	Joyce Hallifield	25	Junor T Baker	593
Joan Earle Broad	239	John Harkin	604	Joyce Hammond	67	Justin Bayless	598
Joan E Milne	43	John Harrold	363	Joyce Hargreaves	529	J Vanson	250
Joan Fletcher	182	John H Israel	227	Joyce Hemsley	142	J V Ford	215
Joan Gallen	363	John J Allan	439	Joyce Hockley	198	J Waller	175
Joan Godfrey	199	John Jordan	127	Joyce Hudspith	195	J W Whiteacre	24
Joan Hammond	81	John Leighton	640	Joyce K Tweedie	310	K Ainsley	605
Joan Hands	114	John London	341	Joyce MacDonald	291	Kamala Perera	496
Joan Hartland	54	John L Wigley	343	Joyce Maud Carter	329	Karen Barron	334
Joan Hawkes	550	John Malley	24	Joyce M Carter	552	Karen Neville	523
Joan Helen Grant	110	John Mallon	380	Joyce Morris	235	Karen Pratt	401
Joan Howes	470	John McPartlin	385	Joyce Mussett	582	Karen Rust	204
Joan Igesund	105	John Michael Scott	424	Joyce Preddle	163	Karen Williams	191
Joan Kelly	170	John Morgan	367	Joyce Walker	32	Kate Everett	153
Joan Kingscott	588	John Morrison	226	Joyce West	174	Kate Johnson	391
Joan L Carter	337	John M Spiers	510	Joyce White	388	Kate Ransom	242
Joan Leahy	107	John Mutton	162	Joyce Woods	204	Kateryna Mazelan (nee Kozak)	537
Joan Lewis	540	John Neal	113	Joy Davies	385	Kate Shkanova	101
Joan Lister	650	John Notley	359	Joy Hall	497	Katherine Hedison	67
Joan Littleworth	535	John Parry	267	Joy Jackson	580	Katheryn Tilling	207
Joan Magennis	359	John Paulley	218	Joy Lenton	225	Kath Gay	50
Joan Marrion	655	John Pegg	296	Jo Young	571	Kathleen Baillie	172
Joan Mathers	365	John Pert	418	Joy R Gunstone	230	Kathleen Biesierkirski	234
Joan M Hopkins	529	John Pierrepont	356	Joy Saunders	40	Kathleen Davey	233
Joan Morris	61	John Remmington	536	Joy Toms	534	Kathleen Day	533
Joanna Butler	254	John Riddick	109	Joy Wilson	92	Kathleen Earle	642
Joanne Burns	88	John Robert Burr	239	Joy Winter	608	Kathleen Gosling	416
Joanne Elliott	479	John Robertson	173	J P Brooks	200	Kathleen Holmes	290
Joanne Hale	349	John Robinson	43	J P Cook	383	Kathleen Keech	464
Joanne L Lancaster	628	John Stuart Yewlett	359	J P Henderson-Long	263	Kathleen Lockwood	532
Joanne Manning	35	John Tirebuck	189	J Pruden	157	Kathleen McBurney	77

Name	No.	Name	No.	Name	No.	Name	No.
Kathleen M Scatchard	28	Lady H	140	Lorna Tippett	361	Maralyn Rees-Molyneux	368
Kathleen M Smith	406	L A G Butler	92	Lorna Troop	250	Marc McHale	624
Kathleen Patricia Peebles	470	L A McIntosh	424	Lorraine Ann Hunting	339	Margaret-Anne Heap	407
Kathleen Potter	275	Lannette Lusk	501	Lorraine De Vanche	281	Margaret Ackerley	646
Kathleen Price	431	Laura Harris	287	Lorraine Gallagher	282	Margaret A Greenhalgh	409
Kathleen Townsley	209	Laura P Williams	318	Louisa Dean	122	Margaret Ann Scott	589
Kathleen Wendy Jones	562	Laurel Willman (11)	114	Louis Don Barrow	206	Margaret Ann Wheatley	355
Kathleen Whitty	529	Laurence E Nicholas	503	Louise Allen	35	Margaret Bailey	604
Kathryn E Needham	387	Laurence Richards	281	Louise Hercules	100	Margaret B Baguley	343
Kathryn Evans	176	Laurence Shelley	456	Louise Jones	376	Margaret Bennett	202
Kath Watkinson	609	L Beddow	315	Louise Jones (?)	353	Margaret Berry	184
Kathy French	464	L Coleman	391	Louise Mills	47	Margaret Burgess	408
Katie Boyd	100	Leeanne Shires	603	Louise Pamela Webster	45	Margaret Burtenshaw-Haines	511
Katie Cheetham	116	Lee Walford	458	Louise Pearce	586	Margaret Campbell	373
Katie Turner	372	Leigh Crighton	240	Louise Pringle	271	Margaret Chisman	375
Katja Kielhauser	80	Leigh Smart	218	Louise Wheeler	266	Margaret Clary	331
Katrina Bride	187	Leila McLeish	520	L Saunders	115	Margaret Cryer	523
Katrina Plumb	474	Lelia Grant	230	L Simcock Daisy	395	Margaret Davies	616
Kay Jude	502	Len Clarke	54	L T Burbery	299	Margaret Deverson	204
Kay L Soord	232	Len Corner	588	L Turner	249	Margaret Fowler	600
Kay Reynolds	644	Len Woodhead	53	Lucinda Hearne	108	Margaret Gleeson Spanos	91
Kay Watts	186	Leonard T Coleman	56	Lucy-May Bloxham	158	Margaret Gregory	507
Kaz	595	Lesley A Stevenson	368	Lucy Browster	585	Margaret Hanning	105
K Crabb	372	Lesley Clary-Sage	397	Lucy Crisp	441	Margaret Harrison	285
K E Evans	504	Lesley Elaine Greenwood	69	Lucy Downes	164	Margaret Hibbert	94
Keith B Osborne	365	Leslie F Dukes	403	Lucy Elliott (15)	583	Margaret Hodgson	619
Keith Dry	329	Leslie F Higgins	274	Lucy Holloway	226	Margaret Hughes	635
Keith F Lainton	252	Letita Hughes (14)	191	Lucy M Kaye	32	Margaret Kaye	223
Keith Garrett	474	Lewis Cottington	253	Lydia E Stanton	607	Margaret Kelly	223
Keith Jenkins	564	Lewis Palgrave	372	Lynda Burton	447	Margaret Knox Stubbs	611
Keith Large	141	L France	491	Lynda Fordham	285	Margaret Lawson	535
Keith L Powell	93	L Fulker	402	Lynda Hill	386	Margaret Luckett	278
Keith Robbins	392	L Gould	406	Lynda Peat	463	Margaret Marsh	60
Keith Skelton	579	L G Stiles	205	Lyndsey Herron	68	Margaret Martin	565
Keith Tissington	28	L Hammond Oberansky	621	Lyndsey Louise Watson	616	Margaret Mary Harrop	293
Keith Wilson	299	Lila Jackson	466	Lynn Buxton	175	Margaret Mary Sherwood	629
Ken Angus	104	Lilian King	637	Lynn Craig	56	Margaret M Cassidy	65
Ken Cox	557	Lilian Loftus	204	Lynne Hope	414	Margaret McQuade	211
Ken Marshall	545	Lilian Owen	486	Lynne Lister	284	Margaret Meadows	310
Ken Millar	607	Lilian Perriman	68	Lynne Taylor	359	Margaret Meagher	218
Kenneth Buckley	507	Lily Pepper	399	Lynne Walden	229	Margaret Milnes	377
Kenneth Copley	249	Lily Radcliffe	354	Lyn Sandford	347	Margaret Mitchell	333
Kenneth Cutts	51	Linda Ann Marriott	82	Lynsay Bestwick	355	Margaret M Lyon	254
Kenneth I Squires	314	Linda Brown	357	Lynsey Bessent	370	Margaret Murphy	43
Kenneth Tropman	217	Linda Fensome	213	Lyn Whitehouse	227	Margaret P Auerbach	497
Kenneth V Jackson	49	Linda Francis	193	Mabel Houseman	118	Margaret Pow	41
Kenny McAlpine	516	Linda Hamlin	284	Mabel McCoy	458	Margaret Randall	411
Ken Watts	564	Linda Hodgson	446	Mabel Wall	560	Margaret Reichlin	28
Kerridwen Niner	527	Linda J Coombes	165	Mac	358	Margaret Renshaw	403
Kerry-Ann Fender	326	Linda Jennings	243	Machiavelli G Dayupay	104	Margaret Rhodes	435
Kerry Catherine Hart	607	Linda Kettle	66	M Ackroyd	459	Margaret Sherrington	609
Kerry Shepherd	430	Linda Meadows	343	Maddie Reade	237	Margaret Sparshott	560
Kevin Collins	342	Linda Tosney	59	Maddoc Martin	362	Margaret Stumpp	519
Kevin J Foulger	402	Linda Walker	490	Madge Goodman	287	Margaret Taylor	436
Kevin McCann	166	Linda Zulaica	335	Madge Goodman	434	Margaret Thomas	112
Kevin Smette	439	Lindsey Jane Way	331	Magdalene Chadwick	267	Margaret Thompson	512
Kevin Welch	358	Lindsey Susan Powell	59	Maggie Andrews	77	Margaret Trivasse	578
K F Hardy	369	Lisa Bristow	444	Maggie Cartridge	105	Margaret Wallace	272
K Hale (15)	103	Lisa Harper-Gough & Steve Wickens	271	Maggie Pryce Jones	617	Margaret Ward	44
Kim Stretton	470	Lisa McKenzie	454	Maggie Sparvell	572	Margaret Wensley	641
Kim Taylor	114	Lisa Thompson	164	Maggie Strong	130	Margaret Willey	230
Kim Warren	557	Liseanne Rix	387	Maggy Rosentritt	54	Margaret Wood	605
Kinsman Clive	397	Liz Dicken	266	Maimie Watson Stokoe	374	Margery Crabtree	323
Kirsha Johnson	365	Liz Edmonds	125	Mai M Roach	336	Margery Rayson	159
Kirstie Clark	531	L Lowe	340	Mair Alexander	544	Margret Phillips	424
K J Wakefield	390	L Muscroft	228	Maisie Dance	209	Margt C Leighton	34
K L Pusey	625	Lola Perks-Hartnell	83	Maisie Trussler	125	Marguerite Pratt	614
K M Brown	341	Lord Ciaran D'arcy	394	Malachy Trainor	52	Maria-Christina	135
K M Clemo	468	Loré Föst	294	Malcolm Dewhirst	116	Maria Dabrowska	36
K N Jeffery	33	Lorna June Burdon	289	Malcolm Fairbrother	330	Mariana Zavati Gardner	460
Kulbir Kaur	628	Lorna Lea	22	Malcolm Goat	153	Marian Bythell	55
K Watkiss	188	Lorna M Evans	654	Malcolm Hole	574	Marian Clark	246
K W Benoy	101	Lorna Moffatt	615	Mandy Holten	441	Marian Curtis-Jones	371
K W Parker	273	Lorna Sim	219	Mandy Salter	585	Marianne Kennedy	551

Name	Page	Name	Page	Name	Page	Name	Page
Maria Pelengaris	237	Mary Froggett	135	May Shaoul	556	Moira Wiggins	351
Marie Ashford	238	Mary Graves	292	May Ward	175	Mojibur Rahman	41
Marie Bagley	558	Mary Hackney	247	May Ward	292	Mollie Carter	446
Marie B McKenzie	377	Mary Hill	193	May Watkins	621	Mollie D Earl	126
Marie Coyles	120	Mary Hudson	22	M Baker	588	Molly Phasey	257
Mariegold Heron	301	Mary Johnson-Riley	318	M Bloomfield	523	Molly Read	91
Marie Gray	276	Mary J Whiteley	98	M Braithwaite	199	Molly Stacey	585
Marie Haswell	447	Mary Lawson	345	M Breslin	162	Molly Wyatt	182
Marie Kelly	82	Marylin Drew	77	M B Tucker	463	Monica D Buxton	102
Marie Wood	421	Mary Linney	234	M Byles	107	Monica Docherty	488
Marilyn Davidson	590	Mary Long	268	M Byles	199	Monica Gibson	497
Marilyn Hine	247	Mary L Smith	87	M C Cobb	415	Monica Gurney	413
Marilyn Jones	393	Mary McGuigan	109	M C Davies	241	Monica Long	601
Marilyn Pullan	446	Mary Murphy (Thurlow)	563	M E C Houlden	504	Monica Redhead	280
Marilyn Wilson	199	Mary Nugent	397	Meg Gilholm	482	Monica Simpson	605
Marion A Lee	597	Mary Pampolini-Roberts	108	Meg Sika	150	Monica Wood	238
Marion Bayliss	493	Mary Parker	307	Meg Stephenson	25	Moon Stone	623
Marion de Bruyn	254	Mary Pauline Winter (née Coleman)	81	Meg Wilson	151	Morag Maciver	641
Marion Edwards	232	Mary Pledge	364	Melanie Burgess	228	Morney Wilson	114
Marion Kelly	180	Mary Plumb	152	Meltem Baykaner	334	Moyra Summers	518
Marion Marston	300	Mary Roberts	636	M Entecott	289	M P Blackwell	437
Marion McGarrigle	432	Mary Robertson	129	Merlene Francois	228	M P Johnson	275
Marion Meikle Mason	476	Mary Robertson	514	Meryl Champion	544	M P Webb	392
Marion Pollitt	606	Mary Rose Dury	469	M F Williams	273	M Rankin	564
Marisa Greenaway	480	Mary Shepherd	122	M G Howcroft	461	M Roe	514
Marj Busby	41	Mary Skelton	577	M Goodland	490	M Sellers	181
Marji Tomlinson	185	Mary Staniforth	461	M Grice	171	M Smale	518
Marjorie Beaven	259	Mary Stoner	521	M Holmes	553	M Turner	565
Marjorie Chapman	156	Mary Taylor	131	Mica Hope Phillips (12)	338	Muhammad Salim	187
Marjorie Cripps	342	Mary Veronica Ciarella Murray	358	Michael Bangerter	339	Muriel Berry	280
Marjorie Haddon	143	Mary Webster	458	Michael B Scribbler	353	Muriel Golding	596
Marjorie Jones	432	Mary Whittaker	466	Michael Carter	66	Muriel Hughes	361
Marjorie J Picton	392	Mary Whorlow	451	Michael Courtney Soper	241	Muriel Johnson	293
Marjorie Leyshon	446	Mary Wood	317	Michael Davidson	435	Muriel Nicola Waldt	344
Marjorie Piggins	626	Matthew Coles	37	Michael Denholme Hortus Stalker	200	Muriel Rodgers	141
Marjorie Poyner	267	Matthew Hustings	134	Michael Hurst	166	Muriel Willa	504
Marjorie Seaman	39	Matthew Tiller	100	Michael J Pritchard	254	M Waller	516
Marjorie Simpson	540	Matthew W Jones	566	Michael K Moore	442	M Wood	337
Marjorie Wheeler	536	Maud Eleanor Hobbs	78	Michael Lyons	532	M Wright	29
Marjory Doyne	127	Maude Newton	455	Michael McKenna	471	M Yaqub Mirza	425
Marjory Price	20	Maura Malone	447	Michael Quarrington	506	Myfanwy Clarke	459
Mark Bailey	95	Maureen Anderson	342	Michael William Molden	50	Myra D Walker	483
Mark Boardman	492	Maureen Ann Baker	622	Michael Wilson	115	Myra Ramsey	617
Mark Cleaver	183	Maureen Arnold	330	Michael Wise	312	Nadine Mackie	272
Mark L Moulds	81	Maureen Dawson	542	Michele Simone Fudge	241	Nancy Robbins	115
Mark Sims	468	Maureen Digges	568	Michelle Hinton	129	Nancy Sheldon	297
Marliese E M Porter	407	Maureen Gentry-Evans	526	Michelle Luetchford	426	Nan Ogg	507
Marnie Connley	176	Maureen Inglis-Taylor	149	Mick Marlow	150	Naomi Mc Ardle	236
Marsha Leone	143	Maureen Newman	521	Mick Nash	274	Nash	275
Martha Fear	538	Maureen Oglesby	143	Midge Bainbridge	303	Natalie Brocklehurst	570
Martin Collins	309	Maureen Peacock	51	Mike Green	450	Natalie Jagger	578
Martin Harris Parry	117	Maureen Powell	248	Mike Hayes	239	Natalie Louise West	91
Martin Hiney	560	Maureen Quirey	39	Mike Monaghan	550	Nathalie El-Korashy	177
Martin Jackson	408	Maureen Reeves	309	Mike Sullivan	555	Nayyer Ali Chandella	575
Martin Norman	493	Maureen Reynolds	302	Mike Vipond	630	Neil Arch	553
Martin Selwood	115	Maureen Roberts	245	Millicent Blanche Colwell	589	Neill Cadmore	648
Martin Winbolt-Lewis	126	Maureen Rosina Batchelor	135	Millicent Hewitt	136	Neil Stirk	206
Marvyn Attwell	431	Maureen Sadler	224	Milly Saunders Farren	517	Neil Warren	170
Mary A Lisowska	593	Maureen Sponar	176	M J Chadwick	517	Netta Irvine	483
Mary Anne Clock	308	Maureen Tooze	182	M Jones	118	N Evans	125
Mary Anne Scott	244	Maureen Turner	561	M Joseph	273	N Gell	615
Mary Antcliffe	455	Maureen Westwood O'Hara	352	M Jukes	83	Niall McManus	329
Mary A Slater	512	Maureen Williams	371	M Lamin	515	Nichola J Keel	484
Mary Baird Hammond	38	Maurice Bailey	38	M L Oliver	204	Nicholas Howard	424
Mary Biggs	467	Maurice Ivor Birch	312	M Lynch	487	Nicky Anderson	477
Mary Buckley-Clarke	367	Maurice Langley	455	M Mayes	554	Nicola Harris	584
Mary Cadman	454	Mavis Abernethy	538	M McLeod	186	Nicola Jade Poulton	649
Mary Cole	398	Mavis R Cocks	384	M McPhee	427	Nicola Plumb	593
Mary Daly	524	Mavis Simpson	368	M M Dolding	361	Nigel Astell	434
Mary Davies	563	Mavis Wilson	424	M Munro Gibson	469	Nigel Chisholm	546
Mary Elizabeth Cowburn	644	Maxine Coughlan	458	M Mustoe	340	Nigel Courtney	203
Mary Elizabeth Hughes	443	May C Jenkins	316	M Nickholds	140	Nigel Hunt	406
Mary Fleming	507	May Morrott	280	Mo Fletcher	85	Nigel Leake	618
Mary Foggin	502	May Murray	71	Moira Round	160	Nina Graham	265

Name	No.	Name	No.	Name	No.	Name	No.
Nina Woolf	346	Pat Bidmead	256	Pauline Ilsley	592	Philip Nind (13)	357
Nita Garlinge	69	Pat Chamberlain	134	Pauline Kavanagh	572	Philippa Adburgham	229
N Lemel	444	Pat Fenton	528	Pauline Kirk	64	Phil Leese	524
N M Beddoes	302	Pat Ferris	220	Pauline Mayoh-Wild	369	Phillip Hunter Davis	192
Nola Small	254	Pat Heppel	190	Pauline M Clarke	310	Phillip Tinsley	322
Noni Fanger	335	Patricia Ann Hendy-Davies	600	Pauline Tattersall	98	P Hunt	472
Nora Veysey	57	Patricia Arnett	198	Pauline Vincent	413	Phyllis Blue	569
Norma A MacArthur	121	Patricia Ayres	382	Paul J Abbott	450	Phyllis Dartnell	202
Norma Davies	416	Patricia Bullock	513	Paul Kangley	372	Phyllis Hall	121
Norma Griffiths	620	Patricia Burgess	173	Paul Kelly	606	Phyllis Henderson	414
Norma Marshman	550	Patricia Cairns Laird	510	Paul Knox	36	Phyllis Ing	127
Norman Bissett	496	Patricia Carr	110	Paul Magson	595	Phyllis J Pearce	601
Norman Brookes	610	Patricia Carter	446	Paul Parkin	401	Phyllis Moore	624
Norman Cathie	121	Patricia Cobb	612	Paul R Baker	306	Phyllis O'Connell (Hampson)	89
Norman Letts	143	Patricia Daly	375	Paul Reece	313	Phyllis Sandiford	467
Norman Meadows	279	Patricia Davis	455	Paul Reynard	301	Phyllis Spooner	86
Norman Royal	243	Patricia Dyer	614	Paul Secrett	482	Phyllis Williams	487
Norma Rudge	402	Patricia Fallace	116	Paul Spender	79	Phyllis Wright	245
Norma Spillett	212	Patricia Farmer	507	Paul Thompson	514	Phyllis Wright	265
Norrie Ferguson	21	Patricia Firmin	653	Paul Volantefitz	226	P Jakes	152
N S Pearce	253	Patricia Frost	561	Paul Wright	636	P J Hale	303
Octavia Hornby	421	Patricia Graham	260	P B James	421	P John Banks	205
Olga Allen	19	Patricia Herrod	64	P Block	58	P Kelso	361
Olga Margaret Moorhouse	71	Patricia Ives	317	P Cockin	453	P L Carvell	606
Olga M Momcilovic	596	Patricia J Edwins	315	P Dunbar	182	Pleione Tooley	291
Olga Ramshaw	465	Patricia Johnson	236	Pearl Briggs	352	P M Ashforth	491
Olive Culshaw	136	Patricia Kennett	140	Pearl Burdock	147	P M H Wood	536
Olive Haycock	417	Patricia Lynne Phipps	591	Pearl Gill	554	P M Jones	464
Olive May McIntosh-Stedman	32	Patricia March	294	Pearl Hammond	78	P Morrill	379
Olive M Kenyon	327	Patricia M Farbrother	263	Pearlina Lindsay	577	P Mullins	423
Olive M Poole	76	Patricia Orton	258	Pearl Johnston-Stewart	79	Poet W Holden	441
Oliver Povey	473	Patricia Penders White	305	Pearl Williams	381	P Potts	495
Olive Smith	531	Patricia Raison	116	P E Darch	519	P Richards	138
Olive Young	142	Patricia Smith	21	Peggy Adams	602	Priscilla Noble-Mathews	381
Olli Suntinen	525	Patricia Taylor	553	Peggy Briston	373	P Smith	495
Olwyn Kershaw	550	Patricia Turner	319	Peggy Day	178	P Walton	622
O M Giblin	376	Patricia Whiting	554	Peggy Finch	277	P Wolstenholme	549
O Miller	545	Patricia Whittle	236	Peggy G Oates	464	P W Pidgeon	390
Oonagh Twomey	181	Patricia Whorwood	440	Peggy Haynes	156	Rachael Wolfenden	96
Owen Edwards	266	Patricia Woodley	540	Peggy Johnson	381	Racheal Shanks (16)	289
Owen Robert Cullimore	652	Patrick Brady	332	Peggy Netcott	51	Rachel E Joyce	226
Paff-Pafford	172	Patrick Davies	499	Peggy Seeley	522	Rachel Kate	387
Pamala Steeden	551	Patrick Gormley	68	Penn Preston	540	Rachel Mary Mills	201
Pam Chappell	639	Patrick Mannion	642	Penny Freeston	64	Rachel McKie	342
Pam Cluderay	210	Pat Rissen	460	Penny Kirby	74	Rachel M Green	313
Pam Eggleston	135	Pat Rogers	201	Penny Rose	395	Rachel M Prentice	425
Pamela Ashton	485	Pat Seddon	254	Penny Smith	176	Rachel Treadwell	477
Pamela Baily	104	Pat Simms	205	Perveez Dadachanji	566	Rachel Van Den Bergen	62
Pamela Butler	604	Patsy Preshaw	85	Peter Antonian	566	R A Hardwidge	609
Pamela Coope	555	Pattie Lopez	638	Peter Belford	31	Ralph Davis	139
Pamela Dixon	233	Pat Todd	186	Peter Clay	301	Ralph H Stephens	71
Pamela Gormley	40	Pat Watson	633	Peter Comaish	614	Ralph Littlewood	161
Pamela Hanover	101	Pat Wharam	109	Peter Corbett	103	Ralph Smith	356
Pamela Harrison	521	Pat Whitmarsh	469	Peter Doole	578	Ramon Gonzalez	387
Pamela Harvey	26	Paula Fox	72	Peter Gillott	653	R Ashcroft	109
Pamela Hawksley Blackburn	520	Paula Larkin	298	Peter Godfrey	527	Ray Chapman	494
Pamela Hopes	166	Paula Walsh	553	Peter Griffiths	236	Ray Crutchlow	559
Pamela J O'Donnell	213	Paul Bowler	122	Peter James O'Rourke	197	Ray Davis	194
Pamela Matthews	251	Paul Darby	419	Peter J Millam	468	Raymond Barber	264
Pamela Popp	371	Paul David Dawson	275	Peter J Sutton	516	Raymond Gurney	545
Pamela Sanders	27	Paul Denver	325	Peter Morriss	225	Raymond Holley	389
Pamela Sandry-Gorman	415	Paul Elwell	488	Peter P Gear	643	Raymond J Hobbs	411
Pamela Slade	605	Pauletta J Edwards	476	Peter Spurgin	388	Raymond Law	505
Pamela Wells	351	Paul Faulkner	42	Peter Towner	449	Raymond Law	506
Pam Hammocks	504	Paul Gamble	389	Peter Vaughan Williams	430	Raymond Spiteri	375
Pam Hornby	374	Paul Gardner	217	Peter Wait	511	Raymond Thomas Edwards	325
Pam Love	149	Paul Green	236	Petya Christie	425	Raymond Wakefield	501
Pam Russell	419	Paul Griffin	549	P Fazackarley	251	Ray Perkins	577
Pam Wood	378	Paulie Pentelow	249	Phil Austin	618	Ray Racy	220
Páraic Folan	300	Pauline Boncey	170	Phil Fox	53	Ray Slater	454
Pat Adams	199	Pauline Brennan	133	Philip Clark	389	Ray Smart	293
Pat Allington-Smith	388	Pauline Burton	154	Philip Dyson	522	Ray Walker	240
Pat Ammundsen	21	Pauline Butler	161	Philip Lowe	66	R Danks	584
Pat Berkshire	498	Pauline E Reynolds	20	Philip M Brown	499	R Darakhshani	538

Name	No.	Name	No.	Name	No.	Name	No.
R D Hiscoke	399	Roger Newton	175	Ruth Lydia Daly	631	Sheila Harris	258
Rebecca H Weir	353	Roger Oldfield	140	Ruth Martin	282	Sheila Harvey	144
Rebecca Keough	241	Roger Williams	101	Ruth M Ellett	170	Sheila H Birkett	478
Rebecca Pine	284	Roger Wootton	208	R V Windett	229	Sheila Jane Hobson	29
Rebecca Purcell	239	Roland Seager	304	R W Cummings	339	Sheila J Hodgkins	604
R E Bilson	621	Roland Torn	72	Sajid Patel	44	Sheila Jones	515
Reg Baggs	182	Roman Suchyj	524	Sally A Turner	630	Sheila Kohn	219
Reg Dyer	589	Roma Scrivener	217	Sally Crook-Ford	505	Sheila Leheup	216
Reg James	22	Ronald D Lush	86	Sally Spedding	75	Sheila Lloyd	328
Rex Baker	404	Ronald Rodger Caseby	157	Sally Thompson	404	Sheila Macdonald	592
R G Sill	181	Ron Bassam	217	Sally Wyatt	258	Sheila Mack	528
R G Sill	321	Ron Beaumont	341	Sal Whatley	606	Sheila Margaret Storr	586
R H Drew	410	Ron Renton	249	Samantha Braum	580	Sheila Moore	331
R Holmes	235	Ron Shettle	493	Samantha Philo-Gill	112	Sheila Scott	125
R Humphrey	171	Ron Whatley	371	Samantha Walsh	47	Sheila Seabourne	124
Richard Ansell	346	Ron Woollard	403	Samantha Williams	153	Sheila Spence	520
Richard Bradshaw	51	Rosaleen Clarke	590	Sam Kelly	29	Sheila Waterhouse	147
Richard Cluroe	541	Rosalind I Caygill	90	Sammy Davis	178	Sheila Watts	112
Richard D Tompkins	411	Rosalyn Hogg	545	Sam Spruce	294	Sheila Whitehead	454
Richard E Stoyles	441	Rose-Mary Gower	269	Samuel Edwards	171	Sheralee Le-Gros	443
Richard Gould	559	Rose Baines	613	Samuel Takavarasha Jnr	619	Shirley Carlton	418
Richard Gunn	154	Rose Horscroft	556	Sandie	271	Shirley Davis	374
Richard J Byers	317	Roselie Mills	558	Sandie Smith	295	Shirley I Straw	99
Richard Layton	40	Rosemarie Reeves	632	Sandra Benson	293	Shirley Johnson	190
Richard Mahoney	260	Rosemary A Shaw	583	Sandra Griesbach	304	Shirley Jones Dwyer	63
Richard Saunders	618	Rosemary Cook	530	Sandra H Seed	395	Shirley Ludlow	76
Richard Stead	551	Rosemary C Whatling	47	Sandra Hughes	356	Shirley McIntyre	100
Richard Stoker	403	Rosemary Davies	337	Sandra J Walker	193	Shirley Monckton-Rickett	544
Richard Tapley	602	Rosemary de Harrow	519	Sandra Madden	116	Shirley Pinnington	347
Richard Young	65	Rosemary England	203	Sandra Pitt	135	Shirley R Thomas	334
Rick Oak	193	Rosemary Graham	330	Sandra W Bridgeman	229	Shirley Thompson	541
Rick Storey	21	Rosemary Harvey	84	Sandy Phillips	96	Shirley W Parker	406
Ricky N Lock	140	Rosemary Keith	567	Sarah Allison	174	S H Smith	43
Rita Arksey	532	Rosemary King	230	Sarah Ann Rees	480	Shula Bailey	401
Rita Hardiman	221	Rosemary Peach	187	Sarah Bingham	336	Sid Harris	127
Rita Johnson	462	Rosemary Povey	286	Sarah Blackmore	324	Simon McAlear	438
Rita Mash	79	Rosemary Sheridan	162	Sarah Buchan Anderson	82	Simon Peterson	542
Rita Pedrick	109	Rosemary Stanford	376	Sarah Croston	381	Simon P Rossiter	651
Rita Pilbrow-Carlsson	115	Rosemary Thewlis	610	Sarah Dodds	322	Simon Richardson	147
Rita Scott	225	Rosemary Watts	502	Sarah Heptinstall	146	Simon Rowson Clark	386
R J Collins	378	Rosemary Yvonne Vandeldt	468	Sarah Howard	75	Sister Trinity Tarr	27
R J Stallon	168	Rosie Heartland	386	Sarah Hutchinson	614	S J Dodwell	386
R L Cooper	291	Rosie Hues	108	Sarah Munro	185	S J Goodman	610
R L Harvey	341	R Osier	443	Sarah Robinson	502	S Joyce	261
R Mills	488	Rosina Choyce	143	S A Sanders	607	S Lester	470
R Morgan	183	Rosina Drury	302	S A Swain	595	S L Howe	521
R N Taber	84	Rosina Winiarski	223	S Baker	179	S M Thompson	522
Robbie Ellis	35	Rossana Pinto	534	S Barnard	142	Snikpohd	467
Roberta A Davies	365	Roula Writer	423	S Bellas	194	S Oldaker	244
Robert A Gould	208	Rowan	320	S Beverly-Ruff	243	Sonia Jones	307
Robert Carson	29	Rowena	338	S C Cowley	302	Sonia Richards	430
Robert Corrigan	531	Roy Akerman	572	Scott Humphrey	521	Sonia Riggs	246
Robert Denis Spencer	303	Roy Burfield	311	S Croxtall	190	Sonja F Mills	292
Robert Doherty	286	Roy Court	248	S C Talmadge	40	Sonya Hynes	476
Robert E Fraser	80	Roy Dickinson	499	Sean Jackson	261	Sophie E Lawrence (17)	62
Robert Fallon	27	Roy Perkins	54	Semra Yeo	573	S Park	498
Robert Hayward	247	Roy Rudd	166	Serena Shores	350	S R Hawk'sbee	471
Robert Henry	347	Roy Stevens	508	S Glover	38	Sringkhala(Lucina Della Rocca)	92
Robert Henry Lonsdale	165	Royston Davies	494	Shajna B Chowdhury	373	S Simcoe	602
Robert Hogg	473	Royston Herbert	165	Shane Hinton (13)	129	S Stalker	432
Robert K Bowhill	93	Roy T Gough	78	Sharon Elton	26	Stan Coombs	33
Robert McIlveen	645	Roy Vaughan	256	Sharon Reaper	620	Stan Downing	49
Robert Newton	630	Rozetta Pate	319	Sharron Hollingsworth	23	Stan Gilbert	318
Robert Peckham	164	R P Candlish	331	Sheelagh Chimes	330	Stan Herbert	417
Robert S Dell	294	R Sturdy	161	Sheena Conroy	436	Stanley G Witty	62
Robert T Collins	110	Rupert Smith	408	Sheila Atkinson	581	Stanley Longbottom	85
Robert Wakerley	651	Russell Hyman	350	Sheila Barton	547	Stanley Moore	470
Robert Warren	194	Ruth Baker	185	Sheila Booth	441	Stan M Tweedie	427
Robert Wynn-Davies	558	Ruth Berry	252	Sheila Buckingham	601	Stan Walton	411
Robin Halder	252	Ruth Brigden	360	Sheila Burnett	198	Stan Whomsley	119
Robin J Grigsby	635	Ruth Connolly	270	Sheila C Barr	508	S Tarr	566
Rod Palmer	267	Ruth Fellows	342	Sheila Fernley-Benard	185	S Taylor	42
Roger Bellamy	390	Ruth Grant	365	Sheila Gilbert	192	Stein Dunne	375
Roger M Creegan	43	Ruth Hartridge	630	Sheila Giles	346	Stella C Smith	328

Name	No.	Name	No.	Name	No.	Name	No.
Stella Haynes	516	Sylvia Rouse	490	Trevor Beach	526	W D Stanley	41
Stephanie Brown	556	Sylvia White	533	Trevor Headley	569	W E Clements	87
Stephanie Harris	627	Sylvie Alexandre-Nelson	347	Trevor Huntington	469	W E Holloway	634
Stephanie Linney	380	T A L	612	Tricia Jones	196	Wendy A Lyon	466
Stephen Eric Smyth	579	Tanzia Haq	165	Tricia Sturgeon	604	Wendy Andrews	380
Stephen Painting	266	Tarn Hows	80	Trish Shepherd	378	Wendy Chaffer	548
Stephen Wooley	340	Tay Collicutt	514	Trudy Simpson	585	Wendy Coulson	201
Steve Blackwell	315	Ted Harriott	81	T W Denis Constance	297	Wendy Day	261
Steve Gunning	181	Tedward	283	U Chaplin	289	Wendy Grounds	534
Steven J Forster	100	Tegid Furzer	492	Una Davies	396	Wendy Milner	141
Steven M Shanks	603	T Elliott	180	Una Thurgill	547	Wendy Scott	218
Steve Randell	428	Terence Leslie	59	Ursula Bayer	312	Wendy Shutler	447
Stroma M Hammond	92	Teresa M Garfield	201	Val Backs	402	Wendy Stark	604
Stuart Delvin	473	Teresa R Chester	303	Val Bermingham	300	Wendy Vidler	538
Stuart Plumley	433	Teri-Louise Caterer	597	Valerie Caine	279	Wendy Webb	279
Stuart Springthorpe	111	Terrence St John	74	Valerie Catterall	456	Wendy Winslet	234
S T Vaughan	398	Terry Bates	606	Valerie Cooper	493	Wenna Taylor	526
Sue Benwell	235	Terry Gilvin	269	Valerie Faith Irvine-Fortescue	338	W Herbert G Palfrey	426
Sue Brown	215	Terry Grimson	480	Valerie Hall	34	W Holmes	213
Sue Byham	366	Terry Lane	284	Valerie Lowe	552	W H Thomas	513
Sue Devlin	425	Terry Rowberry	137	Valerie Marshall	97	Wilfred John Parker	601
Sue Godsell	66	Terry Temlett	323	Valerie McKinley	45	Will Daunt	526
Sue Hughes	333	Tessa Hammond	50	Valerie Smerdon	611	William A Laws	90
Sue Ireland	46	T F Ryan	403	Valerie Thompson	211	William A Mack	300
Sue Percival	159	T Garwood	419	Valerie Willan	409	William A Smyth	419
Sue Rowe	152	T G Bicknell	495	Valerie Zanetti	484	William Birtwistle	88
Sue Smith	347	T G Bloodworth	288	Val Hoare	505	William Dodd	450
Sue Starling	27	The Jaimi	586	Val Stephenson	412	William F Park	404
Sue White	503	Thelma (Slee) Thomas	277	Vaughan Stone	321	William G Evans	253
Sunny-Laverne Sharp (8)	399	Thelma Anne Barton	448	V E Adamson	23	William Greig	465
Susan A Semmens	78	Thelma Hynes	85	V E Godfrey	440	William J Bartram	160
Susan Carole Gash-Roberts	270	Thelma Kellgren	145	Velvet Dusk	405	William Knapton	570
Susan E Roffey	314	Thelma Robinson	333	Vera Banwell	490	William Precey	162
Susan Goldsmith	191	Thelma Smithies	244	Vera Davies	379	Will of Endon	440
Susan Gordon	225	Theresa Carey	82	Vera Ewers	192	Wilma Jayne Gravenor	407
Susan Green	433	Theresa M Carrier	333	Vera Flint	409	Wilma Nicholas	376
Susan Hamlyn	86	Theresa Mead	574	Vera Hankins	310	Wilma Whitla	388
Susan Jane Byers	216	Therese G Gilbert	484	Vera Homer	258	Wilson E Jones	582
Susan Latimer	171	Thomas Hull	128	Vera Lee	547	Winifred Booth	374
Susan Lowe	38	Thomas Jones	309	Vera May Waterworth	287	Winifred Brasenell	38
Susan Macdougal	59	Thomas Murphy	200	Vera M Holmes	421	Winifred Rachel Probert	94
Susan Mary Robertson	472	Thomas Titchener	452	Vera Morrill	586	Winifred Smith	392
Susan M Billington	150	Thomas W O'Connell	237	Vera Parsonage	148	Winifred Tutte	539
Susannah Carroll	595	Thomas W O'Connell	349	Vera Torbet	636	Winnie Milnes	164
Susan Richardson	512	Tim Hoare	34	Verity Holloway	329	Winnie Pat Lee	366
Susan Richardson	579	Tina Sanderson	383	Veronica Bulmer	305	Winsome Mary Payter	535
Susan Skinner	50	T Kemran-Mustafa	23	Veronica Charlwood Ross	259	W J F Haney	66
Susan Straughan-Harding	161	T M McFarlane	305	Veronica Taylor	224	Wlodzimier Kajon	34
Susan Twells	405	T M Slomczynski	55	Veronica Tilbury	634	W McLean	152
Susan Wren	150	T M Wright	228	Veronica Twells	378	W Moyle Breton	348
Susie Belt	494	Tomboy	494	V Harding	598	W Prance	479
Susie Field	345	Tom Collin	163	Vic Calladine	652	W Price	89
Suzanna Wilson	257	Tom Griffiths	316	Vicki Harrold	589	W Stannard	344
Suzanne Joy Golding	298	Tom Hulley	117	Vic Round	93	W Wyndham Lewis	556
Suzanne Reeves	76	Tom Martin	599	Victor Lown	389	W Yagel	297
S V Batten	296	Tom McDonald	360	Vida Taylor	33	Wyn Williams	39
S Woodbine	186	Tommy McBride	255	Vie Tulloch	410	Yasmeen Ahmed	231
Sybil Bourchier Steel	629	Tom Sexton	130	Vikki Silverlock	564	Y Corcoran	475
Sybil Edwards	390	Tonie S Ritchie	513	Vince Hughes	143	Yvonne Forrester	145
Sybil R Collins	73	Tony Channon	228	Violet Beattie	198	Yvonne Lane	548
Sydney Ward	568	Tony Emmott	432	Violet Cook	290	Yvonne Rossiter	149
Sylvan	579	Tony Fox	628	Violet Higgins	344	Yvonne Watkin-Rees	332
Sylvette Gilbert-Sivieude	120	Tony Harris	387	Violetta Ferguson	178	Zandra Collisson	354
Sylvia Anne Lees	442	Tony Hayden	483	Vivek P Sarma	46	Zara Britton	221
Sylvia Clark	475	Tony Hucks	437	Vivian Khan	573	Zeedy Thompson	537
Sylvia E L Reynolds	282	Tony King	228	Vivienne Constantinides	533	Zena Parker	509
Sylvia Fairclough	323	Tony Parkinson	395	Vivienne C Wiggins	314	Zenda Madge	275
Sylvia Farr	301	Tony Reese	337	Vivvi	601	Zing J Rock	79
Sylvia Horder	22	Tony Roberts	259	V Jean Tyler	49	Zoe French	69
Sylvia Iveson	632	Tracey Dixon	283	V J Havis	594	Zoë Hall	87
Sylvia Moulds	243	Tracey McConnell	137	V Scytere	137	Zoe Laing	298
Sylvia Partridge	381	Tracy Brierley	371	Walter Crooks	146	Zoé M Pearce	379
Sylvia Price	289	Tracy Hazelby	415	Walter E Causer	600	Zoiyar Cole	211
Sylvia Reeve	423	Tracy Sampson	313	W A Rodgers (Lonnie)	301	Zoltan P Dienes	37

OF PHANTOM SHADOWS

Passing phantom shadows
Undulate before my eyes,
A youth of pleasant meadows,
Celebrates the early morning rise.

The chasing of ancient rainbows,
An enchanted crock of gold,
The passing of phantom shadows,
Of every story, ever told.

In verdant isolation,
Metronomic time ticks hollow,
Bland of decoration,
In the land of phantom shadows.

Fascinating paths,
Dance the phantom shadows,
Time skips, cries and laughs,
In the land of phantom hollows.

Whence the twilight wails,
Amidst a kaleidoscopic dusk,
A waxing moon sets a sail,
Spiralling phantom shadows dust.

My glass, is half empty,
Some argue: surely, but half full?
But life I lived and loved a-plenty,
And tried to be, optimistically, never dull.

Of phantom shadows
Undulating before my eyes?
Golden memories of golden meadows,
Unforgotten treasure, in celebration of everyone,
Throughout my life.

Glenwyn Peter Evans

CONGRATULATIONS GLENWYN!

Of Phantom Shadows has been selected as the winning
poem in this collection. You win a fantastic *Harrods
Bulgravia Hamper* and we look forward to reading more of
your poetry in the future.

*The Belgravia contains a slection of wine
and spirits, biscuits, preserves, chocolate,
confectioery and accompaniments. Presented
with a natural traditional basket with a
Harrods leather tag.*

CELEBRATIONS WE CAN BUT TRY

Another celebration is here again
Through world's disasters, who's to blame?
G8 summit, world appeal
Millions suffering, starvation, drought
We can but try. Can this be real?

All charities, bringing aid to many
How can we help? I ask myself
Maybe a stall at our charter fair
My friends and I we can but try.

So wool and needles to the ready
Gifts and crafts readily accepted.
So many stalls, so much appeal
Can our work bring personal reward?
We can but try to make things happen at the fair.

Enjoy now, the colourful array
Life's too short let's enjoy our parts
Costumed people all around
Laughter fills this sunny day.

Money flowing, purses empty
Who is winning games galore?
Do we really know the score?
But hopefully our small donations
Will help the underprivileged nations.

God bless our work
Let's hope this century we get it right
No wars, pray peace be ours
We can but try and all people with grace survive.

E Saynor

THE VALLEY OF TIME

We're here but for a while,
to dance, to sing, to love in style.
To worship life and walk the mile
upon life's road with sheer abandonment,
surrendered hearts to suff'ring and enjoyment.

A baby born, a newling at the start,
with open eyes and open heart.
No boundaries, no barriers apart.
She is the world, the world is her
No evil, good, no power.

Sweet child now as you yearn
to find out more, so much to learn.
This is your life, this is your turn
to touch the light, the stars, the moon,
th' eternal sky. The world's in tune.

And as you dance this greatest symphony,
from Heaven to Earth now flows the energy.
Your earthly body tasting eternity.
This planetarium valley our hourly time
is but a part of life, a taste of bread and wine.

We build a wall, defend the woundedness inside.
We think we're safe, and we can hide
that deepest part, our essence opened wide . . .
your healing water gushes like a river
over this war-torn, broken heart . . . I shiver . . .

The fire's out, the phoenix is in flight
and leaves behind the darkness of the night,
faces the sunshine and the light
of truth and peace within, integrity.
Heaven and Earth in harmony . . .

Olga Allen

THE WEST WIND

Like birds before a lowering storm
The clouds flit over this darkening sky
The wind blows strong out from the west
To scatter far with mournful cry.

The waxing moon with watery ring
Now sails on high through fleeting cloud
Its shadowed face, when oft' times glimpsed
Is but a dead world's phantom shroud.

Where no life reigns and all is still
This bleak and barren wilderness
Knows not the lulling western winds
That dip to Earth in soft caress.

By silent marsh with waters still
And rank grass growing by the edge
Where plaintive plovers send their call
The west wind sighs amidst the sedge.

Then onward over the distant hills
To rest awhile in shadowed copse
Yet to rise again in sudden haste
Far fleeing 'ere the night dew drops.

With hasty gust by river's bank
To stir the waters, flowing deep
The ruffled waves dance far and wide
And sink again in murmuring sleep

So - on the rough inclement seas
Far-flinging spume over towering waves
That rush to pound the distant shores
With hollow boom and echo in the caves.

Over land and sea of unknown climes
From rugged peak to sandy bay
This ever vagrant spirit is
The western wind upon its way.

Julia Simpson

NO ONE IS PERFECT

Words of comfort
Is all I can say,
Songs of praise is what I'll sing,
Food on the table,
And clothes on your back
I will provide,
And as long as I am around,
There will always be a roof
Over your head.

When I needed help,
You did hot hesitate,
Or, turn your back on me,
You were my rock,
Without you,
I would never have survived.

Your kindness proved to me,
That people should not be judged
Because of their creed,
Colour or nationality,
Everyone is an individual
And should be given a chance.

We all have our faults,
Good and bad,
No one is perfect,
If we could try and remember that,
It would make life easier
And this world would be a better place.

Pauline E Reynolds

I THANK THEE

Father God, I thank Thee
Thank You for the opportunity
To let my spirit grow
By sending me below to learn
The things You would have me know
And let my spirit glow

Sweet Jesus I thank Thee
For Your gift of eternity
For each drop of blood
Each thorn upon Thy brow
Each lash that Thou has suffered
For my sins, that I may
Enter Heaven now
To Thee my head I bow

Holy Spirit I thank Thee
For Thy promptings and guidance
Which makes a better person of me
Holy angels I thank Thee
For times of protection
And your reminders of God's love
And the teachings on how the Lord
Would have me be

Thank You for the gift of understanding
The power to realise Thy love for me
Even though I be a sinner Thou has love for me
Heavenly Father I bow before Thee
And honour Thee, for Thy gifts of love
And I thank Thee for my free agency
To come to You on bended knee
Offering my love to Thee.

Anne Marshall

THE HEALING BALM OF LOVE

Love helps to heal the murky waters of despair
Bringing peace and tranquillity to a turbulent sky
As I bask in the balm that caresses my inner soul
My heart reaches out to the everlasting love I feel for another.

Not only can love create strength and courage
It can also be a source of contentment within
One of the greatest feelings of all
Is learning to love yourself no matter what transpires.

Healing can come in many ways
To promote well-being and deep happiness
As I live each day with a dose of respect and love for myself
I am able to spread this inner serenity towards cherished friends.

Marjory Price

FLASHBACK

A ten-year-old memory decided to call
He was smart and just as tall
Flashy car with girls in plenty
Things were good, a full inventory
Life was great just having a ball
He was so sure that he knew it all.

A ten second memory just crashed in
Shrunken now and so terribly thin
Flashy car and all girls gone
Where on Earth did it all go wrong?

He thought that he would run not crawl
Now I know he knew nothing at all.

H J Mazza

Marc Chagall - The Dance

Three horns erect, playing for the dance,
two on his head one in his pants; the bull-headed man
entrances as he bows the fingered strings,
of his blue violin.

Men and maids all twirl and prance:
dancing in the dance that makes deposits
that ensure all future life.
Food from the fertile plains, babies from wives.

And for all things that make for full
and satisfying lives.

So they dance and twirling sing
to the cadences of the sounds that the man
with the bull's head coaxes forth
with his bow, from all four of those
vibrating high bridged strings -

stretched tight, tuned to sing
as the voice of the blue violin,
trill after trill the voice, the voice,
the sound of a blue violin,

the dance, the dance.

Rick Storey

Two Trades

I am a poet and a potter,
Whilst the wheel in endless putter,
Through my lips in hurried stutter
Seem to slip,
My whirling thoughts.

Twirling wheel, and whirling phrases
Never ceasing, rarely pleasing.
So the search for true perfection
Will proceed.

Whilst my hand the slip applying,
Through my mind in figures flying.
Pictures of perfection,
Pots of delectation,
Indeed!

Slow the wheel and speed the memory
Turn the pot and twist the yarn.
In the kiln, the pot perfecting.
In the flame, my words rejecting.
Work the clay and start the song
Again.

Pat Ammundsen

Mattins In Springtime

Birds break first light's mute expectancy
With vernal call-signs trumpeting: *the sun is up!*
And excitement that again it's peaked
Like a parent performing a trick for a child
Who demands: *do it again . . . do it again!*

Songthrush, chaffinch, warbler,
Open their operatic throats
To vocalise dissonant decibels
That pre-empt the milkman's tintinnabulation
And commuter-car cacophony:

Arousing laggard sleepers
To an improbable crescendo of silence

Broken by a close insistent cockcrow.

David Sewell Hawkins

Celebrations

Fifteen years of Forward Press
Should be well celebrated
For a young and vigorous editing team,
How long we poets have waited
So let the cheers ring out at length,
Loud, long and unabated
As they go from strength to strength
Admired and highly rated.

Then fellow poets raise your glass
And pray that there is in store
Continued success of Forward Press,
For another fifteen years or more.

Norrie Ferguson

My Poem

What does it mean?
Nothing really, I just liked the words
The sounds, the cadences of metre

What's it about then?
Life, love, joy, death, hate, despair
You choose, it doesn't matter

It isn't a poem, there's no rhyme.
I know, but what do you want, blood?
Because that's what you've got
Torn from the living flesh
A bloody part of me, too painful to ignore
Too difficult to reach another way
Memories, visions, pictures beyond time
Glimpses of light across the void
A ledge of hope in the wall of the unknown

The blood seeps out across the page
But unseen, it drips to the floor.
It doesn't make sense.
I know, I just liked the words.

Patricia Smith

A Christian Quintile

Jesus
Fountain of Life
Beginning and our end,
For all to see, was and will be
Our God

the

God who
Is alive, active
And of the loving kind,
Available, accessible
I am

ready to

Transform,
Complete, renew
Those who turn back can be
Changed, in a moment, into
New robes.

Brian Strand

RECIPE FOR JOY

It isn't just the daffodils that make the spring,
Or the blue sky and the white clouds way up high.
It's not the green grass growing and sparkling with dew,
Or the warm breeze rustling softly, like a sigh.

It isn't even spring just because the new buds shoot,
From the branches of the trees, to turn them green.
It's not the hawthorn blossom, perfuming the air,
Or the forsythia's yellow starshine in-between.

No it isn't quite the colours of the flowers everywhere,
The whole of Nature bursting out in bloom.
The radiance of the sunshine, lighting up a world
That was darkened, in the shade of winter's gloom.

Just imagine all the wonder and the beauty all around,
If there was silence over everything.
No it isn't just the natural perfection of the Earth,
It's harmonious choirs of birds that make the spring!

It's the jubilation of the blackbird, the cooing of the dove,
The cawing of the crows in glorious flight.
The joy of the dawn chorus, heralding the day,
Sparrows chirping in the hedge, from morn till night.

It's thanks to God's love that we're all blessed with this season,
That delights our hearts and minds, through ears and eyes.
He sends the combination of the flowers and the birds,
That makes the spring a wonderful surprise.

Lorna Lea

THE PERFUME BOTTLE

A small perfume bottle
Fashioned for Princess Di
Her daily companion
Handled by her was I.

In palaces I lived
And moved in circles high.
Yet way in far-off places
The poor we'd not pass by.

With king-to-be I lived,
The princes I saw born.
Fulfilled daily duty
Until the fateful morn.

There in a dark tunnel
A blue-eyed princess lay
And from her jewelled handbag
Burst forth into the fray.

Years passed by unnoticed
As 'neath the car seat lay.
Until a great clear-out
With rubbish binned away.

Far in an Oxfam shop
I shone there on display
A wee girl with a bright smile
Excitedly did say,

'Mum, that perfume bottle
Please will you buy for me?
Next week is my birthday
I'll show my friends at tea.'

Ten pounds, the price they paid
Will help Sudan's project
And carry on Di's work
The starving ones protect.

Mary Hudson

SPIRIT IN THE MIND

You, for me materialise
And fill the vacuum
Of my desires;
As another solid
By my right-hand side,
Assembled to perfection
Of my thoughts.

You, hold my hand
In stress and need,
Your movement be
The comfort of my eyes;
Your existence, make
The bliss of every day.

Be my companion
In adventures chase,
Your conversation equal
To my own;
A blessing that will last
The span of life,
And to my hopes
Extend in endless term.

Sad, you are but a ghost
A ghost within myself
With absence of reality;
Just hope, unfulfilled
One of many, waiting
There - if called.

Henry J Green

SUZIE, RENDEZOUS SUR LA PLÁGE

Dusk fell like a mantle of gold tint
on black shadow
As the lone figure crossed the horizon
with easel and brush pressed closed to his breast
Nothing stirred in the sunset brilliance
But the silhouette of the four graces
in the falling darkness
As he came upon the scene of unlooked for inspiration
That likened to 'DéJeuner sur L'Herbe'
on this evening of enchantment
So the night hung suspended in timeless pleasure.

Sylvia Horder

ALL FOR FREE

All for free, all for free,
There is so much in the world to see,
A rainbow arc or a setting sun,
A silent meadow ere morning's begun.

All for free, all for free,
Open your eyes and then you can see,
Blossoms that burst on the orchard bough,
Valleys and streams which with beauty endow.

All for free, all for free,
A myriad of things for our luxury,
The smile of a babe, the stars above,
The light in the eye when love's begun.

All for free, all for free,
Look at the sight of such majesty
As that of a tree high in the air
And underneath bluebells everywhere.

All for free, all for free,
The calm or the spume of a storm-tossed sea,
Chaffinches, skylarks, creatures at play,
We should give thanks for these every day.

Reg James

THE OVER SIXTY CLUB

I have just become a member
Of a very special club
To which we all gain membership
Granted we live long enough
Yet why should 60 signify the end?
It should be a beginning
With time for fun with friends
At 59 one is busy
With work and energetic play
With great enthusiasm
For every passing day.
Then suddenly retirement looms
It seems a welcome state
With time for doing other things
Before it is too late.
The fateful day arrives
We must say farewell
To responsible employment
Energetic sport and fun
It is frightening how quickly
Friends and colleagues seem to find
They must treat you gently
Considered weak in heart and mind.
Yet I still play tennis
With the occasional ace
Finish the Sunday crossword
Albeit at a slower pace.
One does not atrophy in a single day
Life is still exciting
No matter what they say.

B Williams

MEMORIES PASS

Awaken shattered heroes
Foreign lands calling
Heartbeat against heartbeat
Whispering morning sun
Ribbon like bird in flight
Aboard deck sailing
Naturalised exposed freedom
Purplish-blue sea
Reflective dancing light
Ablaze of colour
Reminiscent gracious life
Mesmerising gleaming eyes
Dream within yourself
Smile, laughter, romance
Bittersweet tears
Lovers gone before
Myths of the past
Awe-inspiring ventures
Unleash our fate
Ongoing changing feelings
Scented air, milky-white clouds
Joyous, deep beauty
Far-off places
Affection washed over
Blinding effortless courage
Undeterred faithful desire
Brief predictable strike
Like hook into fish
Fertile delicate breath
Summer shade lingers.

Sharron Hollingsworth

MAMMA IS NOW GONE

Mamma is now gone. Far away to pastures new,
where birds sing beautifully for the few who
understand their lyrics and hum in time to
their sweet tune, which eases the pain that
runs through their veins, to hearts shattered
by those who wish to exterminate and obliterate
all traces of humanity by offering insincere
promises that fail to materialise and end up
being buried alive under old forgotten trees,
that are starved of air - never seeing the light
of day because, like us, they have no say.
No opinion as to how mankind should express its
desires, in barren lands that offer no respite
from prying eyes and over-sized mouths - who talk
the talk in a thousand tongues and take to the
streets to express their ideals but are shot down
like flies by ancient minds, who only accept that
which is true to them and kick-in-to-touch the
new-fangled thinking of a generation that dares to
believe that they can compete in a world where
everything is sold and life is so cheap!
The brave charge forward but are dealt a cruel blow
and are cut down to size, so that this becomes a
lesson which teaches them to accept the status quo
and tow the line that has been passed down from
those who know better and show us the way in which
we must think and stick to our place - by never
answering back or questioning what it is that we
must never, ever know!

T Kemran-Mustafa

THE RIVERS OF MY LIFE

By Findhorn's fast and sparkling stream
I sit and ponder in a dream
Of days gone by
When in my youth
I walked by rivers just as fine.

By Thames I strode
Hand in hand,
With boyfriend bold,
To Kew and Richmond we would walk
And even found some time to talk and maybe steal a kiss or two.

So life passed by
And step by step we found ourselves by Devon's shore
With rivers bounding from the moor.

We settled in an ancient town
And found the dart was near by hand
To give us joy and walks galore.

But life goes on - one's love is lost
So northward seemed to call me on.

So beside the Yorkshire Derwent fair
I settled with a partner there.
A smallish stream it seemed to me,
But never ceasing on its way to join the Ouse eventually.

Once more alone, all loved ones gone,
I travel further than before
To find myself by Moray's shore
And there find home for evermore.

So here I sit by Findhorn's stream
Keeping alive my youthful dream
But alas! my knees are stiff
My hips are false; I shall never do another waltz;
But looking back my life has been,
Full of honey, jam and cream.

V E Adamson

A DREAMER OF DREAMS
(To Whittaker Bradley)

Tell me - what do your eyes see?
Are they filled with a thousand dreams
As you listen to tales told by travelling men
Of places and things that they've seen?

Some men will always be dreamers
And listen to other men's tales
They will never feel the restless sea
Or a strong wind filling ships' sails.

But you were not just a dreamer
You lived the dreams in your eyes
You saw those faraway oceans
And the Southern Cross in the sky.

Yours was a restless spirit
In your heart burned a flickering flame
You stepped out through destiny's door
To a land that was new and untamed.

Now the journey of life is over
Do you lay in that faraway land?
Did your restless spirit find freedom?
Did you hold your dreams in your hand?

Howard Atkinson

THE FROG AND THE LILY

The lily's scent is subtle yet can hold your senses fast
but like the lily blossom her love's not meant to last.
Froggy loved his Lily from the moment that he spawned
he would sit and sing upon her pad from dusk till it was dawn.
Lily truly loved his voice, his song made her heart fond
she was glad that she was singled out from others in the pond.
Now as winter sets in on the water, her withered petals fall
the crumpled remnants of her splendour, drift off beyond recall.
Still Frog he can remember, as he sits on her wilting pad
his voice once filled with love songs, is now subdued and sad.
He lays himself beside her, still wrapped in Lily's fronds
his body soon decays and dies, his melody has gone.
Spring sunshine filters through the trees to replenish the forest pond
new shoots begin to spring and sprout as Lily is reborn.
Her beauty leaves you breathless as she looks over her domain
she spreads her scent into the air to enrapture hearts again.
No thoughts now of springtimes gone, her memory slate wiped clean
she blossoms now for love anew not old ones that have been.
For past loves must remain just that, like dreams in her winter sleep
already she has forgot the frog who died there at her feet.

George Holmes

PLAYGROUND TEARS

The day was bright, the day was dark
No one visited the little park,
The swings stood still and all forlorn
Bathed in morning's golden dawn
No one played there anymore
No children's laughter, it seemed withdrawn
Rust stood out upon the seats
Children playing, sharing sweets
It's all old-fashioned, so they say
There are better things to do and play
The grass was brown, all was dry
No shouts of *hello* or even *goodbye*
It's all gone now, better things to do
Isn't that like me and you?

John Malley

O PULSE OF MY WORLD

Fast moving waters wash me away
Wash me away to my sea!
Wonderful waves love me gently
Powerful waves beat me carefully
Lash my body against your rocks
And allow me once more to be *me*,
Together with you, my sea.
My heart in volcanic upheaval
I'm aware your power can be evil
You corrode metal anchors and hulls
You throw back to the beach old wood,
Crustaceans and Skulls, yet I love you!
I'm your moon and tidal daughter
Living within your heartbeat
Yet you sent hurricanes to destroy me
And slaughter.
Don't exile me for your powerful gain
Like the anchors in slow decay
Part of me spared just for today.
I forgive you for my pain.
Driftwood fires crackle on your shore
Warming the pulse of my world
The push and pull of the Earth at my door
Wash me back to my sea once more.
Please tame your winds to mild
For I'm still your moon and tide child
O pulse of my world.

J W Whiteacre

LONELY THOUGHTS

In the nebulous world of shifting shadows
That shroud the banks of an autumn stream
There lives a thought from long ago -
By a charcoal burner and his dream
To leave this place where ghostly wreaths
Of smoke curl and twist throughout the trees.
Where sounds of things so long thought dead
Strike terror into heart and head -
The thought of something not quite known
Gives way to fear of being alone.
And yet - no need to fear the sound
Of rustling leaves upon the ground
Or birds singing in the trees.
Of insects' murmurs, of humming bees.
The soft and gentle velvet wand
Of a butterfly's wing
Or a lady's hand.
Perhaps my mind has told me lies
And it's only the wind in the trees that sighs.
The ghosts in the woods I should not fear
For now my future's crystal clear.
All of these things I cannot leave,
For the rest of my life I know I'd grieve
To leave the things I've come to love
The fields, the woods, a cooing dove.
The charcoal burner's sitting there,
A gentle smile upon his lips,
He wipes a smut from off his face,
Then stands and places hands on hips.
'My son,' he says, 'you've become a man today,'
Then smiles again and fades away.
So all my fears have come to nought,
I'm staying with my lonely thoughts.

Daniel P Callaghan

THE COUCH POTATO

Our Bobby loves the telly, but aa like ter dance a lot.
Modern, line or sequence, it doesn't matter what.
Bobby peers up from the football with accents firm and clear,
Ses, 'It's ower cad ter gan oot, pet! Trail oot in this? Nee fear!'

'What about the shoppin'? Wu hev nee mince or veg.
A loaf of bread and pint of milk would keep us from the edge.'
'Aa divn't fear starvation while aave got me crate of beer,
It's ower cad ter gan oot, pet, trail oot in this? Nee fear!'

'Well what aboot the aad folk, wu hev ter keep an eye,
Wu need ter check that all is well, wu'll hever ter gan up-bye!'
'Me father's aaful crabby 'n me sister lives quite near,
It's ower cad ter gan oot pet, trail oot in this? Nee fear!'

'The day is warm and sunny, the air is fresh and clear
Wu need ter hav some exercise with a walk along the pier.'
'Gan oot yersel, yer'll like it more without me at your rear,
It's far ower *hot* te be oot pet, trail oot in this? *Nee fear!*'

Meg Stephenson

A WONDERFUL WORLD

What a wonderful world if all could be
As happy as me today.

They could laugh and sing and clap their hands
In a warm and wonderful way.

Pigs would fly and flap their wings
And elephants sing and dance

The blind would see and the hungry eat
And the poor would be given their chance.

The trees would talk and flowers walk
And donkeys leapfrog in the fields.

The fighting would cease and in would come peace
And the sick would all be healed.

Chickens would crow and cocks lay eggs
And bricks would float on the sea.

Mountains would move and deserts cool
And storms would cease to be.

Each pebble and stone would turn to gold
Each thistle a lollipop sweet

And enemies change to shake the hand
Of every stranger they meet.

Dogs would give milk and sheep would miaow
We'd live till eternity.

What a wonderful place the world would be
If all were as happy as me.

Helen E Langstone

MY LOVE FOR YOU

No rose's hue ever wafted before my sense of smell -
ever matched your beauteous frame or none that I can tell.
Though mighty Zeus at Mount Olympia did reign
did dispatch his powers over the gods he did claim.
His magic powers though he could bestow,
would never separate or compare to the bottomless pit of love
stored within my heart's domain forever new.
My love, languishing softly, forever blooming
in my treasure store of love, just for you.

John Gaze

THE SEASONS OF OUR LIVES

Our dawn - the spring - the babe in arms
The four-hour feeds, the rattles, teething
Little jars of food, a cuddly toy,
He sits erect, the spine developing.
Intelligence far outshoots his growth
He recognises people
He's put to bed - all those long sleeps
His batteries recharged for him to yell.

Now summer - the growing child,
The education, the music, the swimming.
The wonder of the youth grown to man
Fulfilled with happiness and striving.
A wife maybe, but certainly a motor
The engine roars with expectation.
From university, some honours worked for
- Still music, writing for a band.
A pram, a cot, box of disposable nappies
The new arrival's coming soon in summer.

The autumn in our lives, the backache
The greying hair, the loss of it, the wrinkles.
The television, writing, golfing.
Investments, being a grandad, fishing.
The timeshare, club and garden
Begonias good enough for showing.
The cauliflowers as big as footballs
The beans like long, green rulers growing.
The music, tapes, old favourite records.
The garage, bigger than a cottage.

Soon winter, not cold for some, but cosy
To reap life's store of industry and striving
Retirement - what it is, is undecided
More like hard work than holiday you know.
An early riser, little sleep is needed
A walking stick will help to oil the hinges
The contact lenses, holiday retirement flat

The family round him - grandson, niece and nephew
It is the winter now, leaves on the trees have withered
But spring is seen, the babe, the cuddly toy, the highchair
Soon it is time for one life's work to be done.

Joan Peacock

A CELEBRATION

I would like to contribute to Forward Press,
To celebrate poetry is my only guess!
In my time I have written quite a few,
This is one that is special and new!

On this anniversary I can participate,
To mark a very special date!
As with all others, I do my stint,
To see my name go down in print!
With all the poets in our nation,
I am just one person in creation!
Putting my thoughts to the test,
Trying always to do my best!
Hoping the editor will like my work,
Not really knowing, I can get some perk!
To win something would be nice,
Though I think it is like the toss of a dice!
So just to prove that I can write,
I will send my poem this very night.
Sending my best wishes to Forward Press,
For fifteen years of great success.

Joyce Hallifield

SOMEONE

someone saved my soul tonight
someone knows my name
someone took the pieces of my heart
and put them together again

someone took me in his arms
someone held me tight
someone showed me passion
and turned darkness into light

someone kissed me gently
someone took away the pain
someone showed me real love
and ignited the flame

someone who takes good care of me
someone who wipes my tears
someone who knows my desires
someone who knows my fears

someone I love so dearly
someone I love so true
someone I worship and adore
that someone is you.

Jean Lilian Bramhill

I SAID A PRAYER FOR YOU TODAY

I said a prayer for you today
    And know God must have heard.
I felt the answer in my heart
    Though he said not a word.
I didn't ask for wealth or fame
    (I knew you wouldn't mind)
I asked for priceless treasures rare
    Of a more lasting kind . . .
I prayed that he'd be near you
    At the start of each new day
To grant you health and blessings fair
    And friends to share your way.
I asked for happiness for you
    In all things great and small
But that you'd know his loving care
    I prayed the most of all.

Sharon Elton

ON THE DESTRUCTION OF THE ESSEX
COUNTRYSIDE

Farewell to my county
    the land of my birth
Man covets thy bounty
    and concretes your earth.

Farewell to the farmland
    and old moated halls
and timber-framed cottages
    with pargetted walls.

Farewell to quiet picturesque places
    leafy, thatched and garden-tilled
as developers snatch these open spaces
    to make them tarmac and noise-filled.

Farewell to medieval timbered town
    with historic church and guildhall,
no longer unspoilt and a place of renown
    but having to yield to the planners' call.

Farewell to the county as destruction is wrought
    by building more houses and vulgar runways
in the sham name of progress, sparing no thought
    for the rich heritage of earlier days.

Alistair L Lawrence

JULY IN CAMERA

In the secluded glory
of this fresh, peaceful morning,
light paints all colours with the sun's intensity;
lending pinks, reds, subtle yellows to the flower heads of roses
which, climbing, spread to enter where the windows lean to see;
clover's soft, green, lucky leaves lie low as mowers pass,
buttercups dot a shaded patch beneath the apple trees,
spiraea is voluminous, almost kneeling to mown grass,
showing bunches of magenta to the searching honeybees.

Here a tall, thick, beech hedge
frames these mounted July pictures
amid the blended fragrance of pre-breakfast morning air;
fruit trees in abstraction as they've shed this season's cherries
though vigorous currant bushes lean down laden with their share;
amongst these leaves hang clusters, beaded bright as polished jet,
such pleasure from familiar scent of bold fruit swinging there,
stragglers among strawberries but plump raspberries ripen yet,
picked for wine, jam and sweet desserts, all delicious summer fare.

In the brightening stillness
of this sparkling summer morning
are two energetic wrens which skip to songs the robin brings;
low in a straight line, aiming for the river's bank-side reeds
flies a heron in thin pencil shape with large, slow, flapping wings;
onto lupins with their fledglings settle sparrows for their feeds
pecking aphids that debilitate the beauty of each flower,
blackbirds guard new nests and young over which the cock bird sings
as ultramarine strengthens before morning's open court's next hour.

Dennis Marshall

SNOWFLAKE

Sunlight on a frozen lake,
A snowflake lost in a winter wind,
I flutter down, skim its smooth surface.
I stand up on my star-like points,
Shimmer, sparkle,
Light as thistledown.

Then I see you.
Across the ice I speed my thoughts,
My everlasting longing.
The magic begins -
My form solidifies, changes.
Arms and legs shape and are strong.
I leap towards you; you catch me,
Hold close my imitation human form,
Then throw me as if you knew
It was only real for a while.

The dance has started,
We whirl and you hold me
With that strength
That turns winter pools to ice,
But there is sunlight in your eyes
And I melt into you,
And in the echo of your thoughts,
The intimacy of your touch,
The pulse of your love,
My body is renewed
Until the dance is over.
I am yours to bend, command, embrace.
Without you I am only ice,
My essence is only winter.
I kiss your mouth and you remember.

Pamela Harvey

MINING

Sweat-streaked, semi-naked
He aims the tungsten tip
Screaming!
The bit bites deep
Into the resistant mass.

He prods the wound
Packing the lethal dressing
Retreats
A warning klaxon
Terrible seconds of waiting.

A dull blast
Tearing, shuddering shocks
Stillness
Rumbling, a roaring agony
A final breath of dust.

Men survey the dripping orifice
The scattered viscera
Crawl
Over skeletal fragments
To harvest exposed veins.

Pamela Sanders

TORMENT OF THE RING

Looking back it was never meant to last
        The flirtatious nature of her spirit
Was imprisoned by the band of gold
        Pressed on her by pregnancy.
The childlike insistence on matrimonial tradition
        Taking no heed of his limited resources
Or her condition
        Sent alarm bells ringing.
Surprisingly she had a flair for motherhood
        From those precious baby stages,
Attentive, caring, almost doting.
        It was he who lacked in words if not deeds
The sentiments to give her
        A more secure awareness of his presence.
The financial struggle to establish themselves
        Bound them together.
A last, free of childcare
        With city job carefully chosen
The opportunity for flattery and adulation
        Her ego craved.
Nights out with the girls became more frequent
        Homecoming later, excuses more trivial.
Encouraging to socialise on his own
        Her breathless excitement, flushed face
On more than one late excursion
        Reminded him of a summer evening
Wrestling playfully on flattened hay
        Her thin cotton dress rucked high.
Jealousy and suspicion were now ripe
        He knew he was being taken for a fool
The marriage was as good as over,
        Tight-lipped he refused to question
Afraid of the truth, his pride still intact.
        Self-doubt also festered
Would a daily show of adoration
        With a weekly bunch of roses
Have sufficed to keep her on track?
        Too late, he would never know
On table, a note topped by her band of gold
        She had left her torment behind.

Robert Fallon

TO THE LITTLE ONE

This time has come, you're on your way
You meet your lovely parents today
Have no fears, little one
Maybe a daughter, maybe a son
For you were given an angel to care
To hold your hand, always be there
A mummy and daddy who love you so
Only love and joy with them you will know
As you enter this world, rest assured
That you will always be adored
Your life before you, love will abound
Enjoying touch, enjoying sound
Little one, as you have lovingly grown
Already so much care you've been shown
From the two who bore you and an angel's wing
Today all your family will sing
I wish you only happiness and joy
No difference if you are a girl or a boy
You have now a nest to build your life
With a lovely daddy and his precious wife.

God bless you
                G Auntie Sue

Sue Starling

MY LIFE NOW

The kiss was like the touch of a butterfly's wing,
But to my heart such joy did it bring.
I asked myself what would it evoke,
For friendship and deeper relations it spoke.
Blue shining eyes of gentleness and care,
As we met occasionally, matters to share.
I felt I had become of a life a part,
And hoped the journey would not bring 'smart'.
For this has happened to my life before,
And from a rift I was left heart-sore.
But now it seems like the flow and the ebb of the shore,
As growth revealed caring and concern more.
I was asked to do things that would use my gifts,
Artwork, writings to precis and help family rifts.
Forward Press has opportuned me poems to write,
And they have printed my small efforts to my delight.
There was teasing as I shared of 'There's more to you than
                                meets the eye.'

Which led to understanding that I need not be shy.
Though we cannot, it seems, often meet,
There are occasions on which we can greet.
There is a link that seems like an invisible line,
Silent thoughts, smiles and handshakes with mine,
There is an appreciation of what I do,
Which helps me feel valued and not my time rue.
For, 'after care of cardiac arrest', restored to health,
All the good experiences have been a great wealth.
Now my life's river gently flows,
Hoping in love, peace and virtue it grows.

Sister Trinity Tarr

ODE TO THE FARMER

The farmer 'e were once a serf,
Though 'e moved up to yeoman,
Still working in the wind and mud,
'Less war called 'im for bowman.

'E 'ad 'is chickens, pig and sheep,
'Is good 'orse and 'is cow.
'E made a sturdy oaken cart,
And walked behind 'is plough.

The muck from all 'is animals,
It fed 'is fields of corn,
And that in turn 'is livestock fed,
And seed for next spring's dawn.

'Is leather, feathers, wool and fur,
From cow, goose, sheep and coney,
Were cured and woven, teased or spun,
All natural-like, not phoney.

'Is timber from 'is copses came,
'Is thatch from this year's wheat.
'Is walls from stones cleared from 'is fields,
For buildings safe and neat.

'Is life were 'ard, but earned respect,
'E welcomed better tools,
And better animals and seeds,
But worked with nature's rules.

But science offered him the world,
With riches past believing.
So back to serfdom he's been led,
With politics deceiving.

Margaret Reichlin

THE GENTLEMAN'S GAME

The game of golf has altered much
Since its first inception.
The clothes, the clubs, the course have all
Changed beyond conception.

A jacket, tie, plus-fours, brown brogues
Were essential for the day.
Your appearance was what counted,
Not the way that you could play.
Now, it's shirts and polo sweaters
And purpose-made spiked shoes;
With trendy, tailored flannels
In multicoloured hues.

Club shafts were made of hickory
With heads of curious shapes.
Each mashie, spoon and brassie
Had grips wrapped in leather tapes.
First steel, then carbon-shafted clubs
Sent that small ball out of sight.
Rubber covers replaced leather
To keep grips dry and tight.

The fairways once were grazed by sheep,
Wire fences round each green.
The course looked like a moorland heath,
Green-keepers never seen.
Large mowers have replaced the sheep,
Each green's well-manicured.
All bunkers look immaculate -
Course quality assured.

The game of golf has altered much,
But one thing stays the same.
No round's been played in eighteen strokes -
But then, it's just a game!

Brian M Wood

THE BEST THINGS IN LIFE ARE FREE

The best things in life are free,
Some may say, 'How can this be?'
But I believe it is very true
There's lots of good things to see and do.

On a nice warm summer's day,
I just love to wend my way,
To the seaside, that's the place for me,
In fact, there is nowhere else I'd rather be.

When I was young, a game I used to play
Was to run into the sea and say,
'You can't catch me, you can't catch me!'
Then rush back before the waves splashed me.

Nevertheless, you could always bet,
The bottom of my dress got very wet,
But I didn't mind one little bit,
It soon dried out when in the sun I'd sit.

These memories I still treasure,
Even now, I derive much pleasure,
By going to the seaside to paddle my feet.
At my age, it is a very special treat.

So when I say, the best things in life are free,
Maybe now, you will believe me,
For the very air we breathe, whereby we live,
We to the Lord our thanks should give.

Irene Morris

PRESS ON FORWARD

Bring out the wine to toast the muse,
With all who share the pen and page,
Poets of the present time and,
The poets of another age.

To Will of Avon raise a glass,
Who might of Forward Press approve,
A people's poet, born to move,
The heart of man and boy and lass.

Let's celebrate the story too,
Article and well-penned letter,
Magazine and anthology,
Let success get ever better.

Fifteen years, we are yet but young,
May it go on for many more,
Let Forward Press have praises sung,
For this is what we write things for!

*'Well, in part. With my best wishes
and good luck.'*

Kathleen M Scatchard

NAPPY TALK

He talks to her in his own strange way,
She does not understand him
But she seems to know what he says.
No verbs pass between them
No syllables or nouns,
Just tenderness of touch
And assuring familiar sounds.
He shouts with all the breath in his lungs,
Words lost in translation
As they converse in alien tongues.
Their language is the same
A primitive verbal storm,
No consonants or vowels rain down
Between a mother and her newborn.

Keith Tissington

GOLDEN DREAMS

Take my hand my darling
And I will lead the way
Through nightly golden dreams
And troubles of the day

Take my hand and hold it firm
Whilst we walk in fairy glens
We'll sit beside a babbling brook
And sleep on beds of fern

Come with me my dearest
Along the winding woodland way
We'll stroll among the bluebells
And watch the fairies play

We'll drink from golden flower cups
Taste the morning dew
And fly on wings of gossamer
Dream of pixies too

We'll sit atop a mushroom
To watch the world go by
See fairies dancing in the glen
Then chase a butterfly

Come with me my dearest love
Where the treetops softly sway
And childhood dreams will all come true
Perhaps some other day.

John W Hewing

I FOUND YOU

Life seemed dull
Just taking things in my stride
Until I found you to have by my side,
You're more precious than diamonds
More valuable than silver or gold
And in my heart you I'll forever hold,
Dreams really can come true
Anything is possible as I have found you.

Diane Harbottle

BEING A POET

'You are a poet,' he said, 'how does that feel?'

'Like nothing on Earth, I think, like I am bleeding words
It calms my system, but fires my imagination

It loses me in worlds of far-reaching desperation
But sends me joyous, flying through the stars

It is as painful as losing someone close
Or as happy as welcoming a newborn son

How I strain for that finished word or meaning
Then rejoice in gaining a simple rhyme

It is like opening my fractured heart for all to see
Yet it feels so good to share the depth of pain

It is all consuming and it bares my tortured soul
While bringing peace and happiness at my lowest ebb

It is like being sad or happy and not knowing which it is
It is my whole life but has no part in my existence

Nothing can beat the feeling of a dam bursting flow of words
But who can know the frustration of a blank page or line?

Being a poet is a punishment and a reward for life's many paths
And how does it feel? Above everything else, *free and alive!*'

Sam Kelly

THE POWER

I am the wind, I am the sun
I am the night when day is done
I am the sea and sky above
I am the clouds that fly like a dove
I am the dawn when morning is nigh
I am the sunlight that lightens the sky
I am the one that lifts men's souls
I am the spirit that makes men whole
I move along amongst all things
I am the power that makes tides fling
Their waves over rocks and sand
I am the force that shapes the land
I make the mountains, hills and vales
I carve the rivers that flow through dales
I am the look in children's eyes
That makes mothers laugh or cry
I am the music and the sound
Which eases hearts and makes men proud
But with all these forces that time brings
What would it be like without all these things?

M Wright

AIRA FORCE

(For Marion)

Past Dockray village the Aira Beck flows;
To enter Ullswater's western shores.
Cascading down the Aira Force,
The water rushes on its course.
We looked upon your towering height,
Admired the chimera's dance of light.
We paused a moment on our way
A trout within the shallows lay.
Your beauty held us in its power,
We knew the names of every flower.
What beauties I have seen tonight,
The sky was like a sea of light.
And though the morning brought the rain;
My spirits felt renewed again . . .
I thought of summers - now long past
And wished this life would ever last . . .

Robert Carson

STILL HERE

I may have died
But I still see
All the tears
You cry for me

Though your loss feels
Too much to bear
It shows to me
How much you care

You thought I'd gone
I did not go
How could I
When you felt so low?

You thought I'd left
I did not leave
I sit beside you
While you grieve

I sit beside you while you weep
I lie beside you while you sleep
With every tear I'm here.

Sheila Jane Hobson

SPRING

I walked along this path for many a day in the cold winter,
With the ground laid bare.
Seeking out the beauty which surrounded it as the floor lay cold
And frost-bitten with tiny glistening specks of white dust.
Life stood still with nature,
But the beauty I found was undiscovered until

A yellow invasion sundered the corner of my eye,
My curiosity worked in harmony as my vision focused on the mass
Of yellow which rose up like a powerful wave.
Blinding out the thoughts I once had, I observed this great blanket
Of yellow which oppressed the ripe bushes in the background.

What was once opaque to the mind suddenly became transparent
Like running water,
The value and quality of time was a gift; not to be undermined.
Previous my thoughts along this cold, empty desolate walk
Were never interrupted by such a scene of beauty,
It was a voluptuous sight, untouched by time.

I dipped my hand resentfully into the unmarked territory
Of the golden yellow basket,
I was a virgin to this skill, between my fingers I felt the warmth
Between us, as the sun glistened romantically,
It moved gracefully, gliding peacefully like a swan on the water.

A low din bellowed with my ears as I picked it, the still moment
Was nestled with a light breeze as their heads swayed.
To my nose an aroma rose upwards as the scent unravelled
My taste, it was sweet, like a moment of passion.
I scurried home the usual way, wearing my yellow possession
Like a weapon of pride. I placed it in safe embedment.

Time passed as I watched my beautiful prize stand proudly,
Basking in the bright tint of the sun, with its head held high.
Puzzled my mind was, when no longer did pride hang over this gift,
Instead I saw a picture of pain and shame as it began to wither
Into a brittle ball, with its beautiful yellow no longer to be seen.

As I thought with the captivity of my mind, I realised the value
And quality of time,
Once my walk was desolated but then fulfilled by my proud daffodil.
I had watched spring pass through its course as I looked on
With the life and death of a daffodil.
I dazed in a tranquil dream, looking at the power nature can possess.

John D Savage

DESTINY

Out of the darkness that hides me
Black as pitch from north to south
I thank whatever gods there be
For my unconquerable spirit
And in these true circumstances
I have no fear, I stand aloft, and
While under this quirk of fate
My heart is heavy, it's full of hate
Beyond this place of wrath and tears
Which brings out the horror of the years
And yet with the menace and fears
They shall find me ready for my peers.
It matters not how I play this game
Change the rules it is still the same
For my fate rests deep down within me
As I am the true master of my own destiny.

Guthrie Morrison

SIREN SONG
(An Ulster Legend)

He walked the sands silvered in the moonlight,
His heart empty as the dried-up shells beneath his feet;
Soon, the sound of singing came ringing
Round the rocks across the bay where the soft sway
Of the sea carried the notes to shore;
He listened, and the magic closed around him,
Embracing, enfolding him in its beauty
Until his soul was steeped in each note, each ripple
Of the tide rolling in across the sands;
When the tide was full - his heart, too -
He turned and saw her, the source of that sweet sound,
The lure no man can resist, the irresistible lips
Pursing for a kiss, the flowing hair
Concealing breasts more fair than any other,
The graceful movement propelling her forward
Through the water; near, closer, clearer came the song,
Thronging his heart, his brain, his being,
Until they were no longer his . . .

The beach lay bare, save for
A strew of seaweed bunched and blown,
Stones thrown up by the tide and the dry husks of shells:
There, where the waves wrapped round the rocks,
The line of footprints ended,
Blended with the silver trail that shone
Under the stars, and in the far distance
A sweeter note than seamews crying
Mingled with the ceaseless sighing of the sea.

Betty McIlroy

OLIVIA'S PRESENT

He was put in my hand all slimy and cold.
He was only a baby but looked really old.
His topside convex, his underside flat,
Now who on this Earth could possibly love that?
Beady eyes and creepy claws
And not a nice colour either.
Not green, brown or yellow, he was neither.
He made no noise, whatever he did
He occasionally blinked, with only one eyelid
A misnomer as well - they call him a 'pet'
But I've seen nothing resembling that title as yet!
What use could he be to anyone, not just to me?
He can't be cuddled or stroked
He won't sleep on the bed
If you took him for a walk, you'd be gone for a year
And the strain of it all
Would leave him half-dead.
Oh dear!
And just when I thought, *what a terrible mistake*,
He stared at me hard, so an effort I did make
I gave him some greens and then watched him feasting
He woke in the morning and gave me a greeting
The same hard stare
But this time with love
Eyes twinkling with glee, ecstatic to see me
My lovely little beastie!
To care about me, seems his only purpose
And it matters no more that he's only a tortoise

Ssshhh! He's sleeping now . . .

C S Hindshaw

THE NET

At first, it was so easy,
We moved ahead,
No resistance,
Carefree.

Soon aware,
A lagging,
And shortly, we moved on,
Though some of the greater ones
Were no longer around,
Somehow, left behind.

I had no problems,
I just bode,
Until it appeared to me,
The opening,
The way through.

Lately it's been hard.
There are more restrictions,
While the new wee ones whiz by,
Carefree.

I'm difficulty.
Now it hurts.
I squeeze,
To pull myself through.

What were my goals back then?
Did I miss the chance
To be singled out
Sifted through nature's riddle,
One of the trillion few
Pure specks of gold,
Carefully sprinkled
On the sparkling shore?

Did I get too large?
Too fat? . . . Impure?
Or too old?

Now I'm stuck
In the net!

F Ian Tiso

CONFUSION

I can't quite explain
The way you make me feel
It's just so amazing
The feeling is unreal

You make me feel I'm glowing
I feel so warm inside
You make me feel so special
Yet these feelings I have to hide

For if I could, I'd be with you
And happy I would be
Life would be so splendid
I would feel contented, you and me

But I just don't know what's right for you
Or even what you want
All I know is that you make me feel this way
And the feeling is one I want.

Gemma Steele

GATEWAYS TO LIFE

There's harsh groans and coaxing voices,
A slap, a cry of pain,
A sharp intake of breath.
The gateway to life
Is breached

Reading, writing, arithmetic,
Trigonometry, English,
Qualifications.
The gateway to success
Is preached.

A pretty face, a smile,
A slim waist, a pert bum,
A quick glance.
The gateway to love
Is unleashed.

Years roll by, kids flee the nest,
Anticipation, jubilation,
Weariness.
The gateway to retirement
Is reached.

Gentle walks on creaking joints,
Grandchildren, memories,
St Peter.
The final gateway,
Life is complete.

C Matthews

A MOST FORTUNATE BEING

I'm glad I am who I am
My throat is not dry
As the millions whose screams are not heard
And oceans of tears
From the suffering
And torture through centuries
By Man filled with the Devil
Knowing only bloodlust.
The fear and horror continues universal
I escape the floods in far-off lands
The deaths in that continent dark, so ghastly
The sea and its constant hunger for victims
The earthquakes in other lands
The machines that fly with imperfections
And crash with helpless lost souls
The contributions I give to alleviate the misery
Yet little help in a hopeless cause
But I survive, I survive
Oh Lord, how fortunate am I
That by accident of birth
And selfishly, I feel happy
By being who I am
The agony of the innocent
Incarcerated for year upon year
The nightmare each night
The injustices prevailing
Some may be helped
But nature is cruel
I view it all from a distance
And happy that I am who I am.

Peter Belford

GOBBLEDEGOOK

In Timbuktu there was a man
More powerful than Kublai Khan,
Who had within his palace walls
Many labyrinthine halls,
Where all the world would go to play
And then they couldn't get away
From that most powerful of men
Who lured them all into his den.

He had rooms full of waifs and strays,
Of women corseted in stays,
Of all those damsels in distress
Who'd got themselves into a mess,
Of knights, forever clad in armour,
The milkmaid and the dairy farmer,
The writer with his quill and pen,
The duck, the goose, the cow, the hen.

When he was hungry, like the gannet
He gobbled most things on the planet.
Then asked himself the pressing question
Which ones gave him indigestion?
Not the nun in sacred habit,
Not the hare and not the rabbit,
Not the soldier with his rifle
Who made his guts ache just a trifle.

The things he found most hard to swallow
Down his throat all dark and hollow,
Were Richard Branson with balloons,
Uri Geller bending spoons,
John Major, Tony Blair and Paddy,
Giant Haystacks and Big Daddy,
Mick Jagger with his rubber lips
And Cher with all her plastic bits.

But what really most upset the man,
More powerful than Kublai Khan,
Was eating all the Ku Klux Klan!

Joyce Walker

FALLING LEAVES

(Written during my term as Oxfordshire County Councillor)

Autumn is upon us
Notice the falling leaves
Everywhere the evenings draw in early darkness
Heart and soul must remain grateful for all mercies

Leaves large or small have lovely shape
Turning colour from green to orange and to brown
Fallen leaves are beautiful wherever they fall and escape
Looking like the ground is in a leafy patchwork decorative gown

The mighty wind blows strong and cold
Now there is need to wear woollen clothes
Cold mighty wind affecting the old
If not properly dressed and out watching the landscape
                                              of fallen leaves

Thoughts of winter approaching before our eyes
Leaves left to rot
Memories of fallen leaves
To be used as compost

If living in Oxford with the many spires
In the passing of autumn and dark evenings drawing in
Obscuring spires viewing for many living in Oxfordshire
For many there will be evenings in

Yet in daylight there is beauty
Of varying shades of autumn-fallen leaves on the ground
Environment of mingled leaf colours drawing the eyes to a duty
To see and appreciate all there is around.

Olive May McIntosh-Stedman

VIC (VERY IMPORTANT CLOWN)

I live in a room of a very large house
High up on a rather long shelf,
I'm not on my own - to my left there's a gnome
And on my right a very short elf.
On the shelf down below is a doll with a bow
While up above is a big teddy bear,
He's a rather soft touch, though he doesn't say much
Just sits in his old rocking chair.
The Russian doll appears to be rather snooty
She just stands in the corner - but my, what a beauty!
With her red velvet coat and black Cossack boots
Even the old wooden owl gives a hoot.

Now, when our little owner lies down for the night
And there's only the moon to give us some light,
We come out of the closet, the boxes and shelves
To dance with the fairies, the gnomes and the elves.
The animals come from the ark two by two
Paddington Bear, Eeyore, Tigger and Pooh
The dolls do the Can-Can; old owl starts to sing
Even the bell on the doll's house rings.
One of the gnomes does some magic tricks
With some string and a brush and a few Lego bricks.
He's really quite good, and I ought to know
I'm a clown by trade - I've done many a show.
But one day the box I was in caught fire
So it was decided that I should retire,
And that's why it is, I sit on a shelf
Somewhere between a gnome and an elf.

But I'm never lonely, quite the reverse
I practise all day my tricks and my verse,
So when darkness comes I am ready to go
To be once again the star of the show.

Diane Howard

AN ENIGMA

Brindle-coloured, body long, just inches off the ground.
Rippling muscles, sturdy legs and massive paws as well.
Intelligence in every pore, and wildly wagging tail.
Alert to all that's going on, alert to every sound.

Nose a-quivering, smiling jaws, with lolling long pink tongue.
Tearing round the garden, flattening all the plants,
Hoping that we'll join him in his merry dance.
Everything is wonderful when you're only one!

We know that he must be with us, to see what we're about.
Into every corner and up the stairs he can't get down!
Rushing back and forwards, tripping up just like a clown,
Ears always flapping madly, and they're often inside out!

How can one resist him, as he turns around to stare
At anyone who's watching him, with one paw in the air?

Inquiring looks remind us that he's ready for his walk.
Receiving cuddles, hugs and pats from everyone we meet,
Enjoying the attention as he gambols down the street.
Do we have to go in now? He almost seems to talk.

Doorbell's ringing, off he goes with eager sparkling eyes.
And if it is the telephone, of course he must be there.
Curling up against your legs or underneath your chair,
Hoping you won't talk too long if on your feet he lies.

Snoring in his basket or fast asleep upon the floor,
His paws relaxed beside him, out for the count you're sure,
Until a sudden visitor comes knocking at the door!

Now if you'd like to know just who this rhyme is all about,
Do note each line's initial letter and you'll soon find out.

Lucy M Kaye

KYM

We cannot see our daughter,
We cannot touch her hand,
The Lord came down and took her,
To what He calls the 'Promised Land'.
The pain, the hurt, the heartache,
For those who are left behind,
We do not think the Lord, to us,
Has been so very kind.
What is life to us without her?
Only memories for us to share,
They tell us that the pain will go,
But please Lord, tell us where.
Lord, we try to be forgiving,
For knowing that You're there,
But You took our daughter, Kym,
From us and left us in despair.
We cannot pray at this sad time,
We don't think that it's fair,
The only peace that we shall have
Is when we meet Kym there.

Aubrey Abram

THE MARBLE MIRACLE

In chalky classrooms of long ago
My mind meandered to your attentive face.
One lesson recalled your perfect beauty
Was that as long ago as thirty-six?
The lily I drew was graceless compared to you
The teacher frowning, shook his head,
'You are too young for the flower of death.'
He taught Latin, dead as any flower.
I gave you the drawing which drew a smile
More beautiful than time or rhyme.
In my mind unspoken words were etched
'I will love that girl until I die.'
Now at her graveside, my face is lily-white
I've forgotten all the Latin, but not this maid
See roses lie upon the ground so cold
I have regrets as I turn away
I never drew a rose or,
Knew her worth or age
I know it now, I see through my tears
And read it on her marble page.

K N Jeffery

THE FORTUNE TELLER

Look into my crystal ball,
She looks at me and smiles,
Her eyes see through my very soul,
And reads my life in miles.

'Oh tell me that my future's bright,
And I will soon be free,
Say you see a lovely calm,
Beyond my stormy sea.'

Her eyes retreat, my spirit bared,
Her face is dark and sad,
'A long and bloodied battle yet,
Before your peace be had.'

Vida Taylor

SO I BELIEVE

A heaven awaits me - so I am told
        When my Shepherd calls me to the fold
All happiness greets me - so I am told
        No want, no sorrow, no growing old
Goodness and mercy is there to behold
        With joy everlasting - so I am told.

Surrounded by glory - I've heard it said
        Loved ones will greet me tho' long since dead
And for all eternity - I've heard it said
        We will be together, forever united
        No more partings, nor tears to be shed,
Every prayer answered - I've heard it said.

Heavenly worthiness - so they tell me
        Is cultivated in my piety.
My Earthly stay will be - so they tell me
        A preparation for hierarchy.
With commandments honoured continuously
        I will inherit Heaven - so they tell me.

But Heaven is here for me - so I believe
        In family, friends and their loving received.
All the future is ours - so I believe
        In the heaven our minds and spirits conceive.
Here is our heaven, we all can achieve
        A heaven where loving is the creed - so I believe.

Stan Coombs

WAKE

I was awake on that day
when you gave me a lick
of your lollipop
and when my hand, now all sticky,
was dragged round a corner
to listen with you
to a Bakelite radio
that sang hoop-te-do.

'Red Sails in the Sunset',
'Can I do you now?'
And Kathleen was taken
home once again,
when singers still treadled
their sewing machines
and Allard and Alvis
made motors for me:
when Crosby still hoped
and crooners still mooned,
Billie Holiday bowed
at the end of each tune;
Sinatra's Hoboken blurred
mistily soft, backing
the piers of Brando's
waterfront loft.

These are the dreams
that now shade far away
and there's only remembrance
I was awake on that day.

Jim Rogerson

MYTHICAL EARTHLY DREAMS

Upon thy misty moor,
Slavishly yet unreach'd,
Hush thou, thou heavenly peace,
Filled with heather amidst
Rumbling fountain springs,
Compassed by time,
Untouch'd by human hands,
Acquaintance, wind, rain, cloudy sky,
Canst best yet innocence be denied.

Lascivious of days gone by,
Rare as thy titlark,
Primitive maids once bathed 'neath
Fountain springs
Imagination beyond speckled dreams,
Saints aroused amidst heavenly clouds,
Heaths, moorland torn bitterly apart,
Twittering 'twas no more,
Foliage green, mystical songbirds
In early spring.

Fragrance upon thy heather hills,
Where at leisure poppies danced,
Heaven thou overwhelming glance
Whistling past, age-old wrinkled clouds,
Thus on the prowl came man,
Ghost-like, riotous, short-sighted distant crowds,
Stone-eyed, clasped-iron hands,
Greed-stirred, tongue-tied nations split wide,
War declared, heaths, moorland, died
Alas, all went to bed to hide.

Gusts of wind, howling roar,
Heaven 'n' sky world opened wide
Foamless red, oceans began to rise,
Amber day, night-chilled sky,
Anger aflame, mantles wrapt in shame,
Humanity thus gone astray,

O' er past consumed, fantasy aghast,
Genius brains consumed worldly gains,
Too much power, 'tis nuclear hour,
Myrtle shame, mythology is not to blame.

Wlodzimier Kajon

THIS TREE

What is a tree? To many people it is many things
A thing of beauty, yes certainly - crooked branches reach
To embrace the world and all that's in it; in
A sylvan woodland glade, a tree stands, offering each
Passer-by shade; somewhere to sit and picnic maybe.
Children may want to climb - to feel the friendly embrace.
This tree - many will not know the name; this matters not;
All are beautiful - ash, oak, sycamore, beech - your face
Uplifted, you drink in the sheer magnificence; what
Is a tree, if not one of the world's wonders? When
This tree is cut down, some are saddened; but you see
A tree never really dies - more beauty, for men
To craft; exquisite things are made - for you - for me.

If this sad old world should one day come to an end
Somewhere this tree will still stand - for it is a godsend.

Valerie Hall

THE STONE CHILD
(After the photograph of a sculpture)

The stone child
is kneeling with
an empty bowl,

her eyes half-closed,
face raised trustingly
to the light,

contrasting with
her unruly locks
and plain, thin shift

from which
fragile little feet
peep shyly out.

Such naïve hope
in hard times
this child has.

Will someone fill
her proffered bowl
for her? Will you? Will I?

Only in our heads
can the questions
speak and echo.

She remains silent
challenging us
being merely

the black and white
photo of a
stone child.

Tim Hoare

IT WAS A LOVELY DAY

It was a lovely day
Quite some time away,
'It's the fight, not the winning
That gives the edge',
My brother says, and he would know,
His journey had already started.

'Feel the air upon your face,
Take it at a gentle pace
Sweet is light at the end of day
That light delays',
My brother says, and he would know,
His journey had already started.

'Like rain upon the ground
It halts our step and gathers fear
But no great mystery is there
Than we already share',
My brother says, and he would know,
His journey had already started.

It was a lovely day,
Quite a time away,
While walking there alone
I heard my brother say,
'Go back dear sister,
Sweet is my journey on,
You know I cannot stay.'

Margt C Leighton

IT'S OVER

I couldn't change your mind
Even if I'd have tried
You would constantly run
Where you didn't belong.

It seemed clear to me
That you just couldn't see
All the love in my eyes
Or the definite signs.

I watched you slip away
I held predictions of the day
When you were no longer around to hold
I stood helpless while you stood bold.

You had a tendency of letting me down
Yet I know you would deny this now
And although you didn't ever realise
Each time you let go, I felt tears in my eyes.

You were too strong to say your thoughts
I often asked but you kept them inside once more
You dismissed my understanding to protect your pride
I tried to help but you pushed me aside.

You once gave me happiness and a reason to live
Now our marriage is over, there's no more to give
I fight through each day but the pain doesn't end
I still wait for you and for my heart to mend.

Louise Allen

HOW MANY SLEEPS BEFORE GRANDPA COMES?

How many sleeps before Grandpa comes?
We spoke on the phone today . . .
He's flying soon on a big silver plane
To stay with us all on holiday!

We are going to show our pictures
Drawn, especially for Grandpa to see.
Then tell him about our pony and toys,
Over a nice hot cup of tea!

How many sleeps before Grandpa comes?
When we can knock on his door and say
'Grandpa, are you awake yet?
We've got our storybooks here to play!'

Oh! How many sleeps before Grandpa comes?
At bedtime, shall we look at the moon?
Then smile, because the moon is smiling at Grandpa,
We can whisper, 'God bless, see you soon!'

Joanne Manning

LIFE

Life
It's to be lived,
Not wasted.
Never waste it.
Life is too precious,
Life is too short.

You'll have regrets,
You'll make mistakes,
Without them you do not live.
You merely exist

And to exist is the greatest sin.
You have a life,
Live it,
Because rest assured
You're a long time dead.

Colette McCormick

POPPIES

Delicate and ephemeral
The poppy stands so tall.
A flower of great beauty,
Boldly coloured to enthral.

In swirls across the meadows
Poppies dance and sway;
Demanding our attention,
Drawing eyes their way.

How is it that such beauty
Should deep emotions flare?
The petals are blood-red.
Sadness fills the air!

Flaming poppy vistas
Replaced the fields of death,
Where thousands of young soldiers
Uttered their last breath.

The blackness at the centre
Caused darkness of a kind
That drugged the lives of many -
Causing stupor of the mind.

Yet, poppies are still blooming
With elegance and grace;
Confidently able
To brighten empty space.

Brenda Artingstall

BROUGHAM HALL
(Demolished in 1934)

I've played music here - this summery day in June
The ageless breeze harmonising through instrumental leaves
And sifting through the ashes of time
Revealing charred fragments of fortune's splendour
Consumed by merciless flames of misfortune.

Power lodged here like a taloned eagle
Elevated above Lowther
Soaring on feudalistic wings across the centuries
To alight on a Lord Chancellor's shoulder.

Fine Art lodged here - chisels cutting mason's magic in stone
Raised elegance under a tranquil Westmoreland sky
Linenfold oak - swathed walls under sumptuous ceilings
Tapestry images seen at Bayeux.

Kings lodged here - regal processions through great avenue
And eastern portal
Louis Phillippe and the seventh Edward
Walked the western terrace as the lowering sun
Burnished the meadows where once raged England's last battle.

Decline lodged here - the turn of a card, the roll of a dice
Determined the warrant of death - but did Victor feel
Remorse or sadness at such loss, such finality?
The gavel's crash echoed through barren rooms and an empty life.

Jealousy destroyed here - Cowper's barbarous hammer and pick
Shattered the mason's magic in stone
Gross wounds to fester and weep above Lowther
Nettle and barbed briar creeping to hide the stinging scar.

I've played music here - this summery day in June
The ageless breeze harmonising through instrumental leaves
My notes dissolve in air and are gone, but the ancient symphony
Engraved in the scattered stones is perpetual.

Robbie Ellis

THE INVENTION

It started as a germ, a little worm of an idea,
Quietly nagging at his mind
For days and weeks it would not go away.
This just might work, he thought.
'Don't be a jerk,' they said,
'Go away and think again.'
But still it stayed inside his brain.
It grew, became a few disjointed thoughts,
That had no form, a foetal mass before it's born.
Nurtured in its mother's womb.
No outward sign but over time
An all-consuming endless line
Of questions asked, and answered too
The theory points to something new.
And still the idea grew and grew.
Then *pow!* And how
The inspiration comes to him
No nagging doubt he shouts it out,
'That's it, I've seen the light.'
He writes the finished theory down
And sits exhausted looking round,
Happy in the afterglow
Of what he wants the world to know.
A source of heat and light for all
He dials the number, makes the call
Trembling as he spreads the word.
He's feted, given rave reviews
His face is worldwide on the news.
As time goes by he's still the toast
Of everybody coast to coast
And yes, it's fun to be the one
That tapped the power of the sun.

Another germ, a little worm
Of doubt inside his mind
The tiny voice becomes a scream,
'This is not what at first it seemed.'
As yesterday we thanked the one
Who tapped the power of the sun
Today we know that we were wrong
This man had made the atom bomb.

Paul Knox

THE WORDS

Nothing lasts forever
Everything falls apart eventually
The working parts grind to a halt
All used up and gone
Except words
They never wear out
The more we use them the better they become
Words perfectly placed their meaning exact
Sit right in sight and sound
Every word like a carefully chosen and honed stone
In a drystone wall
Eternally tenacious words cling to our memory and ride out
On our tongue
Constructing sense out of civilisation
Words have been, are and will be
The soul of communication
In perpetuity.

Maria Dabrowska

COMPANIONS

(From 'The Dripping Tap' collection by Diana Blench)

Peace and love and healing
Walk hand in hand, these three
Bring to me a healing, bring your love to me.

Love and peace and healing
Strengthen me every day
Love brings joy into my life, love is here to stay.

Peace has come upon me
And whatever I shall face,
Whatever storms surround me, peace will find a place.

You have given me these companions
To accompany me on my way
Peace and love and healing, for these three I pray.

Diana Blench

A GREAT MAN

As he lies in state for all to see
This great man of serenity
He was the one who gave us all hope
Now he's gone, John Paul the Pope.

Twenty-seven years ago he was elected
From many Cardinals he was selected
None of us knew what a difference he would make
A great man of God as leader did take.

In the Vatican he made his home
Italy's wonderful city of Rome
Here he ruled over the Catholic world
This saintly man unruffled, unfurled.

Now lying there in his robes of ruby red
His trusty mitre placed upon his head
People in their thousands come to say goodbye
All with great sadness, unashamed they cry.

Illness at the very end took its toll
He tried so hard to keep up his role
Then the Lord took his hand and said,
'It's time to come home with me instead.'

He's now on his way back to his final home
One last journey before he leaves Rome
This great man who touched us all
Goodbye, God bless, Pope John Paul.

Gill D'Arcy

MARIO FENINGER

He plays piano with passion
with a fired molten energy,
the notes lingering in one's mind
long after the fingers move on
in total control of the keys

The intensity and power
of the alive musical word
portraying communication
in absolute absoluteness
harmonising with life's force

Matter, energy, space and time
disappearing into nothing
while the music steals one away
into the realm of pure spirit
then returns one, refreshed, for life.

Corin Jasmine Dienes

YOU, YOURSELF

The waves crash against the rocks
And the lighthouse warns of dawn,
Seagulls circle above in flocks,
And rolling fog is signalled by the horn.

Grass turns from green to white,
Sand whips round the skin,
Wind shatters the bursting kite,
While pushing the racing tin.

The canvas windbreaks hide the travellers,
Ship off the shore bounces in the wake,
Sheltered promenade calls all gatherers,
The calling, to which all but I partake.

Now those waves lap at my feet,
With the stars in the morning sky,
To beg a question of our noble seat,
Question none can answer, never mind try.

Seaweed hangs around our necks,
Saltwater looms in our hair,
All of us, every single speck,
Tell your tale of imagination there.

Can you smell the sea breeze
Weep as the refreshing wind coats your mind,
In it let yourself freeze,
Stay for all time, 'til you find

Yourself.

Matthew Coles

FOR OUR SIXTY-FIFTH WEDDING ANNIVERSARY

Seventy years ago we were just friends
And we discussed all political trends.
There were too many who starved and were poor,
What could be done? We were not very sure!

Maybe there should be a quick revolution?
Though rolling heads did not seem the solution!
In the meantime we both just kept on growing,
While with much love our good friendship was flowing!

Sixty-five years ago, wonder of wonders,
We grew romantic with emotional thunders!
We were too young but we wanted each other
No longer living as sister and brother!

So we decided that we must get married,
But one condition this contract it carried:
We must have ten children or many more,
Family life was what lay in store!

Then this our marriage turned out so tumultuous,
Conflicts galore but still, oh so voluptuous.
We raised five children, just half of the contract!
Doctors did stop us just halfway our planned track!

We've enjoyed loving for sixty-five years
Sometime elated but sometimes in tears
But not a dull moment we have lived through,
Through all vicissitudes we knew love true!

Now that we are nearing the end of our trip,
More into spiritual values we dip,
Make a crescendo of this part of life
Let the finale with much love be rife!

Zoltan P Dienes

SAY IT WITH POETRY

When you want to say how much you care
And don't know quite where to start
Pick up a pencil and write down the words
A poem straight from your heart.

When you need to give someone you love
A present because they are sick
And you just aren't sure what gift you should choose
A poem will do the trick.

When you want to say thank you to very dear friends
And can't find the right words to say
Pick up some paper and write it all down
A poem will save the day.

When you want to immortalise much-loved pets
So you'll gone on remembering
Compose all your feelings into a verse
A poem's the perfect thing.

When you want to remember loved ones now passed
Who are now in our dear Lord's care
And you need to ask Him to keep them safe
A poem's the perfect prayer.

When you have so much feeling locked in your heart
And you want to set it free
Don't bottle it up but write it all down
In the form of 'poetry'.

Denise Castellani

AGEING LOVE

Darling, I love you so much
A look, a kiss, a gentle touch,
If what you see turns you cold
Remember I'm just growing old.
Close your eyes and you might find
My younger image in your mind,
I have eyes and still can see
You too have changed, it's not just me.
What happened to that handsome guy
With a twinkle in his eye,
Brown curly hair and eyes so blue?
Inside the outer shell, it's you.
Don't be put off by my ageing frame
It's really me, I am the same.
Getting old is not a sin
Please search for me, I am within!

Enid Thomas

THANK YOU

Faxes, e-mails, letters too
Come through their sources unto you
You read and study these each day
Of what we poets think and say!
Some you select to print and use
But, how do you people really choose?
It would drive my head astray
To do such work day after day!
So, 'Thank you' each and every one
For a job well-read and work well done.
Congratulations Forward Press
I think your staff deserve a rest.

Beth Stewart

CELEBRATIONS - A WOMAN OF TASTE

(Having been given a box of 'Celebrations' for my birthday)

I think of her with fondness,
As I taste her Milky Way,
Her Bounty's so delicious
I could suck them every day.

Her Topics were so full of nuts,
They took me by surprise
And her Teasers were so tempting,
Wrapped in innocent disguise.

Mars reminded me of Venus,
With all her complications,
A Truffle of emotions
That make or break relations.

Her Galaxy is rainbow-like
With many hues and lights,
Sometimes as smooth as Caramel,
At others, dark as nights.

I am thankful for her sweetness,
A delightful box of lickers,
Next time I wish to have a treat
I'll think of her nice Snickers.

Joseph McGarraghy

ACCOUNT RENDERED

Toad in hole and snake in grass
Nemesis bids you to her table.
For here arranged in ample measure
Each dish sublime to satisfy.

Small fry was I, 'gainst your shark-like ambition
Torn up, rejected, and tossed aside.
Yet the day would come, the moment sweet
As you feast upon the aloe of gall.

Drink deep the cup of bitterness,
Eat well my foe and contemplate
All thy past gains . . . and taste
The flavours I now return.

The ova of spite are poached
The cream of hurts well whipped
All in the basin of discontent
And served with the relish of loathing.

Use well the knife of my despair.
Take up the fork, and thus
Upon the panoply of fear
Partake the fruits of retribution.

Maurice Bailey

IN MY GARDEN

At the beginning of the year
Snowdrops, crocuses and daffodils.
Other bulbs are waiting for
Easter to appear.
Warm days are on their way.
Roses in full bloom.
Sweet peas growing very tall
With fragrance in the air.

Autumn comes and leaves begin to fall,
Golden colours everywhere and trees
With apple, plum and pear.
Lovely chrysanthemums blooming everywhere.
I thank the Lord above for giving us hands
For planting and giving us all His love.

Winifred Brasenell

THE MERMAID'S LAMENT

Strange sea music whispered in my ear -
The song of the mermaid crystal-clear.
Its sadness reached through the midnight air -
A tale of love which none could share.

Her soulful cry tore at my heart -
For she and her true love had to part.
She called to him across the seas,
An echo carried by the breeze.

I knew how she was feeling for
I had suffered like that before.
My own dear love had let me see
That she wished only to be free.

The mermaid called her lover's name
For he had set her heart aflame.
But now she suffers untold pain -
She'll never know such love again.

My heart reached out to bring her peace -
And so, perhaps, my own release!
I'd battle with the mighty wave
And join her in her ocean grave.

Mary Baird Hammond

FIASCO

Paula ran along a Helsinki street
With aching legs and tired feet
From early on in the race
She did set the pace.
With determination and a strong heart
She led from the very start.
Going on to win the race
A gold medal for first place.
She has shown what she can do,
Watched by millions like me and you.
Athens was a different story,
A motorcycle crew stole her glory.
You should see how it feels
To have a motorcycle snapping at your heels.
Back to Britain came the *gold,*
Onto the memory we will hold.
Now we are on a winning streak
Forget the *fiasco* that was Greek . . .

S Glover

CHASE THE RAINBOW

Gather the platinum dewdrops
As the sunbeams begin to creep
And dry the treasure.
Thread them on a whisper of silver
And I'll wear it for you.
Your crown is made of autumn leaves
Gold, amber and bronze.
I gathered only the ones that the sunbeams struck
So they shone with warmth
And glowed with richness.
My bracelet is fashioned
From frost and icicles
Cool against my wintry skin
Luminous against my pale flesh.
Icicles sing a delicate chorus
From the trees and hedgerows
As we sit and wait on the frozen bank
Ready to chase the rainbow.

Susan Lowe

THE ARTIST

An artist conducts with palette and brush
A symphony that comes deep from his mind,
Colours used, so vivid, so bright,
Capturing the sun and darkness of night
The moods that flow from the artist's soul
From violent red to sky-blue cold
Where his brush lands no one knows
Then, within seconds, the colours flow
An explosion of yellows and purples too
A suggestion of gold with red seeping through
Years of torment comes out through the brush
Sometimes feeling he has to rush
To put on canvas just what he feels
Definitely a man who does not yield
Sometimes the painting, just doesn't come right
In temper, his brushes have been known to take flight
Having witnessed an artist in such a temper
And he cut the canvas with a knife down the centre
As a child of ten I just froze in total fear
Cos I thought my dad was going to cut off his ear
The painting in question was of our dear mum
With fear on her face, she was struck quite dumb
As that beautiful painting was thrown across the floor
Broken in pieces so we'd see it no more
So with tears in her eyes, Mum turned and fled
All because the artist starts to see red.

Graham Bowers

A MOMENT IN TIME

Serene and silent, no movement or sound,
Only our footprints on virgin ground.
Hushed and hallowed, all seemed to be,
As we walked slowly, dog and me.

Early morning, quiet and still,
As we looked down from snow-capped hill.
It seemed the whole world was asleep,
As Mother Nature, her watch did keep.

And then against the sparkling white,
Shone ruby red, in contrast bright,
A cheeky robin whistled clear and broke the silence
                                        so sublime,
And captured in my heart forever
A magical moment in time.

Jacqueline Claire Davies

OUR WONDERFUL WORLD

'What a wonderful world we live in,' my mother used to say,
As she stepped into her garden, on a fine and sunny day,
'The birds are joyfully singing and the flowers smell so sweet,
Today, I'll get my washing dry, and cook something good to eat,
We've got so much to be thankful for,' was what she often said,
'But we must always think of others, as some folks don't get fed.'

It is now eighty years since she said those words to me,
And as I set off on my holiday, as happy as could be,
I thought, *what a wonderful world we live in today,*
With tele, computers, cars and planes, to take us away
We now can see mountains, rivers and oceans galore,
Not just the back garden, as my mum did before.

But the birds are still singing, and the flowers still smell sweet,
And while we have plenty, others still don't have much to eat,
So though the world has progressed in oh, so many ways!
Are folk really any happier than in those *'good old days'*?

Marjorie Seaman

REFLECTIONS IN THE GARDEN

Looking at the garden
I admit it is a mess;
The second half of August
It should be at its best!
What can one do when the sun is hot
When pansies shrivel in a sunny spot;
When lovely rosebuds
Rudely awakened by the heat
Spread out their petals
At an irrational speed?
So short is their lifespan
It just isn't true
Some clouds and raindrops
Are all it would take to make them gain
A few days in glory to reign.
It is rather like people with talents galore
Who suffocate the phrase, 'what a bore'!
Come on, let's encourage,
Energise and support the faint-hearted
With a wake-up call;
Or they become like the pansy and the rose
And shrivel up in no time at all.

Josepha Blay

THE QUESTION

When we get to those pearly gates
And meet God face to face
There are so many questions
We might ask of His good grace

Perhaps we ought to ask Him why
He's let this world become
Like a modern day Gomorrah
Filled with violence and drugs?
Why has this world become
Unsafe for children anymore
Old folk attacked and bullied
Not respected as of yore?
Why this world always seems at war
And terrorism rife?
He surely did not mean for us to suffer such a life

Now maybe we could ask Him
About all these awful things
When we have left this careworn world
And can ponder on God's scheme
But these troubles come from man alone
Not God's doing, but our sin;
Of Him, I'd only ask one thing,
'Lord, please may I come in?'

Maureen Quirey

NOSTALGIA

I was born when the sun was younger
When white sunlit days persisted well
Into long, warm, coppery, swallow-filled evenings
When the world was beautiful, long ago, long ago.

One sun-dappled day of my long-ago youth
I closed my eyes to dream and opened them on old age
Fifty years and more had gone by
Fifty years and more of servitude to existence
All gone, all gone in a sigh.

Wyn Williams

QUEEN AND COUNTRY

Sixty long years ago
Peace came to this troubled land,
They went to fight a foe
By land, sea and air,
In mud, cloud and sand.

Few returned to hope and joy,
Many left in soil so grey.
Hope, joy, where are they now?
Shattered again by evil minds.
Our Queen and Country
Stand once more,
To keep such evil
From our shore,
No guns, just courage to defend
Our right to live
The life we give.

Pamela Gormley

THE GALAXY

The swell of the night holds me here
Stationary I am
You revolve around me
On occasion, a flicker
A beat of light
Then . . . nothing
You sway in the rhythm
Everything turns within you
Your arms outstretched
Pulling in more
Capture those things
From beyond the outer rim
They join the rhythm
For I am the centre
My force turns you
Your life in my arms
Spiral is my flare
Stars will shoot
Comets will fly
Meteors will burn
Before I die.

Amy Feather

CHANGE OF ADDRESS

I used to live in a flat at the top of some stairs
A place I loved for many years
But then my knees with wear and tear
Made me decide I should move elsewhere
And then I had some luck one day
A little ground floor flat came my way
In a sheltered housing complex where it's nice and safe
And I'm very happy to be in this place
The warden phones each morning to check you are well
And pull-cords in our rooms can summon help if needed
So our welfare is looked after as calls are soon heeded
I have a little bit of garden where I spend happy hours
Just sitting out there or tending the flowers
There's a lovely big lounge here where we can all meet
For tea, coffee or bingo, a weekly treat
I have made lots of friends here and have to say
I'm enjoying life here in so many ways
And hope to be here till the end of my days.
As for my knees, they have improved no end
Now I have no stairs to ascend or descend.

S C Talmadge

MOONSTRUCK

I stand at my window for hours at a time
Staring at shadows cast by 'Lady Moonshine'
Then along comes a cloud to shroud her sweet face
And briefly she's gone, not a sign and no trace.
Gracefully she returns to bathe the world in light
Changing the landscape into a magical sight.
Silently she glides across the night sky
Her reflection on water shows a tear in her eye.
Wistfully she looks down on the world far below
Her soft, tranquil face has a mystical glow.
Fascinating, intoxicating, she lulls us to sleep
Standing guard like a sentinel, our dreams hers to keep.
Inspiring the mind with her spiritual presence
Many words have been written to capture her essence.
Eternal is her beauty, time cannot erase
That mysterious, enigmatic smile on her face.

Carrie Ann Hammond

DEATH OF A PRINCESS

Her presence was grand, she was mighty and proud,
As she travelled the land, her heart sang out loud,
She was always the star, number one with the crowd,
And the news travelled far that the fog was her shroud.

She was daughter to Stanier, brightest gleam in his eye,
With the gifts that he gave her, one might think she could fly,
Oh, they stole her uniqueness on the grounds of the cost,
But she retained her sickness till the day she was lost.

But for fate's deadly blisters, might she be with us still?
Joining in with her sisters, see them besting the hill,
When demise has no witness, who can pinpoint the ill?
None can prove only best guess what effected the kill.

What a horrendous end after so many miles,
Like a ship on the rocks, hers was called Windward Isles,
The Princess died at Harrow, 1952's fluke,
And her duties henceforth, rendered to the Duke.

Richard Layton

POETS

Aim to show you life the way they see it
Initiate from hidden depths, a thought

Portray an event they want to share
Reach out to touch the heart in a report

Paint a picture so that readers' eyes
Can see it in the words they deign to use

Share experiences of interest
Relate a tale intending to amuse

Illustrate occasions to create
Impressive souvenirs forever stored

Reminisce the changing paths of time
Recalling memories to strike a chord

Capture precious moments and impart
Their sentiments of pleasure, hope, love, cheer

Generate emotions in their words
Leave feelings stirred, a sigh, a silent tear

Hope their words will travel on through time
To be re-read for ever and a day

In books of poetry that publishers
Compile promoting poets on their way.

Congratulations - Forward Press, thank you
For fifteen years of making dreams come true.

Joy Saunders

THE SOLDIER'S SONG

Never knew what happened to him
Don't know how he died,
Only know the family's pain
Their grief and tears they cried.

Born and bred in Batley
Tall in youth and strong,
From a small mill town in Yorkshire
He sang the soldiers' song.

In April nineteen forty-four
Then only twenty years,
He was killed, we don't know how
We saw his parents' grief and tears.

Born and bred in Batley
From Coal Pit Lane he came,
A small mill town in Yorkshire
Frank Kemp was his name.

He gave his life for freedom
The rights of man to save,
He sang the soldiers' song
In Kohima lives his grave.

There, stands a proud memorial
Carved words on which convey,
'When you go home tell them of us and say
For your tomorrow, we gave our today'.

Our years we gave, they were not long
We sang the soldiers' song.

W D Stanley

THE DIFFERENCE BETWEEN HE AND SHE

Beside the obvious, the difference between
he and she is like the throw of dice.
Resting on the facets of life broad or mean
she is a pool of piety once or twice.
Whereas he walks on a tightrope
but stands at ease ready to pay any price.
Like a spell she chants mysteries
whereas he splices his life slice by slice.

She is intrigued by a play of chance
and he likes to win each and every game.
She is tormented by lively thoughts
and he? The bullseye is always in his aim.
Enigma of ages moulded in flesh and bone
she likes to sleepwalk in fortune and fame.
He is the one who takes a flight of fancy
whereas she dances like a flame.

He is only one side of the coin of life
she is the other face to make it complete
if she plays the goddess of creation
and he sails through the ocean of deceit.
Stress of journey on the highway of life
torments her soul day and night.
Where he stands alone, proud and pleased
and she is there to pay with all her zeal.

She complements all there is in his life.
He is so very much immune from strife.
One way or the other in life and death
he is there for her and she is for him.
Where tears merge with happiness
and life flows like the grain of times.
Obvious is the smile on the face of bliss
the difference sleeps at the edge of their wish.

Mojibur Rahman

GOOD FRAME OF MIND

I was born with a good frame of mind,
I walked away leaving my roots behind.
Poor Mum and Dad nearly blew their mind,
Some people said, 'The girl is mad.'
They didn't know I was very sad.
I watched the ships from days to weeks,
I watched the ships from months to years,
Then one day I was sailing away,
I had a dream, I didn't know what it did mean.
I found myself dancing on the music scene.
The music shop I did a hop,
I was dancing to 'hip hop'.
Then I began to feel like jack-in-the-box,
Haunted by the songs of the music beating in my head,
Haunted by the songs of the wind blowing across the seas,
I was born with a good frame of mind,
I walked away leaving my roots behind.
I had a vision, I didn't know what it did mean,
It drove me away across the sea.
Then everything unfolds in my destiny,
I wake up at the break of dawn
To hear the cockerels crowing in the early morn,
To milk the cows and feed the hens.
Destiny keeps playing on my mind,
I unleash these words like music in the air.
Hearing the sounds everywhere, everywhere . . .

Jean Austin

FASCINATING RHYTHMS

Couples close, dancing to the tempo.
Singers crooning, sometimes with gusto.
Violins so sweet, making the music ring.
Pianos the same, also violas sing.
Clarinets and trumpets, fingers moving quickly.
Drums beating, joining with instruments, swiftly.

Those were the days, mellow, really the best.
Making people's legs move with such zest.
Their hearts so in love, beating sublime.
As they were in the arms of the man of that time.
Until they announced, 'Ladies and Gentlemen please,
The last waltz,' before it was time for all to cease.

Marj Busby

ON THE OUTSIDE

I'm on the outside still looking in
Do they see me or feel me within?

Standing alone not wanting to leave
Feeling the pain not wanting to grieve

Cast away out of sight
Not acknowledged unless the time is right

Still surrounded with nowhere to run
Was it like this, when it begun?

This is me, I want to scream
I am alive not a dream

Let me cross over to the other side
I want to join in, don't want to hide

Give me a chance, I'm sure you will find
I am a good person, thoughtful and kind

But no, I'm stuck here on the outside
No one to turn to or in them confide.

Margaret Pow

RSPCA

Working at the RSPCA
Seeing the animals every day
Is the awful pain we see
Just wanting to be set free

They come in sometimes beaten
Look like they've never eaten
The pain we see in their eyes
Owners telling us awful lies

What we do is give love and care
Having a family is what they love to share
We help them find a new home
Somewhere to call their very own

Inspectors seeing how they live
Evidence shows what they hit them with
They give out a groan or yelp
What we do is give them help

We take in cats, dogs and birds
Nothing can explain in words
Hamsters, gerbils, rats and mice
Let's hope next time owners think twice.

If you can offer these animals anything at all
Then don't pass us by, give us a call.

Emma Whitehurst (18)

THE FORGOTTEN HOUSE

The years had left a sullen tone,
Its once proud features now broke and worn.
The façade once a gleaming shine,
Now faded and peeling with advancing time.

How it knew laughter within its walls,
With people thronging through the hall.
All ages came and danced till dawn,
With mirthful laughter, such joyous times.

Perhaps the day will dawn again,
When new life enters the forgotten door.
The house will sing again at last,
Its future secured from a neglected past.

Catherine Atkinson

CLOFORD

I saw the ancient manor house
Historic hall of Tudor fame,
Scaffolds reaching chimney pots -
All shrouded in white plastic veil
Great ghost of bygone generations -
Once a valued cherished farm.
Now, alas, a watery wreck -
Many memories in the mud
Wintry wastelands doom and gloom,
Stony sites where buildings stood.
Not a soul there to be seen
Gone - a busy farming life,
No men now or machinery
Phil's chicken houses derelict
Rotting in the rain.
Happier days - long gone.
Can a new developer
Restore the pride of Cloford Farm?
A wealthy man from London came,
Spent money on the old ancestral place,
To be once more a gracious home
Where laughter echoes round the rooms.
Sadly Phil has gone now,
But the sun shines on Cloford again.

Ellen M Lock

GENTLE REPOSE

Sleep my pretty one and slumber deep,
Bring to a close this troublesome day.
Let all stirring cease and so bring forth tranquillity.

Sleep my pretty one into a deep repose,
Not e'er disturbed by this world's shadows.
But bright and light gives way to flight into another sphere.

Sleep my pretty one and be transported into a world beyond worlds,
For this is not moulded by the skilful hands of man,
But by the great Creator, in accordance with His plan.

S Taylor

COMPLEX WORLD AND SPIRIT

*('O Florida . . . prepare your perpetual Pentecost of golf course
and freeway, shopping mall and car' . . . Gwyneth Lewis, Welsh poet of
2005 Pentecost)*

This painting reminds of
My earlier abstract
'Christabel' by Coleridge.
Two things pursue
Manichaean turned dialectic
Or the world spirit complex.
Abstracts dream
The flutterings
Or fearful moans.
The toothless mastiff
Senses evil
When a bright green
Snake coils around
And swells the neck.
The dove Merton's
Prisoner after matins
Or the illusive
Christabel.

Paul Faulkner

STRESS AND THE PICTURE

When problems overwhelm me
I sit in my easy chair,
I gaze at the picture on the wall
And imagine myself in there.

I lean against that friendly tree
In my face, its leaves caress,
I reach out to its branches
To ease away my stress.

I sit and watch the river
Flowing slowly, quite serene,
I find the solace that I seek
In that tranquil country scene.

I stroll along the shady path -
Its end I cannot see,
It seems to stretch for miles and miles
Into infinity.

I lie down by the hedgerow
Warm earth beneath me lies,
I bury my face in the verdant grass
To soothe my tired eyes.

In my head I hear the birdsong
And the buzzing of the bees,
The quiet whisper of the leaves
As they meet the gentle breeze.

All tension seems to leave me,
How I wish I could remain
In the ambience of calm and peace
Within that picture frame!

D Morgan

WALLACE IS DEAD

(On the 700th anniversary of the death of William Wallace)

There's news come from London of Wallace's death.
They've hung, drawn and quartered him,
Called him a rebel,
And killed him.

A traitor betrayed him, they captured him cold,
They dragged him down south with them,
Put him on trial there,
And killed him.

He tried to protest that he's true to the Crown
Of Scotland. His destiny -
Hero of Scotland -
They killed him.

That king - Edward Longshanks - he just doesn't care
That Scotland's a free country.
He thinks he owns us.
He killed him.

But doesn't he realise that we *are* free,
And freedom is all we want.
Wallace, he knew it -
They killed him.

Now we will avenge him, our hero he was,
He will not have died in vain.
Their fatal blunder -
They killed him!

Joan E Milne

GRADUATION DAY

Capped, gowned and glorified,
They laugh into the sun-kissed afternoon.
Young breasts are flushed with pride;
Careers are mapped; they're aiming for the moon.

Inebriate, they drink
The vintage wine of silver-spooned success,
And teeter on the brink
Of golden, demi-godded blessedness,

Too full of self-esteem
To heed the fateful writing on the wall -
The tyrant in the dream
That murders youth and leaves no pride at all.

S H Smith

SWEET DREAMS

Sweet dreams, my love, may God be with you through the night
I ask He guard and guide you when we are out of sight
Perhaps you'll dream of me as fast asleep you lie
And think again of all the happy times gone by
You mean so much, you're always on my mind
No words I need to tell you of this special love I find
A sleep is but a time we're in a realm of peace
Where everlasting thoughts remain and never cease
So remember I am with you as you slumber through the night
God's angel will embrace you, until the morning light.

Margaret Murphy

WHEN LOVE STARTS TO FADE

When love starts to fade
There is no going back
The things that unite you
Weaken and crack

You wonder what happened
To turn things to dust
Was it me? Was it her?
Was it just lack of trust?

The truth is that nothing
Can hold it in place
Once the love starts to fade
And the end gathers pace

Love has four seasons
Spring is the first
To be with each other
An insatiable thirst

In summer, contentment
And comfortable ease
But the passion is cooling
And soon it will freeze

By autumn, the feelings
That excited you most
Are fading and dying
Love's becoming a ghost

The winter is cold
So harsh and unkind
The love that you shared
Turns to hate in your mind

But time is a healer
You will love again
Maybe not so intensely
As you did then

Is the pain of the winter
Worth the joy of spring?
Your only reminder
A tarnished gold ring

Each broken promise
That you both have made
Tears a piece from your heart
When love starts to fade.

John Robinson

LIFE

Life - returning with the dawn,
That heralds of the breaking morn -
What agonies, what thrills you bring,
To give us joy, to give a sting.

You go forever on your way,
We ne'er recoup one single day -
Back we can look, but never go,
However much we will it so.

To learn from what has gone before,
Perchance we should, not shut the door -
But most times we just fumble on,
How little gained from what has gone.

Those errors which our fathers made,
They should into hist'ry fade -
They come back with a different twist,
Yet more woes on mankind's list.

But despite anguish and our woes,
Despite depression, heartache, foes -
We yet have sunshine, friends and glee,
Riches there for you - and me.

Roger M Creegan

MY STAR

Lamp of the night softly gleaming,
O'er all the world and o'er me.
Star of the morning and evening,
Star of the ocean and sea.

When the twilight brings forth a stillness,
And a hush can be heard o'er the Earth,
A star shines in solitary splendour,
An eye-twinkling moment gives birth.

My star can be seen looking westward,
And as the night deepens, it goes
On the long, glorious journey to eastward,
And as the night wanes, it still glows.

Then with the dawn of the morning,
It shines forth, with a last golden spark,
Vying sometimes with the sun's burst,
A glimmer of hope in our dark.

On mountains in clear crystal dawnings,
I've seen the sun, moon and my star.
My heart and my kind filled with beauty.
I've had glimpses of Heaven afar.

Once my star looked just like a spaceship,
Low in the heavens, blushed with rose.
Once I saw clouds that just look like angels,
And beauty surrounded my soul.

Jean Turner

MAY YOU CONTINUE

So you are fifteen years old, now that's really great
How many new poets have passed through your gate?
You began your life to give writers a chance
To express their feelings and make a stance
Little did you know where that would lead
Publishing poems from people like me
With your list of themes that arrive every month
There's plenty of choice, an assorted bunch
If one isn't suitable there's always another
No need for a writer to get into a lather
There are also the stories that search our brains for ideas
Producing a story that could finish with tears
Your books are really nice and presented so well
They have pride of place on my mantel shelf
So thanks Forward Press and 'Happy Birthday' to you
May you continue to go on for many years too.

Margaret Ward

SPIRIT OF THE WILD

You can see him from a distance
      his head held to the side,
A magnificent white stallion
      too wild for one to ride.
Standing on his two hind legs
      his tail, it sweeps the ground,
Front hooves hover in the air
      but he doesn't make a sound.
He's surveying all his kingdom
      protecting his domain,
Lovely in the distance with his
      lovely snowy mane.
Though I can hold and touch him,
      alas I must comment,
That my spirit of the wild
      is just an ornament.

I Higginson

A BEAUTIFUL ROSE

(Dedicated to my wife)

The Lord gave me beautiful gardens, vast lands too.
In one beautiful garden plenty of fresh flowers grew and grew.
Along the outskirts of the garden, trees stood big and tall,
So when the wind came they would stand firm and never fall.
Amongst the freesias and carnations some pretty daffodils grew.
Amongst daffodils and strelitzias a beautiful spring of water
trickled gently through.
Right in the midst of my garden a delicate and beautiful rose grew.
This rose was so beautiful, like diamonds, unique,
through and through.
Its clarity was like the rubies, sapphires and gems.
Its elegance and beauty continued sparkling days on end.
It was protected by all the flowers starting from the trees on the end.
It was just like a pearl beneath the deep blue sea,
protected in a graceful shell.

This garden the Lord gave me is the garden of my heart.
The flowers in this garden would never grow apart.
The rose that grew in this garden was someone special through
and through.
It was the most beautiful rose the Lord gave me.
The one I found in you.

Forever yours
Sajid

Sajid Patel

THE FILLING STATION

Do we fill the body
Or do we fill the soul?
Do we enjoy the food,
Be it for the physical or spiritual?
I'd rather have a fat soul
Than a fat body. We're on a diet
I hear my wife cry.
I must try fruit and vegetables.
It takes discipline this fate.
I admire anyone who tries.
Keep then our body and soul together.
Get our priorities right.
O' that my worship would be free and spontaneous.
A happy sound indeed for the worshipper
And most importantly a happy God.
Let us all be happy and glad
In the knowledge that He is a forgiving God
And He will accept us if we repent.

Gordon A Cameron

THUS BE THE LAND OF DREAMS

I wandered slowly in a dream
With you, I am sure, I must have been,
Linking thoughts with you, within my scene,
So many words are written of things that might have been.

Yet on reflection, and after contemplation,
Will my wanderings through a dream
Bear relation to the actions that I have seen,
Whilst suspended, floating, through time extreme?

Thus be the land of dreams,
Its gardens and divinity,
The moulding of our minds . . .
Confirmation of life and its fraternity.

Bah Kaffir

BLACK ROSE

She sits alone,
Petals black as night.
A woven nest of twisted
Thorns, lifeless and ready
To crack.

Christian Ward

OUR PRECIOUS LOVE

Why oh why dear Lord above
Must we lose so soon
The ones we love so much?
Why must they always go
And leave us all alone
Without their warm embrace
And their soft tender touch?

For when we were young and carefree
They would walk by our side
Through both night and day
Trying if they could, to keep
Both the pains and sorrow away
For they would hold us so tender in their arms
And embrace us so warmly
In their soft, tender love and charms
And they would always be there
To keep us from harm
Through both the ups and down
In our lives

So why, oh why dear Lord above
Must we always lose so soon
The ones we love much?

Donald John Tye

MITZI

'How can a cat change your life?' some may ask,
Well the answer is simple yet true,
I now have someone to love and care for,
And someone who loves me unconditionally too.

Right from the day I got her,
I know we'd got along just fine,
She's just so loving and so affectionate,
There's no doubting that Mitzi is mine.

As she struts around the house,
She miaows and she purrs,
She treats this as her territory,
She knows this house is hers.

Up until I got her,
My mood was low, to say the very least,
But now I have her to look after,
All those horrid, negative feelings have ceased.

Even when it's night-time,
She sneaks in beside me in my bed,
And often in the early hours,
She'll wake me up if she wants fed.

I couldn't imagine life without her now,
I wish I'd had her long before,
She's such a delight to care for,
I couldn't ask for anything more!

Louise Pamela Webster

FATHER, I LOVE YOU SO

Father, dear Father, I love you so,
Your light is where I long to go,
Your peace and love upon me shower,
Every day and every hour,
I am one with you, as I walk this path so true,
Bless those whom I meet with your light,
That they may see you through me, to guide the blind
Into your beauty.

As I walk my path through life, may those before me
Light my way and teach me to help my 'family' on the path behind,
Where I once trod, when I was blind.
It was time, Father, so lost and alone, no one here
To guide me 'home'
Back to you and your love so true.

But my heart for you was always there,
The sight of your light I never lost,
Like a ship in the night, you guided me across the dark seas,
Thank you Father, for the wind in my sails,
With angel wings I did prevail,
To here and now within your light
I carried your love throughout the night,
But when I leave this place, one thing I know,
Into your arms I will go,
All because
I love you so!

Chris Whooley

THE LAST TIME

Gaunt, was always
The word that fitted you best.
Even from the first time I saw you.

It suited you,
Added a mysterious air
To your devil-may-care
Demeanour.

Tall and slim
To the point of scrag-end, I used to joke,

That was when
We were still in love,
Could still laugh at each other's silliness.

Gaunt, was still
How I saw you that last time,

By then you were
Staring from liver-diseased eyes,
Grinning with cigarette-stained teeth,
Smelling of decay and cheap whiskey.

There was no longer any mystery,
Yet, the devil remained . . .
Uncaring.

Valerie McKinley

I GREW UP

Here you are, funny old thing,
Standing after all this time.
I had such fun, you were mine,
To and fro on your back and away I would go,
To a place only children could know.
And my mother would say, 'That is enough for today,'
And I said I would be back,
So stand up straight, you funny old gate.

Beryl Elizabeth Moore

THE MAGIC OF A SUMMER'S EVENING

As I trod the meadow's narrow path
I saw a swallow skim the drying swath
And heard the curlew's haunting cry
As velvety shadows of night crept in
The moon rose, as the sun left a bloodied sky
And slipped behind the western rim.

And in that fading light of day
I saw a vixen and her cubs at play
As the dew came down on summer's haze
Rooks, with steady purposeful wing-beat
Were eyed by cautious rabbits as they grazed,
As to churchyard elms made their retreat.

A blackbird sang his final lay
His tribute to the dying day
Whilst chewing cud and standing mute, the kine
Cast shadows in the evening light
While from sties came snores from slumbering swine
The sound drifting on the breeze of night.

The big horses stood just by the gate
To rest, and for the morning wait
When the man will yoke them up again,
For dusk had bade the chattering mower cease
Tomorrow more grass will be slain
But for now, half dark and summer's night-time peace.

E D Bowen

THE BLIND MAN

Tap, tap, goes the stick of the blind man as he feels his way around
His world is only darkness, it's only smell and sound.
He paints a picture in his mind of how the world must look
He only knows the world by touch and reading his Braille book.
It is a somewhat lonely life for an active man
His guide dog gives him company and all the love he can.
But sometimes he just wishes for someone to share his life
For someone warm and tender, a kind and caring wife.
It isn't easy making friends, most people don't even try
Sometimes people say 'Hello' but most just pass him by.
He likes to hear the birds sing the beauty of their song
To hear the children's laughter, it helps the day along.
His pleasures are his radio and his records too
Also his tape recorder, it stops him feeling blue.
He loves the perfumed flowers as he walks across the park
The scented stock and jasmine that comes out after dark.
His pleasures are the simple ones that God gives you and me
But he is more aware of them because he cannot see.

Christine Corby

NATURE CAN PAINT TOO

Margaret, my artistic friend, the strokes of your brush like magic
Create light and colour which form your landscapes,
They bring to life the enchanted land.
Serenaded by Puccini's music I find myself mesmerised back
To the hot summer days of my youth
Where butterflies and white doves fly to the light blue sky,
The scent of roses fills the air as they travel over a sea of green,
Passing valleys, forests, and mountains of rainbow.
Created within your imagination, fashioned by your hands.
Who am I to praise your work?
I am only a poet, humbled in your presence.
I look at you and I know it's true; nature can paint too.
Beautiful lady you are a living work of art.

Duncan MacFarlane

TEMPTATION

To steal that smile . . . on your lips
To play with fire . . . burn my fingertips
Temptation
Can't resist this
Have to live this
To lie for . . . to die for . . . temptation

I have pushed these thoughts far behind
I have thrown you out of my mind
Still I keep going back
Again I am fetching back . . .
Temptation
Surrender to this . . .
Succumb to this . . . temptation

Metal and magnet
Moth and the flame
We are the same . . . temptation
I have lost to my heart
You've lost to your mind
We still play the game . . . temptation
Can't resist this
Have to live this
To lie for . . . to die for . . . temptation

There is a thin line
The balance is fine
Between good and evil
The God and Devil . . . temptation
Can't resist this
Have to live this
To lie for . . . to die for . . . temptation.

Vivek P Sarma

THE WINTER CAT

There's a meal awaiting when I get in.
I've glanced at my reflection and look terribly thin.
Winter is here and it can be a bore,
Mousing in cold is a terrible chore.
But please don't sympathise, I don't like that,
After all I am a mega-being, I am a cat.

I have a fur coat that all seem to admire.
A special place at home in front of the fire.
I even have servants who run after me.
Oh drat and bother, I think I've picked up a flea!
Never mind, my valet will attend me with care,
Brush me and comb me and clean all my hair.

When hairdressing's done and I'm perfect again
I'll rise from my spot and go out in the rain.
There's an overhanging bush in the garden you see
And the birds haven't a clue it is sheltering me!
I crouch very still, I daren't even holler
But they always seem to hear the bell fixed to my collar.

I've caught the odd mouse in my time, it is true.
Thought I'd give them as presents, at Christmas, to you;
But you ranted and raved and took them outside,
It wasn't my fault that the bloomin' things died.
Oh, the light has come on; you're in the kitchen I see,
Think I'll decorate your worktops with my 'fleur-de-lis'.

I have to watch you when I come from outdoors
And mud just happened to stick to my paws.
You look so interesting when your face goes red,
Then you seem to explode and chase me to bed.
There's one more thing I have to say and it's true.
You'll never own this cat, for I'll always own you!

Sue Ireland

REVENGE IS SWEET

I always knew you hated me,
I knew you didn't care,
I knew it from the start,
You didn't want me there.
Why I ever bothered
Even trying to be nice,
'You're nothing much to look at,'
You told me once or twice.
I know I'm nothing special,
But I have my feelings too,
You didn't need to hurt me,
I was never cruel to you.
'You're crazy, mad and stupid,
I wish that you were dead,
I hate you every moment,'
Was all you ever said.

I'll grant your wish my darling,
I'll make your dream come true,
But when I'm six feet under,
My ghost will hate you too . . .

Samantha Walsh

IT'S A GOOD LIFE

As I awake, another morn
Stretch and yawn, breathe deep
Winter sun beams through the drapes
It's time to cast off sleep

Look from the window to frosty roofs
Sparkling white and clear
It's just so good to be alive
Watching the day appear

So many sounds in the morning air
Feathered friends arrive
Singing, whistling, squawking loud
In this garden of plenty they thrive

The colours of spring are all around
Bringing new life to the earth
Purple, yellow, white and pink
Nothing can better their worth

Wispy white clouds in a deep blue sky
Cool, clean air to breathe
It means so much just being here
It's not my time to leave

I sit by the fire, my dog by my side
Watching the flames burn bright
Peaceful thoughts fill my head
I'll sleep content tonight.

Esther Jones

HEATHCLIFF

In a corner of blue sky
The forked tree of night despairs,
Flinging its bare limbs wild
Above its heart-shadow's trunk.

Beneath the soil
The knotted roots are
The hope that anchored
Love to the moor.

Its fear creaks in the breeze.
The brown-black darkness
Turns to man.

Louise Mills

THE ART OF LIVING

Talent is needed to pursue any art
Without it we're handicapped from the start
One art demands more than all the rest
The 'Art of Living' is a never-ending test

Is it wise to show completely how much you care
Or be taken for granted that you'll always be there?
Does too easily gained devotion indicate the meek
Breeding future boredom and more exciting company to seek?

Should forgiveness be offered when the doubts remain
That your illusions could be shattered once again?
Is it possible to regain the happiness you once knew
Or decide a new start is best for both of you?

Could too much help given end at the receiver's cost
When they become too dependent and their own confidence lost?
Should you lie to save a friend
If it means others suffer in the end?

When you think you're becoming master of the art
A new experience thrusts you right back at the start
But should your interest and endurance never cease
You'll be able to admire your own masterpiece.

Joyce Atkinson

THE TREE

In 1973 my daughter paid 15p for a tree,
From school it came, Scots pine by name.
It measured inches in a pot
And made its home in a garden spot.
Birds have nested every year,
But now it's not just magpies and pigeons
But squirrels too, by my back window in full view.
The pleasure this tree has given me,
The secrets it's heard and shade it's afforded
Many have died, but their memory recorded
Sitting under the branches in peaceful repose,
Drinking tea and watching the humming bee.
I'm grateful for the year of the tree
When it was our duty to plant
Nearly for free!

Rosemary C Whatling

AUTUMN AND SPRING

I'm nearing autumn - you are still spring
I only meant this to be a fling
But it goes deeper than I thought
Into my life such joy you have brought.

An Adonis who says he loves me
Deep down inside I know it can't be
You promise that you will always be true
I don't know what I'll do without you.

You'll break my heart when you go away
And I'm not sure how I'll face that day
You've given me more than you know
But I'll survive when you have to go.

Don't let it be yet, stay for a while
You are the one who can make me smile
If I were younger we'd have a chance
But I know soon we'll have our last dance.

Ann Blair

HAUNTING MEMORIES

There was a tall lady who lived in a wood
Some folk said that she was very, very good.
Some folk, however, said she was bad.
But when I heard this, it made me mad.

So I waited every day for the lady to pass by
And when I saw her face I could only cry . . .
Then she sat astride her broomstick
And soared up into the sky, black cat and all!

Dylis M Letchford

EVERY SECOND COUNTS

From your first cry - animation in the world,
Until your last cry when you will depart,
Every second counts, your life as unfurled,
To count all the seconds, 'tis a work of art.

For we know not the second when we start,
Advancing knowledge cannot answer that,
The unknown factor as God shall impart,
And so our last second we know not what.

Time is a mystery all of our days,
Time has no beginning, it has no end,
We are little sparks - flash and end our ways,
We terminate as how we wend or tend.

If your mind thinks slow or fast like the trains,
The seconds divide your losses and gains,
Enjoy living water from all the founts,
Then you will know every second counts.

For our beating hearts tick-tock every hour,
Yet have no power to grow a flower,
Fly in aircraft like a bird in the sky,
Plod about on two legs and yet to die.

For you can work awhile or sleep awhile,
And progress your life with all of your guile,
Drinking living water from all of the founts,
Always remember every second counts.

Dennis Parkes

TWINKLE, TWINKLE

Twinkle, twinkle, little star
Shining bright yet so far
So far yet so clear
Makes you look so near

Makes me think of things good
Bright and clear so you should
You are always there
I have no fear

Twinkling in the sky at night
Makes everything feel right
Just a twinkle in my eye
Even when there are clouds at night in the sky

Always there, never fear
Though it may not be clear
Twinkle, twinkle, little star
The brightest by far

Always there for me
Even if I cannot see
Just a clear night
And there you are, twinkling bright.

Garry Bedford

YOU FLIRT AND TANTALISE MY SOUL

I long to gaze within your eyes
And hear the sound of your tender sighs,
As we talk and as we speak,
I long to kiss you on the cheek.

Your winning smile and knowing grin,
That pleasure comes from deep within,
You flatter me with what you say
And dispel my fears in disarray.

How I long that I might kiss your lips,
Like nectar sweet; with longing sips.
To know the thoughts within your head,
Would lead me to my lover's bed.

I know your love it has control,
It satisfies both body and soul,
In my thoughts you'll always be,
Now and for eternity!

You flirt and tantalise my soul,
With little white lies, I'd lose control,
But gently, you lead the way
And hold my love, so it will stay.

Within your arms, I long to be,
Safe and secure for eternity
And when my night it turns to day
I know your love won't slip away.

David Watkins

CELEBRATIONS

The invitation jumped out of the post,
'Join with them, the poets who do have the most'.
She picked up her pen
And found an envelope, on which to write a storming yen
To win a super hamper,
Or at least that's what she hoped.

Celebrations are afoot,
Join with them and raise a glass
Well done to one and all,
In the scheme of things
It's been a ball!

Underlying, all the hard work
The final decision will fall on their shoulders
Cos at the end of the day
It's their call.

But in the meantime,
Well done and keep on writing
To all poets of poems
Big and small!

Gillian A Brown

ACTORS' SONNET
(Inspired following a production of Romeo and Juliet)

Bravo! Hail good thespians of the play,
I salute your flowing recitations,
That in the Bard of Avon's words did sway,
To inflame my soul in thought's elations,
Thus being star'd by this play's noble verse
And 'thralling rhyme, its pitch and melody,
Its pun, its tragic melodrama terse,
And final starry lovers' threnody,
How can I praise enough your acting's worth?
For in a thousand palpitating 'I's'
It has already been given rich birth,
In whistles, shouts, applause and plaintive sighs,
Thus this acclaim gives honour to your art,
But let's acknowledge now, the poet's part.

Barry Bradshaigh

ELY CATHEDRAL

You see it carved in stone
On the sundial in the market square:
'A city built on a hill
Cannot be hid'.

You see it carved in stone
And know it to be true:
The great 'Ship of the Fens'
Cannot be hid.

You see her from a distance
As you drive across the fen:
The single tower standing at the West Front
Like the high prow of the vessel;

And as you get closer
The eight-sided lantern is apparent,
Rearing up amidships
Behind the fo'c'sle.

You see her from a distance
And see her closer too,
Whether you drive up the Forehill
Or the Back Hill.

You enter the cathedral
And repeat the words of Matthew's gospel:
'A city built on a hill
Cannot be hid'.

A city built on a hill
Cannot be hid,
Any more than you would want to hide your light
Under a bushel.

Stan Downing

THE FAIRGROUND

In the amusement park,
All the fun of the fair
Rides on ghost train and Noah's ark.
Carousel, caterpillar, then a chair.

Sideshows, stalls full of prizes.
Toy tanks to roll into slots
Hoopla with its deft disguises
Darts: you had to spear the spots.

Roll your pennies, coconut shy
Fountain shoot and tin can alley
'Four balls for sixpence,' was the cry
Throwing them at poor Aunt Sally.

Fortune teller - Gypsy Rose Lee
Candyfloss, cold ice cream.
Hamburgers instead of tea
It really is a child's dream.

Sawdust balls covered in fabric
On a length of strong elastic
Funny hats with words so comic
Be a brick and kiss me quick.

Sounds of music into the night,
Hundreds of light bulbs shining bright.
For the children at least
A fairground is a feast.

Alfred Smirk

THE RIVER LEEN

The once pristine River Leen,
Now a brick filled, polluted stream,
Where once roach and minnow swam,
Lies a supermarket trolley and a rusting pram.
Where once we paddled with tender feet,
Lies broken glass and an old car seat.
By the Castle Rock it rushed hell bent,
Meandering down to the River Trent,
Through hamlet, village and fledgling town,
Past summer fields and woodland brown.
Crocus bloomed along the banks
And daffodils in serried ranks,
All built over by bridge and road,
Gone is the habitat of frog and toad.
Under factories and houses now,
No longer do the willows bow,
Where anglers dipped a baited hook,
In a crystal clear, winding brook.
'Twas long ago when it was clean,
Nottingham's ancient River Leen.
Now it flows through a man-made channel,
To end its life in a dark canal.

Kenneth V Jackson

PRIDE BEFORE THE FALL

You were loath to go
We knew you couldn't stay
Yet you lingered like that summer
Soft and gentle with each day

Precious time stood still
Stolen nights together
Memories to last
Forever and ever

Somehow you took our daughter
Down the aisle as bride
She knew, you both walked tall
In triumph, joy and pride

That dusk the swallows gathered
Wing by feather on the wire
And every eve for nigh two weeks
Waiting, circling ever higher

You hung on, stretching summer
To the limit of your strength
Till the honeymoon was over
And you could go at length

The leaving was so quiet
Full of hush and peace
Beautiful and painless
A truly rare release

The wire was deserted
The birds had flown as well
And so this time of year
I feel compelled to tell
How with each September's swallows
I thankfully recall
Your chosen time of going
With pride before the fall.

V Jean Tyler

IN THE UMBRA

Fish lie sideways
On the slimy breasts
Of stagnant ponds,
In the twilit eve
Of human blunder.

Blue sky darkens,
As shrouds, like clouds,
Eclipse the sun,
And flowers wilt,
Then wither in the umbra.

Birds drop like rain
From seedless trees
In woodlands stark
With rigor mortis,
Where silence echoes
Through their brittle boughs
Like roaring thunder.

Drab, like winter's
Veil of death looms,
Like penance,
Over cheerless,
Lifeless tundra.

Harry Crompton-fils

THE ZOO

When I was young I was taken to the zoo
All kinds of animals I saw, lions and tigers too
Monkeys jumping up on tyres
Giraffes' long necks bending over wires
Polar bears in their dens climbing up on rocks
An elephant giving rides for the children's pleasure
A lion in his small cage pacing up and down
So sad he looks, I hear him roar, his eyes a-glare
So many people stare - what ever is he doing there?
How cruel, I thought, do we care?
It is really us who keep him there
All these people come here to explore
They pay their money at the gate
And give the animals their awful fate
How I wish I could set them free
And put the people behind the bars for free
A spectacle that would be
For all the animals to come and see.

Kath Gay

ASPEN

When I awoke this morning
my tree was wearing
a headdress of little red catkins.
She will soon complete her costume
with a robe of red catkins.
One day she will lose her headdress
and after that her gown will go.
She will wear a crown of buds
and a leafy cloak will follow.
In the summer her green leaves will flutter.
Birds will twitter in her branches.
In the autumn she will strew the garden
with fragments from her russet gown.
When winter comes and she stands naked
the snow king will lend her a white mantle.
But now she is wearing
a headdress of little red catkins.
It is spring!

Tessa Hammond

UNTIL WE ARE ONE
(A poem for Sophie)

If I could choose a night to comfort me when you are gone
The night would be a summer's night so blue
With silver stars like the fallen tears of parted loves
I would feel your breath against my face
And your sweet smile would make me warm again
Until we are one

If I could choose a day to ease my pain when you are gone
The day would be a winter's day so clear
With sunlight on the snow like fields of melted gold
A nightingale would sing your voice into my heart again
Until we are one

If I could choose a time to comfort me when you are gone
It would be the day you made my life complete
When there was no greater wealth or beauty
Than the sound of your heart beating next to mine
You brought perfection to this world, sleep now my life
Until we are one

Michael William Molden

THERE WAS A LIFETIME ONCE

There was a lifetime once different it seemed to this
when I was a child
There was a moment suddenly I was not
And freedom of the open, happy fields was gone,
then I was captive in a wider world, leaving behind the close up
faces of the flowers, woven nests with ovals of blue and green,
the raindrop hung suspended in the glittering April rain;
there was then the rainbow's promise after thunder,
swallows in still welcoming eaves and sudden laughter.
There was a time of impulsive joy, quick as lark's rise to blue,
and seeking violets in the secret wood's ways and primrosing,
the moment was lived all summer long,
the winter safe by hearth of cottage home.

Which moment was last look on meadow, river
and the encircling lanes?
Which moment did the Gates of Eden close with innocence gone?
There was a moment once I was a child - which moment was I not?

Allyson Kennedy Kiddle

CUTHBERT

Behind the old stone church an autumn sun
dispels its fire on gravestone, grass and thicket,
penetrating history's fallen light.
Across the causeway matin bells ring out,
black against the sky, the priory burns.

We walk the sheep tracks, wander over pebbles,
reeded sand dunes, rocks and tidal pools
to reach the broken stones of Cuthbert's cell.
Here he fought the Devil, built a wall
of peace and prayer, knelt and talked to seals.

All day long we breathe the power he knew
in driftwood, shell, pebble, bird, sun -
beauty that divides and makes things one
and when mauve evening clouds pile the horizon
and light escapes and pours into the sea

and peewits cry and waders tread the shores
wet reflections, scuffing pools of gold,
the evening star flies in like a glass bird
and on the causeway where the tide recedes
from pole to pole the pilgrim's way is clear.

Susan Skinner

THE YELLOW SKIP

We moved into our new house and hired ourselves a skip
    so all our garden rubbish wouldn't make the close a tip.
We went to bed one evening and next day when we woke
    we looked inside the yellow skip and neither of us spoke.
Before our very eyes we saw a mass of alien things
    there were old TV aerials and broken kiddies' swings.
There was a bright green garden fence and miscellaneous stuff.
    The mystery, it deepened, as none of it belonged to us.
We realised at night they came, the alien skip-tippers.
    We never heard a single thing; they must have come in slippers.
Some neighbours asked us if we'd mind if they dumped
    some of their trash.
We said we really didn't mind and asked them for no cash.
    In fact it brought us all quite close, we ended up quite pally.
    The street took on a new name, we now call it Skip Alley.

Maureen Peacock

MAKE THE WORLD A LITTLE YOUNGER

Are we as young as we think when
The world is just an infant?
We . . . born out of cosmic dust -
Seeded just a moment ago.

Are we as old as we think when
The world has seen it all?
We . . . carbon-based entities from
Outer space . . . long ago.

Can we achieve just a little of
What the world achieved in
The blink of an eye,
When as part of that world, we die?

The world is just a child,
Without the arms of its mother,
So let's embrace the world
And comfort it . . . as it grows old.

Kenneth Cutts

ON REFLECTION

Frost and sun fresh risen
newborn upon the autumn air
Red berries in the bottom hedge.
Birds full-throated sing their praise
of morning sun and autumn's breath.
New sights, new sounds and yet
landscape dies when night descends.
Sleep wrapped the snails, birds, beasts,
while scavengers wake to plunder
bins and bulging sacks for food scraps
discarded by the human race
that lesser kind not starve
in days of winter yet to come.
In town shoppers skid and slide
on icy pavements, outside stores
Christmas dressed with frost-laced windows,
intent on gathering festive fare
in celebration of a Birth.
While in streets, propped by railings,
slumped on steps, blue with cold,
tattered remnants of the human race, beg.

Peggy Netcott

THE LOTUS SEED

I believe I have a lotus seed, laying dormant deep inside,
It's resting in my heart space, a space where my hope once died.
The seed is a very precious jewel, waiting to awaken my heart,
A heart that in the past has broken, suffered damage, torn apart.
The seed brings hope, for I believe that one day it will start to grow,
Through compassion and loving kindness,
Tiny roots will be the first to show.
With time the roots will grow strong,
Anchoring the lotus to my heart's ground,
Roots entwined around my heart,
With light and love, my heart will be bound,
A shoot will rise up from the seed, stretching up to merge with the sky,
Growing, rising, travelling with love, as it grows to reach up high.
During its journey will be formed a bud,
Encasing spiritual love and light,
Beautiful petals forming and resting,
Conserving energy in its care of darkest night,
I wait for the day when the flower is fully formed,
And the bud will open wide,
Exposing the beautiful lotus flower,
Which for so long in the bud did hide,
As the perfect petals slowly uncurl, opening my heart up to the light,
I imagine the lotus flower above me, a vision of loveliness,
A wonderful sight,
The numerous petals unfolding, reflecting the many facets of my soul,
Spiritual enlightenment, integration of emotion,
Heart and Earth as one whole.
And so I meditate and patiently wait for that precious day to come,
When my inner being and my lotus flower,
Will be merged together as one.

Corinda Daw

I GUESS THAT I'M A GHOST

I'm not quite sure if I'm a ghost
But guess it must be so.
My family state I've passed away
And surely they should know.

The fact that I have breathed my last
I can't get through my head,
And yet a gravestone never lies.
The damned thing states - I'm dead.

I glide down ill-lit corridors,
In draughty halls I roam.
In graveyards when the moon is full,
I really feel at home.

The front door isn't used a lot,
I walk straight through the wall
And cats which purred around my feet
Don't like me now at all.

A constant chill around me thrives,
Whilst through the night I groan.
My hobbies rest on clanking chains
Or wailing down the phone.

With chat they all review my life,
Whilst I just hang around
And watch them looting all the things
Of one beneath the ground.

It seems I must accept my fate,
So join me in a toast.
To long and happy haunting days,
A full-time working ghost.

Richard Bradshaw

WIND OF PREY
THE PRIDE OF A TUMBLED TREE
(A Christian ethic)

Shadows in the night,
solitude and pride,
in the day, saturated green
with sapling flock,
wind gathering wide.

Wind of prey
upon swaddling bark,
branching pangs,
beneath moonlight dark.

Branches clumsy in different directions,
in springtime leaf or winter stark,
cordially gather.
Trace of age, a compact mould, rooting
scouts enforce to corporeal weather.

Wind of prey,
upon swaddling bark,
branching pangs,
beneath moonlight dark.

Above the earth below,
the ivy lays its roost,
the falling leaves of autumn,
the fertile golden brown,
of the next year's boost.

Wind of prey,
upon swaddling bark,
branching pangs,
beneath moonlight dark.

In stormy wind the tumbling tree
is a shabby shawl
smuggling roots, lever closer to despair,
the trunk a flaking cave,
the inward mellow call.

Wind of prey,
upon swaddling bark,
branching pangs,
beneath moonlight dark.

Windswept clouds, a downtrodden
perception of a tree would ever last.
Twigs and scattered leaves
disperse from gruesome age,
nature's awaiting cast.

Wind of prey,
upon swaddling bark,
branching pangs,
beneath moonlight dark.

Colum Donnelly

AND MORE YES

Inside heart bleeds again
Those raw gifts you bring
Startled, you see my being
Celebrate it all, why not?
Let us rush the thunder
Distant bells and oh the joy
With silence no more
And nature so and no less
Reign as master or law
And dream more dreams, yes.

Malachy Trainor

GOODBYE CRUEL WORLD

Days are black and endless, nothing new to see,
Pain and anger swallows me in, or maybe that's just me.
I don't belong in such a world, I feel I don't fit in,
Whichever way I play it, I never seem to win.

I've lost all my self confidence and wish for me to die
What purpose do I serve to live, it's all been such a lie.
Watching normal people about their daily life,
I'm happy to be out of it, I cannot bear the strife.

It's easier with alcohol, it helps to quell the pain
And then I can punish myself for all I didn't gain.
Mental pain is hard to bear, it cuts your heart in two,
Oh, to be reborn and start again, some happiness anew.

Society demands perfection and I hate how I look,
To see myself daily, is bad in any book.
I'd like to be a Dispirin, dissolve and disappear,
It seems far more preferable, than dealing with the fear.

Perhaps one day I'll find myself, forget about the past,
Welcome happiness and love again, how long will it last?
This Devil's curse consumes me, it strikes day or night,
The power and intensity gives me quite a fright.

And so I say goodbye to another lonely day,
I've got through yet a further one in my own special way.
If I wasn't meant to leave you and go off up above,
You can guarantee, on this Earth, I gave some of my love.

Hayley E Hanson

THE WAR GENERATION
(With thanks to Vera Brittain)

Locked in your time
voices petalled in youth,
flowers earthed in fertile soil . . .
persistent, persistent drumbeat;
letters, poems from the trenches,
your love, your valour, despair,
brother-in-arms lies on brother
mud and mud, through the year.

You the bereaved tell your story
the waiting, the suffering, the pain
of losing the ones you love dearly
your lover, your brother, your friends;
the closing of youth from its promise
the numbness within and within,
a war dragging on, unrelenting,
your work only saving your brain.

This girl in the end is the woman
her light burning with zeal,
fixed with an inner conviction -
peace in our lives come what will.
I feel your pain and your passion,
share your beliefs, your ideals,
you've woken in me understanding
we are close though we never shall meet.

Only in spirit I reach you,
opened, touched by your dreams
and though you've moved on now forever,
I'm one human being you've changed.

Glenna Welsh

AUTUMN WALK

Down the road I walked that beautiful autumn day
The trees stood dressed in gold to greet me on my way
Over the hills and down the dales I wandered on that day
And the splendour of the autumn was with me all the way

I wandered by still waters and gentle flowing streams
And down some country roads I never before had been
Emerging from a shady spot I found the fog descended
And now with all my heart I wished my journey ended

I walked on and on and no one could I see
So I sat down to rest with my back against a tree
I closed my eyes a moment and wondered where I had been
Then right before me the most beautiful girl I'd ever seen

Her golden hair reached to her waist a lovely smile upon her face
With shining eyes this beauty is full of charm and grace
She holds my hand, I hold my breath, my heart is beating fast
I hold her close, her lips touch mine, a spell around me she has cast

A thousand thoughts flash through my mind as I hold her in my arms
Please be mine beautiful maiden for I'm captivated by your charm
She smiles and turns away - oh what have I done wrong?
I open my eyes, my arms are around the tree
And my sweet lass has gone.

Harry Skinn

THE LINCOLNSHIRE FENS IN MAY

How great to be in Lincolnshire and work outdoors in May
Where you can walk with nature and see wonders every day
The cuckoo has now arrived and is looking round for nests
He sings his song so beautiful and never hardly rests

The wild duck has had one clutch and prepares to nest again
The moorhen sits upon her nest in sunshine and in rain
The lark is way up in the sky and singing its great tune
She will lay her eggs in the sugar beet rows and hatch them off in June

The wheat crops they are growing well and are almost 6 inches high
And soon the harrier will return and plunge down from the sky
He will build the nest down on the ground and then he will start to mate
He'll then be hunting from dawn till dusk to feed her she can't wait

The hares they have been chasing around the fields all spring
The little leveretts are now running around and will hide under anything
The plover she has laid her eggs and sits upon her nest
Her mate he dives down on you if you go near he will protest

The cock pheasant struts around and shows his pride and style
His mate is sitting comfortable she has been sitting quite a while
In 3 weeks time she will be proud and strutting with her chicks
May even be a dozen as they start to scratch and pick

You walk along the large drain side and something will catch your eye
It's one of the prettiest birds you will ever see, the kingfisher gliding by
He will perch upon a reed plant and looks so bright and real
Then he will dive down in the stream and come up with a meal.

One of the loveliest sights you will ever see as the river comes in view
Is a swan sitting on her nest so proud and graceful too
But walk too close to the nesting site and you could soon be caught
Her proud male mate is watching you and he guards her like a fort

The woodland floors are covered with bluebells everywhere
Also in some sunny spots the lily of the valley smells sweetly in the air
It's great to be in Lincolnshire and see all these beautiful things in May
I wish that you could walk with me, you would have a lovely day.

Len Woodhead

NIALL'S KITE

The kite was a dragon,
A rip-roarer,
Awash in the flips and fancies of every air tremor,
Blondin on a string.

Its two yellow bows had lodged in the pig feeder,
Triangles in a trough,
Stunting the stunts.

A pop-up breeze, sweet-talker,
Tweaked a cheek, cooing,
Making the kite jump, hop
In a frenzy of flounce.

Niall had come to it in a panic,
Eyes as full as oysters,
Bangs in his chest.

He was the kite-dancer, a Mongolian messenger
Twirling across fields,
Merlin and Merlin tied to the sky,
Crow scaring.

With a twist, a tug, a marionette lug
He bullied out the tensions,
Springing the kite.
Small boy's delight!

Phil Fox

DREAM OF MY LOVE

By night as I slept, the fairy queen came,
'Three wishes are yours, pray give them a name.'
Come happy day, when I'm with you,
Sweetest of dreams will then all come true.

I asked not honour, wealth and fame
Nor for happiness, health and great name,
But only for you, for you, just you.

In dreamland a wave of a wand and behold,
You are beside me gowned in cloth of gold.
Hand in hand we joyfully stroll
Till we rest by sweet leafy bole.

There 'neath the shade of the tropic palms,
Your lips divine as you lie in my arms
Such is the heaven of dreamland.

Dull morning breaks, where is my love?
Gone with dreams on wings of a dove,
Oh for the wings of blessed bird of peace,
For the powers of famed Golden Fleece.

Ne'er again I'd dream the joys I spend with you.
Visions of the night would be sweet reality.

Captain Valentine Daly

MY CHILDREN

The children I had have all grown up and gone,
But my love for them still lingers on.
They're mothers and fathers with ones of their own,
And sometimes I envy them as I feel alone.

I'm luckier than most, I have a husband who cares
And children who love me and also do theirs.
For their children are a part of me,
As I started it, so I have more love as part of it.

There isn't a day I don't think of them
And always will until the very end.

Babs Tock

MY PAINTBOX

Oh that I could paint a picture
Of our old world free from pain,
Wars and famine would be no more
Peace and harmony reign.

Dear little children from every land
Smiling with plenty to eat,
Fresh flowing water for everyone,
Good shoes for poor callused feet.

Every creature to feel the sun,
Cruel battery farming unknown,
Chickens pecking at corn in the field
Livestock would unshackled, roam.

Everything beautiful, happy and glad
Man speaking peace unto man,
Living together in faith and love
This is what our creator planned.

'Twould be the world God had intended
Where milk and honey doth flow,
Lion would lie down with the lamb,
But such peace we will never yet know.

He formed His creation, wonderful, pure
Full of beauteous peaceful love,
But greedy man ruined it all down the years,
Our Lord must be weeping above.

I can never paint this picture
Of God's world and how it should be,
Until man repents and turns to the Saviour
My paintbox remains grey, to me.

Dorothy M Mitchell

EDEN REVISITED

Adam and Eve frolicked naked in the Garden of Eden
That's because there was no one else around to see them
Just for fun they had a little grapple
It wasn't very comfortable, Eve was laying on an apple.

'Shall we eat it?' she did say,
'After all an apple a day keeps the doctor away.'
'No we mustn't we've been told, let's not be that bold -
Who's this doctor anyway?'

The apple was eaten, that's for sure!
And it caused an almighty uproar,
'Who's been eating my apple?'
A voice came from above,
'Not me,' said Adam, 'did I my love?'
'Not me,' said Eve, 'there must be some mistake
It must have been that bloody snake.'

'The snake didn't do it,' said the voice from above.
'You've told me lies, so no more love.
The good life's over, no more living your life in clover
Cover yourselves with the leaves from the figs
No more running naked, you're going to have some kids.'

Two sons they had, but things were never stable
In a fit of rage Cain killed his brother Able.
Banished to the Land of Nod
His feet had gone where no one else had ever trod
On this journey he did not tarry
But when he got there who was he supposed to marry?
To start the world's population
He must find someone for copulation
Throughout his life, he'll find no other
The only living woman, is his mother.

This riddle, remains unsolved,
Perhaps the world just evolved!

Roy Perkins

NORTH WIND

Blow hard you icy-cold wind: blow
Your breath scars the valleys and shapes gorges below,
Ripping tops from mountains like fluffy eiderdown
Trees bow down before you with no mercy shown,

Skin is scoured with vengeance from animal and man
Clouds thrown across the skies and then torn apart,
Hands are raised to protect faces and eyes
Seas rising rain clouds, covering darkened skies,

Wave after wave now pounding wide open spaces
Wind with the force of nature now unleashed,
This is the power of the wind from the north
Blowing wildly, now showing its ugly teeth

Rain pounding with the impact of hammers
Tearing apart the very ground beneath,
Rivers forming deep below, underground caverns moulded,
Torrents forced from their hiding, earth is now folded

This force of nature too wild to harness
Broken trees tossed into the air,
Suddenly all is quiet; all is still once more,
Seas are calm, wind abated, peace has come to
The lonely shore.

Len Clarke

SELF-DESTRUCTION

Man wasn't put on this Earth to fight
As I glance around, dead and wounded fill my sight.
How futile, all this bloodshed and waste of life,
Is there an answer to end this war and strife?

A small child squats with her doll clutched near
Down her cheek rolls a single tear.
She can't understand why her mother can't speak,
Why she lays so still, when her love she seeks.

Just another statistic in this war without end,
All in the name of religion and politics they defend.
How can religion be the cause of such things?
Knowing full well all the pain and misery war brings.

With this new century upon us, let us have peace.
Let man love his neighbour, the fighting must cease.
Let us all live together with love, not hate,
Strive to unite the world before it's too late.

Maggy Rosentritt

IF I COULD CHOOSE

If I could choose a time to die
It wouldn't be in spring
Because then I wouldn't see the flowers grow
Or hear the skylark sing.

But if I should die in summer
I would miss the Earth aglow
The flowers, trees and all of nature
These things I wouldn't know.

But then again to die in autumn
Would be a terrible thing
I'd miss the gold of the autumn leaves
That surely would be a sin.

There's only winter left to die
But what a time to go
To miss the stillness of a winter's night
And the earth 'neath a mantle of snow.

So I'll leave it to nature, she's wiser than me
I think that she will know best
She'll pick the time when I should go
And lay me down to rest.

Joan Hartland

OLD BLUE EYES

When I was born I was bright and new
Blue as the sky on a summer's day
I had millions of relations all the same as me
Blue as the azure firmament.

A million became a hundred, then fifty, then ten
Ten bright blue buttons on a cornflower dress
We went on walks in the countryside
Relaxed in a punt on the river
Loving fingers released us to reveal yielding flesh
Summers passed, our frock became unfashionable
It hung in a dark wardrobe away from the world.

After a year or two we left the dress to go and live in a button box
Mother of pearl told us tales of distant oceans and life at the depth
                                                              of the sea
Crystal enthralled us with images of parties and hunt balls
Brass told us of a soldier's life, trenches full of mud
Dusky, dark-eyed maidens on foreign shores
Our box was bright red with elephants parading on its sides
Like Sheherazade it beguiled us with myths and legends from
                                                    eastern lands.

Children would open the box and study the contents as if they
                                                      were jewels

No jewel, I
Just sky blue plastic, nothing to mark me as different
Brothers came and went, ten became eight, eight became two
Two bright blue buttons in a box.

Teddy was blind
Too much love had robbed him of embroidered sight
My brother and I were chosen to let him see again
To see the sun rise
To see the friendly faces of other toys
To see that special face, green eyes, golden curls
The face of one you love
The face of one who loves you.

Held in a warm embrace, cosy, safe
Sweet breath wafting over us
Two old blue eyes on an old bear's face
Two eyes that hold the wisdom of the world
That understands the unspoken prayer.

T M Slomczynski

IT'S SOMETHING

It's something to know when the east wind blows
That the sky behind is blue
Though the storm drives fast, it will end at last
And the sun comes shining through.

It's something to keep when the snow lies deep
One's heart and spirit in tune
To be sunny and try the whole year through
In November as well as June.

It's something to stand to the work on hand
And carry the share of the load
To keep up the pace with a smile on your face
When we come to the uphill road.

It's something to feel the promise is real
That cheeriness somehow brings
That whatever goes wrong, there's a hope and a song
With God's love at the centre of things.

Edward Brookes

MAYBE THIS WAITING IS GIVING US BOTH PREPARATION TIME

Maybe this is a preparation period.
Maybe all this waiting is giving us both time,
To adjust our minds to these new changes and challenges
Coming to us both as we are merging into one.
There are big and little changes to go through alone and
Together.
Changes you may not agree with; challenges
I may not want to go through.
My life is going to change for certain,
There is a great deal with much compromising.
I am taking a huge gamble.
There is no guarantee it is going to work out.
Finding and living with your soulmate.
It is not always a bed of roses,
It takes courage, dedication, mutual respect and
Spirituality.
Trust, care, understanding and unconditional love.
It doesn't come easy.
We will have to work hard at it every day,
It isn't easy earning any rewards when it isn't there.
People change, I change,
You don't know what person these transitions turn you into,
As a person until you have gone through them yourself.
If you have yearned to become one, with your soulmate,
We are still two separate individuals blessed with God's
Free will, living inside us both.
We cannot earn this from another person.
We cannot take it away from another individual,
Not even your soulmate.

Jenifer Ellen Austin

DARKNESS

She sat in darkness
But she did not notice
Her heart was bitter
But she did not care
Her eyes were blind
But still she tried to see
She did not notice the sniggers rise
He came as silence and tried to call her
He came as moonlight
But was shut out
He came as sunlight
But her darkness ate him
He did not count the price
And then he gave her the only gift any other couldn't
He gave her what would truly break through
He gave his own life so she would get her own back
And from that moment she was his own.

Ann-Marie Spittle

BE STILL

Be still and know that God is here
In your presence now
Sending rays of quietness
His love and peace and gentleness
Are signs that He is watching you
For you are special in His heart
And will be now for evermore.

Marian Bythell

A DEVON SPRING

I know it is a Devon Spring
When I can hear the chaffinch sing
And rooks are calling in the trees
Or wheeling on an April breeze.
In narrow lanes, the primrose peeps
From high-banked hedge, in which it sleeps
The cold-dark through, and comes at last
To flower, when chill Winter's passed.
The apple blossom on the bough
Sends fragrance wafting to me now.
Daffodils gaily toss their heads,
Brilliant yellow in their beds.
The lambs are frisking, woolly-white.
Returning swallows swoop in flight.
When birdcalls through the woodlands ring,
I know it is a Devon Spring.

Diana H Adams

WHISPERS OF CREATION

As I sit beneath the trees
In the shade from the burning sun
All is still - but wait
I hear a rustling amongst the leaves
As they dance to and fro
In the shimmering breeze

I hear melodious sounds
In the woodland
Where I love to stroll
The constant drone of a busy bee
Carrying sweet honey for my tea

Joyous, tinkling notes
Beckon me
As I wander through
This glade of pure delight
A gurgling, babbling stream
Ripples gently on its journey
Down to the sea

Shuffling in the long grass
On a glorious summer's day
I hear a snuffling sound
As a spiky hedgehog
With twitching nose
Searches for a juicy worm
As he makes his presence known

In the dappled sunlight
Soft as a falling feather
A dainty butterfly
Flutters her delicate wings
As she gently alights
Like a lady's parasol
Upon the flowering carpet
Of the shadowed wood

Whispering winds whom we cannot see
But whose voice is truly heard
As it moans in the chimney tops
Sighs in the freshening breeze
Shakes the cascading curtains of leaves
Shouts with awesome anger
Breaking and bruising
Nature's tranquil scene.

O wondrous Creator
Recreate us
That we may hear
The smallest whisper of God.

Frances M Gorton

TWILIGHT TIME

When twilight falls and bedtime calls
For the birds that go to roost
There's an eerie silence for a while
Then all the bats fly out in file
And another world awakens
Slimy slugs crawl across the path
Next morning you find the aftermath
Moths flutter around the outdoor light
Determined to give my wife a fright
Things with dangly legs and wings like lace
Fly up into the burning light
Then fall down into your face
The croaking of a frog or maybe it's a toad
Whatever it is it sounds like fun
In the pond across the road
The chirping of the crickets goes on from dusk till light
It's magical to sit and listen to the noises of the night.

Alan Wilcox

LOVE SONG

We need no balcony, no moonlit bay,
Our love is infinite and here to stay
Not just a brief romantic interlude
A stepping stone on life's romantic way.

For we belong together, you and I
Created - as the very Earth and sky
To share our hopes, our dreams, our lives
As long as God allows and life survives.

To share our health, enjoy the wealth
That being with each other brings
To live each hour, to scent each flower
And marvel at each bird that sings.

Your meeting kiss, your greeting smile that radiates your face,
That lovely face I know so well illuminates each place
We go together - everyone can see that we belong,
Each hidden glance a merry dance, the words that make the song.

An age-old song, a modern song, a lovely melody,
That comforts life and lifts our hopes
And lets our love go free,
Long may it last my darling, forever is too soon
For what can match our symphony, two loving hearts in tune.

Leonard T Coleman

REFLECTIONS

Sense the noisy silence of virgin-white snow
Mile upon mile of an unspoilt calm
Weather-beaten branches knotted and gnarled
Weighed down to the limit as their arms unfold.

Telltale footprints leading to the duck pond
Frustrated beaks tapping at the ice
Small, joyous children daringly skating
Waving their arms as they giggle and fall.

Bright, glowing embers hiss, spit and crackling
Flickering shadows dancing in the dusk
Soft breaded squares very gently toasting
Pierced in the middle by a fork, red and hot.

From somewhere in the distance
Church bells are practising
Inviting its parish to join in prayer
Singers unite in 'The Holly and the Ivy'
Reminding us how grateful we are to be there.

Lynn Craig

CITY STREETS

Emerging from the desolate windswept dawn
Lies a fallen angel
A harbinger of death's decay
In the back street of cities' molten gold
People pass by - bemused and worried
For what will tomorrow bring?
Is there a spiritual foreboding - unfolding light?
The underground is dirty and terse
Waiting for man's changed recompense
In the still light lies a darkened soul
A wasting man cries
Cries of mercy to leave this place
But nothing comes of his plans
For the passenger of light is no longer
There with Babylon burning
Of bundled and flattened epitaphs
Of great and religious men
Unto birth and empire
For time is the eternal warrior
A vagabond of hanged perspectives
Of little and distant blessed dreams
The rats look wondrously toward crisp bags
Meanwhile both the tramps and rubbish multiply.

Finnan Boyle

TO A SNOWDROP

Oh you tiny little thing
    Are you the herald of the spring?
From the ground where you stay
    Looking for the light of day.

Oh you pretty little thing
    Are you the harbinger of spring?
On stilted legs your tiny face
    Ever dancing, full of grace.

Oh you lovely little thing
    Crowned in glory, like a king.
Nodding here and nodding there,
    Looking around you everywhere.

Oh you dainty little thing
    Beautiful as a butterfly wing.
With tiny petals white and clean,
    Ever waiting to be seen.

You arrive out of the blue
    When no one is expecting you.
You surprise us every year
    When we see your form appear.

You are not happy in the house
    Where you stand quiet as a mouse.
Admired at first with pleasing glances
    Then left, forgotten, for other fancies.

You are not with us very long
    But we miss you when you've gone.
Back to the earth, to sleep and rest
    And to return looking your best.

Who gave you the life you live?
    And what more can you give?
It is God who gave you this life's task,
    He gives it to everyone who asks.
Some make the grade but some may fall,
    But still He loves us, one and all.

Joan Smith

MY GOD

Does your God guide you on your way?
                      Mine does.
And help you cope throughout the day?
                      Mine does.
And call you when you go astray?
And tell you what to do and say?
                      Mine does.

Does your God worry when you sin?
                      Mine does.
And open His arms to fold you in?
                      Mine does
And bear with you through thick and thin?
And love you - whether you lose or win?
                      Mine does.

Does your God sometimes cry with you?
                      Mine does.
For things you try and just can't do?
                      Mines does.
And does He share your laughter too?
And sometimes actually laugh *at* you?
                      Mine does.

Does your God shake His head to chide?
                      Mine does.
And leave you with no place to hide?
                      Mine does.
But when cares of the day are cast aside
Does He tuck you up and say, 'Well, you tried.'
                      Mine does.

Nora Veysey

THE SCHIZOID SPREADING
(After Philip Larkin's 'The Whitsun Weddings')

All year, inside the sprawled minds that swept
    For centuries inland,
A low and sloping word was routward kept.
Loud skies flew by, thought-straddled battles, and
Endless voices floating on a cough.
A rattle smashed completely: pleasures dipped
And died; and now and then a spell of sparks
Defaced each week of beauty, truth and wrath,
Until the endless year, now crudely stripped
Encroached upon a hospital stars.

At first, I did not notice what a noise
    The madness made
Each patient that I stopped out: time deploys
The dints of mental illness like a grave.
And round the steeled wards, the groans and skirls
I took for porters hissing in their veils,
And went by pleading. Once I had slept there though,
I heard them, grimacing and screaming: girls
In pastiched torrid clothing, heels and nails,
All drugged completely, watching me flail.

As if out on the end of a vengeful scent
    Raving and complaining
At something which denied *them*. Lost, I bent
Backwardly and forwards, now defamed
And heard the horror once again and shrill:
The brain with bad welts beneath its boots
And furrowed foreheads; nurses proudly cracked;
An Empire shouting sl*t; and then the ferns,
The spitting gloves and tablets on the rack:
The cocoa, coffee; medicated flaps . . .

James Bellamy

CARE OF OUR COUNTRYSIDE

This wonderful Earth was a gift from above
Let us therefore protect it with kindness and love
So in the future, generations to come
Will be able to say they thought of us some

Let us leave to them the birds and the bees
The rivers, the mountains, flowers and trees
So that when they breathe we must ensure
That the air that they breathe is 100% pure

The woods have gone, one no longer sees
The open glades and towering trees
The ragwort, vetch and wiry fern
Have all diminished to the farmer's 'burn'.

From the fields and woods the rabbits have gone
And the trout in the stream well, we have none
No more do we hear the corncrake's call
No more do we see the elm leaves fall

The kingfisher now is almost extinct
The curlew too is on the brink
The trees are stripped down my old lane
Thanks to the scourge of acid rain

The cliffs and the shores to the tern are a haven
The crags and the rocks are home to the raven
The valley and woods where the kite has its nest
Must never be marred by man's greed and zest

What was once protected from damage and harm
Has now all gone under intensive farm
In my generation our loss is so vast
If it goes on like this we just cannot last

So please protect our countryside
And try to save it far and wide
And make a pledge and final solution
To rid this Earth of filth and pollution.

J Jones

JERUSALEM

Where is my Jerusalem?
Just a dream - far, far away.
For all is turmoil, disarray.
My nightmare is reality,
As war clouds gather silently.

In far-off lands I see their fear
As women grieve for those held dear.
Hopeless, helpless is my heart.
So far away I have no part
Of their harsh world and their deep pain.
I'll seek refuge in dream again.

Then I'll see peace unfurled,
Friendship blossoming in our world.
Black reaching out across to white,
Clasping hands together tight.
There are streams running crystal clear,
No pollution with fresh clean air.

Throughout the land such peace and calm,
It soothes my heart with quiet balm.
Then I awake and realise it is but a dream.
Tears fill my eyes for all that's lost and can't return.
Where is my Jerusalem?

Audrey Lay

DAWN

He was old - well past the eighty years, he was a man of words
often of a poetic turn of mind.
He had just been introduced to a newborn baby girl,
the following words flowed with ease from his mind
to pen and paper.
If you can remember the colour of a sovereign that
was the colour of her hair, add to that, eyes as blue as the sea
on a fine day, eyelashes so like a mini-waterfall
in delicate fine hair.
A button nose as the pearl teardrop from a bride's tiara,
a rosebud mouth pursed as if to say,
'I'm new!'
Arms and legs of that newborn, pink that only she could possess
ending in fingers and toes of baby cockleshells.
Now you can tell what the baby was like.
Her name was *Dawn*
for she was born at the break of day,
this was one beautiful baby girl.

Though he was old, he could still appreciate the beauty
of a new *dawn*
each word of this description is God's created beauty.

Erica Menzies

REQUIEM OF A CHILD

The crematorium is so bitter cold and unwelcoming.
It's just like school. 'Be quiet and sit there very still.'
Music, from a mighty organ somewhere, is softly playing,
As we shuffle and squeak in rows we all quickly fill.
In wonder. The silent space feels as if it is the sky
That's full of nothing, patiently waiting for the sun.
For we are here because my little gran has died.
I don't know where she has gone. In tears my mum,
Yet silently. It frightens me, it's so unlike her not to smile.
As we wait, a strange man talks. Others weep and sniffle
In the coldness.
I have Gran in my head. She would think this was vile.
'You're too young to understand,' they said. 'She was very old.'
We watch the coffin, as through the curtains it slowly goes.
To music she didn't like.
I feel her smile. Her funny laugh. Her lovely warm knee.
Mum says, 'She's gone now,' but I don't think she knows
How I saw her pain last week, as she kissed and cuddled me.
I'm not sad, but lonely. Together we had such special days.
'Be brave for us,' she's saying to me softly, 'you're so very much like me.'

George Carrick

THE VISION

It was early one morn,
I was watching the dawn
When it caught my eye,
This beautiful vision up in the sky.

So still and serene,
A vision of Christ!
It was the most wonderful sight
I had ever seen.

I have looked time after time
But all in vain,
Will I ever see His vision again?

P Block

GOD'S FACE

Man is born with just one face
Presented to the world.
That one face can have many faces
Waiting to be unfurled.

The faces can like masks display
The falseness of his being.
But when the 'true' face takes a hold
It's God's face that you're seeing.

Lindsey Susan Powell

THE LEAVES FELL ONE BY ONE

She strolled across the meadow
Bathed in the morning sun
I met her in the shady grove
And the leaves fell one by one

I held her gently in my arms
And said it must be done
So whilst we shared a fond embrace
The leaves fell one by one

As tears bedewed her rosy cheeks
I slung my trusty gun
And as I stoutly marched away
The leaves fell one by one

We shipped aboard a rusty tub
And sailed to meet the Hun
Our hearts were high and full of hope
As the leaves fell one by one

The enemies grim redoubt we stormed
All thought the day was won
But bullets flew in deadly hail
And the leaves fell one by one

Our lads now lie in lasting peace
Their gallant race is run
Let's not forget their sacrifice
When the leaves fell one by one.

Terence Leslie

CELEBRATION

Gather round the fireside glow,
Come from lands both high and low,
Wear ye cloth of darkest green,
So all around may know your name.
Dance with joy, the summer in,
By light and leaf and flowering stem,
Dance and spin an elfin reel,
See the Rood-mass set its seal.
Spin the wheel; chant the rune,
Darksome night shining moon,
Turn the seasons onward now,
Until the solstice meets its brow,
Toast and cheer with merry lust,
Savour ghosts in which we trust,
Strike the chords: laugh and play,
On this day: the first of May.
Hand fast at dawn, feel the dew form,
Being as one on this summer's morn,
Sweetly smell the garlands bright,
Till you are one within the Rite.
Cast the circle, light the flames,
Sprinkling salt, charge Athame,
Looking to the light, when there be fears,
A loving of life shouldn't bring tears.
The breath of nature is the key,
Rebirth, creation: so mote it be!

Josh Brittain

TO CHARLOTTE

Do the wild windswept moors
Call to you, in the darkest hours?
Do they send their friend the wind
To bring you back to them again?

A bleak landscape of grass and heather
Where you and your sisters, walked together
Dreaming of a life, you were never to know
Did you talk about the places, you would like to go?

Though in your grave you lie
You have not been forgotten with time
You still live on, in people's hearts
With admiration for your works.

Happiness, seemed to delude you, most of your life
Except for a few months, when you became a wife
But then my assumptions, are from what I have read
By people who wrote about you, when you were dead.

Oh, I know you loved the moors
The howling wind, held no fears
Was it a comfort to your ears
As you wiped away your tears?

Linda Tosney

THE RISE OF THE SUN

(In loving memory of Jack Bartlett - Grandad)

As you lay there sick in your hospital bed
you looked me in the eye and told me you were dying.
As I kissed you goodbye and left the room
my throat blocked up and I started crying.

Totally helpless is the way you feel
when someone you love is speaking in that way.
But helpless I was not, I soon realised this
as I turned to God and I started to pray.

I asked of God to give you strength
to say your farewells so your suffering was rid.
I said this prayer numerous times
and the following night that's exactly what *He* did.

Now many people think that your journey has ended
when in fact it has only just begun.
For we all know that after the moon has vanished
once again will be the rise of the sun.

You yourself were somewhat sceptical of this
and now God has clearly shown you the truth.
He has returned your 20/20 vision,
your mobility and most importantly, your youth.

No longer are you confined to a hospital bed
unable to appreciate the break of a new dawn.
No longer do you breathe a weak, shoddy breath
but now inhale the air of a newborn.

Overhead is a sparkling blue fountain
and the uplifting sound of jazz and blues.
On your face is a cheeky great smile
and on your feet are your dancing shoes.

You are now free to continue living
albeit in a different universe it sometimes seems.
And until the day that we come join you
we'll continue to dance with you within our dreams.

Susan Macdougal

TO AN AUTISTIC CHILD

Oh Simon, I watch you standing there,
Your small face so absorbed, so unaware,
Your eyes remote on things that only you can see,
In some far distant, sad infinity,
I lean to you and gently call your name,
So many times I've tried to make you hear,
But only once you heard me and came near
And then you really saw me for a while
And we stood heart to heart
And smile to smile,
I saw the recognition in your eyes,
Your slow and gentle smile of sweet surprise,
But then you turn your head and you are gone,
Back to your world of sunshine without care
And my heart aches to walk away
And leave you there.

Barbara O'Brien

DIVINE ACCEPTANCE

There's no need to look for Jesus
For my friend He's always there.
And no matter what your problem is
He'll always listen to your prayer.

There are times when we all feel depressed
We lose heart and start to moan.
Just spare the time to pray to Jesus
Don't try to struggle all alone.

He'll give you the calm assurance
And the confidence to cope.
For if you have Jesus in your life
Then you always will have hope.

We know that Jesus gave His life
To free each of us from sin.
So if your life now weighs you down
Please pray. Please turn to Him.

Gordon Barnett

SALUTE TO ROYALTY

From Hanover to Windsor royal consorts reigned through the years,
  From Sophia of Zelle to Mary of Teck the royal list appears;
But the queen of them all accepted the post when the throne looked
                                bleak indeed,
    Just a smiling wee Scottish lassie so determined to succeed.

Amidst ermine, pearls and tiaras resolutely the path she trod
    Paved the way to a throne at the Abbey for a crown ordained
                                by God;
Throughout World War II she did not flinch when skies were
                                so overcast,
    And stayed beside us all the way right to the very last.

O Mother Queen of bygone days so nostalgically do we recall
    How we travelled safely alone on the roads, nought tragic
                                or ill could befall;
Those days of yore with open doors without the fear of theft,
    When children played happily anywhere, no parents were bereft.

Let the grace of Diana continue to thrive in a constantly
                                changing world,
    Despite cries of 'devolution' the Union Jack remains unfurled;
Should an up-and-coming youngster our hope and honour redeem,
    May William, the second Conqueror, rise to William
                                the fifth supreme.

Margaret Marsh

JONES THE SCRAP

Nothing was too big and nothing was too small,
Whatever 'twas you wanted, Jones the Scrap would have it all.
Mountains of scrap metal and stacks and stacks of wood,
Most of it was rubbish, but some of it quite good.

He'd weigh your lead and copper on scales he vowed were right,
But what *you* found heavy carrying, his scales made awf'lly light.
He'd haggle over pennies and count out every one,
And wouldn't dare look happy until you'd been and gone.

Railway trucks were loaded with scrap metal every day,
But the piles in Jones' scrapyard just *never* seemed to stray.
They just grew even bigger, as dealers one and all
Brought in their loaded lorries to make the piles stay tall.

Jones' home life was quite different . . . everything was *new*,
A villa by the seaside, complete with wondrous view.
No expense was spared . . . he lived life to the full,
He ate and drank and smoked cigars all night without a lull.

His paunch grew ever bigger . . . his breath grew ever less,
He knew his current lifestyle had made his health a mess.
He was heading for the scrap heap - his ticker soon would cease,
It did! Poor Jonesy became another 'Rest in Peace'!

He found himself at Heaven, outside the Golden Gate,
Where St Peter took his name and told him where to wait.
'I'll have to go and ask if you're entitled to come in,
It all depends on whether you've led a life of sin!'

St Peter entered Heaven to discuss it with his Boss,
Who snorted, 'Jones the Scrap from Wales . . . I couldn't give a toss!
We'll have him if repentant . . . it isn't yet too late.'
But Jones had gone to his scrapyard . . . and so had the Golden Gate!

G K (Bill) Baker

THE POWER OF THE MIND

Thought that transcends reaches now perceived
Passing above the barriers of time
An insight propelled into realms now eclipsed
With an invisible link that unites the past, the present and the future

The power of imagination, foresight and inner awareness
From a soul restless in its entirety, searching for the truth
Or inner calm that floats above and beyond
But always out of reach, defying capture
Until the power of the mind is stilled

But then we have no man at all -
Just an empty shell and forgotten dreams
The flame extinguished and only ash.

Doris Hoole

THE MISSING LOTTERY TICKET

'What have you done with my lottery ticket, I just left it on the chair?
It could be worth a fortune, but I don't suppose you care.
The lads will be round in the morning expecting to hear that we've won,
Instead of a rattle to play with, you gave the ticket to our son.
Oh what am I going to tell them? You only get one chance in life,
If we've won the lottery and can't claim it, I might be minus a wife.'
'If that's a threat you can forget it, you're not walking out on me,
Your girlfriend telephoned this morning, she'll be waiting for you
                                when you're free.
So I told her not to bother, she's coming round later today,
She says that she's expecting and wonders just who's going to pay!'

James Ayrey

MY DAD

Wish I'd found time to talk to my dad
About his life he once had.
About his days where he went to school,
Was he good, or did he break the rules?

About his youth, what he did as a boy,
If his life was good and full of joy.
When he left school and ran away from home,
Thought he'd become a man of his own.

Joined the army and went to war,
It was all for us he was fighting for.
Spent weeks in the trenches, guns all around,
Cold and wet feet stuck in mud in the ground.

Never knew just how long they had got,
Getting away, without getting shot.
Must have been hard having no food,
Frightened to stand or even just move.

It was the First World War, so few survived,
But luck was with him, he came out alive.
He must have had many a tale to tell,
How they ducked and dived to miss the shells.

I wish he'd talked about the war,
I think he felt he was being a bore.
Maybe telling was too hard to bear,
Only he knew, because he was there.

If he was with me here today
I'd want to know, not walk away.
To tell me stories about the war,
And what they all were fighting for.

He was a hero which makes me sad,
I wish I'd found time to talk to my dad.
When he went his stories went too,
Part of his life that I never knew.

Joan Morris

RIPPLE

With a dormant mirrored surface
The lake lies still and cool,
And at that given moment
It unravels like a spool.
The hoop-like waves get bigger
As they glide across the top.
And once its move has started
It has no power to stop.
With ever widening circles
The ripple's path will go,
Speeding out across the lake
Its watery life to show.
And with a fleeting passion
It makes its gentle dance,
Because it never comes again,
Like us, it has one chance.
Time moves on and it's no more
This brief encounter spent,
Just for one lovely moment
Its beauty it has lent.
A kiss upon the waiting bank
Will end this magic spell,
It's one of nature's miracles
That we all know so well.

Duchess Newman

OUR LIVES

We did not come into this world of ours
Of our own choice or desire
But we have got to live our lives
Whatever God bestows
Some are rich, some are poor
But we should try and wear a smile
Some are good-looking, some not so
But we cannot choose our style
Some have good health and some not so
But we all share the things of life
The lovely flowers, the singing birds
The darkness and the light
And everything that grows
We all have our ups and downs to bear
But it all makes life worthwhile
If we had everything so good
Life would not be worthwhile
So let's pause a while, count our blessings
God loves us all just the same.

Eileen Finlinson

NOT TO SEEK LORD BUT TO SHARE

Dear Lord much too often
We seek You in prayer
Because we are wallowing
In our own self despair

We make every work
We'll often moan when we speak
An imperative plea
For whatever we seek

We pray for ourselves
And so seldom for others
We're concerned with our problems
And not with our brothers

We seem to forget Lord
That the sweet hour of prayer
Is not for self caring
But to place in Your care

All the lost souls
Unloved and unknown
And to keep praying for them
Until they are Your own

For it is never enough
To seek God in prayer
With no thoughts of others
Who are lost in despair

So teach us dear Lord
That the power of prayer
Is not for self caring
But to place in Your care

All the lost souls
Unloved and unknown
And to keep praying for them
Until they are Your own

For it is never enough
To seek God in prayer
With no thoughts of others
Who are lost in despair

So teach us dear Lord
That the power of prayer
Is made stronger by placing
The word in His care

David Sheasby

A CHILD'S VISION

Have you ever sat down and looked up at the sky
And watched the large clouds as they slowly pass by
And pictured the faces the clouds seem to form?
The faces look angry when there is a storm.

Have you ever heard birds sing as you lie in your bed?
They sound just like tunes as they float overhead.
Have you ever heard the breeze as it sings in the trees,
Or heard the music that's made by the bees?

If you have, you're a child with the world at your feet,
It's a magic you have that you always must keep.
For as you grow up the sounds they all change -
The sound of the storm then will only mean rain.

Amy Cornes Torr

THE STORY OF LIFE

Destruction . . . devastation . . . depression . . .
All these are spread throughout the world
During the tough times in the hot and in the cold
We forget about most living in poverty
We're too busy partying and living it up in Coventry
It scares me to think that such cruelty goes on
And all we seem to do is worry about the little things
What happened to looking out for one and another?
It isn't hard, we bring it on ourselves cause no one seems to bother
I remember a time when everyone cared
Nowadays destruction, devastation and depression are forever
                                        scarred into our minds
Cause that's just how the world is, full of hatred yet full of love
It's hard, it's cruel, but it's the story of life!

Sophie E Lawrence (17)

UTOPIA

Legal robbery is now your best bet
Buy all you want and get deep in debt
We live in a society that says this is the way
To have a good time and let someone else pay
All you do is spend, spend, spend
Cars, motorbikes, in fact, any new trend

Get yourself two million in debt
It's like winning the lottery, you just hedge your bet
Once you get two million in tow
You are in the top class of those in the know
MPs, judges, solicitors and their wives
In this debt ridden heaven you enjoy your lives

When pressure from the lender reaches top bar
Simply go bankrupt, you are now a real star
Rest on your laurels for a full year
It's like having a holiday, you just disappear
Then after a year you start again
And the money comes in like golden rain

So please remember lots of cards
Spend, spend, spend like lords and bards
It's certainly better than going to work
And what is more, it don't even hurt

Now you know why they immigrate
Nearly go mad to get through the gate
Into this country, home of all Brits
Where plastic buys anything, including new body bits.

Stanley G Witty

NATURE

Sun's wash spreads over moonscape moors,
Encircling rocks with loops of light.
Dredged from darkness, an eagle soars,
Above receding realms of night,
Where dim stars fade and flicker out,
Grey clouds edged with a golden hue,
Reflect in streams of teeming trout,
Beneath a watchful water shrew.

Damselflies in vaporous heat,
Dance the sun-dazzled depths of dawn,
Among wet wisps of meadowsweet,
Are creepers of invading thorn,
And when long day fades into dusk -
A pewter moon is webbed in trees,
The low sun is an empty husk,
A red balloon blown on the breeze.

These images of nature teem
Into my mind to fondly keep,
Pale pristine pictures held in dream,
Set in the silences of sleep.

Dave Austin

SEA BREEZES

The swash encircles
the beach corridors and inlets.
And over the rock pools -
pink and emerald and
smooth as a mirror.
The herring gull tugs at the
lyme grass
sprouting from the bald dunes
and stamps in temper
till the cockles surrender.
The bulbous natterjack toad is
oblivious, dozing on his island bed.
While fluttering in the breeze
are gems of saffron poppies
courtesy of the beach treasury.
And the huge breakers roar
and keep their secrets.

Dorothy McGregor

THE TABBY

Curled up in the golden sun
Under the chestnut tree.
Branches forming the shade.
She rests peacefully.
Patches of brown in this autumn season.
Leaves blowing slightly in the gentle breeze and -
The garden seat where she lies of chestnut brown and dark leaf green.
Gold and black tabby blending in with the picture.
A scene like heaven.
It is much richer than the cold, cold concrete of the towns and cities.
So soft, so serene, so sweet.
Not fussy and frilly.
The simplest pleasures in life are the best.
Aren't I lucky to be blessed
With a room with a view
Of the tabby that lives next door to me?

Rachel Van Den Bergen

A Rose

A rose to me,
Is perfection at a glance.
Soft delicate petals
Enfolding, one by one.
As if to enchant
Each passer by.
Whether it be you
Or I, or butterfly.

Roses for love,
Roses for joy,
Roses for sadness shared,
A rose to prove
That someone really cared.

Barbara Joan Shaw

The Track

Clickety-clack, clickety-cluck,
Goes the tube on the track.
From Euston To Victoria,
From East End to euphoria.

Dark is the underground,
Lost people cannot be found.
A man commits suicide,
Everyone rushes for their ride.

The hustle and bustle for the train,
At least in the underground
You keep dry from the rain.
In the underground you push and shove,
No time to view the peaceful dove.

The clatter of shoes on the escalators,
Posh people going to meet their mater and paters.
The whir and click of the ticket machine,
On the underground people just daydream.

On the tube there are everyday folk.
Next stop you want sir!
It's time you woke.

Jacqueline G Harris

Worth Fighting For? I Ask

Remember that day when we both ran off to sea,
Went for our medicals - just you and me.
Seven doctors in total to see if we were fighting fit,
To get a shilling a day, your food and your kit.

A doctor examined your eyes, one for your ears, one your backside,
Looked up the latter to see that you had nothing to hide,
One for the heart, lungs, kidneys, he said, 'Urinate in the trough,'
Then one grabbed your 'whatsits' and shouted, 'Cough!'

After several hours you were declared fit to go and do battle,
Herded away and often treated little better than cattle.
Almost six years going through hell, fire and water,
All that toil, sweat, bloodshed, tears and slaughter.

Then on our return Winston promised homes fit for heroes,
How dare he, they said, and ousted him, those opposition weirdos.
Now sixty years on my monthly rent is two and a half times more
Than the total of service pay that I received throughout the war.

My grandchildren cannot even afford a deposit for a home of their own,
For their further education they have to take out a massive loan.
So our sacrifice and that of our dead comrades was totally absurd,
The politicians, yet once again, have given us the bird.

Our country's housing has been ceded to the property spiv,
Instead of lasting peace there is violence where we live,
The armed forces of a *great Britain* gave their all,
For the overpaid MPs to let our living standards fall.

Jack Edwards

Moreover

Oh how sad the world would be
If we lost all plants and trees.
Where would the birds and squirrels rest,
The butterflies and the bees?
And there would be no fine romance,
For there'd be no single rose
To say we love our sweethearts
Before we kneel down to propose.
A bride's hands they would be empty
As she walks down the aisle,
No dream bouquet to match her gown,
Though she walks with grace and style
And when our loved ones pass away,
We pray to God on high,
But there'd be no special garland
To say our last goodbye.
So I truly hope we never lose
The precious flowers and the trees
They give much more than colour or scent
So let's help to save them, please.

Shirley Jones Dwyer

Hate And War Has Torn Us Apart

Being a shepherd's pie is risky, and hey!
Give me beer and whisky
Because I am going far away.

There is another country
I dreamt of long ago
My journey starts tomorrow.

If tomorrow comes
If it does not
Mother Earth will bang the drums.

Father Time will play the bagpipes
As independent individuals
Become stereotypes.

Hate has torn us apart
The powers that be
Have destroyed our heart.

Where did they come from,
These denizens of hell
Who dropped the H-bomb?

The bomb was in our minds and hearts
The enemy was within
The secret war has torn us apart.

So what do we do now? you say
The only options left
Do we protest or pray?

The media gives us a tiny fraction
Of the truth, and the time is . . . *now!*
Now is the time for action.

The boys from the Mersey, the Thames and the Clyde
Stand up and be counted
The power is now on our side.

Antony Haselton

OH CALL BACK YESTERDAY, BID TIME RETURN

Disappointment is the travel agent ringing back
to say the only flights left are from Manchester
or waking in the dark to go to work
a few hours after you went to bed
then going back to buy the last pair of shoes
that were sold this morning.
Disappointment is being told your cancer has come back
so there are no planes from Manchester.
Suddenly, time caves in;
you wish you were thirteen and could start again
so there might have been a film of the story
you wanted to write.

Penny Freeston

NOAH'S ANIMAL ANTICS
(Dedicated to my 6 grandchildren)

When the Artful Angry Adder Asked the Address of the Ark,
the Boring Bashful Badger only knew it in the dark.
The Crafty Clicking Cricket caught a lift on a Creaking Cart
but the Docile Dawdling Donkey was left Dreaming at the start.
The Ever-Eyeful Eagle Escaped Easily from the ledge,
the Fluffy Fluttering Finches Flew out Fast from in the hedge.
The Grouchy Gruffy Goats were left Gnawing at the Gate,
while the Heavy Humping Hippos Had a Habit of being late.
The Itchy Irksome Insects hitched a ride on an Ibis' back,
while the Jolly Joking Jellyfish Just drifted on a wreck.
The Kindly little Koala with a face that you could Kiss
Leapt up onto the Leopard's back whose Lips you couldn't miss.
The Multi-legged Millipede Meandered through the Mud
to where the Naughty Newts were stuck and had to have a tug.
The Ostrich Overtook the lot by taking massive strides,
but the Podgy Prickly Porcupine Proposed to take his time.
The Quail was asking Questions, 'Who's that holding up the queue?'
It's the Rumbling Robust Rhino who takes up the space of two.
The Sloppy Sliding Sea lion had no legs to take the Strain,
but caught up the Trundling Tortoise who took his Tent
for when it rained.
An Umbrella wasn't needed for the Urchin from the sea
while the Vixen tried to Vanish before the Voyage got underway.
The Weary Wobbling Walrus Was left Wondering What to do
with all the eXcess animals still waiting at the zoo.
The Yak began to Yawn, for he was bored with all the Yelling,
but the Zebra Zipped up his stripy suit and was ready to get going.

All the animals made it to the ark with plenty of time to spare,
and when the rain began to fall, they were glad they all got there.

Audrey Harman

JUST A THOUGHT

Some old masters might agree,
And say along with untrained me
That modern art and sometimes prose
Reminds them of the king's new clothes.
A dirty bed unmade in part
Is called the purest form of art,
And while a pile of concrete blocks
Is meant to knock us off our socks,
It's hard for others to agree,
For them it's difficult to see
That paint on canvas, random thrown
Is an art form they would own.
Can it vie with Gainsborough?
Perhaps one day it might,
But no one told the king the truth,
That he looked a pretty sight.

Doreen P Damsell

WALKING TO SNAILBEACH

My past walked lanes like these,
Through fern and celandine
Seeking work. Small and blackened men,
They mined the coal from pit to pit,
Following change as a fly follows meat.
I am at home here.

Yet the images are strange, negative.
Along these hills a leaden white has hardened
Since Roman times; set into furnaces and roofs,
Ruins bleaching in fields barren of grass.
Here men shovelled stone
Or burrowed under a paradise of flower,
Ghost-white, destroying as they went.

Why do I know this place?
Some memory not my own calls me:
Ghosts of ancestors passing through.
I am not myself alone, but many,
A continuum, a rusting chain.
My links were forged between coal and cars
Among Black Country voices. Sweating women
Hammered my iron in backyard shops
(Brick bicycle sheds now); my beginnings are broken.

I have my legends of course,
Stories told to me by ancient aunts
Knitting time in endless scarves.
Great great grandmama
Bathed her husband in bread and milk
(His skin was stubborn to heal, burnt crisp in a flashback).
Their son swam flooded stalls and died.
Somebody's cousin, brilliant with a piano,
Tried a career playing to the movie halls
The year talkies came out.

I come from a long line of failures
But they changed a nation,
Walked from the Middle Ages into now,
Carrying a whole society.
In this silent place, amongst the spoil heaps
And columbine, my ghosts may stand with dignity.
Waiting my arrival, they watch,
White against white.

Pauline Kirk

THE SPELL

The silence could be felt and heard
Yet no one spoke or said a word.
A shudder passed between us all,
We stood, and waited for the call
That would be to us an exciting sound,
Why we were there, on sacred ground.

The sky turned grey, blue then black,
With quivering breath we all hung back.
Would we see, or would we not
The signs and symbols time forgot?
A circle then we all did make
And joined hands tight, so not to break
The spell we chanted in quiet tones,
That sent shivers through our very bones.
With heads turning left then right,
Eyes pierced darkness in the cooling night.

One could sense and feel tension there,
Our panic rising in the cold damp air.
The spell was broken, we could not stay,
We parted hands and ran away.
We fled towards the city sights,
To the friendly streets with golden lights.

Patricia Herrod

REMEMBER TO FORGET

Remember to forget the injuries done to you,
Remember to forget the wrongs that folks construe
Into your actions that were noble, pure and true,
Remember to forget - it's better if you do!

Remember to forget the gossip that you heard
For if you pass it on more trouble may be stirred,
Remember to forget to speak in haste the angry word,
Remember to forget - remorse is then deterred!

Remember to forget that word - unkind, untrue,
Remember to forget those thoughtless words that flew
Straight as a dart into your heart and pierced it through and through,
Remember to forget - your peace of mind renew!

Remember to forget the faults of other folk,
Remember to forget the nasty words they spoke
That did bitterness, unhappiness and agony provoke,
Remember to forget - new friendships to invoke.

So remember to forget - as your life you live,
But if you should forget - remember to forgive!

Greta E Bray

A WINDOW ON LIFE

As I look out of my window
I can see the children play,
They laugh and sing and run around,
I think they could do it all day.
Then my mind goes slipping back,
Three score years to be exact,
To a time when I was also young
And could run and run and run for fun.
Alas those days they are no more
Because by now my knees are sore,
Yes my knees are sore, my shoulders ache,
I lie in bed sometimes awake
And I think of things I saw that day,
In the little school yard across the way.
I wonder what the future holds
For those dancing, singing little souls.
Sometimes I wish it could be me,
But then of course that cannot be.
In my heart I know it's nature's way,
The old must go, so the young can stay.
So to the children at Grange School
I'd like to leave this golden rule,
Show kindness to the folk you meet,
So you can have a life complete,
Then when you're old you won't feel sad
For after all, life wasn't bad.

Richard Young

END OF DAYS

(This poem was written on 5.5.05 at the side of my mother just before she died. I will always love you Mother and you will always be in my heart. Your son)

We sat beside a single thought of things we've done together,
We looked into the feelings a mother can but feel,
To see the love she holds inside is more than one can bear,
For she is more than gold or gems and all that's on this Earth,
She seems a little stressed at times, but that's what mothers are,
They care so much for offspring that nothing will exchange,
So please don't take away this life there's nothing left for us,
Tomorrow comes so empty,
The days ahead have gone.

Joseph Jezierski

21 TODAY

Where have the years gone?
Big part of your life
Just passes in a flash
And now 21 today.

Time to be independent,
Time to have your life set out,
Time to be a serious adult, scary
21 today.

No more safety net
From your mother and father,
Time to go out and make them proud,
You're an adult now
21 today.

You've learnt the knowledge,
You've learnt life can be tough
But rewarding as well,
You have loved and lost
And had to carry on
21 today.

You will make mistakes
And have your heart broken
But will learn so much as time goes on
And come out the other end tougher, stronger
As this is all life and part of growing up
21 today.

You're young,
There's a lot to see and do
Exciting, scary but never boring.

Happy birthday
You're 21 today.

Gillian Elaine McKinley

ALEXANDRA - 21

As I think of my daughter I think of myself
As she lends immortality to the life I have left
A fantasy of self image looms in her face
As her true identity struggles from my embrace

I ask of my father who died before she had life
To grant her his wisdom which is hers by right
Their name is tinged with greatness humbly viewed
Strong leaders with the strength of stress endured

My mother her guardian angel I ask to remain
That her kindness in Alex may manifest the same
Loved ones' qualities are catalysts to our own
The fruits of our lives are sharingly grown

From her father I give the energy for business
Which leads to a healthy mind and success
A carefully nurtured and expanding optimism
Not diminished by too much criticism

May her grandmother's control and identification of self
Her longevity and comparitive health
Her financial ability to make ends meet
Be there for Alex her loved ones to keep

From myself I offer my God, a husband and children
A loving base with a stable equilibrium
Makes for the ability to feel the needs of the world
As the complexities of a future life unfurl

Blessed with a face of which a goddess would be proud
A strong body and the wisdom of a leader endowed
A strength and courage from her Chinese birth sign given
Life for Alexandra should be well worth living

Margaret M Cassidy

LAST FAREWELL

Coal burning on the open fire,
Flames billowing up high,
Logs sizzling in the amazing heat
As I prepare to say goodbye.

My life is coming to an end,
Breathing is an effort now
But I go with a heavy heart
After that senseless, angry row.

Words that were better left unsaid
As you slammed shut the door,
Bitter recriminations that burnt the lips
That left my heart so sore.

Suddenly there you are before me,
You kneel beside me to say
The words that I waited so long to hear
On this very special day.

For my love, I can't take you with me,
I have to journey alone,
But I go now with peace in my heart
Now we have had the chance to atone.

We made our peace as I breathed my last
I felt your kiss on my cheek.
Going towards that golden light,
The one we all always seek.

I have gone now to a better place
But I will visit one day soon
And watch over you as you dream
Of us dancing to endless tunes.

Sue Godsell

THE SNOWS ARE STILL MELTING

Who will remember, who can forget?
Father forgive, we have sinned.
Furnaces burning deep into the night,
Lives blown away in the wind.

They came in their thousands, their lives in a case,
The rich and the poor all from one race.
Doctors or farmers, their future the same,
With questioning eyes, who is to blame?

Herded in ghettos, so easy to find,
Still unbelieving, their senses still blind.
Loaded on wagons, packed in like sheep,
Winter and summer the sky has to weep.

'Where are my children?' A voice in the storm,
The veil in the temple is suddenly torn.
Monsters in uniforms shiny and smart
Have blinded the world and ripped out its heart.

In cars and on horses they strut and they stride,
Their blood covered ideals they show off with pride.
These Aryan masters who would be so pure,
Can't tell the difference between gold and manure.

Many years later the world still looks back,
Desperately trying to cover its tracks.
'We're not to blame, we did not know.'
Still the furnaces are melting the snow.

Africa, Asia, go where you will,
The uniformed monsters are still out to kill.
Father forgive, for we all have sinned
And lives are still blown away in the wind.

W J F Haney

IN PRAISE OF TAYLOR MADE

The 580 driver, R Taylor Made,
Puts all other drivers into the shade:
Large club head, large sweet spot, effect trampoline
And sometimes my distance is almost obscene.
There is no doubt at all, I am hitting it longer;
It must be the club, I am not getting stronger
But I am confident now, that I can compete,
No longer a pushover, nobody's meat.
I must find a coach, the best only will do.
Butch Harmon, Scott Cranfield, Leadbetter of Pugh.
He must do it for love for the pay will be small,
How much can I offer? Ten per cent of - all!
Stop dreaming Michael, put your feet on the ground,
One day you may play a half decent round.
But the sun is shining, you are fit and alive;
Who knows, you might even break eighty-five!

Michael Carter

SAD WATERS

Souls ride the surf now, where sea horses once thundered,
Poor people scraped a living there and holidaymakers blundered.
Silhouettes, hypnotised by a raging sea,
Paralysed with amazement and awe,
Fled too late in disbelief, as carnage broke the shore.

Paradise was shattered, submerged in sorrow,
Beneath a turquoise sky,
I turn away from the news of a wave and quietly ask why
A fractured sea bed swept their worlds away,
As some looked on as the ocean turned and drowned them
On that day.

Can a continent heal from such total pain?
See orphans smiling, playing in the rain.
A hollowed father clings to his child, encased in a cask of mud,
What life is this? Innocents broken in the brown waters of the flood.
The spirit of man shone through that day, the world took up the plea,
Humanity and hope spoke loudly, for the victims of the sea.

Philip Lowe

CLIMBING THE LADDER TO FAME

When first you write and learn the craft, remember
Don't be too dramatic, keep it plain,
As complicated plots and lots of characters
Reveal an amateur at work again.

It may seem rather obvious in retrospect
For authors love their tragedies and verbs
They say life isn't like that so be careful
Your story isn't bordering on the absurd.

Yet Dinah up the road has been in hospital,
The neighbour's cat run over as she fled,
And poor old Mr Jives a local publican
Had a funny turn and fell down dead;
The bungalow at Pitt Street then caught fire,
The house across the road was burgled twice,
A motorcyclist crashed into our hedgerow
And killed himself (real life's not always nice).

So take it from me, as a writer,
When practising your new craft,
Remember - keep it simple, spare the drama -
Then you might be remembered for your art.

Linda Kettle

BARBADOS

Soft gold sands and turquoise seas
Bright sarongs dance in the breeze
The Jolly Roger's distant beat
Parasols that shade the heat
Palm leaf hats top braided hair
Churches filled with joyful prayer
Hobie cats bob gaily by
The amber sun sinks in the sky
Balmy days and sultry nights
Palm trees strung with fairy lights
Tree frogs call while steel bands play
Limbo dancers bend and sway
Rum punch flows and cool beer pours
Reggae rhythms fill dance floors
Moonlight shimmers on each bay
The ending of a perfect day.

Katherine Hedison

POETICALLY CORRECT?

I'm not sure about similes -
oh yes, *now* I remember,
they're weaker than metaphors,
like snow in December.

I've *heard* alliteration
can get your point across.
What a weary, worried world,
if it became my boss!

I'm quite into *imagery* -
the words reach out to me,
along with *rhyme* and *rhythm*,
I'm a simple soul you see!

I don't like judging people,
or how they use a word -
if it helps them survive in life,
to criticise would be absurd!

My love of words is not diminished
by the approach I choose to take.
Writing is a powerful tool
when new lives we seek to make!

I may not always analyse
each stanza 'by the book' -
but hopefully I inspire some
to give words a second look!

And if along the journey
of writing from the heart,
I teach and learn a little more,
I'll know I've played my part.

Sharing words - *our* words,
in our own individual way,
is just a way of reaching out;
knowing we're valued - and so is what we say!

Annette Borrill

THE NORFOLK BROADS

As your boat glides through the water the feeling is this,
The feeling of freedom to me is sheer bliss,
The things that you see as you get underway
Change quite rapidly day after day.
The wildlife is abundant, a joy to behold,
A glimpse of a heron is worth more than gold.
The wild flowers, the bulrush, a blossom on a tree,
Seems like the Garden of Eden on Earth for me.
The windmill, the wherry, the cruiser and yacht,
All help to add to the pleasures you've got.
The colourful wild ducks and kingfishers too
All help to make heaven on Earth for you,
As you glide through the water on our Norfolk Broads
It's the nearest thing to paradise so just thank the Lord,
The reeds stand on guard all along the way,
They move with the boats' wash and gently sway.
See the craftsmanship of a building topped with thatch,
Seemingly to surpass this there is no match,
As you pass churches, wind pump or weir
It makes you feel you're glad to be here,
The honking of the geese in a noisy display
Will soon break the peace of a beautiful day.
You can laze or just gaze at the beauty put on this Earth to be seen
And enjoy all the rapture be you ordinary man, king or queen.
Be you bishop, pop star, locals, or visitors having a break
The Broads in all their beauty are there for everyone's sake.
The elegant swans hold their proud heads in the air
Gracefully swimming about without a care,
Men sitting fishing try their luck for roach and bream
To catch the biggest one yet is their dream.
With dragonflies and butterflies flitting by
Are sure to catch anyone's watchful eye.
See delightful grebe with young ones on their back,
It seems parental care they do not lack,
Scurrying water hen, coot or swooping gull,
The sheer peacefulness gives you and me time to mull
Over our thoughts and wallow in bliss
To find and enjoy you just shouldn't miss.

Joyce Hammond

THE 3 Bs

Baubles, bikes and balderdash,
a special time of year,
it's nearly time to panic -
it's dangerously near!
Fairy lights and moondust,
the tinkling of a bell,
arguments in bus queues,
the shopping list from Hell!
Fresh mince pies and carols,
salmonella, headaches, strain,
the frostiness of pure white snow
now sadly turns to rain.
'Cyber' toys left on all night -
flat batteries, Christmas morning,
power cuts and tins of ham,
cheap gifts, without the warning.
Chaos in the kitchen,
Dad still in the loo,
then the day arrives at last -
I love it all - don't you?
Relax and scoff more chocolate,
now raise your festive cup,
can someone turn the queen on?
And stuff the washing up!

J Lovell

CAREFREE CHILDHOOD

Our Second World War childhood
Was unbelievably good,
As we didn't understand, being small,
So fortunately, didn't suffer at all.

Girls and boys played together
Outside in every kind of weather,
Or into town for a film or funfair,
A joyful childhood beyond compare.

On summer days could be seen fluttering by,
The translucent, diaphanous butterfly.
Winter brought its own enjoyment -
When it snowed it felt heaven-sent.

Ina J Harrington

ONE WISH

From the outside looking in,
Is this where I should have been?
Am I family, friend or foe?
In my mind I just don't know.

Myself it seems I cannot bear,
My thoughts deep, dark, full of despair.
I cannot let you in to share,
Make you part of my nightmare.

One wish for me it would be,
To let this heart of mine be free.
Leave my pain back in the past,
Life anew within my grasp.

The sky may be blue or grey,
The rain alone won't make me stay,
But to see your smile every day,
To help each other pave the way,

This is the one thing that I crave,
But you alone my heart can save.
A simple thing it would seem,
But you only live inside my dream.

You are not real life at all,
So you can never hear my call.
My dreams are all that I have,
So you may as well take my wish back.

Eleanor Lloyd

WAITING

I'm sitting in the rain
Waiting for the train

Watching others pass
Mine is always last

I sit on my own
Wishing I was home

I hear something coming
It's the train's engine humming

I get on the train
Out of the rain

I'm into the heat
In a lovely comfy seat

Now I'm on the train
My journey starts again.

Lyndsey Herron

A POET'S DREAM

It's a poet's dream
lying by a summer stream
listening to the rippling water flow
while a soft breeze gently blows

Looking up at the mighty sky
as time drifts slowly by
seeing clouds like cotton wool balls
or even snow, which in winter falls

Meanwhile in the grass so high
a little ladybird climbs, not flies
colours brown and black
on its shiny round back

In a birch a lark sings its song
standing on a branch so long
just then a bee buzzes by
right in front of my very eyes

But I'm surrounded by thistles and nettles
not flowers with lily-white petals
or petals, yellow, pink or blue
which in springtime in some garden grew

On this lazy afternoon
in the midst of long grass I feel cocooned
today my sunbed is the ground
as the hot sun shines brightly down

Got nothing to do, nowhere to go
except to relax by the stream, hearing water flow
while the water twists and turns around stones
I'm like a child in a pram, lying here alone

I see butterflies flapping their wings
such pretty little things
different colours, different names
but all butterflies just the same

There's a calmness in the warm air
and I haven't got a care
got no worries on my mind
in this lazy summertime

I'm far from the madding crowd
just gazing at pure white clouds
and lie here is what I intend to do
until this restful sunny day is through.

Patrick Gormley

NEW LOVE - OLD LOVE

Punish me now for that heat long ago,
I saw her freshness, her smooth skin aglow.
Throat-tightening impulse I could not resist,
No turning back then, once we had kissed.

Punish me now, loving slender thighs,
Soft, sunken belly, those doe-like eyes.
The perfumed down on her Venus mount -
Twinned lustful glances too intense to count.

Punish me now just for being a man -
Age does repulse what indifference began.
No longer the spark from the smoothing of breast,
Gone is the passion, the climax, the rest.

I could soar to the sky while you stayed on base ground -
I would suckle and couple with pleasure new-found.
You once were to me, my first love, my first vow -
I still am that man - please don't punish me now.

Lilian Perriman

FOR DOROTHY

'What is a child?' you asked and smiled,

Is it a flower growing free and wild?
Dimpled cheek in bows and lace,
Tomboy with a muddy face,
Pouting lip, flashing eye,
Grazed knee and a hundred questions why.
An energy freak,
A sleepy heap,
Holding hands, teasing the cat,
Inquisitive fingers point at this and that,
Trusting eyes,
Sad goodbyes,
All these rolled into one or more,
This is the child you could adore.
But - just one moment more you'll wish
A million miles away
And say -
'I've had enough today.'
Then a hand will reach across a space,
A smile will cover a dirty face,
Sticky kiss on bending cheek,
Feelings mixed, anger, joy, make you weak.
This whirlwind, this force so wild,
Charmer, vixen, demon, angel -
This is a child.

Barbara Buckley

HOLA TO SPAIN

We are sitting in the airport,
Waiting for our plane,
To take us on our holidays,
We are bound for sunny Spain.

We might go and see a bullfight,
Flamenco dancing too,
But if we don't do any of these,
There are lots of things to do.

Like going to a theme park,
Or just laze upon the beach,
We can do some present shopping,
All things that are in our reach.

Then when our week is over,
And we wait to board the plane,
We can think of what we did in Spain
And head for home again.

Glennis Ecclestone

CONGRATULATIONS FORWARD PRESS

You have reached the peak of fifteen years,
Has there been any blood or tears?
I know things cannot always go right,
Like trying to fit our poems onto pages if a bit tight.

We hope you go on for many years,
Even if we do make you sweat blood and tears.
But never mind, don't give up yet,
You may find a poem or story you like, I'll bet.

So come on Forward Press, just another fifteen years.
I know, I know it's blood, sweat and tears,
But think of the joy you are giving to us
And we will all promise not to give you any fuss.

Zoe French

THE SHIP OF DREAMS

Each night I board the ship of dreams
And follow the brightest star
Along Heaven's silver oceans
To a land so very far.
Past suns and moons and planets
Until I reach that special place
Where I can be with you again
And kiss your smiling face.

It's here I can remember every single happy day.
The things we said, the things we did,
The games we used to play,
The places we would go to,
The summers in the sand,
The times we laughed, the few we cried,
The way you held my hand.

But you're playing here with angels now
Since you chose a different track
And the light you followed took you out
But it couldn't bring you back.
So to keep you always in my heart
And forever in my sight
I board this ship and make this trip
On my dream boat every night.
But the tide too soon is turning
And so I'll blow my kiss and then
I'll wave goodbye and board the ship
To take me home again.
I'll always hear your laughter
As I'm leaving Heaven's shore
And I know I'll make this journey
Every night - for evermore.

Lesley Elaine Greenwood

FIFTEEN YEARS

When it was my fifteenth birthday,
I loved the old poems told by my gran.
Her poems are still in my memory,
So I'll write some myself if I can.

'The Road to Heaven', 'The Newsboy's Debt',
And 'Betty's Quilt', that Gran told,
These were always my favourites,
I still say them now I am old.

My poetry book is like a diary,
Of fifty-five years of my life,
Stories of special occasions,
Holidays, parties and becoming a wife.

Now you've been running for fifteen years,
I'll have to write one about you,
I'm looking at all of your books on my shelf
And I think of the work you must do.

You've made many people feel happy,
When they see their own poem printed there,
They know lots of people will read it,
For your prices are always so fair.

I'll hope to see this in your new book,
To add to the rest on my shelf,
Knowing my new poem is in it,
A poem about me and yourself.

Nita Garlinge

THE DIFFERENCE

View the world and all its differences with joy
To each new experience and adventure, do not be coy
Open up your heart and mind and eye
To welcome every difference - do not sigh
And turn away from new or different things

Grasp with eager hands and venture in
Where others may not go and you will win
A wealth of knowledge others miss
Because they fear the difference
Which gives such wonder and such joy

Do not look inwards but out to new horizons
Don't hold back from entering new situations
See how others live and plan and pray
Find out what the other man has to say
Enjoy the world in all its splendour

Each man has such a lot to offer
In attitudes, ideas and culture
Each new country, culture and religion
Has a special essence and admiration
For each and every one is essential

Edna D'Lima

NOTHING ELSE MATTERS

You gave me wonder
In the dark street
The night you called my name
Your call came thru' the darkness
Strong and clear, I heard the echo of the flame
That leaping cuts the velvet with its fire
Makes brighter the stars
And shames the glory of the very moon
To paleness
Return is instant
I am with you again
Nothing else matters.

Bryn Bartlett

JACK HADDOCK

A local historian lives nearby.
'Catch a bus, a train,' we'll cry.
'Oh no,' says Jack, 'do as you like,
but I would rather use my bike.'

Yet public transport is his pride,
even though he never takes a ride.
A keen photographer is our Jack,
off he'll cycle along the track.

Snap, there's an image before it's gone,
there will never be another one.
Buses, trains, barges in canal lock,
pictures all taken by Jack Haddock.

Tales from people who worked the trade,
tape recordings, Jack Haddock made.
Memories of Walsall would have been lost,
Jack collected them, whatever the cost.

Jack's such a man with tales to tell,
of his youth, World War II, work as well.
A Walsall lad with loads of friends,
plenty of anecdotes, without any ends.

Andrew B Perrins

SOLDIER SON

As he stands on his front lawn
Watching the traffic pass him by
He remembers the good times
And wipes a tear from his eye
He remembers of a world with no pity or pain
And when you walked down the street
Everyone knew your name
But now all he sees is war
And destruction all around
And where there once was a community
Now there's a broken down town
In the silence he remembers
Of a beautiful sunlit day
And a son who was always
Wanting him to play
But that son is off fighting in a faraway land
For some powerful leader who always demands
He sits and he wonders what'll happen to him
Will he become a commander?
Will he ever see him again?
He turns on the TV
But then there's a knock at the door
As he opens it he cries
For there stands his soldier son
With happy tears in his eyes.

Andrew Goldstraw

OUR DESIGNED FOREVER

My secret lover
We make love in silent form
Listen, watch, learn and know
The ins and outs of you
We are writhing till the dawn

How clear you are
Open touches you show me
What I want
How to guide ourselves through the rough
To make a home

Safety, passion, our love and trust
We have enough
We are angels in the morning sun
We are creatures of lust
We are two in one
Deep inside no more no less
You are the one who does it best

A touch that brings the ravenous storm
The pounding of my heavy chest
The fire that builds under my flesh
You create it; you have the power to take it
To make me milky warm
As light as a snowflake
As high as the moon
As dark as the Devil's thoughts

I look into you and see the world, everything I never thought
There is no other that can compete
You are my man
My rock, my feather
My eyes when I am blind
The link when I am not together
Give me nothing
This is Heaven
This is our designed forever.

Bryony Freeman

CAN YOU STILL LOVE ME?

(To my husband John, after a mastectomy in 1968)

I feel as though I know not who I am this day,
My mind has harboured thoughts I find no answer for.
I wish to still this silent scream once more,
But striving only brings confusion into play.

How can you still love me, when most of me is gone?
The spring from which life runs is dry,
Tears of self sorrow run unshed out of my eye,
I am with you love and yet I'm so alone.

My body, mutilated by the surgeon's knife,
Tells nothing of the strife which lies within.
My brain is savaged by a constant din,
This 'war' creates such havoc in my life.

Friends can help but little, though they try,
Life would be so empty, if they did not share my fears,
But they cannot share the scalding tears
Which can't be shed, for even they are dry.

If you *can* still love me, love me more,
You are my anchor, in a raging sea and tide.
Stay ever close and bind me to your side,
Lest I be cast adrift and never reach the shore.

Olga Margaret Moorhouse

SOPHIE

Upon a billboard
Advertising perfume
Is a photo of a lady,
Naked as the day she was born,
Wearing nothing save for her shoes.
There is an aura that she is
Confident with her firm body,
Indeed there is a hint of enjoyment
As she caresses her left breast,
As if awaiting to share that enjoyment
With someone else.

But the stiff-necked
And narrow-nosed
Rose up shouting comments;
'Disgusting, obscene,
Unclean, lewd, degrading,'
Until weak-willed officials removed
The advertisement from the billboard.

How strange that those who condemned
Have forgotten that we are formed in
The image of God.

David A Garside

TRAFFIC AND THE SOLUTION

Above the horizon the sun will peep
Awakening all from the night's sleep
The jam-packed highways all in haste
Turning the tarmac into paste

What is gained by all the speed?
Lots more accidents, yes indeed
The air polluted with the fume
Cars nose to tail without room

How to stop it for a start?
We could go back to horse and cart
A peaceful journey every day
And all this for a feed of hay.

Ralph H Stephens

STATUE OF LOVE

It was many years ago
I was hit by a thunderbolt
A million to one chance
That created a romance
She touched the corners of my mind
Raised the shutters and the blinds
From a cold dark place
That I could never escape

I took an early morning run
Along the beach
I remember the sunrise
The day was a peach
When I saw a desperate struggle
Of someone in trouble
I didn't think twice
As I battled with the tide
For an eternity
As we scrambled to the beach
Her eyes fluttered open
And I was shook and woken
From a sleep

Now I thank the sea
And the roaring tide
For all the beauty
That surrounds my life
Cos our love will always show
Sculpted in the smoothness
Of stone . . .

Frank Howarth-Hynes

HOPE SPRINGS ETERNAL

Rain and wind, ice and snow
January's here with winds that blow
Snow and ice, wind and rain
February's weather just the same

It's March, I see some buds appear
Maybe spring is coming near
April daffs all bright and yellow
Now the weather starts to mellow

In May spring flowers start to fade
And holiday plans are quickly made
Wind and rain, no snow or ice
Sometimes June can be quite nice

July's allotted lots of sun
Then back to rain, that stops the fun
We know that August's just the same
But sometimes we get warmer rain

September sees the nights draw in
The sunshine getting rather thin
October's weather quite appalling
It's mostly rain that keeps on falling

November's always dark and drear
I'm glad that Christmas time is near
Rain and wind, ice and snow
December's here with winds that blow.

I hope that next month's better.

May Murray

AUTUMN

'Open wide,' I say and try to force the spoon thro' lips so thin and dry,
Like purple strips across a page of white notched linen,
Stretched taut to blend with pillow.

What was once a nubile living being, like spring
Has drifted into autumn,
Where fallen leaves have left the skeleton tree, once proud and tall,
No longer full of sap.

Now drained of nature's strength it's become this figure
Lying prone and motionless, encompassed in goose feathers
Waiting for the 'Fall'.

Her auburn hair, like russet-coppered leaves,
Once bounced in step with lust for life,
But taken over now by timeless seasons that move on,
Waiting for no one.

Merciless in speed; concessionless to age!
Spring, summer, autumn, winter,
Moving fast like sunlight flickering on water,
Moonlight dancing on dreams.

Not even time for winter now.
She'll leave with speed as colours change,
And shortened days, like life she loved, draw slowly to an end,
And I can only wait.

Janet Llewellyn

CHRISTMAS LOVE

Love is like a Christmas tree,
It gives much happiness,
It gives the gifts like love alone
With wrappings full of bliss.
The baubles that are shiny
Are like the heart so warm,
That's where love is lying,
Especially on Christmas morn.
Everyone has got that love
Just like the fairy on the tree
And she the main attraction,
She's beautiful like love you see.
Then there is the sparkling tinsel
And the lights that shine so well,
It all glows and twinkles,
Like love, it has its spell.
Love is like a Christmas tree,
It gives to you and me.
It's warm, so kind and thoughtful,
For this is love so free.

Jean Lloyd-Williams

TO ALL DRIVERS

Every day I hear about some accidents, you know,
Why is this you may reply, I simply do not know,
Is it simply tiredness or is it the wife?
We must put a stop to this and try to get things right.
I know you do long journeys to Scotland or Penzance,
You must be fit, not tired, I think you'll understand.
Think of home and your family, keep this on your minds,
Watch out for others, never mind the time.
Then back home safely to the family and the wife,
Keep on trucking and stay alive.

Roland Torn

THE BEACH

Cleansed by the moon's silent strength
The beach lay naked to the dawn,
For within the darkness the ebbing tide
Had with nimble fingers drawn
The pattern of its mood upon the sand.

Soon this empty beach would echo to the sounds
Of children playing by the sea,
Of adults chattering in the sun
And eating ice cream, crisps and tea,
Then leaving litter strewn upon the sand.

But the tide would turn again
And water creep upon the shore
To drag back the summer rubbish
Until once more
There lay the virgin sand.

Joyce Dunkley

ASTESAINTS

Every day now Astesaints sweep onto Astestore floors
Searching for space to pay homage to their democratically
elected god.
What are they? A relatively new form of Homo sapiens
Reared from a very healthy pedigree!
They can be found wheeling tinselled trolleys
Amongst miles of aisles of tempting treats -
Suppliant saplers chanting words of praise!
Tannoy tin sounds rattle new hymns of devotion -
New words and prayers with new connotations,
New rhythms - heavy metal tunes - canned like conurbations!
Like lemons to the slaughter
In frenzied furies they forage and fight -
Greedy grasping fingers clutching at straws of sand -
Plastic people in a homogenous wonderland.
The calculating cold hand unrelentingly
Demands the daily collection, gurgling happily, moving quickly
As its roll of honour transforms totals
Into gigantic towers of tedious perfection.
Reluctantly leaving heaven Astesaints
Emit one final exodus of self-service, chanting in unison:-

O worship our store all towered in glass -
Who could ask more for our daily mass?
Its body is mastic - its head's in a daze -
Pavilioned in plastic and girded with haze!

Paula Fox

QUEEN OF DIAMONDS

I want to shout out ever so loud
My three children make me so very proud.
Graeme, my son of 20 is tall, good-looking and has a heart of gold
From a serious car accident he recovered to ensure his enjoyment
of life will not fold.
Dana is my daughter of 18 who is so full of style and class
No other father could be prouder of his lass.
Bernadette is my youngest at 17
And has grown into a hard-working and beautiful girl
When seeing her many a lad's heart will twirl.
Talking of my three diamonds I just cannot hide
My feelings of love and my utter adoring pride.
All my children have immensely enriched my life
For this reason my deepest gratitude goes to Mandy,
my queen of a wife
Marrying her was the best thing I have ever done
No man could be prouder of his wife, daughters and son.

Graeme Doherty

CORNISH FEST

Four friends set off for distant Cornwall
dreaming of hot pasties on the sea wall.
Seaside and waves and gorgeous sunshine,
evenings with meals and bottles of wine.

They found that the well known 'Fawlty Towers'
had moved to Newquay, among the flowers.
With rubber sheets and dubious meats,
soup and cheesecakes that were *real* treats!

Odours drove them to seek some culture,
taking care to avoid the vultures.
They walked one evening to Fistral Bay,
to watch the seals and surfers play.

The ghosts of Heligan were hidden from view,
among the palms, the tree ferns grew.
Beautiful mystery with deep green ponds.
Paradise, with creepers hanging in fronds.

Eden's terraces adorned the pit -
the spectacular project was quite a hit!
Conservation is their aim
and there's trains and drains, they even use rain!
But among the tropics, glass and biomes,
robins have invaded and made it their home.

Hilary M Rose

A SPECK OF LOVE

There was a glint of heaven in her smile,
A touch of solace in her eyes,
No words were used,
But each the other knew
A speck of love between them flew;
Why should this speck of love not grow
Or blow away in daily strife?
Let eyes between them turn to fix
Whatever comes in love more rife.

Ben Henderson Smith

WHEN I WAS JUST A BOY

When I was just a boy, lad
When I was just a boy,
We didn't have such fancy things
But life was full of joy.
With sugar in a sack, lad
And butter in a pat,
And cheese with wires for cutting,
And Tom, the grocer's cat.
He sat warm in the window
Where customers could see,
And when he caught me looking
He'd stretch his paw to me.

I sit here in my chair, lad,
Here in these modern days,
The old times are so clear, lad
As in the sun I laze.
That grocer's shop with crusty bread,
Broken biscuits in a tin,
A little box upon the shelf
To put the money in.
And when I see your sliced bread
Pizzas like a plastic pad,
Then I recall when I was small,
A happy little lad.

Sybil R Collins

SAFARI, LOCH TUMMEL

An adventure safari up north,
In March, Perthshire Highlands, and cold.
In a Land Rover we journeyed forth,
We were captured, enraptured, but old.

The driver was Scots, in a kilt,
Bow-legged, quietly grizzled and calm.
The track steeped at lunatic tilt,
But none of us came to much harm.

The Land Rover soared like a bird:
Either side purple saxifrage bloomed,
Schiehallion was misty but regal,
A barium mine briefly loomed.

We sighted a lone golden eagle,
A hare, an abundance of ewes,
A wheatear, a linnet, some deer,
And views upon views upon views.

I suppose, had a sheep been as rare
As an osprey or white Arctic hare,
Our hearts might have leapt at the sight,
As they did when we saw the red kite.

For sheep on the run are no rarity,
Resignation, sly smiles, loud hilarity
Greet their terrified run, or the muddle,
As they scamper and crowd in a huddle.

But they're bountiful, clothing and feeding us,
Impressive as well, high and steep:
All the more since the sheep are not needing us.
It is we who are needing the sheep.

G Tapper

GROUNDED

Our neighbour has a secret -

once a fighter pilot,
butterflies are his
thing now

jealous of their wings,
he traps them and pins
them down in a miniature morgue

once a year, I'm summoned
to his shed to view the
multicoloured corpses -
skewered in time

he fiddles furtively with
the sweaty lock, while I shuffle
the dust and watch spiders wrestling
prey in webs that match his scar.

Joking, I ask if he's frightened
they'll fly away -

triumphant, he tells me their
flying days are over -
like his

he says this one is very rare,
possibly extinct now - the one
that outshines the rest, its
impossible iridescence
mocking death

in a kimono of emerald silk
his wife stares bleakly from
an upstairs window -

she had been beautiful too.

Jennifer D Wootton

ALONE

The little boy sat on the step, his head was hung down low,
he was all alone there and had nowhere else to go.
Shoes he wore were battered and unshod upon his feet,
the snow had begun falling, the wind began to beat.
His little hands were trembling, he pulled his legs up tight,
huddled in the corner he prepared to spend the night.
Carriages trundled on their way; no one seemed to care,
people just kept passing by, sometimes they would stare.
He was very hungry, his stomach rumbled loud,
how he wished someone would stop, out there in the crowd.
The tears began falling slowly down his cheek,
he was feeling cold now and he was very weak.
Pressing close into the corner, right against the door,
he felt a strange sensation he'd never felt before,
his body felt all warm, his hands no longer cold;
maybe God was calling him to come and join His fold.
He closed his eyes, a smile caressed his face,
perhaps, he thought, *Heaven was better than this place*.
The cold light of morning found him still tightly curled,
a smile still upon his face, but no longer in this world.

Iris Taylor

ALL I NEED

I have no one
But You Lord
That's all you have
It has been said
I reply in thought
He is all I need
Side by side
We walk the hills
And pastures green
Stroll beside
The silver streams
He guides me
Holds me in the
Palm of His hand
I have no one
But You Lord
That's all you have
It has been said
I reply in thought
He is all I need.

Penny Kirby

OUT OF THIS WORLD

Enter a library and escape to another world
Where in plain sight there is the meaning of life.
Broaden your mind with revelations,
So you can experience revolutions, motivation.
Lose yourself, as you marvel in the stories of old
You may stumble onto a pot of gold.
Give yourself ammunition to go forth,
Study human history, your fellow man.
If to escape from reality is your plan,
Be an intrepid explorer, reach far-off places,
And face any feat,
You can never know what heights you will reach.
Adventure into a fantasy, to a world of your own.
Become a county sheriff, a soldier, an apparition,
Here you need no one's permission.
Learn about teaching, computing, writing and such,
Do a lot of revision and broaden your view,
Then maybe one day someone will read about you.

Elaine Priscilla Kilshaw

THE SILVER BIRCH

Mighty I did stand
Beneath this garden fence.
My silver jacket of bark shone
And I have seen the nests
Of many a small bird come and go.

Then one April morning,
When I began to grow my leaves
A cruel hand cut my branches down
And one by one I fell below.

A good thirty years or more I have stood here,
Gave catkin and buds that became sheltered leaves.
A beautiful show of growth each year
And shaded children as they played beneath,
With their laughter and their tears.

The sparrows and the blackbirds
Chased through my dancing bow of arms.
But know . . .
This chainsaw tears my silver breast
And I am not a mighty sight,
But I am in a silent pain
And gone in half the time of a day's wage.

Carole Morris

RYE

Rye has a fascination for Barbara and me
Set on a hill o'erlooking the sea,
Its erstwhile age of piracy,
A Cinque Port of charm and romance I deem.
The old-fashioned tea room, how oft we'd meet
Listening to stories, tales of the deep,
Such mariners' yarns of old, you ken
Like dodging rough weather and excisemen,
Fishermen's tall stories by the score or more
Like smugglers' rich pickings from some foreign shore,
The Mermaid Inn, antiques galore,
Dusty old bookshelves containing books of yore,
Lamb House near the old church,
I do declare, Henry James resided there.
Thus through the north gate
O'er cobbled streets we drive,
With reflections and happy days
At the sea port of Rye.

Terrence St John

AIRMAN

High above the dusty veldt
where rising banks of cumulus, sparkle white
against the perfect blue of southern skies,
a fledgling airman, young, excited, all alone
practising the art of flight so newly learned,
twisting, turning, swooping, soaring through the peaks
and vales of cotton wool,
onward, upward, reaching for the heights,
exhilarating solitude.

High above the Lakeland fields
where rising fells majestic lie, bracken brown
against the misty grey of northern sky,
that one-time airman, short of wind and boyish zest,
walks with steady tread, calm, content, pausing
every now and then to memorise the view,
or maybe catch his breath,
onward, upward, reaching for the heights,
exhilarating solitude.

G R Bell

BARBED WIRE

The foliage stank
Of blood, mostly theirs
Seagulls, oh no
Rats and tabby cats
Went wild
As the captives filed in
Long lines into the shelter
We have done what is what
That is it.

Then like a mighty fist of iron
It is seen on the TV screen
And reporters report
On the battle scene
Havoc and bullets a-raining
I show we learned to feign
To hesitate and move in again
When the waste is clear
We moved like reindeer
Pawing away like lightning spears
Zooming in we vowed
The enemy crowd
We would give them hell.

Sparkling as do both
An eye for an eye
A tooth for a tooth
And if the stars do drop
Well we will use you
For an elementary prop.

Hardeep Singh-Leader

FAULDHOUSE GOLF COURSE

The yellow sun's slant rays
Light up the green fairways
Where men play on, despite
The coming on of night.

The sun too gilds the rows
Wherein the dead repose,
Divided by a ledge
Of heather, and beech hedge.

Between two cities now
The train ascends the brow
And I too catch my breath,
Poised between life and death.

Diana Richardson

THE COMFORT ZONE

They've chosen PVC, not wood which
Inconveniently needs oil, is prone
Like them to shrink and swell
Depending on the weather.
And tinted triple-thickness glass with
Multi-locks and louvred blinds. The
Kind they've seen in waiting rooms
And cool smooth tiles
And rattan cane.
Fat nests from Wyevale,
'His and hers' in which to brood
Upon the world; to read of dust,
Of sand, and blood. Of Basra's
Pain and lives wrapped
Up in rotten rags. Of those who
Won't see dawn again.

Sally Spedding

FEAR

It was midnight; all was quiet in the graveyard.
The headstones of the dead were casting shadows in the moonlight.
Up in the branch of a tree, sat an owl.
His beady eyes watching down below.

Suddenly there was a piercing scream; the owl flew away.
The dead turned in their graves.
Then ghosts appeared, ghosts of past and present.
Fear of dying, long since faded away.

The scream came from a young woman. Had she seen a ghost?
What was she doing, there in the graveyard?
Had fear taken her soul, or was she already dead?

The church was a lonely place at night,
Ghosts floated around the graveyard.
The young woman didn't know if she was alive or dead.
Fear was in her eyes. 'Why am I here?' she shouted.
'Because you are dead,' came a reply.

Somehow she had known. 'I don't feel afraid anymore,' she said.
'I'm a lost soul, a ghost, a spirit with no feeling.'
'Join us,' came a reply, 'this night nearly ends.'
She looked all around. 'Yes,' she said, 'I think I will.'

Morning came. The sunshine was warm.
The graveyard was quiet. The ghosts had faded away.
Lying on a grave was the body of a young woman.
Here she died. How long ago, we will never know.

David O'Neill

THE LEGACY I LEAVE

I have no wealth dear child to leave
When my travelling days are done.
My riches are a priceless gift
To share with you my son.

The winding roads that beckon me
Through town and village street.
The lofty spires . . . our heritage
Across a vale of meadowsweet.

The murmuring stream, the field of corn,
A cobbled street on a golden morn.
A sleepy village, quaint old towns,
The city of dreams where men in gowns
Have taught the likes of you and me
To travel the road of destiny.
To know the joys beyond all measure
As each and every mile we treasure.

The memory of days well spent
In our land so green and fair
Are all the riches I possess -
A prize beyond compare.

Take them with love, and travel down
The path where you will see
The untold wealth I leave to you
In my humble legacy.

Eileen Combellack

MIRACLE

From the depths of me
You rose, unbidden.
Radiant eyes,
Blue and cloudless as
Sky in summer,
Full of promise,
Like the dawn.

Sarah Howard

QUIET MORNING, APRIL 2000

The sun was shining, one felt the warmth after bitter, cold days,
All around the chapel grass was mown,
Daffodils and small tulips bloomed.
In this lovely old place, sanctified for centuries
With praise and prayer raised to God,
We met together, followers of Christ,
Twelve of us like disciples of old.
Our morning hymn ascended to God.
We listened, there was word and music,
Then quiet, sun streaming through the windows
Dappling the old brick floor with light.
Twelve people, silent before God.
The morning drew to its close,
Candles were lit and prayers offered,
Hands laid on heads in blessing and healing.
It was over, we returned to everyday living,
Twelve people, refreshed and renewed.

Shirley Ludlow

CELEBRATIONS

From the day we are born to the day we die
Our lives are dotted about with celebrations,
To be born in the first place is regarded as a high
But it may play havoc with financial calculations.

The years roll by and the birthdays are marked,
Eighteen is a milestone in the lives of many.
Soon wedding bells toll out and some people embark,
It's an expensive business, possibly more than any.

A house is acquired and regarded as a love nest,
To celebrate this, it is blessed with a house-warming,
Then follow the specials: silver, gold and diamond, then laid to rest
And if the couple are in Jesus, a new day is dawning.

With hand held in hand they receive their reward,
There are celebrations in Heaven over one sinner who's repented,
Now rejoicing in glory in the presence of the Lord
The couple's journey on Earth has finally ended.

It's celebration time for our good friends at Forward Press,
For fifteen years they've laboured through good times and bad,
I'm sure it's been worth all the strain and the stress,
Considering all the joy and success we have had.

John Waby

A POETIC LINE OR TWO

No sound from the wind, but the branches sway
On the trees nearby in the month of May.
Summer has not shown its true colours just yet,
But as past summers go, we accept what we get.
There are countries in the world that never see rain,
And when we get showers, we'll exclaim, 'Not again!'
Without it our plant life would never survive,
The honeybees wouldn't be able to work in the hive.
Our weather will always be a topical subject
As the old adage goes, nothing is perfect,
But while we worry about most trivial things,
Life will go on and church bells will ring.
We will thank the Lord we've got what it takes
And if we are lucky, we will get the breaks,
When I sit here alone with my thoughts and hopes
And if anything should happen I think I could cope,
I have my family, friends and help galore,
With that in mind, who needs any more?

Joseph Broadley

THE SEA

The raging winds tossed the sea about,
It lashed itself against the jagged rocks,
White frothy water flew into the air and the spray tingled on our skin,
The wind blew on as we walked, heads down against the force,
The sun tried to peep out from the dark grey clouds,
The arid ground beneath our feet strewn with black volcanic lava,
Here and there, fishermen cast their nets,
A solitary gull fought its way in hopelessness
Against the gale, then dived in for the catch.
We turned our backs against the sea and walked away, exhausted.

Olive M Poole

MY COUNTDOWN DILEMMA

At last I'm here on Countdown
It really is a thrill
To make long words from letters
And to test my number skill

For weeks and weeks I've pondered
How best to play the game
Which tactics, I have wondered
Guarantee a champion's fame?

One large one and five small ones
Or two big ones and four small
Shall I let Carol make the choice?
I'm just not sure at all

The numbers could be easy
Yet again they may be hard
I daren't lack concentration
Or I might miss 'leotard'

Will my mind go blank and fail me
Or will I do just fine?
Suppose I only manage three
When I want to get a nine?

How many vowels shall I pick?
It could be three or four
I need to press the buzzer quick
To make sure that I score

The conundrum may elude me
I might make a mistake
Will I use a word that's not allowed?
Calm down for goodness sake

But whatsoe'er may happen
I'll have a super time
And should I not appear again
At least you've heard my rhyme

Christine Skeer

A POEM DEDICATED TO CLIFF RICHARD

Although I am merely a Cliff Richard fan
You are indeed a very special man

Your words and music are full of happiness and love
With all good things from above

Your Christian faith is so important to you
A message of love that's so faithful and true

My greatest wish would be complete
If one day we were able to meet

And now Cliff, in words that are honest and true
I just want to say, 'I love you.'

Suzanne Reeves

THE PROJECT

She did not have a drawing,
But she must have had a plan;
She was halfway through the project,
I wasn't there when she began.
She did not need a ladder,
Or any help at all,
It was a big construction
For one so very small.
Working through the dark of night,
Seemed not to have a break,
A diligence not needing light,
For how long it would take.
The precision was outstanding,
She didn't need a rule,
Didn't have to pass exams
Or even go to school.
Then when it was completed,
Her ardour did not ebb;
They were two of nature's wonders,
The spider and her web!

Bill Austin

OLD FASHIONED

I have a love of old-fashioned things,
Like the sweet shop door with a bell that rings,
Opening wide to a world of treasure,
Sweeties in glass jars, scales to measure.

Brass weights, important when you've a penny to buy,
With wide open eyes and hopes so high,
Toffee in tins to crack with a hammer,
It's quiet in the shop, away from life's clamour.

School bell's stopped ringing, minute bell soon will sound,
But in the meantime, with eyes wide and round,
You can decide, which shall it be?
A humbug or kali? All sorts you can see.

Looking back, the memory holds true,
At least it does for me and perhaps for you,
The sweet shop bell rings out over the years,
Times of laughter, times of tears.

O happy days of long ago,
The sweetness lingers and rightly so,
There seemed more time, people would listen,
And at the sight of those jars,
How our eyes would glisten.

Voices that had a smile in their words,
Sweeties that brightened the day,
Echoes of that calling school bell,
Country days of far away.

Hilary Mason

THE WAR IN IRAQ

His tunic was grey, but now wine-red,
He had blood on his hands, a young boy now dead.
His eyes were still open, bright blue like the sky.
The look in his eyes said *why?*
He has left behind him the ones whom he loved.
Men stand and weep, holding his body,
A prayer for his soul the Lord to keep.
People who never weep are fools or frauds,
They know nothing of love.
More sons will die and mothers will ask why.
Will it benefit other lives? Certainly not mine.
Blood will continue to flow like wine.

Marylin Drew

IMPLICIT TRUST

I remember my childhood with love and affection,
There was no need to worry or seek direction,
Nothing could spoil or penetrate my trust
In parents and sisters I loved so much.
I'm sorry I took eleven years for granted,
But the childhood bliss in me had planted
A value of people for the rest of my life,
Opening my heart to others hurting inside.
'Twas said you're an orphan when a parent dies,
I only knew that I cried and cried,
When under a roof fall of coal, Dad lost his life.
My childhood days had come to an end,
I had to grow up, be a responsible friend
To a mum so courageous in her care for five,
Including our baby brother, newly arrived.
His needs and ours were intertwined,
This family bonding brought peace of mind,
Until the child in the cot nearly died one night.
The doctor advised a crisis would decide,
A turning point with help at hand
Was urgently needed, in panic I ran.
In the outside porch I prayed The Lord's Prayer,
Then I talked and cried together to a God who cares.
The baby recovered and I found direction,
For all of my life I am a committed Christian.

Kathleen McBurney

CONVERSATION WITH CÉZANNE

Master, you speak to us in a visual
language. We listen to the power
of colours eclipsing a black palette,
woven oblique brushstrokes
and overlapping planes.

Through juxtaposing patches of colour
you lead us down the ochre path
to where your thoughts become
visible, reflecting the inner world,
not the one before your eyes.

We feel the scorch of red earth,
breathe the scent of pencil-thin
pines framing Mont Sainte-Victoire
and from still life landscapes long
to taste your waxy apples of childhood.

We learn that spirit and reality
are not opposed, the painter's view
is a miracle waiting to happen - how
else do you change a jug into
a wine glass before our eyes?

Giotto would applaud the weight
of your ponderous style, how you hold
anger in check with singing colours,
and discard dimension to disclose
the secret of your chimerical vision.

In the ash of time the critics extol
your milky-blue bathers, knowing
you are the master for all who follow.
So Paul, does dominion dispel the dark
dense stone within your heart?

Maggie Andrews

A DREAM PARTY

I'm sixty today and I celebrate
I have some fun and see my mates
A pile of cards behind the door
Friends arrive with presents galore

A birthday party with a cake
My next-door neighbour kindly baked
My family's here with the kids
We hug and kiss and reminisce

There's lots to eat and talk about
To hear myself I have to shout
They slap my back, I can't stop tears
I've never had such fun in years

A lovely day without a care
The sound of laughter fills the air
'We love you dearly,' they all say
They'll never go, they want to stay

I wake at dawn. What was that?
I'm all alone in my tiny flat
It was a dream and that's a pity
A lonely man in this big city

All is still, no one about
A lovely dream without a doubt
My friends and family, they weren't here
It did not happen. Perhaps next year?

Harry Murtagh

WISHING STAR

There is a place in my heart forever,
Where my love will always stay,
And this is the tribute I would send,
With love, on every special day.

Dear love of mine I was very sad,
The day you went away,
But you are always in my thoughts,
So this I want to say,

Your photograph in pride of place,
Will always keep you near,
On special days I can't send a card,
But I can speak to you in prayer.

My prayer would say, dear loved one,
Although from me you are far,
I look up to the heavens,
And see you on your wishing star.

It is the star that shines so bright,
And sparkles with such zest,
That is how I know, that it is you,
For it outshines all the rest.

Maud Eleanor Hobbs

A TIME GONE BY

The warmth of the sun on a summer's day
Brings thoughts of times so far away,
Daisy chains and sunlit views,
When we were young and life was new.
Not a care in the world had we,
Just eyes for each other, so free.
Now years later, I'm on my own,
I do not feel alone,
For memories of the love we shared
Bring joy to my heart, never to be compared.

Joan D Bailey

SHOES

Yesterday I found your shoes,
I didn't know
I could laugh
And cry
At the same time,
You danced in those shoes,
I closed my eyes
And hummed our song
Very quietly,
It's been so long
I forgot the words,
I saw you,
Felt your arms around my waist,
I touched the laces
But can't touch you,
The dance is over now.

Susan A Semmens

THE ONE YOU HAD TO RIDE

I had a Runwell cycle that lived up to its name,
'Twas made in central Birmingham, not far from Summer Lane.
It really was a bicycle and one that you could trust,
With paintwork and good plating, you knew would never rust.
They only had one colour, it's known as bottle green,
And when you rode the saddle, you did it with esteem.
You got an extra inner tube, some spanners and a pump,
A can of oil, a battery lamp and a saddle bag to hump.
All that you could carry, wherever you did go,
For sometimes going up a hill meant pedalling very slow.
They sold them out in China, Malaya and the East,
Some even went to Africa, though sometimes, but not least,
The BSA and Hercules, the Rudge and Raleigh too,
All did their best to beat the Runwell, well that's very true.
From the factory in Lawson Street, the workers had a pride
In knowing that a Runwell was 'The one you had to ride'.

Roy T Gough

THE TWO TAILORS

My father was a high-class tailor,
Please listen to his story, I beg.
He would like to have become a sailor,
But in his youth he lost his left leg.

He married and had six children,
A family of three girls and three boys.
He wasn't as active as some men,
But he joined in our laughter and joys.

As time went by we moved house,
From one side of town to the other.
Life went on for my father and spouse,
The lady being our mother.

My father was friendly with a man
Whose job was a tailor too,
And the strange coincidences began,
Having lost his right leg, he was only wearing one shoe.

From then on, one pair of shoes was bought
Between my father and friend across the street,
Just plain lace-up shoes were sought,
Because they both had the same size feet.

Pearl Hammond

STILLNESS

Can you feel the breath of an angel
kissing the wind in the deep stillness of your being?
Looking to the night skyline, can you hear the tremor
of the small stream trickling past the reeds?

In the stillness of the night, can you hear a cow
munching the grass stems in contentment?
Do you welcome the darkness of yourself
and the night, as old friends well traveled?

And give thanks with the breath of life to all who dwell here;
and know you are heard?

Did you catch the reply? Did you?
It was the breath of an angel kissing the wind.

Zing J Rock

FOR LONELY WIVES

Dearest husband, dear, sweet soul,
God beckoned you away,
You've passed into the silence,
But how near you seem today.
You haunt the shadows of the house,
I pass you on the stairs,
I meet you in the garden,
You're here and everywhere.
Though your home is in Heaven now,
We are never far apart,
The fragrance of your memory lives on
Within my heart.
How much I remember of our marriage, I recall
How good you were to me, the greatest love of all.
I believe that God lets husbands hover near
When their wives need them,
When in danger, doubt or fear,
For often when I'm feeling sad
A light breaks in the gloom
And I could swear there is an angel
Somewhere in the room.

Rita Mash

A RITUAL BROKEN

The ritual of thirty years has been broken.
Breakfast eaten in stony silence,
No cards exchanged this year.
A silly falling out.
Stress of yuletide revelry no doubt.

Just two cards, small, cheap, insignificant,
But a ritual has been broken.
Yet here we are, the year is new
And all is well,
No abyss, no doom, no Hell.

In fact we are content, reassured.
We have got away with it.
We are still in one piece.
This year we will break with a few more traditions,
Just for the hell of it.

Out with the old, in with the new,
And a happy New Year to all of you.

Frances Roberts

A TOAST TAE RABBIE

On yer feet *if* ye can stan',
I say to each an' every man;
This is nae jist anither booze-up
Wi' yer couthie cronies. Na!
Ye' er here tae rake yer conscience an' tae answer weel.
Could I stan' up tae Rabbie Burns,
That Ayrshire plooman chiel?
His times, his anguish an a' his sorrow,
Workin' in time he couldna' borrow.
Is there a man amang ye at the age o' thirty-seven
Can staun' an' say
'I've had my day,
I'll now bow oot wi' grace;
I've lived and loved and left this world
Wi' words a better place'?
Na! Na! He wis exceptional, tho' whiles he hidna known it
The laddie wis a genius, as weel as bein' a poet.
He left us a' wi' wondrous words, some tender an' some great.
The world's ready for anither Rabbie, bit that's jist up tae fate!

Pearl Johnston-Stewart

NEEDLEWORK

Lonely Miss Smith had a tapestry on the go
Her neighbours found her a right old sew and sew
She would sit by her window, cold and draughty
And lose herself in needlework, very crafty
With needle and thread, thumb capped with a thimble
Her elderly fingers were still very nimble
Her steely-grey hair, wrapped up in a bun
Glistening silver streaks in the afternoon sun
Her hands all crinkled, her face all wrinkled
And doing her favourite hobby, her brown eyes twinkled
Be it a tapestry or pretty cross-stitch
She would revel in the colours, pallid and rich
She sometimes found the canvas very tricky
And with untidy threads she became very picky
There was nothing that she couldn't embroider
But what had made everyone avoid her?
She was picky and crafty and known to wheedle
An old sew and sew, who loved to needle.

Paul Spender

IF YOU WOULD SIT WITH ME

Distant hills I cannot see,
But there is beauty here, for me.
The beauty that every season brings,
From winter's sleep to spring's wakenings.
Where once the ground appeared dead,
Spring flowers a living carpet spread;
And rippling waters of the stream
Awaken me, as from a dream.
The trees no longer stark and bare,
A new, fresh garb of green now wear,
And from the branches boldly sing
Birds in chorus, to welcome spring.
Were I a thousand miles away,
This is where my heart would stay.

Distant hills I cannot see,
But there is beauty here, for me.
There is no place I'd rather be
Than here, if you would sit with me.

Joan Thompson

A SUMMER EVENING

That enchanted hour 'twixt day and night
When shadows deepen in softened light
And mellow to the ear is rural sound
Distant, yet near and all around

The wandering wind gently stirs the air
Carrying scents so elusive and rare
Whispering through the chestnut trees
The warm summer evening breeze

And in it's all embracing balm
Come thirsty men from cot and farm
Outside the thatch-roofed inn to sit
Slaking their thirst as the lamps are lit

The work is done, they take their ease
On rustic benches 'neath the trees
And talk of cows, a cabbage patch
A half-forgotten cricket match

Tobacco smoke in lazy rolls
Rises from the cherrywood bowls
As friendly banter flies to and fro
And contentment rules the evening glow.

Robert E Fraser

THE RHYTHM OF LIFE

Through the rhythm of life runs a golden thread of energy
                   beyond compare . . .
It is found in the world of nature, we breathe it in the air.
To find this precious gift from God, you need a quiet mind,
To open up your heart and search for blessings - you will find.
For all around you every day, in thought and word and deed,
This golden thread of energy can fill your every need.

You will find it in a sunrise, the breath of a new dawn.
The quiet certainty that life renews with each new morn.
Be sensitive to others, the energy is there,
When you with kindness sin your heart and another's care can share.
Explore your favourite flower, its petals, shape and size,
The beauty and the colour will increase before your eyes.

Trees also hold this special gift, seek out their strength and power,
Wander in the leafy shade, enjoy a quiet hour.
Giant oaks, their branches moving gently in the breeze.
Breathe deeply of the clean fresh air and feel your body ease.
Sunshine lighting, warm and healing - touch the soft brown earth,
Peat sweet and clean slips through your fingers, a gift from
                           Mother Earth.

God filled the world with energy, to help us every day,
But in the rush and haste of life, we throw this gift away.
So find a time to be at peace, away from stress and strife,
And tune into this energy - the 'Golden Thread of Life'.

Cynthia Shum

NATURE

When you step on the land you change it,
No matter how quick or small that step is,
Nature can feel it and shudders under the weight.

You step on an ant and that life is gone,
No matter how small life is,
When it is gone, it will never come back.

But the day will come when Nature fights back,
She doesn't care about good or evil,
And she will take back what belongs to her.

Katja Kielhauser

PROSPERITY

Our support network,
family and friends,
provides for our growth.
We prosper
knowing we are loved.
Holding each other
up above the mire,
giving time gladly,
embracing our frailty.
Sometimes we err,
with the best of intention,
feel guilty
for lack of care.
But we try,
making the effort
to understand,
to heal the rifts.
Moving onward together
we celebrate our humanity.

Chris Webb

THE NOW

No longer the mills are cool water fed,
Lonesome they stand in silence and decay,
Across the stygian ferry gone Albert and Ned,
The clicking and crushing, no more in play.

Twin wheels of oak lie mouldering still –
Crenellated spokes like ancient ducking stools,
The stream carries only flotsam to spill,
And iron hubs to elementals that rule.

Deciduous trees kiss bleak mortar in its neglect,
Just one leaded window and one hinged door,
Now only debt to nature finally shows respect,
Once used for the melting pot of the poor.

Time-warped and strange for a future day,
'Shades of Cézanne,' the cries of the now,
Perhaps the works once again allowed to play?
But rustic swains' toil finally takes the bow.

Tarn Hows

AD ASTRA

Show me the way through the clouds to Valhalla,
Guide me at sunset, when angels are winging,
Through the dusky gold twilight, by a gossamer path,
To the first evening star, with the Valkyries singing.

Through the Van Allen belt, to the purple beyond,
On moonbeams of silver, and time travelled light,
Through Milky Way mists and deep oceans of stardust,
To the great hall of Odin, I travel tonight.

Alone, with the ghosts of my comrades around me,
'Midst the night-scented jasmine, and firefly glow;
In my outdated, craft, on this weed-covered runway,
I watch the horizon for Thor's hammer blow.

I am eager for flight, I am tired of Earth,
My time is at hand, and my engines are running;
My sorrow is only for those I must leave,
But my ancestors call, and tonight, I am coming.

John Bevan Stocks

TURKISH DELIGHT

Beside the Bosphorus there sleeps a city
Where minarets shiver in the hazy heat
And waxen white lilies, in cool chastity
Are lemon-tree canopied, scent bitter-sweet.
Chant of the muezzin drifts faint and soulful,
Steals the distant dreams from shimmering domes
Still drowsy in dawning Istanbul.

Biddy Redgrove

GOLDEN DAY

Through special days
From silver, pearl and ruby,
We've marked the years
With celebrated joys.
And now we've reached
Yet one more special milestone,
Our golden day,
Of memories we've shared,
Such love and happiness,
The years have given
To bless us,
As we gather on this day
To celebrate
And share our joy with others,
On our truly happy
Special golden day . . .

Joan Hammond

IMPRINTS

It was the year before the end of the world.
You were doll-like,
With your white sawn-off hair
Like that of a baby,
Even though you were nearly five.

You perched beside me on the kerb
In our traffic-free street.
I did not know your name.
I was never to know your name
Or even which house was yours.
I could recite my own address, though.

And then you turned and kissed me:
I can still feel the softness of your lips
Across the distance of 67 years
And clearly see you
Reaching out to me.

That is all of the snapshot.
But if I were to return to that place -
If any part of it survived -
And find you there sitting at the roadside,
I would know you were the kissing girl . . .

Except that now you are not she.
You will have adopted a thousand
Grown-up disguises
And I cannot go back to my old home,
Where death was soon to rule.

Though they rebuilt it later
You can't recreate a lost childhood.
Still, the kiss remains forever,
Like a spring breeze,
And you will never grow older.

Ted Harriott

CRY VICTORIA . . .

Cry Victoria all the while;
Cry Victoria, do not smile.
Daddy's lost down the mine,
Won't be back at any time . . .

And don't ever forget -
Should you grow very old -
The men that were trapped
In the dark, damp and cold . . .

And don't ever forget
How they perished - they died -
As their kin at the top
Wailed and they cried . . .

Each tear a deep suffering;
Each wail a pained song
For the men that were theirs,
For those that are gone . . .

Don't ever forget, Victoria dear,
Take the memory with you year after year . . .
Let our men not be lost with the passing of time;
Have their names on a list, or in a sweet rhyme . . .

And, Victoria dear, remember too,
The toil of donkey, pony or ass;
And the fate of canaries,
A-testing for gas . . .

Don't ever forget . . .

Mary Pauline Winter (née Coleman)

BENEATH TIP LANE

The shouts of angry men we faced
As through the council gates we raced,
Where untold treasure could be found,
My favourite childhood hunting ground.
A company of gulls and rats,
Catapults and Davy Crockett hats,
This wild frontier of waste we'd roam,
The dust-filled sky in monochrome.
A playground built from man's decay,
Air sickly sweet by heat of day,
This living, shifting land was mine,
A feast on which my eyes could dine.
Those things which people threw away,
That treasure I still have today,
But my childhood lies beneath Tip Lane,
A treasure I cannot reclaim.

Mark L Moulds

FIGHT THE GOOD FIGHT

Politicians laugh and joke
Mindless of their bloodied hands
Verbal diarrhoea their weapon
When defending doubtful plans.

They've blown the arms off one poor schoolboy
Kissed a babe - poor little mite
Offered friendship - offered goodies
When will these people see the light?

To be a recognised war criminal
Ignore international law
Instigate conflict and killing
Be on the side that lost the war.

Alf Cole

I AM HERE

I am your comfort when things seem grey
I hope you feel me near you on this day
Tell me your innermost thoughts
I understand your doubts
I do not judge you
Nor criticise your wrongs
We all need someone to turn to
And I am here with you
To give you strength
To hold your hopes and dreams
If things don't go according to plan
Speak to me, I am your man
I am your guide
I am your hope
I am your spirit
You are my love
You are my reason
You are part of my Earth
Part of my universe

Linda Ann Marriott

RICHES SHARED

We dream of riches
We dream of fame
We struggle to compete
We strive to reach our goal in life
To make our lives complete
I wonder just how many folks
We hurt along the way
The more we have, the more we want
Does it really pay?
Time passes - have regrets
To say the very least
While we sit at our tables
Enjoy our usual feast
It's never too late to change our ways
If we want peace of mind
Atone for our misgivings
By being good and kind
Help our fellow countryman
Who needs a helping hand
Feed the starving children
Dying in other lands
There is more to life than riches
I am sure you will agree
Simple pleasures to enjoy
A contented heart can see

Sarah Buchan Anderson

MY SCOTLAND

There is something about Scotland that I like
Each time I go out for a hike
Along lochs and rivers, or up thro' glens
Climbing gentle hills or muckle Bens
Each so bonnie in its own way
I hope that forever that's how it will stay
For Scotland you are the land that I adore
My country and my home for evermore.

George Wright

CELEBRATIONS

People celebrate all over the world,
Birthdays, christenings and weddings,
But I will celebrate today
Because I'm giving my daughter away.

I know I'll have a big bill to pay,
But hopefully it will be the last,
And years of paying out
Will all be in the past.

Her husband will have to take it all on,
I hope he knows how much she will spend.
He need not come to me,
I have nothing left to lend.

So I'll raise my glass
To wish him well,
And celebrate.

Evelyn Hoy

OUR WEDDING DAY

Our wedding day will be so special
It means more to me than ever
I am with you today and forever and
That's something I will always treasure

Just seeing your face in the crowd
It could be quiet or very loud
I know for sure when I look at you
That you're the one for me and
Our love will go on unconditionally

You mean the world to me, and me to you
And I know our true love will see us through
Together we will make our vows in front of the crowd
'To have and to hold, together, forever,' is said out loud.

I love you more than ever and I'm sure in my heart
That our love will continue, come what may
As I express these true words to you today

'I love you.'

Theresa Carey

MOTHER

The special person,
The friend you need,
When times are hard
And your heart breaks,
She's always there
To hear the tale
The many times
You tried and failed
She listens patiently
As you ramble on,
Offers comfort,
Helps you be strong,
Giving you strength
To carry on,
Treat her tenderly
With special care,
The day will come
She's no longer there,
No one else
Can take her place,
You're left with memories
Of a loving face.

Marie Kelly

THE UNICORN

I saw the moonlight over the sea
As the unicorn flew down
And I felt the magic enchanting me
As I saw the moonlight over the sea
There were silver wings beating silently
As it pawed the liquid ground

I saw the moonlight over the sea
And the waves reached to the sky
And through that wonderful watery wave
The unicorn flew by
Silver and silent it hovered
Silhouetted against the sky

I saw the moonlight over the sea
And I held my breath in delight
For the unicorn was dancing
In the silver sheen of light
Dancing and prancing above the sea
With a mane of silvery white

I saw the moonlight over the sea
And the memory lingers yet
Of the silver shining unicorn
Half mythical, half pet
Sculpted by moonlight, spawned by the sea
The magical unicorn dancing for me

Judy Smith

CELEBRATORY YEAR

F orward Press; cheers, and congratulations!
I t's your 15th anniversary,
F or your poetry publications.
T o the poet a necessity,
E nabling work to be seen in print.
E ven young children can try their hand,
N ow that's a lovely start, don't you think?
T ime to grow with poetry so grand,
H oping to contribute something new.

A ll they need is that encouragement.
N ice for everyone their work to view
N ow they have attained acknowledgement.
I t's great to have the opportunity.
V ery pleased Forward Press can provide
E very type for the community.
R ight from their hearts, they write and confide,
S howing their feelings through poetry.
A lways writing with great endeavour,
R emembering their anthology.
Y es, Forward Press, continue forever.

Doreen Ranson

OVERCOMING

Sighs must go, fret too, yet pray
For hope to chase the tears away;
Unless of *joy* they wet the eye,
Such welcome tears who can deny?

Hope - once more, then *smile* and *laugh*.
Laughter heals the soul's distress,
So happiness gained the sweetest way
Is there yet for another day.

Life's too short, too good to waste
Too long in tears, whate'er the cause.
Like the flowers refreshed by rain
We must *lift* our heads, *forget* the pain.

Lola Perks-Hartnell

WHAT PRICE FAME?

I have always been star-struck,
But never looked for fame,
Meeting Dalziel and Pascoe in the library
Was my famous claim.

I was so pleased to be
Photographed with them,
The popular TV duo to me
Were the 'crème de la crème'!

Years ago, when I was
Doing various office work,
Entertaining with 'comic verse'
Was my little quirk!

If there had been a 'special' period
In their lives of note,
They would give me some personal clues
And then get a poem to quote!

To me it was just harmless fun,
Just for a joke,
But it went down well,
With those particular folk!

Friends would often say,
'You should have kept copies,' of which I regret.
Now I'm in a book from Forward Press, so!
Am I famous yet?

M Jukes

MY ENGLAND

This is my England, my own promised land
And every day, I bless the gift of sight,
The richness I witness, wherever I may stand
All around are scenes of pure delight.

It gives me inspiration, and peace of mind,
Hidden treasures bestowed, close at hand
To gaze at nature's miracles, I am often inclined,
This absorbing beauty is easy to understand.

The serenity of the countryside lies for miles around
Any disconcerting thoughts will quickly disappear
In its complete winsomeness, I am totally drowned
My perspective on life becomes really clear.

The impetus it instils, forces me to write
About the wonders which captivate every day
Held in winter's throes or when spring is in sight,
The heralding of autumn, as summer fades away.

To marvel at the spectacle of clouds, so low
You can reach out and touch them with your hand,
Views across this country give a spectacular show
The opulence of this kingdom is truly grand.

There is something extraordinary about country air
Which invigorates and makes you feel so fresh,
Such splendid surroundings, hard to equal anywhere
Its grandeur can bring a tingle to your flesh.

Watch an early mist rise, the sun filtering through
Observing the sea, and the secrets it must hold,
Morning fields, when grass is submerged in dew
Bringing serenity, when days are long and cold.

Summer with such sumptuous hues,
The wonder of nature's ability to change,
Take in some awesome views,
Which can encapsulate from a distant range.

B W Ballard

THE STRANGE WORLD WE LIVE IN!

'Write us a poem,' said my daughter,
'A poem about love,' said my wife,
'That's not much fun,' said my twelve-year-old son,
'Why not write us a poem about life?
Write us a poem about people,
And peculiar things that they do,
About people who bicker and argue and fight,
Because one of them's Catholic or Jew,
Tell us of blokes who beat up old folks
And take every penny they've got,
And people who try to climb mountains
And die on the way to the top,
Tell us of men who are ready to die
Because they believe in a cause,
And tell us about all the children
Who believe there's a real Santa Claus,
Tell us of folks who go around telling jokes
And try to spread laughter and fun,
And tell us again of those terrible men
Who rule with the knife and the gun.
Please tell me Dad, as I'm only a lad,
Have we any real future in store?
Or is your generation determined to
Make sure that somewhere,
There's always a war?'

Cliff Seaman

MEDITATION

So often I've wandered, their beauty unending
The byways of Rutland when summer has flown;
And grieved at its passing with grey mist descending
As leaves into thick coloured carpets are blown.

The sorrow I feel at another year passing,
Reflecting a life that is all but now spent,
Is harder to bear as the years are amassing
While old age confirms that my youth was just lent.

The churchyard I stop at compounds this great sadness
For there on the tombstones, most faded away
Are memories of loved ones recalled with such gladness
With no one to tend them this bleak autumn day.

For time has eroded in slow even paces
The hovels of surfs and the castles of kings,
Till nothing is left but the faintest of traces
In fields where the lark and the mistle thrush sing.

Perhaps they all too had their fears that proved groundless
For the uncertain future their children must face.
But ours is an age when destruction is boundless,
They knew not the terror of life's ruthless pace.

Where many now live for a life of distraction
That numbs all their senses and calms the real dread
Of the horror of hate, and its hideous reaction
That leaves sometimes no one to bury the dead.

In vain do the voices of reason shout warning
But their message is drowned in an ocean of greed
For few will believe that the holocaust dawning
Has been caused by all those that take more than they need.

Yet when I consider life's splendour abounding,
This moment in time seems like only a game
Played out on a voyage as we each take our sounding.
But a hundred years hence, will it still be the same?

Januarius

THE SAXON KING

(Inspired by a visit to Sutton Hoo)

Our fathers came to pillage and to fight
Driving you British farmers from your lands.
The Roman governors parleyed with our might,
Sought help from our brave Saxon fighting bands.

They gave us land - if we would fight for them,
Such fertile land, our cows and sheep grew fat.
And when the Romans left, we Saxon kings
Brought in our laws that men might know as fact.

We weren't just raiders, pirates, banditry -
We had our gods - unlike your Christian God,
Who turned the other cheek when struck in the face
But war god Woden, guardian of our race.

And now we're kings of Britain, with our laws,
Our wisdom and our justice - stern to you -
But fair, exacting *wergild* when blood's shed . . .
And yet your gentle God, to whom you're true,

Beguiles us. I've a shrine richly endowed
With altars built to Woden and to Jesus,
Your humble God, rejected by the proud,
Who sheltered those who'd sunk too low for shame . . .

And when it's time for Heaven or Valhalla,
With tributes paid to your God and to mine,
I'll join the angels far from Earthly clamour
Or feast in Odin's Hall and drink his wine.

My grave shall be a ship - an 80-footer,
Stacked full of weapons, plate and gems of every kind,
Twelve centuries will pass and then some looter
May find my hoard - myself he'll never find.

Rosemary Harvey

DANCER AT THE EDGE OF TIME

On a custom-built stage reaching out
to mind and soul anxious to express
our reasons for being here despite
smouldering coals of body language,
petty potholes of pretty speech
(or signing) - for any language can
but brush the surface of those nether
regions of self . . . wherein we rage
at being misunderstood

Now meek, mild; now grown wild,
this dance of a lifetime they paid
a high price to see, who have
summoned me here (for a private
viewing only) hoping to be shown
the various steps between right
and wrong - and in so doing,
learn something, at least, about
live art

Gliding with grace, gesturing a plea
to be acknowledged (better still,
recognised) by an inner eye that's
too often inclined to remain shut
than be made to choose a path we'd
much rather ignore. Dancer takes
a bow. Performance over, task all
but ended; art's love affair with life
lent new meaning, purpose

So let's learn, no time to rehearse;
the next move ours

R N Taber

THE FOUR SEASONS

When I think of springtime
I roll back the years,
In my mum's golden garden,
I wipe up the tears.
Then comes the summer
And mountains of hay,
My mum holds my hand
On a sweet summer's day.
Then there's the autumn,
We sweep up the leaves,
My mum lights the bonfire,
So happy those years.
The winter's upon us,
Mum says wrap up warm,
She loves us so dearly
And we came to no harm.
Then came our Christmas
With Mum, round the fire
She told us her stories,
We never would tire.
And so the four seasons
They come and they pass,
We gather her flowers,
Mum's resting at last.

Thelma Hynes

TIME

I visited a friend today, she's living in a home,
Not because of illness, but simply cos she's old.
I spent an hour or two there, we even sat to pray
And then I felt it best to leave, we'd little left to say.
As I turned to wave goodbye and saw her tired frame,
Suddenly I realised that soon I'd be the same.
Where had all the time gone? Who had stolen all the years?
What on Earth had happened to cause these awful fears?
I had only yesterday been youthful, active, strong,
Playing with my children, bursting with life's song,
Always with such energy, so many things to do,
Ready every morning to face the day on cue.
It surely was just yesterday I faced life with such flair,
What had age to do with me? I'd lots of time to spare.
I never gave the smallest thought, to think that I'd be old,
No longer fit, or youthful, never quite as bold.
Age had seemed like nothing, life had been so kind you see,
And there I thought was plenty more, I'd lots of life in me.
Then suddenly I understood this strong and awful dread,
And why the many memories were spinning through my head.
I'd been made to realise, that this important phase
Was not a dress rehearsal, but my own life's final stage.
It wouldn't matter very much how many years I'd spent,
The years we have are after all, the time that we've been lent.
It only really matters what I do and what I say,
The time I take to help a need, the friend I make today.
The frightened child whose hand I hold, the neighbour who's alone.
The stranger on a busy street, the person far from home.
So very fast our time goes by, so quickly do we age,
Never really seeing our life written as a page.
What written here is everything that we will be and do,
So do things right because, my friend, old age will visit you.

Jo Fletcher

FIRST LOVE

First love,
Unrequited.
Seen from afar.
First love,
Unrequited.
Knows not who we are.
Seems unattainable.
Never gets close.
Passed by unnoticed,
Feeling morose.
Meet: just by chance,
Eyes burn with desire.
Life seems to change:
Smouldering fire.
Longed for moment awakens,
Quivering heart.
Thrilling excitement,
Never will part.
First kiss holds such promise
Future of bliss
Romantic fervour,
Chaste, innocent kiss.
Hands held close,
Fingers entwined.
World does not exist
It has been left behind.
Locked in a cocoon,
Sweet passionate embrace.
First love forever
Remembered always.

Patsy Preshaw

THE BRIDGE AT MOSTAR

Elegant
In single span,
Mostar's jewel Stari-Most
Confidently, safely bridged
The flowing river far below
Throughout four hundred years and more,
Resisting man's destructive urge
And nature's hostile forces.

But when assailed unceasingly
By targeted explosive shells,
Unable to protect itself
Or treat its gaping wounds,
It finally succumbed,
The last defiant remnants sent crashing,
As an avalanche,
Into a watery grave,
Leaving unaccustomed exposed void
On the skyline's jagged silhouette
And Neretva's angry turquoise
Sanguine stained.

Yet in the midst of devastation,
Hovering like a ghost,
A short-lived brilliant rainbow
Settled on the yawning breach,
Portentously,
For the broken Stari-Most.

Stanley Longbottom

THE WATER'S EDGE

I walked down by the water's edge,
The gentle waves were lapping by the shore;
I dipped my feet into the tepid sea
And left my footprints in the sand,
As you and I did many years before.

I stood there by the water's edge
And gazed alone across the calm blue sea.
The gulls were circling round above my head,
And children played and couples laughed,
And I remembered how it used to be.

Each day I go to the water's edge;
It's there sometimes, I think you speak my name.
I'm sure it's almost time you came for me,
I've been alone these long, long years
And without you, life is not the same.

One day you'll come to the water's edge
You'll see my footprints in the sand, and call;
And I will come to you, and hand in hand
We'll skim across the green-blue deep
Where we'll share the sweetest sleep of all.

Phyllis Spooner

TIME

Time is something given to all of us . . .
Time to share;
Time to use in prayer;
Time to see our friends;
Time to read our favourite book;
Time to feel the warmth of sunshine;
Time to give to those in need;
Time to look at nature's beauty
Whether it be.
Bird, tree, scenery or flower;
The waves of the ocean;
The ripple on the stream;
The stars in the sky -
Also the moon at night;
The first bulbs appearing;
The yellow of spring -
The snowdrops so angelic;
All this, in *time*, will be seen.

Alice Norma Pusey

LOST CHILD

Upon new ground a young girl stands
With no love to hold her hand
Lost in the confusion of being alone
Young girl, lost child without a home
Who walks upon these crowded streets
With her heavy load upon tired feet
She passes people she's never met
Whilst trying hard to forget
Her yesterday days that come to mind
Where a part of herself was left behind
As she walks alone in this new found place
She bravely wipes the tears from her face
As the blink of an eye takes on all of the view
She kisses goodbye to the place she once knew
Young girl, lost child you will survive
For love will dry the tears you've cried.

Susan Hamlyn

LOVE FIRST LEARNED

First experiences
I like my milk and food
I like my mother's smile
Her arms around me
I like the warmth
Not the cold
I like the sweet spoken word
But not the harsh shout
I like my toys
Not when they're taken away
I like my cuddles and sleep
I like to awake and start a new day
I like to learn
To see, think, walk or laugh
Not to fall or hurt myself
I like to experience new things
I like your touch and smell
I like it when you tell me
You love me
I feel good inside
I like feeling good
I shall do things for you too
That should make you smile
I think that I love you
I think I do.

Ronald D Lush

EVERYTHING THAT LIVES

Everything that lives, that is breathing,
Is a miracle to me,
A dung beetle on the African plains
Is such a marvellous creature,
It is small, but so important to life,
A penguin standing guarding his eggs,
In the bitter cold hurricane-force winds,
And standing on the ice of Antarctica,
A large brown bear fishing for salmon,
Out of the Alaska rivers,
A blueprint clicking together,
The giant jigsaw,
Is it in colour, or black and white
To the eye of the beholder?
Do we bleed red blood,
And is dying as tragic as we think?
Does our soul leap into another skin,
Or am I next to become
A cat, a tree, or a bumblebee?
Everything that lives,
Is it me?

Jan Bevan

LULLABY
(For my grandchildren)

I will capture the moon in a puddle
Keep a rainbow on a silver length of thread
I'll ask the geese for the down from their middles
To make you cloud-covered pillows for your head.

I will build you a castle from candy
Keep jars of birthday wishes, smiles and sunbeams
I'll ask the lark kindly sing with the honeybee
To make sweet music that's fit for a queen.

I will slay all the dragons and demons
Keep wicked witches and wolves from your door
I'll ask my heart be gift-wrapped with gold ribbons
To make sure you are forever loved and adored.

Jo Stock

THE ULSHAW CAT

Our local hero, a ginger tom,
Lives his life with some aplomb.
This one-eyed cat, his name is Moses,
He always seems to come up roses.

Though getting old, he is still quite neat,
He always 'falls upon his feet',
For though well loved, and with no need,
He will often call at my house to feed.

Now Sunday morn, he goes to church
And on an altar seat will perch.
When he has heard the preacher's sermon,
Off he goes in search of vermin.

Soon he returns, now cleansed of sin,
He taps on the window to be let in.
Now it seems his heart's desire,
To sleep outstretched before the fire.

Our friend no longer in his prime,
Has become a legend in his time.
Now with two homes, and everything to hand,
Moses has reached 'the promised land'.

(Sadly now deceased.)

D B Bowes

OLD FRIEND

Old friend you guide me with each footstep that I take
Pulling me to you.
Many years have passed and a great distance has separated us
Never completely forgotten.
There in the shadows you have remained within me
Surrounded by summer memories full of laughter.
They generate a longing to return.
Somewhere I'm always with you.
Sorrow creeps over in time, as does the twilight's faltering rays.

Old friend nothing can remove you from my heart or mind.
Momentarily forgotten, still I hear you calling,
It pains me knowing that I cannot be with you each time.
How the years have changed you.
New people have come and gone.
Some adding to you, though most taking bits away with them,
Changes have been made,
Do you look back at me and see the differences?
No carefree girl in her youth.
A wife, a mother
Carrying with her a history,
A past, both bad and good.

Old friend we sit together, as the day draws to its end
Though a quiet sits over us, it is not uncomfortable
And is borne from years of familiarity
Warm and secure like a lover's embrace.
Still goodbye arrives and I place a smile upon my face
Already recalling the most recent memories we have made.
With each step away I struggle
Hard to quash the aching that is growing inside.

Old friend be strong, we will meet again.
Time and people will have changed us even more so.
I will recognise you. Will you recognise me?
I'm fighting the urge to glance back over my shoulder,
But can no longer resist.
To see you in sunset's glorious colours, burned into my retinas.
Dropping like gold your sands fall into the sea
An ever-changing myriad of blue.

Zoë Hall

STORIES IN MY HEAD

I lay curled up in my bed
Writing stories in my head
Romance and history
Comedy and mystery
All waiting to be written and then read

Lying curled up in my bed
I think of characters we'll dread
Male ones, female ones
Braves ones and timid ones
All waiting to be created in my head

Stretching out upon my bed
I plan the stories way ahead
Serious plots, funny plots
Perhaps my tale should have a twist instead

Getting up from my bed
I begin to write the stories in my head
Romance and mystery
Characters from history
Soon they will be written and waiting to be read

Elwyn Bull

SPRINGTIME IN ENGLAND

It is a joy to know God cares,
Again to see His great repairs,
The grass gets greener every day
And animals just romp and play.

New life springs up just anywhere,
A joy for us to stand and stare,
The birds again sing clear and loud
So happy with less rain and cloud.

Brand new buds again emerge,
With stepping stones along the verge,
Gardens so very bright with colour
Can we but give to God the honour.

The trees grow large and stronger still
This lovely life gives one a thrill,
The squirrels forage the whole year round
And know the longer days abound.

It is a joy to be alive
And taste the honey from the hive,
God always knows just what to give
So that His creation can still live,
He is faithful ever, strong and true
Great love He pours on me and you.

Mary L Smith

THE GIFT OF LIFE

The beauty of your life is told
As each and every day unfolds,
Like the smile of the infant newborn
To greet you like the summer's dawn.

Like the song of birds among the trees
To the soft sighs of the early breeze.
Like the murmur of a gentle stream
That comes to you as you sit and dream!

Like the sound of children as they laugh at play
The sound of the farmer gathering new mown hay!
So each night as you kneel and pray
Thank the Lord for each and every day!

W E Clements

MOONLIGHT FANTASY

Silently she rises
From the dark, limpid pool;
Breasts tipped with silver
Pointing sexily, wanton;
Arms aloft, she sways gently
As the moon's rays
Touch and probe her nakedness
Like a lover's hands,
Remembering . . .
Come dear maid into
The still forest, let me
Adorn your body with flowers,
Garland your dark hair
With stardust,
Make sweet love to you . . .
Dance for me in the moonlight
Then go!
Light as thistledown
O'er a carpet of leaves;
Your tinkling laugh
Fading away
Will haunt me forever . . .
Woodland nymph,
My luscious beauty . . .

Joanne Burns

THE LIVING JEWEL

When the light strikes right across the bay
The rainbow arches the clean blue sky
As the pure water runs through your hands
You view the vast pleasures of the land.

The world lovingly has the moon in tow
As the shooting stars shoot, firing the night
Emotions move from stop to go.
Doesn't it just make you feel right?
Isn't it good to be here today?
So great to be alive
On this living jewel
Floating past the Milky Way

Protected by our atmosphere -
It's safe to dream
Feel real, surreal
The evening beautiful and so clear
Doesn't it just make you want to
Stand up and cheer!

Graham Peter Metson

AS THE WORLD SLEEPS

Silent is the wind, nature is asleep,
In the wood and dale and across the steep,
Darkness envelopes all, and yet
Dyed tints of colour from a golden sunset.

From the passing stream, hear its music rise,
Sweet notes of nature's melodies,
They reach up to the darkening mountain head,
Where the rising moon's floodlight starts to spread.

A shooting star suddenly blazes on high,
Across the blueness of the starry sky,
Swiftly it dies, like some phantom form
Seen in the midst of a gathering storm.

Suddenly stars fade, the night is o'er,
Morning light appears, dark shadows no more,
From mountain top to ocean deep,
The world awakes from its nightly sleep.

Isaac Smith

THE DOLLS OF BESLAN
(6th September 2004)

A cherished doll so lovingly placed -
Its features betraying that played-with look
And the other signs; yet still arranged much
As before its 'liberation' from the school -
Rests happy now.
The doll had 'survived' paradoxically
Despite the life that had not.
It was rescued as a 'belonging',
Its crop of hair hanging
Limply, barely attached like the head
To the charred remnants of the body.
'It was given,' they said, 'for her comfort.'
It is a sentiment that echoes
Through the endless streets of pain.
Through the agony of a town
That once knew another time
When children lived and played
In simple innocence.

A miniature coffin lies bedecked
With the flowers and mementoes - with one
Tattered doll offered as a tender gift.
A return of something that was dearly loved,
And poignant now
In reunion where memories fall with tears
For the mourners to collect.
It is a gathering to witness
A precious thing linking
With a uniqueness - that has meaning
Both in life and the circumstance of death.
'Together now and quietly sleeping!'
And dolls are folded into the arms
Of the children and displayed
Openly to a grieving world.
Time is held in that embrace
Against its further progress.
All history lies undone.

William Birtwistle

THE GIRL I LOVE

By the stream
My love she sits
Where water flows
From the mountain tops.

The sun shines down
Upon her face
And catches her smile
And short fair hair.

Water fresh and clear
Running over pebble beds
And through the valley lands.

Peace is in the air
And the view
Beyond compare.

A space in time
That will never be replaced

For youth has passed
And will not return.

G F Snook

WINDY

The fickle, the feckless, the frolicsome wind
Pestered and puffed on a chill autumn day
Drink's can, discarded, disowned and disused
Rattled and rollicked along the highway.

Wind whistled down chimneys, and swirled around eaves
It hustled and bustled the dry autumn leaves
They jousted and jostled and prettily pranced
Red, gold and amber - all joining the dance.

Hats blew from heads, and cold fingers went fumbling
Whirling like dervishes, leaves came a-tumbling
Plastic bag caught in some wires overhead
No longer a bag, but a windsock, instead.

Chins caressed collars, and skirts went all skittish
Flags on the flagpoles were flappingly British -
So were commuters - but to themselves said -
What a morning! I shouldn't have got out of bed!

W Price

NAUTICAL MEMORABILIA

When I was a lad Ma'am
I too had a yacht
I called her Brittania
Believe it or not.
Every Sunday I sailed her
On the Round Pond
I would visit India and China
And places beyond.
How your imagination runs wild
When you're a child on the Round Pond
The ducks preened their feathers
The swans bowed their heads
And then swam away.
'What a lovely name for a yacht,'
I heard one of them say.
'Tack about Leo me hearties,'
I cried.
'It's Brittania, Brittania!'
I shouted with pride.
I remembered the sad time
I laid her to rest
Scuttled on the Round Pond
I thought that was the best
I look back at the time, Ma'am
When I was a lad
And my yacht Brittania
Life wasn't all bad.

Dennis R Beton

THE TRILOGY

The foundation stones are placed by God,
Each path we take left, right or centre.
The holy seeds from child to youth,
Grow to bloom like healthy flowers,
That glow in the world's garden.
Holy souls then pass to Heaven,
To dwell with the angels of transparent crystal.
Then fountains will sprinkle holy water
Down onto a troubled Earth.
Then the marbled floor beneath our feet,
Will lead us to the path, to a mountain cross.
Then the trinity of Father, Son and Holy Spirit
Takes our sacred hearts,
To a holy city for a union with God.

G Louch

TINA'S PUB

There was a pub called the Vic,
Just up from the nick,
Wherein legions all day had a drink;
The beer it was good, so too was the food,
And the barmaids all gave you a wink.

It was half-past four when through the door,
Came Tina in off the street;
We all gave a cheer
Then choked on our beer,
Her bloomers were down at her feet.

Realising her gaffe she just gave a laugh,
And threw them right up in the air,
Out the window they flew on,
Near strangled a poor pigeon,
And ended up goodness knows where.

A sighting nearby on St John's Kirk up high,
Drew crowds there to get a good view,
They all stood aghast
For up on the mast
Hung the garment, in red, white and blue.

Was all of this true?
Well, maybe, the red, white and blue,
But these tales stay alive, and let our memories survive,
For alas those days that we knew,
Seem so wretchedly few.

As time moves us all on,
The old pub's sold now and gone;
But we can ponder awhile to remember and smile,
You see, of all the pubs we can pick,
We think yet of sweet Tina, and her girls of the Vic.

Alistair McLean

SALLY

I just wanted to tell you about our Sal
A very fine dog and great little pal
Once you have a dog it is never the same
Lots of the unexpected, much love, some pain

Jabs at the vet, paper on the floor
A squeaky, fluffy puppy, waiting by the door
The first time she found her voice, a brand new bark
She showed it off to Brother Tom when out in the park

So clean and understanding everything that is said
The bedroom door, left just open, so up onto the bed
For a quick nap after lunch, to be rested for the greeting
Of family coming home at the end of the evening

For years she was always there, in her favourite places
On the landing, in the garden, lots of cat chases
Gradually becoming slower, and not as much care
Wobbly on those older legs, but the will is still there

As I held her in my arms as I had often done
And carried her to the car for a ride in the sun
Just before Christmas she barked her last
Only a small one, a reminder of the past

After 20 years she is there still
In our memories she always will
Be on that chair or in that part
Of the park or watching the sky as it becomes dark

Was that her by the door, out the corner of my eye
No, just my old boots, in her favourite spot, I begin to cry
A love that lasted so many years still grows and still grows
Sally - how we miss you so.

Phyllis O'Connell (Hampson)

FLOWERS

A rose, a rose, such beautiful flower
In full bloom, it's the darling of the hour
Red, yellow, white and other colours too
In my garden border, there are quite a few

The daffodils are finished for this year
Replaced by wallflowers, at which I stare
Pink, yellow, maroon, and other colours too
In my garden border, there are quite a few

Dandelions and daisies, are all over the lawn
And reaching their full height, one by one
Yellow and white, and some broken ones too
In my garden, and there are quite a few

Window boxes and pots, are being prepared
For an array of coloured flowers, to be shared
Whites, yellows, blues and other colours too
Outside my porch, and there are quite a few

Planting and manuring, go on day after day
Keeping gardens full, and in such a fine array
Colours of the rainbow, and pastel colours too
In my garden and baskets, there are quite a few

The fruit trees will soon be full of flowers
Filling the street, amid the summer showers
Pink, white and such a beautiful smell too
Along our street, and there are quite a few

Winter and the gardens look rather shabby
Rubbish everywhere, including next door's tabby
The lawn is long, and weeds have come through
In my garden and border, there are quite a few

William A Laws

HUNGRY AS THE SEA

The wild wind races from the sea
Over huge waves,
And engulfs the land.
The waves are like white-fanged monsters
Pounding the rocks and shore,
With a loud and fearful roar.

The storm is here tonight
I'll keep my lantern alight,
And logs aglow in the hearth
As succour to the poor souls,
Who may come to my door.

The bell tolls in the church tower
And doors and windows,
Shake and rattle bravely
Holding their strength against the tempest.

The fury of the wind
Takes my breath away,
With head bent
I push my way home.

Thunderously the waves
Still pound the beach,
The spume stings like fire
Yet it is bitterly cold.

The clouds are phantom horses
In full gallop,
Trampling the stars
As they flee across the sky.

Who is this coming up the hill?
A merman from the depth of the sea,
His hair is green with wrack
And in his arms he carries,
A boy child to me.

Avis Nixon

COLOURS NATURAL

Star-white held in gloomy sky
Grey clouds rushing by
Above blue, purple river waters
Green leaves whisper, murmur softly,
Cascading down to the jade green sea.

Yellow sands gleam in the moonlight
Strewn with black-brown bubbled seaweed
Scattered over burnt umber rocks
Spread with limpets, whelks and cowries
All in shades of different hues.

Rosalind I Caygill

THE MEANING OF CHRISTMAS

The meaning of Christmas is hard to define
To some, it just means good food and wine
To children it often means lots of new toys
To mothers it always means more work and noise

The meaning of Christmas gets hard to remember
When commercially it starts in September
The summer holidays are scarcely done
When cards and baubles appear by the ton!

The meaning of Christmas is becoming hidden
Till sometimes a thought will come unbidden
That the reason we celebrate this special occasion
Is because Jesus was born to be our salvation

The meaning of Christmas came one starry night
When one star shone excessively bright
And to the shepherds in the fields
It became an angel who to them revealed
That a baby was born in Bethlehem
Who was to be a king to all of them

The meaning of Christmas when that baby was born
And the three wise men came to see him at dawn
Was to bring him gifts as he lay in the manger
There was so much love, and life held no danger.

The meaning of Christmas, is 'joy to the world'
With love and happiness unfurled
If greed and selfishness could be put aside
Then in all the countries, peace would abide.

Jean Wood

THE EARTH ABIDES

There are weeds and grasses growing now,
Where the roses used to be.
The burgeoning trees are wild and wanton,
Where once flowers bloomed fair and free.
A wild woodland; a rank and rampant waste.
The verdant vegetation has long forgotten,
The gardener and his toil that gave them birth.
Its creator long departed, this deserted domain.
Much time has passed, though the land remains,
Still the ground is a green and growing thing,
For the soil has seen many a long winter,
And the returning miracle of spring.
Time flows; the sun rises; seasons come and go.
Like the turning tide, from midsummer's heat,
To deep winter's lingering ice and snow.
Look on this flowing pageantry and wonder.
Once it evoked much passion and such pride.
The gardener has long since turned to dust,
Regret not my friend and in sentiment lament.
Rather be proud, see how the Earth abides.

Julia Pegg

OBJECT OF WORSHIP

Object of worship ages gone,
Superbly svelte or frankly fat,
Aloof, mysterious and lone,
Disguised now as the common cat.
Try to commune and understand,
Meet with indifference sublime.
You tolerate my proffered hand,
Especially at feeding time.

When in those worlds I'll never know
And stretched supine upon the mat,
I ponder how I've watched you grow
From helpless mite to killer cat
A steel-taut frame, an unsheathed claw,
A quivered flank, a sudden rush
And careless laid before my door
The lifeless form of hapless thrush.

Fresh from your silent, secret night,
The world renewed, your day begun,
You deem it your unquestioned right
To slumber in the filtered sun.
But curled compactly by the fire
Relaxed, replete and faintly bored,
To emulate few could aspire,
Lithe, lissom, lovely - and adored!

Molly Read

ABOVE THE VALLEY

It's on a ledge above the valley that he rests.
A single Welsh slate marks his bed.
The angora goats trim it well.
With wild beds of daffodils and snowdrops,
nodding gently in the breeze.
Seagulls send out a plaintive cry,
the rocks reply in an echoing style,
a man-built stile that shepherds use.
Horsemen took a step from it too.
Its peacefulness remains as that,
of ancient times,
which makes me say, 'I will return to Wales.'
It was above the valley that he saw the wild horses roam,
where the tiny rivers flow.
Saw bright silvery salmon leap in the Tiefi river just below.
A kestrel gliding in full flight, as a hungry hawk is in disgrace,
being marched out to sea by a troop of assertive jackdaws,
all in chorus.
Ten mares in ever movement, sheltering and shielding
as many foals, who sometimes surprise their earnest mums,
by flying off in a frenzy dance, all legs with head and tail a-fleeting.
It is in Wales where the noble beasts intermingle
with the newly sheared sheep with their little lambs
and share the flowing streams as the great beeches
and the stalwart foxgloves are all on guard.
Green of field and green of tree and shades of shades
of colour be, beneath an ever changing sky.
Shapely mythical clouds all vanishing in a flash.
A palish crimson sky draws close to the mountain,
slowly deepening until dark.
A lone buzzard swoops into a dark cloud,
'A soul set free,' he whispered.

Margaret Gleeson Spanos

OUTSIDE LOOKING IN

On a cold winter's eve, whilst walking alone
The stranger he was lost, chilled to the bone
As he rounded the corner on that frosty clear night
The stranger saw before him an awesome sight
On the outside looking in, the house was aglow
With laughter and music, the party in full flow
The magnificent band were playing a haunting waltz
As glasses were raised by the guests for the toast
The large sweeping staircase from the ballroom was grand
Where ladies of elegance in their ballgowns did stand
Chattering and laughing faces full of joy
Like pages from the history books, when he was a boy
Coat wrapped around him down the drive he did stroll
While fluttering around him was the first winter's snow
A last glance over his shoulder caused more of a chill
As the derelict old house stood dark, silent and still.

Jackie Gifford

PERCY

I'm going to talk about Percy, who's a very good friend of mine
I chanced upon Percy whilst still a young girl
So I've known him a very long time
He's a person I've always relied on
He's stood by me through thick and through thin
And he's always arrived in the nick of time, whatever the trouble I'm in
He's always around when I need him, most especially when things
                                                  are quite tough
And whatever the circumstances, Percy will never give up
He pushes and chivvies and urges me on
To do better things than I'm doing
And with so much encouragement, how can I fail to take heart
                                          and keep on going?
Sometimes when I'm weary and life's not much fun
I run around in circles and nothing seems to get done
I just call upon Percy, my faithful old friend
And there I am back on the road again
I've used him quite shamefully over the years, with never a hint
                                                  of remorse
Because the good friend I've just been talking about
Is old Percy Verence of course

Barbara Scriven

LIFE

You only get one chance
To make your dreams come true
To make the most of life
And do what's best for you

It seems like one big ride
That leaves you in a spin
Make your tears turn to laughter
And turn your frown into a grin

Turn all the hatred into love
Life's too short to fight
Make peace where there is war
Turn darkness into light

Life is never easy
It brings lots of ups and downs
But when the tough times arrive
Family and friends will be around.

Natalie Louise West

CAFÉ IN THE CRYPT

With gutt'ring nightlight candles, holly-crowned,
Shadowy corners, intimate, abound,
And medieval Christmas carols round
The cav'nous ancient arches soft' resound.

In from the gray December tree-lit gloom
Come shoppers, students, lovers, all for whom
This 'neath the pavement-level vaulted room
Presents a welcome place, no more a tomb.

But, watch one story, unidentified -
A surreptitious tissue, gently plied,
A hand-clasp loosened, and a kiss denied,
We see a romance buried, for love died.

Jo Brookes

SAFE AS HOUSES

Am I mad
Or just eccentric?
The medical term is agoraphobic

As I feel the world outside is full of fright
That disturbs my sleep all through the night
Until I dream, how amazing
All those different streets that I am exploring
With no fear, no heavy heart
I can't wait for my dream time to start
For my adventures to begin at last
Why does the night-time go so fast?

When or where will I go?
Will it rain, hail or even snow?
It doesn't matter as I step outside the door
As I am not frightened anymore

I feel safe as houses in my sleep
It's the world outside that makes me frail

Darren Babbage

HAVE YOU EVER NOTICED

Have you ever noticed when you microwave a jug
Or when you heat a drink and put it in a mug
That when you open up, the handle's always at the back
And the oven glove is missing from the rack?
Little bits and bobs have a life that's all their own
You go to put them in a drawer, but they decide to roam.
Under a chair is a favourite spot for buttons on the loose
You search for them high and low, but is it any use?
Like chameleons the colours blend wherever they fall
You search and search, but can't find them anywhere at all.
Have you ever noticed when ferreting in a cupboard
The items at the front come leaping out with one accord?
That marble which was lurking in the pile
Came jumping out and quickly ran a mile.
Have you ever noticed, when quietly knitting in your chair
Your ball of wool will jump and roll, then fix you with a stare?
Now shall you rise and clamp the culprit in your grip
Or gently tug the line so that you can continue with the knit?
When vacuuming the carpet and making things pristine
Have you ever noticed, after stowing the machine
That where you thought was spick and span and spotlessly clean
Little bits of fluff and cotton can be seen?
Have you ever found, while reading in a book
The pages stick together and refuse to let you look?
These inanimate objects have no life I'm told
But in my experience they are extremely bold.
Life's little irritations come to plague my life
The Devil surely sent them to give me so much strife!

Stroma M Hammond

I AM HAPPY IN JESUS

I am happy in Jesus
I am trusting in His word
Though shattered by the storms of life
I shall not fear
For He will see me through
He will walk with me
And He will talk with me
So why should I fear?
He tells me I am His own
And that He loved me so much that
He suffered and died in my place,
That I should live a victorious and
Happy life by His grace.
One day He is coming to take me to
His lovely home above
What a day that will be!
The rule is that I must humble myself
To walk with Him.
He is the King of kings.
He reigns on high.
Leaving to go to that beautiful home
I can take nothing with me,
But I can send it on ahead.
I hear His voice saying,
'All this I have done for you.
What hast thou done for me?'
Yes! He loves me.
He tells me I must be faithful
And true to His word
To be His own.
He will take me by His hand
And lead me to the promised land.

Joy Wilson

SUMMER DAYS

Now summertime is once more here
It's time for us to give a cheer
All is warm, so bright and gay
In the countryside we smell the hay
Nights are short, the days are long
Birds fill the air with their sweet song
In the parks it's music from the band
While lovers stroll by hand in hand
Lazy clouds float by in the sky
Enjoy it all we do all try
Summertime has such a tender touch
I love this season so very much
Now summertime is once more here
Enjoy it all, I will don't fear

L A G Butler

GIFT

Gratefully!
Eye pierces the
flower's beauty
imbibing its healing.
Simultaneously.
Slaughtering - suffering.
Humanity.
All where!
Evil prevails
and so does
joy.

Sringkhala
(Lucina Della Rocca)

THOUGHTS OF A BUCCANEER

I was feared as I steered me old pirate bark
Plundering, thieving - in for many a lark.
Way down in the hold chests of treasure was stowed
But me longing for looting - it just growed and growed.

Went right to me head - I was took off me guard
Blasted mutinous crew all held the trump card.
They trapped me and wrapped me and put me ashore
'Twas marooned that they left me - a whole year or more.

How I cursed all the perishers and bemoaned me fate
They had all me jewels and me pieces of eight.
Seemed I'd never again quaff a tankard or two
And tickle the wrenches after supping a few.

I survived best I could and at last I was found
And brought back to me homeland - safe, but unsound.
I've repented me ways - landlubbering be best
Cos now I have found me a much nicer chest.

Silk covered, well shaped and lovely to hold
And when wraps be took off - a joy to behold.
Heart of gold, sparkling eyes, ruby lips, charms galore
And the strongest of clasps - I can't ask for more!

Eric E Webb

DISTANT REFLECTIONS

Ships pass in the night and are then remote,
    The sea is endless upon which they float,
Yet briefly they meet at one time and place,
    Announced by the bleep of a radar trace.

The watch gaze out as the other draws near,
    Passage lights, silhouette, hull and deck gear
Maybe a signal to ask and to tell
    'Ahoy there, what ship, where bound?' and,
    'Farewell.'

Now there's sadness for something that's lost,
    The unregistered joy as two paths crossed,
A primeval sentiment active still,
    Sublimate now to political skill.

And so it is with a heavier heart,
    They witness each other, pass and depart,
All that remains are two wakes that collide,
    Stirring reflections cast on to the side.

Robert K Bowhill

SOLILOQUY

Ah! Dear love you have not died
just flown away like birds at eventide
But tears unshed could fill a mighty dam
flooding it with dreams
of unknown destiny and as I don
a smiling mask and join
the ranks of brave hypocrisy
A parallel, saintly in simplicity
lanterned corners of my heart
where cold wind streamed.

Along the corridors of time
buffeting the grieving heart and mind
But light has spread its silvery hope
flooding chambers of despair.

Ah! Dear love, you are still here
and as I kneel to kiss your marbled brow
Breathtaking beauty of your
thought eventually surrounds . . .

Ann Safe

THAT PAINTED BUS

Yes that painted bus of flowers is ours
You laugh because it is pink
There are so many things inside
Even a shower and a sink.

Yes that painted bus of flowers is ours
It is helping us upon our trip
From Woodstock to Glastonbury
It is a trip so hip.

Yes that painted bus of flowers is ours
Though we sleep outside
For being at one with nature
Helps us with our ride.

Keith L Powell

AWAKENING

Wakes now the sun's warm kiss the dormant earth,
Stirs the reluctant soul to life again;
Now swells the gentle air to symphony,
Notes sweet to pain:
So fill the vessel, even to the brim:
Come pain or joy, lifts up the soul her lips
To drink again.

Now must she drink, and thirst, to drink again
And find all beauty in a moment's span;
All joy, all wonder, mirrored in the cup,
Be it blessing or bane:
Whether it hold of grief or ecstasy:
Come pain or joy, she stands with outstretched hands
And trembles on the brink of mystery.

Daphne Foreman

THE AFRICA CORPS ARE COMING

The cold surrenders, the sun across the desert; blazing,
The hues and shades of the dunes, just amazing.
Desert storms arrive and sandflies are humming,
Check your guns my lads, the Africa corps are coming.

Slide into your Sherman tank, dig your slit trench deeper,
Pray it will save you from becoming an eternal sleeper.
Clean your weapons lads, check your bandages can staunch that
                                    blood a-running.
We dig in and stand, Monty said, 'The Africa corps are coming.'

Strain your eyes lads, check that distant ridge,
Behind you Tobruck, Rommels, Suez Bridge.
A calm prevails, an accordion, a 'little Marlene' a-strumming,
No more marching backward lads, here we stand, the Africa corps
                                      are coming.

Those panzers moving through a thoroughfare of graves,
Moving through the desert, shifting sands, a sea of waves.
So here we are lads, ready to fight, not lying in the sands a-sunning,
That sand will turn red, because the Africa corps are coming.

The Bedouin waits as the northern hordes invade their land,
Soon, they'll scavenge the skeletal scrap, that scar and cover
                                   the sand.

So lads, we, like the bowman of Agrincourt,
Our brothers on the Somme and many battles fought.
This day we'll turn the war and send Rommel a-running,
The dust could rise, the noise get louder,
The Africa corps are coming,
The Africa corps are coming.

Vic Round

THE WINDOW IS OPEN

Never cry in despair
Always travel the desert
Stand tall on a distant tower
A world, around you, in thought
Walk inside that window
The window open to your soul.

Jennifer T Macleod

ACCOUNT RENDERED

Tim Sullivan set sail from Donegal
Unasked, to battle for another's land
And in Berlin, amongst the smoke and pall
He disobeyed an officer's command

Told to destroy a building which still stood
Tim had a flash of Irish second-sight
'I'm sorry Sir, I can't.' The major's mood
To anger flared, his face with fury white

Amongst Tim's friends there was a restless stir
'You heard me Sullivan.' Tim stood his ground
He shook his head - 'I cannot do it Sir
Court martial me - I will not bring it down.'

And as they stood, from the house there came
A German girl, three children tightly clasped
All stood transfixed. Tim breathed, 'By the Holy Name.'
And crossed himself, the Major, awestruck, gasped.

Tim and the girl would never meet again but now the most
Amazing sequel to this haunting rhyme
To those who scoff at spectre, shade or ghost
Living or dead, a girl transcended space and time

Long years on, in a bedsitting room
A saucepan on the stove, Tim fell asleep
The saucepan overflowed, the dousèd flare releasing deadly fume
As evily the gas began to seep

And then - and then, the German hausfrau came
And wakened him. He saw her fading shade
He smelt the gas from the extinguished flame
Across the years the unpaid debt was paid

Winifred Rachel Probert

A HOPE OF PEACE

Why is it so since time began,
That man has fought in every land,
War after war, with nothing gained,
What is the cause, who is to blame?

Religion has to take its place,
Of troubled times in every race,
In all the countries the world o'er,
The Bible seemed to hold the power.

Jealousy next must toe the line,
Corrupts the soul, and twists the mind,
Cause of many a battlefield,
Where many a man his fate was sealed.

Greed would be the biggest sinner,
Always a loser, never a winner,
What one man has, another man steals,
Why is it so no guilt he feels?

Now if every man could be content,
With all the gifts that God has sent,
Then all the world wars would cease,
And give us everlasting peace.

D S Cromar

SHARING TEA

A robin came to visit me,
one day when I was having tea.
He sat upon the window sill,
and sang a song so bright and trill.
To the bird I threw some cake,
which he was pleased to quickly take,
and as he darted like an arrow,
his place was taken by a sparrow.
I passed some crumbs of cake to him
and of a sudden with a whim,
he took to flight and flew away,
his place was taken by a jay.
To the jay I gave some pieces three,
it took them to a nearby tree.
In flew a finch which sat quite still,
I placed upon the window sill
a good sized chunk of tasty cake,
which I had taken pains to make.
The plate was sitting on my knee,
I found there was no cake for me.

Colin Ritton

BUTTERFLIES IN AMBER

Memories come and settle in the mind
And set like butterflies in amber. They
Come with the seemingly mundane, without
Warning. They are the surprise components -

Of ordinary things. A child's dress all but
Finished. The sight of curtains drawn against
The summer heat, furniture gleaming with
Lavender wax or a flowerbed fenced -

In against intruders. Shadows of leaves
On water, unkept daisy speckled lawns,
Wallflowers all bright and grown dense, heady
With perfume, butterflies resting in swarms -

Resting like recalled memories settling
Forever like butterflies in amber.

Margaret Hibbert

THE THRUSH

Oh thrush, I love to hear you sing!
Those liquid cadences and trills
Herald an end to winter's ills
And usher in the spring.

But, build your nest far, far from me -
For feral cats, like tigers wild,
Patrol in search of thrushes' child
Each hedge and bush and tree.

And shun the fieldside hedges too,
For there you'll find, some sunny day,
A noxious cloud of poison spray
Will put an end to you.

Nor choose the roadside verges lush,
For mangled bodies by the way
Tell the sad tale of death each day,
And spell a warning, thrush!

But still, in spite of all of this,
Led on by instinct blind and strong,
You fill the evening air with song
For ignorance is bliss.

So, let what will the future bring,
Your fate and mine be what they may,
Still in the fading light of day
I love to hear you sing.

Dorothy Steadman

A SATURDAY AFTERNOON

(For Jo)

I know what bliss is,
I must conclude,
'Tis your sweet kisses,
With Chinese food.

Mark Bailey

REFLECTIONS OF A NIGHT NURSE

In the quiet hours of night,
        Making sure all is right.
Wanting to make *you* aware,
        As you sleep, we *do* care.
    Quietly, around we creep,
        Checking that you are asleep.
If we find that you are not,
        A drink we'll make, soothing and hot.
Should you need your bell to ring,
        Help and *kindness*, we try to bring.
To help you on to slumberland,
        We *are* willing to hold your hand.
Sounds and shadows, so different seem,
        Perhaps you wake up from a dream.
Morning dawns, then you will see,
        A smiling face with a cup of tea.
As day draws on into another night,
        Please do not worry, or have a fright.
You are in *God's* hands, *and* His keep,
        We watch by as you lie asleep.

June F Allum

CELEBRATIONS

Whatever the occasion
It's good to celebrate
Be that celebration
A birth or special date

A family occasion
Where there's a show of face
To that of jubilation
When remembrances take place

We celebrate the seasons
Take joy in nature's gifts
And pray to the almighty
To give our hearts a lift

We say thanks for our achievements
Of things we may have done
And recognise these
With many joyful songs

But whatever the occasion
It's good to celebrate
A look at the world around us
Shows where we make mistakes

Let us learn from celebration
The feelings it bestows
To make us richer in good feelings
And keep us set aglow

Elizabeth Bennett

THE CROSS-EYED COCKNEY CAT

I'm known as 'that strange lookin' black crors-eyed cat',
and nobody's sure just wot I'm lookin' at.
They stare at me oddly and say, 'Look 'ere mate,
that black crors-eyed cat's just crawled under yer gate.'

The kid from next door then yelled over the wall,
'That cat ain't just scruffy, it's crors-eyed an' all.
Dunno if it's lookin' at me or at you,
cos when it looks *my* way, it looks your way too!'

Then 'enry and 'ilda both gazed at me face.
'Cor blimey,' said 'enry, 'that cat's a disgrace,
so shaggy, bedraggled, 'e's lost all 'is pride.'
An look ere, gasped 'ilda, 'the poor ting's crors-eyed.'

Soon out came the neighbours who live next but two,
'That cat don't look normal,' they said, 'wot finks you?'
The man shrugged 'is shoulders and said, 'Listen 'ere,
that cat's got an 'art just like us - ain't yer dear?'

'Twas then I decided to curl round 'is knee.
I knew very soon 'e'd begin lovin' me.
'Is 'art really melted, 'e saw me anew;
or did 'e see two cats? Cos 'e's crors-eyed too!

Joan Zambelli

BEGGARS CAN'T BE CHOOSERS

He stands there rigid by a post
Holding leaflets, for all to see
Looks so thin, ignored by most
A few pence is a leaflet's fee
Crying for help, doesn't want to beg
He's no beggar, he's clean and shaven
Just a few pence to find a bed
To rest and sleep in any haven
Some stare as they rush by
No thoughts for others homeless, starving
Not caring if he lives, or to die
I slip him a coin, as I pass by
Coming back another, as I say, 'Hi'
Alas, beginning of a new season
Will you spend Christmas all alone!
That alone is good enough reason
To show you care, and to atone

I K Skinner

THE MORNING AFTER

What on Earth did I drink last night
To make my head ache so?
A hair of the dog might fix it
And make the headache go.

But what on Earth did I drink last night,
I'll try and remember the lot,
I think we started with cocktails,
Yes, dry martinis were what we got.

There was a dry white wine with the first course,
A rich Bordeaux with the meat,
A nice dessert wine with the pudding
And then coffee and brandy - neat.

And then there were drinks after dinner,
Of gin and tonics, I think I had three,
After that I recall nothing clearly,
If you want to know more - don't ask me.

So that is the sum of my drinks last night,
I think I've remembered them all,
So what should I take as a hair of the dog?
I don't care - I sure had a ball!

Daphne Hanson

SQUATTER BIRDS

'These birds are such a nuisance,'
The station master said.
Does that mean in consequence
He would prefer them dead?
They flit around the station
Morning, noon and night.
An appalling situation,
All's spotted, dirty white.
We used to wait on platform one,
Diverted now, to two.
Perhaps we could scare them,
Without more ado.
If they flew away then,
All pleasure it would give.
We cannot destroy them;
They have a right to live.
Men have opened up the woodland
Laid a tarmacadam path.
Perhaps that makes us understand
Their change of habitat.
Employed, a man, with hose and brush
To keep the railway tidy.
The only man who likes them there
He draws his wage each Friday.

Bridie Sutton

AS TIME GOES BY

You looked the best I'd ever seen you,
Then all of a sudden you looked unreal like someone
I'd never seen before,

Each day you struggled for breath,
Looking back I know it was for the best,

Your skin used to be so soft, but not no longer,
Your eyes are sunken, they used to be sparkling,
Your body used to be filled with warmth,
But now all that is left is cold.

You took your last breath and you were gone,
Words cannot describe how much we miss you Mum.

Rachael Wolfenden

I NEED . . . COMPASSION

I need . . . a helping hand
I need . . . someone to take command
I need . . . a shoulder to cry on
I need . . . a friend to rely on
I need . . . you to lead me
I need . . . you to feed me
I need . . . comfort in my sorrow
I need . . . help through tomorrow
I need . . . oh, so much
I need . . . your special touch
I need, I need, I need

Each one of us has been there
Each one of us has shed a tear
Each one of us knows how to need
But who amongst us can do that good deed?
We all need others in times of strife
If we helped one another we'd all have a better life

So don't turn away in a nonchalant fashion
But be like Jesus and show some compassion
Help make this world a better place
And do *your* bit to save the human race
Show all of mankind what Jesus would do
Turn 'I need' into 'I can do it for you'.

Eve Hughes

FRONT TO BACK

The postman came with no letter,
I awoke without opening my eyes.
For breakfast, the burnt toast, I did despise
When I dropped it, it wasn't brown,
It didn't even land butter side down!
The fried egg was still in its shell,
The bacon rashers a-plenty, but the pig,
Oh! How it did smell . . . !
I waited an hour, a shower, no rain.
On the train I stood sitting up.
Tried the crossword with no luck, or ink.
I read from a book with no cover, no pages,
There ought to be a link!
At the station, the ticking clock,
Had hands that never moved.
My theory was about to be proved.
Outside a bird took off from a tree,
But it hit the ground. It wasn't me
Who saw the dog bark and heard no sound!
The car it sped right by me,
Its wheels were standing still.
At the pelican crossing there were none,
It really made me *ill!*
I stopped in the park for a while,
To feed the birds and smile at the people
Who weren't there.
They didn't care . . . !

Gerry Dymock

INSANITY

I did not hear the whispers,
People said behind my back, .
Nor saw the side-long glances
That conveyed I'd lost the knack,
Some laughed, some cried, some turned aside
Said, I was one short of a pack.

But I heard the words *they* whispered,
At night while in my bed,
They spoke of flying to the moon,
One night when the moon was red,
They said they would return to me
When I was cold and dead.

I saw the faces float by me,
When tears were in my eye,
And some were mad, and some were glad,
And some just rushed on by,
A few of them were dear to me,
Did smile and give a sigh.

The days just tumbled into nights,
Nights tumbled to despair,
I twisted day, I turned the dark,
I scarcely was aware.
Shadows came and shadows went
I really didn't care.

Were they fiends or were they friends?
Why don't they let me be,
So I can float or I can sink
It's immaterial to me.
Why look, the moon has turned to red,
I can fly to insanity.

Sandy Phillips

SHOPPING

Shopping with Mummy is never much fun
She dashes around, quickly gets it all done
'We've got to rush home to cook dinner,' she'll say
'No time to stop in the park today.'

We have to buy bread, and potatoes too
Fruit and veg, 'cause they're good for you
And then we get meat, and butter, and cheese
'Ooh, look at those sweets - can I have some please?'

'Not now Jack,' Mum says, 'let's buy ice cream instead
You'll enjoy some of that when you're ready for bed.'
I spy Kit-Kats and Mars bars high up on a shelf
If I wasn't so small I could reach them myself!

Now the shopping's all finished; I'll just have to wait
There's Ribena at home - *proper food* on a plate
But my eyelids are drooping, I'm sucking my thumb
It makes me so tired, this shopping with Mum!

Now, shopping with Dad is much better because
We'll ride into town on the top of the bus
Then we'll go to a shop to buy maggots and flies
We'll go fishing tomorrow - a lovely surprise.

Then, maybe he'll get me a new ball to kick
I'm better at football; Dad can't run that quick
We'll eat burgers and chips, or a hot sausage roll
My dad never hurries, he just likes to stroll

Sometimes we take home some cream cakes in a box
I'm happy today - I've got new stripy socks
The shops that Dad likes are the *bestest* by far
Dad's bought me a goldfish; I'll carry the jar

The man's made a handle from dirty old string
And I've been with Dad to buy Mummy a ring -
It's her birthday next week, so we've got her a card -
Too late Dad's remembered - my gran needed lard.

But we're back on the bus now, there's no going back
If Gran's cross with Dad he'll say, 'Just blame young Jack'.
Then we'll all have a laugh, and eat cream cakes for tea
Yes, I love to go shopping - just Daddy and me

And sometimes of course we do all go together
And we have a nice time then, whatever the weather
Buying new clothes or shoes, and a nice book to read -
That makes family shopping a real treat indeed.

B D Postings

AUTUMN GLORY

Russet is the bracken on distant highland glens,
Shrouds of mist caressing mighty towering bens,
Icy is the wind that whispers now from high,
And lingers in the twilight beneath an autumn sky.

Leaves are gently falling by heather covered braes,
Touched by frosty fingers in Mother Nature's ways.
Copper bright the colours, this season of such change,
Like paintings on the landscape, a vision in our range.

Snow-capped the far off summits, majestic now they stand,
Like sentinels they look upon the ever changing land.
Far off in the distance the wild birds plaintive call,
Herald autumn's glory that's free for one and all.

Stark and bare the trees now, undressed by nature's hand,
Mantle green has vanished with autumn's magic wand,
Silent snowflakes falling, carpet now of white,
Glisten in the darkness of winter's coming night.

Alister H Thomson

SANTA'S BEEN

The children are tucked in bed,
Santa's mince pie and milk await,
We wait till they're fast asleep,
Oh no! Forgot the carrot for Rudolph.

Gather stockings laden with goods,
A glass of wine much deserved,
Check to see their sleeping heads,
Lay their stockings by the bed.

Awoken early morning with gleeful cries,
Santa's been, look what we got!
OK children, please five minutes more,
Nip down, put the turkey in.

We give in at six o'clock,
Still tired we've had our lot.
Downstairs bleary eyed,
Look around the Christmas tree.

Shrills of laughter, cries of delight,
'He got my letter,' they choroused together,
'Mum open this, Mum do this,'
Tiredness turns to bliss
To see the smiles upon their faces.

Santa's been, they've undone the lot,
Presents left in crumpled pile,
Can we go out to play?
It's another Christmas Day.

Carol Paxton

THE HOUSE OF LIFE

You knock at the door and then pass through
A door that makes you struggle to view
A life of comfort did start in the womb
Now passed through into a sunlit room
A tiny babe with the world at its feet
You go into the hall of life to greet
The great big world that's so full of noise
Is there for you to learn with ease and poise
To overcome the stresses and the strains
That befalls us all with many more pains
You then pass on into the lounge so light
To marry the person of choice with much delight
Then moving on into another room
And children come for you to groom
Into the kitchen you go to prepare
For them the sweetmeats that only you dare
And for them to progress and climb the stairs
Only to leave you later in pairs
The bedrooms in which were full of years
Are now left empty except for memories you endear
One partner will move to another room
Then life will have its days of downs and glooms
Until the box room seems to be the only place
All memories of your life only you can face
But God is all around your house
With love and understanding in which to arouse
A move to one of higher places
Which we all go to with all creeds and races
The bathroom then becomes a place to lose
All inhibitations and you are left to diffuse
The bad things in life and remember the good
And to forget everything that was misunderstood
You slowly close your eyes and drift
Into the place and thank Him for your gift
Of family and friends, of happiness which was lent
For the House of Life and all its contents.

Valerie Marshall

WHY

Why?
The word pounds the tortured brain
as sobs are muffled into a pillow.
Sleep has fled, as far removed as the east is from the west.
Eyes, gritty and poker flame hot, scorch exhausted eyelids.
The pain is unspeakable, indescribable, the loss inconsolable.
He was to young to die, my father, he had so much more to offer!
The appeal court is silent, the decision final.

Why?
The anguished cry is full of anger.
'If you are a god of love, why allow this pain to rip us apart?'
The pain of loss,
The pain of watching a loved one suffer,
The agony of helplessness as a fighting spirit slips away.

Why?
The word is a whisper now.
Hope is gone as grief takes over.
The tears begin their remorseless trek, eyes redden,
The heart aches and a new pain is born.

'My God, why have You forsaken me?'
The panic in the words reveals the confusion of the soul.
Prayers drift to the ceiling,
Burst like tired bubbles and vanish in a moment.
The final rejection is complete - now God has gone.

Loss upon loss, grief upon grief,
The inner ear is deafened by the cacophony of sorrow.
Night is full of tears and nightmares,
Inner fears return to haunt and mock the ravaged soul.
The spirit is battered, bruised, torn apart,
Burdened by a load not thought possible to bear.

Yet . . .
A whisper of peace seeps through the clamour and clatter of turmoil.
'I know your pain, my child.
I lost my father too - for you.
He didn't die, but turned his back,
The sight of sin too hard to take,
The price I paid for you, to win you back.'

The outstretched hands reveal the scars,
The signs of love so deep that the storm of pain quietens
From within the circle of an embrace
That tenderly enfolds all.

Why?
The question is never answered,
But the wounded Saviour reveals that . . .
God knows.

Georgina Wilson

WHAT IF?

What if one morn' you 'woke to find no birdsong filled the air?
What if you looked around and found no bees or butterflies anywhere?
How would you feel if no perfumed or colourful flowers could be
seen,
No blossom filled hedges or trees about, and no daisies
carpeted fields of green?
What if the bushes and trees bore no fruit, and no nuts or berries
were left to eat?
And all because you killed the caterpillars, grubs, snails and spiders
to keep your garden neat.
Each tiny creature that's born on this planet gives life
so another might thrive,
So we must guard all of the creatures however small
in order that we may survive.

Betty Irwin-Burton

THE EVIL DEAD

In the dead of night when the moon is full
as all earthly mortals sleep,
Up from the bowels of the Earth
the evil spirits creep.
Demons, vampires, witches, ghouls,
the dead who will not die,
The powers of darkness cometh,
the time is drawing nigh.

When the big old oaks bend double
and the willows weep and moan,
And the sheep upon the hillside
seek out refuge until dawn.
When the rafters creak and hinges squeak
and a coldness fills the air,
And somewhere in the blackened night
someone gives a silent prayer.

When darkness shadows steel across the floor
and a deathly silence lingers,
And a latch lifts on an unlocked door
by unseen shapeless fingers.
When a piercing scream rents through the night
followed by a doleful sigh,
The evil is upon us
the dead who will not die.

Pauline Tattersall

THE PRISONER

Nights were long and dark without him,
Desolation filled her heart
Overflowing with the torment
Of the years they'd spent apart.

All the pain, torture, strife
Humiliation he was bearing,
How she wished that she was sharing
Every blow dealt upon him,
Each privation that he suffered
All the hardship he endured.

Thousands died and thousands suffered
On that horrifying railway,
Beriberi and starvation,
Sickness, death and degradation;
But the guards they could not break him.

She prayed on through long, long years,
Frantically obsessed by fears,
Fears of what might soon befall him
If again she'd ever see him.

At last he came, a little drawn,
Skeleton-like, a little wan,
Looking almost ten years older
But blue eyes shining, never bolder.

She'd helped him through those ghastly years
Lived in dread and constant fears
Of whether all strength would desert him
Whether he could carry on.

Now, outstretched arms welcomed him,
He looked upon her friendly grin,
Remembering the sweetness of her,
The strength and courage oozing from her,
All the things that kept him sane
Through three long years of grief and pain.

Mary J Whiteley

THE CHILDREN ON THE STREET

My mind becomes a memory
Of all the happy times.
The growing years of children,
Right before your eyes.
Times move on so quickly
They are grown, and play no more.
It's quiet on the pavement,
No more playing with the ball.
The voices, they have gone too,
And some have moved away.
It all seems very empty,
On long summer days.
But if you close your eyes,
And listen very hard,
You can hear children's voices,
Playing on the yard.
Riding on their bicycles,
Football on the street.
Listening is just wonderful,
Gives your heart a treat.
Oh, those growing years of children,
You will hear for evermore.
In your imagination,
When that football makes a score.
And in your heart, those memories,
Forever, you will keep.
To remember is just wonderful,
When the children played on the street.

Dorothy Marshall Bowen

THE LIPS WHICH CANNOT SPEAK

Certain as the snowflakes, sure as summer rain,
Each and every one of us must mourn and mourn again.
And all will feel a sad regret, week by solemn week,
      Their refrain will surely be -
      My lips they did not speak.

He whispered low, 'Have you come to watch me die lass?'
I should have said, 'Don't be afraid, you know I love you so.'
He lay there, turned to face the wall, quiet then and weak,
      Shock or pain, I do not know,
      But these lips refused to speak.

Lovely as an angel, a smile so tender and so sweet,
She came to me in dreamland, and knelt there at my feet,
She came to say her last goodbye, but frozen, dumb and weak,
      Why, oh why must I possess
      The lips which do not speak?

I sat beside my dear old friend, watched him slowly wilt away,
The faded eyes, once so bright, had seen their last of day,
I heard the whispered words of love, that last long painful creak,
      Manacled with long forgotten chains,
      My lips they dared not speak.

'The mills of God grind slowly, but grind exceeding small'
And when the Grim Old Reaper stealthy makes his call -
Will life on me a cruel vengeance wreak,
      Will I look into the eyes I love
      Yet only see, the lips which cannot speak?

Shirley I Straw

FIRST IN LINE

Since time began and men learnt greed
Coveting food and land beyond their need,
I heard the shields and weapons rattle
Before each and every senseless battle.

At ancient Jericho I was there
When Joshua attacked and laid the city bare.
When David fought the Philistines
There I stood within the battle lines.

Alexander in his savage conquest
Overrunning lands both east and west,
Took me with him to help him fight
The powerful Persian's awesome might.

At Thermopylae and Marathon too,
The battles began, my sword I drew,
When Boudicca defied the Roman rule,
The final end was savage and cruel.

When Harold met William face to face,
Each to annihilate the other's race.
I was in the forefront of the affray,
Alas I did not see another day.

The Wars of the Roses and later yet,
The Civil War with monarchy's upset.
The constant wars against the French,
Where I finished in some lonely trench.

It was Napoleon's turn to despoil and ravage
The European nations he chose to savage,
Until at Waterloo the rampage did end
And gave the countryside time to mend.

In India and Africa I met the call,
Persuaded there to fight and fall.
To lie forever in some foreign field
Because politicians and rulers failed to yield.

To America I made my way,
To fight for right and there to stay
In America's Independence war,
And in the Civil War and more.

In Europe at the bottom of a trench,
Accompanied by Ypres' charnel stench,
Trampled, forgotten, without a grave,
Alongside many others of the brave.

A war to end all wars, the politicians said,
But it was me, not them who lost my head,
To meet my end for a few square feet
Before warring nations deigned to treat.

My duty in later years, I did not shirk
I faced the bloody horrors of Dunkirk,
Of sunny Tobruk and El Alamein,
Monte Casino in the pouring rain.

I belong to each and every nation,
I'm seen at every battle station.
I'm not the one who gives the orders
To storm other country's national borders.

Who am I condemned to die,
Never, never to question why?
I am the common soldier who gives his all,
Forever, always the first to fall.

Remember me who's gone before,
You thoughtless, selfish men of war,
Before you give the final word
That never ever should be heard.

Graham John

WHY?

Why are there names on the seats in the park?
Why does the moon only shine when it's dark?
Why is the world such a beautiful place
When people are slowly destroying it with such a fast pace?
Why do people not live for today?
Why should we still feel the need to pray?
Why did someone invent money?
Why are people with less than us seen as funny?
Why are we told what we should wear?
Why do people feel they have the right to stare?
Why do so many children come from broken homes?
Why are kids losing their way because they are all alone?
Why do we live in fear of attack?
Freedom of speech is what this country seems to lack.
Why are killers still being born?
We don't know who or what's to blame anymore.
Why are young lives still starving to death?
Why do some not know at 15 who wrote Macbeth?
Why can they not find a cure for AIDs?
Why is cancer becoming more common every day?
Why did a young man die because of his colour?
Can we still not learn to love one another?

Why are there names on the seats in the park?
Why does the moon only shine when it's dark?

Georgina May Carey

THE AFFIRMATION

Then I would applaud your skill and pity my faith
Should I embrace these broad 'n' tendered arms
Refined by languid loves
Who sought to flee but, then resumed to trust
In sacred words you pledged
As if the pride were suckled from their minds
That primes your unrelenting need
To validate 'n' feed these flaccid unperfected traits
Once ciphered from the gaits of lesser gods
The ones who blazed a trail
For you and yours to scour 'n' assail
The weak, the humble and the shy
Who gave you poise to pacify
With flick of tongue and curl of wrist
Such beauty is indeed a gift
An amulet to cherish not to bruise
Each fragile ego as you move
From two to three to four to five
Elixirs on which you thrive
And prosper mighty without pause
I wish you fortune on your course my dear.

Louise Hercules

A REPLACEMENT

My parents gave me a stone
To counter my depression.
To make me feel better as
Being sad achieved a possession.

It's strange to feel sentimental
About a small grey stone.
Because of this rock,
I'll never be alone.

I suppose the stone, holds
The same qualities as the object it replaced.
But the rock can't walk out
With any sort of haste.

Steven J Forster

ANTICLIMAX

Along the towpath comes trotting
A dog, in colours a cat would call tortoiseshell.
In his mouth is the slim arm of a willow.

He must have chosen this stick for himself;
No master would throw something so unwieldy.

He looks like the herald of something,
Fulfilling his small role with canine humility.
There should be an exquisite procession behind him -
Chariots or wagons overflowing with bands,
Seeming to follow but, in truth, leading.

But instead there follows a father, dutifully propelling
A resentful pushchairful of baby.
Their eyes are trained on the gravel -
Eyes impervious to trees.

Matthew Tiller

A DRUNKARD'S DREAM

Miss Peabody has passed away; they think she may have drowned
Her deathbed was a soggy mess when she was finally found
Her petard was well hoisted, I think you will agree
That dandelions have caused her fate of drowning in her wee

Let's not forget the benefits she gave in her demise
Where would we be without Miss P and her true sacrifice
If she'd not stumbled headlong, that night so long ago
The dandelions' secret - no one would ever know

The world would be so different, a sadder drier place
We must not underestimate this improved human race
We can drink and have a skinful without that nagging dread
Of waking up six times each night and leaving our warm bed

The dandelions they work their charm as everybody knows
They bring on enuresis, you just lay there and it flows
Damp beds each day are nothing when you've had
                                    a full night's snooze
It's thanks to Lady Peabody that we can sup more booze.

Shirley McIntyre

THE ARTS

What's poetry to me?
What do soft cadences do
With the beauty of their lines
And the timing of a rhyme?
They take me back through years
Which I quickly overleap
To when the sound of Mother's breathing
Drifted me to sleep.

What's literature to me?
What do stories and novels do
With the secrets that they hold
Showing us lives so bright and bold?
They take me back to the start -
I need no longer dig so deep
For when the sound of Mother's breathing
Drifted me to sleep.

What is art to me?
What do fine paintings do
With brushstrokes painting line
From colour so sublime?
Back, they travel me
So time and distance meet.
I hear the sound of Mother's breathing
Drifting me to sleep.

Katie Boyd

FLOWER OF THE SKY

Summer! Long time
Since I felt your warmth caress my tender frame
When will you decide to come again?
Early flowers thrive on your sweet kiss
And spread their petals soft with dewdrop mist
Summer shine your dazzling light
And colour this world for me
Big yellow flower
King of the sky
Enrapture this Earth
With a passionate eye.

Pamela Hanover

A TRAWLER'S LAST TRIP

It was still day but dark as night
An eerie sulphur dark grey light
Lashing rain in a force nine gale
A cruel driving wind as well

The sea was mad and raging high
All hell let loose in sea and sky
With the Cornish coast in sight
A trawler in a losing fight

Waves of water forty feet high
Seemed to crash down from the sky
The spray with gale force fury stung
Like the bull shot from a gun

With hands so cold that lost all feel
In vain the skipper fought the wheel
Then sound of screeching wood and steel
As rugged rocks tore hull and keel

With merciless waves crashing down
The crew in that ship were drowned
The price of fish at times is high
But for that price at times men die

K W Benoy

I WISH I'D BEEN

I wish I'd been a dancer
As good as Fred Astaire.
When young I practised very hard -
My Ginger was a chair.

I wish I'd been a cricketer
As good as Ian Botham:
A bowler and a batman -
But he never lived in Gotham.

I wish I'd been an artist
As good as that chap Turner;
But in art classes at night school,
All I drew were Bunsen burners.

I wish I'd been an athlete
As good as Lord Seb Coe.
What made him take up running?
Well, you wouldn't want to know.

I wish I'd been a poet
Like my favourite, Thomas Hood;
But mine are more like Edward Lear,
Though perhaps not quite as good.

Yes, I write funny poems;
Limericks, things of that sort;
And if you infringe my copyright,
Then I'll see you in court.

Roger Williams

AT NIGHT

Timelessness, subdued in the stillness of parallel worlds,
Bathed in mellow melancholy
I lie in my bed, knowing my happiness he beholds.
He, who is so far away. Not with me. I perceive reality.

The only light - phosphorescent pink,
Spinning its cobwebs around the room.
I think of him. Lips - a luscious, Lucozade tasting drink.
Bodily mellifluousness. Imagine being wrapped in a silky cocoon.

Desire, spontaneity, laughter and thrills
Are all precious gifts of the summer we shared.
Carefree, colourful, that's how one feels
When he is around. Play his tune. Be an instrument to be played!

Disillusionment overcomes, as I lie here alone,
Revelling in solitude I relive every memory of the sun.
Thoughts with emotions mix. Heavy eyelids. Morpheus
                              is my chaperone
Again into the world of sweet odours of opium dens. Fantasies come!

Is insomnia poor excuse for insanity
When reality and dreams are so closely entwined?
I don't know. Love confuses and dares, brings unusual
                              beauty, vivacity.
I miss him. He, who is far, far away. This cannot be denied.

Possessive, and ugly I may at times be
Luring his presence into my being.
In the morning, I know, dream's over, he has to flee
The castle within me. Serene and opulent green.

We dream and we love, we wake and we part,
Thus only in a dream we give and take
The faith, the hope, holding two souls in one heart.
Morning comes. Reality beholds; he is away. Till next night
                              I keep awake!

Kate Shkanova

A LONG WAY FROM TOMORROW

A war I was fighting, to keep this world we live in free
I found myself surrounded, a prisoner were me
To a camp I was taken, full of injured and dead
I met a fellow soldier, who turned to me and said,
'Each day we're getting further away, much further from tomorrow
For some there will be joy my friend, for others only sorrow'

I became friends with the soldier, Old Fred was his name
He said that each day would be tough, survival is the game,
'Smile through all adversity, and never wear a frown
The enemy cannot win, if you don't let them get you down
Everything will be just fine, I see a light shining bright
We're walking through a tunnel, and at the end there is a light'

Each day we were marched for miles, in strong and searing heat
For some it was an ordeal, just standing on their feet
Beating followed beating, we all fought back the tears
While Fred's words of encouragement, were ringing in my ears,
'Always think of home my friend, though you are so far away
Keep a dream within your heart, and you'll be home one day'

Each day the death toll mounted, with others growing weak
I was so numb when it ended, I couldn't even speak
Old Fred never made it home, he sadly passed away
But I look up to Heaven, and I can see him smile today
Though Fred wasn't there in person, his spirit was all the same
And I could see him smiling down, when tomorrow finally came

Dale McFadden

MOTHER'S DAY

Being a mother, oh, what a joy!
Whether your baby's a girl or a boy.
Looking to you to care and provide.
In return, their love they don't hide.
Kisses and cuddles in the early years,
Make things better and dry up their tears.
Years quickly pass and their needs alter.
You hope they'll confide, and they will not falter.
Going out at night clubbing, you hoped they wouldn't go.
And wishing they didn't think they are all in the know.
Disagreements, I'm afraid, there will be.
You only want the best but they can't see.
Trust and faith come with the passing of time.
Harmony will be restored and all will be fine.
Happy days will outweigh the bad.
Children make you so proud and ever so glad.
Each child unique in their special way.
Remembering their mum on Mother's Day.

Anne Sackey

THE COMFORTABLE CHAIR

The chair she sat in was old and worn,
Her face was showing expressions of scorn,
The family wished to change the suite,
And throw the chair into the street.
Refusing to move, no way would she budge,
Determination, we knew she'd begrudge
Parting with something she'd moulded through wear,
That ridiculous, worn out, comfortable chair.
She muttered words of 'I'll go too, if I must,
This chair is part of the family trust.
If your father knew what was happening now,
He'd cause a God almighty row.'
We passed her a gin to appease her a little,
We could see she was smouldering and getting brittle.
She took a gulp, then spluttered more words,
'Pass me a ciggy,' plus a few other verbs.
What in the world can we do about this?
We decided perhaps to give it a miss.
Leave the chair in a corner somewhere
Away from the suite, to miss the glare,
Of glancing eyes that couldn't but see,
The frightful state, and a possible flea.

She raised her glass to be refilled,
Some, we noticed, had already spilled.
The ash balanced on the end of her stub
Good for the carpet, just give it a rub.
We can't believe she was known as 'Duchess',
The house so clean and never a mess.
She suddenly turned and gave us a grin,
'Isn't it time for another gin?'
We thought she had mellowed, but no, we were wrong,
Her words sprang forth, emphatic and strong.
'There's no way that I'll move from my comfortable chair,
I'll die first, rather than send it from here.'
We said, 'Now don't worry, we've given it thought,
This whole situation is making us fraught.
So keep the old chair, if that's your desire,
We can't burn you both on top of the fire.'
So happy she is in her old scruffy way,
Drinking and smoking, so no more can we say.

Monica D Buxton

STUDENT'S UNION
(Mature student induction)

Anticipate what?
Unknown territory - the province of youth.
A dark, empty space
Casual dregs on cluttered tables.
One small group, talking
In half-hearted boredom.
No lectures, no learning,
Their choice is to be there.
The room is caught
Without its dress-up finery.
Stale and static.
It awaits arousal; needs
Something.

Later,
Crushed and deafened,
Strobe-lit and sexy,
It happens.

Celia Saywell

THE WEAKEST LINK, MY ETERNAL NIGHTMARE

It's five-fifteen and The Weakest Link
Makes us laugh from the start of Ann's lobsided-wink
This is just the first round, the questions, a breeze,
But the nervous are shaky and weak at the knees
We laugh from our armchairs - they're such a dim lot!
Two twenties are thirty? No, she's lost the plot.
The woman in black they all seem to fear,
Treat her with scorn! Call her 'M'dear'
A fairly bright soul, I'm egged on by a chum,
Three thousand perhaps? A nice tidy sum
How do I treat Annie? Not too hard, I decide
But I'll give some smart answers, I do have my pride
We stand in the darkness, myself and the dense
I forget to bank money - that's of no consequence
A mere blip - to triple is multiply by four
Did I really say that? Annie smirks at my score
'Jillian, put down your board - I see you like knitting'
'No, actually Chanel let me down at my fitting.'
At least, that's what I meant to say,
But my teeth and tongue got in the way
They laugh at my answers - I surely can't stay?
But as yet I am standing, the laugh of the day
When I go it's with no dignity
No self-esteem, no celebrity.

Jillian Megram

CONSTANT LOVE

The love of a sweetheart
Is exciting it's true
But they may have others
And make you blue

The love of a mother
Is constant and giving
Her love for you
A reason for living

But the love of a child
Snuggled on your chest
Trusting eyes looking upwards
Must surely be the best.

Greta Elizabeth Beevers

UNTITLED

I gave up wishing
it got me nowhere in the end
forgive and forget
I won't defend

here comes loneliness
he's my old friend
so sail away on the oceans
carry me far, just take me away

I cried for a century
I felt the pain grow more
I caught a thousand teardrops
so just close the door

turn the chapter
step off the train
it takes you nowhere

shadow on my face
the mask is torn
nowhere to turn
once you're born

you go on hoping and praying
for the destiny of man and yourself
and all the memories lie forgotten
the dust is swirling from the past

so I lay the ghost to rest and walk the last mile
turn only once, look back
and remember with a smile
that I was here, I gave something
some meaning, in that moment
that moment, that year

David Chapman

THE CERAMIC LEAP

F ifteen years,
O ur ceramic anniversary.
R eaching a delicate time,
W aiting for a gentle breeze to shatter our
A chievements, our
R ichly composed shards of starlight,
D elivered to us through our flowing pen.

P oetry marked by unchanging fragility.
R ight nor wrong nor anything can move,
E xcept our golden thoughts of
S uccess, celebrated as we
S tand to make a glorious leap from ceramic fifteen.

K Hale (15)

HER AND THE MOON

There is a shine to your eyes that's drying:
A reminder of what has faded like a church rubbing.
With it in mind I cling like a barnacle:
Alive or dead, no movement to prove.

So many goodbyes only spoken:
Could leave gold behind easier than you.
Kept taking your hand when you turned away:
Threw you back in the battle newly wounded.

The motion of the stars echoed your leaving:
A turning in a space around everyone else.
Then there was only your moon-like face:
Pulling and shaping me as a beaten wave.

Gary T Pollard

PANIC STATIONS

Starting the day, waking up was the worst part
She would open her eyes and it was there
Waiting for her
Fingers drumming on her brain
Ceaseless hammering in her heart

Painfully alert and paralysed all at once
Prozac might help
Positive attitude will help
Physiotherapy a must
Psychological support a possibility

So much help with treating the
Physical disease
But who is going to help
With her feelings of having her life threatened?

Jill Lesley Gilbert

THE SECRET VALLEY

The deep cleft
Inside shallow rolling hills
Sears and shades
A lush green overhanging firmament;
With a winding serpentine brook
Sneaking in and dark viridian cool,
Hiding its clear head
With perpendicular arching trees.
A lasting cathedral to nature
Grown over sedate years
With tall fern and bluebell nights.

There is a silent secret here
With wafting invisible scents,
And words spoken gently
While hiking through
This camouflaged verdant space
An infinity of fractal motion
Gently waving their heads in chorus
Down in wood-bridged lairs.
And a quiet symphony of bird calls
For no other reason
Than being alive and there,
Singing their songs of joy
To the breasted skies
Whose end is a full reservoir
Of memories.

Unconscious depths
Felt with friends and camera shots;
Walking through cow smells and farmyards
And across sloping fields
Where dead moles were hung.
And on the ridge
The last sight of a light blue haze
Over the Bowland Bay was spied
Drinking in the forever times,
When in old age
We will take refuge
In this small glimpse
Of paradise found,
Realising there was no more to say
For we had come full circle
In that precious day.

Peter Corbett

KARMA APPLE PEOPLE

Black spots coming out
Of the evening sun
A dark hand outstretched
Beneath the tree laden
A slithering twilight shadow
As Heaven played sweet
Among the heavy branches
God's in a formation of cloud
Living with the long lost churches
The world of green sublime
With wisdom's nature old
Time to eat the past
Again and again and again.

John Ball

SOLUTION

When sediment settles, dregs, detritus,
Leaden and heavy, crystal clear liquid remains.
No doubts entertained,
War is mandatory,
Statesmen embroiled,
Arms are engaged,
States embattled,
Reputations made.

Smart bombs destroy,
Houses collapse, water mains burst,
Power lines break, food supply cut.
Citizens helpless, disenfranchised,
Dis everything; dismembered, disenchanted,
Disgruntled, distressed.
Shake the flask, read the runes
Swirling in the cloudy cup,
A solution; a vision.

Jean Greenall

MY CHARLIE GIRL

(Written whilst sitting in the Brighton Metropole Hilton Hotel in June 2005)

Nothing prepared me for the sense of desolation
The feeling of being in suspended animation
Will I wake up - I hope it's a dream
Outwardly calm, but inside I scream

When I was young I had all my life,
Was busy all day being somebody's wife
Now I'm alone, she was all that I had
People I know think I'm really quite mad

'But it was only a dog,' they say without feeling
They don't seem to realise that now my life has no meaning
I'm fooling myself that she is still here
That she'll rush in to see if I'm in my armchair
And as she'd gone blind towards the end
I'd call, 'Over here,' to my dear little friend.

The well meaning people who try to console
Really don't know how I feel at all
And as I sit and write these lines
Surrounded by splendour, great food and wines
It all means to me just nothing at all
All I want back is my sweet Charlie Girl.

Pamela Baily

A PLACE CALLED HOME

Somewhere out there is,
A place called home,
I don't know where,
I don't know when,
But somewhere in the open sea,
Is a land called home to me.

It could be big,
It could be small,
But it doesn't matter,
Because it's home to me.

It's where I'm from,
It's part of me,
To deny it,
Would be to deny me too.

My family's there, my friends are too,
And just like me they can't deny it too,
Because they, like me,
Are from a place called home,
Which is just another part of me.

Fiona Carson

BIRTH OF LOVE

Love! Born in alpha of knowledge
One virtue that is of a universality
An essential emotion that's for all
Love develops the values of Man
To a purer form as a crystal ideals
Love they say, can defeat them all
Hence no known barriers after all
Love has a vision for what is right
Therefore blind for an earthly lust
Virtue that all of creation's shared
Virtue that is mysterious and bare
Along with such decency and care
Love that is unchanging for us all
Therefore endures the test of time
As long as God remains our God
Then there came the birth of love

Machiavelli G Dayupay

THE CRUMMOCK MAKER

His hut stood at the edge of time.

He worked in a jungle of hazel;
empty cornucopias of rams' horns
cluttering bench, littering floor.
I'd find him hunched over his vice,
absorbed in the alchemy of his craft.
Oh, the smells that were there!
Linseed oil and lanolin, sawn horn,
glue, bubbling and gurgling in a pot -
the fragrance of pipe tobacco.
He'd be sawing or shaping a horn;
rasping, polishing, skrimshawing thistles
to sit proudly under the hand's heel.
A marriage of shaft and handle;
a brass ferrule, a lick of varnish -
and a crummock fit for St Columba!

I see him yet in my mind's eye:
back bowed and bent like a ram's horn,
his sparse hair white as thistle-down.
Behind his spectacles
his eyes glitter with the stuff of stars.

Ken Angus

INNER THOUGHTS

Do you look at the skies, see the clouds pass by?
Do you look at some trees, wondering why they're so high?
Does the wonder of all make you stand and think?
Would you miss all this if you stopped to blink?
Do you stand in wonder and look in awe?
Do you think to yourself, what is all this for?
Do you have an answer to what you ask?
Do you say this creation was quite a task?
Do you often relax and close your eyes?
Do you open them up and look in surprise?
Do you wonder why there is rain and sun?
Do you wonder why the world was begun?
Do you really find concern for life?
Do you find there's lots of stress and strife?
Do you manage to cope with every day?
Do you find it easy to go on your way?
Are you really alone with what you ask?
Do you feel like a clown who wears a mask?
If you find all these answers please do tell,
For all these questions are mine as well.

Ena Andrews

ECLIPSE 1999

An eerie stillness filled the air
a twilight settled in
the sky was dim and empty
where all the birds had been.
Grey-silver hue hung over fields
where creatures lay to slumber
completely *fooled* by this miracle
they rested themselves in awed wonder.
We gazed transfixed as a chill set in
and a *slight* breeze rustled the tree
it seemed for a time like the *end* of the world
so little the eye could see.
The moon had covered our bright golden sun
whose light we depended upon,
and blackness prevailed as the moon *spread* itself
and our *familiar* brightness was gone.
As slow as it went, it returned once again
and we uttered a sigh of relief,
it had left us aghast, with *no* words to be said,
what we'd witnessed was beyond belief.
As the sun reappeared
shining down through dull cloud
and the moon glided slowly away,
we *smiled* at the sun and each *other*
so *proud*
to have *witnessed* this *wondrous* day . . . !

Margaret Hanning

HELP ME DEAR LORD

Help me, dear Lord to be honest and true,
    To do with a will, the things I must do.

Neither fretting, nor frowning,
    But with joy and with pride.

Help me remember,
    You're there,
        By my side!

And help me, dear Lord,
    To be kinder to others,

So they too may enjoy
    This day and its hours.

Maggie Cartridge

CELEBRATION OF LIFE

Sitting by the window,
She has no idea of time,
Holding back the threadbare curtains
She peers through the dirt and grime.

Just one corner
Where a hand has wiped the dirt away,
Reveals a sad old face,
Looking out into the day.

The old wrinkled face,
That its ninety-nine years has brought,
Is lifeless and tired,
Forgotten and distraught.

The thin bony body
Shuffles back into the room,
That seldom sees the sunlight,
To shine upon the gloom.

Sitting heavily in her rocker,
She prays to God to bring a swift death,
And as if to answer her prayer
She sighs and takes her last breath.

No one came to her funeral
As she was laid to rest in the ground,
A forgotten grave with no flowers,
Just the earth raised up in a mound.

And yet Mother Nature never forgot
As the grass and brambles grew,
And each spring a primrose blooms
To celebrate her life anew.

C V Perkins

A SPECIAL OCCASION

Congratulations Forward Press
Upon this grand occasion!
Poets from all walks of life
Will proudly afford you a standing ovation

Lots of subject matter
Has come to your attention.
Poems on every subject,
Lots worthy of a mention.

Authors of various ages and
Every denomination,
Poems about worldly events
To people living above their station.

Here's to the next fifteen years,
May you go from strength to strength.
Another mail delivery arrives
With poems of various lengths.

Joan Igesund

INNOCENCE

Little children it's a shame
That civilisation will not take the blame
Your innocence is a picture today
But mankind will change your ways

Our colour and religion
Our class and distinction
The traditions of our families
That stops us living happily

When we learn to live, we die
So learn to live today, don't cry
But smile with an open heart
And show them love can be an art.

Bruce Ripley

EBB TIDE

The fount of joy
No longer wells within me . . .
The lift of heart
That heralded the start
Of each new day
Is now no longer there . . .
The sense of fun
That ran like silver thread
Through the dull fabric of my years;
The eagerness
That was the air beneath my wings;
The love of life
That was the substance of my days
And coloured
All the simple, mundane things,
No longer warm my soul;
And time . . .
That not so long since,
Seemed to fly,
Stands - mocking - at my shoulder,
As with dragging feet and backward glance,
I gaze into the mists and shadows
Of the twilight of my days.

Elizabeth Amy Johns

POT OF GOLD

(Dedicated To Ashley Davis)

I now see the world in bright, bright colour,
no longer black and white, and without you
my visions are blurred, disturbed by lack of light.

Butterflies swim in my stomach,
and turn my mind around.
I feel everything one hundred times more:
every scent, every touch, every sound.

The world is full of glorious passion,
and I'm as high as a drug filled night
But this time I know I won't come down,
not till my life takes flight.

And until that day I'll love you still,
and tell the world and shout.
Give all I have to give to you,
and breathe all that you breathe out.

Jesamine Cook

CIRCLES OF TODAY

Rainbow of colour
Arched half circle across
A dark and threatening sky
God's promise on high
Of calm to follow storm.

Pavements circled with deep puddles
Child splashes through in red Wellingtons
Summer laughter in a safe place.

The Internet circles the earth
Drawing the world population
Closer together in life's survival
Knowledge knits caring people
Together and brings action.
When voices can be clearly heard
Crying poverty from other lands
Hands reach out and pack a van
So that helpless can receive aid
And a debt is paid to humanity.

Freda Grieve

AND SO YOU LEAVE

And so you leave,
- a parting dove,
that flies to warmer shores.
And all alone,
we think of you,
of what we had before.
And holding back,
the bitter tears,
we part for you, goodbye.
So spread your wings,
and like a dove,
to distant lands you'll fly.

Elena Uteva

FROM CONFLICT TO PEACE

Conflict spread throughout the world
Battle banners all unfurled
For six long years the war did rage
Killing folk of every age.

Soldiers, sailors and airmen too
Gave their lives for me and you
Civilians many also died
Millions injured on each side.

At last it came, the world at peace
Fighting, killing, all did cease
Surviving forces all returned
Were any lessons really learned?

We prayed that peace at last would stay
No other fool would stand and say
'I want this and I want that,
My country starves whilst I get fat.'

Minor clashes here and there
When someone wants more than their share
Once again the troops we'll send
To bring back peace, the rift to end.

We've seen the end of two world wars
And prayed that there would be no more
Let's have peace throughout the world
No more the battle flags unfurled.

But until that hoped for day
All that we can do is pray
Pray to God for all our worth
Once more have peace upon the Earth.

Bill Brittain

ICY RIVER

An icy river flows within my heart.
A tide of turbulence that never ceases,
never stays its destructive path.
It drowns the fondness
of past memories, sweeps on
unabated, destroying future
dreams. It seems to ebb and flow,
first letting in transparent
hope, then surging out
in wild defiant mood.
Its cold, rude current sending
shivers through my soul.
My heart weeps adding to the torrent
and drowning my saturated love
betrayed by you.

Aleene Hatchard

PUPPY LOVE

My poor puppy he doesn't know his worth
His owner's in her own world again
The usual self loathing curse

He should be running through the park
Jumping over grass
But she stays home all day
Thinking of the past

He's such a joy to have around
If only she could see
When he wags his tail
And his eyes say *please notice me*

The house is very stark today
Even though the sun is bright outside
No human voice heard from within
And not a single happy bark

And as he sleeps beside her feet
The day draws to an end
What a waste on her to have
Such a loving loyal friend

She's not a bad person
Don't get me wrong
She loves him very much
And wants to be strong

She'd love him to see her happy
And take him out to play
And be the friend that he deserves
To have one day.

Dragana Mundzic

THE BEGGAR

I gaze into his vacant eyes,
And note his pallid skin -
Cross-legged and rigid there he sits -
I hand a coin to him.
Some insults now are hurled at him,
As people pass him by,
'Get up you lazy thing,' they say,
'You people are work shy!'
But then I get on thinking,
As I walk along,
Whatever caused this lad to beg,
What on earth went wrong?
No man in his senses
Would sit all day and freeze,
And those of us who judge him
Should go down on our knees
And pray for this poor creature
Who has given up on life -
And feel sympathy towards him,
When the wind cuts like a knife!
Be thankful for those comforts
Which we all enjoy
And have compassion for this being -
He is only just a boy!
Forgive us when we criticise
Those who cannot cope.
Let's strive in our community
To bring those lost souls hope!

Joan Leahy

HOLIDAY IN TIROL

Picture a village in a valley, deep and wide
Where the lush meadows grow
Great, pine-clad mountains sweep up each side,
The distant peaks covered in snow.

See the houses and shops, bright and neat
Cafés and hotels, people busy everywhere,
The flower-filled balconies line the street,
And the scent of coffee warms the crisp air.

The river rushes onward, over gravel bed below,
A little train bustles with whistle tooting madly,
I long to be there, oh madly, sadly,
But now I m old and can t afford to go.

Amy Oldham

WHY NOT LIVE AND LET LIVE?

There's veg'tables and fruits galore,
Plus grains and nuts and seeds,
So why should Man want even more,
When on dead flesh he feeds?

He also plunders milk and eggs
Without the slightest need;
Mistreating all that have four legs,
Insatiable his greed.

Of course, two-legged creatures too,
And those who have just fins,
Much suffering are all put through
As Man compounds his sins.

Why doesn't it occur to Man
He's merely part of Whole,
Included in Creator's plan
To play a loving role?

. . . By caring for defenceless ones
In ev'ry way he can,
Instead of which their blood just runs,
Providing meat for Man.

This gross barbarity must cease
For sake of all concern'd,
And Man will never find true peace
Until this lesson's learn'd.

Alan Spinks

THE MISTRESS

As if I am fooled by those lowered eyes
That wait, ready to slip into my shoes
At a moment's notice. Her unsung lullabies
Of secret thought disturb the rocky cradle.
Nursing the ignored evidence of my need,
She stirs tea and gossips at her master's table.

As if I am fooled by those insolent eyes
That rake the unknown reflection of my sin,
Proof of my passion that protests against domesticity
To emasculate the man seduced by my lies.
I unbind my hair to embrace the conspiracy
That willingly flings all caution to the wind.

As if I cannot see my destiny in those knowing eyes,
That calculate the price of my uninvited guest.
How many crumpled sheets will mortify
The old man, and place her centre stage?
Will she grow old in my shoes? Her fantasies
Fulfilled, as she preens in cast-off lace;
Mistress of a house, in which I had no place.

M Byles

BETH

Beth has left our Earthly World,
She's gone where all good Border Collies go,
To a canine heaven in the sky,
Beyond the stars that glow.

Her life on Earth now over,
Her days competing in agility are gone,
Eileen has fond memories,
And the trophies Beth has won.

In a canine heaven,
Way beyond the stars,
She's reunited with old pal Kaiser,
In a spot 'twixt Earth and Mars.

Tea leaf Jock can't steal her food,
Cos it's no longer there,
She will not have to struggle now,
Each night to climb the stair.

Mel and Pip will miss her,
Playing on the lawn,
Or going for a daily walk,
Early every morn.

Although she has now left,
Fond memories will remain,
It is with great affection,
We will always speak her name.

Jack Robinson

WHAT IS WISDOM?

Ask what is?

Like rocks building variegated veins,
Like tree trunks gathering rings,
Like onions growing peels,
And skin lining up wrinkles,
Wisdom creeps up on us in layers,
Coats us in sheaths
Wraps us in wreaths
Of love.

Wisdom shines.

Who can imagine the slow process
Of accumulating layers of love?

We glisten.

We gestate wisdom through time. When will it manifest?
How much more love do we need to become wise?

We radiate.

We smooth love into our folds, layer upon layer like face cream, like
lipstick. We press it deep into our hearts. We anoint ourselves with
the practice of love: patience and work.

We are absolutely gleaming.

An onion peels. Skin wrinkles. Grey rocks split into a radiance
Of crystals.
Mountains are lined in the hues of time.
Rivers run and are dry. We laugh and we cry.
We are caught in the miracle of love.

Brilliantly.

Our dreams slip from cocoons
Into butterflies.
We glow wise.

Mary Pampolini-Roberts

I LIVE IN HOPE . . .

I'll describe the dream I had today,
'Tis a dream that shall come true.
Once my overcoat is well worn out
And my life on Earth is thru.
They laid me on a cold, cold slab
They thought my life was done.
I felt sweet angels tending me
And I woke up in the sun.
I walked from where they'd laid me down,
Saw a garden full and fair.
Oft read about the promised land
And knew that I was there.
Looked on colours indescribable,
Such brilliance not known before.
There peace became my garment
As I stood to look in awe.
There I saw the lambs and lions
Just as the Word had said.
Found the truth of every promise
That I many times had read.
I know I shall be singing,
Thanking God for evermore.
Safe, at last, and happy
With no memory of a life before.
From the dream I woke contented.
And 'Hope' had filled my heart.
I have so much to thank the Lord for,
And it's time for me to start.
                    Of course!

Rosie Hues

GIVE ME FIVE

If you are blind
You cannot see
The whole picture

If you are deaf
You do not hear
Both sides

If you are mute
You cannot voice
An opinion

If your tongue
Is cut out
You cannot taste
The difference

If your nose is blocked
You are unable
To smell the goodness

And yet . . .
Those of us
Who have five senses

Are still seeing half a picture

Still hearing one side

Still not speaking out

Still tasteless

Still blocked up

How many senses do we need to have?

Maybe one
A sense of bravery.

Anita McNamee

A KIND OF MAGIC

Resting in the garden
The work, for now, behind
A sense of satisfaction
Fills my contented mind

A voice I heard; I looked around
No one was there, just the sound
Of lilting music, like a song
Filling the air

'Do you believe in magic?' said the voice
Surprised, I looked around my well known space
I must be dreaming, or I'm listening to
Someone from another place.

Longing to hear the lovely voice again
I asked, 'What sort of magic do you mean?'
The voice came nearer, quietly speaking
Though every word was plain

'On the Arctic tundra, in the desert sand
Is the miracle of creation
The magic of the Earth goes on
Untouched by human hand.'

I heard the world's long history
Of life and growth and nature's sway
The rhythmic cycles of the Earth
A never-ending mystery

The voice sang on from earth to sky
Then faded and was gone
But every word I heard will stay
Engraved in my philosophy.

Mary McGuigan

MY NEXT POEM

My next poem will be woven through
With your exquisite threads,
Shining beautiful and golden.
It will be painted with
Bright broad colours,
Passionate and loyal,
Lifted from your palette
Onto my unremarkable canvas.

My next poem will rhyme with our dreams,
Disrupt the beat,
The metre, of unfulfilled wishes.
Images of love, desire and delight
Will alliterate and assonate.
And the drowning sailor
Plucked by you from cold waters
Will be my metaphor.

My next poem could reflect on a tear,
Or illuminate a smile,
Recall the weather
And the time of year we met,
Wonder at crazy thoughts that . . .
But mainly it will be about you,
Because I am the man
You have made of me.

My next poem is this one.
It is dedicated to you.

John Riddick

GEMMA'S WEDDING

There's not many of us around
a bit thin on the ground you might say
disease and disaster have taken their toll
we've learnt to roll with the punches
so a wedding is an occasion
for raisin' a hulie
making a fuss to see the bride blush
it's not her fault there's not many of us around
that we're a bit thin on the ground
so raise your glass
to the lass that's starting
a new branch on the family tree.

Pat Wharam

SEPTEMBER

It has begun

The long shadows seeping through the trees
casting dark fingers across the garden floor.
September sunshine, warm and still, no breeze
to rustle the branches or rattle the door.

It has begun

The nights are longer and start early now.
Extra blanket to combat the chill of cool
as dusk and gentle mist float like white cloud
and stars sparkle brightly in the black pool.

It has begun

The dawn beams golden wings
shrouds the earth with warm breath.
Enhanced, the sounds as blackbird sings,
enchanting still, impending summer's death.

It has begun

The last of the season's cloth is spread,
forest silent, still, dying leaves succumb.
Fruit is gathered, nuts are shed
trees ready to reflect the golden sun.

Rita Pedrick

THE OASIS

There's a little oasis off the A55,
You turn off at St Asaph, it's just a short drive,
A high board fence where the clematis grows
And the smell of the honeysuckle reaches your nose.
One seat in the shadow and one in the sun
Where you can relax when the day's work is done.
The buzz of the bee as he targets the flower,
The sound of the clock striking the hour,
The birds excitedly taking their bath
While the squirrel runs swiftly along the stone path.
With an agile leap he is on the bird table
Snatching the food while he is able.
The red-breasted robin swoops down to earth
And swiftly devours the crumbs on the turf.
Her bright twinkling eye looks directly at me
And with a brown and red flash she is back on the tree.
As the sun's reflection in the fountain gleams
I lay back and surrender to the land of dreams.

R Ashcroft

THE BRIDAL PATH
(For Les)

Forget-me-nots growing in the long grass
Swaying in the warmth of the summer sun
Peeping through the foxtails' pink tips
As they dance in the gentle breeze
As we walk hand in hand along the bridal path
So tempting are they to pick a few
And bend to smell the scent
You reached out to me
For a lover's kiss
To make my heart miss a beat
As we walked along the bridal path
The forget-me-nots are so blue, but not so
Blue as my lover's eyes.

Patricia Carr

ANTICIPATING ANNIVERSARIES

Anticipation had mounted as friends sailed o'er green sea
Blue sky above. Perfect conditions for a holiday spree.
Basking in sunshine, a welcome reprieve
From wet terrain at home. All were relieved.

Suddenly wind began blowing, causing billowing sails.
'No more fishing,' the crew proclaimed.
Pleasure was instantly a forgotten aim,
As breezes whipped the ocean into frenzied waves.

'Quick, head for the harbour where safety awaits.'
Exercising caution, they proceeded while the gale began to abate,
Safely anchored within shelter by a steady quayside,
Ruffled travellers were grateful, and heaved several deep sighs.

With joy do we anticipate our eternal existence?
Riding storms on life's journey, then to blissful conditions.
With God as companion, travelling aright
We'll be led to 'Heaven's Harbour' where there's perpetual light.

Anniversaries are special, usually happy and glad,
Loved ones departed, induce memories sad.
When life is committed to Christ, it's an occasion one cannot forget
Like a ship secure in harbour, our creator provides necessary
                                                    strength.

Annie Harcus

CLIMBING THE MOUNTAIN OF LIFE

Some mountains are high and magnificent. Some are low
Why do people climb mountains? Because they are there
Some are easy to climb, just just green slopes
Others have rocks to climb over or pass by
All climbers of mountains need the help of a guide
To lead them and find the best way.
Sometimes the path is snow covered or covered with a strange weed
Sometimes there are crevices or sharp stones to avoid
At all times a guide is needed to guide us
To keep on the path and not stray from it
Up and up the mountain the climbers go
Looking around at the beauty seen on the way
Sometimes, a bird, a flower, a cloud, or another mountain.
On some mountains several people climb together
On others just one on a rope
To climb is like our journey through life
Sometimes things go well, sometimes there is danger
Pitfalls and the going is tough
We need our Heavenly Guide with us
All the way to gently direct us
Life is like a mountain we are climbing each day
Until we reach the summit and our heavenly home
Where we are welcomed by our Lord and Heavenly Father.

Jean Martin-Doyle

COVE BAY

Wow what a view
And there isn't even a queue
I first see blue
I just want to take a pew
Walk further on
Come on, come on
I'm high up right now
But wow oh wow
There are caves down there
I run without a care
Down and round
Down and down
I'm there, I'm there
I stop and stare
Do I dare
Through an opening
Oh I'm hoping
Yes, unreal, I feel, I feel
This is so surreal
Stones, pebbles, under foot
Still I find the route
The light shines through
And greets me to
The other side
Nowhere to hide
The sea, the, the, the
Look at the rocks, the, the
The pools created by the sea
Just left to be
Little creatures live and thrive
To try and be alive
I look up and see
The grass on a ledge just wanting to be
Sandstone sculpted by the tide
I wish I'd been along for the ride
I have to take it all in
If I don't it will be a sin
One thing for sure
I'll be back for another personal tour.

Joan Helen Grant

CATHEDRAL CLOSE

I nudged and bumped my way along that noisy, crowded street,
Among the unheeded words, wasted against the traffic's beat.
And as the way bent right, I turned left into an alley
To escape the racket, and to let my senses rally.
I passed through a barrier, half-gate, half-door.

And suddenly I could no longer hear the city's roar,
The silence was almost tangible, as of another age.
People walked slowly, quietly, like lineless actors on an empty stage.
The houses, on the edge, looked settled, well-kept, treasured,
As if their owners' lives were measured, leisured, pleasured.

Soaring high above them was the glorious, slender spire
Of the Cathedral, bidding us to raise our eyes ever, ever higher,
Explaining the belief of many generations, in whose eyes,
Heaven is up above, higher than the very skies.
Beneath was the body of the Cathedral, with carvings and
a vaulted ceiling,
Where worshippers wandered, gazing - or paid their homage kneeling.

But even great artists, poets, wordsmiths, lack the supreme facility
To portray convincingly that awesome aura of tranquillity.

Robert T Collins

AFRICA

Africa: hot;
Crispy-spiced-chicken hot
Baked in the centre of the planet
It began there
The story of the human race
Black face
Hairy skin -
Fashion model
These are your kin!
All ethnic groupings share a soul
Each struggled out
From the African bowl
And populated Mother Earth
Where countless species
Had their birth.

This continent of poorest poor
In riches rich
With life galore
Its colours, sights
And sounds and smells
Its fortress
Where dictator dwells
Its shanty town
With starving folk
Is this some kind
Of awful joke?

Awake world
Open up your eyes
This was originally paradise
Cease the turmoil
Cease the fighting
Peace awaits
And it's inviting
There is a way
And it's no mystery
As Bob says,
'Let's make poverty history!'

Jill Hudson

JENNY'S ROSE

Jenny stoops to smell the rose
Jenny kneels in sweet repose
Seasons come and seasons go
But Jenny's rose shall all times grow

Jenny sits upon the seat
With falling lids she falls asleep
Jenny came to feed the birds
But lost herself in dreams instead

The blackbird is so very wise
Whistles sweet up in the skies
He waits for food that Jenny brings
For one whole hour he sweetly sings

Jenny wakes up with a yawn
With arms upstretched she gives a groom
Time to give the birds their food
And hurry home jest as she should.

Irene Crawford

THOUGHT-FLOW PROBLEM

Indulging in a blissful spell of idleness,
I received a communication from Forward Press,
exhorting me to submit a poem, my very best!
Are the fates conspiring against me to deny me rest?

As the letter arrived during a time of fine weather,
I was tempted to dismiss the idea altogether,
but my conscience waged a war of attrition,
until I reached a state of meek submission.

I called upon my Muse to fuel my imagination,
all in vain as Euterpe was away on vacation.
Like a cerebral kaleidoscope, images flashed across my mind,
difficult to encapsulate in words, too vague and ill-defined.

Where is the vivid imagination of earlier days?
When scenes of pastoral beauty could be depicted in ways
that the reader could envisage white horses dancing on an
angry sea
or the delicate tracery of leaves on a silver birch tree.

Anno-domini is to blame, the cynics cruelly cry
as I protest indignantly that my dotage is not yet nigh;
I simply cannot concentrate to compose on a bus or train
for the ringing of mobile phones encroaching on my brain.

Suddenly realisation dawns; solution is in sight.
The struggle to find a topic on which to write
has paradoxically become the theme of this little lay
which I hope will reach the editor before D-Day.*

* Deadline Day.

Alison Drever

CONDUIT

When it flows
Like a herd of beasts
Or a mighty river
Individual droplets running to and fro
Through different trails
Towards the same destination

When it comes
Like a wave of inspiration
Or an explosion of reason
And rhyme
Lexical sculptures
Delighting both scholars and artisans

I am the conduit
I am the gate
When the muse descends
Am I seized by fate?

Are the words mine?
Is the construction complete?
Can I be said to invent
Or to arrange?
Am I a wordsmith
Or an architect?
Am I a writer
Or a builder?

The story is ended
The stanzas run dry
The words on the page
My mind starts to fly
Another inspired moment is born
I follow its lead
I write through to dawn

A slave to the muse
A tool that we tame
A professional task
Or infantile game.

Andrew Blundell

TIME

Time marches on
but when all is said and done
time means nothing to no one
just a device designed
to measure our lives by
like a yardstick or a plumbline
to deceive us enable us to cope
with the otherwise continual monotony
ticking tocking to break up the silence
and make some small sense
of this senselessness and sorrow
giving shape to our memory
to live in hope of tomorrow

Time it marches on
yet the day can seem so long
whilst the night beats swift and strong
tick tock bodyclock still we soldier on . . .

Fiona Clark

AN AGEING KING

Surveying his future as far as he dare,
he glimpses the enemy.
The advancing years, always on the periphery
now marching.

Strong and muscular with inherent nobility,
he stands unflinching.
His green eyes darkened by all he has seen,
now glisten.

He is not prepared, they are here too soon,
their victory inevitable.
A heart that still dreams of the future
now frightened.

But death remains distant, this is his time
to continue writing his history.
A man in control of his own destiny;
now fighting.

Samantha Philo-Gill

FOR JAY

(Inspired by Rudyard Kipling's 'If')

My son, if you can journey
Along life's rocky way,
And to yourself you can be true
And honest every day.
If to all those less fortunate
You lend a helping hand,
And not hate those who cause you hurt
But try to understand.
If you can face adversity
And look it in the eye,
If you can know just when to laugh
And when it's good to cry.
If you can disappointment take
And never let it show,
If you can know when to hold on
And when to let things go.
If then all this you can achieve
And still find time for fun,
Then you will know just what it takes
To be a man, my son.

Margaret Thomas

TRAPPED

In bedsit land when days are grey,
I often while the hours away,
By gazing outward from my room,
Through open window, from my tomb,
But one day, when the world seemed dead,
The sash came down and trapped my head,
So there I was with legs akimbo,
My head stuck firm outside the window,
There I was for all to view,
My head thrust out, my torso blue,
I cursed and swore, I said, 'Begat,'
The sun came out, I had no hat!
And just as things could get no worse,
A passing seagull dropped his silent curse!
It trickled down my neck, confirmed my fears,
By filling not just one, but both my ears,
I shouted, 'Help,' I shouted, 'Please,'
The circulation ceased below my knees,
I thought, *what will I do, how can this be?*
And what if nature makes me pee!
I shouted, 'Someone, fetch a ladder,'
I had misgivings for my bladder,
And, even worse, with fearful growls,
Strange groanings deep within my bowels!
No one came near, my terrors rose,
A passing bee alighted on my nose,
Its tickling feet drove me insane,
And then was gone, followed by rain!
It soaked my head and I began to wonder,
How long this torture, pain and thunder,
Would last, but not for long,
The streaks of lightning proved me wrong,
It flashed above me, like Hell's clapper,
And landed on my baldy napper,
My ears were scorched, my nostrils singed,
I cried in torment, whined and whinged.

What had I done to cause this hell?
Things would be better if I fell,
At least my head would not be stuck,
And my poor fate would be tough luck!

Jim Crook

MEMORY

Lines which to the intellect unbidden
Come, the moment matching and enhancing;
Shared reminiscences to laughter doubled;
When out of sight and time, remembrance of
Occasions of past joys and loveliness;
Recollection of that eager though yet
Tentative first kiss or fingers twining;
Of these consist the stuff of memory,
That endless sourcing of the mind's delight
Which also in its kindliness enwraps
And smothers ancient miseries and griefs.
If at the margins faltering, when names
And numbers for the telephone escape,
Or when you puzzle on the landing for
The reason why you had to climb the stairs
And superficial, trivial things of
Yesterday forget, don't be concerned,
It is the edges only that are frayed.
The body of that precious fabric is
Intact with threads so bright and woven firm
That they will never wear away or fade.

Sheila Watts

CELEBRATION

When I received a letter to enter something for this special date
I couldn't find a poem I thought suited so decided to wait
Put a new one together that would be best
I am pleased with all the ones I've written they'd all pass the test
My poetry became a lovely gift from a very painful life
I struggled hard to survive living here separated as Taff's wife
It was so nice to see how well the poems did
Lifted me from darkest days like taking off a lid
My poems reflected my journey through it all
The good times and the bad times and things I'd rather not recall
But if something good can come from suffering then that's a reward
Perhaps help others like me to say thank You Lord.

Audrey Davies

NIGHT

I see a beautiful, dark blue, velvet sky sprinkled with diamonds
that no one can steal.

The cuckoo, the night owl, the dog fox calling his mate hoping
that she won't be late as he promised to go hunting with her in
Bradgate Park.

We are alright until it snows but then we are in trouble, we cannot
hide our tracks and can soon get caught.

Then we have the poachers to dodge, and their dogs.

My only crime was to be born as a fox.

I see a beautiful, dark blue, velvet sky sprinkled with diamonds
that no one can steal.

' Milner

WHO DO YOU SAY I AM?

You are my breath that awakens me each morning
That sees me through each coming day
You are the mist that dampens my feet
As You guide me along my way

You are the sun that warms up the Earth
Which brings the life back into the sleepy dawn
You are my prayer each morning
Which guides each coming day

You are my heart's desire
And all I hope to be
You are my deliverer, my hope
In all things now and to come

The giver of all things
From the smallest to the biggest
Of all my blessings
You are my hand and heart
That guides my way

That fills me with power
Far beyond this world
You teach me Your wisdom
From Your great book

You open my eyes to see
The beauty that surrounds me
You are the wind beneath my wings
As my heart soars higher than an eagle

That I am nothing, without You
You are God's precious son,
You are my Lord, God, almighty
I worship You, but most of all
You are my best friend
Amen.

E Chapman

GRANT ME A WISH

Grant me a wish, I'd put the world to right
Drown misery and make you feel alright
Plant peace in the garden for all to see
Harvest wealth; spread it over land and sea

Market love on the doorstep of mankind
Leaving sorrowful stories behind
I will imprison the weapons of war
When anger confronts you, I'll show the door

Bring joy to those who long for its power
Friendship builds, increases by the hour
Links with the lonely and finds a new home
Marks a new chapter, a wonderful poem

I'd circulate good health to those without
Silence evil; give affection a shout
Generate warmth to the cold and freezing
Give the confused understanding reason

Kaleidoscope of colour, bless the blind
Out of darkness to light, fill their mind
Return the ability to the lame
Their response in action becomes the same

Honour mother tongue the wish to express
Satisfy the skill, clearing from the mess
Sounds awaken the redundant eardrum
Allow me some time perfection will come

John Neal

THE EAGLE

I watched it glide high in the sky
Its wings outstretched, his eyes alive
Grace and beauty of this phenomenal bird
As he travels at speed
Through this magnificent Earth
Searching for food on this hot summer day
Suddenly diving like a plane
His eyes had spotted his catch for today
Swooping clutching his unaware prey
The strength of his wings is so easy to see
Climbing so high as he touches the sky
Gliding towards the nest in the cliff
Glad to be able to feed her young chicks.

Doreen Cawley

THE RAINBOW

Three days it rains upon the earth
It is no fun
Rivers flood
Fields submerge
There is no sun

Three months it rains upon my soul
No joy or fun
Sorrow comes
Crisis follows
Where is the Son?

One day, the rainbow's on the earth,
Dark skies have run
Waters steady
Fields surface
Here comes the sun

That day the rainbow's on my soul
Dark thoughts have run
Chaos subsides
Hope rises
Here comes - the Son.

David Speed

THE GARDEN OF DELIGHT

Summer is the time of year
The bunnies hop around
Birds are singing joyfully
As the butterflies dance by
In the garden of delight.

Flowers growing everywhere
Grass is flowing, trees are swaying
All the rain has disappeared
The sun comes out to say hello
In the garden of delight.

Fish are swimming beneath the rocks
In the shallow water
No time for boredom, come outside
Everyone is having fun
In the garden of delight.

Laurel Willman (11)

THIS ROOM

There are no windows in this room.
I came here when the leaves were green.
You took my hand to hide the truth.
We danced in silence -
The stone-hearted goodbye waltz.

There is no music in this room.
The only song I hear is yours.
The needle scratched when autumn fell,
To repeat, repeat in anguish -
Farewell, farewell, farewell.

There are no words in this room.
I forget the poem that you wrote.
Too well-read, it crumbled to nothing.
Your loving sentiments turn blank -
Letters have no meaning here.

There are no people in this room
The stillness does not quiet me.
I scream, I pace, I scream, I pace.
I demand some roll of thunder -
Alarm this putrid air with noise.

There are no doors in this room.
No way in, no way out.
Something grabbed me by the hair,
Flung me in and sealed this box -
I won't see you again.

Morney Wilson

THE SILENT POEM

It lies in a drawer, not forgotten
But unseen
A lover of yesteryear, no stranger
Memories to treasure, eyes that
Knew the ocean depths
Of a love so true

Anniversaries come and go
The years have flown, we were
Young and slim the smiles within
Now a photo tucked away
Pain and suffering on your brow
Had taken its toll

The other you, put away
Gently in a drawer
Knowing you, not forgotten.

Joan Hands

WHAT THE MIRROR SAW . . .

The mirror reflects the scene ahead
Of a murder, with someone dead.
Hung from a rope and framed in guilt
It spied all those deeds dealt.

The blood spilt between carpet pile
Soaked the starched shirt in style.
The stop of life leaves a chill
Count the raising breath - it's nil.

It hung above the floor beneath
And saw the knife pulled from its sheath
No one heard the leaked last breath
And no one saw the sudden death.

The uniformed bod peered ahead
And sighed, 'Poor old Fred'.
With no witness to the deed
The doer is all but freed.

If only the policeman thought
We had a witness - then he'd be caught
And he leant a hand against the wall
And knocked the mirror to a fall.

Behind a space where it stood
Was a camera in a box of wood.
Its film intact and ready to roll
To send the killer to the goal.

The evidence was there to see
A woman in a shirt and apron to her knee
She placed poor Fred onto the floor
This is what the mirror saw . . .

The room was a kitchen with pots all around
And the knife sliced quickly without a sound
His blood trickled, escaped to the floor
All this happened behind a closed door.

Poor Fred was lifted up on high
And plonked straight into a pan to fry.
With onions and carrots added with zest
He became the dinner for the policeman and a guest.

Kim Taylor

TIME GOES ON

Spending more time than not
Wanting something more,
Something different
Knowing having something
Else will complete
The puzzle which
After years
Still only has the outline completed.
Start from the outside in
Inside out.
Read the book
Cover to cover
Front page to back
Ending first
Neither matters
Now I am sure
We'll complete it.
Sure we'll find the end
And answer all answers
Question all questions
And
Sing out of key.

Alice Emery

CELEBRATION FOR RUSSELL

My daughter invited me to tea
By way of a celebration you see
But this celebration is just a bit sad
It's different to all of the others we've had
We rejoiced when each of her three sons were born
We all 'wet their heads' and felt sorry next morn
We next got together to christen each boy
And wish them good health and a life full of joy
But the first born was just a bit special you see
With the top of the wedding cake for tea
And now he has grown to a gorgeous man who
Wants to leave home as all young men do
And my daughter will miss him but not let it show
Cos she's a good mum she is letting him go
With lots of good wishes from all of us
And although for his sake we won't make a fuss
This celebration is just for our 'Russ'.

Nancy Robbins

MY GREATEST LOSS

(A tribute to my late wife)

I walk through the valley of shadows
After a lifetime of happiness
My dear one has now departed
And I'm left with emptiness

Through joy, sometimes tears, we travelled
Always there, by each other's side
Living for one another
Whatever life should betide

The happiness I get from our children
Whose mother they've lost too
Sustains me in my greatest loss
For without them I'd not get through

So if you are in this position
Remember as you grieve and despair
There are others whose lives are similar
And who think of you and care

And if you have lost a loved one
And your thoughts are racked with pain
Remember it's not forever
But 'till you meet again'.

Martin Selwood

CROWBAR

I'm a black and sombre crow,
And I think you ought to know,
I'm a barrister at law of high repute,
Spending most of every day,
Litigating in a way,
That affirms that I will always press my suit.

From my chambers upon high,
In the courts of leaf and sky,
I'll engage to undertake a client's brief,
Using subtlety and tact,
I elicit every fact
To ensure my client's seldom come to grief.

When folk see me don my wig,
They quite often dance a jig.
For my presence is of justice, truth and right
And when a trial is over,
Be it Scunthorpe, Leeds or Dover.
The court applauds with all its feathered might.

Albert Hart

MY EAST OF EDEN

In Byzantium I first gazed on thee
my Athena of dark eyed serenity.
From ancient Eden you stepped with grace,
an Aegean princess born from a golden race.
You took my life
and with fragile hands re-crafted me,
a sculptress, a teacher
who taught of a deeper honesty.

Now in these hours of exile
when melancholy haunts my mind,
I'll hide within my memories
and with you
an eternal peace I'll find.

Michael Wilson

LANGUAGE CLASS

We sit, English lips
moving in a most un-English way,
babbling childlike
in front of University graduates;
our mouths mouth sounds
which are a shade too labial
or dental, or nasal,
but the nuances are lost
on graduates - no matter how bright
or formal; the native foreigner
at his side
will soon dispel moot points.
Learned at his mother's knee
they are not even academic
but just well known and loved
expressions of his other land.
But we hug our new-found
symbols to ourselves;
these secret sounds are ours
if we can but remember them.
And if our lips are moved
within the narrow limits
imposed by long usage,
we can bring a smile
to the face of a Spaniard
or Turk, can argue with an
irate Italian or undo
the puzzle-lock of Linear-8.

L Saunders

GRATITUDE

Fifteen years since you went
Baby Ron was one week old
I got two jobs to pay the rent
Mum's jewellery had to be sold.

For fifteen years has Forward Press
Presented us with many a 'thought'
Emotions they ask us to express,
Emotions I've honestly fought

So with bitterness and hate long gone
I feel deep gratitude, not strife
He's a gift from Heaven, my Ron.

He's my pride, my life . . .
. . . My life.

Rita Pilbrow-Carlsson

THROUGH A MOTHER'S EYES

Through my eyes I espy
Rhyme of reasons
Shattered window soul
Crucified convicted mode
Standing solitaire
I weep for thee
Enveloped guilt
Stricken mind
I cannot touch
Thy path of fate
Experience the now
The crumbled gait
Heart-wrenched
Splintered passion
Fibres lay defeated
Pitiful grate
Thy son
Spiritual soul
Faith instill in thee
Pillared courage
Solemnly declare
Knowledge of life
Crux of thy gain
Guidance cometh
Tomorrow liveth hope
Acceptance trust
Sublime love
For matter together
Grow.

Sandra Madden

ETERNITY RING

Here, beside you,
        I'll be found:
Heart-shackled,
        love-bound.
What 'though cares
        our life surround -
Love protects
        our sacred ground
With
        joy profound.

Patricia Fallace

GENESIS

The nascent hour sounds as the vernal cock crows
Whilst a rising radiant aurora coats the earth.
Provenience has decreed that the stirring rootstock
Should put closure upon the winter's dearth.

The fountainhead doffs its icy cap
Satiating meandering brooks and streams,
Adam's wine flows as of vitalities vines
Dormant souls awake from their dreams.

Stretching branches flex their muscles
As waking buds raise their heads,
A smile rides upon the cool spring airs
And vivid flush returns to the beds,

On the breeze drifts a symphonic crescendo
As a chorus of praise is uttered and heard,
Replacing the mourning requiem's silence
For this is the beginning, this is the word.

Malcolm Dewhirst

PS I NAMED YOU HOPE

Did you ever know that I loved you,
That I held you close to my heart?
No one I thought could take you away
Or try to tear us apart.
Did you ever know my anguish
When they told me you weren't here to stay?
They came to my bed, held my hand
And said God had stole you away.
Did you ever feel my body ache
When they told me you'd died in my womb?
That your fragile heart refused to beat
And your body would lie in a tomb.
Did you ever hear my prayers
As they lowered you into the ground?
And their scornful eyes pierced my skin
And the silence screamed too loud.
Did you ever believe the rumours
That branded your mummy to blame?
That she took your life in heartless hands
And caused you to die with no name.
Will you ever believe I am sorry
And I live every moment in shame?
For I pray every night in longing
That you won't hold me to blame.

Denise Stock

HE CARED

My Lord, He came, He cared
He died for me
My own dear Lord
On Calvary's tree
His precious blood
To earth did drop
Did we care?
Did we stop, hurting Him . . .
The people cried
Crucify . . .
The Father turned away His eye
It pleased Him to send His son
For you, for me, for everyone
Jesus showed us how to live
Loving each other and to give
Our lives, our all to God
For that's what He did
By dying on that cross
To bring us back to God
His blood our sins did wash
Oh Lord forgive us when we forget
The day we broke Your heart.

Patricia Raison

THE EVENING PROMISE

Behind the glass I take away every feature of the sundown sky,
Like the grey tree beneath the falling black my mind wriggles,
Upside, backwards and ahead it goes,
Thoughts foaming when leaves plunge on a raw afternoon.
I recall moments I thought I'd never forget.
The cutting breeze awakens my every secret.
The shadowed night casts its dark magic inside my head,
Becoming a colourful canvas of memories from evenings past.
I whisper, 'Goodnight,' to the twilight sky and promise to remember,
Never forget.

Katie Cheetham

SUPERMARKET TEMPTATIONS

It's shopping day and in I go.
I have a list with me
Of all the things I need to buy,
Then, all around I see . . .

Cakes and buns and cream eclairs,
Oh wow! I think, yes please!
I could eat them 'til the cows come home!
Such tasty morsels these.

Ginger nuts and bourbon creams
And chocolate digestives!
Wafers, cookies, lemon puffs!
My stomach's getting restive.

Chocolate, fudge and sherbet drops!
All down the aisles I see
Great mountains of them in full view.
They're calling out to me!

Trifle, ice cream, suet pud!
They're lovely, they're divine.
I see them on the shelves and think,
Come home with me - be mine!

Rice puddings, custard, apple pies!
It's like a fairy grotto.
My shopping cart just yearns for you,
'Go for it.' That's my motto.

But wait, I hear an inner voice.
My conscience calls my name.
'You came in here for *healthy* food!'
. . . But salad's not the same.

Anne Gardiner

AFTERMATH

Flesh revolves and reflects earthly pleasures, encased in glass,
Protected from nil.
Empty skulls floating across permanent blue, drifting slowly to
oblivion.
You can't see the brown earth, it's covered in algae
But beneath the suffocation the insects sleep and dream,
Communism has not been born down there, no choking gas
envelopes the freedom.
Straitjackets do not exist in the world of the free.
But who are you?
Walking on pavements still damp from the previous night's fallout.
Souls that tried to escape, lie rotting in caves, stalactites are no
longer there.
The labour of a thousand years destroyed in one second of fanatical
pleasure.
The trees which once breathed life, gain new friendship with their
gnarled neighbours.
The hills are barren, scorched by the blast!
But the molten earth deep beneath growls in defiance,
Yielding not to the Master who wears an iron gauntlet.
But the rains will lash and the winds corrode, and time; to decay
the glove
The Earth will awaken, pushing forth fingers of life,
First a trickle,
Gaining strength, until it blossoms into a rushing torrent!
Tiny green shoots appear through the blackened soil,
Buds cautiously peer at the sky; sky purified of evil.
The first song of a bird drifts through the unblemished air; and a
baby is born!
Around its neck is tied a label and on it written;
Pity me!

Brian Denton

VOYAGE OF LIFE

Trust is the boat in which we ride
And hope is the mast-head sail
And we travel on, through storm and doubt
In the faith that things will all turn out
And sometimes the journey is pleasant and light
And the winds are very fair
And of the craft beneath our frame
We can become unaware
But sometimes the route demands our all
And overboard must go - the treasures saved
And valued, still, even as we don't know.
But our trusty craft will get us there
To the captain's destination
The further shore and shining peak
Without a hesitation
So we trust to the craft
And sail in hope
Salvation dearly bought
And our journey is what we must focus upon
And how good a shipmate taught
And leave the end to One who knows
Who gave His guarantee
And proved the journey beyond all doubt
At the mast-head of Calvary.

Gill Mainwaring

SCHERZO FOR A SIX-YEAR-OLD

Ding dong, dong ding
I'm sure you all will know the thing
You're sharp enough, I do know that
The sound is just a touch B flat
A little loud and none too low
The little girl next-door, you know
Is having lessons on the piano.

Ding dong, dong ding
I'm sure you all will know the thing
F A C E between the lines
She plays them really mighty fine
Black notes, white notes, with panache
Softly comes a mighty *crash*
Silence then, till once again
There's the sound we've come to know
Of lessons upon the piano.

Ding dong, dong ding
I'm sure you all will know the thing
It's more assured, that sounds quite good
I told you so, I said she could
Practice hard my little dear
Hard upon your neighbour's ear
And one day sweetie you will know
To draw sweet sounds from your piano.

Martin Harris Parry

HORSE CHESTNUTS

They forget how the bricks can hurt
falling from their throw impatient
when time will always provide

these boys want to snatch conkers
before the rest of us are out of bed
like storm-troopers in the dawn

destined to grow into predators
who will drive their tanks or drop
their bombs without remorse.

Tom Hulley

A Palm Cross In My Hand

I'm standing on the Mount of Olives
A palm cross in my hand,
Looking back two thousand years
Endeavouring to understand.
For along this narrow and winding path
Crowds greeted Jesus, with shouts of glee,
Then a few days later the mood had changed
'Kill Him' was their only plea.

I'm standing on the Mount of Olives
A broken palm cross in my hand,
The picture I see of God's great love
Enables me to understand.
We travel the narrow and winding path
As we live our lives each day,
And have a choice to believe in Jesus
Or just let Him slip away.

I've seen the crowds and heard the cheer
When His suffering turned night into day,
And as I leave the Mount of Olives
A breeze blows my palm cross away.

Jean Mackenzie

First Villanelle

The lightning flashed across the sky
As my lover left to go to war
Birds to cover winging by

Would that I could also fly
Take to wings through yonder door
The lightning flashed across the sky

Heart is heavy - eyes are dry
Tears exhausted, flow no more
Birds to cover winging by

To be courageous I will try
Keep hearth and home as days of yore
The lightning flashed across the sky

The time is past for asking why
Or wonder what a war is for
Birds to cover winging by

We'll put our trust in Him on high
His care and comfort ever sure
The lightning flashed across the sky
Birds to cover winging by . . .

Joyce Alice Turner

Discovery

Space
aged them this day.
They were seeking something.
It makes the heart race.

With the light glinting on the wings,
what they found was themselves.
And the world grew at 17,000 mph.

So as the sun shines on science,
and the whole thing reflecting
on the public conscience,
we're gonna walk . . .

I suppose if people are getting up a little earlier and working a little
faster today, it's because of you and people like you. (Of the NASA
astronaut, who was at the controls of the shuttle when it landed).

I'm going to write something. You've inspired us all.

M Jones

My Lovely Sally

I thought at 85
I'd never fall in love;
But as my eyes wonder in deep repose,
A little doggie all brown and fawn:
Lit my eyes.

So proud was I to call,
Her name Sally;
She's like a baby,
With big, brown eyes:
That look at you with love and trust.

She's good at tenting,
And trustful too:
She surely loves you
Through and through.

What gifts of love,
For you to share;
With a gift from God,
Who knows you care.

Mabel Houseman

Dream Of Ane Auld House

The house stood there before me
I think since days of yore
I had a funny feeling
That I'd been here before

The door was dark and solid
The steps were worn and bare
The windows old and battered
Just because on one did care

Even the trees were familiar
They stretched up to the sky
As I approached the doorway
I felt reserved and shy.

I tried the door to open
It slid open with a groan
I went into the hallway
Was I really quite alone?

There was the presence of another
But in my heart I felt no fear
The spirits that were present
Made me feel quite welcome here.

I wandered through the hallway
Ventured up the old worn stair
I went into one of the bedrooms
And what did I find there?

A picture of a girl so fair
Upon a high up shelf
As I gazed at it I realised
It was a copy of myself

Who was she in the picture
Who looked so much like me?
The feeling I'd been here before
Again came over me.

What was it that brought me here?
I cannot quite explain
I knew that when I left here
I would not return again.

I wandered down the stair again
And went into the hall
I left the house and when I looked back
It was not there at all.

E Walker

OUR PATRON SAINTS

St George, the saint of our land,
By your side we proudly stand;
To keep the evil from us at bay
It was the dragon you did slay.

The Irish parade on St Patrick's day,
Through the streets they march away;
With a lot of fuss they leap about;
'It's St Patrick's day,' they all shout.

The Welsh all sing on St David's day;
To him a daffodil they all display.
They then all sing in full voice,
'St David was our greatest choice.'

The Scots all dance on St Andrew's day,
They drink and dance the night away;
The swirling kilt to the sound of pipes
For them St Andrew is just right.

The English are quiet on St George's day,
Going about their business in every way,
But in their hearts there deep down
St George, their patron saint, is found.

Francis Allen

APPLES

At Agincourt the French we fought
There they were soundly beaten
The score then was at least two nought
It was the scrumps we'd eaten
Then when they failed to rally up
As we had done before
They blocked the roads round Calais up
And tried to get a draw.

1066 was just a fix
In spite of what they said
They turned up here at half past six
When we were still in bed.
All English history we know
Is full of quirks and dramas
No Englishman will draw a bow
When still in his pyjamas.

But on the field of Agincourt
We gave it to 'em proper
A lesson they were really taught
And did they come le cropper!
So when the half-time whistle blew
They passed frogs' legs around
Golden Delicious then they threw
Half-eaten to the ground.

The Englishmen stood straight and spruce
The French bewailed their sins
And saw that English apple juice
Did run down English chins.
'Mon Dieu,' the French lieutenant cried,
'There's like le Russet
To help evacuate le bowels
An lubricate le gusset.'

When next with apples you are faced
Buy Cox's, Bramleys, Worcesters,
You'll find that all the others taste
Like last weeks' woolly dusters.
Keep English apples on your plate
Then you'll be pleased you bought
The fruit that English archers ate
That day at Agincourt.

Stan Whomsley

A THOUGHT OF RISKENHOPE IN YARROW

At the head o' the Loch o' the Lowes
At the head o' Yarrow - mirrored the lovely scene
In the late light - green hills mass and form
And autumn brilliance of bracken, and far at
The end - in the darkening water
Polished and perfect, reflected in shimmering
Glass - green meadows and 'Homestead'
Smoke curling up - the still air and down
Through the water - double and perfect
- Alone - shining at sunset - the lonely
Shieling - the white 'Riskenhope'
Long, long ago, so long their sorrows
Now ended, the broken remnant - the
Wasted - the persecuted -
Here in the hills - keep the faith
Paid their strong devotions - up from
White 'Riskenhope' - up from Yarrow
Up still and up climbing the burnside
Deep in the hills, up to the thorn tree -
Far from the valley tracks -
Far from the horsemen of 'Claverhouse'
Hark! To the preacher -
The boy (Renwick) the martyr -
The fair faced - preaching the word
- His last - at 'Riskenhope'.

Isabella Shaw

MY CHILDHOOD CHRISTMAS

I remember so well the Christmases of many years ago
When I was just a schoolgirl, we almost always had the snow
That glistened all around like stars, and carpeted the ground
Leaving our footprints in the snow, we did not make a sound,
As we softly walked from house to house, singing carols to everyone,
The snow still gently falling our footprints almost goes
Lanterns swinging in the breeze, helping to light our way
As we spread our Christmas message to welcome Christ's birthday.
There were snowmen in the gardens, carrot noses and button eyes.
Then at last we reach the vicarage, for hot chocolate and mince pies.
We stand before an open fire warming our hands and feet
Before setting off once more, our Christmas message to repeat
With 'Peace on Earth', goodwill to men ringing out so loud and clear,
And shouts of Merry Christmas and a Happy Good New Year.
These are my childhood memories of Christmas long ago
Christmas tree and fairy lights twinkling in the firelight glow
Hanging up our stockings, too excited to go to sleep, trying hard to
Stay awake, so we could take a peep of Santa in his robe of red,
His sack packed full of toys
For all the village children, all the girls and boys.
Oh what happy memories of Christmases long past
Memories so dear to me, in my heart forever cast.

Brenda Hill

JOE

I'd just like to say, thanks for your loving care.
And thanks for the son and daughter we share.
The years may come, the years my go,
I'm still your Margie, you are still my Joe.

My teeth have all gone, my hair's rather thin.
But you're not to blame for the state I am in,
We've had our ups and downs we know
But I'm still your Margie, you are still my Joe.

I rely on you Joe, on you I depend.
You're not only my husband, you're my best friend.
As we've grown older, as through the years we go
I'm still your Margie, you are still my Joe.

Irene Price

IONIC SONG

Oh, Homer!
Your sea of wine runs deep.
Flooding caves where fishes sleep
On pebbled stones.
Untouched by a tide that barely moves
Beneath a searing sun.

Enchanted isle.
Where once Hellenic heroes, home from war
Displayed athletic strengths.
Wrestling, running, dancing, leaping,
In bronzed and supple arms of maidens, sleeping.
Lips against enticing breasts,
Heads festooned with laurel leaves and flowers
Soon to wake, and dine
On fevered love and heady wine.

Across the bay
The rocks where Sappho leapt.
Lost lovers watched in disbelief.
Then wept.
In the encroaching dusk,
The air is perfumed
By resin from the pines
And myrtle mixed with musk.
Goat bells clang from a distant hill
While the Skopje hoots at the stars.

Dawn is close.
Waiting for a sign
A sun exposed, unclothed by any cloud.
Unabashed, lacking modesty
Will kiss the swelling fruits
Gnarled olive trees produce.
Softening the grapes on vines
Casting shadows 'neath the walnut trees
Competing with contented bees.
Silence broken by the sawing cicadas
And the slap of waves as a caique
Steers towards a deserted shore.

Ann Wardlaw

OUL LAMMAS FAIR BALLYCASTLE

Lammas Fair where you sell your ware.
Come from arts and parts
Rides on horses and carts.

You have your sideshows,
Dancing, singing, to and fro . . .

Tapes of singers
Big Tom, Singing Brickie, John Watt
From country to pop.

At the diamond stand
Plums, fruits and dulse and yellowman.
The towel sale
Promising you a great deal.

Bargains galore
There is lots more.
Clothes stalls, jewellery to your dolls.

Mothers with pushchairs
They are there
Amusements and parks
For children to have a lark.

Chips and burgers van
Ice cream, candyfloss and Coke can
Meet old friends and talk
Go on a seaside walk.

Marie Coyles

BY THE RIVERSIDE

We stepped in doubt, to find the way
To freedom . . . there was naught to say,
Only the river to admire,
Which woke in me a deep desire
To rest, and taste the gentle breeze,
Inching in from hidden leas,
So elusive to discover.

My woollen garment did so smother
Me, so I lay down, to think
Of cool refreshment. In did sink
A lassitude, and soon I slept.

On the placid river crept,
Making little noise . . . slight gurgles
Only, when attention burgles
All one's dreaming, to announce
The cow-hands . . . on their path to flounce
Was their ambition, home to take
These creatures, lapping by the lake,
Whence rose this stream of water cool.

I had no implement, no tool,
Just lay, to rest in this quiet spot.
Onward did my charger trot,
Till out of sight . . . and I was left
Beside this river, heart bereft
Of anything, except the will to sleep.
Onward did the waters weep,
Out of sight, and far away . . .
I slept, with nothing, still, to say.

Charles Hardman

WELL, WELL!

What do we have down on Earth
A year '2000' a brand new year . . .
Will it be pleasant? Or another curse?
Dear gull, my friend, do we really care?

We seem to thrive as we fly,
We quarrel for food that's true but we can escape . . .
Humans? They kill each other, rage and cry
And the treasures of the Earth they rape.

Let's fly away, no need for us to witness
This orgy of science and pain,
Anyway throughout the centuries humans more or less
Survived also. Sunshine, snow or rain.

Come on mate, let's go . . .

Let's soar above the waves and use this patch of the Earth
That a thoughtful: *Zeus* -
Look! Over there, a bird made of metal?
What was I saying? Oh! Aye about a patch made for us?
Tut tut! Not as good as us that 'thing' hey, gull?

Give the humans their due anyway
So let's be magnanimous when we land,
They do try to copy our way,
We'll go down and with our wings shake their hands.

Peace to all men . . . and birds . . .
Hee! Hee! Chuckles *Zeus*.
This is the silliest poem I've ever heard.

Sylvette Gilbert-Sivieude

LONE VIGIL

Each day he sits upon the shore
And feels the wind on his cheek
He tastes the salt upon his lips
And hears the waves at his feet.

He hears the seagulls high overhead
And feels the warmth of the sun
He fondles the tiny wet pebbles
And hears as they drop one by one.

But he cannot see the changing sky
Or the crests of the waves tipped with white
Yet he thrills to the scents and sounds of the sea
And longs for the gift of his sight.

He cannot see the ragged rocks
Or the delicate shells in the bay
So he touches and he listens
As he sits by the shore every day.

Phyllis Hall

UNTITLED

My hip and my heart hinder me
and my head and my hands even worse,
my ankles are bigger for no reason I figure
but I have not as yet ordered the hearse.

A bypass rejected - should I be selected,
was the last thing I wanted just now.
My ambition for longevity with little senility
far outweighs the surgeon's sacred cow.

I've a grand memory for forgetting but never regretting
the times I have spent with the nurses.
With mortality in mind and a most open mind
I'm certainly not interested in hearses.

But my hip and my heart have long been sedated
with pills most people deplore.
So I intend soldiering on and try to prolong
a lifetime supreme - there must be more!

Norman Cathie

THE MENU

I look the menu down and up
To start I'll have French onion soup
A slice or two of garlic bread
The menu list is keenly read
Second course is meat or fish
Chicken pie or gammon dish
Cold cuts, salad or salami
Salmon smoked or breaded scampi
A la carte is minestrone
Au gratin veg or macaroni
Scallops, oysters on the half-shell
Red wine, Chardonnay or Moselle.
Lettuce, cabbage leaves or spinach
'By leaves we live,' a salad sandwich
French fries, mashed or roast potatoes
Peppers stuffed or grilled tomatoes.
Dessert is such a tasty treat
Lemon, orange, sherbet sweet
Chocolate pudding or baked rice
Custard, apple pie with spice.
Finish up with tea or coffee
Cappuccino or fudge toffee
A neat liqueur comes at the end
The menu I could recommend.

Norma A MacArthur

THE SEA WE SAIL

We all must sail the sea of life,
The waves can be smooth or rough,
For some it's a trouble free journey,
But for others it can be very tough.

Some people enjoy every comfort on board,
Their ship gives a passage of love,
Others just stay below the decks
And never see the sunshine above.

Some of us mix with all others aboard
Whilst some enjoy travelling alone,
In each case the journey is their chance,
Each setting their own life's tone.

Some day upon this sea of life
Strong waves will rise and fall,
The worry what tomorrow's tide will bring
Wondering if we'll cope with it all.

We could say that our ship is our family
And sail each day with love all around,
We'll then not suffer from any rough seas
And negotiate life's sea safe and sound.

The waves upon this sea of life
Are what we are, what we do, what we say,
We all have the same destination
Of Eternity, which we'll all reach one day.

So enjoy the journey on the sea of life
For one day we'll come to the end,
Keep the sea calm with our joy and our love,
And that last harbour will be ours to attend.

Harry Ireland

WARTIME MEMORY

We had a happy home life in family harmony,
Our parents showered devoted love and security,
Taught to respect our elders with consideration,
To thank God for our blessings with true appreciation.

Moving at a slower pace before the last world war
Working life was steady, responsible, therefore
There was a quiet contentment and closer family ties
Helping one another when problems did arise.

We only had a radio to keep us entertained
With a toilet in the backyard, miserable when it rained.
Paraffin lamps lit the rooms, no other power had we,
Except the coal-fired cooking range, our only energy.

The declaration of World War II caused turmoil and distress,
Men went to join the forces, brought families great duress,
Women worked in factories to earn a salary,
Wishing for a quick return to sweet normality.

Imprinted on our memories are the sound of sirens warning,
Of German bombers overhead through the night 'til morning.
Dark skies scanned by searchlights to entrap the foe,
Barrage balloons were hoisted a deterrent to flying low.

Surviving on meagre rations no chance of becoming obese,
Afraid in air raid shelters, when would the bombing cease?
So happy the day the war ended, there was dancing in the street,
Held celebration parties, what a welcome treat.
I was only twelve years old when peace reigned once again.
But I still enjoyed my childhood, vivid memories I retain.

Doreen Kowalska

LOVING YOU

My mind takes me back to when we first met,
the warmth of your smile, I'll never forget.
The touch of your hand, the feel of your kiss,
my heart never knew, it could feel like this.
You showered me with affection and love,
my angel sent down, from far up above.
The one in my life, who gives it true meaning,
the moments, the passion, such intense feeling.
You're the greatest thing to happen to me,
realising my dreams, and all I can be.

You're always right there, holding my hand,
to love and support when I'm too weak to stand.
You're my towering strength, my tunnel of light,
unconditionally loving with all of your might.
We've been through it all, the good times and bad,
made each other happy, angry and sad.
But you're always there, right by my side,
filling my heart with this sense of pride.
I never knew I could love in so many ways,
and I know that I will for the rest of my days.

Louisa Dean

ALL IN ALL

Celtic warrior, Celtic knight,
Celtic holy man, Celtic light.
Chalice of life, chalice of blood,
Chalice of the sacred heart, chalice of our love.

Sword of comfort, sword of flame,
Sword of saints, sword of spirits' gain.
Cross of love, cross of shame,
Cross of heartache, cross of His name.

Celtic day, Celtic year,
Celtic sunrise, Celtic sphere.
Mystic lady, mystic man.
Mystic *Lord*, mystic land.

Praying angel, praying child.
Praying virgin, praying humble and mild.
Hearts of diamond, hearts of gold,
Hearts of heroes, hearts so old.

Wanting beauty, wanting sight,
Wanting forgiveness, wanting flight.
Needing me, needing you,
Needing comfort, needing two.

Celtic marriage, Celtic moon,
Celtic faith, Celtic noon.
Secret brother, secret wife,
Secret breath, secret life.

Sacred prayer, sacred power,
Sacred strength, sacred tower.
Shelter in Heaven, shelter on Earth,
Shelter for billions, shelter with mirth.

Hidden vessels, hidden bonds,
Hidden lessons, hidden songs.
Blessed in thought, blessed in deed,
Blessed with grace, blessed in the hour of need.

Holy water, Holy wine
Holy Son, Holy time
Holy streams, Holy food,
Holy rivers, Holy showers,
Holy name, Holy powers.

Catherine Haley

LIFE

Life is such a special thing
Grasp every opportunity that each day brings
We are here for a fraction of time
Be happy, be good and always be kind.

We never know when we walk out the door
What each new day has for us in store
We never know if we have time to say goodbye
To the ones we love most, yes - you and I.

What fate awaits us only God can say
Always have faith and we must pray
For a brighter tomorrow, for hope, for love
And He will guide us - our Lord above.

Christine Hardemon

FRIGHTMARE

In dark trees as I walk with the breeze
I'm filled with a sense of doubt
I thought for a second that somebody beckoned
Then came a sinister shout.

Here in my dreams I can still hear the screams
My imagination is running riot
Running for the door on a moving floor
Then suddenly all is quiet.

Now I'm stood on the street as white as a sheet
Surrounded by faces unknown
As I look through the glass at things from the past
These are the seeds I have sown.

As the shadows are calling I find myself falling
I'm trapped in this dreadful place
In the sinking sands with the grabbing hands
I see the most hideous face.

As I awake in my bed maybe I'm dead
I see white coats all around
With wires without traces and no eyes on their faces
And mouths that don't make a sound.

Locked in a room that's white like the moon
Things are not what they seem
Can't you see it's not how it should be?
Forever trapped inside my dream.

Paul Bowler

THE TABLE'S LAMENT

Here in this dusty place I like
While total strangers pass me by
I wonder what my fate will be
Will someone come and purchase me

I used to be polished with loving care
And placed beside my owner's chair
And every day at half-past three
She used to use me for her tea

But as more fine things she acquired
Of polishing she quickly tired
My lovely surface ceased to glow
'No good,' she said, 'you'll have to go.'

So now in junk shop I recline
No one cares to make me shine
Please someone come and look at me
And take me home in time for tea.

Mary Shepherd

DAD'S POLISHED SHOES

Dad used to march on Remembrance Sunday
Often beneath a scowling grey sky,
He didn't say much as he brushed his best suit
But I noticed a faraway look in his eye.

He carefully combed his wavy dark hair,
A crisp clean shirt would always choose,
And on a spread out newspaper
Vigorously polished his black leather shoes.

Those shoes would shine like glossy jet
I knew it was something to do with the war,
He once told me he'd served in the East
And returned on a boat from Singapore.

A march to the cenotaph head held high
Proud and yet so sad somehow,
But how could I have seen back then
What I see oh so clearly now?

Those cold raw Sundays, sometimes rain
The crowds, the singing, but most I recall,
Dad's polished shoes bright in the gloom
At the end of the day they said it all.

Elaine Beresford

DIAMOND OR A PEARL

There are people in this world that like diamonds
There are people in this world that like pearls
There was someone who liked anything that sparkled just the same
Like the eyes of that sweet old-fashioned girl

No matter what the time or day you would never hear her say
The lonely word of no or sorry I must go
In that old sofa chair - you would always find her sitting there

I guess there will always be a little bit missing
Now that Mum has finally gone away
But I'm not sitting around and keep on wishing
Because I know she wouldn't want it - not that way

I'm grateful for the love that's now gone missing
It will be the finest jewel in my heart
You could never buy this feeling that I'm missing
It will stay with me and fill that missing part

There are people in this world that love diamonds
There are people in this world that love pearls,
But I will always love the eyes that sparkled just the same
From the smile of that sweet old-fashioned girl

I ask you my friend to say which would you choose today?
A diamond or a pearl? Or a sweet old-fashioned girl?
With a love so rare that you always knew would be there
From the sweetest little lady in the world.

Jessie Morton

CHANGE

On taking down the old photographs from the walls,
I observe the beauty of blankness.
And even with the dust lines
And black holes from nail marks
It is wonderfully light and spacious.
And I feel a sense of renewal
As on a fine spring morning
When the world, washed by light rain,
Sparkles with beauty and hope
And the air feels sweetly alive
With endless exciting possibilities!

Jean-Angela Smith

CELEBRATIONS

C ounting all our blessings
E very single year
L aughing through our troubles
E very kind of cheer,
B etter to remember
R egister our thought
A dding written poetry
T hough fifteen years are sought.
I recall small booklets
O nly ones I have today
N ever forget the cards
S ent wherever our friends stay,
I magine there were no outlets
N o way for us to show
P romote our variations
R evise that which we know.
I nspire us with a subject
N othing too austere
T hen we can try writing
  With a glass of wine . . . or beer!

June Barber

LOOKING BACK - TO GO FORWARD - URGENTLY

The words of today burn and explode with new meaning
Seventy-two years ago - when I was ten,
There was hidden screaming
No TV or Internet informed us then!

Then the dogs of war were unleashed
Now again, the canine teeth are bared
From a myriad gun barrels, the cordite smell released
Over continents, human life goes uncared.

For sixty years, the world had the shadow of a mushroom cloud
Now humanity could destroy itself many times over!
While the ocean level may yet provide another flood!
Are we to make ourselves an interplanetary rover?

These are dark forces we face
Yet, we have great powers for friendship and peace
Scientific and technical skills, often misused in a monetary race
Poverty is rife, yet a few million live engorged.

While we recognise the problems ahead
None can escape the daily battle for hope
The desire for life is the force that rules our head
Or we accept, that we have lost the power to cope.

Dave Davis

SPEAKING OF SCHEHERAZADE

Here where Scheherazade told her tales
in tented splendour on cushions of silk
I dream away an Arabian night
as midnight kisses the oasis
and a zephyr from sands
of a silent desert blows warm
perfuming the dark
with fragrance of tamarind and myrrh
illuminating my dreams
returning Scheherazade to my side.
Come my lady
tell me a tale of old Baghdad
let me see again the houris of the harem
dance in their veils of gossamer silk
then walk with me once more
along Euphrates banks
as this night steals away my heart.

Alexander Stubbs

THE LAST FRONTIER
(Dedicated To All In The Conquest Of Outer Space)

The last frontier conquest of outer space
Mankind's final forward, free floating pace
Reach, possess world's light years afar
In Ephemeris grasp the elusive, incandescent star
Ancients of yore worshipped starlit constellation
Wondrous miracle, their idol God's creation
Glistening orbs, stars gleam and shine,
Heavenly diadems in eternal universe shrine
Modern science provides factual proof
Stars Earth-born as our own world in truth
Lustrous reflection of their solar's light
Nestled, as gems surreal, in black velvet night
Mooncast pale luminesce wax and wane more
Powered pull each ebbing tidal shore
Moon nor stars no warmth shed
Daytime by contrast, almighty sun fed
Climatic gentle, sensual or evil phases senses feel
Wind and rain, also form elemental reel
Planet moon, awesome finality, there man has been
Yearning still further explore the cosmogenic scene
Brave astronauts claim compelling awareness, an existence of God
Distant earth shine, enigmatic space lure, praise and laud
Dangerous quest, risking very life, seeming absence of care
Admire brilliant scientists, all involved who share
The final attempt, space rockets to beam
Breach the yawning galactic chasm, is it only a dream?

Christina Harkness

CAPITAL LONDON

London conjures up pictures
Of buildings ancient and grand
From Buckingham Palace to Admirality Arch
Trafalgar Square to the Strand.

The grey stone Tower of London
Silhouetted against the sky
Guarded by Beefeaters clad in bright red
Please the onlooker's eye.

Retracing your footsteps to Mansion House
Where visiting dignitaries go
And all the people in the land
Come to see the Lord Mayor's Show.

The Dome of St Paul's comes into view
Built by Sir Christopher Wren
While by the Thames the chimes ring out
Of our world famous Big Ben.

Then Westminster Abbey, the Houses of Parliament
The corridors of power
From where our country is governed
And watched over hour by hour.

Whitehall; the poignant Cenotaph
Veterans march by every year
In memory of those who won't grow old
Who for us overcame their fear.

St James' Park, Hyde Park
To Kensington's Albert Hall
Where music of great composers
Thrills and delights us all.

Pomp and Circumstance fanfares of trumpets echo
These are the sights and sounds of London we all love and know!

Barbara Fosh

MOTHER EARTH

A higher power has created our wondrous universe and infinite space.
In that vast expanse rotates Earth, our home.
It is blanketed by an irreplaceable atmosphere
which embraces and cushions all.
Pressures of untamed, unparalleled forces are released and explode,
peppering her surface indiscriminately.
The rocks hide their secrets, fossils and precious stones
are petrified in time.
Water in all its guises permeates the crust.
Moisture from the clouds sculptures majestic snow-capped mountains
that hide their towering peaks in envelopes of mist.
All is phenomenal and created for a purpose.
Within the harsh realities of life exists beauty,
which has always been abundant since the dawn of time.
Acting as lungs, the plants texture the surface.
Marvel at the diversity of flora and fauna
adapting and struggling to survive.
Like babies totally blind we cling,
sapping our Mother Earth of her vital strengths.
Don't let her change because we take her for granted.
Are we parasites taking all from our host and giving nothing in return?
Our interdependency on all life forms is paramount for survival.
We must all value Mother Earth,
for every plant and creature is privileged to dwell on her surface.

Audrey Faulkner O'Connor

THE VALE OF EVESHAM IN SUMMERTIME

There is a memory of a path
Across a field, in summertime.
It winds its way to swings and slides,
Goalposts and waiting friends.
All we need to pass the day
In summertime.

The Vale waits silently
Under an August sun.
Only a scattering of birds
Disturbs the summer haze,
Scavenging for food among the maize.

We push and shout and play,
Our noisy games disturb the peaceful day,
But, like the birds, we scatter home at dusk,
To scavenge for food, covered in
summer's dust.

Sheila Seabourne

REFLECTION

Today I have a smiling face
Staring from my glass
Tainted with the frosted ice
And floating in liquid brass.

Yesterday my purse was empty
But every hand was full
Shaking hands on my entry
To a room of merry fools.

Tomorrow, parades will dance inside my head
To snare drums and a thumping beat.
So wrap me up in a cotton wool bed
Before I fall and kiss the king's feet.

Carol Coney

GAZA WITHDRAWAL AUGUST 2005

Jews against Jews,
West Bank evacuation in the news,
Synagogues symbolic and emotional places,
Sacred objects and confused faces . . .
Settlers adamant about their belief,
Their future appears devoid of relief . . .
Political and personal risk,
Today's task must be brisk . . .
Police and army personnel,
Soldiers experiencing personal hell . . .
Settlers sitting on the floor,
Some praying for help once more . . .
Rejection towards Jew against Jew,
Rabbis try to meditate, some do . . .
Others tearfully go towards the gate,
Many worry about their fate . . .
Spiritual and emotional solidarity,
Painful images and unfamiliarity . . .
Immense outrage at intrusion,
Traumatic evidence of today's confusion . . .

Liz Edmonds

THE WINCHESTER CATHEDRAL DIVER

William Walker, diver supreme
Hero of all Winchesterian's dreams
Cathedral on verge of collapse at its east
Subsidence will bring our church down at the least;
Walker descends to the base it is said
Working in darkness is what I have read
Now his work is commemorated forever
His name is the name remembered together
With all of his mates, for they helped as well
For this book to be published his story to tell
How Winchester Cathedral, still standing today
Majestic, inspiring, inviting all to stay
William Walker, here is our decree
That you shall be honoured on a certain day
When all the people in the Cathedral will
Stand and salute their saviour Bill!
Now, on behalf of his grandson Tony
I write this poem as a one-off-only.

Maisie Trussler

WORDS

I tried to write my words upon the wind
But like confetti it blew them all into disarray
I wrote my words in the sand
But the breeze ushered them all away
I spoke my words out loud
They vanished and dispersed with the leaving crowd
On water next, I tried to write
But my words were washed away out of sight.

In metal, I tried to place my trust
But my words merely faded with time and rust
On paper, stone and wood I know
My words will eventually be turned to dust
Is it the words I write
That seem to make them vanish overnight?

Then realising I must begin again to write
Not with ink or pen but with a zeal and passion
I must write my words in the
Hearts and minds of men
Then and only then will my words forever last.

D Seiglow

WINTER

The cool winds,
The frozen snow,
As it was
Years ago,
The lost years,
The day's fears,
Loved and unloved,
Wise and unwise.
It was draughty,
In that big house
Where you and I lived,
A house of myth
Where I read
And read
Beautiful books,
Stories of meaning
Passion and honour,
By love were
We brought here,
May love be the way
Again; never frozen
In those winters of
Loss and hardship;
May love bring us safely through these years too.
Amen.

N Evans

UNDER THE GREENWOOD

Come my fair sweet and pretty one
Sit beside me 'neath this tree
Escape the heat of noonday sun.

I've made a chain of daisies spun
'Twill crown thy beauteous company
Come my fair sweet and pretty one

Why even bees do cease their hum
Cool in clover field they gladly
Escape the heat of noonday sun

My heart dear maid is quite undone
In fullness of my love for thee
Come my fair sweet and pretty one

I'll finish what I have begun
When we in shadow of a tree
Escape the heat of noonday sun

That you and I can soon be one
Will you consent to marry me?
Come my fair sweet and pretty one
Escape the heat of noonday sun.

Sheila Scott

MY SISTER

Though in age we're some six years apart
We grow closer each day by the ties of our heart.
We lead our own lives, go our own way
But you're in my thoughts each and every day.
When I'm feeling down, full of despair,
I know without doubt you'll always be there.
You don't ask questions, you give me the space
I need to recover at my own slow pace.
You're part of my one, part of my whole,
Part of my being, part of my soul.
You don't need gifts of chocolate or flowers,
The joy that you bring is uniquely ours.
When it comes to sisters you're a cut above.
My own special sister, the one that I love.

Christine Collins

THE HEALERS

He placed the card upon the shelf; the girl, her sightless eyes,
Would never see the love it brought and cry with brief surprise.
She sat in silence, while the grief was gripping at her soul;
Her mother fighting for each breath, too desperate to console.

The man sat slumped behind the screens, restraining needs to yell;
While doctors muffled, shuffled feet and wondered what to tell.
The wife of youth and now of age pushed him round the grounds,
The dreams of their retirement now a wreck of mocking sounds.

The chaplain felt the pain around of all that 'Might have been,'
Wondering often how to help; or else to leave the scene.
We care for patients in their beds, relieved to see them leave,
But often fail to notice those who care and hope and grieve.

Spare a moment's thought or prayer for those who stand and wait,
Those who yearn, the ones who learn to share and bear the weight.
Be gentle with the mother who, for want of tears to weep,
Stays by the bed of her dear son a sleepless watch to keep.

Remember all love's bonds that get so tangled in life's storms;
The loss that draws the wayward heart, and helps strong ties to form.
Remember that the human heart may weaken, wander, wane;
But also waken, pulse and fly aroused by others' pain.

The ones who walk the corridors, who sit in wards and yearn,
Discover sweeter springs of care well up from what they learn.
The rhythms that immerse their lives, the ups and downs they feel,
Go to form those pearls inside, and healing gifts reveal.

Martin Winbolt-Lewis

THE DAY THAT MOVED THE WORLD

The Earth moved off its axis
On the day that shook the World
When the earthquake 'neath the Ocean
Unleashed a Tsunami fast unfurled.
The wave sped across the Indian Ocean
At 500 miles an hour
And many unsuspecting countries
Were lashed by its mighty power.
People on the beaches
Were sucked into its spell
And flung back upon the shoreline
In a living/dying hell.
The waters swallowed up the land
And all that stood thereon
And bashed the buildings all to naught
And most of life was gone.
Over two hundred thousand died that day
There were left but just a few
In coastal regions of the lands
That had come within its view.
The people they lost everything
Their loved ones, homes and livelihood
But they found in all the chaos
Great humanity that was good.
For the mega force of nature
That moved the axis of the World
Unleashing unknown terrors
As to their deaths were many hurled:
Also moved the hearts of people
Across the Nations looking on
And many deeds of loving kindness
Amidst the horrors really shone.

Mollie D Earl

JED

When you were a little lad
You brought me a chocolate Flake
And you'd hang over the fence with your sister
And say, 'Can we come in for some cake?'

The next years you fetched me field mice,
So they'd be safe from your cats,
But your cats made friends with my dogs
And the cats brought me dead grey rats.

You must have released dozens of frogs
Into the sanctuary of my pond
And while you were emptying my biscuit tin
We seemed to form quite a bond.

You'd sit in the big old chair by the fire
Drinking hot choc from a mug,
And the eldest cat packed his bags and moved in
And slept on the fireside rug.

Now you're a man and you tower over me
When you stoop to give me a hug,
But you still sit by the fire in my back room
And drink mocha choc from a mug.

Frankie Shepherd

AFRICA

The clouds are heavy with impending rain
while the wind sings its song again and again.
The land lays waiting open and dry.
River basins rippled; empty, as the days go by.
Shrivelled scrub shimmer in the dusty haze
of the sun's ever-remorseless rays.
Bleached bones stare with empty eyes
waiting to be filled, while the eagle cries,
its wings spread, soaring over barren land,
searching for scurrying creatures in the sand.
Rumbles of thunder rent the air
giving hope to those who despair . . . then . . .
heavy drops of rain start to pattern the ground,
at last the christening as the rain comes down.

Elizabeth Morton

BEAUTY

Does beauty sit upon a shelf
And think of no one but herself?
A pretty package wrapped with pride
Can hold a selfish heart inside.

Some people hold their teddy tight
And then they cry into the night,
Some people don't like their eyes or nose,
Their ears, their hair or hands or toes.

A loving heart that beats within
Is beauty deeper than the skin,
Such beauty seen within your eyes
Might be your loveliest surprise.

The land of pleasant dreams is the place
You learn that beauty is not a face,
Because of good things that you do,
Your heart of gold will come shining through.

The lesson that you'll learn is this,
Selfish does what selfish is,
But you are beautiful because,
Beauty is what beauty does.

Josie McClung (11)

TRU'ANT

On my way to school I decided not to go,
Instead I went a-walking to where lovely flowers grow.
My mind it started thinking for I knew it was not right,
I remembered what my mother said,
She said, 'Be home soon tonight.'

Too late, I thought as the school bell in the distance I did hear,
The teacher will be counting all the children now I fear.
I sat beside a little stream, the sun was warming me.
I closed my eyes and lay my head against a big oak tree.

The day was full of promise, the sun was shining bright,
But when I woke the sun had gone and the day had turned to night.

My eyes filled with tears, I knew now I'd been a fool,
My parents would be worried sick,
Oh I wish now I'd gone to school.

Jack Holt

THE PASSING OF TIME

She sits before the mirror now, her eyes reveal the truth,
How cruel time has ravaged all her vanity and youth.
She was so conscious of her looks, her smile has lost its sun,
So sad when one remembers how she looked at twenty-one.

Her skin is pale like water it's so starved of sun and air;
Those lips that once kissed babies are no longer soft and fair;
Those trenches on her forehead give each wrinkle, fold and line,
A dignity and presence when you're nearly eighty-nine.

She sees her hair is astral grey which once was Titian red.
Th'injustice of old age has left its mark on every thread.
Her hands are stiff, arthritic, and no longer soft and warm,
Those long attractive fingers have lost all their shape and form.

Her burdened shoulders sagely stoop, her sticks strain at her feet;
Each breathless step she walks with care her slow, unsteady beat.
She cannot bend to touch her dog that lies beside her chair,
Or give each room the semblance of a 'newborn' mother's care.

She cannot hear the soughing wind that courts the early dawn,
Or those bel canto blackbirds on the dewy-crested lawn.
The robin daily sings upon the open window sill,
Not knowing when its song is sung its notes no longer thrill.

The effervescent sparkle of her eyes has lost its blaze,
Like flames of dying embers they no longer cheer the gaze.
She's watched her beauty passing like the moon when on the wane,
When curtain calls have ceased then she'll be twenty-one again.

John Jordan

PROGRESS

Seven years ago I took up my pen
And started to compose poems again,
My first poem was published in the school magazine
When I was about the age of fifteen.

I did not start again until I was eighty-three,
It was your advert in the paper that tempted me.
And now through the powers of Forward Press
My desire for writing I cannot suppress.

I hope to continue for at least another five years
Then I shall be one hundred, oh I hope I'm still here.
Thank you for the help and encouragement you give to me
And all the other poets since you began in 1990.

May you continue to print all our work
Because I can assure you we poets won't shirk
To support you all in the future years,
So I'll say good luck, God bless you and many cheers.

Phyllis Ing

IN MEMORIAM
(For Peter, La Bassée, 1940)

It echoes through the land, a sudden cry!
The white sun is trapped by a small pool of melting snow.
A frozen branch of moss leans sideways
pushing the rimmed dark leaves aside.
The years have passed,
and still the dipper flies from stone to stone
and sparrows vaguely flock in search of food.
So life, which is one moving scene from place to place,
moves on . . . counts . . . calculates,
and seething, drops into a muddy ditch,
love . . . life . . . and laughter.

Two years ago . . . pain reeks along the narrow road
stretching its gaunt arms around the green moss-covered trees,
yelling its way through all the twisted bracken stalks . . .
'And these shall come again,' shrieks Life
'Two years ago today,' spits Death.

Field mice, magpies, pigeons whirring by,
a horse plunging in a madder coloured field,
gay faces,
large strong hands.
Laughter . . . life . . . then death.
And yet leaves flutter still,
fish in sunlight swim in clear, cool, bright water
and lilies flower in tiny ponds.
Sometimes the smell of the sea
comes slowly over the pale sand . . .
. . . but the cry is all over the blue sea.
The cry is everywhere in the world.

Marjory Doyne

THE ROSE

When I behold a perfect rose
I think of you my wife
And see unequalled memories
Through all our married life

I see a heart that is strong and true
Encased with love and caring
Surrounded by a velvet cloak
Like a rosebud so comparing

When tears like rain on petals fell
And our grasses were not so green
Through winds and storms and troubled times
You stood solid and serene

Like the rose your love is a fragrance
That has scented through all of my life
I will cherish and love you forever
My rose, my love, my wife.

Sid Harris

AN ANNIVERSARY ACROSTIC

A nother year has passed away for a
N ew one to encroach upon our consciousness. Greater
N ewer hopes and expectations fill our minds, perhaps more
I ntense and ambitious than those we've thought of hitherto.
V isions of new aims and aspirations
E ncourage us to feel that there could be better things in store.
R ough it may have been at times in inclement conditions, with
S torms and troubles to upset the senses with minatory peril.
A new year, or even a new day, fresh and clear, can soon
R evive the strength and embolden the spirit.
Y ear by year we can be thankful for the past and hopeful for the
future.

Gwilym Beechey

VINCENT MY BROTHER

Your eyes of madness in deep despair
Pierce my heart with scream of ghost
And though you shot away your dreams,
Your rainbow shines from barren walls
This vision of beauty haunts my soul.
Church that stands under sky of Prussian blue
And stars keep watch over holy ground,
Fields of green grass rooted in earth
Blood red poppies move in the breeze.
A gypsy girl with dusky brown skin
She smiles at you with precious touch
With innocent eyes you looked upon
This woman with sweet embrace.
Those swirling clouds in torment spin
Over a village blessed with sound of bell.
Your name was called from shadows cold
Aflame with images of lightning celestial bliss.
You spoke in tongues with fire of love,
To strangers lost in that strange land.
Vincent, I bleed for you, do not bleed for me
Ablaze forth our hearts to Heaven's sweet domain.
We brothers of the sacred brush
Washed in precious images of France.
Dark cloud of eyes that follows you
Through fields of wheat in joy do sing.
You a child lost in a storm,
That silent night you cried again.
In that asylum you wept jewels red
On a grave in garden white with snow
You walked in black and were baptised in fire
And anointed with the tears of sorrow.
The nuns looked on in shocked surprise
Upon this man rocked with naked pain.
Vincent do not grieve with sorrows born
Because one broken seagull lies on the shore.
Oh spirit of mystery with scent of love
Those yellow sunflowers smile for you.

Thomas Hull

THE HEARSE

The hearse moved slowly, in front of me,
Ahead, her coffin, I could see,
My heart, so full of pain,
Should I not, see her again.

Tears filled my eyes, for the want of she,
How I wish, it could be me,
Lying where, the flowers are fresh,
In the back, of that lonely hearse.

The hearse wound, along its way,
People stopped, as if to pray:
Heads bowed down, eyes cast low,
Knowing where, it did go.

The hearse took, that long last ride,
How I wish, she was by my side,
Loneliness, I feel in here,
Please be with me, oh my dear.

The hearse took her, to the grave,
By her side, she will save,
That lasting, place for me,
Is where I long, long to be.

The hearse, now empty, does ride home,
I am standing, here alone,
But one day, it'll bring me too,
And, I'll lie, next to you.

J Lanigan

FOR EACH OTHER

Treasured vow
Personally sworn
Together now
Marriage born.

Gentle touch
Smile returned
Unspoken word
Lovingly earned.

Ever supportive
Patience untold
Encouragement, give
Desires unfold.

Visions shared
Consideration too
Criticism spared
Loving you.

Time together
Talking abounds
Companionable silence
Completeness found.

Attentive listening
Thoughts discussed
Mutually finding
Equal trust.

Laughter joined
Kindly meant
Sometimes tears
Fleetingly spent.

Regrets unknown
Contentment now
Faithfully shown
Treasured vow.

Gerard Chamberlain

CONGRATULATIONS

My hat rests on the table, still yet holding the brim,
Awaiting to make the three hurrahs to welcome the founder in.
The day is set for accolades for those with forward vision,
Who can gainsay such style and verve with cynical derision?

With wide response of swelling verse to meet the selected day
Bringing forth a flood of talent surging to have their say,
Coaxing thoughts from wilted pens to ensure deadlines are met,
Trading words in lexicon gamble before the stanzas are set.

Despite the hectic hustle and swirling responsive choice,
Ideas are not mustered at a whim to seek a viable voice.
Being a non-competitive type and merely just a tyro,
The whirligig of wind and bluster is strictly for an autogyro.

The blandishments to raise the style I find are quite a damper
So, with due deference I am, thus, not looking for a hamper.
Suffice to say that if my verse can sway the eyes to read
I have gained some satisfaction to satisfy a personal need.

Let me be in no illusion, my verse is merely a meagre stint,
Though surely this is not a race to grasp some place in print.
So my message goes, to all who surely can aptly guess:
'Good luck to all and best wishes to those producing Forward Press!'

Jack Patterson

POETRY

Reading - talking
Listening.
Writing thoughts,
Meeting friends.
Getting ideas.
Dreaming -
Posting letters,
Waiting delivery.
Excitement -
Published!
Well known? Known less . . .
Getting chance.
'Forward Press'

J Ferguson

A ROMAN SONNET

Rome, the wonderful eternal city,
From the air we saw the Colosseum,
Threw a coin in the fountain of Trevi,
A bus tour in Rome, herself a museum.
A visit to Keats' house was a real boon,
We saw Tosca's Castel St Angelo,
Mad traffic and a quarter silver moon,
Photos of Piazza del Popolo.
The highlight was a prayer in St Peter's,
The holiness was present all around,
Saw the Spanish steps, finest of features,
For the entire day, we were both spellbound.
We flew there for lunch on low budget wings,
When you've had cancer you do crazy things.

Mary Robertson

WEEP NOT FOR ME

I can hear a mother weeping
On a hill called Calvary
Where our dear Lord and Saviour
Died, nailed upon a tree,
They say it was for sinners
That he hung and suffered there
Was he innocent or guilty?
Did those sinners really care?

With a sword wound in his side
A crown of thorns upon his head,
'Father please, please forgive them,'
Were the last words that He said.
Mary must have often wondered
What wrong had Jesus done?
I will weep for His poor mother
For the loss of her dear Son.

Many years have swiftly gone by
Since that awful dreadful day
Many sinners have been saved
But some have lost their way,
Why did He die for sinners?
Why did He die for me?
For His mother's ghostly weeping
Lingers still on Calvary.

Glory be to God the Father
Glory be to God the Son
Praise and thank Him for His mercy
And the love that He has won,
Weep not for me for I'm the sinner
Weep not for me I kneel and pray
Please forgive me O my Saviour
I was wrong, now I obey.

Jean-Ruth

SKINNER

(Inspired by William Blake's 'The Tiger')

Tiger, tiger, black as night
In the day, he is bright as light
He hunts all day
To give his victim a horrible fright.

He does hunt high and low
With his huge eyes all aglow
He sees a victim in the grass
He jumps at it with teeth like glass.

Now he is fed
He's off to bed
He needs to rest
So tomorrow he can beat the rest.

In the morning he stretches his limbs
Ready to hunt for his dinnertime things
Do you know what he is called?
His name's the Skinner, so you have been warned.

Shane Hinton (13)

FRIEND

Tap, tap every morning I feel Echo's paws
Softly touching upon my face
He is saying, 'Mum I am hungry,
Feed my tummy with all and sundry.'

It is said Siamese will attach
To one person to meet their match
I chose Echo, Echo chose me
We are the best friends that could ever be.

Echo talks non stop all day
'Mom look at me! I want to play.'
Woe betide if he is ignored
Because he will strum his vocal chords.

I cannot resist his big blue eyes
He cannot be naughty even if he tries
I would be lost without my friend
No other feline could ever contend.

Michelle Hinton

THE PLACE WHERE I LIVE

All is quiet and peaceful
No stress or violence
Trees in the fields, flowers blooming
Rabbits playing, foxes hunting
Pheasants, pigeons free to fly
A little girl plays on the swings
Strolls home for her tea and bath
An elderly couple sit in the garden
Cottage door and windows open
The milkman, postman, bus driver
All have a cheery greeting
Girls and boys enjoy their disco
No drugs or drunks to cause trouble
The word 'war' has no meaning
Each one to his own religion
This is the place where I live.

Doris Warren

How Precious Is Life

The rain falls like tears upon the windowpane
A young life snatched away with no reason, no blame.
A child cut down whilst in its prime
Makes no sense, no reason, no rhyme.
The sun shines through black clouds, the teardrops glisten
As the wind sings a song through rooftops, through trees, for ears
to listen.
Never again will this child walk in sunshine or in the darkest night
To show how much, how precious is life.

The rain now ceased yet the window still holds
The tears of a million glistening drops on a morning unfolds.
The child whose laughter can no longer be heard
Will play on a conscience, unspoken, not uttered a word.
And so as the autumn leaves fall to the ground
Naked branches of trees all dewy wet, beneath their clothes just a
mound.

The child who had so much to live for
Gone now no longer to walk through this door.

And so as the window its tears clearing away
As starts the beginning of a brand new day.

But low the rain falls again, how many tears can there be
The conscience arises as wet birds hurriedly flee.
Oh the tears of life, the storms of true love
A child snatched away into a manic storm up above
Will there be no end to this heartache and strife
But then to remember, how precious is life.

Now comes the anger as thunder loudly does roar
A conscience pricks as tree branches do fall.
A mighty fist takes a final blow
Questions of why, no answer as the tears still flow.

There seems no end as once more the chilly wind cuts like a knife
To finally recognise how precious is life.

Maggie Strong

Natural Theatre

A cavernous emptiness
Hewn by the arduous toil
And passions, by men
Of yesterday.
This monolith of
Strange peaceful
Emptiness,
Vast as the dawn.
Grey rock, weathered
By time.
Quietness. Solitude.
Broken only by the wind
Whistling through the trees.

This natural theatre
Where are the players?
The stage is empty.
Only my thoughts can see
The changing scenery,
Hear the music
Played with love and emotion
By people
Searching for perfection.

G Burgess

On Life's Highway

It's not what you do, it's not what you say
It is so very true, on life's highway, I love you
We both live in a world of trouble and strife
With sorrow to be found, in all of the countries
Take for instance what nature did, oh boy how I wish
We could together my love, to make things come right
For the troubles that are in our world today fight
The devils that rule the countries and peace in sight
What a lovely world that would be my love all things bright
Let us live for today, think about tomorrow
I steal your heart but never steal or not borrow
It's not what we say, it's not what we do
It's always our love for each other loving wife and mother
We fell in love and did, yes darling, did discover
We, my dear, you bet were made for each other
On life's highway, you are and will always be my lover
It's not what we both say, not what we do
Forever and ever my love, I love you, on the 14th February
'Valentine's Day' my darling, you will always be
My love my mate, my loving said 'Valentine'
Always together, will always suit me just fine.

Tom Sexton

Here Life

When life has ceased to let your gaps
Fill up with aspirations
When you are here and dreams are there
To stare as fascinations
It has become your endless space
That doubt has left you yearning
When all it is looks clear as light
And has sometime been burning.

Whenever you can feel the doubt
And stall at what's forgotten
Look out and see it's not a time
To sigh or throw your lot in
While many people bottle up
And many wane in pity
You can be sure there is a price
To all that's smart or witty.

This is a symbol or a thought
From someone who has noted
That simple habits, easy dreams
Are real, not sugar coated
So let your mind go on its way
And tell your heart to wander
Along its sparkling quest for life
Allow it time to ponder.

There are a million faceless birds
Who fly in flocks of purpose
All striving for the unknown place
Where predators won't surface
You feel the ground and glimpse the sky
Anticipation grips you
How can agendas line your path
And bind with ties that lips do?

You are a splendid vat of hope
Without your joy, we're frightened
Call out your song and let them go
Be resolute and lightened.

Cherry Hullock

SLEEPING

If I was back in Eden times
'No fear'
I'd have in me
The grass would be my blanket
Leaves would cover me.
I'd lay beneath the twinkling stars
The moon would shine on me,
Crystal clear water
Clean air I would breathe
Until morning light appeared.

Mary Taylor

THE PORTRAIT

She waits in the wings brush poised like Monet's
Paint palette overflows with flames, gold and reds.
As soon with a flourish while awaiting her cue
To be called with her canvas - autumn season is due.
Impatient yet eager she's waited so long
As summer kept autumn on hold with her song.
The mists met the trees still shimmering green
Reluctant warm sunshine - autumn sadly deceives
But with gentle persuasion she starts on her quest
Quietly at first brushes tip the first hedge
To enhance changing colours, this is her pledge.

Like the circle of life increasing the pace
With reckless abandon the desire is to race.
Provide vivid colours - magical powers unfold
Unseen we all wonder this joy to behold
Eager and forceful exhausted yet proud
Her picture complete - takes a bow from the clouds.
We watch and we wait her skills unfulfilled
The carpet is yet to be laid as leaves yield
Crisp 'neath our feet - colours still bright
Autumn lady delivers another delight.

Do we all ever wonder this dream to inspire
As small eager fingers trace colours of fire.
This artistic reflection lay dormant and new
With a smile she retreats - her work is on view.
The lady's portrait of colour was long overdue.

Irene Siviour

CASUALTIES OF WAR

Yesterday I heard a man cry
He sobbed just like a little kid
He was afraid of the future
What lay in store for him
And his family.

All around him lay
Broken bodies of men
He had known for years
They lay in the rubble
Of empty shell casings
And blood and s**t and snot

Yesterday
I wept with this stranger
I too sobbed just like a kid
I am fearful of tomorrow
Even though I'm now dead.

I Stoles

AN ENCHANTED EVENING OUT

A visit to an Australian restaurant with a lass
Turned out to be an experience without surpass
The atmosphere was romantic, the food was good
My chicken was tremendous being cooked in wood
My companion was lovely making me feel proud
Interesting conversation with laughter so loud
The service and wine could not be beat
The hills were magnificent as viewed from my seat.

On the journey home we saw a wonderful sight
The most beautiful loch shining in the night
It was as if the car knew it had to stop
As I pulled into a spot verging on a huge drop
The birds were chirping in the trees around
Ducks swam at the edge of the swampy ground
When the lass moved closer and planted a kiss
I knew then I was in for a night not to miss.

We kissed and cuddled for ages that night
Our romance had blossomed and it felt right
Eventually I drove the lass home to her house
Kissing goodnight being as quiet as a mouse
Then home I went and quickly off to bed
With sweet dreams filling up my head.

George Alexander

NATURAL HAZARDS

A super-bug, a super-bug
Mutates from bird to man,
And doctors only shoulders shrug
As death flies man to man.

The global heat, the global heat
Will change the way we grow
As agriculture can't compete
And dusty deserts blow.

The next ice age, the next ice age
Will then take o'er the globe,
And any left from desert's rage
In icy shrouds will robe.

The cosmic ray, the cosmic ray
Will burn us through and through;
So cancer cells will have their day
Until we perish too.

The Yellowstone, the Yellowstone
Will blow its top one day;
Then those nearby as one atone,
Their ashes fired in clay.

An asteroid, an asteroid
Is spinning through our space,
And it is one we can't avoid;
Farewell the human race.

So we must go, so we must go,
While life with death competes,
Where Dartmoor streams still sweetly flow
And vigour fills our streets.

Godfrey Ackers

LIFE IS LIKE THE SEASONS

Life is like a year -
Full of seasons, all most dear.
It opens like the early spring -
A newborn babe - awe inspiring.
As spring unfolds in the countryside,
Fields, flowers, birds and animals preside,
So the baby grows into a child,
Blossoming in character, meek and mild.
He has characteristics all of his own,
As has every animal when full grown.
After spring comes summer, with hot sunny days,
And the boy grows through his teenage years.
He blossoms forth into a man of pride,
Caring now for his own true bride.
All feels good like the summer sun,
He watches over his family, every one.
Then as the years pass by, so the summer fades,
Trees lose their leaves in the autumn shades.
His family age and begin to diverse,
His son goes to college, his daughter's a nurse.
Time moves on into autumn tide,
And he's left once more at home with his bride,
Growing quietly into a Darby and Joan,
In the autumn of life, now his children have gone.
Adjusting once more to the season of life,
Just happy to be with his dutiful wife.
As autumn brings in dark nights once more,
And the wintry weather knocks on the door,
So the couple grow older - no more do they roam,
Together they await the Reaper, who'll take his harvest home.

Jean C Pease

DESIRE

I listen to silence,
Trapped in thought,
Awoken by your tender touch,
Your lips pressed so softly against mine,
I speak, you whisper,
Let our bodies escape our mind,
Let our souls unite in passion,
I seize your hand,
Your heartbeat, I feel against my chest,
I slowly stroke your face, a passionate kiss,
Lust boiling over,
You place your soft finger against my lips,
I shiver, I spoke, you speak,
Let us be free,
Let our mind break free from our fears,
While we swim in the sea of love,
You hold my waist, I gaze into your eyes,
We both lean in and fall into a world of forbidden enjoyment,
Craving your smell, seduced by your touch,
Fierce connection,
Unable to control my feelings
I let go,
We explore new places of pleasure,
I feel your breath against my skin,
We endure new heights of passion,
The explosion of love occurs,
And silence again,
I open my eyes searching,
Missing your caress,
Anger appears,
And you disappear.

Alicia Francois-George

A COUNTRY CHILDHOOD

I wish England was like it used to be,
When we had scones and jam and cake for tea
We sat and discussed our school day,
When homework's done go out to play
Scrumping apples, climbing trees
Sometimes stung by angry bees,
Church on Sunday, hymns to sing
Thank You God for everything
A day by the sea, we went by train,
Fingers crossed, don't let it rain
Building sandcastles, a donkey ride
Paddling in the ebbing tide.
Tired and sleepy home by ten
Life was very different then,
I know that I was truly blest
Because I saw England at its best.

Brenda Peel

STRANGEWAYS RIOT APRIL 1990

Strangeways Prison, grim and bleak,
     Prisoners rioted
          It's news this week.

The governor, the warders,
Taken by surprise.
As violent men turned on them
Such hatred, in their eyes.

The hardened few ran amok,
A riot had started throughout the block.

Rampaging and wrecking
Was all they had in mind
Up onto the roof they went
To plead to all mankind.

What will they achieve with all this abuse?
More deaths, more violence, what will they choose?
And when it's all over, will they atone?
Or carry on, like Al Capone?

E Gosney

AGIOS FAYENTES' BELL

Proud it stands on hilltop high
Watching over sea and sky,

Held by wooden stakes and hope,
Giving life and bringing hope.

Forged in nineteen fifty-four
From the remnants of the war,
Meant to be a monument
To all the lives that then were spent.

Surrounded by the rubble scree
Of earthquake back in fifty-three,
When lives were lost upon this isle
And where we linger now, awhile.

The bell that peals but little now
Sees passers by who ponder how,
This place so quiet and serene
Was once laid bare in nightmare scene.

I like to think that we now know
Something of the long ago,
When Agios Fayentes' lonely bell
Echoed out its tale to tell.

John Cook

LATE LOVE IN A SUMMER GARDEN

It must be more than twenty years at least since I performed beneath
these trees.
Nervously striding through the grass inexpertly shouting
Shakespeare to the sky.
How many times in melancholy dreams have I returned?
Lysander seeks his Hermia in the wood near Athens still.

It was my first time acting in a play, hers too, she told me shyly at the
start.
The old hands encouraged us, treated us as friends, called us fellow
thespians.

Took us to the pub and bought us drinks,
Flirted gently, gave tips on acting in the open air

Each night she cautioned, 'Lie you not so near,'
As she (reluctantly I thought) pushed me away.
Each night we danced off hand in hand into the moonlit wood,
Applause still ringing in our ears,
Hugged each other rather longer than was strictly necessary,
Joyfully swapped congratulations and enthusiastic thanks.

I had it all planned, at the party after the last performance
I'd ask her to go out with me, a meal at a little Italian restaurant
I knew.

But the last performance done, she quickly left,
I heard soon afterwards she'd moved away, no one knew where.

Many other parts I've played since then, a seedy pimp, a holy saint,
a don,
And as the hair grew thin and the waist grew large, frustrated
Husbands and ignored,
Exasperated dads,
Even a bear once, and I have the photographs to prove it, a nun.
But never again have been, or found, a true love, until now.

When fat buffoon Sir Toby fondles, woos his Maria, cuddles, kisses
And caresses her,
The youngest wren of nine, twice deserted and divorced, but comely
still.

Tonight's rehearsal done, I'll drive her home,
I will not make the same mistake again.

Brian Ford

THE CHILD

Come child, take my hand
Together we'll explore the labyrinth of life
Stumble on the steps of early years
The falls, the searchings, bruises, tears
Lessons learnt.

Come child, choose your path
Conform, rebel, be friendly, fierce
Each way erodes an early innocence
Each choice for you
Proves new, a fresh experience.

Come child
Face the maze of friendship, jealousy
The pain of learning life can hurt
Excite, depress or thrill
One path is flat, the other undulates.

Cross the bridge of adulthood
gently loose my hand, touch fingers
release you
In the maze's core
The lessons learnt.

Pauline Brennan

THERE ARE NO CLOUDS

Cast off the mooring ropes at bow and stern
Head out into the early morning mist
Hoist the big mainsail, free the jib, and turn
Feeling the filling canvas make her list

The venerable diesel chugs and splutters
Its smoky wraith lingering in our wake
We weave our way between sloops and cutters
Cleaving across crests beginning to break

Waves slap the hull and slither down the deck
We've left the strident seagulls far behind
The lighthouse beam pales as we pass the wreck
Whose rusting iron ribs still groan and grind

We round the point and catch the tidal flow
Astern, a fresh Force 4 lends us its wings
No engine needed now. I go below
And listen to the sounds that silence brings

An inner peace surfaces in this calm
Quietly floating all one's stress away
Silence with stillness - a heavenly balm
That heals the damage of each crazy day

I go up top and breathe in salty air
Now, far away from the jostling crowds
I adjust my eyes to the sun's bright glare
And scan the horizon - there are no clouds.

Alexander Blackie

MY LITTLE FLOWER

Roses are red
Violets are blue
Daffodils are yellow
Daisies are white
You are indeed my little flower
For sure a delight
Such a beautiful sight
My little flower beautiful and bright
A little flower from a bud grows
To be a bright flower
You a little girl from a baby have grown
To be a beautiful girl
Yes my beautiful little flower
My beautiful angel princess
Colourful and bright a pure delight
You are indeed a beautiful sight
A pure delight
My little flower Jordana
You do certainly brighten up the day
With your beautiful smile
With your beautiful laugh
My beautiful Jordana angel princess
Just like a little flower
So beautiful and delightful
You Jordana are beautiful and delightful
Yes roses are red
Violets are blue
Daffodils are yellow
Daisies are white
You are indeed Jordana
My little flower
My angel princess.

David J Hall

FORBIDDEN LOVE

My dearest love, I should not tell you how
I long to hold you close and oh so tenderly.
It's wrong, I know, to want you as I do
But I can't help the love that burns inside of me.
I dare not ask, my dear, that you return my love,
I know that you my own can never, ever be,
Soon you will leave me only memories
Of those sweet moments when I held you close to me.

My love, my love, words just cannot express
The love for you that fills my overflowing heart.
I lied, my dear when I said I could check
The love I've felt for you right from the very start.
My dearest, dearest darling, loveliest, sweetest one,
I've never dared to tell you how your many charms
Bring joy to me and bitter sweetness too
Each time I hold you in my eager, trembling arms.

Don't take from me the joy that you can give.
The days we do not meet are days so full of pain.
I count the seconds till we are alone
And I can hold you close inside my arms again.
Don't ever think, my dear, by casting me aside
That you can save my breaking heart from pain and grief,
The moment's past when I could turn away
And only in your arms can I find sweet relief.

And so, my love, I ask you only this
To let me have such love as you feel you can give.
Please darling, please, I ask that I may have
A touch, a kiss that I from day to day may live.
Too soon now you must go, dear God let time stand still,
Make every hour a day, make every day a week.
My dearest darling, make me happy now,
For soon instead of kisses there'll be teardrops on my cheek.

G Baker

UNTITLED

The memory of that day we met still lingers in my mind,
Time spent together, precious moments fill my thoughts
But fate was so unkind, the time had come
To say goodbye, left an emptiness in my heart
'Cause all I want is you my love and never more to part.
My love for you grows stronger each passing day goes by,
Tears fill my eyes with sadness and I begin to cry.
I cry because I've lost my love, I knew for many years,
The only things I now have left are *memories and tears*.

E Brooks

WIDE AWAKE NOW

The vandals now
Live with the goths
And other sackers of Rome.
Their painted
White knobbed skin
Parades the sunny pavement
From the council estate
To the shops.
Their shouts and stone throwing
Raise no phalanx
To defend us
For we treat them as our own,
Pretending there are no barbarians
Only those less fortunate
Than ourselves.

Matthew Hustings

NATURE'S PEACE

The evening was still
And still the river,
A silver mirror
Imaging high
Quiet hill and sky.

The cool air around
Bore only such sound
As seemed to be
Part of tranquillity.

Broken by croak of frog,
Hidden in reed and bog;
And the muted trill
Of a mistle thrush.

Then - deepening hush
As creatures settle;
Undisturbed by man,
To peace of natural habitat.

Jean McPherson

HOPE RECYCLED

Once upon a time
When the world was young
We lived, laughed and loved.
The sun always shone
And daisies grew on the embankment.

Wars came upon us.
Battles like loves were lost or won.
The world grew up!
Cynicism was born
And innocence was gone forever.

Leaders smile benignly.
They talk, shake hands
And promise to change the world.
The songs they sing are not new,
But still their rhetoric impresses us.

The world has aged, and its
Battle scars are many.
But in our optimism we are still young;
The sun still shines.
And in blissful naivety
Daisies still grow upon the embankment.

Pat Chamberlain

MY LOVE

As I lay down my weary head
Hoping to sleep, but no, instead
I lay awake thinking of you
And of our love, so warm and true.

But as the night ticks slowly by
I wonder what went wrong, and why?
Why did you have to go away?
Left me alone to face the day.

I know our love will never die
We are forever - you and I.
I will wait for you, come what may
For you to help me on my way.

Knowing that you'll be there for me,
To renew our love eternally,
Gives me the strength to carry on.
Until my life on Earth is done.

Antoinette Beards

MORNING AWAKES

Like a mantle cloak upon the dew
The early mist appears
Rising slowly in full view
Then suddenly disappears.

While the golden morning sunlight
Awakens the break of day
The clouds in flight
Slowly fade away.

And in the morning air
Refreshed by the early dew
Flowers begin to stir
While songbirds herald the day anew.

J Mangan

THE QUEEN MOTHER

Inestimable, inimitable, beautiful lady,
Revered by the world, adored by the nation,
Your 100th birthday,
We greet with elation.

Your feathery hats,
The special wave of your hand,
Your dignity, your grace,
Acknowledged, through the land.

Your courage, compassion -
Pain and grief you've been through -
Bereavement you've suffered
But your faith remains true.

Your understanding of everyone,
Your wonderful smile
Warms all our hearts
In Queen Mother style!

We all hold you high
In the love of our hearts
For the loving understanding
Your radiance imparts.

Jane Finlayson

OUR FATHER

Sitting around him in a circle,
Someone asked, 'Teach us to pray
As John taught his disciples.'

He thought for a moment, then began:
'Our Father,' - we repeated after him,
'Who art in Heaven,' *how sublime*, we thought.
'Hallowed be Thy Name,' - *what beautiful words!*
'Thy Kingdom come, Thy will be done,
On Earth as it is in Heaven.' -
We smiled and nodded our agreement.
'Give us this day our daily bread,' -
Somewhat embarrassed, we remembered
The times we'd forgotten to buy some.
'And forgive us our trespasses as we
Forgive those who trespass against us.'
Peter shifted uneasily, and we all
Looked shamefacedly at each other.
'And lead us not into temptation
But deliver us from Evil.'
Judas flinched, as if a nerve had been touched,
And averted his gaze.

'Father, forgive us -
We know not what we do.

Maria-Christina

GOD'S WONDERS

All things are as nature did intend
The lambs with all their fleecy wool
Go skipping over dale and hill.
He made the flowers that smell so sweet
That grow so prettily around your feet.

He made the bees and all small things
And also little birds with wings.
He made the moon and stars so bright
That twinkle brightly in the night.

God also made the beasts
And animals mild
That live so peacefully in the wild
And also the little child.
How grateful I should be
That He made all these things for me.

Sandra Pitt

WINDOWS

Open windows beckon sounds and smells from cluttered streets
And those who have lived long, gaze out at their diminished world.
Big Mac litter swirls and swivels like a frisky pup,
Then dies killed by the crannies of the corner shop.

The Refuse Monster with his fetid breath eats early in the morning
Devouring with his jaws of steel the remnants of the Big Mac meal.
Then stately Left-Hand Drive majestically in his wake
Rotates his brushes overriding grit and dirt.

And those who gaze upon a now diminished world
Embrace the dawn with ever-open arms,
The sound, the sight, the smell of newly laundered streets
Delights, refreshes, renews, rejuvenates.

Mary Froggett

SPECIAL OCCASIONS

Twenty-five years have passed
Since the day we said I do
Twenty-five years we have spent together
And I still love you
It is our silver wedding day.

Now another twenty-five years on
We have spent together
Where have fifty years gone?
And I still love you
It is our golden wedding day.

Now sixty years we have spent together
And now we are getting old.
A long time has past since we said, 'I do,'
And I still love you
It is our diamond wedding day.

Maureen Rosina Batchelor

GOLDEN YEARS

Ooh, celebrations, how I love them
Lots of garlands, balloons and strings
Mountains of food and all good things
Sunshine and flowers
Dressing up for hours and hours
Dancing with the one you love
Birds flying, are they doves?
I did it all when I was young
So bring on the dancing girls and
Let's have some fun.

Pam Eggleston

AUTUMN

Red, brown and gold, the leaves are falling down
Soon they will be scattered all around the town
Shiny, brown, conkers peep through their jackets of green
They are the biggest I have ever seen.
The horse chestnut trees stand majestic and proud
And red hips and laws grow all around
Bushes of holly are in the hedgerows
They are fine bushes that ere grow
Their red berries are a symbol of blood
Shed by the Lord up in Heaven above
Now He reigns in perfect glory
We can all recall the story
White mistletoe is also seen
Amongst the bushes so serene
Oranges, leeks and tomatoes red
These are the produce we are fed
Chrysanthemums, pink, yellow and white
They all make a very splendid sight
Crusty rolls and large brown bread
These for the *Harvest Festival* bred.

Beryl O'Brien

ANNIVERSARY 1945-2005

We must never forget the debt we owe
To the brave young men, sixty years ago,
Off they went to fight a war
In a faraway land called Japan.

They were worked to death from dawn
To dusk without any food - not even a crust,
If they tried to escape and were caught by a guard
They were made to dig their own graves and hung on a tree,
There to remain for other prisoners to see.

Unspeakable torture they suffered for years
And they bore it all through blood, sweat and tears.
Their bodies were scarred and oh so thin,
But their courage was strong and filled to the brim.

I was a girl all these years ago
When this war was being fought far away from home,
And so it turned out the war was won
In that far off land called *The Rising Sun*.

Anita Todd

THE KITTENS

Five little kittens adorable and sweet
Five little kittens playing at my feet
Five little kittens with your eyes of blue
You're full of tricks and pranks I simply don't know what to do.

Five hungry kittens sardines for your tea
Five little kittens as happy as can be
Five naughty kittens climbing everywhere
Swinging from the curtains, and clawing at my chair.

Five noisy kittens you really are a scream
Five busy kittens are you running out of steam?
Five sleepy kittens curl up in your bed
So I can watch you tenderly and stroke your tiny heads.

Five little kittens entwined around my heart
You have grown so rapidly and now it's time to part
Five little kittens each go your separate way
I've grown to love you all so much, if only you could stay.

Millicent Hewitt

UNDER-ACHIEVER

Surprising, how many at the funeral.
Nowadays you'd call her an under-achiever
Always on the edge of a dither.

Of course the boys came first with father, they always
Did in those days - education too.
Girls washed-up and mended and cleaned the boots
And donkey-stoned the step and ran the errands.
Boys got out of everything..

We were brought up not to shove ourselves forward
And to keep out of the papers.
I didn't take any notice - you know me -
But Sophie, she was too shy and hated her freckles
And got pushed around.
She took it to heart, this 'turn the other cheek',
Never stuck her neck out, nervous of meeting people
Then she would feel a drip and cry buckets.

She did have her bits of talent, yes.
Once a musical visitor heard her trilling
In the next room and thought she was the wireless -
Offered to have her trained but she shied away,
Frightened of opportunities. Not the right time,
She said, she was needed at home - but she never told mother.

She could paint too - distinguished, someone called her -
But never made much of it. It was the children
Then, I remember, made it the wrong time.
She hid behind a wall of excuses,
All tense and tangled up.

At seventy-four she couldn't hold a brush
And her voice croaked. Everyone managed fine
Without her. She knew she was nothing
And often had damp hankies.

Then the Lord had need of her.
So that was all right. It didn't matter at all
That she was nothing. She didn't have to waste
Good dying time feeling inadequate.
I hope it can be the same for me -
The acceptance, I mean.

Olive Culshaw

THE POWER

You'd better stay, don't have to run
You felt the pain, now feel the sun
All the good work has been done
You are the best, you are the one
Back to life you come
From out of the darkness
And into the sun
There's nothing to fear now
You are the one
Chosen by God's angels
To preach what you hear
You have the strength now
You have no one to fear
You've been reborn
You have the power
Live your life, give your life
Year after year, minute after minute
Hour after hour
When you're gone and your spirit is free
We'll remember that you conquered over Satan's might
You have the strength
You have the power
You were blind
But you saw the light.

A P Richardson

PRUSSIAN BLUE

There was a gentle crescent moon
Where I walked along with you
In a land where the darkest night
Was a shade of Prussian blue.

White horses rose up from the waves
And pranced upon the shore
The sea receded back again
Much calmer than before.

Strolling through enchanted groves
Mixed fruits grew on every bough
Daisies opened at our feet
It all seemed right somehow.

The air was filled with lilting song
A nightingale sang from every tree
And in the coppice on the hill
Wild deer that did not flee.

Rabbits were scampering unafraid
They fed on moonbeams from our hands
In the stillness of the hour
Foxes frolicked on the sand.

Hypnotic scents from fragrant flowers
Under their spell I walked with you
There was a gentle crescent moon
And the night wore Prussian blue.

June Worsell

CREATURES OF THE UNDERWORLD

In the glowing of the sunset, showering colour all around
There is much to be remembered, of the life that's underground.
There are creatures in the darkness, that do their daily toil,
They seldom see the brightness as they live beneath the soil.

We do not see them working as we would wish to do,
For they are very timid and run at sight of you.
They build their homes and shelters, each little piece an art,
And toil and sweat like we do, for each must play their part.

They too have many problems as day by day they live
And also have the hardships this world of ours can give
And in their life they've enemies for this they must prepare
'Cause wind and rain ne'er asks them what time to come and where.

So each must be in readiness, for weather's hoary hand
And make the homes they live in strong and firm beneath the land.
Not only weather keeps them inside the little homes
For in the waking daytime, the ignorant human roams.

It's not because they're cruel, they just don't understand
That 'neath the soil they're treading exists another land.
These creatures have a life to live, much similar to our own,
They can't protest like we do, or give a fearful groan.

Their homes just go on crumbling and tumble round their ears
As we walk in the countryside increasing all their fears
So when walking in the paradise of all these creatures small
Please watch your step, it's not too much to ask you after all.

Errol Johnson

THE DEATH OF SOCIALISM

An ordinary house brick with a red ribbon tied around it.
Placed in a bulletproof high security glass cabinet.
Kept in a building secret from the general public.
The thing that makes this brick special isn't the red ribbon
But because it was made from sand found on Mars.

V Scytere

THE WEEKEND

Weekends are a busy time
Loads of washing on the line
Lawns are cut and gardens dug
Spray-gun out to kill a bug
Cars are washed and polished too
Kids fed up with nowt to do
Perhaps we'll take them to the zoo
Tomorrow if it doesn't rain
A visit to the beach again
My goodness what a pain
Roll on Monday
But all's in vain
Next weekend will be the same.

Terry Rowberry

MIDSUMMER

Midsummer day, the sun is high
Above is blue, a cloudless sky
Sit quietly in the cool, cool shade
Enjoy the beauty God has made.

Wander slowly across the lea
Nature's flowers are there to see
Watch bumblebee and butterfly
Maybe a dragonfly float by

Pause by the pond, yellow flags abound
Hush! Very quiet, not a sound
See from the reeds a moorhen glide
Two tiny babies by her side
A sparkling fish leaps, down again, *splash!*
Kingfisher darts, blue lightning flash.

Stroll lazily through the woodland trees
Feel a cooling summer breeze
Wood pigeons cooing, rustling leaves
See lacy shadows sunlight weaves.

Rabbits scutter as you near
Make a sound and they disappear
Bright-eyed squirrel escapes up tree
Then sits to watch, 'You can't catch me.'
There's brush-tailed fox, don't think he'll stay
One scent of you and he's away.

Amble back to the cool, cool shade
Reflect on the beauty God has made.

Dorothy Margaret Smith

WALK TALL WITH ME

Walk tall with me on the lakeside of love,
Come walk along the meandering paths of the lake
Of flowing waters, gently moving with their glimmering reflection
Of the deep flourishing love, of your heart.
Come trust in me.

Come listen to the melodious birdsong,
Whispering softly, *I love you.*
Accepting you as you are,
The tune of care and compassion, entwining two hearts as one,
Branches stretching out to the world, singing of God's love.

Come fill your heart with laughter and be happy,
For that's what love is about!
Sharing your pathway with others,
Leaves not a single doubt.
That God is love.
Get in touch! Connect yourself to His line,
Why not give him a shout!

Tracey McConnell

THE LAST BIOGRAPHER

I am the minder of his fame,
Researcher of his soul,
Keep watch while rash historians
Evaluate his role.
As enemies become our friends,
And friends become our foes,
While battles are turned inside out,
As scepticism grows.

Like driftwood from the Internet
Tides scatter and replace,
New facts collide with memories
In history's vast space.
The last biographer works on
Till all have had their say.
Official secrets, faded, tired,
Clutch grudgingly at day.

I am the keeper of his fame,
Researcher of his soul,
Companion in the loneliness
Of Judgement's final toll.

Gillian Thomas

THE UNHOLY MATRIFUNNY

Throughout the ages all marriages
Were known as the holy matrimony.
But today many ended up costing bags of money.
At first that love was sweeter than honey,
But afterwards it just went funny.

Relationships are always breaking down
In the country, in the town.
For all kinds of different reasons,
Minds are always changing,
Just like the four yearly seasons.
While some are chopping and changing,
Some are rearranging.

This one was named convenience, marriage,
It works like the horse and carriage,
Sometimes slow, sometimes fast,
But never ever seems to last.
Another one named pay to stay
Which doesn't last a single day.
Another one named come what may
Which taught the sinners how to pray
Or how to find another way.
They made their vows to say I do
Knowing that they were untrue.

After endless counselling and much discourse,
Many still went through with divorce.
A marriage could climb into the brain,
And cause someone to go insane.
Committing murder or suicide,
Also some to run and hide,
From those in which they did confide.
Many are enjoying true love, lasting marriages,
While some continue to live like savages.
It's sad when our holy matrimony becomes unholy matrifunny,
Costing millions of bags of money.
We can't blame the lawyer nor the judge,
When matrimonial love turned to hate and grudge.
For they neither cheat nor rob,
They are only doing a job.

P Richards

THE SHELL

The clear water
The shell just out of reach
It looks so beautiful down there
I go deeper and deeper.
The waves are high, taking the shell away, further from me
But I want that shell so much.
It's not like the rest, it's special.
Now on the shore they are calling me to stop, don't go further
Don't . . .
But I don't hear
I don't want to hear
I have my own dreams.
The shell whispers to me
Calls to me
Makes me forget my fears
Promises things I've always dreamed of.
And a passion makes me plunge into the cold depths
Fighting, striving, almost drowning in the wreckage of life
Doing all I can to find that elusive thing
But it drifts further and further away.
And I think if only I can reach that bit further
Do that little bit more.
But the more I try, the more it drifts away
As though mocking me with its beauty.
As if to say, 'Here I am. I am Adonis but you can never touch me.'
And when all is lost, when all is desperate
All I can do is watch hopelessly
As a young, powerful sea claims its prize
And you are lost forever.

Christine Rowley

WHY ON EARTH?

We are all born into this world naked and new
Destined to struggle and work, apart from a few
Life dishes out the cards of the game
To most obscurity and to others some fame.

Fairness is not present at the first moment of life
Lots are fit and well, while a few are dealt only strife
We take for granted our sound limbs, hearing and sight
The less fortunate put up with their plight.

So as life for you goes on and good things become great
Remember the ones not so lucky and think of their fate.
When you have toothache or just a bad hair day
Given the choice would you choose their way?

Don't moan about the weather or trivial things
Count your blessings, enjoy today and what tomorrow brings
Savour the richness of life all around
In nature so many things to be found.

Take in the beauty of a blue sky summer day
Relish the clouds that throw rain your way,
Enjoy the good fortune of being able to do
Anything you want for others, and for you.

Look in the mirror and like what you see
A good hand was dealt to you and to me.
In the great scheme of things on this Earth
For some reason we are all different at birth.

A level playing field is what we all need
Enough food to spread around and to feed
The starving young kids mankind produces
Every person on Earth, all have their uses.

But the reason of life's lottery is not yet clear
Religions try to explain, but trade mostly in fear
Thank your lucky stars you are OK from birth,
When the less fortunate can only ask, why on Earth?

Carl Nixon

7TH JULY 2005

8.49, commuting for 9am start
On underground train 'midst London's heart,
The crowds above jostle, weave and dart
To sign on time sparing late night depart.

Carriage's rhythmical swaying leads to daydreams,
Holidays, dating, musical themes,
Innocent workers, would-be Hakim,
Judged and found guilty our British regime.

Grim suicidal bomber shouldering rucksack
Mingles unnoticed hand under sack,
8.50 detonates! All pitch-black!
Explosion burst! Where he once stood bomb flak.

Immediately driver led with soothing flashlight.
'Everyone follow, keep me in sight!
Leave injured for doctors' skilled insight,
Paramedics helicoptering to site!'

Those uninjured aided travellers slightly hurt
Sprawled in carriage debris, shocked, inert,
Passengers' future, sharp-eyed, alert
For terrorists using force to subvert.

8.49, some travelled to work by red bus,
Others detoured if station delays sussed,
One spotted 'hiker's' rucksack flap fuss,
Raced downstairs as bomb blast blew top from bus.

Loved ones winged quietly to celestial gateway,
Remembered, recalled, more loved each day,
Always young in memories will stay
Freely returning in songs or word play.

Hilary Jill Robson

THIS QUIET ROOM

I sit alone in this quiet room,
As darkness softly falls,
Where the dim outline of pictures,
Seen like shadows on the walls,
And I think of my three sons;
Of days that used to be,
For the distant past still lingers,
In an old man's memory.

Once again, I hear, from this quiet room,
The voice of a clarinet,
Playing a favourite concerto,
Or a stately minuet,
Then an oboe plays a haunting tune,
That brings a wayward tear,
And a flute soon adds its silvery tones,
To the music that I hear.

For my sons were all musicians,
And played in concert halls,
I hear them still, if I listen,
As darkness softly falls,
But my thoughts are tinged with sadness,
When I sit here all alone,
In this quiet room filled with memories,
Of sons who have long since gone.

Ralph Davis

RAIN-GOD

Born of the rain the statue cries
When it pours, stood here so long,
For 3000 years it's been worshipped
And adored.

At one with time now showing its age,
Cracks have appeared in this silent sage.

Thousands have gathered to show their respect,
To marvel at this wonder the ancients have left.

Shrouded in mystery you remain an enigma,
How did they build you, and what were you built for?

Thousands of dawns have passed you by,
Thousands of sunsets have said goodbye.

And still you stand in your jungle home,
A silent sentinel, a testament to a time
We'll never know.

David Horan

BIRTH OF JESUS

Mary and Joseph travelled all night
For somewhere to stay,
There was nowhere in sight!
Tired and weary
Starting to despair,
Then finally someone answered their prayer.
A stable they found,
From a long distance,
Is this a dream or is this existence?
There a beautiful baby boy was born
Not a time to be forlorn.

For in the eastern sky a star was shining.
Filled all around with a bright silver lining!
Not far from it
Three pairs of eyes are looking,
These three kings are in for a booking,
People arriving from everywhere
Is that baby Jesus?
Ssh, it's rude to stare.
There He lies in a manger of straw
The newborn King,
A perfect picture to draw.
So this is why we celebrate Christmas,
The Son of God's birthday,
Christ mass.

Charlotte Penfold (19)

I MIGHT HAVE BEEN

I might have been, the poet who told his tales in verse.
I might have been, the actor with Shakespeare to rehearse.
I might have been, the general leading armies for a cause.
I might have been, the high court judge laying down the laws.
I might have been, the doctor who fought against disease.
I might have been, the captain who sailed the seven seas.
I might have been, the athlete as our flag was proudly raised.
I might have been, the dancer whose skills were always praised.
I might have been, the famous star who filled the world with song.
I might have been, the honest man who righted every wrong.
I might have been, the little child who sat upon your knee.
I might have been, the guiding hand when it got hard to see.
I might have been, just anyone, it's difficult to say.
If *they* had left me with my *life* not taken it away.

Felix McCabe

AMBER EYES

I stand so tall with bark so tough,
I stand so broad, always in a rush.
To look inside would be so dark,
To search within would leave its mark.
My rings are tight away from view,
From ages past, from me to you.
Within the rings my child does lay,
Behind the bark to live each day.
The roots go deep within the soil,
To draw life's breath from our eternal coil.
It's only when the shell feels pain,
Does the amber run like a tear of rain.
Within the gold the child is seen,
His past and present, all he's been.
He watches out and knows so well,
The cost of dreams he wants to tell.
The branches stretch to touch the sky,
To find potential in the amber eyes.
The oak stands strong through wind and rain,
Through sun and breeze to keep me sane.
My life the oak will see the end,
It's kept me well and stayed my friend.

Ricky N Lock

THE THINGS I TOOK FOR GRANTED

The things I took for granted -
Long ago when I was young:
The bluebelled, primrosed woodlands
And fields in which to run.

The tadpoled ponds to skitter on;
The stepping stones, those summer songs;
The laughing brooks, those first love looks -
Have sadly all but gone.

Oh! Take me back sweet zephyr wings,
Take me back I pray;
For the things I took for granted -
Have sadly gone away.

Was life so full of innocence
Seen through the eyes of youth?
Or was it just enlightenment -
Having had first sight of truth?

Still my heart and soul will always stay,
And my spirit fore'er in fields will play:
In woodlands that the golden primrose gild,
And glades that royal bluebells filled -
Are with me to this day;
For the things I took for granted -
Have sadly gone away.

Roger Oldfield

DARKNESS

Like lost demented souls, tossed
by dark swirling water
drifting aimlessly with wind, tide
and silent undertow.
Weird, worthless debris,
like prehistoric predators, reptilian shapes
with amputated limbs, sun-bleached, white,
half buried in the sand.
Now cast high on a desolate shore
above the sombre, grey sea,
they sit in defiance of the journey,
to redeem their loss.

James Fraser

LOVE'S NEW MOON

We wandered along on the wet firm sand
Hand in hand by the light of the moon -
The light rippled with the ocean waves
As they washed quietly in on the pebbled seashore.

In this beautiful moment as we strolled in the moonlight
The stars shone bright around the dome of light
Efficacious in its brilliance -
In the stillness you could hear the crickets -
As they clicked their even song.

In this nocturnal time, a time, so like -
Being at the threshold of a new time -
Shared with new love.
At the beginning of a new relationship
With nature, with God, and with man.

E Montgomery

WINTER CHRISTMAS SUNSHINE

Darkly shaped mountain skies besides shimmering
Winter sunshine exotic days like this
Busy Christmas shoppers gives a lilt to their
Steps such fine weather one can hardly miss
So much to do, no hassle but excitement for quite a few
Seagulls flying to their winter abode
Darkness is falling towards the end of the cool of the day
Kittiwakes are trilling they soon will follow in the same way
Nature's beauty so amazing which is beyond our grasp
Winters on this planet inspire all our thoughts
What more could one ask?

M Nickholds

WINTER

Clear night, starlight,
Moon bright, silent might;
Signs that winter now is here . . .
Trees are naked, stark, austere
As they stretch towards the sky;
Their leaves on the ground - to die.

At times white frost envelops all within
Its reach - a sparkling brilliance, a velvet sheen.

An eerie she-wolf call
Echoing through the night,
The tu-whit tu-whoo of the owl,
Little birds shelt'ring till daylight:
A snapping twig, a creaking bough,
Winter is surely with us now.

Patricia Kennett

LET ME BE THERE

Am I not yours for good or woe
How else can friends prove true?
Tell me what breaks and brings you low
And let me stand with you
So that when the night falls tremendous
When the last lamp burns low
And one of us or both of us
The long, lone road must go
Look with your dear eyes into mine
Give me a handshake true
Whatever fate our souls await
Let me be there, let me be, there with you.

Lady H

FLOWER IN THE FOREST

Visiting a forest glade
All alone and in the shade
A solitary flower I did see
Neath a spreading walnut tree.

A beautiful orchid of azure blue
Speckled with spots of a yellow hue
A brilliant sight beholds the eye
Giving pleasure to the hoi polloi

Further on for all to see
Festoons of ferns 'neath a Christmas tree
Red berries of holly and ivy too
Late November, Christmas soon due.

Driving home for toast and tea
I quite enjoyed my jamboree
It lifts the spirits the forest glade
Especially the orchid in the shade.

D Squires

NO LOVE TO HOLD

As William Wordsworth put it!
Child is father of the man.
This child is a very fuddle man
And affected by lack of childhood love

Which damaged him completely.
When he reached for those apron strings
Was pushed away with waxy belligerence
And crawled to a corner to bathe his wounds.

Found solace when he joined the army
And fought for Queen and country
During the Korean war
Which was after a spell at racing stables.

Nowadays tries to block out
The bad memories of yesteryear
Indulging in strong beer and spirits
While listening to classical music on another planet.

Francis Hughes

YORKSHIRE

Yorkshire great county of the North,
Acres of moorland, heather and gorse,
A walk through the Dales, sights not to miss,
God's picture painted by angels kissed.

City, town, village, all worth the seeing,
People warm-hearted, think of others' being
Families deep-rooted, help one another,
Parents, grandparents, sister and brother,

The folk in these parts are proud, loving, true,
Work very hard when the work's there to do,
Times sadly change, Yorkshire will live on,
Her arms outspread, reaching for the sun.

My own roots go deep, born a true Yorkshire lass,
By gum have to say it, my people have class,
Dialect reight luvly, when I speak it feels good,
My heritage a part of me, I thank Him above.

May the white rose of Yorkshire bloom for evermore,
Its perfect petals, win hearts by the score,
Let all lads and lasses continue the line,
Then future children will walk the Pennine spine.

Muriel Rodgers

DELIBERATELY PROVOCATIVE

You make men your audience
Know how to work a crowd
They love your naughty laugh
Especially as it's loud

I don't play along
Bigger things to worry about
Petrol going up
And getting this government out

So that makes you provoke me
You seem to love me under stress
Think because I'm angry
I'm oblivious to how you dress

Weak men cannot handle
How you act like 'Jack the Lad'
Playing them at their own game
Being risqué and bad

Believe me I'm not weak
You could never be more wrong
When it comes to protecting you
I'm very, very strong

And behind the big bravado
I know you can be shy
Though few would believe
Or ever understand why

They've never seen you vulnerable
They've never seen you cry
But that's when I want to hold you
And never say goodbye

Keith Large

CHINESE PERFUMES

Puzzle me,
A riddled opium scent.
Upon huge red leaves
And orange stems.
Satin brocade dragons,
Whisper joyous whimsies.
Languorous oils,
Jars musk rimmed,
Patchouli pungent,
Steeped velvet.
Novice, cast thorns away.
Master, fill a soft palm.
Scatter the groves of cedar
Where beauty
Is a humble wind.
Cathay sail
Virgin junk's
Pristine jade water
Girdle the white,
Drizzled peaks.
A temple box,
Buffed pebbles,
Incense infused,
Willow-patterned attar.
Anoint, our contemplation.

Wendy Milner

KEEP FIT

Keep fit, that's the key to life
As it's good for you, as it's simple
Exercise to follow, keep fit and
Be healthy.
It will grow on you, it will keep you young,
And beautiful inside
It should be practised for all walks of life,
It could be for few times, or more,
As it keeps your heart feeling happy, 'Happy.'

Dancing with music is good
For you, to enjoy, keeping fit is vital,
As it helps you to maintain a good lifestyle
When you are old and grey
Keep fit and stay healthy,
And the world will be bright and sunny.

F Jackson

REASON TO BE

I sit and watch the heaven's door
Open up amid the clouds,
Like lightning bolts the sun bursts out
To reform and restore
All living things on the Earth's floor,
I stand and feel vibrations
From the very core
Reclaiming my soul to leave no doubt,
I walk and hear the crackle
Of autumn leaves underfoot,
The morning mist now cleared,
Every sight and feeling tells me
I should not have feared,
This new day has arrived
And I've done more
Than just survive,
I've seen the sun and it's given me
The very reason to be.

S Barnard

WHAT ARE WE?

Within the structured orbits of our reality,
Meditations, helices of spirituality
Break the metered bonds of here and now;
Like heavenly stars forming the plough
Freshly tilled our stardust's harvests yield
Awareness, comprehensions, truths revealed.

Anchored links, gripping gravity entwines
Earthbound illusions of our narrowed lines,
Yet latent horizons have always been
Shrouded in unconsciousness, unseen.
Ripples of possibility, quantum wave
The thinker is the thought in essence brave.

The phantom shapes of consciousness dance
Resculpting peripheral images of chance.
As joyous songs pervade such actualities
Resonating harmony's capabilities.
The eyes of the soul again behold
The ensuing stardust trails men unfold.

Music of the mind blends with every key
Recalling ubiquitous melodies set free.
Forever is born from perpetual death
Harmonious infinities given breath.
Time through men's lives made manifest
Stars of eternity at our behest.

H D Hensman

THE MILL

Tucked in a corner
In a Yorkshire town
The mill stood proud.
Flagged yard,
Men loading sacks,
Lorries waiting around.
Friendly wave, go inside,
Magic for a child.
Massive space,
Sneezy dust
From flour and grain.
Peaty smells, jutey sacks,
Footsteps all around.
Ride down the chutes
A special treat. Sleeping cats
Dreaming dreams
Of scurrying rats.

The mill is gone but
The magic lives on.

Eva Harper

ROUND THE CLOCK TEMPERATURE

You give me fever.

Y ou raise up my temperature high
O verwhelmed by this love am I
U ntil stars fail to shine in the sky.

G uess that I had no defence
I t was love, with no recompense,
V iolas and roses I bring just for you,
E uphoria of my heart is yours too.

M emories of bliss, how they shine,
E ach evening, our love was divine.

F orever my darling, you'll know
E xcursions to romance pleases me so.
V iolas and roses I bring just for you
E ndlessly hopelessly devoted it's true
R ound the clock fever, persists over you.

You give me fever.

Joyce Hemsley

THE MIRROR OF THE SOUL

The eyes are the mirror of the soul,
How true, when we are angry they
                    are as black as coal.
They fill with tears, when we are sad,
And are belligerent, when we are bad.
Some eyes just sparkle, shine, and are
                    full of fun,
This is how our hearts are won.
There are some blue eyes that glint like steel,
These show hearts that do not feel.
Soft brown eyes mean a heart of gold,
And a warmth of spirit will unfold.
Blue eyes, that are wide, and shine,
Are beautiful till the end of time.
The love in the eyes of a child,
Can change form gentle into wild.
Eyes that are sincere and dream all day
Are unusual and kind in every way.
The benign eyes of the elderly,
Endear each one to you and me.
But the eyes that come from Heaven above,
Are the eyes of a man and woman in love.

Olive Young

FITS LIKE A GLOVE

So much oxygen, but I still cannot breathe
This box is empty, but to move, I heave
The air feels like gas and the box feels like lead
Imagining, yet unvisioned inside this full head
This concrete we walk on, this earth that we live
With hand like fist, not taught to give
Taught to have and keep for ourselves
Leaving our children to choke on these shelves
We need to fill our children with joy and with hope
Instead we teach them to fight and show them how to cope
To make a point you need to make a stand
To refine this life and create a new land
Fashion becomes when just one person dares
Yet a freakish creature if no one shares
So what will it take for this world to know *love?*
Find it within, so it fits like a glove.

Marsha Leone

THINGS THAT WERE, THINGS THAT ARE

*(This poem was dedicated to my mother who lost her sight through diabetes,
and is now no longer alive)*

In my world of darkness, for now I cannot see,
I was once well sighted to see both you and me,
My hands that were once busy, made things with loving care,
Are now so still and idle, blindness I cannot bear,
My white stick helps me, if only I could see,
What is that buzzing by me? Perhaps a bumblebee,
I miss those beautiful colours I saw when I had sight,
The world is so dark now, without the bright sunlight,
Those that see must help me now to go from place to place,
Where is that blessed bathroom? I have to wash my face.

Rosina Choyce

PEGGY

The little lady looked so frail,
her eyes so red, her face so pale,
her hair awry, her wrinkled skin
almost transparent, paper thin.
The sprightliness had disappeared
on that grey day so greatly feared;
the day her husband breathed his last
and left her grieving for the past.

'It's so final,' she said, and wept
some more, knowing she must accept
death's heavy hand, the loss, the grief,
as though some strange but clever thief
had crept into her house at night
and stolen from her all the light
of life's fire, leaving her alone,
abandoned, lost in her own home.

The ticking clock, the empty chair,
the rails of clothes just hanging there.
The people came but now they're gone
and silence reigned; it felt so wrong.
The tears returned; with heavy heart
and faltering step, she made a start
towards tomorrow, on her own
when she would face the world alone.

Marjorie Haddon

WATER

W ater, water
A qua cool
T urquoise coloured
E ver pure
R iver roaring, it's fantastic!

Emma Towes-Phillips

DANCING SHADOWS

Like dancing dervishes on a snow clad lawn,
On a moonlit night, a ballet's born.
Flickering leaves on a waving bough,
Become dancing shadows in the evening glow.

Twisting and tripping over bordered lawns,
Nature comes alive in black and white forms.
A lull in the wind and 'still' they all stand,
As if being conducted by an unseen hand.

The elongated shadows from the midnight ball,
Start to perform on the garden wall.
Twirling and cavorting with snowflakes in the wind,
Never seeming to tire or rescind.

Crunching of feet on the frosted drive,
Morning has come and the dance won't survive.
The sun may come out on the glittering snow,
Perhaps the shadows, we'll never know.

Norman Letts

FEARS

Some people dread phantoms and beasts of the night
And others hate reptiles that slither and bite.
There's some dislike earthworms and frogs, toads or rats
And many not enamoured of mosquitoes or bats.
Huge numbers loathe spiders and caterpillars too
And the lovers of slugs are decidedly few.

There's strong men turn pale and go weak at the knees
Just thinking of cockroaches, beetles or fleas.
Some can't stand being idle but others go berserk
At the very idea they should go out to work.
Then there's numerous souls who become quite appalled
At the thought of growing fat or much worse going bald.

It's not just us humans whose lives are so fraught
There's all the poor creatures who are hunted for sport.
There are hens kept in batteries, sad veal calves and lambs
And dear little piglets brought up to be hams.
But quite unlike us since the time life began
They've had little to fear except 'civilised' man.

Vince Hughes

THE FOX

Who startled who the more,
The fox or I?
Sitting on my bench as evening fell
And dusk was nigh.
The moon was hidden behind the cloud
Like peeping out from a shroud.
Beautiful fox looked at me
Russet and cream, with amber eyes
That looked at me
And I at him.
He turned and ran
Whence he had come
Dropping his bone as e'er he ran
Our close encounter at setting sun.

Maureen Oglesby

EARTH SPEAKS

Man, listen a while and, I shall speak!
Millions of years did pass
Before you and your cattle
Trampled the grass.
Moving on from there
Man has shown less and less care.
Briefly he has badly blundered,
As my precious, bounteous but
Limited resources he has plundered.

My work took not just
Seven days and seven nights,
But millenniums of aeons before
For conditions or life, it was right.
From a swirling, spiral nebula,
Emerged things most peculiar.
Masses of hell-hot gases,
Finally coalescing into vital elements.
Without these, there would be no life.
Neither flora nor fauna,
A world barren, painted into a corner.
Probably drab grey, or possibly red,
Certainly not green and blue.
Definitely no place for you,
Ignorant man, indifferent
To any sensible plan.

End now pollution, to relentless
Exploitation, find a solution!
Man you must use gumption,
Or face expulsion from this my planet,
For you are more greedy and
Rapacious than a gannet!

This, my message must
Be globally relayed,
I, Earth, sadly, badly need aid!
Without a healthy me, you have
No destiny, other than extinction.
Use gumption or forego even last unction.

Graham Watkins

BRAVES OF THE SEA

The wind was strong, the waves were high
With black thunderclouds parading the sky
Flashes galore, the wicked lightning
Made being at sea, so very frightening.

But there were some there, fathers and brothers
Fighting the sea, to save all the others
They crewed their boat, just volunteers
Striving for lives and showing no fears.

The lifeboat cut through, and under the waves
The shipwrecked were yelling, calling the braves
Tensions were high, all calmness gone
But fighting for lives urges them on.

With Sou'westers on heads, protection from rain
They answer all calls, again and again
Once on their way, with courage and tack
You're sure they will get there, they never turn back.

While battling the seas with gusto and zest
Lifeboatmen are sure to give it their best
Sometimes they fail, but mostly they win
That's when they return with an almighty grin.

Frank Harper

SONG OF PEACE

As the people sang their songs of peace
Their memories filled the sky with pain
And the heavens wept and washed their face
Of tears and blood with driven rain
Let terror die in dark disgrace
And never haunt the Earth again.

Peace people peace
Let the world start to care
Peace people peace
Make it here and everywhere
Sing this song of peace
Let your heart have its say
May the music never cease
Sing it now and every day.

As the people spoke their words of truth
Justice and freedom filled the sky
The heavens screamed of nature's proof
As wet leaves blew in the sun to die
Let liberty remain aloof
And always ask the question why?

As the people prayed the air was still
With grace and love and conquered fears
No bullet, bomb nor power to kill
For all of Heaven and Earth declares
That grace and love must drink their fill
When war is over the peace is theirs.

Bill Campbell

WHAT IS A POEM?

A poem's a piece of life wrapped up in rhyme,
It's a few words of wisdom frozen in time.
There, curled up inside are the gems of ideas
And diamonds of happiness, thoughtfulness, fears;
Gold nuggets of drama, experience divine.
They are dreams of the future, footsteps through time.
So read and enjoy them and breathe in their power.
A poem's a treasure, a heavenly flower.

Sheila Harvey

MY BEST EVER POEM

A poem is wanted
It is not easy to write one on demand
It has to come from the heart.
The heart has many nuances, happy and sad
Like a diamond with many facets.
We live in a different world - the good old days are gone
Although it is debatable
Good and bad times we all have experienced
Dreadful wars and dreadful diseases have befallen us.
Now another word is looming above *'Terrorism!'*
The fiend who will bring destruction.
We don't know the time and we don't know where it will strike.
We can hear the rumble of thunder in the sky
And it might just pass us by.
We can see a large bag at the corner, was it discarded
Or is it packed full of nails?
Will it explode and bring destruction to many waiting there?
We don't know what is in store for us?
We can just hope and pray it will pass us by.

Gusty Cotterell

A Unique Pontiff

An inevitable situation yet no one was quite prepared.
The death of Pope John Paul II, a deep sadness flared.
All faiths, all nationalities, all the Earth united in sorrow.
Unaware of the successor that will control us from tomorrow.
With dignity, his eminence showed courage and grace.
Humanity and humility to all the human race.
Over a quarter of a century his tireless campaigning.
He travelled the world, very little countries remaining.
In his native Poland, he has left a vast void.
Adored, revered, treasured by the tabloid.
A requiem mass mourned the passing of the Pope.
Throughout the globe there was compassion and hope.
That the great man himself who suffered such pain.
A saint, an example of an extraordinary reign.
Has he left this world a better place?
No wars? No violence? No grief? A calmer pace!
Tranquillity, unison, tolerance and peace?
An end to traumas, prejudice to cease.
Millions and millions have been moved by his presence.
A unique ingredient that was his essence.
Peace to the world - we are all concerned.
As he enters God's realm a lesson is learned.

B Thomas

Hope

Be cheerful and carry on
For day is not yet done
To fight the good fight
With all your might
In the midst of life do not give in
Hope that you will be awarded
And that you will move forward
The good you have done will be known
And among friends love grown is shown.
What sometimes seems not fair
Means that you have to persist with care
Try harder to achieve to gain,
Your ultimate aim
And for a start
Win many people's hearts and souls
What you have to say may be short and terse
Secure in a poem in verse.

Allan Mapstone

On Holiday

It's really hard
To know what to do
New opportunities
Are so very few -
When we discovered
We were both eighty-two
It seemed so logical
Well, wouldn't you?
We climbed the hill
Arm in arm
Parkinson's Disease
Caused us no alarm.
We kissed 'goodnight.'
He was so sweet
Our walking sticks
Kept us on our feet.
Dorothy Parker had a
Name for it
Which I can't remember
But perhaps I will
By next September -

Thelma Kellgren

A Man's Nobility

The lives of men of greatness
Through history unfold
But many men of greatness
Their story never told.

He could no longer work or write
And yet he taught me more
Than many men of action
As patiently he bore
The burden of those endless nights
Immobilised by day
A man of so much courage
With lifeless limbs like clay.

In spite of his infirmity
And physical restraint
From him I heard no murmur
Of pity or complaint

His humour and the smile he showed
Gave me the eyes to see
Amidst such suffering and the pain
A man's nobility
Shared with a little lady
Who gave to him her life
Yet said she was no heroine
Simply a brave man's wife.

Cecil Lewis

Your Little Ones

It seems like only yesterday
You were sitting on my knee
I turned round for a moment
But now who's this I see?

An adult, not a child anymore
To hold eternally
What happened to the years gone by?
I really just can't see

You would always make me pictures
While smiling happily
That little world you lived in
I always longed to be

But every day, when you wanted to play
There was always something to do
Somewhere along this life I lived
I never found time for you

The ironing could have waited
The tidying and dishes too
But you always did come last
On a long list of things to do

It's too late now, the time has gone
On my knee you'll sit no more
Just an empty house and memories
And a phone call I wait for

So take the time while you have the chance
To cherish your little one
For tomorrow comes sooner than you think
And then they will be gone.

Yvonne Forrester

THE HAUNTED HOUSE!

The deserted mansion,
Is a terrible place,
Where skeletons rattle,
And ghosts do chase!

My friend went to the haunted house,
She didn't come back that night,
People said that the vampire,
Had killed her, with his evil bite!

I decided to go and look for her,
So I set off into the night,
With only the moon for guidance,
But I got the most awful fright!

For the haunted mansion looked ordinary,
Under the moon's golden glow,
But hidden behind the crooked door,
Was a *real* horror movie on show!

The dead had risen from their coffins,
Stumbling around the room in a trance,
Vampires and ghosts guarded everywhere,
But I decided to take a chance!

Vampires bared their teeth at me,
Ghosts chased me everywhere,
Witches flew above me,
The dead chased me into their snare!

I was trapped,
In a pitch-black room,
Cobwebs entangling me,
Then something moved in the dark and gloom!

What happened next was a complete blur,
A vampire flew at me . . . it was my friend Gem!
She bit me in the neck,
And the next thing I knew, I was one of them!

Gemma Musgrove

MY ONE AND ONLY LOVE

For me, there will never ever be
A love as caring and strong as he.
My life has been the richer far
As his love shone out like the brightest star.

I always was the light of his life,
And if I was ever really in strife
His strong arms would encircle me,
My tears would stop and clearly I'd see.

'No need to worry, my love,' he would say,
'We'll always get through,' despite all the fray,
Together we'll stand, sorting everything out,
For we know that love is what life's all about.

This caring, kind and gentle man
Was my whole life for a thirty year span.
No better husband could I ever have had,
But now my life is empty and sad.

God came and took him away you see,
To reside up in Heaven and look down on me,
To watch over me alone on this Earth
But not quite, for he left me someone of so much worth.

That's right, our dear son, now a grown handsome man,
Who will cherish his wife, as part of the plan
To carry on love, and care and content,
Making sure that our lives have been very well spent.

Doreen McDonald Banks

A BROKEN PEG

I've secured my charges high on the line,
Held them firm while the wind did whine,
Towels, shirts and stockings good,
I've held them with strong legs of wood.

One day a gust of mighty force
Tore me from my normal course.
I felt a snap and down I tumbled,
Into the grass I ungainly stumbled.

I'd lost a leg and in stunned horror,
I knew life couldn't be the same the morrow.
I lay in the grass there all forlorn
Hoping I wouldn't be left alone.

Laying so frightened and unheeded,
Thinking I would ne'er be needed,
To rot and decay ignored by all,
Was a thought to me which did appal.

I still had use, if only one leg,
Though my days were over for use as a peg.
I was lifted one day by a hand so warm,
Grubby and stained as from a farm.

But no, to a greenhouse I was carried,
Laid on a peat bed there I tarried.
Warm and cosy I felt at ease,
Hoping the warm hand I could please.

Into the peat my leg was buried,
To lift tiny seedlings so unhurried.
Holes I made in tidy rows
To drop the plants in so to pose.
To grow and mature as God intended,
Sharing in nature's colours splendid.

Dibbling holes is my new employ,
Watching the shoots grow I enjoy.
From wet and wind I've changed my work,
My newer tasks I never shirk.

Though tragically I lost a leg,
A better job I'd never beg.
Content and calm in temperature steady,
I am with my one leg - ever ready.

Walter Crooks

LEST WE FORGET - A NOTE TO REMEMBER

I am not life, I am not death,
I ask you who am I?
I am the birth of dying lives,
The graves of living born to die.
I am the crib of breaths of new,
Six shadowed feet beneath the ground,
I am the end of children's song,
Sung silently, heard not a sound.

And the colours fade from all of eyes,
As last young hearts bleed final cries,
Tears drain away to a black and white world,
Lost in war's stream of eternal goodbyes.

Empty now of hearts of love,
But full of empty shells above,
Tears falling now, in place of rain,
Cleansing souls of children slain,
For there's nothing left now, not a sound,
Death walks upon his burial ground.

And to this very day we shall always remember,
The demise of our youth, on that silent November.

Sarah Heptinstall

TOWARDS THE LIGHT

The dark of night
Beyond the stars,
Deep, infinite
In its unfathomable power,
Fills my soul with an
Intense, primeval longing:
And my soul, destined to the
Rhythms and mysteries of life.
Reawakens to a new understanding,
Of belonging and acceptance.

And the darkness deepens
Into a breathing presence,
Caressing my closed eyes,
Going down to the depths of
My heart with a feral leap,
Releasing its mortal beat,
And my soul, in obeyance to
The mysteries and power of
The immortal within it,
Rises to meet the feral leap,
Pausing for a fleeting moment . . .
Then wing away, beyond the
Darkest dark . . . towards
Eternal light.

Colleen Biggins

A HERO ABANDONED

Contemporaries rise and fall:
Our classic masters gain re-call,
Enduring through the ages
Our nation's worth in pages
Withstands the test. Win overall.

Obsessed by words, yet not by fame,
Wholehearted effort casts a name
In print; to leave behind when
No other man can bind them
By jealousy or mortal bane.

Prophetic words of William Blake,
Made rivals' tempers squirm and shake;
'Simple, dull and quite insane,'
Any word to cause him pain,
Financially, the man to break.

His lyrics with the young would stay
Like 'Pop Star' idols of today.
A rebel from the normal,
He hated what was formal.
Convention thrust (too soon) away.

The revolutionary fears
Of bloodshed; carnage veiled in tears
A no-win situation)
From youthful adoration;
Perhaps, antagonised his peers.

Years later, Yeats could see his worth;
Gained pleasure from Blake's lyrics' mirth.
Revised editions soon became
With William Blake, a household name.
The great man's honour, in rebirth.

Pearl Burdock

AURORA

Currente calamo . . .

She has lilies of the morning
on her brow, the slow white
of the rising sun:
in her are moon and sun
of pure, of unchanged time
of apple days.
In the diamond-down
of her eyes
such dream-desires,
these shut,
these open sapphires.

In her cloud-mind these seasons
are her rosary: unmade the world,
the lion summer tamed,
soft July a weeping autumn.
She is silken of another sun
her laurel choice the first Olympus.
Will this sky tremble
on the shadow land,
unmoving as
her sylphan hand?

Simon Richardson

THE CIRCLE

Everybody has a circle,
Drawn around their life,
Some only have inside that circle
Daughter, husband, wife,
Some go further, taking in their friends and neighbours, too,
Others' widen further, to include both me and you.
Think about the first circle,
Ever drawn on Earth,
The one that was, long, long ago,
When life began its birth.
God made it to include all men,
Whatever skin or creed,
He made Earth round, to include all,
His example we should heed.
When we stop loving one another, the damage is not done
To the other person, whom we slight,
Ourselves we scar, for it comes back to us,
So let us watch that we
Draw such a circle that we cannot see
The end of it, then we shall prove,
That love's the force that mountains move.

Jasmine Grace Geddes

LATE AUTUMN DAY

Dark clouds hang in the sky,
Wind whistles like a sigh.
Rain drenched sheep in the field,
The bracken sways, to the wind it yields.

Sombre feels the deserted moors
Lightened only by the hips and haws.
Eerie stillness, not a bird in sight,
The hills are hushed, as at night.

Cold rain and deepening cloud,
Covering the landscape like a shroud.
This autumn day, no longer bright,
Just, the deep dark clouds of night.

Sheila Waterhouse

PENSION DAY

Monday is my pension day,
I'll get my coat and hat.
It's cold outside, I won't delay,
Getting this and that.
The Post Office is rather full
I dare not crash the queue,
But once I get my pension
My shopping I will do,
Inside the Co-op I will go,
I'll buy a pot of jam,
And for my tea, if not too dear,
I'll get a tin of Spam.
Sixpence dearer than last week,
I'll not put up with that,
Instead I'll buy a tin of meat,
To feed and spoil the cat,
Across the road I'll make my way
Into the butcher's shop,
And if it isn't much to pay,
I'll get a nice big chop.

Oh! deary me what a price,
Never mind, it will be nice,
It was so dear the chop he sold,
I really thought it edged with gold,
I must go home, my purse is thin,
I look inside, there's not much in.
I wonder where my pension went,
I cannot think what I have spent,
I can't have reason to complain,
Till pension day comes round again.

Vera Parsonage

THE SECOND COMING

I gaze out longingly through the latticed window.
The tall slim trees no longer bare,
But decked in the whitest of white mantles,
Beckon to me to join in their evening of excitement
And expectancy,
Like messengers of the night
Announcing this spectacular event.

I lift the latch and venture forth into the cold
Night air
Which freezes me through and through.
But no matter; my task must be fulfilled.
And so begins my trek as my thoughts, like a
Captive audience,
Are drawn, as if magnetized,
Towards the ultimate goal.

The cool crisp air chills my breath as I run
Through the fields of white, as yet unblemished,
Snow.
The starkness of the scene bewilders my thoughts.
Breathless, and in anticipation,
A welcoming light draws me closer and closer
With a warmth more serene.
In the stillness the echo of a call.

Can this be the long sought-after goal?
So long-awaited but what a reward!
A light to extinguish others . . .

The light of His love.

Carol A Alvis

THE LANE

I love to walk this winding lane
That smells so fresh from summer rain,
Thick hedges rise, then wildly run
To meet above and hide the sun,
But here and there will break to show
A wall, where ferns and ivy grow,
And sometimes if I really try
To make no sound as I pass by
I'll see a wren dart from the wall,
And hear the blackbird's chattering call.

It narrows here, and winding still
To where tall elms stand on the hill,
That have the very best of view,
Where I can sit and watch anew
Bees that rush from flower to flower,
And cows that wait the milking hour.
As I gaze beyond the cows
Between the elm tree's lowest boughs,
The blue sea stretches far away
With white sailed yachts upon the bay,
And giant rocks where seagulls scream,
And glide with ease on winds unseen.

There the town lies by the bay,
A million people come, they say!
To see the gaily coloured lights
And gaze in awe, at all the sights,
Or lie upon the crowded beach,
If there's a spot in easy reach!
Join the queue for fish and chips,
Or candyfloss, or pleasure trips,
And all the streets are crowded out
So one can hardly walk about.

But here red poppies gently sway,
Here the thrush sings every day,
Here there are no thoughts of time,
No ambitious heights to climb,
Just peace of mind and joy remain,
To walk with me, this winding lane.

J Feaviour

SECOND WORLD WAR

Sixty years since the end of the war, where many had never seen anything like that before.

'Peace in our time' was the Chamberlain cry, as he landed back home from Hitler's goodbye. The Prime Minister returned with promises in hand, while the Germans were planning invading Poland, and while we all waited for much better news, the gestapo had started degrading the Jews.

Into the forties, at the height of the war, it became so difficult to cope anymore. So many killed and too many maimed, it became heart-breaking to have them all named. Everyone prayed and went down on one knee, in the hope that the Lord would set the world free.

Along with the Yanks and Colonial power, the war took a turn for their finest hour and side by side with the Soviets, Ghurkas and all, the timing was right for the Germans to fall.

Our brave men and women went to this war, with some of them many
times before, but when the call came to defend King and Queen, their bravery and valour were there to be seen. Those who took part would never forget, the terrible loss and sense of regret.

When finally the end came after six years of hell, those that survived had their own stories to tell. But whatever they thought during those dreadful years, it was hardly surprising it all ended in tears.

D Bainbridge

MY SONS

Flesh of my flesh
You have crossed as I did
That turbulent sea of childhood.

You have escaped as your father did
That slippery, hooded serpent of youth,
Your journey most arduous has ended.

But a new one has now begun
With pastures anew far afield;
So, my sons do not look back.

If ever henceforth
Obstacles come your way
And you feel my need,

I will be there beside you
In the hour of your need
In a blink of an eye,
For the eyes of my mind are on you.

A Jamil

TO A DEPARTED HERO

In the warmth of an April evening, my face to the sun,
I walked on the beach. It was Sunday. I was alone.
A slight east wind was blowing. My spirits were gay,
I hummed cheery tunes to myself and thanked God for this day.
Snatched from my long rounds of work, from the whirr of the town,
To the right of me rose the rolling, billowing Downs,
An echo, reflection of that lapis lazuli blue
Which, with the tide on my left, receded then grew.

My thoughts of poetry then abruptly were halted;
I became conscious that, as I strode gaily along
A tall quiet form behind in my shadow was walking;
I glanced quickly round - he was fair and slim and so young.
I retarded my steps and soon was rewarded - he passed me,
But dropped back again in a very few seconds from then.
The seafront was crowded with hundreds of gay laughing people,
For the war news was good - let he alone among men
On this glorious day when all the world was rejoicing
Seemed sad and dejected and solitary in his despair;
Yet with his head held high he accepted his fortune
And carried his burden with noble and capable air.

I sat on a seat by the beach and once more he passed me,
But yet thoughts of him could not be dismissed from my mind.
I slowly arose, to return, to wend my way homeward;
I had hardly advanced a few paces - he again was behind.
I turned up a lane, then stopped, and as he came level,
I slipped my hand into his and after a while:
'Why did you think that I, out of all these, could help you?'
His looks of deep anguish gave way to a radiant smile,
But reply he gave none, only held my hand in his firmly.

We walked on together, far from the noisy throng;
A deep sense of gladness, of strength and of peace fell upon me,
My heart within me was ready to burst into song,
I had done nothing, yet I had done all. I know not
How to express the thoughts that fled through my brain -
If I were to die in my slumber that very evening
Yet, young as I was, I would not have lived in vain.

Soon we arrived at the road in which I was staying,
Yet the thought of our parting was not at all bitter to me.
On reaching my gate he kissed my hand very gently
And went on his way. And I? I went in to tea.

Maureen Inglis-Taylor

THE WELSH DRESSER

Mother had a dresser and she polished it with pride.
From all the shelves above it, to all the drawers inside.
Each plate and cup was dusted, each ornament displayed,
Were pointed out to visitors, as on some grand parade.

All the little pieces brought back such memories,
Of day trips to the seaside, of winds and briny seas.
Some were labelled Brighton and Weston-super-Mare.
All meant such happy memories which Mother longed to share.

There were teapots, all best china, and collected through the years
Meaning, oh so many things, bringing sentimental tears.
A brass lamp shone and polished, reflected in the sun.
With glass chimney and wick with oil, to light when day was done.

She kept it as a memory of 'As life used to be,'
In one of the Welsh Valleys, and before electricity.
But one fine day came woodworm and the dresser had to go,
All the nick-nacks on it, no longer could she show.

The house seemed strange without it, and an empty space was seen.
And bare wall now was visible, where the dresser once had been.
An air of gloom fell on the house, it was so hard to bear.
Mother, silent with crossed hands, showed just her depth of care.

But, then we found the answer came, and soon, against the wall,
Installed with careful placing, a glass cabinet so tall.
Mother changed that moment on, a smile lit up her face,
And each proud piece was then restored, back to its rightful place.

Gwyneth Pritchard

LOOK FOR ME

Look for me at dead of night when the world is fast asleep
Look for me at early morn when the mist begins to creep.
Look for me when the birdsong is almost too sweet to bear
Or when the autumn leaves are red and the fox leaves his lair,
Look for me when the wind sends clouds scudding across the sky
And when the teeming rain which follows brings tears to your eyes.
Perhaps your mind will turn to me and all you left behind
Because you said that we were through - how could you be so blind?

Even if I don't see you, I'll know that you were there
The movement of a curtain, the whisper of a stair.
Or your lips touching my face as you murmur my name
I'll look back and tears will flow but I'll be glad you came.

Pam Love

ROUGH SEAS

Oh turbulent troublesome restless sea
Out of the depth you came
That we may be disturbed on our journey today
Why choose today to come out to play
All this is caused by a breeze
Making us ill or feeling not at ease.
Each wave higher than the last
Who will overcome this fight?
The boat or the sea
The boat speeds on relentlessly
The children run up and down the stairs with glee
Whilst older folk have to walk so carefully
Oh wind and waves cease and be at peace
Just before we reach the shore
The wind dies down and we hear no more.

Yvonne Rossiter

A DICKENSIAN ODE TO THE FIELDS OF ABEL MAGWITCH

Cathedral Bells rang,
Over Whitstable 'n' Rye,
Bells of Canterbury,
Of hops,
Of orchards and incense.

For Micawber sat and snorted,
Taking his porter and wine
Whilst young Pip would run through the
Old Curiosity Shop,
Greeting the spirit of Magwitch,
In the fields and marshes beyond.

Whilst Boz
Mused on Twist,
For whipping his incredible whiskers,
He travelled to the rhyme of the Dim
Church line
Reminiscing then,
And reminiscing long,
Over Little Dorrit,
Camden Town,
And The Marshalsea.

Andrew Fry

A WOMAN'S JOB IS NEVER DONE

Is she just a woman wanting it all
Or a woman who has it all but no insight
Continues searching and seeking
What she's already rejected
Always believing there is something better somewhere

Convincing herself that there will be no wars or famine
Once she's fed and watered everyone else
Tidied up after all and sundry
Tucked the kids safely in bed
Everyone's happy, she will be happy
She will have quality time then
Read a book or write her life story

Only her corner of her world is lit
The rest shrouded in silence and darkness
She can't disturb her sleeping army
With a late night cup in one hand
A pen and paper in the other,
Only to start planning for the next day
Other people's lives -
A woman's job is never done

Is she a woman wanting it all
Or a woman who has it all
But does not believe in herself
Celebrating and cheering her friends and family
Her own award, down to luck
'Oh it's nothing; anyone could have done it!'
Convinced that someday, somewhere, someone
Will discover her talents
Her life will be celebrated then

Woman, the truth is that there is no better time
To acknowledge and celebrate life than now
If not now, when?
Stop wasting time, wait for no one - not even a soulmate!
You all right where you are
Acknowledge it
Celebrate your life in the most audacious way
Care to join her? It's about time!

Meg Sika

CLOWN

There's a clown with his hand on the dead man's handle;
Capering, cavorting, congenital fool
Who exalts himself in the public eye,
Who shapes and moulds the public will.
He attempts an acrobatic leap
But tumbles flat on his shadowy face;
He opens up his mouth to speak
And falls again, tripped by his tongue.

This clown wears no elaborate mask
Or costume, baggy and bizarre;
He's dapper and grey and he smiles like a snake
As sweat drips through his open pores
And his easy tears give birth to lies.
His muscles tense as cameras flash
And he's stormed by questions from the crowd.

A clown who doesn't know he's a clown,
A fool who doesn't know he's a fool,
A poison dart in the heart of the world,
A ticking bomb, a waiting plague.
He's an instrument of deadly force
Who kisses his children and prays to God,
Crosses his fingers behind his back,
One eye on the lens and one on the clock.

Mick Marlow

SNOWSTORM

Night fell in an icy wind, driving through the streets,
Bowing and blowing over the hills,
Tugging at the billowing clouds,
The theatre rocking and tilting in the gale,
The gothic moon flying high above a rogue sea.
The strange conductor raised his wand in a fanfare of snow
Tearing the membrane of the livid sky
And jumping free in the chains of the storm
This was no opera, this was punk!

Someone cleared the evidence away before the dawn
And set the sun up early in a laundered sky.
Grass and shooting bulbs lay mute beneath the snow
Only glum brambles pushed through to make a sound.
The day passed in a scraping of spades
And a river of fallen stars.
The sun grew sleepy and tangled in the trees
But deep inside the dark and white cathedral wood
Birds chattered and beech trees wore ermine stoles
And their pine partners were crystal princes.

Susan Wren

BLOSSOM ON THE VINE

Life is fleeting yet eternal!
For one brief moment we are the blossom on the vine.

A tiny seed is planted and grows
into a vine from which a fragile bud appears,
nurtured with life giving streams until
such time it is ready to burst forth and blossom.

It reigns delicate, bold, embracing
the sun, clinging, wavering in a gentle breeze,
falling earthward when storm clouds appear.
Too soon its season is over; all is scattered.

The blossom is gone . . .

but the vine does not die; it sleeps
content in God's garden, then awakes to bloom again!

Susan M Billington

HOLY WATER STOUP (ST PETER'S, WENHASTON)

How many fingers
Have dipped in this ancient
Bowl of stone?
Misshapen, slightly tilted,
Set in a niche
Beside an arch leading into the church.
Now resting in bright sunshine,
But open to all the elements
Of wind and rain,
Since centuries long gone.
How many fingers?
Some in haste
Some in despair
Some in hope
Some in fear
Some in superstition
Some seeking grace
Some with relief
Some in disbelief
Some in penitence
Some in disgrace
Some with fortitude
Some in gratitude
And some out of habit
Have dipped and traced the sign
Of the cross at this place?
God alone knows.

Anne P Munday

RED ROOFS IN SUBURBIA

Looking down from the top of the hill,
My neighbourhood sprawls before me.
Houses red roofed and busy, where people
Get ready for work in the city.
Children squabble and chatter and text their friends.
'Are you ready for school?'
There are dreams to fulfil.
It's the start of the day.
Other houses are quiet
With just a few creaks as arthritic elderly
Stumble from sleep.
A young mother rests by the side of a cot.
After pacing the floor until crying stopped.
Next door someone answers the phone, now tears
In their eyes they're completely alone.
Queues at the bus stop.
Crowds at the station
A husband running late phones a worried relation.
The hospital covers acres of ground, buildings fighting
Each other for light and for space.
Corridors bustle with fast running nurses.
Slow shambling patients with hollow grey faces,
Enter with sadness.
Most come out smiling, renewed and uplifted.
For others the future's uncertain and misted.
The bus takes them home to their loved ones again.
Trusting science and skill to combat their pain.
In the far distance the river is seen.
Is boundary fast moving and sparkling grey green.
Suburbia ends and London begins.

Christine Clark

DEPRESSION SPEAKS

I am the darkness, I am the void
That you run from but cannot avoid.

Doomed to an existence of despair,
I will lure you into my lair.

I prey upon your sadness and insecurity
My venom seeps in and steals your purity.

I will rip out your soul and devour it whole.
You'll walk the Earth empty, a fire without coal.

I will imprison you in your very own mind,
There will be no sanctuary for you to find.

No faith can save you from my power
I will torment your every waking hour.

Each day I'll get stronger and you'll get weak
For you there will be no sunshine, no happiness to seek.

An abandoned building left to rot,
Open to vagrants to abuse what little you've got.

Eventually I will be your only friend
Until death takes you in the end.

Helena Jaksic

GOD'S CREATION

As we look each day around us
We can see so many things,
Things for which we must be thankful,
Which to life so much joy brings;
Thank You Lord for rain and sunshine,
And for flowers and trees which grow,
Thank You Lord for all the beauty
Which on this earth You bestow.

Thank You for the sea and sky, Lord,
And the birds and creatures too,
Thank You Lord for nature's beauty,
Where we see Your love anew.
For our food and clothing, too, Lord,
Doctors, nurses, teachers too,
For all those who serve us daily,
We would give our thanks, and do.

We would also like to thank You
For the life You freely gave,
That we all might have salvation
From all sin our souls to save.
Thank You, thank You, dear Lord Jesus,
For the blessings that You give,
Help us Saviour to be grateful,
Each and every day we live.

Anne Gray

THE SOUL FLIES FREE

The soul flies free -
Help us to understand
And let it go.
Held as we are.
We grieve and strain
Not comprehending
That there is no loss or parting -
Only freedom.

He is not changing.
Only being as before,
But now able to give even more
All that he was
To all who still are -
Freely and with love.

Meg Wilson

Too Late

(This poem is dedicated to my late mother who died a month ago)

Nobody knows when that day will come
As on that Saturday morn the telephone rang
'We've got to go now,' she said
I looked at the man standing by my side and he knew at once

We got in the car and made our way
We did not speak or laugh like we normally did
The journey so quick it was as if we'd flown

Walking up those stairs seemed like a mountain high
And through those doors so quick to find
But no words I wanted to hear, no hugs or kisses for me this day
But only silence and peace.

For there she lay my mother so dear
No words could I speak, only tears of sadness
For I was too late.

W McLean

A Country Church

Among memorials and epitaphs
And ghosts of graveyard gatherings,
Where meet untidy footstep-trodden paths
And pilgrim's inspiration clings,
Serene upon her hilltop habitat,
Superior in her design,
She stands steadfast, though enemies have spat
And stoned her walls, she stays divine.

Solitude behind the heavy door,
Parish pride in tidiness
And polish greet the passing visitor,
History hides in each recess.
Antique plaques displayed with prominence,
Gleaming brasses catch the eye
Immortalising past inhabitants,
Much-thumbed hymn books idle lie.

Her windows watch, in isolation, Time
Transforming nettle into flower,
And flower into brick as houses climb
Towards her dominating tower.
Museum of marriages, of birth and death,
Guardian of grief, lamp of laughter,
She is the first light and the final breath,
She is Before, Now and After.

F G Ward

Time

Time travels like a little pill
That comes into its own to still
And calm emotions that traverse
With power and voice of verse
Which claim attention to allay pain
Like a sigh at any time again and again
So take a deep breath and allow
Your peace of mind to take a bow
Accepting truth for a moment in time
Will prove your love is sublime
And guide thoughts with grace
By giving timeless memories space
Knowing life has the power
To rise and bring a happy hour
Like any spring or summer shower
To bloom within, heart, home and flower.

Beryl Hall

What Is Summer?

A cloudless azure sky as far as the eye can see
swallows darting through the air and gentle hum of bees
the scent of roses, lavender and pinks on the breeze
as I sit in my garden, that is summer to me.

For young children going to the beach is a perfect day
building castles on warm sand beneath a golden sun
splashing in and out of the clear water is such fun
licking ice creams whilst watching sailing boats in the bay.

The older generation remember summers past
especially those of the Second World War years
when many women worked on the land hiding their fears
for their men by toiling long hours bringing in the harvest.

Some people enjoy trekking across the open moors
striding through heather and gorse or climbing a tor
others play tennis or cricket hoping for a good score
or ride all the roller coasters at Alton Towers.

Why is it when we think of favourite summer days
it is glorious weather with not even a haze
yet in reality clouds often hide the sun's face
with rain and lightning chasing thunder in an angry race.

When this happens we must close our eyes and pretend
we've been transported to where we want to be, then
it can be summer any time in our dreams
for life doesn't always have to be how it seems.

Sue Rowe

My Special Day

'It's nearly time,' I hear someone say,
Between the hustle and bustle of this busy day.
Door slam, people leave, 'See you there,' they call,
Oh! I can hardly breathe.
I can hear Dad calling to me, 'Are you ready love?'
In barely a whispered voice I say, 'I'm coming.'
I take one last look in the mirror,
At this person who is me.
Looking forward now, towards my future,
Of the person I hope to be.

My white satin dress with embroidered flowers and pearls,
My veil of see-through lace.
With my hair held high in curls,
I carry tiny white flowers and rose pink bouquet.
I will walk arm in arm with my dad now,
On this my wedding day.

So proud is my dad, so proud he is of me,
I'm glad we have this moment together, so special.
Our hearts so full of memories,
So lovely, so cherished, this day is going to be.

Mary Plumb

Our Loved Ones

If only we could have one wish
We know what that would be
We would ask the Lord
To open the gates for you
For us to see
We would put our arms
Around you
And give you all our love
Then ask the Lord
To take care of you
Up in Heaven above.
God bless.

P Jakes

AUTUMN VACATES

Flickering candles
Scattering winds
Autumn vacates
As winter begins
The darkness slowly
Clawing its way
Casting long shadows
In the middle of the day
Fog silently forming
Its presence unnerves
Distance deceptive
Car horns can be heard
Beam of a headlight
Visibility zero
The bitter night air
Biting
Right down to the marrow.

Samantha Williams

KISS

You flew out of my life one day
Unseen forces took you away
To a place they say was better for you
But the kisses you gave me they took away too.

When I cried in the night for this ache in my heart
For this physical longing which tore me apart
When I craved for your touch, for the loving I miss
I could not now go on and I begged for your kiss.

Four years have now passed and I sit here alone
Some of the nights an abyss here is shown
Into which I must fall, but try to survive
As I crawl out and clutch at the thought, I'm alive.

I still wait in darkness alone, for the kiss
For the beautiful meeting of lips and the bliss
And just as I feel this pure joy will not come
A small child, wet lips on my cheek - 'Love you Mum.'

Elizabeth Williams

WHO AM I?

Oh my God
Who am I?
Another raindrop from the sky
Another pebble on the beach
A slithering writhing
Clinking leech
If I should ponder till seas run dry,
I shall never know just who am I
Day after day
Year after year
The world is filled with hatred and fear.
But what am I?
Amongst them all
Another shadow
The night doth call
Oh my God,
Just who am I
To sit in judgement beneath the sky
When I knew that Thou art judge over us all
But You are the flower of Heaven and I
Am the weed against the wall.

Christine Kitchen

QUEEN ELIZABETH II GOLDEN JUBILEE

The people of our nation, were filled with zest and glee,
To celebrate our Majesty's Golden Jubilee;
Street parties were a climax and took some organisation,
But it only seems like yesterday, since Queen Elizabeth's Coronation.

Red, white and blue bunting was visible from far and wide,
With Britain steeped in pageantry, folks filled with joy and pride;
The homage of the people is certainly not a mystery
For those Jubilee celebrations will go down in history.

The grounds of Buckingham Palace, staged a concert
for classical years,
With majestic orchestration, a delight to the human ears:
The conductor moved his baton, with such style and dedication.
Whilst the musicians provided music with no signs of trepidation.

A pop concert provided music, with rhythmic renditions,
All artistes fully enjoying, such appealing conditions;
Comedians and comperes kept the crowds on their toes,
As the notes reached by singers provided memories from shows.

The skies above the palace were clear without a cloud in sight,
This helped provide an atmosphere of individuals joy and delight;
Concorde and the Red Arrows, flew past with their royal salute,
With dignity and stature, for Queen Elizabeth, so resolute.

As crowds waved flags and banners, to Elgar's musical story,
They raised their voices with heads held high,
singing 'Land of Hope and Glory,'
Fireworks lit the evening sky, followed by a Union Jack laser display,
A memorable event has come to a close, but will live with us
for all our days.

Malcolm Goat

DEEP WITHIN MY SOUL

When you see me smiling
It isn't always what it seems
I sometimes wake at night
Because of my bad dreams
We've all lost someone
At sometime in our lives
But the biggest loss of all
Is the one that's hard to hide

Deep within my soul
Lies a sadness that won't leave
Memories that hurt me
More than anyone could believe
My tears they flow so easily
When my thoughts turn to you
I hold up my hand to God
And hope that He will see me through

A part of me has died
Will I ever be the same
Will I step out of the darkness
Into the light again
My ever flowing tears
Won't wash my blues away
I wake up every morning
And pray for a better day
Don't look on the outside
The pain lies deep within my soul
Won't someone take it from me
So that I can once again be whole.

Kate Everett

GEM OF GRANDEUR

Serene and silent, an English valley,
Swathed in rolling pastures green.
Spiky conifers stand tall and proud,
Warriors of war, remembrance of ages past.

Nestled 'neath a cool blue sky,
A scattered hamlet quietly sleeps.
Around the Gothic church, tombstones grey
Silently hail the stroke of seven.

'Midst dappled shade, the dank musk smell
Of lichen creeping round a sickly oak.
White wood anemones take a peep,
Their petals moist with the morning dew.

Golden rays shimmer through leafy glades,
Over weathered rocks ripples a silver stream.
On yonder branch, with tail cocked high,
A wren proudly sings his own symphony.

Over the hills a weary tractor toils,
Ploughing deep furrows to scatter the seeds.
Fiery and red, the sun majestically rises,
Revealing a beautiful English valley.

Diana Frewin

VOICES OF THE ADULT CHILDREN

I am your hero
Your bright as light and special child
See how successful I am
Count my achievements
Look how I am perfect for you
How hard I strive to do things well
Surely you must approve of me
For I am an extraordinary child:
When I grow up, I will be a leader,
My boldness hiding my pain.

I am your mascot
Your sunny, sweet as honey child
See how funny I am
Count the ways I make you laugh
Look how I ease your pain
How hard I strive to make things better
Surely you must approve of me
For I am the life and soul of your life:
When I grow up, I will be a clown,
My humour hiding my pain.

I am your scapegoat
Your ear-splitting, defiant, noisy child
See how boisterous I am
Count the ways I misbehave
Look how I can be angry for you
How hard I strive to accept the blame
Surely you must approve of me
For I give you an excuse to be mad:
When I grow up, I will be a bully,
My coldness hiding my pain.

I am your lost child
Your hush-hush-hushaby quiet child
See how reclusive I am
Count my books and playthings
Look how I stay out of your way
How hard I strive to do things by myself
Surely you must approve of me
For I am no trouble at all:
When I grow up, I will be nobody,
My silence hiding my pain.

Carole Wale

WHEN DAYS BECAME YOU

Once, when days became you
I could have died loving
The very air you dreamed on;
Now, the thoughts that spread through
The whisper of your brow ever creasing
Flew away the beauty, now forever gone.

What lines were worries that crept
Over the fine loveliness of your face
To mark the coming of an age:
What fears with the night wept
That made your heart cold like bit and brace
To fire my love to smoulder forever in a cage.

Your walk still has a young girl's grace
And from a distance I can picture you
Among the blowing grass like a winter sun;
And were I to run as if in a race
Through the hedges like a swallow flew
I would see your young beauty gracefully burn.

For you hold yourself well and proud
Ever careful to remain young as possible
Hiding your neck behind a scarf of flowers;
As the undertaker hides behind a shroud
And shadows ring your eyes making them susceptible
To the death on your shoulder-boughs.

Richard Gunn

A DAY OF HORROR

The world is full of people on the move
On the way to - who knows where?
Flying to make the distance shorter
Seeking excitement, dare?
Now, we have hatred, destruction in our midst.
A few only remembering God in His Heaven
The one who made us, died for us
In perfect love, our sins to bear.

We have it all, or so they say,
Wealth, health and brain.
Yet, on September 11, 2001, we saw horrific things
Appalled by the sights and sounds, the grief
And pain.
Man's inhumanity and all it brings,
Deliberately planned in ice-cold blood
Calculated, a madman's ploy

What does it achieve, save making us all wake up,
Believe
And not take for granted this era's joy.
Are we self-complacent with the right to expect, get
Unheeding another one's need?
The world grows smaller
Should we who grow older have made it a better place?

It's all there really.
Room for all - breathless beauty, fantastic wealth
The Lord, in His wisdom, created it first.
May He forgive us for what we do.
He is in this place.
He sees. He hears. He cries.
John chapter 11 says, 'Jesus wept'.
Please God, wipe dry our tears
And turn not Thy face away.

Pauline Burton

SUNDAY 21 AUGUST 2005

On jaunts to air-conditioned shopping malls
where products seem divorced from animals,
what toddler or teenager can recall
seeing slim mill - chimneys belch smoke - or fall
suddenly, tremendously to the ground?
Much more recent development around.

From within high-rising or low-squatting
buildings, on hazy days, someone's spotting
a ghostly chimney's smoke spewed overhead -
from such a mill - or somewhere else instead?
Whatever has been remembered somehow . . .
this bright Sunday people are shopping now -

or standing near to the town Cenotaph
to honour someone in a photograph.
This August morning many call to mind
those millions dead World Wars left behind . . .
cumulus cloud collecting in the sky -
not that dread mushroom shape towering high

that still invisibly threatens all life
because we see no end to human strife -
though swiftly people and places alter -
our belief in any future falter . . .

cloud drifts forward for there is no stopping.
Meanwhile, most people carry on shopping.

Chris Creedon

A SPARK IN THE NIGHT

Deep in the woods, through the thick of the trees,
Small beings are hidden, concealed by the leaves.
At the foot of an oak, among toadstools in ring,
Is the entrance to a realm where the fairies all sing.

For unseen to those humans who do not believe,
Are the most delicate of creatures you could ever perceive.
They glide on the air, the sun through their wings,
Their purpose and nature is of various things.

For there are those like Berry and Newt of the lake,
Who spend all of the day in search of trouble to make.
And Acorn and Firefly, whose intentions are good,
Light the way for small children who get lost in the wood.

There's Twiglet and Sparrow, who build fairy huts,
Out of branches and mud and a hollowed out nut.
And Chestnut and Willow and Small baby Tad,
Whose home is a log on a large lily pad.

There are the elders, the wise ones, Chalcedony and Poke,
Who are guiders and watches for all fairy folk.
So if ever a fairy should be lost or afraid,
And their bright shining light should grow dimmer or fade,
The elders will call to their pure fairy hearts,
And will guide these small spirits to the safest of parts.

For the realm is a sacred and magical place,
Where great care must be taken to preserve this space.
For the trees and the grass and the rocks and the stream,
All the natural wonders make this fairyland dream

So when the sky turns purple and the night grows near,
If you truly believe, they will appear.
As the fairies' favourite time is surely the night,
When the outside world is still and the moon shines so bright,
And music and dancing shall through the woods ring,
And a small choir of voices as the fairies all sing.

So if you should see one such beauty, a spark in the night,
Make the wish of your dreams . . . and hold on to it tight!

Jennifer Campbell

THROUGH MY EYES AS A CHILD

My sister and I were playing while our parents discussed the war
We didn't understand their worries but callers were always at the
door.
My father was asked to 'firewatch', I didn't grasp that at all
As the cold dark nights were coming, *we* would watch the fire with
curtains pulled

My father made frames for the windows covered with thick black felt
These were put up every evening, with my brothers help
We were told it was to keep the light inside
But outside with gates and lamp post we'd collide

And then this strange man called, a tin hat on his head
He had six boxes for us, the enclosed to 'try on,' he said.
What fun - I thought he'd brought us presents
But inside a mask - that smelt unpleasant
I hid behind my mother and refused to try it on
The family were wearing theirs but I didn't see the point

Then we had sheets of iron delivered and little bunk beds
Another thing I couldn't understand, we already had a greenhouse
and shed.
Later a lady called to say my sister and I should be sent away
She mentioned evacuation, and they would arrange where we'd stay
My mother wasn't keen, saying she would think it over
The war had started, darker nights, it was now October.

We went to stay with an elderly aunt, in a village near Cambridge
Who lived with her well spoken friend, in a very old vicarage
Her father was the vicar there, and her brother followed him
She said to call her Miss Banton and patted us on the chin
I could never get her name quite right and called her Miss Bantam
With eyes closed she'd say, 'I'm not a chicken, it is Banton not
Bantam.'

There was just one large classroom in the village school
Children from five to eleven sat in rows on stools
We would learn our times tables and take it in turn to read
Wishing it was half-past three, when we would be freed.

I very much missed my parents and the family
Christmas was very near and I thought, sadly
Father Christmas wouldn't know where we were
But my aunt and Miss Banton were a kindly pair
Knowing Christmas would be here soon
Had a big tree and presents in the dining room

We had a lovely Christmas, morning service in the church
Christmas dinner and presents, hidden sweets for which we
searched.
Boxing Day morning we were given the news that we were going
home
Our dad was coming, as without us the house had been like a tomb.

The months that we had been away, there hadn't been one air raid
'Whatever will be will be' my mother would always say
We were very glad to be with them, our books and dolls around us
Neighbours, friends and even teachers hugged and made a fuss

The Blitz started the next year, and was very loud and noisy
But I won't go on anymore - as that's another story.

Dorothy Edwards

LE SHUTTLE

High tech confined
We rush under the sea
Emerging in a wilderness of rails
And rattling exit lanes -
The ultimate triumphant victory
Over La Manche.

Down the straight poplar road,
Brass sun burnishing the graves,
Flat fields and marble monuments
Commemorating the unnumbered souls
Dead on the beach or slaughtered in the mud;

The bronze shield of sun now gilds each cross,
Down through the names that sound a litany:
Arras, Armentieres, Omaha and Sword,
Till blood red sun dips, bleeding shadows
Soft into the twilight, and the moon
Stands over France, stilly admonishing
Man and his brilliant, bold technology,
Built on that useless, bloody carnival.

Peggy Haynes

MY LOVE

In every poet's life you will find
The fairer sex is in his mind
He reasons talent from above
Any verse to his own true love

He can choose the words that will contain
The loving messages from his brain
To tokens of his deep devotion
Showing in words of fevered emotion

In his eyes she has no faults
Can he surmise the way he's taught
The touch of their lips
And he is caught

While he admires her every whim,
She must prepare to come to him
Years may pass from young into age
But she's the centre of his stage.

He will fulfil her every wish
At her call or touch he'll sigh
And for her love he would die
But in return he will explain
No holding back or no refrain

Not to fail to let him know
By little touches or eyes aglow
Then he is hers no one could take
She's the one his heart could break.

E Hockley

A VINTAGE YEAR . . .

Summer fruits, harvest from a winter sowing,
Sunlight dancing on crimson strawberries.
Lush raspberries, with gentle dewdrops glowing,
Trees laden, their fruits near ripening.

Bees, nectar-drunk, a blackbird's melody.
Our cottage garden, high summer in July.
The ambient air, so placid, stress-free, and
Blossom scented. A baby's happy cry.

A blanket spread beneath a pear tree's shade.
Chubby arms waving, merry wreathing smile,
Tiny toes, so kissable, with sunbeams overlaid.
A bumper harvest, from last autumn sown!

Marjorie Chapman

CHRISTMAS DREAMS

Our two little girls remind me of the Christmases we knew.
The excitement shared on Christmas morn was there for you and me.
We hardly slept the night before and couldn't wait to see.
Just how many parcels were in our sacks and what the gifts would be.

In the early hours we'd be awake and giggling and talking lay
Longing for the changing sky and to see the break of day.
We couldn't wait and out of bed both of us would get.
Until a voice we knew and loved would say, 'Oh no - not yet.'
And then dear Mum would change her tone and say, 'You can open
Just two each.'
So in the sacks we'd rummage to see if we could reach -
The presents we were hoping for
Our lists were written with care
Some things for ourselves and some games for us to share.
Such happy moments we have known together all the way
Our lives have always been entwined and even to this day
We're joined in Christmas love and Christmas wishes by the score,
There can't be sisters anywhere who love each other more.

Barbara King

THE DOVE OF PEACE

Smooth of wing - a gentle thing,
Its olive branch, an offering,
Hoping, ever hoping still,
Its role of peacemaker to fill.

From land to land and shore to shore
It takes its message, evermore
Striving to break the mould of hate
Mankind has made through spate on spate
Of wars and greed and racist strife,
Of bombs and guns and thrust of knife.

And still by lust for power borne
Man rushes on destruction torn,
Heedless of all who try to stay
The killing and the sad affray.

The dove of peace - it hovers by,
Ignored - rejected - crucified,
Its message of hope and freedom spurned,
Will we never learn?
Will we never learn?

Annabel Barnes

LADIES AND GENTLEMEN OF THE PRESS . . .

For fifteen years you've been reading our verses
Fifteen years of elation and curses
Fifteen years of being excited, enthralled
Fifteen years of being downcast and appalled.

You've arrived each Monday, buoyed up with hope
That this week you'll find a Keats or a Pope
Or a work whose brilliance stands out a mile
Or something so silly it just makes you smile.

You've sorted, sifted, discarded with pain
And tried to be thrilled by those that remain
You've changed format and print and staff as well
Expanded, prospered and managed to excel.

From post room to editors and those in between
Who cope with the haste and daily routine
From those who've been published accept this toast
To the staff of the press we love the most:

Cheers! Here's to the next fifteen years!

Betty Nevell

TOMMY THE CHAMP
(Love Nan and Grandad)

Tall, blond, slim and handsome,
That's our Tom
Courage is his middle name,
That's our Tom.

Excelled at all sorts,
Champion of them all,
Not in our wildest dreams
Did we know
He was heading for a fall.

A fall not of his making;
Fate dealt him a bitter blow,
Struck down with a rare illness,
He took it in his stride,
Champion that he is,
He fills our hearts with pride.

Spirit undimmed,
A fighter unsurpassed,
Give him some luck Lord,
That's all we ask.

Keep fighting Tom
We know that you will win,
For whatever life throws at you
You'll take it on the chin.

Alas, our Tom's fight for life
Was all in vain
But we remember his courage,
It will help us ease the pain.

J Pruden

TO GIVE

I long to build something from nothing, sweet Jesus,
To give back a little of what I got from you.
To find the time to go out and help others.
Do with their lives what You wish them to do.
Change one thing and just make it better,
Give someone hope in a time of despair,
Cut the bonds that have someone fettered,
Give them the freedom their life to repair.
Feed the wasted body of a starving stranger,
Pluck from someone their avarice and sin.
Led from the wrong path a soul that is in danger,
Plead for You to give them strength that comes from within.
Seek in my own life quiet and contentment,
The gift to forgive those who have done me wrong,
Harbouring not anger, hate or resentment,
Help the weak to grow firm and strong.
Look to nature for peace and for solace,
Fight for good environmental change
Helping the wildlife and natural progress,
In growing crops and saving animals' pain
Accepting all people as one family,
Making no difference to colour of skin,
This is the way all folk get homily
And truly the way peace can begin.
Take with gratitude whatever I am offered,
Give to the needy all that I can,
Ask for advice when I need it,
Try to help others to understand.
When I am wrong have genuine regret,
Plead Your forgiveness and mercy to man,
Not a lot, Dear God, to ask when I am asking it from You.

Eithne McCrossan

THE RIVER NILE

We cruised up the Nile in the early spring,
There's never any rainfall in Egypt -
Golden sun poured down from a bright blue sky.
But the nights were cool and purple and quiet
And magical when the moon shone silver.

Across the tranquil waters of the Nile
Life is much the same as ever it was.
Small villages - dogs and goats are there.
We watched as camels raced along the shore
Urged on by jumping and arm-flapping men.
Women washing clothes at the water's edge;
Small boys waving as the boat passed by.
Date palms flourish and the sugar cane grows

We relaxed in this timeless atmosphere.
The sun struck flat and the wind blew briskly
As we pushed north to ancient Thebes - Luxor.
A mixed group on board, spending the morning
Dozing in the sun, reading and talking,
Or watching the water change with the hour
From mercury tinged with polished silver,
To sea-green with luminous streaks of gold
And then deep blue sparkling with diamonds.

In Feluccas we danced over the water,
The sails dipped and curtseyed as the boatmen
Jumped merrily over us clutching at ropes.
They sang as we sailed and taught us to sing
The Nubian folk song in their own tongue.
We marvelled at ruined temples and statues,
Colourful paintings on ancient stone walls.
All sorts of artefacts stored for hereafter,
They dwelt in tents, built palaces for tombs.

Huge statues of pharaohs, dwarfing us all.
Karnak Avenue of Ram-headed sphinxes.
Such age-old places and strange-sounding names -
Akhenaten, Ramses, Nefertari,
Hatshepsut and boy King Tutankhamen,
Will be engraved on our hearts forever,
Evocations of ancient Mysteries.

Beatrice Wilson

SNOWDON'S CREST

From the Royal Goat Hotel's door
On Beddgelert's lush valley floor
Where two white rushing rivers meet,
Near Prince Llewellyn family seat,
Winds a worn trail to Snowdon's crest
That rhododendrons now infest.

Up its slopes, for part of that way,
Walkers wander about each day
Past faithful hound Gellert's grave pile
To where fine pines marching in file
Meet defeat, on scree and mine spoil,
In rhododendron's toxic soil.

Many hikers made of sterner stuff
Will stride on, though the going's tough,
Racing the steaming rack rail train
To the rundown top shop's terrain.
And join its sleeping knight hero
Where rhododendron's growth's zero.

There pleads King Arthur, tales tell,
His blade beneath a deep lake's swell,
And where now frozen in grey slate
Senior fossils with him wait;
'Don't let your heritage degrade
Through poison suckers that invade!'

Ronald Rodger Caseby

DEATH

Death is a nothing,
It's not all that bad.
Only those who are left,
Are the ones who feel sad.
Tears are shed at the parting,
There's a feeling of gloom,
But it's a far better thing,
Than lying ill in some room.

Death is a friend,
Though it's hard to believe,
By the ones who are left,
They're the ones who will grieve.
When it comes there's a stillness,
A feeling of gloom.
For the people still left,
Sitting there in that room.

Death is the healer,
Of all things that are bad.
When it comes it's a friend,
To those people who know,
That they've suffered enough,
That it's now time to go.
It's the ones who are left,
Who are red-eyed and sad.
Because now that it's happened,
There's a feeling of gloom,
For those people still left,
Sitting there in that room.

Jack Blades

A GARDEN OF REFLECTIONS

The warm scented roses of love surround, my garden of deep peace
which holds no bounds,
For it has been planned for summer days, to make the most of the
sun's soft rays.
This is my garden of love.

A path to walk while deep in thought, where on the wind trailing
scents
are caught,
Of lavender sweet and lilacs blue, dainty wisteria with its gentle hue.
This is a haven of love.

Sitting quietly under the laburnum tree, I thank the Lord for I have
the key,
Which fits this wonderful garden of love, given to me from
Heaven above
Oh! My garden of love.

This perfect garden has a pond, but still I can see those roses beyond.
The dragonflies, frogs and butterflies play and the fat bees bumble for
most of the day.
A garden of pure joy.

Through the mint green door - dare I disturb! Grows the parsley,
thyme and the basil herb.
Small crazy paving between culinary patch is where we gather
a fragrant batch.
A garden of recipes.

Aromatic seasonings lead to the dell, with cool leafy trees and
the blue harebell.
Wild flowers profuse and the chaffinch nests, now this is my favourite
place of rest.
My beautiful garden of love.

Lucy-May Bloxham

SHADES OF SUMMER

The twisted branches of the gnarled old tree
Made mottled shades where the sun could not be.
A three-legged cat hopped wearily by
To find a cool hedge where in peace he could lie.
Out of the dried grass a dog raised his head,
Too hot to chase, he watched instead.
So the cat moved out away from view
To find a place where a slight breeze blew.
Now the warm day is passing away,
The tree comes to life, birds make the leaves sway.
They feed their young with hungry beaks,
Then settle down and everyone sleeps.
The dog and the cat have gone to their home,
To seek food and comfort, the tree is alone.
Now the shadows are silhouetted with light
From the magnificent still of a dark blue night.

Barbara Twort

THE MISSION

A future spacecraft travelled far,
To the planet of a distant star.
An unmanned probe found in space,
Came apparently from that place.
A voyage of discovery through deep space,
To try and contact an alien race.
The system reached left no doubt,
There it was the third planet out.
Shuttle ready with crew to man it,
In standard orbit round the planet.
Orbital scan, then they land,
But no life found just rock and sand.
The evidence found solves the mystery,
These friendly aliens, now just history.
With war and planet violation,
Came total self-annihilation.
As the star ship travels back through space,
A question asked, what was that place,
Well, just for the log, for what it's worth,
We do believe they called it Earth.

Bob Marsh

MIRROR MIRROR ON THE WALL

When I look in the mirror, who exactly do I see?
Definitely not the face of the young girl I used to be!
When did all those wrinkles appear and look at that big frown,
No wonder I often feel depressed, out of sorts and so down.
That old face can't belong to me, inside I still feel twenty-one,
Always game for a laugh, so many places to see, people to meet,
so full of fun.
Why did the years pass by so quickly been and gone in a flash.
I realise before I know it, it'll be time soon, to claim my OAP bus pass!
Then I really will feel old and realise my time on Earth is nearly
done,
But looking back, I can remember some happy times with family
And friends, now sadly gone,
My face shows all the happiness, the joy, the hurt, the many tears that
I've cried,
I know I can't hold back the years anymore, no matter how hard I've
tried,
So I'll just have to grin and bear it and as they say, grow old
gracefully,
Or book in for a course of Botox, or better still a facelift, no that's not
for cowardly me!

Dot Ridings

FRIENDSHIP

When we were young,
We played, we three,
At games together, happily,
We went to the park,
And took our tea,
Went on the swings and acrobats,
We loved our fun, with balls and bats.
When we were teens,
And went our ways,
We kept in touch, on our birthdays,
And now we are a special age,
We keep in touch, just we three,
At Christmas, birthdays, still you see,
We are here today, to celebrate,
Dear Marjorie's special eighties date,
We are good friends you will agree,
Marj, Kath and Ena,
          Yes, that's me.

Ena Field

THE DAFFODIL

Tall and straight
Statuesque golden sceptre,
Gently sun kissed diamond -
Figment of man's desire
That blossoms through early spring
By roadside
Country lane
Or babbling stream:
All marvel at such beauty,
This jewel in nature's crown . . .
The daffodil.

Arthur Pickles

SCALING MOUNTAINS

We bravely walk on glass.
While others play
we boldly tread our fears
to conquer Everest.

Each has their
own mountain to scale,
individual and unique.
We lend support
but the task
is ours alone.
We place our footsteps
where feet have gone before,
recognising toeholds,
handholds.
And we climb.

The height terrifies us.
The chasm beneath our feet
beckons enticingly.
It plummets,
calls to us
like a siren in the night
but we use the ropes
and resist.

Each mountain is different but
we bravely walk on glass.
While others play,
we boldly tread our fears
and conquer life.

Sue Percival

EXPRESSIONS OF GOD'S LOVE

Not like St Paul and his on the road to Damascus Revelation
but every day of my life there has been the realisation
that the love of God encompasses me - I always know
that whatever occurs is for my good and wherever I may go
is covered by His grace however many times I fall short
of His expectations - He is always there to exhort
and to comfort me for the failings. From the day of my birth
I am sure if I was the only sinner on God's wonderful Earth
He would still have sent His Son, Jesus, only me to redeem,
this is a very personal matter from God to me, between
just the two of us so how can I fail to adore
the Saviour who loves me so much He gave His only Son for
me and, of course, all the people on the Earth He created.
Whatever happens in my life His love has never abated.
Although to fathom His mysteries is not what I am here for
and now I am growing older the list of those 'gone before'
is lengthening year by year - until it sometimes seems
there are more over there waiting for me (I see them in my dreams)
than are left here, so I know that when God calls me to be by His side
still supporting me, by His grace, in His love I'll forever abide.

Florence Broomfield

THE AARDVARK AND THE ZEBRA

The aardvark and the zebra are many poles apart
They're at either ends of the dictionary and nowhere near the heart
But the aardvark has one advantage and for that he's pretty sure
There ain't no other animal that's gonna come before
While the zebra seems to be content and knows his proper place
The aardvark sitting up in front will never interface
I think when God was typing names like dogs and cats and mice
When he got to aardvark he hit the A key twice
And being Lord Almighty he's never wrong it's said
So now the dear old aardvark will always stay aahead.
The zebra's still a placid beast and never can be goaded
He knows his place he knows his price p'raps that's why he's been
                                                          bar-coded.

Don Hunt

THE FADING RAYS

Cast the rays of autumn sun
upon the shady hill
where we two lovers hand in hand
discover at thy will

The downward side of nature's call
retreating like the rays
the evenings warm
until the sun has set
and calm repose the day

Until the dusk
when the sleeping world
of animals come to prey
the vixen with her cubs
so young
forage to live their way

The silent night cast shadows
the owls hoot eerily
the world of nocturnal creatures
have their turn to play.

Margery Rayson

NIGHTMARE

Dreams are only fragments
Of yesterday and before
Dreams keep us reminded
Of an ever open door.
Dreams can be so frightening
They can wake you in the night
Dreams can be consoling,
Refreshing and contrite.
Dreams could be a warning
Of impending doom to come
Dreams can foretell disaster
A change of life for some.
But looking on the bright side
And you've had all you can take
Then use your sense of common,
And bleedin' stay awake!

John Topham

VAUGHN WILLIAMS' LARK

I've seen his lark ascending
Just a speck against the sky
An oscillating shimmer
Of black transmitted white

With shafts of golden sunshine
Breaking dark and stormy clouds
And a hint of distant thunder
Rolling through the Cheshire gap

I've heard its radio crackle
And oddly splintered notes
Cast out in muted splutters
Cross the blue spheroidal light

And it seemed to float forever
Like a new celestial star
Suspended in the ether
As if time was slowing down

Then its enigmatic tumble
In a jink of feathered twirls
To a wide expanse of stubble
With flints like broken bones

And it seemed this was an essence
That would linger for a life
And I knew the inspiration
Vaughn Williams had in mind.

C Goldsmith

GREAT OR GOOD

Oh! How I wish I were a man! What wondrous things I'd do,
I'd write such books that all the world would read them thro' and thro'
The fire flashed before his eyes, as if he thought it hard to wait;
His mother whispered, 'First be good, then if you will, be great!'

The boy sprang from his mother's side with footsteps light and gay
But dreams of fame were with him still, amid his childish play!

Years passed away and he had grown at length to man's estate
Alas! He cared not to be good, but only to be great.

He wrote, men read, the world around was ringing with his name,
His early dreams had never reached to such a height of fame,
Yet would he sigh, as if within his heart felt desolate, as if
It were a weary thing to walk amongst the great!

'Ye humble ones,' he cried, 'who tread the path of duty well
The peace of mind I may not find stoops down with you to dwell,'
I would that had I lived like you, content in low estate,
Oh! Could I have my life again, I would be good, not great!

Moira Round

FAITHFUL FRIENDS

Our hearts were broken one sad day
When George the Cavalier passed away;
He'd been our friend for ten long years,
When our George died we both shed tears.
The Vicar came to talk us through our grief,
His kindly words of comfort brought relief.
We thought it nigh impossible to find another friend
But way up at East Runton our search came to an end.
Four little golden bundles lay huddled in a pen
The problem was which one to choose,
The Lord was with us then!
A black-faced puppy left the pen, whatever all the fuss,
We named him Dougal there and then, for he had chosen us!
Lhasa Apso was the breed, the first we've had as yet,
Friends to Monks in Monasteries, all way from Tibet!
We felt that God was with us at this time in our life
As He is with us all the time through sorrow and through strife.
God read our situation, He met our deepest need;
He guided us to Dougal, a miracle indeed.
I often marvel every day, especially of late,
How can a dog so very small fill a void so very great?

William J Bartram

EXIT

Hello World - it's me I'm here!
Have you forgotten my very existence?
Have I forgotten that I exist?
Do I breathe freely?
Does my heart beat with joy?
Or does it beat with monotonous regularity?
Maybe I wish it would stop
Perhaps I need to be in a different place
Where? Heaven or Hell?
Which is it now?
What do I think?
What do you think?

Day breaks, night falls
In-between, turmoil reigns
My mind is weary
My soul despairs
Is this it, is there more than this?
Do you answer yes?
Please tell me then, where do I look?
Will you help me?
Will I find what I am looking for?
What am I looking for?
Does the answer lie in the grey shadows?
Dare I move forward?

Goodbye World - the task is too great
To exist in your world is too hard
Will I find that different place?
Will I be as lonely?
Who will care?
Now that I have decided, the numbness eases
The pretence is over
The game stops
My needs can be satisfied
I am finally in control
Cradled in the grey shadows my heart stops
At last, *Peace!*

Barbara Blyth

AUTUMN ANTICIPATION

This year,
Air of anticipation,
As miserly summer slowly departs,
Clinging on.

Bringing hope within sundown's shadow
That somewhere beyond rain torrents,
Windy storm,
New form.

Seasonal change,
Constant, uncertain flux,
Paddling pool clearing,
Bringing frosty fresh
Greetin' morn'n all.

Loss of flood drain,
Kindred help.
Moving on,
Searching everywhere.

Autumnal sleepy air,
Dreamy dusty snowfall there.
Finding the innocent Chil'e
Waiting for reason why.

Lady oracle no cry,
Just try,
Justify falling apart,
Wi' Heid achey pain.

Rustle their leaves,
Finding the angels warming falling love
Cosmic enveloping,
Different solar system,
Under same sky.

Fiona Gunn

THE VIGIL

I can't believe you are dying,
Or that soon will close a door
On a lovely soul, who loved his life
For ninety years and four.

Yet the love you gave us Daddy,
As on life's path we trod
Has naught compared to the love you gave,
Jesus Christ - your God

So along with fastening buttons
And teaching us all 'fair play'
You gave us lessons in loving Him
You taught us how to pray.

Now as your eyes are closing,
Your earthly life soon o'er
We know that God is waiting there
Behind the closing door.

The new life waiting for you
Our mind can't comprehend
The glory of the face of God
A life that has no end.

Be with us always Daddy
On our journey through the years
As we wait to meet again in Heaven
Please help us dry our tears.

Pauline Butler

THE LETTER

Softly, the letter dropped on the mat,
Would I, if ever, dare to read,
I'd been expecting some news for so long,
When he went away - so silly - we agreed.

Every time that he sent me a letter,
Writing on envelope would never be his,
So - courage my girl, go pick up the missive
Shaking hands tear at flap, what would be inside this!

So many have died, they will never come back,
And many that have, scarred in so many ways,
If he makes it back, will he be any different?
But he's coming! He's coming! I'm counting the days!

The damned bus is late, hurry up, hurry up!
It pulls up at the stop, I'll be on time, no more grief
Hurry up, hurry up, I won't make it to station,
He alights from the train, tight in arms - such relief.

Ralph Littlewood

MEMORIES OF KERNOW

The moon was full, the tide was high,
The water gleaming bright, unfathomable in the clear moonlight
Softly lapping against the fleet, waiting to sail on its retreat.
Beyond the harbour, over the bar, out in the bay lies
St George's Isle, ethereal, bathing in silver moonlight,
Gleaming and glistening like a precious jewel.
On rooftops and cliffs the gulls await the coming dawn.
The streets are empty, not for long.
When day dawns they will echo with visitors chatter,
Off to the beach with a pasty in hand.
By next high tide the river will fill with craft of all shapes
And sizes, offering trips, way up the river or out to sea,
Fishing or self drive, all are on offer, and if you are
Lucky you may see Nelson the seal.
When evening arrives, the seafront will echo with songs of the sea
From a Fishermen's Choir.

R Sturdy

A MOTHER'S PRAYER ON STARTING NURSERY

He's going off to the big wide world
Going without a care
But, I ask you this wide world,
Please listen to my prayer
I'm sending out my little boy
Please allow him to explore.
But when he searches looks and finds
Wide world I do implore
Treat him with all the kindness
That in your heart you find
And allow my little boy
To softly fill his mind
To drink from cups of wisdom
And the knowledge fill him up
To explore with all his senses
Don't allow him to give up
And send him safely home again
To tell me what he saw
When I will love and care for him
And quietly shut the door.

Susan Straughan-Harding

LOVING FRIENDS

There's a corner in my heart
It's special for friends
I've been blessed
Along my way
Giving courage that I've lacked
Inspiration, certainly needed that!
Friendly people sharing themselves,
How happy can life be
Knowing never far from me
Truly very comforting
Their fragrance as a rose
Lovely friends known
Much appreciate
My precious moments
Corner in my heart fulfilled
Bubbles over, remembering
Loving friends memories.

Rosemary Sheridan

THE JOURNEY OF LIFE

Life is never simple
Confusion and stress must flow
But listening and helping one another
You'll put on an awesome show.

Each one of us is different
We'll all fall down some day
But through all that misdirection
Persistence will show you the way.

Everyone has skills and strengths
We must work as a team to succeed
But as long as we all stick together
A happy life you will lead.

Sometimes in life we reach turning points
And don't always know what to do
But once you've listened to everyone else
Remember to listen to you.

The journey of life doesn't have to be hard
As long as you make the right choices,
Be happy and kind to family and friends
And listen to each others' voices.

Elizabeth Banks (17)

BENEATH THIS TREE

We gathered here beneath this tree,
When you were young.
Our salted tears that fell upon you,
On that day,
Have long been washed,
By changing season's toils.
And loved ones who were here,
Beneath this tree, so long ago,
Have made the lonely journey
To be near you.

No summer suns have kissed your lovely face,
Nor snowflakes, soft, caressed against your cheek.
The seasons pass and we are older now.
As autumn paints her prelude
To the winter's song.
You, my son, are here beneath this tree.
Forever beautiful, forever young.

Glyn Davies

THE MAN I LOVE

The man I love
Is rather a bore
Drops his things
All over the floor
Wakes me up
With his awful snore
Brings me no flowers
Never closes the door
But he's told me things
I haven't forgot
Says that I'm lovely
When I know that I'm not
Gives me a kiss
When I'm feeling low
Wouldn't be without him
I'm a fool, I know.

William Precey

FORGOTTEN LAND

Roof timbers bent with age
Wearily rest on granite walls
Doors and windows flap in the wind
Eventually falling to the ground

Inside a past life can be seen
Wood and stone a rusting stove
A view of the fields now overgrown
No more spring crops to be sewn

Creaking farm tools rattle and whine
Collapsing with the passage of time
Skeletal crows hang from a fence
Bounty paid in shillings and pence

Spoonhill Wood mysteriously sits
Its secrets wrapped in weeds and vines
Big old oak trees still enchant
While watching over its habitants.

Farmyard animal, sounds no more
Cobbles grace the courtyard floor
The pigsty smells a little sweeter
The cesspool dry and full of creeper

Weary bodies laid to rest
No one willing to take the task
The hustle of a working farm
Gently succumbing to peaceful calm.

John Mutton

SPRING AWAKENING

When the days lengthen
And the sun's rays strengthen
And the sleeping world
Of nature comes alive
When the garden greenery
Discards the black robe of winter
And the snowdrop in the garden grows
Then spring is in the air
The birds begin to pair and nest
Their chorus fills the morning air
And nature is soon at her best
As winter's chill is left behind
And spring prepares to greet the summer

M Breslin

IN A KENT GARDEN

The garden was still, almost silent,
It was the end of a very hot day,
The best time to be in a garden
When the night creatures come out to play.

I sat perfectly still - heard a hoot of an owl
And the monotonous collated doves call -
Then it all started happening, just as I'd hoped
It was playtime for one and all.

First a wee mouse - had it been in my house
I would have screamed and shooed it away,
But out in the garden it's different
And I watched till it scampered away.

A rabbit came next - nervous at first
But realising I meant it no harm
It ate its fill, then hurried off
To the bank at the back of the farm.

The star turn in a show is always last
I hoped it would be so tonight
I'd waited long and patiently
But oh what a pretty sight.
In the hedges I saw a movement
And there in the evening light
A vixen and two cubs emerged
Much to my delight.

They played for a while without a care
Then a mouse disturbed the evening air,
They vanished quickly out of sight
Maybe they will come another night.

Constance Dewdney

THE SLEEPERS

Buried deep within the earth
In the country of their birth
Lay the dead of ancient wars
Sacrificed for many a cause.

Over moor and over valley
Long-forgotten warriors lie
Roman, Celt and Norman noble
All in anonymity.

Men of Lancaster and York
Pike and bowmen, young and old
Left behind their grieving loved ones
To perish on the snowy wold.

Puritan and Cavalier, in the fusel's deadly hail.
Faced the cannon's belching muzzle
All were buried where they fell.

Centuries of mortal conflict
Stained our land with human blood
Faceless victims long forgotten
Buried deep in field and woods.

As you walk our country byways
See the sun on roof and spire
Hear the lark sing in the heavens
Soaring ever higher and higher.

Woolly sheep graze in the meadows
As they've done from ancient time
Such a scene of rural beauty
Gives a sense of peace sublime.

Passing time has cleansed the landscape
Every trace of strife is gone
Deep within their secret places
Silent sleepers slumber on.

Janet Cavill

PRECEDENCE

Past the wretched,
appeal until the worst,
the fathoms of desire,
arrest before the possible, like words
that are sung and squeezed of all thought, of that
which precedes me.

I, and the vast,
welcome them to undo the heavens,
sewn through the clouds of irreversibility,
and all that which precedes me.

Opium my heart,
sanctioned through silicon tubes,
and entered amidst the backdoor of gravity's boots,
hounded by criminals who sing, 'Hail that
which precedes you.'

And failed I am,
failed to lay on thoughts of monastery,
of thoughts of flayed and wasted spent,
of drabs of spit and motion loss,
sacrificed pills of a prisoner's cost,

I am, failed I am,
left wondering why I focus on dexterity,
when I see, only to my discretion, that
which precedes me.

Tom Collin

THE OLD CEMETERY ALTON

No slow processing mourners, faithful families
Tending loved ones' graves;
No grateful lovers, finding an escape
From nosey families.
The gate stays locked against the vandals.
Elderly ladies steer reluctant dogs
Between the yews, now grossly overgrown;
Graves untended, bearing mundane messages,
Extolling worthy merchants or a mother
'Now at rest' from years of drudgery
And wifely duties.
Toppled tombstones, long since fallen angels
'Midst ghastly rain-stained artificial flowers -
All as dead as those who lie beneath
Its close-cropped grass - the duty of the Council.

And yet - just once a year its life returns;
Under the hedges, round the sombre years
Carpets of vibrant colour - daffodils
Sporting amongst the snowdrops and the crocus,
Conscious of their so short time to stay,
To leave their message with all sleeping here
'In hope of the Resurrection.'

Joyce Preddle

TO MOTHER

Cherished possession, a mother's love,
Borne in the heart, unshakened
By the bitterest strife, it shall prove
A guiding light, never darkened.

Dulled though it be by constant touch,
Awakening comes, with separation
To stay, just as such;
A bond of deep appreciation.

George Beckford

PRAYER OF HOPE FROM NATURE

The badger, the otter,
the bird family,
all other wonderful
nature spirits.
Wonder and look
at man.
'What are you doing
to our world?'
the birds say.
'I sing a beautiful tune,'
The animals say,
'All I need is a little food.'
The trees and grasses
and flower,
give fresh air and beauty.
The sun gives by day,
the moon smiles by night.
Oh the man in the moon
always smiling.
The lion so majestic and proud.
All the nature's spirits,
all help man to see.
A cat sat on a lap.
A candle glistens in the dark,
giving light, hope, peace
to a soul of sight.

Robert Peckham

OUR MEETING FOUNDERED OVER MONEY

Hard, that Arthur Murray dancing teacher!
Firm on price, although I did beseech her,
Please become my foxtrot promise-keeper
For tuition charges somewhat cheaper.

Overlooking Leicester Square, the dance space
Shone with mirrors showing my enthralled face
And Ms Tutor's educational striding.
Disciplined her movements, sharp or gliding.

But our meeting foundered over money.
I could not afford the dance-struck honey.
Stuck she to the Murray standard charges,
Set to upgrade *wealthy* waltzing barges.

Now that ballroom dancing's geriatric,
And Astair's not here to do his hat trick,
Still I can't forget that slinky siren.
One free lesson and I felt like Byron.

Allan Bula

SMILING

Smiling is infectious,
You catch it like the flu!
When someone smiled at me today,
I started smiling too.
I passed around a corner
And someone saw me grin
When he smiled I realised
I'd passed it on to him.
I thought about a smile
Then realised its worth,
A single smile, just like mine
Could travel round the earth.
So if you see a smile begin,
Don't leave it undetected
Let's start an epidemic,
And get the world infected.

Eunice Brown

THROUGH THE EYES OF A CHILD

Through the eyes of a child
I saw the future
Through the eyes of old age
I saw the past
Children's eyes made memories
That to old age would last.

Through the eyes of a child I made -
Sandcastles on the beach
With buckets and spades -
And saw aeroplanes out of reach.

Through the eyes of old age I saw futures shattered
As war spread through the land,
And death and destruction came
On that once pleasant sand.

Through the eyes of a child I saw love
From parents - they gave their all
Through the eyes of old age - I read papers
Some children - not loved at all.

Through the eyes of a child I saw -
Years and years of change
Growing-up - becoming adult
Making decisions - reaching an age.

Now through my eyes of old age
My memories would fill a book
But I yearn for the days of my childhood,
I can hardly remember - where do I look?

Winnie Milnes

MY TREASURE ISLAND

I follow the footprints that lead to my heart,
where the thoughts of my treasures take place and start,
I pack my soul's suitcase with things that are me,
my memories, faith, friends and family,
I hop on a boat that floats the sea of love,
and reflect on my treasures from God above,
I look at my strengths and the things I adore,
my heart skips a beat as I arrive at the shore,
I throw in the anchor that stops the bad thoughts,
and jump on the island to begin to be taught,
the lessons taught can be hard to understand,
but I have my strength and God's sheltering hands,
I dig up the treasure deep down inside,
for I should speak out and develop my pride,
I find my chest and reveal the rare stone,
for I am my island and my treasure's my own.

Lisa Thompson

FRIENDSHIP

We are the countries of the world,
You and me.
In the early ages when we first met,
We were inseparable.
We were as one.
But over time we split apart,
And drifted away
To settle in separate corners of the globe.
Even now we force wars
Upon each other.
Whatever happened to
Our unity?

Lucy Downes

THE BEST

Each thought is the best of the moment,
Each action the best of its time;
Past, present and future are in it.
They make up this life of mine.
One day at a time I decide what to do
And as long as I am sincere and true,
There can be no regret of past thought or deed.
For recrimination there is no need
From each thought and action I learn by degree.
It is another step forward in life's mystery.
There's no going back, no changing the past.
What was done, was done, and forever will last.
With each new insight understanding will grow
So onwards and upwards I shall go.
When at the end of my life I can say:
        'I have done my best,'
Then with peace in my heart
I can accept my well-earned rest.

Helga Dharmpaul

ONE LAST CHANCE

Just twenty-four hours now left to go
The world will end . . . and *I'll* have to go.
I've got no choice, so it's no good swearing.
Just pick up my heels
And decide what I'm wearing.
I've paid the gas and electric too
I've got no debts . . . so that will do?
But what about my Auntie Flo?
She has a birthday tomorrow, you know.
Oh dear! I wish I had more time
My head's in a spin, and I don't feel fine
I wanted to go and see a friend
I also had my coupon to send
Alas the time . . . it goes so fast
And what in the world am I thinking of
I don't do the lottery and I don't have gas.
I've dithered about and lost the time
So I'll give in and sit and waste the time
I put on the kettle and make some tea
And end my days in ecstasy.

Mary Kirkland

A COUNTRY WALK

A bright sunny day to set the mood
Lightly clothed and stoutly shoed
In sweet harmony along we stroll
An atmosphere to please the soul

Climbing stiles to new pastures green
Rabbits, birds and bold foxes seen
When hummocks loom we climb the heights
King of the castle we claim our rights

Until challenged we tumble to the ground
And tenderly wrestle below the mound
A picnic by a flowing stream
And then a nap perchance to dream

We wake and stroll along some more
The sap of life at pleasure's core
Gentle caressing of a summer's breeze
Tender soft kisses as a lover's tease

A perfect harmonising treat
Till at last our homing feet
Once more return along the way
Rejoicing in a perfect day.

Royston Herbert

THE EXTERMINATION

The malt is supped, it's time to go,
        Clip clop, clip clop tally-ho,
The ritual line of scarlet menace,
        Is rarely tested by fences and hedges.
Tempered notes drown wild bird song,
        But not the unsung plea: *Why me? Why me?*
Run, run, you pure born of ancient damn,
        Blissful with your world.
Run, run as fast as you can,
        Snarling death is briskly snapping at your heels,
Caution to the wind,
        No friends, no redeemer no angels wings for you,
Trumpet sounds that terrify,
        Relentless, they are relentless,
The baying hounds from Hell proclaim they are fast drawing near,
        Be quick, be quick or this will cost you dear,
Run my fine red fauna, run until you drop,
        Those led by blood and fed by blood,
Soon feast upon exhausted flesh,
        Pitiful screams don't appease their shameful lust for gore,
Dead now, gone now, nature's own stealth is no more,
        Torn into a thousand sinful shreds,
While the jeering merciless,
        Daub your brave blood across their barbaric foreheads.

Robert Henry Lonsdale

HOW THE WIND BLOWS

Listen real close for the winds whispering tales,
Great stories of adventure, of boats and their sails.
It'll tell you of pirates, those jolly buccaneers
Of sailing the ocean, sailors' loves and their fears.

Perhaps there's an island with treasure to find,
Or is there a shipwreck, in the back of your mind.
Who knows what the wind's seen as it blows by and by?
Gathering many stories as it swirls through the sky.

Ever it moves across land and sea,
Seeking out news for you and for me.
Dragons and knights, for a fair maiden's hand,
Do battle together all over the land.

Then there's the great whale deep down in the blue.
Calling out messages, for me and for you.
Dolphins, seals, lobster and crab
Have told him stories of that Captain Ahab

Blowing through your hair, caressing your face.
Telling its tale to the whole human race.
So take heed and listen, to all that it says,
For each story is different in so many ways.

Linda J Coombes

SOMEWHERE IN THE WORLD TODAY

Somewhere in the world today,
Poverty is growing restless,
Everything everyone is getting bombed,
No one can stop it.

Somewhere in the world today,
Stealing is getting atrocious,
More teenagers are skipping school,
Innocent people are losing their lives by *murder!*
And no there's no way to stop it . . .

Tanzia Haq

MORE THAN NATURE

Blinded by a paragon of effortless flight
To feel this once is to live a thousand blissful lives
In such comfort one can hardly complain
In such comfort we sleep at night.

The rising of the sun and clearing of the mists
Covers the land in a thin golden drape
While chasing away the bleakness of the night
You lay awake waiting to be kissed

As the midday sun warms the ground
The life around signs a joyful tune
While those who listen absorb in awe
The delights of such a beautiful sound

Weakness in its reach is felt by all
In our world there is no such thing
For our light never fades
Like melodies of the dove's call

So every morning and every night
We lay together in love forever
Listening to those beautiful songs
Forever blind from such an effortless flight.

Michael Hurst

TREASURE TROVES OF THE SECRET WOODS

Walking through woods dark and deep in shade,
Springtime's golden brilliance stirs from winter hibernation
Here is peace and solitude.
Yellow primroses greet me with a gentle smile
Tread gently as you stroll along
Lovely fragrances of spring's rebirth, another springtime
Splendour to remember as I take a walk on the wild side
Happy am I to roam and tread familiar paths of ferns so old
New soft green moss, crusty mould amongst grey weathered old
                                                         stones.
The winding paths ahead, here in my secret wood
So serene and still with wild flowers reveal hedgerows that sparkle
                                                         bright
In early morning a dew spotlight.
Mossy banks if I feel weary, to rest awhile
Perhaps to inhale perfumed fragrances of nature's artistry
Amongst the glory of the secret wood's treasure-troves, often unseen
For sure my eyes do see each primrose that glistens for me.
Now it's time for a fond farewell as I select a path to take me home
Paths that no one can ever call their own
Out of the secret dreamy woods
When time stood still for one alone
'Timeless beauty'.

Pamela Hopes

POEM FOR PEACE

How wonderful this world would be
If everyone lived in harmony
To see a smile on every face
No matter the colour, creed or race
Vanish hate, greed and desire to destroy
The beauty God bestowed, for us to enjoy.
He created men and women, so brave and clever
We must all do our best, and try to endeavour
To live in peace, make heaven on Earth
Prove to our Master our very worth
Let God's love be our inspiration
To build once again a peaceful nation.

D Gilson

MEMORIES OF CHILDHOOD

Those good old country memories,
They are with me all the time . . .
Those beautiful country memories
Do enable me to pen in poetic, lyrical rhyme.
Memories of those carefree childhood times,
When to every boy and girl . . .
The adventures and thrills and spills
Would have us all in a whirl.
With trees to climb and swings swung high,
Then carts and bows and arrows . . .
The rivers and streams and meadows
Did make for one a route to those borrowed barrows.
Places to go and hide-and-seek,
And things to watch and see . . .
Such was one's upbringing,
When there were no video games and we didn't have TV.
We always heeded that golden rule,
Respect for one's neighbours and their livelihood . . .
But, when we played pranks, we were often chased -
And at times chastised - but it was for our own good.
Mummy's home-grown home cooking,
And Daddy's home loving ways . . .
Those good old country memories
Will remain with me all my days.

Kevin McCann

INTERRUPTED RACE

My sin was the worship of the golden calf of athletics
All my free time was train, train and compete
Sunday mornings I ran past the church where I should have been
                                                avoiding the satanic
But my aim was to win pot after pot and join the elite.

Not only running but rowing in the bow of a delicate shell
And shooting Barnes Bridge on the Thames was my delight
My shoulders and abdominals were put through hell
But after showering and downing a pint I was ready for a big bite.

Then when I was gone forty I found that I cold race walk well
So it was London to Brighton several times a very long way
The one hundred and fifty miles stint at Nijmegen gave me a gong
                                                that I must tell
but it was the five mile races at Battersea Park that made my day.

When I was fifty-eight my body one day refused to run anymore
I was frustrated and in despair since this was my pain.
I was in amateur dramatics back at the church I began to explore
I enjoyed acting the baddie even in the Ghost Train.

Like refuse my trophies are in a big black bag which now rests in the
                                                loft.
To see all those people jogging reminds me of yesteryear's stamina
I am no longer a disciple of athletics since the calf I have lost
I follow as a disciple of Christ and feed daily on his manna.

Roy Rudd

LIFE

When you stop and think
And wonder why
That your life
Has passed you by
And if it makes
You feel so sad
Think about your life
And all the times
That you have had.

Alan Green

MOMENTS OF LOVE

When we experience moments of love,
considering that love does not grow on trees,
do we really appreciate that moment, or
is it, for us, just a flash of a passing moment,
to lie dormant in the mind, or perhaps
be captured by the unconscious mind, used
at a later date to entice real moments
of love, pleasure and happiness.
Do we make use of our experience of
love and pleasure, or do we leave
unfulfilled on long, beautiful summer evenings,
the hours which seemed to us that there
might be a hint of love and pleasure.
Yet, such beautiful hours are not, by
a long chalk, wasted. When new moments of
love present themselves which would ordinarily
pass by, leaving the base for a solid consistency
of a rich orchestration, prolonging themselves
into classic examples of love which we
capture now and again through our unconscious
mind. This love continues to exist and is
sent via that stream from the unconscious
into the conscious mind, becoming great moments
of love and pleasure.

Gerard Kenny

WHY?

Do anyone please tell me why
The ones I love are born to die
They reach old age then say goodbye
So tell me true, do I so lie?
Wish I could tell a different story
Yet we all die without hope or glory
From now straight to my precise death
When from this life I'll be bereft
For birth and death
Come to us all
And death is as natural
As nature's call
Yet won't know what
When said and done
For life is like
A shining sun
Our blinding origin
Beyond our sight
As life is day
Then death is night.

Jack Georgion

REVELRY

The sea, the sun, the stars are fun
And everything is merry,
All combine to celebrate
This fifteenth anniversary.

It's summer bright, it's day long light
Let's put the streamers out!
So hang the garlands, throw the feasts,
Make music, sing and shout -

Here's to the future trains of thought,
In sentence, prose and rhyme,
Together thrill with happy plans
And have a jolly time!

A Audrey Agnew

BOOB JOB

I'm gonna have a boob job
If I can raise the cash
The Doc said it's impossible
To get it on the 'nash'

I've had enough of padded bras
That push you up and out
No more little bee stings
I want boobs that knock you out!

A lovely pair of knockers
At least a double 'D'
Voluptuous and sexy
With a cleavage to the knees

So I'm saving all my money
For it costs a tidy sum
I've given up the chocolates
No fags, just chewing gum

The sacrifice is worth it
For if one day you see
A beautiful, gorgeous, sexy
Bouncy busty blonde
(In a mini skirt and tottering
On stilettoes in Romford Market)
That'll be *me!*

Amelia Dunn

FIRST TIME AWAY

Father and I, to the station did go,
The railway station, with luggage,
We met others,
With fathers, mothers, sisters or brothers.
We board the train, say goodbye
To babble and gabble, all the way.
On and on we went.
At Penzance station, stood a bus,
Just for us.
A manor house, where we were to stay,
Loomed up before us, on the way.
Washing, dining, then into double bunks,
To heave a sigh, to hear a cry,
Their first away, like mine today

As Churchill said,
'Work on the farms,
In the fields,
On the land,'
We were now in the army.
The women's land army,
To do our best,
You all know the rest.

Eveline Nash Gaging

ELLA DE'S BIRTHDAY

In a different time at a different place
One golden Friday in a room filled with fun
The expectant excited smile on Daddy's face
Time to laugh with friends, play games and run

On Daddy's birthday when he was two
Chocolate covered face from treats and cake
The look on your baby face, my heart will break
Today is Ella De's birthday and she is two

With your angelic upturned face and blue eyes
Dressed in a princess fairy dress for your birthday tea
Hidden in pink boxes, presents all a surprise
Happy to be a part of your special day and your nanny.

June Witt

No Poppies

No poppies for us
it would be so very nice,
if on your Remembrance Day,
you would spare a minute
to remember us, your four-legged
soldiers of the wars,
the horses, dogs, donkeys and
pigeons that flew with messages
through fire.

We also laid down our lives
in those dark days of war,
no remembrance day for us
yet we give unconditional love
and loyalty without demand
to all mankind, even when we
get shot as well as you.

No war memorial statue
for us, well, perhaps a few
we carried men to war and
it filled us with terror too,
with shells, bullets that flew and swords
that stopped us, as we laid down our
lives with you.

So it would be nice to
know that when poppy petals
fall, you will spare a thought
for us, who are the victims
of mankind, cruelty and because
we think of you.

Julia Holden

The Sounds Of Nature

These are the sounds I love to hear
So soft and soothing to my ear.
Of nature's offerings every day
Like - wavelets running in the bay

And like the soft wind in the trees
I find the humming of the bees
Uplifting to my weary mind,
The sweetest balm for humankind.

Just listen to the lark above
Its brilliant song is full of love.
The song thrush and the blackbird tune,
Enrich us till the end of June.

The lowing of the cattle too
The cock that greets the day anew.
The sheep their lambs so softly call,
The rustle of the leaves at Fall.

Contrast these with the manmade noise
Of roaring engines - the traffic voice
The garden mower, the roadside drill,
Loud noise, the silent air to fill.

How crass Man is compared to *God*
Whose creations all who see - applaud
Do we really think that we are fit
Upon this wondrous Earth to sit,

This heaven here on which we dwell
Will soon be made, by man, a hell.
Of nature's sounds - a running brook,
Of mountain views on which to look,
Of waterfall and flowing river,
Pray God, these will remain forever.

Dorothy Hill Bradshaw

The Ring

Hooked-up from the depths as if fished from the sea
A mud-matted chunk amid soil and stones
Which, seeped in a vinegar solution
For weeks in one of Mother's old clay pots
Like a limpet-like nugget of dark soil
Till the hunk of mud and soil slowly sank,
Revealed a bright, buckle-shaped, hallmarked ring
Buffed and burnished bright till it came up clean.
Now, the silver shines; a ring worn proudly
Close to the knuckle, like a second-skin:
Weighing-up its worth; its hallmarked value
Secondary to its prized permeations -
Its soiled scratches hinting at history
Unknown, previous ownership: real worth;
A fluidly flowing fish from the earth -
Quicksilver, slightly bent and buckled, but
Sparking something - like an electric eel -
A close-comfort sterling-silver circle
A newly-netted bright hand; a real catch
Close to the pen's flow and coming up clean.

R J Stallon

Crushed Grass And Vintage Wine

Crushed grass and breeze-borne blossoms,
The early summer sun.
The hum of busy insects,
The sparkling river's run.
Softly scented silken skin,
A young love newly won.

Moments of pure pleasure
As our limbs entwine.

Sheepskin laid on Axminster,
Glowing logs on fire,
Soft minor keys flowing from
An acappella choir.
Flavour of a vintage wine,
Old love that will not die.

Memories to treasure,
Crushed grass and vintage wine.

Ian McCrae

Day, After Day

Each day my mind drifts towards thoughts of you:
What is she doing?
Who is she doing it with?
And why can't she be doing it with me?

Each night I dream about you.
Don't get me wrong, it's nothing sordid!
But we are together:
You are mine, and I am all yours.

Each day I wonder when I'll see you next.
I look forward to, and cherish,
Each moment that we spend together
And when that final moment is over
I begin to anticipate the next.

I often find myself relaying our conversations;
I can remember every discussion that we've shared.
Some of them hurt, and are best forgotten,
But you said them, so how can I?

Day, after day, after day, after day
You are constantly, no permanently, in my thoughts.
Some would call it an infatuation . . .
I prefer to call it love!

J M Everingham

LOVE TRIUMPHANT

You hinder me to tear me down
A constant predator that wafts around
I am wary of your earthly existence
My final enemy to death persistent
Not an alien, for you began with Eve
You are the Devil, I'm not deceived,
Your purpose is to break my soul
Yet I shall reach my final goal
From my body worn to the limit
With final breath I shall then be free
To meet with God who welcomes me
To cross the path to evermore
No more to fear when at death's door
Another door, to whatever awaits
To the purest love no room for hate.
To meet my loved ones, I have faith
Love reigns supreme at the Golden Gate

Joan Prentice

CHATTING

What do we talk about when we meet?
'Morning Sally, how's your feet?'
'It's too hot for me, how about you?'
'I can't stand the cold, it might give me flu.'
'Come to think of it dear, I'm not too well,'
'Got these twinges again, giving me Hell.'
'Seen Mrs Perkins since she had her op?'
'I do believe she can only hop.'
'They took a lump off her little toe,
And now she thinks it will never grow.'
'My doctor says I'm not to worry,
To go for a walk and not to hurry.'
'Bye-bye Sally, see you soon,
I'm off to a meeting this afternoon,
Just to have some tea and chatter,
Hear some news, things that matter
Like the weather, winds and rain,
Or how's your ulcer dear, again!'

G Drew

WHERE ANGELS PRAY QUIETLY

Sweeping past rainbows
I fly my dreams up to Him
All on coloured kites

When faith faces fear
Turning thoughts above the clouds
Catches His strong light

A rose petal falls
On water and the angels
Pray there quietly

Dispelled disbeliefs
Folded into paper boats
Slowly float away

Swift flights of angels
Through thin air, fulfil frail prayers
Trailing on ebb-tides

On rain-darkened days
They soar, feather-light, my prayers
In bright kimonos!

Colette Thomson

GROWING OLD GRACEFULLY

I look at my skin
as I write this down
It's now all wrinkly
and turned a soft brown
I look out my window
as night turns dawn
I cover my eyes
and I stifle a yawn
It's raining outside
and the wind's rising high
shades of blue infusing the sky

I want to dream of beautiful fields
where the sun shines down
and snaps at our heels
I can smell the roads
they've just been turned
thick, dark liquid
like buckets of thick, black lard
With abundance of vitality
energy and youth on our side
we jump on our bikes
and go on a ride
I can smell the flowers
the grass and the rape
We throw back our heads and laugh and play
and point out landmarks along the way
Our youth my dears we would like to keep
But alas it's not so, we have to sleep.

When I wake up from my nightly rest
I choose the memories that I love best
I'm not educated to a high degree
and my words are not laurels
as you can see
But I'm glad to have shared
this thought with you.

Dorothy Rowe

A WALK IN THE PARK

Tranquillity is all around me,
As I take my stroll through the park.
The sun's rays peak through the tall, elegant trees,
Caressing their leaves with its golden rays.

There is beauty to behold -
From the fragrant bushes,
To the delicate flowers,
Which cover the surroundings.

A rustle can be heard -
Two squirrels appear,
Foraging for tasty acorns,
Before chasing one another up the tall oak tree.

I walk on -
Birds can be heard up above -
Their melodious songs,
Bringing tears to my eyes.

A family of rabbits can be seen,
Munching on the juicy, green grass.
There is a sound -
They stop to listen ears erect,
Before running to hide.
Their fluffy, cottontails disappearing in the undergrowth.

I look back -
My walk is complete.
I stand in awe and wonder, for one last time,
Admiring the surroundings before me,
Before I bid a fond farewell.

Debbie Nobbs

A STORY FOR THE TELLING

A ray of light, shone in the room,
Bringing sunshine into the gloom.
Showing the dust where it lay
Or shimmered in the ray.
Cobwebs hung, here and there,
Sadness was everywhere.
Who had lived here in this dank house?
Did they have stories they could tell?
Did they know happiness, and sorrow?
Who knows what lay here within these walls.
Away from the road that led to falls.
They would have known the sound of water,
Bouncing in amongst the boulders,
Falling with such grace and power,
Bringing wealth to sheltered ground.
Why did they leave, no one knew,
Nor indeed could they say, who.
Maybe they lived here, long, long ago,
Too far back in time for anyone to know.
Hidden away here a mystery,
Behind brambles, nettles, even a tree.
Stumbled upon by a mere chance.
A story for the telling.

Grace Maycock

21ST CENTURY TREADMILL

Modern races
Not snail paces
Internet superhighway
And the byways
Doing it my ways
And the grill
Of the treadmill
As we rush
To the crush
Of the getting and the gain
Society driven insane
And we worry
In the hurry
Money screams
Of the dreams
Out of reach
As we screech

To a halt.

Ruth M Ellett

BAG OF ALL BELONGINGS

Who will buy my dear bag
Of ephemeral joys
Mixed with some mischances
Mistakes, misdemeanours
And angers that are heavy?

Who will desire a bag
Of misplaced hopes, passions
Unreturned, then disdained,
A few soft smiles, at odds
With broken confidences?

Who will require a bag
Painted with bright sadness,
Filled with Pandora's range
Of sinfulnesses,
Of aching unhappiness?

Joan Kelly

TRUTH BEHIND THE EYES

Confronted by a woman
Her clothes all torn like rags
All of her belongings
Wrapped up in carrier bags

I look into her tearful eyes
Her eyes of emerald green
I start to see a part of her
Something I've never seen

I notice there's a softness
Behind a hardened skin
A hint of vulnerability
A caring soul within

This woman has been deeply hurt
Cut down to the core
A woman who just needs some love
So she won't hurt any more

She needs to feel some purpose
Some meaning in her life
The kind love of a caring man
To take away her strife

She wants to have no worries
No hurts, no cares, no fears
Security in future times
A life without the tears

She's too proud to admit it
She needs no helping hand
She's lived her life like this for years
On her own two feet she'll stand.

Neil Warren

A NEW WORLD TOMORROW?

When God looks down He must be sad,
His anguished angels looking on,
Wonder where to lay a hand,
So many hurting, so much wrong.

He knows what drives the desperate
To do His wicked deeds,
The world has caused His problems
And it should sort His needs.

He sees the worldwide fighting,
Hears terrored prayers for peace
And wills Man, love His neighbours
Then wars would surely cease.

It must worry Him when greedy
Take more than their lot,
Guilty, without conscience,
And do not care a 'jot'.

This fruitful world of plenty
Was made for all to share.
None need thirst or hunger
And room for all is there.

He must long to see us all content,
We should have learned by now
It's in us all to change the world
And everyone knows how.

Pauline Boncey

MAN MOST EVIL

It's sixty years since they entered the gates,
And discovered how thousands of souls had suffered such
terrible fates.
Humiliated, terrified, stunned and abused,
Every plea for mercy, cruelly refused.
They had been abducted from Europe far and wide.
To become victims of the largest ever act of genocide.

To qualify for such a fate was hardly something new,
Just the simple fact of being a Jew.
Gypsies, the handicapped, the mentally ill were also on the list.
Strangely when rounded up, very few felt the urge to resist.
Family after family seemed to accept their fate.
Perhaps subdued by the strength of hate.

A mother's instinct is to keep their children safe from all harm.
How do you cope when babies are ripped from loving arms?
Children torn from mothers, husbands torn from wives.
An evil regime that didn't give a damn about their lives.
Human cargo delivered by train after train.
Cries for mercy ignored again and again.

Maybe the lucky ones died shortly after being unloaded.
The unlucky ones, were worked, starved and constantly goaded.
Beaten, stripped, shorn and forced to cower,
Death came slowly, gassed in a mock shower.
Their corpses then buried in putrid mire,
Or burnt in ovens or on an open fire.

No food, medicine, sanitation, nor even room to slumber.
Even their name was replaced by a number.
The young, the old and the weak were first to die.
With survivors too weak to cry.
Starvation, dysentery and typhoid,
A slow death from one or the other was hard to avoid.

Still there are sheds full of glasses, suitcases and human hair.
All these years later their desperate despair, still hangs in the air.
Today the camps offer an insight to immense suffering and pain.
You would think it would never happen again.
Bosnia and Serbia to name but two,
Show what evil men in the name of religion will do.

R Humphrey

SHORT CUT TO THE SUN

There are two winters that advance upon me now:
One of days diminishing,
The other a diminishing of days.
Both dwindle into dark,
A shortening - less light, less life.
Autumn makes small flames at first, and then
The fire spreads, consumes the green:
Even as your illness touches only here,
Then there, this function fails,
This difficulty comes.
Next spring
Is waiting ready in the sealed buds,
Ours, of souls, we have to take on trust;
Faith winnowed by cold winds and
Hope shrivelled in the frost
Of unsent letters and unanswered phones.
I see a single track, stretching to some point
Past my sight's seeing,
Which I must walk alone.
For some of us must walk this winter through,
Whilst others, like the swallows flying south,
Take the short cut to the sun.
Do not be in too much of a hurry
To start this final flight.
I have no wings: my future is on foot.

Susan Latimer

A SECRET CRUSH

I would fight for your honour
I would give you my soul
I would hold you forever
So you're never cold.

I would run a great distance
I would swim all the seas
I would climb all the mountains
Just for love's mystery.

I would shut out the darkness
I would keep in the light
I would bind us together
Like the stars in the night

I would shield you from sickness
I would give you my care
I would comfort you when lonely
And clothe you when bare

I would help you when troubled
I would aid you when sad
I would protect you when frightened
And calm you when mad

I would grasp all emotions
I would show you my love
I would glide into your heart
Like a majestic white dove

Let me drown in your laughter
Let me die in your arms
Let me love you forever
So my soul can be calm.

Samuel Edwards

THE PLAY

The stage is set - the scenery's right, the actors take their places,
The props are made, the script's been learned, the make-up's on
their faces.

The stage is vast - 'tis all the world, the scenery is the Lord's,
The actors are the human race, the script's our spoken words.

The props - possessions gained in life, the face we show - our
make-up
The drama's long – a lifetime show, our parts are there to take up.

Each scene, a different phase in life, to perform, we are delighted,
The acts - tragedy, comedy, tears and mirth, the story - how we
write it.

The curtain rises - all is new, the scene - a kindergarten,
The One above observes the play, his spirit seems to hearten.

Scene follows scene, act follows act, some players leave, more
enter.
The starring roles change actors too, as others take the centre.

As time goes by excitement grows - a birth - a death - a wedding,
And scenes of comedy, when the stars slip on the path they're
treading.

The final scene is with us now, the curtain there to lower,
The actors bow and leave the stage, our drama now is over.

The One above has seen the play and heard the words we've
spoken.
Now comes the time that we await - His write-up as a token -

Of whether he approves or not, the drama we've enacted -
And whether 'tis a prize we'll gain, or a punishment be exacted.

However let us act our parts, perfect them to the letter,
Assist all others to improve - and the play - let's make it better.

And so to earn the grand applause, the actors show their worth
And hope their drama can be done forever - here on earth.

M Grice

GARDEN RAPTURE

Country garden
full of life
beautiful tints
devoid of strife
let my fingers
touch your soul
allow the breeze
across my brow
to gently fondle
my wrinkles slow
now perfumes blend
with new mown grass
twittering birds chat
as they fly past
buzzing insects
are nature's sigh
viewing her kingdom
from on high
all this and health
makes living unique
what other wealth
is there too seek
that gives such joy
as sitting quietly
in restful garden
enjoying nature's melody
at the age of ninety.

Harold Brawn

CHINKABOO

It's the same every morning
The first thing that we do,
A cup of tea, sit,
Look out on the garden,
Watch the birds flitter to and fro.
Wogan on the radio
Rambling on with the usual
Rubbishy stuff.
We don't talk much
Just watch the birds, pecking
Seeds and nuts that we put out.
The birds know our garden,
Always something there to eat.
Sparrows, starlings, blue tits, blackbirds
A thrush, a woodpecker now and then
A robin, a wren, inquisitive,
Keeping a careful eye on things.
One morning we sat there quietly,
It was a miserable day, dark clouds
Drizzle, not many birds about.
Suddenly my wife cried out
'Look over there, there's a chinkaboo.'
I jumped up looking all around,
Never seen one of those before.
'Where, where?' I cried. 'I can't see it,'
Looking across at my wife.
Laughing, tears in her eyes
I said, 'Stop messing about,
Tell me where it is, before it goes away.'
With a great deal of effort
She puts her arm on my shoulder
Then points up to the sky.
Eyes sparkling,
'All I said dear, was look,
As the clouds opened a little,
There's a chink of blue!'

Grahame Garfield Evans

WHITE FLOWERS

White flowers
I bring
Recalling hours
We spent together
In laughter
In tears.
White, pure
Like the gift
You gave of
Yourself, flower
Of your personhood
Unfolds now
Beautified in memory.
Seasons turn,
Warmth and calmness
Touch me here
Where you rest in
The heart of holiness
Reaching me
Quietly and in peace.

George Coombs

THE AID WORKERS

They came from afar,
Having travelled thousands of miles;
Over snow-capped mountains they came
Returning home.

They came from afar,
Over wealthy cities and desert sands;
Through cloud and rainstorm, past forest
Lakes and glens.

They came from afar,
From working amongst the poor
Whose homes were built of rubble;
Who experienced the cold of winter
The heat and drought of summer.

They came from afar
To see those they loved;
To rest in green pastures
And be re-energised, refreshed and renewed
Far from the poppy fields.

Kathleen Baillie

THE POWER OF THE POEM

If you write a letter by hand, or typewriter or computer
To the Pope, the queen, a king, TRH or the Holy Ghost
When retired which you can post on your scooter
But damned lucky if ever you get a reply in the post

But simply try writing a clever poem just to show 'em
God knows why, but you nearly always get a reply
I have in my files famous replies from Prince of Wales,
He loves poems from down and under
Others like PM's, Holy Peters, presidents, dissidents
Always reply many in the sky some asking why?
But always the power of the poem grips the mind
Leaving nattering on mobile phones way behind
But if you need money that is not funny
At ninety-seven I will soon be where there is none
Our PM for sure he always replies . . . 'Do I take my gun?'

Paff-Pafford

FEBRUARY SEA

Drifting seagulls floating by,
Etched like arrows in the sky.
Birds of white
In silent flight.

Heaving, undulating sea
Not bound by land, moving free.
Grey green ocean,
Timeless motion.

Reflected sun and shimmering light
Rolling waves with crests of white,
Attack the shore
With rushing roar.

Crashing down, midst foam and spray
Endless, endless, through the day.
Awesome power,
For hour on hour.

The restless motion of the sea
Conveys a menace for all to see.
Majestic force,
Of nature's course.

John Robertson

DAYS OF MY CHILDHOOD

close my eyes and drink in the scent of flowers,
The heady perfume of roses, honeysuckle, lavender.
become aware of the gentle hum of the bee, collecting pollen.
And the beautiful song of the skylark rising ever higher in flight.
And I dream of hot summer days, 'neath a cloudless sky.
dream of my childhood long since gone.
Days of warm memories, of constant sunshine,
Playing in the meadow in grass knee-high,
Running and skipping through lush greenery,
Days spent paddling in the cool stream,
Trousers rolled up and dresses hitched high.
Days spent quietly sat in long grass
Idly making daisy chains.
Days of harvesting, collecting brambles for jam,
And climbing the trees in the orchard for the apples.
Days of playing hide-and-seek in the copse,
Or swinging from the branches of the trees.
And summer nearly over, we'd help with the harvest,
And at the end of day, tired and happy
We'd ride home on the hay cart.
Days of bliss, of laughter, of innocent fun
Days of my childhood long since gone.

Patricia Burgess

THE MOTORWAY

There is no beginning there is no end
I see in the distance every single bend
Three lanes, four lanes maybe five
I concentrate fully to stay alive
Day and night there are always cars
The central reservation with its taut iron bars
This way, that way what a hullabaloo
Stuck in a traffic jam on the M62
The humdrum sound lulls my ears
The AA man always allays any fears
Bridge after bridge sign after sign
As last my slip road
Motorway, I resign.

Ivana Cullup

MEN

What can we do with them?
Can't live with them
But can live without them
They are noisy and loud
They stand out in a crowd
They like beer and football
They like to think they know it all
Their friends are just as bad
Enough to drive us women mad
If women could emulate men
There would be no need for any of them
To live in a world free of men
To be free of all the noise.
What would we do without the boys
We could drink and party
Be always merry and hearty
To live life without a man
Who could think of a better plan
No matter how hard we try
Man will always multiply
If only we could find a solution
To man's evolution
A carefree world it would be
Women ruling for eternity.

A Reilly

OWL'S ROOST

If only we could still be there,
That lovely cottage - standing where
The fields of flowers are just like a carpet in the spring,
The memories all come flooding in.
The massive walnut tree (still so old)
Providing the squirrel of rusty gold -
With a winter store of sheer delight -
Collected in the dead of night.
Then in the morning, eager hands collect them all.
From the hole that's made by the privy wall.
There are trees to climb, to shout and sing,
Helping out with rooks' fierce din,
The baker man with a horse and cart
Whistling his way with a merry march.
Stopping to let the horse drink from the stream
Listening to the songbirds scream of their delight -
but as yet unseen.
They all congregate at the top of the tree
And look up to Heaven - feeling the breeze
They are thinking it's wonderful to be alive
Giving pleasure to all - as they make a dive,
To the field where 'owls roost' once majestically stood.
Making me stop and think of memories so good.

Iris Brown

THE IMPRESSIONIST

I'll paint you a picture on canvas so plain,
Show it to you, but to no one again.
It's in black and white, like the story I've told,
Not through rose coloured glasses, nor tinted with gold.
The painting is abstract, you clearly will see -
Look at it closely, the subject is me.

Brenda Nicholson

JILTED

Climb malice mountain, swim the swollen river of rejection.
The ache so deep it blinds all reason.
Get even? Get that hate and throw it in their face?
Kind words become just sympathetic swords twisting inside
A bleeding heart.
Pity only fuels hate's fire, debilitates and drains the soul.
Alone on bended knee, tears will keep the swollen river flowing.
Age will not consider this infection, though in youth its drama
Magnified.
The cure lies in another eye.
The tempest leaves its signature, nothing new? Bedraggled and
Abandoned like a pair of worn out shoes.
Finding the antidote something to appease, when from loves
Poisoned chalice we have drunk so greedily.
The cure lies in another eye.
As umbilical cord was severed our fight alone began.
Mind without preconception.
The great jug of life poured down our throats, all the feelings
And beliefs involved.
What comfort have we now? To what now can we hold?
The cure lies in another eye.

H Loseby

PUSSY CAT ALRIGHTI

A tale has been told of Alrighti West
Of how he moved house, he thought it was best.
Now Righti could sleep and not know a thing,
Small mice played around him, they would make quite a din.
They jumped on his tail and blew in his ears and sat on his head.
Then laughed thro' their tears
But the pussy slept on and did nothing but snore.

Now the mice told their friends of the games that they had,
They played ring of roses and hid in his fur -
Hide and seek all the night - he did not even stir
They pulled funny faces and were rather rude,
And even blew raspberries as they gobbled his food,
But the pussy slept on and did nothing but snore.

Sometimes they had picnics when the moon shone bright,
Mice sat all around him all thro' the night,
Then they tickled his tummy and his whiskers would twitch,
They couldn't stop laughing till they fell in a ditch
And the pussy slept on and did nothing but snore.

Then the mice told the rabbits; one night they all sat
While the mice had a party, they all wore funny hats.
Some mice had small whistles made from stems of the corn,
Some had little acorns which they banged till the dawn.
They ate all the blackberries fresh from the trees
And nearly got drunk on dandelion tea
And the pussy slept on and did nothing but snore.

It was such a grand party and the rabbits agreed
They would all have another as soon as could be,
Now the rabbits told hedgehogs, and hedgehogs told owls,
The owls told the bats and the bats told the cows,
They could come to a party to have fun with a cat -
But only if they all bring funny hats!

So one warm summer's night they all happily came
To a wonderful party and played lots of games -
And I have been told it was quite a sight
To see creatures so happy, dancing all thro' the night.

This was so long ago and the tale is still told
By all of the animals wherever you go.
It will go on for ever and ever more of how
The pussy slept on and did nothing but snore.

Joyce West

CHILDHOOD MEMORIES

Contemplating childhood is a thing I often do
Remembering the things I did as in the world I grew
Visits to the sweet shop with pennies clutched in palm
Where we could just indulge ourselves without a single qualm
I often think of liquorice rolls and coloured aniseed
And jars of sticky toffee, which I always seem to need
Rows and rows of coloured pop all lined up on the shelves
With Dandelion and Burdock and Vimto for ourselves
I often think of chukky eggs all warm from under hens
And visits to the farmyard where we had many friends
I remember lots of piglets feeding from their mother sows
And wandering into shiphams where they were milking cows
The scents and smells of farmyards are with me to this day
Of lovely chestnut horses and playing in the hay
Of helping at the harvest making cornstooks in the field
And frightened little rabbits so scared to be revealed
I well remember Mummy in a chauffeur driven car
Being driven off on shopping trips to distances afar
And Daddy in his pinstripe suit with bowler hat and cane
Being driven to the station to catch his city train
I still remember bedtime and the fun we had between
A lovely story by the fire and cup of Ovaltine
And Friday night was senna-pods in case we hadn't been
So we would end the week up with our innards nice and clean
The kneeling down to say our prayers the goodnight kiss and hug
Before at last the light went out and we were warm and snug
The smell of brekky cooking when we woke up at morn
The getting up and rushing down 'twas so good to be born
We had a lovely playroom completely filled with toys
With one end for the little girls and one end for the boys
There were china cups and saucers so that we could all have tea
With all our dolls and teddy bears in our own nursery
There were dinky cars, Meccano and lovely Hornby trains
And boxes full of balsa wood for making model planes
We had a splendid rocking horse and dolls with thick black hair
And books and games and jigsaws and a lovely rocking chair
Going off to parties with velvet cape a flowing
In pretty silky party frock with apple cheeks a glowing
Hide and seek and postman's knock and pinning tail on donkey
And jumping up and spinning round until we all felt wonky
Going off to school each day when holidays were over
Carrying my satchel as I sat in Daddy's Rover
Those dreadful navy knickers with elastic at the knee
And those ghastly vests and bodices that really bothered me
On looking back it seems so strange the plenty that we had
When there were those with nothing who oft in rags were clad
We used to see the women who lived in Scotland Road
Wearing their huge shawls to try to keep out bitter cold
With children often shoeless running up and down the street
With me myself in patent pumps upon my lucky feet
But now things are so different for the State has come to aid
The people who are short of cash are certain to get paid
So no more shoeless children and no more shawl clad mums
And no more destitution in over crowded slums
But I was oh so lucky such a lucky little girl
For I had simply everything – but not one single curl.

Barbara Hampson

SEA OF SOULS

I have wandered across the plains, my feet bloodied and torn,
And marvelled at the beauty of the Earth at the rising of the dawn.
I have quenched my thirst and drunk deep from the well,
And lamented the fate of those languishing where they dwell.
I have heard forgotten souls buried beneath a thousand layers,
Washed free by the rising tide of their tears.

Sarah Allison

MY DEREK

My dearest husband passed away
I think about him every day
The little things he used to say
Will stay with me forever and aye
We used to ride on our bikes through the county lanes
In the sunshine and the rain
We had great times just us two
We can never have them again
We went for walks with Benji along Lowe Hill
Our beloved dog we love him still
Life is so short, we are only borrowed
We do not know what will happen tomorrow
I think about the good times we had together
They will stay in my heart forever and ever.

May Ward

A MIND LOST

*I wrote these words for my cousin Madge, who ended her time
in a care home on October 16, 2002)*

As you sit with spoon in hand, before this lady once so grand,
Who cannot now for ravages of time, control her body or her mind.
This lady once with husband walked, holding hands they never thought,
That fate would stage a terrible blow,
She now wears make up just for show.
Do you know just how she feels? As you sit with spoon in hand,
Before this lady once so grand,
In younger days she won a race, yet now needs help to wash her face,
Do you know just how she feels, as beside her you now kneel?
Then gently ask of days gone by and wipe a tear from her eye,
Words of comfort, hold her hand, getting up you now stand
Beside this lady old - yet grand.

Caroline Halliday

SMILE GOD LOVES YOU

We are on a journey, a journey through life
And it's made up of happiness and a little strife
If you're feeling all alone and don't know what to do
Just ask Jesus into your life
Don't feel lonely or afraid
God is only a prayer away
Hallilu . . . Hallelujah

Tune into the channel, the channel of life
And the picture you shall see, will be bright
Smile to one and other and share your cares around
And you will feel a warmth in the inside
Don't feel lonely or afraid
God is only a prayer away
Hallilu . . . Hallelujah

The world belongs to God, He made it for you and me
The sky, the sea, the flowers and the birds and bees
And when you see a rainbow high up in the air
You know that God is spreading His love everywhere
Don't feel lonely or afraid
God is only a prayer away
Hallilu Hallelujah

So . . . don't feel lonely or afraid
For God is only a prayer away
Every day smile and say
God loves me today
Hallelujah . . . Hallelujah . . . God loves me today.

Waller

FIRST LIGHT 2002

At crack of dawn, crisp with rime,
Not far from Closeburn, the New Year's morn,
Cold crow crouched on his crooked branch,
Watching his world for weaklings and carrion,
Sees us silently slip on our way.
Our first footfalls in frosty Dumfriesshire,
Stridulate softly on sugary snow.
Like fish in Deucalion's flooded forest,
The moon is trapped in a tangle of trees.
To each field and every hedgerow,
A dusting of snow adds delicate detail.
Beneath a flush of fire-glow sky,
The pallid hills lie, piles of ash.
Along the lane in a lodge forlorn,
Ghosts who gather to gaze through the gloom,
Offer no greetings to guests at the door.
A cow-man alights from his car at a gate,
And bag on his shoulder bellows for his beasts,
Black as coal brought last night,
With whisky and shortbread to welcome the New Year.
The whole herd hurries, heeding his cries,
To appease their hunger with pelleted fare.
Their coats all steaming they crowd round the manger.
Then to Kirkland Cottage, cold as its hearthstone.
Ears are nipped, numbed the fingers,
As draughts blow through dry-stone walls.
Yet the rhythm of our strides rouses the spirit;
We breathe more deeply; blood runs warmer;
Bracing air banishes lethargy,
Distance decreases, dull wits revive.
Since early exertions excite the appetite,
Turning our tracks at Templeland Mains,
We head homewards, happily anticipating
The savour of cereals, sausages, mushrooms,
Toast with honey, tea piping-hot,
Eggs and bacon, breakfast at Trigony.

Roger Newton

FOR DEAN

I had you just a little while,
And you belonged to me,
I watched you sleep then start to smile
But it wasn't meant to be.
You were a funny little chap -
A miniature old man!
And if I could have you back again
Then I'd give all I can.
I used to sing and dance with you
And this you used to love,
I wonder if you sing and dance
Now you are up above.
It is so many years ago,
You quietly fell asleep,
I have no photos of your face
Though your memory I'll forever keep.
So little son, I write these words
Although we are apart,
You're never very far away
Because you're in my heart.
I had you just a little while
But it was never meant.
I loved you - then I lost you,
'Cos you were only lent.
              God Bless
              Love Mummy xx

Lynn Buxton

THE DEMOLITION OF WALES

What happened to our coal mines,
And our determined hardworking men?
With faces so black, coming up the shaft,
With a proudness in their eyes, we'll never see again.
What happened to our steelworks?
With men working blast furnaces,
Immensely hot and humid,
But always with a cheery smile,
As they crowded over public bars,
To replenish lost fluid,
Always in their working clothes,
And always thankful to be employed.
Who cruelly cut these fine men down in their prime,
After a lifetime of dedication to their work?
Not a thought for those who gave their all
To the companies' time,
These works have now been dismantled,
And made into museums or grassed over fields.
The Welsh heritage we were so proud of,
Has been forsaken by cheaper foreign deals.
We are reaching a third generation of unemployment,
To gallant men who toiled for a pittance,
Who still walk around our villages,
With black scars and hacking cough as witness,
Their determination gone, the same way as their jobs
Told there was no more coal left in their pits,
Yet we knew the coal was as plenty,
As any of the government's lies,
It's been twenty years since being thrown on the scrap heap,
Yet you can still see the sadness in their eyes,
The jobs they went by the thousands,
Through all our valleys and dales,
We were so proud of our hardworking men,
Who kept our fires burning and our furnaces alight,
But proudest of all is to say they all lived in Wales.

Kathryn Evans

A MOTHER'S SONG

What shall I give my children by way of a legacy?
A helping hand when things go wrong - strawberry jam for tea,
The soothing lilt of a bedtime song, a little of all that's me -
And even when they have grown too big - the comfort of my knee.

What shall I give my children to show them that I care?
A large firm hand round a smaller hand - respect when they kneel in
                                                                    prayer,
The patience to try and understand; time to brush their hair,
And when they come wearily home from school - the certainty *I'll* be
                                                                    there.

What shall I give my children to teach them all *I* know?
The chance to discover beautiful books and how new babies grow,
And why the Pimpernel hides its looks, and why some things just
                                                                    glow
Like candlelight and cathedrals, and butterfly wings and snow.

What shall I give my children, for them to remember *me* by?
Praise for their small achievements - sympathy when they cry -
Courage to bear bereavements or weather a stormy sky,
And the memory - of a happy home - to keep in their hearts - 'til
                                                                    they die?

Maureen Sponar

THE LEGACY

I awoke to an eerie silence
All was calm, not a breath of a breeze
The rays of the sun streamed into my room
announcing a new day beginning.

At a loss to tell why the silence
disturbed my innermost sense of peace
I arose from my bed to greet the dawn
and welcome the warmth of the sun.

Everything seemed to me sublime
as I gazed across the morning scene:
the clouds, the hills, the forests and fields
each in their own way calm and serene.

And yet, the picture was incomplete
I looked to the skies, the fields and the woods
Not a bird could I glimpse in all that vast
array of nature, so calm and still.

The forests eroded, the fields stripped
bare of hedgerows and copses where birds
would roost and nest and raise their young
and their demise is our great loss.

Anne Sharples

DEAR FRIEND

Thank you for your letter.
It came the other day.
Made me feel quite happy -
With what it had to say.
A celebration.
Fifteen years in operation.
For ten of those I've known you
You made me feel quite proud.
Accepting *me*
My work in print.
I'd joined your joyful crowd.
So now, sincere wishes I do send
For many, many more successful years.

I raise my glass.
As others will. I'm sure.
                    To Forward Press
                    'Cheers.'

Marnie Connley

SPRING PANOPLY

Bunched on slim stalks,
tight-furled buds dangle
puckered rosebud lips
offering a kiss of welcome.

Canopies blush beauty,
full-blown, short lived
cherry petals. Pink froth
becomes a tidemark
on trim emerald turf,
fallen blossom
marking ebb and flow
of capricious night winds.

Matching ruffle-edged flounce
adrift alongside wall or path
extends its rosy glow
to soften harsh perimeters
with flower-strewn edging.

Penny Smith

THE WIND, FRIEND OR FOE?

I lay on the beach at Woolacombe
Listening to children at play.
A gentle breeze caressed my cheeks
And blew all my troubles away.

Out in the bay a yacht was seen
Sweetly gliding along,
The wind provided its only power
It was strong, but not too strong.

Somewhere out in the Irish Sea
A strong wind, ground was gaining.
A mass of black cloud was gathering
Soon it would be raining,

From Sennen Cove the wind roared on
Gaining strength as it went.
Until it reached Mother Ivy's Bay
And then its force was spent.

Trees were uprooted, phone lines pulled down
No place was there for the faint hearted,
Finally the anger of the wind cooled down
Calm returned and the clearing up started.

In Noah's day the rains came down
Forty days and nights in all
But God sent a wind after that time
Only then did the levels fall.

The Israelites fled from Egypt
The Red Sea looked deep and wide.
A strong east wind parted the waters
The ground where they walked was dried.

Eddie Turner

FOLLOWING MY DREAMS

Following my dreams
For twenty-seven years
Happiness and laughter
Regrets and tears

I followed the light
In a long endless line
I know it was there for me
I realise it was mine

Feelings of happiness
Joy and success
People always told me
I deserved nothing less

The light is so powerful
So warming, so near
My anxiousness diminishes
I am no longer in fear

I reach out my hands
They feel warm to the light
My dreams are becoming reality
I need no longer fight

It is my inspiration
That wonderful light
It continues to guide me
Such a beautiful sight

The light is so precious
So much more than it seems
It has given me strength
To follow my dreams . . .

Nathalie El-Korashy

DANCE OF THE INNOCENT

She stood for a moment, tiptoe in the doorway
Then sprang in the air her arms lifting high.
She danced in the spotlight beamed down by the sun's rays,
And laughed as she whirled singing, 'Look at the sky,
Blue, gold and beautiful and I'm free from care,'
Blossoms from apple trees pushed into her hair.

Poised in the centre, a moment of silence,
Her hands stroked the green leaves brought in from the garden,
Her face still and thoughtful, the laughter receding,
'I'm sorry, I should not have come, beg your pardon.'
A dark cloud had covered the bright golden sunbeams.
The blossom and freedom now part of her daydreams.

The spotlight returned on the girl and her shadow,
A breeze rustled through as the cloud moved away,
Her feet began tapping then faster and faster
She whirled with her shadow, 'I'm Princess of the May!'
Her face glowed with happiness, renewed now with gladness
Trampling over her deep moving sadness.

'I'll bring you blossom,' she laughed as she swayed out.
Gone in a moment as if never there.
The joy and the dancing, the blossom and laughter,
On the floor one leaf shed out of her hair.

This we accept and enjoy in the ballet,
Remark in a film or approve in a book.
Yet this was a real girl who danced in my workplace,
This unacceptable, uncomfortable. And look
I see through the window her body dejected
Led to the ambulance, mind and spirit neglected.

Yet how often have we almost bowed to the impulse
To hop on the pavement or skip in the rain,
To sing at the bus stop, to dance in the library,
To laugh loudly when shopping? Yet are we insane?
Normal behavioiur? Now there's a fine line
Of standards acceptable - in her world or mine!

Ivy Gallagher

MY LOST POEM OF SPRING

Dear oh dear how annoying,
Wherever can it be?
I've looked just everywhere
But my poem I cannot see.

Wherever has it gone?
Is it in the bin?
No! I looked very carefully
But my poem is not within.

Is it with my other poems?
No! I've looked at every one,
But still I cannot find it!
Whatever can be done?

I've looked high, I've looked low,
I've looked in nook and cranny;
But not a sign do I see!
It certainly is uncanny!

Oh well! I'll write another one,
It will not be quite the thing,
Oh I wish that I could find,
My lost poem of spring . . .

J Legg

ANGELS

Can you hear the angels singing?
As softly as a summer breeze

Can you feel the love they radiate?
To help put your heart at ease

Can you feel their tears that quietly fall?
Just like a gentle summer rain
While they share your pain and worry
And help to pick you up again

Can you hear the music of their harps?
Sweet and joyous, loud and clear
A message sent to calm the soul
And chase away all fear

Can you see their tiny footprints?
As they walk alongside you

Can you feel the beating of their wings?
As they help carry you on through

But it doesn't matter if you can't
Because angels are entrusted with our care
They hold aching hearts so tenderly -
You just never realise that they're there.

Dino

THIEF IN THE NIGHT

He came like a thief in the night
And went like a streak of lightning
There were scratches, bumps and bangs
It really was most frightening.

The bird feeder was bitten through
The nuts lay on the floor
Again it happened, the next night too
And the same as the night before.

Who was the intruder causing destruction?
Who was the stealthy thief?
When I looked the very next day
It really was beyond belief.

There before my eyes the culprit lay
With beady eyes and bushy tail
His coat did shine a silvery grey
Then the squirrel just scampered away.

We now take the feeder in at night
And the birds have nuts in the morning
They'll certainly be gone if a squirrel's about
So let this be a warning!

Violetta Ferguson

THE FAMOUS GOLD HILL

What an exhilarating thrill
By going up the cobbled stones of Gold Hill.
Making your legs move arduously more and more
It is assuredly a great joy when one reaches the top,
And seeing all the landscape magically lying there like patches
Of green and brown
With the growing of the crops.
Also with the farms sitting cows
So peacefully the sun all day long.
This part of Wessex to me is most colourful to see
And will always remain my heart strong.

Sammy Davis

NOWHERE AND NO ONE

I live in an unrealistic world where nothing is as it seems.
Instead I spend my days living out your wildest dreams.
In an unforgiving place where nobody cares,
I sleep through the hours stalking your nightmares,
In a forgotten thought I can be anyone I choose to be,
But in a memory, I can fulfil your fantasy.
I dance with the angels on clouds so black,
It's not the body but the mind I attack,
I may be trapped by the walls of life,
But one day I will overcome trouble and strife,
In the hearts of men so evil,
I bring them destruction and eternal upheaval,
In history where all did wrong,
Now for you I will forever hold strong
For all those who share the same pain as me,
I shall take you to glory that you will see,
And with those whose life they stole,
I stand in darkness, waiting for their sinful soul.

Jonathan Gilbert

LIKE THE AIR WE BREATHE

To our Momma, you're our strength and our reason, the things
we need,
Our passion, our life, like the air we breathe.

A comforter when we couldn't sleep, with fairy stories and acorn cups
Stroking our hair, turning bad dreams to good.

Treating us to things for no reason at all,
Even with soggy trainers, picking us up after a fall.

Your thoughtfulness seeps into our lives with loving notes and tales,
Like the air we breathe, you're the wind in our sails.

Steering us wisely but with freedom to move,
Open arms, open heart, with you there's nothing to prove.

Accepting and tolerant, as there's no denying we're a bit odd!
Listening attentively before giving us the nod.

So amusing, so able to make us both laugh,
Like the air we breathe, you are part of our path.

Debbie Harris

THE WRONG SIDE OF THE WINDOW

Down on the dance floor, a kaleidoscope
Of shifting, shimmering colour; bridegroom, bride,
Attendants, younger guests in swirling motion
Swept on the tide of music.

Up in the gallery, the less athletic
Delight in double vision; the far wall -
Fashioned of glass - projecting images
Against the midnight sky.

Gluck's blessed spirits dancing in the air?
Aurora Borealis? ('Merry Dancers'
Northerners name them). Beauty incandescent -
Numinous revelry.

Out on the balcony beyond the window,
Taking the air in spite of threatening clouds,
Stand solid, sober folk apparently
In earnest conversation.

And if we elders feel nostalgic envy
Of young high spirits, deeper our compassion
For stolid, serious folk who cannot see
The dancers in the sky.

Peggy Day

THE BLANKET TOWN

Over three hundred years of history came to a close
On the nineteenth of July two thousand and two,
Never again would the blankets be made
The loyal workers no jobs to pursue.

The name of Witney was known the world o'er
For the finest blankets to ever be made,
And the town that had prospered all those years
Said farewell, and thanks, to a much-loved trade.

The fleece from the sheep was spun into wool,
Then into shuttles the bobbins were placed
Back and forth, they went on the giant looms
In the weaving shed where they once graced.

A town where once several mills flourished
Only one still carried the name,
The Early's sign was extinguished that day
To all it seemed such a shame.

The mills were scattered all over the town,
But now houses have taken their place,
A superstore stands on the site of another,
One large chimney just left as a trace.

Never again will Witney be known
As the place where the blankets are made,
To become just another town on a map
As the memories of the mills fade.

Jo Robinson

HECTOR HICCUP

Hector 'hiccup' couldn't stop,
Hiccuping all the way to the shop,
Susie 'sneezer' went with him,
(Together, sneezing and hiccuping.)

Hector:- 'Stand behind me and sneeze, Suzie do,
The shock might just stop me hiccuping . . . Sue.'

But, oh – (just then Inspector Harris appeared up the road with)
'wot's all this then . . . *ello . . . ello!*'

Harris took out notebook and pen . . . for . . .
A policeman on duty, must observe the law . . .
(So he wrote down their names, addresses and all).

Harris, you see, was over zealous,
And had recently become a trifle jealous,
Of his colleague, Inspector Axeltree,
For every one of Harris's arrests,
His colleague made three!

And Harris felt he must to his duty, apply devotion,
That he must match this 'target' of three,
(For promotion.)

But then . . . Harris, yet scribbling in his book,
Reluctantly realised that no crime had been undertook!

And 'no offence' was taken from our afflicted pair,
But, what's all this, then . . .?
If you would care - (you who read these silly words)
The sneezes and hiccups were no longer
To be heard!

For as a result of Harris' arrest,
The hiccups and sneezes were now put to rest!

The pair were so delighted and made friends once more,
With Harris that (over eager) man of the law
Chuckling away, the three at tea,
Were Harris, Hector and Susie . . . !
(Minus Hiccups and Sneezes, and . . . let off . . . *Scoff free!*)

Andy Field

BING

Living deep within the country I decided that a dog was the very thing
to make me feel secure.
So I phoned the home for strays and within a few short days,
they called me back to say they had the very dog for sure.
He was only five months old with a nature kind but bold, he'd had
owners four who somehow couldn't cope.
For this six stone half breed hound a home needed to be found,
I began to think I was his only hope.
He was handsome, huge and black and there was no turning back
When his big brown eyes looked into mine and said
'Please give me a new home, I promise I won't roam, all that I need
is a meal, some love, a bed.'
He liked my house, it's true, but it needed a re-do, so he tore the
Curtains down, tore them to bits.
The rugs and cushions too were not the proper hue but he liked the
Taste and soon had them in strips.
My shoes and socks and welly soon went into his belly,
He munched his way through everything he smelt,
My new hat, my delight, vanished overnight to reappear next day
neat piles of poo and felt.
His appetite gigantic began to make me frantic but I couldn't bring
Myself to say farewell.
With his six stone on my lap this soppy drooling chap
Sat watching telly with his ever rumbling belly.
We just had to find a way to end this hell.
What he needed was employment to add to his enjoyment,
My husband said a guard-dog he might be,
So off to work he's gone with his lunch box and his bone to guard
His master's lorry he'll be free.
I'd have staked my last pound note this plan's no antidote but to my
Amazement he has proved me wrong
Teeth saying, 'You'll be sorry if you try to steal this lorry,
I'm a guard dog, see my teeth, I'm very strong,'
Now with his new job of work he no longer goes berserk - just
A minute, where's my box of chocolates gone?

S Baker

AFTER WORDSWORTH

From childhood, Wordsworth's gift of eye and ear
Ascribed to natural objects, mountains, woods
And waterfalls, a sense of the sublime;
A source of strength that led his adult years
To jettison the social round and turn
Again with Dorothy to well-loved scenes,
And find among the outcast and the poor
An adaptation to the commonplace
That fostered human dignity akin
To nature's elevation of the mind.

It was his sister's Journal first observed
The dancing daffodils along the shore,
That gave him consolation later felt
When memory retraced the lakeside walk;
Desire to see into the life of things,
Romantic passion to capacity.
Gave balance to emotion and deep thought.

More people than the towns can now sustain
Require the spaces where wild flowers grew;
Although the bond between all living things
Transcends commercial rivalry, ideals
That Wordsworth followed all his life must bow
To conservation's law, and nature once
The teacher must be taught, and mystery
Give way to project skills. Yet anyone
Who sees wild daffodils untouched, will find
They stay forever on the inward eye.

Angela Butler

AUTISM

I never wanted to be this way, I think when he was making me
God had an off day
Did he nip outside for a quick cup of tea and a fag
And when he got back forgot where he was and put my brain in
                                                              wrong?
Just look at me, I am tall, good looking, clean and smart
But I can't understand things and this puts me apart from other
                                                              people.
I try so hard to please everyone, but it doesn't always work out right
People keep telling me what to do, this makes me very cross
I know what I am doing,
They say they are giving me advice, but I think they are criticising.
It makes me so angry that I get upset and do silly things and then
There's more trouble
Mum tries to understand and I don't want to let her down but I can't
                                                              help it
They tell me I have autism, but I don't understand that either
I think God put a bit from a spin dryer in my brain
That's what makes all my thoughts whiz round and get jumbled up
Not all the time of course, but just sometimes
There must be a button somewhere
And somehow it gets pressed and off goes my brain, round and
                                                              round
They send nice people to talk to me, they try to help, say I mustn't
                                                              Worry
They tell me to be laid back, does this mean I have to lie on the floor?
It really is very confusing to an autistic person like me
So if you speak to me or see me around
Don't laugh or make fun or shout if I don't get things right
Remember God was having a bad day when He made me
He has them you know
Sometimes He puts people together the wrong way and they come
Out too small
Or their arms and legs don't match
I think God isn't perfect; He has His off days like all the rest of us.

Marion Kelly

LIKE FATHER, LIKE SON

Richard, my son,
You were the family face,
A true composite of forebears,
Or familiars, like me,
Of Grandad, and others
You were too young to know.

Features and characteristics
Defined as of old,
In profile, or smile,
Or colour and boldness of eye,
Reflecting past generations long gone,
And lives left largely untold.

Yet, old genes were reborn
As if new,
Transcending our mere mortality
And time flown,
To be recast in a uniqueness
That was you.

And now, despite your tragic
Very premature demise,
That heredity has not died,
For within that gorgeous little son
Of your own, within Cai,
The quintessence of family lives on.

Andrew Farmer

IN MY HEAD

In my head I'm still 18
Young, fit, bright and keen,
Slim, full of fun and flirty
To me then being old was 30!

In my head I'm 21
My teens too quickly gone,
Successful in my job
Happy with my husband Bob.

In my head I'm 35
I cradle my first child,
Now I live a mother's part,
Contentment fills my heart.

In my head I'm 48
Always rushing can't be late,
I must slow down my pace
Try to remember life is not a race.

In my head I'm 55
I hold my first grandchild,
A darling little boy
To fill my heart with love and joy.

In my head in 69
Look in the mirror at each line,
Gone is my auburn hair
A reflection of my mother standing there.

Now I'm old and grey
Feeling tired every day,
But I can close my eyes and dream
For in my head I'm still 18.

T Elliott

THE GREAT ESCAPE

My nan has an orchard
And in it were some sheep.
They shared it with the apple and plum trees,
Which around they would peep.
Clinton and Terry were their names,
And they used to fight.
They would kick and ram each other,
And they would even bite.

But one day they got together,
And hatched a little plan.
They thought they could weaken the fence,
But there was no fooling my nan.
She brought in reinforcements,
To fix the damage done,
But the sheep were determined,
That night they would run.

So under the cover of darkness,
They had a go once more.
They pushed and shoved as best they could,
And the fence fell to the floor.
They were out and away,
As fast as they could trot.
But did they know where to run?
They most certainly did not!

They were found looking sheepish,
Grazing in a nearby field.
So they had very little choice,
Other than to yield.
Clinton and Terry had had an ordeal,
And they were very tense,
So maybe the grass isn't always greener,
On the other side of the fence.

Jemma Pinkerton

BE STILL AND KNOW

I have put weeping in the wind
Comfort in the sun
Beauty on the wing
Music in the treetops
Secrets in the rich earth
Thoughts in the mind of man.

Oceans vast and wild and teeming
I have tamed to touch the shore
In time and tide - rules of creation
Set in place with mighty power.

Moon and stars and galaxies
Movement fills the universe
Light and darkness hide-and-seeking
Pain and struggle under flowing
Hope and life fulfilling.

Death is but a disappearing
Absence finds a deeper presence
Gone from sight but truly living
In the heart of the beloved.

I have put weeping in the wind
Comfort in the sun
Beauty on the wing
Music in the treetops
Secrets in the rich earth
Thoughts in the mind of man.

Oonagh Twomey

PENMANSHIP

To perceive and understand, penmanship the written word.
Whose once deciphered and declared intent, becomes an open
                                                    book
The punning use of wordplay, by a skilled and witty hand.
Phraseology of the wordsmith, clever devised and planned.
Whether pointed arrows on shafted wing, their discontent to stir,
Or words of love and harmony that soothe away their sting.
Will set our readers on a tour, whose sensory perception we invite.
Engaging them in craftsmanship their participation our delight.

Edna Sarsfield

A CELEBRATION

Stand and deliver is the call,
Do it now or be up the wall.
Pen to hand let us start,
Engage brain to be smart
From the pen ink does flow,
Look how quickly the words do grow.
No time to sit and think,
Quickly now before the brain does sink.
Eyes like a typewriter be
For catching mistakes you see,
A deadline to be caught
If not, no books to be bought.
Printing press up and running,
The editor patient but gunning.
Top speed now, no delay,
We have got to catch our celebration day.
Fifteen years, that's quite a lot
And no one tied in a knot.
So thanks for all you do,
To make the book come true.
So just for once, may I say
Do have a good Celebration Day.

R G Sill

ALL SOULS' NIGHT (2ND NOVEMBER)

Outside the November wind sighed,
I heard her voice whispering slowly
And crept quietly to her bedroom door.

Ninety-six, she lay quite still but for the gentle
Tapping of frail fingers on the counterpane
Whilst moonbeams played like a halo round her silver hair.

She spoke names, Virginia, Tom,
Raised her hand and beckoned them closer,
I tiptoed through the bedroom door
And broke the spell, eyes opened, she smiled,
'I talked to my dead - the Holy Souls.'

Abina Russell

COBBLESTONES

Among a labyrinth of
cobblestones
a man with a rose walks slowly by.

Wind sweeps along the alley streets
swirling the dust beneath his feet
as he turns down
a misty thoroughfare . . .

Underground the city crawls
to a deadpan beat that never rests
tired eyes
            expressionless
the void sinks into his soul.

He clutches the rose.

Hanging on to a subway train
the weight of the day leans on him

needing only, to see
her face . . .

And escaping from the world below
he traces a path on the
cobblestones of his hometown

(its sunset dwindling like a childhood past)

and touches the gate
handing his love, this special rose

that lights her smiling, sparkling eyes
in the softly falling rain.

Steve Gunning

RENEWAL

Life's stolen hours nectar flowers, breeze blows a whisper away.
Fronds of tender bowers ties the still dark towers of dreams
Starlit night golden rhymes dulled by time passing
Sweet gentle rain falls softly on my face.

M Sellers

LEAVING

Dark have been my dreams of late.
A cloak of loneliness hangs heavy about me.
The leaving is the worst.

Arrivals produce rapturous embraces
And kisses from lips that breathe fire into my very core.
But the leaving is the worst.

The time spent with you is
A joyous symphony of just being.
But the leaving is the worst.

The leaving is always the worst.

David Lees

RETAINED IN SCARBOROUGH

September's image night inside
lit through café shades
spread dotted and suspended
above the diners' heads
mirrored on both sides.

Peopled interchange of pictures
all sides reversed, returned
arriving, staying or departing
while the waiters serve
acting into chorus lines.

Chosen dishes table-spaced
vision synchronise of cutlery
with each copy doubled
as other seated customers
thread mimes of conversation.

Windows forming night without
right angling to reflections
allowing mostly streets below
of garlands lighting bulbs
and harbour in perspective.

Lighthouse shape inactive
withheld from mirror place
touched by shadow form
in floodlight mauve halfway
unmagnetized beyond the pane.

Night reflections keep within
walls of shine opposed
electroned copies taken over
to reproduce and animate
reversed in rows forever.

Reg Baggs

THE PRISONER

The face speaks volumes
No need for words
The strain often shows . . .

The hands are restless
They never sit still
Busy doing nothing . . .

And the eyes . . .
The windows to the soul
Are closed!

They look - but remain distant.

The distance of pain, regret and fear.
Fear of not knowing what the future holds . . .

P Dunbar

THE CHRISTENING

There I was alone, in the middle of the crowd
While all around me, voices, high and loud
With glasses raised were toasting this new birth
And I felt like the only one on Earth
Without a loving partner by my side
And needed, oh so much to run and hide,
I was invisible to one and all
And could not for the life of me recall
Why I was standing in this foreign place,
And then I caught the look upon her face,
My lovely niece with new son in her arms,
Her look of pure love satisfied my qualms
And set at last my grieving soul in peace
Because of that expression on her face.

Joan Fletcher

SEARCHING

Dark, heavy burdened clouds
Block life's source
Moisture becomes uncontainable

Troubles released
Life evaporates despair
Colour, texture, radiance

A noticeable contrast

Is there a deeper message?
Perhaps . . . for me

Through despair lies hope

Behind darkness lies light
Death leads to life
Nature remains in constant balance

Perhaps

Today she will make her choice
Today

Anabel Green

SINBAD

He looked so outstanding and had such appeal
From the moment you saw him your heart he would steal.

A coat like a husky yet soft to the touch
His eyes pools of amber that told you so much

His nature was perfect gentle and sweet
Children who met him were swept off their feet

If you threw him a ball he'd take it straight home
To his own domain where he loved to roam

He was king of his garden and our garden too
A hole in the fence where he would come through

He would come in the house and cause such a stir
With dozens of cuddles just beyond compare

Though sixteen years passed he never grew old
Harder to take was the heat and the cold

On November the 7th he just went to sleep
Without any fuss not even a peep

I can look through the window and still see him there
Running and playing magnificent flair

What wonderful moments for us to recall
Of a special alsation who just had it all

We all miss you Sinbad and hold you so dear
Though your beauty's at rest your spirit's still there.

Maureen Tooze

SHE SLEPT HERE

Sweep the chamber floor sweetly clean
Polish the windows clear and bright
Hang the red brocade bed curtains
For our wise good Queen Bess will sleep her tonight.

On down mattress lay sheets of silk
Stand silver candlesticks for light
Deck the shelf with Tudor roses
Virgin Queen Elizabeth sleeps here tonight.

Take away the soiled oaken stool
Perfume the wig stand for delight
Softly play the viol and lute
Our royal queen sleeps here tonight.

Remove the wine flask and the cup
Re-arrange the tapestries aright
Whisk away chalk white face powder
Queen Elizabeth I slept here last night.

Molly Wyatt

EINSTEIN THE GENIUS CAT

Einstein is a clever cat
Of that there is no doubt
And if you have a problem
He's the one to sort it out

He sneaks into the classroom
In the middle of the night
If there's a sum upon the blackboard
He'll work hard to get it right

Or if there is a spelling
That you really cannot do
He'll clasp a pen in his right paw
And write it down for you

He's been known to have a long debate
On the theory of relativity
And to explain quantum physics
Makes him squeal aloud with glee

So if you're stuck with homework
And it's giving you some trouble
Call very loud, 'Where's Einstein?'
And he'll be there at the double.

You'll get a gold star for it
And you'll be top of the class
Just remember to leave some milk for Einstein
In a champagne glass.

Ali Pickard

SAGA OF THE LEAF

I watched you fall from a tree -
So began a merry journey.
You fluttered all down the road -
Far away from your treetop abode
Then bumped into a dog that barked
As if you were hell-bent on a lark!
After this you fell into a puddle -
Got wet and were in an awful muddle.
The postman waved you aside with an arm -
Still you didn't come to any harm.
Some schoolchildren hurrying past -
Noticed you twirling and started to laugh.
Then a waft of wind carried you high -
As if to mimic the birds in the sky.
Then, a bit soggy, you came to grief
As you landed right under my feet.
So I picked you up and dried you off -
Carried you carefully 'cause you were soft;
Brown, yellow and reddish stains -
Decided to keep you and give you a name.
So now you're called Fred and in a book -
Pressed you well with a new look.
You lie with Shakespeare though rather torn -
The leaves of the *Tempest* you now adorn.

Christine Stallion

LOVE'S JOURNEY

Come walk with me my darling down memory lane
Where everything is different yet everything's the same
We have always been together we have never been apart
We have always loved each other right from the very start
Now our days are numbered our lives are nearly through
Hold my hand my darling I am still in love with you.

R Morgan

VOYAGE THROUGH THE UNIVERSE

Ripples of energy
Dance to the creator's tune,
Vibrations that echo throughout the universe,
In which light and colour interact,
Spiralling,
Spinning,
Leaping,
Flickering.

Swirling clouds of beauty,
Sounds defying description,
Evolved from its unknown origins,
On a voyage of discovery,
Linking the spirit,
With elements of the alpha
Which rejoice in their creator,
The essence.

The origin,
Rapturous in its unfolding,
Casts fragments of itself,
Born from the void before time existed,
Interconnected fibres
Which ebb and flow
In perpetual motion,
Back to the source.

Exquisite planets and stars exist,
Fingerprints of God,
A celestial orchestra,
Echoes through space,
The beginning into infinity,
Universal symphonies,
Masterpieces of the divine,
Omnipotent presence.

Ann G Wallace

REAR-VIEW MIRROR

Will you sit in my car?
Will you drive on my birthday?
It ain't no good shaking your hair
Cos it's only your eyes I ever see
There's desire, my love, in the way you look
A terrible beauty holding on to me.

You can be blonde, you can be dark
Makes no difference to me
Mountains will clasp clouds the same colour
For they are so unquestioning
Rain will fall like tears
Nature will make rivers of us all.

The greens of our valley will meet us
That wooden greeting we pushed open
A linnet's song that quickened our hearts
And those rusting red lips that parted
How many times must I glimpse you
For you to uproot me?

It ain't no good washing your skin
Cos it's only your eyes I ever see
Watching the redwoods move with us
Tall grasses grow from your body
Blonde hair incandescent through my hands
All that's left is the view.

Mark Cleaver

DARKNESS OF THE NIGHT

In the darkness of the night
Lonely lovers cry with broken hearts
Cherished memories are all they own
Their darkest hours are before dawn.

Tomorrow a fading memory of the past
Where smiles are fake, pretence hangs heavy
When reality becomes surreal
Words of truth are lies unspoken.

Seduction is the name of lust
Where bitterness reins supreme
Many facets of deception and desolation
Madness the prize, humiliation the trophy.

Winners or losers rewards are the same
Tears tarnish the spirit, drown their souls
Love is the symptom desire the cure
Delusion in the darkness of the night.

Margaret Berry

THE RIVER OF LIFE

Come and join us
At the river of life,
Which is free for all,
Take this gift of life.

The river never runs dry
But flows freely,
The water is refreshing
And tastes so good.

Here you will find
Riches in abundance,
Everlasting peace and joy.

All troubles and worries
Get washed away,
Here there will be happiness
Much joy and peace.
Come to the river of life.

Julie Smith

AWAITING RETURN OF THE LIFEBOAT THE LOVER

Statuesque she stood, drenched, bedraggled hair plastered against
                                                    her face.
Leaning into the wind, unseeing eyes staring out there into space.
Brown plaid shawl clutched with skeletal fingered grip
Wet taffeta skirt, wind billowed, outlined her hand-pressed hip.
Insensitive to the scouring searing sand, lashing salt spray.
If asked, uncertain, if it were today, tomorrow, or even yesterday.
For one who stood so still, cold undoubtedly, senses dead
A hot summer's day was imprinted in her mind, her 'Ted'.
The flattened corn, the love nest, the shyness after the frenzied
                                                    embrace.
The tender look, the soft kiss on her brow, the work-roughed hand so
                                                    gentle on her face.
Her 'Ted' belying the loutish behaviour he outwardly portrayed
The pitying glances of seemingly another lass betrayed.
The involuntary plea, 'Dear God! Bring him back to me.'
The sun-kissed corn, the howling gale, the maelstrom sea.
Statuesque she stood, drenched, bedraggled hair plastered against
                                                    her face.
Leaning into the wind, unseeing eyes staring out there into space.

A Quinn

GREAT YARMOUTH SONG OF THE SEA

I walk the shoreline
At the break of dawn.
Curly waves of ringlets kiss the shore,
And hand in hand as lovers be,
They twist and turn,
Dragging back the seashells
And singing a song of love and ecstasy.

White horses line the skyline,
Like soldiers on parade,
Enjoying the sound of music
That the ringlets and seashells have made.
The sun wakes up
And floods the scene with delight.
The sea changes a pearly blue,
A reflection from the sky
That once was, a grey and dark night.

The tide moves along the Golden Mile.
A favourite spot it will always be,
For Mum and Dad and family.
They forget the waves of ringlets,
Who grow in confidence,
Like the fish do in the sea.
They become soulmates,
And soulmates forever be.

The promenade attracts attention
In the heat of the rising sun.
People crowd the pavements
To risk a gamble and enjoy the fun.
Some prefer the market,
For bargains they might see.
Others prefer a pint of beer
To quench their thirst,
And some prefer to swim the mighty sea.

The temperature has dropped,
As evening draws in
The curly waves have come to rest.
They gave us music,
They gave us song.
Now it's up to the couples
In the evening light,
Hand in hand, as lovers be,
To carry on.

'What can I give
To a town that rose out of the sea?
I admire their efforts; and their history!
My heart I would give.
My heart to thee.'

E Peaford

AN ANGEL'S WHISPER
(For Mam, Brenda Margaret Frowen)

We glimpsed an angel's wings
As silently we wept
And then we heard a robin sing
Close to where you slept
And as we bowed our heads
In reflection of the love we'd known
A gentle voice whispered
'You are not alone,'
And we felt the kiss of the wind
As we closed our eyes in prayer
Asking for a sign you were still here
And where you lay
A feather came to rest.

Jan Maissen

THE HANDS OF JESUS

Not white hands, are the hands I love the best,
Not perfumed fingers, with jewels dressed.
The hands I love, are bruised and torn,
With nail prints, for everyone lovingly borne.
Yes, for all the world, they were nailed to the tree,
After falsely being tried, without one plea.

Roughened and coarse at the carpenter's bench,
His early years at home had been spent,
But those hands were later in love, often used,
To touch the leper, and blind confused.

Gentle hands were placed on the heads
Of little ones dear to the master wed
He lifted them up, on His knees in love,
And blessed them there, despite disproof.

The dead were raised at the touch of His hand,
The dumb did speak, the deaf did hear, the lame did stand,
Restored to health in body and mind,
Forgiven by Him, and sin put behind.

How humble those hands, as the feet He washed,
Of His disciples, He knew without cleansing, were lost.
Yes, lost in their sins, as all of us stand,
Unless washed in His blood, and upheld by His hand.

But *those sinless* hands, used so much in Galilee
Were cruelly torn, when nailed to the tree,
Yes, nailed to that cross on that stark hillside,
For the world: you and me, He suffered and died.

But hallelujah, He rose and ascended on high,
To His home in glory, by His Father's side.
But one day, there we shall see Him again,
If born of His Spirit, and we remain
True to His word, in obedience and faith.
We shall see those hands and surely be safe,
Yes; safe forever in those keeping hands
Having eternal life, with God our Father, and all His band.

Ruth Baker

ANGELS WEAR WHITE FEATHERS

Polly and me had just got wed
When I marched off to war
'd seen barely eighteen summers
'd not left home before
swore to serve king and country
made a solemn vow
t was a bit of a jape
And a bit of a lark!
But I'm not laughing now
saw my best pal Billy
Killed by an enemy shell
A bit of a jape a bit of a lark
But now he's blown to Hell!
As I looked around the blood filled trench
saw all my comrades . . . dead
And with screams and shellfire in my ears
turned tail . . . and fled
The padre saw my stumbling flight
And led me back somehow
A bit of a jape a bit of a lark
Nobody's laughing now!
My Polly got a letter one 1918 morn
Blind terror was my only crime . . .
But I was shot at dawn.

Marji Tomlinson

GRADELEY GOSSAMER

It is difficult to hale the taste of gossamer.
We devise goluptious goddess like visions
Discerning beauty;
Graminaceous hale in art and literature.

Harmoniously tantara
Respects courteous attentions
Devising with
Wisdom delightful,
Flimsy substances
In autumn
November time.

The grassy excellent robust liking
Harmoniously gyve the godet
Southerly sough
Agreed upon
The southing.

Sarah Munro

BURNING EMBERS

A red glow rises where the forest burns
To make a livid scar across the skies.
The air that once was sweet of smell, now turns
To irritate the nostrils, mouth and eyes.
A black offensive smoke first billows high
Then covers all beneath in choking cloud.
And trees once voiceless can be heard to sigh
Or tremble as they stand with heads now bowed.
This once was England's green and pleasant land
Here, where the sap has dried within the heat
'Tis but the work of someone's careless hand
That brings untimely death to all around.

Another time, another place, we find
A country stream no longer bubbles free,
Polluted by the chemicals that bind
Each atom as it struggles to the sea.
We give so little to our heritage,
But rather feel the need to devastate
That which supports our life through every stage.
Let us draw back now, before it is too late.

Sheila Fernley-Benard

LIFE'S PRICE . . . LIFE'S COST . . .

Life is a loan:
What you borrow is time,
No limit it seems, at the start,
Silver in months, years are in gold

Life is a lease:
A length of time limited,
Fixed and sure from the start,
Silver in seasons, ages in gold.

Love is a lending:
That seeks no return
Compounding each day from the heart,
Silver in reasons and values in gold

Death is a debt
A bond that is broken
No interest in life from the start,
Silver in sorrow heartbreak in gold.

A Brady

FORTY YEARS AGO

Forty years ago was when I first saw you
Forty years ago that was when I knew
That you would be the only one for me
But alas it was never to be
For you never smiled or even said hello
Now forty years on and still you don't know

They say in time, I will forget
But up to now I haven't yet
And to be honest I don't really want to
I'd rather spend my time thinking of you
And when I close my eyes I still see you there
With your blue eyes and hair oh so fair

I often wonder what you are doing now
And wish you would think of me somehow
But I doubt you even remember my name
Or would recognise me if you saw me again
For you never smiled or even said hello
Now forty years on and still you don't know

For forty years I've wished and hoped in vain
That maybe one day I would see you again
But now it don't seem if that will ever be
And I doubt if you will ever think of me
So I'll just hang on to this dream of mine
As I know no better way of passing my time.

Eileen Kyte

REMEMBER JESUS LOVES YOU

The world can seem a lonely place
When you feel in deep despair,
Remember Jesus loves you,
He is always close beside you, He is there,
When the long nights seem even longer,
And you don't know what to do,
Remember Jesus loves you,
And He will see you through,
When you feel you've hit rock bottom,
And you don't feel you can cope,
Remember Jesus loves you,
He is your future and your hope,
At times when things seem too much,
And life doesn't seem fair,
Remember Jesus loves you
And He really does care,
It may feel that there is no one
Who has suffered as much as you,
Remember Jesus loves you,
And what He went through,
He was beaten, tortured, died in pain,
But for you He would go through it all again,
And if you have no one in the world
That you feel you can turn to,
Remember Jesus loves you.

Pat Todd

PATIENCE

Patience is but a lure
To draw us back from immediately wanting more
Wait wait the doubters preach
Pushing us away from the happiness
We should hold on to
And give our all to
While it is within our reach.

S Woodbine

LAMP POST FEVER

What is it about a lamp post
That makes a dog go wild,
And nearly dislocate your arm
As he yanks you like a child?
It matters not that he has passed this way
So many times before -
It's so important that he lifts his leg
And leaves his mark once more!

That post was once so clean and new
With paintwork oh so shiny
But now it has lost its lustrous look
Through dogs both huge and tiny!
They sniff the base and wag their tails
Then give a bark or two,
And as they teeter on three legs
They christen their personal loo!

Once a year the council sends
A man with paint and brush
To rid the post of stains and smells,
For this loo will not flush!
He dons a mask and rubber gloves
To keep the germs away -
With a good rub down, and a coat of paint
That post will last for aye!

So when you take your dog for a walk
And see a lamp post bright
Try to think how it must feel
When dogs make it look a sight.
Those frequent showers of acid rain
From canines large and small
Can blister and corrode the paint -
It does no good at all!

Yet what goes through a doggie mind
Is very hard to know,
It may think a daily watering
Will help that lamp post grow!
So when you're propelled towards it
At a very ungainly speed -
Just clench your teeth - say a prayer -
And hold tightly to that lead!

M McLeod

POEM FOR DAVID

Golden headed, loving boy
I value him
Calm and peaceful
Full of ideas
Genius with hyper energy
I know how hard you work
I know how hard you try
Wait for me here
I do not know your address
I've thought about the acer for your memory
I've tried to pray for an answer
I've imagined wonderful things
That have not yet happened
Every footfall that is yours
I open my door now but no one there
I look for you in cars that pass
I see you in all sorts of ways
You're up in the air
Are you frightened of me?
No need to. I love you
I always shall
More than I love my life
I know you are with me.

Kay Watts

THE FISHERS

As the tide ebbs, bare ribs,
Skeletal fingers, beckon
Above the shallow water,
Blackened and threatening,
Like the remains of some
Primeval animal,
Vainly attempting to escape
The clutches of the deep and glaucous mud,
Old as the Ice Age, ever ready
To swallow unsuspecting innocents.

There was a boy once . . .

From the shore a lonely
Fisherman casts his line,
Patiently waiting for the flounders
Which skim the surface of the mud
Or settle on the softness.

There is a moment between ebb and flow
When all is still; even the cormorant,
Sleek and black and watchful
Frozen like an etching.

And then the gentle sucking as the tide
Turns round, softly at first and sending out
Hesitant feelers
That scarcely break
The surface of the water;

And then the channel fills, the reeds
Sway gently as the water edges round;

And as the water deepens
The cormorant dives, elegantly
Silent and deadly, and breaks his fast.

The fisherman reels in his line
Baiting the hook and sending it
Singing out again across the water.
He will wait patiently;
He is the intruder here.

Meanwhile, the bird has had his fill
And settles down again upon its perch.
Motionless as death.

Dorothy Davis-Sellick

OUR LITTLE TORQUAY TRAIN

Our Torquay train has now been renamed,
And is painted red, white
As The Herald Express and you can guess
Which way it goes round the town.
Does it still pass the pier, that's seen better years
Pass the park, and the green surrounds
With a painted face, on the front of the train
Along the front and down the lanes
Past the fair, is it still there?
Does it still run in the rain?
Will it stop, at a certain spot?
And how many now, does it contain?
To admire the view, as it goes *choo-choo!*
While the miles it starts to gain.
It's there for everyone to use
So why not send in your happy news
Of the train that gives a picturesque ride
Round the town and down a lane
Back up the hill and round again
Our little Torquay train.

Rosemary Peach

DARLING DAD
(Written 30.11.04. The day Dad sadly passed away)

You slipped away so peacefully
To Heaven which is pain free
We held hands as we said our goodbyes
We both cried!
You knew your time was nigh.

Your rolling tears I wiped away
Mine will flow forever and a day.

You have departed, but you haven't gone
The bond between us will always be strong.
A precious dad, a true friend
Truly from beginning to the end.

Unconditional love a rarity
We both cared for each other unreservedly
God is there to guide you through these
Pastures new
Welcoming you with open arms.

Saying, 'Hello son welcome in,
Meet old family and friends
Your life on Earth is complete
Rejoice, be glad, there's no need to be sad

Be strong, come and see
Come rest and sing now in Heaven with Me
I'll take care of you son
Come, come with Me my precious one.'

Gwennie Jones (Nen x)

NO, NONE

The devil theory and other things
Suggest that there might not be a next year.
Dormancy will ensure all is then a blank.
After New Year's Day - nothing.
Or perhaps no New Year's Day after the 31st.
No new Blondie concert. No trade and commerce -
No stock market.
No Dow Jones or FTSE or anything.
No summer, no Wimbledon.
No priests or pimps, Pope or porn.
No political or social agenda.
No Jim, Tom, Cate or Miranda.
No latent period to wake man.
No Earth next year, never again.

Muhammad Salim

SONNET ON WHISTLER'S 'NOCTURNE IN GREY AND GOLD'

A blue-grey mist hangs dormant on the lake,
It stains the sky and clouds the watery glass,
It pulls me nightward in its doleful wake
And lays a liquid cloak on which I pass.
At dead of night the painter draws the shapes
Of skulking keels and half-remembered masts,
Of pinnacles and towers, which when he wakes
Emerge through silken paint and distant pasts.
Our ancestors looked on this with disdain
And in such mournful scenes, their hoodwinked eyes
Saw only paint flung to no mortal gain,
The painter, like the fog, they'd demonise,
For me the fog enrobes a gentle night
Embroidering the dark with threads of light.

Katrina Bride

OUR CELEBRATION

A celebration of calm and peace,
An end to wars and hate,
No more bombings, pain, torment to cease,
This my vision to allow us all to celebrate.

No more loss of lives often too young,
Around this world such hurt, too much to bear,
A song of celebration from each heart sung,
Is this so out of touch to let each other care?

To take a hand inside of mine of yours,
Reinvent words like love, tolerance, understanding,
Lay down demons to snarl no more, reflect, pause,
A world of celebration attainable with true meaning.

K Watkiss

THE PENCIL

The tree was tall and beautiful
The birds' nests were its crown
Then axes, saws and lumberjacks
Arrived and chopped it down.

Stripped of branches, leaves all gone
It lay there long and large
They rolled it to the river, then
Towed it down behind a barge.

In the mill they shaped and sawed and cut
Small pieces to provide
That ended up 7" long
With graphite down inside.

They sent them to the paint shop then
For colours bright or pale
And after sharpening up the point,
On to the shops for sale.

The golden letters on each one
Read 'Pencil H' or 'B'
Young Johnny just now starting school
Said, 'Yellow please for me.'

In class, with paper on each desk
The children all sit down
Johnny takes his pencil, draws a tree,
With birds' nests as its crown.

Enid Gill

MY BROTHER'S PET

My brother kept a little pet
Sidney was his name
Inside a comfy cardboard box
And often out he came
Every day running loose around the house
I always thought his little pet
Must be a tiny mouse
I used to run out too
Before he hid as usual
Inside my outdoor shoe
Always was the left one
How could I have known
Inside were baby spiders
Now the eggs had grown
I realise now that Sidney
Was the mother holding fort
My brother suddenly he
Became my only thought
Picked up my shoe in anger
Bad deeds in my head
Went up to little brother's room
And tipped them in his bed.

Jacqui Morgan

BEST GET A MOVE ON

Best get moving,
My day can't start,
Without me.

Wonder what would happen
If I didn't bother,
Would my day cease to exist?

I suppose it would,
Without me it cannot be here,
It's an awesome responsibility.

B Smith

THE DANCE CONTINUES

Advancing and meeting,
Greeting, and then retreating,
Life is just one long dance -
A comedy of chance,
Urging heart and brain
To feel love again
As we come together
In soft kid or leather,
Or drift with aching heart -
You going your way,
I going my way,
Until the band's stream comes to us again
In life's sensual hot swaying;
And each best of the band
Pulsing and saying
Love will understand!

Dan Pugh

DOCTOR I DO NOT FEEL WELL!

I have got a cold and a rotten chest,
Ring the surgery, that's the best,
On tenterhooks, I wait with fright,
When the bell goes, that's for you all right.
My heart is banging like a drum,
Thinking my last day has come.
Get stripped off, I wish to test.
I bet the Doc's laughing at my vest.
Breathe in, breathe out, hard and soft.
Is it worth stripping for a cough?
Sometimes I get in such a tangle,
Look as if I have been through a mangle.
To get out of that surgery I really must,
My feet will not even hit the dust,
My bra is now on back to front,
My vest and things are hanging out.
No tights upon my legs at all.
They're in my pocket in a ball,
Our doctor is quite a man,
Doing his best wherever he can.
To remember names and all those pills,
For this and that and every ills.
My body's all to hell I guess,
Doc's studying what he can do next.
I hate going up to see him at all,
'Why haven't you been here before?'
'I do not like to waste your time.'
'That's what I am here for, never mind.'
Scrabble in and scrabble out,
'Take these, you will be better - no doubt.'
I only wish that was true,
Will you never make me twenty-two?
Guess not.

E Witt-Way

INVERNESS LADY

Inverness lady, great friend of mine
Times spent with you, the sun does shine.
Happy am I, you call me a friend
Knowing in my heart, our friendship won't end.

Walking through the woods, we hear the birds sing
The wind is in your hair, like a living thing.
The years I have known you, have given me joy
You the great lady, and me the small boy.

Your laughter to my ears, is a sweet note
So for you this verse, I carefully wrote.
To thank you for your friendship, and joy through the years
May our friendship be eternal and not end in tears

Ian R Woollcott

CHRISTMAS DAY

Shuffling along the dreary London street,
Her coat pulled high against the bitter sleet,
Looking for a friendly face, there was none.

Christmas lights twinkled in shop windows,
Gifts wrapped in gold paper,
She could just window shop for now,
There is always 'later'.

The local park swamped in snow,
Hungry birds hoping for a scrap of human kindness.
Where was everybody?

Trudging home sadly, lonely flat waiting;
Sparse but clean, hoping to see a friendly face,
But there's nobody . . .

Julie Hinson

THE LITTLE PEOPLE

I searched through the heathers of mountain and glen
By the moon's silver light, through pasture and fen.
Under the waters that fall to the lake,
And between shady grasses that shimmer, and shake.

I asked of the wise ones that live in the wood
To give me some answers - that is, if they could.
I asked of the squirrel, the rabbit, the fox,
'Is it true that the wee folk live near, in a box?'

'And is it true that the little ones count stars at night
Just in case some are missing when they've set them alight?'
'Are goblins wicked and pixies quite tall?
Compared to the elves, who are no size at all.'

'Do they eat nuts and berries from winter till spring,
And bathe in the mist while spell fairies sing?'
'Do they dress in bright colours and sip from the dew?
And are the garments they wear, woven by you?'

Not one of them answered and all showed disdain,
As much as to say, 'Don't come here again.'
I turned from the forest and down to the pond,
Where lo and behold shone a magical wand.

Then out of the woodland came skipping and running
Scores of the little ones, skilful and cunning.
They lifted me onto their tiny backs, and centipede fashion
Began making tracks to my home in the village, quite far away.
They invaded my garden - they are still there today.

I've got used to their company, I like them around but I
Don't understand how my homestead they found or why
No one noticed them coming this way, for
Hundreds of people pass by every day.

Frederic Davies

SEARCHING

Your kitten has been out for a long time. Too long.
You go through the house, just in case he's sneaked in
As he sometimes does and curls upon your pillow for a snooze.
He's not there, nor in any other favourite spot.
You move to the garden, heart beating just a little faster.
You search, you call him. He's not there.
You go indoors and wait some more, studying the path,
Waiting for him to come trotting along, the way he always does.
It's well past his breakfast time.
There is a sickness in your stomach.
A bad feeling you can't explain.
You go out into the road to walk around the block.
Maybe he's just lost
You feel the pain already
But nothing can prepare you for that third road you turn into.
For there he is, a small white shape lying at the side of the pavement.
Not much blood, but oh, how his head hangs lifeless over your arm
When you pick him up.
Some kind person has laid him carefully upon a grassy bank
By a pathway.
You cradle him gently as you carry him home
And you are numb with sadness for what you have lost
And what will never be again.
In the years to come, that sickening moment will return
Bringing back the sorrow which you felt
On the day your kitten died.

Frances Burrow

SHIPS

I came here on a Highland Omnibus
And explored this state
Like one who comes upon a church
Of living stone, alone,
And catches breath at such serenity,
Then, touched by God, that instant,
Gains knowledge that his life
Can never be the same.

Transmogrified, my wine was turned
Into water from a peaty burn,
Heady in its purity but cold.

Senses turning somersaults,
Fear and longing, solitude,
Mingles with the loneliness
In space that still holds spirit force
For melancholy, masochistic tears

As on the shore, I wait for them;
Columba, Claymore, Clansman,
M S Caledonia
Edging by the Lismore light,
Bringing far flung children from the west
Or lovers with an aching heart
To pass me by, unnoticed in the throng.

The wind, a song,
A howling seabird Banshee song
With words just shapes before my ears,
My mother tongue, yet not my mother's tongue,
I did not come from here.

Teach me, please,
Deny to me the knowledge that my teacher's dead,
Plant the Gaelic chanter song
In minor keys, deep within my alien head.
Hypnotise me, bring it out.
Let all my magic words, unearthed, be said.

John Tirebuck

MIGHTY MELODY

Etched against the sky
Craggy peaks in rosy hue
Welcome the morning.

Washed by dewy mist
Wispy clouds play hide-and-seek
Surprising shadows.

Scoured by waterfalls
Steep ravines chatter and chime
To froth in silence.

Mirrored in deepness
The sky ripples in response
Across rich canvas.

Wrapped in mystery
Chameleon of seasons
Sings a siren song.

Mighty melody
To open the heart and soul
Of man and mountain.

Shirley Johnson

MARY REFLECTS

It seemed like just an ordinary night,
When, suddenly, my room was filled with light!
I became aware of a stranger, standing near,
And my heart was pounding fast with fear.

'Mary!' he said. 'Please don't be afraid,
For you are a highly favoured young maid.'
What sort of greeting was this? thought I,
From a stranger who seemed to fall from the sky!

'Mary, you are chosen to fulfil a task
That no one but God Himself could ask.
You will soon bear a special son -
None other than God's Anointed One!'

'But, how can this be? Oh, how can it be?
For I am not wed, and only ten and three!'
'When God first made this blesséd world,
His Spirit hovered, with wings unfurled.

'And before you have lain with any man,
This Creator Spirit will fulfil God's plan.'
I could not grasp it, but this I knew -
This stranger was surely speaking true.

'I see a manger, I see a hill;
This mystery seems to be God's will.
My mind is made up - you are free to go,
I am willing to serve, and it shall be so!'

Next day, dear Joseph came to call,
And I tried to explain and describe it all.
Poor Joseph was shocked, and didn't know
If he should marry me, or let me go.

Then, after a while, he took my hand
And said, 'Mary, I do not understand
All the mysteries of this blesséd life,
But you shall surely be my wife!'

With that my heart began to sing,
'Lord, I accept anything the future may bring!'
Then, God's gift to me unfurled,
And my son grew up to save the world!

David Wilson

LIMITATIONS

Alone,
But with others,
I sit before the flay of knowledge:
Centrifugal thrown,
The atoms of wisdom
And edicts bombard me where I stand in the way
I own,
Not the mind of reception I wish,
But soak only fragments that appease my tone.

Would I not be of a happier way
To have reached and gleaned the harvest of fact
That passed above my head?
And would I be now, where I would be then -
Did fate decree my stay?

Alone,
In hand with others,
I sit upon the flay of knowledge:
Centrifugal thrown,
Few atoms of wisdom
And edicts strive to escape my brow.
I own,
To the mind of reception I've known;
It is the way of the harvest that would not be sown.

S Croxtall

TAKING TEA WITH NEPTUNE

A slip of a girl and a world of seas,
Sole companions, more often, enemies,
For ninety days cramped in a fragile shell,
Wind and waves took her to the depths of hell!
With each rising wave, loneliness grew,
No land, no signposts, seagulls - a few,
While biting cold swamped her from bow to aft,
Determination and sheer guts captained her craft.
Her emotions surfed from one day to another,
Watching constantly mast, sails and rudder,
Like the waves, reaching the pinnacle of elation,
Next plunging into troughs of desolation.

Southern seas were cruel and foreboding,
To starboard at dawn icebergs perilously floating
Seemed to be sucking her into their icy grip,
How few women could face such a treacherous trip!
When her upper sail needed instant repair
She shinned up the mast in utter despair,
Battered and bruised she returned to her pillow
Sleeping away fear of spume and billow.
On Christmas Day still sailing into the unknown,
She wrote greetings on balloons and filmed for home,
Cramped in her prison she tried hard to be jolly,
Tucked into a small Christmas pud topped with holly!

Antarctica behind her, Cape Horn she came around,
Her joy was ecstatic and knew no bounds,
Now her stalwart yacht sailing north knew the foe,
Half the voyage over, halfway to go!
At the equator she gifted Neptune, God of the Sea,
Sprinkled waves with ginger nuts for his tea,
With the biscuits her fears dispersed on the foam,
Full-knowing a Higher Being was guiding her home!
At times she rejoiced in the peace and wonder,
At spectacular dawns and sunsets took time to ponder
Of her minuteness in this vast highway of mystery,
Yet Ellen MacArthur had earned a place in history!

Pat Heppel

SILENT PROMISE

Sleep so peacefully little one
For many journeys have yet to come
Tucked up safely in your bed
With little monkey by your head

Fear not your dreams, for I am here
I will banish, all that fears
I'll wish away, all things that harm
To keep your innocence, and gentle charm

For you I would like so many things
Of castles, cakes an playtime kings
But as you grow up through the years
Remember son, God always hears

A tiny piece of world you'll touch
So treasure all, you love so much
If all could love, as I and you
Then hopes of peace will follow through

Remember son, the 23rd Psalm
I promise then, you'll feel no harm.

Susan Goldsmith

CRY OF THE UNBORN

Predestination ruled that I should live.
Had this not been good cause bereft of other -
Companionship of sister or fond brother?
In dust here must I lie
While up above me fly
Exulting in their freedom, birds together?

Whose is the choice to slay me in the womb,
My bones and body to a certain end
So intricately formed? Do comprehend,
O Mother! Let me live -
Then I might also give
My life for brother, sister, country, friend.

Pray, who'll preserve my body and my soul;
Provide the panacea for my plight?
No libertine, no fraud, no proselyte,
But one who fears the Lord,
Assimilates His word
And bears His laws and liberties to light.

Christine MacLeod

AM

Walking without shadows
In the morning mist,
Viewing from above
From the still place of my soul.

And yes the goddess sings
With the joy of spring,
Watching with kind eyes
On us the human kind.

Remember it is not a race,
Just a gentle path
Where we may stumble now and then,
But what is that if not nature's intent?

To bend with the wind if you can
And flow like the stream,
Even water
Can round the sharp edges
Of the rocks of life in the end.

Karen Williams

SONNET FOR MAX

The beaming boy holds out his arms to me,
A gesture full of trust and love and faith,
His eyes aglow with questions, I can see.
He knows that I will keep him sure and safe.
Our days together mark an easy pace,
We play and talk or read and walk
And always, smiles alight about his face.
He makes up crazy stories - I revel in his talk!
I hope that he'll remember me, as I
Can now recall my nan, my strong support,
My rock. I hope his future thoughts will fly
To Grandma - words she said and what she taught.
His daddy was (and is) my sunshine boy
And now this shining child becomes my joy.

Carol Richardson

ENGLAND

Rain soaked hills
Trout filled rills
Fresh green fields
Cow's milk yields.

Tall stately trees
Dressed in leaves
Sun dappled glades
Where deer graze.

God made bowers
Full of flowers
Heather glad moors
And birds outdoors.

Land of chimes
Of past times.
The future holds
What England moulds.

By some adored
And some abhorred.
Not all bliss
England is this.

But with dawn
Of summer morn
Who shall compare
With England fair?

Beryl M Malkin

MY LITTLE SISTER

My little sister she is really happy,
She is just into pants
So throw away the nappy.
She is now in a bed
Out of the cot,
Her name is Charlotte
And she smiles a lot.
After dinner she eats
Lots of sweets,
Then she is tired and falls
Straight to sleep.
She likes playing with teddies
And dollies too,
Big ones, small ones, and Winnie the Pooh.
Her middle name is Lily,
Her dolly is called Milly.
My little sis
She's the one you can't miss!

Letita Hughes (14)

ONE RAINY DAY

It is time to sit and ponder
Reflect upon the day
Where I am and where I'm going
And have I lost my way

I wish that I had travelled more
So many sights to see
All the wonders of the world
Have just eluded me

Don't misunderstand me
I've led a joyful life
My family are my backbone
I've loved being a mother and a wife

Today I'm fired up with ambition
I want to write a book
Sail a yacht around the world
And seek adventure just like Cook

I want to go hot-air ballooning
Watch the sun rise, admire the sights
Swoop in a helicopter over the Grand Canyon
Even though I'm afraid of heights

I want to visit the Niagara Falls
To swim with dolphins, feel alive
Go on safari in the African jungle
Embrace danger and yet survive

I'm invigorated by these exciting dreams
My determination now is strong
It is surprising how your thoughts can stray
When it's been raining all day long!

Christina R Maggs

THE COMING OF DAWN

As I wake and wonder
What dawn will bring forth,
Then I wonder of a new beginning,
The sun peeping through the dawn
Brings forth all the brightness,
As the darkness fades away.
It's time to start afresh and get going,
To renew your life and go.
At dawn you think and say,
Although life is passing by,
You can look to health and happiness
            To another dawn.

A F Hiscocks

SANGUINE SHOES

In sanguine shoes
I walk these blues
Through cornfields ripe and sunny,
And by the gate
I dip my fate
In golden urns of honey.
Across the miles
I learn to smile
Through all that brings me down,
And in this place
Across my face
I wear a winner's crown.
To all who bleed
And feel the need
To lose their heavy blues,
Do not hide
Come step inside
These shiny sanguine shoes.

Andrew Hobbs

LIFE'S PERPETUAL BEAT

Birth sparkles to existence
Life ceases at the finish

Sunrise begins the light
Sunset snuffs the day

Seasons come and depart
Flowers bloom then fade
Leaves turn then fall

True love glistens, passion heat
Burning bright; never diminished
A fragrance blossoms, which never plummets

Phillip Hunter Davis

INSPIRED BY NATURE

Take a look around you at the beauty of the Earth,
The sea, the land and sky
The amazing effect of each subject
Makes you really ask, 'Why?'

As we gaze at a clear, blue ocean
Do we question, 'Who painted it blue?'
Lush, green fields, trees of russet and gold
That's the magic of nature come true

The fragrance of flowers, scents of blossoms,
Exotic colours on butterflies' wings,
Even the blending of colours in a rainbow,
From nature comes all manner of things

Birds and bees, all living creatures,
The wonders of nature appeal to all
One answer, written in the Good Book
'The good Lord made them all'.

Vera Ewers

TO A DAUGHTER

If I could teach you one thing, what would it be?
How not to make the same mistakes as me?

To live in the present and not let dreams rule.
To make the right choices while you're still at school.

To be true to your faith when your heart's full of doubt,
To let in compassion, but keep anger out.

To nurture ambition but never be cruel,
To be generous to others but don't be a fool.

To be kind to yourself when your dreams turn to dust,
To keep just a few friends you know you can trust.

To believe in yourself when no one else dares.
To know you are loved when it seems no one cares.

To search for the silence when the world seems too loud.
To develop your own style, don't follow the crowd.

To keep your ideals when your strength's almost gone,
To do the right thing, not the popular one.

To see that your fate is for you to decide,
To know that you hold all the answers inside.

To look to the future, but learn from the past,
To treasure each day as though it's your last.

But more than all this, more than anything else,
I hope I can teach you to just be
Yourself

Sheila Gilbert

HARD LABOUR

I am naked, warm,
Suspended in liquid animation;
Comforted, cosseted, cocooned.
Unknown forces guide me, turn me;
Eyes shut, fists clenched, head down,
I am ready for action.

There is pressure; pushing and pressing,
Hour after hour after hour;
Tightening and relaxing, compressing and contracting . . .

Hours turn to minutes, minutes turn to seconds,
Pressure increasing; noises from outside:
Moaning and groaning, pushing and panting . . .
Break through!
One more push and . . . whoosh!
I am expelled.

Hardness beneath me,
Rough hands grabbing me, lifting me, flipping me,
Cold air shivers me, loud noise deafens me,
Harsh light blinding me . . .
Exposed! I cry.

Soft hands swaddle me; gentle arms coddle me . . .
Know that smell . . . know that voice . . .
Look into her face can't focus,
Eyes swimming in my head;
Weird shapes surround me. I cry.

Something soft in my mouth; can't grip it, lose it,
Frantically search for it; I cry.
Try again . . . can't do it . . . too hard;
Eyes closing . . . tired . . .
Job done:

I am born.

Janet Greenwood

THE FAIR MAIDEN OF SPRING

The sun, is the gold of your hair,
The carpet of bluebells, your eyes,
The velvet of green grass, your dress,
Your brown shoes, the sparrow that flies.

Your hair is awake before me,
Filling the world with its gold,
Dancing around the daffodils,
Giving new life to the old.

At your eyes, I stare with amazement,
The beautiful, cold, silent blue,
The air is heavy with perfume,
The promise of new life is true.

Sometimes, when I tread on your dress,
It feels like a cushion of air,
Giving the mountains their beauty,
Shaded sometimes, by your hair.

Your shoes, they are my alarm clock,
Their song brings new life to the day,
In the woods, the parks and the gardens,
They always have so much to say.

Spring, you did not just happen,
No, you were a gift of love,
Thanks be to Him who created you,
Thanks be to our God of love.

Sandra J Walker

POEMS

Each poem I've written
Was a work of art,
Each poem I've written
Came straight from the heart.
The topics are all different,
No two are the same,
Like things in history
To soft gentle rain.
Like tiny babies
All wrinkly and new,
To old whiskered gentlemen
Or the odd cat or two.
But to write down my poetry
As it comes from my heart
Is to thank Forward Press
For my poetic start!

Linda Francis

BILGE

He was proud when he bought his first car
Came to take me out providing it wasn't far.
The fastest she could go was sixty miles an hour
Forty was a struggle; she simply lacked horsepower.

The engine was clapped out; needed a lot of oil
Had to take some water, worried she would boil.
A board covered a hole caused by rust
Spot welding was needed, that was a must.

He decided to take her to the garage next day
To have her re-sprayed and the rust cleared away.
She looked so smart when he fetched her back
Not a mark on her paint, she was shiny black.

After a number of years had passed us by
He looked at the car and gave a big sigh.
I could see that he would hate
Having to sell old his Morris 8.

Mary Hill

COMPUTER, COMMUTER

Same train different day
Online offline online offline
Same car same way
Black, black tar journey far
Stand at station queue ahead
Train is late still in shed
Moving slow not getting far
Wished I'd took the comfy car
Traffic jam snails pace
So much for the human race
A real pain here comes the rain
Sometimes wish I'd took the train
Now at work what's to be done
Looks like more computer fun
Log on, log off, log on again
Think I might have finger strain
Had enough time to go
Oh good oh look is that the snow
Car breaks down need a tow
Take the train beat the rush
No chance mate they're stuck in slush.

Rick Oak

CHY-AN-DOWER

Choose any lane in Cornwall, they all will take you there.
Into a wondrous world of dreams that everyone can share.
There's mystery and there's magic, take the blinkers from your eyes.
It's in the land, it's in the sea, it's in the clear blue skies.

Holy men on sandal'd feet once bestrode this savage land.
They taught the wild-eyed Cornish to reach out and take God's hand.
From all around the world they came, these Saints of high degree.
Churches, towns and villages, took their names for all to see.

Ghosts of ancient Kings and Princes, myths of beasts that prowl
the moor.
As numerous as the grains of sand that lie upon the shore.
King Arthur and fair Guinevere, and Lancelot of the Lake.
Their place in Cornish folklore, for evermore will take.

Tales of wreckers, on the jagged cliffs, bright lanterns lead the way.
Poor sailor men lured on the rocks, who with their lives did pay.
And smugglers in the dark of night, staggering o'er the beach.
Hiding brandy, rum, tobacco, out of revenue man's long reach.

How rage the winds, and angry seas that beat around the coast.
How brave the men who sail these seas, where sudden death is host.
How wild the heath lands of the north, hear now proud miners tell.
How tons of rock and tin were mined, scratched from that granite hell.

Now, south o'er rolling pasture land and wooded valleys deep.
Past Truro, on to Falmouth Bay, sleepless watch the castles keep.
Small boats now work the Carrick Roads where once proud
galleons lay.
While tourists ride the salty waves through every sunny day.

Then turn you west past Helston town, and onward
through Penzance.
Then finally, when you reach Land's End, it's an awesome
sight perchance.
White crested waves pound on granite rocks, salt spray fills soft air.
Three thousand miles of water now that seals and dolphins share.

The tourists then with cars piled high, turn east for hearth and home.
Past Bodmin Town, and cross the moors, where the fabled beast
did roam.
But if the Kingdom chooses you, it's unwise to say it nay.
For you'll ne'er re-cross the Tamar, and in Cornwall you must stay.

G Hunter Smith

JEANNIE

I watch her smiling as she sits in her chair,
Watching the television, with a blank stare.
Ask what she's watching, says she doesn't know,
Her eyes say it all, but her smile makes her glow.
She's had a few strokes, which have left her this way
The curse of the cigarette has had its day.
The feeling has gone in her right arm,
But doctor says, 'No need for alarm'.
As I look at her now, she fills me with pride,
This disaster has left her, nowhere to hide.
But through it all she never complains,
The sound of her laughter will always remain.
Not even a shadow of what she used to be,
Can only be remembered by the ones who can see.
A hardworking woman, a mother and wife,
A granny and great granny whose been cheated of life.
A shoulder to cry on, a rock for us all,
She will always in my mind be ten feet tall.
This woman I talk about is not without flaw,
She happens to have me as a son-in-law.

Charles Trail

SOUNDS NICE

I like to hear my little dog bark.
When I pick up his lead, and take him to the park,
He jumps up and down, then runs wildly around,
And comes home exhausted, and falls flat on his belly.

'Tis great to hear my father shout,
As he watches the football on the telly,
'Kick it, man, get stuck in there, lads,'
What makes me think, his side is not winning?

On Wednesday I listen for the ice cream man,
The music I hear as he drives around,
Right outside our door is where he stops in our street,
Mum says, 'We will have ice cream for tea'.
I say, 'Three cheers'.

It's good to hear the paperboy whistle, as he comes down
The street on his morning delivery, I look through the window,
Sometimes he will blink, has he something in his eye,
Or just a friendly wink?

On Friday I listened for the postman, walking down the street,
Big boots he wears, to save wearing out his feet,
I opened the door and said, 'It's my birthday today,'
He handed me the letters, all addressed to Sally May.

I love to hear the church bells ring, calling Mum and me
To say our prayers, we kneel on our hassocks,
And say, 'Thank You God, for the sights and sounds we all enjoy,
In this beautiful world we live in'.

Robert Warren

A PLAY OF TIME

A play of time the stage is set:
The winter long and lingering tries to stay
But snowdrops struggling through the ground chases it away
And soon those daffodils, the golden herald of spring
Welcome the boxing match the mad March Hares will bring.

The hedgerow, white with blackthorn flowers
Fine backdrop for the chorus of the day
Welcome the cuckoo to the scene
As thrush and blackbird trill a symphony of May
Then rose of summer blushing pink
Perfumes the bower: in shade we sit
To laze away this summer day!

Through rising mist, the huntsman's horn is calling up the hounds
And autumn leaves of red and gold are drifting to the ground:
The orchard's picked: this cider gold, in wooden casks will lie
Too soon ten trillion flakes of snow, will fill the winter skies;
And underneath this silent shroud the summer seed survives.

Ray Davis

I'LL NEVER SAY REMEMBER ME

I'll never say remember me
If remember me be pain
For what is lost in yesterday's love
We'll never see again.
For we will never capture lost love
For lost love lies in the past
So sweet, so tender was first love.
But was never made to last.
This is now my second love
And it will always be
Lasting as the years go by
In a cherished sweet memory.

S Bellas

PRECIOUS ONE

(For Nyles, with love Nanna Gloria May 1999)

How beautiful you are
Flaxen hair so fine
Shining in the sunlight
Eyes so clear and curious
Skin unblemished and milky
Except for a faint blush
On plump cheeks
Lips with cupid bow defined
Pink and soft
You laugh as you climb the stairs
Ahead of me
Half turning to be sure I am following
How different from the time we
First met a year ago
Then fighting for your life
Every breath taken by machine
Tiny chest heaving mercilessly
Everyone's joy at your birth
Completely overshadowed
With fear indescribably excruciating
Now my heart is at the sight of you
So full of pride at your progress
That I feel it must surely burst
I thank God each day
And pray for His presence
With you always.

Gloria D Hollister

ME

Each day a little older
'Cos time does not stand still
I wish I could grow younger
But know I never will.

The years go by much quicker
Or so it seems to me
Than when I was a teenager
With loads of energy.

Things have worked out great for me
And everything is good
I wouldn't change my life now
Even if I could.

Now I'm not so nimble
But wiser I might be
And I've got something precious
A loving family.

Beryl Upshall

WHEN WE WERE SEVENTEEN

Every day . . . enchantment
Just to hold your hand
Every hour . . . excitement
They say that love is grand
Every moment passing
Just knowing you are mine
When you're in love and seventeen
Each second is heady wine

Time flies by so quickly
And young love fades away
The years can make a difference
For that is life's way
Now you pass me in the crowd
Have you forgotten what might have been?
If we had stayed in love
Just like we were at seventeen.

Joyce Hudspith

COMPOSED THOUGHTS TO CELEBRATE

Easy notes can make good tunes,
They can be 'cool' on mobile phones.
Lots of note repeats are boring,
A varied mix sends humours soaring.

Unique tunes can't be defined,
Melodic logic comes to mind.
Yet success can't be contrived,
Rare vibes confirm best form arrived.

Trying to explain all this,
Is still very hit and miss.
'Surfing' keyboard permutations
Can bring ecstatic celebrations!

As a poet and musician
I enjoy a merry mission.
Sharing works on page and score,
Yields much appetite for more.

Clive Robson

GOD'S SON

Jesus is God's Holy Son,
Pure and simple
The beloved one
Miracles and healings He has done
Bringing love and peace to everyone

Calming the waters
For the fisherman
Thorns on His head
For a crown
Simply dressed in a white gown

He comes to us
When we are down
He eases our sorrows
And soothes our brows
And through our sufferings,
He still is here,
Carrying us to higher spheres.

Jessie Moody

RED ICE

Who doesn't look forward to springtime?
After winter's white mantle turns green
Songbirds return to our gardens
Hoping nests that they build are unseen.

Who doesn't look forward to springtime?
With flowers in bloom everywhere
Their colourful shapes and sweet fragrances
Send feelings of well-being everywhere.

In springtime we all think of Easter
Religious thoughts, are they really sincere?
Is Calgary just a childhood memory?
Buried deep and too busy to care.

Who doesn't look forward to springtime?
Ask the seal, whose mother lies dead,
Whilst our children seek out, those hidden Easter Eggs
Northern ice turns bloody and red.

Mother Nature gives life every springtime
For the Harp Seal it brings death every year
Hunters return with their hammers and picks
Leaving a carcass-strewn, bloody thoroughfare.

Who doesn't look forward to springtime?
When clocks move forward in time
It's a pity these hunters don't do the same
Instead of supporting this fur trading crime.

Clive Goldsmith

WATER MIRROR

Searching for hours.
Wet, numb feet.
Shiver in the shade.
Michael and Melissa.
Painstaking.
Rock pools watching.
Toes gripping.
Fingers delicate.
Touching sealife.
Gathering in shells.
Bucket held.
Digging spade.
Rods with nets.
Little, fast movement.
Eyes fascinated.
Muddy water.
Hand massage.
By goblins and gremlins.
Slimy green pigment.
Rubbed in gently.
Coughed by fossil rock.
Spiky, slippery.
Seeping seaweed.
Emerald shrubbery.
Growth of.
Entanglement.
Crust of the seas.
Sand and grit.
Rubbing vigorously.
Healing salty aroma.
Hardened then washed
Hands vigorated like new.

Tricia Jones

THE SOUND OF SILENCE

The sound of silence is the break of day,
The curtain of night is swept gently away,
The soft morning dew, and sunsets' blaze,
Nature's morning and evening silent praise.

The sound of silence is an opening bud,
The stillness found in the heart of a wood,
The cathedral hush of a forest glade,
Nature's shrine to beauty in dappled shade.

The sound of silence is the tranquil air
Of hearts in harmony with God at prayer,
No murmuring or softly spoken word,
Yet from the depth of silence it is heard.

In the silent moments when thoughts take flight
Into realms of beauty, peace and light,
The spirit soars on faith's extended wings,
The heart rejoices and in silence sings.

Edith Stell

HAPPY 15TH ANNIVERSARY

Congratulations! In fifteen successful years,
'*Following the famous footsteps*' of Keats, to Master Shakespeare's;
With competitions, themes of reflections, nature, crime and passion,
Authors are enthralled, at seeing their prose in publication;
The creative artwork for the chosen imprints, in glorious array,
Our success is measured beyond compare, in every possible way;
We thank everyone at Forward Press for their expertise
                                    and administration,
To promote our work, with the greatest respect, and admiration.

Irene Greenan

RE-VAMPING OUR LOCAL CO-OP

A week's busy reparation
We, customers, blind, impulsive, urge elsewhere,
The aged, elderly - seven days desperation
More need of a gesture and pointing 'over there!'

Thought and sincerity came to our aid;
Newsagents' shop adjoining giving thought -
Slitting shelves by magazines helping the grocery trade
Railway modeller interspersing Golden Shred, all aid not taught.

Following the week of food essential drama
Within the existing building precincts
To come behold! A middle ages cathedral calma,
Aisles of shopping, suggesting these links.

All the assistants under manager Mark Deacon,
Surely well named for the altars of shopping
Such intense symbolism, a beacon
Warning that a central tower will be stopping.

Oh, back in the days of my youth,
Mummy holding my hand, crossing the road
To that huge, unkempt corner Co-Op, by truth,
Twice weekly I suffered this goad.

Jim Lucas

ANIMALS IN WAR

(This was presented to Anne HRH. The Princess Royal to mark the unveiling of the 'Animal in War Memorial' on 27th November 04 in London and now hangs in the Imperial War Museum.)

Could you this once
On Remembrance Day
Remember us, before you pray?
For we were soldiers too
The animals who died for you.

Dogs and mules and horses
Some carried you in war
And as the shells and bullets flew
It filled us all with terror too
For we are flesh and blood like you.

Dogs under fire took messages
Though one in six got through.
And no one gave a second thought.
Most never even knew.

And dogs to save the human lives
We searched for buried mines
Thus dying opened up the road
So you could cross the Rhine.

We dogs were sacrificed, 'we had no choice'
For we were sent to war which then sufficed.

We long-eared chums in Burma
In Wingate's teams of mules,
We climbed the stone on mountain tracks
To carry loads of guns and tools upon our backs.
When wounded still we carried on . . . anon!

Some died of cold in Flander's Fields,
Or drowned in mud at Passchendaele
It happened 90 years ago, remember, tell our tale.
And now in War we serve you still
You have our trust to see us through.

But, no poppies for us?

Gordon Paul Charkin (War Veteran)

THE FRONT ROOM

I was born in a terraced house
Downstairs front room
The glow of the new electric light
Illuminated the dim room.

Brothers and sisters seven in all
Mother and father always on call
The house was damp and very small
Often the plaster would fall off the wall

We all lived together like peas in a pod
One brother repaired the shoes and kept us well shod
All helped out as best they could
Decorating and DIY we all understood

Years later the lads started to drift away
The army called, they had to obey
Mother and father were there many years
Until one day
The front room was dimmed and filled with tears.

Anthony Hull

ANNIVERSARIES

Special days are remembered,
Private moments celebrated,
Public anniversaries,
Occasions, time related.

There are places that evoke
Our ghosts from the past,
Amusing anecdotes,
Striking chords like a blast!

Calendar dates, we'd forget
But memory is too strong,
Golden days recalling joy,
Events returned by a song!

Life is all anniversaries,
Dreams that lived or died.
Happiness or sadness,
When we laughed, when we cried!

Time records our lifespan,
Thro' the clock upon the wall.
While hearts record our memories,
That anniversaries instantly recall!

E M Eagle

THE GRACEFUL PRINCESS OF THE ROSE

Enraptured in the moment of desire
More than the sky of blue or the sapphire,
Springtime revealed a blossom to inspire,
A blossom young and worthy to bestow
Upon the gentle soul where blessings go.

Enchantment was enhanced within the light,
Completely beautiful, a welcome sight
Of slenderness and splendour to excite,
Enfold me in a dream while joys impart,
The heart that thirsts for love thirsts for the heart.

Alluring, delicate bouquet, love knows
She is the graceful princess of the rose,
Exceedingly with fragrance to disclose,
My welling pleasures flow with gratitude
Rejoicing in the silent altitude.

From panache that's observed there's no retreat,
My vision of her posture's hard to beat
And love's achieved elated ways to greet.
Proximity showed favour presently,
Emotion, movement, captivatingly.

Peter James O'Rourke

A CORNISH RIVER

The Molingey stream is such a wonderful scene,
As it meanders to Pentewan, and the sea.
Wildlife you can share, without a care,
Let's all know that, we are free.

The rivers in spate, even though spring is quite late,
The ducks are still building a nest.
White throated dipper acts the clown,
And just nearly gets his feet wet!
On aphids he feeds, and bits of weed,
As he flits from stone to stone.

Above in the sky, a heron flies by,
Looking; anyone's fish to take.
Gaudy feathered jay, with a lopping flight,
Is looking for his dinner in the bright sunlight.
Then just as quick as that, the weather turns black,
A sudden *flash of thunder*,
Lightning rents the sky.
Mother Nature warns her little people,
A deluge is very nigh.
Down sheets the hail, and life giving rain,
Into the river, then the sea to drain.

But 'oh,' that Cornish fresh air!

Geoff Von-Heizon

TEARS OF A CLOWN

No use pretending, little clown
No need to wear that funny frown
Gone is the laughter and the cheers
At last you can shed those silent tears.

Without your pal the chips are down
You're no longer funny, little clown!
Throw away your make-up and false nose,
No longer wear those baggy clothes.

The little clown looked so forlorn,
Holding the collar his pal had worn,
Just then he heard a loud short yap;
And in bounded a scruffy little chap.

Where have you been, my little friend?
Without you my life's at an end,
The dog licked his hand as if to say;
Master I am home to stay.
They top the bill in every town,
'Yes that scruffy dog and the little clown'.

Isabella Pownall

LIFE'S EXTENSION

Have you ever heard the beat of angel's wings?
And then the melody of heavenly strings?
Just when you're busy and life's too quick
To take such an eternal trip.
And then to find, oh joy of joys
This time they've passed you by
The lights, the bed, what nurses say
Confirm that you're alive today.
The days pass into weeks and months go by
Now what a joy to walk, gaze at the sky
A simple thing like clouds above
Or friendships which are akin to love
And finally to see your mate and know
That just for now you didn't have to go
Enjoy the sun, the rain and touch a hand
This is indeed the Promised Land.

D M Pentlow

A POEM FOR STEWARDSHIP

We come, we are ambassadors for Christ and for His holy church,
Not for ourselves we speak but for Him.
His words are in our hearts and on our lips.
Forgetful we may be of much He gives,
But yet we do believe, that we should speak
Of all His goodness, and of His great works for all mankind.
Is it too much to ask that we should offer Him
Some token of our thanks for all that He has given,
In healing arts, in wealth of harvest yield,
Our lives, the beauty of the Earth
Which though man may do his worst
Does yet bring forth a bounteous wealth.
In man's creations He shows forth His hand,
And brings us to our knees in adoration -
Not of man, but of His works.
We are His hands to work, His feet to bring the gospel,
His heart to beat with sorrow and compassion
At all the wickedness and misery of the world.
We are His voice to speak His word,
To sing His praise unto Eternity,
If we the pillars and living stones do fall -
Then falls our church,
And Jesus Christ our Saviour came in vain.

Patricia Arnett

THIS LAND, THIS SCOTLAND

This is the land, where eagles soar
On majestic sweep of wing.
This is the land where deer do roam,
And birds do freely sing.

This is the land of purple heaths
That stretch so far, so wide,
With grouse and capercaillie,
And hares on mountainside.

A land where lochs reflect the hills,
And regal mountain peaks stretch tall
Snow-capped against a clear blue sky -
So *soft* the rains that fall.

A land where sheep meander
On lonely Highland ways.
A land that's full of tumbling streams,
Grand castles, gentle braes.

A land where mists swirl in the glens,
And beaches beguile with silvered charm -
Where all is quiet, remote and still,
No urban rush, just blessed calm.

Joyce Hockley

THE WITCHING HOUR

The witching hour, the moon shines bright,
Black broomsticks fly the sky tonight;
They land on Borders bookshop where
Small children stand in line to stare,
Eyes wide with scarce concealed delight.

We elders contemplate the sight
Of books piled high to left and right,
The reason we all queue to share
The witching hour.

Oh Harry P, your gallant fight
'Gainst Voldemort's minions and his might
Unfolds as page by page you dare
To bring your magic spells to bear,
For little ones whose faces light
The witching hour.

Sheila Burnett

THE BRITISH ISLES

English lakes and Yorkshire dales,
The craggy mountain tops of Wales,
Scotland, land of hill and heather,
Stunning views, in sunny weather.
The Emerald Isle, so fair and green,
Charms you back there, once you've been,
All make up 'The British Isles,'
That none can match o'er many miles.

The Isle of Man with horse-drawn trams,
No worries there of traffic jams!
The Isles of Jersey and of Scilly
Beckon you, just willy-nilly.
The misty isle, the Isle of Skye,
With Cuillin hills that stretch so high,
Endearing place that lures you there,
Splendour for all to see and share.

The cocktail isles in all their glory,
Rhum, Eigg and Mull, of folklore story.
Coll, Staffa, and Iona too,
That sacred isle with much to view.
And oh, what fairer sights to see
Than Isles of Arran and Tiree.
Unspoilt beauty stretches out,
That tugs your heart, without a doubt.

From Shetland down to Isle of Wight,
And in-between, no fairer sight.
The flora, fauna, rocks and all,
And birds that haunt you with their call,
Enchanting place that sure beguiles,
None other than 'The British Isles'.

Violet Beattie

FOOT AND MOUTH

Where did this sickness come from
Carried in the air?
Just to even think of it
Makes my heart despair.
Lambs and calves newly born
Hardly lived a day,
Slaughtered by the thousands,
Their bodies burned away.
Pigs, sheep and cattle
No more roam the hills,
All lost their lives to this disease
That pains them, and then kills.
Some people aren't affected
By what all this may mean,
Until they want some lamb or pork
Or beef that's nice and lean.
Then they'll have to pay the price
Of meat sent from abroad,
No more homegrown produce
That they can freeze and hoard.
The farmers have lost their livelihoods,
Some never will survive,
A lifetime's work gone down the drain,
Will take five years to revive.
I wonder sometimes in this life
Where man's priorities lie,
Spending millions on studying outer space
While earthly creatures die.

Evelyn Osman

ADIEU

He felt a touch on his shoulder
So light; yet firm and kind
He paused for a moment; felt colder
Then a thought like a flame seared his mind.
He knew without doubt who was waiting
Knew that he had to go.
Knew he'd no time for farewells
That this was the end of the show.
Just for a moment he knew it
Then the flame in his mind died away
And his spirit soared freely forever
His form would return to the clay.
Just for a while he was saddened
Then his heart was filled with joy;
With a surge his spirit was gladdened
As if he were a boy.
He looked down at the form he was leaving
Then gazed upwards in wonder and awe
At the friends who were waiting to greet him
All those that had gone before.

Pat Adams

MARIA

am Maria, named after Ave Maria, an elderly, Spanish,
                                        peasant lady.
My ancient home is the theatre of my whole existence.
As a child learning that important catechism from my parents,
Those questions and answers that help to unravel the journey to life,
Learning to understand the different moods of nature,
Working in the fields, taking a laden donkey to market,
Drawing strength from my church and its religion,
Graduating to marriage and family and their independence.
I thank God for my life,
And now the theatre is a cinema of memories that sustain me.
Do not be misled by my wizened face, for the will is as strong
                                        as ever,
The mind keen, the memories so sharp,
As if they are projecting every day onto a screen.

Joan Godfrey

DEAR MOTHER

(In memory of our dear mother Ellen)

You are my mother
And the lady I love
You remind me of
The sweetest white dove
I dream and I cry for you
Every night and day
I hope my tears touched you
And sent you on your way
I pray your soul soars
Across the blue skies above
With my dear old father
Your only true love
Now you are both gone
It has left me in dismay
But oh how I know
We'll meet again one day
Sweet memories of you
They shine in my heart
Oh mother, how I wish
That you didn't depart.

Marilyn Wilson

THE OLD FACTORY

As I walked past
The old factory
It brought back
Many a memory

It's been closed now
For many a year
To my eye
It brought a tear

Everything was spic 'n' span
And brass polished
Now it's
To be demolished

I low happy I was
To work there
All that's left
Are the memories I share

I remember
All six floors
That are now
Behind closed doors.

Frank Tonner

SWORD OF THE SPIRIT

True, deep beauty
Is the sword of the spirit
Piercing the hardness of life.
The true, deep beauty of creation
Is a healing answer to strife.

See a wee rabbit
Formed like a snowflake,
Prickled with claws
And a sparkling face.
A true, deep beauty of life.

See the pure flowers
Studding a meadow,
Flowers in trees
Against a blue sky.
A true, deep beauty of life.

True, deep beauty
Is the sword of the spirit.

M Braithwaite

SONNET IN BLUE

The brush clouded the clear water sky blue
As the artist swished and twirled number three.
The object of her art draped over the settee
In his old birthday suit - with all on view.
Her passion filled the room, coloured the canvas
As her two dimensional lover took shape.
Lovingly the artist sought to recreate
A distant gaze that sought forgiveness.

Though he said art and love should be inspired
Her creativity and love soon felt rejected.
The brush, and the paint, and the lover retired,
Like faded love, cobwebbed and neglected.
She covered over in an attempt to erase,
The empty reflection that warped and crazed.

M Byles

BY THE RIVER

By the river rolling fine,
I lie down in the cool, fresh grass,
On the waves the sun's rays shine,
Shimmering as stray boats pass;
I rest my head and breathe a sigh,
And raise my eyes up to the sky,
Where birds on wing, their chorus blend
In tuneful sounds from end to end;
There's nought to hear but these, I find,
Save for an aircraft's distant drone,
I shut my eyes, true bliss so kind
Descends upon me, all alone;
Tranquillity flows through my soul,
Seeking my young heart, its goal,
To enter in and clear the weight
Of life's harsh hustle, dwelling late;
Enveloped in the waves of peace
I find the beauties of the Earth
Apparent, captured with great ease,
The oldest treasures since our birth,
Unobtainable before,
Yet so close but yet ignored,
Elusive only to the mind
Which makes the eye so very blind!

Alison Lingwood

THE UNICORN

There's an eerie kind of feeling
When the sunlight shafts the trees
The mist it hangs like gossamer
Making droplets on the leaves . . .
The air is filled with newness
It holds excitement - like a birth
A kind of expectation of what
The day will now unearth . . .
For there are folk within our midst
Who remain truly open hearted
And can still imagine a world gone by
With creatures long departed . . .
For if you close your eyes you'll see
What most think is just a 'horse'
But the 'horn' protruding from her head
Is evidence - of course . . . !
This unusual kind of vision
Stands now in full view
I hold my breath - and wait awhile
Don't know what I should do . . .
The forest where she can hide is dark
But there really is no doubt
I want to shout - there's a unicorn!
But the words just won't come out . . .

Anne E Roberts

IN TIME

A gentle breeze
Upon my face
Of the silent tear
There is no trace
In solitude I dwell
Under the old chestnut tree
In time . . . will my sadness leave me.

Christa Todd

FORWARD PRESS FOR EVERMORE
(This classic poem is respectfully dedicated to all of the editorial/poetical staff at Forward Press themselves)

From the very start they have consistently published
Supremely excellent poetry of the most exceptional literary merit.

- From that actual time onwards,
We have always all moved greatly forward
With our most definitive collections,
Individual offerings, and poetical reflections.

- Thereby truly bringing
None other than the written word itself to creative life.

- For the very emphasis has always
Been firmly placed on
Real masterful cadence, couplets,
And whatever else has genuinely withstood
The full test of time.

In short,
Perfectly harmonious, yet clearly poetical
Licence to progress with
The ever solid,
Seriously authentic,
Completely imaginative,
Deeply rhythmical substance.

Way beyond
The concise literary realms of
The substantially visionary,
Powerfully dramatic force to
Flourish with remarkably wonderful pride,
Securely harnessed at the
Very core of 'Forward Press'.

Michael Denholme Hortus Stalker

FORGOTTEN CHILD

The little child just tottered round
No joyful play or uttered sound
His face no sign of joy or woe
Just round and round the room he would go
No one to kiss or hand to hold
No cosy hugs when it got cold
Life for him was oh so hard
No parent's love or birthday cards
This room his world, outside so strange
The darkness inside would never change
When inside they came all white and clean
The light behind so menacing and mean
Their arms outstretched so strange but warm
He knew right then they meant no harm
From the corner he crawled his body all bare
Arms held out wide, so much love to share
Through his short life this was all he had seen
Now suddenly outside he felt so alive and clean
This room he thought was all there could be
Now outside in the sun, the end, no more misery.

J P Brooks

EVE KALI

The sun rose and danced
Zig-zagged across the sky
The Sundance Kid 2
A thin white line moon
Shaped head and shoulders,
3 times the goddess came down.
Brown uniform, smiled, rapport.

Thomas Murphy

Autumn Comes . . .

About the time that autumn comes,
Before the trees are bare, but
Colourfully bathed in red-brown hues,
Dappling the ground beneath,
Earth begins her restful slumber.
Frost nips at the early morn,
Gone is the warmth of the summer sun.
Higher, the moon does rise.
Insects, birds and animals too,
Join in this hibernation,
Kites and eagles once flew high,
Lustfully over mice and shrew filled,
Moorland and scrubland broad.
Now all are barren, apart from . . .
Occasional washes of purple heather.
Ponder this if you will,
Quaint cottages with rose covered walls,
Rooftops thatched, not uniformly tiled.
Sunshine, bright but not warm,
Turning windows into glinting lights.
Under hedges, nest woodland creatures,
Vast fields which once grew grain, now . . .
With winter approaching, they're fallow.
Xylophones are no match for the music of bird songs,
Yearly migrants have long departed.
Zealous squirrels are hiding autumn's rich harvest.

Helen Steel

The Evening's Host

What do you see sitting up there without appearing to have
                                                a single care?

Do you watch the world below as it passes you by
                                        completely unaware,
Or do you fill your time each day listening for each little sound
                                        that could be your prey?

Day or night you live in a world that is your own,
Moving silently through the sky often undetected without even
                                                a groan.

At night you move swiftly with a silence so deafening,
You could almost be a ghost.
Occasionally the silence you will break with a ghostly call
That wakes the night as if to announce that you are the
                                                evening's host.

A creature of the night you are,
A picture of beauty and elegance is what we see,
But a mystery your mind still remains as you sit up there in your tree.

Wendy Coulson

Death Of A Black Swan

Her beauty enhanced the lake that winter,
Contrasting with her snowy-white cousins.
From all around they came in their dozens
To see the fine exotic visitor,
Coloured as if by an artist, tinter,
Of the lake's monochromic denizens.
But someone nurtured an evil mission.
Someone so twisted with hatred so bitter
That he must destroy that beautiful bird
And deprive the people of her splendour.
Taking aim with his crossbow he fired
At the black swan with neck gracefully curled,
And nobody was there to save her.
She shuddered and without a sound, she died.

Teresa M Garfield

Granddaughter's Wedding

At last the special day is here
The guests arrive from far and near
The bride, so beautiful and serene
In gorgeous gown - fit for a queen!
With proud Dad, she rides in gleaming coach
While bridesmaids chatter in the church porch
The groom waits nervously to see
His lovely, radiant wife to be
The mothers of the pair look grand
And grans and grandads stand hand in hand
The vicar starts the ceremony -
Amid the flowers - a sight to see
And soon they're pronounced 'man and wife'
And wished a long and happy life
Off to the reception in a grand marquee
Where everyone has a lovely tea.
Then it's the toasts and speeches too
When the best man tells a joke or two!
The band arrives for the evening's delight
And everyone dances on through the night.
The happy pair leave for their honeymoon
And the band then plays its final tune
A day to remember forever and ever
And, 'Thank You God,' for the perfect weather!
We thank you for a perfect day
Which couldn't have been better in any way!
We wish them joy and happiness forever
And a long and special life together.

Pat Rogers

15th Anniversary Of Forward Press

I started off a few years ago
Poems of this, that and others you know
Parents, and Grandma, gardens and pets,
Tragedies, royalty, I've 'done it' you bet.

I have enjoyed every minute
It's brought me such joy
And I hope to all readers
Man, woman, girls, and boys.

I've always loved poetry
It touches your heart,
It brings writers together
Who all take a part.

They all work hard at Forward Press
And the end product we see,
Is simply the best.

I could not single one out
As being my best
That would be unfair
To all the rest.

So this, guys and gals
Comes to you from me
Cheers! 'Happy Anniversary'.

Rachel Mary Mills

Congratulations

This is a chance for me to say
Best of luck for your special day
For all the poets just like me
Who pen our words for all to see
To see it printed brings success
We owe it all to *Forward Press*.

Isobel Clanfield

CELEBRATE THE LOVE OF LIFE

Our relationships, which mean so much accomplished with love,
Patience, understanding, toil and strife
Good health, which none can be without
Support of friends, shared experiences, some happy,
Some sad, some painful, treasured more as the days go by
The world rushes on bent on destruction.
The answer is in the waves of creation
Out of it is built a new dimension.
Brothers clasping hand of brothers
Sisters clasping hand of sisters
Looking out for each other
Helping where we can, this is the hope for all mankind.
Then one day what was Martin Luther's dream will be a reality
All will learn to live in harmony and peace,
No matter what colour, nationality or creed.
The salvation of all mankind lies in Christ Himself.
Celebration of Forward Press
What wealth of words must have passed your desk
Thanks for the years we have enjoyed
Let's have music, food, wine and song
With all the writers and poets.

Elsie Moore

SADNESS IN FASHION!

I had a dress; a favourite dress
I wore this as much as I could
For special occasions in wintertime
When I wanted to look my best
Sadly one day a hole appeared
After many years of good wear
In the armpit the dress began to tear
My favourite dress was beyond repair.

I had a coat; a green winter coat
I wore this as much as I could
In wintertime when the wind did blow
And the snow would fall if it could
The coat had warmth, the coat had taste
From Selfridge's London it came
Sadly one day the lining tore and split away
After many years of good wear
I was obliged to give the coat away
To a secondhand shop
I treasured that coat and shed many tears.

I had a little black dress; it was better than the rest
The dress stood out a mile and made the gentlemen smile
Cut to the knees, it was the 'swinging sixties'
With fine panels that floated as one strolled
I wore this for dinner dates and parties
Amongst the London elite; the chic
When I wanted to look my best
In the taxis of London and the hotels of the West End
The restaurants of the capital discreet.

I had a kaftan; a fantastic kaftan in the Christmas of 1974
When I was pregnant with my second child
In the February he was born
The kaftan was graceful and elegant it fell to the floor
To my toes and covered my bump in the way I applaud
In the shades of the Union Jack I felt complete and adored.

Both the little black dress and the fantastic kaftan
Eventually had their day although I was loathe to give them away
I remember with pride the little black dress
And the fantastic kaftan nostalgic of the Jet Set.

Margaret Bennett

SHOPPING

Another outing to the shops looking for something to buy,
But for everything I seem to like the price is much too high.
Maybe I'm being too fussy but this dress seems much too short,
In every other way it fits, perhaps I could take up sport.
No, the dress doesn't look right, let's try another shop,
All this running around is making me feel that I shall drop.
The neckline of this dress is too low, it shows far too much of me,
At my age it would really be quite unseemly.
Oh, to be young again and not care what I wear,
I used to dash around the shops without a care.
I'd better find my daughter; she may be having a spree,
She is so like the way I used to be, you see.

Phyllis Dartnell

OUR HOLIDAYS

Come, let us hurry,
As I packed our bags in haste.
The day's finally come,
And we have no time to waste.
I can hear the train,
I heard the kids shout with glee.
The guard waved his flag;
We'll be there in time for tea.

What a week it was,
As we paddled in the sea.
Laying on the sands,
Oh, so happy and carefree.
Eating candyfloss,
Had time to visit the zoo.
Riding on the fair,
What a lot of things to do.

The sun shone all week,
Not a cloud up in the sky.
The week has ended,
And now we must say goodbye.
Slowly traced our tracks,
To the station down the lane.
Cheer up, never mind,
We will soon be back again.

Antoinette Beards

APPLEBY

Appleby-in-Westmorland -
It's really quite unique.
Always bright and friendly -
It's rarely cold or bleak.

It's in the heart of Cumbria,
Along the Eden Valley.
The river's really beautiful,
It makes you want to dally!

The trees are green and plentiful,
The willows gently sway.
The banks are full of flowers, wild,
So colourful and gay.

Hills and mountains all around,
Magnificent is the view.
Climbers come from counties wide
To see what they can do.

The sky is filled with countless stars,
The moon is shining bright,
A gentle breeze sways in the trees -
It is a lovely night!

Joan Packwood

AWESOME NIGHT

Beneath a counterpane of stars
So clear and bright I feel both low
And lifted up as I recline
On folding bed in desert night.
The burning fires of midday sun
Are now replaced by chill so sharp
It brings recall of childhood's thrill
On winter's day when all was still
With frost, whose silent spell insists
We marvel at the magic scene.
Too soon the dawn awakes and noise
Begins a ripple through our camp
As bustle slow returns to drag
Us back to here and now. Perhaps
We need to glimpse a desert sky
At night to see ourselves aright,
As tiny specks within a vast
Expanse of universe. And yet
We're called to transmute awe and angst
To love that raises souls to realms
Beyond the reach of furthest stars,
As inner light defies both death
And sense we're all alone, bereft
Of hope. That tiny spark of grace
Within is worth entire embrace
Of all that's seen or just inferred
Of wondrous spread of time and space
And diverse creatures they have spawned,
Including selves who hear the call
To rise above our lowly births.

Henry Disney

ODD SOCKS

Where do all the odd socks go?
To the land of single socks?
Think of those left behind
Exposed to those hard knocks.

Is there a club for single socks?
If so, where do they meet?
In a local Parish Hall
Or a pub just down the street?

And what do those odd socks do
When they are alone?
Do they mope and while away
Waiting listless by the phone?

I know that some are lucky
And find their other pair
Walking side by side
In left and right footwear.

They say that some stay alone
Never to be used
Meeting up with other odd socks
Similarly abused.

So spare a thought for those odd socks
As you throw one in the bin
So and find the other one
And also throw that in.

Nigel Courtney

THE NEW MILLENNIUM

People from all over the world
Have been planning with anticipation,
To welcome in the new millennium
Which calls for a great celebration.

We shall reflect on the past years
The highs and lows,
Make our New Year resolutions
And try to keep those.

Quite what the new millennium
Will have in store,
There is a tremendous feeling of optimism
But no one can be sure.

There will be fireworks and parties
Dancing and singing,
The bubbly will flow
And the church bells will be ringing.

Let us all get together
The elderly and the young,
To herald in
The new millennium.

Ena Page

JADE'S SMILE

Her sweet smile just bubbled with happiness
Like a fountain all sparkling bright
And the glow of the sun through the raindrops
Made the smile even more a delight.

Sweetest child, with the radiant smile,
You chase the clouds away
And bring the sunshine to our lives,
You brighten up our day.

Though many times we grumble
When dreams we don't fulfil,
How can we know the heartache
This child is hiding still?

Like the beauty of the rainbow
And the green of a summer glade
All these come together
In the smile that belongs to Jade.

An inspiration to us all
So stay and think awhile,
This child can neither speak nor walk,
All Jade can do is smile.

Beryl Heathcote

DESOLATION

Heart-bled I walk in dry rock land
Across vast plateaux of no streams,
Through gorges of lick-dry dust,
A place of long dead dreams.

No eagle's cry or lark's full song,
No lambs or walkers here,
But souls of ghouls, lost in time,
Amongst the ash of bones.

Arid sticks of life once spent
Amidst the fecund roar
Of daily life's perpetual round,
Reduced to hoarse wind-soar.

Through wasteland country thus I flee,
Hands held to grasp no more;
To wander ever with the dead,
Bewildered by the core

Of current life day's demands,
So near, yet distant - so
I watch in separate space and time
And quietly let it go.

Rosemary England

THE OLD ARMCHAIR

In a corner of the dining room
It still is standing there,
With cushions worn and faded,
It's Father's favourite chair.

Whenever he came in the room
If you were in his place,
You rose and gave him back his seat
And did it with good grace.

As father of the family
He considered it his due
To have the armchair of his choice
And you thought that way too.

Though Father died some years ago
The chair's still standing there,
For me to put my feet up
When I have the time to spare.

And sometimes when I'm sitting
In the chair, and half asleep
I hear a footstep in the hall
And to my feet I leap.

My memory goes rushing back
And for a moment there,
I think that it is Father,
Come to claim the old armchair.

M L Oliver

MY UNIVERSE

Outer pressure, inner force,
All come together to endorse
Energy, creating vital heat,
And fire within performs the feat.
Exhaustion is cleansed there too
By cooling waters flushing through
And each corner, each vital part,
Is nourished by the heart.
A single cell will be revived,
The will, will surely provide,
Guided by the spirit's speak,
So sublime, so unique.
Peace with self transposes,
Sympathy and mutual love discloses.
I will control my universe
And sweet harmony will disperse.

Margaret Deverson

FUTURE

We all have a future
But no one knows what does lie in store,
It can be very exciting
Finding out! What is just behind the door?

We have all had a bad time
When there has been a tunnel
But there has been no light,
We all say, 'We can make it,'
And prove it by putting up a fight.

We all have dreams
That we want to do,
And if we really want it bad enough
It is said, 'That it will come true'.

Karen Rust

A MOTHER'S LOVE

My mother, you have left me,
Gone to live with Dad above,
You've taken all your earthly charms,
But left me all your love.
You were always there to turn to
When my heart was full of woe,
Your loving arms would hold me
And you'd show the way to go.
Oh Mother, how I miss you,
Your sweet and lovely face,
I miss your strength and wisdom,
Your power and your grace,
I know you'll never leave me,
You are always by my side,
But how I wish that I could see you
As my tears I try to hide.
I know we'll meet again some day
So I must be patient now,
And wait to feel your hand in mine
And kiss your loving brow.

Joyce Woods

PLEASE STAY

Do not desert me on this night
As I fear the lonely silent hours
Stay with me till morning light.

Lie with me and hold me tight
Speak softly words of love
Do not desert me on this night.

I know I do not have the right
To keep you by my side, but
Stay with me till morning light.

Hold me close and calm my fright
And gently stroke my hair
Do not desert me on this night.

Lend me your ear to my sad plight
And grant me this one wish
Stay with me till morning light.

And when the dark at last takes flight
I will surely let you go
Do not desert me on this night
Stay with me till morning light.

Jeanette L Durk

A SUMMER'S DAY

Beautiful roses, smelling so sweet,
And honeysuckle along the street,
The sky so blue and the sun so bright,
To be out today is pure delight.
Trees moving their 'hands' as if to pray,
It really is such a lovely day,
In the park, with the river close by,
The river gulls soaring in the sky.
The children playing on the soft grass
And cheerily waving, as I pass,
They are precious to the Lord above,
Let us all show to them His great love.
Thank God for all that is good and true,
Thank Him, too, for His true love to you.

Lilian Loftus

SADness - Winter

Blackened leaves on sagging stems are comforted by diadems,
Cold fashioned from the eve before, as winter's mantle covered
More than gravel paths, now crusted white, whilst restless corms
Defy the blight, can't wait their call from suns unseen:
Attempt to gild the Earth with green.
Skeletons cling to spidered beech,
Menacing rose thorns fill the breach, darkly defiant,
Awaiting springwood, static aggression with no velvet hood.
Rangy witch-hazels unsheathe flaxen claw,
Those less than robust succumb before thaw;
Snow-laden conifers half shield the rest,
With late autumn colour very hard-pressed to weather the spears
Of the next daunting rain; hazard's dank drummers:
Purveyors of pain.
No languid alert from collared dove as steel-eyed kestrels hunt above
Scuts retreat from fallow field, with hawthorne margins,
Nature's shield.
A creaking hinge on tipsy gate does nothing more
Than agitate the downcast frame of one-time sprite,
Assuming weeds for filched sunlight;
But Pandora's box can lift a heart,
As dawn and dusk grow more apart,
Then spirits may well soar to sing as bursting burgeons herald spring.

L G Stiles

My Children

My children, thousands have I borne like seeds from thistle downs,
And some have scattered o'er the world to bloom in foreign towns.
Some left their roots in letters, in science and in arts,
But none as loving as the ones who gave to me their hearts.

Traders, soldiers, men of God, still leave my homes each day,
With messages of peace and hope, they wend their glorious way.
To far and distant fields they go, by air, by sea, by land,
Ambassadors of my hometown to shake a foreign hand.

My future lies with you, the young, yes you, both white and brown,
For soon your praises will be sung, when history's written down.
So let discrimination cease and live in fine accord
And be the ones to lead the way, and let the world applaud.

Jan Caswell

Love Is

(This poem won an area competition judged by Barbara Cartland)

The welcome home when you return,
Two loving arms for which I yearn.
A tender look, a loving smile,
A hearth that's warm when you stay a while.
An open door, a well-worn mat.
Coat hooks for you to hang your hat.
Love is all these things for me,
Whenever your love returns to be.
Enclosed within my arms again,
From out of the cold and in from the rain.
To sit a while together at last,
Thinking of the days gone past.
My love for you is deep as the sea,
Shining out for all to see.
Now you are gone I sense you near,
I love you still, you are so dear.
The jewelled stars will shine down from above,
Telling you of my deep love.
You hold me still, though we are apart,
For years ago I gave you my heart.

Alice Stapleton

Love And Let Live

Let me not impatient be
Because she is so slow,
Let me not think secretly
I wish that she would go,
Let me listen silently
To memories of yore,
Let me not say angrily
'I've heard it all before,'
Let me treat her lovingly,
Be kind in every way,
Because I know and for sure
I too may be old one day.

I R Maybury

The Unseen Friend

One morning very early, I asked God, could we talk?
I told Him that I loved Him and would like to take a walk
I felt His presence near me, His arms around me tight
He knew without my saying, I'd spent a lonely night
I'd lain in bed for hours just waiting for the dawn
Not knowing who to turn to, just feeling so forlorn
Our conversation started when I clumsily began
To tell Him of my sadness, and my search for 'Who I am'
He listened to my sorrows; He listened to my fears
His arms were still around me as I shed a thousand tears
The sun was shining in my room, outside the birds were singing
Suddenly I realised the telephone was ringing
I dried my eyes, composed myself and reached out for the phone
The familiar voice that answered me proved I was not alone
I chatted for a little while to someone very caring
Plans were made to meet that day so we could do some sharing
I thanked dear God for being there and showing me a way
To help another person live through another day
The friend that I was meeting had been engulfed in grief
Now it was my turn to offer comfort and relief
I knew we two would share this day and help each other smile
We would put aside our sadness just for a little while
My conversations with my God I know will never end
I am so very grateful to have Him as my Friend.

Pat Simms

A Right Honourable Madam Speaker

(Dedicated to Betty Boothroyd ex-MP and ex-Right Honourable Madam Speaker)

'Stick to the point, Mr Squeaker,'
Shades, echoes and memories of post-war years
With Hyde Park Corner's soap-box speaker
(And the great issues of mankind passed us by).

'Point of ordah, Madam Speaker,'
'That is not the point,' cheep, cheeps our MPs
'Honourable Membah misses the point,'
Declare right honourable membahs
Point-scoring their way through debates
(And the great issues of mankind pass them by?)

'Time's up!' declares Right Honourable Madam Speaker
With much finale and so much final panache
(As only an ex-Tiller dancing girl can can-can)
As one side's sexes roar their last appreciation
And the other sides stay strangely meanly silent
(And the great issues of mankind and womankind
Passed them by on the other side?)

*A new housemartin has long since flown to speaker's chair
Borne on a blasted heath's discretional, impartial air
Nigh, nay well gone 50 years of shared public Common(s) shame
Ted Heath and his band - but what's in a name?*

P John Banks

TO MARY, MY PRECIOUS ANGEL

Mary, I love you in full adoration
I give you my devoted heart and meek soul
And all my passions in timeless betrothal
Your wish being mine I kneel at your disposal
O Mary, you will always be my angel

I do as you command me to do always
I seek sewers of divine Aureole Seas
I must drink of your loving cup endlessly
I must savour your delicious Tooki stews
Mary, I love you in full adoration

I buy you gifts in gratitude for Tooki
Fancy chocolate boxes to your boudoir
Please give me your Tooki sanctions forever
In eternal moontide seas of Aureole
O Mary, you will always be my angel

I adorn you in silk robes of indigo
I place a crown of sapphires upon your head
Decorations of pearls and rings of diamonds
Showers of scented violets and lavenders
Mary, I love you in full adoration

I enjoy your delights constantly coming
Stir my taste buds with your piquant honeycomb
Inflame my nostrils with your pungent perfume
Flush me in Aureole Seas beneath your throne
O Mary, you will always be my angel.

Louis Don Barrow

MUM

(Words will never be enough to show our love for you, but I know you loved reading my poems so here's one for you to celebrate your life)

A great, great person,
Full of love for everyone,
The best mum we could have hoped for,
The only one we'd ever want,
The best wife Jim could have hoped for,
The only one he'd ever want,
So good,
She was like a second mum to many,
Caring for others more than herself,
An emotional person granted,
Only because she cared so much,
Any way she could, she would,
A cup of coffee the best,
A held hand, a big cuddle,
Always willing to give,
Always there in moments of need,
A happy, caring person,
This is my memory,
The years of pain now gone,
A relaxing life she now leads,
Up there with Grandad and Penny,
Knowing our every thought,
Knowing how much we loved her,
Life will continue,
For that is what she'd want,
We'll do our best for you now, Mum,
Your body may have died,
But Carol Elizabeth Stirk,
A loving mum and wife,
Will never die.

Neil Stirk

A SPECIAL ACHIEVEMENT

One day I was thinking
There was something special
I would like to do
So then I began to sponsor
A little girl of just eight
Her name was Ramatu
She lived her life
Very different to the way
We are used to
And for Ramatu to go to bed
Hungry was never anything new.
Ramatu was African
Living close to Sierra Leone
In a leaking shack with an
Extended family they all
Shared this home.
Her parents were peasant
Farmers with crops failing
All the time
Because the rain seemingly
Never reached them on time.
With sandstorms each November
Making life more difficult for them too.
I still have the letters and photograph to treasure
So today, Ramatu, I send my very best wishes
All those many miles away to you.

Janet Weatherhead

NURSERY TALE

(Based on nursery rhymes)

Sleeping Beauty fell asleep.
Little Bo Peep lost her sheep.
Humpty Dumpty had a great fall.
Cinderella went to the ball.

London Bridge is falling down,
Jack fell down and broke his crown.
Pussycat frightened a mouse under a chair.
Johnny's so long at the fair.

Mary, Mary's garden is in bloom.
The cow jumped over the moon.
The little dog broke out in laughter.
They all lived happily ever after.

J Cross

LOVE'S AND LIFE'S DIVINITY

Crafted out of hills and lakes, with depths that defy all comprehension
Love and life's creation taken to ultimate indescribable dimension,
Strength only ever known in those that are brave and true,
Gentility borne on hands that can mould a vision that's bold and new,
Spirit ethereal in its form, ascending to heights none has dared to scale,
Honour and integrity that would make most good men pale
To insignificance . . .
And yet, you encapsulate life's divinity and take me, small and frail,
Into your heart.

Annie Morrice

LONDON LIGHTS

The streets of London call to me
There's no place else I want to be
With sights that fill my mind with awe
Just makes me wish for more and more
Buildings stretch both far and wide
And still I walk and sometimes ride
Taxicabs are all around.
Big red buses stand so proud
These sights to me are dreams come true
My visits here are rare and few
But when I leave these precious sights
My heart will stay with London lights.

Dorothy Haywood

MY MATE ALB

(Dedicated to my mate Albert T Creese)

So! You took a bow and bailed out, not locally though where all
                    your old mates would remember one last shout.
'Cheers, Albert, cheers, Bunny, good luck on your journey, it won't
                    be the same without you about'.
Not that much has been seen of you since you've been
                    Thailand bound.
But I don't blame you for the new life that you found.

I wonder though that you knew something? - that it wasn't
                    going to last -
So you decided to enjoy what was left to the very last gasp.
Or did it come out of the blue and grab you by surprise?
Hardly giving you time for wherefores or the whys?

When that letter of mine, to you, returned and scrawled across
                    the front
'He died in February' - The words so cold and blunt.
'He died in February' - No! That cannot be true.
Then I cried Alb. Honest I did, as I realised it was the end to
                    you and me.

What became of the dreams, the aspirations of your long gone past?
Alas! The ideas of our youth were born, yet never born to last.
For youth, so fickle that when a new thought falls in place -
Fifty years that might have been were lost - gone without a trace.

We may have made a fortune or become bums along the way?
We may have had adventures that we'd talk about today?
We may have done some things that were better left well hid?
But, Alb! None of which would be better than the birth of
                    my tea-pot-lids.

Fifty years ago - we'd race each other etching plates.
And the Mirror crossword! Who'd be first? 'Me of course,' you'd state.
We were just like brothers you and me though I supported
                    the Lilley-Whites and you a Gunner be.
I should have been your last call - I certainly had the right.
I should have visited you out in Thai. My careless oversight
Because sometimes the grim old reaper surprises when he calls
                    in an early lease.
And you heard the words he uttered, 'Come in, Albert T McCreese'.

A M Doubler

A LOST SOUL

The wails of the wind whisper stories I cannot
Chattering raindrops tell of times I'd forgot
The world is grey, even the sun avoids my gaze
And the nightingale sings a lament of past days.

The rose gives no scent nor pleases my eyes
Echoes of a bright dream shine black through my mind
I struggle through silence a smile on my face
As the tears in my heart burn my dreams to waste.

Catheryn Tilling

AN ANNIVERSARY SMILE

Your smile has never wavered
Through the fickle flux of years,
Although I know at times
Your spirits ebbed quite low.
Your laughter clear and heart's good cheer
Have bubbled year by year.
Your care, your tenderness,
Your love, your strength
Have somehow all endured
And shining flow with warmth
From deep inside, a hidden source,
A secret spring you kindly share,
More brightly than mere smiles
On laughter's shallow shore.

Brian Christopher Wilkinson

HERON DYKE

It was a good day for fishing, to go after pike,
And my mind was settled to try Heron Dyke.
Where the bullrushes danced to the tune of the breeze
And I could sit sheltered 'neath white willow trees.
And watch the kingfishers, on blue spangled wings,
Dash past to their nest by the old cattle rings,
Where they'd built a home in a hole in the bank
Just half a hand's breadth 'neath the old water tank,
Half hidden behind a bullrush's clump,
Undeterred by the clank of the old water pump,
Where they'd snatch at the ruby-red demoiselle fly
As it flittered and fluttered its dainty way by . . .

Or stabbed at the water with poniard-like beak
To take to their young 'uns the bright silver bleak
That gambled their lives on the surface to feed
On flies, and on flotsam, (and paying no heed)
To cold eyes that watched from the dyke's depths below,
Of pike that, sans warning, could death there bestow.
For big fish were in there, down in the green weeds,
With great jaws a-grinning and eyes like stone beads.
Ah! They lay in ambush, in water's cold sheath
With great jaws hair-triggered, and a thousand sharp teeth.
Ah! Big fish were in there, of that I was sure
And knowing the water I thought I could lure
A fish or three,
Maybe four,
Perhaps even five!
For as all anglers know (in matters piscernal)
A good swim of water makes hope leap eternal . . .
Oh ah! Doesn't it just!

John Whittock

GOD'S BRIGHT LIGHT

As in all things beautiful and bright,
God made the world,
Then gave it light.
Then dark for rest,
Within the night.

In Heaven with happiness galore,
Dwell with *God*, if good,
For evermore.
As with all the planets
God created,
God is never ever over rated!

Dorothy Mary Allchin

QUESTIONS UNANSWERED

Why does 'The Wrath of God'
Descend upon the good,
Oft more so than the Evil?
I'd tell you if I could!

Why do evil people
Seem to 'get away with it'?
Doing, saying, what they wish;
They just don't care one bit.

Is ever good rewarded?
We'd like to think it is;
It may be on occasion
But the decision must be His.

We've got to think there's reasons
For the sufferings of the Good;
Maybe it's just one big test -
It'll turn out as it should.

We'd like to think there's something
Beyond this world of woe;
Something to be hoped for,
Somewhere sweet to go.

God must decide these things;
We're in His hands, you know.
We like to think good deeds
A better life may sow.

Roger Wootton

IT'S A GLADIOLI WHAT THE SUMMERTIME BRINGS

It's a gladioli what the summertime brings,
What about the roses, the sunflower too
The purple loostrife and evening primrose,
And then there's the Hollyhock,
The blackbird goes hop, hop, hop, scuffle - worm pulled
From the grass and snail and slug,
Sings his blackbird song in the morning,
Again in the evening,
And as we get older we appreciate these things,
Watering with a watering can,
Or watering with a hosepipe, with a splash at the tubs,
The hen blackbird comes pecking for ants,
And the water makes flowerbuds with a splash.
I got you, laugh it all over, get me one back,
That can prove one thing or another,
On a heatwave of a hot summer,
Bringing out the blooms, with a little watering
Over on a hot summer's day,
Blackbird sitting on an open cut nest,
And we all like to suntan in that way,
And as we get a bit older, we appreciate these things,
It's a gladioli what the summertime brings,
The blackbird singing, with his hen on the nest,
Black he chuckles, and his hen goes to the water bowl for a suckle,
Then the blackbird goes hop, hop, hop,
Scuffle - worm pulled from the grass,
And a snail and slug, he sings in the trees,
With flowers and bees,
With some of us not well,
And stay at home is what one sees,
And as we get a bit older, we appreciate these things.

Robert A Gould

BEN CLEUCH

We are climbing, climbing, climbing
        To the summit of the hill,
Now we're sitting close together
        Taking in green nature's fill.
Now our eyes are looking outward
        To the shining, silver river,
In the silence we remember
        The divine, eternal giver.

Suddenly the rain is falling,
        Falling, falling all around,
Just as quickly it is over,
        Oh! The freshness of the ground.
Then we see the arc of magic,
        It is just beneath our feet,
We are sitting on a rainbow,
        The vision takes away all speech.
We are covered with the colours,
        Painted by the hand of God.

We are running downward, downward,
        Downward to the earth below,
We can see the sun is setting,
        Telling us that we must go.
We will climb up other hillsides,
        But this one will stand apart;
We have seen a glimpse of Heaven
        It is imprinted on our hearts.

Jessica Boak

STOLEN

Beautiful;
I would not envisage this in a dreamy delusion -
it is not a hazy hallucination!
Confirmed by sun shining from blue skies
beautifully blemished by white wisps;
it's a paradise I'd never imagined.

Serene sound;
sprinkling, splashing, dousing, washing -
nourishing water hushing like silk over stone,
traversing without care, for it is free!
A smell so cool and fresh, cup your hands
and taste its innocence.

Air, water, flower and stone in harmony create perfection.
The Garden of Eden's far richer relation -
flourishes of heathers and trees and grass,
Shangri-La's European cousin, but this one is real -
a green utopia of untouched elation.

Breathless;
if I wasn't below the clouds,
I'd believe this was Heaven.

Though;
to see the skies angered,
overcome by grey,
to see this gentle brute
escape its boundaries and power!
Rains fall - thunderstorm!
Water bounds like petrol bombs,
coarse crashing irrigations
against a rocky facia floods the plain!

The falls have stolen my heart; my heart can stay.

Alex Harford

THE LOSS OF EDEN

The world You made is changing, Lord, from purity to sin,
Eden is slowly dying, Lord, badness is oozing in,
The scarcity of woodlands, that helps this earth to breathe,
The killing and the mayhem, that makes this Eden bleed.
And yet, dear Lord, You sit and watch, the acts of fellow man,
To see if we will change our ways, I know You hope we can.

For, Lord, You are a loving God
Forgiving of our sin,
How long before Your trust runs dry,
Before bravely stepping in?

To help us come together, to change our sorry ways,
Or must we keep on going down this road to darker days,
Till all the land is barren, no silvery moon to shine,
No birds in flight, no animals, humanity in deep decline?
For we are foolish, cannot see the harm that we have done,
Destruction of the planet, the killing of the sun.

Yet, Lord, You are a loving God
Forgiving of our sin
Let Eden rise, before your eyes
Dear Lord, please step right in.

Kathleen Townsley

IN DAYS OF OLD

In days of old when knights were bold
And dragons ruled the Earth
Where peasants did as they were told
For fear of evil wrath

There was a knight and good was he
He fought with strength and valour
He settled right, he slew bad knights
And was a dragon slayer!

Until one day along came one
Who was as mighty and brave as he
Last boldest, bravest dragon
That you would ever see!

This bold one said,
'Let's fight for right together, you and me
With strength and fearless cunning
A mighty force we two could be!'

So dragon and knight they fought for right
They rid the land of wrong
And made the world in which they live
A magical place to belong!

Christine Pointer

MUSIC

Music is the only thing
That keeps my soul alive
Without it I don't think
I would very long survive.

This world would be so very sad
Without the sound of rock and roll
And so many would be out of work
And queuing for the dole.

So keep on playing all that jazz
Folk, classical and pop
And the world will keep revolving
And will not want to stop.

Music is the food of love
So play on for me
And soothe my tired and weary soul
With a haunting melody.

Janet Larkin

TRANQUILLITY

In the heart of the countryside
I have found an inner peace
All the pent-up longing of past months
To walk through pastures green
The scent of the briar-rose wafting in the breeze.
And the light fall of snow on the hills of brown
Makes a perfect background for tiny, white-washed cottages
Nestling in the down far away from the noisy town
Far from the endless pace which is the plight of the human race.
If this be depression then I shall ever be
As my heart would break if they took these thoughts and
sights away from me.
All the poets of past decades wrote of the beauty and
glorious delight
From the splendour of the dawn to the stillness of the night.
If one only took time to stand and stare
There would be no wars or strife to bear;
How futile life itself would be
If one would have no time to rest beneath a tree
To gaze upon all God's creation
The things He has planned
And placed for all to wonder by His almighty hand.

Gwyneth E Scott

THE OLD ORCHARD

The blackbird is singing for the last time in the old orchard.
The final crop has been picked and stored.
Tomorrow the bulldozer is coming.

No daffodils will nod their golden heads under the blossoms
Next spring
Tomorrow the bulldozer is coming.

For more than seventy years they have fruited,
Planted with loving care
By hands that had known the horror of the trenches.
Tomorrow the bulldozer is coming.

Apples, pears and plums gathered each summer
In that old orchard.
Through good years and bad, war and peace.
Tomorrow the bulldozer is coming.

Old orchards and little people have had their day,
Bureaucrats must have theirs.
Big combines need this one acre.
Tomorrow the bulldozer is coming.

So turn over in your grave, Dad,
While your daughter weeps
Weeps for the loss of an old orchard.
For tomorrow the bulldozer is coming.

Maisie Dance

THE SWEETEST THING

His face shone out at me,
Like a soft sunbeam piercing a cloud.
His eyes sparkled and glittered;
They were stars, clear and pure.
His lips curved, flawless,
Red roses fresh from spring's dewdrops.
His body was lithe and muscular,
It felt like a panther ready to pounce.
Now only the memory remains,
His delicate touch upon my back,
The voice of honey in my ear;
My sweetest thing was gone
Forever.

Charlotte Meredith

THE POLAR PRINCE

The Polar Prince sits lonely and sad
Behind bars at the local zoo,
With nothing to do except beg.
Mud in his once milk-white coat,
Fur bedraggled at his throat,
Waterhole filthy and yellow.
Poor beast assaulted by heat and flies,
What memories stir behind your soulful eyes?
Do you dream of Arctic snows,
Dark green waters, icy floes?
Splendid bear with blank expression,
Victim of man's cruel aggression,
Padding restless around your cage,
Are you filled with impotent rage
Against the Homo Sapiens who come to stare
At the occupant of an unnatural lair?
Sleep, and keep your dreams, white bear.
Swim in a moonlit sea,
Joyous and free.
Splash through the shallows.
Shake your great shaggy coat.
Then on ice cream paw
Make tracks along a silvered shore.

Ellsie Russell

WHEELS

I'm no good with wheels
Can't ride a bike,
I don't drive a car I'd much rather hike!

When I became a mam
With babies three
I needed 'L' plates on the pram for me.

Bumping over pavements,
Freewheeling down hills.
When I'd arrive back home, I'd have to take a pill.

Supermarket trolleys
Drive me to distraction.
One of these days I'll end up in traction.

Now meals-on-wheels is welcome
If I become disabled. But 'til that day,
Say, 'Wheels away!' and just eat at the table.

E Thorpe

I'M A NAUGHTY DOG

I've been in such trouble with mistress and master
Just 'cause I knocked over a bucket of plaster.
And why did I get a very sharp pat?
Just, 'cause I upset the family cat
When I sat still I still got a moan.
Just, 'cause Gran tripped on my favourite bone.
And why did Mum say, 'You'd best say your prayers'.
Just 'cause the master fell down the stairs!
I didn't see him and he didn't see me.
The carpet and I are both brown you see!
But weren't they proud of my very loud bark
When I stopped a burglar without leaving a mark.
Now I know I'm quite popular despite all of this
'Cause this morning my nose got a very big kiss!

Pam Cluderay

CAKES AND LEMONADE

A special event this coming year
Installed rich furnishing of brightness here.
Curtains and drapes with swags and tails
Unfolded a drama of storm-tossed gales.
That woollen cloth of bunting red,
Swayed like tassels in twirling thread.
Stretching along its highway there,
Cobbled streets stopped in a curve to stare.
Balloons full-blown with coloured string
Brought gaiety and life to the crowded ring.
Sam promised me he would not be late
Participating as others in township's fete.
Men bowler-hatted wore buttoned spats,
Their wives they escorted in wide-brimmed hats.
Box-kites flew high soaring above,
And lasses went dancing which flustered a dove.
Trestles from sheds were brought to the party,
And long forms, not chairs, for folk so hearty.
Weather so fair as Martinmas Day
For fun on a farm when making hay.
Cakes homemade and deep custard tart,
Long sausage rolls, then a Queen of Heart.
Lemonade and sherbert that old-fashioned way
Kept children chatting that live-long day.
The mayor and mayoress in regalia so fine,
Spoke on the rostrum from time to time.
After those speeches extending so wide
Came ponies who trotted for children to ride.
Along then a band with music for marching,
Its rousing tunes setting souls astirring.
At the close of that day the weary went home
To re-kindle the joy of freedom to roam.
Celebrations are made for a blending of hearts
That look to the future whilst remembering the past.

Arthur Ford

BEN - 1993-2005

It's time for you to go, old man
And free yourself from pain
To me you've been a loyal friend
Like no one I can name

My love for man's best friend
No one can understand
The bond that grew between us
Not I, had even planned

Always close beside me
As we walked for hours on end
You were my canine confidante
And never did offend

You knew when I was hurting
From illness, and in pain
You came and sat beside me
So your comfort I could claim

You never liked the rainy days
As we set off for the park
A doggy 'caped crusader'
With a deep and manly bark

You simply loved the seaside
Where you'd play and dig for shells
And frolic in the water
Then return all fishy smells!

I miss my big black Labrador
And all your little ways
You're gone but not forgotten
As I contemplate my days.

Brian Henderson

ANCIENT OAK

A great, ancient oak on the edge of the wood,
For many, many years, there it has stood.
Bare are the branches at the onset of spring,
Somewhere the birds gather to parade and sing.
A carpet of bluebells covers the ground,
Squirrels and rabbits scurry around.
The early morning chorus, just before sunrise,
A huge, golden ball appears in the skies,
Filtering rays of light through the trees,
Gossamer threads, catching the light in the breeze.
Searching for food, a vixen and her cubs,
Blackbirds and thrushes probing for grubs,
Rowdy rooks, with screeching chicks,
High in the trees, in a nest of sticks,
Birds building nests of twigs and moss,
All woven together, criss and cross.
A watchful roe deer, with her fawn,
A wonderful sight in the early dawn.
Now in full leaf is our ancient oak,
Giving food and shelter, even to folk.
Butterflies with delicate wings,
Toadstools in a magical ring.
The late summer brings sudden storms,
But the month of September is still warm.
The glory of autumn, with leaves of gold,
A magnificent picture to behold.
A carpet of leaves now covers the ground,
So still and peaceful, there's hardly a sound.
The days are shorter, food is sparse,
Woodland in winter can be very harsh.
Snowflakes falling in the still of the night,
In the morning sun, it sparkles so bright.
For many, many years, this ancient oak has stood,
Now laden with snow, at the edge of the wood.

Zoiyar Cole

QUILL POWER

The thrill of the quill gives me endless delight
On virgin-white paper, my friend will soon write
The nib will caress and the black ink shall flow
And speak of great passions or places to go.

The quill can be harmful and mar someone's life
And be much more deadly than any sharp knife
The quill has the power to refresh and heal
The frailest of people who've had a rough deal.

My father could leap from his wheelchair right now
And drive a fast car if the ink would allow
Then laugh at a policeman who's really near by
And found that his car is now high in the sky.

The mute could cry out in such glorious voice
And not be ignored and just given no choice
The stressed could escape from their anguish and pain
By sleeping in boats on the calm River Seine.

The quill can give comfort to those in despair
Who've lost a beloved, or pet in their care.
The ink will immortalise in such a way
To strengthen those people to cope with each day.

The thrill of the quill is a wonderful thing
You could ride a white horse with such beautiful wings
Then run up the steps of a fairytale tower
And shout from the top to proclaim your quill power.

Connie Garrard

THE SEA

I hate the sea
For its evil and deceit
I recall how it welcomed you
While gently enticing you away from me
So cunning, in not revealing its true intentions
I watched the sea play with you
Like a cat does its prey
Why did it grab you
And hug you so tight?
Leaving me breathless,
And you without breath.

Ian Benjamin

MAKE ME SMILE

Put a smile upon my face,
Just the tears to replace,
Make me happy for a while,
Please make me have a smile.

It's so hard not to frown,
When I'm feeling so far down,
Lift my spirits, make me high,
Oh please don't make me cry.

I just cannot explain,
What goes wrong inside my brain,
The pattern's always the same
I know I'm not to blame.

There's just no answers to be,
With depression you see,
I'm just a terrible slave,
Please, please help me be brave.

Give me courage to go on with my life,
Let me be strong through everyday strife,
May there be no more sorrow,
Let me look forward to tomorrow!

Margaret McQuade

PORTHCAWL

A little voice in the distance quietly asked,
'Won't you take me to Poofcawl?'
Looking towards where the sound had come from
My glance caught the window in the background
And I could see it had started to rain
It was pouring down

This question had come from my eldest grandson
Eager to revisit this seaside town
His mum had taken him there before
Where happily he had played upon the shore

Lots of memories he had stored within
Ghost rides with his Aunty Jean
Splashing about in the sparkling sea
The sun's reflection casting a blinding gleam

Sandcastles built with skill and flair
The fun pretending being a knight of the realm
Donkey rides across the sands
Fishing in rockpools full with crabs
Grubby face and grubby hands
The end of a perfect day

Once again I heard that voice ask,
'Won't you take me to Poofcawl?'
His pronunciation for that town
He found it hard to get his tongue around
After all he was only a six-year-old.

Valerie Thompson

THE BLACK SHEEP RETURNS

The old house stands bleak and empty, decaying it defies the world
Almost hidden by nettles and weeds, no longer children's
                                        laughter is heard
Returning to see my old home again, before it becomes too late
Rotting wood surrounds the old house, where once stood a white
                                        fence and gate.

The willow tree, looking dejected, still remains, nearby is a child's
                                        rusty swing
Struggling through this wilderness with mounting excitement,
                                        my heart begins to sing
The happiness this old house once held for me,
                                        will remain in my heart forever
Playing by the stream, climbing apple trees, these are the things
                                        I still treasure.

Childhood days when life was carefree, I will always remember this
Coming back here to capture those precious times,
                                        has been perfect bliss
Peering through cobwebs on a dirty windowpane,
                                        an open fireplace I see
For a moment the room becomes alive, with all my family waiting
                                        for me.

The illusion quickly disappears; I am alone on the outside looking in
As the past comes flooding back, it breaks my heart then the
                                        tears begin
Now it is back to reality, I must leave this long ago happy world behind
The old house cries out for me to stay,
        but only ghosts from the past did I find.

With only these memories for companions,
                        travelling alone I lock out the past
This part of my life is over and gone, this visit will be my last
Leaving the old house crumbling, the garden withering away
                                        will soon die
Having turned back the pages of my childhood, all that remains
                                        is goodbye.

All the love and laughter has gone, my place is no longer here
The black sheep returned to the fold, but there was only
                                        loneliness I fear.
Thinking of things that might have been, are just beautiful dreams
Long ago I chose my own destiny, and it was not as bad as it seems.

Brenda Casburn-Colvin

THE UNKNOWN SOLDIER'S MESSAGE

When the battles were thick and fast
And the bullets flying round,
Oh! The heartache and the sorrow,
When my mates fell to the ground.

What am I doing here?
What's this madness all about,
When this mess is over
'Three cheers, ' I'm going to shout.

Then out would come a photo,
Of a British country lane,
I'm doing it for Blighty,
Hope it stays the same.

I'll hug, and hold, and kiss you all,
And never let you go,
But first the fight and capture,
Of all the ruddy foe.

Be happy, content, peace on Earth,
That's my message to you,
It wasn't meant to be,
That all *my* dreams come true.

B Strickson

BILL AND BEN

Here comes Bill and Ben
Two arrogant Yorkshire men
From God's own country (so they say)
Across the Humber bridge
To picturesque Lincolnshire
Arrogant and blunt
As some Yorkies are!
From across the bridge afar
Ee-by-gum here they come again
Those two blunt Yorkshire men.
Wallpaper and paint is their game
Bill and Ben are their names.
There's Viv and Dan-Kelly and me
We sell the paper and the paint
Then make the tea
And clean the floor -
They say, 'If you don't like it
There's the door!'
We have a joke with Bill and Ben
But only every now and then!
All names have been changed
So we don't get shown the door!
As home across the bridge
Ee-by-gum Bill and Ben go!

Norma Spillett

TIME THE WORLD GREW UP

If I was to go one hundred miles up,
No boundaries would I see,
It seems to me,
That the countries look the same.

We are all human beings,
With a life to live,
But everybody does not see it that way,
But they should,
Beneath we are all the same.

Let the skies be filled with peace,
No jet fighters would we see,
It's better like that,
Living in harmony.

All the world join hands,
Whatever colour you are,
Colours blend, violence would end

We are sliding off the back of the 20th century,
Into the 21st
Twenty-one, coming of age,
It's time the world grew up.

Africa, Asia, Europe,
North and South America,
Australia, Antarctica,
All hold hands.

Adrian Starbuck

MY SOUL

I let you down
I failed
I did not know what to do
Confusion reigned
The pain in my mind and heart
I am sorry,
But it's not enough
It took another to put it right
To make it better
My soul was sick.

A Shanahan Brooks

THE SECRET GARDEN

There's a patch at the back of a plain little house
And no one would know it was there.
Just a small hidden plot, not a park or great lot,
In the back and beyond of somewhere.

There's a high fence all round this sheltered ground
Enclosing a garden so rare.
With love cultivated, in tenderness created
With gentle touches and lavished with care.

It is here that she spends her contented hours,
Tending and caring for her fragrant flowers.
Individually planted by her loving hand.
Each one placed just where she'd planned.

Not so much in long straight arrays,
But more akin to wild hedgerow displays.
She cares not for plants in regimental row.
In random blooms she prefers them to grow,

As if Mother Nature had cast them there,
To push through the soil and sweeten the air.
With roses in passion climbing the door
And lupins to tower and insects enthral.

White allyssum scattering over here and there,
Clumps of lobelia reaching for air.
Petunias, pansies and marigolds too!
Pinks, carnations and violets blue.

Multiple shades of red, pink and blues.
Bewildered assortment of textures and hues.
Enchantment to catch not only the eye,
But also the bees, wasp and butterfly.

A garden of contrast, dappled with shade.
Greens glowing in sunlight, brighter than jade.
A garden like this gives so much pleasure in life.
But much more when tended by my dearest, sweet wife.

W Holmes

LOVE

Without intent
I turned to see
Stirring the air across from me
The perfect female rhapsody
Stealing my breath with her poignancy
And melting my thoughts
With her gentle warmth
Which on the breeze lingered over me.

I looked
Upon her mystery
Which claimed her very subtlety
And was now possessing me
Pulling my heart
Which longed to be
Carrying my love
Which had but all been won
Into the arms of victory.

I moved
Compelled overwhelmingly
As I saw her beauty facing me
And the world flew by as she welcomed me
Her eyes sparkling
With sincerity
We laughed and talked
Kissed and walked
With love our only company.

David Pike

FATHER'S DAY TEARS

Father's Day is here again, time to show you care
For all the things your father's done, and for always being there.
The path of life is oh so long with happy times and sad
And through it all the one who cares, is your dearest dad.

So to all of you this Father's Day
To all who have a dad
Repay to him the love and care that he has always had.
For once you lose your father, you've lost a part of life
That helped you through your troubles and your strife.

Don't take him for granted for one day he won't be there
Show him now you love him and that you care
For on this Father's Day, I'll thank my father
For all in life he gave
Father's Day tears will fall, as I gently lay
My card and flowers upon my father's grave.

Pamela J O'Donnell

OCEANS CALL

Fire-licked skies as the sun sinks low,
      Tranquillity stirred from tequila's glow.
Silver glitter on calm, deep amber seas,
      Flightless backdrop, no birds, no breeze.
Horizons stretched far-panoramic views,
      In sepia, in colour, in black and white hue.
Hovering of lone, on distant lands where heart's stitched,
      Wordless whispers beneath canvas, these sails soon will reach.
Sense of venture as miles, languish between shores,
      Navigation from tropical and onto glacier floors.
Candlelit flicker from the brief wink of a star,
      Negotiated seclusion, as the yacht races the dark.
Repairs carried out as the rigging is scaled,
      Undeterred by Atlantic rough storms and severe gales,
Circumnavigate countless miles untouched,
      Achieving a dream still uncaught but in sight.
Though spirits aroused greeted home mists of dawns rise,
      As flora and fauna rests on sore eyes.
But restless by day, missed adrenaline of nights,
      Soon adventure again beckons under fall mast by twilight.

A A Murphy

A RECIPE FOR CARING

Take a little happiness
Build up on it each day
Take a little love
And send it on its way
Take an empty heart
And fill it with a smile
Take a lonely hand
And hold it for a while
Feel a warmth surround you
And help those all around
Take a troubled soul
And lift it off the ground
Take time to give a smile
To people that you meet
A nod, a wave, a quick hello
When passing in the street
A recipe for caring
Sharing through and through
A little bit of thoughtfulness
Is all you need to do.

Linda Fensome

FOOTPRINTS IN THE SAND

Footprints in the sand,
When were they made?
Why after so many years, did they never fade?
Was it just to let us know
That someone was here before?
That people once thrived,
Upon this distant shore.
One day perhaps we'll discover,
Who inhabited this place
Were they the original species
Who started the human race?

Edward Hill

TEARS OF LIFE

I shed a little tear today - it was school and my first day
My mother brought me to the gate then turned and went away,
I ran into the playground and felt grown-up and brave -
Until I saw my mother's tears as she turned round to wave.

I shed a little tear today, my very best friend died
I've no idea why this was - I just want to run and hide,
Grandad is old - but not my friend, why did this have to be?
I still have other friends, but it was always him and me.

I shed a little tear today a little dog I found
A hungry, scraggy little thing just wandering around,
I picked him up and hugged him, then took him home to Dad
I've got another best friend now so life is not all bad.

I shed a little tear today, my girlfriend went away
And left me with a broken heart to struggle through the day,
I'm told that 'I am only young' and 'life's not all like this' -
Why can't we pick the good times and make the bad times miss.

I shed a little tear today - a happy little tear
It was a happy wedding day, the best day of the year,
Many happy tears were shed that no one even saw
And when the day was over - Mom and Dad shed more.

I shed a little tear today as I stood beside the grave
I didn't care who saw me - I was suddenly quite brave,
I thought of all the happy years oh! how those years have flown
Please help me Lord to carry on now that I'm on my own.

I shed a happy tear today - I held a baby girl
A warm and smiling bundle, more valuable than pearl,
How can I ease the heartaches that she'll meet through the years?
There is absolutely nothing - she has to cry *her* tears.

Some days are easy, some are hard, but all of life is good
It's not all 'easy-going' as we all thought it would,
Tears are part of living; you must be brave to cry
So just be bold, don't hide your tears, because *they* never lie.

Jim Pritchard

REFLECTIONS

Silent,
        Reflecting,
Sunlight,
        Dancing on water,
Like stars.
Wishing on tears,
        For caresses of love,
Missing,
        Those magic moments,
When our actions
        Spoke louder than words.

Jean Caldwell

TWILIGHT ENTWINED

Day and night highlights a symmetrical white and black,
While wandering down a dew wet and moss-laden track,
A mud-marked path freckled with toadstools and mushrooms,
All seemlingly encased within misty night-time glooms,
But in such bracken-stirred woodlands, nightlife prevails,
With glowing fireflies revealing sloping slugs' slimy trails.
Damp dew-licked leaves reflect their own incandescent hue,
From the star's creamy white to the river's rainbow blue,
For sapphire moonbeams illuminate bubbling brooks,
While chiming, chirping crickets sing in rocky nooks,
Boisterous, night flying brown bats chant their ultrasonics,
While yellow-speckled bugs murmur blissful oblivionics.
From bright, breeze blown buttercup scenting sweet maybes,
To bare-backed beetles dawdling dandily in bosoms of daisies,
Through to the distant humming of a darting dragonfly,
And the percussion of a moon-seeking moth fluttering by,
They will majestically capture you, magically in the night,
Spellbinding you with seductive sorcery, stotting your sight,
Because of all the romantic wonders that mankind can find,
There are none greater than the eurhythmy of twilight entwined.

Dale Mullock

JUSTICE?

I can take a life, kill somebody's wife,
        Perhaps an innocent child,
And an old man or woman so mild,
        But they can't and won't hang me,
        Maybe I'll even go free,
I could spend a spell in the clink,
        If they can prove I'm not over the brink,
Then again if I am they won't give a damn,
        What's a life? It's not their strife,
        So I can use a knife,
It says in the good book I know,
        And God has ordained that it's so,
        That a tooth for a tooth and an eye for an eye,
And it's only our Saviour,
        Should decree when we die.

Emily M Dixon

CHAZ

We have a large black dog
Labrador retriever says the pedigree catalogue,

He's friendly and bright
But easily takes fright,

He eats food twice daily
More often if he could gaily,

He's reached seven years old
Still very playful and sometimes bold,

Never leave a slipper or trainer about
They'll be chewed to pieces till there's nowt,

He likes a run every day
No matter what the weather he'll go anyway,

If people are about in the dark
He will give off a deep and loud bark,

Chaz is his name
Life here is never the same,

Too late to swap him for another
The daft dog thinks I'm his mother.

Angela Cooney

UNTITLED

It was winter in the garden,
The plants looked cold and dead.
The bushes showed stark branches,
And no flower raised its head.

Yet now I stand here gazing
At a world that's been transformed.
There's beauty in each tiny blade.
It's cold, but my heart is warmed.

In the night the snow came down
To turn the black to white.
Each twig is clothed in cotton wool.
I'm enraptured by the sight.

There's tiny footprints on the lawn
Where birds have searched for bread.
Each mark is clear and pointed
Like a little arrowhead.

I see a fox has passed this way,
His tracks precise and neat.
A line of beads upon a thread,
Such dainty little feet.

And now the sun is shining
To add its special glow.
It spotlights on the fishpond
Where goldfish lie below.

Their frozen forms hang waiting
To feel the touch of spring.
But now they dream their fishy thoughts
And do not heed a thing.

Out the front the snow is churned
It's colour dimmed by sand -
But here, within my garden
Is a winter wonderland.

Jacquie Russell

A PRAYER FOR APRIL 30TH

Dear God, just for myself I make this plea:
Hold April in Your hand a moment more for me,
That I may wonder 'ere the wonders flee.

Snowdrop and crocus long have gone,
But daffodils could surely linger on.
The windflowers, like a drift of snow
Sway gently on the forest floor below
And blackthorn also clothed in white,
Says spring is surely in our sight.

The creeping ivy may confuse
The shyer violet does the light eschew.
No gold of man could ever shine,
As bright as your own celandine.

What do the bluebells say to me?
A drift, a carpet, and then a sea.
Queen of the woodland, there you reign,
To lift my winter soul again.

The blackbird sings at break of day.
The starlings splash their bath in play.
The hedges green, the new-mown grass,
How does this always come to pass?

This magic month, so quickly to depart,
Hold in Your hand that I may write it on my heart.

Judy McEwan

LONELINESS

Crowds of people everywhere,
But I can only stand and stare.
Each going their own way,
Life's game to play.

Will someone talk to me?
Or is it they do not see?
They always rush past.
Perhaps someone will stop at last.

But no, they never do,
Every day through and through,
So, I hurry back home,
Again to be alone.

Perhaps one day a friend I will meet
It would be such a treat,
But as the years go by,
My only companion is the sky.

The clouds look down on me
Do they really see
How lonely it can be
For someone like me?

J V Ford

LOVE

Love is a very precious gift that money cannot buy
You can't make someone love you no matter how you try
We love our brothers and sisters and our mum and dad
But do we ever tell them of this love we have?
You might say, 'But they know we love them'.
Surely we don't have to make a display!
Well I suggest, try giving them a big hug, it will go a long way
And learn to say I love you as you go from day to day
Mums and dads, please tell your children, even when they're
                                    grown up by the way

Love is a basic human need
To have caring friends we all like to succeed
Remember what our Heavenly Father said is true
Love one another as I have loved you.

Helen Johnson

THE LAND OF MAKE-BELIEVE

In the land of slumber when I lay me down to sleep.
I travel to a dreamworld where my secrets I can keep.
The voyage to my subconscious takes me to a wondrous place.
A land of myth and magic where they seem to know my face.
The highlight of the landscape is a castle standing high.
And in the blue sky up above the dragons learn to fly.
Fair maidens in the courtyard are escorted by white knights.
Who sit astride black stallions in their armour shining bright
Alongside is the meadow where the unicorns are born.
With long white manes and on their heads a jewel-encrusted horn.
Just beyond the meadow is the woodland and the stream
Where fairies make their magic using starlight and sunbeams.
They share their glen with leprechauns, with elves and pixies too.
Who tend the woodland wildlife and create the morning dew.
The land of myth and magic is beyond your wildest dreams.
Where anything is possible and nothing's what it seems.
On arousing from my slumber I leave fantasy behind.
In reality the magic sleeps in my subconscious mind.

Sue Brown

GERALD MOONEY: GLORIFYING THE POOR

(Dedicated to Dad who died alone of a heart attack 14/8/1978)

Bar that lonely landmine tripping drugs way,
From following the impoverished mind,
Over every footstep, so dead,
So weary, so sore, to Heaven, it hugs:
Shining gold of love, no second-hand mugs,
Within one's self, untouchable, is bled,
Prayer to God, unless touched by bed,
Love cannot touch us: there shallow slugs,
Minds inflammable, wishes burn hearts,
We understand little of the simple,
The lonely, explosions smack starts:
Treading brains in Hell, Satan's dimple,
So weary, so sore, from Heaven's gate,
Shine, gold of love, prayer never to late.

Edmund Saint George Mooney

MAKE ME WHOLE

Shattered hopes,
Lonely night,
Single tear,
Fleeting light.

Broken body,
Tortured soul,
Needing you,
To make me whole.

Kiss on lips,
Hold my breath,
You bring me back,
From brink of death.

Love is true,
Love is near,
Your reflection,
In a tear.

Hold me close,
Don't let me fall,
Into where
I'll feel no more.

Want your love,
Want you near,
Whisper in
My drummed-out ear.

Hold me close,
For evermore,
Or at least
Until the dawn.

J S Gillespie

EBONY . . .

I stand at the gate calling,
My black mare is grazing.
The summer breeze is shifting,
A westward wind is blowing.

The summer scents are filling my senses,
The meadows are rich and rare.
I stand at the gate calling,
Ebony starts walking.

The summer sun is high above,
The bees around are buzzing;
The pools are rippling down the stream,
And Ebony my mare is there.

Susan Jane Byers

BRITISH SUMMER NIGHT

British summer night
Fine rain of midnight dew
Drunken brawling fights
Of men who've had a few
A taxi comes and passes
With women p****ed on Pimms
Tattoos on their fat asses
With tans upon fat limbs
And so I sit and wait for
Myself to become sober
The time has now grown late
My drunken state is over
As rain begins to fall
The heat of tarmac steams
And lights sheen on the floor
From taxis torch light beams
As I walk I get soaked
With misty morning rain
I stop to light a smoke
Then I walk on again
I walk with twilight skies
And clouds all tinged with red
I'll say my last goodbyes
Because I'm off to bed.

Jack John Georgion

VOICES OF LIFE

A river is like a voice, which flows to the mouth
It twists and bends, gurgles and laughs
Expresses emotions and gives little gasps
People will listen and take heart when they hear
The swift flowing sounds from the voice of the river
High and low like the ebb of a tide
Sweet words are emitted that ripple and ride
It's a wonderful feeling to be able to express
The inner feelings we must not suppress
So flow, flow as much as you like
There'll be rocks and bridges to withstand your might
Words come like rain constant and flowing
But no one knows just where you're going
It rushes forth to refresh our minds
With words of expression to suit all kinds
So little river keep splashing and talking
We love your sounds when we're out walking
The golden hills will rise and fall
With echoes of pleasure, which come to the fore.

Jo Taylor

LOVE IN THE BORDERS

Basil pined for Rosemary growing in a pot
He cast her loving glances and cried, 'Forget-Me-Not'
Now she was quite flirtatious, her eyes would often stray
To where her love Sweet William grew just across the way

Poor William loved another, who shared his flower bed
A haughty Black-Eyed-Susan of whom it must be said
She scorned her ardent lover, she wouldn't give him Thyme
No Canterbury Bells would ring, no union sublime

So William sought another to ease his aching heart
He spied an Amaranthus, then felt a Cupid's dart
And so like Snow-In-Summer he melted at the sight
Of tearful Love-Lies-Bleeding, the source of his delight

Now Rosemary was jealous, determined to try harder
Perhaps a Red-Hot-Poker might dampen down his ardour!
Love that's unrequited will evermore exist
Then feelings that are clouded become Love-In-A-Mist.

Sheila Leheup

40TH ANNIVERSARY

It was a long time ago in '48,
That you and I had our first date.
The news of our marriage on them we sprung,
They tried to tell us we were too young.

Two years on we tied the knot,
On a day in August I have never forgot.
But 40 years on we are still together,
I loved you then and I will forever.

You mean more to me than you really know,
Although there are times it may not show.
We have shared our tears and a great deal of fun,
And we still call each other affectionately 'Hun'.

The lovely children to me you endowed,
To have you and them I am really proud.
And what more can I ask for out of life,
Than my children and dearest, darling wife?

Our life's been sunny, never shady,
And to me you're once, twice, three times a lady.
So as we celebrate this special day,
There is something more I would just like to say.

A thank you that comes from deep in the heart,
To all our friends of our life you've been part.
To Russell, Gavin, Charlotte, Michelle, Richard, Derek, Yvonne,
For without all of you today couldn't go on.
And to you, 'Hun,' in so many ways,
My love today, tomorrow, forever, always.

Ron Bassam

SEEING IS BELIEVING

The face in the mirror, what do I see?
That silent reflection, is it really of me?
There are lines caused by laughter, other lines too,
Left by sorrow and sadness, seeing life through . . .

I can look angry or give you a smile,
Pull funny faces; pretend for a while.
Be someone famous, or very glam . . .
Well, maybe not . . . I'll stay as I am.

My face in the mirror then starts to annoy.
I keep moving back to when only a boy.
Then I rub on the glass, hoping to see
The face of my youth, so clear and line free.

But it does not happen, and never can.
The face in the mirror is one of a man.
The mirror is clear, the reflection is true.
Accept the image . . . it really is you.

Kenneth Tropman

THE QUARRY

Countryman, do tell us
What has happened here
the old forsaken quarry,
Why do shed doors swing to and fro,
unlatched, unhinged,
the grass-swept wind,
While ragged trees stand vacantly?
The rabbits make their paths and do not care,
The sheep have crows upon their backs,
And no one ever enters here.
Was money lost, was someone hurt
To make this place so bare?
Countryman, tell us
What has happened here?
Why must we stand and stare?

Paul Gardner

HARVEST SONG

Some sun, some rain, some warmth, some chill.
Grass becomes adorned with morning jewel
Shining to Sol's smile in dwindling days
While nature with her paintbrush plays.
Masterpieces extended during night,
Leaves gilded hues match dramatic red
Majestic purple joins humble brown
Foretelling what must come quite soon.
Berries glow to feed the feathered flock
Wind's murmur stirs the crop to drop.
Plump nuts for squirrels in the wood
Who busily store their winter food.
Baled hayfields bristle stubble now
Till ploughs arrive feeding gull and crow.
Muddy streams chuckle, bustling on,
Flirting and frolicking with each stone.

The countryside yawns and takes repose
As voices rise in harvest praise.

Roma Scrivener

MEDITERRANEAN EVENING ALONE

In sea swallowed, sun lost evening loneliness,
As twinkling lights replace that blaze of day
Whose rainbow hues now calm seas caress,
And then in silence slowly fade away,
I ponder deep - and this soon dimming view
Is brighter made by loving thoughts of you.

Calm sea, so briefly bathed by colours that you drowned
When bounded by horizon, where once that sea met sky
But now as twilight deepens where none is to be found,
And space of Earth and space of Heaven each other now deny;
Gone is the light your earthly arc to show
Whilst deeper thoughts of love within me grow.

Then pensive through a lonely glass of wine
I view my life and what perchance remains,
And watch consumed the wax that measures time
As glass reflects those gently flickering flames.
Yet musing time, and what with it to do
Means naught to me without those thoughts of you.

As evening coolness now gives way to night,
And silent calm becomes that moon-flecked sea
Which, saddened not by loneliness, so dances bright
That broken is my thoughtful reverie
I wish for you such deep tranquillity
As brightest moon upon the calmest sea.

Douglas Bryan Kennett

REMEMBRANCE DAY

We'll not forget the lives so bravely lost
On foreign soil or in the ocean deep,
Where souls are resting from their arduous toils
No more to be awakened from their sleep.
We bow our heads in deep remembrance now,
With silent thoughts of all their grief and pain,
Hoping that one day, in perfect peace,
We'll all be reunited once again.

We'll not forget the reason for their death,
The agony and heartache, which they shared;
We offer them a simple floral wreath
In gratitude for all the young lives spared.
For we've enjoyed the freedom which they won
Yet could not share the triumph of the day.
May rest eternal be their great reward
And memories in our hearts forever stay.

Janet Jones

LOVE IN THE COUNTRYSIDE

The hillsides filled with roaming sheep,
The cornfields filled with manure heaps.
The rivers filled with choice of fish,
For ramblers, pubs give first class dish.

The hedgerows filled with choice of flowers,
The woodlands have some secret bowers.
The country lanes spread o'er our land,
Need careful drivers with steady hand.

The badgers leave their setts at night,
The mess they make, a ghastly sight.
The fox and deer, so oft do roam,
They search for food some way from home.

The birds build nests in hedges and trees,
For them the whole wide world is free.
The seagulls leave the sea when wild,
They come inland, give thrills to child.

The beauty of the hills and dales,
The thrill of being in wind and gales,
The joy of wandering in snow-filled drifts,
The countryside filled with heaven-sent gifts.

John Paulley

SCOTTISH HILLS

The craggy mountains call me
To walk their stony paths,
The rivers rushing wildly,
Splash cold, as I go past.

Sweet purple heather blankets the ground,
With yellow gorse in varied mounds,
As peaceful silence, grows all around.

Another world I find I'm in, of beauty so extreme.
I look in awe and think that this, can only be a dream.

Whose footsteps do I walk in?
Who has passed this way afore?
Proud Scottish men and women,
Whose clans, there are no more

Memories of their history, heard in local tongue
Stories of the lives they led, forever will be sung.

Wendy Scott

THE PILGRIM

Being in Movement.

Crossing the restless sea,
Climbing the craggy mountain peaks,
Stepping the pebbly sandy shores,
Following the sinuous river,
Imprinting the fields, the flowers, the grass.

Arriving.

To stay still;
Quiet;
In peace;
To speak, to hear,
To Be

To carry the message from one to the other
The body in movement
The essence in
Connecting
People with places.

Jane Bingeman

FACE TO FACE WITH HEARTACHE

Through the open door, she entered into the shop
Newspaper rolled, taste buds dead, about ready to drop
Coffee aroma filled the air, she ordered with some thought
She sat back, feet up, knowing her life she had to sort

Her husband had just left her after marriage of 34 years
She'd cried until her heart broke, fighting back the tears
Her mind was in turmoil, her brain worked overtime
She kept reassuring herself all would turn out fine

Why me? she asked herself time and time again
Please take away the pain strains and relieve the pain
You walked outa' the door and outa' my life
How could you do this to an honest, everloving wife?

Running away with a girl old enough to be your daughter
You've nothing in common and a lesson will be taught ya'
The attraction is obvious it's just that plain to see
You'll fall like a conker falls from a tree

What am I gonna do? There's no smile upon my face
Loneliness surrounds me in this big, empty space
I lay the table for two then realise you're not there
In life and love things don't always turn out fair

The clock strikes on the hour, I watch with tearful eyes
No respite, I'm hanging out my tears on the line to dry
I'd better face reality, nothing really goes away
Rebuild my life one step at a time, take it day by day.

Leigh Smart

DAY OF CHANGE

We are a nation who tolerate each other's way of life
Going about our daily business without causing strife
Day after day passed for us in a happy mixture of work and play
In vain we were warned that ahead of us violent trouble lay

But we did not really believe it, not in our green and pleasant land
Like the proverbial ostriches we buried our heads in the sand
A stunned nation watched in disbelief first reports of bombs on TV
And found it hard to understand how suddenly this could really be

So many people had started out on their routine day once again
Little knowing it would end in horror, devastation and great pain
Loss of lives and terrible injuries, the grim pictures we all saw
Just one day changed so many lives, that day and for evermore

We will try and carry on our normal lives, those who are able to
With stoicism we will struggle on to do the things we normally do
But on our streets police are armed and vigilant, alert and aware
Gone are the days when we lived each day happily, without care

In the name of religion came that terrible, fateful day of change
To cause such carnage because of one's beliefs is certainly strange
May we win through the hard times with wisdom and tolerance
Yet be strong enough against terrorism to take a determined stance

Hopefully the blighted lives will heal and return to near normal
And in this country peace and love will come again to us all
And we will cease to look with suspicion at every stranger
Offering the hand of friendship, without expecting danger.

Margaret Meagher

WE POETS

We poets are all strutting our stuff
Writing about the gentle,
The meek, the coarse and the tough.
Poet's wear varied faces
As we walk through life's different paces.
But each poet makes up one whole.
As we go *forward* and celebrate poetry
One and all.

Anita Hopes

THE MIRROR'S TALE

I'm sure I must be round and old . . .
As that is what I'm being told
When people come and stare at me . . .
 just stare back - incessantly!
They come each day - in ones - or pairs -
 hear their footsteps on the stairs -

They visit me in the evening as well,
And when I hear the sound of the bell
On the creaking door that leads to my room,
 know someone else is coming to groom
And preen or make funny faces -
From the door to me is just six paces . . .

The grown-ups vary in their approach to me
Some are sad - even melancholy
As they gaze into my all-seeing eyes,
They're aware of the truth - I tell them no lies . . .
It's sad to see the wistful gazes
Of people growing old, who are longing for praises
As they used to get just a few years ago -
But they can't hide from me - for I just *know* . . .

The children's visits are much more fun . . .
Their faces are shining - reflecting the sun.
Their eyes are bright, inquisitive and bold
As the grown-ups were before they got old . . .

Sometimes I'm 'misty' and wiped by a sleeve
Of a boy with 'spots', who cannot believe
He will ever be able to talk to a girl . . .
'If I could but speak, I'd say, 'Give it a whirl . . .'
There were others before you who felt just the same,
And realised later - when they'd grown and found fame -
The mirrors are friendly - and not there to judge . . .
But are handy - when used to wipe off a smudge
That's annoying your mother - who thinks of her son
With such loving pride - so be happy - have fun . . .

The girls have their problems too - they've been here
And have felt just like you - they too had their fear
That noone would want them, they thought they were plain
But after a while they were smiling again . . .
For they met someone kind, who made them feel good
And they turned into beauties - as I knew that they would!
Every mirror has a tale to tell!
From infant to old age I wish you all well.

Sheila Kuhn

A TRIBUTE

The collection at the Smith
Was a treasure to observe
Children in line were singing
Of Scotland's heritage and worth

Robert the Bruce, home at last in State
Through the ages of lofty peaks
A wealth of loyalty displayed

Lord Mayor in attendance
So he could see and comprehend
The atmosphere of achievement

While Moira Lawson baked the cake
A celebration of worth for all
He conducted the party to oversee
A treasure and name to vie
The childhood standing by.

Jean Bald

MYSTERIES OF LIFE

What lies far over the mountains?
Or lives behind the hills
Mostly hopes that are out of reach
And will never be fulfilled.
What is behind the sunset?
The translucent golden light
It appears to beckon *to me*
As it welcomes *in* the night.
There's something there behind a cloud
A mystery to unfold
The galaxies and universe
Hold more than we are told.
What lurks beneath the black holes
That once were brilliant stars?
For nothing lasts forever
Not even Jupiter or Mars.
What happens at the break of dawn
When Earth beholds the light?
The glory of the early morn
Brings nought but sweet delight.
If all these mysteries did unfold
Would life be just the same?
Knowing that we are Earthlings
We'd find *something* there to blame.

Gwen Ellis Hunt

AT YOUR COMMAND

'It's time to get your hair cut,'
My wife tells me today.
'You truly look a scruffy mutt'.
I really must obey.

'Darling, not too short now,'
She shouts to me again.
I wave and give a little bow
And flick my hairy mane.

'Morning, the usual, Sir?'
He greets me with a flair.
My answer is to concur
And sit down in the chair.

'Weather's not so nice this week'.
(I wish they wouldn't natter).
Severed hair falls on my cheek,
I suppose it doesn't matter.

Ears, nose and eyebrows
Are treated just the same.
'There you go,' the barber crows.
Isn't it all a pain?

I call out to the Lovely One,
'I'm home, come take a view'.
'Yes, very nice, the lawn's overgrown,
That needs cutting too'.

Douglas Bishop

CHILDREN

Listen to the stories of those who fought and won,
Glorify the war dead, for they were all some mother's son
They gave their lives for our freedom
And their sacrifice we respect
So tell *your* sons and daughters
Lest we forget, lest we forget.

Lorna Sim

MY SPECIAL BROTHER

Gordon, you were the little brother I loved with all my heart
We shared so many happy times until death forced us apart;
Mum and Dad never recovered from losing you so young
Taken home to Heaven, your life had just begun.

Until you came into the family I was the only one
I was so glad to have you; it's no fun just on your own;
I guess you were quite special right from the very start
Little did we realise how soon we'd have to part.

The years have passed so quickly since you closed your eyes
                                              for good
But our love for you has never died and so it never should;
Kevin and Mark can't recall the special brother that we had
But I know that you are watching us along with our much missed dad.

You lie resting in a cemetery so very far away
But the miles don't make any difference as I miss you so each day;
I often look at Robert and picture you instead
Wondering how you'd look now but the picture's in my head.

Gordon, all I have are memories and photos to recall.
That special little brother who I miss the most of all;
Kevin and Mark I love to bits but they cannot replace
The very special brother who had an angel's face.

I speak to you so many times wishing you were here
But only having memories of you makes missing you so dear;
If I could walk to Heaven and visit you each day
I'd gladly hold you in my arms and never walk away.

A sister's tribute.

Pat Ferris

THE FAMOUS FRIENDS

(A vignette c.1740, Metcalf Sculpsit)

Beneath a dramatic, cloud-flecked summer sky
The dusty road winds down from Ullenhall
Between the great oaks of Arden's greenery
To broad vistas and avenues of Barrells Hall,
By grove, shrubbery, stepped lawns and urns beset,
Where Henrietta, Lady Luxborough roves
With fellow landskip improver and poet,
Essayist William Shenstone of Leasowes;
Above, on grand terrace mellow flagstones
Richard Graves, a clever satirical novelist,
Holding a hefty, yellow calf-bound tome,
Chinwags to Anthony Whistler, neo-classicist.

Some way off, sitting pensive on a stone,
Gazing o'er the fair vale, notebook in hand,
Our old friend Somerville we now discern,
Edstone's hunting squire, local big Whig,
Justice of the Peace, famed poet of 'The Chace'.
In mid-distance on mossy woodland ride,
Another poet, Richard Jago no less,
Walks over from Snitterfield, preoccupied,
Towards him, doubtless eager to express
A new verse subject, line or mere idea.
Down in this lower corner, through the gates
Lord Lyttleton drives his speeding chaise-and-pair.

This eighteenth-century coterie all complete,
What will the *cognoscenti*, literary aesthetes
Now assembled here, decide to do today?
Alas, despite the heat, we simply cannot say,
Because the engraver froze the scene ice-still.
Likewise, I find it impossible to delineate, tell
At this great distance both of time and space
Which one, if any of them, is 'Genius of the Place'.

David Daymond

GLORIOUS DAY!

The sun is up. Another glorious day begins.
Time to step out and cast away the old sins.
To climb a mountain, walk along a beach
Strive to achieve things far beyond my reach.

To love all men, of every race and creed,
And cleanse myself of selfishness and greed.
From this day on, to make each moment real
And every task, pursue with honest zeal.

To reach these goals, I can no more delay
No dwelling on mistakes of yesterday;
But strive each day to love my fellow man
And share with all, the Lord's eternal plan.

On that day when *my own* sun does not rise
I pray, my friends; you'll see it through my eyes
And think of me as one, who strove to fully live
Each glorious day the Good Lord had to give.

Brian Croft

BY CHANCE

Like a meteor in the night
You pierced my heart with sharp delight,
Like a rumour from the east
Unnerved me to a fierce unrest.

One afternoon of wind and rain
You came, by chance, to my poor room,
Circled your skirt upon the floor
And tricked oblivion.

So learned my hopes to sing
At whisper of your name;
Winds of a wild romance
Fanned my dry heart aflame.

Hopeless, masochistic pain
That loving you, you'd love again
I dreamed, and dreamed in vain.
Fate played a shifty game
That summer long; puffed out my flame
And choked my song.

You went your way.
Since when
When I come home
A handful of dry words upon a page
Is all I own.

Ray Racy

ENGAGEMENT

I am my beloved's
And my beloved's mine
Two hearts are united
Two lives are entwined
Two hearts are committed
To place the Lord Jesus first
I know of no greater blessing
For two sweethearts here on Earth.

For 'twas God who planned it
That man should not live alone
It was God who so delighted
In bringing two to be as one
And with an open Bible
Sanctified by prayer and praise
May your lives be so blessed
In your earthly 'paradise'.

Doreen Reeves

REMEMBERING THE GOLDEN JUBILEE

Our queen has reigned for fifty years, a cause for celebration,
For she has served with selflessness and real dedication,
And so the people came to join the parties and the cheering,
As she embodies qualities that others find endearing.

She's shown stability and strength amidst the agitation
Of shifting values in the world and change throughout the nation,
Yet with a gentleness and grace she's carried out her duty.
When meeting folk from far and wide her smiles have lent her beauty.

Two concerts in the palace grounds were eagerly attended,
With bursts of brilliant fireworks before the evening ended,
Like waterfalls cascading down to crowds that stood enraptured.
In memories and videos this fine display was captured.

The carnival gave great delight, a sumptuous procession
Of 'butterflies,' and tiny tots who moved with self possession,
Of dancing girls and men in masks, exotic in their guises,
A day of singing, laughter, fun and full of glad surprises.

The fly past was the final show: in a precise formation
They soared above the waving flags much to our admiration,
With Concorde and Red Arrows last, they trailed their clouds of glory
Of red and white and royal blue - the moral of this story:

With all the speeches and parades, each service of thanksgiving
Has brought a sense of unity and here where we are living
The cultural diversity can be an education,
So we can say with open hearts that we are a great nation.

Anne Greenhow

THE FLOWER OF LOVE

In the parched, stony earth, a seed is planted,
Tenaciously, a delicate, hardy flower grows,
Drawing through its roots the well spring water
That flows, deep below the surface.

All men delight in its fragrance,
Feeling a wonder mixed with fear,
Tasting its smell as a connoisseur with trepidation,
Savours the bouquet of a rich and heady wine.

With heightened sensitivity man notices
Its minutely, perfectly formed, tender petals.
No man dares to pluck it from its natural surrounds,
So it remains and grows.

Sometimes it is uprooted and burned,
At others, dying beneath the relentless, withering sun.
For a while thriving then destroyed, at the first onset of a storm.
Though blooming, it is marred, bent awry, it grows misshapen,
But, on occasions, stalwart it grows.

The flower is able to weather the most relentless of storms,
The disease infestations, which hamper and plague its existence,
Until it grows not as a flower, but as a flowering hardy shrub,
Putting forth new shoots, offshoots and offspring,
Providing shelter and protection for all men beneath its leafy boughs.

Damien Plummer

RICH REWARD

Into a small country church one day,
A tired visitor came to pray.

Down she sat, upon the pew,
Sad and weary, old Maisie Drew.

'Dear Lord, please help my poor son Stan,
He really is a kindly man. Please help him, angels, if You can?'

With this simple prayer she shed a tear,
Then turned to see an angel near.

A glimpse of gold, a joyful heart,
Meant a rich reward for this elderly mother's devoted heart.

Tara Britton

THE ORCHESTRA

The violins said to the orchestra, 'We really don't need you,
We can do it all ourselves for we are quite a few.'
The cellos said, 'You need our help for where would be the bass?
You are high and fiddly, you really have no case.'
The double bass joined the fray, 'Without me you've no ground,
I anchor the whole orchestra, I'm the best thing around.'
The flute and piccolo started up in high, quivering voices,
'We always have the melody, we are the people's choices.'
The oboe, clarinet, bassoon put in a plea to be heard,
'We give colour and texture,' they quickly observed.
The brass said quite strongly, 'When the music needs to be loud,
We come in with our mighty power and the audience is wowed.'
The drum took up the argument and banged away with strength,
'I keep the rhythm going, I can play at great length.'
The triangle joined in next with its tinkling note,
'I can be heard above everyone with my shiny, silver coat.'
The castanets and maracas each had their say in turn,
'We are effective for colour, of that everyone should learn.'
The xylophone clattered out its thoughts as its hammers struck
The keys, 'I am suited to fast music and do all I can to please.'
Mr Sopranino, the conductor, came and tapped his baton on
the stand
When there was total silence, he started them with his hand.
Gone was all the squabbling and saying, 'I'm the best!'
For they all played together, even down to the rests.
The music they were playing was a lively symphony,
The whole was made of every part joined together in unity.
And so it is with people, it's not the individual part
But working all together and doing it from the heart!

Rita Hardiman

WESTMEATH FAR AWAY

With sheer delight, my heart takes flight,
And soars back home today,
To meander o'er your hills once more,
Dear Westmeath far away.

Down memory road, to my old abode,
I wander 'neath the hill,
Oh, sweet Rathshane, I'm home again,
By that grand old corn Mill.

That lovely place, by the old Mill-race,
Was home sweet home before
I love it still, and always will,
No heart could love it more.

With line and hook, I fished the brook,
Beneath that lordly hill,
In the dappled shade, the elms made,
By the quaint old corn Mill.

Though I had no reel, nor wicker creel,
Yet I enjoyed it all,
The working wheel, the smell of meal,
And the rainbow o'er the fall.

In my lovely dream, I see your stream,
Where sparkling waters flow,
And the brightest green, I ever seen,
Where lush green meadows grow.

And if I'm blessed, with a last request,
Let it be, dear God, I pray,
To wander o'er, your hills once more,
Dear Westmeath far away.

James Baxter

WHAT A CLOT!

This morning I woke early . . .
Did all my daily chores!
Washed and dried my flowing locks . . .
(To look as good as yours!)
Gathered my belongings -
Glasses, purse and phone,
Got into my car to start my journey . . .
All alone!
Going like a rocket . . .
Down the three '0' three . . .
Thinking that when I arrived . . .
I'd order up some tea!
Reached my destination
Spot on half-past ten . . . !
Thought it would be really good . . .
To see you once again!
Found a perfect table
So I could keep an eye . . .
Just in case I missed you . . .
And you would sail right by!
Got a little anxious, the clock was ticking on . . .
Our meeting time had now been reached . . .
Passed me by . . .
And gone!
Didn't have your mobile, so tried to ring your mum
(Hoping that she just might know) . . .
The reason . . . you'd not come?
Waited until ten to twelve . . .
Hoped you were OK . . .
Then I'm afraid the penny dropped . . .
It wasn't . . . *the right day!*

Jill Alcock

KITES IN THE SKY OVER TIANANMEN SQUARE

Built in the centre
of what is now Beijing
lies Tiananmen Square
defining the longitude line
of the city centre,
a focal point for Mao's tomb
and final place to rest.
Above, his portrait hangs to leer
down on his people
crowding the square in holiday mood.

Children swarm,
Mandarins
in bright coloured clothes,
orange, jade, scarlet, turquoise, blue
a rainbow of delight
as they fly their kites,
true replicas of
spirits of devils, spirits of gods
they scream their joy
as wild dragons, fierce birds
prey on flowers of peace
tangle their swirling tails
to dominate the skies.

Freed from despotic rule,
Mao now long gone
yet still his smile
casts its shadow on
Tiananmen Square.

Elizabeth Hackman

THE CHRISTMAS ANGEL

When God decided to send His Son to Earth
The question was 'Where should be the birth?'
He sent His messengers around the planet
To seek a place just right for the event

Except the littlest angel thought too small
Who stayed behind to wait in God's great hall

Soon smallest angel, bored, went off alone
To seek a haven for the child to come
And soon got lost, confused amid Earth's babble
Then wandered, unannounced into a stable

There to rest

Later the angels told God where they'd been
They told of wondrous places they had seen
All thought theirs was the right place
How to choose between them? This was not the case
Smallest angel came, a tale to tell

'I was tired and cold, lonely as well
When I wandered into a stable bare
Mary and Joseph welcomed me with care'.

'That is the place,' said God, 'for My Son's birth
Where love abounds My Son shall visit the Earth
And find a place to rest'.

Dolly Harmer

MY LAD AT CHRISTMAS

Be quiet, my lad, can't you see,
I'm busy with the Christmas tree.
But, Mum.
Be quiet, my lad, and pass that here,
I'll be ready for Christmas, have no fear.
What with Grandma coming and Auntie too,
Can't you see there's a lot to do?
But, Mum.
Be quiet, my lad, and stop playing about,
You only know it makes me shout,
All the presents now under the tree,
Goodness me, it's half past three.
But, Mum.
For goodness sake what's the matter, my lad?
You should be happy and not so sad.
But, Mum,
It's the turkey and it's on the floor,
And it's just been eaten by the dog next door.

C Boneham

ST EDMUNDS

It's one hundred and fifty years old
Standing still, so proud and bold
As soon as you enter in
A calming of your thoughts begin.

It's so peaceful and tranquil there
A haven for all to share.
Inviting us to come to shelter
Away from life's mad helter-skelter.

To sit to think of God above
Who cares for us with unstinting love.
Who tries to guide us on our way,
To enhance our lives day by day.

As we leave this church so small
We give our thanks one and all.
How lucky to be able to worship still
At St Edmunds, the little church on the hill.

Helen Lock

I THINK OF YOU

In the stillness of the early morning
(amid birdsong and gently rustling leaves)

In the warmth and fluffiness of a purring
ginger-white kitten,

In the crisp cool freshness of an autumn wind
as golden yellow leaves fall softly to the ground,

In the solitude of a car parked by a quiet
woodland.

On a journey home alone filled with beautiful
memories,

In the gently fading sunlight as a late summer's
evening turns to dusk,

Within that inner silent space between life's
trials and turmoil

Always,
          Ever,
                    I think of you.

Jennifer Densham

THE REDWOOD'S STORY

Here I stand like a garden sentinel.
The most long-living tree of all
Life isn't easy you can tell
When I keep on growing so very tall.
I dwarf the other trees around
But gladly I have found
That I surpass all the local trees
In dress, in figure and in deeds.
Of course I could be a Christmas tree.
No other tree can claim that honour but me.
My green hair grows up so very high
And my great ambition is to reach the sky.
I shelter homeless birds and insects rare
But I am puzzled why I am still there
Other trees have not survived.
Countless people have also died.
Despite the dark, dull days that autumn sends
And the long winter's gnawing winds,
Happily I realise why I am still here
And therefore I must never fear.
I know Mother Nature takes good care
And keeps me standing tall and fair.
I am looking forward to the buzzing sounds
And summer's golden sun that has no bounds.

Margaret Kelly

ROSES

It all began with roses around our own front door:
He grew them and he tended them -
They couldn't ask for more.
For many years they flourished,
As did our children two,
Ever stronger, ever taller, as they wont to do.
Now other hands must tend them,
Although it breaks my heart
That I am here and he is not:
I thought we'd never part.
He's gone where none can follow,
But he's never far away,
For while kids and roses flourish,
With me he'll always stay.

Janet Bowerman

DIGGING MY GRAVE

I am digging my grave with
My spoon they say. I look back
Over a lifetime of see-saw dieting.
There was never a time
I did not have a weight problem.

Low fat milk, low alcohol drinks
So that my friends think
I am a weirdo 'on the wagon'.
The constant disappointment on
The scales and the low self-esteem which
                                        Follows it.

I eat to live not
Live to eat. Food has lost interest.
If a plate of food is
Placed on a table I will eat it,
Automatically, in all probability.
Just as long as I don't have to cook it.

The constant knowledge that
Whatever I eat will turn to fat
Is depressing enough.
The lucky ones without weight problems
Look on with veiled indifference.
Lucky,
They will never know the
Humiliation of the overweight.

Hilary Moore

JUST A THOUGHT

In our centuries old beautiful and troubled world . . .
It has been said,
'Every thought has been thought,' and
'Every word has been spoken'.

Pathos, dramas, love poems, ballads and sentimental songs,
Operas sung rising to fill holes in the skies
Odes, ditties, soliloquies, tributes and obituaries . . .

Words as different patterns, shapes and colours
Soft as velvet, searing as acetic acid
Tumbling like odd sized marbles in an empty box
Used and played with time and time again
Written profusely . . . capturing speech and thought
Diverse as ever changing moods and different skins
Echoing to and fro . . . bouncing off mountains
Always about us, some in strange or familiar guises

If all the words in all the nations joined together . . .
They'd wrap the world in a warm cloying poultice
And hang together like low chattering clouds
Making a cacophony of sound . . . which would deafen the ears.

Why is it then, there are no words or sounds
So deafening . . .
As the silence of an empty room?

Margaret Kaye

THE GIFT OF A POEM

The poem lay on the table among
Her things; the printed text became a song.
His words took on a life force of their own,
Rich in tone, with the strength of a full-blown
Field of golden corn ready for reaping,
As gentle as a babe quietly sleeping.
They murmured to her again and again
With the soft persistence of falling rain.
They dropped like notes of music on her ears,
They touched her soul and mingled with her tears.

Rosina Winiarski

PURR-FECT BLISS

Here I lie content,
Content in this moment of time,
Here upon the grass,
So cool beneath my furry frame,
Upon the grass,
Where tiny flowers shyly peep.

Here I lie content,
The sun caresses my body,
So soothing, so warm,
This is heaven,
This moment in time,
Where I perchance to sleep.

Veronica Taylor

STEPPING STONES

Tread lightly as you go along your way,
No one knows what lies beyond the bay,
Think twice before you have your say,
Harsh words will only spoil our day.

There are stepping stones across the stream
Where murky waters deep and dark may seem,
No place to stop, to plot, to scheme,
Step by step to find the sunlight's gleam.

If you should fall along the way,
You call but no one hears
What you have to say or even,
Know your fears or see the tears.

No one knows what the future has in store,
Each new day is different from the one before.
Yesterday has gone, and that's for sure.
The future, the present, only knock upon your door.

Other folk like you have fallen,
But still they try to get back up.
Some stay down for longer
And some have better luck.

So put your best foot forward
And carry on your way.
There's always a new tomorrow,
There's always another day.

Maureen Sadler

ENSEMBLE

I am forced to write poetry
I am coerced to write verse
Soon an end will come to this melee
Living with these lines
Certain things are none too fine
Lack of spontaneity can but only lead to dismay

Here then is the devil's altar
The very bridge on which I falter
The very line with which I seek to pray
For a better future
One without a tutor
To dismiss my soul if she may

I look into the jet-black sky
And presently I wonder why
I always dread the forthcoming day
It is up to me to try
I have heard as time goes by
It is only me who knows the way.

Cliff Holt

NEAR TO WATERLOO BRIDGE

I saw you,
Simply standing on a doorstep.
Young, lean,
Looking ghostly. Dressed
In the thinnest of clothes -
Trousers, a T-shirt,
No shoes . . .
The day was cold.
Sunday. London had rid itself of people -
Near to Waterloo Bridge
London was deserted.
My man and I were on our way home.
In a merry, merry mood.
We had spent the day on the Thames.
Good food, a few drinks.
Light-headed, we had danced the hours away.
I saw you, I said
'Did you see that guy?'
We walked by.
I kept looking behind me,
Aware that you had moved -
You frightened me.
Suddenly the river wind
Pressing against your chest
Revealed small breasts.
I saw the figure
Of a woman -
You were no threat.
You crossed the road.
Slowly, so slowly.
Silently drifted away.
Expressionless.

Claire-Lyse Sylvester

RAMBLINGS

Recovering from a bruising fall,
I missed my daily constitutional.
To raise my weary bones at all
Became a tricky task quiet convolutional.
O happy day when I could roam at last
Around the block with walking stick,
And dream sad dreams of journeys past,
As my joints gave loud rheumatic click.
In my short walk I spied 'For Sale'.
In fragrant bloom, multiplying as I went,
The coloured billboards left a trail
Of agents' smiles of great content.
And double-glazing met my gaze,
A new style - I tried in vain to spot it,
An archaic cheer I tried to raise
For those who hadn't got it!
A magnolia tree, in glorious bloom
'Til someone dug it up to make more room
To park his foreign car.
Some eating places now in view
Indian tandoori, Thai, kebab the palate savours,
Outside the Chinese take-away a queue
For Peking duck, sweet and sour, and oriental flavours.
Around the block its joys can bring,
No time for stay-at-homing,
The shortest walk a wondrous thing,
Just let your mind go roaming.

Jack Scrafton

This Wonderful World

Who is it makes the wind to blow?
And who the smallest seed to grow?
Whose power, design and careful plan
Turns helpless babe to full-grown man?

Throughout the world what do we see
But boundless creativity?
And could we live in total light
Without the respite of the night?

The oxygen we breathe in air -
Who makes sure it's always there?
Or blood that runs within our veins -
How come that it our life sustains?

How can the sea just ebb and flow?
And far-off stars remain aglow?
Whence comes this ceaseless energy?
Who keeps things going endlessly?

The colours that we see around
And all the treasures underground -
Who thought of them and made them so?
Who stops the world from spinning slow?

Why should a flower come from a bud?
Or cattle need to chew the cud?
If these were left to me and you
I fear what chaos might ensue.

Most would say the answer's clear:
Nature is the engineer.
But though my spelling may be odd,
This word to me just spells out *God*.

David Varley

Letting Go

Love held him tight
As hand clasped hand,
I would not let him go.
I was the voice of reason, wisdom,
Watching my seed grow.
Yet time marched on
And loosed the bond,
Slowly gathering pace -
He strained for independence,
To run in his own race.
Now still the rock
On which he leans,
Crumbling, yet holding fast -
My child grows wise
For future years,
While I cling to the past.

Joy Lenton

Mystery

'Twas Christmas and I heard Dad mutter,
'What does one do with brandy butter?
I have never heard of it put on bread'.
And he stood there, scratching his head.
'It's brandy, so do I put it in my drink?
Oh, I don't know just what to think!
It's butter too, it says so, see -,
Why is it such a mystery to me?'
I said, 'You put it on your Christmas pud'.
'Christmas pud? Well, that's no good.
On Christmas pud I put some cream
It goes down smoothly. Like a dream.
No, I'll have it for my supper
On cream crackers, with a cuppa'.

Susan Gordon

In The Land Of Ptolemy

I stand amidst the dust of time, where from the desert sands
                                    there rise
In majesty such structures grand upon the land of Ptolemy
                                    and his progeny.
Yet even old before his time stand these monuments of
                                    another's line.
Each shimmering tomb a gaunt reminder of the seed of
                                    ancient Egypt's womb.

The sand grows hot beneath my feet, I taste the rising morning heat,
And in the shadow of history these edifices of mystery
Scream to me of ages past, of kings and queens of a kingdom
                                    so vast
That though long centuries have passed their names endure,
                                    their legacy lasts.

Oh great pyramid I see just what I am meant to be,
I cannot help but wonder at your splendour for it is just that
That brings me here to stand before these stones, these tombs,
                                    this portal
Into another time and place, where pharaohs walked with
                                    godlike grace.
For though the sands of time have flown, and many desert
                                    winds have blown,
I stand in awe of what I see, I salute your enduring majesty.
Here in the valley where the kings are no more,
I blink in the sun, touch the shimmering heat, and peer through
                                    history's door.

Brian Porter

High Peaks

I enter its silence
And breathe in its tranquillity;
They have stood the ravages of time.
These purple-headed peaks
That carve their silence to the sky;
These grey stone walls raised
Up like altars in praise of God.
Here the centuries pass marked by virgin snows.

God created these moors
With their wild openness,
These peaks that lie bleak
To their belonging
This land tended by stubborn men,
Wresting a livelihood from
The harshness of its unyielding.
There are those that endeavour,
Those that minister this land;
Those whose shadows pass
Fleetingly the rocky outcrops
That have stood a million years.

Peter Morriss

Holidays

What a wonderful time of the year
To get out into the fresh air
We'll play some old fashioned games
To have a nice bat and ball game
Then a game of hopscotch
Then to skip with the rope turning
Chance to play marbles together
Hands up to play two baller
To see the children with smiling faces
It is the simple things
That are the best.

Rita Scott

SEEING OURSELVES AS OTHERS SEE US

I am sitting on a seat
And seven pairs of eyes are beginning to stare.
I know I'm not paranoid and I don't need to care
Because I am the model in an art class, you see,
And that is the reason they are looking at me.

Silence descends like a cloak.
They look at my nose, ears, eyes and my hair
And then do some measuring in order to prepare.
They start with trepidation and some with dread,
With crayons and pencils to draw my head.

I look at the portraits being drawn,
As every twenty minute I get up for a break
To prevent any stiffness, a pain or an ache,
The faces vary in shape - one eye has a squint,
But of my features and likeness there isn't a hint.

Rachel E Joyce

AUTUMN - A CELEBRATION

Winged messengers speed swift across the sky
As nature's festival its joy proclaims.
Above the stormclouds, southwards, swallows fly,
Whilst far below, the trees erupt in flames.
The wild wood, rapturous, glowing in its glory,
Spent leaves cascade, as from a golden pyre,
Great sacred oaks, huge branches russet, hoary
Blaze up - their twigs like fingers to a fire.

A sensuous time of harvest, fruit and flowers,
Gold wheat and corn, the bounteous gifts of earth,
Whilst nut trees, laden in their leafy bowers,
Await the lick of frost at winter's birth.
Like shrivelled parchments from some ancient books,
Behind the tractor's rows, the black birds fly
And to the cawing of the straggly rooks
The brown earth turns beneath the seagulls cry.

And as the sunset darkens from the east
We'll see what offerings frosty winter throws -
As gaudy in his coat of black and white,
The felon magpie struts the rutted rows.

Lucy Holloway

LAST MAN STANDING

*(Dedicated to Hans Mullen, Hermut & Angelike Boak, Ingrid Friedrichsen,
Helga Angalike Fitz and Paul Volante)*

It seems not so long ago, we were full of fight and hacked away at the
Stasrzi Polizi in East Berlin,
Even I who took the brunt from the interrogation by Honikar Polizi
I've still survived,
But one by one we all have to die,
But *not* by the hands of the Stasrzi Polizi.
But God has taken them one by one.
Now I am the only one left to tell the tale, of how we fought so all
of you could live on,
Only I remember the deeds and pain that we did endure
all those years ago.
Only I, the last man standing remembering the love and pain we
shared behind that Iron Curtain we came.
My bones are all weary. I am sad to say,
And when life is all said and done and no one left to carry on.
And now how I long to be in my Fatherland.
If only I could lay there to rest,
Beside the five of the very best,
My friends in their Sunday best:

Paul Volantefitz

JUDGEMENT

We think we know the answer
We think we know the cure
We think we know the answer
But then we're not too sure

We think of this and think of that
The truth we know nor care
Sound judgement to me it seems
Stands mute like some forgotten dreams

Your judgement delivered with unkind cuts
Against a host of ifs and buts
Judge not that ye may not be judged
Ye live in a world of ifs and buts.

John Morrison

NEVER FORGOTTEN NAN

What can we say about our Nan
The best you'll ever find
She always had the time for us
Her endless love divine
The lullabies she sang to us
When we were very small
Her gentle hands upon our pain
If we should ever fall,
'Let's kiss it better,' she would say
And then the pain would go away.
The gifts she had and shared with us
Will stay within our hearts
As long as we can say our prayers
We'll never be apart
So when we're sad and feeling blue
We only need to think of you
The word forgotten won't exist
With the memories you've left behind
So! Nan take with you all the love we can give
From you family and your friends
And with these words
God bless you Nan
Eternity never ends.

J A Alcock

SRI LANKA - ISLAND OF MY SOUL

Etched deep within my memory is a time so long ago
When you and I walked on the golden sand.
Blue skies and glorious sunshine, the whispering of the waves
As from the crystal sea they rolled to land.

Tall and graceful palm trees swaying to the music of the breeze
The faces of the people chocolate brown
Smiled a welcome for the tourists - each and everyone
On their island in the sun. No need to frown.

Inland in the busy town chaotic traffic hurried by,
And in amongst the chaos was the charm
Of elephants and bullock carts and a hundred honking horns,
And no one seemed to come to any harm.

There were dancers in the temples and the constant beat of drums
And Buddha's watching over - so serene,
While colourful, costumed islanders brought perfumed lotus flowers
Devout, they offered gifts. Oh, wondrous scene!

Forever etched in memory is this island in the sun,
And then the great tsunami took its toll
In this paradise, in this happy land. There is devastation now
And tears fall for the island of my soul.

Barbara Dunning

A GLIMMER OF LIGHT

So often in this modern world
  Aggression seems to rule
And bitterness between two sides
  Begins each day in school.
Neighbour fights with neighbour too
  And countries hate each other
Gangs join force to set off bombs
  With aims to kill some others.
No corner of this world is free
  And people live in fear
Today could be that dreadful day
  When they might pay so dear.
Strangers are viewed cautiously
  And sometimes others too
We even suspect friends at times
  And wonder - what is true?
All this fear makes life so grim
  Not knowing who to trust
The thing we need is honesty
  So talking is a must.
But thank God all is never lost
  There are still kind folk near
So life is not all doom and gloom
  There is *some* kindness here,
And this will lighten up the dark
  Which seems so heavy now
Perhaps that light will soon increase
  If we can teach them how.

Elsie J Sharman

FAIRIES BRIGHT

The sky above is smoky blue
The stars above are shining thru,
I lay here looking up to the sky,
So clear thru my window on high.
Bewildered by the vastness of space
A silhouette I see of a magnolia tree,
Blowing in the evening breeze
As it sways to and fro,
The stars flicker,
A dancing light around my room,
Imagination starts to flow,
I imagine the dancing lights are fairies bright,
With feathery wings and colours so bright,
They're dancing for me,
Oh what a pretty sight.

Jenny Johnson

MY CAT - MONGI

He is a black and grey tabby with only one eye
Amazingly enough he still manages to get by.
He looks after his territory - day and night
Never ever worrying about his poor sight.

Other tomcats in our close come nowhere near
Is word had got around it is him they should fear.
His hunting technique is 'simply watch and wait'
Sooner or later the little mouse meets his fate.

Indoors he will come for a rest and a doze
A little bit of fuss and a stroke on the nose.
Soon he will purr, it is the sweetest of sounds
His world is complete for our love has no bounds.

Jan Whitehouse

SPRING MADNESS

March hares are mad,
They emulate the movement
Of blown blossom,
Floating, drifting,
Dancing, free of care.

Birds go beserk,
Waking at first light
They shrill out, lists
Of tasks to be performed,
Build nests, lay eggs, hatch young,
Feed and succour fledglings,
Teach them how to fly,
And daylight hours seem short.

All life is mad in spring,
Thrusting towards the sky,
Ignoring bitter winds,
Frost's deathly finger touch,
Eager for light and warmth
Impatient for the sun.

Youth in swelling spring
Dances with outstretched arms
In some enchanted fantasy,
Embracing life's abundance,
The bitter and the sweet,
Mad as a March hare;
Frantic as a songbird;
Fragile as blown blossom.

Hazel Wellings

WARTIME MOTHERS

I think of mothers with tears in their eyes,
Finding them hard to suppress, when saying goodbye.
Kissing their son's for the very last time,
Not knowing if the war would be won or lost,
Nor aware of the outcome and the terrible cost
The scenario repeated many thousands of times,
Their darling boys having become young men,
Some would come home but God knows when!
Thousands would remain at the scene of the battle,
Headstones reminding us of conflict and valour.
Do we care for the mothers, or does it not matter?
For the mothers, a life wondering what might have been,
Our darling boys killing their darling boys
And their darling boys killing ours.
Headstones in faultless regimental lines,
Flowers and tranquillity setting the scene.
A slight figure stooped over a headstone there,
Dressed in black with silvery hair,
Tears rolling down her wrinkled cheek.
Years have passed, the pain remains.
No mother should have to visit the grave of her son,
Especially one killed by another mum's son.
She turns away with tears in her eyes,
Treading the path that she's trodden before,
Her mind in a state and thinking of war.
Over the years, she's had to bear,
All of the sorrow, does anyone care?
Memories of her boy, so vivid in her mind
Putting up with the sorrow and untold pain,
Neither side seemed to have made any gain.

John H Israel

LIGHT SENSATION

What colours are in Heaven?
Will music be my guide?
Or will lucky number seven
Be coloured on t'other side
Will thrushes sing so lyrical
Have tones purple deep and mystical?

I hope pianos are played in Heaven
Domino keys no black nor white can hide
Yin and Yang may be in Heaven
Pure light never to be denied
It may not be so farcical
To find this colour's ephemeral

Shimmering angels play sweet harps - as given
By golden breath the ether sighed
In marble halls amongst all brethren
Accompanied by great Welsh Choirs
This colour surely magical
Even for the puritanical

Will saxophonists number at least eleven?
Only time will tell and this we'll bide
In truth as God himself forgave them
Who jived away a life denied
So be not blue nor get hysterical
When this hue lights us metaphysically.

T M Wright

FIRST DAY OF SPRING

I woke this morning early, before the rooster's cry,
Before Auroras passing - to light the morning sky.

I lie in expectation to hear the Mavis sing
As leader of the chorus, to welcome in the spring.

With pleasure mounting in my soul I heard the sweetest sound,
The air was filled with birdsong, melodious, pure, profound.

I threw the windows open wide, to let the music swell,
And then I opened up my heart and therein let it dwell.

I watched the sunrise paint the clouds with glorious rosy hues,
As it, the giver of all life, this first spring day imbues,

New growth to start, new hope to come, new dawns for us to see,
A beautiful reminder of nature's constancy . . .

L Muscroft

CONVERSATION WITH A CAT

I met a cat by Ballard's Gate,
As through the dampened grass it came,
Paws poised before each careful step
To shake the raindrops from its fur.
Then stopped to stare with great, green eyes
And greeted me as all cats do.
From that moment we were friends
And so would be until its mind
Was drawn to sights I could not see.
Meantime I stooped and stroked its back
And talked of things cats understand,
Like chasing mice and harvest moons.
Falling leaves that let them play
As once they did when they were young.
Of scraps of fish, and milk, and cream,
Of fireside rugs on a winter's night.
Companionable talk, until, at last
The cats' attention strayed beyond.
A flickered tail and it was gone.

Tony King

RESPECT

R egard others, honour their feelings deal with your own insecurities
E liminate your fears and envy, everyone deserves good virtue.
S ingled out for your dress code is nonsensical and
                        absurd behaviour.
P oise with a good value towards others mothering love is a
                        great step forward.
E ach one pay attention to their transgression aggression is
                        an onslaught attack.
C onsideration creates compassion, passion and enthusiasm
                        are what you need.
T oo many good people are robbed of their confidence leaving
                        them elusive by deceptive ones.

Merlene Francois

A CELEBRATION OF SPRING

Here come the days of spring, the birds are on the wing,
The burgeoning life is spreading in the air.
The snowdrops we adore, are on the woodland floor
The carpeting of bluebells, claim their share.
Forsythia and aconite, indeed a gladsome sight,
With primrose and anemone sublime
Contrast their colours fair, a sight we love and share,
While heather clumps, their bells will sway and chime.

The winter's passed away, the snow has gone astray,
The north-west winds have now been lulled to sleep.
But strangers e'er beware and think you have a care
And let your secret sense a watch to keep.
The forecast man may say, 'You'll be all right today
I see no earthly reason to be scared'.
Before you shed a clout, be like the wary scout,
Remember well the maxim, 'Be prepared'.

There may be nought to fear, the sky is blue and clear,
The friendly sun shines bright and warms the day.
But be you well aware that cloudless skies bid fair
To let Jack Frost his icy hand to play.
Now these are shameful thoughts that put you out of sorts.
Let's look upon the bright side of the scene.
The crocus is in bloom, it dispels the winter gloom
And daffodils are ever so serene.

God's gift to man is this - there is everlasting bliss
If we recognise the wonder of His ways.
Through the beauty and the strife and the changing face of life
His Hand is clear in all that one surveys.

Tony Channon

OLD AGE NEVER COMES ALONE

I'm old and I repeat myself often
I suspect that I am a bit of a bore
I tell the same story over and over
And it's usually about the war
I get anxious about appointments
Or simple trips out or visits
I can't seem to cope with life anymore
It's not a lot of fun for me
You younger ones laugh or lose patience
Whilst I just love having all these anxieties
They're what makes my life worth living
Could it really be the onset of senility?
Yes, I'm old and so will you be one day
And your memory will start to fade
Hopefully the world will be a more tolerant place
That makes room for the old and frail.

Melanie Burgess

DRUGS IN OUR TIME

I remember when life was so good
In our green and pleasant land
Before drugs took a hold
Life was really grand

Drugs destroy our children's lives
Before they have had time to live
To learn the beauty of the world
And all it has to give

Don't spend your young lives getting hooked
Waiting for the next quick fix
For the quick fix of drugs never lasts
And like a fish you will soon be hooked

The beauty all around us
Is there for all of us to see
It doesn't cost a penny
It's all completely free

The beauty of the skies
The flowers and the trees
All God's living creatures
Are there for you and me.

Sandra W Bridgeman

I STOOD ON THE THRESHOLD OF THE NIGHT

I stood on the threshold of the night,
On the edge of night, on its very rim,
Beneath, a deep and dark abyss,
Above, the stars cool, blue and dim.

I stepped straight into the bowl of night,
Into its deep and cavernous room,
While the sapphire stars, aloof, austere,
Cast their pale blue gaze o'er the muffled gloom.

I sailed through the jet-black sea of night,
Through inky oceans of solemn space,
And I plucked the stars from the firmament,
Dark waves swept in to cover their place.

By the pallid gleam of my lamp-light stars,
I sailed back through that ebony orb of night,
I stepped over its threshold once more, and found
Myself returned to a world of light.

To my pale cool goddess whose jet-black hair
Cascades around her as she lies,
And before her I cast the cool, blue stars,
To reflect deep and dark in her cool, blue eyes.

Barry Jones

CELEBRATION

I never thought I'd say
But I'm sure you'll all agree
Forward Press is the answer
For the likes of you and me.

We love to write our stories
Our poems for one and all
Let's join the celebrations
And really have a ball.

There's Seven Wonders of the World
The eighth I'm sure you'll agree
Is for Forward Press's great success
And a happy 15th anniversary.

Let's drink a toast and wish them well
For many years to come
For Forward Press's founder
Ian Walton a glass of rum.

Emma Hardwick

TO A SHY LOVER

My love,
Let's put away the masks,
And drop the proper phrases.

In this velvet dark,
Where touch falls soft as Cupid's wing,
Souls can speak without speech,
Hearts can heed without hearing.

Love is thoughtless of time,
But still time passes.

Therefore I say:
Waste not this night,
But let us haste to know each other.

Philippa Adburgham

THE SEASONS

Look around and you will see
Seasonal beauty constantly.
A dull winter's day, when the cold winds blow
Covering our town in a blanket of snow.
Transforming bare trees, and carpeting the ground
In a pure white shroud that deadens all sound.
The breeze becomes balmy and the sun warms the earth
There are buds on the trees, and the land gives birth
To daffodils and crocus, what a sight to behold
The fresh colours of spring begins to unfold.
Glorious sunshine and soft April showers
Fill all our gardens with beautiful flowers.
Songs from the birds, and buzzing of a bee,
A cat lies slumbering in the shade of a tree.
These herald the coming of summer at last
The coldness of winter is in the past.
Crops ripen in the fields, and fruit on the trees
But damp misty mornings, and a cooling breeze
Tell us autumn is here, and the colours will change
To reds, browns and orange, a fantastic range.
Days become shorter, there's frost on the rooftop
The cycle of the seasons will never stop.

Lynne Walden

A NURSERY RHYME FOR ADULTS

Mary had a mobile phone,
It glowed a greeny glow
And everywhere that Mary went,
The phone was sure to go.

She used it all the live-long day
To talk to her friend Marje
And when she went to bed at night,
She put her phone on charge.

Tom, Tom, the tycoon's son,
Stole a Jag and took it for a run.
Imagining himself at the Goodwood Races,
He put the Jaguar through its paces.
He drove the car like a bat out of Hell -
Now he's cooling off in a prison cell.

Jack and Jill ran up a bill
Against their credit card,
And on the day they had to pay,
Times, they found, were hard.
Poor Jack had but half-a-crown,
Jill was depressed and feeling down.
Between them they incurred a might debt,
Which, as far as I know, isn't settled yet.

R V Windett

THE GIFT OF FRIENDSHIP

When we were young
You ran and laughed,
I sat and dreamt
A thousand dreams.

We moved away and
Many countries separated us
But we still wrote and talked
Just as if we were near.

When sadness and loss came my way
I found you there to welcome me
Your warm embrace,
Your friendly smile.

Now that we are older
You still run and have fun
I sit, read and remember
The dreams we once had.

The dreams have now gone
But the greatest gift of all
Is here with us to stay.
Thank you my friend,
May our tomorrow be like today.

Lelia Grant

DAMP DISCUSSION

I met an old lady the other day when I was travelling on life's way,
She sat down with me while I was enjoying a cup of tea.

She had certainly done a lot of living,
No way did I begrudge the time that I was giving.

Jim said this, did that, went on so long,
It seemed her son could do no wrong.

I left her with my ears a-bristle,
In her voice was a croaking whistle.

And my face was wet, because, in the course of all her chat,
With every word she spoke, she spat!

Joy R Gunstone

THE WISDOM TREE

The dawn gives way to morning splendour
Shining her light on the wisdom tree
All her leaves are made of silver
And her fruit is poetry
Bluebirds shelter in her presence
Raindrops kiss her silver boughs
Spiders weave a web of wonder
Sprinkled in a golden shroud
Soon the day has almost ended
But the tree shines through the night
Angels came and breathed upon her
And the tree became pure white
Through a haze of golden moonglow
Diamond beads of dew appeared
Shining like a giant halo
A sanctuary for beast or bird
Suddenly from out of nowhere
A voice spoke with authority
I am the light that shines in the night
I am the poetry
I am the Lord of the Universe
I am the wisdom tree.

Gloria B Rogers

ZIMBABWEAN TSUNAMI

They came; those army trucks with men in riot gear.
Their orders; all the squatter camps and vendor's stalls to clear!
Destroy the lives of people struggling to exist.
Give no warning; just burn, break, loot and as a final demoniac twist,
Browbeat them into tearing down their cardboard shacks
With their bare hands. Chop-chop, no time to pack.
Secrete a battered kettle, pot, a blanket, clothes,
Then with wailing babies on their backs,
Force them to tramp the dusty roads
To seek a place to sleep, to scrounge a scrap to eat,
To weep and shiver in the winter cold.
Who are these faceless men, who carry out their orders grim?
Brain-washed thugs, trained to obey a despot's brutal whim
Are they not brothers, husbands, uncles, sons
With cherished wives and mothers, maybe precious little ones?
Can they not feel the shock and terror they inspire
As they tear-gas, raid and set on fire, poor people's huts
And hand-carved wares. Do they not care?
How can one aged, power-crazed man,
Destroy not just the fertile land,
But lose compassion for his kith and kin
As retribution for a vote he did not win?
The doubly homeless cry out loud, unheard and plead for help.
The cancelled paper debts will never feed
A people starved of dignity and hope, of basic human rights
Displaced in fright to catastrophic flight,
Politically free but yet unfreed.

Rosemary King

APRIL MORNING - FRANCE

I push open the shutters
And the cool morning air, mellow as wine,
Washes over me.
There's a hint of woodsmoke on the breeze,
And from the forest a cuckoo calls.

In sombre rows the vineyards wait for spring,
While the jazzy fields of rape zing with colour.

In the garden a crowd of irises reach for the sky;
The first rose dares to peep;
A hare lopes through the long grass,
And in the woodpile adders sleep.

Margaret Willey

DAY BY DAY

We work and play
To save and pay
For that day

Then we have to wait
For another day

We go shopping for food
And clothes
The next day

Some days seem to go fast
Some days seem to go slow

On the seventh day
We pray and ask God
To give us strength and will
To go on day after day.

Jim Miller

ARSON ATTACK

(On Penney's cottage, Upton, Torquay)

The spark that flew in the dark of the day
and coloured the evening sky,
surged through the thatch and blackened the beams
of history, and for what and for why?

For five hundred years the old home had stood
quiet in its changing vale,
sheltering those who toiled and grew old
adding their lives to its tale.

Peaceful and picturesque close to the soil
thatched with skill, built by hard-working hands,
already a home when the Tudors and Stewarts
were ruling over our lands.

In a vale of farmland, minding it's own
crouching low, part of life, death and birth,
coping with change as the centuries fled
and roads and cars covered the Earth.

A landmark to all who travelled its way
linking future and present and past,
then the roaring red flames furled
their smoke-stinking cloud, leaving onlookers aghast.

Sadly revealed, wrecked, roofless and maimed
neglected, with no loving care,
after five hundred years a criminal's hand
took five minutes to lay it bare.

We mourn that the mindless exact such a toll
for no reason, with nothing to gain;
for some things have worth of more value than coin
and whose loss causes nothing but pain.

Brenda Heath

TWO THOUSAND YEARS

From dirt track roads to motorways
Two thousand years have come and gone
From fighting with bow's and arrows
To the dreaded atomic bomb.

Once man travelled on horse back on his journeys
But now it is in petrol driven limousine
Once journeys could have been on a chariot
Now we speed along almost too fast to be seen.

Once man sailed on the sea in galleons made of wood
Which where powered by slaves galore
Now days it is in luxury liners carrying cars and all
Powered by diesel engine on the bottom floor.

Once people lived together in places called hamlets
And had to grow all there own food on the land
Now most people live in grand style houses
With superstores everywhere, all at hand.

Once messages were sent by smoke signals
Or by horse back riders, across dangerous land
Now mobile phones can reach us anywhere
And send photos with MP3 music in your ear.

So what happened over two thousand years
What has never changed at all?
Can you guess, can you think
Of anything that has not changed at all.

Yes. God's love is still the same
Revealed in Jesus Christ, God's Son
Two thousand years might have come and gone
But Jesus is still mankind's number one.

Alan Hatton

POETIC PRAISE

The heady scent of wisteria
Invades the evening air . . .
Red roses from the one you love,
White lace, and promises.
Angels singing in perfect harmony,
Wedding vows and holy matrimony.

It's the ripple of excitement
That makes me want to worship you,
The eternal nature of God who sees
My past, my present and my future,
The timeless treasure of a faith that's sure,
That makes me want to follow you all my days.

Cathy Mearman

FLOWERS

Flowers,
Forlorn beneath me
Catastrophic petals
Blooming in my eyes
Beauty,
Cut deep in every stem
Bloom to your fullest
Enhancing your smell
Passionate and discreet,
That's what you are
Your colourful personality
Withdrawing within,
Say goodbye,
My erratic one.

Yasmeen Ahmed

AND OTHER PRETTY DARLINGS

Understandably
We are jealous,
And envious of their skill
In multi-dimensional
Movement:
Without the aid
Of cumbersome
And inefficient machinery.

We resent
Their easy utilization
Of the air
Which we can only breathe
Or pollute.

Their single-minded,
Naive cruelty
Is alien to our
Complicated aggressions;
Having no roots
In devious enjoyment;
No aftertaste of joy
Or inverted sorrow.

But behind all else
The illogical fear,
The primeval
Instinctive terror;
Engendered doubtless
By their
Reptilian origins
And our own cultural
Heritage.

The serpent syndrome.

Jeffrey A Pickford

BEING RESCUED

My heart is straining within me,
But I am breathing.
I wait for your life to begin,
Myself to be leaving.
Your will to be done,
My will to be none.
Your angels will surround protecting me,
Your kingdom will be found resurrecting me.
Into a place safer than this,
No betrayal in thy kiss.
My soft thoughts may gently flow without the anger strangling,
Sweet love ever so strong may grow; I won't be left just dangling.
For they arms will be ever so tight,
Keeping me from losing my sight,
For thy hope defends my flight,
I trust you will be with me day and night.

Kay L Soord

CHILDHOOD DAYS

Life as a child was the best,
Go play on the street with all the rest,
Knock-a-door run, and hide-and-seek,
One, two, ten let's take a peek.
Skipping, frog-hopping, tin-can-alley,
Let's have a race, who'll win the rally?
Sledging in the snow on our mum's tray,
If she catches us what will she say.
Climbing trees down on the wreck,
Being careful not to hit the deck,
Jumping top to bottom in a pile of hay,
Nothing now would spoil our day.
Bonfire Night we enjoyed the most,
Beats a trip down the coast,
Twinkling pretty sparkling lights,
Whizzing up at speed to great heights.
'Time to come in now,' Mum would say,
'Oh, ten more minutes please, for us to play,'
'Sorry, time to rest your weary head,
It's time for bath and bed.
Jama's on and say goodnight,
Kiss on the head and sleep tight'.

Jacqueline Appleby

A VERY BRIEF ENCOUNTER

I saw you on the cross-country train
When I was travelling south
And when you smiled and said, 'Hello'
My heart was in my mouth

You were so good looking
With fair hair and a gorgeous smile
And I was experiencing feelings
Which had lain dormant for many a while

I find it very difficult
To describe what I was feeling
I only know that one look from you
Could send my senses reeling

All too soon I reached my journey's end
And we had to say goodbye
I wonder what the outcome would have been
If I had said I had something in my eye

Who knows, perhaps our paths will cross
When I travel south again
Until then I will have my memory
Of a very brief encounter on a train.

Jackie Richardson

SUMMER

Spring's way into summer comes
With lengthening days
Eyes in greenness steeped, and sun's
Assertion of strength.

The lark lifts, frees her voice high
In blue transparency
Hangs poised and dazzles the eye
To the edge of wonder.

Sun, leaf, lark and I are one.
Desiring nothing
Stimulated, sustained, walk on
While the sun paces.

Idris Woodfield

DON'T TRADE IN YOUR DREAMS

A new day, a fresh start
Time to mend a broken heart
Let your smile shine through your tears.
Say goodbye to doubts and fears.
Leave behind those sad ties
Look ahead to new skies
Don't trade in your dreams, for beyond the clouds are sunbeams.

The tree of life has to grow,
You and I both know
There's always another day and sky
Don't ever let hope die.
Like a candle burns at night
You too can shine your light.
Don't trade in your dreams, for beyond the clouds are sunbeams.

Like a shining morning star,
That's beckoning from afar,
It's a great big world out there
For someone like you to share,
So with hope in your heart.
Step out for a new start
Let your smile shine through your tears.
Say goodbye to doubts and fears
Don't trade in your dreams, for beyond the clouds are sunbeams.

Marion Edwards

MUCH ADO ABOUT NOWT

In olden days, bygone days
When Shaky were just a pup,
As he walked the mean streets
Just who should he meet
But the guy next door called Dave.

Says Dave to Bill, 'My you're lookin' very neat,
In your fine cocked hat an' hose
Has a rich relative just died an' left you some dough
Or have you got a real job at last?'

'Why Sirrah, by my breeks, you've got a damn cheek
To ask such impertinent questions to me,
Now, because I'm such a gent, I won't clonk you on the donk
And leave your honkin' plooky hooter in ruins.

But, between you and me and the wall with no ears,
I'm with the dreamiest toff in creation,
And now I don't scrub, or sew,
That's just a nonny noony no
An' the name o' me fellah is Bacon.

Archie Hardie

REMEMBERING

Beneath a lean tree of newborn green,
Against a sky of Wedgwood blue,
Our old age collie panting at our side,
We lay back . . . remembering.

Away from the TV, away from the car fumes,
From shopping trolleys and gossip . . . here was silence,
Only broken by the bleat of a sheep
Or the screech of a stray gull
And the tireless tossing of stones
Up the beach by the tug of the tide.

Sixty years back on a day such as this
We met after five years apart
At Waverley Station a bit before eight.
I stood there dejected, but still had to wait.
The train was five minutes late.
With a huffing and puffing the overnight giant
Emerged from the tunnel and came to a stop.

Windows opened, doors slammed. A mass of young men
All uniformed, tanned and looking the same
Poured out on the platform and jostled me by.
Out of that mêlée how was I to see
Your face in the crowd? But you recognised me.
Eyes met for a moment, then followed a kiss,
Quite shyly at first on your broken lip,
Sunburnt on the journey from prison camp.

We look back in thankfulness on your return
Unimpaired by the war while others were not.
Today full of gratitude the least we can do
Is to share round our happiness all our lives through.

Kathleen Davey

BODIES IN THE SAND

Are they really merely ordinary mortals?
Offering valiant deeds in sacrifice
For dreams trodden beyond hope's portals
Where a grave's silence can only suffice.

Did he place willow to ball, hear the crowd yell?
Did she cross volley into waiting net?
Did they feel wind against taut sail?
Did both shed tears for a love ill met?

They are our brave,
Names chiselled upon honour's scroll.
All things cherished they gave
That we may grow old.

Remember them as warm summer rain,
Sweet fragrances held upon spring's early breeze.
Remember them as ice-cold champagne,
Enjoy views they shall never again see.

A prayer for those they leave behind,
The child of smiles, tasselled hair fair.
Wife trying not to give loss any mind
And mother, face grey as thinning hair.

Empty space at table laid
No soulmate to share embrace.
Bedroom silent, no reason for draw shade.
Mirror reflecting a single pain drawn face.

Framed image at centre mantle
Filling space at Yuletide.
Raise a toast for King and Queen safe in high castle
And those taken upon misfortune's low prowling tide.

Gordon Starr

HARD TO LIVE

It's hard to live and feel the vibes
No loving presence at your side
No one whose prime concern is you
A sunny Sunday makes you blue.

It's hard to live and be alone
No one answering their phone
You try your best to no avail
To give your heart but only fail.

And years slip by and things decline
If people ask, you say you're fine
'Cos that is all they want to hear
Their time for you is short, that's clear.

It's hard to live and be unloved
In a sea of strangers pushed and shoved.
A waste of space as you grow old
And the sunny Sunday soon turns cold.

J Kattenburg

AUSTRIAN HOLIDAY

High in buttercup mountains
Dolls' houses appear far below,
Numerous wild flowers, vivid
In colour make a fine show.
Our little steam train chugs
And pushes us joyfully along:
Contentment seems to be
The theme of the song.

The cows graze in rich
Mountain pastures at will
Their tinkling bells echoing still.
Pine forest grows in evergreen abundance.
Over the rocks streams leap and dance
Into the waterfall's frothy light.

Brown horses stand with manes creamy white
And a lone boy flies a colourful kite.
The crunch of boots as ramblers march on,
Heavenly joys to think upon.

Train journeys and mountains,
Birdsong and flowers,
A wonderful way to spend
Long happy hours.

June Coral Dye

LOVE'S CARE

Because your sadness adds to mine, I try
To spare you pain, to shield you from the woe
All sentient beings born for death must know,
I mourn to see your hopes as bright stars die
On your dawn-altars, watch the heaven-high,
World-spanning rainbows of your brave dreams glow,
To fade so soon . . . I long to stop the slow
Descent of night upon your changing sky.

Is this love pure that seeks in saving you
From sorrow's pain, to ease its own despair?
To catch your shining thread and weave a new
Garment of light a little while to wear,
Casting its black aside? No, love *most* true
Would make your happiness its only care.

Pamela Dixon

MY GREAT LOSS

I commit myself to paper as I write upon this page
Trying to come to terms with internal emotional rage
The rage that makes me feel that my whole body is in pain
When I conjure up your picture again and again

I watched you getting better from the illness that you had
And everyone was pleased for you and really very glad
But fate can play some dirty tricks and really turn the knife
Especially when it really meant the taking of a life

We gathered around your bedside and helplessly we stood
We tried to show you love and care and hope you'd understood
But little did I know that day that you had felt so ill
Ill enough to give up on the hold of your life's will

Now when I open up my arms I find this empty space
A space that is not for refill and never to replace
For it is hard to lose your mother whether young or very old
Leaving only empty heartache and memories to hold.

Wendy Winslet

FIFTEEN YEARS WITH FORWARD PRESS

Congratulations Forward Press,
Let's raise our glasses high.
You really are a great success
There's many reasons why.

'To me' you've been a special friend,
And here's a little hint.
You've helped me turn my thoughts to words,
And see them all in print.

Your story is a special one,
That should be read and told.
And here's to many future years,
You're worth your weight in gold.

You've given me lots of confidence,
Much pleasure - what is more.
I always get an extra thrill,
When your letter pops through my door.

So carry on oh writer's friend,
And celebrate your success.
With this poem comes lots of love,
To wonderful Forward Press.

Mary Linney

WINTERING

Clumps cooled in the stacks,
Crouched in clouds,
Cold now, and Siberian winds blow:
It will snow.

Snow, like it hasn't done in years,
Snow, that accumulates with tears
From a bitter winter,
Sobbing with the memories -
Be warned -
A palimpsest to devastate the swarm.

Flowers tremble,
Petals bending under frozen water;
A subterranean bloom,
A translucent tomb
Should the blanket fail to warm the sleeper.

The first flakes,
See the tracks that they make,
In the grey sky,
White butterflies.

Graeme Vine

THE LESSON OF LIFE

We buy a ticket for our destination,
When we go on holiday.
We start off with determination
With some knowledge of the way.

We need no ticket to enter this world
Quite unknown is our destiny.
The road we must take is not unfurled
But it will lead to eternity.

On the road of life there is no return
It is only a single track.
The way may be rough there are lessons to learn
And never may we turn back.

For the first few miles we are led along
With few decisions to make.
We move along with the weak and the strong
Being advised which road to take.

We travel along our uncertain road
With many a steep hill to climb.
Often we carry a heavy load
And life is far from sublime.

We come to some crossroads, which to take?
Cannot make up our minds what to do.
So much depends on the choice we make
Hard times we may have to go through.

Thus the pattern of life goes on to the end
With dangers and pleasures in store.
To dark despair the wrong choice may you send
If the right one, of life you could ask no more.

D Huff

CONGRATULATIONS

Congratulations on this your fifteenth year,
You've published lots of poetry, a joy for us to hear.
Poems that bring us laughter, some that are so sad
But of the thousands I have read, none have been really bad.
Your books give us inspiration, to get our minds in gear
So that we can send you more poetry, year by year by year.
Congratulations to your editorial staff, they all work very hard
And on this your anniversary, send them all a card.

Ivor Percival

REFLECTIONS

The mirror hangs upon the wall,
Down the passage in the hall.
A glance at her on going out,
A frown and then a little pout.
Mascara smudge upon a cheek,
Cannot have that, a date to keep.
Oh no, a hair is out of place,
Must hurry, must hurry, have to race.
Maybe she's going to her fate,
As off she goes to meet her date.

Gleaming, glistening is my face,
Whoever looks in I will trace.
Yesterday the face was happy,
Eyes shining, looking natty.
Stricken face and tears that fall,
Waiting for that absent call.
Reflections of a heart that's broken,
Words that never will be spoken.
I can be good, I can be kind,
But I can always read your mind.

Kathleen Biesierkirski

BORN AGAIN

Still held so tightly
Within the dreams of youth
My body tired and aching
Craves the summer
When this fantasy reveals
A day with no beginning
That stretches out beyond the winter
To a sunset that calls us
To reflect upon our lives

Satisfied
And ready for the night
Our hearts
Now freed from a past
That fed our nightmares
And our minds
A single golden thread
Binding us together
Surrounding our lives
A cocoon within which we can grow
Until the day that we are born
And we stand together
As delicate as saplings
That still remain
After the great oak has fallen
In the storm.

James Olley

TEMPUS FUGIT

Tomorrow has this alarming knack
Of turning into yesterday
Fast enough to make us keen
To spend today very slowly,
If only that were possible.
Time, however, that calculating wizard,
Of calendars and clocks,
Is not to be dissuaded
But sends all our futures
Into the past
Whilst we are otherwise engaged.

David Lucas

FIRSTBORN

I remember when I first held you and looked into your eyes,
I promised you then that my love would never die.
The years they passed so quickly or at least to me it seemed,
And soon memories of your childhood were just a colourful dream.
Then you started changing, but it wasn't for the best
Your mood became so dark and cold,
Every day was another test.
I begged for you to tell me what I had done wrong,
Where was the son I loved so much, where had that child gone?
You said you couldn't cope with the pressure, with the pain
Then you slammed the door that final time, as I cried out your name.
For months I didn't see you, I felt lost and so alone
Just waiting for that moment when you might call home.
Then the phone call came,
A friend of yours he said.
His voice was fraught and tearful and I could feel his distress.
So now I hold you once again, but your body is cold,
And the needle marks in your arms confirm what I've been told.
And as I stare into your eyes and I see only death
You softly say, 'I'm sorry Mum' as you draw your final breath.

E Holmes

DEEPEST THOUGHTS

Oh to hover with the lark
In cloudless sky, dipping and weaving
To follow skyline and to mark
Shadows on vales and hills cleaving.
Kissing the clouds as we ascend
Angels we greet on gossamer wings
Wishing this joy would never end
Nor the wonderful peace it brings.

Joyce Morris

FRAGRANCE OF CHILDHOOD

I wouldn't want to be young again,
Tossed on the sea of adolescent hopes
And fears: now soaring on thermals of joy,
Only to plunge tomorrow in troughs of pain.
That boundless trust in friendships bright and new,
Founded on sands of inexperience,
Reaped betrayals which like thunder loomed,
Till shrunk to insignificance, as flew
The chastening years . . .

Yet when nasturtiums gather on the wall,
And Shirley poppies bloom all silky frills,
Their scents are redolent of long ago,
And childhood's blue and golden days recall.
With Grandmother I walk long streets that led
To her allotment by the railway line,
Past the deaf girl leaning on her gate, mute
With vacant smile, hear Grandma's kind words said.
Her humble love for earth and growing things
She taught with carrots, peas and marigolds
That clustered round her shabby little hut,
Where summer swallows passed on midnight wings.
The song of her content then fills my ears,
And warms my heart like my own scented loam,
As in a dream I clasp her work-worn hand,
Look into her blue eyes washed wise with tears.

Elinor Wilson

CATHERINE AND HEATHCLIFF

Tonight you are my Heathcliff
With your tousled hair so black,
And I resemble Cathy
Well, I might do . . . from the back.

When once we roamed the moorland
It were really quite a shame,
Some poachers tried to shoot us
When they thought that we were game.

I look towards the steely skies
To seek a wheeling hawk,
But here instead a rotten rook
Just gives a piercing squawk.

I call to you across the moors
The cruel winds snatch your name,
And once again me posh coiffure's
Been flattened by the rain.

I'm sitting here with freezing feet
Upon a floating log,
And all because me brand new shoes
Got sucked into a bog.

Me words may never sound as nice
As Emily Brontë's do,
But given half a chance I'd reach
Some Wuthering Heights with you!

Sue Benwell

MY DEAREST FRIEND

My dearest friend
I have a secret, I hold close to my heart
I no longer see you the way I did
You are no longer a friend
My perception has changed, my heart too
A flower has bloomed, winter has ended
You are the sun, I've been longing for
My days are now bright and beautiful
My world full of light, once so dark.

My feelings have changed so has my world
Thank you, I am no longer in darkness.

Paul Green

CROWDED ISOLATION

I feel alone
But to be truly alone
One must be surrounded by friends
Yet have no common ground or common mode of communication,
That is my location.

I feel devoid of sympathy
Yet empathy wells within me
I've experienced all their losses and all their joys
Yet I cannot bring myself to share their bereavements
Or find mirth in their achievements.

I am surrounded by human beings
But feel entirely alone,
A rogue amidst all these clones,
An anomaly in the giant graph of life
That causes the chief mathematician angst and strife.

He tries, as do I,
To find an explanation for my existence but, like me,
He finds no solution for this problem,
So, I lie in bed alone,
Dreaming of the day when I find home.

Naomi Mc Ardle

PETALS ON A POOL

How well I remember
The first time we met
Just a moment in time
I'll never forget
In solitude standing
By a small still pool
'Neath the shade of a tree
So peaceful and cool
The scent of wild flowers
Wafting on the air
And a feeling inside
That someone was there
Gazing into the pool
My heart leapt a pace
On seeing reflected
A man's handsome face
His smile was quite charming
With warm loving eyes
Totally enchanted
I stood hypnotised
Alas, fragrant blossoms
On a soft breeze borne
Disturbed your image
Leaving me forlorn
For there was only me
A romantic fool
Weaving dreams around
Petals, on a pool.

Patricia Whittle

NO REGRETS

We all make mistakes, we all have regrets
At times we all fail, in the goals that we set
Not intending to hurt ourselves or another
Looking back over years, the truth we discover
How foolish we've been, oh the pain it has cost
To the things we can't change, and the years we have lost
The bitter tears we've shed, of remorse
If only we'd sailed on a different course
But we didn't know then, what we know now
Wisdom we've gained; in our hearts to allow
To reflect and look back, learn from our past
For not all is lost in the dye we have cast.

Patricia Johnson

SAINT GEORGE

Sadly, since year three-o-four
England's George has been no more;
April saw him lose his head,
Ever since he's been quite dead.
Nothing not a dicky-bird
Ever since that twenty-third!

But scripture tells us something quaint,
That England's George, if trusting saint,
Must sleep - for incorruption's sake -
And in the resurrection wake!
Then, saints elect will death disdain,
When Christ returns to Earth again.

Peter Griffiths

COVER HER BONES

Part of the walkway straggle we stare intrusively
At various artefacts so carefully displayed,
One shield boss, a torque, nine chipped and ancient spears
Then, shuffling down the line, at skeletons
Of what, a bored guide told us were 'Fragile
Bones of a young female found close by
A Saxon warrior's remains, Jute maybe.'
These two the focal points of a display
Fund raising officially to desecrate
Perhaps three thousand graves and so reveal
What could historically be a most important site.

Headlined - Amazing Archaeological Breakthrough -
Research will tell of tribal settlements
Their age-old customs and their daily lives
And scholars will debate their likely wars
The length and terms of their uncertain peace:
But look at these long buried bones and think
Perhaps they should remain untouched, unseen,
Holding their own the secrets of the lives
They led, the deaths they died. These bones, once clothed
In living flesh, are now become dry curiosity.

Idly we speculate; was she the warrior's beloved,
A captive princess from some conquered tribe,
Victim of ritual murder, rape, assault
Or simply just a girl who died too young,
A girl of no particular account,
A private person who'd abhor this revelation.

We're fascinated by such distant time,
Exposure after a thousand shrouded years
Urges, almost, a vulgar scrutiny.
But please not here, not this especial place.
Strangely, we think of her with tenderness
Accord her remote respect that she can never know,
Leave her in peace, don't violate her grave,
Cover her bones, yes, leave her resting so.

Gillian Howarth

THE WEDDING DRESS

Can a dress speak
How did my eye catch you
Among the cast aside fripperies?
Who had worn you
Then carelessly left you
Under the market stall canopies?

You were a bride
Princess, ballerina
Beautifully tragic lost maiden
Pirouetting,
Church pillars exalting
Cloth caressing heath, moss laden.

Such indulgence
As I slipped into you
Unsure where flesh ended, you began.
I held one rose
You commanded no less,
Wind pushed out your silks, your glory shone.

Erica Roach

FOR YOU

It must have been hard for you all those years ago
I can only imagine for I can never truly know
Were you a lonely and frightened child, my love?
Feeling the hurt and pain as you tried to rise above

Did you ever wonder what you had done wrong?
To be without your mother's love, to have to be so strong
A little child should know the power of security
And know someone is there, even for eternity

But now after so many years I still see pain in your eyes
Afraid to want something good in life, afraid to criticise
For will the past come back to haunt you? Best leave it alone
Best put on a brave face, don't want others to see you moan

Yet you were only a child, you did nothing wrong
You couldn't have known that then, you deserved to belong
And there is a place for you here on this Earth
Don't let anyone tell you different or bring down your self-worth

It's time to forgive yourself and let the self-hatred cease
Let go of the guilt, it is undeserved, let it be released
Feel the rage for all that you did not have back then
For all who treated you badly, all you wish to condemn

But remember, these are your feelings, to others they can
do no harm
Though kept within you they can, so maybe it's time to disarm
Feel what you feel for as long as you need, my love
Then you will be free and I'll watch you fly as high as a dove.

Maria Pelengaris

NORWEGIAN MOON

Yes, so tempting was your moonlight's potion . . .
Drinking deep the
stolen brew,
Glass tears
gone . . .
a
secret,
our laughter,
so merciless,
setting golden drops, stars of my heartache.

Carol Ann Darling

SUNNY DAYS

A friend called Alex said to me,
'Would you like to come to Everleigh?
It's over the downs, not far away.'
I replied, 'Why not, it's a lovely day.'

We stopped at Marlborough to change bus,
Then walked round town, the two of us.
I took him in the charity shop,
Then started buying, I just couldn't stop.
Things to hang upon my wall,
Dress to wear for the Christmas ball.

Then straight into the fairy shop,
Like a little girl, my eyes did pop.
He sprinkled fairy dust on my head,
And I had a little twirl.
'We best get going,' Alex said,
'If you want to catch an earl.'
'Catch an earl do you think I can?
I will be happy to catch a man.'

Through electric gates, down a tree-lined drive,
It felt so good to be alive.
Would you like to walk and see the view?
Or drive down slowly, it's up to you.

We got to the Manor, the west wing I think,
And Nora showed me round,
I was feeling in the pink
Then something made a sound.
A big red rooster and his hens
Had come to say hello,
Broken biscuits is what he wants
Nora told me so.

Walking barefoot through the estate,
To the magic woods, I couldn't wait
I might see rabbits, maybe a deer,
Or the little people with wings so sheer.
There is so much more I want to write
But your brother said, 'That's all tonight.'
So I must close this little poem,
And pick up my stuff and get off home.

Maddie Reade

THE ORANGE ACCOMMODATION

The rooms were plain.
The décor was always the same.
The streetlight shone its dull light;
Casting black figures in the night -

Guests with no name or invite.
Mundane evenings spent in this place
Emphasised its bricks and mortar.
Unmollified with any silk or lace,

Basic with fittings for gas and water.
No television or telephone,
No welcoming mat to call it a home.
No name above the door in stone.

Only two hundred yards from the city
Whose contrast in sight and sound was very busy.
Even the *Craft Centre* had items so pretty.
Yet in this place was simplicity,

And lived a quiet and wise man
Who kept his orange home in a state of peace.
No detail changed since council planning began;
As it was, since he first obtained the lease.

Thomas W O'Connell

TEMPTATIONS OF EVE

All he sees is luscious lips,
Flowing hair, swinging hips.
Skin so soft, skin so fair,
He wants to touch, will he dare?
Deep dark eyes like pools of green,
Bewitching him into a dream.
Hypnotised by her fine form.
Awakening of a jewelled dawn.
Her spell is cast, web is spun,
Waiting for her prey to come.
A siren so alluring she,
In her arms he wants to be.
Eyes half closed, soft breasts heave,
Around him, finest silk she'll weave.
Enchantingly, she'll draw him near,
Velvet tone of voice he'll hear.
Seductively the vamp moves in,
A clever sorceress who'll win.
Drawing him nearer to her lair,
Sweeping back her tawny hair,
Well caught into the age old trap,
A fine cocoon of silk she'll wrap.
Victims sucked 'til parched and dry,
In a spellbound trance, waits to die.
It's over now, she has gone,
Heavy in heart, knowing wrong.
The temptress came by name of Eve,
With her web she will deceive.

Monica Wood

AUTUMN

On moor and heath
The north wind blows
A messenger of winter snows
In unfrocked trees
A night owl cries
Its mournful cant
To crystal skies,
A distant church bell
Chimes away
And brings to end
Another day
The countryside will slumber soon,
Whilst riding high the autumn moon.

Ernest Jones

WAITING

Each day is a test.
On edge, I make it through
One more, my
Nerves frayed.
Perhaps I shouldn't trust you,
Shouldn't be so patient.
Good things come to those who
Wait, but I've waited
Forever,
My patience is wearing down
Till each second ticks away
Like thunder,
Striking me down.
Not sure if you will hurt me,
I hope, I pray
My time will come.

Jennifer Wright

IN THE BEGINNING

(Genesis 1)

In the beginning there was God,
Alone in His Heaven, Three in One;
Then God said, 'Let there be light'
Let it shine forth with power and might,
The greater light to shine by day,
The lesser at night, to light the way.'
Evening and morning were the first day,
Thus did it happen in this way.

The Spirit of the Lord was there
Living, moving, showing His care;
Separating the land and sky,
Preparing it for you and I.
Up above He put the heavens,
Lighting the stars in their millions,
Sending forth His heavenly light,
Showing forth His power and might.

He made the flowers and the trees,
Yielding up their fruit and seeds;
He made the waters teem with life,
With fish and mammals they were rife;
And the birds to fill the sky,
Soaring up above so high,
And great monsters of the deep
And everything that walks or creeps.

It was the end of the fifth day,
Everything was done God's way.
He looked and saw that it was good,
With many plants and trees for food;
But then God, who is all seeing
Said, 'Let's make a human being!
Let us make him like we Three,
Someone to love and walk with Me.'

So God made humans in His likeness,
But did not give them all His highness,
Though to angels they are lower,
Yet God crowned them with His honour;
Gave them rule o'er His Creation,
Said they were to have dominion.
On the seventh day God rested,
Pleased with all that He'd invested.

Irene Hart

SUCH A SACRIFICE

When I count how well I'm blessed, o'er seven
Decades, in this sunlit global world, and
That special talent, which I delight to
Air, alive in me, eagerly seeking

Rhyme and verse in which to paint a picture,
I pore over: can I perchance, too, give
Pleasure to my Maker, my Saviour, who
In the twinkling of an eye gave me my

Being, my walking legs, my voice, my sense
Of sight, smell, taste, touch and hearing? Speaking
Of His world can I not portray praise and
Glory and heartfelt gratitude to one

Scourged, crowned with stabbing thorns, crucified, and
All the while, His mother weeping, beside?

Marie Ashford

WEAVERS' CHANT

Weave . . .
The terracotta of the earth
Into our mixed and varied strands,
Green of dashed tears and spring leaf-mirth,
And the dumb colour of the furrowed lands:
Dim tint of oak's awakening leaves,
And rainbow colours that the sky conceives.

Weave, with the cautious craftsman's hands,
Strong and tenacious, care and not care,
Broad earth-colours in wide bands
On loom that spans in air,
Shuttle of rich and mingled mirth,
Singing the songs of our strange earth.

Weave in the russet autumn flame,
The dying green of grassy hills,
And mushroom colours with no name,
And the no-colours of the rills;
Umber and blue and naughty of shadow:
Gold of rich sun on a hay-meadow.

Weave in the eldritch mauve of night:
The peacock tint of night birds' wings,
Speckle of owl - moon lantern-light
That seeps in silver-gilt, glimmer of things
All of the misty evening's tincture spilt:
Flicker of fire, all elfin green that sings,
Shimmer of stones in Excalibur's hilt.

Weave, weave -
Out of the seas that leave
No living or dying
As they laugh or grieve,
The vanishing colours
Of the skies' wide air -
Cerule or white or dove-wing,
Aureole hair
Of evening.

Weave . . .
Till the human heart perceive
The beauty and joy and voice of everything
Past praising!

Elsa Ivor

THE DAWN CHORUS

An angel dances to the dawn chorus
A silhouette, a ray of light
Where shadows fade
Shards of light filter in
Leaving only beauty in its sight

If a cloud should stand its ground
The tide of warmth shall overcome
A rainbow paints the morning sky
Welcoming the merging sun

The tree branches embraced
Like entwined hands
Trying to capture this majestic scene
Before them is this new day approaching
Autumn brown transforms to green

The wind whistles, almost in tune
As dew-drops shine like chandeliers
And as we awake from our slumber
So disappears all our dreams.

Rebecca Purcell

THOUGHT CRIMES

No doubler yellow lines,
No cameras trap the unaware,
No tax evasion and steep fines.
Just loneliness, a life unfair.

No child molester, hated paedophile,
No exploitation or victim of neglect,
No drugs distort and guillotine a smile.
Just silence and no fellow to respect.

No chance homicide or by design,
No rapine lust, a virgin body soiled,
No taking things not already mine.
Just no inner peace; calm, tightly coiled.

No company corrupt, no phoney bill,
No bent official open to an offer,
No hand-biter, sticky fingers in the till.
Just distant moon and stars to fill the coffer.

No ethnic cleansing, no brutal torture hooks,
No persecution for belief, no burning books,
No frozen gulag or steamy Camp X-Ray.
Just no-choice solitude; one more uncertain day.

What law ordained that giant, crashing wave
That freed me from all these things not right,
But severed me from friends and family I so crave.
Survival is a balsa raft; no haven yet in sight.

Mike Hayes

LET'S CELEBRATE

For fifteen years of Forward Press
Publishing new poems that impress
Let's celebrate.
For opening doors to poets new
Bringing fresh works for you to view
Let's celebrate.
Giving those unheard of a voice
Widening the spectrum of choice
Let's celebrate.
For each and everyone of us
Who find composing not much fuss
Let's celebrate.

For Forward Press we shout, 'Hooray!'
For encouraging us to have a say
Whether poetry or prose is our sway
We'll celebrate with you today.

Joan Earle Broad

IN PASSING

Weep not, dear heart, nor grieve me
For our love is deep and true
Think of all the love you gave me
And the love I gave to you

Cry not, dear love, nor worry
For our love is both strong and deep
Think of the happiness we have had
And sleep in the deepest sleep

Try to smile for me, my beloved
Think of me holding your heart
Think of me being close to you
And nevermore being apart.

John Robert Burr

THE EAGLE'S WAY

He soars, he circles,
He rides the thermal wind.
Aloof, with feathers rippled,
He hunts, on golden wing.

Feathers of fantasy,
To flow, swoop and peel.
Too cruel, the beak savages.
Comes death, comes the meal.

No need the packs scent,
As the antlered stag.
One dive, one kill,
With one talloned grab.

No set lordly table, wild his hearth,
Calm he graces.
Rules valley, loch and heather,
Reigns cold rugged places.

Glaring eyes scan,
Search for weasel and stoat.
Sweep castle and crag,
Pierce harbour and moat.

Far below, his menu.
Teeming life. He decides.
The rabbit, the mouse,
Who lives, who dies?

Centuries long gone, now
Times nest on the edge.
He mates for the future, trusts
Granite's, sheer ledge.

His protection is fear,
Few hands seek, interlope.
His betrayal, the climber.
The ice axe, the rope.

Gordon Wilson

THE CATFLAP HOUSE HOTEL

I moved into a cottage, in a quiet cul-de-sac,
Neighbours to the left and right, and facing front and back.

Sometimes waking in the dark, I'd feel alone and bleak,
That feeling left me suddenly! In fact less than a week!

For some ambiguous reason, only felines can foretell,
My tiny home has now become, The Catflap House Hotel!

Across the nation everywhere, when darkness lingers down,
Doors are opened late at night and kitties hit the town!

A common misconception, cats like being out all night,
I've studied this most carefully; the cats say I am right!

Cast out kitten Snoopy, fluffy, black and white,
Flies inside and cuddles round the heating tank all night.

A ginger tom young Toby sneaks in from next door,
Eats his fill, then commandeers cushions on the floor.

Tortoiseshell Kira, sits haughtily, as if to say,
I need a lot of stroking - all night will be okay!

A tabby thug old Tigger makes other felines flee,
A nightly truce then sprawls himself, upon my best settee.

Smokie, a laid-back stray, lies on the front door mat,
Creeps in as the door is opened, snuggles up to another cat.

Pepsi and Koko clamber round, when I fall into bed,
Shared with Portia the Persian, wrapped around my head.

Those who think cats hunt at night, or wonder where they roam?
Check the Catflap House Hotel; they've booked into my home!

Leigh Crighton

THE MANOR

I know a place where friendships grow,
Where folk respect each other,
Where conversations freely flow
And benefit one another.

The venue has a rural charm,
With lawns and trees surrounding.
The atmosphere is one of calm,
With peace and quiet abounding.

Here are the homes of older folk
In search of tranquil pleasure.
Coffee mornings, time to joke
In happy hours of leisure.

More formal options, too, abound:
Evenings of classical music,
And others with a lighter sound
Are pleasantly therapeutic.

From time to time excursions are made
To locations of general interest,
With occasional lunches and teas in the shade
And plenty of places for leg rest.

The buildings themselves are a source of delight:
Purpose-built flats that are varied in size,
An old manor house, with liveries on site
And lounges for functions that residents devise.

This is the place where we now reside,
Untroubled by council or planner,
We just please ourselves how well we provide
For our comfort at home in the Manor.

Ray Walker

THE ONE AND ONLY

In the green, green peace
Of the deep forest glades,
In the scent of the heather
With skylarks on high,
On the strand where the
Lone white egret wades,
With the proud, dark sweep
Of the hills to the sky,
I will come back to you
And you to me.

In coppiced oak woods
And wetlands wide,
Where the bog myrtle grows
And the bog-cottons blow
And the pilgrim butterflies
Hover and glide
And the bright yellow asphodels
Beckon and glow,
I will come back to you
And you to me.

In sunshine and laughter,
In sadness and tears,
In things to come after
And yesterday's years,
At the place where we'll gather
Before we embark,
Bound for tomorrow . . .
Into the dark,
I will come back to you
And you to me.

Archie Buchanan

TO CREATE AND SHARE, WHAT CAN COMPARE?

What comprises a poem?
Format can be organised, structured or without pattern,
Fit an earthy agenda, or appear distant, abstruse, mystic,
        like the rings of Saturn.
Meaning may be classical, traditional, avant garde,
        experimental, futuristic.
Expression gentle, forceful, vague, descriptive, vulgar,
        educational, artistic.

Length is typically varied, from a few couplets to epic,
        a marathon recital,
Scope is challenging, boundless, skill extends to discovering
        a fitting title.
Reason ranges from political, romantic, advertisement,
        simple enjoyment,
Authors equate to aesthetic or financial gain, if really fortunate,
        employment.

Poets like painters, capture a moment, preserve a memory,
        mood or event,
Fashion literary compositions to inspire emotion,
        construct a verbal monument.
Transport us from the mundane to fantasy, wild imagination,
        sensual bliss,
Frighten, comfort, cheer, provoke, unsettle, or correct
        what we find amiss.

Musicians work with poems, a master captures their beauty,
        form and flow,
Endearing rhyming sentiment is blended with exquisite
        harmonic arpeggio.
Poetry can dance, skip, delight, elevate, exalt us with its motion
Raise our spirit to divine realms of worship, praise, gratitude,
        devotion.

It celebrates the joy of living, makes us tearful, pensive,
        happy, rejuvenated,
Releases us from routine, the commonplace, to a state unfettered,
        liberated.

This communication is popular because of its concise, compact
        interaction,
It can focus on thoughts; provide pleasant interludes as opposed
        to distraction.

So, the writer harnesses heart and soul to make their
        subjects appealing,
Hopes the reader finds stimulus and pleasure,
        warmth and kindred feeling.
We all have individual preference in regard to topics
        we promote and address,
Gain encouragement, reward, and incentive thanks to expertise
        from Forward Press.

Dennis Overton

CHRISTMAS

Christmas this year is a change from the past
With family spread out in areas that are vast
The family has expanded with lovely additions
All caring for each other without any conditions
The miles between us have increased of late
With children seeking a life far beyond our gate
Therefore Christmas now will be emails and phone calls
Certainly different from train sets and dolls
For dinner and tea just the two of us
Loving each other there will be little fuss
Chatting and laughing with thoughts overflowing
The day will fade slowly with a tear maybe showing
With my family all happy I should ask for no more
Only Christmas to me would be their knock on the door.

Rebecca Keough

OUR JOE

It's hard to live without you,
Our loyal trusted friend,
I couldn't say goodbye to you,
Because this is not the end.

I know you are in a better place,
Now you no longer suffer pain,
As memories of you I recall,
My tears begin to fall again.

Little Joe, I'll always miss you,
And your playful happy face,
Home is not the same without you,
A sad and lonely place

I pray God takes good care of you,
As you loved us over the years,
I miss your welcome at the gates,
My eyes still fill with tears.

My heart it yearns to tell me,
To no longer cry,
For I was lucky to know our Joe for
Thirteen years of my life!

So I'll now recall your happy face,
How you made our world such a wonderful place,
May God bless you our Joe, as He blessed
Us with you thirteen years ago!

Michele Simone Fudge

TASMANIAN RAINFOREST

Stark white trunks thrust in death throes
To the sky naked in their shame to
Topple to the forest floor in timeless patterns of renewal

Their life is spent but all around a
Myriad of greens of moss and fern
Lichens and liverworts leech a living from the mountain soil

A primeval tapestry of pencil pines and
Graceful myrtle sway in the soughing breeze
Ever restless anointing and caressing stirring
Mystery in their virgin wilderness

On the shady slopes above the snow line
The Huon pines stretch heavenwards
Some as old as Christ himself twisted
And gnarled yet with crowns of pride
Steadfast in the firmament

And everywhere the sound of water the
Fulcrum the life-giver endlessly infusing
Nourishing nature's eternity
Drawing the circle between life and death.

M C Davies

WHAT IS FOUND THERE?

Gathering all in the sky, those metal shapes,
Free as the wind, or with guidelines,
Are difficult to focus on, yet look closely,
In their own wise stillness they are here, and they are here.

Michael Courtney Soper

UNCONDITIONAL LOVE

The little girl had long dark hair with rarest glints of gold
Her eyes were big, delphinium blue, and she was eight years old.
A happy child and thoughtful, who adored her sisters and brothers
The eldest girl in a family of six, she was known as
                                        'The Little Mother'.
There were always errands that had to be run and plenty
                                        of jobs to do
With James aged six and Margery, four and Dorothy, not yet two.
The other two boys were nine and ten, the eldest, her favourite,
                                        was Jack
There was never enough money so Mum had to work, but of love
                                        there was never a lack.
It was 1913, in April, the day when her father died,
A heart attack they called it, and everybody cried.
And everybody was concerned, what would her mother do?
With six children to feed and clothe, well, it's not like one or two!
A family meeting was arranged and an aunt came that day
She was married, no children of her own, but her home
                                        was miles away.
Her husband was the landlord of the Tile Sheds Inn
'To help, I'll take one off your hands,' she said, 'we are all kith and kin.
The eldest girl will suit us fine, it's one less mouth to feed.
Put her things into my bag, no more than she will need.'
So on that day, the little girl with eyes delphinium blue
Lost not just her father, but her mother and whole family too.
She was taken to live with people unknown in a place that was
                                        strange and new
'I must be grateful,' she kept telling herself, 'but I wish my aunt
                                        had picked two.'
She did not want for material things; her uncle and aunt were kind
But she was bereft of all that she knew, it was love that was
                                        hard to find.
Until the day she found a friend with dirt all over his face
His home was in a dreadful mess, and his manners a disgrace!
But he was always there for her, she never felt in the way,
He made no demands, never scolded and was content
                                        with her all day.
She called him MrJackieboy, I don't have to tell you why,
He was never too busy to listen, even when she wanted to cry.

They shared an unconditional love; she knew his heart was big
And no one else really loved him, for he was a saddle-back pig.
But he was her very bestest friend, she loved him like no other
She was a lonely little girl of eight, she told me - she's my mother.

Betty Brown

MY TWIN AND I

Were we really young once -
Full of vim and vigour?
Wearing lovely dresses
Made to show our figure.

Cycling through the country -
Romping in the hay.
Dancing at the youth club
At the end of the day.

Yes, we've snaps to prove it -
(Mainly black and white)
But they bring back memories
In the restless night.

Old familiar faces -
Some are gone forever.
Reunited in our dreams -
Forgotten? Never!

B Haworth

MOVING ON

I stand, alone.
At the base of my brain,
The top of my spine.
A thousand questions endlessly cluttering my head.
Afraid and unsure.
Lost and unspoken.
Forgotten and unloved.

You were able to read my thoughts once,
And I could read yours through your eyes.
Opening up the world before me, you taught me how to love.
My heart was yours for the taking,
I blindly gave into your feelings, ignoring my own in the process.
And now? Where do I go from here?

I will myself to move on,
A million chances that had eluded me, now take hold of my mind.
I embrace the life I gave away so foolishly.
Once more believing in dreams and fairy tales.
Unhindered I can reach out,
To take the risk and fulfil a destiny of my own design.

Falling into myself and teaching my heart how to live again.
Here I am -
Unafraid and certain.
Found and undaunted.
Remembered and loved.
I stand, alone.

At the base of my brain,
The top of my spine . . .
See me!

Kate Ransom

A YORKSHIRE MINER'S LASS

Born and bred in Yorkshire,
When we all were poor,
We had few possessions -
No need to lock the door.

We were a real community,
Few people owned a car
And the village bustled -
No one travelled far.

A horse and cart pulled up outside.
We wished each other luck -
With shovels at the ready,
To scoop up the horse muck.

It fertilised the gardens:
Life was much simpler then.
Women were as God intended
And men were real men's men.

Children knew how to behave
And if they dared back chat,
A clip around the ear'ole
Soon put paid to that!

Machines then replaced people
In this modern time.
The pit and coalite plant closed down
And jobs went down the line.

No more a close community,
The pit site is now grass,
But I'm still glad that I grew up
A Yorkshire miner's lass.

Janet Hewitt

THAT SPECIAL MOMENT

Those wonderful words, 'I love you' from your lips did flow.
Those wonderful words, 'I love you' were all I wanted to know.
I knew my prayers were answered the day you told me this.
I held my hands about your face and I thanked you with a kiss.
'I love you too my darling,' I replied in ecstasy.
I felt the warmth of love that flowed between both you and me.
I felt my body tremble from the excitement in my heart.
I thought of all the hours that we'd spent in vain, apart.
I wish that you'd confronted me the minute that you knew.
Because - I've gone around in circles, not knowing what to do.
This feeling that's so mutual is burning like a fire.
This feeling that's so strong inside has left us with desire.
Nothing in this universe can kill the love we own.
Never has a love this strong ever before been known.
We kissed each other tenderly, and held each other tight.
The comfort that we felt from this definitely felt so right.
This special moment in our lives will always be a treasure.
The moment, for the first time, we both felt so much pleasure.
Thank you for confronting me in this beautiful way.
You've left a very happy person standing in dismay.

Linda Jennings

KAI'S LITTLE BIRD

Kai was maidservant of long ago
She worked in an inn,
God bless her so.
She washed the feet of the tired travellers
And served them with wine and food,
Kai the servant girl,
All of them came to the inn,
Samaritans, Pharisees and Sadducees and Romans
From the governor's palace,
Tribunes and centurions,
All came to Kai the maidservant girl.

All marvelled at the little brown bird she kept in her cage
Who sang its heart out at the least voice,
Everyone marvelled at the little bird in the cage
That only obeyed Kai
The maidservant girl.
The apostles came to this inn in Jerusalem for
Wine and talk and listened to the little bird sing
And came to see Kai the maidservant girl.
Then one day at sunset there was a great tempest over the city
And the curtain of the temple was cut in two,
The Christ Lord was being crucified.
The little bird escaped from his cage and found himself at Calvary
Where a drop of the Saviour's blood stained his breast,
At length he returned to the inn
Where Kai took him in,
And now you see the robin redbreast, a descendant of Kai's
little bird all over the world as a poignant memory.

Gerard Allardyce

BLESS ALL THE REST

Jessica and Holly were the two we had in mind,
When we said our nightly prayers -
Please God take them home and be so kind
As to let them forget their earthly cares
Now, they're making rainbows Soham sometimes sees
Picture one each end, angels so beguiling -
Or with dear God upon His holy knees.
The children are happy now and smiling -
We know they're loved by the very best,
And pray dear God
bless all the rest.
Amen.'

Sylvia Moulds

IF THE PRIZE WAS YOU

In this life there are many winners.
Seeking each and every prize
From seasoned performers to raw beginners
Limelight dazzling their wide eyes
But in my humble estimation, adulation, capitulation
I'd consider such a coup
Would be to start anew
If the prize was you.

If the prize was you I'd skim the rim of the Grand Canyon
Then I'd swim across Lake Mead
Each and every night at Disney
Main Street parade, I'd lead
I'd blast off in rocket ship without a thought
Explore the vast universe as an astronaut
There is nothing I could not do
If the prize is you.

If the prize was you I would be the greatest athlete
And at each and ever Olympic game
Come first in every entry
Be the carrier of the flame
I'd chisel out a face at old Mount Rushmore
Till my hands were bleeding and were sore
Then sit and enjoy the view
If the prize was you.

If the prize was you there'd be nothing more for me
                    this world could hold
I'd sell my soul, trade my heart, for that pot of gold
Say you love me and I'll spend eternity crossing the desert sand
Take my hand
Understand
I'll be happy my whole lifetime through
If the prize was you.

S Beverly-Ruff

MOMENTS

If I could only hold
The moments when
The light first tiptoed in
Across your primrose lawn,
To touch upon your sleeping cheek
And awaken
The morning first seen,
Just in case
A lost tear should form
To spoil the opening view.

To call the early breeze,
To move upon and keep
Your golden dream,
As if it were
The first opening crocus of spring
To be held
In cupped and caring hands
For all time;
And to hold the moments
Like the delicate petals,
Without the cruel crush
Of final parting.

Norman Royal

CHILDHOOD MEMORIES

Now past three score and eight
I remember playing outside the garden gate
Childhood memories
Must not step on pavement crack
Hopscotch also was a must
Now past three score and eight
What's the time Mister Wolf?
Sheep, sheep cross over another call
Childhood memories
High in the sky kites would fly
Children gambolled on grass so dry
Now past three score and eight
Try to catch tiddlers in the brook
Heads down in comic book
Childhood memories
Now with memories, I lean upon the gate
I would love to do it again, but it's too late
Now past three score and eight
Childhood memories.

John Edney

END OF AN ERA

The hush of silence lingers
It is present everywhere
So real that you can feel it
As it hovers in the air.
For over twenty years we've lived here
With our family of four boys
This house has been the centre
Of companionship and noise.
But now our sons have left home
Youth inevitably do,
So we are moving to a smaller house
That's more suitable for two.
This place is just an empty shell
It is a home no more
We'll take our memories with us
The last time we close the door.
As we wander around, we visualise
A face in each empty room
The house is dead and gives of vibes
Like the silence of the tomb.

Mary Anne Scott

THE BEGGAR

As I was going to church one day
I met a begger on the way,
His clothes were old, so tattered and torn,
I looked at his face, it was so forlorn,
He gave a small grin when I smiled at him.
'Where are you off to?' he cried,
'I'm going to church, how about you?
Would you like to come inside?'
He held out his hand and put it in mine,
We both walked down the very long aisle,
We sat in a pew and said a small prayer,
The organist came and sat on his chair,
As he started to play the beggar stood up,
I thought to myself, *what now?*
He started to sing, you could hear a pin drop,
What a beautiful voice this beggar had got,
We both walked out to the bright daylight,
He doffed his old cap and said, 'Goodbye,
Oh, what a grand day I've had.'

Thelma Smithies

ROOTS

Wherever you travel through life
From a small child to adulthood
Try on your journey to do
Something to make you feel good
But do not forget your roots
Even if you aspire to great heights
In a job that you have got
Try to keep your feet firmly aground
And remember the ones who have not
And do not forget your roots
You may have done better than others
Making you swell up with pride
Bur remember the ones left behind
Even though they have tried and tried
And always remember your roots
If you come from a family of workers
Remember they have given their all
So as you might climb up the ladder
Being there as your anchor lest you fall
So do not forget your roots
Look at yourself as a tree
Without roots you are nothing at all
So now and then remember your roots
They are your best asset of all.

Daphne Fryer

GRANDCHILDREN

I love my two grandchildren
They are the world to me,
Joey is six, Amy is two,
I'm proud as proud can be.

I'm sure they think that I'm their age,
Able to run and jump,
'Catch me Nanny,' Amy calls,
Then falls over with a bump.

She keeps me on my toes alright,
I try to stay ahead,
'Nanny, look at me,' she says
As she bounces off the bed.

I wish I had her energy,
An absolute live wire,
She's funny and adorable,
She never seems to tire.

She's started going to nursery now
Of which she's not too sure,
But give her a few more visits
And I know she'll like it more.

Joe is such a clever boy
(He gets it all from me),
He's bright and friendly,
Polite and kind,
Good parents are the key.

He wants to play the trumpet,
When he gets a bit more puff,
Earplugs may be useful here
'Cos practise could be tough.

Although they run me off my feet,
They really are a tonic,
So what do I do at the end of the day?
Have something alcoholic!
Cheers!

S Oldaker

THE FORGOTTEN

Please feed our children.
Abandoned inhabitants
Of once fertile land,
The grandeur of this place
Speaks death to us,
The brutal blaze of sky
Cupping the careless crystal of the sun,
Burning our eyes
To sunken sores,
Our bodies to dust
That falls in whispers on the plain.
We are the forgotten.
No crop no crumb
No root no seed,
Children eating dirt -
Now there is nothing.
We wait, with dignity
An invisible shroud.
For the love of Christ,
Please feed our children.

Joan Briggs

CLOUDS

Look up to the sky
What do you see?
Clouds!
I have seen a chariot
Racing among the dark
Of promised rain.
A sailing ship surging
Through the bluest of blue.
A rainbow
With colours of every hue.
And in the evening we behold
Sunset;
Colours of orange, purple and gold.
Comes the night
And the moon is bright
Surrounded by stars,
Each twinkling orb
Shining with all its might.
Then at dawn
The sun begins to rise,
Once more the clouds are visible
Before our very eyes.

Doris Mary Miller

MY BEST POEM

To know that God above
Created you for me to love
He chose you out from all the rest
Because He knows I loved you best
Had a heart so warm and true
But now it's gone from me to you
Like care of it as I have done
For now you've two and I have none
If go to Heaven and you're not there
I'll paint your face on the golden stair
So all the angels can look and see
What you my darling meant to me
And if you're not there by judgement day
I know you've gone the other way
So I'll give the angels back their wings
Gold harp and other things
And just to prove what I would do
I'd even go to Hell for you!

Clarke

WINDOWS

The eyes work for people as windows on the world
With them are observed all the wonders to behold
The sea, the sky, flowers trees and living things
Bringing joy and pleasure, but sometimes painful scenes.

Other kinds of windows, with sizable frames
Are fitted with shapely transparent panes
Of double glazing unbreakable glass,
For us to glance and observe as we pass.

Through these apertures the sunlight gleams
With strong, bright, warm, brilliant beams
Lighting up a dull, grey, gloomy day
And we sincerely hope they have come to stay.

The daylight shows people about, on the street,
Dark night-time, mostly lovers meet,
Blinds are drawn, they cover the view,
It's warm and cosy, inside, until the dew.

Also lovely churches and cathedrals shine
With beautifully coloured, ornamental designs
On windows of outstanding shapes and sizes,
Magnificent, to the glory of God, deserving of prizes.

Phyllis Wright

PERSEVERANCE

To be clever is a bonus
In each and every way.
To use the talents we are given
Makes life richer every day.

It's hard to learn when you are young
With distractions all the way.
From computers and TV games
And enticing outside play.

Who wants to study history
When the sun is in the sky?
Or study Will Shakespeare
In the English of his day.

Stick it out and pass exams
And one day you will find,
That learning and struggling
Have organised your mind.

Then all the things you loved at school
Like art and handicrafts
Will become your precious hobbies
When you have the time at last.

Cassandra May Poultney

FREE SPIRIT

Now I am free, now I can fly
Over the treetops and up in the sky.
My spirit can soar in clouds above
All I feel now is peace, and love.
No more pain, now my body has gone
Yet I'm still alive, my life goes on.

So don't feel sad, or cry for me
I'm happy now, and I am free.
Now I'm with you, *everywhere*
Turn around and I'll be there.
You'll hear my voice, inside your head
And you will know that I'm not dead.

Maureen Roberts

'SOOTY', THE MILLENNIUM CAT

A new millennium, they said,
Our cat's alive - he should be dead!
He's lived for twenty years you see,
That's one, four, '0' for you and me.
A cat of very high esteem;
A cat who *always* gets the cream;
A cat who never shirks his duty;
The millennium cat - whose name is 'Sooty'.

His fur is soft and long and black,
And lies quite flat along his back.
His legs are bent and won't go fast,
His hunting days are in the past.
He's ready to retire and rest;
His sell-by date is past its best.

But he's a special cat - I know,
And 'picks me up' when I feel low.
His gentle eyes and lovely face,
Transport me to a better place;
Where everything is good and kind,
And worldly cares are left behind:
Where wealth and money have no hold,
And love is worth much more than gold.

So many people have no time,
Their life is just an uphill climb.
They never pause to look around,
To see the sights or hear a sound,
Or watch a sunrise from the hill,
When everything is calm and still.

But 'Sooty', the millennium cat,
Will lie for hours and do just that.
He'll sit from dusk until the dawn,
When daylight brings a brand new morn.
And then he'll curl up tight and sleep;
I pray to God his soul to keep.

A new millennium at last,
With hate and violence in the past.
This human race must forge ahead
And learn to love and care instead.
There'll be no hunger and no greed,
And we'll have everything we need.
This is the only way to be,
In this our brand new century.

These peaceful thoughts passed through my head,
As I was lying in my bed,
With my companion curled up near -
And suddenly it seemed to clear.
These thoughts transferred to me like *that*
From 'Sooty' - the millennium cat.

Avril T Hogg

POETRY

Poetry is not just words; it springs out of the mind,
Sometimes coming from the heart with words you cannot find,
Some words express a fine spring morn,
Or sunny summer's day,
Or golden autumn's sunshine brightening our way,
And in the cold dark winter we can often find,
Pleasure in our verses and sometimes peace of mind,
Your books have given pleasure to readers just like me,
For you print not only words but our thoughts you see,
Thoughts of golden happy days some alas now gone,
Words to mourn a loved one as time marches on,
So happy anniversary and may you always be,
There to search inside the hearts of simple folk like me.

C Growcott

INSPIRATION FROM PSALM 46

There is a place
Where rivers run
And burning amber
Shines the sun

Here wars will cease
The bow will break
Man will no longer
Quiver and shake

The sword will be broken
And man will love
Their hearts will change
And peace will prove

His kingdom come
Will see no wars
Or shattered hearts
Behind closed doors

God is in the midst
In this holy place
In Heaven we shall be
Looking upon His face.

Sonia Riggs

AN ODE TO FIFTY YEARS

A Wedding Day is a happy day
With all the trimmings along the way
It shows just how two people care
Having a lifetime together to share
When it comes to your own mum and dad
Without a doubt it is compared
And the happy memories you've both shared
With all the life's troubles along the way
July 14th 1951 was your special day
And when the years sway to and fro
And each anniversary comes and goes
To reach fifty years of marriage these days
Is a real achievement in many ways
You've both been very kind,
Thoughtful and generous to me
I couldn't ask for better loving parents
So I hope, Dear Mum and Dad, today
Will be a Special Golden Wedding Day.

Marian Clark

TIME SCALE

The days may still be long and bright
They keep the summer at its best
But migrant birds are well aware
That time has come to leave their nest.

Sometimes I wish to be like them,
To have strong wings and fly away
From the approaching autumn months
Into a full blossoming May.

To fly back to a younger age
That restless, free world of a kind
To live through all the joys of youth
But with a grown up, wiser mind.

On the tireless wings of dreams
I may be trekking every day
But in the real world around
It is the birds that fly away.

Anthony Gyimes

An Ode To The Novice Golfer

A little birdie tells me, you're learning to play golf
I know it isn't easy learning all the strokes
You pick me out of your golf bag and place me on the tee
Out come the driver and iron - take your pick
Either one is all right with me
Practice your swing and loosen up
Oh no, he's hit me and I've landed in the rough
Pitch me out and see where I land
I think I am heading for the sand
Get your wedge and swing me through
Hmm - the water's coming into view
Along he comes and scoops me out
He's called my parentage into doubt
The largest iron comes out of the bag
I he gave me a whack - boy is he mad
I went flying through the air - as if he didn't have a care
Only to find I was on the green
I really though It was having a dream
He lined up his putter but swung too hard -
                    missing the hole by a yard
He tried again only to find - he'd putt it back to the other side
The bogeys were out in full force - I didn't think
                    he would stick the course
After more strokes I finally went in
All he could muster was a sickly grin
He picked me up and put me away, muttering,
            'I've had enough of you for today'
I think he was feeling under par
He headed off to the clubhouse bar
Having a drink, nursing his pride - trying to explain
                    why the shots went wide
Tomorrow is another day - all refreshed ready to play
I'm already sitting on the tee
I'm keeping my head down, *so is he.*

Marilyn Hine

Make Each Day Count

Many, many moons and years ago
When the living was much more slow
A young boy fell in love with a pretty girl
And drove her heart into a whirl
They were both so young in their early teens
Deep in love with so many dreams
Their love was very special in every way
t remained as wonderful as their first day
Though there had been upsets with their peers
Their love never faltered throughout the years
Although the times were very hard indeed
For now they had young of their own to feed
Along life's way facing problems and fears
Sometimes causing pain and many tears
Some were sad tears, some were purely joy
During the years that passed them both by
Every morning since their wedded bliss
He would wake and say I love you with a kiss
t was a love that had grown so very rare
Which only these two could ever share
Then one day to illness they had to part
That's when the pain and heartache began to start
She clutched her grown children to her tender breast
Now a middle aged woman she laid her man to rest
She had no jurisdiction upon her man's fate
So love each other tenderly before it becomes too late
While you have each other show that you care
Love and make each day count while you are a pair.

Angie Farrow

Among The Woods In Spring

I love to stroll among the woods in Spring
Where violets and bluebells grow, to hear
The thrushes swell their song, and then to muse
Beside that running brook where wild thyme flowers
With maiden scent as newborn buds unfold.

Sweet robin's wistful song, with purest strains,
Blends with blackbird's fluting warble graced
With trills, delighting me with melody
As, rapt in contemplation, I now glide,
As though on wings, through labyrinths of green.

A crooked little footpath winds its way
Through oaken glades where grey-brown squirrels leap
From trunk to trunk, and as I creep in stealth
Among those spreading roots a furtive vole
Peeps out, then dives into his secret burrow.

From hornbeam aisles to beechen shades I pass,
Where foxes delve and badgers play at ease;
Then onward to an open clearing where,
Stretched upon a sunlit velvet lawn,
A vixen feeds her young, secure from harm.

And now to woodland's deepest heart where, close
Beside that running brook, I linger long,
Quite over-canopied by verdant boughs
Whose drooping branches burgeon, green with sap,
Distilling Spring's fine fragrances anew.

And there I stand beneath that virgin arch
Of overhanging greenery, entranced;
And there, beyond the crystal stream, alone,
A sacred fawn, exhaling, leads the dance
To hushed Creation's harmonies new born.

Robert Hayward

October Morning

How I love the beauty of the morning,
On a fine October day.
With woods, fields, and hedgerows, dressed in every hue,
I cannot count the colours, so wonderful to behold,
Flame and green, bronze and rust, blended in with gold.

The sun shines from an azure sky,
That's streaked and flecked with fluffy clouds,
Defining the colours, bathing them in a gentle light.
A balm to the distracted mind, my cares are sent to flight.

Blessed with sight to see, how can I not love this scene?
To carry into rainy days, imprinted on my memory.
Look around you; we are on a higher plain,
The bliss of nature makes us strong again.

Mary Hackney

The Wrong Place (Finsbury Park Bus Station, 1974)

Amid the rasp of hastily-applied carbon fibre disc brakes
The bellowing cough of the unloved throng
The spattered grey girders
The torn, drifting print
The guttural sounds of people, just people
The slipping past of something not quite tangible
The drear monochrome of another same day

The thought suddenly struck . . .

This isn't where I should be meeting you, my love.

Ade Macrow

MY GARDEN OF REMEMBRANCE

The scent of wallflowers in the spring
Bring bittersweet delight;
Bright, clustered blooms of red and gold -
A wondrous heaven-sent sight!

Rich reds recall her ruby lips,
Glad golds evoke her hair;
Fresh fragrance, after April's rain,
Prompts pangs of love once rare.

The sight and smell of those sweet flowers,
God's gift each year to all;
Such splendour transcends human arts -
Their power will never pall.

As Wordsworth lauded daffodils,
Enriched by radiant rhymes,
So, annually, my gillyflowers
Strike chords of joyous times.

Young love is now a memory,
Grown cold for many a year;
At Eastertime, come shower or shine,
Those flowers induce a tear.

Roy Court

LAMENT FOR THE SNOWS OF KILIMANJARO

I saw a sad photograph the other day
Showing Kilimanjaro with snowless summit.
The photograph was taken from the air
And a carpet of foamy white clouds
Mocked the grey and barren crest
And in a mere blink of time the scattered snow
Will dissolve like the skin from a rotting corpse
And no more feet will crunch on magical white.

So next time you drive feel a little shame
For it's not just others who are to blame.

How sad Johann Rebmann would be today
For snow lay deep when he stood here,
The first European to discover a place,
Bedecked with snow two hundred miles from the Equator.
Mawenzi and Kibo peaks peer pitifully out of the clouds
Invisibly shorn of their claim to fame
Now just an ordinary rocky mountain
As it was eleven thousand years ago.

And the people who stare from far down below
See it with no glistening crown of snow.

Guy Fletcher

MALVERN

Since first I climbed green Malvern's Hill
The memory of its beauty lingers still.

As I looked across to Brecon
O'er the quilted Vale of Severn,
Methought I saw a glimpse of Eden
If not a vision of Heaven.

Then gazed I o'er Colwall nestling deep
Within the shade of Hereford's wooded Keep.
As the sun lowered on distant Brecon Hill,
Malvern's everlasting beauty lingered still.

When at last I reach my journey's end,
I can at least to myself commend
That go I may to the farthest metropolis,
Ne'er will I see a fairer sight than this.

As I gaze from afar at the green-clad hill,
The memory if its beauty lingers still.

Jack Purdom

AUTUMN DREAMS

Beside the fire the old man sat,
his body worn with work and age.
His face which rough winds, sun and time
had weathered like a parchment page.
With hands which in his youth, so strong
had guided many a plough horse team.
The joints now gnarled as the oaks he'd felled
with axe so sharp, with eye so keen.

But in his soul, he can't accept
that life for him is drawing in.
He gazes in the fire and dreams,
as in his heart he's young again.
He climbs once more the steep hillside
which towers behind the farm, to gaze
across the fertile fields, with woods
and homesteads rising through the haze.

Then, like a monarch, proud he stands,
while from this high, vast, lofty throne,
his eye surveys both beast and land,
hard work enabled him to own.
The chestnut horse that gallops by
in free, exultant, agile flight,
reminds him of the many colts
he'd bred and tended day and night.

A log falls down in the grey stone grate,
and in his chair the old man stirs,
but soon returns to his world of dreams
as the wintry wind whistles through the firs.
Yet, as the morning light creeps through
the cracked and dusty windowpane,
there's an air of stillness in the room,
as nature wakes the world again.

The sheepdog bitch lies on the hearth,
awaiting the morning's first command,
but no sound comes from her master's chair,
as she licks and nudges the gnarled old hand.
For spread across that wise old face
is a smile of contentment and peace.
For he has completed his aim in life,
and well deserves to rest at ease.

Maureen Powell

ONLY MEMORIES REMAIN

After the dreams, the morning does rise
And sleep is abandoned by night

The dependable dawn arrives in the sky
Residing in a moment of calm

The populace awake for another charade
Another day in the company of chance

New memories await to covet the day
To steal every hour for their own

The morning proceeds after the breakfast brigade
In a frantic and irritable mood

The afternoon wanders without malice or haste
Acting like a welcoming host

The evenings so quiet inhabited by peace
Till the epidemic of sleep does return

The memories are born, groomed and stored
All filed till required once again

The morning has gone, the afternoon's left
The evenings vanished into the dark

And after today only memories remain
To live in the conduits life.

David Bridgewater

HAPPY, HAPPY, GRAND PAPPY

To hold my grandson in my arms
Is like childhood again for me
Through his eyes full of excitement and wonder
At all there is to see
At five years old he is already
The brightest flame to enlighten my life
He teaches me how to pull funny faces
And laughs as we frighten my wife.

He likes to swap places with me,
I'm the boy and he's Grand Pappy
I ask him to teach me to count,
That really makes him happy
He can count from one to twenty
Without even taking a breath
But when asked to show me how to draw numbers,
He acts a little deaf.

As I draw numbers for him,
On purpose I draw a backwards figure three
He spots in an instant, 'that's not right,'
As he snatches the pencil off me
He draws the figure correctly,
With a contented smile on his face
'That's the right way little boy,'
He laughs, 'Now let's go and have a race.'

He's the youngest Beatles fan I know,
A bath time favourite since he was two
Far better than the bang, bang rave music
That his mum and dad are really into
As soon as we set off anywhere in the car,
It's, 'Grand Pappy put the Beatles on'
His heads starts nodding and his hands are drumming,
He really is a clever little one.

Kurt, that's his name, has a phobia,
He definitely doesn't like the dark
He sleeps with the bedside light on all night;
I'll switch if off just for a lark.
But every morning when I get up
You can guarantee he has put it on again
Who switched my light out? I bet it was you Grand Pappy,
You always do the same.'

Now I have a powerful torch with its beam
You can see a very long way
Kurt finds it quite an adventure to go out at night
With the torch to play
Kurt loves to walk with Millie our dog
And hold her on her lead
A dark night walk with Millie and the torch
He finds to be very great fun indeed.

Kurt is my only grandson,
I have a granddaughter too called Katie
A granddaughter of nearly two now,
That's nearly two going on thirty
My daughter Sharon and her husband Phil
Have made my life so sweet
With Carol my wife of over thirty years,
Grand Pappy's life really is complete.

Ron Renton

NIGHT TRAIN

I glance up
Across the aisle
She smiles
Remains
A faceless stranger
I stare out of the window
My ghostly reflection in the darkness
Oddly comforting.

Paulie Pentelow

THE VIGIL

Under the flickering lamp he stood,
Watching traffic rolling by.
Waiting for her to come,
One bus, two, three bus, four.
Time is passing slowly, should he wait,
For one bus more?
Is it the cold that keeps her in,
Or is it that he unknown has sinned?
If this is true then pray forgive him,
For to offend was no intention.
When will he see that smile again?
Its memory last forever.
Time is passing, it is late,
It does not seem he'll see his date.
Homeward on his weary way,
Just his thoughts for company.
Blackened is his honoured quest,
If ill intentions they behest.
No help from anyone he'll get,
But even for him there is hope yet.
He'll pray to her and hope she hears,
For to him she's very dear.
And in its own way,
Let's hope love finds a way.

Kenneth Copley

VILLAGE LIFE

Village life was the life for me
Trouble is I'm now eighty-three,
Time gone by when we felt free
To come and go as we please
A policeman always on the beat
No cars around, you used your feet.
Shops on the corner
Or down the street
Local hall where friends could meet
Children playing in the street
No need to fear they would be beat.
Railway station up the road
Trains on time with heavy loads
Waiting room with a fine coal fire,
Porters cleaning platform with hearts desire.
Most important, people came around
Vicar, schoolmaster and Sergeant Brown.
Church or chapel on a Sunday
Ladies with their lovely hats
Men and kids in Sunday best
Always knew what was good or bad
Made them happy and not sad.
Baker, milkman, coal man too
Would deliver all the goods to you.
You would pay them at the door
Never afraid to ask for more
Horse and carts are now the thing of the past,
The fuel they used was hay and grass.

L Turner

THE PRICELESS PRICE OF LOVE

About one million years ago
When I was here on Earth
I found the price of love
And know what love is worth

Love can't be bought
Love can't be sold
Love's better by far
Than silver and gold

Love produces all the art
Realises all our dreams
Provides one with a healthy heart
Sends water for our streams

The lame find they can walk
The blind find they can see
The dumb find they can talk
Love is that heavenly

Love is the greatest power on Earth
The source of all that's good
We all should know what love is worth
And if we don't, we should.

J Vanson

DAYS NOW ARE SLIPPING BY

Days now are slipping by faster than ever before.
Things are forever changing, changing sometimes for the good,
Changing sometimes for the bad, but it's always changing.
Love and hate, friend and foe, life and death, come and go.
Families added to and subtracted from, coming and going by
                                         night and day.
Growing up and moving on, leaving empty spaces
                        that's so hard to fill.
Hold close to all your dreams and thoughts, before they're all gone.
A lifetime of lessons to stand you in stead, of joy and of pain.
Now pass them down to the young to help them build themselves
                                    a better life.
Pass down your memories so they will live on after you're gone.

Christopher Bean

BARREN BEAUTY

Jagged mountain valleys
Shrouded veils of cloudy white
Clear cold windless skies
Bathed in mystical half light

Rocky granite outcrops
Black against a golden screen
Dressed in gowns of purity
Where only gods have been

High peaks of barren beauty
Disrobed by lifted mist
Reveals the naked glory
When by the sun they're kissed

Flaming orbs of fiery red
Held in awe as darkness falls
The cloak of velvet softness
Kept close by granite walls

Moon smiles as he watches
Ghostly games the shadows play
Shamelessly they giggle
At their childish display

Distant sounds disturb the silence
Of the mountains in their dreams
Years of patient waiting
Soothed by cooling gentle streams.

Alison J Mannion

A FRESH NEW IDEA

What is there to celebrate?
Not a lot, you'd say,
But I remember many things
About the month of May.

Dancing round the maypole
Weaving in and out,
Red, white and blue and yellow
Ribbons all about.

Tall, hairy shire horses
Brasses all ablaze,
Gaily dressed with rosettes
For the big parade.

The Boys Brigade, the striking drum,
The happy majorette,
Scenes return from childhood,
I never shall forget.

So celebrate in memory
The days of long ago,
To brighten up today's world
Let the old traditions flow.

Jean Carroll

REMEMBER

Remember all those times, dreams did come true,
When hand in hand we walked, our hearts alight,
No obstacles along the way could blight
Our oneness, no discordant past to rue,
Or ruin pledges blessed, with hope anew,
Our days fulfilled, the shadows put to flight.
Remember places, plans, a future bright,
When courage from each other's hearts we drew,
To take a chance and happiness accrue,
Happy our sharing out the gladness.
When did the 'us' turn into 'me' and 'you'?
Let memories alight away the sadness,
And hand in hand, our pledges blessed renew,
Joyous in recherishing the gladness.

Lorna Troop

PETAL OR METAL

On the streets you may see me every day
Trigger pressed and the contents start to spray
I can be imitation or I can be real
And inside my coat I can be concealed
I'm around giving people smiles and cries
And nearly always there when somebody dies
Buy me, sell me, throw me away
I can change minds and change what you say
You can purchase me, whether you're a saint or thug
Can be surrounded and killed by a slug
You can hold me when you've done something wrong
And in the wrong circumstances I won't be around long
You can put me on a table or on a shelf
With lots of others or by myself
If I'm not careful I'll end up scattered
If dropped on the floor I'll end up battered
Just by staring at me I can communicate
I may even be carried on a first date
My weight light or heavy, my texture can be smooth
People who carry me often have something to prove.

A R Pemberton

IN PRAISE OF THE HEBRIDES

A wanderer winding from the south
First hied to the far Hebrides,
Much moved opened his minstrel mouth
And sang such sun-born strains as these,
Watching the gentle waters play
Upon the shore at Stornoway:

Hail, Lewis Isle of peat-flats low
And peak-stark ridge to raise the sky,
Coasts of keen winds but seldom snow
Where swart shags dive and hawks wheel high;
Where but a blessed light shines clear
And captains may a safe course steer.

Fair Harris Island furthermost!
Of white gold beaches, steepest scars,
The happy shore of Horgabost
And roads more right for goats than cars;
In vale and mountain dear delight,
Whoever sojourns in your sight!

St Barrie's Isle! What memories mine
Of smooth-stoned cairn and treeless turf,
Forsaken cell and strange-kept shrine,
Wide waters crowned with curling surf,
In wedlock one with Vatersay
Across the waves to find a way.

Cumaean Sybils, close your books,
And Smyrnan Sages, sing no more!
Imbibe the Hebridean brooks
And dance the Superborean shore!
Forsake, my muse, famed isles of Greece:
Here let your poet-soul find peace!

Barrie Williams

UNTITLED

'The stone is cold beneath my head
The pavement makes a rock hard bed
All around me I see
Christmastime festivity
Decorations in the shops
People pulling out the stops
Mouth-watering turkey, goose and wine
Such a happy Christmastime
Sparkling lights upon the tree
Inside my head I scream, *help me*
Just in case you didn't guess
I am one of life's homeless
People rushing stare with fear
Do they think I like it here?
Huddled in the shop doorway
Cold and fearful where I lay
Don't they know I have no choice?
Homeless folk don't have a voice
To cry out in reproof
'Please someone give me a roof'
To shelter from the icy rain
Can no one ever feel my pain?
Suddenly a star appears
Celestial music fills my ears
The star is filling all my sight
Getting larger, burning bright
Warmth and peace surround me
Loving arms have found me
In the morning as I lie
On the pavement where I die
The establishment will say
One less mouth to feed today.'

Pamela Matthews

THE SMOKERS

From John O'Groats in Scotland
To Lands End in the south
You'll always find employees
With cigarettes in mouth

You can see them through the windows
Of any city street
At predetermined meeting points
Where others they will greet

They will be there in the morning
And when their day is done
Never bothered by the weather
They smoke through rain or sun

A tightly knit society
Their movements always planned
With their leader giving signals
That all can understand

They move as one towards the doors
A common theme in mind
To puff upon that cigarette
That helps them to unwind

When you add up all the smoke breaks
Non-smokers never win
For they have to man the workplace
Till the smokers file back in!

Charlie McInally

MY BARGAIN HAT

I just nipped in to browse
And there it was, a bargain at a pound.
The hat with pink roses on the band
I really fancied that
But not today, will call again
To see if it should be still there
Available for me.
Must visit my special friend
With birthday to match.
On the way I visit a garage sale
A bargain to catch.
A summer suit, cream with pink flowers to match
I purchased this and other things
Now to find that hat.
In the shop I go
What did I see?
The hat awaited me
A perfect match
At the bargain price of 50p!

P Fazackarley

NEIGHBOURS

An Englishman's home is his castle
The pundits tell us that,
But why not let the drawbridge down
Put *welcome* on the mat,
Most people are gregarious
Recluses very few
So make friends with your neighbours
And have a chat or two,
We all need help occasionally
And who could ask for more
Than to accept a helping hand
From the folk that live next door.

Eric Chamberlin

The Last Episode

A meteor hurtling through space
Will end the earthly human race.
A race is on to fill an ark
A frail craft that will embark
On a long journey across space
To find another earth-like place.
What can I do to get a chair?
Will they need my skills out there?
No, let's be honest, not for me
The voyage across that heavenly sea.
My humble skills the Earth won't leave.
To play Adam to a spaceship Eve.
A wild party might be fun
Or end it quickly with a gun
But no; because I really hope
To see the way they end my 'soap'.

Keith F Lainton

Holiday Time

'Linen supplied,' the advert said,
So there will be sheets upon the bed.
But of towels there was no mention made
So don't expect them to be on the towel rail, tidily laid.

'Spacious chalet,' the advert said,
So there is sure to be more than one bed.
But no mention was made of two bedrooms or three
So are you sure there'll be room for me?

'Five minutes from sandy beach,' the advert said,
So there's no need for sandals or shoes as seaward we tread.
But no mention was made of loos or tea-bars
So will we be able to get tea and a Mars?

'Quiet and peaceful,' the advert said,
So maybe it will not only be quiet but totally dead!
But no mention was made of movies or funfairs
So what! It's holiday time again so who cares?

Ruth Berry

The Family

Mothers are like wheel hubs
They're the centre of family life.
Dads are like the tyres
Strong and faithful on the outside.
The spokes are the children
That make the tyre whole.

Mothers in their kitchens
Make it a happy place to chat.
Dads in their gardens
Find this the way to relax.
Kids, they like to make things;
All are occupied.

When one part is broken
Or a spoke falls out of line,
This causes problems
To the others left behind.
Now all must work together
To remain intact.

Mothers keep on caring
Even when the going's tough.
Dads keep on believing
As you read the Word of God.
Kids, just help your parents
Showing them God's love.

J Stillwell

Rohan, Ode To My Son

Oh, bundle of joy, born literally late in the month of Valentine
You epitomise the embodiment of this time of passion!
Your long, perfect infant form ushers forth a new latent branch to
                              my existing paternal compassion.
Your strong neck which you can prematurely support a few weeks
                              after your birth,
Coupled with your strong grip as you cling onto my finger and
The incessant battle with infant colic which you have now overcome,
Are signs of a nascent, strong persona for whom I will have no
                              future worries about . . .
Cool, calm and placid, you are a total antithesis to your boisterous,
                              strong-willed sister Natasha!
Often, it is even difficult to imagine that we have a nursing baby
                              in the house;
So quiet, serene, an enchanting that you are!
As I look into your intelligent, baby brown eyes
Framed within your cherubic, Churchillian face with your wispy,
                              brown duck's head-like quiff,
Listening to your premature baby babble from just two months old,
I realise that your developing mind will not let you speak to me
                              prematurely with that fertile mind of yours.
Pray tell, if you had the power of speech, what would you say to me?
The senseless slaughter that goes on in the name of humanity
                              perhaps?
Your angelic, beatific smile, reminiscent of my own, which lights
                              up any room
Will be a constant reminder after I am long gone
That by carrying the family name into the next generation
You will secure my own immortality!

Robin Halder

Remembrance Sunday

The Great War it has been named,
But was it great for the dead and maimed?
All those young men who gave up their lives,
Leaving behind, children, parents and wives.
Their country called them into battle,
They were killed needlessly, just like cattle.
Mown down like the grass on the lawn,
Their bodies mutilated, ripped and torn.
They had no grievance against the foe,
But they had to return blow for blow.
Europe was unable to make peace,
And so the fighting did not cease.
They volunteered for their country's sake,
But, oh, how many hearts were to break!
They left full of patriotism, happy and bright,
But many came back without their sight.
We should remember our dead with pride,
For all of us they bravely died.
Young men and young women too,
Gave their lives for me and you.
And yet it happened all over again
In spite of all the carnage and the pain.
In 1939 yet another World War,
More lives lost, blood and gore!
On foreign battlefields they lay dying,
Their families grieving, lost and crying.
So we wear our poppies on 11th November,
And all those brave young people remember.
Yes, honour them on Remembrance Day,
And for their brave, young souls do pray.

Grace Harding

BLIND MAN'S BLUFF

The call to arms spells honour of the free,
Pursuit of courage hails the troops to war
With ransomed souls and power for chivalry,
In combat bold our pride we can't ignore.
A nation's hopes and fears portray the cost
Of sacrifice, the incisions never heal,
What price for freedom found? We ask the loss,
Proud hymns to pain and folly will reveal . . .

When all is done there are no times of peace:
The memories never fade, but silent woe
Stirs hatred for brutality - the foe.
There is no silence in the wake of strife:
We educate, and learn to face the past,
The bitter lessons never wholly last!

Frank A Zwolinski

LOOKING FOR DUP

I came downstairs so quietly
I did not wear my shoes
But Mummy said I wakened him
And so I know it's true.
For Mummy never tells me lies,
That's not the thing to do.

I have looked in every bedroom
And under every bed
I have looked in every wardrobe
And where the meter is read.
I have looked in every cupboard
Plus the cloakroom in the hall,
Looked in Daddy's garage
Then his toolbox, though it's small.

I don't know why he hides from me
He must be Mummy's friend
But if I keep on looking
I will find him in the end.

I know I woke him yesterday
Because I bumped downstairs
Bumped into the kitchen
Then I bumped into my chair
I must have startled Mummy
For she dropped her breakfast cup
She turned to me
Then smiled and said,
'My darling's waken-dup.'

Lewis Cottington

ELECTRA IS SINGING HER POETRY AT TWILIGHT

She is suspended in eternity's web like a muse whose dreaminess
Has become a vision cast into an oblivion which weeps for night.

Those spectres which haunt her are like frost's tossing words,
The whispers which are wandering with the moon's sadness,
Electra strokes into these oceans like a fire licking darkness,

Become engulfed in this stormy humming which is an
Echo pulsating through a dusty lunar scope of awaking.

Her poetry is like fertility as the dawn rises with yesterday's dew,
Quivering in patterns for these mornings dappled with moisture,
The enigma which radiated like the wind embraces forgotten mist;

I stroll into her swaying fields of corn flickering with a shadow,
Her pen begins to scribe like a wave in verse for echoing twilight.

S Pearce

TO SPEND ONE MOMENT WITH MUM

The lawn it seemed to stretch for miles, so green it lay before us
New flowers covered every inch, and a blackbird sang its chorus
The quiet it seemed to greet us there, as sadness bit our hearts
Yet one always feels much better when from this place departs

We know we've done our duty being here today
Then we whisper a short prayer for you, where here we'd love to stay
Among the silence we can think, of what you were in life
And through it all love never dies; sleep just ends most
                                        pain and strife

The Lord He called to you one night, and come daylight
                                        you were gone
We found you there with a smiling face, but the spirit and you
                                        were one
The time had come for you to leave, no time to say goodbye
On this your best yet holiday, to that city in the sky

You did your bit and now you rest, beneath these lovely trees
I can hear you gently talk to us, your voice on gentle breeze
God's garden is your pleasure now to tend each plant with love
I'll leave you now but back I'll come, stay safe with God above.

E Bollington

THE FAMILY HOLIDAY

Vapour trails across the sky
People going places, I don't know why
Some going to visit family and friends
Some are glad when their journey ends

It must feel good to be in the air
Going to foreign lands, it doesn't matter where
People taking holidays in the sun
Lying around on beaches, having fun

And then one day, it's back home again
Back home to England, and our summer rain
But it's nice to look back at the times we had
With the kids, and Mum and Dad

We can't wait to see the photographs
The kids pulling faces just for laughs
Well, that's what should happen, but it's such a sin
Silly old Dad, forgot to put the film in

Well never mind, it's in the past
The sun is shining at home today, but it won't last
There's always next year to try again
We are hoping to go to Spain

But it's no surprise, Dad's coming too
So it will no doubt be disaster number two
The holiday will soon be booked
On flying now, the family is hooked

So off we'll go to a different place
Same old kids, same old Dad, same old face
The holiday time is here again
So off we go to sunny Spain

Everything is all systems go
Where are the passports? I don't know
All our efforts are all in vain
The old man always gets the blame

We've got to get off the bloody plane
Perhaps next year we'll try again
Don't cry
Goodbye.

William G Evans

STORED MEMORIES

I've been to many places
And travelled far and wide
The memories I'm holding
Are buried deep inside

There are many rooms inside my mind
I try hard to recall
Which one holds special memories
Or does one room hold them all

I find a key, unlock a door
I step inside the room
The memories come flooding out
As though swept by a broom

Memories of yesteryear
Of good times spent at school
When we used to laugh and play
Or sometimes act the fool

I open up another door
And quickly close again
There's too much sadness buried here
I do not want the pain

I look and find another room
And when I step inside
It's full of special memories
Which filled me with such pride

Now I know where they're all stored
And neatly put away
I'll leave the rooms all safely locked
Until another day.

Margaret M Lyon

LOST GIRL

Tears on my pillow a forceful sorrow in my heart,
Wishing the world would go away, so I could make a fresh start.
Looking in the reflection of a girl I once knew,
Though the mist grew thicker in the rainy dew.
Look into my window try and find my heart,
You may have to look deep, the coverings are sharp.
But somewhere down there through the wire concrete and damp,
There is a flame still burning in my withering oil lamp.
So try and find my courage, love and will is there,
Lighten up my flame that is your final dare.

Joanna Butler

CALENDULAS

Her friends did not give her flowers.
Winter left her garden spent and frosted.
She did not need plants
But a boost - a health farm -
A hot tub to wallow in
And to restore her mind.

She wanted orange -
Not calendulas
The sun changing to red,
As it dipped below the hill.

A make-over - yes, the painter would mix.
He listened quietly - yellow and red -
Adjusted the quantities just right -
A perfect magician.

She noticed his eyes change colour -
Included it in her mind-set.
'I can see you love the sunlight,' he said
'And tonight your dreams will be of warmth.'

Nola Small

MASK ON THE WALL

A mask on the wall
Hides a once beautiful race forgotten!
A sad one with limbs like cotton.
The haunted eyes say, 'Give us food!'
The hungry cry, 'Give us water, we are dry.'
The scorched earth can no longer produce corn
The mother has no milk for her newborn.
Bellies swollen, limbs like sticks
Stagnant water full of disease
Broken bodies, broken souls
Hearts are aching for one's child
The child that won't see morning
The mother, the father, the son
Dead and gone forever
Because no one cared enough!
All that is left of this proud race
Is a mask on the wall.

Pat Seddon

QUESTION TO THE ANSWER

Words, thoughts ideas
Cascade
Down a knowledge deficit
Funnel
Through a gap in understanding
Drain
Into a pool of questions.
Seek, hunt,
Track and trap that answer
Elusive
Always round the next bend
Never sighted
Obscured from view.
So intent
On capturing the answer
Did not occur
No one gave a thought
Listen
Very closely
To the question
For
From within
The answer whispers.

Michael J Pritchard

NEVER, NEVERLAND

Those who visit Never, Neverland
Are dreamers through and through
They never face the facts of life -
Just ride: those magic carpets in the sky!

In that mythical Never, Neverland
Where only dreamers roam -
Within their facile state of mind
Reality has flown way out of line!

Step off that magic carpet,
Remove those blinkered specs.
Then, you'll see more clearly
And become - like one of us!

We know it's only make believe
And that we shall never see,
That mystic Never, Neverland
That only dreamers see!

Marion de Bruyn

LEGACY FROM A LOVED ONE

Our years together have all been good
So please don't grieve for me,
Go on with your life as I wish you to
And please don't grieve for me.

There's been so much that we have shared
Through all the constant years,
The memories I leave will always be there
And won't wash away with your tears.

Remember the things that made us laugh,
The silly and private things,
Our pleasure in each other's company,
The joy that closeness brings.

Never think that you are alone
Because I'm not there to see,
When a voice in your heart says,
'Life is for living'
You'll know that the voice is *me*.

So go on your way, the first steps are hard,
But once you have started, you'll see
The way ahead will get easier with time
If you don't stop to grieve for me.

Edna Cosby

FORGOTTEN WORLD

I envisaged a ferocious relentless rainforest fire,
That was escalating, way out of control.
A small magnifying lens, that had been left behind carelessly,
Just ignited the large Amazon bowl.

I could smell mahogany embers of tall trees being scorched,
That alopeciad the lush Brazilian terrain.
There were cultures, villages, whole villages wiped out,
I perceived flames, as my face felt rain.

My heart was touched deeply; my raw emotions ran reckless,
By the capitalists making vast fortunes from wood.
Those unsuspecting disadvantaged Third World poor,
Were left abandoned and homeless in the mud.

I caught sight of an Indian tribesman, who was scarred,
His burnt hands cupping water to his singed lips.
He was carrying his means for his very next meal,
A simple blow-pipe with the darts of poisoned tips.

He was tasting black water, that had been flavoured by ash,
Trying to quench a thirst, amidst the billowing smoke.
He was coughing up sputum, that was stained tarry black,
He was gasping and starting to choke.

Those trapped animal screams were deafening to my ears,
I smelt aromas of the raw roasted skin.
Pandemonium outbreaks in this disappearing world
Amidst the clattering, clamorous din.

Alas! Hark the herald angels are silent,
I fear I no longer hear their sweet songs.
All that these destitute people had held scared once,
Have absolutely nowhere now to belong.

There was haunting sounds from a dear Jesuit's flute,
Shedding teardrops through the ballads he played.
Down on both knees, facing the heavens above,
Bible clenched in his hands as he prayed.

His cloth habit had fungus, forming from the mildew,
His eyes scanned columns, as if a cathedral nave.
Pleading to his god for those unfortunate people,
Pleading if they and their sacred land could be saved?

Tommy McBride

A SONG

I hear this song in my heart,
It sings of sadness and of joy,
It sings of pain and relief,
It is never clear to hear yet it is there.

This song is special but all people know it,
It helps us in bad times and in good,
It never leaves our side,
It stays with us for our life.

So sing this song with me you all know it,
Let the world hear our joy don't hide your heart,
All the happiness of the world will be open to us,
It is the song of celebration.

Beatrix Kielhauser

MEMORIES OF LIFE

What will they find when I am gone?
A house full of 'rubbish' to them.
There are old clothes and hats and papers galore,
So much kept and looked after, for when?

Over eighty years I've collected junk
(Couldn't bear to throw it away)
There are childhood memories hidden here
I could take out and look at one day.

My aunt's beads - Mother's wedding veil,
And baby shoes still in the drawer.
My father's cap badge from his service life
And souvenirs from the war.

There are photos and letters from years long ago
And papers and magazines too,
From a letter date they relate to research,
Even menus gained from a cruise.

Then clothes in the wardrobe remind me of times
When I dressed up and wore pretty things.
The dress that I wore at my special 'dos'
And the hats bring back memories too.

So what will they do with the books I bought
Even the ones that I write?
They won't mean so much when they look at the shelves
But to me they have been my life.

Some letters they'll find tucked away in books.
I valued the contacts I had,
They were written to me by the authors themselves,
So look carefully through if you can.

I am sorry and sad for the mess that I leave.
It's too painful to clear it away.
Give some to my friends if you want to, of course
We may meet again one day.

Doris E Pullen

PLEASE

If I die with no goodbyes
My love for you all
Will never die
For in Heaven
I will love you still
Although my presence
Will be nil
So promise me please
Whatever it takes
Take care of each other
For Mum's sake.

Doreen Day

BIRD IN JULY

The sun ashines.
The roses bloom.
A garden's joy
And joy's perfume.

I hear in tune
A bird in song.
Do not tell me
That she is wrong.

For she is right.
Her sound, my sight.
A jewell'd means
Of hope's, delight.

Bird is happy.
And so am I.
May long her song
Embrace the sky.

May her glory,
Though small she be,
Accompany those
Who walk unfree.

Hywel Davies

PAINTING A SUMMER'S MORNING

Ghostly grass phantom fields,
A pale grey wash over English wealds.
Dissected trees that weep false tears
Skilfully applied by mist; now fears
That the lemon watercolour sun
That overslept, will have to run
Undignified, to take his place
And start the day with perspiring face,
So splashing with the palette's paint
Each solitary leaf, without restraint.
Never was a monarch so bejewelled,
(That we could only watch enthralled)
The change to multicoloured hues
That filled the senses 'til they, imbued
Could properly greet the wondrous dawning
Of an Essex, summer's morning.

Roy Vaughan

REMEMBERING

I remember the sweet sickly smell
Of burning tea,
It was the overall impression
Left with me to store in my brain,
As dockside warehouses
Met reality of war,
And parts of the East End
Were no more.
To my childhood mind it seemed
As if a giant screamed
For his pipe filled with leaves,
To throw flame from one side of his mouth
And a dense ring of cloud from the other
To proclaim he could and would smother
The streets below.
The odour clung to dress and jacket sleeves
Long after the fires had subsided,
Long after the sting left the eyes
And the double sided ache lost its pain.
Why should that smell rather than the destruction
Remain in my mind
To recall childhood experiences of war?

Pat Bidmead

OUR YORKSHIRE MOORS

Windswept moors, bleak and heather-strewn, the
Sheep teetering as they graze between rugged limestone rocks,
Some giving birth beside ancient stone walls,
Built by broad and reddened hands.

The shepherd's shrill whistle directs and guides
His dogs, who circle the obstinate flock,
Barking commands, gently nipping wayward heels
Into the sheep pen.

Meandering streams drape hill and dale, like silver ribbons;
Crystal clear, they bubble and gurgle over stones
Smoothed through centuries of nature's sculpturing.
Gushing spring waters burst from wells
Once sacred to the Druids, offering welcome refreshment
To the thirsty traveller.

On misty, slate-grey days, the spirits of prehistoric man seem to
Permeate the jagged rocks, the bracken and gorse.
Ancient Pagan spirits battle with
The early saints as,

Javelins of slanting drizzle jab into the earth.
The savage, brooding beauty is etched in the heart,
The soul, the mind.
Beloved are these, our wild Yorkshire Moors.

Betty Morton

FEAR AT FLANDERS

'Jump into the trenches lads,'
I hear my comrades shout
'Try to get to cover
The enemy's about.'

I hear shouting all around me,
I see a soldier fire his gun,
I am rooted to this spot
As I have nowhere to run.

Shooting from my right,
And shooting from my rear.
I say a silent prayer
As I know the end is near.

Men are dropping everywhere,
I can hear their mournful cry.
I may be just a poppy
But I know I soon will die.

B Cotterill

THE PLEDGE

Marriage is a pledge between lovers,
Made on their wedding day.
A vow to help each other
Along life's rocky way.
When things go wrong,
Learn to forgive and forget.
Losing the one you cherish,
Can mean a lifetime of regret.

Don't risk those years of love
On a sudden surge of lust.
Resist that flight of fancy,
Don't break your bond of trust.
On the other side the grass
Always seems a better shade of green.
In truth, the grass is greener
Where you've already been.

Ernest Barrett

SIMPLE OFFERING

I entered our church today,
Seeking peace to think and pray,
But a loud voiced woman and children chattering
Disturbed the peace, my solace shattering.

By the pillar stood an elaborate stand,
Of bright yellow flowers, from a foreign land,
Well arranged with great precision
But further noise enforced my decision.

So I left the church and left the flowers,
And seeing hedge-parsley, remember the hours
I'd spent in a bare simple church,
Which was well tended, but hadn't much.

A faithful parishioner dusted and swept the floor,
Shone the brasses and pews, it didn't need more.
Then she gathered hedge-parsley and put it in a jar,
High on a narrow window ledge to be viewed from afar.

The narrow church placed amidst fields,
Where farmers counted their animals and yields,
Offered in its peace and simplicity,
The gift of deepest undisturbed serenity.

Suzanna Wilson

CO CO

She was small and black,
And I loved her so,
My poor, little Co Co.

We found her in a little backyard
Covered in fleas.
Her life had been hard.

Through all the years that followed,
Wherever I happened to be,
Co Co was my companion,
Keeping me company.

In old age, though, full of pain,
That brave little dog
Carried on the same,
Doing all she thought she should
Just as long as she could.

Only memories linger on,
Now my little pet is gone.

Irene Millington

RAIN PLEASE

Please God just a little rain,
To help to cool me down again,
It's not that I do mind the heat,
But oh my poor aching feet,
Hot flushes on top of this,
It's not really what I call bliss.
Thunder bugs there are now,
Clinging to my wet brow,
Is that a little cloud I see?
Oh dear God You did hear me,
Now a tiny drop of rain.
I don't want to be a pain,
One day I'll moan because it's hot,
And then complain because it's not,
It's raining now quite a bit,
Washing roads full of grit,
I think we've had enough thank You,
No more I say, that'll do!

C Iverson

CONTENTMENT

I've never really had much luck with fame.
Through good or bad, I've tried to stay the same.
For I am just a common working man,
Being content throughout my own life's span.

But I do worry about some other folk,
Who always tell me that they're stony broke;
I wonder if I'm suffering from greed,
Because I have a lot more than I need.

My motto's always been 'Pay as you go'
And if I could not pay, I did not go.
When offered plastic cards, I'd say, 'No thanks,'
That way there's no repayments to the banks.

So why do people get so deep in debt?
And cannot pay for goods they've bought . . .and yet
They'll still spend out on things they can't afford
Like several holidays each year, abroad.

Dear Lord, I thank You for Your earthly plan
In making me a common working man;
I don't need wealth, to feel so rich and free,
So please, dear Lord, make others rich . . . like me.

Alf Godman

TIGHTROPE

Life is a balancing act
don't you think?
Each time we blink
a tear from the eye
there's an up-turn to climb
one step at a time
Sleeping with sadness
to wake in the sun
A grief overcome
A half empty cup
with hope filled up

Maintaining a balance
Hostage to chance
On the tightrope we tread
stretching ahead
A steep drop beneath
Too easy to fall
But the light of God
above it all
To contend with the worst
so the best to exact . . .
A very delicate balancing act.

Jo Lee

FIRST BORN

This little body light but strong so close against my breast.
Whose rosebud mouth that greedily demands and gives no rest.
A downy head; a velvet cheek; I need to gently touch.
Humanity so tiny that relies on me so much.
This part of me that wondrously is now a separate being.
Whose little hand can grasp my own but eyes yet still unseeing.
Will get to know me and to love me as I watch her grow.
Joyous times ahead of me because I love her so.

Second born

I cradle him within my arms this feeling once again.
The joy and wonder of it all forgetting all the pain.
Contentment here within me now; confidence abounds.
Understanding all the little unfamiliar sounds.
Knowledge now on how to rear him comforting his cries.
A joy again to touch his cheek and gaze into his eyes.

Molly Phasey

Is Love Just Wishful Thinking?

Is love just wishful thinking?
Is happiness a cloak
That's wrapped around the misery
Of someone you don't like?

Is jealous an ugly thing,
Possessiveness an ugly sin
Born of wanting full control -
Full control of everything?

If marriage is a union
Blessed by God in church -
How come there's so much divorce?
How come they don't all work?

Is one man's joy another's sorrow
Is his ride to success made smooth
On the back of a tired and starving mule
Too desperate for the carrot to refuse?

Is love just wishful thinking?
Is jealousy a sin?
How come life makes so many victims
Why can't everyone win?

Patricia Orton

Just A Few Lines

Celebrate life
Enjoy all you do
Give out your goodness -
It will return in due course to you.

Make friends, treat them well
Be happy - who can tell
What future and luck is forecast for you
Just do your best, be honest to all
Then you'll have memories
Full of love - to recall.

Celebrate a baby's smile
A lover's gift, a husband's style
A mother's love and father's too
Celebrate life and its goodness for you.

Vera Homer

Chin Up

Buttercups show true love
I hold one up to you.
Buttercups are sweet and true
And this I ask of you.
This I ask and honesty
In everything you do.
I hold a buttercup to you
But you my love aren't true.
Your love is fragile like the petals
That so easily fall
You are one among the many
Who cannot hear love call.
Buttercups will true love show
But if you gather as you go
And if you gather many
Will many tell you
Yes or no?
Many masses on the hillside
Many in the valleys low
I hold a buttercup to you
It tells me buttercups don't know.

Constance Roper

My Pain

(Dedicated to Jenny Sim)

The pain is so intense
How shall I cope?
Shall I ignore it?
Or wish it away?
Tears come to my eyes
As I realise I can do neither

It grips me internally
It is like a lion . . . devouring its prey
It claws at my body
Drawing blood

Shall it be my blood . . .
Just to endure . . . it takes all my
Strength . . . I am immersed in the hurting
I cannot emit victory over it . . .
Body and mind

It's enough to send me
Running into the night
Running scared . . . bloodied trail
Caught up in a net . . . it comes in waves
My agony . . .
My existence . . . my being

Prostrate tasting the earth
My tears mingled . . . with my . . .
Sad heart . . . producing a state of the art . . .
Graphic diagrams of suffering

Do you think . . .
It will ever end . . .
Coming to its sorry conclusion . . .
That's the question . . .
What's the answer . . .

Sally Wyatt

From The Heart Of The Earth

The lifting up that men saw just as shame
This Jesus showed, was glorious, healing truth
For those who raised their eyes to see the light.
The Cross became a crown, the lifting high
Became a throne of God, Golgotha's height
A way into the holiest place of all.
He faced the darkness of Golgotha's night,
The lonely cry, the bitter anguish keen,
The black, dark gloom of death, He faced all this,
And found the morning rise, a cloudless dawn -
A new life surging mid the spring's bright flowers.
And joy was born, created fresh from God.

But Mary could not see; her tear-filled eyes
Could only long to keep Him there in sight.
'My God and yours, your Father and yet mine.
I go where you belong, to help you rise
To newer truth and greater riches far.
I go that I may come and stay with you -
An endless fellowship, eternal bond.'

The pain of parting lifted, glorified
In ceaseless, deep communion with God.
For we shall never know what God can give
Until we yield that which we hold so dear,
And loose the grasp on that to which we cling,
And find the thing we yielded, given back,
Refined and purified - a sacred gift
From God.

Sheila Harris

THE CORNER CAFE

Midday - the door swings open,
An old man shuffles to his table.
A waitress, with bleached complexion
Tired with kitchen condensation,
Rearranges the plastic roses
As she awaits an order.

Alone - his friend no longer comes.
Her Pekinese was banned
From steaming up the plate glass windows
And snuffling under tables
Where well shod clientele
Tap impatient heels.
This is where he once talked business.
His past achievements could cut a swathe
Through present idle chatter.

Some days, when out of step,
He was running across the Downs
Through clouds of blue butterflies
Into his mother's arms;
Relapsing into a world of nursery rhymes.
Or conjuring up the girl on a silver bicycle
With long brown legs under short flowered skirt,
Now slowly riding out of view -
Her name forgotten down the years.
A sun-deck on the pier
Where once he fell in love,
Only to lose her to another.
Bright blonde hair and sapphire eyes
Flicker and recede.

Sometimes he heard a laugh;
Envied an intimacy
Of which he felt no part
As minutes dragged to hours.

Lunchtime over the café empties.
The old man nods in the corner;
Parchment white as the tablecloth
Waiting for his tea . . .

Veronica Charlwood Ross

GOLDEN DREAMS

I remember a year of my childhood
And the golden dreams I used to dream
Whilst wandering along a seashore
Or by a mountain stream.
I spent so many lonely hours
Beside a field of corn
Listening to the skylarks
In the haze of a summer morn.

I wandered o'er the dunes
And raced the ebbing tide
To search the rocks and pools
Where crabs and things might hide.
Into my private world of solitude
Companionship I did not seek nor care
For dreams I dreamt in childhood
Were dreams I would not share.

They were such very special dreams
To me so precious and so dear
That I locked each within my heart
To remind me of that year.
But like the melodies of songbirds
Or waves upon a shore
Those golden dreams of childhood days
Are lost for evermore.

Gwen Liddy

TOGETHERNESS

We had such fun and laugher when we first met,
Then the many dates which we always kept.
You came towards me, my heart would leap,
Our romantic date we then would keep.

Somehow I knew we were meant to be,
As I waited eagerly for your face to see.
More walks, more fun as we went on,
Until the day ended and night had come.

My true love you were to me,
I thought that I would always see
The blue of your eyes, your loving smile,
Wonderful gifts God gave you for a while.

The sound of your voice, your loving kiss,
Now only memories of all of this.
You were my love, my dearest friend,
I will always be with you until the end.

Evelyn M Harding

SPRINGTIME OR FALL?

How will it be, when my Master comes nigh,
Will there be n'er a place, I can hide?
How will I stand, when He takes hold my hand,
And a life's at the ebb, of the tide?
When will I know, when my Saviour will show,
Will it be in the day - or by night?
So will He be there - in winter's despair,
Or the advent of spring's comely light?
Maybe, it's proper - that I shouldn't know,
When that time's due, to pay me that call.
Just to carry on still - and abide by His will,
And enjoy every hour - to the full!
And when one special day,
When He has His way,
And offers me His outstretched hand,
I'll know - that it's time, then,
To finish this rhyme, and simply,
With grace,
Understand.

Tony Roberts

FIRST LOVE

Every second
You are away
I dream of you
All night and day.
At your quick step
My heart beats fast,
Your crooked smile
I see at last.
We cycle up
To Windy Ridge -
Picnic on plums
Beneath the bridge.
Hand in hand,
We laugh and run
Along ribbed sands
In blazing sun,
Fling ourselves down
In dunes to dry.
Knowing our love
Will never die.
Once more we lie
In sweet repose,
Entwined like petals
Of a rose.

Marjorie Beaven

MUM

She gently swept a curly tendril across her brow,
In a hasty gesture, deep in concentration
Pushing the dolly stick in a vigorous motion
Lost in the hot steam, a long ago picture.

Her smile was never far away on her unblemished face,
Her personality such she would never shy from a challenge or dare.

One summer's day when the sun was high,
The barometer rising minute by minute.
Mum peddled home in a glossy fake fur
Her covenant prize for morning's toil.
She did not seem to notice
How passers-by just stood and stared.

My mum was forever on her feet
She seemed to have boundless nervous energy
Never enough hours in the day to complete her menial tasks,
But through adversity and joy
Her composure remained, an inner gift.

I loved her then when I was a mere child,
Adulthood strengthens your emotions.
Our roles have become reversed;
I nurture, she's the dependant childlike figure.
Family bonds are strong not easily fractured
By the passing of time, not one small rift.

Heather Lynes

LONESOME TED

Poor Teddy's mouth was sewn on upside down,
And his forehead had a permanent frown.
Feeling rejected and utterly glum,
He observed from the shelf for a perspective chum.
Teddy was made on an industrial estate,
It was up to the factory to decide his fate.
Two girls got a warning over poor old Teddy,
Because their hands were less than steady.
Their concentration was very poor,
Because they got drunk the night before!
Teddy was imperfect because of that,
And for three years on the shelf he sat.
But he received some news this afternoon,
And he's off to the children's home at the end of June.
There is a moral to this little bear's tale,
If manufacturing a teddy cut back on the ale!

Caroline Dean

MY LITTLE STAR

You are the smallest star
In the universe, I have chosen you.
As time goes by
Life will change for
Better or for worse. I will
Look to you for guidance
In you I will place
My trust, if a dark cloud
Shall appear and suddenly
Spoil my view. Then I will
Wait and wait forever to
Catch a sight of you. Dark
Clouds don't last forever,
They never ever do and
When they disappear again,
You will come into view.
For me, you will always shine so
Bright and forever be my
Guiding light.
My little star of hope.

Richard Mahoney

PORTRAIT

My grandmother wore long skirts,
She was small and neat,
Her silver hair worn in a bun
Was long enough to sit on,
And I was allowed to brush it as a treat.

Before I slept on drowsy afternoons,
She would sit and hold me, humming
Like a lone melodious bee,
Until I was gone into the dreams
She murmured in my ear,
I was secure then without fear.

She could move quickly
On black shod silent feet,
Or make a room a refuge from the cold,
With hands grown old and warped
With serving.

To go outside she wore a shawl,
Black and wool warm drawn around her
Keeping out the cold,
She often held within its warmest fold,
Against her breast, babies and kittens,
And anything which needed rest.

She wore a hat on Sunday,
And I remember how,
Gloved hands interlocking,
We went to church.
I watched her face,
She had serenity and grace.
And she was kind,
She understood a sigh
And could always find
Time to comfort.

She is I know a part of me,
And when she came to die
I was bereft, with only memory
Of that to ease the way to living.

My grandmother wore long skirts,
With movements like a sigh.
My grandmother wore long skirts.
Now so do I.

Doreen M Neu

DAD CAME IN FOR A CUP OF TEA

'Dad came for a cup of tea,' you said.
But when you'd made it, he had gone.
I thought you were dreaming as the stroke stole your mind.
I humoured you. Was I wrong?

I watched you wither before my eyes.
And tried to make sense of your words.
They tripped from your mouth in a tumble
Like flocks of squabbling birds.

Twenty-five years since Dad left you.
Cruel cancer had taken him then.
You carried on bravely, got on with your life,
Full of faith, that you'd see him again.

The last day I sat there beside you,
The light in your eyes had grown dim.
That night you were freed from your burden of life.
At last, you could go be with him.

Patricia Graham

A LESSON WITH JAMES

(Especially for James - born 10.08.2000 at 12.45pm)

I have learnt since your birth
There is nothing more precious on Earth
Than you.
I have learnt to be unselfish
Because you are everything I cherish.
I have learnt to be more grateful
Because you are perfect and beautiful.
You are my everything
My darling.
A joy to behold
A story waiting to be told.
I have learnt that patience is a virtue
Something I never had before you.
I have learnt to appreciate life more
I never knew motherhood before.
I have learnt when you are sleeping
You are safely in my keeping.
I learn new things every day
You are developing in every way.
I have learnt to enjoy childish games
With you, my darling son, James.
I have learnt there is nothing finer than the gift of motherhood.
And if I could
Dear James, I would
Have you over and over again
No matter how great the labour pain.

C A Keohane

PARTY ANIMAL

Out in the street, I am the egotist . . .
I take the beat everywhere I go . . .
And I don't care though I could offend, you know . . .

I'm going to be a party animal . . .
Too wild, a bit tame . . .
But inside and outside, I won't change.

Hello to you, I am the egotist . . .
I take mystery to everyone . . .
And I don't care, though, to rebel is having fun.

I'm going to be . . . a party animal . . .
Too wild, bit tame . . .
But inside and outside I won't change.

Wendy Day

BEAUTIFUL WORLD

If the smile on your face lights my darkness
And the taste of your lips is like wine,
When you speak, your voice soothes and caresses
This troublesome heart of mine.

When we dance, you set my heart racing,
When you walk, paths are covered with gold,
The touch of your hand feels like gossamer wings,
In your arms, I don't want to grow old.

If your hair is the sun shining brightly
And your eyes are the rock pools that sing,
And your scent is the air I breathe deeply,
What a beautiful world I live in!

E Joyce

A LOVER'S USELESS LAMENT

He has a group of discontentments, miserable sighs
That keep the wretched sleep from out the poorly creature's eyes;
Yet when at rest his love will take the daft sap in her arms
His mind can dwell on nothing but her undisputed charms.

It serves no point to sometimes let the paltry inner mind
Think about her failings, for all of humankind
Could never be devoid of such; we are not perfect, ever;
Such little inconsistencies are constant as our weather

And that, as we all come to know
Will vary from the arid heat to winter's arctic blow;
Red sands from the Sahara will sometimes fall in rain
Which boring global warming's used as threatenings to explain

In spite of timeless changing facts, denied always by some,
That climate as a variable of our uneven sun
Was ever thus, except of course to those who are demented;
Has been ever since our worlds and planets were invented.

So what slight point could ever hope to get to be achieved
By relating to one's own true love what littlenesses grieved,
Or of some slighting tardiness, perhaps, in one response
When all a suitor needs, at any time, is once

To settle and enjoy with her a moment's utter rest,
To gaze at her and stay his head upon her perfect breast;
To talk with her and walk with her as long as he is able;
To bed with her and bawd with her and sup with her at table.

Sean Jackson

THE PURPLE OMAN MOUNTAINS

When the purple Oman Mountains
edge the ochre sand,
I'm haunted by the beauty of
that proud and ancient land.

The searing sun moves overhead
on its westward way -
black goats, a-scatter, nibble wide
from youthful bright-eyed sway.

But later in the heat-haze day
subtle change occurs,
distant features come to life,
the arid harshness stirs.

The lengthening evening shadows
intensify the scene,
revealing all the hidden depths
lurking in between:
they heighten and delineate the
tracings in the dunes,
drawn by tireless whispering winds,
now stilled, in mystic runes.

The pink and purple jebel shades
compliment the sky,
until they fade to silhouette
against the flames - and die.

When the purple Oman mountains
edge the ochre sand,
I'm haunted by the beauty of
that proud and ancient land.

Edward Fursdon

My Best Friend A Gentle Giant

A man who is attentive and protective to those close to him,
Knowing him, you will find, animals and birds bring out
                              a tenderness in him,
A softness which is loving and kind.
An intelligent man, a man who has strong political views.
A great interest in his daily life
To read the 'Guardian' and give support to Labour's strife.
An endless knowledge of jazz artists and films galore.
A library brain, a computer store.
Dates of events on life's unknown path
Happy and sad times that have long passed,
Stored information, which is right, you can bet
Others may not remember, or wish to forget.
Centre of attention he likes to be
A dream to appear, tan-faced on TV.
To dream of a big band playing, as he rides his trolley
                              through the store,
Crowds applauding and fainting on the floor.
He awakes to sing, 'I've got you under my skin'
Just to dream - he's not him.
A sincere man, who can trust, and love, it's seen in his eyes.
One can reflect how he feels and he deserves likewise.
He may be as big and as strong as a tree,
But his well-being is very important to me.
I know he will read this again and again
And wonder, 'Am I really this gem?'
But before you put my rhyme to rest,
I have to say - Sinatra's the best!

Janey Wiggins

Stepping Stones

Step, step, stepping-stones a journey through her life,
Tick, tock, striking clock beating out the strife,
Baby come, baby go, bright-eyed toddler to and fro,
Teenage spots, heartbreak days, blushing bride can't wait to say,
I will, I won't, I do, I don't.
Lovers of the moment will never be apart,
Grow roses round the garden with a valentine for her heart,
Lazy, crazy summers, dark, stark winters,
Chopping up logs, and picking up splinters.
Lady in waiting to make her life complete,
Nine months later, she greets those tiny feet,
Heaven on her doorstep, a bouncing baby boy,
No amount of riches could ever bring this joy.
They rode the swings and roundabouts, took long walks
                              on the beach,
He was there beside her, but somehow out of reach,
Storm clouds are brewing; it's raining every day,
Broken hearts and promises have driven him away.
Valentine has left us and now we're all alone,
You're all that I have left my son until you're fully grown,
Another brown-eyed wonder is tugging at my heart,
But you are only loaned to me, so one day we must part.
The sands of time are running out and the man's no longer a boy,
Take comfort in the love we have, step back, and savour the joy.
Now the years have passed us by, I'll cherish every day,
Goodbye my little soldier, who loved me come what may,
It's time for change and pastures new,
So don't look back I beg of you.
Step, step, stepping-stones are almost through for me,
I've lived my life the best I can, so what will be, will be,
That ticking clock is starting fresh, and now it chimes for you,
Go find your world on that stepping stone,
Seize the hour, live the dream and stay true.

Jan Yule

The Far Distant Hills

In gardens I have often strayed
To meditate and dream
And wander amid the flowering shrubs
Whose scent is pure and clean.

With great tall trees around me
Spreading their limbs of cooling shade,
As I recline beneath their boughs with
Thoughts of happy days.

The glowing sun shines from Heaven
Above, on fields and meadows green,
And all is bathed in its wondrous
Light a sight to behold, so serene.

And clouds roll by like great ships in the sky
While birds of the air soar skyward above
And the trees give a sigh as the breeze rushes by,
How beautiful is this garden of love.

Then my thoughts ever stray to the far distant hills,
As I remember the old days gone by
When I was a youth and in my prime
I used to have a very grand time
But now I'm old and not so young
I am now enjoying the evening sun.

So as I lie beneath these boughs
And gaze at the azure sky above
I close my eyes and thank the Lord
For this life of mine which is full of love.

John Collard

The Good Old Days

What's happened to the little things
That each day would bring?
The milkman calling, 'Milko!'
A newsboy whistling
The policeman on the corner
Showing anyone the way
What's happened to the little things
Can anyone really say?
Wherever is the newspaper
That comes with fish and chips
The oranges all red and sweet
That haven't any pips?
And where is the baker
Who had a corner shop
With big, jammy doughnuts
And a lovely crust cob?
What's happened to the little things
Where did they all go?
The blackbird that woke us in the morning
Red robins and the snow.
A fishmonger with his barrow
With whelks and wriggly sprats
An old lady sitting in the doorway
With her little dog and cats.
A street where one could walk
Without fear of being mugged
People saying, 'Good morning'
And children being hugged.
There's no end to the simple things
We seem to have lost sight of
Especially the little word l.o.v.e
That spells love.

Hilda Griffiths

TSUNAMI

I lie on the beach, beside my mother,
In the warmth of the sun.
Listening to the joyous sounds of children
Playing in the sand.
The surf gently ebbs and flows
As it bubbles along the shore.
I raise my head to watch
My father and my young brother,
Splashing in the sea.
I stretch out my hand to stroke Max, our dog,
Who is lying beside me. He is not there,
And my hand makes empty circles in the air.
I get up, and walk away from the sea
To look for him, but no dogs bark.
Suddenly the sky is dark.
The sea becomes a convulsive mass,
Tempestuous and boiling.
A white wall of water, several feet high,
Explodes onto the shore.
I see my mother rush into the sea,
Shrieking to my father and brother.
Time after time the sea rises up,
And then crashes down again,
Propelled by a giant, unseen hand.
I run towards a tree and clutch its branches.
The sea encroaches,
Opening its jaws to engulf me.
Deadly and menacing.
It retreats, just a little,
And I am left, clinging and dazed.
I hear the awful screams of the dying.
A man appears and grabs me,
Lifts me on to his shoulder,
And stumbles to higher ground.
An eternity passes.
I lie still and quiet, in deep shock, but safe.

I know that I will never see my family again.
Not even Max.
But life must be renewed,
And I shall have to learn to live,
All over again.

Eve Turner

TO THOSE WE LEFT BEHIND

Happy we 'pals' of battalions from villages borne of love
And sweet tender mercies; unlike here entrenched
With the foe, grey mists on the horizon, silhouetted hove
Of sallow composition; subdued and drenched.

Between us, in 'no-man's-land' a barren waste
Of limbs stacked high, orchestrating the way
Of death, foreshadowing yet even still the taste
To come, and soon; at the break of day.

Our friends, our fathers, uncles and brothers
In arms; cleaving the ground of crimson red
Left on the battle-scarred plains, with their mothers'
Voices ringing out; as bells that toll the dead

Then slowly faint whispers are heard amidst the grave
Of brown and grey; 'Is that you John! Bill! Fred!'
'Is that you 'Jurgen! Rommel! Hans!' You the brave
Who fell, still living amongst the dead.

The shroud of death that covers distempered cries,
Now lifting as 'both' find their heroes of 'cause'
And naked transgression remains; signature of lies
And deceit; like whores, showing no remorse.

J Clark

CELEBRATIONS

The fifteenth anniversary of Forward Press
Let's celebrate!
How pleased I am to have been chosen to forward a poem,
I hope is the best.
Will that fantastic Harrods Hamper be mine?
If so, on what will I dine?
Biscuits, cakes, jars and bottles, many goodies I see
All in a hamper waiting for me.
If I don't succeed this time
Then perhaps next time
It will be mine.

Patricia M Farbrother

WHAT FUTURE POEMS

What future poems
Lie pregnant in the undergrowth
Of the mind?
What stars
Will ultimately shine
From a dark sky?

Secretly now,
In fertile darkness,
Like worms busy in soil,
They seek nourishment,
Waiting impatiently
For rain to flush them out.

What fiery ecstasies,
What mighty, ponderous thoughts
Will be translated?
Sonnets or villanelles
Perhaps will push them
Into eternity.

Or, will they dazzle
For a day, then dwindle
Into worms again,
Making false promise
Of the energy
Which strove to give them birth?

Elsie Hamilton

IN THE SPIRIT OF THE TEAM

Working together is -
Sharing the responsibility,
Helping each other to
Achieve that goal
Knowing that many hands
Make light work, that
Two heads are better than one,
And that together,
We are beautiful.

Working together is -
A glass raised in partnership,
Felicitation or commiseration,
And a great sense of team spirit,
With the knowledge that any problems encountered
Can be overcome.

Working together isn't just that.
It's being together,
Caring about each other,
Loving our world and being
At one with it and ourselves.

It will go on working -
If we stick together.

J P Henderson-Long

PEOPLE

People, people, what can we say about people?
Do you know? Who can tell about people?

Each one's so different, yet each forms the whole and
That whole's only part of another sum,
That's yours and mine and his or her sum.

People sleep at night to dream about tomorrow or yesterday
And you know we can see so far,
See it all and more, never choose not to.

People move far and further and break free from this notion
That we're only here today and gone tomorrow,
There's no hope, but amazingly believe we can achieve
And that the onus is on us and with belief we'll reach our destiny
And that's to be a witness and take control of all we see
By understanding fully minutia to eternity, for with knowledge
We will banish all inertia and accelerate away
From mediocrity, equip ourselves with clarity of mind -
All danger in perspective human hands can tell the time

Early in the morning, our days have just begun,
The children of tomorrow can face the loving sun
And gather round and gather round let everybody see
We're as great as any force, brute force can't harm humanity

We were born into the darkness, but then walked into the light
Reading meanings into nature, seeing further than the night
To demean us is pointless, turn it round and get it right
There's no end to our achievements, it's the people with the power
in this time

People, people there's only Earth and people
Every him is a brother; every her is a sister,
Moving closer together, watching out for each other
Walking into the future, greeting each new adventure.

And people seeing people, one another's
All we've got and all we're getting, in the end,
When time is done, know there's more of us to come,
From up in Heaven, new inhabitants of that emerging star
Are shining even brighter than the star that shone before

And people, in sadness but in hope!
Looking down and all around
What is this we've been put in? It
Makes us wonder what to make of it and ask him does he know?
Oh, but who could blame us,
For we the lonely, may be grown
But we're still children in our hearts.

Raymond Barber

LATCHKEY KIDS

Children of the rich and of the poor
They all belong to someone.
Each one looking for love and joy
Like any normal girl or boy.
The children home from school
Searching for Mum to talk of the day they have had
But Mum is not always there,
Putting on a smile trying to hide the disappointment they feel
In this world of material gain,
Home come the parents, children want to talk,
'No, not now dear my TV programme is due,
Go to your room and play, there's a dear!'
You parents, your child feels put out
Give some of your time and talk to your lovely children
After all they are the aftermath of your moments of love.

David Bromage

A MOTHER'S LOVE

So gentle, so mild, still nought but a child.
To be chosen was scary to the virginal Mary.
Understand it she couldn't deny it she wouldn't,
Overwhelmed by the honour of the charge laid upon her.

To Joseph then came Angel Gabriel by name,
Told him he could wed with no shame on his head.

For nine months she carried Him, her son,
In a manger laid Him, with joy overcome.
Gazed at Him lovingly, tears in her eyes,
Her breast He sucked hungrily, stilling His cries.

The years quickly passed, He grew up so fast,
Soon He would leave her, making no demur.

Her heart grew so heavy with sorrow
Knowing what would happen tomorrow.
The darkness was total, the sky rent with thunder,
'It is finished,' He cried, as the veil tore asunder.

She knew He was dead; the night was so long,
But the tomb it was empty, oh where had He gone?

They all hid away behind a locked door
Afraid of the mob and of the law.
Then their fear turned to joy and delight
When Jesus appeared in their sight.

He showed them the scars of His pain
Then they knew they would not doubt again.

They grew strong in their faith, and brave,
Still proclaiming His word to their grave.
Mary praised God for His son,
Knowing His will had been done.

Jennifer Stella Smeed

THE MEANING OF LIFE!

There's only so much in life you can learn,
From each narrow turn
We surely must learn
I never learnt
I tried but I couldn't see
The total devastation waiting for me.
Life is a lesson
Or that's why they say
But the boredom of life, just got in the way,
Too many hours, not enough time
Confusion is stressful
It spins round in my mind.
Sometimes my thoughts get out of control
But with each new day
Another story unfolds.
The things that I do
Make me who I am
That one tiny ant, running round in God's hand,
From each little corner
The difference I feel
Like skinning an orange of its orange peel
Age it comes quickly,
My bones feel it worse
Thirty-five going on sixty
What lessons have I learnt
Live life to the full,
Live it now, live it true
'Cause the meaning of life is, it won't wait for you!

Beckie Royce

THE RHYMING DOCTOR

When you're sad and downhearted
And feeling so blue
There's a small book of poetry
Waiting for you.
Just lazily browse
Through the pages awhile
And you're sure to find something
To bring you a smile.

Take a small daily dose
And I think you will find
The cares and the worries
Start slipping behind
Try Wordsworth or Brooke
Or Pam Ayres for sure
A small book of poetry
Is a wonderful cure.

Then when you feel better
And not so alone
Try penning a few simple
Words of your own
For somewhere there's someone
As lonely as you
And a happy wee verse
Can cheer others up too.

Beryl Williams

THE FORBIDDEN KINGDOM

You spoke to me of a fairytale place -
A kingdom, where rabbits reign supreme.
Visible only by night.
I took your hand with childlike enthusiasm,
Begging you to take me to this place.

Silently, expectantly, we wait -
There is nothing, only an eerie stillness.
Then as if by magic, they appear -
Rabbits
Hundreds of them, protected from man,
In the safety of this Shangri-la.

We stand enraptured -
By this nocturnal entertainment.
Unaware of the uninvited spectators,
The performers continue
Their rabbit dance, by moonlight.
We are mysteriously mesmerized.
Until, almost as if the music of the dance
Had been brought to an untimely end -
All movement stops.

They sit motionless, aware suddenly of our presence.
Hundreds of pairs of eyes stare back at us.
A menacing mist starts to rise from the river.
I clasp your hand tighter, in fear of something
Unknown to man, which would seem to exist in this place.

We are running breathless, now,
Towards our escape route.
Chased, by the invisible threat.
The road and civilization, appear before us.
The pounding of our hearts can still be heard.

'A voice would seem to speak -
Enter the Forbidden Kingdom,
At your peril!'

Nina Graham

PANDEMONIUM

I'll tell you today about the war,
No not the big one, the one in our house,
It all happened really because of a mouse.
Someone tried to hit it, but hit the tap
Out gushed the water, and filled Granny's lap.
She was shelling peas and up they went flying
All over the place, one did not know where you would find them lying!

The bowl hit the cat, who was by then wet,
Poor thing got knocked out, being old needed the vet.
For the noise he had made, we thought he was dying.
We wrapped him in a towel, to help with the drying
The mouse was still free and running around,
He was all wet and looked half-drowned.

Those trying to catch him, kept bumping together
I felt I was at the end of my tether,
What with the floor being so wet
And the water still sprouting just like a jet.
For the stopcock, it just couldn't be found.
I remembered it was buried under the mound,

Which the children had made, when friends came to play
I was going to clear it sometime today.
It would have to be now, to turn off the water,
I called to my son, and also my daughter.
As they were digging to find the stopcock
The spade broke in two, when hitting a rock.

(Oh well it was old) and just our luck
To break when most needed to move all the muck.
Then we looked up and there on the table,
Sat the mouse watching, and when we were able
To stop laughing, and clear up the mess.
It had turned out quite funny I must confess.

Phyllis Wright

UNIVERSAL TOLERANCE

As the light dims, dreams drift unbidden through my mind,
Those golden visions of the might-have-been,
Rich, joyful memories of an enchanted youth
When even the impossible appeared
To be within my grasp,
Scenes of unimagined beauty draw my phantom footsteps on;
Mountains and valleys filled with perfumes of delight;
A tumbling stream that flows with diamond droplets
Shiningly evocative of happiness and peaceful days

Oh let me sleep in ecstasy untroubled
By the savage history we're writing in this age . . .
Marvels of science bring the news
Of cruelty and death into my quiet room.
Millions of sufferers with hungry eyes and frightened children
Drag their tortured bodies awkwardly
Across the blighted plains and drive on by terror
Stagger over mountain passes
Hostile in their arid bareness,
How can the God of love and kindness
See this desperation and withhold
The power of His omnipotence
To soothe and save these hordes of anguished souls?

Dear God as I enjoy the bright light and the
Warm embrace of gentle sunshine, listen, I beg you,
To the urgent prayers that crave your intervention
To alleviate, or better still, to end this agony.
Flood the parched earth with understanding,
Fill the most evil hearts with sorrow
At the grief they cause and bring us all
The gift of universal tolerance.

Flora Hughes

THE CRYPTIC CRYSTAL

Hard, unyielding and powerful
You lie, heavy in my palm
Yet it is not cold that I feel
But a strange warmth and calm

Your harsh, flashing faces
Sparkle and repel the light
Or do they absorb mystic energy?
And hold it safe and tight

Sharp razor-like edges
Without sympathy you wield
But there's' more to you than meets the eye
In unfathomable depths concealed.

I stare at your glittering facets
Which allow me to peek inside
What enigmas do you hold within?
What secrets do you hide?

Your stony appearance belies your nature
You are only acting a part
For within your impenetrable exterior
Beats a fiery, passionate heart.

Louise Wheeler

WINDOW SEAT

As I sit alone in my window seat,
I muse on life's rich pattern,
Behind the old lace curtains
That hide the world away.
Which pattern will I choose?
The window mirrors an image, face to face.
As we really are . . .
Before we look to fault our peers,
No whitewash, no lies will hide
The foolishness of our shallow lives
To meet the future without regret, or tears,
Somewhere, there's a record of our ugly side.
As I gently let the curtain fall,
I think of the reflections through my window
Before looking through another,
And if I do . . . ?
I will be in humble humility.

Liz Dicken

HST THROUGH HUNGERFORD

Rain-sleets flow
From a sodden sky
To saturate the day.

Barriers fall and slow;
Ephemeral words in reply,
Warn, to stand clear, away

Now, from the platform edge
Where expectancy and danger lurk;
As ever, hand-in-glove.

A sullen silence hangs on that ledge;
Then breaks, all in a minute's work;
Shattered by the haul and shove

Of turbocharged power and scream,
And cold-hard metal on compressed air;
It splits the town apart,

Then fades, like a dream,
On; to a separate future, while I stare
Across these lines of force and heart.

Stephen Painting

IRELAND

Little koala,
Perched in the cold waters
Of the great Atlantic,
Bred wild, tortured in captivity,
Your fur is warm and thick.

Head and body,
Divided as mind and soul,
You clutch, and remain cluttered,
Your ancient face bares the toll.

And yet you smile,
Your laugh resonates above all,
Always little,
Forever standing tall.

Declan Mullan

TODAY

Time is of the essence, one should feel each precious day
Take note of nature's treasures freely on display
See the mountains proudly stand,
Listen to the wind, at no one's command
Watch the mighty sea as it ebbs and flows,
And the tiny stream, swiftly passing through.
Green acres and dells, ageless rocks, with stories to tell
The smell of the earth, the hush that comes when evening falls
Morning dew, that lasts no time at all
The ruffle of corn straight and gold
People old and new, with tales to be told,
Photographs to share
Look around, live for the moment,
Enjoy, have fun
There is no guarantee tomorrow will come.

I D Welch

WHERE IS WALES?

The EU ends at Offa's Dyke
The cover on its book declares,
Beyond the dyke is Heaven's own land
A land through which we send our prayers.
Come cross the dyke by nearest road -
A sign will say in Heaven's own speak
'Croeso' (Welcome) to you strangers
Who wear a daffodil or leek.
Saxons, Franks and Goths are welcome
To the land beyond the map
Where Earth and Heaven are all caught up
To close the intervening gap.

Now hear the singing of the saints
Cwm Rhondda, Blaenwern, Calon Lân,
Is it not the sound of Heaven
Which lasted since the world began?
Now cross the bridge to Mona's Isle
A breeding ground for poets rife
And note the quirky longest name,
Know you another in your life?
Then make your way to Snowdon's mount
And climb the peak. When you are there
Then feel the nearness of your God,
Tell Him the EU is just where?
So, learn the language, stay awhile
'Ere you return to EU's guile.

Owen Edwards

REFLECTION

To stand on the side of goodness,
As an act of trust.
To persevere in trying to do right.
To be kind: to keep one's heart and mind,
Open to the spirit's touch,
Perchance one is found worthy.
To have done with old hatreds and prejudices,
Is not this the nub of the matter?
If I would find a symbol,
Perhaps it might be this warm light
In the frosted grass,
Of these winter aconites
Friend what would you choose?
How travel?

J Cox

RESOURCES

A thousand ages in Thy sight
Are like an evening gone.
In the millennium must we fight
For this world to be as one?
Hedgerows gone and soil erosion
GM's fine or crop abuse?
Field tests just controlled explosion!
All can find some good excuse!
Then, will there be grass beneath our feet?
Will minds stretch out to reach the sky?
Know wayside roams to waters meet
Or watch a barn owl learn to fly?
Shall we just look so straight ahead
With prejudice and fear?
And wildlife flees from man its dread
The Good Book is quite clear,
For beauty on our planet earth
Mankind and nature must unite
Lord, guide 2000 from rebirth
Ere zero age cries out in plight.

Beryl Mapperley

CELEBRATION

August 2005 is the month for being alive,
To join in all the fun of joining words to cut and run,
For it is an anniversary of the Forward Press.
So here we are all ready to start,
Forming words together is a fine art.
An art that started long ago,
Way back when words were formed
From letters all jumbled and so
Here are a few that I hope will do
Justice to this poem all rich in verse,
And the English language which when spoken correctly,
So affectively smites the ear drums.
A pleasure to hear, so celebrate with style
For quite a while and think of all the poets you have created,
What a wonderful glorious feeling inside,
How proud you must be to look and see,
Your work all over the place,
Such a lot of people writing to celebrate,
To celebrate the birth of your verse.

Magdalene Chadwick

NATURE'S SONG

I sit and listen to nature's sounds
The song of the robin, the whispering breeze,
The rustle of leaves as they circle down
Till in heaps they lie upon the ground.

The chatter of magpies, the babbling brook,
The sharp harsh call of the black, black rook.
The call of the fox in the early dawn,
The hoot of the owl sounds so forlorn.

Spring into summer blends
The babbling brook on its way it wends
Through meadows lush and fields of grain
Welcoming the clouds that bring the rain,

The squirrels swing through the trees once more
Gathering food for their winter store.
Gaily the stream goes babbling along
Joining in on nature's song.

Marjorie Poyner

IF ONLY

Some attempts are pretty dire
Some of these - you can, admire
Some mimic McGonagall at his best
Leaving you, laughably depressed.

Some turn of Milliganesque
That would leave John Lennon - distressed
Or would have Master Will - turn in his grave
Or make the Marquis DeSade - even more depraved.

Some would make Oscar 'Wilde'
That anyone could conceive - such a child
I feel that there is a Thomas Hardy verse, deep inside
Oh to create another Frankenstein's bride!

It makes my quill - tremble at the thought
To uncover some epic ode - I had long sought
But alas - shock - horror - dismay, this
Like Long John Silver's treasure - remains, buried away.

Perhaps a Sir Galahad - venturing on a dragon quest
At some fair maiden's - request
Will gallop his way - onto this poet's page
Will prevent me - strangling my typewriter - in lack of inspirational rage.

Rod Palmer

TIME

Time lays a carpet behind the 'Now',
Only heads turned to the past
Can comprehend the pattern,
For 'Now' covers the form with clutter
Of little anxieties,
And forward faces peering at tomorrow
Lose the coherence of the whole.
Promises are hopeful buds,
But only in the past
Unfold their secret petals
To exude in memory
Their fragrant atmosphere
'Now' lives.
But in a line of indefinable narrowness
Blurring in its unmeasurable hurry
The present reality
Slips like quicksilver
Through the fingers of my sluggish mind;
The only real to me,
Lives in memory.

John Parry

HOLIDAY MEMORIES
BU-BU-IS CHIHUAHUAS!

Away on our annual holiday we all go,
But who will be there we don't know.
Meet some new friends or some old,
We go back because on Chihuahuas we are sold!

From behind the bar we see his beaming smile,
'Hello my friends it's been a long while.'
With his rounded belly and his big hat,
You can't beat a greeting like that.

To all the good looking ladies,
You hear him say, 'Will you have Bu-Bu's babies?'
You ask him for a coffee and what do you get
'Anything in Spain is possible, did you forget?'

We ask him for a drink to take away,
And he replies, 'Special price for you today.'
We offer him a drink, and what does he say,
'First drink, in this glass today!'

Bu-Bu is of course his name,
And year after year he remains the same!
'Peanuts for the monkeys,' we hear him say,
As he puts a dish down and walks away!

'For my children, for my new house,'
He'll soon be saying it to someone else.
'The bar is open,' we hear him say,
'Sorry the sun in Florida today.'

It's raining outside, so in the bar we sit down,
Is that a cockerel? No, it's Bu-Bu being a clown!
He always seems happy, and never sad,
Thank you Bu-Bu for the lovely holiday we've had!

It's time now for us to go home and say farewell,
With tears in his eyes Bu-Bu says, 'Are you not well?'
With a big cuddle and a shake of his hand,
We leave Spain and return to our homeland!

Dereck Palmer

DON'T CRY . . .

Don't cry because you can no longer see
The outer shell that you thought of as me.
There's nothing to fear,
I'm standing so near,
And only my costume has ceased to be.

The dreaming starts at the moment of birth,
This complex drama we act out on earth.
The show does go on
Long after we're gone,
Tragedies, comedies, sorrow and mirth.

I'm right by your side and holding your hand,
The weaker you feel, the closer I'll stand.
Whatever you do,
My soul's there for you
With love infinite as the sea and the sand.

I am part of every breath that you take,
My voice is heard in the music you make.
Others' eyes may show
A smile that you know,
Bonds of laughter and love that death cannot break.

Don't weep at the turning of every page,
Time has no meaning when we leave the stage.
Let comfort be found,
Believe I'm around,
Spirits together through every age.

Gabrielle Gascoigne

EMILY

Such beauty I'd not seen before
Deaf and blind and so much more.
Yet in that child was a holy flame
From her peace and tranquillity came.
Her visit to our grey world was short
In her presence humility was taught.
To step from God's garden for a while
To give peace with her gentle smile.
The child was full of heavenly grace
Our world could never be her place.
The beauty of Emily will never fade
By her touch calm and peace was made.
Yes Emily was to pass away
She had to go she could not stay
At nine years old she said goodbye
And was gone like a beautiful butterfly.

Mary Long

FROM MARS TO EARTH THE FINAL
DESTINATION

Mars used to be a beautiful planet
But the inhabitants ruined it, dam it
They were not interested in the planet's health
Only making money and earning wealth,

They extracted all its minerals, oils, fossils fuels
As well as all its diamonds and precious jewels
Now you look up to the stars to see what looks like a red planet
This is what its inhabitants done to it, dam it.

We have a beautiful planet; look what's happening to ours
Did they planet hop to come to live on ours?
We have problems with our ozone layer
Are they doing it to ours what they have done to theirs?

Think of all the reasons why the space station is there
And what is happening quickly around us here and there
Has our world a future or is it now too late?
Will it be the Martians who decide our fate?

Allan Joseph Smith

PATHETIC FALLACY

Standing alone in an open field
Breeze teasing the dry blades of grass
That dance around me
And tickle my calves

On my own in an empty field
Starting at the shadow trees
That stretch before me
And into a closet forest

A path winds through the roots
That writhe across the ground
And over mounds to trick and trip me
And cover my face in dirt

Kneeling down beside a sliver
Of a river, home to stones
My reflection ripples up at me
And doesn't meet my eye

The endless blue sky has dived
And vanished into the water
The cotton wool clouds gone -
The sky is only dark.

Carly Bareham

WAR AND ME

'The war has begun, the war has begun.'
I shout, scream and cry to my mum.
'Why did it happen? I don't want to go.'
But my dad tells me the things I should know.
'Tonight you'll pack a suitcase with your gas mask in a box,
You can take some food, a drink and even your little toy fox.
Then Gracie and you will meet at school and travel out of town,
Because you'll be safe from guns and bombs without
                                    hearing a sound.'
'Mum, Dad, do you love me? Or is that why you're sending us away?
Because I don't want to go, please can I stay?'
'We don't want to leave you, but all you need is love,
So every night when you're away, pray to God up above.'

My sister and I live away we have no more fears,
But every day without my mum and dad I cry many tears.
I really miss my family, my home and my friends,
And one day I know that this awful war will end.

The war has ended, hip, hip, hooray,
I'm glad my mum told me to pray.
As I come home to see my mum and dad
I see my mum's face looking awfully sad.
I run over and she kisses my cheek,
She is thin, bony, pale and weak.
Then suddenly she tells me my dad has died,
The house has been bombed and we sat down and cried.
Why did this happen? My dad is not here,
Tears fall down my face, he was so dear.
Then I think to myself, what was this fighting for?
Because this hatred, lead to a brutal war.

Helen Towner

SOULFUL BROWN EYES

Capering over the mud splattered path,
Joyously snuffling the decaying tawny leaves
The dog is at one with itself and the universe.
A large, slimy puddle beckons enticingly,
Yielding to temptation without a qualm
The mischievous canine plunges into the ooze.
Reluctantly obeying his owner's whistle,
The begrimed dog runs towards her
Generously sharing his coat's filthy cargo.
The words of irritation die on her lips
When confronted by a pair of
Soulful brown eyes.

Rose-Mary Gower

THIS GIFT

He knew that I was hurting,
Somewhere deep inside.
Said that he felt the tears,
I have silently cried
'I'll catch you,' he said,
When he knew that I would fall.
I'll be here beside you
To help you through it all.
I'll be here to listen,
To all you have to say.
Let my love enfold you,
In the darkest hour of day.
Call me when you're lonely,
When your heart fills with despair.
Take this gift of friendship,
And know I'll always care.'

Deanna Dixon

THE MIRACLE

I saw this lovely flower,
Sprouting from the ground.
It really was a miracle,
For guess where it was found?
Not in a beautiful garden,
Or a colourful flower bed.
But amongst a rubbish tip
Was a lovely shade of red.

Everything near was colourless,
Dirty and smelly too.
But then I saw the flower,
What a fantastic hue.
I wondered how it got there.
Was it from a seed?
Maybe a bird dropped it,
Whilst it was having a feed.

No matter how it got there
Amongst the rubbish tip.
It made a colourful display,
Where the flower now sits.
So if you think your life is dull,
Just take a look around.
See if you can find a flower
Sprouting from the ground.

Just think about that flower
He is now alone,
Among the dirt and rubble,
It's not really his home.
So, if you have a problem,
And don't know what to do.
Find a lovely flower,
And thank God that it's not you.

Doreen E Hampshire

AUTUMN TIME

Birds merrily singing in chorus in the silent early morn,
Chirping and chirruping tuneful melodies, as a new day is born.

Length of days now shortening, shrouded in mists and autumn dew,
Dancing and swaying autumn leaves,
Rising, drifting as light winds blew,
Fluttering and with freedom and ease
As they fall, creating a richly woven tapestry
Reflecting the beauty of creation,
In nature's adorning finery.

The warmth of summer recedes, gives way to the autumnal
                                    cooling air,
The beauty of the season there to ponder, reflect and share.

New term begun anew, back to school children wend their way,
Chattering, hopping, teasing, laughing, sharing memories
                                    of their holiday.
Tales of visits to parks, or zoos, or of playing on the local sands,
Others telling of adventures having flown to far off lands.

Like the birds in the trees, we can find a song to sing,
Listen for the laughter of children, the sweet joy it can bring.
The gentleness of autumn can brighten each and every day,
Reminding us of the beauty in each other as we travel
                                    along life's pathway.

Terry Gilvin

THE END

Staring across a luminous landscape
Senses beating in time with a chill breeze
Icy waves leave the shore
Winter descends and bolts summer's door
Forever.

Falling, falling

Spinning in a whirling void
Stranded in unexplored space
But where exactly am I?
At the heart of the big bang
Or just drifting in time.

Falling, falling

Blackness surrounds me
Pushing, dragging, suffocating
Sudden, piercing flash explodes around me
Too close, but I can't turn away
Body ensnared, ready to implode
Thoughts reach out and claw at the unknown.

Falling, falling

How far to go?
Corona winks at me
An eclipse splits in two
As I look down
At my life's review.

Falling, falling

Maybe I need a spiral shroud
To cover me and point me in the right direction
Time shudders and stumbles to a halt
As I am catapulted into another dimension
And reach the end of organic ingenuity.

Andrew Ryan

TOO LATE?

Where will I go next?
I'm confused and alone
I've no more a place
I can call home
There's nobody here
That I recognise
Just crowds of people
With tear-stained eyes
I never did listen
To the warnings I'd heard
I was told what would happen
But I wasn't scared
I never believed
That Jesus would come
Just in a moment
To take Christians home
But I found out the hard way
That it was all true
And I realise now
There's nothing I can do
I just can't escape it
And whatever my fate
It's all my own fault
I left it too late!

Ruth Connolly

TEARS FOR RWANDA

Our bones lay bleached upon the ground
The birds don't sing, there is no sound.
You were our neighbours and our friends
What evil brought this terrible end?
But when you shut your eyes at night
Sleep doesn't come, only terrible sights.

Our pain has now gone away,
You have to live with yours every day.
The world just turned its back on us,
And now we crumble in the dust
As horror filled those terrible days
All we could do was cry and pray.

Cathie Booth

FOOTPRINTS

Footprints,
In the sand, in the street,
In our life,
Normally tell a tale
Of where we've been,
Of where we've come from,
More often than not I'm proud,
Some might brush away the mark
With a sweeping hand
As not to be reminded,
Of a dark event or two,
But me,
I'm English . . . no, I'm British,
And once again . . . I'm proud,
So let the footprints lay,
For all to see,
In the sand, in the street,
In our life, in our country.

Chris Silvester

RAIN ON DRACUS

I sheltered beneath the large beech tree
That grew on the steep, now muddy hill
Running down from the village road
The tree and I now stand together on Dracus.
As her dripping curtain shields I remember
This is where I lived long childhood days
I wait in silent dreams from yesterday.
At last the pouring rain has spent
Its drenching torrents
Now quenching the dry, thirsty ground
Of this receding summer's day
Closing itself in creeping darkness
Musty in the steaming undergrowth.
I look up at the tree to watch
Large water droplets fall
Cascading through the beech tree leaves
Good timing Mother Nature
You meant that drop to refresh my face.
Cows moo in relief, steaming off
The trickling wetness of
Irritating rain meandering through short hair
Skin annoyed now on passive animals.
Dusk, and blotchy cowhides move in greyness
Along a mysterious bushy Dracus lane, and on
To mill around the witch's stone
Spookily stood in the fairies field
I too am home, cowslips to pick tomorrow.

Susan Carole Gash-Roberts

IMAGINATION

As I sit here on my balcony
Gazing out across the sea
I can imagine so many different places
Many cultures breeds and races
I don't need to take a plane that flies
All I have to do is close my eyes
My mind will take me where I want to be
So take my hand and come with me

First stop Cairo with cabal bars
We'll ride on camels, visit street bazaars
Cyprus on those moonlit nights
Beautiful sunsets, rapturous sights
Singapore with crowded streets
Rickshaw rides in sultry heat
Corfu and Crete, the isles of sun
Surfing, sailing, oh such fun

Italy, a touch of Heaven
Means that you'll be surely driven
To want to return to those beautiful lakes
Caldero and Garda what pictures make
Those awesome dolomite mountains, so high
That they magically merge into the sky
Then we are on that London bound plane
To theatres, Kew Gardens and Petticoat Lane

All those places your mind can see
That it's almost like reality
Open your eyes and we're right back there
To a star spangled sky so dreamy and clear.

Sandie

FOR ETERNITY

As we irrational mortals trudge through life;
We must face many a trouble; many a strife.
We ask many unanswerable questions;
Most of which originate from doubtful notions!
I cannot stand questions such as these;
And they're as irritating as a complicated weave.
Is the big bang theory plausible; or did we merely originate
                                        from the sea?
Or perhaps there is in fact a God and is it a he or a she?
Is there such a thing as a miracle?
And do I have the right to be cynical?
But despite all my doubts; I do believe one thing;
Something of which softens this life; and makes it embellishing.
We all shall face that terrible pain; one of which is inescapable;
To lose one so dear; the anguish is so palpable.
But fear not those who mourn,
For you must remain strong; even though you feel torn!
We will lose our lovers, our siblings; our father and our mother;
We may feel they have left us forever.
But the truth is they are merely waiting for us;
Whether it be in the next life, or in the heavens above.
Forget those stressful questions and notions;
As all that really matters are those with whom we share our devotion!
We must learn to cherish our mortal existence;
As our end is not too far in the distance.
Enjoy your life on Earth while you still can
For it is not too long before you body shall rejoin the land.
But you shall awaken once again by the sensation of love,
And rejoin those you hold dear in another life; or in heavens above.
We should cherish life; however short it may be,
As we have plenty of time to spend with those we love;
                                        for the rest of eternity.

L Barnes

NINKATY-NOO

In the land of Ninkaty-Noo
Where girls are pink and boys are blue
Where birds ride cycles and cats drive cars
There's moonbeams dancing around the stars
That's when I stop and think of you
When I wander into Ninkaty-Noo

Ninkaty-Noo is my special place
Where I sit and imagine your smiling face
Where rhinos sing songs and hippos too
Now you know I'm in Ninkaty-Noo

Take my hand and I'll take you there
To my special world without a care
Where flowers sway to a disco beat
And snowflakes dance in the summer heat
Now let us see what we can do
In my land of Ninkaty-Noo

Lisa Harper-Gough & Steve Wickens

UNION

There is a door
And it opens
Before.
I stand
And insert the key -
A talisman -
And it takes me
To thee -
At the house at the edge
Of green sea
That swirls
Beneath
The arch of the castle
Of Cornwall at Tintagel
Where we live
With Magdalene and Jesus
In harmony
In perfect matrimony.

Louise Pringle

QUESTIONS

How could Christ come to dwell on Earth
Stooping to such a lowly birth?
How could He leave that heavenly throne,
With only a stable for His home?
How could He come from the Father's side,
Finally to be crucified?
How could He bear to dwell below?
Only because He loved us so.

How could He live with sinful man?
Because He was willing to meet God's plan.
The word became flesh, for all to behold,
His perfect life on Earth unfold.
How could He bring us back to God?
Redemption's pathway He alone trod.
His glory shone, that all may see,
In Him, God's love and purity.

How can we comprehend such grace?
By faith look upward, into His face,
And know the peace that He can bring,
When He is accepted as Saviour and king.
So praise His name, because He came,
In willing hearts to live and reign,
Rejoice again this Christmas time
And honour the Babe, as our Lord divine.

E Phillis

JACARANDA BLOSSOMS

On this hot summer's afternoon,
As the cool breeze filtered through the huge jacaranda trees,
Fern-like leaves rustled, sending showers of a colourful array,
Violet, blue and purple blossoms fell like confetti to the ground,
Lining the streets and pavements,
A romantic setting for sure!
Beneath the trees expressionless faces wondered,
Secretly, hoping to catch a blossom or two.
For as the tale goes, catch a blossom and make a wish,
For it might just come true.
It's an adventure for young, spirit-filled people,
Fantasising about a dream.
Just like those dreamy shampoo adverts
Running amongst a carpet full of cool, bell-like flowers,
Tossing them into the air.
It felt like paradise.
Then, 'Cut!' A rumbling from above.
The heavens opened and blessed the land,
It's the late afternoon showers.
A beautiful mass of colour converged together,
Flowing like a meandering stream.
All was not lost for tomorrow would be another day.
A dream embarked upon a season never to forget.
It's time for seeds to glide with the wind,
Anchor and nestle amongst earthy shades of autumn,
Finding nourishment and protection from those chilly winter months.
Spring would bring life again,
Reaching far beyond our wildest dreams.
A tree blowing in the breeze,
Watching, yet another tale,
Bringing joy to the moments of summer.
Life's little treasures.
A season for all.

Nadine Mackie

THE FREE SPIRIT - YOU

For whom am I weeping?
It is surely for me,
When I recall yourself lying tired and weary,
I shall try not to be selfish and weep for me.

Instead,
Beyond the mists of despair and pain,
Distinctly I see you
Beautifully strong again,
Determined, resolute, racing around,
Physically, mentally, covering ground,
I shall try not to weep but recall you sound.

Countless happy times and laughter we shared,
The numbers who loved you;
Really cared,
Who looked forward to hearing
Your good sense and droll humour,
Without patience to listen, to gossip or rumour,
I shall try not to weep but remember your summer.

So many have used the same word 'special'
Above other folk,
Unusual, especial,
An envious legacy,
Joyous mem'ries too,
I shall try not to weep knowing God released you,
To become a free spirit,
Rendezvous with real you,
The one and only we all loved and knew.

Hilary Jill Robson

IN TOUCH

Tourism is a touching experience.

A group with the tenuous link
Of choosing alike
Spend time together, coaching and being coached
Their rippling life circles touch briefly
They will not keep in touch.
But day by day, they
Build a holiday together
Linked by those limited times
Spent, scattered through towns
Following guides through galleries
Discussing the weather and
Families left behind.

The guided tour.
We hang on every word
Snap cameras when instructed
Keep to the strict timetable.
In time allowed
By guide and driver
We discover for ourselves
Places romanticised in picture and in history
But time allowed is short
'You have fifteen minutes . . . '
'No time to go inside . . . '
'Make sure you're back on time . . . '

Not enough time for the longed for exploration
Not enough time to climb or wander
Just enough time to cross the road
And *touch*

It is a kind of compensation
An aide memoir
A link with past creators.
Roughness of stone
Coolness of slate and marble
Weathered and worn with age,
Surfaces of history.

How many and whose other hands have touched
And felt as I?
That special momentary touch
Bringing a sense of communication
A sense of satisfaction
A touching experience.

Margaret Wallace

DREAMERS

Oh Isabel, sweet Isabel
My beautiful Queen of Spain
You came to me at moonlight
And the world was young again.
The night was filled with passion
Your lips so soft and warm,
But alas for lonely dreamers
I awoke and you were gone!

My life is cold and lonely,
Each day so dark and drear,
My heart yearns for the dreamtime
When you, my love, are near.
Come back to me my Isabel
Come back to me once more,
Bring warmth and love and passion
And stay for evermore.

A E Garrod

NARCISSUS

One of a host,
Without conceit would tell,
Of its six petal star,
Behind a gold trumpet and bell.

One of a mass,
Would extol its fluted,
Corrugated rim,
On the horn, quite muted.

Did Dorothy squeal in delight,
Descending on that collected, magical sight?
Thus prompting her brothers,
Hidden prose to flight.

One on a stem would vie to be,
The pride of the blooms,
Swell that majestic head,
And emanate, intoxicant, sweet perfumes.

So did William really stare
At that crowd of yellow,
And golden glare,
. . . Beside the lake?

K W Parker

THE PALM TREE

The palm tree stands tall, magnificent,
Its strength and stature, lovely to see,
As we look up, it's likened to our Lord
Steadfast, strong and growing beautifully.

Always there even in the wilderness,
To shelter from, to comfort, to feed,
Those who seek help and guidance
The palm, like God, strength in need.

In distant lands they used it in design
For followers visiting the temple.
Who would come to love this beautiful tree
To see its strength, to share its example.

Oh Lord, dear Lord, how we love Thee!
Help us like the palm to be strong.
Upright in our lives, an example to others
Giving and sharing love, all our days long
Amen.

A Pincombe

A SUMMER EVENING

Birds dipping and weaving, in a cloudless sky.
Soft breezes, rippling through the trees,
A lonely seagull - with a plaintive cry.
An old man gardening on his knees.
The buzzy bees, darting from flower to flower.
Working so hard - afraid to waste a minute.
Must be so tired, in this their final hour.
Pollen drenched, they now may rest, this is their limit.
The sun will very soon be out of sight.
Leaving the earth, dry, hard and warm.
Soon the evening and gradual fading light
Will cool my hot and weary form.
I sit now upon my garden seat.
Refreshed and cooled, in this calm night air
Amid the borders, blooms seem to compete,
With fragrances and myriad hues, beyond compare
I thank the Lord for giving me this day.
For the wondrous privilege to behold
The miracle of life that will forever stay
Our Maker's gift of beauty, thus bestowed.

M F Williams

ST VALENCIENNES VALENTINE 1918

I fell in a septic sea of mud
Drowning as the sun my face deserted
My eyes sealed ears deaf to thee
Winter hands my bones now caress
No sweetheart embrace in this lonely hall
We stand erect and face the stars
Numbered by stone in still eternity
Forgotten as my valentine's kiss.

James P O'Keeffe

FORWARD AND PRESS

Forward, forward, forward ever
Backward, backward, backward never
Promoters of arts are minimal
On the coast of arts' ocean,
Countless sculptors and painters
Uncountable wordetchers and wordweavers
Amidst wordsmiths on the shore of arts
Had extinct their sacred count
Since their imaginations are not appreciated
But Forward Press acutely persisted
On assisting and appreciating
Arts through her branches of imprints,
Poetry Now publishes poetry
For the pleasure of the people,
Anchor Books publishes poetry
By the people; for the people,
Spotlight Poets promotes poets
Truly through their poetry,
Whilst WomensWords wages war
Against the mutilation of women's right
Via publishing WomensWords,
Triumph House, New Fiction and StrongWords
Also are imprints of Forward Press
Firmly stand in the *Commercial Art City*,
Peterborough in the United Kingdom
Dominant of Remus exotic House.

Aderemi Adegbite

MAKING RIPPLES

You dropped a pebble into a pool
And watched those circles start
Then from one small centre it opened up
Just like our hearts.

These circles they multiply
Into many, many others,
It's like the efforts to the poor
Our sisters and brothers.

These ripples stretch across boundaries
As we all join hand in hand,
Making friendships work by giving
Throughout God's magical lands.

Feed the children, stop this hunger,
Make of it what it ought to be,
They are pining watch them dying,
Look into their eyes and see.

Drop those pebbles of heavenly goodness
Into God's open-ended pond,
Making, many, many ripples,
To help all those of whom we can.

M Joseph

ONE OF MILLIONS

The ground, where I stand,
Is the bed, where I sleep,
And the roof, I call home,
Is a blue plastic sheet.
Plastic that once,
Held a package or two,
The sort that was sent,
From a store, just for you.

The water, I drink,
I get from a stream,
Where cattle once wallowed,
Mosquitoes now teem,
The water that once,
Was so clear and so deep,
Squelches with mud,
Barely covers my feet.

The food, that I find,
Doesn't come every day,
For I'm not always quick,
If a rat runs my way.
A rat, that is looking,
To eat, just like me,
They've a right to be living,
A life; hunger free.

When did I last eat,
A three course meal?
For me, that's a dream,
It's a vision; unreal,
It's a thought, that I hold,
When I try to sleep,
And the corn that I planted,
I pray I will reap.

And the mounds of earth,
Down there, by the tree,
Are the graves of those,
Once my family.
They're all dead now,
Leaving me all alone,
Don't let my life end,
As just skin and just bone.

Leslie F Higgins

ENDINGS

It's the lucky one who doesn't have to die alone
Cloistered in a lonely bed
 - Thrown, like bones, to the gods of war
Led like a lamb, by the hand of man
To a leafy lane where a life is wrung to its close.
It's the lucky one who passes plain
And full of grace
 - Who has the spell of love
To help him look Death in the face.
But, what of the one who cries in fear
 - Who reaches for a kindly hand
When none is near?
Who helps the timid, quailing soul
To face what the brave call glory?
Pah! It's only a story!
There is only the hellish dying inch by inch
In pallid rooms and leafy lanes
 - Or a savage smiting in some foreign land!
The dreams of gods demand a death
Yet fail to look yours in the eye.
All turn away their knowing face
 - Withhold their saving hand.

Barbara J Mitchell

ROCK 'N' ROLL SESTINA

When Bert got fed up delivering coal,
Which served just to save him from drawing the dole,
He felt his life was in a bit of a hole,
He didn't seem really to have any goal
So one night, he chanced it, and off quietly stole,
To try to become a star of rock 'n' roll.

He knew not the first thing about rock 'n' roll,
His only experience was delivering coal,
So into a Soho coffee bar he stole,
He felt he could earn more than drawing the dole,
So rock 'n' roll stardom became his new gaol,
It seemed many parts went to make up the whole.

The coffee bar seemed like a bit of a hole,
But the place was alive, throbbing with rock 'n' roll,
It seemed the place to start achieving his goal,
To get him away from delivering coal,
And obviate the need to start drawing the dole,
Make a fortune, and buy his girl a nice mink stole.

She'd look such a treat in a furry mink stole,
And his life would no longer be in a hole,
And he wouldn't need to sign on for the dole,
If a rock 'n' roll star was to be his new role,
So much more prestigious than working with coal,
And all this for just aiming at a new goal.

So just 'cos he needed to find a new goal,
Away from his former profession he stole,
So as not to spend many years just humping coal,
And sinking into an unspeakable hole,
He elected to try his hand at rock 'n' roll,
To avoid the need for signing on for the dole.

There wasn't much future in drawing the dole,
Any more than there was in delivering coal,
There's much more prestige when you sing rock 'n' roll,
Which is why quick away from his old past he stole,
To avoid a life spent being stuck in a hole,
He set out his plans to achieve his new goal.

If the goal in your life's to get out of a hole,
And you don't want to hump coal or sign on the dole,
There'll always be someone to say that you stole
If you strum a guitar and you sing rock 'n' roll.

Mick Nash

THE MIST AROUND THE MOON

She emerges through the dawning
Like a gossamer of old
With the gentle breeze caressing
Through her shimmering hair of gold

And she trails her whispering colours
From the palettes of her youth
Like the everlasting flowers
That recall such days of truth

She can drift across the seasons
Till the fields are white with frost
On the edges of those visions
Where the borderlines are lost

But her eyes still hold their beauty
Though her features fade so soon
As they melt into a mem'ry
Of the mist around the moon.

David Gasking

Two Worlds Collide

They came, we witnessed; oh how they conquered
Seducing minds and hearts too long blinkered
Vulnerable youth, Africa's tomorrow
Ambassadors foregoing their sorrow
Children bridging a gap between nations
Their faith a rainbow of inspiration.

Third World with a generation purged
By AIDS the twentieth century scourge
Leaving children orphaned before their time
To hunger resigned - a sad pantomime.
Images washing over TV screens
In denial we blank out the scenes
Famine, drought - nature's criminality
First Worlds' denial of reality
Rejecting our impotent helplessness
Too little too late, situation hopeless.

Air palpable with poignant hopefulness
Beguiling eyes belying deep sadness
Youthful faces alight with optimism
Sweet young voices spanning a chasm
Stunned audience rise in acclamation
Homage for talented delegation
Rising above their country's privation
Tentative steps towards countries salvation

Ashamed we rush home to hug close our own
Thanking God such horror they've never known
Mindful every three seconds a black child dies
Of dehydration under blazing skies.

Kathleen Potter

Blessed Earth

Extremities stripped to an icy glare,
The land of dreams is falling,
And written in the passing air,
Landmarks devoured in mourning,

Aplomb the world for all its contempt,
Against mankind's plea of peace,
And fallen soldiers on a land of resent,
As into the air fly our tempted geese,

The moon is rising from our dusty wells,
Refracted glow from the god of night,
And witches reach out with candid spells,
Beneath the veil of the morning light,

Peaceful revolt in the eye of the storm,
Sailed vessels prominently rising,
And a disguised peace in winter is born,
For summer's sand is slowly dying,

The dreams of man whittle away,
In the salty air above the sea,
And the cliffs of beauty die not fray,
As the gods rise in a tender degree,

The whitewash climbs above our eyes,
As the smell of summer falls below us,
And once our cliffs get crucified,
No gravity will spare the buried dust,

Floating hopes and dreams devour,
The aching rights of yesterday's plight,
And we may fall from hour to hour,
With an army that has no power to fight,

Among the fallen dust angels will rise,
Like the waters that used to evaporate,
And blessed earth will crucify,
All those that changed its fate.

Paul David Dawson

Spring

Spring! She is the season in two parts
The growing seed - the purest heart.
The vital grain that ever feeds
The earth and all mankind's new needs.

Alive and potent, yet so mild
She gently nurtures nature's child
The corn, the wheat, the fruit and flowers
She endows with all her powers.

Yet soon she will just fade away
Deep underground her past to play,
She procreates with every breath
Goddess of generation and death.

M P Johnson

One Smile, That Smile

One smile from those deep, dark sensuous
And enticing puppy dog eyes.

One smile, so powerful and all becoming,
So beautiful, tender and enriching.

One smile to turn a dull, cloudy and rainy day
To warm sunshine and blue skies.

One smile is all it takes to make life seem so precious,
So special, so worthwhile.

Oh, how I miss that stunning smile, once seen daily,
But then my love departed for pastures new.

Since then, that smile has eluded me for too long
And the memory is slowly fading away.

I would travel for hundreds, thousands of miles,
North, south, east or west, love knows no bounds,
For just one glimpse of that smile.
Oh that smile, that smile

So, just name the time and place, my love, and I will be there . . .

Nash

The Old School Gate

Standing at the old school gates taking in the view
The years have passed on by, yet nothing here seems new.
Closing my eyes for a moment I can sense the classroom smell
Letting my mind drift back I remember those days too well.
The best years of my life my mum would always say
How long before I realised, it really was that way?

How I loathed all the homework, the uniform, the rules,
Looking back they helped to give me life's most useful tools.
I learnt to share, to stand my ground. I learnt how to compete,
Inside those gates I learnt to fight, I learnt to take defeat.
I learnt to work, to concentrate to go out and to win
I learnt that going forward was never giving in.

Inside those gates I learnt to love as only teenagers do,
I learnt that teenage hearts can easily be broken in two.
I remember the first boy who took me on a date
Meeting me at half past three, outside this very gate.
True love, I gave my heart, I knew what it all meant
Two months later I realised, my heart was only lent.

Standing here I watch all the children running past
I want to stop and tell them this time just will not last.
Life moves on so fast our world is spinning on
Blink twice and you'll find your teenage years are gone
Into adulthood and its worries, you'll find it's all too late
Waiting for your children outside the old school gate.

Zenda Madge

SWEET DREAMS

I have a super mobile phone
That will not let me be alone.
I lost instructions that I had
And now the thing drives me mad.
It rings to tell me I may snooze
When I'm about to watch the news.
I go to bed to rest my head
And all I get is noise instead.
Music is what it is called
Their voices should be overhauled.
A lullaby by Brahms, it seems
Would send me to the land of dreams
Or walk with Straus in a Vienna wood
This I know would do me good.
So rearrange your programme, make it a success
Then my night's sleep would not be in a mess.

Herdis Churchill

THE LEGACY OF WAR

The legacy of war -
Is that you see no more
The ones you loved.

Sent to a foreign land,
Uniformed - gun in hand.
Licensed to kill.

You hate the foreign land
And now with pen in hand;
Write 'I'll be home.'

But then a sniper's gun,
Gives you no time to run
Shelter or hide..

Too true - you'll soon be home.
Dead - and no more to roam
The killing fields.

Elwynne

WHAT IS A MARRIAGE, WHAT DOES IT MEAN?

What is a marriage, what does it mean?
A marriage is two people bound together by their love
It is giving one to another unconditionally
And trusting that someone will always be there
To wipe away the tears when they fall
Marriage does not always run smoothly
But a love that's strong will hold together in the hard times
And be magical in the good ones
It is being able to forgive and not bear grudges
And always saying 'we' instead of 'I'
Knowing what the other is thinking by just the look on their face
A gentle smile that says, 'I love you' without uttering a word
It is arms holding one another, reassuring and safe
And gentle kisses out walking in the summer rain
Laughing at silly things, little jokes only you both can understand
Being in a world all of your own
Where nothing else matters except being together
But most important of all marriage is a partnership
Sealed with a kiss and a band of gold
May your marriage and the love you feel for each other today
Grow with each passing year to become
What marriage means for both of you.

Jacqui Watson

YOU HAVE BEEN CHOSEN

(This poem was written for my special friend, Brenda, at the beginning of her battle with cancer. After a short, courageous struggle, she lost the fight, so these words are dedicated to her memory)

You have been chosen;
there is no prize,
no great surprise.

You have been chosen;
you have no voice,
no other choice.

You have been chosen;
you are the one,
dusted and done.

You have been chosen;
no reason and no rhyme,
it is your time.

You have been chosen;
your spirit's strong,
you've done no wrong.

You have been chosen;
there is no fete,
no grand debate.

You have been chosen;
you can fight,
He'll see you right.

You have been chosen;
lovely, inspirational you,
you will win through.

Angela R Davies

UNWANTED GIFTS

Friends seek for gifts more suitable,
For my advancing age.
And so I'm given cardigans
Of baby blue and beige.

I get teacups labelled 'Grandma'
With sugar bowl and jug.
But I have to say, this grandma,
Would prefer a funky mug.

They aim to make me happy
With some soap-upon-a-rope.
But the thing I've always wanted
Is a kid's kaleidoscope.

I'd like drawing books and pencils
In a psychedelic case.
And a set of water colours
Would put a smile upon my face.

Bed socks and carpet slippers,
Might be suitable and cosy.
But some technicolor make-up
Would keep me colourful and rosy.

Those chocolates bought at Christmas
Don't sit well upon the hips.
I'd prefer some Jelly Babies,
And those fizzy Sherbet Dips.

But perhaps it's time to settle down,
To do just what I'm told.
Time to wear those fluffy slippers,
And disgracefully grow old!

Marie Gray

VICTIM OF ANTI-SOCIAL BEHAVIOUR

I want them to know what they're doing to me
The pain, the suffering, the hell, can't they see?
They dish it out both day and night
I dread the dark, I dread the light.
Please make them stop.
Please make it abate.

They have no respect for their fellow human being,
They torment, intimidate,
Normal life they negate.

It's been three long years, this merciless campaign
Of verbal abuse and derogatory claims,
Of footballs raining on my car,
Swearing at me and calling me names.
Hammering my door and false accusations,
I want my life back
It has to stop.

Parental responsibility is visibly absent
Children learn by example, that is apparent
Anti-social behaviour is the end result.

They're out of control,
They do not care
Not one iota, about anyone, anywhere.

They will not break me.
They will not succeed.
They will not drive me away
I am here to stay.

Judith Aubrey

THE OLD MULBERRY TREE

If only I could be there again,
Dreaming, while plaiting a daisy chain!
Under shade of that old mulberry tree
Oh so long ago, now only a memory.

Steamy summer days were spent dreaming,
Watching the swallows fly by, so low.
In the distance children screaming!
The meadow, a shimmering green glow
Dotted with daisies, a most beautiful scene,
Muffled cowbells in the distance, so serene!

That old tree, stood proudly up high,
On a riverbank, as if to pierce the sky.
The lazy river flowing gracefully with its tide
Quietly meandering through the countryside.

Balmy days were spent, idling in its shade
Watching the pink flamingo wade
Through mudflats, uphill, on meadow to graze
As time stood still, like lost in a maze.

Sailing yachts on the river, passing each other
Lazily stirring the water causing it to ripple
Exchanging greetings and the odd tipple!

Listening to frogs croak, the reeds sway
Swallows darting, flamingos flying away,
Here, swans were leaping, causing a splash
All competing for their daily food to catch.

I often wonder, if that old tree still stands,
Up so high on the beautiful river bank?
So gracefully giving shelter and shade
To any passing stranger, daring to invade,

A most wonderfully serene place on Earth
Forever a treasured memory, deep in my heart!

Anna Elliott

MR BONE, THE BAKER

Jump on the bus straight after school
How far has he got - the lovable fool!
There's the cart, with Billy feeding
From his nosebag, gently swinging

I hear Mr Bone, he's laughing with glee
Having delivered the bread, it's time for tea.
Billy and I begin to move on
We know the round and it's very long.

Fill my basket with all sorts of things
White, brown and black bread and bun rings
Seeded rolls, cakes, so many kinds
It doesn't matter; we've left baker behind!

Take what you fancy, have a good look
No money now, baker writes in his book.
We both climb up to sit on top
Billy slowly gets into his trot.

Clip clop, clip clop, go Billy's feet
Making our way down the High Street.
All of a sudden a car passes by,
Billy rears up and starts to fly!

Away we go, no stopping him now -
My foot hard on the brake . . . *Wow!*
Bread rolls and bun rings all over the road
The doors have come undone . . . *oh no!*

Children run out from their houses to see
Quick, pick them up, something nice for tea!
It's all over now, Billy has calmed down,
Back to his trotting, through the town.

Soon we are finished; to the stable we go,
Fresh hay for the horse, Baker shouts 'Whoa!
A great big rat is in there feeding,
Baker lifts the pitchfork and rat is bleeding!

I feel a shiver, making my way home,
There's never a dull day, working for Mr Bone.
Mum has the milk on - I like it hot!
'Did you bring the bread with you?' 'Sorry, I forgot!'

Peggy Finch

MILLENNIUM DREAM

A cardboard box no longer home
Drug-crazed violence off the street
No orphan children rubbish comb
In ragged clothes, with bloodstained feet

Hunger pangs forgotten now
Brother share with brother
No barren soil beneath the plough
Infants suckle broody mother

No man entombed in prison cell
Crime exists no more
Each fortress now an empty shell
Virtue the ever open door

Eternal peace cease savage war
No flower of youth cut down
Mankind obeying nature's law
On bloody death all men shall frown

The Hiroshima cloud was cast
Man's destructive force completed
Remain a memory of the past
Embrace now the once defeated

Millennium beckons hope-filled heart
As one with friend and foe
On life's stage each man his part
The seeds of love to sow.

Thelma (Slee) Thomas

Then And Now

When I was young, and so naïve,
Embracing change without a qualm,
I moved from school, then job to job,
Devoid of thoughts that brooked alarm.

Security was not my aim.
Instead, adventurous pursuits
Predominated in my life,
With scant concern for home or roots.

I took both these for granted then,
A base inherited at birth:
But now I know that home and roots
Take life from time, and love, and earth!

Familiar things make up our home,
Reflections of our dwelling there:
The house, its rooms, the memories
Of laughter, tears, of love and care.

Their garnering requires time,
A place to be, to settle down
To live each day, to foster friends,
To learn our way about the town.

Then come those years when time seems short,
When age suspects it cannot cope
So well with unfamiliar things:
When what we fear defies our hope.

I know not if it's gain or loss,
The insight that the years bestow,
But youth to age grows circumspect:
Was more intrepid then than now.

Increasingly we eschew change
That robs us of familiar things.
Does even thought of Heaven quell
The anxt of loss that promise brings?

John Beazley

A Moment Of Time

An old man shuffled along the path
Keeping just in the light of the sun
His thoughts were still bitter and dark
As his mind wandered back one more time.

His love had left him when he was young
His children had grown up and long gone
His heart once full of passion and life
Was now - oh so cold and so sad.

Then, perhaps by some chance, or by fate
He noticed an old lady approaching - so slow -
As she came nearer, they both stopped and turned
Was it possible? Oh yes! It was *her!*

Even after all these years, they both knew.
Tears trickled down his old wrinkled face
The old lady - dry eyed - she just bowed
Then she looked up, but no words were said.

They both had their own private memories
Which they both thought were now all dead
Their eyes met again, for one brief moment
But they just looked and then turned their heads.

Transfixed in that *moment of time*
The old man turned and walked on his way
When he reached home he was very distraught
The agonies of time would not go away.

Then he gave out one last cry of pain
And after all these years, at long last
To end this long *moment of time*
He lay down and died from his broken heart.

Margaret Luckett

The Wrights Brothers - Achieving One's Goal

The Wright brothers Orville and Wilbur
Two exceptional men of the highest calibre.
Without them, we might not have powered flight
We could still be peddling around on our bikes.

By day in Dayton, Ohio, they ran a shop for repairing bikes
Tinkering with their glider through the night
Devoting all their spare time and energies
To turn their dream of flying into reality.

With their knowledge of bikes and technical expertise
Fabricated their flying machine with ease.
Though their first experimental glider was unstable
Sorted the problem out by adding winglets and cables.

Their passion for flight knew no bounds
Modifying their prototype to maximise every ounce.
A flyer that's worth its weight in gold
The high drama at Kittyhawk was about to unfold.

On 17th December 1903, they decided to give it a try
One hundred and twenty feet distance was achieved by that first fly-by.
Their dream of flying had come true
Soaring like birds in a sky so blue.

The Wright Flyer was only the beginning
Not until Yuri Gagarin, outer space was the ceiling.
Orville and Wilbur Wright had led the way
Travelling by jet planes is here to stay

The space shuttle has taken mankind to even greater heights
Lest we forget, the Wright brothers were once repairers of bikes.
No matter who we are, it is said that 'Fortune favours the bold'
The Wright brothers showed that, with commitment,
anyone can achieve their goal.

Jim Tan

Resistance Was Fruitless

I resolved to pluck a blackberry
And felt its resistance.
Its silent protest
Rippled in the autumn breeze.

Determination powered my hand
With feverish excitement.
Eagerness forced my will
Into an orgasm of greed.

The fruit of my desire
Was young and immature.
A vigorous stripling,
The berry exuded spirit.

Wearing a mask of exaltation
I was blinded to its youthful colour.
Enraged by its militancy
I grasped its neck as a yoke.

Enslaved by my power
The victim clung to its bearer.
Mutely pleading for resilience
Its strength was eroded.

Fingers stained by battle,
Conscience blemished by voracity,
Resistance was fruitless.
I raised my victim in triumph.

Valerie Caine

* Weddings And * Funeral(s)

* weddings and * funeral(s), it must be fifteen years,
and now my suit, although it's best, is mothballed full of fears.
I cannot open wardrobe door and wreathe its dust in sheets
without recalling trousers creased into such varied seats.

If I could live my life again, a new suit I would buy
so that my bedroom no more lived endangered by a sigh.
I would ensure a jolly cloth, to make me laugh out loud
and to each ceremony skip, less starched but much too proud.

The vicar's quip, 'You're much too late,' or, 'Wedding's booked
                                        next week,'
and I could grin from here to here, as Fred's most festive freak.
My grandaughter, most whitely miffed, by my recounted tale,
might pat me on my ageing pate, hiss, 'That suit's now for sale!'

My walk, unaided by a stick, though serious gait might show
I turned up with mournful stare for Mother's Romeo.
The ex, now there's a thought, so fine, such sport could flow so free
I chose right: annoying grief; or smile and whoop of glee.

* weddings and * funeral(s), I think I know the score,
seems to me the voting's rigged, now I've passed sixty-four.
The sums grow more conservative, so when it's time to go,
I've slept through wakes till no one's left - but vicar - for my show.

I've made a deal, I've now struck gold, there's one last special gig,
I must wear my suit again, I'll dress it with a fig.
My birthday suit will suit me fine; don't dress me in a shroud.
I've spread the word to guarantee my launch attracts a crowd.

Meanwhile my suit's upon a Guy, that soon goes up in smoke,
lost a few pounds for charity, a stylish hippie joke.
* weddings and * funeral(s), my ratings can't go down;
pop, jazz and jive, hop's beaming nude: the finest swinger in town.

Wendy Webb

Mother Of All Mothers

She issues her one-way tickets then collects what is due:
being neither ocean nor pond, mountain or molehill;
impersonal as a cameo sculpted from blanched ivory.
Hot-blooded or cold and aloof, a conduit for forces
urging her choleric blood into abnormal courses,
to destroy on a Biblical scale of frenzied savagery.
Endowed with a huge appetite, her guests always meet the bill,
unaware they are the fare on her farewell menu.

At times soft as summer zephyrs where ripening stalks of corn
mature at their ease alongside the barley-bearded stem
a lilting Aeolian harp sighs from a windy hill;
soft as the downy feathers of her fledging nightingales,
the quiescent murmurings of tiny infant quails.
Mother of all mothers, everything bends to her will:
each day starts with a paean of praise and ends with a requiem
for her extended benefice conceals the poisoned thorn.

Senses dull as intellect fades and the deep dark valley nears
while winter's savage moment white waits its turn in the wings
the abyss gives that parting kiss finalising life.
Running the full term gauntlet or the axe that truncates years
she ignores our joys, our loves and hates, the sum of all our fears.
The pushy exodus usher signals to the exit midwife
those souls meant for the shredder to emerge as vibrating strings
tuning distant heavenly harps to the music of the spheres.

Norman Meadows

Half Forgotten Memory

As I sat dreaming here one night
by the candles' flickering glow curling tendrils of incense
drifting through the light.

I thought I heard my name like a long whispering sigh
trembling through the smoke remember me . . . remember me . . .

A half forgotten memory, a fugitive shadow, hovering,
clinging to my subconscious mind like strands of silken cobwebs.

Music from another realm trailing through my dreams.
Stirring an echo in my soul of a long forgotten love.

A face takes shape, then dissolves into nothing
leaving me feeling bereft, yearning for I know not what.

Who is this spectre of the past that calls my name?
From the swirling mists of time who is this shade
who haunts my dreams like a half forgotten memory?
Remember me . . . remember me . . .

Brigitta D'Arcy-Hays

Untitled
(Dedicated to the Father and His Son and to the Holy Spirit)

When I get up in the early morn
I see a bright shining image as pure as Thee
For I am a spirit from God up above
Joined together with His Son in pure love
Someone who's trusted and true to the end
He is forever . . . my faithful friend
He is the one that can depend upon
From the start of each new day
Until the darkness comes, laying down the bright new sun
From morning till night
And my whole lifetime through
He promises me that he will do all that He can do
For me and for you
So shall it be, so open up your heart and shout it out loud
That there is someone who stands out in the crowd
Who is filled with pure love
Someone that is sent to be with us from up above
And He will be with you too in every place and everywhere
And in everything that you do
For He loves you.

Jessica Wright

The Generator

Our house is called 'Sunnybrook Cottage',
We have to generate our own wattage
We happen to live near the banks of the Severn.
In summer you know, it's close to Heaven.

In winter, it can be quite a bind
Years gone by, we had to wind
But now we have a 'Start O' Matic'
When the lights come on it's quite dramatic.

Whenever we have a thunderstorm
Often you know it's quite the norm
To have a blasted power cut
Everyone's in darkness, but
At 'Sunnybrook Cottage', to our delight
The lights in every room are bright
And we can watch our telly, still
Guess what! We won't miss 'The Bill'.

Flora Denning

OUR PLACE IN LIFE

We each of us have our place in life
It may be big or small
Everyone has their own special niche
So there is room for us all.

Sometimes it seems so pointless
We're sure we'd never be missed
If we just gave up and ended
Our struggle to exist.

Most of us rise to courageous heights
In times of stress and daring
But the ordinary living from day to day
Often seems so wearing.

We cannot all climb mountains
Paint pictures, write or sing
We wonder if it's worth it
We can't do anything.

And yet we all are needed
However small our part
Because by being just ourselves
We're all in someone's heart.

So remember, you're a vital cog
When you feel ready to drop
And if one small cog falls out and breaks
The Wheel of Life would stop.

May Morrott

CADISHEAD MOSS

Jewel in the city's crown
Is the verdant moss.
In early morning veiled by mist
Until by wakening sunshine kissed
Revealing fertile fields
Of peaty earth that treasure yields.

Rows and rows of celery
Stand in sheltered butts
Teasing the air with perfume rich.
The blackbirds fly from ditch to ditch
Where their nests are hidden
Not far from a worm-rich midden.

Cos lettuces for London
Webbs for Manchester,
Spring onions and radish grow
And weeds that have avoided hoe
Share rich soil together
Soaking up the sunny weather.

The smoky smells of autumn
Signal summer's end.
Potatoes picked and safely stored
And added to the fruitful hoard
Of blackberry and plum
Rich harvest of the summer sun.

Swallows seek the warmer climes
But I am content
To hibernate and close my door
Till spring, and when my life is over
I'd love my ashes spread
On rich moss soil at Cadishead.

Muriel Berry

FAMILY AND FRIENDS

We met as friends,
(for this be thanks)
with genial smiling faces
between the generations;
and love sat at an adjoining table
observing the scene unseen . . .

A gentle discourse started up,
a mild exchange of careful news
(like neighbours),
smiles soft and safe, rarely
a muted eagerness,
but warmth was mislaid;
and love still sat at an adjoining table.

Small masks shone undisturbed,
nothing broke the art of harmony,
such is the power of self deception;
and love still sat
though shrinking slightly,
at the adjoining table.

In fond farewell
lip met lip with gentle kisses,
a child embraced and love looked
hopefully over.

With deep relief, the car moved on;
no head turned in fond farewell;
and love
having sat too long
moved finally away.

Monica Redhead

THE PRIME MINISTER

We were invited to Number 10
We were chosen from our school,
To meet Tony Blair the Prime Minister
We thought that rather cool.
Outside we all took photos
With the policeman who was good fun,
Then we made our way inside the house
So glad that we had come.
We were shown into a large room
And given glasses of juice and wine,
As we waited for the Prime Minister
How quickly went the time.
Then the doors opened and in he came
Smiling, talking and shaking hands,
It was a very great honour
We did feel rather grand.
He then went on and made a speech
He said a big thank you for all we do,
He said we were very valued
For all our hard work too.
A photographer was taking pictures
The ladies flocked around,
It was hard to get near to him
You had to stand your ground.
Someone said it was like being with Robbie Williams
The Prime Minister replied, 'Not quite.'
We all had such a good laugh
It was really quite a night.

Diane King

TIDE-FIGHTING

Our footprints make dents in the damp, drying shingle,
Receding sea rollers a low fading rumble.
Behind rocky outcrops, in southerly breeze,
The sun breaks out early round rows of Welsh hills,
Fractures and sparkles through thin-branching trees.

'There was never a morning like this,' said my dad,
As on to firm sand we stepped out in the sun.
'Conditions are perfect for fighting the tide.
Gather the family, shovels and buckets
And build us a castle the waves cannot tumble.'

A low rising mound, within acres of sand,
The keep for the castle to make a last stand.
Breakwater strengthened with boulder and post
With channels deflecting the currented waves.
But the sea, with its ripples, had been here before.

All day, flying shovels. Shoulders were sore.
From rocks and from sand we remodelled the shore.
Up rose the keep, with a slab on the top.
Gullies were deepened, diverting the flow.
The sea watched in silence. It knew where to go.

We sweated and laboured, the sun on our backs.
No pause for siesta, but ate sandy snacks.
Here was definitive tide-fighting drawn.
Hours to the evening, from wind-perfect morn.
That sea was approaching. 'Prepare to defend!'

Perhaps the waves noticed our day's laboured sweat,
As it swirled round the gullies and gnawed at the break.
Our spades wielded frantically mending the holes.
There's space for just one on the fast crumbling keep.
My spade is defiant, tho' mindless seas crash round my knees.

From above, after sleeping, I look down to the beach
Where the generic battle was fought.
Barely remaining, a ring of smooth boulders, a rise in the sand.
My dad should be here, to share in my tear.
His castle too, so he ought.

David Light

OH I WISH I COULD BE AN ASTRONAUT

Oh I wish I could be an astronaut
And go up into space,
And climb aboard the shuttle
That flies at such a pace.

Oh I wish I could be an astronaut
They wear those padded, crisp, white suits
Have really flashy helmets
And amazingly heavy boots.

Oh I wish I could be an astronaut
And look down upon the Earth,
It is the most incredible sight
Makes you realise what life is worth.

Oh I wish I could be an astronaut
And fly amongst the stars
And maybe in the future
I get to go to Mars.

Oh I wish I could be an astronaut
And fly around the moon
But just like any trip you tend to take
It would be over all too soon.

Lorraine De Vanche

CHILDREN'S WAR GAMES IN 1939/40

I imagined it would be dark
In 1939.
I imagined the sky would cloud over
And dogs would cease to bark.

In the event the dogs barked
The sky was many times pieced by light.
As a child it all seemed exciting
The whine and roar of aeroplanes fighting
The disturbed nights and thumping crashes
Better by far than the itch of children's rashes.
But I didn't think sweets would disappear
Unless you had a coupon book!
Somehow you didn't feel a mother's fear
That never again would we be able to look
At the face of the man of the house
Who donned a khaki cap or wore a band upon his arm.
Or when the house across the way
Vanished, as we in shelters, sang a psalm.
With the house, playmates too, went away.

When we played war the prisoners all went free
And those shot dead, got up
And walked home to a dried egg tea.

In 1939/40
I imagined it would be dark
And it was, with windows blacked out
And no signposts, to find your way about.

At night I used to stand on the doorstep
Watch shells burst into flowers over the park
And think about the spark of shrapnel falling
Of how I would collect the silver grey metal
The following morning, with friends calling
To compare their collection of nose cones
And shell bases, pulled from the city pavements.
Nearby factories made us into bombing zones.
Somehow we didn't think like that in
Playground arguments.

In our wars nobody actually disappeared
But, of course, when adults play games
Things go wrong, ugly heads are reared
Strange, funny, haw-haw voices issued from the wireless
Hitler, Georing, Gobbels became household names
Later the whispered landing of a man named Hess.

Suddenly a country called France, fell
And we were standing alone.
Being British we made a victory from defeat
As the ships from Dunkirk cast a magic spell
So did the words of Mr Churchill in defiant speeches
Calling on us to fight in the towns and on the beaches.

Now it did seem dark
Even the youngest heart could feel
The chill of fear.
We realised this game, was for real.

John Aldred

HOPING YOU STILL CARE (GILFACH GIRL)

Wash away my heartache but not with my tears
Warm me with your gentle touch and your sweet kisses too.
Guide me back to your love once more
For I need you now just as I always have
If you ever doubt my love for you
Reflect upon the poetry that I once wrote
Look into my eyes, feel my thoughts and live them out
Pray tell me what I wish to hear.

Laurence Richards

LATE AWAKENING

I didn't hear the alarm,
So I tried to keep calm,
Rushed to the shower
It's cold, there's no power
Knock my toe on the leg of the bed,
Put both feet in my tights, in only one leg.
The milkman usually comes early
But oh, not today!
It's just my luck he is still on his way
The shoes that I really wanted to wear,
I can only find one, out of the pair.
Hoping that nothing else will go wrong,
Then only one earring, where's the other one gone?
Blamed the whole mess on the night before,
Then just when going out of the door
Realisation was slowly dawning
It isn't Monday, it's Sunday morning!

Jean Dutfield

NEW BEGINNINGS

The things we want are never found
Grasping in the night, dawn is long awaited.
Then clear the day, a new morn
Where mists of apprehension fade.
Sun illumines, revealing thoughts
Caught up upon the changing winds.
Dry days, by gentle rains assuaged,
Then comes the rainbow.
Yet forever, night becomes day, day night,
Do not let memory's darkness,
Override the light.
Reflect in calmness,
With exuberance anticipate.
The labyrinth of life,
Is always solved through faith.

Ruth Martin

TIME IN THE LIFE OF A FARMER

Time to get up, the cockerel crows
At 6 o'clock in the morn
The farmer's off to milk the cows
And a new baby calf is born
It's 10 o'clock he's off to lunch
A cup of coffee and a roll
And back to work he's off again
To feed his mare and her foal
Now dinner time it's 1 o'clock
Just finished clearing the yard
Then quickly take some hay to the flock
He's been working oh so hard
After dinner he feeds the pigs
And checks the hives for honey
It's a busy life being a farmer
But that's how he makes his money
Half-past three already
The cows need milking again
Hurry up and get it done
As it looks like it might be rain
Six o'clock has come round once more
It's supper time for the farmer
His wife has cooked a delicious meal
Now it's time to rest his feet by the fire.

Lorraine Gallagher

LONDON

London, sweet London,
we feel your name with pride
London, sweet London,
forever you'll abide

The river keeps rolling
as endless is her plight
guarding and guiding
her city into light

Showing us her heritage
so steeped in history,
the pomp and the pageantry
are there for all to see

London, sweet London,
we feel your name with pride
London, sweet London,
forever you'll abide

The people and the palaces
at its foundation lies
where nations meet nations
so rich in enterprise

This city, this capital,
this home of England rare
will always be a treasure,
a joy beyond compare

London, sweet London,
we feel your name with pride
London, sweet London,
forever you'll abide.

Janice Honeybourne

SOME MOTHER'S SON!

'Ignore him!' she heard people mutter,
As someone's son lay in the gutter.
'Just pass on by, he's not worth it mate,
And anyway it looks too late!'
'Disgusting!' yelled two well dressed blokes,
'Let's hope he just lies there and chokes!'
An old lady shakes her head and shrills,
'I blame it on the booze and pills!'
Some school kids passing pause to stare . . .
Then spit to show *they* just don't care.
'Bring back National Service, that'll get 'em sorted,'
A retired old soldier then retorted.
'Build more prisons for the scum . . .'
Jeered a teenaged mother with her infant son.
'He was here last night,' an old tramp hissed,
'He's either stoned or Brahms and Liszt!'
A grandma shouts . . . 'Keep away from that!'
Yet yesterday she fed an old stray cat.
A ticket warden, on his rounds,
Quickly looks upon the ground . . .
Then says out loud, 'I know 'im mate,
He lives on that there council estate!'
A posh voice pipes up loud and clear . . .
'Isn't that just what *I* said, my dear?'
And not one single person that passed him by,
Though quick to condemn, did not ask why . . .
Why someone's son should end their days,
With hateful words and indifferent gaze.
For . . . no matter what he'd been, or done,
That poor lad was still . . . *some mother's son!*

Sylvia E L Reynolds

IF

If I could fly
My feet well off the ground
And see the world from up above
Pursuing all the wonders to be found.

If I could reach the stars
And feel their icy touch
Or swing from branches of the highest tree
Savouring things that mean so much.

If I could look into the tiniest flower
Seeing through eyes of the humble bee,
Or stand on mountain tops
And look towards the grandeur of the sea.

If these are dreams,
Flights of fancy, differing from my life,
But I am here, an ordinary person
Happy to be a mother and a wife.

Jean Humphris

LITERARY BLONDE

My hair is blonde
To look at me
You'd never guess or know it
That secretly I am in fact
A writer and a poet

OK, so Dickens needn't fret
His high seat is secure
And I'll not challenge Betjeman
Ted Hughes or Evelyn Waugh

But on a good day, pen in hand
And when the juices flow
I'll pluck a topic from the air
Sit down and off I'll go

OK, I'll win no Booker prize
Who gives a toss, who cares
For I'm peroxide poetess
The prejudiced beware!

Jacqui Dunne

SOUTH OF YESTERDAY

Remember south of yesterday
When everything was young
Never a thought was given
To life and what may come
Today is now your future
Cherish all it brings
Let it be an adventure
Ignore the petty things
It's rather like the seasons
Summer, spring and winter snow
All are there for a reason
As you will surely come to know
Be certain each day is precious
Memories must never fade
Address all problems knowing
They are only man-made
Remember south of yesterday
When time was there to borrow
How quickly the future passes
And we are heading north of tomorrow.

Edward

A WORD OF WISDOM

A word of wisdom to the wise
And those who want to listen
Appreciate just what you have
Not what you think you're missing

Look for love where it exists
From those who hold you dear
Don't crave for what you will not find
In an anxious life of fear

Rejoice in what is good and true
Don't be blind, open your eyes
Realise your wealth and fortunes
For they come in many a guise.

Georgina Paraskeva

FLOWERS

The petals of the flowers
Close up tight
Sky turns dark
Brings in the night.

The flowers sway as the
Cold wind blows
Tightly closed to keep
The cold outdoors.

Soon the sun will shine so bright
Bringing with it warm delight
Petals open one by one
Showing their colour to everyone.

Bold and bright
So tall they stand
Bringing colour across the land.

Happy faces smile to see
Such beautiful flowers
Open for all to see.

Tracey Dixon

THE BRIDGE

Only last week, walking by the allotments,
Now greened by summer,
I came to where the bridge
Crosses a weedy stream.
Three wooden sleepers, salvaged
From a defunct mineral railway,
And slippery with algae,
And I remembered my father,
Gone these past years.
Memory shows him tall, straight-backed,
Proud to share his knowledge
Of field and water, plant and bird.
In his company
This bridge became a shrine
Every exploring walk converging
On its weathered planks,
And we would cross from mundane to magical
In a few short strides.
Not this day.
The magic had gone, like my father.
The other side of the stream
Was as ordinary as this,
And the wooden bridge
Was just that.

Eric Holt

I Wish I Could Fly

Sat in my garden, lots of thoughts in my head,
And looking at the view from my seat,
I wish I could fly way up in that sky,
What wondrous things I would see.

Tiny little people running around like ants,
Trees so small they look like plants,
I would soar across the mountain tops and take a pinch of snow,
I'd fly across the sea and spot the islands so far below,
I would follow the great whale swimming in the ocean blue,
I'd look in awe at the Great Pyramids and the Grand Canyon too.

I would wonder at steaming volcanoes,
And Niagara Falls beneath,
And when I grew tired, I would fly back home,
To the wonderful sights awaiting me,
The beautiful hills and valleys of Leeds,
I see from my garden seat.

Lynne Lister

Cycle

Ash
Substance
Birth tube
Life
Life's work
Travel to work
7.7.05
****
****
Subterranean
Death Tube
Ash.

Linda Hamlin

Season's End

The sky is grey
The earth is cold
The ground is wet
The trees are crying because the branches are cracking
The cracking branches are saying their goodbyes to the falling leaves
The wet grass embraces the dying leaves
The dying leaves have left their home until next time
For a new season is awake.

Ines Newell

A Game Of Cards

With cards in her hand and a smile on her face
The game of life she plays,
With friends all around and family too,
Life is lived each day.

The years go by, the limbs they seize,
The eyes are not the same
But still the game of life she plays
As she travels from day to day.

Then when a call from above is heard
The cards she stacks and takes,
To play with God in Heaven above
As a new day begins to break.

There, lost friends she finds and family too
And the game once again begins
In God's care she plays from day to day
With a smile upon her face.

C Kelly

An Everlasting Sleep

(On the death of a favourite cat)

The draped sofa that was her comfort cleared,
her blanket folded lovingly and stored;
the spread of dishes by the kitchen door
gathered, caressed and washed;
these shoulders that had borne a Pharaoh's daughter
sink in a favoured seat to spread deserted lap.

Over the thin December days
the well-judged spring uncoiled
that once described a pyramid;
and with that shortest day we guessed,
but would not recognise, the signs
of Beauty in the throes of death.

It seemed the shortest week that took
a healthy appetite to nought,
that would not let her take or keep
the sustenance of life. She fought
the pain with dignity and pride until
the vet decreed an everlasting sleep.

On that black table our black Beauty lay,
white tips of paws outstretched,
haunches as firm as frailty allowed
and sphinx-like, never flinched or moved.
Then as we cried, she wheezed and purred
to recognise our sad goodbyes.

Now in the house we find those empty haunts
wherein she sat and washed or curled and lay,
unnaturally tidy, still, unruffled.
Behind our morning curtains no wide eyes;
on evening driveway no high tail,
no greeting, rubbing, rolling, loving.

Save in the deep-eyed mind, are guarded
secrets of a thousand whispered purrs.
And in the starlit deserts surely
Beauty wanders there.

Rebecca Pine

I Love You Like A Warm, Wet Summer Storm

I love you like a warm, wet summer storm
I love you even on a bad day that we sometimes share
I love you even when you snore very loud and make funny noises
I love you when you put rollers in your hair and look like some alien
creature from Star Trek, once removed you look gorgeous with all
your long, dark, flowing hair
I love you when you tease me
Although I get angry, you always laugh and calm me down
I love your zest for life and positive thinking,
'Things could be worse,' you say
I love you for the two beautiful children that you gave to me
Your endless commitment to their well-being above yourself
I love you when you dance salsa and other men look at you
Men have the privilege to dance with you for I am not a jealous man
On the subject of jealousy, I suppose I should love you for that too
Although it took me several years to understand that was your way
of saying you love me
I love you when you cry, your emotions get the best of you
Never the one to be predictable
Always a challenge, never boring
I love you when you sing me a lullaby and stroke my hair
To feel like a child
What more could a man want?
When the rain stops
I'll carry on loving you
Te quiero mucho.

Terry Lane

DREAMING

I dreamed I was completely weightless;
Moon-walking somewhere out in space.
My metallic suit was grey and shapeless,
Yet I moved with a certain style and grace.

I blatantly defied earthly forces of 'G'.
Danced, light as a feather, on ceiling so tall.
I had never before known the meaning of 'free'!
Even tears of joy I could not get to fall.

I watched meteors stage a firework show,
Before an audience of twinkling stars.
I gathered a harvest moon with The Plough;
And watched Jupiter line up with Mars.

I reached out to catch a bright shooting star.
It passed by me at such a great speed;
I gave chase in my lunar-modular car,
At a pace which, I hoped, would diminish its lead . . .

It sparkled and twinkled its path thru' the sky;
Its tail a bright blur or hot, flaming red.
As I watched its trail, at last, I knew why
It would seem so minutely small from my bed.

I witnessed the sun rise up and shine;
A magnificent sight; too good to miss.
I floated on air at the end of a line;
Twisting and turning . . . that way and this . . .

I dreamed I remembered way back, a long time;
Floating, in just the same way - in a room:
Moving and breathing in waters so calm
They could only have been in my mother's womb.

I gazed all around me, in wonder and awe,
At millions of stars in an endless clear sky.
I recalled The Creation . . . and that's when I saw
That I believe in one God . . . and know why.

Doris Sproston

A FISHY TALE

It was just an ordinary day,
nothing different in any way.
Out on the boat the fisherman went,
to catch anything he was hell-bent.

Casting his line he hoped for the best,
to catch a tuna was his quest.
Settling down and checking his gear,
he sat in his chair and had a beer.

Suddenly an enormous tug on his line,
the fisherman hoped this was a good sign.
'I've got a catch,' with an excited squeal,
he straightened up to wind in the reel.

His hands shook and his mouth was dry,
'Reel in quicker,' the others did cry.
Up she shot, the enormous shiny brute,
eight foot long, eyes black as soot.

'Oh my God,' the fisherman cried out.
'It's a monster,' the others did shout.
The fisherman's beer stung his dry throat,
as he tied his marlin to the side of the boat.

On the dock she hung like a giant tower,
cameras clicking, he felt like a star.
He told tales about his marlin for many a year,
ending up twelve feet long, after a few beer.

Margaret Harrison

CELEBRATION

It's celebration time again
Let's pray it doesn't rain
Time for barbecues with family and friends
Plenty of gossip and latest trends
A balmy night with soft lights
Just right for getting tight
A glass of wine in your hand
Come and sit, no need to stand
Go on, top it up, the night is young
In fact it's only just begun

The barbecue is nice and hot
Just look at that lot
You can smell it a mile away
What a fantastic celebration day
Chicken, burgers and sausages too
That's enough, that will do
Mushrooms and garlic bread
You would think we had never been fed
Maybe just enough room for a little more
Whoa, that's enough for four

The wine is flowing like water
Shall I have one more, did I ought to?
Yes, life's too short to say no
I'll have one more and a potato
I've eaten so much I'm feeling fat
Go on, just one more sausage and I'll stop at that
Now here's the sweet
I'll have just one for a treat
Barbecued marshmallows, yummy
Bananas and hot syrup, just look at my tummy

The celebration is well under way
We could carry on for another day
Music playing, bodies swaying
Laughter in the crowd
Some getting a little loud
One sure thing, there is no doubt
This is what life is all about
Doing nothing taxing
Just having fun and relaxing
Under the moon and stars
Celebrating with a few jars.

Barbara Geatches

FLIGHT

Wouldn't it be lovely if only I had wings
I would be able to escape from all the mundane things
The everyday monotony, the common household chores
The polishing, washing up and hoovering the floors
There would be no excuse for missing work
No need to queue for cancelled bus or train
I could provide my own transport
There and back again
Imagine the birds' comments
Commotion and the fuss
They'd twitter, 'He must be a new species,
He's certainly not one of us.'
Holidays would be wonderful, permanently cheap
Whatever time of season, it would be constantly off-peak
But the best advantage ever
Would be when the neighbour from next door
Dropped in just for coffee
And stayed for evermore
Imagine their astonishment
When you said without a lie
'Sorry I'm in a hurry.
Must dash I've got to fly.'

Lynda Fordham

Populus Nigra Betulifolia

Huge and handsome, black poplar trees flourished
For many hundreds of years in England.
From their substance came cruck-frames for houses,
Farm wagon bottoms and scaffolding poles.
Known to John Constable, he portrayed them
In 'The Haywain', his much displayed landscape.

They thrived in field hedges so long ago.
Then why have their numbers now diminished?
Over selection or disease? Not so!
Habits and habitat are the culprits.
Land cultivation overindulged in;
Changes in environment the results.

Rooted twigs', branches' and fallen trees' clones,
Their grey-green leaves shimmer and dance in spring.
The dark fissured bark is like wrinkled skin
On an old and much loved human face.
Birds go to them for roosting and shelter.
We should look on them as our heritage.

E Joan Knight

The Autumn Of Life

From green to red,
Gold and brown,
The leaves on the trees
Come tumbling down.
On the ground,
Wrinkled and dried,
They lie for children
To kick aside.

My hair has changed
To grey from brown,
Parts of my body
Come tumbling down.
My skin has become
Wrinkled and dried.
In the autumn of life
I'm kicked aside.

Jackie Barker-Smith

Success In Marriage

Many couples these days on their day of marriage
May like to come along the street in a horse and carriage
This is a scene all the guests would like to see
Everybody will hope the couple will be as happy as can be
Both of them will now have a new style of life
One will have a husband, the other will have a wife
There will be new responsibilities for each one of them
They should support each other, treating one another as a gem.

Marriage can be a journey, containing many a hard task
A couple should be aware that all they have to do is ask
Ask each other for help or advice on what to do
This should apply to all couples all the year through
Also, if one of them is at home or in hospital feeling unwell
The other one should visit often and have something good to tell
They will help each other, that is a fact for sure
Whether their partner gets rich or happens to get poor.

Most couples would like to have a family some day
It is important to talk and both people have their say
There are some facts that have to be taken into account
Are they too young and in upbringing what would be the amount?
Couples and indeed everyone should always remember to never
Go about all though their lives holding a grudge forever
A person could die from a disease or be killed by a lorry
And then we all know it would be too late to say, 'I am sorry.'

Robert Doherty

The Queue

Do you remember
How we used to queue?
Sugar, butter, syrup
That two ounce of Typhoo.

We always have been tidy
Willing to stand in line.
In all the other countries
We would outshine.

Up there in the city
We still had bowler hats.
In 1943
They drew the line at spats.

The canteen at the Ministry
Was used most of the time.
Except when 'Pass' inspection
Stopped us in our prime.

The market in the city
Sold all sorts of fruit.
The queue so very chatty
As we stood there for our loot.

The time was long ago now
And all were pleased to share.
The smog, the rain, the blackout
Included in the fare.

Rosemary Povey

Wave Of Despair

(Tsunami)

A solid wall of water appeared
unannounced to alter the shape of the world
like a drape unfurled,
God knows from where or why.
Nature at its worst has cursed the eastern lands
placing sorrow and sadness
in the palms of human hands.
Can water be solid? Can it leave such squalid
decay and stench?
Destroying villages and human life,
parting mother from child and husband from wife
while running wild, evil untamed,
bodies un-named - dissolving in the heat of the sun.
Who deserved this kiss of death?
Who asked for their very last breath
to be sucked out by the force,
of water unstoppable in its course?
God give us the strength to rebuild the lives
of all those who strive
to bring back normality to all who are caught,
fraught with frustration
in this wave of despair, for yes, we do all care.
The terror of not knowing if our end is in sight
Do we pretend that we'll be alright
or imagine perhaps the dark of the night
will bring fresh disaster
once more to cast
a dark shadow,
to fill us with terror
all due to an error
of nature?

Jackie Johnson

CELEBRATIONS

C elebrations this year two thousand and five
E ntries on this occasion to the Forward Press
L et's send in our best poems
E veryone will be a success
B iggest and best poetry book it will be
R eady to show it's our anniversary
A poem written for this occasion
T he ones written by members of the team
I an Walton, Forward Press founder
O n top of this special edition
N ow is the time to show
S teve Twelvetree his dream.

Vera May Waterworth

RECIPE OF LIFE

If I could sit upon a branch
and watch the world go by,
of all the things I see below
What would I change and why?

I'd change the lives of millions
who live in dread and fear,
of weapons of destruction
men in power hold so dear

I'd change the lives of children,
the vulnerable and the old,
that hands supposed to love them
won't make their blood run cold.

I'd change the minds of huntsmen
who upon the horse cavort,
coats of red match blood of fox
ripped apart for sport.

But if each of us could change
the world the way we choose,
whose will would be the greater,
and if the recipe of life is changed
will the dish taste any sweeter.

B Ratcliffe

SANITY!

Where's it gone?
Did I throw it away?
How frustrating,
Been on my mind all day.
It must be here somewhere,
I'm sure I had it around,
can't put my finger on
can't hear a sound.
It shouldn't be so hard
To keep it I think . . .
I've read all the articles,
I've been to my shrink.
I've helped myself out
Practised calmness and all,
How can I now face?
Life's supposed to be a ball.
It's not in the living room though there are my keys.
It's not in the kitchen, oh I must pay those fees.
It's not in the bedroom, never a need to look there -
It's not in that mirror, no matter how long I stare.

Emma Eliott

AUTUMN HARVEST

A taste of autumn in the air,
The nights they grow soon dark,
Children raiding conker trees
Are echoing from the park.
Leaves in hues, red, green and gold
Scattered all around,
Acorns, tempting squirrels
Are carpeting the ground.
The last of the blackberries
Festooned in silvery thread;
The berries of the hawthorn bush
Are now a warm bright red.
Here and there a rose hip too,
Glimpsed through shedding trees,
The wind softly moaning
As it rises from the breeze.
The warmth of the fireside
As we close out the night,
The reading of a bedside book
Before we douse the light,
The beauty, joy and comforts
Provided for you and me,
A crispy frosty morning
In my mind's eye, I can see.
The joyous hymns of harvest time
That make the rafters ring,
We give up prayers of thankfulness
In every psalm we sing.

Madge Goodman

WELCOME TO THE ACORNS, WEYMOUTH

You enter the door of the Acorns,
Not quite sure what to do next -
There are so many things to do,
Much more than you'd expect.

There's always a discussion of 'What the Papers Say',
Or if you are artistic
You can colour a picture your way.
You don't *have* to *use* paints if you don't want to,
Coloured pencils and pens are there too.
Even drawings are supplied,
See how easy things are made for you.

There are also quizzes and other things,
If you want to use your brains,
But if you feel more energetic
There are lots of different games.

Some people like to go cooking,
And when the cakes are done -
The result is sold in the main hall,
The money goes to our amenity fund.

The fund helps pay for our outings
When the warmer weather comes,
And we end our trip in a *pub* for *lunch*
Then return home with nice filled tums.
We have to thank Therese for all our lovely trips,
She spends hours checking different places -
To make sure there's room for all to sit.

Laura Harris

CHEQUERS FROM COOMBE HILL

Come and see, come and see
Your presence passes over me as you climb
New spirits and souls of our time
Following generations' well indented grooves
And elegant equestrian hooves.

Come and see, come and see
Come and sit on my monument steps
Reflect the men remembered and their deeds
Was their fate planned long before, maybe
At a clandestine cloistered Chequers assembly?

Come and see, come and see
Subbuteo golf figures on the green
A silent snaking train slithering on the scene
Albatross gliders optically vying for space
Against silverfish planes of grace.

Come and see, come and see
Robust ramblers, farragoes of families, dogs abound
Tailwagging, some in packs as if to hound
Jacob coated coloured kites, strain to soar
From string wrestling children, as of yore.

Come and see, come and see
Rothschild's houses, their whispering wealth.
Music, beauty, art and commerce felt
Habile Halton's hangers harbouring hidden power
Sympathetic of our day and hour.

Come and see, come and see
Kaleidoscopic seasons, harbinger hazes
Of halcyon days, herringbone horizons
Bracing breezes, autumnal awe, thistledown clouds
White ethereal magical masque, viewed from the gods.

Come and see, come and see
Come ponder the imponderable
Dream dreams, catch the intangible
Down there is the struggle for survival
But here, here is for our soul's revival.

Brigid Nicholson

LIGHT OF THE WORLD

I had a funny feeling that the sky could fall tonight,
That the sun and moon would darken and the stars would lose
                                                    their light
And some of us would wonder and some be filled with fright.

And as the darkness deepened and the minutes sauntered on
Those of us with perfect sight found all our sight had gone.
I had a funny feeling but I think it was just me
That those who had been blind from birth all at once could see!

So as the darkness deepened and the time just lingered on
Some people started praying and some burst into song;
But some were very frightened and found the dark too long.

Some knew that they were living and some thought they had died,
Some were full of laughter and some knelt down and cried,
And some were filled with longing as a bridegroom and his bride.

Some people searched for torches to brighten up the night
And some reached out for switches to try a little light,
And others looked for matches but nothing would ignite,

And still the darkness lingered on and on . . .

Then I had the feeling that a brighter light returned;
There was no need for candles or lanterns to be burned.
And all at once we knew then that the light was here to stay
For the blackness of the night became an everlasting day,
And Jesus had returned as if he'd never been away,

And all at once the darkness had all gone!

Jill James

CREATION

From the depths of glorious Gloucestershire
My pen and I create,
Verses, steeped in personal experience.
Some dark, from days of depression.
Others a breath of fresh air,
Peace of mind, happiness.
How strange the moods of Man
Can change so quick, like a summer storm
Announcing itself with a crash of thunder!
Meanwhile the mighty Severn rolls on.
Black clouds subside, distant lightning
Fades, like mortality.
Wheat fields welcome back the warm summer sun.
So I continue the fight.
Seeking solace with words.
They say 'The pen is mightier than the sword',
Beware the lady of the lake,
Who holds Excalibur!

T G Bloodworth

THE BOOK MY FRIEND

The library is the place I live
It's always been a part of my life
Right from three when my parents joined me
Reading came naturally to me

I've been lucky, called a bookworm
Reading a book a day at times
'What do you find to read about?' I've been asked
'Anything and everything,' I reply

I'd rather read books about sci-fi
Or biographies or something real life
Not romances cos they are silly
Get enough of that on telly

To get lost inside a book is bliss
To find a magical world like this
Absorbed from cover to cover
Sitting in a corner reading for hours

Growing up through the years
Learning all the time, from each book
Hardly able to fit in anything else
Tearing myself away, I have to eat

When in book reading mode that is
Still going to the library every week
Scouring the bookshelves each time
Which ones shall I choose?

I'd love to keep them all with me
As every one has a place in my life
Once read, holds a special memory
My books, my friends for life.

Janet Jannaway

REMEMBER . . . REMEMBER . . .

Remember, remember, they said on the radio and TV,
Remember, remember . . . could they mean me?
I was a war baby in those dark days,
Absent Mum making guns, Grandma says.
Dad doing his duty somewhere far away,
Grandad was fire watching, fears to allay.
The indoor shelter with neighbours inside,
The outdoor shelter, smelly, dark, people hide.
The noise, the screams, the fear and woe,
The bombs descend on friends and foe . . .
Remember, remember, so they do not forget . . .
But have they learnt? I doubt it yet . . .

Carol Hudson

THE ANGEL OF DREAMS

She glides down from her point of sight
And effortlessly takes flight
Her wings shift the air as she surveys the scene
The night is a kingdom and she is its queen

The first child on this cruel night
Is a young boy who was picked for a fight
He wishes to dream of his mother long passed
So she grants his wish as he whispers, 'At last.'

The second is a young girl of 13
She is the sweetest child you have ever seen
She wishes to dream of a happy place
But destiny chose a much worse fate

And last is a baby of innocence and wonder
Whose parents believe in an absolute blunder
Yet this child shall dream of a world of peace
A place where wars, famine and violence will cease

Why not make the last dream a reality
Send away all men with no sense of morality
Because peace is something that can't be taken by force
Just get rid of violence and let nature take its course

Racheal Shanks (16)

UNFAIR WORLD

Unfair is this world that from one's eyes judgements are made,
condemning a book by its cover, never reading a page.
What would life be like if we were all the same?
A duplicated body, but what colour, creed or size?
Even from the beginning, we begin to victimise.
We are each born differently with a blueprint of our own.
Would you really want to be as individual as a clone?
A constant mirror image mimicking your every deed.
Reap what you sow if you're prepared to throw the seed.
I for one would not like it; I guess you wouldn't too.
Next time don't be so quick to judge, for the one who's judged
may be you!
Look with your heart and not your eyes. Looks are deceptive,
they tell you lies. Trust in your feelings and not the disguise.
He looks a tough man, no worries, but all alone he cries.
Everyone's an individual - that's their given right, but for that
individuality, why do we have to fight?
For we are each born differently with a blueprint of our own.
Would you really want to be as individual as a clone?
A constant mirror image mimicking your every deed.
Reap what you sow if you're prepared to throw the seed.
I for one would not like it; I guess you wouldn't too.
Next time don't be so quick to judge, for the one who's judged
may be you . . .

John A Turner

SOMERSET COAST

A million stones, shaped by nature's hand
Fascinating; this coastal land!
There, indeed, all time stands still,
The endless waves have their own will.
Sometimes serene, then wild and loud,
Sometimes sea-mist like a shroud.
Seabirds hover and wing their way,
What a truly lovely day!
I walk for miles - so much to see,
All stress is gone - here I feel free.

J Chaplin

WHAT DO I KNOW?

I am pale skinned, grey haired and old.
I am downhearted and have a cold.
I cuddle up, sneezing, close to the fire,
I long for a beach with a sunbed for hire.

I switch on the telly in hope of some fun,
I see bodies on a beach, not relaxed, but on the run.
I watch with dread as the reporter speaks,
I hear a tale of a wave that freaks.

I forget my cold and fail to cough.
I take it all in, I can't get enough.
I shed a tear that is not for me,
I grieve for the lives never to be.

I am ashamed of that miserable me,
I phone the number to answer the plea.
I give as much as I can afford.
I do not pray, I know no Lord.

But if He or Allah or Buddha is around,
Let's hope that in Asia He'll be found.

M Entecott

A POET OF MODERN VERSE

Live Poet, live -
And turn your morbid thoughts
Away from tales of sorrow and perdition.
Be joyful -
You, whose writings others read
And from them learn the state of Earth's condition.
Why talk of death, of plague, and strife.
(We know that they exist)
But yet above all other things
Do we still not have the precious gift of life?

Wake up Poet, arise;
Cast off your gloom, start living once again.
Spread out hope, not fear, amongst rich and poor.
For is it not a better creed to preach
Than all your awful predictions of war?
Sing but in praise
Of life and all things living;
Of sun and rain, of fruits and flowers and field.
And sing out in praise of the caring and the giving,
That all their works a noble peace may yield.

Sylvia Price

HIGH ON A HILL

High on a hill, a gentle breeze blows
As I look across the panoramic view below
Bathed in sunshine the land and sea
Make a beautiful picture, an artist's dream.
Tiny yachts sail on the distant blue water
Boats on the horizon cross the sea to Cornish harbours.
The curve of the bay, edged by the towering coast
Shelter sandy beaches and hidden coves
Masses of trees in all shades of green
Surround houses, schools, hospitals and farms.
A patchwork of fields as far as I can see
Slant down to the cliffs above the sea
Sun glints on glass as cars travel the roads
A train passes through the trees, its sound echoes.
From clayworks below smoke spirals to the sky
Each way I turn something catches my eye.
Colourful rooftops amongst trees of green
Blue sky and blue sea, it's a glorious scene.
High on a hill, on this summer's day I see,
A part of Cornwall in all its glory.

Lorna June Burdon

OH DEAR

'Oh dear', has been said so many times,
'Look for the silver lining'.
This too has been said so many times
By people who've been beset
By problems, sometimes many.
So please don't think you
Are the first person to have any.

Anne Trapp

WOODLAND HARBINGERS

Primrose

From undisturbed seclusion 'midst the tangle
Of long-grounded boughs and last year's lifeless leaves
There shines out in a strong determined hue
That ancient pointer to the forest's age
Which e'en before its pillars lofty grew
Stippled the temple floor with flecks of gold
The glowing-out-of-dimness trim primrose.

Windflower

Ring the woodland changes now
And let the glades of forest-virgin snow
The Milky Way white wood anemones
Thaw spring's chill and spartan symmetry
Into softer lines of emerald leafy loveliness
And let Creation's new life find a myriad forms
Reflecting Him whose spirit knows no bounds.

Bluebell

The shy-at-first sheer mesmeritic haze
Unlaid brush-stroke of celestial hue
Shapes now into those carillons of praise
Whose silent chimes ring out perspectives new
And fast transform the landscape's slate-grey face
Into a Van Gogh palette of vibrating blue
Glade-gathered glimpses of God's boundless grace.

Christopher Rudd

CELEBRATIONS

We celebrate the things in life
That bring us greatest pleasure
That help to smooth away all strife
And bring joy to our leisure.

The happy bridegroom proudly stands
To greet his lovely bride,
The glad exchange of golden bands,
The words 'I do' and the knot is tied.

The beginning and end of every year
We greet with celebrations.
We eat too much and drink too much
And end up with palpitations.

We fill our glasses, raise them high,
Excitement fills the air,
We hope that trouble passes by
And that future days will all be fair.

And now we raise our glasses
To a fifteen-year-old 'brain child'
That grows in stature as time passes
Let's drink to *poetry and time beguiled*.

Kathleen Holmes

PEOPLE WATCHING

Watching other people,
As they go about their day,
Is a wonderful occupation,
Though there isn't any pay.
First find yourself a vacant bench,
Near the centre of the town,
Make yourself quite comfortable
And settle oneself down.

Look

People pass, where do they go?
Most loaded up with shopping,
Out of 'Woolies' into 'Smith's'
Then into more shops popping,
Men stand outside shops alone
Whilst wives spend all their cash,
Children for a toy just moan,
Or want a toilet dash.

Then

Wonder where she buys her clothes
And how does she dare to wear them?
Should she wear her skirt that high?
Hey! I sound like Mother Hen,
Well she is definitely no chicken,
More like mutton dressed like lamb,
Far too old to wear such clothes,
I am glad of who I am.

Now

Take pity on the young mum,
How her child is screaming,
She has no control over him,
Well that's how it is seeming.
In my days we gave a smack,
Now that's against the law,
Bless her! Now she's cuddling him,
That's what mums are for.

Now it's time to venture home,
Today's people watching done,
Another day not quite alone,
For watching can be fun,
No one ever talks to me,
Or even knows I'm there,
Unaware of my occupation
That anyone can share.

Violet Cook

GOD BLESS

A little smile she managed and I knew it was the last
That dear old face of hers was almost still
But written on it signs of all the life which now was passed
I recognised so much, against my will

The tragic times of life were clearly etched upon her brow
The poverty and hardship that she knew
I hope it's all forgotten as she quietly leaves me now
I tell her how my love for her is true

I trust as she lies sleeping there is joy among her dreams
Anticipating those who've gone before
As calm descends to wrap around her, like a cloak it seems
No need for her to struggle any more.

Dorothy Blakeman

THE WIDER PICTURE

For fifteen years we have been writing in verse
Of happiness, sadness and we sometimes even digress
To thinking how to improve the way that we live
With thoughts of equality and being more willing to give

For the short time we are on Earth while just passing through
We have become so materialistic as we strive to accrue
Useless possessions like a passionate greed
More than we can use or will ever need

Those that still care should use their free choice
To lay down some guidelines and be a strong voice
Tackle every problem and show a better way
To change our behaviour that seems to have gone astray

To love one another and show some compassion
Share what we have and set a new fashion
Give thought to the growing lack of respect
That leaves us uneasy and that we have come to neglect

Good luck with the fifteen years' celebrations and future success
Look forward to reading the entries in the next Forward Press
With tales of their experiences and ideas that we always enjoy
From participation by all ages, from manhood to boy

Joyce MacDonald

METAMORPHOSIS

The little tadpole in the pond
Has no idea
Of all the land that lies beyond
Its tiny sphere.
It cannot know or guess
That, in a month or less,
Its tail will go
And legs will grow,
And it will learn to live on land
A life that's changed.
How could a tadpole understand
What God arranged?

The caterpillar on the wall
Is unaware
That one day it will cease to crawl
And take to air.
A lovely, graceful thing,
It will become a-wing,
And flutter by
In summer sky,
Free from the life it knew below
Upon the land.
How could a caterpillar know
What God has planned?

And we, whose lives are mainly spent
In frenzied quest
Of all the things that represent
For us the best,
Are told that, when we die,
We shall not dormant lie,
But rise anew
In altered view.
We know not how we shall be changed,
But we are blessed
Because we know what God's arranged
Will be the best.

Pleione Tooley

NOT ONLY IS IT A CELEBRATION

Not only is it a celebration,
But also a great poetry invitation,
To highlight the free art of poetry,
For achieving its anniversary victory.
It's the Forward Press consistency,
In its struggle to advance the art of poetry.

Poetry is the art of thinking, imagination,
High literary musical expression
And professional ability of concentration
To create an attractive masterly selected word,
That satisfies the audience and
Readers and lovers of poet's word.

Be it a poet, could master the art of poetry,
But still a poet needs a publisher of poetry,
Who takes it from isolation to public world of poetry.

So poetry advances by publishing of poetry,
That's the task of Forward Press,
To make poetry one of the lovely arts,
Advancing its role in the world.
Poetry is riches of mankind,
Poets are the vanguards of civilisation and humankind,
Throughout the past, the present and
The forward generations advancing the art of poetry,
Happy congratulations for Forward Press and its great family!

Jalil Kasto

YORKSHIRE, WHERE'S THAT?
(Yorkshire is attempting to kidnap Nottingham's Robin Hood to boost their tourist trade)

Robin Hood's a Yorkshire man?
Nay, lad, nay.
Strong i' th' arm
And weak i' th' head?
Nay, lad, nay.
The man who took on our sheriff
And all of King John's men
And outfought them
And outwitted them
Again and again and again.
Strong in the arm
That might be so
But weak in the head,
Oh! No, no, no.
Geoff Boycott might be a Welshman
And Freddy Truman may be a Scot
But our Robin a Yorkshireman?
I tell you he was not.
Where did you get that from?
The Last of the Summer Wine?
That's just good comedy fiction
And if you watch it that's just fine
But don't believe the characters
When they start to spin a line.
You were overrun by Vikings
And might recall those pillaging days
But don't think you can come down here
And practice Norseman ways.
You might carry off Sherwood Forest
Or steal our ancient oak,
But to claim Robin's home was Yorkshire,
That's gone past a joke.

R L Cooper

One Day In Kippford

We sat on the 'Wee Pier' in Kippford,
with the warm sun on our backs.
The tide crept up the mudflats
filling the trails and the tracks.
It covered the neatly etched footprints,
that ran to a stranded boat.
Very soon that vacant craft would be
lazily bobbing afloat.

Stones of glistening granite
lay basking in the sun.
We watched the relentless water
cover them, every one.
We counted the yachts in the Estuary,
as they gradually drifted free,
held only by their anchors,
beneath the invading sea.

And like those yachts that gently
danced in the playful breeze,
we just let time drift away,
with our elbows on our knees.
The sails would flap and toss,
as the fresh air passed them by.
Seagulls laughed overhead
as they soared in the clear blue sky.

Patterns drawn on the wet sand,
showed where birds had scurried.
A canvas of short-lived pictures
where man and dog had hurried.
Too soon this scene before us
was totally hidden from view,
gone like our time at Kippford,
a rare time with nothing to do!

Sonja F Mills

Together

A poem does not have to rhyme
Though I think it reads like a church bell's chime
Give love to the world and you will receive love back.

The world in parts is a horrible place
People fighting because of a race
One side's a boy with happiness in his eyes
The other is a girl, frozen beneath wide open skies
One wishes, one wishes, the battles will cease
One wishes, one wishes, we can all live in peace
I have seen hatred burning in people's eyes
Their faces bursting like cherry-red skies
How much longer can we take the lies
Before world leaders realise
The world is all but one place?
No need for starvation in any race
Food should be flown all over the world
Instead of insults constantly hurled
What would the world be like as one?
Lots of laughter, lots of fun?
I am not at knowledge to say
Though hope sometime I'll see the day
People join hands from every race
To build a peace sign spotable from space
One day I hope we can all look back
Look back as one not white or black
Peace to the world

Gary S Morton

A Typical Eastwood Family

A thout ya wornt gooin owt, las nayt ya towd mi that ya wont
So dunna botha comin rownd cos anutha chap I fownd
Mi fatha got sozzled las nayt an Motha oh got stroppy
Oh hit im wi a rollin pin an nok'ed im owt cowd
A dunna wanta be arownd wen Fatha wakens up
So owt a guz an hid me sen rayt quik, fast as a cud
Wen Fatha wakened up me motha kept her distance
The nasty sod was moanin of demons in is yed
He banged his fist on't table an said, 'Giz a cup a char.'
'Dunna stand thear like a lemon, wot's up wi ya? A dunna bite.'
'I not a bad owd codger so cum on giz a kiss ya gorgess silly bogger.'
I waited till he'd gon to wok befor I showd me face
Me motha was glad to see me so we had a cup a char
I got me sen a job in a busy factory, it dunt pay much,
but it's bet than nowt
I cold do wi a winter coat so I'll ata save up worra can
Till I've gorra nuff to buy one.

Christine Cook

Untitled

(Thoughts on seeing some felled and uprooted trees in a field in Scotland, June 1982)

O noble giants
Sad am I to see you fallen thus -
Your arms still leafy-laden
Now spread upon the ground,
No more to sway or rustle in the breeze
Or give cool shade for weary travellers,
Why should you suffer such indignity?

Poor gentle giants
How I grieve for you -
Your roots and very being now exposed,
Your life supply cut off
Ere you fulfilled our age-old purposes.

Even your dead are often left still standing
And beautiful in silhouette against the sky.
But you, like warriors upon a battlefield,
Lie still.

Poor fallen giants,
You don't deserve such ruthless desecration,
'Twere better far to be struck down
By lightning, fire or workman's searing axe
Than to lie naked in that lonely place,
Robbed of your vital contact
With the Mother Earth who held and nurtured you.

Lie still in pain
And let the touch of Earth give gentle peace.

Mary Graves

My Prayer For Benji, My Dearest Dog

My Benji at night-time when I say my prayers
I pray for God to keep you in His care
It is very hard to bear this loneliness
For you are not there for me to caress
Gone are the days when we played together
We used to go to the Roaches - you would dive in the heather
Those days are gone now, I am so sad
You were the best pal I ever had
The love we had for each other no one could ever know
My days seem to go very slow
I still look for you every morning and night
Without you Benji things don't seem right
I hope my dear God will help me
Because I am no good on my own
Without you Benji it does not seem like home.

May Ward

MY LOVE

The sun shines bright on a summer's day.
The sun shines bright and hears me say,
'My love has gone. O my love has gone.'
And I weep, 'neath the sun for my love.

I walk along at the edge of the sea,
Waves lap my feet as they say to me,
'Your love has gone, o your love has gone.'
And I weep by the sea for my love.

The moon rides high in a velvet sky
The moon rides high and hears me sigh,
'My love has gone, o my love has gone.'
And I weep, 'neath the moon for my love.

Days, months and years have passed away.
Now only my heart can hear me say,
'My love has gone, o my love has gone.'
And I smile when I think of my love.

Muriel Johnson

BEAUTIFUL ELINOR . . .

Where have thee gone my sweet Elinor?
It seems so long since we were made to part.
There were those who said I was not worthy,
Now nothing can mend this broken heart.
We walked under an arbour of scented jasmine
And vowed our love beneath the stars.
Yet every day is filled with yearning,
To be wherever thou are . . .

Beautiful Elinor, thou art like a breath of spring,
With raven hair as black as ebony and skin as soft as snow.
And bright, beguiling eyes of sapphire blue,
A beaming smile that promises many wondrous things,
Ruby lips that set all young men's hearts aglow . . .
I will search all corners of the Earth for thee
Nothing in Heaven or on Earth can bar my way.
And when at last I find thee I shall hold thee close
Forever and a day . . .

For ours is not a fickle love that is brief in passing,
But a love so profound that it reaches in and touches the soul.
A love that surpasses all other,
One love to last a lifetime through.
One that will remain constant and true, for all time . . .

Jilly Tynan

A POEM FOR AUTUMN

I love the autumn; I love the colours of the leaves
I love the gold and the russet and the yellow and the brown;
I love the green that hangs on to the bitter end
When the cruel November frost finally wins the battle
And all, but a few, lie dying on the ground.
Yet the mighty trees, though naked, are merely sleeping;
And will wake again next spring.

I love the autumn; I was born in that season,
In September when the fruits are mellow and the sunset golden.
When gentle winds swirl the fallen leaves around, chasing them
                                             into corners.
Children in the park run and kick the leaves from their tidy
                                             hiding places.
When swans and geese noisily migrate to warmer climes
And lights are lit early on buses and trains, in shops and in homes.
The autumn brings a feeling of peace; I love the autumn.

Sandra Benson

THE UPPER ROOM

They went into an upper room we're told,
An ordinary cold bare room.
They met with many misgivings and fears,
In an atmosphere heavy with gloom.

Their leader, in dying, had let them down
They hardly believed that He'd gone
Nor could they accept His appalling death
And questioned what they had done.

They knew they'd betrayed Him, knew they'd failed
As they gathered to fathom it out.
They went into the upper room disturbed,
Obsessed and possessed by doubt,

While they were hiding, because of their fear
He came through the closed, locked doors,
He stood 'in the midst' and He showed them His hands
Just saying, 'My peace is yours.'

They saw the marks in His hands and his side
From wounds that had been so bad.
When it dawned on their minds who it really was
Then those disciples were glad.

Great peace flowed from His presence there
As the Spirit came with His breath
And love outpoured from His mended heart
As the blood had flowed at His death

They went back to that upper room once more
After they'd watched Him ascend
To His Father in Heaven, from whom He'd come,
And they knew it wasn't the end.

For He'd told them He'd come again, one day
Dispelling the whole world's gloom.
He asked them to always watch and pray,
As they did in that upper room.

For two thousand years His disciples have met
In church, cathedral and home
But no greater blessing has been dispensed yet
Than that in the upper room.

Ray Smart

A CELEBRATION WISH

A gloomy day in January,
A couple of years ago.
On reading the newspaper,
In the fireside's glow,
I saw an advert jumping out,
For poems from one and all,
Send your entry to this address
Your poems, short and tall,
The content is up to you.
Yes, you could make the choice.
Then if you are successful
One of the lucky ones,
£1,000 in prizes, waiting, to be won.
So, I took my pen to paper,
As I'm not one to shy away
The offer of a prize like that,
On a dark and dismal day.
I succeeded in an entry
Into the book that year,
But it was with regret, no £1,000 I fear,
Several more I entered,
Published, yet never won,
So on this anniversary celebration
Hope this one wins the 'ton'.

Margaret Mary Harrop

ESSEX SUMMER

Essex lanes are brimming now
With seas of cream and green;
Queen Anne's lace and meadow sweet,
Hawthorn white and wild rose pink
Suffuse this fairest scene.

Town fêtes and village fairs teem
With myriad stalls of cakes, jams and flowers,
Stacks of books and mounds of bric-a-brac.
Merry games and furious fun burst
From Flitch, Morris, seaside and castle towers.

Our history shines through roads and homes
In names from ancient days:
Epping, Roding, Mistley, Colchester and Grays.
Sunlit saffron pargeting vies with golden thatch,
While over all church steeples call to eternal ways.

Patricia March

THE LIFE BEYOND

You live on in my memory
Though people count you dead
Your pictures show you as you were
Before you quickly fled.

In me you live again my dear
In me you never die
For you are here with me, dear heart,
Not far beyond the sky.

For life and death are really one
In God's great company
Where He is present, life is there
Yet hard for us to see.

So let us live by faith, not sight
Hard though that may seem
The two are one in God's great scheme
The Three in One great team.

Robert S Dell

IN MEMORIAM

My dearest Julian, my only son,
Why did you have to leave so suddenly
That August night two years ago?
You had no premonition that the day
Would be your last one here on Earth,
That you would not return to us
After your brass band practice.
There was no time to say goodbye,
I could not tell you how we loved you.
Your life cut short at forty-five
For no apparent reason.
No accident befell you, no illness struck you down,
You just collapsed . . . and died.
You had so many things to do,
Songs to sing, places to see
And so much love to give -
(They say the good die young!)
We miss you so and not a day goes by
Without a memory of something said or done.
My tears are never very far away
And grief lies heavy on my aching heart.
You were so special and I love you so -
My darling Julian, my only son.

Ann Linney

ABOUT TURN!

A change of shape if only that one could
A change of attitude that is understood
That past harm that now is healed
A new happening unexpectedly revealed
See what has happened with your own eyes
That big change that cannot be disguised
See the worth now shown
Different from what one had known
The so great change in someone's heart
That now sets that person apart
That's cured the one who seemed so ill
That brings about an enormous thrill
Would you help out - if you thought you could?
To carve, to reshape a 'block of wood'
To show the value in a life now earned
It has come about - a worm has turned!

John 'El' Wright

SUMMER DAYS

I once knew a cricketer for whom summer was his life.
Whilst on the clubhouse balcony every weekend sat his wife.
He batted, bowled and fielded in flannels crispy clean
And in his imaginations was the greatest ever seen.
He knew his average, every ball and every run he scored.
Prepared his bat with loving care as the linseed oil he poured.
The winter months he hated, football was for fools,
Instead he dreamt of summer days and went to cricket schools.
There were books to read on cricket and dice cricket games to play
And with very little coaxing in the snow he'd often play.
But summer was his favourite time, no cold weather man was he.
This was the happy cricketer, that cricketer was me.

Sam Spruce

GOD'S ARTISTRY

Beautiful is the countryside.
A picture painted by God's hand,
In a myriad of different shades
On His canvas - sky, sea and land.

A pallet of many colours
He mixes with great care
To illuminate the landscape
For His people everywhere.

Nothing will clash, everything blends in,
Brilliant, varied, dark or shade.
Each season a kaleidoscope
Of the harmony He has made.

The trees, the hedges and the grass
Are in greens of attractive hue.
Clouds and sky forever changing
Their mobile tints amid the blue.

Gloomy storms upon the seas
He paints in neutral, brown and grey.
But blooms shining like rainbow's spectrum
Will lighten the darkest day.

Artists may paint pictures
Which can be viewed from near or far.
But they can never match God's work
No matter how fine they are.

What a dull outlook it would be
If all were in black and white.
So, thanks to God for His artistry
In colouration for our sight.

Loré Föst

THE HOMELESS

Just spare a thought, in your warm bed,
For those without a home, full of dread,
Filled with anxious despair, this day may bring
More untold misery - more barbs that sting,
When a partner leaves home without any care
For the innocent, some babes, souls laid bare,
Will struggle on and never find courage, the heart
To carry on with lives so rudely torn apart,
Among the homeless.

A father tries hard, a loving mother weeps
As they go separate ways, neither one sleeps
And little suffering children pay the price
When the bills are not met, tears cannot suffice,
For the money runs out - a home to be sold,
Another once happy family, out in the cold,
With nowhere else to go, maybe one shabby room,
Their unhappy lives overshadowed by gloom,
These, the homeless ones.

A mother, so despairing, may try to end life,
A father, once bright, never knew such strife.
Why then have they quarrelled, been led astray
Unthinking of the little ones who have to pay?
Who do not understand why so much stress
Should bring everyone this great unhappiness,
To make them feel so wretched, so insecure,
So unworthy, unable to cope - too much to endure,
Little homeless waifs!

Spending their childhood, feeling lost and alone,
In a damp, unpleasant, run down, mouldy 'home',
Called 'emergency housing', this is their plight,
Breathing in germs, inhaling coldness, every night,
Just spare a thought, when tucked up in beds,
How secure you are - not living in dread
Of harmful elements, people, to spoil your life,
Who resent how you live and turn the knife
On the homeless ones.

Julia Eva Yeardye

SUMMERLEAZE

Summerleaze, Summerleaze
You put me at my ease.
For if God has a face
Surely it's your chiselled landscape?

Rocky forehead, ruddy cheek, jutting jaw
Sandy pallor - ever changing expression
Sea meeting sky, your eyes
The river - mouth.

How do you wear your hair?
Rocky outcrop.
Your smile, the warm day sun
Greets me as I come over your brow.

Plunge into the Cornish tankard
Fishermen cast their nets
Rescuing me from your embrace
Intoxicated by the smell and your grace.

The wind whistles a merry tune
Bobbing boats acknowledge the 'Rock'
Birds as the crowds flock
To hear the voice carried over yon' hill.

Summerleaze, Summerleaze
You bring me to my knees
For surely there is a prayer
To give thanks, for I've been there!

Cecilia Hill

POURQUOIS VOUS FRAPPEZ?

To beat a wind
and whip it white
as lips,

silver like,
on a salver salivating
winter,

sharp shark shivering nights,
sober as John the Baptist,
acidic as Salome.

This hill is my plate
complete with rim,
a ridge shining under light,

thin as eagle's wing,
beating
narcissistic reflections inside a pool . . .

Graham Fairbrass

SOLDIERS, HEROES AND SONS

The battlefields are all red,
      From all the terrible blood that's shed.
We call them heroes because they're dead,
      But they are some mother's son.

They lay down their lives, so others can live.
      In love and harmony and to give,
A peaceful future for us all,
      But they are some mother's son.

They lose their spirit, they lose their limbs
      And ask the Lord to forgive their sins,
So as not to die in dread and fear,
      But they are some mother's son.

They award them medals, but what good are them
      When they are dead soldiers and not living men?
It's just to say they're heroes,
      But they are some mother's son.

Why do we have to have all this killing,
      Just because these men and boys are willing
      to give their lives if need be,
To protect their country from the enemy,
      But they are some mother's son

We are all grateful, God only knows!
      For these fine soldiers, our heroes.
But they are men and only young boys,
      Yes, they are some mother's son.

Sandie Smith

OUR WORLD

Do love and life go hand in hand?
When the road gets tough, there is no path,
No harbour for shelter in hostile land,
No kiss to calm the coming wrath.
But hope sincere will help us through,
Renew our trust for times to come
With friendships fostered, loyal and true,
Families, closeness, joys - a home -
So do not question love that's built
On time, and stands the test of life
For unlike blooms that fade and wilt
With decadent traits it is not rife.

Evelyn D Alvis

WHEN TIME FAILS

After the spring,
Summer impassable;
The seconds creep
Through the stalled minutes
Of an unmoving hour.

They hang like beads
On a counting-frame
In a remembered schoolroom,
The unaltering chamber
Of the day.

The room is shuttered
Against the future,
Against the storm outside,
Where tomorrow is spun by the wind,
Woven by the rain.

Can the honeyed flower
Survive?
The lily face
The downpour?
Bees find shelter?

The music of spring was broken,
Time froze with the tune
When the string snapped,
Severing past from present,
Melody from silence.

We are still sitting
In the same room;
The seconds hang
Like wooden beads
Across a wooden frame.

Dorothy Buyers

SUMMER MAGIC

What was that sound? I stepped from the path
And peered into the dark fastness of woodland,
I heard the faint chimes of a clock in a distant tower.
The evening shadows hid an army of creatures
Moving around me. The soft wing of a moth touched my face.
Then, in the still air, the stirrings ceased, the wood fell silent,
There was a strong excitement of anticipation,
As from a nearby bush came a plaintive cluster of notes,
An evocative call tossed in the air, a flow of melody
Piped as from a faery flute. The wood was bewitched
By the sound. Even the screech owls were silent.

The nightingale pursued his overture, trilling gently
As he composed the song for us. Short bursts of phrases
Interspersed with silences floated through the night air.
Then a brilliant cascade became a sparkling allegro,
A tumbling of notes from the very heart of the singer.
Immersed in the sound, I recalled the echoes
Of a vanished horizon, the world in the passion of its youth.
The song poured from primeval woods into the new millennium
Now upon us; the same sound, the offering of the bird
To its creator. A gift of love, indeed.

Lost in my thoughts in the beauty of the scene,
The litany of praise was fading into silence.
The woodland creatures resumed their nightly foraging,
I heard the soft brushing of feet and the harsh cry of a vixen.
In a daze I retraced my steps in the moonlight,
The clear plaintive notes still fresh in my ears.
A symphony of joy in the thrill of being alive
From a little brown bird on a sweet summer night.

Beryl Louise Penny

WHAT CAN I GIVE YOU?

I can give to you
Nothing but hope -

For I can give to you - or any other -
No more or no less than what I am.
The man I am is not another -
Others' feelings are often a sham.
I am thus, now - more good than evil -
Between God and the Devil,
Because life made me so.

Youth was a quest with many false alarms
And, later, maturity still contained mystery.
Middle age was a stealthy march like a man-at-arms
Or like a fog-encircled cruise on an unknown sea.
Sometimes there was sorrow
Or a hopeless tomorrow
To face - unwillingly to know.

Yet there was a deep and abiding
Bedrock of a love of life beneath it all
And I knew no way of hiding
All I had tried to be as I followed the call
To simply trust in myself with Him always
And do the best I could in all my days
Until it was time to go.

So I can give to you
Nothing but hope -
Because you'll be given to bear
No more than you're able to bear -
As God and the Devil help you to grow
Better at living each day!

S V Batten

A PAGAN PLACE

Listen, you disbelievers,
Do not scoff and turn your face.
There is a devouring power held,
In every slough, burn and stone,
Within this alien, pagan place.
Just lay your hands on this chill rock,
Potency of time locked in its heart.
Or hear this ancient oak tree moan.
Winter wind thrashed in the dark.
This moor has seen eight thousand years,
And will see many thousands more.
Though blasted cold by winter's tears,
Frost hard, to spring's raw, slow thaw.
This is a place of hills and onerous sky
Where only the rugged, dun folk roam.
With its boggy mires and windy heaths,
Where baleful, coal-black ravens fly
Over woolly, wandering upland sheep,
And a lone shepherd's crumbling croft.
This is not a welcoming place,
For some foolhardy man to dwell.
A lonely place, a mystic place,
Long snared in some pagan spell.

John Pegg

UNTITLED

Believe
Hope and
Pray
Is the best
Love, every day.

Gerasim

UTOPIA

Throwing my coin into the wishing well
with a dream I have to tell:
Let all the people of the globe
enjoy fulfilment of their hope
That peace will reign forever after
each to rejoice in song and laughter
bliss to be bestowed on all
happiness on hand at call
No more worries, no more grief
Trust in hearts and firm belief
In mutual love and human grace
To make the world a peaceful place
All this might be a timid clue
For my dream to come true . . .

N Yagel

CHARLIE

Charlie is my darling,
I'm quite sure he knows he's mine,
When he scampers madly into the room
Tail a-wagging - eyes a-shine,
It's the comfort of my lap he'll seek
Then plants a kiss upon my cheek,
My heart, entranced, begins to sing
Yes, Charlie is my darling.

Just a mongrel puppy he may be,
No claim to a canine family tree,
Yet his looks are really quite unique,
Face full of mischief, coat black and sleek,
His intelligence shows for all to see,
As good as any pedigree.
He will 'Stay' and 'Sit' and 'Fetch' and 'Bring',
Yes, Charlie is my darling.

His character does have its flaws,
See those scratch marks on the doors?
Those fringes nibbled from the mat?
Naughty Charlie - he did that.
He misbehaves when he's left alone,
Barks whenever I'm on the phone,
And yet, I forgive him everything.
Yes, Charlie is my own darling.

Nancy Sheldon

OUR CHURCH

The pews are not ornamental but plain in our church,
But the people have made long cushions for folks' delight;
There is no wonderful rood screen in our church,
But banners which people have worked with all their might.

There is no wonderful scroll-work in our church,
Just a plaque or two to commemorate some of our dead;
There is no beautiful altar in our church,
But a sturdy table with flowers on instead.

There are no wonderful statues in our church,
Just a cross behind the pulpit giving off light;
There are no beautiful paintings in our church,
But the drawings the children do. My, what a sight!

But there is a wonderful feeling in our church.
We all belong and are all of one accord.
We love, care for and rejoice in one another,
And always give thanks and praise to Christ our Lord.

Lilian Mounter

CHILDREN OF THE DARK

They, all of them, were children of the dark
Whose inner light glowed in their world around.
They taught me great endurance, patience, skills
Which in our seeing world are seldom found,
Their fingers gently traced the blind school wall
Or tightly gripped the banisters of stairs
Feet walked so firmly, on familiar floors
Courage and inward strength was truly theirs!
Their sense of touch and smell was so acute
It compensated for unseeing eyes,
Whilst to each tiny sound their ears were tuned -
No visitor could take them by surprise!
They painted wondrous pictures in their minds,
With colours bright, which they had never seen,
Described to me in words so vivid, clear!
The magic of some wonderful daydreams.
Ripples of laughter could often be heard,
When humour overspilled into a room
No self-pity in their presence was found
Their natures would dispel the darkest gloom.
Those children of the dark brightened my life
With a spark which for me will never dim.
Now, when I am faced with failing sight
Their courage brings me strength and peace within.
God bless them all! My children of the light.

Barbara Saum

THE LOVE OF MY LIFE

The sea, I really love, in all of her magnificent moods
When calm and smooth she seems as a sheet of glass,
But we know by the tides, she never really stays still
As when those mountainous breakers against the cliff smash.

The ocean on a moonlit night is a most wondrous sight
Like the movement of the tide as it ripples on the seashore,
Then because of the storm, giant waves have turned the sea white,
You cannot believe it to be the same sea that you saw before.

Those lovely cool soft summer evenings, after that long hot day,
Then watch that magnificent sunset followed by the moon's glow.
The winter, those cold days, the frost, the snow and the ice,
Nature's promise: a new spring and warm summer will surely follow.

Another great love is the garden, at times the working seems hard
When after all that forking, turning and planting those seeds,
The protection, fertilising, and when dry all that watering,
How is it possible you get all those persistent weeds?

But the garden is a most wonderful friend, and kind in its way,
The benefits by far outnumber all the weeds and those parasites,
The work may be hard and nature sometimes extreme and unkind
But she always repays, the flowers and vegetables really delight.

Good health is the real blessing that allows you delights like
Another great love of my life, to walk where nature really is free,
Through wonderful woods among all those shrubs and wild flowers
And those fabulous cliff paths with views out over the sea.

All these wonders of nature that are ours because we are free,
The explanation for my feelings is because I really love life,
But I am sure this life and all its wonders that nature allows
Would mean very little to me without the real love of my life;
My wife!

T W Denis Constance

MY OLD BRUM

(In memory of Tommy Noakes)

Oh Brum you've changed so often
Over the many years
And you have brought me happiness
As well as many tears

The old Bull-ring had such character
With its barrow boys and all
And the muscle man wrapped up in chains
Who tried to beat them all

One man lay on his back
With a slab placed on his chest
And his mate would hit it with a sledge-hammer
I think you know the rest

The blind man selling matches
He was there for many years
And 'Holy Joe' we all did know
Shouting out his prayers

Yes Brum you've given me lots of fun
Especially as a boy
And now you've changed just once again
And your buildings reach the sky

But I wish you well new Brummagen
Go forward as you will
Because I am a true Brummy man
And I love you still

It's many years since I've been away
And in my prayers you'll stay
And I will always love you 'Brum'
Until my dying day.

Bob Lowe

LIFE WILL GO ON REGARDLESS

Life has a way of surviving
Under all circumstances
No matter what befalls
One, searching, searching
Will in the end conquer
The will to live is the mother
Of all that happens in life
Take heed of all that you are doing
At all times of the day and night
Keep your wits about you
Then if trouble comes your way
Fight it tooth and nail
Give it no rest and promise in your heart
To master it come what may
Never feel you have let yourself down
Whatever happens stand your ground
Leave no stone unturned
You will conquer in the end
Then one can say truthfully
Life will go on regardless

Alma Montgomery Frank

CARNIVAL

Your eyes were shining
Your smile was too.
When you took that walk
I was proud I knew you.

You had a march
You had your chance.
I could not get a big enough glance.

Zoe Laing

INSPIRATION

I went to the woodlands yesterday
Where the tall trees reach for the sky
I waited for inspiration
And thought it had passed me by

All I could do was survey the scene
No verse to me would come
I watched the shadows grow and fade
And heard a bumblebee hum

Blues and greens were all around
White blown blossom clothed the ground
Oh what a pity not to tell
The magic of Mother Nature's spell

But now today it comes to me
Verse after verse my pen flows free
To tell of the flowers, the beauty, the sky
I find inspiration did not pass me by

D George

THE BEST THINGS IN LIFE ARE FREE

We only have to look around,
Then so clearly we will see,
There is so much that does abound
The best things in life are free.

The blue of sea, the sky to match,
The gentle breeze caressing,
The sound of seagulls we can catch,
Our life is one great blessing.

The countryside so lush and green,
In the fields are flocks of sheep,
There's so much beauty to be seen
We know God His vigil keep.

The children's voices loud and clear,
Some are working, some at play,
To us these sounds are very dear,
And we hear them every day.

To have our loved ones round about,
Just to know that they are near,
Makes us want to laugh and shout,
Every day of life's so dear.

Money cannot buy these things,
None of these gifts are for sale,
Life's so good to us, it brings
Happiness, so much detail.

How very thankful we should be,
This world's a wonderful place,
We only have to look and see
That God's made the human race.

Suzanne Joy Golding

AVERSE TO DIETING

Thick chocolate biscuits, sweets, cherry pies
Burgers, milkshakes, chicken nuggets and fries
Not quite 'Diet Trials' nor Atkins at that
Just wicked indulgence, oozing in fat!

Not a calorie wasted nor even disliked
It's a pity I've broken the exercise bike!
Well maybe next summer I'll go to the gym
Going via the chippy, to break myself in!

Well what's all this diet stuff for anyway?
Good health, nice figure, I've heard them all say
Who knows, I could possibly give it a try
After, of course, that last apple pie!

Paula Larkin

TRAVEL (STATIC) OR BY THE BOOK

Travel broadens the mind,
Or so, I have often heard said,
But frankly, it only broadens the mind
If the travellers themselves are well read!

So take a book and a chair
And quietly repair
To your favourite spot in the garden,
You'll find in a while,
You'll travel in style
All your thoughts on movement will harden!

Leaping stiles with a bounce
Like a duchess you'll flounce
Down the road to a distant horizon,
And there you will find
It's all in the mind
The book is the place to keep eyes on!

What need I of airport and baggage?
When seated in chair
I can still take the air
And vegetate just like a cabbage!

So your thoughts will run on
But remember the sun
As you allow all your limbs to take root,
For in less than an hour
He'll show you his power,
You'll end up a glowing beetroot!

If this travel appeals,
Movement, no wheels,
Your mind can roam free as it will,
No queues or bad news
Will hold up your cruise
And the blues you can definitely kill.

So take a book in the shade,
You're not on parade,
So relax with a cool drink inside you,
All that strenuous measure
To find holiday pleasure
Can be found in that small book beside you!

Graham K A Walker

LONG WAY TO GO

Out of the plastic playground
Into the big wide world
Just treat it like a playground
That is what I heard.

Rhythm plays a part
And rhythmlesness an art
But from you whom I know
The place where I will start

Lessons here to learn
Eagle in the sky
You pull me to ecstasy
When I feel the high

I'll dance with you in recklessness
Into the day we'll see
Until that hour cometh
We'll drift within the seas

L T Burbery

MY LOVE

Though time is here
Between our years
And our ways are far apart,
Strange patterns of life,
Do cross in ways
And meet within the heart.
In you I find,
A love to share,
Though words are hard to say,
I hope within your heart,
You'll see my love,
In a very special way.

David Shepherd

THE AWAKENING

The old house stood empty, alone and forlorn.
Talk, love and laughter were gone.
The ghosts of the past were occupants now
spirit and stone were as one.

I walked through the hall and ascended the stairs
the past I relived like a dream;
savouring happy days, recalling the sad
and mourning the might have been.

I moved with despair from room to room
wiping a tear from my eye.
Why am I sad when the times were so good,
what is the reason why?

A coward I stood at the door of my room
but the urge was too strong to deny
and aided by strings of invisible force
I stepped inside with a sigh.

An old wooden box stood alone on a shelf,
my sad heart was flooded with joy.
How could I forget those wonderful days
when I was a carefree boy?

I relived again the dreams of my youth
as I handled each treasure with care.
A medley collection, a story for each,
a memory for all that were there.

I buried the box near the old apple tree,
The sun was high in the sky.
It shone upon my windowpane
and the old house winked his eye.

Amy Shelton Goodall

MY GARDEN PRAYER

I love my little garden Lord,
Which You have given to me.
I thank You for this haven,
Where You can set me free.

I pray each night to give me strength,
To sow more wondrous seed.
And for You to bless the pretty birds
Who fly right in to feed.

I bless You for my sight and smell,
To enjoy the flowers so.
And all the bees and butterflies
Who gently come and go.

So bless my little garden Lord
It gives me peace and joy.
For I have prayed each night to You
Since I was just a boy.

Keith Wilson

THE LEGACY
(Remembrance Day reflections)

No brief now held for monarch nobly grand,
nor zestful clamour of their unreserved obey,
who in proud uniform once stood in fine array,
honouring fond loyal tryst, in march command.
Unflinching, strong, no hint of doubtful sway,
they held fast, died and forfeited the dream,
but now in eerie quiet of the tomb, they scream
a message poignant, piercing earthly clay.

A wish that counsels but judicious thought,
entreating those who yet have lingering breath,
for as ancestry precedes their generations' death
they lie, attesting how such waste was bought.
What man or men did light the fuse, and then
in macabre motion set, those awful deeds
which now are prey, as truth's own spectre feeds
on why those wars were born, and born again?

The silenced throng roars out in loud proclaim,
the text undaunted by the sod, and yet deaf ears
in scorn, pay scanty heed to unfeigned fears,
of those who paid the bloody price of fame.
Their valours urge an end to bogus gloried fray,
for xenophobic minds endure with evil to invest;
whilst from quiescent privacy the fallen's sole behest,
pleads Man to ploughshares turn, and ne'er to stray.

William A Mack

MY LOVE'S FULL RECOVERY

My real love is the flame burning itself.
The faux fair coin of love flipped never true.
Yet, flipped once for you, though the love's still cheap.
Fractured will, cracked soul, cheap thrill, all you.

Love twice told in six turns of the annual.
You were there, with no tear - your page unworn.
The other: loud love; heat cooled in cheap change.
Love for free, not for me, I crave the thorn.

Take my sword, carve out my fake passion.
Engrave afresh the real version in me.
I've coined all these tales, now you close the book
From this point: my love's full recovery.

Josh Morrall

AUTUMN HOMECOMING

Autumn garden, blooming still
Indian summer, blessed sun,
Shining down, mature and friendly.
And still the brightest marigold,
Stands ablaze with golden pride.
Tall and dainty late anemones
Dance and sway in glad array.
Deeply bronze, sunburned rudbekia,
And autumn glory sedum proud,
Flowers burnished 'neath the sun.

Look there, a dainty clematis
Dares to open new made buds,
Mistaking sun for springtime.
See there, a dancing fuschia tall,
Awaits with dread the autumn frosts.

But best of all in the distance, I spy
The dear autumn gardener, busy at work,
Clearing the leaves, tidying the grass,
Endless the jobs at the close of the year.
But glad the homecoming when winter is near
And autumnal glory a joy to behold.

Marion Marston

A TIME FOR LOVE

Perchance, shall a time for true passionate perpetual love, so
inconceivably, disappear?
Or, for another eternally enticing moment, amiably, it shall
remain here?
Ever so indiscriminate; in no more than a mere spontaneous sphere;
'tis my sincere heart, I quaintly ask; so fervent, yet tenderly dear.

Whilst I lie here, upon the ground, thinking such thoughts yet to
be found,
Watching the tranquil birds, amongst clouds, aimlessly floating around,
Ever so gently I deem a resolute sigh, as infinitive time, so unknowingly
passes me by;
Yielding no esteem for the affectionate, or compassions, towards the
relentlessly shy.

Can the romance of time dare to mime, with the lyrical poet whom
can
infinitivally rhyme?
Or would it be a crime, for the worth of a dime, to be compared to
love's infinite prime?
As when time notoriously cares to choose, one's cordial love to
enticingly use,
Upon the peerless lovers seeking the love, which they inevitably lose.

For if desirable emotions were so very fast, for relentless time to be
curiously cast,
whom would not desire true love, to be as ardently vast, as time
eternally goes past?
If alternatively so, love was formally slow, where would such desires
eventually go?
To such a place perhaps, where there are no foe. A place one day
I hope to know.

'Tis impetuously so, that I shed a tear; how from my romantic heart,
one might hear;
How I pray that true love shall hence graciously appear, and remain
much closer than near,
For as my truly passionate perpetual love is sublime,
It shall as eternity never end; and retain immortality, for all of
love's time.

Páraic Folan

HOME COMFORTS

Dreaming spires in a warm summer haze,
Is Oxford, my city of beauty and grace.
Gentle walks in old college grounds,
With exotic contrast in botanical gardens displayed.
Then tea on the riverbank in the afternoon shade,
Watching punters idly drifting, in a soft magical way.
I know I am home in this beautiful place,
And forever will be, for I'll never stray.

Val Bermingham

BY THE FIRESIDE

The fire glows within the hearth
This freezing winter night . . .
It is so cosy sitting here
By the fireside warm and bright.

In sheer bliss my cat and dog
Lie in comfort by the fire . . .
They stretch their paws in great delight -
And of this warmth they will not tire!

Old Jack Frost can do his worst
For we are here together
Watching the golden dancing flames,
So never mind the weather!

D Townshend

I WISH

There was a time when I didn't like my dad.
But then, how many young boys do?
He was either out at work,
or telling me what to do.
'Don't do that. Do as you're told,'
was all he ever seemed to say.
All he ever did was work,
with no time left for play.
It was Mum who bought my toys and sweets.
It was Mum who washed and ironed all my clothes.
It was Mum who gave me all the cuddles.
It was Mum who wiped my runny nose.
It was Mum who chased away the monsters,
that used to lurk beneath my bed.
It was Mum who left the light on and said,
'Good night, God bless,' and gently kissed my head.
It was Mum who organised Christmas and birthday treats
and still found the time to give me siblings along the way.
And what did my dad do to help?
Absolutely nothing! He just worked all day.
So I never really liked my dad when I was young,
and that included my teen years too.
But that was then and this is now
and now I know the things that I never knew.
Now I *know* why he was tired and grumpy.
It was because he had a father's bills to pay.
His hours were long because the pay was small,
with little time left over to spend in idle play.
The smacks and moans I suffered
were not dished out for fun.
But to guide me on my way,
because he loved me as his son.
Some people never realise,
the things that they didn't say.
And by the time they do,
the loved one has passed away.
Luckily I was not one of them,
my dad became my friend.
I had told him that I loved him
long before the end.
And I held his hand and kissed him goodbye
on the day he passed away.
No, I never liked my dad much as a boy,
But how I wish that he was here today.

Peter Clay

MY TRIBUTE TO 'THE QUEEN ALEXANDRA' HOSPITAL HOME, WORTHING

As I sat and looked across the sea,
In the distance the 'White Cliffs of Dover'
Many memories came back to me,
Dame Vera Lynn loved to sing to the soldiers,
Her songs will go down in history,
In the 'Queen Alexandra' I spent some days,
A soldier told me of life on the Burma railway many years ago.
The days he'll never forget.
So many lost their lives,
No more to see the sun set
Wheelchair bound and cannot walk,
They give a smile, but some cannot talk,
A wonderful staff, caring and kind,
As beautiful a home as you could find.

Sylvia Farr

LOVE

As I was walking down our garden path
A smile came upon my face, I had to laugh
It was something you said the night before
I think it was, I'm not quite sure
'I can't imagine a world without you,' you said
The things you talk about when you're in bed
'Do you think we will meet again on the other side?'
'I've thought about that myself,' I replied
'I think we will, I hope we do
I can't imagine a world without you.'

W A Rodgers (Lonnie)

BUTTER SIDE DOWN

There it lies, butter-side down.
My reflexes, dulled by bleary dawn,
Failed to snatch the wayward slice
Which went abseiling down my dressing gown.
The browned, moist crust,
Clad in its thick, dairy coat,
Came to an undignified rest
Upon the chessboard-patterned floor.
My body sags in acceptance
Of the end result.

Paul Reynard

ELUSIVE

Elusive as quicksilver
A candle in the wind
A mirage in a desert
A song some never sing
When you think you've grasped it
In your hand
Like a thief it slips away
And the emptiness that's
Left behind
Will never go away.

All fall beneath the
Spell it weaves
Weak or strong
No one is free
Freely given you soar
On eagles' wings
Withheld you're
On your knees
Yes love is such
A fragile gift
Often lent but
Seldom owned
And broken hearts
And unshed tears
Are the interest
On the loan

Andrew Fox

ON WANDSWORTH BRIDGE

Let there be no next episode for me.
I can only stomach scattered moments
Of Heaven: like the grey afternoon
On Wandsworth Bridge when I watched the broad sweep
Of tarmac, felt at home with enormous hoardings
Showing beer, and red and green garage scene,
Looked up with awe at thick dark cylinders
Of coopers plant, observed dun pavement, mustard sky,
Grind of traffic, slap of rain.

Mariegold Heron

ONLY TWO MINUTES

For two minutes in November we pause to honour those,
who gave for us their valued lives whilst vanquishing our foes.
Heroic acts of brave young men in telling brings them fame
but many died, their war untold but heroes just the same.

Alongside brother, brother fought and friend, alongside friend,
they joined together, fought together, comrades to the end.
On monuments throughout the land, the facts are there to see,
a massive loss of brave young men who died to keep us free.

They died in trenches in the field; they died from cannon shell,
from rifle fire and mustard gas and other forms of Hell.
They gave their all that we might live in freedom, without fear,
some too young to understand the reason they were there.

Comrades in arms they fought to win, their cause so justified
and side by side they faced the foe and side by side they died,
and rank on rank their crosses stand in graveyards overseas
memorials to their sacrifice and there they lay in peace.

So is two minutes long enough to honour men as brave?
So is two minutes long enough to recall what they gave?
Too short a time to mourn for them whose lives were bravely lost,
just who they were and what they did at monumental cost.

That first Great War was long ago and harder to recall
but records show how much we owe to those who gave their all.
Such wars are fought time and again with more young soldiers killed
the causes are both just and good but their life's blood is spilt.

Remember during that Great War one year on Christmas Day,
the front line troops laid down their arms and met their foes halfway.
If on the battlefield a truce on one historic day,
then how much more a longer peace if we our trust displayed?

But bitterness from former times and earlier conflicts fought,
perpetuate hatred in a present nation's thoughts.
This generation bears no guilt for what has gone before,
to forgive and understand this fact could subdue thoughts of war.

That right must triumph over wrong is justifiable cause,
to quell the terrorist and fiend that we may end all wars
and peace worldwide will reign at last, the final battle fought
then those, whose lives we honour now will not be lost for nought.

S C Cowley

THE HEART OF A VIOLIN

Oh! violin I hear your strings of sorrow,
Don't break your heart oh! violin,
Play, play, play me a melody of happiness,
I want to hear you laugh and sing.

Oh! violin I hear your strings crying,
Yet you sound like angels serenading the moon,
Have your strings been wounded like mine,
Or is there something you cannot play?

Oh! violin of love, let me caress your heart,
I hear you, strings throwing fragrant flowers,
Petals floating with coloured sounds,
You carry me through rainbows.

Oh! violin do I feel the vibration of your heart,
Or are your strings crying again?
Don't cry oh violin, dance, dance, dance with your strings,
Play, play, play me a melody of rainbow love.

Oh! violin do I hear strings of joy and delight,
Oh happy violin, play, play, play to me,
Laugh, sing, dance with me,
Fly me, with you on rainbow clouds.

Rosina Drury

GRANDFATHER CLOCK

Minutes speed around you, Grandfather Clock,
The seconds chase, they pass and mock
The hour that marks the timing of the day
Only to tease and race again the circular way.

Your hands reach out to point the passing hour
Accusing relentlessly if we should cower
Under the burden of the worker's load
Knowing we are late down the hard disc road.

Then Time hovers over us a hangman's noose
Waiting to strangle if we should lose
Ourselves in a moment of contemplation
Dragging us down to eternal damnation.

Once caught there is no chance of reprieve
Time's tentacles cling, we cannot leave
To renounce Time's cause and claim oblivion
To bask in the sun of life's meridian.

So Grandfather Clock, count the time if you please,
We can't cope without you though you taunt and tease:
Keep your kind old heart ticking, let passing hours chime
While we count only the minutes sublime.

N M Beddoes

THE DEMOLITION MAN

Most of the time
She knows he loves her
In his own fashion.
Quietly.
Except every once in a while
When he does a demolition job
On her emotions.
Crumbling them neatly to dust
Like any old chimney stack.

Most of the time
His good points shine over
Their marriage like a light.
A beacon.
Except every now and then
When he does a demolition job
On her happiness.
Eroding it slowly and surely
As any sea-lashed coastline.

Most of the time
She's happy with her
Lot in life.
Even content.
Except every once in a while
When he does a demolition job
On her dreams
With his own brand of mental cruelty
Delivered with a smile.

Maureen Reynolds

HEARTS

A heart is such a tender thing,
So easily bruised,
An unkind word or cutting look,
It feels it all, love is such a healing balm,
A touch, a glance, a squeeze of hand
To the poor, lonely soul,
A million dollars could not buy,
Rare indeed, is this sweet and lovely thing,
One heart that to another talks
In dear sweet harmony.

J Sweeney

LOVE'S CASTLE

Curses flying fast and low, follow the train as it melts the snow.
'You won't leave,' she said.
She fired the bullets they handed round,
Took more than her share, tried to shoot you down.
You stood, but bled.
Talked with her friends, reloaded her mind,
Found you again, fired blind.
You took the hits.
Kept a hold of the dream, of what had been,
Refused to feel
The now
She knew you would not leave,
Sealed in with the glue of grief, how could you?
Walled in with the crystals of memory, how would you
Break free?
The castle would fall
The nightmares became real at last,
As you looked with seeing eyes and, saw it all.
'You won't leave,' she said.
The castle shivered, the crystals cracked,
The castle fell.
Curses flying fast and low follow the train
As it melts the snow
She mouths and screams in the curling steam,
Stands in the melting snow.
Watches the red tail light.
Never thought you'd go.

Robert Denis Spencer

TWO VISITS TO LIBYA

Springtime, two thousand and one:
Colourful salads,
Spicy bean soup,
Bottled water, fizzy cans
In modern hotels.
Blossoming almond trees,
Low-lying mint and rosemary;
Warm breezes waft their aromas
Round sandstone ruins.
Keen twitchers spot
A redstart, a crested lark,
A tern dive-bombing
Into heavy blue seas.
Every day more interesting . . .

Any season, nineteen forty-one:
Bully beef,
Weevil biscuits,
Gallon of water a day
For all needs.
Winds stir up sand
Round the live-in truck,
Bringing whiffs of latrines.
Soldier kills a scorpion
With his lighted ciggy,
Helps to bury pals
Burnt while playing cards
In a lorry that was bombed.
Every day more harrowing . . .

Julia Perren

WALKING

On Hope Cove cliffs,
I pause;
the view is calling
through the grass
that grows at the cliff-edge.
It creates space
to hear the voice of river bed and tree,
to feel the beckoning of sun across a field,
to fall with fresh meltwater deep
to some unknown place,
to step a little forwards,
fly upon the backs of birds,
and touch the weight of clouds
to see below
small dots of sheep,
small dots of men.

Back in our crowded valleys
turn from the flock
a moment, and be still,
to think about the
calling of the view.

Midge Bainbridge

LET'S CELEBRATE

A border, bare brown earth is all that's there
Weeds dead, buried, frozen for the months ahead
Lawns crisp and crunchy like a chocolate bar
Firmly in place like gel spiked hair
Trees stripped, beautiful sculptures against the skyline
Hedgerows with only the holly bearing colour and fruit
A glimmer of hope, little white, nodding heads of the snowdrop
So delicate in harshest of weather
Daffodils, tulips herald spring
Lambs skipping, birds parade and flaunt
Love is all around, let's celebrate
The clouds race across the sky, rain unlocks the earth
Sun's gentle teasing, warming their backs like a wake-up call
Until high and oh so hot
The border a riot of extravagant colours beneath its rays
Swallows iridescent and always on the chatlines
All too quick the sun lowers its blinds,
Hosepipes, watering cans are needed no more
Lawnmowers, strimmers hibernating in the shed
Colours change, golden, crimson autumn winds blow
Dreary days, dark nights, oh thank goodness for Christmas lights
They brighten up our wintertime
New year is here, promises and new hopes.
The cycle of life starts again
So go on, let's celebrate.

Teresa R Chester

PERCHANCE TO DREAM . . .

When dreams alone,
Can lift you higher than
You've ever known,

But down to Earth is
Where I want to be, with
Feet on terra firma.

Let the fairies fly by night,
With wings that beat
To bring daylight,

Then I can wend my way
Like streams - guided
By fairy moonbeams.

P J Hale

THE LATE JANE CLARKE

I really hope that, one day
When I head for church on Sunday,
I shall be there for the opening words of Mass;
For, despite the best intention
(And I now collect my pension),
I have always been a dilatory lass.

As a child I lagged behind
And I found it most unkind,
Struggling in my mother's vigorous Catholic wake.
For she set a cracking pace
In the Sunday morning race,
'Get a move on, Jane,' she'd cry, 'for Heaven's sake.'

Blame the nuns I had at school
Who said it was against the rule
To arrive at church too late for the collection.
That I'd massed improperly
If I missed the offertory
And I'd have to go *again* to reach perfection.

So here I am, a whirling dervish
Running late for early service
(And it's been put back to 8am since Jan)
Frantic glancing at the time
In my usual pantomime -
Drink another cup of coffee if I can!

The unholy rush to town
With the minutes counting down
And more traffic lights en route than I can mention;
But as I slither in,
With a 'mea culpa' grin,
I relax - I'm just *ahead* of the collection.

I have told my younger son
When my life is finally done
That I expect a little speech beside my bier.
I just hope his voice won't falter
As he stands before the altar.
I just regret I'll not be there to hear.

'Friends and family,' he will say,
In his best funeral way,
'Today she got to Mass with time to spare.
She's here, not in the foyer;
She's heard the introit *and* the Gloria
And, with luck, she'll even hear the final prayer.'

Jane Clarke

I'D SAY

'God knows best is the truth,' I'd say
So all I do is kneel and pray
Then subdued my fears, no more I fret
If God wills so, my needs are met.

I ask not precious gems or gold
But to see springtime unfold
To see the dawn break through the night
Although I loved those stars so bright
See racing clouds across the sky
Feel the wind as it passes by
Hear the wondrous sounds the songbirds make
Eyes to see the flowers awake
Watch breakers on the moonlit sand
Feel the gentle touch of a friendly hand
The leafy lane, the sun, the rain
The sylvan lake, the pebbled stream
All this is real, not just a dream.
These things a joy both night and day
God's answer to my prayers I'd say.

Roland Seager

THE FLEET-FOOTED VISITOR

You came with the approaching storm
Split the clouds, mocked the sky
Blew raspberries at passers-by
Plucked the apples, shook off the leaves
Ankle deep under the trees.

The fleet-footed visitor
Rushed through my residence
Flew back and forth from room to room
Left doors ajar, overwhelming
Whistling out of tune.

Helter-skelter up and down stairs
Curtains fanning, waving like a flag
Sheets of water running down the glass
Curling smoke round the chimneys
Flying down the drive.

Howling, shrieking under the skies
Wheeling, lifting, soaring birds
Over meadows full of fresh scent
Over clear streams and twinkling grass
Till the moon came overhead.

Breathless, lingering, dying wind
Standing still ready to drop
At length giving up his full strength
Out of the storm a soft breeze was born.

Beth Izatt Anderson

BLOSSOM TIME

Blossoms, pink-white upon a cushion grow.
        Foam jewels set against a blackening sky.
They stand, goblet cream where
        Not long since the icy wind did blow.
Jewels, jewels, light on dark,
        How fine; how grand a stance, employ.
Soon to dance upon a breeze,
        Flutter down, quiet at ease.
Then we'll see the fruiting tree
        But for now, petalled waves upon
            A land-locked sea.
Dance your dance of foam-like glee
        This is my beloved land: I see in thee.

Clive Cornwall

CELEBRATION

Waters awash with fine jewels from the sky,
Waves trimmed with lace set in crinoline style,
Seagulls on wing chant the sea's lullaby,
This beauteous Earth the heart cannot deny.

Familiar sea creatures in silhouette mystify,
Sand, worn like silk shoes, caressed by the sun,
Cliffs, the brave titans, protect with their samurai,
This beauteous Earth the heart cannot deny.

Trees proudly majestic their sway gentle and shy,
Flowers, like a prism, reflect true rainbow smiles,
Raindrops, the tears when a cloud needs to cry,
Oh this beauteous Earth the heart cannot deny.

Serene moon-kissed lakes look like lapis lazuli,
Darkness a shadow wearing shimmering shroud,
Stars, borne of magic, cast their spell from on high,
On this beauteous Earth the heart cannot deny.

Sandra Griesbach

Condemned Man

I'm the condemned man,
I'm hanging from the gallows,
My feet don't touch the floor -
You'll never see me hanging around here anymore.
I've been found guilty - of that you can be sure
Yes, you'll find my heart nailed to the door
I've paid the price - no immortality for me
The noose around my neck as tight,
As tight, as tight as it can be
You lit the blue touchpaper,
You've blown me to kingdom come,
You don't want me anymore,
I've nowhere else to run.
I'm facing the firing squad
Concentration in their eyes,
When the bullets hit me
There will be no more sighs,
Just remember one thing,
I'm honest as can be,
I don't deserve my destiny,
Or tainted death that awaits me -
Or the gallows hanging from a tree
You're the love of my life -
Will death release me?

M McFarlane

Colourful Memories

As I sit and rest awhile, into my garden I gaze.
There looking back at me in resplendent glory
Are beautiful flowers, proud, among the sun's rays
Each flower, each bud, my memory stirs, each one tells a story.
The drooping lilac, a fragrance divine.
A thank you gift from a dear friend of mine.
Honeysuckle trailing along the fence.
Filling the evening air with its lovely scent.
Evening primrose, swaying in the breeze, standing proud and tall
Gladioli, marigolds, clematis, sweet peas, memories of them all.
Bulbs, cuttings, seeds, each one from relative or friend
The colours of my roses, gorgeous pink, yellow and deepest red
Each year I remember loved ones as the buds unfurl and bloom
A vase of roses brought indoors, the fragrance fills the room.
Poppies pink or shades of red, above the pansies wave their heads
Primroses, violets, foxgloves, wallflowers
The wonderful memories, such happy hours
The young Cox's apple tree bearing its first fruit
The raspberry seeds I planted, now showing their first shoots
My heaven on Earth, to rest and remember, the times I loved the best
With loved ones and friends, from present and past
Colourful memories forever to last.

Gertrude Schöen

Diana

You gave your love with so much grace,
And gone on to a better place,
Like a butterfly you spread your wings
And soared away to higher things.
Your memory in our hearts we keep
And often have a silent weep.
Your love and kindness will be told
As new generations all grow old,
A treasure within the heart down deep.
A beautiful lady now asleep.

Patricia Penders White

Art At The Royal Academy

'The Academy,' calls the bus conductor and I alight
Push open the revolving door
And mount the steps in keen delight.
I stare at art's expression.
A viewer, I attempt to learn
Why boot-fair wooden objects on a shelf
Profess to be wondrous in itself;
I scan the oils in reds or blacks on white,
A triumph if the swirls are right?
But just what do they bring to light?
Or the Alhambra, two for the price of one
Or 'Anarchistic Punkadell'
Or Y-fronts - who can tell?
Or Urban Owl, over ersatz . . .
Much relieved, I spot landscapes,
Now these I do appreciate!
To the models I relate
A craftsman spent hours on them to make,
They remind me how, when, as a child
I made some out of boxes, with great pride.
Then I come upon a room
Where waves are painted on some tiles;
Description scrawled on walls in rhyme
Tell us what their meaning hides . . .
Shall I go to the Academy next year?
Of course I will, under modern pressure
To renew art's know-how
And to modernism bow
Maybe next year there'll be on the wall
Beauty displayed for all?

Veronica Bulmer

Ghost Soldier

England in cold blood you murdered me,
The murder was unjust,
And my spirit will not rest,
I was only seventeen and had given you my best.

England in cold blood you murdered me,
It seems like only yesterday,
That I climbed down from Mother's knee.

At fourteen I answered Kitchener's call,
Fought some bloody battles,
All to no avail,
You said I was a coward,
When my nerves began to fail.

Then at seventeen when I could take no more
And I'd given you my best.
You said I was a coward
And put a bullet through my chest.

Then a shadow fell across my face,
To see if I was dead,
I heard it say sorry son,
Then put a pistol to my head.

There's one thing that breaks my heart,
To my mother I'd brought shame,
And old friends, they say to my father
Where did your lad fall
We can't see his name on any war memorial?

My spirit will not rest,
I was only seventeen
And had given you my best.

Brian Bateman

FACE FACTS

No tears for what is lost,
The past a day away,
And life is moving forward,
You choose to move or stay.

Move can change perspective,
And bring the past to light,
For who would ever want to stay,
And join the losing fight?

Better to have loved and lost,
And live another day,
Than choose to stay and fight the past,
And then just fade away.

Emma Jane Glenning

MEMORIES

Pytchley Road, so long ago,
We played as children down the road.
The fun we had, so innocent, so pure,
So long ago . . . now no more.

Tescos, MacDonald's and others
Are there now, built on the ground
I played on as a child.
Memories so fond, I just can't seem to let them go.

I was walking down the aisle in Tescos the other day.
Pushing my shopping, I was miles away.
Memories of Alan, Diane, Brian, Paul and others
Came to me as a shriek of laughter so bright and pure.
No! A squeal of a laden trolley passing by.
Back then we were so free.
. . . And now?

Paul R Baker

TRIUMPHANT SPRINGTIME (WITH ORCHESTRA)

Birds silent in threatening biting winds
As trees take on this merry-go-round of challenge,
The vicious winds unrelenting
Refusing to return to winter past
And elements in complete disarray
Ravaging this tortuous scene,
Verdant blades of grass shivering with expectation.
And now, at last, the appearance of rain showers
That refuse to retreat, taking on the battle of resistance,
But in spite of strengthening winds the sun makes its presence known,
Claiming its rightful place
In preparation for wonderful springtime.
Snowdrops with their tiny drooping heads
Peering cautiously above ground
And bursting daffodils opening with great pride
Joyfully shaking their golden heads of beauty,
The tiny heads of snowdrops nodding in firm approval.
Tempted rosebuds, so delicate,
Unfolding now with petals of great artistry
Accompanied by fragrance wafting on a gentle breeze,
Calmness and serenity transforming all around;
With bursting buds opening,
Delicate leaves fluttering,
Fledglings twittering,
Daffodils trumpeting,
Snowdrops conducting expressively,
And bluebells ringing their tinkling bells.
This wonderful show of beauty accompanied by music
Announcing the arrival of magical springtime.

Irene Grahame

THE ARISTOS

The name of my cat is Fleurie.
Her friend is Jehosephat.
Together they sloop their milk and their fish
On their personalised kitchen mat.

Tails up and 'whoops' into my garden,
They jettison through the cat flap,
Poke noses among sweet peas,
Chase butterflies,
Cuff bees (and each other):
Two bimbos in a luxury habitat.

Claws in the oak tree bark
Presage a romp and a lark
On their trampoline of branches, twigs and leaves,
Scrambling birds into full flight,
Pulverising me with fright
As I contemplate the high cost of firemen's fees.

Under the summertime yellowy moon
'Miaow' yodels Jehosephat.
'Mi-ee miee miee-aiow'
Fleurie crescendos back
In 'sharps' which register flat.
A long-suffering owl from its nocturnal roost
Lets out a disdainful hoot
And my military neighbour from his garden next door
Chucks out an old army boot.

In time the night-gig terminates
And cats, birds and insects are still.
Then soft pads are heard on the utility shed
'Neath my wide-open window sill.
A quiet mew, and a graceful leap
Brings a furball onto my bed.
A warm nose nuzzles against my cheek
And Fleurie curls up tail to head.
This is my animal home at last
Despite her prodigal will.
This is my adorable acrobat
My loyal aristo-cat still.

Elise Henden

MUSIC

Is ought so lovely as the gentle sound
Of music drifting on the summer breeze?
A human heart expressing its emotion
Like the soft wind sighing to the graceful trees.

Magic fingers rippling o'er the keys,
Lending earthly notes a joy divine.
A choir sweet and clear as ringing bells,
Around my heart these mysteries entwine.

Such ecstasy, such rapture have I known,
How music can enthral a humble heart.
'Tis life to me! For music so divine
Does all the wonder of the world impart.

I live my saddest moments o'er again,
But music softens grief and eases pain;
Each heartache is a chord, but softly played,
All tears now charmed by memory's sweet refrain.

The happy moments of my life return,
Thrice blessed by music's own sweet heavenly spell;
The web is spun and I am bound within;
A captive in a strange enchanted cell.

And every tune a memory holds for me;
Every note sweet moments does recall;
I pray that gentle music I may hear
Until the curtain of my life shall fall.

Caroline Byron-Johnson

LITTLE JOHNNY WRITES

Little Johnny sat down to see what he could write,
He got a pen and paper and a notepad that was bright.
Then he started writing to see what he could do,
Johnny wrote a story, well one or two.

Wow! What an adventure little Johnny had.
He knew that his adventures would make him very glad.
Tarzan with a rhino chasing after Jane,
A man with a pistol claiming he's John Wayne.

Little Johnny smiled at the work he now done,
He thought that his stories would make him number one.
Little Johnny laughed, he was having fun,
By putting pen to paper his teacher said, 'Well done!'

Caroline Lake

LIVING WITH THE SEASONS OF THE SEA
(For Freda)

The exhilarating feeling of spring is in the air,
As the first watery rays of sunshine appear.
Many rare and curious things are seen,
On the beach where the spring tide has been.
Plants and twigs plucked from strange islands.
Rope, bottles, the odd shoe from foreign lands.

Warm summer waves arrive, bearing milky white tops,
Carrying jellyfish, crabs, shells and bottle tops.
Hordes of holidaymakers invade the inviting shore.
Rubbish infests the golden beaches once more.
Hot grains burn, and the relentless sun is hard to bear.
Inflatables, jet riders, sandcastles are everywhere.

Autumn arrives with cool breezes and pleasure.
Most visitors have left; the coast has given its measure.
Along moss covered steps the soft waves happily slap
Leaving them gleaming and clean, as the seashells tap.
Breathtaking sunsets that colour the sky with fire,
Revealing the vast energy of nature, that will never tire.

Winter seas are fierce and powerfully wild
Crashing angrily over barriers where sand is piled.
With ice and snow and torrential weathers,
Putting lives at risk, seamen at the end of their tethers.
Invincible, treacherous, beautiful and free,
The intriguing, fascinating, wonderful North Sea.

Mary Parker

PEGASUS

The stallion appeared, coal-black and gleaming,
To carry her off, up into the sky.
His thick mane caressed and behind him streaming,
Caught by the wind as he continued to fly.

Into the clouds as a surfer in sea-foam,
Bursting forth later, part of the night.
Fleet of foot was he, swiftly making for home,
Aware on his back, he bore the wee mite!

Amongst the galaxy is one brilliant star,
On the fine forehead there was the same.
For earthbound mortals it is too far,
But the little girl recognised it when he came.

Glad she was to climb up on his back,
The waiting time over, the farewells said.
She clung to him loosely, it was just a knack,
For her strength had diminished as she lay in her bed.

The stallion was sighted still travelling on
But nearing the end, his task almost done.
Soon they will hear a heavenly song
And be bathed in the rays of a brilliant sun.

Daphne McFadyen

ANTHROPOLOGY

Much concerned with anthropology,
Credit did John much deserve.
He asked, 'In what terminology,
Can I God and others serve?'
The whole sphere of scientology
Never to the man appealed,
After trying some technology,
He found this was not his field.
As a doctor of pathology,
He might cure much disease,
Be an expert in neurology,
Seek to put folk at their ease.
Should he study criminology,
Misbehaviour day by day,
Find the answers through psychology,
Show why people go astray?
In a college of theology,
John, at first was all at sea,
But found, through bibliology,
How salvation was to be.
From the world's sad demonology,
He began to sinners lead,
Persuading each to make apology
To the Lord in all his need,
See him join in some doxology,
With new friends in songs of praise,
Discovering true Christology
And God's blessings all his days.

D J Price

FACT

You see a newborn child,
You smell his skin of silk,
You experience awe and wonder;
You hear him cry for milk.
It's the only way to show his need,
His mouth, wide-opened,
With innate sound, his plead,
That cry for help;
He searches, nuzzles her warm, loving breast
For life-sustaining food.

Parent, do you hear it?
Doctor, neighbour, nurse and friend,
Do you hear it?

Today the cry grows louder
Across waves of keen transmission.
You hear the newborn child,
Almost smell his skin of silk
You also 'feel' his hunger,
You hear that cry for milk.

Today that mouth cries louder
Yet, growing weaker every hour,
He is someone's precious offspring
With a need for food and love,
Arms of warmth to nurse his weakness,
Shelter him from cruel bleakness
In a world so slow to act
To endless dire, piercing fact,
Today.

Sonia Jones

DIETING

How often when window-shopping in days gone by
We would check out the style and give a sigh
If only we had the cash and figure too
To purchase those clothes for me and you.

But money was scarce and those pounds there
And if we tried them on others would stare
With that tell-tale mirror reflecting at us
Better hurry along and catch the next bus.

Then we made that decision to lose some weight
And joined a class before it was too late
Those diets seem to work so we'll give it a go
Avoid tempting foods and always say no.

Classes have started and so have we too
Instructor keeps telling us what we must do
Weigh out that food and eat ourselves thin
Checking the fat content on side of the tin.

We have stuck it now for a month or more
With that scale sitting there close to the door
That tell-tale electronic message it gives out
Not a bit of wonder we just want to shout.

We have lost half a pound or maybe one
We'll be going for years before it has gone
Others more successful than we are
Better start walking and forget the car.

I think we should stop for we're getting nowhere
Paying out cash weekly we just can't spare
Just admit our failure when it comes to food
For that chocolate cake was really good.

Imelda Fitzsimons

A DIETER'S LAMENT

It's hard to be on a diet
When you're hungry all the time
My husband says I will look great
When I am eight stone nine
I find it very difficult
I really want to say
Please let me have some chocolate cake
I'll start another day.

But I have joined the diet class
And have my points to count
I only have eighteen a day
It's such a small amount
No more Jelly Babies, nougat fudge or treats
But just a plate of salad, adorned with different meats
I miss my crusty doorsteps, especially buttered toast
I only have a tea plate
When I serve the Sunday roast

I have my diet cookbook
To help me every day
To conjure up a low fat meal
In quite a different way
Don't mention entertaining, or going out to dine
The bubbly is forbidden, so too, a glass of wine

But when I reach my target weight
I will be filled with glee
That's when I will be going . . . on a mammoth
Shopping spree!

Angela Soper-Dyer

FOR ALEC
(Born 1st July 2005)

We saw you on the scan print, soft and sweet as a kernel,
Curled safely in our daughter's womb
One little hand, the left one, reaching out,
Fingers spread, straining to hold our hands,
Or so we mused, wishing we could hold on to you
And travel with you for your whole life,
Protecting you, keeping all harm at bay,
Yet knowing this would keep all life from you,
The pain, and the joy.

Now we hold you to us, listening to your baby breath
Filled with awe at your tiny perfect face,
Your soft little hand spreads at our touch
Tiny fingers closing on ours, comforting us,
As if to say, we can be with you for a while, along your way,
And you will hold us dear, as we hold you,
Your soft honey flesh and precious future
Cupped in our hands and hearts, our darling,
Our little nut-brown boy.

Mary Anne Clock

THE JOURNEY

Holiday time at last
The train running fast
There it was on the rack
My case as usual fully packed
A seat booked by the window
Such excitement, as views flew past
Too quick to really wonder
Who lived in that house?
Who worked in the factory?
Everything sped by
Then meeting companions sat next to me
Was really such a joy
As they came from abroad
And I learned from them
And they from me
As we viewed the scenes together
Of sea and sand go speeding by
Wonderful Durham Cathedral
All this and more
On that happy journey
To bonny Scotland
A special place
In my heart.

J Nicoll

FIRST LOVE

Remember those happy times we used to meet,
Under the old bridge along Canal Street,
How my heart sank if you were a bit late,
But I knew you would come, so I'd stand and wait.

As you came up the hill my heart leapt a mile,
I'd see your beautiful face and beaming smile,
Hand in hand on the towpath we'd walk,
Content together we'd laugh and talk.

Enjoying the countryside just you and I,
We didn't see anyone else passing by,
Engrossed in each other we'd plan and dream,
We had such ambitions at seventeen.

We'd live in the country, have a dog and a cat,
A duck pond and chickens, simple things like that.
Spend time with each other, we'd never part,
We believed in our dreams, they came from the heart.

Christine A Lee

Jig 'O'

There's a monster living down by the flow,
One day you will meet him
The Dreaded Jig 'O'
Spawned way back by goblins and gods,
What were they thinking, the stupid sods.
It's narrow and dark, there's no room to move,
If you've ever worked there, you know you've nothing to prove.
We have all suffered sometime, and have tales of woe,
Of our trials and experiences on
The Dreaded Jig 'O'
Nothing on the jig is ever greased,
I swear it's not fit for man nor beast.
There's a dungeon underneath with rancid air,
I'm sure there's something horrible living down there.
You can bang your head and pinch your hands,
If you drop anything, who knows where it lands.
Some people say it's gremlins below who cause most of the damage
On the Dreaded Jig 'O'
But there is a man with a claim to fame,
I'm sorry but I can't divulge his name.
We had loaded the jig and everything was fine.
The spars had gone in, there was plenty of time.
He was raising the plug, just before lunch,
It was approaching its berth, when there was an almighty *crunch!*
Everyone on the jig stopped work to cringe and stare,
At the lonely soul saying, 'What the f**k happened there?'
To the shift leader's office he was 'bing-bonged' hailed to go,
To receive his penance for the damage to
The Dreaded Jig 'O'
He was a hero for a while amongst the men,
But a few months later he did it again.
But we can only thank him for shutting the jig for three weeks or so,
Because this meant we were free from the clutches of . . .
The Dreaded Jig 'O'.

Thomas Jones

Anthropology

Creation's six long days elapsed
     And life on Earth appeared -
Each man and beast and living thing
     Created whole, not reared.

But science, strangely, seems to think
     That somewhere in the gloom
Infinitesimal fluxions did
     Enable life to bloom.

Enough! For God created all.
     Now Adam, self-propelled,
And single-minded Eve, brought shame,
     For each one had rebelled.

So Jesus came, the Saviour,
     His flesh and blood to give,
That we, partaking, should know love,
     That, through it, we might live.

Now people venture forth upon
     Earth's ever changing face
Each one of us with aught in mind -
     Achieving it through grace.

For God intended us to do
     Whatever we do best -
Some do it well and others try
     Before we're laid to rest.

Death's vice-like grip will be appeased
     When we, in shrouded place,
Awaken to the call of Heaven -
     Then see God face to face.

John Goulding

Do It Yourself

Stripping, scraping, making good
Preparation - sanding wood,
Brush or roller, paper, paint,
Having fun - you know I ain't
Ready pasted, whichever I buy
You know I hate this DIY.

Sawing, planing, drilling holes,
Handles, hinges, curtain poles
Nailing, chiselling, screwing tight,
Pin it down and get it right
Hammer or pliers whichever I try
You know I hate this DIY.

Bricks and mortar, building walls
Plastering on stairs and halls,
Artex, stipple, ragroll too
Take your pick, it's up to you,
Rough or smooth - please tell me why
You know I hate this DIY.

Digging, raking, planting seeds,
Mowing lawns and pulling weeds,
Pruning, trimming, edges neat,
Bedding flowers, small and sweet,
Back-breaking work, you'll hear me cry
'You know I hate this DIY.'

'Get the pros in,' you'll hear me say
Then a shock, big bills to pay
So have a go and do your best
To put all your skills to the test,
You'll be rewarded by and by,
And soon you'll love this DIY.

Maureen Reeves

This Love

This love
This white-hot flame
Fuelled by infinite energy
Perpetually the same
Yet sparkles with diversity

This love
This treasured gift
Increases with each giving
Its value somehow lifts
As the giver is receiving

This love
This mutual care
Remotely need perceiving
An extra sense, so rare
Across all distance cleaving

This love
This immortal soul
A delightful fusion forming
Makes two halves one whole
Each to the other calling

This love
So long neglected
Yearns for its consummation
To see its hope perfected
Complete, one soul, one passion.

Martin Collins

MIZPAH

God gave to us from His own word,
This password only you and I would know
A signature used only between us
Mizpah - significant - in joy and woe

Many years have come and gone
Our Heavenly Father, teaching us His way
Holding up in the storms of life
'How long Lord . . . maybe today?'

Often reminding us of the vision
Standing together, looking to you
The most important part of the equation
Lord, what would You have us to do?

Teaching endurance, patience
Showing us the rejection, resentment - all there
Swirling deep down in the subconscious
'Be still,' You say, 'I care'

Mizpah - 'The Lord watch between us -'
We'll hold on to the vision when we roam
Keep us ever one in You, our Saviour,
Till eternity - when You call us home

So we'll be ever with the Lord
Who walked this way, perfect one
Till that day - only the Father knows when
We'll stand in glory - hear His 'well done'

Alice Carlin

THOSE MIGHTY DAYS OF STEAM

Longingly he relives his boyhood dream,
Pen and notebook ready at hand.
Keen nostrils await grand aroma of steam
Only an enthusiast could understand.
At last she's coming down the line,
Greyish clouds from her funnels pour.
The Flying Scotsman arrives on time.
All so well worth waiting for.
In her coat of Brunswick green
Name in brass that shines,
This incline she takes with ease
Number 4472 he reads just fine.
Nothing compares to travelling by steam
Authentic sound of wheels on track.
Drivers and stokers, all part of the team,
His memories are all flooding back
His book and pen he packs away,
All the details he must now record,
Looking forward to another day
When steam returns to the neighbourhood.

Margaret Meadows

SEASONAL VERSES

The summer sun shines
Bright and hot on sandy shore
Where people get tanned.

In autumn leaves fall
Golden yellow, orange brown,
Bonfires, fireworks spark.

In winter it snows,
Twilight comes early; wind blows.
The cold nips our toes.

Birds return in spring
To nest, and nurture their young
From egg to fledgling.

Pauline M Clarke

A VIEW ON LIFE

My life has been a mixture
Of good things and of bad
In fact just like all of you
With happy times and sad.
But the joys outweigh the sorrows
We are all so richly blessed
With food and friends and fellowship
And a home and bed for rest.
So, why do we sometimes grumble?
Why do we sulk and frown?
Just because some little thing
Has caused us to feel down
Trust in your Heavenly Father
And hold your head up high
Thank God that you are living
You don't know how soon you'll die.

Vera Hankins

ALWAYS SO MUCH MORE THAN JUST

I hear you say you love me
And I know it comes from the heart deep within
What have I done to deserve you?
Always thinking you were the prize I could never win

How lucky am I?
Dreams coming true, real love recognised
Never thought that I could be standing
With you to have right by my side

I don't care if it's fate or not
Because I know it's gonna be forever
There can be no other way
Than you and me together

It's as if we're meant to be
The only answer is us
In love so completely
Always so much more than just

A love I thought I'd never find
You've let me discover
You have my heart, my soul, my all
Never shall they belong to another.

Elaine Donaldson

UNTITLED

Remember, oh remember
The green, glass, gleaming water
Falling
Falling,
Lost to our sight;

The rain's incessant beating;
The urgent, ancient forest
Thrusting
Thrusting
Into the night

And moonless secret darkness;
And we were witless calling
Calling
Calling
For dawn's respite.

Remember, oh remember
The rainbow raptured morning
Singing
Singing
Hymns to the light.

Joyce K Tweedie

PLUTOLATRY

The white man thinks he's very good,
that all he does is right.
He doesn't like those darker skins,
the ones that are not white.

He confiscates, or steals their wealth,
gives them his own diseases.
What right has he to take his fill
of their riches which he seizes?

All Africa has suffered the yoke
of alien cultures and customs.
The black man's life is sadly changed,
for the white man's laid his time bombs.

In India too he stamped his mark,
curtailed their every thought.
Drove them hard like underdogs
and crushed the ones who fought.

In North America he stole the land
from Apache, Commanche and Sioux.
Their nomadic lives were altered then
by the things the white men do.

The Amazon Indians are threatened
and most have already been taken
away from their homes in the jungle
and their lifestyles are forsaken.

Forced into camps and reserves
and denied their natural needs.
Tribes like the Kreen-Akrore
who are Stone Age in their deeds.

For the white man sends his roads
across their territories.
Builds paper mills and factories
and destroys their wetland trees.

All people should live in their own way,
not 'Civilized' or treated like dirt,
and the white man should stay in his cities
and not cause the coloured man hurt.

Daphne Richards

BUTTERFLIES IN A PROVENÇAL GARDEN

O'er lavender hedges
The butterflies hover.
They come for the nectar
They find in sweet clover.

Then flickering, fluttering,
Up through the airs,
Nimble, mercurial,
Dancing in pairs;

Parting and meeting
and playing in flight,
Dashing and tumbling
Down from the height.

Swift to the savoury,
Slow to the mint,
Pausing and questing
They shimmer and glint.

Orange and yellow
And speckled with spots.
Bronze and vermilion
Freckled with dots -

Admirals, peacocks,
And swallow-tails too -
But best, to my fancy,
The small baby blue.

Evelyn Westwood

MY CHANGING WORLD 1925 TO 2005

Back in '25 when I was born
No radio, TV, just gram' with horn.
No welfare state to help the poor
Half-starved kids: no shoes they wore.
Hols were trips to the sea
Or maybe field picnics, locally.
Then in the '40s we went to war;
Altered our lives to the very core.
Men went away: turned the world around.
Jobs for the ladies then were found.
The atom was split and they dropped the bomb,
(Cancer available to everyone!)
Moon and space conquered - to what avail?
Satellite messages replace the mail,
Microwave cooking; washers save time,
But 'idle hands' seem to increase crime.
Mum has to work to pay larger bills
Young men are 'stressed' so make their wills!
Brainwashed children are sent out to kill,
Think being martyrs is a heavenly skill.
Increased pollution causes global 'warm',
And organ transplants are now the 'norm'
Although modern wonders are here to stay
The price in the end is a high one to pay.
Let's look at our values: just stand and think . . .
The *end of the world* . . . are we on the *brink?*

H M Birch

SIGHTS AND SOUNDS OF AN OLD ENGLISH FAIR

Under a great canopy of lighted sky
Roundabouts and stalls and shows congeal.
Brazen music . . . a grinding, blaring symphony
While the crowds surge and sway, surge and sway
And break . . . pushing, catcalling and screaming.
The fizz, fizz, fizz of spinning lights.
Merry-go-rounds, galloping nowhere, whirl and whizz
Through fusillades of excited shouts.
'Cross me palm wiv silver an' I'll read yer 'and Ducky!'
A skeleton dances, rattling dry bones . . .
'Coconuts . . . coconuts . . . knock 'em dahn ter win.'
The big wheel turns above the motley
And couples climb the sky . . . up . . . up . . . up
To brush the stars.
'Come and see the bearded lady . . .'
Stalls laden with rock and cakes,
The puffed up nothingness of candyfloss
And the biggest, stripiest, blackest and whitest humbugs
                                    in all the world.
The enticing lure of hotdogs
Fried onion smells that tickle the nose and saliva drools . . .
The drone and dirge of dodgems . . .
Crash! Bang! And blue sparks fly.
The music overall . . . *tink plonk plonk, tink plonk plonk,*
Tink plonk plonk, tink plonk plonk . . .
'At 59 stone and 4 pounds, this mountain of flesh
Is the fattest lady in the land.'
Rushing, glorious madness . . . eyes shut tight . . . hair streaming . . .
Impassive attendants' swarthy faces
Jingle and chink their harvest.
At the boxing booth the flat-nosed pug
Revolving gum . . . stony faced . . .
'Five pahnds fer the man oo can go five rahnds wiv battlin' Bertie . . .'
Rubbish clutters the ground . . . lolly sticks . . .
Ice cream cartons . . . paper . . . lick . . . suck . . .
'Put that down, Willie, you don't know where it's been.'
Grubby fingers grope for a last coin . . .
Just time to savour the final, magical moments.

Roy Burfield

MOTHERS

I oftimes recall
Her love and care upon us all
And I hid behind the mother's skirt
Lest I from Father's wrath be hurt
Her loving eye would be upon us
Her loving hands would care
Seeming without too much fuss
Held sway by her watchful stare,
With joy her heart it must have been moved
When we the Saviour's love for ourselves had proved
Then on bed of sickness and pain
Her shining example of faith came to me again,
It was my mother's faith, that day
That stopped me wandering so far away.
A shining example my Saviour would know
Oh, how I would be like her, for him also
Thank You Lord, for mothers and fathers too
In toil and sickness their love came through
Their faith an example they passed on
Their love was a link You designed all along
This I know, and I would fain
Believe that I shall see them both again.

D Mason

NO SOUNDTRACK

I have heard your feet by night
where trees and chimney pots are sleeping
and the moon is bright on diamond water;
in dim dawn's grave with promise
softly awaking,
in waves soundlessly breaking at the feet
of cliffs;
in the magic of windless afternoons I
have heard your secret soft footfall;
in the sheen blue shimmer
of a high silent tarn,
the evening dream of byre, barn
and hedgerow by quiet woods,
in grey brooding ridge and hill . . .
where all is still your velvet tread
caresses,
blesses,
and the green Earth song replies.

John Allison

UNDECIDED

Survey the scene before you if you will
Is it full of promise for happier days ahead
Or are you gazing back in anger or regret
At what might have been if all had gone to plan?

Should you live each day as if it was your last
Go hang-gliding or what else you think is scary
Or sit at home and brood upon the time
When lack of action was the order of the day?

Perhaps a bold approach would suit the current thought
Should one be careful, or throw caution to the winds
Or take the middle road and ease your troubled mind
Across the broad acres of your future life?

Alan Marten

MY BUSY, BUSY WORLD

People as clever as me, cannot be expected to find employment
As, I go to bed very late, and equally get up, very late.
For me a teasmade by the bed, is a must.
My first task of any day, is to try and work out
What work today I am absolutely, not going to do!

Once the feet are back on terra firma, for the day.
The journeys to and fro have to be reduced
So collect every item I need to survive, in just one trip
Will the two-day-old clothes, last another day
Or will I have to go to the launderette, at last?

Breakfast is another chore, as choices make you tired
Weetie Bangs, porridge or bacon sandwich?
I have none of this, just stale bread to toast.
Now there is a trip to the supermarket and launderette
Or it's beans on stale toast, once again.
Dirty clothes pile up on the bathroom floor.

I must go back to bed and work out what I need to do
To survive yet another week, of pressure and toil
Is it launderette or supermarket first?
Who can we get to help, to take the dirty washing out
Or get the shopping back? Unpacking is another job
But a cup of tea first, whilst I work something out?

Michael Wise

CONTENT TO SERVE

Humorous assistant in a high street sweet shop
Serving happy children on their way from school
To a handful of chocolates, liquorice, lollipops
Chewing gum, toffee bars
And iced cream fool

Overweight innkeeper with an obese beer gut
Continually swearing in a drunken rage
At a bar full of beer swilling thugs, drunkards
Louts and soccer hooligans
All; under age

Hell fire preacher in a carved oak pulpit
Wrathfully rejoicing, singing songs of praise
To a church full of disbelieving, pious gentiles
Hypocritical of Satan
And his sinful ways.

Maurice Ivor Birch

HOW

I've forgotten how
to bake a cake
my mother knew
my grandmother knew
but I've forgotten now

I've forgotten how
to milk a cow
I once knew
when I was a child
in my village
running wild
but I've forgotten now

I've forgotten how
to beat my brow
I've known
so much humiliation
so much frustration
so much treachery
now I want to be free
but I've forgotten how

Ursula Bayer

GOODBYE MY LOVE

It's hard to say goodbye to the one you love
Deep down you know they have gone to a better place
Waiting for you to be by their side
But life must go on
And our task fulfilled
God gives us strength to carry on
Come what may
When my task is fulfilled
I only hope
God takes me home
To be by your side.

E Bevans

A POEM SPOKEN

A poem
spoken
comes alight
with a life
of its own.

It's like a fire
of small dry sticks
of brown and black
and grey events
set alight
by the flames
of words
dancing
in ever changing
shapes and colours
sad mauves
to bright gold
curling and leaping
alive and beautiful
transient
ephemeral
suddenly complete.

In the silence
the grey ash
transformed now
by the dance
living on.

John Foster-Turner

AFTER THE EQUINOX
(Denton Woods 1984)

I watch the falling gold of the escaping year
For summer's milked memory I shed a lonely tear
Sweet birdsong once coloured the sky;
Now northern winds echo in their fadin' cry
Eloping again with the migrating sun.
Oh swallow, I wish with you I could come
Soaring to the heights of paradise
To a land that has never heard of ice.
Evolution? Why cannot I fly away
From this sky of gathering cloudy grey?
Where now is summer's acoustic breeze
Which danced joyfully through singing trees?
Canopies sagging with a season's treasure
Summer's finalé and most fruitful pleasure.
Even the squirrel has more sense than we
Tucked warm in the hollow of the old oak tree;
Through snow and storm he hibernates
Dreaming the north of Europa thro' all winter's fates.

Paul Reece

FOR PAT

You are the only one for me.
I hope you understand,
that even when alone
I take you by the hand.

You are the greatest friend I know
the one I love so much,
and when we are together
how much I need your touch.

You always say the sweetest things
your thoughts are deep in mine,
I will never forget you
you are my love divine.

There are times we can love
and times we love to hate,
but darling I do believe
our love was meant as fate.

The first time I saw you
the first loving kiss,
I knew we'd be forever
entwined in loving bliss.

And if you ever leave me
I know my life will end,
because with you my darling
I have a lover and best friend.
(Yours always)

Tracy Sampson

PICTURES

Look towards the horizon on a spring morn.
See for yourself the beauty of the coming dawn
Watch the light appear, see it grow as it lifts
The darkness from the valley below.
See in the sky the different hues
Pale yellow, grey, orange and blues
You have the best pictures here to see
Painted by nature, entirely free.
Watch the sky throughout the day
The cotton wool clouds dance in play
It never stays the same for long
A picture is there and then it is gone
Along comes another to take its place
Very rarely does it present the same face
If you try to paint the sky on paper
You will find it quite a caper.
For the clouds move along and the colours alter
Enough to make any artist falter.
You paint your picture, very nice 'tis true
But where you have put cloud it has now turned blue.
I paint pictures in my mind
These are true, and the very best kind.
From day to day you can add some more
And in your mind neatly store
You do not need pictures on a wall
For nature has provided them all.
This poem could go on, there is no limit.
Enjoy the sky and the pictures in it,
From dawn to sunset in all its glory
The sunset - yes, that is another story.

Rachel M Green

DEATH IS LIKE A CAR

The car continues going
Even though we cannot see
And the custom just remains
Itself outside of memory

Death is a relation
To a certain time and place
To eternity it's nothing
In a line of endless grace

I've loved you all so much
That I've known eternity
Vast and never-ending
Deep within the thing that's me

Time is like a river
And love a clear, still lake
That holds the sky within it
Crystalline and yet opaque

And I have had that gift
In an abundance that is rare
With you and with my husband
Who's both gone and everywhere

I felt the awesome beauty
Of the end of earthly breath
I've had a rich, full life
And now a peaceful, shining death.

Amanda Sinnick

THE IMPERIAL DRAGON

The imperial dragon, all smoke and fire,
Of which he never tires.
With black wings and such-like things,
And eyes that glow, at friend and foe.
His claws so sharp, in day or dark.
He flies at speed, at no one's heed.
And when he lands, the earth resounds
With loud bangs and crashes,
Which seem to go on forever.
The imperial dragon is the emperor's true friend
And of which he will defend until the bitter end.

Kenneth I Squires

AUNTIE

Auntie didn't seem to mind that her floors weren't very clean
Or that her copper or windows didn't shine, sparkle and gleam
She would smile when we chose lemonade, instead of creamy milk
Her hair was long and grey but felt of finest silk

She always smelt of summer, when flowers scent the air
Her complexion like a velvet peach, so soft and very fair
We always called her Auntie for we never knew her name
Auntie just loved to join in all our childhood games

Delicious were the buns she baked us, for a special treat
And didn't mind at all if crumbs dropped to our feet
She would tell of the fairies that came in the dark of night
To collect all the crumbs to feast upon, before the dawn's bright light

Auntie's stories filled us with such mystic wonder
During summery sultry days heavy with rumbling thunder
Little ones would stop their crying in the warmth of Auntie's arms
Coloured jars of sweeties, were her magical charms

She captured all us children with her gentle heart
Loved us each in different ways, that a little piece of her she'd part
Upon each of our special days, which Auntie gave to all
Lies a posy of summer flowers, until the autumn's fall.

Susan E Roffey

MISSING YOU

As I try to come to terms with your passing away
My fruits of passion and love, rot, moulder and decay
You were all to me
And forever will be
The apple of my eye.

I cried a tear, it seeped down my cheek
I wearily rested and fell into sleep
Please let me dream
So it might just seem
Not to be true.

I'm your knight in armour and arms, heavily laden
You are my fair-haired lass, a beautiful maiden
I'd put dragons to the sword
To free you from your Lord
Who now holds your heart.

The bright morning sun starts to take rise
I stir from my sleep but keep shut my eyes
I want to still sleep
Where here I might keep
My dreams of you.

I reach out my arms, you are not there
I'm hoping and praying yet clutch nothing but air!
I lay and embrace
This empty space
That once held you.

Andrew John Stevenson

TO WHOM IT MAY CONCERN

To whom it may concern, I'm wishing to complain
I was in your store a while before and I bought myself a brain
At that price I could not grumble for I bought it in the sales
And it came complete with a red receipt which said, 'It never fails'

I took it home that afternoon; removed it from its pack
And tried it on for size - back to front and front to back
I really thought my luck was in . . . it was the perfect fit
Maybe now I could be blessed with humour and with wit?

I wore it for a few weeks and everything seemed fine
Then things started to go pear-shaped and I wished it wasn't mine
I went to see the doctor who gave me lots of scans
He said, 'For you, dear Vivienne, we have so many plans.'

He took me to the theatre; not the type I'd seen before
It was not to see Hamlet or a play by the comedy store
It took some thirteen hours to negotiate the veins
To take out such a tumour they really 'picked my brains'

To the Office of Fair Trading I think I'll take a walk
Tell them all my story of how I could not talk
I was like a little baby . . . had to learn it all again
Unless I get a refund for that faulty specimen

I won't make further purchases from this dodgy store
Just ask yourself this question, would you go back for more?
I think I'll keep the one I've got; it's served me all these years
Sure, I had my ups and downs . . . but now I have no fears.

Vivienne C Wiggins

CELEBRATIONS

Today is a special day as everyone can see,
We are here to celebrate your fifteenth anniversary.
For every poet who has accomplished and achieved their very best,
Has all their work published by the Forward Press.
Full of inspiration as well as peace of mind,
For all the poems that I've read were a joy to find.
So here we raise our glasses to celebrate the best
For everyone's achievements as well as the Forward Press.

Clare L Pantling

TANK BATTLE

Suddenly there is a loud bang
The tank shakes but is standing firm
It's not our turn, but my ears rang
Twenty mil', no need for concern

Again the tank quivers like jelly
That is an eight-eight going past.
'Missed!' said Commander Tim Kelly,
'See if you can spot him, and fast.'

That chopped a tree down at rear
Now the die is well and truly cast
We will get him so have no fear
Of that one I felt a great blast.

'Gunner, I've got him in my sight.'
'Load AP, is the firm command.
'Fire! We will give him a real fright
Show him our gun's in big demand.'

'I hit him Serj, right in the centre
The shell bounded off into the air
The AP is supposed to enter.'
'Try again but with a bit more care!'

The gun is fired with a sharp crack
Turret is filled with acrid fumes.
'I've hit him again, he's fired back'
Bang! And the engine flames in flumes.

'*Bale out!*' the commander's loud shout
I traverse the gun to the centre
So that the two in front get out
That one shot made a hole to enter

Hundred yards away, tank's ablaze
Got him with my very last shot
As the crew just stand there and gaze
The tank's ammo is making it hot

We turn and run along a lane
As bullets start to fly around
Screaming mortar shells; what a pain
Send us sprawling onto the ground.

We survive, and get back to base
'What are you doing?' the Colonel asks.
'Nothing Sir,' we reply, 'casualty case'
'There's a spare, get back to your tasks!'

Beddow

TIME

First comes - the Time of Birth,
Recorded as we appear on Earth.
Ever after we are ruled by time,
Hearing clocks that tick and chime.
'Do I have Time?' I often say
As I rush about throughout the day.
We all know just 'how Time flies'
We've said it many a time with sighs.
Always rushing here and there
Never any time to spare.
''Time stood still' - now there's a thought!
Time to do all the things I ought.
Sadly, 'the Sands of Time' run swiftly out
Ere we discover what this life's about.
'Time and Tide wait for no man'.
Each is allotted his life's span.
After we take our very last breath
The doc records the 'Time of Death'.
So when at last, Old Father Time calls,
The play has run and the curtain falls.

Patricia J Edwins

THE TENT

The sirens whined and wailed,
Outside the aeroplanes droned, and the bombs fell.
But under the blankets and sheets
All was warm and well.

The sheets made a 'tent'
And with torches aglow
Four little faces played
Snakes and ladders and ludo.

They had a secret hoard of biscuits and cheese,
As they shuffled the cards, and threw the dice with ease.

The giggles and laughter were heard through the hall,
When suddenly, they'd hear a footstep fall.

All was quiet, they mustn't be heard,
The grown-ups would think their games 'absurd'.
They were oblivious to the horrors about,
And always afraid their secret would be found out.

Many a plot and plan was made in the 'tent'
By the two little girls and two little boys,
Trying so hard not to make any noise,
They would carry these childhood memories wherever they went.

Sixty years on, and most of their lives spent,
They'd still recall the nights in the 'tent'.
Their games, their plans, now live in the past,
But to this day, their childhood memories
Of the dark days of the war will always last.

Anne Roberts

ELUSIVE MOI!

When the phone rings
Where am I?
On the loo, in the bath
In the garden
End of path.

When I answer
Just too late
Phone put down, and silence reigns
Finish off, what I'm about
Ring back later, caller out.

Ann Homewood

GUY FAWKES

Now Guy Fawkes' name was Guido and it's just four centuries hence
And kids across the country make demands for fifty pence
For a face mask on a condom which they've tied upon old rags
Asking, 'Penny for the Guy mate? 'Cause we need to buy ten fags.'
But this Guy without a neck has had to shoulder years of blame
Whilst his beard became a legend we all forgot his name
Even with that maxim which taught us to remember
A night when nothing happened on the fifth day of November
Yet still we light the fireworks shooting colours through the sky
Tie rockets to the neighbour's cat then watch the pussy fly
But the night they captured Guido he was taken to the tower
Tied upon a rack where they'd stretch him by the hour
And his sentence was extended which put inches on the man
Whose effigy of latex now lies limply in a pram
And the final days of Guy Fawkes were spent in little ease
A tiny cell that cramped him so his chin would touch his knees
Chained up in this dungeon where they kept him fed and watered
So he could live past Christmas to be hung and drawn and quartered.

Steve Blackwell

SATURDAY DAD

Once, we went to the zoo
as a treat.
Now it's where we always go,
Dad and I
on Saturdays.

'Dad, couldn't we
go somewhere else
today?
Sit by a fire perhaps?'

'Sit by a fire?
Your mother's fire?'
So cold the voice,
cold as the autumn air.
'She doesn't want me there!'

I try to say,
'But Dad, you went away -'
The words won't come.

We reach a stream.
Beyond it, children play
on swings and climbing frames.

'Let's cross,' I say.
We try . . .
but the gap's too wide.

May C Jenkins

THANK YOU FORWARD PRESS

I woke up this morning and a letter I see
I picked it up, it's addressed to me
It's from the people in Peterborough called Forward Press
They need another poem, I'd best get dressed
Well I have some paper, I've got my pen
Do I write about now or way back then?
Oh what can I write? What shall I say?
Or should I put it off till another day?
Cos I've written about me, I've written about you
This time I need something fresh and new
I've written about the wind, the sea and sunshine
And I'm really quite fussy, I like them to rhyme
But this time I'm stuck, please help me someone
It's their 15th anniversary, there's a prize to be won
I don't have that long, there's a deadline to meet
To win that prize would be such a treat
I know, I'll just write a line at a time
I'm certain my poem will turn out fine
There's some good poets out there, it's gonna be tough
And Forward Press don't mind if it's written in rough
They set it out in a professional style
They've published for me for quite a while
So I'd like to thank them for the work they do
Cos for me they made my dream come true
Their job must be difficult and often tense
Please publish my poem, you know it makes sense
I thought the words would be hard to find
But I've ended up writing what's on my mind
I've done my best, that's all I can do
Does it get published? That's up to you
There's just one more thing I need to stress
Well done to you all at Forward Press!

Dawn McClarren

CIBBER'S FRIENDS

I heard the sound of angered feathers
and cobweb chains rattled in the wind,
where gravestones walked in heavy guise
I realised why and how they'd sinned.
Those chalk white scars on rolling downs
distilled in voids like children cry,
disclaimers smooth the blockheads rant
unseen, unmoved and this was why.
That sparkled peril on diamond's tusk
in ghostly form a wit be told,
high bridges crossed by tawdry friends
who judge and tease to leave us cold.
Such hollowed pardon dislikes mankind
their weakness stalks low dreaded pains,
in quieting mood where calmness smiles
know yet they shall why Dunciad reigns.
Now hang the titan's scabbard fast
where wordless mists thro' windows drift,
some ardour dulled and vigour waned
ungainly souls mimic to lift.
What beauties singe in rings of fire
that chokes black air and struggles free,
these plaintiffs bark and bark forever
all their world is what we see.
Now raise a chalice sublimely fill
hark not those traits their ways shall die,
while cardinals sleep mellow light to spill
on vanities dream, as I pass by.

Tom Griffiths

POETRY

From the heart - through the pen
To the page - comes the word,
Listened to - remembered,
Treasured, as it's heard.

The poet sees, with artist's eye
Beauty of earth - colour of sky.
In language clear, then asks of you
'Listen, ponder, are these words true?'

Poets, the thinkers of this modern age
Reflect on life along the way.
Their words which the sea of fancy bore,
Echo with sound of beauty and awe!

They've all been reborn into a fairy land
Finding happiness, sorrow, close at hand.
No longer needing to rhyme all their verse
Because now it can be written of course.

With education came books - row on row.
'Oh proud Homer, would that you could know.
Some people still prefer verse to rhyme.
Quite like a child beating a spoon to time!'

Poetry implies some experience -
Feigning perhaps, inexperience!
Plus clarity, wonder and awe.
Making life seem richer than before.

Inarticulate in a crisis, words fail.
Not so the poet, whose voice we then hail!
To scorn imagination is to be,
Like the blind, refusing miracle of sight - *to see!*

Daphne Young

SALVATION

When all hope is lost
And you're at the end
Your prayers will be answered
Sent wrapped in your faith
Because in God you have a friend
Always there in your darkest hour
Returning His love in exchange
For the prayers that you gave

When there is no way out
And you think no one cares
No one hears your screams
No matter how hard you shout
There is always someone there
God alone can see your dreams
No matter how desperate
Your lonely life seems

Salvation comes in many guises
But there is only one for you
A different one is made for each person
They come in all shapes and sizes
Because everyone is unique
Everyone's salvation is different
Dependant on what you seek

When you pray for salvation
What you are given
Maybe not what you want
But it is delivered by divine spirit
Sent out to help you along the way
To give you strength for your journey
So you keep to your allotted path
Because throughout this life
Everyone has their part to play

There is a reason
Why things happen as they do
Even if it isn't clear
Why they happen to you
In that instant of realisation
You know you've found salvation.

Richard J Byers

TIMING

My timing was not perfect
As I joined the queue
The Post Office was due to close
I was behind another two
The guy in front turned around
He had heard me sigh
I looked into his cool calm eyes
Wow! I thought, *oh my!*
He was such a handsome man
With blond hair and eyes of blue
Tanned and fit and rugged
His smile was fetching too
I was truly mesmerised
My heart just missed a beat
I felt like I was falling
And looked round for a seat!
Could this be love? I thought
But I would never know
For his turn in the queue had come
Time for him to go?
But timing in this life
Really is the key
I was queuing for my pension
And he was twenty-three!

Mary Wood

BALLAD FOR PETERBOROUGH CATHEDRAL

(After Charles Causley)

Once we found Charles Causley
So far from his Cornish home
When he wrote of Catherine of Aragon
And the place to which he'd come
To meet his old friend Jumper Cross
Who was killed by a six-foot shell.
Charles had two ghosts for company,
With Queen Catherine as well.

That monster with the flaming beard
Had put Queen Catherine aside
To spend her life away from court
Because an heir she could not provide.
The farming folk knew. They took her hot food
In the last of her days in a cold damp room,
But she lies in a Cathedral now
And deep under stones is her tomb.

We know that there was a railway line
And a frozen fen nearby.
We know that Charles and Jumper Cross
Watched the Flying Scot go by.
Now the Flying Scot has had its day,
But the Fen remains, the Cathedral stands.
Queen Catherine rests here - in Peterborough
Far distant from Spain's sunny lands.

Patricia Ives

IN APPRECIATION

We know we should be grateful
For good deeds that men do,
But I include our canine friends
When gratitude is due.

They'll happily train to be our eyes
When we no longer see,
And if we should become stone deaf
Our ears they'll also be.

If property's in danger
They'll faithfully stand guard
And protect it from intruders
Without a paid reward.

They'll act like Holmes and Watson
Detecting smuggled drugs
And bravely defend lawmen
'Gainst armed attacking thugs.

Dogs help in many rescues
In situations grave,
Through fire and smoke and water
A human life to save.

I really do feel thankful
And my gratitude extends
To those whose patient know-how
Trains our faithful doggy friends.

A I Cotter

HEARTACHE

My heart cries out for you
in the middle of the night.
I know you will never come
and will never even write.

You left me for another,
you said that we were through.
Without your arms to hold me
what will I do?

I just loved you so
and thought that you were true.
How could you dismiss this love
once shared by we two?

Now, I'll shed no more tears,
my life must go on.
Some day I'll find another
to build my life upon.

Julie Brown

WHAT IS A FRIEND WORTH?

A friend is someone faithful who you can tell your troubles to,
They are always there to lend a hand no matter what you do,
When troubles come along to make us feel so sad and low,
That is the time we need our friends to help us see them through,
Friends stick to us through thick and thin no matter what we say,
Even when we reject them and send hurting remarks their way,
It's better to have friends around you than to wish you had,
Being happy with your friends is much better than being sad,
It's easy to make an enemy but hard to keep a friend,
Make sure the friendships that you make never have an end,
Old friends are usually the best, they know our little ways,
They've stuck to us through good and bad and sad or happy days,
It's nice to make ourselves new friends, especially when we're down,
But we must not forget the old friends when the new friendship
has grown,
The value of a new friend must be tested for faults untold,
The value of a treasured old friend is more precious than pure gold,
Throughout my life I've promised to try to make a new friend
each day,
But always I try to remember not to turn the old friends away,
The old friends will be everlasting, on that you can always bet,
As strangers passing along the road are friends we have not met,
We are all God's children, whether we be coloured black or white,
Everyone is just the same in Our Lord Jesus' sight,
So remember that He is with us, our loving, faithful friend,
Although we forsake and hurt Him, He will be with us to the end,
Try to be like Jesus was, when He lived upon this Earth,
Put your heart into making and keeping friends, you'll never know
their worth.

Stan Gilbert

WHY NOT

A poem is a lovely way
To put your thoughts in rhyme
And write of happy days gone by
Of incidents in time

Recalling children's laughter,
Having lots of fun
Joining in their antics
Playing in the sun

Yes memories are sweet and fine
When you pen them in a rhyme.

Hazel Michell

ETERNAL BOND

Why me?
Why poetry?
Allows thought processes unleashed,
rolling in so fast,
to be penned to loved ones.
Dreams of days gone past.

Memories so precious,
memories best forgot,
hopes and aspirations
captured on a page.
Written, unreservedly,
to an audience on a hidden stage.

What for?
For who?
Part of my confusion
needs to be released.
Unspoken, but sincerely meant,
feelings I have for you.

They told me that you died,
but, I know that can't be true,
because I feel your presence,
you are always in my heart,
you are sitting close beside me.
No one can ever tear us apart.

Eve McGrath

NIGHTFALL

Slowly the sun descends in glowing shafts of gold.
Shadows of falling night creep softly through the trees.
Mysterious forms enter each silent place
Shielding night's creatures in their wanderings.
The golden flow of sunset leaves behind
Dark silhouette of every leaf and tree.
Now we shall enter into the unseen world;
This is a magic place, tread softly, do not disturb
The silent denizens, the spirits, at this peaceful time.
See how the evening primrose lights her gold lamps
Calling each moth to sip her nectar sweet;
Lighting the garden through the darkling hours
Until dawn breaks; spirits and moths fly home,
And hot sun rises once again, with burning ray.

Mary Johnson-Riley

EDGES CRISP AND CRINKLY

I know that when the leaves have changed,
With edges crisp and crinkly,
Autumn has returned.

The sun is languid in the sky,
Illuminating two butterflies,
Apache dancing overhead,
Searching for a winter refuge.

Velvet cobnuts are ripened in the hedges,
And the spiny fruit of the sweet chestnuts
Are bristling, ready to burst
To reveal the marron nuts, inside.

The stiff umbels of hogweed stand proud,
Bereft of their petals.

Above me, skeins of geese are
Honking and yapping as they fly
On the top sails of their wings,
Slimbridge bound.

I shudder silently in the cool
Feeling the touch of winter
And meditate about the upcoming spring
And the next blossoming of nature.

Laura P Williams

DREAMING

I was thinking the other day,
How hard life can be.
Each day is a struggle,
And how I'd like to break free.
I'd love to win the lottery
And imagine how life would change.
A beautiful house in the country
An open fire - burning in the range.
Maybe a couple of horses
Running free on the land.
How life would be perfect,
If our fate was planned.
But here I am just dreaming
And reality stares right back.
I enjoyed my little wander
But am now back on track.
I take a look around me
And realised that I'm quite blessed
And that dreaming is an antidote
For when you're feeling stressed.

A Leeson

A TRUE FRIEND

A true friend is one who will always be there,
With a shoulder to cry on,
Someone who will care
If your dreams don't come true, this time or never, the hope that is
                                        gone for ever and ever.

One who will stand by you through thick and thin,
And help you to bear the trouble you're in.
Who will laugh at the world of cynical fame
And make you laugh too at life's double game.

A true friend never lets you down,
One you can rely on,
To smile, not wear a frown
Someone who will know, when it's time to go,
And not hang around when the pace is getting slow.

A true friend is precious,
Whatever may befall,
How fortunate we are, to be blessed with one at all.
So we must play our part,
And cherish from the heart.

Rozetta Pate

AUTUMN GOLD

Autumn has clothed the forest with gold
A spectacle of splendour for all to behold
Dying leaves flutter like birds from the sky,
Flashing their colours as they float by.

Walk in the forest to see the sight
The trees have shed for our delight
The forest ablaze like a funeral pyre
Each step crackles like the embers of fire.

The trees' once mighty umbrella of green
Unadorned in this magical scene
Standing like soldiers at ease
Waiting for spring and the bursting of leaves,
Enjoy for a moment this magnificent sight,
Over all the mystery of a starlit night.

Claire Bartholomew

MOONBEAMS

Moonbeams shine across the sky
Brilliant light as bright as day
Cumulus clouds surround the moon
In burnt orange and grey
Like volcanic rock that moves and sways
Twinkling stars shine bright
Making patterns across the sky
Moonbeams that light up the night
Making shadows leap and bound across the ground
Spiderwebs shine like gossamer wings
The leaves on the trees shine bright in silver and gold
With gold dust sprinkled on hedges alike
As moonbeams light our way
The life at night is on the move
Sliding away from predators of the night
Insects and mammals alike
As nature's way life goes on
Such wonders the moonbeams show
Till the rise of the sun
With its brilliant light
Blows the moonbeams away.

Patricia Turner

THE OTHER EMIGRANTS

Dry your tears.
The farewell concert is concluded now
And 'God Be With You Till We meet Again'
Sung soulfully to send us on our way.
Prayers for our safety have been offered up;
Hands have been shaken; promises exchanged.
'Please write to me' 'Oh yes, I shall, my love
As soon as I arrive and settle in'
'And don't forget me'
'No I shan't, my dear'
'God bless you. Think of me from time to time
As I shall very surely think of you.'

Do not cry.
The parting will not be so very long.
I'll send for you to join me very soon
And we shall be united once again
To make our home together over there.
We shall do well: fortune will smile on us.
The poverty and struggle we have known
Will fast become a sober memory -
The background to our new and prosperous life.
And we shall watch our children growing up
In easier places and in better times.

Now smile for me
So I shall not remember you were sad.
Taking your courage as a part of mine
I'll carry it forever in my heart.
My spirit rises to the challenge now
The trunks are packed and I am set to go.
My hopes and my ambitions both are set
To that bright future I shall make our own.
Tomorrow, the adventure will begin.
Tomorrow, in the morning, I embark
On the incredible, unsinkable 'Titanic'.

*(Written in memory of the author's two uncles, Fred and Edgar Giles,
who left Porthleven to emigrate to America and perished in the Titanic
disaster. Edgar's girlfriend, who was to have joined him later,
cherished his photograph until she died as a very old lady)*

Elsie Balme

THE NEW YEAR

The bells are ringing for the old year,
And the soaring rockets fly,
As you hold my arm so tightly,
With burning tears and a sigh!

And when the party is over my love,
And the silent moon, she regains the sky,
Then, I'll tell you once more, that I love you,
My love, as the old year passes by!

Anthony George Teesdale

MOONLIGHT

Through mystic shadows of the night,
The moon throws stark white light.
Her radiance is beautiful and free,
A carpet of silver she makes the sea.
To the lovers who wander on the shore,
Silver-capped waves sigh once more.
Sleep, she softly seems to say,
For soon will be another day.
All the world sleeping lies
As moonlight hours fly by.
Now she slowly goes her way,
So welcome in another day.

J Brown

MAIDEN AUNT'S LAMENT

We lost our sweethearts in the war,
But must we mourn for evermore?
There is no one to share with me
A sentimental memory.
No one to give me flowers or chocs
Or jewels in a dainty box.
When will there ever be a date
For maiden aunts to celebrate?
On the feast of Valentine
No cards - there is no man of mine,
No wedding anniversary -
Silver . . . gold . . . not even three!
When Mother's Day comes round again
Another pang - we envy them.
And now Grandparent's Day! Whatever next!
I'm really feeling rather vexed.
At Christmas time, no kids to say,
'This year, Mum, come with me stay.'
So, will there *ever* be a date
For maiden aunts to celebrate?

Dorothy M Parker

WET SUITORS

Half closing my shaded eyes, I saw
Three black suited bodies lying inert,
Languid, in the salt sea air,
Skins glistening in the June sun,
Bellies burning on the scorching sand,
Flippers idly fanning each other.

Seaward squeals changed the scenario.
Hoarse barks and grunts escalated
Into roaring, ribald play.
With a humping of shoulder charges
They rose up, jostling bodies
Surging towards the beckoning surf,
Diving and frolicking into the path
Of the three watching, waiting females.

The illusion sealed itself
Into my mind, and closing my eyes,
I sank back into the soft, hot sand.

Rowan

CELEBRATIONS

Life is full of celebrations,
Private events or countrywide,
Bank holidays or family 'occasions',
Full of elation, merriment and pride.

We celebrate the birth of Jesus,
The beloved child of Mary,
Every Christmas singing carols,
Honouring a newborn baby.

Then comes Easter - a time for sadness
Jesus hung on a cross to die,
But He survived and joined His Father
In that wonderful place on high.

Events concerning our dear Queen,
Jubilees both silver and gold,
Beloved every time she's seen,
A monarch we are proud to uphold.

Guy Fawkes gave us firework day,
At Parliament house, he was aiming,
On the fifth of November we light up and play,
To celebrate Mr Fawkes' *own* burning!

Birthdays, weddings and retirement
Historical moments - good and bad,
We know how to celebrate and remember
All the *momentous* times we've had.

D M Carne

JUST A DREAM

I had a dream the other day
I had walked along the Milky Way,
Up to the heavens, beyond and far
Able to touch each twinkling star.

Was this the way to Heaven, or only Mars
Drifting upwards along a path of stars?
Passing the moon and its bright light
Upwards and onwards through the night.

What a wonder this journey was for me
Full of surprise and tranquillity,
At last I felt at peace
No more worries, what a blessed release.

Just me and the stars, the night and the moon
Don't let this dream end, not yet, it's too soon,
Don't send me back to Earth for a while
The stars and the moon they make me smile.

Jean McCoy

IT'S NOT CRICKET

Reclining in the chair
Beside the field
I shut my mind to the irritation
Of the voice that droned on.
The heat oppressive
Prohibited concentration
Sleep was an option
The action uninspiring.
Eyes gradually closed
While still tracing the flight of spin
Then shut at the last sound
The resounding thud of bat on ball.
The clapping aroused me
Disorientated and scared
Stewed but not dream free
Struggling back to reality.

In the local close by
I smilingly lie
And agree to all the plaudits and praise
Lavished on the hero of the hour.

C O Burnell

WELLS

Wells are deep, deep as minds,
Deep as thoughts, intentions sometimes.

Men fought over them, Died for them.
But they never really dredged the depths,
Drew up the heart of them, only toyed with
The drops of moisture, sweat upon the surface
Telling tales of deeper water.
Easily distorted droplets
Charged with poison.

It turned brown
Down below. And rotted.

'How many wells make a river?' they say
And, 'Oh well!' swearing on its depths,
Knowing they cannot be searched,
Shrugging at what's hard to control
And can't be done.

How many rivers of shrugs have flowed? Search and see
Maybe there's a lizard there living free
Untouched by brooding waters.

The skin on the electric wire can be touched with impunity.
What's beneath cannot, for it could maim or kill.
My skin is thin from years and ages past
And still, it lives like the live wire from the plug,
Sensitive, dependant on deep waters
Stirred beneath, available for drinking.
But who would dare?

Diane Burrow

METAMORPHOSIS

Swimming, hunting in the murk, his prey outpacing,
Or lurking in the forests at the fringes of the pond,
Pirate of his ocean with his six oars racing
Pair of peering searchlights piercing, probing far beyond;
This life can now no more its span extend -
The two-year voyage is nearly at an end.

Upon the gently swishing, swaying haven of a sedge
The weary heart of this segmented hull secures a mooring
So close beneath the gently lapping surface, near the edge,
Final peace within the seeming folds of death ensuring.
Body, shrunken, grizzled, stiff and still
Submits at last to death's embracing chill.

But then the unbelievable unfolds before the eyes
As signs of life move secretly and stir within the shell;
The wrinkled body splits and shuffles off its drab disguise -
The prisoner in full splendour is emerging from his cell
And climbs to greet the unfamiliar air
While blinking in the unaccustomed glare.

Segmented hull transformed to form a jointed fuselage
The oars as six-pronged landing-gear so cunningly restored,
The searchlights probing, testing, fearing only a mirage,
Reluctant to believe in such a world to be explored
And stunned at the immensity of space -
The dragonfly rests on the water's face.

The eyes and legs the same, the body has its segments still;
But strength renewed, extended vision, new and strange the mode
Of drawing breath, the gift of wings and blessed freedom will
Permit this startling, sparkling, dazzling being to explode
Its beauty on a gasping world - perfection;
The mystery and truth of resurrection.

Vaughan Stone

MY PLEASURE

It's nice to walk down a leafy glade
A leisurely stroll in the shade.
Down by the twinkling, murmuring, steam.
Walking as if in a dream.
Taking in nature's sounds and sights
Gives a feeling of such delight.
Fish darting as I move along
So fast - they have gone.
Rabbit stamps his back feet
White tail bobs a warning threat.
Pheasant rises with raucous call
Narrowly missing the stone wall.
A flash of blue and red
Kingfisher taking food, fledglings to be fed.
Dragonflies, blue, yellow and red
Hovering, darting amongst the reed bed.
A black and white flash, Dipper hunts his meal
As under the water he does steal.
Willie Wagtail hopping from rock to rock
Catching flies, there's quite a lot.
Pigeon cooing from the tree
Come on Baby come to me.
The rookery is in full caw
As youngsters call for more.
The magpie dips in flight
Is there something bright?
To my right a badger's set
Too light to see them just yet.
I feel someone watching me
It's a barn owl on a branch above me.
A strong aroma I smell
From wild garlic in the dell.
And there in front of me
A carpet of bluebells I see.
Wood anemones scattered amongst the rocks
Showing off their pretty frocks.
The oak, the ash, and sycamore trees
Whose branches and leaves make this avenue for me.
That makes my stroll so leisurely.

R G Sill

CLARIFIED HEART-SEARCH
*(With dictated corrections inserted by Sarah M (patient) and
Kate Singleton (occupational therapist))*

Hearts touch and hold an astounding expanse,
Breathe in to the worlds of each other;
Reflecting emotions, through currents of chance
Or through bonds strong enough to discover.

We each spread some aura, with indistinct borders,
Much wider than we realise.
Imprinting a blessing, averting disorders,
Creative as healing sunrise!

If life seems too dark for a brighter tomorrow,
When turnings feel worthless and bare,
The happiness others have they do not borrow,
We all have some love, hope or flair.

If storms blow and shatter, leaving bleak hurts,
There is promise, because, through our pain
We are finding responses; whether cruel or inert,
And from that stance there are blessings to gain.

At times pleasing others is not the best key!
Holding values, yet leading astray.
Genuine purpose can transform, will set free,
Helping future and past interplay.

Emma Louise Taylor

THE SIXTH OF MARCH

This is a day: this day holds hidden meaning
Within the deep deserted past it reaches
Beyond the rugged, southern shingle beaches
Toward a pair of hopeful lovers leaning,
Against their young and optimistic shoulders.
They're pointing out to sea, the waves are gleaming,
The girl is full of smiles, the boy is dreaming,
They walk for hours there, among the boulders,
And wonder where the path of life is leading.
Yet fate would intervene, and us would sever,
But in that windswept, southern beach I never
Met with anyone half so dear as Heather.
     My own sweet blonde and melancholic lover,
     In times and places we shall not recover.

Fraser Hicks

TUNSTALL BOY

There's a rainbow over Tunstall, just a figment of my mind
Clouds roll over Burslem, the years are in rewind
Scrolling through the decades, faces come and go
I call them on my mobile but they aren't to know

Lightning struck at Westbourne Drive
Katy Beans is still alive
I scoured and scoured the internet
Then remembered where we met

Northern Soul at The Torch
Making love on the porch
Disco nights at The Place
I remember face after face

Thunder rumbles in the park
Bright lights shimmer in the dark
Children laughing in the corridors of years
These older eyes are filled with tears

The clock in the square sounding the hour
That summer day when I picked you a flower
We played our sounds on vinyl forty-fives
And swore our love for the rest of our lives

The juke box still plays a favourite old track
Bars filled with strangers now, no going back
Places seem familiar and some faces too
Just memories remain and my photograph of you

Phillip Tinsley

NATURE'S JEWELS

I care not for diamanté crowns
My diamonds in the skies are found
Black velvet clouds sprinkled with stars
Venus, Pluto, Saturn, Mars
In Heaven's mansion windows bright
To light the paths of angels' flight
The rain that falls upon my head
I care not for my watery tread
But see the glorious flower beds
And mantled green trees overhead
The silver light of Lady Moon
On hills and valleys to festoon
Cast magic threads like fairy wings
On wild wood flowers and mountain springs
Nocturnal movements come to life
In the deep dark secrets of the night
Reaching for life's golden dawn
When the new bright day is born.

Eileen Hope Hesselden

MY SON

My son I have cherished you
From that moment in time
When you first made your entrance
Into this world of mine

My son I have cherished you
Through those early months
Rocked and cradled you
Through those teething grumps

My son I have cherished you
Through those early years
Your first day at school
Wiped away the tears

My son I have cherished you
Through those teenage days
Watched you grow tall
And change your ways

My son I cherish you
You're a fine young man
A son to be proud of
As proud as I can

My son I cherish you
With all of my heart
I'll love you forever
Like I have from the start.

Gill Lawrence

HOPE

Where can I find the hope I need?
What reasons have I to live?
Why struggle through each exhausting day
Till I've nothing left to give?

Hope will always be with you,
A shining gleam each day;
A candle in a darkened room,
A star to guide the way.

But I feel so tired and lonely,
My soul is grey and bare.
All hope just easily fades away
When I'm overcome by despair.

Hope is a loyal and trusty friend
To save you, lest you drown
In a flood of black and frightening thoughts
That threatens to drag you down.

Confusion overwhelms me,
I'm ready to give up the fight.
I have no hope to carry me through
This endless, ghastly night.

What force has been protecting you,
Kept you fighting for so long?
Hope is buried deep in your heart,
Its warmth has made you strong.

I cannot find this hope you describe
Or believe that it exists;
My world and vision are dimly blurred
By thick and gloomy mists.

Hope is found and seen and felt
Amidst great sorrow and pain:
Just watch the evening's setting sun
And believe it will rise again.

Sarah Dodds

GLOBAL WARMING

Summer will never end,
Even now the whole day is heat heavy
And pendulous from room and stair
Leaning from limp walls.
Within this house
The weighted air is impenetrable.

Searching for the smallest breeze
I try a walk in the garden
But there the tattered leaves fall,
Limp, pock-marked and stained,
Leaving a weary stalk, a wrinkled flower.

Here forever and ever the nasturtium plants wind,
Trailing on along a dusty path, I follow them
To where the hanging baskets sway,
Sway to mesmerise,
To conjure up the elusive rain.

Above a filmy sky, a fiery sun grills to shreds
The few last fading strips of cloud.
Outside I watch as passers-by slowly pace the burning road
And city streets hoarsely aspirate a thousand metallic fumes.

Sylvia Fairclough

SOMERSET

I love this green and pleasant land,
this land of sunshine, sea and sand.
Where sea is blue and grass is green
and everywhere an artist's dream.
Where leather thwacks on willow bat
and people talk of this and that.
Where jackdaw cries upon the wing
and mistle thrush its song does sing.
Where gentle waves lap on the beach
and children for their spades do reach.
Where butterflies touch every flower
and church clocks chime at every hour.
Where roses bloom round cottage doors
and rushy mats grace old stone floors.
Where cats sit proud on window sills
and village doctor cures all ills.
Where postman still his bike does ride
and nobody has ought to hide.
Where rippling brook flows down the hill
'mid rows of golden daffodils.
Where rainbow trout come up for flies
and dragonfly so smoothly glides.
Where horses snort and lambs do bleat
and dogs lie panting in the heat.
Where seasons come and seasons go
and time goes slowly, oh! so slow.
Where nothing changes, year on year
and oaken casks still hold the beer.
Where scarecrows o'er the corn do watch
and warn the pigeons not to touch.
Where rabbits bob their fluffy tails
and hay lies neatly stacked in bales.
Where life moves on at steady pace
and envies not the city's race.
Where people love this mortal life
and happiness reigns over strife.
Long may this contentment last,
in Somerset it's never past.

Terry Temlett

INFINITY

I love the sky in all its moods,
How bright it shines,
How darkly broods,
Pillows of cloud in a deep-blue sky,
Seen from a plane
As above I fly,
So feather-soft and white they seem,
I walk upon them in a dream,
Each step is silent, left then right,
A canopy of blue, a quilt of white,
Then, as I walk upon the shore
The skies light up, with sudden roar,
And black clouds scud
As if to run, from raging flood
Of pouring rain, and lightning's flash
And rush and bump, and tear and crash,
And blinding rips of red,
And orange, yellow, flame-like spread
Across a black and angry sky,
So huge are they, so small am I,
Then in a field of golden corn
I watch a day so newly born,
A pale sun rises, fresh and damp
Before the dawn has lit its lamp,
In sky as blue as babies' eyes
All glorious, the sun will rise,
The world awakens, birds will sing,
What will this lovely morning bring?
Then slowly, at the close of day,
Before the light has gone away,
Bright bars of gold and red and blue
And colours bright of every hue,
Will change, and change before my eyes,
Light up, and glorify the skies,
Then as the sun, reluctant, fades,
The night shuts down its velvet shades,
Then lights the stars, like candles bright,
To glint and sparkle through the night.

Margery Crabtree

CONSERVATION CONVERSATION

'Rape!' he cried, she sighed,
'What's happened to the countryside?
Where are the hedges round the edges
and the sedges by the riverside?

Machines grinding over the hills
preparing to fill the overfull tills -
and *all* against God's will.
The farmers cry, 'Why, why, why?'
as they toil beneath God's crowded sky.
'So many forms and a price too high
to work in the countryside.'

Do-gooders think mink must be free
in the countryside.
No longer voles in watery holes beside the canals
and rivers wide that wind their way through
the countryside.
Where are the moorhens and the coots?
'Animal Rights' don't give two hoots
that the birds that crossed water from
side to side, are no longer seen in the countryside.
The mink, now free, so murderous
prey on fauna, once indigenous to our countryside.'

'Look at that field so yellow and wide!'
'It's *rape* that covers the countryside!'
She sighed.

Barbara Stoyles

THE SCARECROW

If I were made of flesh and bone
And not of sticks and straw
I could journey to Niagara
See New England in the fall.
Do you suppose I want to dream?
These feelings are a curse
Who fashioned me in human form
Could not have done much worse.
Tears cannot flow from button eyes
I have no heart to break
This mouth can't scream, these ears can't hear
I'm just a sad mistake.
My fingers are but bundled sticks
That can't caress a maid
Know when I dream heroic deeds
I never am afraid.
Dismiss this outworn overcoat
Lacking style, cut or shape
Think ermine robes, fine leather boots
And a purple velvet cape.
Forget this hair, like hedgehog spines
Wind-taken, falling down
See raven locks, a flowing mane
Topped by a jewelled crown.
Don't watch me hidebound in one place
Close-fixed for evermore
But ride me on a charger white
And cheer me off to war.
Yet here I stand, each breeze to flap
My rags to scare the crows
But, Oh, my makers can't dictate
Where imagination goes.
Not summer's heat, nor winter's frost
Can disturb my reverie
To find a sorcerer who can make
A human man of me.

Sarah Blackmore

THIS DATING THING

What can you do living on your own?
Do you spend all your time living in your home?
How do you make friends, it is not easy to do?
That is why I have picked the phone up to ring you

The dating page is full of different kinds of men
How do you choose, can you pick ten?
Waiting for someone to ring is a nerve racking thing
Oh please phone ring, ring, ring

Will he be tall, fat or thin?
If only this phone of mine would ring
You listen so careful of what he will say
Wondering if he is going to ring today

The moment has come and he has made the call
He gives you his name and says he is dark and tall
We arrange to meet say, perhaps for a drink
Where can we go? Come on think, think, think

The day has come it's time to go
Into the unknown to meet a man you do not know
Will he be there like he said by the door?
What will I say to him, shall I say hello?

There he is all dressed and he really looks tall
He is going to look at me and think I am quite small
The evening goes well we hit it off full swing
I am so pleased I turned to this *dating thing*

Cynthia Scott

THE WOMAN

She trudges down the endless road
Ragged bag with heavy load,
How her shoulders drooped and sagged
Under the weight of her laden bag.
Her feet are swollen and distorted
Each step, her face, with pain contorted,
Miserable day, miserable feet
Trudging down the empty street.

At last she reaches her front door
Thanks the Lord, a few steps more,
Opens the door with a rusty key
Oh what she'd give for a cup of tea.
Once inside undoes her coat
Unwraps the scarf from round her throat,
Hangs her things upon their pegs
Got to rest her weary legs.

Sitting down on a kitchen seat
Eases her shoes from her swollen feet,
She lets out an anguished cry
No tears left, her eyes are dry.
The scruffy cat comes through the flap
Jumps up on her bony lap,
She doesn't mind he's all she's got
Thank goodness he doesn't eat a lot.

The cat jumps down, goes to the sink
Hoping she will give him a drink,
She gets up to empty her shopping
The cat's around her jumping up, hopping.
She finds his food, feeds him first
Forgetting about her own thirst,
Once the cat's fed she makes the tea
Happy to have some company.

All alone in this big house
Her, the cat, an occasional mouse,
They rattle around like stones in a can
How she misses her old man.
He died last year, she's on her ownsome
Old, widowed, and very lonesome,
No neighbourly faces over the wall
No one to talk to, no one at all.

She washes the dishes, turns off the light
Going to bed early tonight,
Up the stairs with heavy tread
Her swollen feet felt like lead.
Has a wash, put on her nightie
Flannelette, nothing flighty,
Pull the sheets and blankets down
Snuggle under the eiderdown.

As she lay there trying to sleep
She quietly has a little weep,
Give me strength to carry on
Now my lovely man has gone.
Just then her scruffy cat came in
And nestled under her wrinkled chin,
She listened to his friendly purr
Not alone, now there's him and her.

Dorothy Fuller

THE VALLEY OF PEACE

Take me back to the valley of my youth,
To places of innocence, people of truth;
To the land of my fathers, land of my birth,
To memories of summers of laughter and mirth:
Where blue skies met grey skies and tears sometimes fell
But not in those summers I remember so well.
I remember the days when a goat-like kid
Would scramble up hillsides as I often did.
When my way was my way, I went as I pleased,
The way of a small child so simply appeased:
A young boy who battled with boulders and won,
His Everest conquered he stood in the sun
Surveying his kingdom, beloved domain,
Displaying disdain at a cloud's hint of rain;
Listening to sounds give the news of the day,
The river, the trees or a train on its way;
The grind and the churn of the old water mill;
Hearing the *baa* talk of sheep on the hill.
All this from my watch point astride hard-won ground
But next day new vistas were soon to be found;
A lake like a secret secreted away,
Found more by good luck and a path gone astray.
Or caves carved discreetly, invitingly cool
But inside wet feet from a well-hidden pool.
And how well remembered occasional shocks
When fleeing from adders emerging from rocks:
Thus never forgetting sensations of fright
When noises so strange pierced the cool air of night;
Awaking to sounds of the dark loud and clear,
The wind or an owl giving nocturnal fear;
Arising next morning bravado returned,
To find new adventures, so much to be learned.
Those years were the finest, those years were the best,
The reason I ask just one final request.
Take me back to the valley or my youth,
To places of innocence, people of truth.
Drive through the mountains, cross a bridge on a bend
And come to the place where the journey will end.
Pass through a village built of grey stone and slate,
See the church not too distant and stop at the gate.
Let this be the end of a promise you'll keep,
To bury me deeply and let no one weep.

Paul Denyer

WORDS WRITTEN

Words written on parchment scroll,
In rhyme and verse our history told.
The sweep of their quill an ancient craft,
Written words speak, lighting up the past.

Words with Celtic brogue and lilt,
Record the battles and blood that's spilt.
Warriors who marched across the land,
A time when armies fought hand to hand.

Words proclaiming law and ancient order,
Written by monks who were the recorder.
Kings and queens of their coronations,
Of bishops and bards their nominations.

Words written, not printed on a press,
Each letter an art drawn to impress.
To emphasise with flare and passion,
Each verse in rhyme was the fashion.

Words, an art in their own right,
Telling of joy and man's plight
Chanted in verse and in rhyme,
To be remembered for all time . . .

Alan J Morgan

DOLLS IN THE ATTIC

Two antique dolls of long ago, faces worn and old
What stories they could tell if only the truth be told
Made by the finest craftsmen for children in the upper class
Their eyes so dark and mysterious were only made of glass
Curly locks of auburn hair, long dresses of satin and lace
Buttoned-up boots and white socks all had their own special place

Sitting upright on an old settee in an attic filled with gloom
This could be their shrine for life, condemned to this dark little room
Property has its problems when the need for maintenance is at hand
Work that is being carried out covers a wide and varied band
Renovations that are taking place made the dust fly everywhere
Those dolls of old seem unperturbed, at the top of that rickety old stair

Alone in this small dingy room that time itself had forgot
A young man carrying out the restoration work certainly has a lot
Sitting there motionless, the dolls monitoring his every move
Nervously glancing back at them, what else has he got to prove
The dolls' lifeless appearance - their stare never seems to tire
Fixation in their eyes of brown are like flaming balls of fire

The attic clock ticking away, his nerves now feeling the strain
Feeling their eyes bearing down on him like heavy falling rain
A mirror in that darkened room one morning he casually glanced
Staring back at him, their eyes - as around the room they danced
His eyes questioning what he saw, their faces full of evil and hate
What crime had he committed? He needed now to retaliate

Some say the reflections in the mirror never tell any lies
In his inner-most self he could hear their taunting mocking cries
His body began shaking violently as into a cold sweat he broke
An examination later told he had experienced a minor stroke
Tests were carried out on him for information they could learn
His problem lay in the attic as the dolls waited for his return

His condition deteriorated rapidly as in that hospital bed he lay
The dolls' eyes never leaving him, staring at him night and day
Nightmares he would suffer, as in his sleep he would scream
Seeing those faces haunting him it only happened in his dream
How can two dolls be accountable for this young man's plight?
We shall never know the answer, as the young man died that night.

Raymond Thomas Edwards

THE JOY OF CHILDREN

What would life be without children?
Always loving without hesitation,
Deep innocent eyes and purity,
Excited, filled with anticipation.

Their thirst for knowledge, insatiable,
Their kisses expressions of devotion,
Ever demanding constant attention.
Continually evoking intense emotions.

Smouldering embers of life's tensions,
Are very easily extinguished,
With an innocent hug and a cherub's smile,
All worries are instantly relinquished.

Children's laughter reverberates,
Happy rainbows we share together,
Shafts of light that illuminate my heart,
Sweet sensations to remember and treasure.

The dismal iniquities of age, vanish
As with them I play again as a child,
No worries or fears, so unpretentious,
A tonic, their imaginations, laughter and smiles.

Yes, what would life be without children?
Always eager to demonstrate their affection,
Able to transform any gloomy atmosphere,
Sparkle like jewels but tarnish with rejection.

Celia Auld

SAVE THE WORLD

What of our children's children, what of their worldly plight?
No lush, green fields or clean water and only a 24 hour night.
Let's stop this devastation, instead let's plant the seeds,
That will save for the next generation, a land that will meet their needs.
Stop the rubbish mountains that block landscapes and mar the view,
Cease chemical emissions that make holes in our skies of blue.
Halt testing of nuclear weapons which pollute our oceans wide,
Pick up all your litter please, clean up our countryside.
Stop industries' chimneys burning our precious fossil fuels,
Don't raid Earth's crust for minerals, for riches and for jewels.
If we don't curb our actions and cease stealing from Earth's well,
There will be nothing left to sustain us, only an empty shell
We need to clean our act up or bit by bit and by and by,
This wondrous place, this world of ours, will just lay down and die.

June Briggs

SPRING (A CAUTIONARY TALE)

In springtime when the sun's warm kiss,
Awakens Mother Earth's desire,
The surging sap begins to rise,
And kindles nature's loins with fire.

Spring is when a creature's fancy,
Wholly turns to procreation,
Birds and bees and beasts in tandem,
Seeding the next generation.

Spreading tender fleshy petals,
Seducing bees that buzz and hum,
Blooms that tempt the bees to enter,
Are pollinated as they come.

I was still a flower in bud,
My blossoming had just begun,
He was tall and strong just like a
Young sapling growing in the sun.

The sun's kiss warmed our skin that day,
And walking in its warm caress,
All our senses were besieged by
Springtime's full luxuriousness.

Mankind, he is nature's master,
He does not hear spring's lusty call,
Standing amidst all this nature,
I thought myself above it all.

The long grass whispered in the wind,
'We're all subject to nature's force.'
The blushing flowers nod their heads,
'Yes, nature always takes its course.'

The sapling pulled me down to earth,
The long grass tickled my bare thighs,
He held me in his sun-warmed arms,
For in boys too the sap will rise.

I blossomed under his warm kiss,
And opened like a blooming bud,
His embrace loosened all my limbs,
And kindled sparks throughout my blood.

Nature designed both boys and bees,
And like the bees who enter blooms,
She gave boys a cruel weapon,
She gave them stings to inflame wombs!

Mother Nature knows her business,
When flaunting her bold springtime charms,
Next spring I will walk the meadow,
With a small baby in my arms.

Kerry-Ann Fender

THE MONEY FAN

I wish I had more money
I'm tired of scraping through
So sick of 'can't afford it'
And always making do
I'd really love to lay my hands
On some ready cash
I wish I had a treasure box
Or a safely hidden stash
If I won the lottery
I know just what I'd do
I'd spend my whole day spending it
My dreams could all come true
I'd never look at price tags
I'd buy what caught my eye
'Will that be cash or credit madam?'
'Cash,' my quick reply
I'd holiday abroad of course
At least five times a year
People would all stop and stare
They'd say, 'Just look at her.'
For I would flaunt my wealth
Each day a shopping day
Spending all my pennies
'Til I'd frittered it away
For you can't take it with you
Enjoy it while you can
I'm so in love with money
I'm a greedy money fan.

Joanne Reader

POSEIDON

With thunderous roar, the mighty god Poseidon
Erupts from the sea
His chariot drawn by twelve white stallions
Who with streaming manes and flaring nostrils
Splash and crash their way across the ocean
Pounding the waters with their powerful hooves
In response to the lash and thrash of their angry master,
Whose very breath incites the winds to further fury,
His voice the threatening thrum
Of the drum, drum, drum, drum drumming
Of the sea.

Waves race for the shore in terror
Attempting to find refuge in the caves
Where they slap and smack against the walls
Swilling the contours of their gaol
As though to find escape from their imprisonment
Only to retreat in defeat, leaving whirlpools
As their desperate footprints
And the echoing thrum
Of the drum, drum, drum, drum drumming
Of the sea.

Against the steely sky, seabirds wheel and weave
Blown hither and thither by the storm
A kaleidoscope of grey white souls,
Shrieking, screaming, keening, grieving,
Their forlorn cries of melancholy
An elegy for all lost souls
Their accompaniment a deep pulsating thrum
The drum, drum, drum, drum drumming
Of the sea.

Juliet Borland

ESCAPISM

I have climbed many mountains if you care to know
Icicles growing like crystals in my beard
Filled up my lungs with air as pure as virgin snow
Elated, as the morning sun appeared

I have drifted around the planet in balloons
Observed from above the busy biosphere
Landed in wilderness among lions, baboons
And smiling crocodiles, blood as cold as fear

I have crossed, braving the formidable Neptune
Oceans and seas infested with great sharks
I have been left stranded on a lost island dune
Having to light fires with wooden sparks

I have been offered as punishment to vultures
For having loved forbidden Amazons
My existence is littered with great adventures
Experiencing incredible liaisons

Entertaining powerful kings in my castle
Giving their queens the ultimate caress
Having famous knights dining around my table
Sometimes, too, eloping with a princess

Some of you who know me well will wonder
How I managed to live each episode
When I never went this far, never mind yonder
Having not even set a foot abroad

To travel the whole world, do what you most desire
Achieve feats well beyond comprehension
And live your wildest whims what you simply require
Is educated imagination

Imagination sprinkled with piquant spices
Will transport you through a panorama
Of places where rewards follow sacrifices
Where fantasies are not anathema

On the screen of your mind you watch your own fable
Escape real life and its tribulations
In dreamy language build your own Tower of Babel
Writing your own personal conclusions

J-C Chandenier

ANNIVERSARY YEAR

The fundamentalist fanatics
Plotted their murderous explosion
But were fortunately foiled
In the nick of time
Four hundred years ago this year.

The arrogant tyrant's invasion plans
Came to nought at Trafalgar's battle,
And so Britain became
A great world power
Two hundred years ago this year.

The evil tyrant's cruel philosophies
Came to nought, and peace started her rein
In western Europe
If not everywhere
Sixty years ago this year.

We knelt by the altar on our wedding day.
I've been blissfully happy ever since
(Or so my wife is
Always telling me)
Forty years ago this year.

Brian Edwards

LAMENT FOR BIRTENSHAW

I sit beside my window
And look up to the sky -
An ever changing picture
I watch with a little sigh.

The colours are so lovely
Turquoise, gold and flame
Then a lively cloud comes dancing
And the shade's not quite the same.

An hour has passed and slowly
The sun sinks in the west
Showing that all the treetops
With rosy glints are dressed.

The wildlife is delightful
As on the wing they go
Singing out their praises
In the day's sweet afterglow.

The hills are not forgotten
Indeed they cannot be
For they in evening's jewellery
Are decked for all to see.

The dappled light is playing
On fields of differing hues
Revealing limes and olives
Purples, browns and blues.

I thank the Great Creator
Whose work is witnessed here
Bringing joy to many
Because the view is clear.

Alas! Man's hand is casting
Dark shadows over this
He threatens massive building
To wipe out all this bliss.

He wants to blot out beauty
By developing this plot
But history, truth and justice
Cry out, 'No - surely not!'

I sit beside my window
And look up to the sky
Is it any wonder
I sigh and sigh and cry?

Olive M Kenyon

CRICKET

How I loved those lazy, leafy afternoons
Of leisure, leaning at the cricket green,
Lost in meditation, drifting between
Slow hours and the sound of teaspoons,
Endlessly listening to the easy tunes
Of leather on willow, as if time had been
Suspended. Oblivious of unseen
Shadows, I dreamed away those sleepy Junes.

Life's like that: there, through the livelong day,
They tossed and pitched their talents; while here, I,
Absorbed in the game and the present fray,
Watching the wickets falling steadily,
Discovered it too late to join the play.
And now the time to act has passed away.

D W Fincham

CHOICE

By some siren call
Should I have been tempted
That good reasons should forestall
And deny the thought then expended

That I am to be borne
On some current fruitless to fight
My past from my future torn
A consequence pointless to flight

It is but a hinge of fate
An untutored choice
A choice in random state
Between fortune's favour and failure poised

Choice has an element of chance
Oft' a stab at future with a broken cane

Brian Norman

NO ONE

Look upon this Earth no more
You who lived here once before,
Did you leave your mark upon this land
For generations to understand?

Why no, there's nothing of you here
You left no one to shed a tear
No sign of ever having been
No gravestone words 'in memory'.

You came into this world my 'friend'
And left without a trace,
Of ever having been a part
Of this, the human race.

You're buried in a pauper's grave
For money had you none
For in our greed and selfish life
We are what we become.

A Pope

ANNIVERSARY

(Dedicated to my dearest husband Rodney)

The time has swiftly flown
Oh where have they gone, those fifty years?
We have shared joy in abundance
Also shed many tears.
God gave us two children to love and cherish
Through good times and storms of alarms.
I felt so very blessed
When I held them in my arms.
You are my soulmate and my friend
Our love remains in heavenly bliss
As these golden years unfold
I remember our first kiss.
We now find we are laughing
At the things we do and say
Am I going out tomorrow
Or should I have gone yesterday?
Fifty years of memories
Gently they unfold
Please God don't let this world demolish
Into oblivion and lose other folks years of gold
Because like phoenix rising from the ashes
Our love will forever hold.

June Jefferson

CHICKENS

What came first, the chicken or the egg?
A question as old as can be.
It may be a problem for most of you,
but it's not a problem for me.

Try and imagine when the Earth was all new
and the creatures all freshly made.
Sitting out there all alone
an egg that nothing had laid.

In the heat of the sun it started to hatch,
with no clucking of hens all around.
As he climbed from his egg alone and scared,
no comforting mum to be found.

So don't you see it's logical
that the chicken must have been first.
It was only Adam and Eve that sinned,
the poor chicken hadn't been cursed.

Since those days the hens have thrived,
we have so many today.
So people like you who love them,
are glad it worked out that way.

They come in all shapes and sizes
and that's the way it should be.
There's nothing like a new laid egg
boiled softly for your tea.

There are big birds and there are little birds
and some that are in-between.
From Plymouth Rocks to Bantams,
their colours must be seen.

There are Rhode Island Reds and White Leghorns,
Buff Orpington and Sussex too.
The range of chickens is endless,
the choice is up to you.

So if at times you're lonely
standing out in your yard.
Just look around at your chickens
and smile, it won't be hard.

Stella C Smith

THE WIND

Oh, how still
So quiet so tranquil
The trees so motionless
I hardly dare breathe
The flowers are like statues
Like painting on a canvas
The grass is it real
Or just an image of my imagination?
How can I tell?
Nothing moves
Can I walk? No I hardly dare talk
For fear of awakening this calmness
It's like a spell has been cast
Almost like an idle ship on an idle shore
Hardly daring to move for fear
Of rippling the glass-like ocean
The clouds they hang in the sky
As if unsure of which way to go
Has time really stood still
Or is it just that the wind
Has not awakened yet?

Sheila Lloyd

I Closed My Eyes

I closed my eyes for a second
No it was longer than that
I dreamed that I was famous
But I soon awoke - drat.

It always happens when eyes are closed
And the dreams begin to show
Mind putting pictures together
And real, they seem to grow.

I closed my eyes today
No it was last night
But then again, I really can't remember
Maybe yes, that's right

I closed my eyes for a second
No it was longer than that
But maybe I was just dreaming
Oh no, not again - drat.

Niall McManus

Lost In Time

Your anniversary is here of 15 years
With you I celebrate, because through
You my mark is left, through you
My words are preserved and kept
My thoughts and words are now in print
For my future generations to forge a link
The thoughts that could have been lost in time
Are printed clear on past times
Had my words not passed to you
The treasures in words would have been out of view
So with the help of Forward Press,
Are now preserved and kept.

Joyce Maud Carter

Cast-Offs

I drove a hail into some wood the other day
And hung upon it odds and ends
Things which had outlived their usefulness
Perhaps one day I'll look up at the nail and say
Why was that stuff not thrown away?

They drove a nail into some wood the other day
And hung thereon the Son of God
They feared His teaching meant the end
Of ruling classes, for indeed they'd heard Him say
Come unto Me I am the way.

That driven nail, meant to extinguish dangerous foe
Has hung eternity in reach
For all who realise the flow
Of His great love cannot be cast aside. For each
Believer He's the only way.

Keith Dry

Heaven Would Roar

Softness
        A dream from which I should never have woken
In a dark field of stars
        In the shape of his shining face
died
        Abandoned by the feathers in my wings.

Verity Holloway

Poem For Peace

Reach out and take your neighbour's hand,
Speak words of love, not hate.
Share what you have with those in need -
Learn to communicate.
Send to poor countries tools not guns.
Teach them to plough and sow.
Bring water and crops to starving lands,
Let all the wide world know -
We are all on Earth through God's good grace -
No one should have to fight for a place.
All have a right to the bounty provided:
Let nations share, not be divided.
Folk should grow old with love and care,
Knowing that help is always there.
Children must smile and play with ease,
While we all dedicate ourselves to peace.

Ellen Day

Homesick

I want to see a highland glen where the burns run crystal clear
And to feel the surge of love in my heart for a land I love so dear
I want to stand on a heather hill and think back years ago
'Til I see those Scottish clansmen marching thru Glen Cue.

The sound of pipes and beating drums will fill me with elation
As I make history come alive by my own imagination
I'll see the battles long since fought and watch the red blood flow
That nourished Scottish soil for thistle and heather to grow.

Deep emotions will sweep o'er me and my eyes will dim with tears
As I watch those glorious highlanders ghosting through the years
The brilliant red of tartan will emblazon the hills like fire
And the haunting lilt of Scottish tunes will echo round the shire.

As the eagle's shadow spans the glen and the sun begins to set
I will leave the past to glory and the present to retrospect.

Janet Petchey

The World Through My Eyes

I look at the world these days,
It hurts when my eyes see
The pain, the hurt and suffering,
When will this world be free?
Children without food, crying for a crust,
Malnutrition, Aids, a life of flies and dust.
Ethiopia, Niger, where are these countries' powers?
Living a life of luxury, in their ivory towers.
Then there are dictators, world rulers of rich and poor,
Instead of giving food, they buy tools of war.
You never hear of presidents or politicians going to war with guns,
They say we must do our duty, prepare your precious sons.
Now in the shadow of evil, we have the terrorist,
Everyone and anyone, could be on their list.
Everyday people going to work, children in their school,
Evil suicide bombers are the killing tool.
Where will evil end? When will murder cease?
So all can live in harmony, a whole world live in peace.
Love is what is needed, love for one another,
Instead of taking up the gun, killing someone's brother.
Forget colours, creeds or whose religion's best,
Naked all we are born, and fed from Mother's breast.
Equal are we all, open your eyes and see,
Blood and flesh and bone, one day will be free.
My eyes look at this world, inside my heart is crying,
Seeing hunger, the hate and war
And watching God's children dying.

Carl Fricker

TRIBUTE TO ALL WAR-TORN COUNTRIES

I've just seen a film on the TV
What horrific sights they showed to me
Men, women and children blown to bits
Guns and grenades made sure of their hits
How can we let these wars go on?
Has all humanity truly gone?
Can men hate and kill each other?
People that they once called brother
Who once lived side by side?
Lived, loved, laughed and cried
What seeds of hate can one man plant?
That makes him seethe, rage and rant
That greed and jealousy rears its ugly head
So soon he wants these people dead
Such barbaric atrocities he will reap
Upon the innocent, defenceless and weak
They burn their homes, rape and pillage
Everywhere, town, city and village
Some escape, but oh, so few
Cold, starvation, take some of them too
When will it end? I hear you cry
If only nations would really try
To share their land with one another
Clasp hands and call each other brother
Help the poorer countries make a living
Give and not count the cost of giving
These wars go on it's time to cease
Let men learn to live in peace
A fervent prayer I send today
help us oh Lord, show us the way

Sheelagh Chimes

CELEBRATIONS

Celebrations of every kind, abound
For life is full of joy.
I feel lucky to *be*.
Lucky to be me!
I'm healthy, whole, happy
And *free!*
We live in a wondrous world
With beauty all around -
The sounds and smells and sights of nature
From shore to sky, throughout the lands.
And all those close to us
Who fill our lives with love.
We need to think of all of this.
It *is* our bliss.

Rosemary Graham

NO COMPANY

On our own, you and me,
Absolutely no company,
Having five minutes, taking time out,
No crying children, or an angry shout,
This is the start of the rest of our life,
Me, you, husband, wife,
Children married with families of their own,
This is being on our own.

We dreamt of this when the kids were small.
Don't remember bad times at all,
When we struggled to make ends meet,
Making sure the kids had the odd treat,
Made sure they always had a holiday,
Spending all your holiday pay.
You remark how quiet it is, and I have to agree,
We decide to pop out and visit our lovely family.

Maureen Arnold

ANNIVERSARY

You have been dead a year and I am numb.
Thoughts of you unbidden come
Of how you were long years ago.
Love and laughter - your hand is mine, just so.
That loving smile,
All mine for just a while.

Oh, I would blot out the failing years,
The sadness and the bitter tears;
The knowledge of the end
When you, my love, my dearest friend,
Would have to journey on alone
And leave me sadly on my own.

But I must carry on from day to day.
Press on regardless, as we used to say.
And maybe in a dream sometime when
I least expect it, you might come home again,
To hold my hand and smile at me
In the way that once we used to be.

Eileen M Lodge

EQUINOX

Red, the setting sun
his yet still fierce breath
sears the drifting sand.
Lays a trail to follow
unmapped by human hand.

Blue, the rising moon
with cool and tranquil grace
bathes the dunes below.
Near, and yet so far
from her beloved's afterglow.

The twilight sky above
reveals their doomed romance.
To always lead and follow
in time's eternal dance.

The day in equilibrium
balanced by these two.
The passion of the red
the serenity of the blue.

Malcolm Fairbrother

INVADED

For 22 years I exist in a body suffering extremes of hormonal hell,
As the tumour pressing on my skull grows larger, so do I,
My arms and legs remain slim and I resemble a lemon on sticks,
My face turns round and red, my skin is taut and stretched,
I exude a smell of male testosterone
And grow body hair to match,
I develop a 5 o'clock shadow.
My reflection is not I.
I cannot have this syndrome, it is too rare.
As the years drag by
I am so depressed; perhaps it is all in my imagination.
My body aches through carrying the weight of the world.
Then, a diagnosis, a hope, a cure,
22 years of misery,
Two years of tests,
Two hours of surgery.
Now I look in the mirror and see what I want to see,
Me.

Beverly Maiden

EMOTIONS, THE COLOUR WHITE FAIRYTALE

Two white doves glide through the white sky.
A pair of white butterflies, flutter in the light breeze,
Dancing in the warm fresh air that we breathe,
So elegant, like ice skaters dancing.
A pair of white doves in love, that stay together for eternity.
Playing the game of kiss chase and hard to get.
Two white swans gliding through the lake,
Dancing together like they are doing the tango.
White blossom drifts in the air like confetti,
White roses smelling as sweet as honey of the bee.
White clouds drifting softly,
Looking like candyfloss that you feel you could eat.
White daisies sitting so prettily, white tulips standing tall like soldiers
With the white woolly sheep grazing on the lush green grass.
The white unicorn's standing tall,
Guarding the carriage like a king with his queen,
Waiting for the prince and princess
To carry them to the church on their wedding day.
With white air bubbles drifting in the skies,
With a mixture of colours of pink, blue, purple,
The angels by their sides sing in the choir, God on their side.
Time is for eternity.
With silver rings they are wed.
The kiss of innocence,
Their bright eyes blue and their smiles of sweetness.
The day is passing now,
Married, the bride and groom,
It is unconditional love they have for one another.
With the skies turning to dusk, one silver star shines on
With the full moon glowing like a torch.
Yet the night is still young.
Raindrops fall like tears, shining in the moonlight.
With a pond so near you can hear the frogs croaking in the midnight
Sitting on the lily pads, talking to one another.
A fairy sits on the edge on the damp grass, with a wand in her hand.
The wind growing colder.
Now, sitting on a toadstool, the fairy wishes it was her
When a frog said to her, 'I will be your prince.'
And with her wand he was.

Lindsey Jane Way

AUTUMN

Gold and russet leaves, a faint dampness in the morning air,
Trees mellowed in the early sun,
For autumn draws near.
The hedges glistening with dew, heady
With a touch of scent
And the many shades of colour,
With a summer well spent.
Faded blossoms and crumpled flowers,
Grey clouds in the sky.
The coolness of the wind telling
Summer's passed us by.
Autumn glory bedecks the countryside anew,
Nature has put on her newest dress
With which to woo.
The winter flowers, springing into life again
Carpeting the wayside, and a distant bird's refrain.
Breaks the silence of an autumn morning
And with it, a new world is gently dawning.
That too will change to cold and rime and snow.
When winter takes over and north winds blow.

P Candlish

ODE TO LARRY GRAYSON

He was such a funny man
One look - the walk - his hand
For forty years he trod the boards
Success - at last was his reward

He told the stories as only he knew how
'Hey! Ho!' As he touched his brow
'Look at the muck'
'A-up-me-duck'

Apricot Lil his friend *Everard*
Slack Alice was his trump card
Names of the people he made up in the town
Jonah the Milk, his whistling renowned

As Nuneaton commemorates his anniversary
Ten years in 2005 - January
'Shut that door' you would hear him say
You gave him your generous applause
'The Generation Game' on TV
His book about the war

'What a gay day' this will be
Something I'm sure you will agree
And remember - the good times
He had shared in your life

So if you are looking down on us Larry
As the *star* now from up above
You once said you wanted to be loved

You made us laugh at your silly jokes
And the way in which you spoke
And now as we look up to the sky
Till we meet again it's - *goodbye - goodbye.*

Sheila Moore

CELEBRATING A REBIRTH

My frail octogenarian husband
Had a day-long blood transfusion.
It began after a lengthy delay,
As in the department there'd been some confusion.

Attended throughout by five dedicated nurses,
In an armchair comfortably seated,
The hours slowly passed and a substantial repast
Broke the boredom, and found him repleted,

At home I was anxious - my mind all astray,
While I absorbed myself in some art;
The clock seemed to be going backwards,
As I thought, prayerfully, with a full heart.

I prepared drop-scones for our tea,
And place the hall chair in front of the door.
Prepared for a long wait to welcome him home . . .
Suddenly he was there! It was just after four.

'It's amazing!' he said, 'I feel so well . . .
My mind is alert, and my legs are stronger!
I can now see much more clearly,
And my balance is wobbly no longer!'

We rejoiced together at the marvels of science,
And for our hospital had nothing but praise.
His quality of life is now greatly enhanced:
For his new life, we'll give thanks all our days.

Margaret Clary

SILENT FRIENDS

Alone I sit in the darkness of a winter's night
Watching, waiting, for . . . something . . .
Silence so evident as the land sleeps
Broken only by the call of a bat
Hunting for its prey . . .
A church bell tolls the hour . . .
Who else had heard but me?
Icy frost ghosts encircle my body . . .
Yet burn my face and hands
Though I am not afraid . . .
I have friends . . . with me . . .
Though they are many
They do not speak . . . only smile
Here in their millions
To give some light to the darkened heavens
As I sit . . . watching, yes;
Silent smiling friends
Whose names I am still learning
As I watch . . . and wait
The Great Bear of courage
Guides a plough over the night sky
I am comforted by His presence
The eyes of Perseus and Seven Sisters
Watch . . . as I do; and I feel a warmth
A triangle of friends join in perfection
Followed by Aries . . . I sit and hope
Secret Andromeda has within, his own galaxy
I have not met yet . . . I am filled with wonder
Orion The Warrior guards all
On their journey with sword and shield
So brave . . . I enjoy his appearance
Beautiful Sirius shines with such brilliance
To light the way . . . for all
I know not darkness
So proud the Big Dog behind his queen
Always faithful . . . I know all is well
To be alone . . . yet not
I have watched and waited
With my friends the stars for a glimpse
Of something . . . 'Travellers' maybe
From some distant galaxy
A universe, so vast in her glory
Holds the secret
I sit alone . . . with friends
So silent, yet smiling at me
Giving light in the darkness
Until . . . dawn breaks
I am happy to know my friends will return
To smile upon me . . .
As I watch . . . and wait . . . for . . . something

Jeni Pierce

THE FULL MOON

(To KB)

When travelling home upon a summer's night,
Along a road with many a standard light,
They saw the darkening clouds above the ground,
Casting their heavy shadows all around.

A gentle rime of silver then came through,
On edges of the curving clouds in view,
And soon, the full-blown circle of a face
Smiled down to make the world a joyful place.

The power of its gaze was touched with love
While shining brightly in the sky above,
And while the couple said their fond farewell,
They truly sensed the full moon's 'magic' spell.

Yvonne Watkin-Rees

LAMBS TO THE SLAUGHTER

With bilious dread I mark the ticking clock:
Though miles away those silent, smoking skies
Instil somehow awareness in my flock,
Presentiment of imminent demise.

Invisibly infecting lamb and calf,
The daily creeping on another batch
Prompts euphemistic parlance out of *maff* . . .
'Containment', 'take out', 'prudently dispatch!'

Those victims of the holocaust, almost
Despairing meekly, herding to their captors' 'Raus!'
Required belief their deaths were never lost,
A meaning to their lives in such chaos.

Today they say they must initiate
A cull of healthy lambs - they've been advised!
A shepherd needs some hope to palliate
The pain as sturdy beasts are sacrificed.

They say that once, engendering rebirth,
A blameless lamb of God to death was led:
I've heard He marks each sparrow's fall to Earth:
And might He hear my slaughterman's fell tread?

Patrick Brady

SUBCONSCIOUS RIVERS

Of times gone by of days we seek
the moment that we find
the universal point of space
our brain has tried to hide
into the vast unconquered paths
of thoughtful bursting banks
flowing through subconscious rivers

Our ears alight with freeing sound
opening imaginary gates
sending an impulse of varied thoughts
questions, answers, debates
through our eyes we see the sights
of thoughtful bursting banks
flowing through subconscious rivers

Into the depths of staggering waves
our mind it slowly seeps
until we see the golden gate
inside our soul it keeps
then through the arch our boat it sails
between thoughtful bursting banks
flowing through subconscious rivers

Behind the gate is their escape
we do not really know
to come so far is such a feat
exhaustion fills our souls
to open up our eyes
would surely snap us from this dream
and bursting banks would flood the rivers

New strength lifts us from our sleep
to look inside the maze
what do we see I do not know
in wonder we only gaze
we press our souls against the walls
where they're about to burst
and flood our heads with drowning rivers

Alan Johnston

THE CLOUDS ARE THE SEA OF THE SKY

The clouds are the sea of the sky says I
The clouds are the sea of the sky
Skipping clouds on the bluest hue
Suddenly blown by an angel's breath
For more images anew, images anew
Within your own sea spectacular
Swimming, soaring, sweeping free
Mountainous cotton wool waves
Dance and weave with glee
Now, broken by breeze and draught
The wind whips up a storm
And clouds become an angry mass
Thunder dark, grim, shattered and torn
Into swirling rage and battered shape
Where rain lives with snow and hail
And all the elements combine
To make the sky the sea somehow.

Then, standing here on man-made planes
Nature's birds in flights of fancy
Viewing prismed clouds in sunrise, low sunset
That trigger thoughts of romance
I gaze up into a starlit sky
Where clouds now, a gentle embrace
Surround the sparkling gems on high
And caress the moon's new face.

Sue Hughes

SAINTS

Saints like Peter, James and John,
They loved Jesus, every one
They worked in kind and gentle ways
And followed Him throughout their days.

A Chorlton

MY FRIEND

I walked along the beach today
The storm had swept the sand away
Ridge upon sandy ridge lay bare
Speckled with shells, crinkly and rare.
The waves lapped gently, held serene
Tamed once more by might unseen
The fury of the fear filled hours
Banished by a gentler power.
The bluest sky, so full of light,
Reflected all that's pure and bright
The clouds snowballed across the heights
Gossamer light and dazzling white.

I proudly walked without a sigh
Uplifted by the signs on high.

I walked with you today, my friend
Along life's pathway, round each bend
Down the slippery slope of fear
Up to the mountain top of cheer.
The voice that stilled the tempest storm
Now calmed our hearts from fear's form
I said, 'Be still, wait patiently,
I am the *Lord* that healeth thee.'
We skipped, we danced, we laughed with glee
And lifted voices joyously.
Set free from fear, made whole again
To stroll along life's earthy plain.

We proudly walked without a care
Lifted by that answered prayer.

Thelma Robinson

BLACK ROSE

I have a little black rose,
As black, as black could be.
How it got its colour,
No one knows you see.

There's not too many of them,
They really are quite rare,
So when you give this rose away,
It shows them that you care.

My black rose has a power,
But what, I do not know,
It seems to lock my sorrow,
Perhaps to make it grow.

In the weeds and brambles,
Where the soil's hard and dry,
My little black rose grows there,
While all around it dies.

So when I'm at my lowest,
And think I can't go on,
I'd go to where my black rose is,
Its power makes me strong.

Dominica Kelly

KIDS' HOLIDAYS

We had our grandchildren for a holiday
'Are you mad?' I heard people say

These four young people made our days
In their own special ways

They gave us joy
Three girls and one boy

We were woken by four smiling faces each day
Eager to see what we were doing and where they would play

Is it the beach, finger painting or the park?
Don't leave us in the dark

Hooray! It's the park; then home for tea
We will miss them, when they go, my husband and me.

Margaret Mitchell

THE CYCLAMEN

It sits upon my window sill
Better than any anti-depressant pill
As I sip my morning cup of tea
I am fascinated by what I see.

Rising above the mirror pot
Sits a bulb or corm, I know not what
From the crowded centre shoots push forth
Growing and jostling for all their worth.

At first I cannot really tell
If leaf or flower is emerging well
But very soon it is clear to me
The difference now easy to see.

The leaf at first is closed, dark and small
As it opens and grows it turns lighter and tall
The upper leaf pattern inspires the best art nouveau
Or the finest lace formed in a circular row.

What thrills me even more
Is the way the twisted petals rise and form a core
With arched head that backwards bursts
Like Japanese fans, bright pink at first.

As leaves and flowers fade and die
New shoots form and vie
For their deserved place in the sun
The cycle of life continues its run.

Theresa M Carrier

THE ROOM

I'm stuck inside a room
The room has many voices,
I can't help feeling confused,
Though I don't have many choices.

I try banging on the wall
A window I cannot see -
I know better than to cry,
Because tears won't set me free.

I wish with all my heart
Just to be let out,
And resist the burning urge
Just to scream and shout.

I see a glint of silver
I see the silver shine,
Engraved upon a key saw the word *mine*.

I picked the key up slowly
Turned it in the lock,
Finally I heard a click
I froze in utter shock.

The door would not open
There had to be a catch,
I should have guessed, I should have known
That there'd be strings attached.

I was told to right my wrongs
By a voice, so stern and clear
And that if I didn't succeed,
I'd be trapped forever, in here.

A sigh of relief swept over,
Almost knocking me to my feet,
A sigh so pleasant,
A sigh so sweet.

I needed to get out
So again I turned the key,
That I had found on the floor,
The one I know was meant for me.

As I stepped outside the room,
I heard humming like a song,
Then my eyes saw people
That had been waiting for me . . .
All along . . .

Meltem Baykaner

A CERTAIN FEELING

Loneliness is -
Not a tangible thing.
It's just something that's there
From summer to spring.
There's nothing to touch,
Yet it's something you feel,
There's nothing to see,
But you know that it's real.

You can be in a crowd -
At a party maybe,
Where the music is loud
And the wine flowing free.
But deep down inside
The feeling's the same,
Loneliness is
The name of the game.

Shirley R Thomas

COUNTRY CHILDREN OF YESTERYEAR

Cheerful, chuckling, chivvied, chided,
Sometimes chirping, like chubby chicks;
Compulsive and continuous chatterboxes -
Sometimes cheeky, seldom churlish,
With faces like chunky Cheddar cheese,
Or cherub-white Caerphilly, if you please;
Some, with hair of chestnut colour,
Of a charming, chestnut colour,
And champions in their own right, when at ease.

Children of the countryside, relaxing
In lush, green clover contentment;
Then, innocent and most intent,
As quiet moment oft, were spent
In making chain upon chain
Of delicate, green-stemmed,
Yellow-faced, white-hemmed,
Petalled daisies;
Oblivious of the world around,
True, perfect peace they all had found.

Then, racing and chasing across the field,
Quite unaware of its vast mineral yield,
Towards the briar hedge beyond,
But pausing by the duck-filled pond
And gazing at its many birds,
Of neat-blended, beauteous colours,
That waddles and straddled and skilfully paddled,
With ease, if you please, to the other side.

They'd see the gentle stream meander,
Or catch a glimpse of goose, or gander;
They'd pick long grasses, country flowers,
Indulge in long idyllic hours:
Then, home again, the day was done,
Such children's innocence was fun.

Glan Grey-Jones

BE HELD FAR FROM HOME

Argh - thirty-six hours to go
and I am in near-hysterical mode,
mid-shopping frenzy heightened
by hideously desirous children
and not knowing what arborio is.
Shall I stick to Italian or try French?
Emergency dip into hidden cook books.
Émincé de choux rouges braisés -
I can do that! Can't say it out loud,
but how difficult can it be?
Stumble home, laden with the store's finest,
shocked at the prices (nothing new there!)
Ensuing riot of preparation takes precedence
over family, work, telephone.
Restless sleep, then only twelve hours to go.
Slight panic as focaccia and brioche
confuse chef into European faux-pas,
then Chardonnay (African) intervenes.
Children go, husband snoozes, supine;
hair dries itself into interesting quiff
over pans in the culinary sauna.
More Chardonnay - I *will* relax, darling.
Rice is fluffy (Delia, you saint).
Doorbell rings, deep breath, more lippy.
Perhaps Rick Stein's next year?

Karen Barron

ROTTWEILER, THEY SAY . . .

They say . . . that you're evil
The Devil's own dog -
I say a worshipper of the Devil
I clearly am not

They say . . . that your eyes
Are piercing and cold -
I see only eyes
That are loving and bold

They say . . . you're a beast
With intent to do harm -
But your eyes have a gaze
That is gentle and calm

They say . . . that you're hard
Have they not stroked your head?
To not stroke your head
Must be something they've read

For your head is of velvet
So soft to the touch
Something which pridefully
I do very much

They say . . . when you speak
They wish to run a mile -
Can they not see it's been said
With a loving Rott smile?

They say . . . that you're evil -
But it is they who are evil
For blackening your name
And causing you pain

You look up at my face
And I see you ask 'Why?'
As I look deep into your eyes
All I can do is cry

For you were born with a curse
Maliciously given by mankind
A curse that would be
Far better left behind

A dog from the Devil?
Or a dog from above?
The Rottweiler I love
Definitely a dog from the Lord up above

Amanda Hawes

ENDEAVOUR - A SONNET

My soul has soared to heights surpassed by none.
Yet still I stand alone 'midst thoughts of you;
The joy we found still warms like noon day sun,
Your tender touch so soft . . . long overdue.

So many miles between our lips does find
Me caught 'twixt timid loops that do condemn
The need of sanity and peace of mind
To hold each precious moment by its stem.

Tis madness that we cannot be as one,
Yet still I love in hope, with fierce belief
That someday, when we will our fears outrun,
Surrender to our needs with sweet relief.

One truth alone stands brave to verify;
Of creeping common sense I shall not die.

Linda Zulaica

ONCE THERE WAS A SPRINGTIME

That spring before the war,
We strolled the meadows, my love and I,
Where the cowslips rang their yellow bells,
And milkmaids and kingcups nodded shyly
In the happy breeze.
He would laugh boyishly . . . fling out his hands
And say, 'Peaches . . . just look at these!
Isn't this world a wonderful place?'
I knew a vague touch of fear in my heart . . .
Thinking if he really understands
That soon we'll be at war, and have to face such sorrow?
He would laugh again, 'I believe tomorrow
Will be a lovely day, nothing is in vain,
I can be patient now spring is here
And primroses survive the night's fierce rain!'
When I mentioned the shadow of a coming war,
He shook his head in disbelief
And took from his pocket little envelopes of flower seeds
To scatter on the green banks along a Sussex Lane . . .
'If it should come to that,
My sowing will not be in vain,
Other men who walk this way will reap the joy,
See the flowers of hope growing
Along these lanes and in the fields
Where this same sun will be glowing.
And the moon look down in the time
Of peace again.'

Later . . . in another May,
I walked along this much-loved country way,
Thinking how the flowers would bloom
And nod
Along the lane . . .
Smiling for that laughing boy,
Who would not walk this way again.

Noni Fanger

LADY WHY DO YOU SMILE?

When all around is sadness
And life is harsh and vile,
Why do you look so far away?
Lady, why do you smile?

Deep, deep, within the heart of me
Well hidden from all view,
Is a moment of pure happiness,
The glory that I knew.
But now that I am getting old
And time is running out,
I'll share with you my secret smile
And say what it's about.

Long years ago when I was young
And to hopeful dreams I clung,
We rode and rode, my love and I
And watched the night slide slowly by,
We rode until we left behind
The sight and sound of all mankind.
The space was huge, all we could spy
Was grass below, above was sky.

The horizon was not flat and stark
But roundly curved in gentle arc.
We sat atop on this strange world,
We two, as wonders fresh unfurled.
We watched the splendour of a newborn sun,
Flames shot through the sky, our day had begun.
Then into my heart forever to stay,
That daybreak of wonder is with me today.

Helen West

AUTUMN SOLSTICE

Blue tits visit Elder Tree
Her branches fully laden
Bramble fruit for all to see
A banquet for a maiden
Hawthorn berries darkest red
Alongside wild roses
All give healing it is said
As well as pretty posies
Next to ripen Apple Bough
With fruit to heal the sick
Come gather up her bounty now
Or choose a lucky stick
'Neath Hazel stand with open hand
To catch a tasty nut
This wise man of the woods
Will open eyes which have been shut
Amid all these our sacred trees
The Oak will be the grandest
He lives at length to give us strength
Just as nature planned it
Great Mother Beech is here to teach
And give us welcome shelter
She rustles as you pass beneath
I'm sure that you have felt her
From woodland now to open field
Fetch corn, oats and barley
A time for harvesting their yield
For folk who know the country
Let's give thanks for autumn then
With all the gifts she brings
This joyful time for food and wine
While happy bird life sings.

Deborah Hall

MEMORIES

Christmas 1937 - and I was quite impressed
To learn of baby Jesus' birth - (some years before) I guessed
I looked up to the heavens - and searched for brightest star
And wondered at the shepherds, who'd followed from afar.

Christmas 1947 - though poor, was full of joy
A stocking with an orange, nuts, an apple and small toy.
I thought a bit about the babe, whose gifts seemed weird to me
And wondered if He'd ever known the thrill of decking tree.

Christmas 1957 - nursing now and caring
Midnight Mass and mistletoe and Christmas Day a-sharing
With patients, (surgeon carving bird), emergencies to tend
And wondered if in teenage years, He'd had the gift to mend.

Christmas 1967 - with babies of my own
The happiest times of my whole life, the best I've ever known.
The house was filled with laughter and more expensive toys.
I'd little thought of 'lowly cribs', indulging my own boys.

Christmas 1977 - teenagers now, my three
Clothes and hi-fis, aftershave and girlfriends round for tea.
Nowhere to sit post washing up, the lunchtime plates and pot
And so recalled, 'no room at inn', but happy still I'd squat.

Christmas 1987 - a grandson of my own
The crib the centre of our lives, the seed of future sown.
The baby stirred, all gathered round, a-worshipping anew
Recalling the three shepherds, who worshipped baby too.

Christmas 1997 - and I am all alone
Reflecting now on 'Noels' past, all happy, but now flown -
To far flung areas of the world, they all now live abroad
I follow star to where they are and I am reassured.

Mai M Roach

THE VILLAGE AUCTION

The village auction, oh what fun
I was making the tea and we had a good run
The auction started with a swing
I stood, alert as I had, not a thing
'A tea trolley,' the auctioneer announced
'I will give five pounds,' I made a pounce
'We don't need that dear,' the auctioneer replied
It was my husband Brian, I nearly cried
By then the audience got quite amused
And life on the whole got a bit confused
But I outdid the highest bid
And a tea trolley I gained for a few quid.

Cyn Jordan

PRESSING FORWARD

There's an atmosphere of anticipation
Of rejoicing and celebration
A milestone has been reached
And many are a part of this
Fifteen years of writing and sifting through the odes
Many a poised pen and some lost for words
The best put in black and white
So in press we can read
But for the ones that didn't make it
There's no time to bereave
So, see it's a celebration
These early years have seen
Many tears and learning
But fun times there have been
Now a great prize is up for grabs
So, editorial team,
Cast your eyes, award the prize,
The best, the cream!

Julianne Clarke

TREASURE IN CLAY

You look deep inside you
And you see the stain
Where your sin has scarred you
Again and again
But God asks you to love Him
And give Him your pain

You look deep inside you
And you know such shame
Though never quite certain
Why you take the blame
But God asks you to love Him
And carry His name

You look deep inside you
And feel a disgrace -
That you can't be worthy
Of the Father's embrace
But God asks you to love Him
And minister grace

You look deep inside you
But can't see the treasure
That God has put in you
Pressed down, in full measure
But God asks you to love Him
And live for His pleasure.

Sarah Bingham

A Reminder That One's Birthday Dinner Should Journey Back In Time

I have a friend, her name is Jane
Last week she took me up Wood Lane
To see the fields, of days gone by
Which were farmed, by Dad and I
What memories came back to me
My brother's initials on a tree
That was so many years ago
I wouldn't find them now, I know
The fields have gone, replaced by trees
But they still bring back memories
Before the war, the land was grazed
Horses, sheep and cows were raised
The orders came, we had to heed
This land must grow crops, for people's needs
George had gone, to war to fight
My life changed, over night
Instead of mowing and carting hay
I now had to learn another way
Of working, and using our old fields
Hoping they would give us some good yields
I went to work with 'Nancy' and 'Flower'
Trudging on from hour to hour
No tractors had we, to do the jobs
But I got by, against all odds
I loved that life so long ago
First to plough and then to sow
Other jobs came in-between
But life went on, it was serene
Not like today, all rush and tear
But plodding on, we still got there
What memories, to live again
Many thanks to my friend Jane!

Jessie Bishop

My First Acceptance

My first poem accepted
The joy of not being rejected

Acceptance makes up for the piles of paper thrown on the floor
I hear my children ask, 'Dad why is Mum
Again behind the locked door?'

Hours of writing not now written in vain
To me this is an honourable gain

There for all my family to have a look
Mum's proof of a poem printed in a poetry book

A Wood

Between Friends

Dear cousin, we grew up together,
remember laughing at your japes.
Playmates in all sorts of weather,
and involved in endless scrapes.

Our lives followed different roads,
Meeting up at family gatherings.
Where your true feelings showed,
and compliments were flattering.

Now we keep in touch by letter,
detour down through the years.
Life could have treated you better,
you were unlucky in love, my dear.

We have remained good friends,
though long ago you hoped for more.
Trusting our friendship never ends,
affectionately yours.

Rosemary Davies

Because You're Mine

It can be painfully revealing analysing one's own feelings,
but mine are very easy to define.
Quite simply, what I need is a purpose, which indeed is
to care for you, and why?
Because you're mine.

That day when I caressed you, I knew I would possess you,
your soft brown eyes, your jet black hair so fine -
and that we'd always be together for untold years - if not
forever, eternally, and why?
Because you're mine.

I took you home to my place, hung your picture by the fireplace,
poured a drink, then went outside to clear my mind;
then as the daylight ended and into night it blended,
you came to me, and why?
Because you're mine.

So what now my lovely lady, full of grace and oh, so stately?
Because you're wonderful and beautifully equine,
I'm going to leap upon your back, so you can gallop
down the track with me astride, and why?
Big horse you're mine!

Tony Reese

An Octogenarian Friend

I see her tottering by on Zimmer frame,
that lady once so elegant and spry;
it flashes through my mid-aged mind - that there,
but for the grace of God, go careless I.
How nimble were those hands which now are swelled;
they knitted, bathed the baby, baked a cake.
Many the times they patted, stroked or clapped
for joy - more often now, they only ache.
Those eyes, now dim, have sparkled with delight
at some achievement of a child or wife;
now they are deeper sunken, tired and red,
until a memory stirs them back to life.

When young and active, normal, in good health,
we little think how fast-approaching age
can alter one's appearance, attitudes
and tolerance of life at that last stage.
I am resolved this will not be my lot -
I'll exercise and read and smile and play;
but should my mind wear out before my frame,
thankfully I'll not know the night from day!

Joan L Carter

God, The Universe And Everything Sonnet

Who lets the Earth hurtle around the sun?
Who keeps the stars on their fiery path?
Is God the mechanic who makes things run?
And should mankind avoid His awesome wrath
Or is the universe a clockwork game?
Wound up at the outset and left to spin
Begetting new lives without any aim
Save procreation so that their genes win
The survival race kills all at the last
The stars will wink out as time races by
Will a lonely God think about the past
Or as He has lived so should He too die?
Or will creation - absolutely cold
Be a dark bubble for God to behold?

James E Cragg

EQUALITY?

I am black and beautiful
What are you staring at?
Just because of my skin colour
I'm just as human as you.

I am mixed race and magnificent
What are you staring at?
Don't call me half-caste or coloured
I'm a person not a thing.

I am Asian and adventurous
What are you staring at?
My faith and my colour -
Doesn't stop me being nice.

I am white and witty
Why aren't I being stared at?
If you had heard and not seen me
Would you think of me as different?

Mica Hope Phillips (12)

A THANK YOU LETTER

Dear (as I think myself) Friend,
Sunday was all
Heaven-kissing hill-walking, though
We had to descend
After receiving Holy Communion,
Even to the summit of Mount Keen,
With crowds of clouds . . .
Some like the Valkyrie
And others grouped - like the Grey Man -
On ranges deep as David's eye blue.
Thanks be to Lord Glentan -
Ar for Laird's-eye-view
Of Lochnagar - zebra-like. Thank you.
Love from Valerie.

Valerie Faith Irvine-Fortescue

ME - MAYBE

I am here yet can't find me
Lost myself, what could this be?
I am standing here yet don't
Know the place, I look in the
Mirror and I don't know the face.

I am frightened and very scared
I don't know what will happen, I
Don't think I will be prepared.
So I am going to sit down in this
Corner and wait for what will be,
I hope I find out really soon,
Because I just want to be me . . .

Elizabeth Mary Turner

PARTING . . .

Take your hand off my chair
I find it uncomfortable sitting there!

Take your coat down off the hook
I want it gone next time I look!

Take yourself and all your lies
I can no longer look into your eyes!

Take it all and close the door
You don't belong here anymore!

Now you've gone I'll be OK
I will, I will, I will, one day!

Rowena

THE NORTH EAST NEUK

This corner of Scotland is the place tae bide
Be it hills, land or at the seaside
Fishing ports all round the coast
Sandy beaches some can boast
Gardenston, Crovie, Pennan or MacDuff
The homeward bound hill leaves ye fair oot o puff
Dolphins, seals and fish in the sea
Sometimes difficult for us to see
Looking over at Mormond, Knock and Bennachie
The hills will aye be dear ta me
Inland farmers working land
Machinery now to lend a hand
Delgaty woods - fresh air for a walk and break
The castle has a tea room with delicious home bakes
There are forests and woods with squirrels and deer
You have to be quiet, to see them come near
Stone circles at Strichen, Aikey Brae and Collerlie
They are there all the time, so you dinna need tae be early
Castles in this area are high on the scene
When you visit them they are fit for a queen
If you prefer to follow the whisky trail
There are many malts around here for sale
Deans and Walkers shortbread are afa fine
If ye dinna worry about yer waistline
Baxters famous for its flavours of jam
Also make soup with pea and ham
Pastimes are many be it tennis, golf or run
Sightseeing, picnics, horseriding or skiing can be fun
The Prop of Ythsie I climbed when young
I thought the last step would never come
The monument at Culsh if you've been you will agree
When you climb to the top, you can see the hills and sea
Capercallie, grouse or partridge are found among the hills
If you are there and see one, it really is a thrill
Spey Bay there are walks by the bay or inland
Seeing osprey, swans or gulls close at hand
It's up to us all to go out and see
Be it the beauty of the countryside or waves in the sea.

Gwen Dunbar

A HAPPY NON-STICK

I'm glad I'm not a woman,
I'm glad I'm not a man,
I'm just happy to be what I am,
A non-stick frying pan.

Get plenty of rest these days,
While microwavy does the cooking.
I can rest and sleep all day
And keep myself good looking.
Being a non-stick
Makes my life okay,
I don't have those metal pads,
Scratching my skin away.
Now and then they get me out,
When they fancy a fry,
So glad when they finish,
And I can say goodbye.
My pan life could have been worse,
I could have been born a chip pan,
Never have a moment's rest
From some greedy chip fan.

You can see being a non-stick
Why I am content
I am not out of shape
Like some pans I know who are bent.

D G Field

DREAMS

Dreams may occur when you are in a hypnotic unconscious trance,
In the midnight hour pictures run through your mind,
                              visions begin to enhance.
Your body and soul are taken over as you lay in slumberous mind,
As you travel to another world, enchanting you may find.
You may have past life regression therapy
                    finding tranquillity and peace.
Recurring spirits are far from beyond
Enlightening desires and destiny with a magic wand,
Hallucination interrupts your state of rest,
You look so dull and motionless, unaware of the test.
Your body is a state which the soul seems to have passed
                         into another state of being,
Lying limp and lifeless, not aware of what you are seeing.
You are in a phase of looking half-dead, people may say just weak,
Counting down from ten to one, life you start to seek,
Lighter and brighter, eyes open wide, you begin to take a peek.
You are now awake from a deep, deep sleep,
                and have just regained your physique.

Lorraine Ann Hunting

CAGED

In the centre of a small whitewashed room
is a rough-hewn wooden easel.
On it a canvas.

A young man -
shoulder length hair,
coarse coat that touches the ground,
stands, still, before it.
In one hand he holds a palette,
in the other a brush.
On the wooden floor are splashes of colour -
purple, yellow-ochre, vermilion . . .

A young girl stands near the easel,
a little back and to its right.
She wears a simple smock of kingfisher blue,
square at the neck - not hers:
hers is flung over a stool
in a dark corner: greasy, stiff with dirt,
patches of stale sweat under each arm.

She is very still;
slanting emerald eyes fixed.
Only the rise and fall
of her breasts say she's real.

Light from an unglazed window
high in the wall
holds her in a cage
of gold and blue.

Each day for a week she has stood in this cage
moving only with the light.
She hates being still -
is frightened to move,
frightened of the young man
who curses if she moves.

Tomorrow she'll go back
to the market where he found her,
spend his florin, laugh at him
for not having slept with her,
sell her olives and grapes, forget
all about his silly picture -
have men - bear children - grow old.

In a cage of gold and blue
there is a girl with green eyes.
I stare at her.
I hold her in my stare.

Michael Bangerter

SO GOOD TO BE ALIVE

Just give me a breather, some space of my own
As I sit with my memoirs I'm not really alone
I can pick up a photograph, get lost in time
Transported in sentiment, glorious moments all mine

Never feel sad because I have grown old
I am still your mum, no longer confident or bold
Now and then I need a nudge when memory fails me so
But I am still around to greet you as you come and go

My eyesight is a problem, I take treatment constantly
These joints of mine get tender and controlled is my BP
Whilst the thyroid hormone tablets are really trouble free
And the dentures need no fixative, they are in harmony with me

My hearing aid has long-life batteries, worthwhile you see
These support tights are a godsend, buy two pairs get one pair free
Life is so worth living, its purposes are many
Just give hope to all who need it and to those who have not any

Blessed are the good in heart and peace to those who strive
To make this world a better place, it is good to be alive.

Barbara Tunstall

INSPIRATION

Steamy night dripping with stars
world is hushed, except for crickets
gladsome thoughts pepper brain -
heart flutters - as cascading leaves.

Life's blessings congregate in joyful mind
current worries obliterated
and fade behind an August moon
there to rest till the 'morrow'.

Enkindled thoughts flame and intensify
God's gifts are recounted
euphoria is becalmed
new inspiration flows in abundance.

Alex Branthwaite

VINCENT

The story of Vincent Van Gogh is a sad story to be told,
He was a brilliant artist who never struck gold.
Never sold a drawing or a painting in his life,
He had to battle with so much torment sometimes in his life.

He was a man who put his love into his works of art,
He was a man who painted and drew from his heart.
Whether it be his sunflowers or a miner down the mine,
All Vincent's works were always very fine.

Painted and drew for pleasure for himself and for me and you,
Pure paint straight from the tube on to the canvas too.
Vincent was driven and lived for his art,
Mixed with the poor and played his part.

While he was here he couldn't sell a thing,
Now he's gone his praises we sing.
What an artist, what a lovely man,
No one can capture life like a Van Gogh can.

Painted and drew so many things, even himself,
People who are very rich own a Van Gogh, it adds to their wealth.
His art sells for fortunes now,
What a difference from the days when he was here, wow.

So let's all hail Vincent, appreciate his art,
It's the legacy he left us when from this world he did depart.
Let's all enjoy Van Gogh, such a wonderful man.
A true friend to many including Cézanne and Paul Gauguin.

R W Cummings

ORIGINS

It was a night - the sky laden with stars
Lit by the lamp - the moon
My sister was born
My coming delayed
With the birth of the sun at dawn
My mother had struggled to give her breath
Not knowing that I was due
But, what of my father
My grandmother, great grandmother?
They're part of my history too
I came from the earth
What colour my skin?
White, like the earth,
As breath was breathed in
I'm one with the plants, the birds
And the trees
The animals too and their histories
I'm one with the wind
That sings through the trees
That sings of the origins of all of these
I am the universe and it is me
Everything moving and growing I see
Language also of this is a part
It is a dance, the dance at the heart
The heart of our life, the core of our being
Created in love
By a Father all-seeing
May I remember that I am a part
Of this boundless universe -
A beat of its heart.

Brenda W Hughes

WITHOUT LOVE

How could we live if love did not exist.
Am empty shell with no anticipation
Or tender word to cause pulsating nerve.
To find no peace in the body's inner core
Or feel no quickening of the heart inside the breast.
My life has taught me many lessons
Each morning I embrace the dawn
As a mother her child newborn,
And with a smile love radiates forth.
Every day I breathe your essence.
A love so intense
You are my life support
The creator of all things.

M Mustoe

BLUE SKIES

I can see something in the distance,
A light in the darkened tunnel.
I can finally see a future,
It's there before my eyes.
There's a sunny day with lovely blue skies.
There's love in my world,
As I look into your loving eyes.
There were grey skies all of my days,
Until you came along.
My sadness went away,
My sad poems became love songs.
You will always be on my mind,
You put a sparkle in my eyes.
That's why you will always have a home in my heart,
Until the day I die.

Stephen Wooley

THE ANGIOGRAM TEST

When you're in trouble with your heart
Get to the Royal Brompton from the start
They get the cameras near your chest
And have you dressed in a long blue vest.
There's also a camera overhead
Wish they were taking my photograph instead
Before you go, your thighs you shave.
Those were the hairs you used to have
The nurse says, 'Now this will feel cold'
Now you're not feeling quite so bold
The doctor says, 'I'll deaden this part here.'
I thought, *bet this will feel quite queer.*
The doctor said, 'You'll feel a scratch as the needle enters in
Then a plastic tube is placed in the artery within the skin.'
The Doc then put in some dye
He had already told me why.
The dye makes you feel quite hot
Makes you think you have, but you've not.
The artery has the wire inside
You can hear voices as they guide.
Right into your heart it goes
On the telly there it shows
Then says, 'Your breath now hold'
Hey! this theatre's really cold
You can hear the cameras click
When you know they have done the trick.
Your breath comes out with quite a gush
The doctor wants a bit of shush.
Breathe in, breathe free
About 8 times it seemed to me.
Then suddenly the test is done
Have I lost or have I won?
It seems that I am nearly all blocked up
I will have to have a serious op.
Still if all comes right
I will be able to sleep OK at night.
Maybe gone will be the pain
A normal life will be again.

L Lowe

WE WILL REMEMBER THEM

We wander freely o'er our land
We should remember and understand
Our brave soldiers went to war
For freedom and for so much more
We will remember them

We see the poppies in the fields
Swaying gently in the breeze
Young men that were oh so brave
Poppies now lie on their grave
We will remember them

So many sons who left their mums
Marching gaily with their chums
They little knew what was in-store
Until they faced the blood and gore
We will remember them

Fighting in a foreign land
Trying hard to understand
The daily struggle, conflict and strife
The terrible senseless loss of life
We will remember them

So when we wander o'er our land
Think of the gallant, glorious band
The young men who faced their fears
They gave their lives for our future years
We will remember them

Barbara M Beatson

VICTORIA STATION CLOCK TOWER

I stand among this modern time
Where once I overlooked the yesterdays
A bygone age of horse and cart
And crinolines
Where speed and need to rush was not as now
My face was clean and bright
My hands were guiding arrows, pointing
Towards destinations, homosapiens had in mind
Time passed by and speed of need of progress
Cluttered up the streets
And horsepower, built into the metal frames
Of modern carts
Made the punctuality of time a factor
I was only part of life
For I, the watch tower
Of a way to destinations far afield
Saw the changes of a style of life.
I am so lucky to be here
For part of me has gone
Platforms to the world I shared
Have disappeared and in their place
Are stables for the horses of this modern age
I stand among this modern age
But memories are mine
I'm overshadowed, this I know
But I can smile
I knew the quiet way of life
I see the hectic everydays of now
But, here I stand, my fingers crossed
For time goes on
My fingers point the way
To where
But memories are mine.

R L Harvey

VELVET MOON

If I could take the velvet from the moon
And lay it as a carpet at your feet
With roses from the Orient at noon
In southern skies the dawn and dusk would meet

Oh! bring your lovely countenance to mine
Your ruby lips, an ornament divine
In fiery kiss let them with mine entwine
In love's great book we shall our names combine

If peaches were the fruit of paradise
Like one, your fair complexion would entice
Of Earth's great crop of men, oh! there just might
Be he who is the one to take delight

Onward through this wonderland I wander
Through passages of endless, ageing time
My heart for you does grow ever fonder
On higher planes of bliss it now does climb

The fires of love are growing oh! so bright
My arms around you, holding you so tight
Starry heavens blazing forth their glory
Adding further contours to love's story

Where have all the dreams gone, where departed?
The agony of love, the ecstasy
Blest the day that saw our love advanced
A rainbow in our lives for all to see

Velvet from the moon could thus be spun
And majesty the Earth to it could lend
Ah, yes! the battle would be justly won
Our lives together then would never end.

John London

CHRISTMAS INVITATION

Thanks for your invitation,
You're very, very kind.
So now I'm thinking what to wear
I must make up my mind.
I know that I must look my best
And be a shining star
For in the festive season
This is what we are.
Red's a Christmas colour
I think I'll settle there,
With a long and slinky see-through dress
To match my underwear,
With a feathered hat to crown it
And bright green fringes there.
I'll go and buy a robin
And put it in my hair.
And just because it's Christmas
Two fluffy pom-poms last
To decorate my head-dress
And make me look the best.
They'll wobble at the table
And make me look quite fast
Because my dress is sleeveless.
Bright bangles will I wear
To match the wobbles on my poms
Just simply for the dare
I can't put on my high heels
My toes have nobbles on
So trainers it will have to be
If I can get them on
They'll say I'm smart
Or look a tart,
And giggles will abound.
But hey! it's the festive season
And that's a very good reason
To look one's best
And blow the rest
Even if it's treason.

K M Brown

A SEASON OF ICE-ELATION

Like madrigals the overture of songbirds
Dawn orchestrated clear melodic trills
Reverberate throughout scarred echo chambers
Wind gouged from ageless purple shadowed hills
Uncompromising glacial chill pervades the countryside
Emphatic affirmation summer's sultriness has died

Splayed out against a bleak, benumbing daybreak
Gaunt sentinels their topmost branches spread
Morosely dark, directing and imploring
They dourly usher in the day ahead
As almost imperceptibly the lightening skies unveil
The marshes and the moorlands where the lingering mists prevail

For winter is a seasonal enchantress
Arrayed throughout in finery of white
Transforming the most featureless of landscapes
With power to aesthetically delight
She sculpts the snow; and laminates with ice clear mountain streams
With crisp, fresh glacial breath, she underscores her pallid themes

A scintillating silver-sequinned hoar frost
Applied by nature's adept stylish hand
Turns bright lactescent white, once verdant meadows
Where wind-whirled leaves perform their saraband
Anticipating spring, the trees deciduously stripped
Stand silently, like actors suddenly bereft of script.

Ron Beaumont

WOULD YOU CREDIT IT

She looked very fetching as she stood in the dock
Wearing sparkling diamonds and designer frock
But she was there to account for her grand spending spree
'It wasn't my fault Judge,' she cried pleadingly.

'The bank's sent me cards allowing me credit
That's why my account accrued all this debit
The first thing I did was go on a world cruise
Where I ate all before and drank all the booze
Second was the new boobs and cute little bot
To complete the picture I had some botox
Then purchased a house in the land of Peru
I wouldn't mind spending some time there with you.'

The barrister speaking on her behalf
Turned to the jury said, 'It's easy to laugh
How many of you here today, are in debt
All of you I'd hazard a guess
It's the fault of the banks, you must agree
This poor woman was clearly led astray.'

The prosecution council sarcastically replied,
'My heart bleeds
Ladies and gentlemen are we expected to believe
This so-called innocent didn't know what she was doing
She's so sharp as a tack, for all her billing and cooing.
No shopping trips for her at Tesco or Asda
This free spender preferred to shop at Prada
She had no collateral and lived on low pay
Whatever she spent, she knew she couldn't repay.
Come, come, you're intelligent people
Her excuses you must admit are decidedly feeble.'

'Don't besmirch this lady's name,' the Judge intervened
As angrily towards the jury he leaned
'The banks are to blame encouraging mad spending sprees
Let's end this case, set her free, if you please.'

With a cheer and a clap she was out of the trap
The judge whispered, 'Come with me for a meal
With my platinum card we should get a good deal.'

Rachel McKie

ATTITUDE

Why do so many people have an attitude to life?
They moan and groan about so many things,
When in this world there is so much strife.
They complain about the weather
When there is pouring rain, and storms about,
Yet, when the sun shines and it is very hot,
In the house they sit and pout.

Why don't they look around them
And take note of what they see?
The flowers in the springtime
Bursting forth for you and me.
A word of kindness, as you pass along your way
Will make all the difference to someone else's day.

A bit more tolerance and understanding
Towards your fellow man, no less,
Would help to ease the path of life,
And banish all trouble and stress.
Just try hard to lose your attitude,
Don't begrudge other people the good things they've achieved,
You could be the same as them, if in yourself you believed.

Marjorie Cripps

THE TECHNOLOGICAL AGE

Like them or loathe them, they're all the rage
A bit complicated for folks of my age.
The art of writing has gone by the way
It seems that progress is made every day.

Life is moving at such a pace.
It seems to me we're on the rat race.
A song comes to mind, and please don't scoff!
It's called 'Stop the world and let me off'.

You walk down the street, and not a greeting.
There they are arranging a meeting.
Someone speaks behind you - are they addressing me?
You turn around, they're oblivious, you see.

Now they're taking pictures, dear me, what next?
Words abbreviated, so they can text.
But however much we grumble and groan
There's just no escaping the mobile phone.

Maureen Anderson

LIFE'S GUIDANCE

Little baby, you've come into this world
With such hope, expectation and love
Your mind is like a blank canvas
Your parents the artists with the brush

They will paint your future before you
And guide you along the way
And if you ever stumble
Will pick you up, brush you down, and pray

For God has put you in their charge
And with His help, will give you the best
Of love, understanding and friendship
They will welcome you into their nest

When the time comes to leave them
They will send you on your way
Because they will know that you will do well
With the guidance they have given day after day.

Ruth Fellows

JOY OF LOVING YOU

Sitting here dreaming in a land of nowhere,
Living in a land of blue, no heart to care,
No kisses that are gentle, given in the night,
Pavements that are blue till the dawn's light,
Golden was my sun, you were there by my side,
Tears that have flowed, dark nights I cried,
Who knows the hearts of the lonely, they hide away,
In the land of lost dreams, they will always lay,
Moon in a starlit sky, in the heavens above,
Only the angels on high, know of lost loves,
Angels above watch over, those hearts so alone,
Walking the streets of blue, never finding a home,
Pain in a heart that aches, hiding themselves away,
On their beds of blue dreams, they will always lay.
No stars in a dark sky shine, dark are their nights,
No happiness, no loving heart, no night delights,
Life goes on they say, carrying their pain well,
Hearts that are broken, no love beside them to tell,
Joys of loving you, never again will I find,
Forever darling, you will remain in my mind.

Kevin Collins

HEATHLAND IN SUMMER

Whispers of white cloud floating across a clear blue sky
The sun warm and inviting, as you stroll through
                              heathland countryside
Brown fritillary butterflies gather on the ragwort's yellow heads
Bracken that stand even taller, with their fronds of fern widespread
Woodland ants in convoy, following a well-worn trail
A lizard dashes across your path, showing his shiny scales
Burnished bronze of the sun beetles, running under your feet
                              in the sand
Bees collecting pollen from wild flowers, in this beautiful unspoilt land
Rabbits chasing everywhere, scurrying into their tunnelled maze
On the breeze, the perfume of heather, one mass of purple haze
In the treetops' canopy a robin sings his heartfelt song
Staging a special performance, as you slowly stroll along
In this quiet setting you feel a sense of peace and calm
The flowers and the wildlife, in the heathland's summer sun.

Linda Meadows

THE KINGFISHER

Along the stream
We made our way,
At first it seemed dull
A band of grey,
When a bright jewel's
Unerring flight
Shot like an arrow
Beyond our sight.
Ere the eye could focus
He was away
Was it a vision
On this dull day?
We caught *but* a glimpse,
What *had* we seen?
The river's bright king,
Metallic green.

Barbara Brown

MEMORY LANE

There's a wonderful highway called Memory Lane,
It stretches way back through the years.
And as we grow older we walk down that road
To remember our laughter and tears.
We see the dear faces of folk who have gone
And places where once we had been
We remember these loved ones as we wander on
To gaze on each sweet homely scene.
Sometimes we go back to our own childhood days
When we were all school girls and boys.
With a penny to spend on some Saturday sweets
It was one of our own special joys.
We remember the games that we played in the street
With our friends we had such lots of fun.
With hopscotch and skipping and marbles as well
And other games out in the sun.
It could be some music or maybe a song
Reminding us of our first dance.
And the young folk we danced with, remember the one
Who brought us first taste of romance.
Yes, a wonderful highway is Memory Lane,
In the future perhaps it may be
Other people will wander, remembering there
And come looking for you or for me.

Margaret B Baguley

DOG ON A CHAIN

Little dog on a chain,
A heavy, short chain.
Confined for life inside a box,
A filthy, bare prison of a box.

He cringes there - hungry, sad and afraid,
His instincts to love and to serve repressed,
Denied his God-given right to be free
By ignorance and human cruelty.

He hears above the windsong in the trees,
He sees the myriad stars that light the heaven,
The free birds as they soar the open skies,
But only living death dwells in his eyes.

Robbed forever of his puppy days,
His youthful strength confined in misery,
No human touch, or voice to call his name,
Heaven sees it all and whispers 'Shame - shame.'

Little dog on a chain,
A broken chain.
Free from the obscene travesty of his cage,
Running wildly through the sweet morning meadows.

Free! Freedom of flight, freedom of motion,
The blood in his veins pounds like the ocean,
A startled old donkey brays as he passes,
Chasing the wind-sprites along the grasses.

Running and trumbling like a brook in flight,
Living his life in a day and a night,
Just for a while - oh, such a little while,
And Heaven sees it all - and gives a smile.

Ann Dempsey

FINAL MOMENTS

Dawson delays as gold encroaches,
After Johnson's surge.
Wilkinson waited, for he knew
That on the pitch his skills would glow,
A: swerve, a jink, a shrug, a show.
His composure, as the kicks he takes;
Hands clasped as if in prayer,
Trinity of man and ball and bar.

Dawson releases for the drop kick,
The ball must kiss the ground,
This mystical link with nature
As boot connects with ball,
Head over heels between the posts.
Greenwood embraces kicker,
They're bringing the World Cup home.

John L Wigley

THE EMERALD ISLE

Hedgerows with wild daisies and cherry fuchsia adorn
every roadside in the Emerald Isle
As bluebells bloom profusely on every byway.
Green fir trees stand erect on every mountainside.
While patient fishermen sit silently
On every lake shore to enhance a glorious day.
The surroundings of the Kerry Mountains
With their majestic peaks
Contracts with the lush grasslands of the golden vale.

On a balmy summer evening our green isle is like paradise,
With the Lord Almighty
Casting the shadows of Heaven over this lovely land.

Eileen Treacy

THE OLD GARDEN SHED

The old garden shed
could hardly be seen.
It was covered in brambles
and trees, like a screen.
A holly bush merrily
grew by the door
and mice scuttled,
busily on the floor.
The spiders had claimed
the window space,
with a mass of cobwebs
just like lace.

How many gardeners
had worked within
these walls of stone
so stout, so strong?
I'm sure each one
could tell a tale
of bygone days,
and lawns so green
and the loveliest roses,
ever seen.

Whence came the tools
stacked by the wall?
The ancient buckets
large and small.
Jars full of screws
all rusty red.
A claw-hammer handle
without a head.
Flower pots too
all idle and still.
A rusty old key
on the window sill.

The bramble fruit are ready to eat.
The wasps and the birds
will have a feast.
What memories cling to
this sad old shed?
Wait?
A faded name on the window ledge
and a date,
when the first rose bloomed.

Violet Higgins

THAT FABULOUS ERA

A lifetime ago you captured my heart,
I thought at the time that we'd never part.

A dream of a boyfriend with shoulders so wide,
your girlfriend and lover just bursting with pride.

The very first touch of your lips upon mine,
such feelings were scary but simply divine.

Enveloped in love and wrapped up in desire,
my body alive, lit up by this fire.

That wonderful ache where my heart used to beat,
soaked right through my being with such tender heat.

Now many years later I think of that time,
that fabulous era when you were all mine,

and I smile at the memory, how lucky I am,
for the one who replaced you, my wonderful man,

has given me stillness and made me content,
this soulmate and lover must be Heaven-sent.

Muriel Nicola Waldt

RED ROSES

Heaven sent red roses,
Surely summer's own fire,
From the days of Moses
Of which we'll never tire.

Red, red roses - beauty!
Delightful to behold:
They don't have a duty -
Just joy, to young and old.

Done with a master's brush,
Painted with colours sublime;
Folding from the green bush,
They'll be here for all time!

Giving people pleasure,
Only by being there;
Memories we treasure,
Of our red roses, fair.

J Millington

COMMENTS

'It will get easier,
As time goes by the pain will fade'.
I hear those words so often
And I think to myself
Most cruel statement ever made.

When the love of your life is taken
The hurt you suffer goes deep.
You listen to people's kind words,
Well intended I'm sure,
But it's comfort you want to reap.

'Think of the happy memories'.
More comments given to you.
Again you have to listen
But take no heed,
Those people don't have a clue.

Well over a year's gone by
Since you lost the love of your life.
The pain never leaves you.
The hurt sustained.
Silly comments cut like a knife.

'I know how you feel but . . .'
You can accept your loss.
Immortal words again
From someone so unreal
They only make you cross.

If people leave me alone
In my own time I will respond.
My own Darly has gone
And I accept that fact
But my grief reflects a loving bond.

'You'll come through this,
When you're ready you'll know'.
Words of wisdom really meant
From a close relation
Who realises I'm feeling low.

I stand here with tears in my eyes.
Head bowed in reverence and sorrow.
I weep at the grave where Darly lies.
How can I face the morrow?

W Stannard

A NEW LIFE

Ten little fingers,
ten little toes.
A tiny rosebud mouth.
A perfect button nose.

A precious little bundle
to cherish and hold.
To love and protect
in the family fold.

Sometimes it's hard
as life passes by
to watch them grow,
and see them cry.

But we're always there
through good times and bad.
To make them happy
and no longer sad.

We have to stand by
as they struggle to cope.
We offer our love,
comfort and hope.

Too soon it is time
to let them go.
It hurts so much,
but we don't let it show.

They always return.
They always come home.
As they know in their hearts,
they're never alone.

Susie Field

MYSTERY OF TIME

Looking fifteen years ahead in nineteen-ninety
Was like looking in a mirror
Where there was not a reflection,
Everything was in the dim and distant future.

However, time and tide have a habit of moving onwards,
Relentlessly, we are at the behest of time.
Who can depict the future so finely?
Much treasure could be the reward!

However, not knowing what the future will hold
Can be a blessing in disguise,
Disappointment can be followed
By one disappointment after another one.

It is willpower and stubbornness that will see you
                    through the day or night.
At your lowest ebb, all hope is gone, or so you think.
A blackbird has young in the nest,
Catching your eye, you are amazed at how he
                    struggles to feed the young.

Deep within your soul a chord is touched,
If a defenceless bird can be a survivor
Then so can anyone; if you can take a leap in the dark,
There is always the belief a vision will come to pass.

Open your eyes, look around, can you see?
The beauty is there waiting to be found
The smile of a child, the welcome from man's best friend,
The blue of the sky, dotted around with white clouds sailing by.

It is all the little things one treasures,
There is not a day without some pleasures,
Looking back, like a flash, the years have gone,
Disappearing into the past, will future years be so slight?
Only time will tell us!

Mary Lawson

A SPECIAL LOVE

In a world of many changes
Tears had fallen, loved ones gone.
Two lonely people feeling wasted,
What was this that life had done?

But then they met, stars started shining,
Flowers blossomed one by one,
Perfumes sent their senses reeling
Once again they found they loved.

Feelings hidden, long forgotten,
Came cascading to the fore.
Years rolled away, they became young lovers,
A love so wondrous to behold.

Summer was a start, beginning,
Something lasting, something true,
Love would keep them close together,
Spring, autumn, winter too.

I am witness to this story,
Stella was a star as named,
She had beauty forever blooming,
Caring, softness, this never fades.

Don was once a fighter pilot,
Bombed the famous River Kwai,
A man of courage, hard to equal.
He survived, came back again.

Two people's fate has jointed together,
Lots of laughter, lots of fun.
If there are winners in this life
I'm certain they have won.

Barbara Brannelly

THE CARE HOME

The sharp smell of incontinence
And ancient bodies
In an overheated room;
Like abandoned dolls
Left in the high back chairs
Each body sadly lolls
In an unnatural way
On bent and bony shoulders,
The head drooped there to stay.

Some hold a well-worn handbag on their knees
 - Though never now to hold their own latch keys -
Perhaps a few old coins in a simple purse,
Some faded photographs of long-dead friends,
A handkerchief embroidered with a name,
A good luck charm and other odds and ends,
Relics of life that once enhanced their days,
Active and happy, useful in many ways
Before old age crept on to leave
Them prisoned in this life of no reprieve.

        Some kind relations visit,
        Try to break through
        The veil of muddled memories,
        Old life so tangled with the new.

The care assistants bustle round,
Rouse them to drink and feed,
As best they can see to their every need,
Prepare them for their beds,
Kindly call each by name
Though to these time-warp folk
Night could be day,
Or day be night -
To most they simply seem the same.

Helen Laurance

THE WHITE LACE BLINDFOLD . . .

Is there a place for us among the stars of night
or on some unlit soaken bank, in time
that holds no fear of what is wrong or right,
but simply speaks a truth of peaks we climb and
feelings that are ours and ours alone . . . ?

And should my heartsent fingers trace a path upon
your trembling skin, cause such sweet sighs once
cast aside, yet reawakened by love's wrath so what
if coming home for me is there between your thighs
and Heaven will not hear the word deny . . .

Does time pass far too quickly, or become the place
we seek and in so doing never pass at all, while white
lace blindfold covers both your mind and those sweet
eyes and, daring any god or man to criticise our fact, our
life, our very souls, we claim our prize . . .

Richard Ansell

SHE'S THE ONE

You are the moon and stars that shine in the night,
You are the sun that shines so bright,
You are the autumn leaves on the ground,
Your love I feel is still all around.

You are the snowflakes that fall silently from above.
You created lots of happiness, laughter and love,
You are the birds that sing in the trees,
You are all these lovely things to me.

You are the one who gave me lots of hugs and kisses,
All these things about you, I am missing.

You are a rose that smells so sweet,
You were the one that people would love to meet.

I know one day my time on Earth will be done,
Then I will walk Heaven's stairs,
And be back with my mum,
She's the one.

Janet Hover

ARCTIC BEAUTY

Bare rocks
Quilted with brilliant colours
And swathes of softest moss.
Seagulls and terns
Whirl and dive.
Geese fly overhead
In neat formation
Necks outstretched like arrows.
Towering glacial monuments rise
Piercing the bright blue canopy above
Laced with puffs of scudding cloud.
The sea is calm and tranquil,
Icy, still,
Mirroring blobs of virgin white
Gliding silently.
Tinged with sunlight
The landscape basks
In a soft warm glow
From the rising sun.
Bare rocks
Quilted with brilliant colours
And swathes of softest moss.

Nina Woolf

ODE TO JAMES DEAN

(On the anniversary of his death, Sept 30th)

I never was a fan, James Dean, I didn't like your style,
I thought you brash and cocky, full of your own conceit.
Your pouting mouth disturbed me not, you did not fill my dreams,
Your pictures never graced my walls, I was indifferent.

Your death, although it saddened me, was not a personal tragedy,
I thought how sad to die so young and got on with my life,
But then one day I read a book, about your life and death,
From there you crept into my heart, into my very soul.

Fair-haired and young, with dreaming eyes and enigmatic smile,
You started a cult up there on the screen for angry
                              young men like you.
You became their rebel without a cause, looked up to and admired.
The one love in your life became your silver dream machine,
Sleek and streamlined, fast and true, it became a part of you.

Man and car became as one, along the highway smooth,
Eating up the lonely miles, you and your dream machine.
On that fateful day in September as autumn touched the hills,
With fingers gold and misty breath, your time was running out.

A fatal mistake was made (not yours) although it was your destiny,
You died together on that highway bleak, you and your
                              silver dream machine.
Your place of death became a shrine for those who loved you most,
Leaving you their love and tears, you and your dream machine.

You are gone, but your legend lives on, and will do for all time,
Eternally young, you'll never grow old,
Rest in peace *James Dean*

Sheila Giles

MOTTISFONT ABBEY

'Of course I'm coming back!' they seem to say,
Those brushes and the pot, the pillar just half hides.
It's all a con, no that's not really fair,
Trompe d'oiel it's called, a visual sleight of hand,
No brushes, no paint pot, no pillar come to that -
Not in 3D - illusion magical.
On other sides bold shields hang on the walls,
Smoke from a flambeaux slowly spirals up.

The Munich years - all Britain holds its breath
And hopes umbrella and a Homberg hat
And trust, goodwill, can keep the Stukas out.
Life goes on - the River Test flows by
As it has done since men with clubs and spears
Had hunted here or later when the monks
Who walked and prayed and gave their lives to God.
And here our artist strolled beside the Test
The weed all streaming like Ophelia's hair,
The lazy trout held balanced in the stream,
And here he saw, as only artists can,
The pictures slowly forming in his mind
Until, when ripe, translated into paint.

Young man's dilemma - if there must be war
Then with it comes the chance to prove yourself,
To know your fears and yet to win your spurs.
This is why peaceful men will go to war.
And always there's the guise - the patriotic one,
Or, to be honest, 'all the friends have joined!'
And so it ends, far from the peaceful Test
There on a battlefield in Normandy.
Bocage and booming guns and blazing tanks.
He wagered life and lost the final bet.

The room remains unfinished - always will,
The artist's tools stand waiting on the ledge.
Against the odds they say, 'I'm coming back!'

David Griffiths

AFRICA - DARK AND DYING

(Who can or will save Africa?)

Africa is as old as the beginning of time
Still here after world empires went into decline
The nation seems unlucky in all forms of life
Nothing but poverty, disease, hunger and strife
Whatever aid you pour down Africa's throat
You might as well give to the fettered goat
Real people of Africa are dying on their feet
While those who are in charge sit on a comfy seat
Spreading the wealth around so everyone has a share
Is something that's unheard of, it does not happen there
Not that it seems to matter what the world thinks
Some African nations still live in camps that stink
Other nations have tried, help Africa in every way
But the inner workings of the country are just a power-play
What can be done for these people in despair
When their very own leaders don't help to prepare
Letting this country die a lingering death
Should never be allowed, but giving fresh breath.

Robert Henry

SYLVIE'S SURREAL SONG

I am a woman and a dreamer, a poet, a singer of secrets,
                              a watcher of seeds,
Between extra-lucidity and madness
I am a tightrope walker on a rope as thin as a hair, ample
                    as dawn and cutting as a razor blade
Dancing my dream awake at wolf-light time
My inner child rules
I want to open every morning the eyes brimming with awe of
                    a child on holiday in summertime.

Walking in the forest was like entering a prayer,
A cathedral of trees, enwebbed in the dappled light,
Sun and leaves, green and gold,
Nature spirits dance, beckoning me

I'll shape shift with the river flow, honouring LA Vouivre
And finally rest with the blackbird between the palms
                    of an angel with peacock wings.

Sylvie Alexandre-Nelson

DISAPPEARING ISLE

Grey sky, grey sea, wind whistles angrily.
Waves pound ashore
Then recede, sucking, hissing,
Dragging sand and shingle
Into the murky depths.

Wind roars, waves crash against cliffs
In a furious assault until, defeated, they
Collapse into the heaving mass.
Lost forever.

A house that once stood firm and proud
Now clings to the hilltop's edge,
Deserted and dilapidated,
Until one final onslaught decides its fate.
It tips, falls and is gone -
To lie broken on the ocean bed.

As future generations paddle here,
Enjoying leisure time as we once did,
Will they consider how things used to be?
Will they know what lies beneath the sea,
Resting there until eternity?

While the waves march ever onward.

Sue Smith

FLIGHT OF FANCY

A sad caterpillar said
As he looked at the sky,
'I wish I had wings so that I could fly'.
But his body was so that was low to the ground
And his legs very many on which he walked 'round
It was true he could climb and sit in the flowers
And there he would daydream for many long hours.

His brothers and sisters
Were content with their lot
They'd chew on the cabbages
In the vegetable plot
But still that sad fellow had ideas of flight
So in cabbage and lettuce he took no delight.

Then one day to dismay
He became long, hard and round
No longer with feet that touched solid ground
And sleep he fell into late summer
To spring
With really no idea of what future would bring.

Life has surprises
Can you believe with your eyes?
On waking next summer
He had wings - just like flies
So if you too have daydreams
Of your very own
Remember his story
And maybe yours
Will be won!

Lyn Sandford

A LAST REQUEST

When I come to the end
And take my last breath
Don't say, 'I've passed away'
Say I've kicked the bucket or popped my clogs
Just died, never passed away
For to pass away seems to wipe you out
As if you had never existed
How can that be, when you've lived a full life?
Well, these words I have always resisted
Think of the memories you have left behind
They will never pass away
Something precious to family and friends
Who will think of them every day
A favourite photo or gift from you
Will keep your memory bright
For you will never 'pass away'
Still remembered, while not in sight.

June Davies

WEIGHING THINGS UP

A look in the mirror gave me a fright
Something was certain, I needed advice
Would it be easy? No, just sacrifice
If I wanted rid of my cellulite.
I hadn't noticed my clothes getting tight
Stretchy waistbands allowed another slice
From that day on, salad I would suffice
To be strong-willed and curb my appetite.
I couldn't believe the size of my rear
So the only answer was exercise
I'm not saying I didn't shed a tear
But getting on the scales won me the prize
So now it's only compliments I hear
With my healthy look, for I've dropped a size.

Shirley Pinnington

SURVIVAL OF THE FITTEST

A tiny fly flew past my eyes,
You'd best vanish fly if you are wise.
My fermenting wine you'll not taste,
Be off now fly - in serious haste.

In the garden there is much to see,
Flowers and birds, and a bumblebee.
A soft furry body and gossamer wings,
From flower to flower the pollen he brings.

To speak of the wasp - on the other hand -
A bold striped body - looking quite grand -
But is not so friendly when he's around,
He stings for no reason is what I've found.

The garden pond with several fish,
A treat to see - but how I wish
The big grey heron would not drop by,
Or the neighbour's cat who expects fish pie!

The fish in the pond are catching midges,
A croaking frog on a lily pad wishes
He'd been awake to enjoy such a meal,
Not realising now how hungry he'd now feel.

Little green aphids, and some that are black,
Stick to the plants and are on the attack,
Eating away - but not for much longer,
Ladybirds land - and are very much stronger.

In May comes a bug that lives just one day,
Hatching out - for hours of play.
Finding the females with whom to perform,
Creating more Maybugs is simply the norm.

A spider's web embraces a hedge,
Silky fibres reach out to the edge,
Diamond mist shines on each delicate strand,
A home and a food store - so well planned.

Not just for beauty is this wondrous sight,
For the spider waits for a fly to alight
On the sticky fronds - not knowing its fate
Is to end up on the spider's meal plate.

A web then is spun around the fly,
After its captor has sucked his blood dry.
Then spider retreats, taking care not to fracture
His web, then hide till the next fly he'll capture.

A lazy slug slides - leaving his slimy trail,
No house on his back like his cousin the snail,
Oh how they are ugly - though not really their fault,
But to save the cabbages - the weapon is salt.

The deed is done and the slugs must perish,
The cabbages now will surely flourish.
Close by a worm wriggles through the soil,
Writhing and twisting ending up in a coil.

A blackbird peeps out from within a tree,
'Oh wriggling worm I have my eye on thee,'
Swiftly he flies down to the ground,
Locating the worm - precision - no sound.

A yellow beak with worm dangling,
A slimy trail, a web with silk strangling -
- Tiny flies - of which some are green,
And now not a Maybug to be seen.

A tiny fly flew past my eyes,
'Twas the one before - to my surprise,
Round and round my head it flew,
Then landed in the fermenting brew.

The tiny fly had beaten me,
For in that brew for all to see,
It was supping in that great big jar,
Turning the wine into *vinegar.*

Some battles are won and some are lost,
Then we sit back to count the cost.
Whether it is insect, beast or man.
Self preservation is each one's plan.

Christine Tracey

MY GARDEN OF MEMORIES

In my garden of memories I'll grow bright poppies red,
The colour of the blood that on a foreign field you shed.
Fragrant rosemary I'll plant in remembrance of you,
And sweet forget-me-nots with flowers of misty blue.
Crimson roses will bloom beneath the blue, summer sky,
To show that my love for you will never die.
The heady, evocative scent of chrysanthemums will
            fill the autumn of my years,
And I'll remember our spring, when the daffodils danced,
            and smile at the memory through my tears.

Anita Cooling

NATURAL ALLURE

Dartmoor is my mistress . . .
She beckons me from afar,
The beguiling contours of her body
Guide me to her like a star.

A provocative figure on the horizon
Fills my soul with deep emotions,
The steep tors demanding much vigour,
I cannot resist her fascination.

She crooks a finger like a siren,
Once again I need to explore,
From the clitter of her summits
To the deep bogs of her floor.

Lost in the folds of her ample bosom
Then following her lengthy streams of life,
Her passions are violent and sudden . . .
Too wild and dominant for a wife.

One moment splashed with colours
With the bright sun on her face,
Then scowling . . . black with anger
Swiftly becoming a dangerous place.

She whispers . . . soft and enthralling,
Her warmth a pure delight,
Then shouting with claps of thunder
Her storm clouds descend like night!

In spring her misty veil is lifted
To reveal a summer dress of green,
In autumn swathed in purple heather,
Her winter wrap is a frosty sheen.

Never sure of the state of her welcome
When I am enticed by her once again,
Will she envelope me with desire
Or drown my ardour with rain?

Whatever mood she is suffering
I cannot repel her magnetic force,
To gently touch her lone granite crosses
Or be torn by her tangle of gorse.

Dartmoor will always have lovers in plenty
All to be humiliated and spurned,
Generations of 'suitors' proposing . . .
But she will never, ever be tamed.

W Moyle Breton

LOVE'S REWARD

'What is love?' I hear you say
Love is not measured day by day
Or month by month or year by year
Love is the essence of all so dear
Love is the grief of a loved one's death
Love is the sigh of a baby's breath

Love only gives, it never asks
For thanks, returns - it never masks
The pure, clear light that dwells within
Us all - it only seeks to win
Over the dark that oft does creep
Into our soul - where we do weep
For erstwhile loves of long ago
Love enters in when we let go
Of all past hurts, old grudges, pain
Love falls on us like gentle rain
To wash away the dust and grime
From all old wounds, they're gone - 'tis time
To heal, forgive, move on once more
And hear the waves lap on the shore

To laugh with joy at all life's blessings
Not count the cost of all our lessons
Like misers counting all their money
Love sweetens life - it is the honey
That soothes our fevered heart and mind
Love's never cruel - love's only kind
For when we lay at the end of the day
Ourselves to sleep - we need not pray
For love - as love is free
Love dwells in all - in you and me.

Gina Bowman

THE MORNING RUSH

I recall as a young lad the *morning rush*.
Racing for the number fifty-something bus;
It spiralled from yonder at a slow hog -
Diminishing a queue, as it merged into the fog.

Each seat filled on the top deck,
A regular passenger would self-consciously check
The back of her hair with care,
Stamping out a butt and whilst

Rising to negotiate the stair bend.
When the bus passed a shade outside an arcade,
Some passengers stole a glance at their reflection.
The conductor would inspect who paid
Before reaching the station.

Many feet turned in like *Rambert's Swan Lake* for the
                              students' stampede!
Felt despondent - a factory worker for a pittance.
What an exciting life they would lead and possess
When exchanging cape and gowns for examination stress.

The unwritten rule not to look back,
Even when the bus meandered on its track.
Shoulders gently swaying side to side,
Passengers creasing newspapers between each glide.

Now you hear pagers or mobile phones in front and behind,
Bound to follow a monologue when spying a road sign.
Buildings have altered or have been knocked down,
But the bus' route is perennial on its way to town.

Thomas W O'Connell

PARTING

I watched you go
        You did not cry
I held your hand
        As we said goodbye

You closed your eyes
        Took your last breath
Your pain was all over
        As you welcomed death

I cried for you
        Now the pain is in me
My broken heart
        Will never be free

Another day passes
        My life goes on by
I think of your memory
        As I sit here and cry

I remember the good times
        There were many we shared
And I always knew
        That forever you cared

In time you grew weaker
        And I cared for you
I promised I would be there
        When the moments became few

I did it for love
        Is all that I can say
Your life has gone
        Death has taken you away

I will carry your memory
        Right here in my heart
Until the time comes
        That I too must part.

Joanne Hale

BEHIND THE CURTAIN

Trouble is hidden behind the drawn curtains,
Problems that no one wants to disclose,
Quarrels and bitterness often encountered,
Cruelty even, behind closed doors.
There are no questions, life appears normal
Neighbours aren't even aware of despair,
Children's pained faces ignored or forgotten -
Where are the people to show that they care?
Such is the state of the world that we live in,
Selfishness, cruelty, often denied,
Life is not meant to be lived in such horror -
Those who are guilty have no sense of pride.
Marriages broken, faithfulness squandered
Breaking the chain that can't be repaired.
Surely the time has come for new thinking -
Bringing back happiness families shared.
Poverty, once was blamed for life's problems,
Now there is wealth and luxury too.
Maybe it's greed that is ruining progress -
Sharing with others is what we must do.
Words are so easy, it's doing that matters,
Pull back the shutters and let the world know -
Working together can sort out life's problems,
And through our actions may happiness grow.

Glenys Moses

WAVES

Waves
Cascading over me
As I lay on the shore
Each and every one, icy
Each one a salty, bitter tear
But then again, a fond memory
Of you and me, just you and me.

Let my body be immersed
In the raging sea
That brings you back to me.

19 and 34,
No age, no age,
As I try to turn the page of my mind
Back to that time,
So special, so divine.

The tides ebbs away,
As I lay
I see you standing in your favourite red dress
By an old shipwreck
Calling me.

I stumble and fall,
Amongst the rock pools
The lead weights and fisherman's thorny hooks
Slicing my feet
But I always knew that one sweet day,
Again we'd meet.

As I get closer to you
Your vision begins to fade
Yet another 'dreamtime' charade?
As the waves swallow me up,
Down or . . . ?

Russell Hyman

MIND BOGGLING

High upon a tower black, shrouded by mist and fog
I knelt upon a concrete roof to converse with my God.
Some questions needed answering to ease my boggled mind
I hoped He'd have the answers which myself I failed to find.
What of this place called Eden, this garden way up high
A spiritual place of beauty between the earth and sky,
Where You created Adam, from whose rib You sculptured Eve
Then told them not to fornicate, now this I can't believe?
I really fail to understand, for if the story's true
Why did You give them organs which allowed them so to do?
You must have known biology among the other things
For You gave the elephant its trunk and the mockingbird its wings.
Now Adam and Eve were newly made, the human race beginners
And immediately designated the first of the earthling sinners.
Now they were cast out on this Earth naked, side by side
And being the only inhabitants, went forth and multiplied.
I hope dear God, You understand why I have a boggled mind
I really do assure You, I don't mean to be unkind.
I do not seek to tear the book of Genesis asunder,
But it seems to me that life began with one appalling blunder.
This blunder then was multiplied at an alarming pace,
Wars, plagues and pestilence beset the human race
And in the very midst of this we had the Virgin birth,
Was it such a good idea to place Your Son on Earth.
He tried to teach the world of love and He was crucified
Yet making love was Adam's crime when he made Eve his bride.
Dear Lord You have not answered the questions of this bard
I've been up here for hours and the concrete is quite hard,
I'll speak to You again my Lord when I've left this world behind
And maybe with a bit of luck, You'll ease my boggled mind.

John Tovey

PROPHETS IN THE WILDERNESS

When all has been said long ago
by wandering prophets in the wilderness
what is left to say?
But still frantic striving and suffering goes on
despite all the cant and know-how.
Sadly I feel that we all miss the point
and go on hurtling in all directions
and raving in a meaningless way
spinning way off the point.

God gave us free choice perhaps to see
what we would do.
If the world seems more evil
can we blame God?
It is difficult to disentangle the
rights and the wrongs.
It is easy to fail and despair
but God wants us to try,
and to love at all costs,
and not to heed the material world.
We are here not to judge but to help
and serve God and each other.
Feel compassion for those who don't make the grade,
and learn humility when we may
easily forget the path we came along.
On the way have a care . . .
By the way have you given of yourself
with all your heart?
Have you thought of responding differently
this time around?
Why not give it a try?
You won't be punished for
trying a different approach.
Give yourself a break -
enjoy a bit of peace -
listen to the prompting of your heart
instead of incessantly calculating.
It is easier on the soul
and you will discover joy.
God is as good as His word.
Listen to His voice as the prophets did
long ago in the silence of their hearts.

Barry Broadmeadow

BLACK IS BLACK

The cirrus white flees from the azure skies,
Retreating iron blocks the sun a while,
Relinquishes its grasp, like lids of eyes,
So hair can catch gold rays and daisies smile;
But somewhere in the violent, caustic sighs,
As moss, where warmth will never kiss the tiles:
Black is black.

Red gingham cloths on tables twitch and jerk,
And yellow wines catch glare and shadowed forms,
Of breeze-borne butterflies and dancing skirts,
While pink surrounds the orange sinking orb;
But somewhere under knives, damp ashtray dirt,
A button missing, blouse just slightly torn:
Black is black.

Blue velvet of late evening beckons stars,
And lamplight glows replace departed day,
While spirits of bronze drinks and happy hours,
Flit through dark green of lawns, where daisies pray;
But in the multitude of mental scars,
Tangled in silk, white moth pendulums sway:
Black is black.

Serena Shores

SICK AND TIRED

I feel so down but I won't shed a tear
I feel so low for my dream is nowhere near
This is the last place I ever want to be
Sat at work . . . wrapped up in my misery
I feel so exhausted and I just can't think
The tears are building up; they'll fall if I blink
I know in my heart where I wish to be
I know in my mind it won't come so easily
If I get any more run down I won't be able to get out of bed
If it gets any worse I fear the effect it'll have on my head
It already seems like it's going to explode
Certain people here just add to the load
How I wish I could take out my aggression
Getting away with it would be the perfect blessing
But I'd never actually perform such acts
Expressing my feelings is just pure facts
Thoughts and feelings swirl in my head
Staying here in this place is my ultimate dread
Let me get away; I want to go to Wales
I'll give all this up if all else fails
I can't stand this torture for much longer
It's not true about what doesn't kill you making you stronger
This life is killing me from the inside out
And I've lost the plot of this poem, what's it all about?
Sometimes I wake up and ask *is it real?*
Sometimes I cannot tell with sight, taste, sound, smell and even feel
I'm so tired it's like I'm in a dream
I'm so tired I cannot even scream
I'm so bored of these chores and repetitive tasks
Please release me from this place, is it too much to ask?
We could be happy 400 miles away
The way we're going, we'll never see the light of day
I'm sick of these same old faces
Take me to different places
Don't know how long we'll have to wait
I have no idea how long this career move will take
All I know is I can't wait much more
I keep imagining me walking out this door
Forever
And never
Coming back.

Craig Stewart

CAN YOU BLAME ME?

Can you blame me for loving the sunset,
Or the moonrise o'er shimmering sea?
Dark waves crashing high where wreckful rocks lie,
Or the seabird's shrill cry; drifting free?

Can you blame me for loving the seaspray
From the tail of a whale as it flips?
Or the sight of a four-masted schooner
Breezing out on its faraway trips?

Can you blame me for loving shell myriads
Pebbles tumbling on shingling shore?
Or the kelp's swaying strands, caressing the sands,
Set in tempo as 'white horses' soar?

Can you blame me for loving sea creatures,
Ocean mists beneath sky grey or blue?
For these treasures of fabulous features,
Can you blame me *Sea* - for loving you?

Elizabeth Joyce Walker

QUEEN ANNE BOLEYN

What were your thoughts as on that day
Your head on Tower Green you lay,
Of circumstances past?
When as a queen you took your place
To that sad time you fell from grace
It was not meant to last.

For you became the second queen
When Catherine had left the scene
Then came your own death-knell.
You were so trusting and so sure
Not knowing what you would endure
You simply could not tell.

Why did fate have to be unkind
To let your name be so maligned
When you had no redress?
But quietly you did display
The courage of a queen the day
You felt the sword's caress.

But oh, what grief you had to bear
To be acquainted so with care
And leave your infant child,
Not there to see her live to be
A famous queen in history,
This daughter meek and mild,

Fair Anne of just a thousand days
Accused in oh so many ways
You did not stand a chance,
Adorned in silk and jewels grand
Adored and fêted through the land
Abandoned at a glance.

The name of Anne Boleyn will be
Remembered by posterity,
But always with a sigh
That one who was so young and fair
With highest hopes, without a care
Was destined so to die!

Moira Wiggins

MY LIFE

When I was young, life was simple.
I hadn't a care in the world.
From the start of day till I came in from play
My time, like a flower, unfurled.

How grown-up I felt as I started a job
And took home my first meagre pay,
But then, quite by chance, I found office romance
And soon I was doubly engaged.

My twenties brought marriage and housework
My thirties, a baby or two.
The following decade disappeared in the shade
Of A Levels, mood swings and 'flu.

Ah, light at the end of the tunnel.
My fledglings are leaving the nest.
The bickering has stopped, the volume has dropped,
Now for a long, well-earned rest.

But what will I do with my freedom?
I simply do not have a clue.
I could paint pretty scenes, write poetry in reams,
Or visit the bears in the zoo.

However I spend all this 'me' time
I know I will not waste a jot.
I feel totally reborn as I lounge on my lawn
And fully content with my lot.

Pamela Wells

THE GREATEST LOVE

If we look for love
We will find it all around us,
Like a big circle of love.

Love in every bird, every
Beautiful flower and tree.
Love in every living animal.

Love in the countryside
In the mountains
And beautiful skies.

Love in the rainbow
After the storms.
This is the love of God.

The greatest love
One can ever have.

Julie Smith

4TH DRAGOON GUARDS IN THE GREAT WAR

We were utilised ahead, us and our horses
There before infantry, as good preparatory forces
We helped Allied Forces to win the Great War
Five million strong, the largest army, by far.

Our Cavalry patrols, fought on the Western Front
Coldstream Guards, 4th Dragoon Guards, all to confront
With our Infantry - Bavarian boys, in German uniforms
Anyone who would fight - death didn't need to conform.

Barbed wire, invented in Texas, then mass produced
Military brains undated it, closer barbs, not to be seduced
This slowed down the Cavalry - deep in its tracks
Plus more modern firearms, meant more bullets in backs.

Many of us trapped, horses and men, cruelly caught
Dead, or mutilated by wire, as they courageously fought
Those who hung there, too dangerous for others to retrieve
Dead from the elements and rats - not from injuries received.

French guns, firing 24 shells, each minute, every hour
Were modernised by others, to give a heavier metal shower
More ammo, always needed, more food, much faster orders
New ways, all invented, to help us all, to move forwards.

A British idea, always carrying most of our fresh foods
Bully beef from Port Fray Bentos, all helped; kept good moods
This food, kept us at the front, we lived in the trenches
So, no let up in fighting, we held up all our defences.

Our generals now used the 'Mark Three', newest telephone
At one time, speaking to nine other leaders, not for contacting home
Troops now moved by train, connected to much larger stations
This complex system, built and used, by men from many nations.

The trenches, deep - four hundred and fifty miles long
All built by soldiers, and manned by the very same throng
By then, masses of army volunteers, conscripts, recruited
Five million soldiers fought on the Western Front, never disputed.

4th Dragoon Guards, now dismounted, fought in the trenches
A three year deadlock - the length of fighting from benches
Those 'benches' were dead soldiers, who, though dead, had uses
Then the Allies hit back - strongly fought enemy abuses.

December 6, 1918, 4th Dragoon Guards, all remounted
With help from infantry, tanks; enemies pushed back, discounted
These guards had the honour, leading Allied Troops into Cologne
This was the end of the Great War, those alive could go home.

Maureen Westwood O'Hara

THOUGH HE SLAY ME

('Though He slay me yet will I trust in Him' Job 13.15)

It did not seem so serious an illness
The after-days come like the days before;
And yet a voice, the moment there is stillness,
Tells me there is a watch upon my door.

My soul was none to beat against the night
To freedom some far-distant from the Earth
Home that I knew, the colour and the light,
Here only in the planet of my birth.

And here below - let those who could, unravel
The mysteries of immortality -
Enough for me I had the world to travel
Under the stars and clouds - footsore maybe

But with a quiet heart, content and more
To let the days their promises fulfil,
Taking the open sky and, as before,
With tempered axe and trusted rope - the hill.

(O hills of brown and many a shade of blue,
O hills with whom how many a dream began;
Whether or not I shall return to you
The heart returns where once the footsteps ran!)

Of outward certainties now dispossessed -
The sense of fitness snapped like parted string
That once enwrapped my senses - can I rest
Without possession of the unseen thing?

Must I who dreamt so often in the past
To perfect the surrender of my will
As oft awake to find myself shut fast
Within the house of self a prisoner still?

There was no stage inside those walls of stone
For masquerade as master of my fate,
No offering of pain that could atone
And all excuses inarticulate . . .

Certain it is that when I come to die
I cannot meet that dark insolvency,
Nor on its failing hold my hand rely -
Except another hand unholdeth me.

I have crossed many rivers. Now I pray
To meet my Saviour at the final brink.
Slain long ago was He; that we today
Might recognise His Hand. And though He slay -
If but the stroke be His - I shall not shrink.

Edward Jackson Smyth

ON REACHING THREE QUARTERS OF A CENTURY

I never thought the day would come when I'd be seventy-five,
I thought if I reached seventy I'd scarcely be alive.
But here I am as large as life and gamely hanging on.
I think that most of me's intact, though some of my teeth have gone!
My hair is slowly turning grey and growing rather thin.
My eyesight isn't what it was.
I've wrinkles on my skin,
My hearing's also on the blink - I can't hear what folk say
And I really have to stop and think what I did yesterday.
But I'm not giving up just yet, though some folk think I should
I've still got lots to offer and most of it is good!
So I'll march bravely onward still glad to be alive
And who knows, one day I may say, 'Today I'm eighty-five!'

Pearl Briggs

TRAMPS' BARN

I, John Ellonby, who am a tramp
and sometime called Vagabond,
aware of a goodly barn in the dale of Mungo,
repaired here in the snow to sleep this night
knowing as I do the dalesmen good and bad.

Of the Shaws, two brothers and a sister,
she stricken,
sitting in their slate-floor kitchen,
a lamb rescued this icy hour from death
drying in the oven, for now alive till later cooking.

Of James Foot and John Lyne, who did show
their droll cousin Smeth a circus,
persuading him there the creature swinging
by tail a tiger was, and a camel be an elephant,
for such was their humour and spiteful with it.

In this dale, too, Jonathan Brierley
of Wetland Hall who did sell his calf
to buy his childer food a treat
for their Christmas
but drank himself coinless with all he had.

As well as Ida Langstart, spinster,
who with sister now dead
did walk arm in arm to farms and cots
to scrub floors and lay out straight with
washing those bodies stiffened in the night.

But mostly, farmer Isaac Slee, old and greedy,
who does burn away his time ready to take
with him every foot of land the day he dies,
and will be remembered in this dale a cruel man
though his tombstone says otherwise.

All these here are known,
as with the Lamberts who comely are
and good to wanderers with soup
and this their barn where I lie
a winter night thankful of two coats.

To all I say Amen and vow that nothing
will I thieve from here, not chickens,
nor cow's milk sucked from the udder,
nor any washing frozen and unwatched
for it is a goodly dale that has such a barn.

Irvine Hunt

ALL ALONE

What I'm most afraid of
is being on my own,
Not being on my own, exactly,
But being all alone.

I've been there before you know,
Didn't like it one small bit,
If it happened to me again,
I know, I couldn't endure it.

The last time, I was younger,
And still had my health,
Now I'm older, and your health
Really is your wealth.

So, both youth and health
Are gone now,
And what terrifies me most,
Is not being on my own, but
Being left here, all alone.

Rebecca H Weir

COFFEE STAINS

Coffee stains on the window sill
Goin' down slow
Turnin' the lamps off
It's time don't you know.

Blue turns to green
And back in-between
Playing the scene
On black and white screen
Goin' down slow.

Virginia's midnight lullaby
Unrehearsed
Unrehearsed
Undertow
Goin' down slow.

Frank's song told it
Dim and low
Over the rim
To overflow
Goin' down slow.

Velvet flipside
Somewhere to night hide
Flowing with the ebb tide
Dripping from the rooftops
Crazy like the night hawks
Goin' down slow.

Back to readin' the dictionary
Just to make the rhymin' easy
Lucky to be here
With a mind so slight
But clear
And eyes that shade to tally
Along a dark blind alley
Wishin' it would grow

From *goin' down slow* . . .

Michael B Scribbler

MY AUNTIE EMMIE

My auntie Emmie was kind,
She will always stay in my mind.
She made my feelings warm and bright,
I think of her all through the night.
Auntie Emmie is there when I see a feather,
I know it is her because she was very clever!

Louise Jones (9)

DREAMS CAN COME TRUE

Many years ago when I was a young bride,
I left my native Lincolnshire, my husband by my side.
We came back home to visit many times throughout the years
And vowed we would come back for good
When retirement days were here.
Six years ago that dream came true
And we made the journey home,
Silver and ruby weddings past and golden still to come.
We left our family behind, but they are all grown up,
And come to visit often as they all said they would.
We are so very lucky to have our dreams come true
And in the evening of our lives to come back home with you.

Alma Sutton

A MYSTICAL GARDEN

A mystical garden where the sun meets the moon,
Incandescent colours roll on by,
Under a glorious blue sky, a painter sits adamantly,
With his artist's palette, of every hue in oils,

Wonderment, where nature's birds fly with magical wings,
Where rain falls down in torrents,
Which floods the earth below,
Like golden bridges, nature's aura shines,

Whilst shooting stars revolve in glory,
Which enthrones God's living light,
Lovely power that awakens the heart,
With spirits in the sky, only dreams tell you why,

Messengers inspire in poetic verse,
The soul reached in learning,
Higher wisdom brought by a guardian angel,
The realms of Heaven burst outwardly with love,

Where beautiful thoughts are sent forth,
Doves scatter the four corners of the Earth,
Angel beings smile their warmth,
While fairies pose with violets,

And nature sings a golden story,
Where bouquets and flowers lay undisturbed,
Glorious carnations abound,
Nearby, mermaids gather beautiful tulips and roses,

Reds and whites, that smell divine,
Dipped in magical aromas,
This true home, where royal oaks stand proud,
Where large ashes have fallen,

Nine planets, like stepping stones,
Rotate magnetic forces,
Where orchestras play sweet music,
Transparent rainbows fill the air,

Atlantic cities stand like time frozen,
Unseen eyes sparkle in rays of light,
Crystals glisten in a fountain of hope,
Whispered secrets are spoken in lovely soft voices,

Where little people dance in a ring of posies,
To welcome you to a wondrous home,
A mystical garden where God loves all,
When love is returned from every heart.

James S Cameron

TRUE LOVE

(Dedicated to my lovely husband Bob)

No words could describe
My love for you
The joy I feel with you
By my side.
Knowing you're there for me
Lightens each day
As we share our memories
Our hopes and our dreams.
Grey clouds are banished
Just by your smile,
Blue skies are promised
Just by your touch.
Who would have thought
When first we met
The path we had to follow
But I can tell you this my love
It's a path I've joyfully followed.

Zandra Collisson

I'VE HEARD IT SAID OLD MEN FORGET

I've heard it said old men forget: Can that be true
Of those who saw the dogs of war
Loosed raging on Mons, Ypres, the Somme:
Who, night on day, heard Death's voice say
Names that still brought tears with the thought
Of how and when Death struck them: men
Who'd smelt Death's stench on air, in trench
Year after year: who'd tasted fear
When down the line word came - the time
Had come: those who had fought on through -
Who'd touched the scythe that life on life
Had reaped - and yet had spared theirs? Let
Them say old men forget. I can't believe they do.

Diane Elizabeth Maltby

THE BELIEVERS

Deep in the vestibule of one simple man's oriel runs time,
        Passing over many times, each mistake creating new ones.

Believing is a reason not to believe
        And I sense that you feel this too but will not change
        Until some dumb-ass chances upon our mistake,
        Playing with fire, drowning us out in its sorry wisdom,
        Letting us cling and hope to the remains of each single day.

I cannot feel any more or less then you did and cannot break free . . .
        No matter how hard I try.

I am standing before you with nothing to hide
        But feel threatened by the endless castrations of ill intent
        Running down the darkest corridor in search of new light.
        Look at me now! I am fire and ice scaling a cliff steeped
                                in all this history.
        I am like you but do not want to admit it.

Watching effortless strangers pass me by, I struggle on.
        Hold the light for me, as I want to reach the other side with
you.
        Do not let go. With each step I am winning for a while
        But when I fall there is nothing to catch me. Why am I here?
        My feet balance on the edge of slate and sand
        Feeling my weight break the very foundations of where I am
from.
        Why am I here?

If there is a simple answer I do not know it,
                        but I am a believer in something
        That keeps on bouncing me back to your door
        Tempting me with your fate, enticing me outside in a cold grey
rain
        Tempted by the sun and moon and stars,
        Holding joy in those moments. I am a believer in something . . .

A cradle rocks by the grate but it is not for you or me,
                        it is for someone else.
        We are someone else's baby forgetting that we were once here.

I am a believer in something. Why am I here?
        When the stars flicker in the silence I look for you
        Dreaming in the rushes of our childhood.
        I am a believer in something . . .

If I etch a star into the darkness perhaps we will both see
        And travel lightly on the finest wings, changing the very
perspective
        Of a life that gathers scars like falling mist.
        We who were the believers in something.

Lily Radcliffe

THE CLOWN
(Based on Leoncavallos' Pagliacci)

I make you laugh, until you cry. But me?
I just wanna die.
Lonely out there beneath the big tops,
I might as well be a one-eyed Cyclops,
Children giggling at my ungainly ways,
My mind don't feel funny.
It's an intricate maze.

If I sang a song, it would have
A gruesome refrain.
About flowers dying in the rain.
Not knowing when the sun will rise,
Tears trickling from a love dove's eyes
Look up to the heavens,
And see thunderous skies.

Please find some sympathy
For this heartbroken fool.
Who brays like a jackass,
But ain't no stubborn mule.
Think of me when you sleep at night,
Don't look in my mirror,
It's a haunting sight.

I'll wager you have dreams of joy,
Skipping through rainbows,
No nightmares to employ
And when you wake up in the morn,
You're refreshed and happy, not forlorn.
I wish it was sad for all you too,
Then we'll all be totally blue
And humbly so.

Gary Monaghan

PARADISE LAND

Looking out across the horizon, the sun is setting fast,
I want to capture it in my mind so it will always last.

My feet are sinking into the cold wet sand,
While looking out at a faraway land.

The clouds drifting along, floating free,
Wind blowing in my eyes, I can barely see.

Palm trees swaying in the gentle breeze,
Birds freely flying across the seas.

What a wonderful place this is to be,
A Paradise Land, I don't want to leave.

Lynsay Bestwick

SILENCE

In silence Man conceives his grandest deeds,
In solitude productive thoughts are born.
A power unseen supplies the strength he needs,
His greatest acts are fostered in the dawn.
The quiet communion with the mystic force
Breathes benediction on a mind at rest;
Is the well-spring to a hidden source
Of sparkling water, the fount of all that's best.
But often in each thumping, blatant hour,
Surrounded by the sterile, shallow things,
Serenity is lost, secret of private power,
The salient strength which softest silence brings.
It may be when we find this perfect peace
That love will enter Earth and strife will cease.

Dorothy Stirland

MY LIFE
(The very best moments in the life of Charles Peachey now aged 87 years)

The house where I was born, didn't have a lawn,
Or garden to grow nice flowers,
We played on cobbled streets, washing lines, full of sheets,
And we had to shout our mothers, if it showered.

Skipping games, shuttlecock, leap frog, and whip and top,
We had to make our own enjoyment then,
Games of marbles, lost and won, but we did have lots of fun,
'Sometimes' I wish those days were back again.

One game was 'kick can squat', you didn't need a lot,
Just a tin and four or five good mates.
We'd play till nearly dark, then walk up to the park,
But got back home before it got too late.

Once a week we had a bath, now it makes me laugh,
By the fire in a tin water container,
There was a rush to get in first, and the winner did get cursed,
And they couldn't put their feelings any plainer.

I'm neither clever, or a fool, at fourteen I left school,
I thought my life would be in clover then,
Instead of days of milk and honey, I worked all week for little money,
And I knew I'd have to think, and think again.

Mam and Dad moved house again, to Silsden here we came,
To a bungalow 'with a bath and hot water'
There never was such times, we could hear the church bell's chimes,
'Twas here I met the 'old town cryer's' daughter.

Doris is her name, I fell in love, I'm not to blame,
I took her umbrella - so I could ask for a date.
She said, 'I'll tell my dad.' Boy did I feel bad,
I gave it back, but I knew I'd met my mate.

World War Two has past, it's over,
Now there's bluebird over Dover,
And I go looking for 'my umbrella girl'
I'm so glad it's yes she said
And we both went off and wed,
Now after fifty years my head's still in a whirl.

Charles Peachey

THE LANGUAGES OF RIVERS

Gently flowing persuasively,
sparkling with irresistible allure,
reflecting amazing light and shade
or rushing by with alarming force
- rivers appeal.

Coolly trickling nonchalantly,
weaving so deftly crystalline patterns,
instantly glistening gems so pure
these moments change to dark torrential tides
- rivers speak.

Strongly rushing tenaciously
bringing an inexplicable grandeur
disturbing animals, fish and birds
yet seeping in and renewing life,
- rivers feed.

Simply speaking creatively
painting scenes artistically moulded,
whispering luminous words and sounds
what secrets are shared expressing love?
- rivers inspire.

Wildly diving menacingly
moving with irrepressible power
caressing silently hills and dales
such journeys smell sweet and replenish streams
- rivers travel.

Margaret Ann Wheatley

ON MALTA'S SHORES

No calm or smoothness of the sea today . . .
Waves attack the rocks,
As the surf mounts high
In mountainous, rhythmic surges
Over lava beaches, hard and bare,
Worn into uneven surface
By the changing moods of the charging water!

In turns, angry or shimmering green
Or indigo, as dark as night;
Or even, when flowing calm as in the summer,
Blue as the sky reflected on those days,
Behazed by blazing sun;
Warmed then by the hottest rays
Which now are dimmed by looming clouds.

No sun today, no heat, no haze, no calm
To soothe the tumultuous torrents!
The sea is expressing its wildest mood
In thrashing, crashing, lashing,
Bashing, smashing, breakers -
Thundering in its ceaseless might
On Malta's north-west shores.

Perhaps 'twas like this, all those years ago,
When St Paul was shipwrecked somewhere near this point,
Maybe where the island, with its ancient memorial
Keeps its lasting watch on the passionate sea
Which caused the historical disaster
Recorded for all time
In Biblical tale and in Malta's history!

Yes, the same sea, which nearly claimed his life,
Still roars out in continual pattern!
And it will thunder on until eternity has run
To work out God's almighty plan
For His whole world and all the beings
Of His wonderful creation:

Nothing else can calm or control
The ever-changing, contrasting moods
Of the tideless Mediterranean Sea!

Donoveen R Alcock

MY LIFE

Many moons have come and gone
In the fullness of my life
How many hopes have all gone wrong
Causing grief and strife?

I love my mother, father, sister too,
Nephews, nieces all, though few
My life was good, whilst I was young
I grew up happy, well and strong.

I had few hobbies, because I was shy,
I had to stop the blushes, I had to try,
So I went for lessons in drama and speech
I might even have been able to teach.

I danced and I acted in many a show
The lessons were worth it, I wasn't so slow
Musicals, drama, comedy shows
Always dressed in different clothes.

I have given the theatre 37 years
Now at this time, there are some little fears,
Fears I might forget my lines
This is not like my golden times.

When will I have the thought that I may stop?
I wouldn't like to be caught on the hop
The world of theatre has given me life
Some might say, it was more like a wife!

John Pierrepont

THE HERD BOY'S SONG

Within the arena's terraced bowl
Swarming throngs clamoured in acclaim
Of their chosen champions who vied
For victory's rich crown and fame
And transient notability:
Ursine strength and sensual beauty
Were both, as virtues, much esteemed;
By artifice attained when denied
By parentage and often deemed
The noblest sight in all creation.

> And, on a distant, lofty hill, a musing sage
> Listened to a herd boy's song
> Telling of a golden age
> When all men walked in cosmic grace, at one with God.

Vampire lusts gorged their bellies on men;
Corruption's foul dwale ran amok;
Power, gold and pleasure took their toll
From those whose feet were not on rock
But deep in desire's soft, shifting sands:
The crying of children filled the air
Where earth lay barren 'neath the sun,
Man fought with man, brother with brother,
Until the sands of hate had run,
Yet thought themselves the image of God.

> And, on a distant, lofty hill, a musing sage
> Listened to a herd boy's song
> Telling of a golden age
> When all men walked in cosmic grace, at one with God.

Time's erasing hand passed o'er the world,
The great arena's bowl lay crushed,
All things sensual were decomposed
And lusting's brazen tongues were hushed.
Fame and renown were empty echoes,
The age of man withered away
And lonely, sighing winds swept the Earth
In the light of a bright, new day.

> And, in the vaulted halls of space, an ageless sage
> Wept to hear a herd boy's song
> Telling of a golden age
> When all men walked in cosmic grace, at one with God.

Ralph Smith

SOMEONE SPECIAL

I hear your voice
I see you smile
I sit and talk with you awhile
Then I awake and you are gone
But thoughts of you still linger on
Of happy days we spent together
We thought it would go on forever
Those lovely walks down country lanes
We even walked in showers of rain
Nothing mattered, you were there
To give me love and really care
Someone special, that was you
That's how I will remember you
For God had plans, He took you home
He broke my heart, left me alone
But I can dream as dreamers do
Until the day I'm home with you.

Sandra Hughes

THE SPIDER

So many different webs he weaves
spanning doors to windows and eaves.
Walk past a tree, or bush, or shrub, ,
and lo and behold, they are such.

The wind can blow, and rain can fall
but the spider's web withstands it all
how can they be so strong, I wonder
to stay through hail and thunder?

The sun shines on them, with the dew,
casting more different pictures for you.
All types of patterns the spider casts
how many? we wonder, they are vast.

J Dawe

THE OAK TREE

For centuries now the mighty oak tree has stood
On a desolate meadow where once was a wood
Your untold beauty you bring especially to me
Not a blot on the landscape like many just see

You had been surrounded by hedgerows, shrubbery and trees
Now all felled by man or died from disease
You've survived all the elements of frost, snow and storm
Your trunk severely weathered and branches all torn

In spring when your buds come forth in the sun
Your forest-green coat has just begun
Birds find you a safe haven so they're nesting here
Whilst many grey squirrels from your trunk-holes appear

Your foliage clad boughs, they spread far and wide
In the summer you shade me and wildlife can hide
As you shed your cupped like fruit of tiny acorn
We hope many more grand oaks may be born

In autumn your elegance you cannot deceive
The colour of deep green has gone from your leaves
As they turn to russet, gold and dark brown
Falling like a paper carpet onto the ground

In winter your outline is like a ghost in the dark
You stand completely naked, your branches so stark
Then with the fall of snow you are draped in white
King of the winter wonderland you grace with delight

Oh tree you are such a wonderful creation
May you continue to be the native of this nation
Not only sanctuary and shelter you give
Because without the tree how would we live?

Linda Brown

MY DOG

My days with her were so full of fun
Running, playing, shooting the gun,
But now that she is old and grey
And cannot run, skip or play,
We'll sit together in the sun
And sit so close we are as one,
Deep in thoughts of those yesterdays
My furry friends those were the days,
But now we sit, then we walk,
Take a drink and have a talk
And take things slow and easy,
For time is getting short for you
And I want it bright and breezy.

Hilary Tozer

THE KEEPER OF MY HEART
(In memory of Earnest Deane Casbeer, who died 12th May 1978 in Okinowa)

Once in a while a man comes along, so different from all others
When I was a girl this man came to me, my hero, friend and lover
Through good times and bad my love never changed
He quite simply was the best.

He wore his uniform, stood so proud, always gentle, never loud
Often his duties called him away but I knew he'd be faithful,
                                        he'd never stray,
Through good times and bad my love never changed
He quite simply was the best.

Time passed by, our love grew strong, I prayed we'd never part
Then with a daughter we were blessed, so quickly she stole our hearts
Through good times and bad my love never changed
He quite simply was the best.

Sadly one day his orders were changed, he had to cross the sea
But right from the start I knew the score,
                                his career could not include me,
Through good times and bad my love never changed
He quite simply was the best.

We kept in touch by letter, his daughter of course he adored
But sad to say when she was six, two officers came to my door
Through good times, through sad my love never changed
He quite simply was the best.

The shock and sorrow I felt when I knew, my hero had taken his life
Just our child and me left to face the world,
                                how would I survive the strife?
Through good times and sad my love never changed
He quite simply was the best.

His memory lived on as I sang his praise,
                                now I was left with our daughter to raise
Her daddy, my hero, my first and true love,
I told her that with tenderness he'd watch o'er her from above
Through good times and sad my love never changed
He quite simply was the best.

Time has passed since he left us, his daughter is now a wife
And at night when I pray I give thanks to the Lord
That this wonderful man entered my life
Through good times and sad my love never changed
He quite simply was the best.

Often sadness comes over me as I think of this man I miss so
I long for my name to be on the list, I'll know then it's my time to go
I'll stand at the heavenly gates and knock as my
                                loved one opens it wide
As I stand and gaze through my tear-filled eyes
Feeling love that's been put to the test
I'll say, 'Darling I've loved you, I've missed you
You quite simply are the best.'

Audrey Tully

MY CAT

My cat will hate ice cream and cake
And sweets and chocolate too
Mice and fish is the dish
My cat prefers to chew

It is no joke my cat hates Coke
And beer and orange juice
No wine, no Lilt, just plain white milk
That cows and goats produce

The food I choose, my cat will refuse
And I guess that is that
Smelly dead mice really don't sound nice
But that's what suits my cat

Philip Nind (13)

DESERT STORM - THE GULF

The sands they drift and move every night
To uncover the bones of the past.
For the men who have come to fight
And found this valley their last.

No flowers or grass to lay over them,
No headstones to give them a name.
For the sake of Christianity,
These young knights they all died in vain.

Sure is our turn to stand in the valley,
With our memories of home in our hearts.
The tears they roll down our cheekbones,
Our nerves are falling apart.

For the shells they fall all around us,
And the bullets to our ears they do sing.
A song of deafness and darkness,
A place that has tempted us in.

A call it comes down the line,
As we gather our courage within.
As we stand and gaze at frightened foe,
The battle it commences again.

Now the valley is deadly silent,
And the dying have drifted away.
To a land of hope and of splendour,
A land that's so far away.

To lay in a land of drifting sands,
Where our souls were torn apart.
Where friend and foe lay toe to toe,
Their bodies all torn apart.

Now back at home and all alone,
With just memories of the past.
Where politicians took our lives
And tore them all apart.

Will we forgive or will they learn
That man is not a toy,
That trust and understanding
Could have saved a mother or boy?

Mac

WALKING WITH MY FATHER

We walk down a long, cinder lane
drawn like a pencil line
between green meadows,
and when the summer sun
sits on the black wheel
it's the moment he leaves me,
one hand grasping the Thermos,
the other ruffling my hair.

It's time for his daily ritual,
the round tag and oiler,
time for his last taste of fresh air.
Soon he'll be on his knees
shovelling, throwing back,
shovelling, throwing back.
And I just keep thinking
of falling rocks and gas
and the sight of blood on coal.

Because Hell's down there,
filled with graveyard dust
and the black spit of dying men.

And in the long, cinder lane
I hold a dandelion clock
and blow the hours away.

Gerald Hampshire

JUNIOR SCHOOL MEMORIES
(The playgrounds of time)

Within my mind, I have walked your playgrounds,
Which are now locked in time.
Though when I was a child, I never knew they would leave.
The games we always played, I have replayed them too,
Though it isn't quite the same, when you can only glance back.

Teachers, playmates, all of whom have gone.
They leave only imprints,
Add to things we only speak about.

Within your classrooms,
There were things we used to learn, things which
Would be very useful in our later lives.
End of the day stories were to be enjoyed,
As the class would all behave themselves.
Pay close attention.

When the summer would come,
Your orchard was open,
We'd love to sit upon the grass,
Play between the trees.
Back then, summers were wonderful.
Could have stayed all day long,
Wandering around our playgrounds in the warm, sunny breeze.

Yes, those were the days. Part of our childhood years.
Now they are locked within time, if only I had the key.

Within my mind, I have re-walked your playgrounds,
Which are now locked in time, though when I was a child,
They were firm beneath my feet.
The outings we shared, I remember those too,
But it is never quite the same
When you are only looking back.

Packed lunches, trips on canal boats,
Both of which are history.
They leave only imprints, add to things we write about.

Upon your playgrounds, we would run, dance and jump.
All around your buildings there were places where we would hide.
Playing hide-and-seek was a regular break-time fun,
Trying very hard not to be seen, so as not to
Give ourselves away.

When the summer would come, your orchard was open.
We'd love to play upon the grass,
Swing upon the trees. Back then,
Our summers were wonderful,
Could have stayed all day long
Wandering around the playground in the warm, sunny breeze.

Yes, those were the days, part of the schooling years,
Now only existing in the past,
They are under lock and key.

Kevin Welch

PRAYER OF GRATITUDE

Dear Lord, each morning when I awake
I thank You for each breath I take
I look around, eyes open wide
Take in the beauty to be seen
As my heart fills with pride
Sometimes I may forget, Lord, just for a little while
As humans often do
Within the hours of the day
But within the stillness of each night
I pray and share my thoughts with You
When daylight hours are through

Mary Veronica Ciarella Murray

CHRISTMAS

I'm here all alone, the fire's embers aglow
The candles they whisper, didn't you know

Father Christmas has been, he was thinking of you
He's left something special, tied up in blue

He saw you asleep and whispered your name
How did he know you wanted that game?

The doll and the teddy both needing a name
The magic of Christmas is with us again

It's time to awake, his work has been done
While you gently slumber, your face he looks on

Come now arise, wipe the sleep from your eyes
Look at the end of your bed

You'll find a surprise when you realise
Father Christmas has done what you said

Lynne Taylor

AN ENGLISH SUMMER

At the gathering of the clouds,
Sunday - day four of the second test,
An English storm brews in the crowd,
The south-easterly wind blowing sixes west,
'Come on Freddie, bowl from around,'
Because those Ashes are choking our summer flowers,
Let us hear those stumps ripped out of the ground,
At the end of the summer, victory will be ours.
We've forgotten those run-outs we shouldn't have missed,
And appeals that end in, 'No, no, no,'
We can read the deliveries from Shane Warne's wrist,
They end up buried through England's meadows.
From the top of the order through to the tail,
Aussies fall like ash between the fingers,
That quick tempoed waltz of flying bales,
Not a single batsman stays and lingers,
What is the summer without fields of straw?
What is a contest with no sweat on your brow?
They say they can win without Steve Waugh,
Dream on Australia, you're in 'England' now!
We're the new number ones, the home of cricket,
From our smoky power plants to the centre at Lords,
As Harmison's yorker takes another wicket,
The whole world hears the English roar,
And when your countrymen greet you, after the plane has landed,
And they ask you the questions you don't want to be asked,
'Why the long faces?' 'Why are you empty handed?'
Just tell them you were rubbish, and totally out-classed!

Ian McNamara

MY LADY'S HAIR

My lady's hair looms large in life,
It causes worry, angst and strife.
A fringe, a bob, which cut, how long?
Advice is sought, what's right? What's wrong?
Some time with mirrors, talk us through
Alternate styles, oh what to do!
At last decisions must be made,
Who will come to my lady's aid?
Procrastination, thief of time,
But better him than fashion crime.
So we will wait another week
Solutions then again to seek.
Meanwhile my view of hair is this,
A set of wigs would be such bliss.

John Stuart Yewlett

SAD CAFÉ

She sits at the café table
by herself but not alone.
Her thoughts are with another
as she looks at the telephone.

She slowly sips her coffee
lips trembling on the cup
framing the rim with a crimson bow
tonight he's out of luck.

Too late to change her mind now
a tear falls from her eye
it's over now, what's gone is past
why did he have to lie?

He stole her heart and made her think
their lives would always blend.
Such love as this was theirs alone
why did it have to end?

But soon she found his love was false
he'd found another flame
and like a moth he circled close
who else was there to blame?

He knew their special café
where first their lives had crossed;
she listens for the telephone
is her past and future lost?

The patron mops the table
and clears the cups away
it's time to leave, he gently hints
no reason now to stay.

She picks her bag up from the floor
and rises to her feet
closes the door behind her
and steps into the street.

Her lonely footsteps echo
in the alley among the bins
within the darkened café
a muffled telephone rings.

John Notley

IN THE WILDERNESS

Out of the dark cloak of time
Silently it came
The burning hand of pain
Mysteriously it touches him

Among the grey shadows he sits
In an air of resignation
His heart yet beating with
Each pressing breath of life

Breaking the silence I hear
His voice, 'Come sit beside me'
Turning I meet his gaze
And walk towards his world

In the wilderness of pain
He wraps me in his close embrace
Softly he says, 'I'm tired'
And my lips speak, 'I know'

Here his warmth holds back the night
And as I sit within his shadow
In a sanctuary of pure peace
He holds me in his gaze

In the dim light our hands touch
His warmth spreads through me
For he presses my hand in his
And love spills

Joan Magennis

REQUIEM, 9/11

Under the rays of the rising sun
September morn did creep
Onto the place below,
A sight to make one weep
For underneath grey swirling clouds
There lay a dead, a scorchéd land.
And yet, as I watched with tearful eyes
I felt again hope rise
For from those clouds and with those clouds,
A lovely angel came,
Her golden tresses flowing,
Bright flowers in her hair,
With pure white wings and arms all bare.
I waited, dazed, with frozen limbs
As she glided up to me,
Then softly did she speak.
'Grieve no more for all those lost
For they're now safe from harm,
So start anew, rebuild this place,
And from the ashes make
A monument for all to see
And honour at the cost.
It will be hard; the road is long,
Nights longer, lonely too,
But I'll be there with you.
Gather all men to sweat and toil
For in that way then you will foil
The ones who planned this act.'
I felt her touch, her hand so light,
She kissed me on the brow
And through her eyes I saw
A veritable host of souls
All walking proud and true,
And I knew then what we must do.
The sun burst through, and as it did,
She disappeared from view,
And I saw again that scorchéd earth
Where we must work anew.

John Alexander Harrison

POETRY

Poetry: once I liked not at all.
Always sad, liked not to play ball.
Lovesick lovers moaned their ill fate
Contemplated sliding in lake.
Mourners mourned ones they did not hate,
'Cheer up,' said their mates for our sake
for the fifteenth anniversary
Forward Press book of poetry.
Poets abound,
Are all around;
Thinking, scheming,
Noting, watching.
Please, now bring out
Good - with no pout.
Cheerful, happy.
Look for beauty
For it abounds
Like the poet.
So be snappy
All you Forward Press poets
Fifteenth is here - be in the best
Forward Press poetry book ever.

Ruth Brigden

UP A GUM TREE DOWN UNDER
(In a slow, drawling Australian accent)

We met at the jetty just outside of town,
At my place that I called Gum-tree Creek,
She was all that was pretty, with her hair hanging down,
And my legs that were strong became weak.

We flirted awhile, puritanical style,
It was there that I asked for her hand,
When she consented, the bans were presented
And in three weeks we would walk down the aisle.

But it was not to be, I was too blind to see,
It was not love that this Sheila was after,
It was her madness for gum, which I thought was dumb,
But it gave her a strange kind of laughter.

You see I owned this plantation, and my sole occupation
Was the gum trees all over my land,
But there'd been devastation through a vile infiltration
Of a virus, and I'm now left with sand.

When word got about that my gum had run out
She withdrew her seal of approval,
For she thought that my gum would bring in a large sum,
When it didn't, she arranged her removal.

She said, 'I'm leaving you, Blue,
I'm going away, I need to find a new patch,
I'll have nothing to chew if I get married to you,
No point in us hanging the latch.'

'Why must you leave?' I said with a sigh,
'Don't you know that you've stolen my heart?'
She said, 'Please do not grieve, just say 'goo'diy'
You'll soon find yourself a new tart.

But there's something that I've got to do,
You've always known that I love it,
It's something that I want from you,
And my mind is made up to have it.'

She kissed me long, then broke away,
She said, 'I'll see you, Bluey.'
It was not just my heart she stole that day,
She stole by bladdy chewy.

Tom McDonald

MY FEARS

So many feelings that words just can't describe.
I'm happy I found you, so glad you're in my life,
But I'm so afraid and so completely scared,
For this much emotion, I'm just not prepared.

Maybe everything is moving a little too fast.
That week we shared together, forever I wanted it to last.
You said we would see how we go,
So why is my head protesting to these feelings that show?

My heart is crying out desperately for you,
But my head is saying, *girl, please think this all through.*
I need to move on and stop living back then.
I can't always wait to ask why, how or when.

If I could go back in time, I would erase
The nightmare that's causing me to go through this phase.
I like you a lot, that I cannot deny,
Maybe it's time I gave my heart another try.

Nothing in this world could make me fully forget,
Although as long as I'm with you, things can only better get.
And gradually in time, the fears I hold will fade
Because of the happiness together we will have made.

Jennifer Smith

WAVES

Beating, retreating
Wearing, depleting,
The core of the rock
Revealed.
Gravelly, grating
Never abating
The beat of the wave
On the shore.

Shimmering, shivering,
Swelling.
Gathering resources.
Powerful pressure
Pounding the beach . . .
Stills to a lullaby
Cradling the swell
Hushed and subdued.

Lapping, rippling,
   Saving its strength
   For the onslaught.
   Every seventh
   Is the big one.
Watch it rising
Out at sea,
   Imminent.

   Accelerates, accumulates
Agitates, recreates
Catastrophe
Surfing, surging, running
   Ground-swelling trough
   Wrecking, breaking.
'Eternal Father strong to save',
Never underestimate
   The power of the wave.

Muriel Hughes

IN THE WOODS

I've lost my voice. It wants
to sing in tune, tongue tap
iambic rhythms, weave
romantic quatrains caught
threading the cranial loom.
Finesse fragility
unmans my pen, confines
the winging words. No sleight
of hand or arcane art
delivers them. Maze mad,
I wander thicket paths
that briar the brain; quagmired
with woodless trees and sloughed
with loss. Desolate here
no shoots from rotting fruits
arise nor sapling growths
unfurl their palms to spring,
just thought, birds fluttering
in the wind; ghosts that haunt
the psyche, whispering.

M M Dolding

PASSING THOUGHTS

The early mist drifts slowly into space
And leaves the silence undisturbed,
For just a little while their heritage is theirs
The mouse, the worm, the vixen and the bird.

All creatures, happy, busy, unafraid
Revel in this vacuum of peace
For all too soon this joy will turn to dread
When noise and fumes invade their private place.

The road that's being made to skirt the town
Has rent the earth and broken all its shell
With gay abandon trees were all chopped down
Their pride and branches shattered as they fell.

The noble eagle, circling high above
Offended by the sights and sounds he hears
Longs for the things that he has grown to love
And what will be his fate in future years?

Carried on the wings of wind, this mighty bird
Alights, and perching on the highest tor
Safe at last he bows his noble head
And ponders - and wonders - why? What for?

P Kelso

THREE BRAVE MEN

The call was there, 'Go into space
Land on the moon and see its face.
Then on from there to distant stars.
Maybe to Venus. P'raps to Mars.'

It began long ago, this urge to explore.
(Some even think it happened before.)
But for us it was 'now' and for three brave men
Who'd left for the moon and danger - when
From an unknown source, the machine they were in
Was badly damaged. Now, how could they win?
So far away, out there in space,
From help on Earth, where began the race
To correct their course, to give them air.
To conserve all the water they had up there.
To keep their morale from getting low,
Those three brave men, who'd said they would go
Away to the moon, do all they were told;
Then return to Earth. But now they were cold.
For their heat had gone, and much of their power,
And God only knew how they felt out there.

Far away on Earth men worked like mad
To feed the computers with all they had.
To send the results to those men on high,
So they would come back. So they would not die.

And they came back home, with little to spare,
Those three brave men, who'd been 'up there'.

Eileen Coates

HUSH

I awake on thunderous raps at my door.
The song thrush had long been drown
by synthetic overtones.
The short summer day puts to bed
the quiet carbon night,
for the morn I wait,
on pencil words, a break,
then sleep to the spirit song.

Ber George Barter

REACH OF THOUGHT

The world spoke, as we journeyed through,
We listened intently, amazed at the recognition
Of the gift we were given.
Marveling to the blending of nature and Man's skills.
Creating a universe with immense culture and pride.
A world filled with knowledge, and astounding discoveries
Still to be made.
An adventure of reality, revealing wisdom of thought, to the many
Changes of climates. Adapting to the time changes. A result of Man's
Creation *The Meridian Line*.
Atmosphere of transposing colour of cultures
Varying in depths of intensity.
Scenery which filled our being, with an awe-inspiring feeling
Of spiritual value.
Our world, our gift, to nurture and love, with appreciation.
A visionary awareness, captivates the imagination, with immense
Grace, filled with gratitude, for the gift of all living things,
And their active part of existence.
Acceptance confirmed, 'Yes, *God* is good.'

Lorna Tippett

DAVID AND GOLIATH

Preface

O'er the rugged hills of Judah, high above old Bethlehem,
Where sheep were wandering about, a boy was guarding them.
A sibling of one Jesse, and the youngest he begat,
A dreamer and utopian, and as lithesome as a cat.
Upon a day, upon a task, to Elah, Jesse bound -
Him with provisions for his kin, abreast some far warground.
And this the story he presents, to them, in disarray -
How he rid him of a predator who wouldn't go away.

O why wert ye so fickle when that girt Goliath came?
O why didst thou fain flee the ranks, and straightaway cry for hame.
To he, a man ten times of me, alone stood I tiptoe
And looked him eye-to-kneecap there, and told him where to go.
He laughed, 'Ho-ho, ho-ho' he boomed all through the deep valley -
Swirling his hefty sword, and brought it crashing where I be.
I dodged and swung my slingshot up and hit him where it hurt,
He ended eye-to-eye of me, all stretched out on the dirt.

O why wert ye so fickle when thou sees what I had done
As all Goliath's men amok, like headless chickens run.
And there stood I, my sling in hand, defiantly unfazed,
E'er looking at the giant head - it's bulging eyes englazed.
E'er looking at the obelisk upon its temple, where
My stone had hit perceptibly to fell the tyrant square.
Yet still afeared wert ye not so, thou seest how well he's dead.
Heed ye no more his maddening, I bring ye wine and bread.

Addendum

Goliath was a pole apart, six mean cubits and a span,
Formidable and furious, a mighty fighting man.
Champion of the Phillistines, with sword and spear and shield
Who chafened all the Israelites to combat in the field.
'Come fight me to the death,' saith he, 'hath anyone the zeal -
Come let me cut they flesh from thee, like strips of orange peel.'
Thus David, son of Jesse, came, a shepherd through and through,
And slayed that irksome warrior, as a shepherd lad would do.

D Haskett-Jones

UNTITLED

Though worthier judges praise this skill portrayed
With blank surprise my first few thoughts were filled
When on thy work my wondering eyes were laid.
Oh, have I done thee wrong? Thou who art skilled
To show in depth of line and charm of tint
A vision of the future, thanks to thy virtues?
Nay, I applaud those signs of challenging thought,
Those lines and forms of indecisive matter,
And outlook so original, so daring,
Yet 'tis no wonder that someone did fling
They work reversed with, doubtless, heedless thought.

And so, with charmed mind I seek to know
The drams thy restless mind hath brought to birth,
The secret bonds with things unseen that grow
Into the work surpassing skill on Earth.
Oh, may thou ever satisfy thy power,
Grasp hold of art's bold privilege and let
Thy fancy range with freedom and with scope;
And though this generation may forget,
Yet future nations may on thee bestow
An honoured name for all the world to know
A genious thought and ne'er gave up to hope.

Audrey Sizer

RAIN

Rain is not gentle
Not anymore
It drums on the pavements
And knocks on the door.
Its power is so forceful
Its pathway so strong
It fills up the rivers
And moves trees along.
It floods in the fields
It seeps through the doors
And everything yields
As it rains more and more.

Where are the April showers?
Soft and refreshing
Reviving the drooping flowers
Watering the meadows
Gentle and soothing
Bringing sunshine as well
With colourful rainbows
To say, 'All is well'.

Alison Watkins

ARABIAN DAY

By the kerbside squatting with whittling sticks
For use as toothpicks
Flies from face he flicks

Hennaed beard a brilliant red
Eyes flashing 'neath turbaned head

Teeth a brilliant white
As he munches on a date

Traffic roars by, no camels to see
Squatting on bended knee

Baker dough kneads
Whilst the legless beggar pleads

Charcoals smell burning in a grate
Barbecued chickens on the plate
Turbaned men stroll by
Swatting away every fly

Women cocooned from head to foot in black
Conversation they don't lack
Babbling like a storm-fed brook
Eyes flashing over every stall

An old man creaks and shuffles slow
Before the scorching nazma's blow
Sun scalding hot
He doesn't give a jot

In every doorway shaded
Merchants squat, wares paraded
For all to see
Haggling filled with glee

Carpets from many lands
Their multicoloured strands
'Trees of Life' line the wall
Outside a budding Zidane kicks a ball

Wind-blown papers amidst the heat and dust
Old Toyota sick with rust
Muezzin calls shopkeepers to pray
Tribute to their one deity.

Maddoc Martin

REPLY TO WILLIAM SHAKESPEARE'S 'ALL THE WORLD'S A STAGE'

'Tis true! The world's a stage
And all the people in it are but players -
With one long drama only to unfold -
No practice runs - no matinees - but only
One unrehearsed performance, through the scenes
In all the stages that each life involves!
But, 'no man is an island' and, alas
Our lives will, and do, impinge on others too.
In fact, so many things impinge on our performance
That few can give an Oscar-winning show.
For most of us, that effort proves too much!
But, as the proverb says, 'Hope springs eternal'
And so, we struggle on, from stage to stage,
Expecting the next one to be better than the last!
Now, as I pass each day, my mind is thinking
Of all the yesterdays I've seen so far!
'Cause I've reached the final stage or my performance,
The rest is all behind me - and I'm tiring!
Yes! Some were happy days, and some were sad,
And sometimes too, along the way, I reckon things were bad!
But now! My glances are all backward cast;
And shadows from way back fall on my path!
And looking now, I reckon I can see
That I tried to make a difference - that was me.
It hasn't all been easy, I confess,
But I taught my kids to strive, to do their best
For people all around them, and give help
To those who need it, as they journey on!
My part in life's great drama's gone unsung!
I have not conquered Everest, nor won
World Cups, Olympic Gold, Nobel prizes or such like,
But, I've played my part - I hope - the very best I could,
And more than that, I simply could not give!

Elizabeth M Tumilty

UNTITLED

Close your eyes and visualize
A peaceful, quiet scene,
A little stream trickling by,
Or a waterfall so serene.

A misty, shrouded mountain top
Up there in drifting clouds,
Wings outstretched, a bird floats
In clear blue skies.

The rolling waves on the sea,
The miles of golden sands,
Or just the swaying of the trees,
Rocked by a gentle breeze.

The warmth of the sun,
The fragrance of the flowers,
The dew on the leaves,
Left by the showers.

The colourless raindrops falling
From a darkened cloud,
The same as the teardrops
That overflow from our eyes.

Let your thoughts and mind wander far and wide,
There's beauty all around us,
To touch, see and hear,
To soften our sorrows,
To lift the darkest cloud.
Find peace in what's around us,
Let the ache in your heart cease.

Joan Wright

SEAT OF LEARNING

Moving across sands of time
Ploughing guidelines in poetic rhyme.
Sowing seeds of wisdom
For generations to read
There's a wealth of knowledge
For those who will heed.
An ocean of love, patience galore,
Helps pupils learn from a tutor they adore.
Give them directions on how to build
A wholesome society that will
Good fruits yield.
Praise their efforts however small
Encourage them to heed erudite call.
Regardless of colour, creed or race
Or whatever else may be the case
Every child is a precious gem
Deserving of protection from
'Satanic mayhem'.

Audrey Luckhurst

ON SEEING GOD

We cannot look into the eyes of God,
or see His face, lest we die.
Read about Him daily in His word
you will see that He is nigh.

Awesome majesty surrounds His throne,
and enter we dare not do,
because He is holiness so supreme,
and sin cannot enter there.

His eyes are too pure to look at sin,
so He sent Jesus down
to this sinful world to make a way
where none was before.

Through the love of His dear Son,
a door is wide open now,
and we may freely enter in to see
the place where there is no sin.

John Harrold

THE SONG

Stood in my garden beneath a black velvet sky
I see moths drawn by light, dance till they die.
Watching sparks fly from the warm kitchen fire
Hearing cows gently lowing as they turn in the byre.

The rustle of field mice as they try to hide
From the cat and the owl who are both eagle-eyed.
The soft cluck of hens as they settle to roost,
Whilst the sly fox creeps nearer, his pantry to boost.

The piercing howl of the tomcat seeking his queen
She answering back with an echoing scream.
I smell the clean air as the rain softly falls
At peace with nature as she beckons and calls.

Suddenly silence and across the night air
The sweet sound of singing, melodic and rare.
Lifting my heart and caressing my soul
Each note perfection, rounded and whole.

Whence comes this beauty, what wondrous thing?
Has God given this gift to perfectly sing?
The smallest of creatures, a little brown bird
The song of the nightingale was the music I heard.

Joan Gallen

The Spirit Of Christmas

The thief climbed down the chimney of an orphanage.
Tommy had been waiting up all night.
'Is that you, Santa?' he asked excitedly,
for this poor soul had lost his sight.
'Yes, yes it is,' replied the thief nervously,
as Tommy's face lit up with joy.
When the thief noticed Tommy was blind,
he asked cunningly, 'What would you like, little boy?'
Said Tom, 'I would like a wheelchair for Julie
and a hearing aid for my friend Mick.
I would like Jesus to make Emma well again
because the doctor says she's very sick.'
The thief, who had been looking apprehensively for the safe,
suddenly became overwhelmed with grief.
'Why are you here, son?' he said compassionately.
'Where are your parents?' asked the thief.
'We are all unwanted,' Tommy answered matter of factly.
'Our parents have thrown us away.'
The thief choked back the tears
thinking desperately for something to say.
This man had spent a lifetime in prison,
but now his heart was beginning to melt.
A surge of love welled up inside of him,
an emotion he had never once felt.
'Is there nothing you want for yourself?' he enquired.
Tommy smiled and shook his head.
'No, I'm fine,' he answered cheerfully.
'Christmas is about giving,' he said.
'Can I get anything for you?' Tom continued.
'I suppose no one ever thinks about you.'
The thief bowed his head humbly.
'No,' he said sadly, 'no, they never do.
But you have given me my best ever present,
you've restored my faith in human nature,' he replied.
'I had forgotten the meaning of Christmas
and the spirit in me had died.'
Tommy ran slowly, carefully towards the thief,
with his arms outstretched wide.
They both hugged each other tightly,
the thief knelt down and cried.
'You're here not because you're unwanted,' he whispered,
'you're here because you're a wonderful, special little lad.
And if God could grant me just one wish
I would ask if I could be your dad.'

Colin Winfield

Life Is For Living

Springtime is here and the flowers in bloom
Blow away cobwebs, the dust and the gloom

Life is for living
So the critics say
You have to grasp it with both hands
Before it slips away

Life is for living
Those ambitions to pursue
Dispel the negative thoughts you have
The world is open for you

Life is for living
Put positive thoughts into place
Take chances and the challenges
That stare you in the face

Life is for living
We take each day as new
This God-given gift is in our reach
And there for me and you.

Jean B Yates

Life's Measure

If I can look and see,
Yet not perceive;
Listen and hear,
But rarely understand:
Should I experience
But scarcely feel:
Or like exceedingly
But never love:
Of music please my ear
Yet never thrill my soul:
Fine words inform my mind,
But fail to reach my heart:
I have not lived,
But pallidly existed,
The glory missed -
A heaven not attained.
Letting life pass me by,
So fearful of the depths
Where wonder waits
Just for the taking.

Mary Pledge

What Is An Angel?

We think of angels up in Heaven above
Also angels are people who help others with love
The doctors and nurses working long hours to tend
Accidents and illness, their aim is to cure in the end

The firefighters and rescuers who risk their lives
With one thought for others to survive
Soldiers, sailors and airmen fighting wars and evil
Police who protect us from villains and upheaval

The ones who visit the sick and bereaved
Sharing their worries, with those who are grieved
The ministers and all who preach God's will to win
Friends who are always there, through thick and thin

The parents who go without, caring for family
Voluntary workers, they are earning for charity
Those who are thoughtful to all mankind
Giving time and devotion by being kind

All who are helping in times of need
Ones who will do some kindly deed
People who are not afraid to let their feelings show
These are some of the angels here below

Elizabeth Mary Dowler

A Good Day

Some days are fast and some are slow
What to do, where to go?
What to learn and seek to know?
What to hide and what to show?
In the storm or singing cool
Bright with colour like knitting wool
Sea breakers dance and ebb and flow
In the boat we pull and row
Will you not come back again?
In the sunshine and the rain
Hearing the water go down the drain
Do everything with might and main
Link together, tie with chains
Days of grief, of joy, of pain
Come to me and sing again
Meet me in the road or lane
Music melodies, glad refrain
You spoke to me, I am glad I came.

George Camp

QUESTIONS!

Do spiders really have kidneys
And nails at the ends of their toes
And ears at the top of their heads
To eavesdrop on each other's woes
And big bundles of wire in their bodies
With which to weave fairy tales
And occasionally when they are hungry
To entrap the unwary males?

And do they really like house-flies
When they buzz around and around
Greeting them like long lost buddies
Cuddling them till there's no sound
And sharing their meals with each other
'Til there's no more of their guests to be found?

Keith B Osborne

MUFFLES

The lead still hangs where it belonged,
And cannot be denied,
Though its owner is no longer here -
For months ago he died.

Muffles was a cross-breed,
In shades of brown and grey.
And in the heyday of his youth
He loved to romp and play.

He tried to match my every mood,
This faithful canine friend;
He sensed my joys and sorrows
In his own way - to the end.

But if I need to be reminded
Of this most loyal pet
I think about the walks we shared,
And this I can't forget.

And now I walk those paths alone,
My footsteps take me there:
I see his shadow by my side,
His presence everywhere!

When I reflect on this dog's life,
On aspects large and small,
I learnt so much from knowing him,
The dearest dog of all.

Joan Mathers

PLOCKTON AND SKYE

You know me well enough
To understand
There will come a time
When I won't leave this land
It beckons to me
Even when I'm asleep
The call is so strong
It cuts very deep
The need is so vast
I forget all my fears
It burns in my veins
Like a river of tears
It's been smouldering in me
Since I was a child
If I were a cat
It would be the call of the wild
Come rain, snow
Wind or sunshine
This is my Heaven
It will always be mine

Ruth Grant

A MILLION MILES APART

In my eyes you still sparkle,
Even if in yours I don't,
You may think I'll be back,
But running to you, I won't,
I'm always comparing others to you,
You were my perfect guy,
Lazing around thinking of you, as the world passes me by.

Freedom from your face,
A maze from your heart,
A river from your soul,
A million miles apart,

There are so many reasons why I can't be with you
Thousands of fields away,
Distance is growing wider every single day,
I still think of you as the one, my first love was you,
I will find another, where our love will follow through,

My heart keeps on beating,
It was a volcano from the start,
A lot of build-up and time,
Then spreading a million miles apart.

Kirsha Johnson

THINK OF ME THEN

Remember me in quiet moments
When the day's demands have all been met,
And your thoughts released, are free to wander
Over memories we won't forget.

Remember me when shadows form at sunrise;
When lightning flashes pierce a darkened sky;
When with softened breath the zephyr lulls you
Or a rainbow's colour spreads its promise wide.

Remember me in the twilight hour
When melancholy takes its toll,
Or when with joy an early sunbeam
Wakes a response within your soul.

Remember me when you hear sweet music,
When the plaintive strum of harp strings sounds,
And woodwinds echo, lush and calming,
Seducing with soft falling founts.

Remember me as the seasons change,
In the chill of winter, in the haze of summer,
On a soft spring day when your steps are gladdened,
Or with autumn's song your heart is saddened.

Remember me when life is ending,
When dreams and memories, sharply focused,
Return to mind - then you'll recall
The moment when our pathways crossed -
Think of me then.

Jennifer Vine

OH THAT IT COULD BE

Oh that our world could be a happy place,
And all its people with one smiling face,
And love for everyone; no matter colour, creed or race.

Oh that each one said, 'Would I to me, have this thing done;
Then starvation, torture and wars
May not go on, and on.'

Oh that when tears were shed, most were tears of joy.
In a world we cherished;
With no neglect, or intentions to destroy.

Roberta A Davies

THE STRAY

The first chill winds of winter blew
As she crouched against the wall
Her once lustrous coat was matted
She remembered the days she'd walked tall.

The much loved pet of a kind old lady
Until death had taken her away
Her life had been a happy one
But now she was just a stray.

Her stomach rumbled with hunger
As she surveyed yet another street
She had walked for miles that day
With nothing at all to eat.

The birds twittered noisily above her
As a door opened not far away
A lady came out to feed them
Then turned and saw the stray.

The lady noticed the sorrowful eyes
And her bedraggled state
She held out morsels of food
Which the cat hungrily ate.

She followed the lady into the house
Where a young boy stroked her fur
The gentle hand upon her back
Made her slowly start to purr.

Her wanderings had taken her to them
She was grateful for her new home
The family were good and kind to her
No more would she have to roam.

Dorothy Baines

MUM AND DAD

Looking back when I was a child
With loads of love and security
A kiss goodnight
Made all things right
I loved being in our family
I had a holiday every year
No matter how little money
Ice cream each day
After sand, sea and play
And love as sweet as honey
I was cared for so very much
Growing up in those remembered days
So long ago
Where did it go?
My wonderful childhood phase
The roles have now become reversed
The cared-for now the carer
My dad and mum
Now eighty-one
Thought of daily with a prayer
Their days, they must be numbered now
Twilight years are rushing by
Both a treasure
Love too great to measure
And the question I ask is, 'Why?'
Why do I have to lose them?
Why do they have to go?
But in my heart
We will never part
They'll be there always, I know.

Sue Byham

THE INNOCENT CRY OUT

For many years I have roamed free
With humans always after me
We have swum the seas around the world
Skies around us have unfurled

To the highest pinnacles of mountain range
To the deepest leagues, so strange
Ever decreasing in our numbers
How many more summers?

In the deepest jungle there is no safe haven
'Nowhere to go,' cries the raven
The coldest waters cannot save me
Everywhere, Man seems to be

With toxic waste, and every other kind of pollution
Does nothing for our population
Every year our numbers wane
Every year so many slain

No matter what and where we are
It's no good wishing on a star
If we have feather, horn or hide
This is the reason why we have died

Young or old, it matters not
If we see man, we've had our lot
Money is what he sees in us
So there's mountains of bones, what's the fuss?

So if they felt a little pain
It's all to our gain
Year upon year, we are slaughtered
With mountains of money our lives are bartered

In another million years or so
Maybe Man
Will have no place to go.

Jeanette Jackson

CREATIVE GIFT

He put creation deep in me, the joy of lovely things,
the whole of nature that I see, but also angels' wings.
He made my hands creative for I long to be like Him -
create, restore, make beautiful, the essence of these things.

Yet I see war, destruction, waste, whatever can I do?
The ugliness of sinful man comes clearly into view -
the love God gave has turned to hate, man cannot now create,
but if I pray and seek God's face, my turmoil will abate:

He'll use me for His glory and to show His perfect will -
a good example in a world where evil's reigning still.
I cannot do all this alone but when the Lord I trust,
His Spirit flowing through me helps me do the things I must.

I'll share in His creative acts, His beauty showing through
so God gets all the glory then, yes this is what I'll do.
I love the Lord with all my heart - how can I love my brother?
Just be the Good Samaritan to get on with each other.

My actions are creative when they're healing, when they're kind.
No matter what the outcome is, this brings me peace of mind.
Creation waits, creation groans - the broken must be healed
and there shall be rejoicing when God's glory is revealed.

I'll let His Spirit intercede for He knows what to say -
the Lord gets all the glory when the Father has His way,
so I shall keep on listening for what He'd have me do -
once more I'll see the Lord at work creating something new.

Winnie Pat Lee

MOTHER EARTH

The long grass shimmers as the breeze touches it
On a summer's day.
A carpet of yellow, 'tis the buttercups
And the ladies' fingers too.

The swallows dart and flit,
Catching flies to fill the ever-hungry mouths
Of the second hatch of chicks.

The trees are all majestic, swaying in the breeze,
The beauty and magic of Mother Earth you see,
Never failing to please.

When the world seems like it's going mad,
The industrial and commercial mouths ever wanting more,
It is welcome to see Mother Nature unobstructed in her glory,
Without the jaws of so-called 'progress' destroying every fibre.

The powers that be don't understand
By destroying Mother Earth, we are destroying ourselves,
For Mother Earth and all that's on her
Is one and all.

Catherine M Simpson

LOVE'S WONDROUS AFFIRM

Once we laughed in each other's clown,
Danced a warm moon, in St Tropez,
And the book of love read crazier words,
But I stand before you in disarray.
Will the loving dreams flow from the past,
The awkward smiles be ones of charm,
To free the dance of rigmarole,
And brave this heart, from daily harm?
The word of justice bears your name,
I'm only strong by softer cries,
But reel the full blows,
And not oft, before your eyes.
Let the mad dog dine your meal,
I'm more to humble, if not your friend,
The shadows and the quite unease
Are borne deep, not to offend.
So rally me, by fairer grace,
A kiss will surely blame our doubt,
That's fair by far,
Kiss again, unruly out.
Let's not shy, in repeated words,
But grab the dreams by joy enough,
Our asking hearts to be redeemed,
We have tenderness to fight it tough.

James Spoors

NOVEMBER

If you could be here with me now
Sat in that empty chair,
Cocoa mug with both hands grasped
Firelight glinting in your hair.
Then I would listen to the tales
Of the exploits of your youth,
And this cold November evening
Would pass quicker, that's the truth.

If you were sat there, slippers crossed
And smouldering in the hearth,
And once more wonder at your face
As it wrinkles when you laugh.
But you've taken that long journey
And we'll never meet again,
So I'm stuck here on this cold
November evening in the rain.

John Morgan

DIVINE EMBRACE

Majestic glory is in your garden,
The beauty of colour in divine embrace,
Caress the petals from the rose from Eden,
Touch the blossoms of hydrangea lace.
Admire the sweetness of a pansy's face,
Wander thro' the pleasures of a green lawn,
Feel the peace around you in the new dawn,
Stroke the purest lilies in their frills,
Caress the fuchsias' hanging bells,
The beauty of colours surrounds you,
Sprinkled like pearls, shining with dew,
Tiny white daisies with a golden eye,
The azure blue sky, clouds drifting by,
Cast your eyes to the waving trees,
Stretching arms feel the cooling breeze,
You feel warmth around your fingers,
A 'presence' a 'love' that seems to linger,
You feel caressed, you are the 'flower',
Majestic peace in a floral bower,
Majestic glory is in your garden,
Your hands caressed in the flight of birds,
Beauty of peace in whispered words,
Filled with glory, filled with grace,
Your heart is filled with divine embrace.

Blanche Naughton

THE DRESDEN LADY

Strong in any crisis.
Rarely ever got it wrong.
She could be, for others,
Collected, brave and strong.
Always had solutions
To the puzzles in each strife.
Undoing others' knots,
Made all their bows sit right.

She, the tree,
Where all could safely nest.
How well she played
The leading lady's part,
Silence, kindness, courage,
She made it look an art.
But when the theatre dimmed
She changed, to play the clown.
Alone, with only darkness,
The small things brought her down.

The dust motes of distress
Could scratch like pointed knife,
Spreading hairline fractures
Along the lacquer of her life.
Stress bent her spine a little,
Made her tilt a little left.
And the tiny, unimportant things,
Now made her feel, bereft.

For herself, she found no answers:
Looking out at life, she found
One hair upon the pavement
Had the power to bring her down.
The passé Dresden lady,
A little less than whole,
A figurine, with faults concealed
Between the crafted folds.

Mary Buckley-Clarke

UNTITLED

What do we see, you ask, what do we see?
Yes, we are thinking when looking at thee
We may seem hard, when we hurry and fuss
But there's many of you, and too few of us
We would like far more time to sit and talk
To bathe you and feed you, and help you to walk
To hear of your lives and things you have done
Your childhood, your husband, daughter, son

But time is against us, there's much to do
Patients too many, nurses too few
We grieve when we see you, so sad and alone
With nobody near you, no friends of your own
We feel all your pain and know of your fear
That nobody cares now your end is near

But nurses are people, with feelings as well
And when we're together, you'll often hear them tell
Of the dearest old gran in the very end bed
And the lovely old dad, and things he said
We speak of compassion, love and feel sad
When the time has arrived for you to depart
You leave us behind with an ache in our heart

When you sleep the long sleep
No more worry or care,
There are other old people
And we must be there
So please understand us
If we hurry and fuss
There are many of you
And too few of us

Frances Maguire

ON RETIREMENT

Where have all the years gone?
Yesterday I felt invincible, eternal,
Today I'm vulnerable
The traumas and fears of adolescence
Don't seem to have been that long ago.
Yet it was a different world, a different planet.
How could things change so much in just one lifetime?
I've gone from a phone in my street to a phone in my pocket.
From sitting listening to a wireless
To flat screen TV with surround sound,
From Brownie box camera to digital photographs.

Where has the summer gone?
Yesterday there were crocuses and snowdrops,
Today the flowers have faded.
The burst of green shoots and new life of spring
Don't seem to have been that long ago.
Yet it was a different world, a different garden.
How could things change so much in just one season?
It's gone from buds to dead heads on flower stems,
From sitting listening to birdsong
To the noise of wind and rain in the leaves around.
From fresh spring sunshine to autumnal haze.

Another season will come and go
Will there be as much change?
What prospect does the future hold?
Gnarled twigs and desolate landscape,
Or glistening frost adding new dimensions to the emptiness,
Winter blooms and berries, more subtle glows and hues?
A new beauty waiting for the ready eye,
A blank canvas, this garden will not retire and die.

Maralyn Rees-Molyneux

THE IDYLL OF BARRA

How I wish I were on Barra where my worries float away,
Where time seemingly stands still
And everyone has the time to give you the time of day,
Where the peace and tranquillity wash over you
Like waves upon the shore,
Where silver sands, the translucent sea
With hues of green and blue,
Along with the friendly people are all there to welcome you.
It's where there's a unique airstrip governed by the tide
When hopefully on a clear day
You can go on an exhilarating return plane ride
That lasts in total for about an hour unless the weather closes in
Then you may be stranded in Benbecula, not my favourite place
But still peaceful and seemingly a million miles
From the hectic rat race,
Barra is beautiful, small and compact
And the serenity of a summer's day
Can really help you along the way,
Though of course there are the winter storms
But there are summer ones too
But it's just the place to escape
And get away to when you're feeling blue,
You can watch the seals bathing on the rocks,
An otter on the beach or even dolphins in the sea,
You can listen to the waves lapping on the shore
Like a gentle melody
Or when the gales blow and the storms brew
You can watch the waves pounding the rocks
Whilst on the beach the salty foam will spew
You can admire the flowers of the different seasons,
The golden hue of the wild iris, primroses of pale yellow,
Pink sea thrift to name but a few,
They're all there, and more, for you to view
As are the rock pools and the sea so crystal clear,
The seasons may change
But the Barra magic weaves round you all year,
It's a beautiful island and in my heart, thoughts and soul,
I hold it very dear.

Lesley A Stevenson

TREADING WATER ON A RAINY AFTERNOON

'We could always try rewrite Cinderella kids,'
I announced to two grandchildren whose eyelids
seemed to be giving in to gravity.
Of course they wanted to know why,
'We like the proper Cinderella,' they said with a sigh.
'Okay then, we could talk about the mice or the pumpkin instead.'
Adam gave me a strange look, but Rachel nodded her head:
'Mice are cool Grandma . . . they make great pets,
You can dress 'em up and feed 'em, they hardly ever need the vets.'
I know working with children and animals is not for the faint-hearted
but by now I was beginning to wish that I'd never started.
Adam asked about pumpkins - where they came from,
where they went.
'Sainsbury's,' I mumbled, but he knew I was ambivalent.
The children smiled indulgently as they watched me bravely trying
to sell a storytelling game that no one there was buying.
Not even the Ugly Sisters, Prince Charming, or his merry men
could put my Jackanory skills back together again.

Suddenly Adam noticed the rain was over and done,
the sun was shining, and now the fun
begun earlier in the yard could be taken up once more.
I helped them into their coats, then stood watching at the door
whilst they played together with reckless narrative ease -
their afternoon inertia disappearing on the pantomime breeze.

Mavis Simpson

No Band Of Gold

It was there in the newly mowed cornfield
That he first saw the dark haired Gypsy maid,
As she danced by herself 'neath the oak tree,
Twisting, twirling about in its shade.
Her long hair, black as the raven,
Tossed loose in the warm autumn breeze,
And her skirt with gold stars on crimson,
Billowed up and swirled round her knees.

And as Carmen danced there she was barefoot,
William's heart was telling him that he
Had fallen head over heels for this vision,
A blithe spirit, abandoned and free.
Every day he went back to the cornfield,
But sadly she never was there.
Only the solitary oak tree,
A symbol of his growing despair.

But his prayers did not go unanswered,
For one day in the boughs of the tree,
Gathering mistletoe to sell in the market
Was the girl chosen to share his destiny.
From that day on they were always together,
Walks in the wood hid their secret romance,
But if ever their paths crossed in the village,
Neither gave scarcely a glance.

She had dreamed of a Romany wedding,
But she knew now that this could never be,
She'll have no band of gold for her finger,
But a token that no one could see.
So he pulled a sharp knife from his waistband,
And deftly drew blood from his wrist,
Then gently he cut Carmen's wrist too,
Their blood mingled, they embraced and they kissed.

When Carmen's family found out, they were angry,
Her brother Bruno said, 'Send her away.'
So they packed her off to her grandma in Spain,
And told her that's where she must stay.

Heartbroken, stunned and bewildered,
William searched for his love near and far,
But all that remained from their short 'marriage'
Was a lock of black hair and *that scar.*

Bill Dovey

The Albatross

Above the south's quick flowing tides
Straight through the torrential rain she glides
When every other seabird hides
The albatross flies bravely

When mighty storms ceaselessly blow
Where the ships of men will hardly go
Their only fate the depths below
She wings her way so carefree

She's the mystic wanderer of the seas
The legend whispered on the breeze
Her airborne presence sailors please
The goddess of the ocean

So proud, so sleek, so born to fly
The majestic glider of the sky
If a million years or more pass by
She'll rule in lonely splendour.

K F Hardy

94/20

I walked in at a bad time
Oh we rowed; out fell
So many bad words.
Loud, so the neighbours whispered
Gossiped
Spoke in disbelief.
And there were some that even knew
What I didn't want to know.
Violence burrowed behind the curtains;
Gosh, the blades
The shrieks. The horror.
A blur, it initially became.
But the guilt
Was the war
Then my memorial
Amen.

Emma Bone

A Mother's Love
(In memory of Michael the beloved son of Margaret and Robyn Dewhurst)

When a mother loses a son it's the saddest thing on Earth
The love they shared together just kept on growing from birth
He filled her life with so much love
An angel sent from up above

Each day you watched him grow with pride
With the feeling of love no mother could hide
He came to you when he needed a friend
You were always there for him up to the end

How can you live when he's no longer there?
His life cut so short, it seems so unfair
His beaming smile would light up your day
Life seems so empty now he's gone away

But remember the happy times you both had
It would break his heart to see you so sad
He's gone to a place where he'll suffer no more
One day he will meet you at Heaven's door

Where he'll smile and take you by the hand
To a place they call 'The Promised Land'
So don't let the heartache cloud the view
Of the beautiful son that you once knew

He's with you in spirit though you cannot touch
But he knows he was loved so very much
Just think of the precious times you both spent
He knew what a mother's love really meant

Pauline Mayoh-Wild

Love

Love is a whisper on the wind
Love is a hope that never dies,
It is a dream that never fades
It is the rainbow in stormy skies.

Love is strong and old as time
Love does not break or buckle with strain,
It sees you through the darkest night
It shows the sunshine through the rain.

Love is constant, love is true
Love is what I've found in you,
It is a joy that never dies
It is the light I see in your eyes.

Jane Oliver

DON'T CRY FOR ME

When I die don't cry for me
let my ashes in the wind blow free
Through the grass and daffodils
in the streams and o'er the hills.

Don't cry for me, I'm not dead at all
when you see a flower bloom, or a snowflake fall
I'll be there like a gentle breeze
in rustling sound of leaves on trees.

Don't cry for me when I'm dead and gone
please let my memory live on and on
In those I love and leave behind
the joy and happiness in life I found.

When I die don't cry for me
what is meant to be will be
Think of times we were together
for love is strong and lasts forever.

Don't cry for me when I'm dead and gone
remember me and I will live on
A quiet moment . . . a gentle smile
think of me for a little while.

Christine Rank

A TOUCH OF SURREALISM

(In memory of Dalí, Master of Surrealism)

Dalí as a young artist
decided to have a go
at self promotion in England.
The big plan was
that in London,
Dalí would stand on a podium
in the middle of Trafalgar Square
and deliver a speech
in Catalan language.

Helped by his entourage
of Catalan secretary and friends
he dressed up as a deep-sea diver,
including helmet and oxygen mask.
The heavy headgear came last
and was then screwed on.

Soon Dalí began to gesticulate and
to say things no one could hear
- but that was to be expected.
When his face changed from pale to red,
it suddenly dawned on the public
that a purple face was not part of the act.

The oxygen was not connected
and Dalí was suffocating!
Swiftly the helmet was removed
on time for the artist to welcome back Life!
He closely escaped
from a surrealistic death.

Jacqueline Gonzalez-Marina

LET LOOSE - GET GOD

Loose me from these bonds of being busy all day long,
May I discard the rubbish that distracts my mind from You,
The magazines, the tele and the endless, mindless songs
That fill our lives with nonsense that detracts from loving You.

Fill us with Your peace, dear Lord, and Your everlasting love
That enfolds us in Your caring arms and forgives us when we sin.
Reshape our lives to fit Your plan of putting others first
And make us more like Jesus for the world to see His Face.

Elizabeth Hawkins

BELIEVING

I have to keep believing,
One day that I will find him,
That he is really out there,
Somewhere,

I have to keep believing,
That one day I'll have a baby,
A child that I can nurture,
And be their special mother,

He's out there somewhere waiting,
To be my Mr Right,
He's handsome and he's funny,
We're meant for one another,

We'll live happily together,
And have those lovely babies,
We'll nurture them together,
And be a happy family,

Somewhere, some day,
Happiness is waiting,
I know that I will find it,
Eventually,

I have to keep believing,
It's all waiting round the corner,
And one day it will happen,
It will be at last my turn,

If I just keep believing,
Some day, somewhere,
It will be my turn,
To fall in love.

Lynsey Bessent

BLOW, WIND, BLOW

The weather is nothing new
It has been around long before me and you
Rainstorms, snowstorms, hailstorms too
The winds will blow and it will rain
And sometimes it becomes quite a pain
The birds don't sing when the weather is rough
They seem to know it's getting tough
Thunder and lightning we all agree
Not to shelter under any old tree
Flooding too, we do not want
And when the rivers do subside
We are left with a very muddy countryside
The forecasters try to let us know
But it turns into the weather comedy show
When it's wrong what they forecast
The wind changed direction
And they were far too late for a correction
With all the knowledge we now possess
The weather makes it look a mess
Winds will blow for evermore
And shake the barometer on the wall
It is still the same as it was before
The weather is still its own law
It will do whatever it likes
And we won't change it
It is an element we just can't beat
In years to come it might give way
And then the sun will come out to play

D H White

HOPE FULFILLED

People with nothing but anger and grief -
When hurricane force engulfed like a thief -
Their vibrant city of music and song,
Where they were happy with family bond strong.

Now, devastation and all treasures lost -
Houses, like playthings, by wild winds were tossed,
All vestige of hope did floodwaters take -
When many lives lost were claimed in its wake.

But strong helping hands by brave human force -
Rescued the stranded - a great comfort source.
Hope returned slowly to people bereft -
They would rebuild from warped remains left.

Money and time it will take we all know -
But from the rubble new city can grow -
With government aid and their strong control -
And when people mend in body and soul.

Until that day - that future tomorrow -
Generous world aid will lessen their sorrow -
Gifts of compassion for them in their plight -
Will help and encourage them fears to fight.

Foundations firm for new buildings they'll lay -
People once anxious can then safer stay -
In vibrant city restored and alive -
With sound of music they'll gladly revive.

Marian Curtis-Jones

A STITCH IN TIME

There's a reason why hurt finds our hearts
Why tears make their homes in our eyes
Life's like a fraying, loose seam, come apart
We can mend it or turn a blind eye
So take a needle to that fraying, old seam
Stitch it tight so it never comes loose
It's frayed because of the lies and deceit
It fell apart when it found out the truth
For the times you felt afraid, stitch double!
For the times you smiled and laughed, stitch once!
For the times you feared, times of trouble
Don't lose your grip or those times will have won
Take your time to do those deep repairs
When life became so tattered, so torn
When your broken heart could no more care
You felt so weary, felt so worn
Stitches don't have to be that perfect or neat
As long as you one day attempt to mend
That fraying, old seam that's so much in need
Of some repair, some love and some friend.

Tracy Brierley

CELEBRATE

Everyone should celebrate
Achievements great or small
There's times we've fallen by the way
And now we're walking tall
And memories are made of these
These moments are so few
And so I lift my champagne glass
And say well done to you.

Pamela Popp

ODE TO THE MACKEREL

Of all the fish I have met - and ate,
The tasty mackerel beats all,
Even the skate.
Oh, I'm partial to cod, haddock or sild,
And sardines are delicious,
When they are grilled.
A kipper for breakfast is also fine;
A bloater at teatime is simply divine.
But I desire mackerel early or late,
For them I'll give up everything -
Including whitebait.

Can't stand cockles or crab-bake
And I'm still unsure about tuna and hake.
Still, I'm willing to sample something anew,
Like shark-fin soup or octopus stew.
But anchovy, prawns, salmon or trout
Is food I can easily do without.
And turbot, huss, dab or eel
Don't contribute to my seafood meal -
A special fish I met and ate,
The shimmering, succulent mackerel -
It was worth the wait.

Ron Whatley

THE GOLDEN ONE

Mary and Tom, it's fifty years since you were wed,
This is the Golden One,
Such happy years together,
Sharing family and fun.

I hope to make a visit,
Flying across the miles,
To visit Staten Island,
Where there'll be many smiles.

Trying to play Jeopardy,
I find it very hard,
I'll probably have a snooze
Or pop out into the yard.

Just being together will be great,
So much to see and do,
Families will have changed,
As I have altered too.

I'm a little dumpy now,
My hair is turning white,
Let's hope I get a bit more slim,
I really am a sight.

Never mind, I am still in one piece,
And thanks to Mr Large
For giving back my life anew,
All this and at no charge.

So I give praise and thanks to God,
For His love and care,
In giving me a second chance,
To lead a pretty normal life
And to plan another year.

With love and best wishes
Sister Maureen (Mo)

Maureen Williams

LIVERPOOL'S MERSEY AT SUNRISE

The River Mersey's majestic way
Is wound through lush green fields,
Pastures where once a now fading memory,
Who toiled the land with bare hands and plodding horses.
Morning time in clear air filled with whistling birds
And cows who chew the cud while a magpie plucks lumps of hair
For a nest to keep her featherless babies warm
In the chill of the night
And the dew of the dawn.
What remains of the big house lies dormant now,
Half ruined by time
But once a proud man turned the key
In his magnificent new abode,
And years later another walked out the great door
For the last time,
Leaving its fading architecture to the elements
That have now taken
Their toll from the great dwelling of stones found and made to fit
And create elegance along the banks of the mighty lady Mersey.
England's flowing jewel of water, clear and fast flowing
Full of life beneath its shimmering ripples
Of perch and pike, trout and eels and silvery salmon
Whose mighty leaps take an ailing body upstream
To its hatching pool,
And new life from death beneath the ripples.
But the river flows on and on oblivious to the beauty
That it passes and creates along the way.
A wiry mare calls to a flighty foal that leaps and bounds
Across a field full of daisies and buttercups.
And strawberry fields naturally blooming in the ditches
Hanging heavy with pure pleasure of red berry so sweet
As the sun comes up across a rocky hill
Where cattle's stearny breath moistens the horizon.
The mighty River Mersey majestically looks on as it passes by
On a wholesome journey
And England proud starts another day.

Paul Kangley

HORROR SHOW

The newborn dead on arrival
A young rebel a fist for survival
Pretty speeches can't disguise
The guilty silences and fake smiles

Lost footsteps in desert sands
Revenge and rumble in forgotten lands
Western minds built the divides
And armed all sides

Crocodile tears are televised
Mass media sell me lies
Evil tyrants on foreign soil
Or those back home who would trade our blood for oil
A multinational education
Designer dreams
GM Liberation
As they stuff their face with another Big Mac
The power marches on the people back

The newborn dead on arrival
A young rebel a fist for survival
Paralysed poverty grips
The working eat from sub-minimum wages

Robbed tax of millions
For company cars and dead Palestinians
You stand in line, you'll get stabbed in the back
The power marches on the people back.

Lewis Palgrave

UNREQUITED LOVE

In my thoughts, you see what I see,
You read my mind as if it were your own . . .
To be near you feels so natural,
To be with you is to feel secure,
To be with you is to feel love.
If only dreams could be captured.

There is nothing incriminating in my dreams
Except a pure and simple desire -
The desire to walk down a familiar street,
You wanting to place your hand in mine,
Parading proudly for all to see.
You and me.

Caroline E Ashton

REUNITED

Waiting,
Time just ticks away
I'm hoping for a letter,
But dreading what it will say.

Praying,
God, let him be OK.
Let the war be over
Let him come home today.

Wishing,
For his body next to mine
To hold him close and watch him sleep
For everything to be fine.

Dreaming,
At last my dream's come true
He's standing at the door
The war is finally through.

Waiting, praying, wishing, dreaming
They don't need to happen anymore
For the pain we've been through, now back together,
We can be each other's cure.

Katie Turner

A CHILD'S GIFT

I sit and watch my brother play,
But he to me is miles away

He's found some sticks lain on the ground,
And with them a new world he's found

The twigs no more mere bits of wood,
Have been transformed into Robin Hood

Leaping from the grass and stones,
He somersaults, his aim he hones

And lands amidst the baddie guys,
Catching the Sheriff by surprise

A fight ensues, the air is tense
Filled with action and suspense

But hero Robin the Sheriff stumps
And from the battle comes up trumps

I never cease to be amazed
How little children fill their days

From all their toys they have to choose
With simple things they can amuse

Perhaps adults from them can learn
Us, who for contentment we yearn

Enjoy the wonders of creation -
Try using *your* imagination!

K Crabb

THE CREATOR'S PALETTE

Traversing the time zones
Across every archipelago,
Peninsula and continent;
Beautifully variegated dawns and sunsets
Emblazon and adorn the skies,
Splashed from the Creator's palette.
Wow!
Momentarily thrilling and
Delighting a billion senses.
Dreamy twilight fading into dusk, or,
Dawn's sun bursting into full brightness.
Just a few more hours, and yet
Another fantastic cyclic display.
Wow!

Azariah Ephratah

MY GARDEN

Sit yourself down at the top of my garden.
Come and enjoy the view!
glety piglety Old Town Hastings,
I love the place, I hope you do too.

Sit your 'bot' on the bench at the top;
You can just about see the sea.
Watch the sunset beyond West Hill . . .
Feel her warm the bones of you and me.

Pretty little summer house . . . especially
When the apple tree's in bloom.
Blossom drops, leaves turn green . . .
Summer's here, all too soon.

No wonder he wrote Alice in Wonderland . . .
Looking down from the top of the hill.
glety piglety Old Town Hastings . . .
Got to have your flowers on the window sill.

Many an evening is spent sitting . . .
Watching the seagulls fly past.
Glass of wine in hand -
Listening to an old folk band . . .

My garden . . . peace at last!

G Maynard

WHAT DID I SEE IN YOU?

My life has been a nightmare, I don't know how I've pulled through
I really want to run and hide each time I think of you
You're big and fat and ugly with warts all down your chest
And when you get undressed they poke out through your vest
Your trousers need a wash and your filthy shirt is frayed
Oh how I've wished you dead, I have prayed and prayed and prayed
But no one up there listens, they pretend they just can't hear
You smell so flipping awful, they can't bear to come too near
Your shoes are a disgrace, they're all scuffed and full of holes
The smell of cheese is dreadful as it seeps out through the soles
And then there is your nose, it's all twisted like a snare
It drips those awful dewdrops from a mass of greying hair
Your eyes now they are something else, the good one swivels round
The other is glass so always stares down at the ground
Your hair is thick and matted and maintains its own livestock
You couldn't get the muck out if you washed it round the clock
Your fingernails are grimed with dirt, I just can't bear to look
And when you poke them up your nose you make an eating hook
Whatever did I see in you, why can't I run away?
Then thankfully I wake from sleep to face another day.

Jackie Davies

SLEEPING WITH THE LIGHTS ON

Tumbled curls upon the pillow restlessly toss and turn,
Eyes stare in fear at the shadows and my arms yearn,
To comfort him and say,
'It is only the moon shining through the trees,
Boughs swaying, dancing in the breeze.'
Sad little boy, sleeping with the lights on.

He is but twenty, but see how in anger his fist is clenched!
Bureaucracy had extinguished his plans and drenched
His promising life in a pool of sorrows.
Officialdom, despair are encircling his life in gloom -
He feels that there is no hope in this dark and dreary room.
I understand too well why he is
Sleeping with the lights on!

Lined, grey, sad face, turned to the wall,
Too tired to weave his dreams, just waiting for that call,
Weary, lonely, old man, life has not been kind to you I fear,
What have you to show now death is near?
Your fate the man with the scythe!
I know why you are
Sleeping with the lights on.

Peggy Briston

UNFAITHFUL I WAS

I want to tell you, my love,
That my heart always belonged to you.
I can even give up my life for you.
I won't ever betray you, sweetheart,
I swear on my love.

I never imagined life would take this new turn.
I just don't believe it . . .
. . . How could I be disloyal to you?

Darling, now I seek justice,
Please forgive me, I got carried away,
I was insane,
Curse me, I ignored your simplicity.

I wish to love you more than ever before.
My love . . . at your feet I want to lay Heaven and Earth.

You can snatch away my peace,
Snatch away my joys, and let me have all your sorrows.

Please stay with me forever,
I shall never make this mistake again.
I shall never be unfair to you.
My heart will always belong, only to you.

The tears falling from my eyes tell my stories,
Please don't consider my tears worthless.
These tears shall wash away the stains
And paint them again into the colour of love.

Shajna B Chowdhury

HOURGLASS FIGURE

There are slimming clubs and diet books
To help you to improve your looks;
Tips for bust and waist and thighs
To trim you down to ideal size

I've tried them all, but sadly fail
So you will understand my wail,
'I fear that I now know my limits -
But my hourglass figure is still 90 minutes!'

Margaret Campbell

A STROLL ALONG THE RIVER

As I sat along the river just the other day,
Staring at the boats and yachts, and a life that still could be.
An old man stood facing me, appeared from I don't know where,
From what direction did he come? Was he ever really there?
He spoke of a reunion, young soldiers he'd fought with,
Fifty years ago or more,
But he pictured them as seventeen years old,
And remembered all the horrific sights they saw.
I watched him battle with himself, to act like he'd forgot,
How him and his young soldier friends,
Forced to watch the nurses who were shot.
A sad old face, painful memories in his eyes.
Bewildered with a system, that's filled him full of lies.
Our eyes stared quite intently, before he shuffled on his way.
I wanted to run after him,
With something comforting to say.
To tell him that we'd learnt, it wouldn't happen anymore,
Where prejudice is a thing of the past,
Like greed, like power, like war.
Another time. Another life, another world maybe,
I often think of that old man,
And his ghosts he shared with me.

Jan Anderson

MEMORIES

Somewhere there, down Memory Lane,
I felt the heartache, once again,
When reading old letters, from days gone by,
Which bring a teardrop, to the eye.

Tears were shed, this sorrowful day,
Of memories, along the way,
Just looking at the letters, and having a cry,
About happiness and sadness, and wondering why.

They will go on forever, and always last,
These few sad letters, from the past,
Although they bring back, all the pain,
The love in these letters, will remain.

For the writer of these letters, a lovely soul,
Has earned his reward, and found his goal,
And so I'm glad, I looked in the past,
And know he has found, his peace at last.

Winifred Booth

SPRINGTIME

The hedges once again are dressed in green
The first young leaves on hawthorn now are seen
Daisies lift their heads above the ground
And 'neath the hedgerows plant life does abound
Newborn lambs lie sunning in the fields
Catkins shake their pollen-laden heads
Everything around looks new and clean
As Mother Earth awakens from her bed
Chestnut trees their sticky buds unfurl
Blossom opens out into the sun
Birds fly round in one mad whirl
To let us know their nesting time's begun
A blackbird sings his love a tender song
His joyful notes ring out so loud and clear
The winter days that were have passed and gone
And all the wealth of springtime days are here.

Maimie Watson Stokoe

THE HILL

The hill seems longer today
Push hard on your stick.
Ahead the dogs run and play
A buzzard hunting high and fine
Up above the snow line.
The hill seems longer today.

Great red stag snorts in defiance
At you the lone usurper
To his world dominance.
Push hard on your stick, don't falter,
The hill seems longer today.

Sit and rest awhile in bothy small,
As snow begins to fall.
Ponder on life and love,
For you have enjoyed it all.
The hill seems longer today.

Head falls on to chest,
Sleep then to dream.
Lost in life's quest,
Gone into death's long rest.
That hill was longer today.

E C Inkpen

ABANDONED

I came home from school one day
To find my parents had moved away

It wasn't because I was a bad kid
They just didn't like the things I did

Could it have been the mice I took home
Or was it the snake that made them roam?

Was it because I scared Aunty dead
By putting the gerbil into her bed?

I was taken into foster care!
A new mum and dad to share

They seemed so very nice
But wouldn't allow the snake or mice

They asked me to helped with the washing up
I accidentally broke a cup

I accidentally set fire to my room
Nearly died, overcome by fumes

Later I overhead them say,
'No wonder her parents moved away!'

Pam Hornby

CARING FOR A CARER

Thank you for your caring
And the kindness of your heart
I never, ever would accept
That we were worlds apart

You showed me such compassion
And encouraged me to be
Interested - motivated
Discovering the real me

If fate had drawn a different hand
Our life journey to pursue
You could have been me, my friend
And I could have been you

Shirley Davis

PEOPLE SAY . . .

People say, 'Make the most of your life,'
But this I did not understand,
Until I lost someone close to my heart,
And I lost that 'guiding hand'.

People say, 'Take a chance,'
But I used to ask them, 'Why?'
Now I know, you only get one life,
So we must do it all before we die.

People say, 'Never give up,'
But sometimes it's hard to keep going.
If only I'd done this a few years ago,
My life may have kept me glowing.

People say, 'Try to be strong,'
But this I can't always do,
As I so miss the ones I have loved and then lost,
And I always will do too.

People say, 'Life does go on,'
But this I can't quiet always grasp.
Cos life's not the same as it was anymore,
Without those dear ones we've loved from the past.

People say, 'You must make them feel proud,'
And this I intend to try,
As I know my dear dad is watching me now,
From the biggest, best star in the sky!

Patricia Daly

A STANDING OVATION FOR DENISE WRIGHT

The tall and slim compere announced
That Denise Wright was going to sing
There was a standing ovation
A real cause for celebration.

When all was quiet, the curtain opened
Onto a pretty garden scene
Denise sat on a floral swing
With microphone in hand she began to sing.

When Denise Wright was only seven
People would say she's come from Heaven
Big, blue eyes, fair, curly hair and a sunshine smile
A soprano voice that could travel half a mile.

One day, when she was eight
She was not well, her mother said,
'Something's wrong, that I can tell.'
With a soft and gentle voice,
''s meningitis!' said Doctor Fry,
'She'll lose her legs or she would die!'

After months of struggle and despair
Lots of courage and tons of care,
Much bravery and much talk
On artificial legs she began to walk.
This is a story and it's true, I am so glad I told it to you
Guess who is singing at the King's tonight?
The indestructible Denise Wright.

Raymond Spiteri

TOY SOLDIERS

Playing war like all young boys
He fired and discharged the lead
The other boy fell and went down in a heap
But nobody cried, '*Bang, bang,* you're dead'.

A child soldier has been killed by another
A symptom of war and its cost
For one grieving mother, a life full of pain
For the killer, an innocence lost.

Eoin Dunne

YESTERDAY . . . AND TOMORROW

I dreamed of a garden
As familiar to me
As my right hand
Yet when I awoke
I could not picture it in my life
It was by no means grand
But a place of simple delight
And quiet meditation.
I knew every leaf,
Each flower was as distinct
To me as if only
Yesterday I had tended it
With my trowel

Where, oh where is it?
Did I, in some former life,
In some quiet other setting
Care for and love this garden?
Were there other children,
Other parents, another dear husband?
Will there be different flowers
Waiting for me in some, as yet,
Unknown bower of quiet thought?

Margaret Chisman

MEMORIES OF LOVE

Melodies fill the silent air,
Recalling how you used to care,
Once more plays that sad refrain
Of hopes that were to die in vain.

Days of laughter, nights of love,
Stars like jewels in Heaven above,
Now gentle raindrops fill the sky
And mingle with the tears I cry.

Promises so quickly made,
Only then to be betrayed,
I sit alone and contemplate,
Blind delusion, or just fate?

Let numbness overtake me now,
Too easy to recall our vow,
The rosy dreams in misted eyes,
They could not see that love was lies.

Anne Wilson

AN ODE TO THE WIND

Softly flows the gentle breeze,
Through the woodland o'er the trees.
Softly flutters russet leaves,
Falling gently, blown with ease.
On it sails o'er land and sea,
Stirring waves more rapidly,
Feeling strength, and mobility,
Blowing waves more frequently.
Tossed ships on waters deep,
Find it hard, their course to keep,
Blown with fury, water seeped.
Heave to at anchor, still, it travels on
Whistling its eerie song.
Tossing cables, tearing along
Ripping through houses, swift and strong,
Raging seas and falling trees,
Havoc in its wake, it falters.
Awakes the dawn, fresh, clear skies,
A raging heart softly sighs,
Peace, be still, God is nigh.

Irene Lee

SHADOWS

Shadows on the ceiling of my mind
Images of what is left behind,
Through the windows once shone light
Now the days are always night,
There are shadows,
On the ceiling of my mind.

Sorrow in the corners of my heart
Memories are tearing me apart,
Chance to give and to believe
Without fear to be aggrieved,
There is sorrow,
In the corner of my heart.

Anger burning deep within my soul
Festers and infects my being whole,
Hollow vessel devoid of form
Decompose the very core,
There is anger,
Burning deep within my soul.

Annette Clarkson

THE SCHOOL OF LIFE

Sparkling blue easel
For white splodges to dab themselves on.
Bright constant in the middle,
Shows off its function and powers.

Green fingers flex and stretch
Before they start their painting.
Unseen hands splash their colour about,
Often with only the slightest touch.

This carries on for a while,
But the constant fades as the painting nears completion.
The colours also diminish
As new ones take their place.

Sparkling turns to navy
And bright to not so bright.
Millions of faraway constants congregate
In worship to the not so bright.

But which do you like better?
And why don't they teach us these things in normal school?

Louise Jones

A WRITER'S THOUGHTS

God can see me sitting here
Inspired by the beauty of trees,
The colours of summer and
Autumn mixed in the leaves.

God can see me amongst flowers,
The wild ones that grow in fields.
Bluebells, buttercups, milkmaids
And the delicate pink anemones.

God can see me feeding the birds
With bread and biscuit crumbs,
To supplement the wild berries
For the tiniest feathered ones.

God can see me looking at
All the beautiful natural things.
And I sense Him always near
In the glory each season brings.

God reveals Himself in sunsets
And the glorious rainbow's hue.
In all these wondrous things
I am sure I can see Him too.

Rosemary Stanford

HAPPY BIRTHDAY, MA'AM

Ninety-five and going strong
Oh happy, happy day,
You still have a lovely face
And smile that seems to say,
'I love to be near my people
Be they young or old,'
You exude radiance and warmth
As the years unfold.
There are millions of us
Who send to you our love,
And may God bless you
As He looks down from above.
Happy, happy birthday
To a lady oh so grand,
Revered by the nation,
Captured by a waving hand.
You give us inspiration
On a buggy or a throne,
We send you loving greetings
To *you* and *you* alone.

Esther Hawkins

IN THE BEGINNING

In the beginning, when Earth floated in space
And the sun, moon and stars settled in place,
Darkness heralded the night, light dawned the day
Galaxies of stars traced the Milky Way.

Millions of heavenly bodies did abound
Out in the universe circling around,
God moulded them all with His powerful hands,
Their purpose enshrined in His mighty plan.

He gave us Earth to make it our world,
One of those beautiful planets of old,
Perfectly balanced, yet so fragile a frame,
Out in the universe there to remain.

God's creation is beauty, boundless in love,
From the depth of oceans to stars above,
Throughout the day and throughout the night,
His work is seen in the greatness of light.

Wilma Nicholas

WINTER IS NIGH

All around the trees are bare
Summer flowers are all but gone
But underneath the dark brown earth
Spring bulbs are lying in the warm
They lie there all through winter long
As the north-east winds do blow
They lie there almost forgotten
Till green shoots start to show
First of all the dainty snowdrop
Fills us all with cheer
The purple and gold of the crocus
Then the daffodils appear
Not everyone likes the winter days
It makes many a poor soul feel sad
But when the spring sun begins to shine
It makes us all feel glad
That winter days are behind us
And the trees are decked in green
Spring flowers are in the hedgerows
Where the winter snow has been

O M Giblin

SPRINGTIME AND ME

How springtime ignites the plant resurrection,
Dressing the earth for microscopic inspection,
Dormant in the ground seeds laid for a season,
Why should they rise again, is there any reason?

Our Creator designed seed to grow according to kind,
To make the Earth ornate, beautiful and well defined,
It brings joy to the spirit, and a spring in our step,
As a new life begins it brings hope and yet . . .

What a guarantee for those who lost loved ones in death,
Yes from the dead they will rise, and take new breath,
As the first man Adam brought death and disgrace,
The second Adam, Jesus, redeemed the human race,

With this guarantee before our very eyes,
God tells us how from death His Son He did rise,
For those with faith and trust in God,
Belief in this guarantee is not very hard,

As surely as spring the resurrection will take place,
A time when God and His Son will judge the human race,
God's word makes clear death pays the penalty for sin,
Through the resurrection season new life will begin.

That's why when springtime comes around,
And we see new life breaking through the ground,
My tears of mourning become tears of elation,
I whisper, 'Thank You, Jehovah for peace, and salvation.'

Barbara Jermyn

STARTHOUGHTS

I   On a clear night when the world is still
    go off alone to some quiet hillside
    and gaze up at the sky;
    then - listen with your heart -
    hear the symphony of the stars
    and harmonise your life to their music.

II There are more stars in the known universe
    than there are grains of sand
    on all the beaches of the planet Earth,
    think about that.

III The stuff that fills the space between the stars,
    that lights and fuels the fires of suns
    and causes strange winds to blow on unknown worlds
    is the stuff that you and I are made of;
    we are as related to the stars as we are
    to our own parents,
    we are part of the cosmic family of creation.

IV Promethean galaxies wheel their eternal way
    through the cosmos;
    they are beyond my reach
    yet still they touch me.

V   If in my dreams I could plant seeds
    wherever my thoughts roamed
    there would be gardens,
    glorious and alive,
    among the stars.

VI The seasons elicit dreams
    we will never lose,
    not even among the stars.

VII The stars are bright tonight,
    each again in its allotted place
    pointing the way for us
    if we could only follow.

David Morgan

THE OLD SWEET SHOP

Often times when I am all alone
Fond memories I recall
Of the old sweet shop I knew as home
When I was very small
In my mind's eye I see it still
The old sweet shop at that top of the hill

The windows were large and filled with sweets
And once inside there were hundreds of treats
Children's faces would light up in surprise
At the wonderful sight before their eyes
To choose a favourite was always a pleasure
In the old sweet shop so full of treasure

There were humbugs, herbals, peppermint rock
Aniseed and spearmint chews always in stock
Pear drops, wine guns, coconut ice
Tea cakes, liquorice and pink sugar mice
Fruit drops, chocolate drops, coconut chips
Jelly babies, fudge and sherbet dips
Sherbet lemons, strawberries and cream, pineapple rock
All of these and more at the old sweet shop
Dolly mixtures, bon bons, barley sugar sticks
Troach drops, toffee and red cherry lips
Yes, in my mind's eye I see it still
The old sweet shop at the top of the hill.

Barbara Mason

THE ALLOTMENTS
(Dedicated to my late husband John)

I saw God at the allotments today,
And I would have knelt down to pray,
But the mud was thick around every brick,
Of the path where I wanted to stay.
So I spoke to God instead,
All I needed was to hold up my head,
He heard my words, I could tell by the birds,
As they sang their songs away.
If we speak to God each day, even though we may not kneel,
We shall be in tune with the sun and the moon,
And will always be able to heal.
I saw God at the allotments today,
In the flowers and the fruit,
He was there holding hands with those on the land,
And He blessed each planted *root*.
I'll see God again tomorrow, when I see someone free of sorrow,
For the sorrow was there for the lack of a prayer,
So speak to God today and tomorrow.

Margaret Milnes

SUCCESS
(Through Forward Press)

How many times I've thought, *is that the phone?*
And rushed to find it's just a distant bell.
How many times I've sat here all alone
Just waiting for the post - and it to tell me
That my poems have been accepted and for once
Not been rejected.
I wonder will I always wait in vain?
And ponder - have *you* ever known the pain
Of sad rejection, grief and expectation?
When you so desire a joyful acclamation
For your crafted, skilful recitation
And the word 'successful' printed on your brain.

But truthfully I've never failed to gain your admiration;
And wish you all the very best for your fifteenth celebration.

Marie B McKenzie

FOR THE LOVE OF GOD

God is omnipotent, that is very clear
In human form, upon a throne, and also everywhere?
I cannot comprehend, perhaps my mind's not so lucid
One ponders if in ancient times it was understood by a Seleucid
Before our birth are we issued with a quota
Of God from generation to generation, the tiniest iota?
If so we are all family, from less than a grain of sand
And we should respect one another from each and every land.

Trish Shepherd

TRICIA DEAR

8.45 on this bright winter's morning,
The sun is streaming over my left shoulder,
Giving me the best possible light
To read again, and again, quietly,
In the stillness of my living room,
The treasured scroll, your words of gold.

You gave me the scroll, almost furtively,
Last night, my last night on duty,
At the hospital, after 30 years of service
And devotion to our cherished patients.
I did read it then, alas, too quickly,
To absorb the thoughts behind the words.

And now, the first lines had barely
Penetrated the depth of my soul,
When I felt the emotions welling
And bursting all over my being.
You plucked hard and strong
At the strings of my heart.

Before the pizzicato was over,
The tears were rolling unashamedly
All over my cheeks and face,
Spreading a soothing balm.
Tell me, dear, what catalyst
Did you use, with such brutal force,
To break down my defences
And render me utterly helpless?
Some 20 years on, the sadness of retirement
Has vanished, and made way for another life.
One chapter had ended, another had just begun.

Andrew E Cox

BED AND BREAKFAST

At the bottom of our garden grows a laurel thick and lush,
It was put there many years ago when just a tiny bush.
It lends a certain elegance, with its top shaped like a dome.

As it stands there in the garden like furniture in a room.
At dusk the birds all gather to roost inside the bush,
They flutter and they chatter, but eventually there's a hush.

But early in the morning it all starts up again
With chattering and flap of wings the bush comes alive and then
Suddenly, one by one the birds depart very much in haste,

Others fly out after them as if they were being chased.
Well, the bush got quite untidy so I trimmed it here and there
And I peered into the darkness
Where the branches were quite bare,

There hanging in the darkness I saw to my surprise
Big, black, luscious berries about a cherry size,
So I think I know the reason why the birds all like to stay
Overnight in our laurel bush, it seems,
They have breakfast on a tray.

Elsie Mather

SEA LEGS

Steam ships, dream ships
a ragged wicker sail
running along the garden
that is the coast of the swale

Tramp ships, vamp ships
a flat jagged raft
all along the seabed
an old sea salt sailing
a cramped motor craft

Out along the estuary
setting up a sail
panting, awaiting
the sound of a wail

All to come shoreward
sea legs found
who would tip the harbour master
the cost of a pound?

Ladies in waiting
at some shore door
customers a-plenty
among maids who
come a-filching
that is the cost of amour.

R J Collins

WHEN WINTER COMES!

This year the old plum tree excelled itself
With crowded blossom on winter-bare arms,
Snowy-white flowers clustered
Against the blue, blue sky!
This tree had waited thirty years
To put on such a show . . .
Then came the wind and rain
From summer's storms -
The plum tree has long since
Thrown its blossoms on the grass,
Its ragged leaves, and plums . . .
But we will remember how it was -
When winter comes!

Veronica Twells

SPRINGTIME

I'm counting days to springtime,
My favourite time of year
When days are warm and mellow
And air is fresh and clear.

I'll hear again the blackbird
See birds upon the trees
The crocus peeping through the earth
And feel the gentle breeze.

I'm counting days to springtime
When everything is new
There'll be the scent of blossom
And sparkle of the dew.

The early morning birdsong
The rustle of the trees
A time for new beginnings
Spring is all of these.

Pam Wood

KIDS

My daughter's quite a character, never thinks before she speaks,
She's obviously never heard the saying, look before you leap,
She engages mouth before her brain, and jumps in with both feet,
I really wish she'd take the time,
Before embarrassing herself for keeps.

The first day that she went to school,
She learned a brand new song,
She said it was called, 'Tin of salmon', I think she got it wrong,
We asked her to recite it and in time we understood,
'Sing Hosanna' was that song,
We wouldn't change her even if we could.

One day while in a sweet shop, I noticed 'Bon Bons' in a jar,
I hadn't had these for ages, so I took them to the bar,
But my daughter in her pushchair
Decided that she wanted just a few,
And promptly shouted as loud as she could,
'Can I have some condoms too?'

As she grew much older, she learned to read and write and spell,
But while in a supermarket I suddenly didn't feel very well,
She leaned into the freezer and pulled a turkey out for me,
And promptly said in front of all,
'Can we have this b*****d (basted) turkey for tea?'

I really don't know if she'll change, for her sake I hope she tries,
To be a little quieter when she speaks, and hope she never lies,
She'll always be my little girl, no matter how old she gets,
If only she thought before she spoke she'd have no real regrets.

F Baker

HEADS AND TAILS

Trying to tie down someone to a script,
Is like trying to leash a will o' the wisp.
So much to say in a head full of words -
Tripping over each other, vowels and verbs.
Not making much sense of the time, but
Then somehow it all starts to rhyme.
Hearts full of love for one another,
Saying words never used to any other.
Trying so hard to be understood - puzzled,
Afraid of being misunderstood.
Words are so special with meanings so clear -
But are they the words we want to hear?
Telling us how to behave in our lives,
Who says I am wrong in my desires?
The answer is in our hearts and heads.
The heart knows the right,
But the head - goes to left.
The battle is in us, we all know the way
But, in the end, will the script be the star
Of the day? Or will our heads once again,
Rule over the roost -
Making decisions against all the rules?
Heads or tails! Someone has to lose -
But in the finale, would we rather choose
Living or dying? How brave must they be
Choosing to die - no more to be, here in this
World; no beauty to see. This life is a gift, from
The greatest of beings. Just live it and love
All the will o' the wisp.

P Morrill

MY HOLIDAY

As a child, rather small
I remember sitting on the harbour wall.
I'm older now but it still beckons me
That Cornish town beside the sea.

Screeching gulls, busy docks,
A cottage garden, hollyhocks,
Towering cliffs, crashing waves,
The lifeboat station, lives to save.

Fresh mackerel, real pasties,
Winkles and crab,
Lobsters and saffron cake
Are there to be had.

I have walked around the Lizard,
Seen tall ships in the bay,
Been to Helston Flora
That really was a day.

Sat upon the green and
Listened to the band.
St Kevern has won prizes
With concerts through the land.

My friends they always welcome me.
'Come any time,' they say.
A quick chat on the telephone
And I am on my way.

Betty M Dunne

HELP!

How did we get in this bog, Celt? How *did* we get in this bog?
The 'footpath' sign *did* point down here,
The yellow way signs *were* good and clear.
But we've gone sadly wrong somewhere, I fear,
For we're *really* stuck in this bog.

I'm up to my knees in mud, Celt,
You are up are to your tummy in mud.
My trousers are awful, all smelly and brown;
If I pull one foot up the other sinks down.
And don't look at me that way, dogs can't frown.
Tho' we're *really* stuck in this mud.

If ever we get from here, Celt, if we ever *do* get from here,
We'll aim over there to those big grey boulders
Where the tough old bracken will come over my shoulders.
Then we'll forge ahead like two brave soldiers,
If only we're not *really* stuck here.

And then when we've got our breath back, Celt,
When we've *really* got back our breath,
We'll retrace our steps and reverse that last lap.
And look for the road - that's these dots on the map.
Just another five miles - 'There's the car!' How I'll clap,
How I'll cheer, if I've *really* the breath.

Vera Davies

WAITER, WAITER . . . THERE'S A FLY IN MY SOUP! (OR SOMETHING TO THAT EFFECT)

I found a slug in my food
I thought, *that was rather rude*
It wriggled about, as I gave a great shout
To the waiter at the other end of the room

He quickly rushed over, his face twisted with horror
As he whisked the plate away,
'I'm so very sorry, I'll fetch you another.'
I said, 'No thanks, just a brandy today!'

Zoé M Pearce

HEAVEN ON EARTH

Do you think it could ever happen
That the world could live at peace
That the blacks and the whites
The browns and the yellows
Could be loved by their fellows
And even united in grief
The short and the tall
Not ridiculed at all
To be fat or be thin
Would not be a sin
Be able to plan ahead
Be never without bread
To sow the good seed
And match with good deed
Rise with the lark
Without caustic remark
Put a smile on your face
For the whole human race
If all's right with the world
Could Heaven be on Earth?

James Rodger

CHRISTMAS IS HERE ONCE MORE

The firelight is glowing
Outside snow is falling
Children are snow-balling
Friends are calling
Christmas is here once more

Church bells are ringing
Choirs are singing
Fir trees and holly
Everyone's jolly
Christmas is here once more

The stable, a manger
Jesus our Saviour
Cattle lowing, wise men bowing
Shepherds and their sheep
Christmas is here once more

A star on high
Angels nearby
Nativity, activity
Christmas is here once more

Wendy Andrews

FRIENDSHIP

No matter how difficult the journey.
No matter how hard the road,
Your journey will be made much easier
If you have someone to share your load.

If each day to you seems march harder,
And you don't know which way to turn,
If there is no one there to guide you,
Then you have a lot to learn!

Friends all around should help you,
That is, if their friendship is true,
If not them, whom do you turn to?
The answer is up to you.

But you can be sure of one thing,
That somewhere along the way,
There's always someone to rely on,
Just act on what they say.

G O Parry

LIFE WITHOUT WORK

A life without work, for some, is to shirk
When the dole is the tops for the bottom
Excuses, excuses, not to be signed off
Justification being no more than cough

The lies to the dole are stretching my soul
In old days we'd be working the coal
Lumps and tar wouldn't alter any retreat
Pride and honour being not a treat

The fortnightly untruths to the job centre
Are tumbling, my mind
The staff being inspiring and kind
The workers knowing the unemployed are blind

The lies to the dole being good for the dishonest soul
Unemployed fish, swimming a bowl
Happy, left unbothered, alarmed when questioned

Life for some without work, is not one to shirk
Knocks to the ego and respect irk
Conscience only knows those with pride
The dolers care for an easy ride

Life can be easy or hard, depending
How you play the signing on card
The fiddlers do well by being lost
The too honest claimants count the cost.

John Mallon

ARE YOU REALLY AWARE?

Do you really know what you're thinking about
As you drive down that familiar road?
You've done it before and you'll do it again,
But are you really aware?
Busy changing stations on the radio
Or cassettes or even CDs
A quick chat on the mobile phone
Planning tonight or even next week.
Talking, laughing and joking with friends
Shouting at one of the kids,
But are you really aware?
So much out of habit like brushing your teeth,
Getting dressed or combing your hair.
A quick gear change here, foot down on the gas,
A cursory look in the mirror . . .
What did you see when you looked in it?
A woman by the side of the road.
'What's odd in that?' you might say
But just look again, reverse back for a while
And you will see what she sees.
A small wooden cross, the mark of respect
And small bunches of beautiful flowers,
Tokens of love from those bereaved,
But are you really aware?
Maybe the driver was as careful as you
As they drove down that familiar road,
Laughing and joking as you have just done
Maybe not . . . no one knows.
'I'd never do that' - 'It won't happen to me'
You might say, but just wait a while,
Remember so far what you've noticed
Since you first got inside your car
To drive on this journey to . . . who knows where,
You may never even arrive.
For as much as you may think you've seen these things
Look again, are you really aware?

Stephanie Linney

THE SALT OF THE EARTH

God bless you, boys, for all you've done.
It was unknown the road you trod,
never knowing where the darkness led,
or how dangerous the spot or sod.
You were real heroes, strong and brave,
who fought the foe, your country to save.
Patriotic to the core,
who fought for King and lore.
You hugged and kissed the ones you loved,
then said goodbye, with an aching heart,
around about tear-filled eyes,
mingled with glistening smiles.
Parents with lumps in their throats,
about their offspring would often boast.
No one knew how they secretly yearned
as they prayed each day for their safe return.
What they suffered,
only those in the midst of battle could relate.
When help reached some, it was far too late.
But memories are forever golden,
so of them they are oft times spoken.
Their fun, laughter and humorous banter
has proven memories are forever,
and always ready to be recalled.

Peggy Johnson

THE SOLITARY RIDER

Sultry winds a-blowing across the arid land
Tumbleweed comes tumbling amidst the swirling sand
Ere the solitary rider with head bowed low on chest
Passed by the lonely ranch house in the desert far out west.
A jackal screams with a mournful howl
That echoes through the night.
A rattler rattles and slithers away hastily out of sight.
The night is alive with fearful sounds:
Sounds that are strange and weird.
The rider stopped his horse and then he slowly raised his head
He pushed his hat back off his brow and scanned the night ahead.
When suddenly a flash of light and crash of exploding sound.
The rider was lifted off his horse and flung upon the ground.
No movement save the sigh of the breeze
And the scuffle of tumbleweed
And the rider lay just where he fell
And there was no one to pay heed.
But when the first rays of sunlight broke across the brow of the hill
The sheriff and his deputy came to examine the kill.
Tis disaster he said for a man to be dead
But he should have remembered the law,
An eye for an eye and a tooth for a tooth that is why he is no more.

Arthur E Crisp

BAPTISM OF LOVE

Delight me with Your baptism of love.
Entice me 'til small waves of tenderness
Lap round my ankles temptingly and sweet.
Persuade me to adventure deeper still;
Immerse me in the loveliness of You

Til, yielding to that all-embracing flow,
Metamorphose into love itself,
And tell Your love with unrestrainéd joy,
And do become that thing I long for most,
Which may become to You a sweet delight.

Sarah Croston

LIFE IN THE CITY

Wednesday and Saturday were market days back then
And if you came from out-of-town the last bus left at ten
Thursday was half day closing, I remember it with pleasure
And Sunday was the day you could wander round at leisure
But city life has changed to seven busy days a week
Pavements resounding to the hurrying, pounding feet
Shops, banks and market days and buses by the dozens
Multi-storey car parks and mobile phones buzzing
The pace of life gets faster, money pours into the tills
Fast food and faster cars and plastic to pay the bills
But step thro' an archway, away from the milling crowd
Back to antiquity and to the history books so proud
For there stands the Cathedral that spans thro' out the years
Its overwhelming beauty can stir your heart to tears
Walk into its splendour - feel so human and so small
A special part of city life that's there for one and all
Sit for a while and feel the nostalgia in your blood
This golden crown of Peterborough is made of stone and wood
Centuries of history are steeped within these walls
And maybe if you're lucky you'll hear an old monk call
In this hallowed place there is peace all around
An oasis of tranquillity in the centre of our town
Echoes of yesteryear have a reoccurring theme
But in this growing city you can buy whate'er you dream
For alongside this haven flows commerce bold and gritty
In the ever-changing patterns of life in our fair city.

Sylvia Partridge

A BEAUTIFUL PICTURE

In the parlour high on the wall
Hangs a beautiful picture admired by all
It hangs there in a frame of gold
That's worth a lots of money I've been told

It's of a beautiful lady in a gown of blue
But who was she? How I wish I knew
Her bonnet's trimmed with ribbons and lace
And a fan almost hides her beautiful face
And what I can see, it's peaches and cream
This lovely lady looks like a dream

But was she really like she looks
Like the ladies in old story books?
Did she not grumble in those long gone days
As she fumbled with corsets, bloomers and stays?
Her lovely hourglass figure's not natural you know
Those whalebone corsets must have hurt her so
What of those boots buttoned up to her knees?
And those stiff, starched petticoats? No comfort in these

Yes she looks lovely but what a price she had to pay
That lovely lady of yesterday
But I still think girls should look like girls
With ribbons and lace, diamonds and pearls
But maybe our young ladies of today have it better
With their trainers, jeans, T-shirts and sweater.

Pearl Williams

COME THE QUIET NIGHT

Tumult, turmoil, hurrying day,
Never a moment to think, you say;
Head in a whirl, feet in a rush,
Oh for a minute of soundless hush.

Strange then how one's thoughts abound
In the midst of chores and endless round.
Come the quiet night to set them down
On migrant wings you find they've flown!

Priscilla Noble-Mathews

SUNSET

Shadows flit along golden sands,
Deepening feathers of darkness,
The sun an orange orb hanging low
In the sky,
Patterns of colour vivid seeming tangible,
Heralding another glorious dawn.

A breeze stirring the gorses,
Whispering in the grasses' secret words,
Everywhere in the coming twilight,
Small creatures scurry by,
Another day comes to an end,
Rays of colour and light spectacular to the eye.

The orange orb disappears,
Soft velvet darkness in its place,
Peace transforms the countryside,
An owl hoots its melancholy cry,
The time for thought, for meditation,
To a new dawn, to a new life beginning.

Elizabeth Hiddleston

KILLING TIME

The tiny golden grains of sand slip through my fingers
As the gale-force winds ferociously snatch them away
I'm frantically searching for my haven
No warning sign as I claw through the undergrowth

The lion is preening itself preparing to pounce
Forever extracting endless whiskers
Visions of tiptoeing around shards of teeth
Creases that have passed the point of no return

I'm trying to run, to escape from myself
I feel so helpless and trapped
I doubt the nightmare will ever cease
A sense of submission lurking nearby

Suddenly I realise I must strive to overcome this fear
I will fight the demon head on
I never give up that easily without a fight
And if it's to the death, cést la vie!

Diane Haworth

ORGAN MUSIC

Soft and gentle it calls
Recalling memories
A mediaeval wedding in flowing robes
Or 21st Century flowers, children,
Joy and sadness.

Loud and strident
Rousing patriotism
Past victories, here by the sea
200 years since Trafalgar,
60 since VE Day.

Hymn tunes woven together
Reminding of life
Patterns like the tapestry interwoven
Gold threads shining in our lives
Through the darkness.

Saints crowding round
Restoring faith
Some in stained glass, tales and tunes,
Others, our family and friends,
Surrounding in prayer.

Anne Sankey

CHATS WITH A CHIHUAHUA

Come, little dog, sit on my desk,
I know you are asking for a caress.
You mess up my papers, my pens go awry,
And yes, I can see the plea in your eye.

It must be soon, your actions say
When you could make time for walk and play.
Sorry, Gizmo, I've work to do,
Letters to write and pay a bill or two.

In your doggy world life is always fun,
You can please yourself to bask in the sun.
We humans are busy planning our day,
Come on, just a short walk, your eyes seem to say.

You've won, little lass, I'll rise from my seat,
We will walk to the park, your friends you can meet.
I glance at you, and, with a sigh
My work I resume, and let sleeping dogs lie.

Patricia Ayres

SONG OF THE HEART

She tried to sell a song to my heart
Yet the tune won't even start
As our time was set at the wrong tempo
The silence offers its own crescendo
I never expected any applause.

I've witnessed the same song turned into another version
Such originality is pure in honesty and devotion
But the key change of society is given a new setting
While I fret over the same solo that's never changing
Its reason is its cause.

She tried and tried and still the same note would hurt
Any persistency sees determination can only flirt
If the love song could ever be a classic
A deeper meaning found purpose the more romantic
The coda of love to begin.

I've searched for the personality that lasts longer
The rhythm of life that shares a beautiful aroma
So will such music be more than the last chord
The final piece of orchestration a legacy reward
While the song of the heart shall always enter in.

Alex Billington

SURVIVAL OF LOVE

I fell in love at twenty-two
With a sailor dressed in blue
We married, became man and wife
Settled down to share our life

The years went by and he did roam
Far, far way from home
Not just for a month or two
But two years he went with a crew

Life was great for a while
Our sons made us smile
Then off the rails he did go
I tried not to let it show

The things he did I took on the chin
No, I never did give in
All through the years my love was there
Although people used to stare

From the navy he did leave
Still wearing his heart on his sleeve
We made 50 years before he died
So that's how long this love survived.

Jean Bradbury

SOUNDS OF SUMMER

I sat in my chair, my eyes lightly closed
Listening to sounds as the birds sang above
The lowing of cattle, the curlews' shrill cry
As they dipped and circled the bright, summer sky.

The faint breezes stirring, the bees' lazy drone
From the distance the sound of some neighbour's phone
The sound of an aeroplane in the blue sky above
The bark of a dog and the coo of a dove.

The trotting of hooves from the lane just beyond
Croaking of frogs as they flipped in the pond
The smell of the lavender, honeysuckle and rose
Sweet-smelling herbs and fields freshly mowed.

I opened my eyes and in the once bright blue sky
Dark clouds had appeared and heaving a sigh
I gathered my thoughts, books as well
And made it indoors as the rain gently fell.

G Bree

THE STORY OF JESUS' BIRTH

In deep ecstasy
the most beautiful Queen
gets absorbed.

A mystery of love
the Father in Heaven
has disclosed.

Mary is enraptured
by His tenderness
and smiles like a rose.

After sleeping
in Her virginal womb
the Baby is born.

Lulling
the tiny, enchanting flower
She covers Him with kisses
and tears,
like dewdrops at dawn.

Fabian Montanaro

WHISPERS THROUGH THE NIGHT

Through the whispers of the night
The nightingale sings her lullaby
She flaps her wings, and takes flight

Sweet phrases, are heard, at twilight
When her valid, rich notes, echo high
Through the whispers of the night

Across her throat, shows beams of white
Her bill pointed, when she flies by
She flaps her wings, and takes flight

Beauty is seen, underneath the moonlight
As the moon moves, around the sky
Through the whispers of the night

An owl peeps down, from the height
And stares with her deep, dark eye
She flaps her wings, and takes flight

Her soft wings, spread, to her delight
As she watches, the nightingale fly
Through the whispers of the night
She flaps her wings, and takes flight.

Jan P McGovern

EMOTIONS

Let me dream, and through dreams
Put sorrows far behind me.
From the loss, with all the pain of losing
Faith and trust in mankind.

I ask where blame lies, all in vain.
When the anger and the tears are spent
For all the heartache and the sorrow caused
My heart cries out, oh please repent.

I try to recollect just what went wrong,
The decay of all the things that we held dear
There was a time when everything was golden
Just when the failure starts isn't clear.

Time to start again without reproaches
But no one's here to share an anxious day
To ease and help a very troubled mind
In all the fiction stories sinners pay.

'Tis said with time, that all our sorrows fade,
Perhaps the guilt lies here within my heart,
In time maybe, one sees it all more clearly
Remembering all the good times at the start.

Now it's time to turn the pages over
From experience one can only gain
Life's too short for recriminations.
Only time and understanding kills the pain.

J P Cook

THINK HAPPY THOUGHTS

Whenever you are feeling low and nothing goes quite right
Don't let it drag you down some more, instead put up a fight
And just to help you on your way, to get on top of things
Think happy thoughts and feel the lift I promise you it brings

Think hot and sunny days and sandy beaches far away
Think of the very favourite place where you would like to stay
Think walking in the moonlight with the person whom you love
With nothing else to share your space except the stars above

Think fondly of the good times shared together with a friend
In fact just think of any way your time you'd rather spend
Think only of those things that bring a calmness to your day
Think happy thoughts for they will always help you on your way.

Tina Sanderson

APRIL'S BIGGEST FOOL

'Look out the window,' you said with a smile,
'There's a snake in the garden the length of the Nile,
I know you hate snakes but go look if you dare.'
So I looked out the window, but nothing was there!

Two hours on, I was doing some chores
When I saw a small mouse scurry out of the door
Well, I jumped up so high that my head hit the roof
And I stood on the table not daring to move.

When at last I came down about 10 minutes on
The mouse had, thank goodness, apparently gone
So with no time to lose, and a good friend to meet
I walked out of the house and my heart skipped a beat!

'Where the heck is my car?' I shouted out loud
I ran round in a panic and soon drew a crowd
Then just as my neighbour was phoning the police
My *good* friend appeared madly waving my keys.

'It's alright,' she told me, 'your car is quite safe
And the mouse was not real and there wasn't a snake.'
It was then that I realised (although it seems cruel)
That today was the first and I'd been April Fooled!

Carol Biddle

THE VERGES IN SUMMER: BIRTH

Shoulder high the verges of mixed flowers bright
Their varied colour merges suffused with brilliant light

Meadowsweet's cream crumbly blossom 'gainst the purple vetch
Swathes of ghost green bedstraw luminously stretch

Sharp, spiked, tough, bold thistle pushes high its head
Leaves of rusty sorrel within the green turn red

Harebells, blue bellflowers, tremble in the grass
Whose feathery seeds show flaxen or softest sweet pink mass

Yellow-centred daisies display their virgin petals
Alongside tapering towers of spiky stinging nettles

Plates of sturdy hogweed above all others stand
Tempting iridescent flies to cease their flight and land

In hedge with curving fingers blond honeysuckle grows
Rambling high abundantly beside the pink wild rose

Probing climbing bindweed's tightening tendrils twine
Round and up for fleshy cup to utilise a spine

Sprouting with full vigour light creamy coronets
The elder bush is smothered by frothy flowerets

Clumps of strong, stout ragwort stiffly stand below
Golden in the sunshine dazzlingly they glow

In light against a background of trees' green foliage
A moving, dappled mass of leaves, a rich, dark curtilage

To these fine flowering forms the black dour soil gives birth
Producing and revealing the glories of the Earth.

J Faith

A MOUSE'S VIEW ON LIFE

Scurrying here, scurrying there
I dare not stay long anywhere
Dive into my hole, puffing and blowing
Family cat waits there, eyes aglowing

A hairy paw comes feeling in
Me in corner, make myself thin
He missed me this time, paw withdraws
Oh how I'd hate to be caught in those huge, huge claws

A mouse's lot is not a happy one
Creeping out, looking for a nourishing crumb
Incase old puss feels like some fun
Eyes alert - whiskers twitch, dash - run

Furtive and yet quick, a mouse has to be
Why did the creator make me - like me?
Oh how I'd love a gentle pat
Sweet purring sound from friendly cat

Have mice lives ever been like that?
Where a mouse could rest on any mat
And morsels left where humans sat
Some people might love me, how's about that?

Wishful thoughts, as I sit in my hole
Searching for food, my only goal
Dodging the cat with ugly claws
Looking for breadcrumbs, even apple cores

A piece of cheese - now there's a treat!
Now that would make my day complete
My wishful thinking makes me glad
As I sit hiding in my skirting pad.

J Howling Smith

FINDING ME

I haven't really found anywhere that I can truly call my home.
I've lived in many places throughout my life . . . yet still feel alone.
There's a feeling of quite never belonging . . . like a table
                                    without a chair,
As a gypsy I keep moving on . . . seeking here and there.
These feelings began when I was a child and they've left me
                                    feeling lost,
This emptiness has stayed with me . . . at such a heavy cost.
So many questions, a constant longing . . . I have this need to know,
I've looked so hard for most of my life . . . my quest continues to grow.
Why did this all happen? Did I do something wrong?
These crazy thoughts have stayed with me like an endless
                                    playing song.
They must have had their reasons as to why they gave me away.
I wanted to look into their eyes, and hear what they had to say.
Did they ever think of me, the daughter they hardly knew?
When all my life they've been with me . . . I have to know the truth.
Do I look like him or her? My mind is curious and wild,
I've longed to hear them say to me . . . 'You're still our precious child'.
They must have conceived me with their love . . . yet gave me
                                    to another,
I need to know why she let me go, I'm hers and she's my mother.
I can't move on in my life till I hear what's rightfully mine,
While I'm waiting on the answers . . . I'm standing still in time.
So many thoughts, unanswered questions, that's all I've ever known,
I surely deserve to know the truth . . I feel I'm on my own.
No one really understand me just what I'm trying to say,
Trying to find my way back home, like a child who's lost her way.
How could she take me in her arms and hold me to her breast,
Yet give me up to someone else . . . like a cuckoo in the nest?
I don't know them . . . yet I ache for them . . . and hope that
                                    they love me.
None of us can change what's happened, my life was meant to be.
But I have the right to ask them why and try and heal my heart,
They can't deny the past to me . . . of each other we're a part.
I need to know the answers and set my spirit free,
By finding them maybe I'll understand I'm really finding me.

Jackie Phillips

HALLOWE'EN

Witches, witches on the prowl
Watched by bat and tawny owl
Get too close and with rage they'll howl
On Hallowe'en

On their broomsticks see them ride
Wild hair streaming out behind
Mischief's what they hope to find
On Hallowe'en

Night-time filled with their cackles and screaming
Magic spells that's what they're weaving
Humans are best safe indoors I'm thinking
On Hallowe'en

They dance with trolls and goblins too
Their black cats spit and snarl at such a view
They'd rather hunt mice - they'd catch some too
On Hallowe'en

Shivering mortals stand and stare
Then shut their eyes tight and murmur a prayer
Those witches they get just any-old-where
On Hallowe'en

And if one should fly quite close to your house
Stay very still, be as quiet as a mouse
But remember - they're only on the loose for Hallowe'en
And then it's all over.

Mavis R Cocks

A Candid Wintering

('As he pores over his task, the writer's breath forms a film of ice over the paper on which the pencil frequently skids.' Captain R F Scott's Diary, from 'The Voyage of the Discovery'.)

Now that he is blizzard-lulled to ice
he cannot tell if this is land or frozen
drift-base. Floes warp within
his blood-straits, haul and yet compress
him, tick and hiss towards the watch's promise.

The stertorous ebb of others' breathing,
an iceberg salving, is candid wintering.

The narwhal wind, incisive and crevasse
deep, chuffs and tusks into the canvas.

Shut eyes flake out an Anarch's universe,
a bewilderment of snow manoeuvres.

Now base supply confuses steerage, storage.
The howling pack, the multiyear, will prise
apart the ribs unplugged by oakum, cordage.

Yet with shimmering costume, balletic promise,
the Aurora convinced him otherwise,
was both the destination pole and harness
with which he hauled survival over ice.

The pencil glissades. The fingers, nacreous,
though mittened, are meant to guide, to crystallise
what happens on a breathcold, frostfield page.

Until the nightfall of the cracked bell
annuls the watch, compounds the stricken hull.

John McPartlin

A Letter To Her Majesty The Queen

Her Majesty, the Queen! Answer me
Tell me, how can I get in touch with you?
I forgot to introduce myself
I'm that young, of great promise
I've heard that your castle is the heaven of peace
And your garden open to outsiders
I'm a bottle-fed child, I'm beginning to cut my teeth
I'm that orphan crying out in pain, enough to wake the dead
I'm that boy in the street, I've no diploma hanging on the wall
But I've an answer to everything
You mother of gloomy weather, diamond of the first water
Tell me, where are your good readers?
I'm that bartender, I'm that thinker,
And my words burnt to a cinder
Her Majesty, the Queen, answer me! I'm in a towering rage
I'm that writer and my paper's yellowed with age
I'm that bird of good omen, prisoner in my golden cage
And my innocence sold into slavery
I'm that busker, I'm always playing my own accompaniment
And the story of my life is quite romantic
Her Majesty, the Queen, believe me!
You can't see the wood for the trees.
As you come to me to see how the land lies
You, Her Majesty, the Queen! In that island of difficult of access
You're all sweetness, pureness and light, your woman whom I trust
You who have a power to act, I'm in hell of a mess
Allow me to sing in your beautiful streets,
To roam round your green wood
That will do me a world of good
I swear, Her Majesty, the Queen! To sink in my second childhood
To distinguish truth from falsehood
Her Majesty, the Queen! Forgive me my trespasses
And all my wishes for your happiness.

Lacene Rahmouni

Night Owl

Night owl howling inwardly,
hooting ouches of silent pain,
eyes blinking too wide and big
and scanning the screen-dark
for prey, some unsuspecting theme
to trap under talons and hold
for beak-ripping, dissecting,
the odd bits left for others
to make something of and consume
like offal, haggis, or white pudding,
a few herbs and verbs mixed in
and served up as a savoury dish
with my own personal je-ne-sais-quoi.
Bon appetit!

Adrian Brett

What's In A Dream?

Kaleidoscope images,
Sensual pigments,
Past life flickers
Converge in a sea of swirling,
Perplexing, wondrous fantasy.
True feelings emerge, surpassing
The mask of dormant troubles,
Heart pounding, waves of
Gyrating muscle force my chest
Into fearsome palpitations.
A sense of suffocation blinds
My existing thoughts,
Drowns the music of tranquillity
And sends my head reeling with
Indefinable panic. Why? For I am calm.
Heat bathes my extremities,
Composure contacts my inner being,
Touched to a state of paralysis,
Who shrouds the light, floundering to
Blind my vision seeping beneath a
Darkened cloud? Dazzling hues take me to task
In seeking the answer.
The reason for rooftops,
Silhouettes and shadows?
Another world merges and saturates
My soul with thankfulness.
The ultimate repose. Pursuing figures,
Please let me stay, remain
In my shuttered dream,
Along with this being, are we destined to meet?

Geraldine Frances Sanders

The Resemblance

Spring brings new life to all around
The evidence is shown on tree and ground
The summer's beauty with flowers in full colour
Is the climax of the year, so we discover.
Autumn's bronze and yellow bring a deep glow
The long days are waning now we know
Winter is here with twigs oh so bare
Bringing frost and cold but hope in the air.

Like seasons, humans start with life anew
Everything around them bears a rosy hue.
Youth comes with all its energy and glow
Trying to brave each turn and conquer every blow.
Maturity is wiser, calming the hurried pace
And knowing past mistakes were caused by haste
Age spans the years and lives for each new day
With faith and hope trusting God's promised way.

Joy Davies

MY GOD

My God, my God, I cry to Thee,
Why have You forsaken me?
To know 'tis I, the Chosen One,
Must bear the pain of love undone,
How long before this life I flee?

Will You not take this cup from me,
And send forth help to set me free?
Will You not save Your only Son,
My God?

The taunting crowd cries out, why He
Cannot redeem Himself, but see,
He lifts His head t'wards Heaven's sun,
To You, my Father, to You, I come,
My God.

Geraldine Taylor

ODE TO TRUTH

('I tore myself away from the safe comfort of certainties, through my love for truth - and truth rewarded me'. (Simone de Beauvoir)

Your eyes rest upon random letters.
Random letters make random words.
Random words combine to make random sentences.
Eyes rest on a random sentence.
The sentence speaks to you.
Random words, 'myself',
'Tore . . . away',
'Safe comfort',
'Certainties',
'Love for truth',
'Rewarded me'.
I see both the complexity,
And the simplicity of life,
Inherent in Simone's words.
The strangeness of her quote,
The very truth that lies within,
The very certainty therein,
That tearing myself away
From my former existence,
Through my love for truth,
For my self-respect,
For my growth as a woman,
In my hope for a future life,
Was the way forward for me.
Random words - a random sentence
A guide to life.
The truth.

Rosie Heartland

TRUTH

Respect your happiness to the full
But where is it you may ask
Where the heart lies I may answer
Not in the purity of dull.

Cherish the moment of bliss
But where does this dwell you may wonder
In the realm of the elated sublime I answer
Not in the realms of saunter.

Embrace the life of inner beauty
But my questions have made me weary you answer
My answers are not for yourself but your spirit
And you too can find them all within yourself.

Simon Rowson Clark

ON COVEHITHE BEACH

So hasten now to leave the beach
Where warmth and light are dying,
And seabirds mew their mournful cry
Where shallow pools are lying.

So take the darkening paths that climb
As peevish wind comes swirling,
Sculpting the dunes to patterns new,
A-teasing, scouring, whirling.

So come away and leave behind
Those whispering waves a-dancing,
For silent shapes, of shadows made
Seem suddenly advancing . . .

No faltering step, no backward glance
At some dark secret hidden -
Lest nameless, nightmare things you dread
Should leap the waves - unbidden!

Joan Brocklehurst

FINGERS

What remarkable things our fingers are,
They can thread a needle or push a car,
They can stroke a cat or bang a nail,
They can cut a shape or point a trail,
They can hold on tight or thrust away,
They can strike out in fear or indulge in play,
They can write a book or wash a face,
They break a glass or comb hair in place,
They can draw a line or splash on paint,
They can play a tune or bless a saint,
They can express love or tremble in hate,
They can wave goodbye or beckon fate,
They can do a million things all the time,
Even write poetry that has a rhyme.
We take them for granted and never think
Without them we would flounder and sink.
Dear fingers, how we appreciate you
For all you enable us to do!

S J Dodwell

MYSTERY TOUR

We're going on a mystery tour
To somewhere we've never been before

We might see a forest or even a lake
I don't know how long it's going to take

Just sit back and enjoy the view
And stop making such a big to-do

Let's look out for some cows or sheep
There's one on the road, *beep, beep, beep*

Phew, that was a bit too close to call
And we almost hit that dry stone wall

Never mind, let's carry on
The lane is clear and the traffic's gone

I think there's a picnic spot coming up soon
We should have lunch as it's nearly noon

A stunning vista at a tranquil spot
Look over there, a sailing yacht

We finish our day with a little roam
And now quite tired we head off home.

Lynda Hill

ON THE POINT AND LINE

Yes, that could be so, possibly.
But perhaps lines are hosts of brave
Points holding hands tenaciously.
And curvaceous, in the way that a wave
Crests and falls; or as tenuous
As enlightenment; or the heavenly
Transfigured souls, ethereally

In appointment with intangibles,
Learning whole worlds of new angles;
Or honing dulled scripture; or nervy doodles
That know not where they came from, why they thrived;
What's the meaning or the purpose intended,
Or how and where it will come to end.

And maybe, extraordinarily,
Short lines are single minute
Points, just momentarily,
Yet swift to change and reunite
As if long lost to real friends;
To recreate and, to celebrate
Being, and more, continuing
Behind all beginnings and ends.

So, teaming with subatomic division,
The sublime astronomic gathers, each line
As each point, blending magnetic cohesion,
In all eventuality; when true to time
And cosmic sound, hands in many ways enjoin
Kingdoms, dance to the rhythm and rhyme!

Ramon Gonzalez

LOVER'S WEATHER

'Rain? What rain?' I cry!
I cannot see the rain,
Who cares the weather through the windowpane?
I have my love, and when she sits by me
Then all is sun and sun is all I see.

What wind? I care not for the wind,
It cannot chill my heart, nor cool my flame
My love is heat, it burns and warms within
It takes more than the wind to cool my skin.

Forget the weather, never mind the storm,
I have my lover's kiss to keep me warm,
And so, held in her warm embrace,
The weather cannot touch me in this place.

Tony Harris

JUST US TOGETHER

What can I say after all this time?
We've lived with dreams, some yours, some mine
Many battlefields both charging crossed
Not all were killed, not all got lost
We'd live to fight another day
Love seems somehow to be that way

Life can play dull, full of routine
We often want to stop and scream
Looking over the fence we tend to stare
Is the grass really so green over there?
Thoughts we've both had you would agree
Thank God we're too old now to jump and see

We've grown together in some ways apart
Yet you're still engraved deep in my heart
You'll find me close, never far away
And that's how I want my world to stay
I may not show, not all the time
How very proud I am you're mine.

Rachel Kate

ANGEL

For I will watch you day and night
And never let you out of sight

For you will never be alone
For I will be your sand and stone

For I will help you through your days
I'll help you through in many ways

Don't grieve for me, for I'll be here
I always will be standing near

For I am the air you breathe
And therefore I'll never leave

I always will be in your heart
I always have been from the start

For I am your path of light
I always will put things right

For if one day you're feeling down
You know that I'll be around

Smiling down from Heaven above
Embracing you with wings of love

When times are bad, and you cannot cope
I'll be your guide, your faith and hope

I hear you when you kneel and pray
For I walk beside you every day

Liseanne Rix

TIME

Time is a curious thing
It starts by seeming endless
As a child a month was like a year
Birthdays and Christmas would never come, I feared
There was always time to play
Hundreds of hours in a day

But now I am older time goes so fast
Another birthday and Christmas just passed
No time to play
No time at all
To do all the things I intended
Time is a curious thing

As a child time was slow
My body was fast
Now that has reversed
My body is slow and time is fast
Time has turned itself around
From slow to fast in the blink of an eye

It would be ideal for body and time
To be in tune with each other
A youthful body and racing time
Growing older and slower together
Body and time going hand in hand
Instead of the opposites taking command.

Kathryn E Needham

STAR

Star,
Oh how you sparkle,
Star,
Oh how you gleam,
Your cousin is
The shooting star,
It flies so high
In the sky.

Corinne Kelly (8)

PRAYING IN HIS NAME

Through Jesus we make our requests
By His compassion stirred
Adopting His own attitude
And trusting in His Word.

The disposition of the Lord
Is what we seek to find
His sound, His light, His atmosphere
With these we fill our mind.

Straight be the wishes of our heart
Like arrows to the mark
Like birds that seek the watering place
Like torch beams through the dark!

So we become enveloped by
The answers to our prayer
And caught up in the joy of One
Who loves to show His care.

Peter Spurgin

MIRABEL

There are green buttons on the figs
The poppies bloom around my feet
The stones return the warmth of beneficent sun
The sound of bells re-echo from walls of golden brown
Warm breezes rustle the grass
My contentment is complete

Neighbours now aged and feeble prepare to leave
They forsake their earthly paradise
Built with such loving care so long ago
Made lovely by their art
Now need more care than beauty and warming sun can bring

When will the day come for me and him?
How can we bear to part with all
That has been given us in this fair place?

Eight hundred years ago when it was formed
Did other people long since dead have such sorrow?
Perhaps the short lives they led
Prepared them better for such partings
Or from their ceaseless toil
Or did such departure seem a great reward?

Pat Allington-Smith

FORGOTTEN WOMEN

Where are the women who mothered a nation,
Who cared for the men who are old,
Who invested their lives in love's expectation,
And wept when the young left the fold?

Where is the love that was promised by men,
And the arms that would ward off the fear,
And the kiss of affection when passion subdued,
And grew colder with each passing year?

They wait in the homes that were fashioned with love,
Enduring emotional hunger,
With no purpose left, they see in his eyes,
Desire for a woman who's younger.

Their beauty has faded as age dropped the net,
In the torture of silence they weep,
And the men have forgotten the care and the love -
The depth of desire is skin deep.

Men have measured their love in material worth,
For sex, youth and beauty they thirst,
But the sad and abandoned are called on once more,
When the old men come home to be nursed.

Wilma Whitla

RECIPE OF LIFE

A mother is so many things
From the time a child is born,
The busy days, those sleepless nights
Yet another day has dawned.

We teach them all the things in life
To dos and don'ts, right and wrong,
Hoping from the day they start
This is how they mean to go on.

The essence of truth and honesty
Self-discipline a must,
Knowing they go with head held high
When into the world they're thrust.

We listen to their stories
That tell of a broken heart,
Laced with tears and sadness
When from a love they part.

A good measure of love and understanding
We hope they will always be,
A proud figure in society
With a mind of their own that's free.

To have a sense of humour
So essential is this spice,
Also the milk of human kindness
Go forth, my child, through life.

This recipe of life, I gave mine
The flavour of which lingers on
Rich with a sense of fulfilment
Passed on from generations long gone.

Joyce White

DAYDREAMING

I would like to have been an artist,
I would like to have been a king.
I would like to have been a lady with a wide, gold ring.

I would like to have gone to China,
And walked along 'The Wall',
Or been captain of a 'Tall Ship'
Sailing oceans all.

I would like to have been a sculptor
Chipping away at stone,
Or roamed in some dark continent
Braving it alone.

I would like to have been an astronaut
Journeying to the moon,
Kicking up a heap of dust
At stroke of lunar noon.

I would like to have travelled Egypt
To view the mighty tombs,
Or wandered with the Bedouin
Among Saharan dunes.

I would like to have lived in India
With the British Raj,
Or baked in the heat of Africa
Watching the rhino charge.

I toyed with going to Persia
Before they changed its name,
Or trekking in Afghanistan
Before the Russians came.

But as with every daydream,
Regret, is how we pay,
For never doing anything,
And letting 'life' get in the way.

Frances Neale

KEEPING IT TIGHT

(In honour of Ian Williams, Skipper, Eskley Cricket Club)

When tactics are talked before the game,
And the batting is ordered name by name,
The advice from the Skipper is always the same:
'Just keep it tight, boys, just keep it tight!'

When the visiting batsmen are flailing the cherry,
And piling up runs and making merry,
The Skipper's instructions will never vary:
'Keep it tight, boys, keep it tight!'

When the bowlers are dropping it awesomely short,
And chances put down which ought to be caught,
The Skipper shouts out with a sort of a snort:
'Keep it tight, boys, keep it tight!'

When silly mid-off has been struck once again,
And still stands resolute though racked with pain,
The Skipper exclaims as he laughs like a drain:
'Keep it tight, boys, keep it tight!'

When he's run from third man to deep long-on,
And the batsman has flashed - and that's four more gone,
The bald-headed sparrow still sings his song:
'Keep it tight, boys, keep it tight!'

When the umpire's deaf, and blind, and mad,
And every decision he gives is bad,
The Skipper consoles the disgruntled and sad
With: 'Just keep it tight, boys, just keep it tight!'

And I've heard it said, and I'm sure it's right,
That when he's in bed and asleep at night
He's heard to groan with all his might:
'Oh! Keep it tight, keep it tight!'

But, sad to say, there'll come a day
When the Grand Old Reaper will have his way,
And Parson and Wardens and folk will say:
'Just screw him down and make sure it's tight!'

Raymond Holley

THE POOL

This glassy layer
That still so still repeats
The trees and sky above
Below
Where coots and swans
Inscribe their journeys
Oh so slow
On other days
Stirs and impatient waves
Rush here and there
In frantic haste
Before all calms down and once again
It ripples gently
Like breath-blown fur on cats
And then on days when summer's high
Its blue, still face
Has many eyes of lily gold
Looking skyward oh so gently bold
While village youth with nets
Dip and sweep
And wide-eyed wonder
At what each sweep reveals
From bulbous tadpole to tiny frog
To fiery stickleback
With jewelled eye
Revealing nature's complex simplicity.

Paul Gamble

ALL FOR LOVE

The Earth began with a big bang
Life by a thread did hang
Starting with a seed so small
Bringing forth from love, life's little ball
Creatures of all shapes and sizes
From the dawn of time to the first sunrises

Tears of joy for the first newborn
Even for the lion and the unicorn
From the stars that twinkle at night
To the sun that shines so bright
Giving flight to the wings of the dove
Beauty all around, given to us with love

Battles fought from age to age
To satisfy some great rage
Put your swords away
And let live for another day
Let us all become the mender
Our swords to love we surrender

So ring out those bells and let's hear the cheers
Sending out the message so everyone hears
Today is for being merry and bright
Let's all fly as high as a kite
Throw out the old, tattered and torn
This day for *Kevin* and *Dawn* a new era born

With a band of gold they plight their troth
They seal their new bond this is for both
Not till death will they part
Because their love is from the heart
The future is untold
But is theirs to take and grab hold.

Philip Clark

THE QUALITY OF OUR LIVES

The quality of our lives
Is bought with thought
Though rarely rooted
In the soil of self

Rather
Is it raised from seed
Nurtured
In the spiritual sanctum
Of the mind
Where the need is seen
For others of our kind
To love, to laugh
To care, to share
To strive for happiness

And if this quality
We would raise
And hold on high
We must forever toil
To keep the waters of the mind
Crystal clear
And free from evil of the kind
That nurtures jealousy, distrust
Enmity and fear
And brings us near to dwell
Forever in the halls of Hell.

Victor Lown

UNTITLED

I sit in my chair, and compose a rhyme,
I think in poetry all the time.
Look out of my window, and see the trees,
Fly with the birds, and sing with the breeze.
I see the sunshine, it makes me smile,
I'm lost in my dreams, for quite a while.
The buds are bursting, the grass is so green,
Now winter is over, I feel like a queen.
As I sit in my chair, I know it is spring,
When the sun starts to shine, and the birds start to sing.
It's my favourite time, I'm happy to say,
I'm still alive to start a new day.
My dreams are now shattered, with the sound of the phone,
I know there is someone, I'm not alone.
It's a friend to say, 'Will you come to tea?'
I'm back in the world of reality.

K J Wakefield

PRIVILEGE

We are your history enjoying your today
And we have time to be with you,
To read to you, contort ourselves to play
A just-invented game, time to supply
The answers to your frequent 'Why?'
                              Since you were born -
A distillation of your parents' deep
Abiding love, of many generations drawn
Together down the ages to be you -
We have held your baby fragrance, petal skin,
Exquisite infant fingers, seen your crawl,
Triumphant totter, sturdy walk, heard you begin
To talk. Now, soon, a canvas new, your school
And pride in drawings, Christmas plays. We shall be there
Involved, supporting, privileged that we
Are part of you and you of us. So much we share.

John Wedge

A MEMORY FOR ALL SEASONS

You will never be forgotten
Though you've gone so far away,
For I think of you with love sincere
Every lonely, lonely day.

I think of you each morning
As off to work I go,
I think of you each evening
As I watch the sunset glow.

I think of you in springtime
When the bird is on the wing
And wish that you were here with me
To hear the skylark sing.

I think of you on summer days
When to the sea I go,
Your face is still before me
It's as if you say hello.

I think of you in autumn
When the leaves fall off the trees,
It's as if I hear you sighing
So softly like the breeze.

I think of you in winter
When the world is grey and cold,
Oh yes, my thoughts are with you still
And full of love untold.

Sybil Edwards

ON THE MOORS

Scruffy ponies huddle together
against the hedge,
slight shelter from the bitter wind.
Their eyes red-rimmed, watering,
empty bellies rumbling.
Ears prick up,
Old Farmer Joe trudging across
empties a sack of windfall apples
at their feet.
"Ere I be, you poor old beggars,
ain't forgotten you.'

Iris Long

WE HAVE IT ALL

Have you ever wished for pots of gold
Or a beautiful mansion with wealth untold?
People at your beck and call
Priceless pictures on your wall,
Then look around, you'll be surprised
You've all those things before your eyes!
We all have riches beyond compare
A happy home when family's there
Always there to lend a hand
If you have a problem, they understand.
My priceless photos on the wall
My favourite ones when they were small
The love I feel when I see each face
No length of time will ever erase,
I have it all!

Jean Lowe

NIGHT'S MYSTERY

Subtle shading down of light
and then darkness:
absolute or starred or moon lit.
Sounds amplified or hushed:
for owl and badger business-time
for others sleep and forgetfulness.
Sleep unravels and ravels day's concerns.
'Sleep on it,' we say: night's erasure.

In this silent, lightless world
a baby was born - a morning star:
a body raised from death's sleep -
the harbinger of eternal dawn.
And night's mystery is our rebirth.

Roger Bellamy

TO OLIVE

Late autumn sun, whose precious beams
With beauty does the Earth enfold,
Paints every leaf and every tree
And tinges darkening clouds with gold.

Could I but hold this moment safe,
And arrest the transient light,
But alas my poor heart knoweth
The brightest day must end in night.

The dusk's chill wind is ever rising,
Portends an early winter's frost,
And through my fingers time is slipping
As another day is lost.

P W Pidgeon

ECT

Pinioned to a hospital bed, for
Electro-convulsive therapy
Drugged, deserted, and speechless,
With wires attached to the wrist,
Other ends go into black box at bedside,
The hum of electric currents, brown
Faces gazing down at patient, and
On floor two squatting attendants
Waiting with stretcher, as nurse
Leans over patient and speaks,
'Open wide, bite on this.' 'This'
Looked like a rubber dog's bone,
Then to the rising hum of electric
Currents, body contorted into
Violent spasms and convulsions
And enforced epileptic fit, then
Complete and utter oblivion.

Later patient wakes in hospital
Bed, in hospital ward, mind a blank.

Duncan Robson

SEEN FROM A WARM ROOM

Are we ever prepared for the joke of snow?
It sometimes lies
I've played the games with sledges and slides
white, sculpted men with coal-black eyes
now a coffee in my hand, I lick the edge of marmalade toast
and watch
a group of tricky youths with fists of hard, sealed snow
and hear the razzamatazz of Rap and laughs that ripple
through cold air

She sees them too and grins
a big, stout woman with reddened cheeks
a scarf tied under her several chins
impervious to cold and the weight of her sack
she engineers her bike to lean against my window
waves and fumbles in her billowing clothes
brings out a cloth
she stands and puffs, breathes deeply then blows
the wind takes up her tune and scatters her papers
like geese in flight
The game is on, lads, catch and count
slide and grab and stuff them back
she glows and blows and waves and goes.

Kate Johnson

DEAD IS THE SOLDIER

still is the soldier in death
in this green Flander's Field.
Once, a strong yet gentle lad
who shyly waved goodbye;
then donned a khaki uniform
and came to fight and die.
Alas, for him no welcome home,
no mother's warm embrace;
never to hear her call his name
or touch her tear-lined face.
No more to walk a country lane,
or sit beside a stream;
or hold a lover tenderly
or plan some future dream.
Here among the poppies,
caressed by butterflies;
in the quiet of eternal sleep
this son of England lies.

David T Wicking

SHE EMPTIED A CITY 2005

Katrina cast her spell that day
Yet, mighty nations would not dare,
Rough waves she brought to wash away.

The population cannot stay
In New Orleans all watered bare,
Katrina cast her spell that day.

On people often heard to say
Our city full of Jazz and flair,
Rough waves she brought to wash away.

Like some beleaguered, tragic play
All politicians to ensnare,
Katrina cast her spell that day,

Those left alive down would not lay!
While most all vow to return there,
Rough waves she brought to wash away.

Of the dead? She will rock and sway
For that all people must beware,
Katrina cast her spell that day,
Rough waves she brought to wash away.

L Coleman

UNTITLED

I am just a simple soul
Playing in life a minor role,
But if all of us in our own small way,
Helped each other through every day,
Filling our lives with loving and sharing
The spiritual knowledge of God,
And the way He is caring.
Lift up your minds from the material greed,
Pray for inner strength
And how to sow the seed,
For then you feel you have done what you can,
And become a more gentle
And tolerant man.
So as you kneel to thank your Maker
For helping you to be a giver not a taker.

I Vale

WHAT DO YOU WANT FOR CHRISTMAS?

'What do you want for Christmas?' I asked my little son,
'What do you want for Christmas? A car, a fort, a gun?
You are too young to realise, as you play there with your toys,
That somewhere in this world of ours,
Guns are killing girls and boys.
I hope and pray that as you grow you'll forget the warlike games,
And to live in peace and harmony will soon become your aims.'

'What do you want for Christmas?' I asked my daughter small,
'What do you want for Christmas? A doll, a bat and ball?
To you it's still like magic - this happy time of year.
Oh may it always stay this way, and not be spoilt by fear.
I hope your generation never has to feel the pain
Of loved ones going off to war, you might not see again.'

'What do you want for Christmas? You world of weary men.'
'What do you want for Christmas?' asks the Babe of Bethlehem.
'Do you want peace and brotherhood, and love for all mankind,
Or do you still want foolish wars, that maim, and kill, and blind?'
He can give us wondrous gifts of tolerance and peace
But first we have to find the way to make the fighting cease.

E Crowhurst

HEARTBREAK

In life some words are like a sharp pin
That punctures the heart and lets sadness in
And so it was as the doctor explained
What was wrong with my son and why he was pained

He'd reached midlife's span with minimum ills
Reasonably healthy and seldom on pills
Enjoying his life with wife and three lasses
Then dark clouds descended like loads of molasses

'His ongoing lifetime will be but short,'
Said the doctor and waited for our natural retort
But stunned as we were and with hearts beating fast
The only words uttered were, 'How long will he last?'

Through our mist-filled eyes and haze-clouded mind
We heard the doctor explain how the problem did find
And, sadly, all ongoing tests only increasingly stated
How badly my son's health had deteriorated

Life has to go on even though full of heartbreak
And we must treat each day for everyone's sake
Just like it was before the bad news was found
And fill them laughter, joy and love all around

'Tis true that no one said life would be easy
'Tis true that some days life could be queasy
But for occasions like this no words can console
The heartbreak that's caused not by pinprick but pole.

Archie Livingstone

HOW NOW?

How many waves make an ocean?
How many blues in the sea?
And if I eat another small chocolate
Will I store one big calorie?
Why does a cuddly black kitten
Grow into an ugly black cat
And eating nice things like chocolate
Make skinny people get fat?
How many slopes on a mountain?
How many steps do we climb?
How many letters and full stops
To produce sound reason and rhyme?
Can we measure the love in a lifetime
The plans, the hopes and the dreams
The smiles, the laughs and the wrinkles
The efforts, the backaches, the schemes?

I could spend all my long day just puzzling
Tide and the clock we can't fight
So I'll just stroke the little black puss cat
And hope that he won't turn to bite.

Winifred Smith

CELEBRATIONS

Balloons rising . . .
Champagne bubbles popping
Curled cucumber cooling
Music and dancing
Fragrant flowers towering
Butterflies flitting
Fountain showers
Faces beaming
White teeth gleaming
Finished writing
At an end.

Irene Patricia Kelly

ABERFAN

The little town of Aberfan has left a tragic mark,
That grim October morning, the weather bleak and dark,
The rain came down in torrents, the wind was blowing wild,
As children walked towards their school,
The children meek and mild.
At nine o'clock that tragic morn, there was a mighty roar,
Men knew it wasn't thunder, as they rushed towards the door.
They feared the worst would happen, that grim and darkened day,
And sensed a coal-tip sliding, they were numb in every way.
The coal tip was so angry, like a wild, demented giant,
And started sliding down the hill, so black, so cold, defiant.
Gushing, swirling, rushing, the blackened mud rushed through,
Everyone was helpless, there was nothing one could do.
Children now were screaming as they saw the blackened slurry,
Engulfing all their village school, there was no time to hurry.

Children they were buried 'neath stone and ugly coals,
Rescuers were fighting hard to reach these poor souls.
Panic now engulfed the scene, with men and women crying,
Digging on relentlessly, they did not give up trying.
Some children they were rescued, still screaming for their mates,
Why did this have to happen - why was it their school gates?
As long as I shall live on Earth, I can't forget this day,
A children's generation was so sadly snatched away.
The landscape now is verdant, where giant coal-tips lay,
Though landscaped and much greener,
The memories they will stay.
That day of devastation, so cruel, full of hate,
Why our little children - why did they meet their fate?
There'll never be an answer, as we look toward the sky,
And people all around the world still ask the question *why?*
They'll never be forgotten, and life will carry on,
We'll always see them smiling, in Wales their land of song.

Marjorie J Picton

SPECK OF HOPE

I shiver,
        There's no going back
I'll deliver,
        As I know I'm on the right track
Each time I peer
        They appear that much clearer
Each time the fear disappears
        As they inch that much nearer
Just as the setting sun
        Is swallowed by the sea
The words are out there
        And they're coming to me
Fresh as a new dawn rising
        The only speck of hope
            On my horizon.

Keith Robbins

VIGIL

Your hand I hold to share the pain
All else I have to offer
Are ears to lend when you complain
And heart to know you suffer.
A plea that He once crucified
Who rose again to live
Will now enfold you in His arms
That He may comfort give.

M P Webb

CRIMSON

(A poem for the love of my life, Fiona Spark)

On this chilly Canberra Saturday,
Your beauty is bathed,
By crimson . . .
The colour of a dying, summer sun.
I ache to steal your picture . . . per se,
Not your heart, or your life,
Just this image of your beauty undone,
A moment I wished to capture to paint some time far away.
I ask politely,
And quickly perhaps without thought,
No . . . I have lost and you, you have won,
You cannot keep the beauty I saw in Bungendore that day,
I can, I will,
Forever deep until this life is lost and run.

J S Liberkowski

A FIREFLY

Nature's lamp, dainty, distinctive and bright
In shadowy places illuminates the night.
Quietly following its chosen path
Leaving no traces of its fleeting light:
A jot of beauty with no aftermath.

Anonymous, unheralded it comes and goes,
Impossible to entrap its tiny glow.
Yet my treasure glows forever
Beguiling, daring my love to follow,
Holding fast my heart in gentle tether.

Petite, precious and incandescent,
My lamp's flame is ever-present.
Emanating from her delightful frame
Her lovely aura is heaven-sent.
Carole is her name.

Allen Jessop

BATHTUB BLUES

My bathtub spoke to me tonight.
I hate to admit it but it did.
It was rather rude, really.
At first I thought I was hearing things
It said, 'Boy, you have an ugly bottom!'

I was affronted.
I didn't know what to say,
So I put in more bubble bath,
And laid on my stomach.
But I couldn't hide it.

Then it spoke again,
'Heh, and your face is just as ugly.
As a matter of fact I can't tell them apart!'
I thought, *what? Who bought this tub anyway?*

I could tell by its speech it was old,
But I kept my mouth shut, and pulled the plug.
It drank as though there were no tomorrow,
Then it belched and went to sleep.

That's when I realised it was on a binge,
So I needn't take it seriously.
But I think I'll wear my swimming trunks tomorrow,
And perhaps put a washcloth over my face.

Nick Porter

CAT

I love thee, O Cat,
For achieving unity between the realities and the trivialities
    of life; for retaining regality when discovered indulging
    in a fish-entangled dream of cream with whisker-twitching
    anticipation.
I love thee, O Cat,
For the height of the lithe lightness that leaps to the
    inconsequential feather; for the depth of the deep contemplation
    that muses on the hidden truth buried in the huge universe;
    for the breadth of the untouchable serenity of feline peace.
I love thee, O Cat,
For thy perfection in a world imperfect which makes thee not
    a lover but Love, not a hunter but Fate, not a killer but Death
    itself.
Because I have loved with Love and fought with Fate and am
    doomed to Death,
I love thee, O Cat.

Catherine Gregory

THROUGH THE LOOKING GLASS

On display in the mirror frame what can I see?
A rather strange woman looks back at me.
Face, which is care-worn, strong, yet round.
The beauty of long ago, now not there found.
Ears that are hidden, because they're too big.
Hair tied behind them, a less glorious wig.
Eyes, which are deep-set, now hooded, less clear.
Jaw, which has double chins hanging, I fear.
Nose rather large, with freckles now sprinkled.
Lips less defined, and neck lined and wrinkled.

Where has she gone, that creature so fair,
With shining green eyes and lustrous long hair?
Where are the keen eyes, smiling lips and good grace
That boys, long ago, sought quickly to chase?
Where is the swan neck, the nose, oh so haughty,
The very quick wit and the humour so naughty?
How and when did she leave? Where did she go?
When last did I see her face all aglow?

On display in the mirror frame what do I see?
A rather strong woman looks back at me.
Beauty is timeless. Experience the true measure.
Memories and a life well lived is rich treasure.

Christine Frederick

INNER CHILD

Inside my head lies the child in me,
The little child the world can't see,

A hidden spirit,
A hidden waif,

Inside my head the child is safe,
Weaving dreams of futures past,
Weaving dreams that cannot last.

Inside my head the child serene,
Accepting changes seen, unseen,

The wise child knows that it must live,
To learn to love, to love to live,
This child endures in spite of me,
This child grows to inspire me.

A place, a time, insight of me,
A space, this space,
Where the world can't be.

Marilyn Jones

How Sweet The Taste Of Jesus

Oh how sweet the taste of Jesus
When just a seed He first bade us
To be one with Him, free from sin
To purify and wash us from all dross.
By His blood He made us clean
By His grace He took our cross
Sweat His blood under a crown of thorns.
Bore our pain, ridicule and scorn
Took upon Him all our shame
Took our curse, hung and died, for us
Just that we might be the same.
Unto us with love He came
His arms outstretched His heart laid bare.
He weeps for us, will we heed His call?
His love so sweet, yet He tasted gall
He surrendered to death for our need.
Will we surrender to Jesus our life to share?
Let the warmth of His love nurture our seed
Come before Him and stand
Reach out and grasp His outstretched hand.
Will we echo His plea?
Father, forgive us for we know not what we do
Jesus, build in us new hearts in the fullness of You
In humble adoration we bow low
As we behold the promises You decree
Beloved Jesus, You did it all
In You, and through You, 'It is finished'
May the glory of You shine here below
And Your love in this place be furnished.
Release the power of Your Holy Spirit from within us
Oh how sweet, how sweet the taste of Jesus.

Jenny Minor

Deluded Mind

On and on went the sycophant
blatantly unaware of the sickness
he was causing, or was he?

So deeply embroiled had he become
in the world he had created for himself
that he could no longer tell fact from
fiction.
Yet still he carried on unaware
of the sickness he caused passers-by.

Persecution mania was his favourite
he'd play this to the hilt if there
was a captive audience.
Yet they too became sickened in
the end.

Then came visions of grandeur believing
he was above the rest yet he still
felt the need to creep.

Now truth and lies were mixed together
like an unbalanced pudding.
Yet still he carried on.
And on the odd occasion, one
would catch a glimpse of the eye
of deception, so calculating, so very
aware -
For this soul, there was no
return. Only endless mind games
and black, black holes of misunderstanding.

A J Marshall

My Childhood Wartime

(Read out on air by me with Bill Buckley, 'Tea At Three' guest on BBC Southern Counties Radio also BBC Essex Radio)

I remember the day Neville Chamberlain gave us the news
It gave my mum and dad and me the blues -
We sat round the wireless to hear what he had to say
He said war had been declared on that Sunday -
The sirens sounded and there was still everywhere
To think what was ahead of us we did not dare -
We put up the blackout and checked our gas masks
My mum was busy with so many tasks -
Dad went as usual to work although it was hard
When he got home there was a letter from the Home Guard -
The letter he got had OHMS on and gave Mum a fright
She thought Dad had been called up and would have to fight -
I went to school with my gas mask in a box
Mum gave me dripping sandwiches and I had holes in my socks -
Our school was bombed and the ceilings came down
There was terrible damage all over the town -
Croydon Aerodrome had planes that went up to fight
They even chased Germans from the sky at night -
We had Anderson shelters that were put in the ground
As you slept on the bunks you could hear every sound -
Ration books, identity cards and things in short supply
The Germans were relentless with their bombs from the sky -
Sticky tape was put on the windows just in case
Hitler dropped one of his bombs and blew glass in our face -
Stirrup pumps, water buckets and sand bags were at the front door
Walking down our streets you could see everyone was at war.

Eddie Owers

The Rainbow At Ely

I saw a rainbow in the eastern sky
It was as pretty as it was high
I don't seem to see them as much as I did
Or perhaps I don't look as often as a kid

Maybe that's the reason grown-ups don't see so much
Because as we get older we start to lose touch
Children are forever looking all around
Left and right and even upside down

Then one day they get all mature
And find their vision has become obscure

The rainbow at Ely made me feel young again
Special and happy and free
In future I'll look harder for rainbows
And maybe they'll look harder for me

I hope so.

Lord Ciaran D'arcy

My Family

I have got seven lovely daughters, also I have got four boys
When they were all much younger they had loads and loads of toys
There were dolls and prams and footballs strewn around the floor
Whips and tops and marbles, one could hardly get through the door

They are all more or less grown up now with children of their own
And now my family has dwindled, there's only one son left at home
I'm a widow and thought I'd be lonely
I miss him and always will too
But now there's the grandchildren, all twenty-eight
So I've no time at all to feel blue

The love that surrounds us is wondrous to see
What more could you really expect?
After all I'm a mum and a nanna
And this then is my family.

Jean Skitrall

THE FIELD OF HONOUR

Running for cover,
Arms held wide.
In fear of war,
With hearts to hide.

A silver blade,
Cuts deep and cold.
Blindness and
Relief it sold.

Shoot to kill.
Shoot to ease.
Hands raised high,
And on your knees.

Calling out,
Across the dark,
The voice you hear,
Grates cold and sharp.

Watching now,
For movements, still.
A chance with God,
And a gift to kill.

Rally cries,
On deaf ears fall.
You do your best,
And they want it all.

The trigger squeezed.
Warm death descends.
Upon your aims,
A heart depends.

Flowers drift,
On winds of change.
Caught in fire,
Or out of range.

It does not matter now,
You fear.
For all you've killed,
Are hopes held dear.

Gordon Finlay

MEMORIES OF THE PAST

Looking back across the years,
To days that used to be,
Remembering those far-off times
When there was so much poverty.
Outside the local labour exchange,
My dad would join the queue,
To sign on for his dole money,
Like thousands of others did too.
For years they were signing on,
Recession had taken its toll,
There were never any jobs around,
They had to sign on the dole.
But many will remember,
How it used to be,
Struggling to make ends meet,
To feed a family.
Things were cheaper in those days,
There was very little money,
Often we had bread and jam,
For us there was no honey.

Jenny Rose

THE FINAL CALLER

I am Death
I will know when to call
I am Death, you can't escape me
I live in you all.
I am Death, you may delay me
For a while or so but
I am Death and when I say so
With me you will go.
Your journey towards me may be
Arduous, painful and long but
I am Death, you can't forsake me
You must go where you belong.
I am Death and I may take you
Before your life's begun.
Yes, I am Death and however
Painful my job is never done.
My name is Death and in spite of it all
I will be the last one to call.

Sandra H Seed

SECRETS

I've got so many
Blockages in life
As well as in my mind

I've to clear a lot
Of clutter from
My house
Inside and out

These have given me
Conflicts now
Which are a lack of
Connection with others

Bric-a-brac has
Always followed me
Around when I've
Moved from place
To place.

Tony Parkinson

UNTITLED

I too
Have seen the blue mountain
Change
To grey
And
Melt away in mist

I too
Have seen the valley fading
And have traced it out
For comfort
Fingering the wet face
Of the darkened ghyll

I too
Have waited for the hardening rock
To return
Again
To echo the sharpness
Of a welcoming sun.

L Simcock Daisy

THE MAN WHO PASSES BY

What kind of world is this, where hate and want and fear
    Oppress so many of the people here?
Where men of the same blood take bombs and guns and knives
    And burn and maim and kill and terrorise.
Where staring eyes gaze sadly, without tears,
    In stark remembrance of bitter, dreadful years -
Numb, devoid of hope, they wait
    For death, in bleak acceptance of their fate
    This is a world where heartless, powerful men
    Exploit the weakness of the poor and ignorant, and then
Live out their days as if in some unfeeling trance
    Whilst those four horsemen make their ineluctible advance.

Here, on this sheltered, scept'red isle we feel apart
    From war, starvation, tyranny; with thankful heart
We bless our way of life, but we are blind
    To a corruption of a very different kind;
A way of life where wealth is worshipped as the whole
    And the body has more value than the soul.
For we are judged, on this still lovely Earth
    By beauty, intellect, material worth
Society pursues these 'gods' with great persistence
    Because they seem to represent our whole existence.

Pity the poor, the ugly, the desperate, homeless ones
    Whose 'staff of life' consists of rich men's crumbs;
Pity those who never have been loved, who then
    Become unlovable and grow to fear all men.
Pity those who in a world of thoughtless greed
    Are made to struggle for each basic human need
But what of him, the man who passes by,
    Who does not spare a thought, nor give a sigh?
Desolation, loneliness, misery, despair -
    Do not concern this man - he does not care.
The cult of self awareness, the doctrine of success
    Encourage him to live a life of studied selfishness.

Happiness to modern man means riches, property and power . . .
    They beckon him, they urge him on,
They tempt him, hour by hour.
    Pity him, this gold brings no true pleasure
But envy, covetousness, lust in fullest measure.
    Unmindful of his soul's great need of Christ
He eagerly pursues his hedonistic flight.
    Yet all about him lie the means for his redeeming
But he is blinded by self-love and deaf to all their pleading.
    He clutches all the while at trivial things,
He stumbles and he trips
    Whilst rushing, headlong, toward his soul's apocalypse.

Una Davies

AGORAPHOBIA

My head; spinning with allusions,
my mind; fighting through confusions,
my heart; delicate as lace,
my hands; covering my face,
my eyes; blurring all I see,
my legs; collapsing under me,
my breaths; growing ever faster,
my thoughts; flirting with disaster,
my spirit; watered down and weak,
my outlook; overcast and bleak,
my body; losing all control,
my parts; begging to be whole,
my life; a jigsaw missing pieces,
my hope; that confidence increases,
my goal; to put it all together,
my chances; a little like the weather.

Andrew Clough

WINTER WARMTH

Snow's muffling blanket coats the land,
bleaching fields and trees,
blacking out street lights, domestic stoves and radios,
leaving only Heaven's bright eyes
to wink at candled windows.

Inside intimate rooms, warming flames
leap and glow, defeating the gloom;
exchanging grey smoke for white flakes
above the chimney tops.

Feigning a former age, children sit on cushions,
with cards and counters,
playing Ludo, Snakes and Ladders, Snap,
as if TV and computers were disinvented.

The firelight's warm, homely gleam
spreads the smell of toasting bread
and a tin kettle, steaming on a trivet,
calls like a bird, to tea.

Catherine Curtis

DIANA

You had beauty
Along with grace
You had a lovely
Smiling face
Warm, compassionate
Loving too
That's why the people
Cared for you
But suddenly
Now you've departed
You've left a nation
Broken-hearted
William and Harry
Are grieving too
But we know your love
Is shining through.

B Holland

A WINTER LANDSCAPE

A soft, white scattering over the land
As if a giant sieve in a giant hand
Has sprinkled a fine sifting of icing
Over each tree and field.

The hard, brown Earth beneath
Striped with furrows straight,
The labour of the farmers
Working hard and toiling late
Into the night, into the winter,
Their work openly revealed.

And the trees silhouetted against the greying sky
Intricate workmanship by a skilful weaver,
Leafless, rounded, lacy, skeletal,
Displaying the monotone beauty of a winter's day.
Understated elegance, wispy, ephemeral.

And so the landscape that could seem so colourless
Is touched with winter's softening, beautifying glaze,
Is lit by sunshine's sparkling, glowing light
Transforming each field and tree, hill and stream
Into the frosted glory of these snow-filled days.

Jenny Dukes

INCANTATION AT HELICON

(Erato's whisper to Hermes, pausing at Hippocrene)

Once stranger on the strand,
The beauty of you,
Precious pearl within the golden
Stretch of fountained reach,
The measured choice of your given kiss
Of flying fancied spindrift touch,
Is spun into my soul.
As Pegasus struck rock
So you brought forth release,
The springing of the sensual draught,
Refreshing succour to thirsting need.
The cool blue shade of you
Eased my burning brow,
And flying with you for a treasured while
Expanded seen to liminal dream.
Now, pausing in your flight
Across the sky to other worlds,
Know as the wind blows,
Whispers of this truth
Will permeate the universe,
Befitted rapture, imbued in being
Will scream in stormings,
Be borne on howling tides,
Sigh through memory, drift in darkness,
Be found throughout all time as constant,
Love.

Lesley Clary-Sage

AS IT PASSED ME BY

When I was laughing, singing, dancing and a bit shy
It passed me by
I try to remember the many things I was doing
And I wish I had realised what it was
As it passed me by.

But I didn't even notice it
Oh how it did fly
As it passed me by.

Now when in my armchair I sit
I recall the days when young and fit
And I know it no longer passes me by
Because it has gone, that is true
Yes, what passed me by, it was my youth.

But I didn't even notice it
Oh how it did fly
As it passed me by.

Chris A Davidson

BEQUEST

It was,
they say,
an arranged marriage,
but she nagged
and he scattered
his seed o'er the land.

When everything in the Garden
ceased to be lovely,
they stomped out of Paradise,

leaving Milton material
for a great epic,
but little success with marriage.

Mary Nugent

TRANSPOSE

Route away from the urban grim, hassles.
Curve upwards, roam a grey road.
Pass white hamlets, nurseries bloom.
View purple ranges shrouded in mist.

Tall silver bark trees, Mountain Ash.
Eucalyptus vapours heady, strong
breathe in. Silence enfolds, fulfils.
Breezes whisper, ancient splendours.

Bell birds echo staccato notes.
Magpies warble trembling throats.
Kookaburras mimic all, ruptures silence.
Animated lush fern, fronds flaunt.

Silence! Dry wood crunches, hush!
Soliloquy! Interlaced branches speak,
trickling stream answers alone, overflows.
Earth-filled Heaven, alights the soul.

Dorothy Grey

THE PASSING YEARS

The years go swiftly by
But in their passing
They bring the minds of thoughtful people
To various ways in which they could help
To stop the upheaveals
Which are shattering the wondrous beauty
Of our Father's creation

The surest way to live
Is by 'The Gospel of Christ'
And the result would be far reaching
For it would teach mankind to be
Thankful for their daily bread
And not waste God given time by thinking of ways
By which they could outdo their neighbour.

E Hodson

THE SEA

The sea!
The giant sea!
Its ebb and flow
is all we know.
What is it thinking?

So gentle,
yet so fierce
            as it crashes
                     across the strand
and invades the land,
            bringing fear . . . and death.
What is it thinking?

It is our friend
When, with bucket and spade,
            days have no end.
This morning it was far away,
now it comes near.
We are told to wish it goodbye
            until . . . next year.
What is it thinking?

It is time to go.
We must hurry
            but we dawdle
                     as we prepare
and watch the sea
            lapping a lonely deckchair.
What is it thinking?

Kinsman Clive

DREAM MAKER

Little man, with funny feet
Bowler hat, and baggy seat
Bendy stick, all fall down
Charlie Chaplin, wears the crown.

Stan and Ollie, double up
Pickfords, drink from loving cup
Buster Keaton, Keystone Cop
WC still the top.

West and Harlow, wink the eye
Valentino, makes them sigh
Silent horror, with no scream
Hollywood magic, sells the dream.

Laughter maker, wartime tale
Sweet romance, men from jail
English, Yank, some from France
Lively music, makes them dance.

Moviola brings a tear,
Sometimes fun then it's fear
Camera rolls, dream makers
Behind the glitter, money takers.

On the screen, a laughing face
At the bar, all heartache
Plastic kisses, on the screen
Lonely Girl, a movie queen.

S T Vaughan

TRAMP'S FIRST CHRISTMAS

I felt lonely that festive time
when my heart and home were lost
My actions and deeds of time just past
how could I have known the cost?

I wandered about, searching my soul
thinking of all I had done wrong
I looked through the window, they were having a ball
and heard the birds sing no more song

Alone on the floor, in that dreary place
with no food to fill the hunger
The ache, the pain, tears on my face
I lay for three days in sombre

Alone in the dark, at New Year's break
my face had just dripped a tear
With no one to laugh, no hands to shake
and no friends to wish Happy New Year.

Al Whittle

SALISBURY CATHEDRAL

As you go around a corner
You see before your eyes,
The towering spire of Salisbury
Soaring upwards to the skies.

Such beauty takes your breath away
And tugs at head and heart,
Such glory and such grandeur
Makes one wonder where to start.

That many hands could carve and work
And many give their lives,
To build this glorious edifice
Of worship and of love.

You know that even as you stand
In awe and feel the glory,
That somewhere in this church's soul
Is an everlasting story.

Mary Cole

FAIRIES

There are fairies at the bottom of our garden,
That's what my grandma would say,
I believed her then, and I believe now
That they live just a dreamworld away.

They can only be seen through the innocent eyes
Of a child, or by those who believe
In the whisper of wings in the morning mist,
As they flit through the webs spiders weave.

Their gossamer wings sparkle like dew
On the grass, in the first morning light.
As they dance through the flowers, and chase butterflies,
They twinkle like stars in the night.

They hold all the magic of a child's first dream,
All the wonder of a wish that 'might be',
The enchantment and mystery of imaginary things,
That charm and delight those who see.

So take care when you go down your garden at night,
Listen carefully; you might hear them laugh.
But you won't see the fairies if you don't believe,
So take care if you stray from the path.

Alan W Davis

AUTUMN

It's my favourite time of year
When golden leaves on trees appear
When leaves are falling from the trees
And dancing in the autumn breeze
When Mother Nature's in her gown
Of autumn gold and golden brown
And children running through the park
Are rushing home before it's dark
And the wind, so clear and fresh
Sends tingles through your face's flesh
All these things, for me are true,
It may mean something else to you.

David Wallace

SOLDIER OF FORTUNE

I have led a hundred soldiers against a terrible foe,
I have plundered whole villages and done more than you will know.
But I have saved a baby from all of this,
Found in a house on fire, his life I could not dismiss.

But you have asked for mercy, and today is judgement day,
Someone else has to ask for your forgiveness, before I let you pass,
Is there someone you have saved worthy of this task?

I have led a thousand soldiers,
And done more than you will ever see,
I have demolished whole towns, the one in charge was me.
But I have saved one small boy,
I found him amongst all of the mess,
I dug him up from the debris, now I am here to confess.

But you have asked for mercy, and today is judgement day,
Someone else has to ask for your forgiveness, before I let you pass,
Is there someone you have saved worthy of this task?

I have led a thousand armies, across terrible terrain.
I have obliterated whole cities, and never felt the pain.
But I was killed by a young man, I recognised from long ago,
I asked him for his forgiveness, if he gave it I do not know.

But you have asked for mercy, and today is judgement day,
You have been forgiven by a young man, who said to let you pass,
Pass, Soldier of Fortune, for this judgement is your last.

Emma Lockyer

WILL YOU BE THERE?

You are so sweet,
You are divine,
I wish you could be
Forever mine.
You're in my heart,
And always close,
You are the one
I love the most.
So will you be there
When I'm on my knees,
Asking you to be mine please?
Will you be there
To hold me tight
So I can make it
Through the night?
I'd be so pleased
If you'd love me so,
My feelings are strong,
And we've far to go.
So please give me this,
And make it true,
Cos there will always be
A me and you.
My entire future
Lies with you,
I love you so much,
Please say, 'I do'.

Lily Pepper

THE RIVER IS FLOWING

I know the river is flowing from my deck;
The trees are rustling in the breeze,
And a violet rose petal floats by.
A whisper in the air, little fairies play with the spring water.
One fairy caught the violet rose petal and gave me it.
And I have had magic powers ever since,
But I've kept it a secret with the river-fairies ever since.

Sunny-Laverne Sharp (8)

LUNCHTIME RECITAL

He sat in isolation,
Avoided by the well behaved,
Respectable music lovers, who
Ensured an empty seat was left
Each side of this newcomer to
Their Friday feast of Sweelinck
And Ruppe.

Could he too love music? This
Tattered remnant with greasy beard
And dank, crusted hair?

Yet his silence was contemplative
As he searched the programme with
Battered magnifying glass and
Thin, wavering fingers. As the great
Harmonies bathed him with swelling
Sound he did not notice the sidelong
Glances from the washed and the well fed.

Had he too eaten? Or had hunger fled
As his pilgrim soul filled
With a prelude of Paradise?

Bronwen Vizard

NUMEROUS FELICITATIONS

It's with pride and the greatest of adulation, a pleasure
I put these thoughts into verse
Heartiest of 'congratulations' are offered amidst all mirth
To the Forward Press who have corrected and nursed
So many aspiring poets and assisted them in their work
All owe a debt of gratitude, from this they will never shirk
If it were not for their kind understanding
Perhaps we would not be?
It is marvellous to view in print and read so eagerly

May all further success continue in those years that lie ahead
With many further aspirations as the contestants' thoughts are read
To all staff we raise a glass of 'bubbly' as we salute you all
Especially to the founder Ian Walton
May he prosper and never fall
Your publications are delightful as we celebrate and cheer
Those volumes that are produced and the poets hold so dear
To see one's name in print as we poets reveal our thoughts
Worldwide is your fame as poets travel
And hence wondrous reports.

On this special occasion as we celebrate your anniversary
We that contribute give credit in its entirety
To a remarkable staff who are employed so courteous and kind
To those many unmentioned even those that bind (the books)
Designers and the minor staff who play so many parts
Our thanks at this special occasion which includes their art
I could go on describing as this typewriter flourishes along
To wish the Forward Press most sincerely in verse or in song
Continuation with such merit and satisfaction proved
To grow even more strong as progress ensues.

Regards and many, many 'congratulations'.

R D Hiscoke

THE RUIN OF BEAUTY

An epitaph for tomorrow
Being written out today
To build to future sorrow
And turn all colours grey
When we see all tarmac widen
Smother flowers and weed
All this we tend to pardon
So we can get more speed
When we see the last three hued fall
With its eggs and nest
We'll see the landscape bare
Except where power pylons rest
The spreading cement is spilling
Designs all out of hand
Man's rape of beauty killing
God's green and pleasant land.

Joan Patrickson

DIVINE LOVE

Upon the saving Cross I see Him in His awful agony,
And in His eyes is that reproach?
No! They are full of love for me.
Oh! How can I repay such love?
No sacrifice is asked nor deed,
And yet there is a gift
Though small,
I can give my heart, my all!
For as He gave His life for me,
I will live my life for Him.

Jeannine Anderson Hall

ONE SMALL PIECE OF DOWN-LAND

I sat in sunshine in a place where join
Men's habitations to the countryside
Yet green and fair. Here moments do bestride
Ages and intervening time purloin;
These four yards of grass overlie the ground
Where now some forty years of kin deceased,
Aligned as on parade, their souls released
But by stark stones kept, mem'ries lost and found.

I and my brother, two among the last
To know these folk, all sev'n - when we expire,
Who without them never were, ancestry
Ourselves shall be. Our children gain new past,
Since allied with other clans they conspire
To build our future of their progeny.

C J Hewish

DESERTED

Shrieking seagulls soar
through a clear blue sky.

Waves lap.

A lone crab sidles
hurriedly from a nearby pool,
across the deserted sand -
then over rocks and hardened driftwood
towards the sea.

On the horizon, a boat bobs
in the translucent green water,
smooth white sails catch the breeze.

I sit on a sand dune
watching warm sand between my toes.
Sea grass whips the air around me
and the salt spray stings my face.

I feel alive, but peaceful,
in this tranquil place - here
I can think, clearly.

Helen Marley

FLOWER ARRANGERS

God is the first arranger
        Of flowers great and small.
He put them on this Earth for us
        To grow and love them all.
Not just exotic beauties
        That come from hotter climes
But violets and daisies
        And graceful columbines.
Cow parsley and celandines
        Like little yellow suns
Peep shyly from a grassy bank
        And convolvulus that runs
Around the trunks of trees
        And up the garden wall,
Just waiting to be admired
        And noticed by us all.
Then walk into your local church
        And say a thankful prayer
For our faithful flower arrangers
        Who use their art with flair.
To the glory of our Father,
        Who loves us all the best
And when your back starts aching
        You can take a well earned rest.

Beatrice Jones

WINGS OF FRIENDSHIP
(The Spirit of RAF Burtonwood)

RAF Burtonwood opened in 1939
With the Battle of Britain, it was just in time

The American air force arrived in '42
Waving their own flag of red, white and blue

To assemble the aircrafts and give support
To the war in Europe that was being fought

The airbase, as it was known
Became Little America, home from home

Spitfires and Bombers, the planes of the day
All took to the skies from the airbase runway

Life in Warrington then changed for a while
And we got used to the American style

The GIs taught us how to dance and sing
Along to music that they called Swing

The Berlin Air Lift, a major role was performed
Through the Cold War era, and later, Desert Storm

All the above is now in the past
But the friendships made were built to last

The gates finally closed in '93
Leaving us wondering of what will be

Soon unveiled as the future plans
Of this once exciting, busy land

Burtonwood Airbase will always be
A special place in Warrington's history

So fly high the spirit of RAF Burtonwood
Fly high, as only you could.

Alison Robinson

HEARTSTRINGS
(Dedicated to Alan)

I've tried so hard to put you from my mind -
I've distanced you by staying well apart
Yet deep within the shadows do I find
My love for you grows stronger in my heart!
I hear scintillas echo from the past -
Reminding me that others played a part!
But you were first and then you were my last
And in-between no one had won my heart!
The future then would seem the place to go
Yet why am I resistant to depart
Into the arms of one I've come to know?
Is there unfinished business in my heart?
These heartstrings will forever be caressed
While hope springs so eternal in my breast!

Arlene Skerratt

A ROSE

A rose, a full blossomed bud,
Growing alone on an overgrown shrub.
Holding its face to be kissed by the sun,
Before the wind blows and its petals are gone.
Just for a while its glory is seen,
Its perfume lingers where once it had been.
Now only the stem and thorns are left,
The rose that once was, is now only a hip.
Brightly coloured, and full of seeds,
Shaking its head in the breeze.
The rose lives on,
Its story is told.
Tinted in dreams with pale,
Pale gold.

Aileen Andrews Jordan

THE FIRST FALL OF WINTER SNOW

Oh, land of magic all aglow,
Transformed in the silent night.
Oh, fairyland flaked with snow,
Alight with brilliant paint of white.

Grassland, meadows, cornfields,
Leaning chimneys of rooftops old,
Coated now with snow that shields
Your nakedness from winter cold.

Rosebuds shrivelled within winter frost,
Sleeping blooms in muddy earth.
Blessed land we treasure most,
New fall of snow, gave life new birth.

Frozen icicles, snowy white,
Tingle sweetly like silver bells,
Shine with sun, tinsel bright,
Fragrant perfume, nature smells.

Church clock tower tall and high,
Robins, red breast on tiny feet,
Timid, hopeful, brave, yet shy,
With happiness new day they greet.

Frozen streams are resting still,
Ducks and swans spreading wings,
Giant wheel of watermill,
A calm peace from nature springs.

Clear blue sky with warm sun,
Blessed land forever glow,
A magic day has just begun,
With the first fall of winter snow.

Shula Bailey

THE LAST WORD

Mother, do you love me?
Father, do you pray for me?
Sister, do you understand me?
Brother, do you speak my words?
Friends, will you look at me?
World, do you hear me?

Mother, will you love me till the end of time?
Father, will you pray till time's end?
Sister, will you tell them who I really am?
Brother, will you tell them the words I speak?
Friend, will you let them see the true me?
World, do you know me?

For you brought me to this world,
With hopes and dreams I knew what I was.
You loved me and prayed for me,
You gave me joy and happiness,
You gave me words to speak.

For now I'm gone, the love I shall leave behind,
The prayers answered and words spoken.

Don't love me for I have gone,
Don't pray for me for I have heard your prayers,
Don't mourn and cry for I have left you love,
Don't sit in darkness and memories for I have sent you my words,
Yet I'm gone, yet I'm here in your dreams.

So tell the world
The words I speak,
For I have forgiven,
Will you?

Paul Parkin

SORROW

The constant motion of life around him
seems unreal, and the long moment of his
suffering rushes around and around in
circles; making each day akin to its
brother, and as his pain engulfs him;
he does not seek from within it, sympathy,
condolence or understanding.

He is doomed to be solitary, but because
of it has no bitterness against the world;
from which he seeks only simple but great
things.

The sea, trees, flowers, brother wind,
sister rain and the golden rays of the sun,
for he has left behind the encumbrance
of endless repetition. No longer is he a
Philistine in a mad, conceited and rushing
world. A place of pitiless greed and coarse
brutality, and as a mere spectator of life;
looks upon the broken heart of the world;
as from his sorrow comes love. Which to him
is the only truth.

A E Mae

SPIRITUAL FLIGHT

Spirit soaring high above Kinder Scout
Arms spread wide
Like golden wings

Gliding from ridge to valley below
All senses alive
Tingling within

Smells of nature wafting by
Ever changing greens
Of fields and trees

Wind rushing by in urgent call
Streams of sunlight
Pouring down

Distant echoes of ramblers free
Earth and sky
Singing in harmony

Sailing on the air's current
As an eagle free
In spirit go I

Karen Pratt

PEACE IN THE WORLD

We all long for peace in a world gone mad,
With bloodshed and fighting and people so sad.
Mothers without sons and wondering why,
And can't come to terms with it as hard as they try.

Why do people hurt each other? They call it a cause,
People so angry and trying to settle old scores.
Starving children who stare with empty eyes,
Tummies so empty you can hear their cries.

Surely we could live together in harmony not strife,
Surely we should value another human life.
We just live in hope that this terror will go,
But when and how we cannot know.

Barbara Ann Barker

BUTTERCUP MEMORIES

I used to run through the bluebell and buttercup fields.
Head over heels us kids would run and enjoy the sun,
Picking the flowers for our mam.
The clover, the grass were so special to us.
We didn't have to look over our shoulders and rush.
We had the delights of playing in hay,
And making grass skirts so we could play.
The stream was our dream,
Catching fish in our jam jars tied with string.
Oh yes, and we knew how to sing.
Home to Mam for bread and jam,
And if you were lucky a slice of spam.
No biscuits for us or orange juice
But plenty of stews that were good for us.
(And lots of steamed pud).
We used to make pretend perfume with the rose petals
And pretend we were posh and special.
Yes, we enjoyed our childhood
Though we didn't have much,
But we had our mam and that was enough.

Connie Lunn

THE PATH OF LOVE

Butterfly, as you flutter in the afternoon breeze -
Where have you been today?
Over hill and vale and on hill top high

    Flying like a bird in the breeze -

When I think of your beauty and how delicate
You are, as the soft breeze carries you along
The shadows of the afternoon lengthen and say . . .

    God's *love* is like a *song* -

So sweet to your ears and soft on your brow . . .
Music to your soul within
When you open your heart, to let *His* love in -

    Then your *love* with Him will begin . . .

So, butterfly, as I watch you flutter
Your wings along the path of love . . .

    In my heart I say, 'yes'
    God's love is like a *song* -

    So please teach me how . . .
      To sing.

Val Backs

DAUGHTER OF THE DANCE

The wind whispered manna on marble lakes
And upon the town sent the swarming flakes,
Until the tumultuous thick grey slate
Cracked its broken rock beside heaven's gate
And fists sprinkled their glowing purple flames
Upon the mountains and their velvet names,
Like brothers sleeping deep in ancient dreams
Of warriors hidden by laughing streams;
Sweet as she who grew flowers in my brain,
Poured dreams into my lap like winnowed grain;
For those violin smiles would never cease,
I saw the Spirit of love, joy and peace
Was deep in the eyes of every glance,
Held captive with a daughter of the dance.

Kevin J Foulger

THE WALLED GARDEN

Early autumn,
The moss-encrusted wall
Safeguards the ripening fruit
From predatory foe.
At dawn
Sun-promised rays enrich the scene,
Gold-painted earth
Shines through the lifting haze.
The gardener
Stirs within his cottage walls,
Refreshed from sleep
He plans the coming day.
Along the path
With eager quickening step,
Helpers from the hamlet
Gather for the fray.
Nimble fingers
Pick the pears and plums,
Plump red berries gathered in
Before the setting sun.

Norma Rudge

FACTORY LASS

Not for her the status of staff
Nor salaried in office spick and span
Dress of gingham with ribbon adorn
Denied for a drab apron worn.

Factory Lass her labours began
Endless race against time clock within
Her daily task would alone conjure
Tumult of sounds then did endure.

From early morn till eventide
Obeyed the master's call
Meagre wage for daily chore
Tender years, alas forbade her more.

Workdays ceased, time clock lost its awe
Home and rest, then Sunday await
Factory Lass emerged like butterfly born
In dress of gingham with ribbon adorn.

Harold Taylor

THE SECRET PLACE

There is a secret place of velvet-black
And cobwebs wet,
And when my world is grey and drab and cold
And I am wearied of fast growing old
Then here I hide.

The door disguised as oyster shell of smiling lips
And opaque windows shield the moisture lurking
Impassively conceal the pulses jerking
And my heart's beat.
This corner of my heart is mine alone,
Mine own retreat.

'Tis then I face the world with surface smiles
The world knows not
That in my secret heart I bow my head
I banter as I'm bid
But in petal peace and lightless quiet of mind
My soul is hid.

L Fulker

WAVE THE WAND OF FREEDOM

(New PC words for the music of 'Land of Hope and Glory', part of Sir Edward Elgar's
Pomp and Circumstance March No. 1' op.39)

Wave the wand of freedom
Wave the dove of peace
Bless the worldwide nations
Make all bloodshed cease

    Broader still and kinder
    Kindled with new love
    Make each nation wiser
    Richer with our love

Spreading ever further
Constant through the world
Let each person witness
See the power of love

    Fondly let us greet you
    Take from you your trust
    Clasp each hand on meeting
    Giving you our trust

Wave the wand of freedom
Wave each dove of peace
Bless each worldwide nation
Make the bloodshed cease

    Broader still and kinder
    Kindled now with love
    Make each person wiser
    Richer with new love.

Richard Stoker

LAND OF MY BIRTH

We travelled over lands, both near, and far
But nothing could I find
Not one thing more beautiful
Than this dear land of mine;
    I know, the weather . . . so unpredictable
At times how hard the wind doth blow
Then at times to my surprise
A blanket of deep snow
From day to day the sun may shine
Giving to us the warmth - amid the rain
Then before we realise, all is fine again;
    We never lack for water
To quench a dried up throat
Unlike many in far-off lands
So many should I try to quote;
    Nor seldom do we see typhoons
Or whirlwinds with their force
Clearing the way of everything
Standing on their course;
    Whilst earthquakes devastate the lands -
Around the world, both far and wide
Many drown beneath the waves
Brought in by the angry tide;
    There are countries where the land is so dry
Parched by the lack of rain
Nothing grows, most die . . . hunger and the pain
So I thank the dear Lord of mine,
Giving to me, the land of my birth
I realise, and I'm grateful
To sanctify its worth.

Leslie F Dukes

MOMENT OF TRUTH

We came out from the jungle by the estuary
knee deep in river ooze, our faces grey, cursing the leeches
and burning them off one by one with butt ends.
Bursting through the last trees by the shore
we saw a sight like theatre when the lights go up,
sun blazing down on a beach gold as Oz
licked by a sapphire sea, a painted paradise.

It was spontaneous, uniforms scattered on the shore,
rifles flung beneath a coconut tree, forgotten.
That afternoon we frolicked in the shallows of the sea,
limbs white in sunlight, naked, fragile, free.

Acting our age we kicked a ball,
waiting for it to fall and hoped it never would.
We lost it all too soon, kicked too far it fell
among some rocks, and searching there we found the smell,
a fat dead pig, guts swollen with gas
lying there, rotting in Eden.

What was the truth about this place?
Was it that moment of magic in the sun
when we were transported back to Eden's paradise?
Or the pig left rotting on the shore,
that taste of Hell on Earth?
Subdued we dressed and quietly left the place,
even the jungle seemed more welcome now,
a place where sunlight and decay both play a part,
but a place we could rely on to be neutral.

Ron Woollard

THE NEST

High up in nude branches of a tree
I saw a bedraggled nest.
No thing of beauty
this windswept nest.
And yet, and yet, my mind
flew back to spring
when in its heart lay warmth and love,
with the gift of life it had been blest.

On a winter's day, in a muddy lane
I saw a neglected house.
No sign of life,
no children's cries,
and yet, and yet, my thoughts
flew back to other years,
here was I born to warmth and love
with the gift of life I had been blest.

Deserted house, deserted nest,
your work is done,
love lingers on.

Margaret Renshaw

TIME THE TYRANT

Time calls you from
Your fields of play,
You must obey.
Your destination. Clay.
Time calls in May
Or in winter's chill.
Obey you must
Destination. Dust.
Your once bright star
Is dim and wan
As you flee to
The arms of oblivion.

T F Ryan

TREE LAMENT
(Inspired by Rudyard Kipling)

Most trees are felled in their prime
British soil to adorn
Who will blister in the midday sun
without oak, ash, only thorn?
Sing oak, ash, with thorns in our flesh
Where's the clean air? Lungs consume fumes!
Gone the glade, providing shade

Oak enhanced the forest of Sherwood
feuds near Nottingham began
Ash of the loam was Marian's home
when Robin was her man
Thorn of the downs plus new towns
Supermarket plonk, replaces pubs and beeroffs!
Majorettes waving candyfloss sticks
gone the glade, providing shade

It's no use thinking we can change things
soldier on, see what tomorrow brings
Sing oak, ash, with a sore burning rash
gone the glade, providing shade.

Jennie Hudson

GRAND CANYON

The world split wide and left a ragged scar,
Which though too old for legend, myth or creed,
Men sculpted into palaces and domes
As if transfiguring those chance designs
Could bind them to our selfish fantasy.

There is no drama here, no metaphor.
A silent, cosmic fissure, ocean deep,
Defies our facile instruments of words,
Constructed image, symphony of sound
With which we would distil significance
From that primeval vastness, self-defined.

So why invoke the artifice of reason,
The messages of faith or tools of art
To pen within the cage of consciousness
A presence that existed before mind,
But one that we can take into ourselves
As naked spirits, happy just to see?

Rex Baker

CONSCIENCE

If conscience is the guide we follow
Can we now repent the wrongs
Sometimes unknowingly we caused
To those we love
Which now are history?
Does not the conscience of the deed
Repeal the hurt
And clear the book of debt
Owed to all the wronged
Into whose life we trod?
It is unlikely to change the way we are
The wounding in our wrath
Could I my faults dispose?
With eager will, I would
Conscience is the guide of right
Which knocks when what we do
Does not equate
When causing hurt
Unfailingly we feel shame.

William F Park

MY LOVE

This message comes with all my love,
To thank you the way
You have brought happiness
To each and every day.

Thank you for all the loving things,
That always mean so much.
Your smile, your kiss, your tenderness,
Your warm and caring touch.

I think of all the quiet times,
When we were all alone,
Magic times for sharing,
A dream all our own.

The memories of sweet yesterdays,
And most of all it's true,
Thank you for the special joy,
I found in loving you.

Love was the warmth that filled my heart,
Whenever you were near,
Love was the joy you brought me,
Whatever day was here.

Love was the world of happiness in loving you,
Which I know will be forever true.
Your love, you, and all you did each day,
Meant more to me than words can ever say.

D Kirk

CHRISTMAS

Moonlight, sparkling on the snow.
Candles, in the windows glow.
Christmas trees, with fairy lights.
Children's faces, lit up with delight.
Toys, balloons, and gifts, galore.
Carol singers, at the door.
Charities, asking for a few pennies more.
We, try to do as much as we can.
For, the aged, the blind and the homeless man.
For, children's charities and animals too.
They, all need our help and donations too.
It's, Christmas and the angels sing.
Praises, to our newborn king.
He, came down from Heaven above.
To teach us all the meaning of *love*.
And, we'll continue to adore.
And, love Him *for evermore*.

A merry Christmas, everyone.

Isabella Anderson

A GARDEN IN SPRING

Colours splashed on earthly canvas,
masterpieces happening,
nature's palette,
mixed with raindrops,
capturing the joys of spring.
Brushes held by moonbeams' fingers,
cloths of sunlight, steeped in dew,
smudging, stroking,
adding sparkle
with a touch of stardust, too.
Works of art, so rare and precious,
free to view, not locked away
in a rich man's dusty strongroom
hidden from the light of day.

Sally Thompson

CELEBRATION

They said it's a celebration, you really can't ignore
Must do something special now you've reached the ten
And three score more
Did they buy my wincey nighties before the pension book
And talk to me so slowly with that patronising look?
They think I've booked with Saga for a slow trip on the Nile
I've got some get real news for them, this oldie's still got style.

I've bought myself a Lurex skirt, worn above the knee
Added some matching trousers, 'cos veins don't look good on me
My hair's streaked red and purple with colours that will glow
Plastered on the Panstick, hope the wrinkles still won't show.

Spent hours in the mirror perfecting every move
I can strut with the best of them, I'm really in the groove
I've got myself some ecstasy in case I start to slow
At my birthday celebration where the call is *go, man, go!*

I'm sure that I'll be noticed; they'll remember I was there
As I dance around me handbag and wave me knickers in the air
I'll be stupendous, I'll be spectacular, yeah, I'll really be too much
Recorded local history
The night I kicked the 18 to 30 disco into touch.

B J Davis

AEON

My orchard blossomed, in the moonlight
'Neath the darkly-brooding flame
Of other stars, soft stole the midnight
Each flower bore thy deathless name
Lilies, paler than the corpse-kissed
Roses, like the blood of mortals
'Ere long, thou swoon'd upon the wraith mist
Of desire's night-scented portals
And all that evermore existed
Were the witch-jewels of thy gaze
By the Morpheus, we trysted
In a violet-opiate haze
The starry wisdom of thy race
Saw the marshlights turn to neon
The sacred-geometry of thy face
Haunts the wraith mist still, sweet Aeon.

Velvet Dusk

WHISPER IN THE WIND

As the wind blows it carries to me,
The smell of pine, echoes from the trees.
Faint whispers that are carried in the air,
Voices from the past, but nobody's there.

Childhood memories of places I have been,
Now left far behind. They seem but a dream,
Pictures and images, stored into the back of my mind,
Released to tell a story of a life left behind.

Memories of children playing in the sun,
The air was filled with laughter.
Life was so much fun.
Now we're older and wiser too,
But the children are still playing as we used to do.

Schooldays were the best days of our lives,
We learnt to work, to play, we were so alive.
When we left, some moved away,
Losing contact with friends we saw every day.

As the wind blows it carries to me,
Memories of what life used to be,
Voices from the past, that are no longer there,
But the memories are just a whisper in the air.

Andrew Brian Zipfell

COMETS

Stars, flowers, stones,
dead poets forever young,
you are visiting our dreams
again and again,
weaving new lifelines.

Men, women,
children, you who came
to violent, untimely death
throughout our history,
forever bleeding - and singing.

You who travelled
from every horizon,
to prisons, to death camps,
from Santiago to Siberia,
from Granada to Baghdad . . .

All of you speaking a sacred language,
so many more following your searchlight.

I think too of the unborn poets
who might have opened their eyes
if their mothers and fathers
had not been slaughtered
in futile fights, in crazy conflicts.

Flying into eternity,
you carry on talking to us.

Antoinette Marshall

SHADOWS

Shadows on my ceiling, shadows on my wall,
shadows made by firelight are the cosiest of all,
logs in the hearth akindle and the moving pictures start
to bring back thoughts of yesteryear I hold within my heart.

The *Man in Black* whose chill voice came from out the radio,
and asked two trembling sisters
had they *turned the lights down low?* The
questioner had no answer as within the shadowy room we sat
with breath abated for weekly tale of doom!

Though God has played *fast forward* with my life of long ago, I still
return to the child's bedroom where I loved the firelight glow;
I lay on downy pillows and gazed above the door,
where a shadowy world of islands strange were waiting to explore.
Or when the measured candlestick, we trod the darkened stair,
shadows of hobgoblins lurked - we always saw them there,
and so with hearts athump we'd reach the safety of our bed,
we prayed those brooding shadows were angels watching overhead.

So when my children blithely say the good old days were bad,
I meditate on what they've got compared with what I had -
their life is bright and neon lit; no shadow of a fire,
and their radiated *Servowarm* is all their hearts' desire,
but I smile for I know that they're missing out,
for there's nothing anywhere that I'd swap for those shadowy
firelit years and the glow on a loved one's hair.

Dorothy Brookes

CLOUDS

Clouds floating up on high, then with one puff they float on by.
They're not there to stay too long, they just go slowly drifting on.

And some clouds look brilliantly white;
They look as if they've been washed at night.

I wonder from those clouds I see,
If someone is looking down on me.
Now when I ponder upon that sight,
I see clouds in a completely different light.

Susan Wells

LILIAN

In my dream I saw her -
Back in the vista of the past.
I was ten, and Lilian eight,
I stood transfixed and watched
My childhood faraway friend,
Glimpsed through an open garden gate.

In my dreams I saw her -
Through a sunburst of secret shadows,
I watched her run and leap at overhead
Boughs, too high above her reach.
In my dream -
I sensed all colours, scent and sound,
Grasses swayed beside the narrow lane,
Ethereal dandelion seed heads blew around.
What was the time of day?

In my dream I saw her -
Dark hair tumbling down her back,
In her short, green dress,
Her long brown legs and feet,
Danced in scuffed shoes.

In my dream she saw me -
She turned awhile to tantalise,
Before dream shadows enveloped her form
And face.
It was then I saw the light in her dark eyes -
And I recognised a ghost of a smile.

Kathleen M Smith

25/3/05 - 6AM

I awoke to the sound of the birds in the trees,
What a sweet sound it was.
As I lay in my bed I thought,
Savour this moment because you never know
When it could be your last.

I lay there continuing to listen to the sweet
Sound of the birds on the morning air.
What a joyous sound they were making.
Then I remembered what day it was, Good Friday,
The day our Lord Jesus Christ was crucified.

Then my thoughts turned to Carol, our lovely Carol,
Who's never done no harm to anyone, who's
Carried on her fight against her illness,
And I feel sadness in my heart of how
She has suffered and hardly complained.

The birds continued to sing sweetly in the trees.
My thoughts linger with Carol and I send
Out my prayers and healing thoughts to her,
Knowing that this is the most I can do for her now.

Sweet hour of prayer my
Loving thoughts are with you, Carol
And I've watched you battle so bravely against the odds.
May you be gently laid to sleep and
When your earthly body is no more,
Your spirit will find peace and be free of pain.

Never fear your crossing of the Great Divide,
For those loved ones who have passed before you
Will be waiting with outstretched arms,
To gather you up and comfort you.

Irene Morgans

THERE'S NO GOODBYE

There's no goodbye, Molly, we're not apart
We are one in all we do
For true love will never depart
My life evolves around you.
This world has little meaning if you were not there
Without your love my hopes would die
Each thought we have is ours to share
Of these facts I would never deny
I cherish you in loving mind
Two souls can meet in divine love.
What greater glory can I find?
What greater testament is there to prove
We're in two worlds yet they are one?
My thoughts dwell in our togetherness
The actions that we have done
Evolves in spiritual success.
Our spirits climb the gradient path
To where eternal bliss is ours to meet
Entering the path to aftermath
Where all seen is so sweet
But you are my guiding star
Your love I carry all my life
It will journey us on far
Molly, my darling wife
Each day I feel you nearer
To the day we will finally meet
And to me there's nothing greater
When our trials have been complete.

L Gould

CELEBRATION

Now is the time to celebrate.
It's that time of year.
Another anniversary date;
Let's give a great big cheer.

Let us raise our glasses
To all friends old and new.
To health, wealth and happiness;
Prosperity in all they do.

Let's hope that many more years,
Shall pass along the way
To add quiet contemplation
To achievements of the day.

Shirley W Parker

TONGUE-TIED

I would that I could open up a book
that sang of you a symphony in sound.
I would that I could clean the clearest brook
and steal the words within its whisper found.
I would that I could fathom in your look
the soaring spring wherein my heart has drowned.
For, ever since the day when first I took
your hand in mine, 'twas then I knew. The ground
dissolved beneath my tongue-tied feet and shook
the addled rafters of my brain. The pounding
of my heart stood still, on tenterhook,
for fear you were a dream that might rebound.
        I have no words that ever could suffice -
        nor dare release you to their sacrifice.

Nigel Hunt

CHRISTCHURCH RIVER WALK

All around the moor I see -
There's sky, the earth, the dogs and me,
Bronze of bracken, red of hawk,
Moss and lichen, teasel stalk;
Along the shore at high tide mark
Amidst the wood and rotting bark,
Bits of plastic, fraying cords,
Rear marram tufts like Celtic hordes,
Bracing themselves with flying hair
To fight the fearsome winds that shear
Through grass and plant and battered tree.

The black crows stalk the river's edge
Bordered by banks of rustling sedge,
And far out in the estuary reach,
One giant's leap from sandy beach,
Seabirds mass on mud flats bare,
Probing the reed for brackish fare;
Soaring up and wheeling high
They turn and dip in sunlit sky,
Caught and held in beams of gold
As day becomes night's frosty cold,
Then rest, to find tomorrow's pledge.

Deirdre Hill

THE ANGEL OF LOVE

The angel of love lives in the heart,
I know that this is true.
He speaks to me daily, offers advice,
And tells me what to do.

Dispense God's love to the people you meet,
Their lives will be changed you'll see,
For love is kind, and soothes the mind,
Do this work for me.

Hugs and kisses can mean so much,
Take up the challenge, my friend.
Love is a potion, keep it in motion,
Till life comes to an end.

Margaret-Anne Heap

GRANDMA'S LAMENT

The years have flown by - how you must have grown,
I try to remember your face.
The small child who hugged me must now be a man . . .
You're sure to be tall - that's my guess.

How I wish I could see you and hold you so close,
As we did in those bygone days.
But, you may not know me, I've changed so much too . . .
I pray that your memory stays.

My hair once was flowing, curly and dark,
Now it's wispy and heavily grey.
I carried you easily, long years ago . . .
Now I'm older, and ache more each day.

Bat and ball in the garden - our favourite game,
You'd smile now to see me, I'm slow.
If you could just reach me, I know I'd feel strong . . .
With your hand in mine, life would flow!

But if you could see deep inside me, you'd know,
My heart's full of love for your touch . . .
You'll know me I'm sure - on that day when we meet,
Darling Grandson, I miss you so much.

Wilma Jayne Gravenor

I WANT . . .

I want to be loved
for who I am,
not what I do.

I want to be respected,
because I've earned it
not because I'm old.

I want to be held in high esteem,
because of my brain
(oh yes, I have one)
not because I cook a good roast dinner.

I want to be spoiled,
because I deserve it
not because I demand it.

I want to be admired,
because I am average,
not because I'm a beauty.

I want to be appreciated,
because I am me
not because of etiquette.

I want the rose to bloom all year,
because it is my favourite
not because science will probably find a way.

I want the world to be reborn,
pure, innocent and with a conscience
to start afresh - for all our sakes!

I just want to be loved

because . . .

Marliese E M Porter

ODE TO WILDLIFE

As I gaze from my window each morning
What a wealth of great beauty I see.
In the garden and pond
And in woods just beyond
So much wildlife just waiting for me.

On the bird table sits a young squirrel
For his breakfast he patiently waits.
Always first in the queue -
But to give him his due
He will leave some behind for his mates.

Round the edge of the pond birds are bathing
Must be more there than up in the sky.
Oh what heavenly bliss!
As the sun plants a kiss
On a frog who pops up for a fly.

In the woods at the top of the garden
All the badgers now peacefully sleep.
They'll be down later on
When the daylight is gone.
If I'm lucky I may get a peep.

Tell me, where would I be without wildlife
That abounds in my garden all year?
Butterflies, birds, frogs, bees,
Badgers, squirrels, all these.
I'd be quite lost without them I fear.

Hazel Russell

I'm Not Gone

I am not gone while you are here
So keep me close and have no fear
I am in every breath you take
I am not asleep I just won't wake
I am the gentle breeze you feel
I am not gone while you are real
You'll feel my presence all around
I am not lost, just can't be found
Every place you visit just wait and see
Some small thing will always remind you of me
So please be happy, don't mourn too long
I may be dead but I have not gone.

Elsie Cooperwaite

Poetic Rambling

I took my poem for a long walk
down a quiet, country lane.
What were the simile and meta phor?
I thought it looked like rain.

I lost an iamb in a hedgerow
and a magpie flew off with my dactyl,
a robin made a nest of my stanza
beside a flowering cranesbill.

We saw a couplet of frogs
on the edge of a Skeltonic,
but though they croaked with delight
their friendship was purely platonic.

The track was rutted and dry
and my sonnet got a bit dusty.
My haiku blew inside out because
the wind had turned quite gusty.

My verse by now was quite blank, so
I plucked a rhyme from the bluebells.
My caesura turned tail for home where
I penned a few villanelles.

Lucinda Hearne

Twenty-Four Hours In Winter

The watery morning sunrise
Gives way to January grey,
Horizon blends into the mist
That hangs over rain-sodden clay.

Stark silhouettes of winter trees
Stand silently in the haze,
A few lonely seagulls screech overhead,
Sad reminders of lost summer days.

Tired little sparrows and blue tits
Hop about looking for food,
Saving their song for better days
When their voices will lift our mood.

As evening falls, an air of quiet
Brings with it the threat of snow,
And we shiver in the eeriness
Of the skies now half-lit glow.

Tomorrow may bring us an icy start
And a brand new landscape to view,
A brightly contrasted etching,
All clear and crisp and new.

Margaret Burgess

Endgame

I am the hot
hoover
of your soul
I am the sea that time
forgot
the ancient water
flowing
down your spine
I am
the glacier that
engulfs you
that cracks the corners
of your lips

I am the dead
I am
the quick
I am the stealer
of your wit
the flame of life
goes bit by bit
the evening dress
the dancing shoes
you have no choice
you cannot choose

for I myself
am deaf and dumb
I hear no cries, I hear
no pleas
only the huge white
sheet of silence.

Rupert Smith

For The Last Soldiers Of World War One

You will be hallowed in the annals of our time.
But there is a passing over, a fated letting go.
Another epoch turns to twilight's shadow, as
Memories close; like stars extinguished up in Heaven.

We do not know the sound of gunfire everywhere
Nor will we feel the red-stained mud upon our skin.
No mortal man or child will ever comprehend again -
On troubled, grainy news reels, what terrors lie within.

Go, you faithful servants, noble warriors, passing the horizon.
No longer have you history's burden on your shoulders -
Free again, and pure, as in more youthful days;
Forever skipping down a cobbled lane without a care.

Martin Jackson

Stay In Touch

I wouldn't mind if you called me
In the middle of the night
With your softly seductive Irish lilt
And unmistakable infectious laugh
Like music to my ears
Provoking a rush of distant memories
As if yesterday
Of intimate pillow-talk
Disclosing secret thoughts

No . . .
I wouldn't mind if you called me
In the middle of the night
I only hope I'm home
If you do.

Dawn Croft

MILLIE JORDAN

(29th July 1920 - 29th October 2004 (aged 84))

Wife, mam, nanna or great nan (sister, aunt or friend),
Millie was one person you could turn to,
On her you could always depend,
Each person has their own special memories,
Of a woman so brave and strong.

This is not the end of her journey,
But the beginning of a brand new one,
She's made sure that we are settled,
And helped us on our way,
Giving us the inspiration,
To be who we are today.

Through her love of music, she's shown us,
How to appreciate everything,
And through her words, that she's written or spoken,
She's proved that life is everything.

She's travelled to the places she loved,
And opened her heart to us all,
She's shown us the strength to carry on,
And to keep on standing tall.

We're all proud of our special lady,
She's a credit to us all.
And one thing to remember always is
She loved us all - with her heart and soul.
Now she's been reunited; with all our loved ones from the past.
The memories of Millie, Bob and Madge,
Will forever last.

Jayne Prime

SLIM - WITH A SMILE?

A friend of mine she is trying to slim,
But, no way, she says, will she go to a gym.
She likes to walk for just a few miles,
Across the fields - the ones without stiles!
At home, I know, she tries to exercise,
Aerobics and the like, to tone hips and thighs!
My friends says she has pounds to lose,
So I told her, 'First you must keep off the booze!
Those tempting white wines, an occasional red,
The lovely pale sherry that goes to your head.'
Then there's large cones of ice cream - with blackcurrants inside!
And gorgeous cream teas, and chips that are fried.
Large apple pies and gateaux are a sin,
Also juicy pasties, the ones with meat in.
There are other foods we're told we shouldn't touch,
Many don't care about that very much.
So, why shouldn't my friend enjoy her ginger crunch,
Or, lots of cheese with a salad for her lunch?
Well, I think it would be OK, say, once in a while,
Mixed with lots of willpower, exercise . . .
        And, dare I say, a smile?

Jeannette Kelly

AN AUTUMN EVENING

Renegade clouds are still and silent
as if sheep were grazing
straying from a blustery moor.
Angrily the breeze molests the trees
leaning through foliage, its wrath erupting.

This sulky evening disappears
trees silhouetted in the dusk
and sunlight arrives with day
melting night-time dreams away.

Herbert Wilson

GOD BLESS ENGLAND

There is something in the air,
One can feel it everywhere.
The miracle of life descending
Bringing hope and joy unending.

Spring is gracious and very kind,
Hope is renewed and pulses unwind.
England is forever beautiful,
God bless her and be ever dutiful.

The Earth is bursting with its pain
So let us have faith in every new day.
There must be something in this life
To spur us forever on our way.

The freshness of grass and daffodils,
A mystery of every recurring faith.
The world goes on and has its fall
Giving the seasons their rightful place.

To be seen at their best in England,
The flowers always know when to grow
Giving delight in early spring
Till the last days of autumn frost.

Valerie Willan

SCOTTISH MIST AND SUN

She comes down the mountainside
So silently, so softly, so coldly
She glides down
And weeps in the shoulder of the hill.
The trees and ferns weep with her
And the landscape is blurred by her tears.
She loves not the sun!

He is coming!
From afar he is coming,
Everything he touches is made new.
Earth loves him!
She opens wide her mysteries
To make perfume for his breath,
Then laughs with ecstasy.

This wondrous happiness
Offends our lonely one.
She starts to draw away
And then to fly.
To the top of the mountain she flies,
And crouching there, sulks,
Swirling her veil.

Vera Flint

LOVE

Love they say is patient,
Love they say is kind,
It sees beyond another's faults
For love they say is blind.

Love takes away the me and mine,
Instead it's us and we,
Yours and mine is ours now,
For love is unity.

Love will not diminish,
Or rust and fade with years,
But will gain its strength from
Time, laughter, joy and tears.

Love is God's own gift to us,
A present from above,
He gives us peace, He gives us joy,
But first He gives us love.

Margaret A Greenhalgh

TIME STOOD STILL

One blissful spring day in the early morn,
I stood at my window and watched the dawn
Come creeping up over the distant hills.
And I listened as the birds began to fill
The air with song, what joy, what awe,
Nothing so beautiful had I seen before.

At last it seemed the world was awake
The sheep and the cows, the ducks on the lake.
The farmer at work with his horse and plough,
The flowers in the garden all taking their bow.
The children to school came wending their way,
Laughing and shouting so happy and gay.

For a while I stood and watched the beauty unfold,
Nought can compare with the work of our Lord.
The beauty of nature all around me lay,
No words can express my feelings that day.
The years have rolled by but to me it seems,
That wonderful scene is now part of my dreams.

Eva A Perrin

REMEMBERING MUSSEL TIMES

Barnacle-encrusted, sea-rock-fresh
Nurtured in clear north waters
Clustered blue mussels.

Three generations shout, 'Great Gran,
The tide is low,
Can we go, can we go mussel gathering?'
Bare feet and buckets
Searching the seaweed and clean shores
For the large, the succulent.
Rinse in the sparkling shallows
Tweak out the stubborn beards.
And sharing the bucket handles
Tripping, shouting, laughing
Alert Great Gran.

The fire is hot, the big pan empty, waiting
Tumble the shellfish in.
How quickly bivalves open
Gifting plump orange sea food.

Now the burning question
How to serve the feast?
Round the kitchen table
Hot from the fire?
Or sweet marinated for tomorrow?
Coated, fried in sizzling oil?
Or bubbling in a French moule soup?
Such squalls of conflicting choice
Such precious summer memories.

Vie Tulloch

FLOWERING JEWELS

As the air came in, feathered intricacies
Echoed in green glass wind chimes
Opening the emptiness that became
Of dark confessions
As muffled music played
With plant curling gentleness
I remembered our togetherness
Under white seagulled clouds
And losing our laughter in daffodilled lanes
Touchable hands
Singing our footsteps in the sand.

Edward Tanguy

TWO SWANS

Two swans on a satin lake, gliding through the mist.
Side by side.
So unaware of the world at large, gracious, elegant, beautiful.
An inspiration for a ballet, making the spirit soar.
More breathtaking than a painting.
Side by side.

Brenda Robinson

BLINDNESS

When I first thought of blindness,
It certainly made me feel sadness,
How can folk cope that are not sighted?
Then I heard of help for the blinded.

There are many types of illness,
With sometimes a cure for the helpless,
So progress for all those sightless,
Need never lack support by the righteous.

War with its victims, lies exposed.
How many are those so involved?
Young or old in battle fought,
Surely not forgotten as an afterthought.

How lucky are the blinded these days,
With help at hand in so many ways,
Dedication has ways to help the blind,
Not least with helping hand to understand.

With games like dominoes and talking books,
Large print reading books and Braille,
Then talking cassettes and music never fail,
Will make life less tedious for all.

So let's pay a tribute to those involved
With all the efforts that are entailed,
Their every bend to help any that are blind
What a poor world without their aid.

Bill Burkitt

LINES TO A RETIRING PRELATE

The Angel of Destiny took up the 'phone
Somewhere in outer space.
'Bring all the documents,' said he,
'In the Herbert Potter case.'
'OK, Chief,' said the silver voice
Of a trusty celestial aide;
And as she hunted among the files
The heavenly music played.

After a long and arduous search
She found a bulky tome,
Giving the Bishop's history
Since the day he first left home.
The Chief perused it with a smile
And once out loud he cried
As his eye caught the words, 'I'm no martinet,
But I could be, if I tried.'

The Angel of Destiny took up his pen,
Turning a brand new page;
And in suitable words agreed that our Friend
Had reached retiring age.
Good health and happiness attend him,
And serene be remaining days
With his pipe and his pouch - and the pension
A benevolent Government pays.

R H Drew

TYLER

My dear little grandson
Tyler's his name
Loves to play pirates
It's his favourite game
He's Captain Hook
I'm Peter Pan
And with Tinkerbell's pixie dust
We fly to Neverland
He digs for treasure with his mate Smee
I run and hide
So he can search for me
He makes me walk the plank
A hundred times a day
But I wouldn't have it any other way
Just to hear him call Nanny
Tugs at my heart
And I feel so very lucky
That in his life I'm a part.

Margaret Randall

DIDGERI DOO

(Inspired by Roger McGough)

Ducks quack in a pond
Monkeys swing in a zoo
Boats sail on the sea
But what does a didgeri do?

Girls wear skirts
Rabbits have their hair
Boys wear trousers
But what does a didgeri wear?

Babies eat mashed up stuff
Kids eat lots of sweets
Grown-ups eat bananas
But what does a didgeri eat?

Babies crawl around
Kids run away
Grown-ups read the paper
But what does a didgeri play?

Volcanoes squirt out lava
My brother can count up to 2
Rock stars like to rock
But what does a didgeri do?

Ellie Rose Guillory (10)

WINTER WINDS

In the grip of winter's blast
Shrieking seabirds bouncing on
Bitter, biting winds
A passing ship with twinkling lights
Pitching, tossing in the night
Raging seas of freezing foam
Lashing the pier on rusting stilts
Barren slopes above the shore
And coastal roads deserted.

In the grip of winter's blast
Empty parks, street lamps shine bright
Shedding light on windswept pavements
The silent stare of a lonely tramp
Idle newspapers float in Heaven's way
Wafting sounds of a distant hooter
In the cold night air
And everywhere is deserted.

Raymond J Hobbs

MY SHELL

When I've left this twisted frame
Do what you will, treat it with shame.
Cast it in a muddy ditch.
Sell it to the nearest witch,
Let her use it in her spells.
Hang it up until it smells.
Throw it in the deepest sea,
This carcass is no longer me.

Rip it up, tear it asunder
And feed it to the noisy thunder.
Put it through a shredding machine.
Hide it where it can never be seen.
Now I'm living in Heaven or Hell
So throw it down a deep, deep well.
Kick it, punch it, burn the thing.
Hang it where the wasps will sting.

Throw it in the nettle patch.
Use it to watch the maggots hatch.
Dig a hole and throw it in.
Pack it away in a plastic bin.
Roast it up until it's tender
Then shove it through a kitchen blender.
Throw it in a river. Tear it up in pieces
And send little bits to my nephews and my nieces.

Richard D Tompkins

MORNING

It is most odd without you,
I cannot work it out.
You should be here when I awake,
Or somewhere round about.

I cannot hear the radio -
You always switch it on:
The house is very quiet yet
You're such a noisy one.

The dog must surely hear me,
Each time I move around,
But I know I am quite certain,
I can't hear a single sound.

Of course! I know what you have done,
You've gone to make some tea
But how did you get out of bed,
Without disturbing me?

Oh God, forgive me, for You know
It's for myself I grieve,
And trust that only You will see
The teardrop on my sleeve.

Stan Walton

PERFECT HEAVEN

I wonder if it rains in Heaven,
Or does the sun shine each day?
And when it's our time to go,
Will someone show the way?

Where no war is fought,
No blood is shed
No rich man,
No poor man,
Where everyone is fed.

To stand by one another,
Hold hands as one.
Live as your God intended,
The way life begun.

Deena Howard

A Jubilee, A Celebration

Let's have a party
A huge celebration
Pack 50 years into a weekend
You can use my back garden
Invite a few friends round
Serve strawberries and salmon roulade

Let's have proms at the palace
A pageant of music
A galaxy of fireworks and stars
We'll have Handel, McCartney
Trail beacons, sound fanfares
Jubilation for those golden years

Start with ducks in the park
In waddling formation
Taking the quiet salute
Then a gold coach procession
And dancers in costume
Pomp and ceremony comes easy to us

Let's have a banquet
And toast a few speeches
We'll invite the Lord Mayor around
Colourful flags waving
And cheering street-liners
With thousands of voices in song

We'll light up the palace
And take a few encores
Mega stars reach for the sky
A choreographed fly-past
Is how we shall end it
An extravaganza on high.

Val Stephenson

Ode To A Pill

Little pill, here in my hand,
I wonder how you understand,
Just what to do, or where to go,
To stop the ache, that hurts me so?
Within your covering lies relief,
You do work alone in unbelief,
You sink in regions there below,
As down my throat, you quickly go.
But what I wonder little pill,
How do you know, where I am ill?

And just how do you really know,
Exactly where you have to go?
I've got a headache, that is true,
My broken ribs need attention to,
So how can anything so small,
End my aches, in no time at all?

Do you work alone, or hire a crew,
To do the good things, that you do?
I'm counting on you mighty strong,
To get in there, where you belong,
Don't let me down, and please don't shirk,
Do your undercover work.

So down my throat, be on your way
And end my aches another day,
Don't take a wrong turn, is my plea,
As I can't take another, until after three.

Irene McBurney

Happy Days

When I was young my aunts seemed old,
Though only in their twenties.
They would all come down at birthday times
To bring their gifts a-plenty.
The birthday song was sung by all and candles all blown out,
Cousins and friends all having fun, eating grub and playing about.

We often donned our wellies and down the brook we went,
Catching tiddlers with our homemade nets -
Ma's stockings heaven-sent.
We always got a foot full and often dropped our jars,
The poor little fish a-flapping, were rescued by our ma.

We would catch sticklebacks and robins, an occasional catfish too,
We caught these in a special place which only a few friends knew.
We took our catch home in our jars and in a bowl they'd go,
Along with some fresh seaweed, they would last a month or so.

We swung our socks above our heads to get the water out,
'Cos Ma had enough washing to do and more would make her shout.
We hid our socks out of her sight, until they all had dried,
But if we fell in and got soaking wet,
Our bums hurt more than our pride.

We loved to go scrumping for apples
And across the field we would go,
A furrowed field planted with taters, so running was no go.
We would stuff 'em up our jumpers till we couldn't stuff no more,
Till the farmer stood there with his shotgun,
And we didn't scrump no more.

At the end of the day we were sat on that table,
Bowl, flannel and soap was the way,
Ma would wash us all clean and put us to bed,
Unaware of our antics that day.

Looking back we were really naughty,
But kids were just kids in them days,
Door knocking and scrumping were part of life,
But we grew up with mended ways.

I would not change my childhood, what lovely times we had.
We had spirit, were robust and healthy, I have memories,
And I am so glad.

Dorothy-Ann Cluley

The World

The bumblebee pollinates the flower,
The lion on Serengeti National Park.
The lonely walk amidst the trees,
Past the lily pond.

A bumblebee amidst bumblebees,
The flowers of colour, blow in the summer breeze.
A door with which we see the world.

Where gnu and lion and elephant thrive,
The old lady who sits in the chair.
Multicoloured cars passing by, here, there, everywhere,
That rainfall onto the canopy of trees.

An oak tree from an acorn does grow,
From every bee, a daffodil or dandelion will show,
Its face amongst the grasslands.
Every door that opens, tend us onwards from those we know,
A tear for those no longer here.

An open door, there sits a chair,
The bench at the end of a green open field,
A view beyond of a city/country scape.

Barry Powell

FARM LIFE

Remember in olden days gone by
Which you may recall with a sigh
The large and weary shire horse
Pulling his cart as a matter of course
And the pigs were in the sty.

The chickens and geese must be fed
The cows from the field were gently led
To give their day's supply of milk
Their coats to touch, like woven silk
Then back to graze they tread.

The fields are full of barley and wheat
Of potatoes, turnips and sugar beet
The aged man with his ox drawn plough
Knowing just when to reap, just when to sow
Making blisters on his hands and feet.

The farmer's wife is making dough
She wipes her hand across her brow
As she mixes, flours and kneads
On her forehead are sweaty beads
As she waits for her bread to grow.

There is a meat pudding in a cloth
A pan of hot and steaming broth
The cats are lying on the old stone floor
Her faithful dog is by the door
As with her scrubbing she tries to make a froth.

Now in these more modern times
We are more used to the combine
And the up-to-date farm machinery
How I think it spoils our scenery
Of the old farming days when they were in their prime.

Pauline Vincent

A GARDEN OF PEACE

There's a garden of beauty
I cannot express
Where there are flowers abundant, that colours caress
How can I tell you of the beauty I've seen?
For God in His mercy has given me this scene
The trees in their glory wave gently in the breeze
Sheltering blue birds and growing with ease
Streams of nectar with white columbine
Sweet-scented roses with our Lord's love entwined
So please, God our Maker, give us this peace here on Earth
For we love You most dearly, our God who gave us riches of birth.

Jean Ford

NEVER GIVE UP HOPE

Never give up hope, never give up hope,
There may be something good round the corner:
Life is an adventure, a wondrous dream,
Though sometimes things go wrong
And everything looks black, or so it seems,
But - never give up hope, never give up hope,
There may be something good round the corner.

Never give up hope, never give up hope,
There may be something good round the corner
Life is a journey, each day there's something new,
We encounter many things on the road,
So, trust in God, don't be blue,
And - never give up hope, never give up hope,
There may be something good round the corner.

Diane R Duff

A PRAYER FOR MY FAMILY

Oh! Lord, please help me to see,
What family life should really be,
To talk with Mum, and share with Dad,
The problems, which they've never had.
To listen to their point of view,
Then may they listen to me too.
So we can strive, so we can be,
The family that You'd have us be.
Full of love, not hurt or pride,
Just working together side by side.
And as we grow together in love,
We seek Your face in Heaven above.
You'd have us all unite as one,
So we could say, Your will be done.
Oh! Lord, help me, my family too,
To come to love and walk with You.

H Gladding

THE MEETING

We meet in the great hall of the station
Where people endlessly come and go
A cavern of hazy watery light
Sparkling speckled dust rising with the scuffle of feet
Coming in from the street
We feel lost midst the other fleeting floating shadows
Mirrored in the windows as they pass quickly out of sight
Our secret thoughts like timeless whispered thoughts
Of generations of travellers
Climb steeply into the domed canopy above
Prayers in search of an answer
Then we at last find one another
Humbled by the tumult of the crowded station we waver
Tentative with one another, heeding each other's silences,
Each other's gestures
Until smiling transparently we feel as one
At peace in a whirlwind of travellers
Time stands momentarily still
Beautiful but unreal this consecration in a station
Before we rush on

Monica Gurney

THE CELLAR OF ENVY

Alone
Prisoner
In
Iron
Shackles
Cold
Dark
Cracking
Walls
Of
Claustrophobic
Gloom
Image
Of
A
Fly
Outside
On
The
Windowpane
Escape
To
Freedom.

J Ashford

THE CLOCK

A clock, a heart, the two combine
A beat, tick-tock, yours and mine
The two forever intertwined
A clock you said a gift to you
Belonged to your Great Grandfather
My Grandfather too

The words I hear spin in my head
A gift to you is what you said,
'A family heirloom from me to you
Then pass it down that's what you'll do'
The generations down the line
Will hear the heartbeat - yours and mine
Each time the clock ticks, tock, tick-tock
Then chimes rumble deep from within the clock
To speak each hour to those who hear
Its voice rumbling, chiming, year after year

To become an old friend for the family
You're never alone with a clock you see
For every time it chimes, it speaks
It tells a tale of family peaks
Of a father giving a gift to a son
Who in turn to his daughter he passed it on
This daughter, then gave it to me
To carry on down this family tree

And when in the silence of night you hear
The gentle tick-tock, in your ear
'Tis only the clock letting you know
That time goes on, not fast, not slow
But gently, tick, tock, tick, tock, tick-tock
This timeless never-ending clock
That brought together two hearts combined
Two hearts forever intertwined.

Lynne Hope

THE AUTUMN LEAVES

The artist sits on the cold stone steps
Beside the grown-over dam
Then leans back to view his scene before bending over
To dip-and-mix the watercolours to blend in exactly
With what he sees near to him and far to the west.

All takes shape and forms with each careful brushstroke
Delicately weighted
To deliver the correct depth of colour onto the pale paper.
Falling and fallen leaves cover broken tree limbs that are
Thrown towards ripe clusters of chestnuts
Autumn-after-autumn.

The scene fixes in the cold north wind
That now plays with the helplessness
Of the artist's overturned water cup; it spins aimlessly
On its narrow, unbalanced, hollow-dented base, tapping
It's out-of-tune song on the well-worn village steps.

John Doherty

TRIPPING THE LIGHT FANTASTIC

Dolly was my partner as we danced and whirled away,
The garden was our ballroom on Grandma's washing day.
We polkaed like professionals, our waltzes were a dream
And the splendour of our tangos the most dramatic ever seen.
The second 'Fred and Ginger' my dad was heard to say
They really were such happy times on Grandma's washing day.
I never thought that I could dance,
I was blessed with two left feet,
But Dolly had three wooden ones
To make our partnership complete.

Jean Reynolds

THE ACTOR WHO THINKS IT WAS WRITTEN FOR HIM

What is contained in that fat head: suggest
An alternative opinion to the star and stand aghast
At the intrusion of the self from the bloated hugeness,
Eyes popping as a bugbear
That buffoon who shakes the bells;

Where did he purchase his grand monopoly?
An apprentice spoon-fed on textbooks and inward guttering.

At once, you decipher the thousand voices, the possession
The difference in pitch - a tone for each class of man:
Boomtown, high gay,
Deep sinister etchings on a cracked
Landscape of a lost instrument
The trumped up orchestra for
A personal bow of
Allegiance to the art.

With whom do you speak with a quick look and half-turn?
Over the shoulder
Somebody more important to him is coming.

Were we once not good friends? Faustus, Macbeth, Caliban
Were we not destined for greater things?
A freedom not found in a six month run.

Take a thorough look at the stature of the gibbering clown,
Hand on heart as if to give authenticity to a glib act -
Ambition before a calm soul as the monster stalks him,
Holds bursting each limb of electricity, pushing outwards
To the nodding of heads
The 'encore', 'bravo'.

Behold my accusation: discuss
Each tuned word and metaphor of dead princes
Rotting with blue bellies, purple and swelling -
Ready to burst with contained secrets, only for you

To suckle upon,
Growing fat like a dead cow
As you melt under that spotlight.

Stuart Springthorpe

A WOMAN'S HOGMANAY

Well here we are, it's Hogmanay
That very special Scottish day
The lobby is shining - it looks like glass
She's polished the wood, and buffed-up the brass
The bills are all paid by their due-by date
It has to be done, they mustn't be late
The table's all set with the cake and black bun
And every savoury under the sun.

Her man as usual has done his bit
Every drink right down to a gin and it
Is arranged on the sideboard just like a bar
She feels he's gone a bit too far
The cocktail shaker looks ill at ease
The whiskey though is sure to please

The washing's all done, and put to air
Her back is breaking, it's really sair
Just enough time to slip into her dress
And comb through her hair it's really a mess

A knock at the door, and here's the first fit
The tiredness has gone, by a smile she is lit
She opens it wide and welcomes them in
Can't hear yourself think for the laughter and din
It's the start of the party and all of the fun
Goodbye to the old year, the new is begun.

Phyllis Henderson

MOTHER

Generations are spreading more widely apart,
We live longer, life moves faster, but at heart
Old age is not fun
When life's nearly done
All I need now is comfort and care; but for a start -

Deafness has plagued me for many a year
Modern gadgets I *don't* want to fit in my ear
Old age is not fun
When life's nearly done
I'm lucky my family still holds me most dear.

Wish my memory was better, it's truly hard work
To hear, to converse - what's the day of the week?
Old age is not fun
When life's nearly done
So I smile and I guess and try to look pert.

I forget if I've eaten my tea or I've not
They bring more bread and butter, and another cup, hot.
Old age is not fun
When life's nearly done
Did I say that already, or have I forgot?

I wish I was home, but I never say so,
Something inside me just states I can't go.
Old age is not fun
When life's nearly done
Think I'll stay here - it's the only home I now know.

They change me and wash me and put me to bed
My thin hair is put tidy, pinned back to my head.
Old age is not fun
When life's nearly done
But at least I'm alive, well cared for, *not* dead.

pp Mother (aged 95)

M C Cobb

SUICIDE

Moonlight over shimmering waters,
Waves break over rocky shores,
Darkness wraps itself around you,
Claiming mind, body and soul.

Sun rising on a misty morning,
Cold air over dew-soaked grass,
Your body lies still, so cold in death,
Your soul released to a better place.

In life you were a tormented being,
No hope, no dreams, just hanging on
To a threadbare life so full of sorrow,
A self-inflicted nightmare of the first degree.

The outstretched hand you refused to take,
The offers of help you pushed aside,
You chose to wallow in your own self-pity,
And finally paid the ultimate price.

What price for those you left behind,
Selfish in death as you were in life,
A self-destruction no love could change,
Spineless to the bitter end.

Is your soul now free in a peaceful place,
Or still wandering, a tormented being?
Will peace ever give your soul a chance,
Or will the tentacles of hate keep peace at bay?

The distant questions and guilt of loved ones
Left behind, wondering what went wrong?
Were they to blame for the way you were feeling?
A hurt so deep, can't right the wrong.

Tracy Hazelby

HEMISPHERES

Daylight had shrunk to marshmallow dough
Night-time had settled down to a silvery glow.
The ocean was turned up like a French letter bed
And the seagulls were quiet, plump and well fed.
The sand was all shifted, sifted and clean
No trace of the holidaymakers
And where the rubbish had been
Gaunt and rugged the cliffs reached their bones
Across the shore
Ebony sea pods crept up from the sea floor.
The silence now swallowed the north, the south,
The east and the west
And flowering plants drooped their heads for night's rest.
Time seemed to trickle away like treacle with long beats
Showing one the value of how slowly time seeps.
Daylight had shrunk to marshmallow dough
Night-time's settled down to a silvery glow.

Christine Wells

OUR GARDEN

Please do not grieve for me when I am gone
See it as the pain I was in, I am now free
Don't let your heartache and tears linger on
Know that I walk beside you, and protect thee

Please do keep your memories locked up in your heart
Shed only a happy tear when you think of them
Think? Of my leaving you, as only time spent apart
Know I wait lovingly, patiently, 'til we meet again

Please take care of yourself and all we hold so dear
Know that 'I love you darling, I always have, I always will.'
Take care of the garden we tended
See the roses bloom each year
Smell their perfumed scent when the nights are long and still

Please pick our favourite *rose* and beside me let it lay
Know the sweet aroma ascends all the way to Heaven
And . . . when the time has come, together, forever we will stay
And we will both tend this beautiful *Garden of Eden*.

Irene Reid

DOWN BY THE RIVER

Down by the river.
A voice seemed to say.
Come by the river.
Come out to play.
I walked to the river.
My pack on my back.
Down to the river.
Through an overgrown track.
I sat by the river.
So still and so calm.
Down by the river.
Where nothing would harm.
A girl by the river.
Lay on the green grass.
Down by the river.
Where she let the day pass.
So nice by the river.
My childhood place.
Was down by the river.
A magical space.
Down by the river.
Come by the river.
To watch water race.

Pamela Sandry-Gorman

BOYS BESIDE A CHESHIRE BRIDGE

I'd give anything to go train-spotting again -
A mile to the bridge, at the end of the lane.
Here, we would spend many an hour
Jotting down numbers propelled by steam power.

The bridge was near to a dairy farm -
For cattle to cross away from all harm,
Through their pastures expresses roared past
With a wave from each driver - his eyes forward cast.

After milking was over morn and night
We'd spot a furious steam-snorting sight;
Rejoining the herd was *the most splendid bull*,
Thank goodness, like us, *his* cup was full.

The names of the engines taught us lots of things,
Of Regiments and Warships and subjects of Kings;
Provinces and Empire, many an island's name -
Oh Gilbert and Ellice - here comes the next train.

When quiet returned to the countryside
Ambitions for the future the boys would confide;
A dream of mine was to finely dine
At a first class table along this line.

A century before boys had initialled our bridge,
Saw open-air crews throw coal at partridge,
Saw Grand Junction stock, and 'Columbine' too,
Spotted 'Cornwall' and 'Hardwicke' fresh out of Crewe.

I daydream at times of those rapturous days,
Of the Spotters now gone their separate ways;
I'd give anything to go train-spotting again
To the bridge by the farm at the end of the lane.

James Conboy

UNCLE RAY/ANOTHER DAY

I never knew you
But we cared
That you were not really here
To see your family grow aright,
All because of that fateful night
That your plane was lost in flight,
All because the world did fight,
All because, all because . . .

I have loved you
But never knew
All the pain they put you through,
All because the armies fought,
All because the world cared nought,
All because, all because . . .

Another day we celebrate,
Another day it's not too late,
There stands a man on Calvary,
Another day it's victory.

Another day He's risen again,
Another day He's coming again,
And maybe you can meet Him too,
All because He loves you so.

Thank You, Jesus, for the cross,
Thank You that You never lost,
That great love that You shared,
That great love that kept You there,
On a tree at Calvary,
Thank You, Lord, You died for me.

Christopher J Symonds

NEVER SAY NEVER AGAIN

A dream that never wakens
Is a dream that takes no chance
A flower that never opens
Is a flower with no fragrance

The moonlight never shining
Is a moon with no romance
Snowflakes never falling
No winter to enhance

A heart with no true feeling
Is a heart without desire
A diamond with no sparkle
Is a diamond void of fire

A hope, that never fades away
Is a hope we keep in sight
Perchance to dream, just once again
For ne'er to change to might.

Audrey Addison

POPE BENEDICT XVI

As white smoke twirls from the Cistine Chapel
Hail! Hail! We have a new pope to acclaim
The huge bell rings out strong from Saint Peter's.

The name he chooses Benedict XVI
Long in our hearts will remain.

As oft' in history long ago,
Benedict XV was a revelation to behold,
So let us hope Benedict XVI is strong,
May he reign ere long.

Good luck as on your journey you go,
Help nations in many ways
Evil must be forever overcome.

From your palace the Vatican
As you look down on Rome,
May God guide you all the way,
Prayers of nations comfort you always.

Kathleen Gosling

MY WIFE'S GARDEN

My wife's garden tells a story,
of summer heat and rain,
with vegetables and flowers drooping
next year will be much the same.

The autumn is very changeable,
I'm sure my wife's getting slower,
she's out there with her pruners,
fork, spade and sometimes mower.

The winter weather is a killer,
but spring brings things to life
then a nasty frost is in the air
so I cover up my wife.

The promise of a fine Easter
then winds rip through the trees.
The apple blossom is scattered,
still my wife picks up the leaves.

The summer is now upon us,
my wife has done her best,
she's now watering *our* garden
while I have a well-earned rest.

Norma Davies

FULL CIRCLE

The perfect
Company of silence within
Past, present and future.
Embracing the whole and nothing
In the endless union of space,
From which we all came.

To hear
The harmony of original thought,
In the comfort of our material home,
And connect to the place
Every wheel of life returns -
Full circle.

Josie Hodges

THE HARD LESSON

From school, I often played truant,
I never wanted to learn,
in geography, I had no interest,
and history was always a yawn.
Logarithms, square root, and algebra
were subjects that caused me to squirm,
and mathematic equations
were things I just couldn't learn.
Their logic always escaped me,
and so I was useless with them.
Nouns, verbs - transitive, and pronouns
were always a puzzle to me.
Adjectives, adverbs and parsing,
their meaning I couldn't explain,
while semantics, and declensions
would just put my head in a spin!
But I wish I hadn't played truant,
I should have stayed there to learn,
as now I am Jack-of-all-Trades,
but unfortunately, Master of None!

E M Lang

IN ISOLATION

Here in solitude I do lie
No friendly faces pass me by
Cut off from all my former friends
Is it now, here, where my life ends?

Memories I have to keep me sane
All alone I find peace not pain
This war I joined so full of hope
Courage I thought would help me cope

So young am I, a smileless face
On foreign soil my resting place
All I have seen has been so vile
Will time show it has been worthwhile?

Fleeting thoughts passing through my mind
Of years ago now left behind
Thoughts of pleasure and of sadness
Years of hope and utter gladness.

How will the future years unfold?
Will there be answers now untold?
Will peace prevail through all mankind?
May each and all his soul will find?

Irene Foxcroft

MEMORY

Something remembered
Then quickly forgotten
Even though
Racing thro' the head
Until the door
Slams shut
With no key.

Yet what was remembered
And is now forgotten
May have been important
Or perhaps not?

Godfrey Dodds

AWAKENING

The seat beside me empty now,
A vacuum left unfilled,
Tender moments victims too
Of wounds that have not healed

Thoughts abound in fruitless search,
Seeking out the reason why
Some ethereal whim or random fate
Should lack the patience so to wait

Why she, who sought so little more
Beyond the love of those held dear,
Why not some more kindless soul
Whose passing might have reaped less toll?

But what if this, this life so called,
Were nothing more than sham or fraud?
A dream perhaps, a state of mind,
Mere moments in some other time?

And now at last some light I see,
This shallow, flawed facsimile
Is not a life but dream instead,
Reflections of a life ahead

Reality, a different kind
Of life beyond the slumbering mind,
But there for when the sleeping's through
There for when the hurt ends too

Life's grand finale plain to see,
Some terminated fantasy
A time to wake and nudge 'death's door'
Her hand and mine will clasp once more.

Stan Herbert

JUST LOOKING AT AUNTY ROSE

I stood by the piano,
Watching Aunty Rose,
She sat there playing every tune she knows,
Sometimes she would glance
And smile towards me.
I was just a small girl
She was so lovely to see,
In her silken blouse with pearls
She crossed her silk clad knee,
When she turned and smiled
She was the entire world to me
In the smoke-filled room
With everyone to see
When she turned and smiled
There was just Aunty Rose and me Olive.

Olive Haycock

OUT OF THIS WORLD

From across the dining table
Sparkling eyes enraptured me.
Unerring flight of cupid's arrow
Turned my senses into jelly,
I was lost and 'all at sea'.
All through the meal he signalled to me
Hardly eating anything.
He made me smile by pulling faces.
Then I laughed out loud, and people
Turned to look; I choked in shame.
But the sweet course was upon us,
So I dived into the choc mousse
Avidly, and sought my refuge
'Sparkling eyes' were smiling gently,
We resumed our 'eyeing' game.
Then he winked, and I was captured
Once again in magic's thrall.
People now were drinking coffee
Some were leaving, and then we were
All alone - we both laughed loudly.
Then he held his arm out to me
Gently led me from the scene,
We just danced to Latin rhythm.
No need to talk, I was in Heaven
Or maybe it was just a dream!
The ship was scarcely undulating,
So we walked along the deck.
Moonlight added further magic;
Gentle breezes stirred my hair,
We were locked in Heaven's care . . .

Dulcie Sharland

KENTISH ORCHARDS

Pride of Kent, the Kentish apple
Majestic colour, flavour fine
Joy to the discerning palate
Fit for kings and queens to dine.

Some may feel a sense of sadness
About an era we could boast
When the wayside Kentish orchard
Wide varieties would host.

Blenheims, Newtons and Lord Derbys,
James Grieve, Gladstones, Beauty of Bath,
All with their distinctive flavours
Scattered through each orchard path.

Even the Cox's Orange Pippin
Prima Donna among those grown
Battles 'gainst inferior apples
And commercial undertone.

Yet the glory is still present
Blossom time in May displays
Kent's own annual panorama
Unsurpassed for many days.

When in autumn fruit for harvest
Guilds the trees with colour bright
Orchards gleam in golden sunshine
And present a glorious sight.

England's garden in the south-east
Especially apple orchards there
Will delight, give pleasure, focus
Loveliness beyond compare.

John Pert

NAMED

(A poem for unborn twins)

They are named;

Their names
Are waiting to be pulled
Over their first cries
And worn for life

Two beating hearts
(cradled by a third)
Tick off the days
Of a blank calendar

Beating the tock of a clock

Tiptoeing towards summer
(holding my breath)
I hold onto their names
As incantations

Pencilling in autumn's auroras
And Christmas stars.

Shirley Carlton

A FEW DISCORDANT NOTES

A time when loving silence stood for speech
Persuaded them that every thought was shared.
In harmony they took their marriage vows
Rejoicing they were now, forever paired.

Then words were traitors signalling dispute.
Ill-chosen jests that hurt the sensitive,
Received retorts that were not soon forgot
And thus grew ever harder to forgive.

Yet still were times when, armistice declared,
They smiled on one another for a day.
Like many marriages, with weather changed,
The hurts were then resolved in lovers' play.

Now both are old and deaf, few words intrude
Upon their newfound peace. The neighbours see
Them sitting hand in hand, on summer days,
Content again with silent harmony.

Griselda Scott

NATURE'S WAY

My consciousness flows with the gentle ebbing tide
Quietly caressing the silver sand
Motions of soft waves breaking on shores
Where its only intruder is man.
Warm salty breezes clear my mind
Transporting my thoughts to a better time.
The loneliness and tranquillity
With each step I take dig deep in my mind
My memories flow with the ever-resuming tide
Precious and sad, fast flowing tears that blind.
Softly in the quiet dawn my thoughts are of you
The deep hurt is still there, the loneliness is all around
In everything I do, in the emptiness of this new day
Still quiet as you now lay,
Your golden hair a vision with each new sunray cascading
Down from Heaven to greet this brand new day
Your laughter fills my ears brought to me by windswept pines,
Listen to what they say
Tall and serene like a copper birch or a sweet-smelling
Blossom tree cascading like confetti
At a spring wedding in May.
Quietly as I pray when this lonely day is done
Only by the knowledge that nature and you
Will always be one.

Carol Irving

RAINFOREST BLUES

The forest's music echoes in my head
From raucous hornbills to cicada's whine,
With chattering cute gibbons overhead
Where great lianas coil and intertwine
And tree snakes hide among the trailing vine.
The jungle's canopy is at such height
It shadows ground, pales gleams of veiled sunshine
And lures me to these forests of the night.

Intense humidity weighs down my head,
Like ball and chain it clamps about my spine.
Through sweat-filled eyes I stumble, watch my tread
Avoiding where thick twisted roots combine,
Intrigued by how the clinging raindrops shine,
They glisten, hanging from wet leaves like lights.
Frail dripping cobwebs make a silver shrine
And lure me to these forests of the night.

The all-pervasive heat fills me with dread,
But music, magic, are the anodyne
That soothes: I'd choose no other place instead.
The sight of hairy apes sends me supine,
I softly move, observing tell-tale signs
Of recent presence, fearing sounds of flight.
The challenge and the tracking skill combine
And lure me to these forests of the night

Where I am trapped and held by their design.
Despite the humid heat they're my delight,
Their wonder, sounds and scents around me twine
And lure me to these forests of the night.

Pam Russell

INSIDE

Inside,
Where we are,
Deep inside.
We address ourselves
In quietness.
The human condition exactly where it is.
Yet further beyond,
Beyond our thought,
Feelings, or knowledge,
In the deepest charm of quiet solitude
Is the inaccessible light.
That which transcends our own perceptions of God.
Which is love divine.

Paul Darby

THE DAY THE ANGELS CAME

I held her hand as she passed away,
As the robin sang at the break of day,
And morning cast a sunbeam on the lawn,
The angels came and she was gone,
But love's still there like the fragrance of a rose,
That never dies or sleeps but only grows.
It's there in evening's mellow hush,
In the sunset's gentle blush,
For oft' in twilight reverie,
My love will come and 'bide with me,
All in beauty as a bride,
Is it an angel by my side?
Then she departs before the dawn,
And casts a sunbeam on the lawn,
A robin sings at the break of day,
I hold her hand as she slips away.

William A Smyth

DEWDROPS

Dewdrops on the rosebuds.
Grass wet beneath my feet.
The stream gently flowing
Making patters, and ripples
Beneath my feet.
Swans swimming by.
The white neck held so high
Sun is gently warming
And shining through the trees.
I walk!
I dream.
Where would this world be
If no water, no sun, no moon
No wind, which brings the rain
For us to save the world He gave?

Beryl Manning

IN MEMORY OF DIANA

I pray to You my Lord above
To ask You why You took away the one we all love
You took her life in such a tragic way
What sin had she done that this was the price she had to pay?
She worked so hard to help the poor
And bring comfort to the ill
What we have been taught is Thy will
Surely You already have enough
Heavenly angels with You up above
That there was no need for You to take
The Earth-angel we all love.

T Garwood

CLOWN

(This poem was written for my one and only granddaughter when she was small. She loved to play and talk to my stuffed clown, Cocoa Chanel! He is still around to this day and although Abbie is nearly ten-and-a-half, she still loves clown)

My nose is round and very big,
And it's attached to me.
My mouth it *smiles* all of the time,
I'm a *happy* clown, you see!
And with my little human friends
I really have a *ball*
Doing cartwheels off the bed rail,
And, sliding down the wall.

I'm loved and kissed and cuddled,
And I sleep right by the side
Of my *number one fan Abigail*,
And here I'll always bide.
I even go on holiday,
Which fills me with such *pride*,
I'm the *luckiest* little fellow,
Though I'm stuffed on the inside!

I have a *funny* wardrobe, yes,
It's all *too big* I know,
My baggy trousers hang on me,
But, do I care? Well, *no!*
I'm just *clown*, and I am *happy*.
As *happy* as can be,
And even though I'm *just a toy*,
My *Abigail, loves* me!

Heather Overfield

NIGHT BEACH

Racing along the beach,
Barefoot in the sand,
Flying with the wind,
Above the very land
Which seems to melt
Away beneath my feet,
Sand trickling through my toes,
Warmed by the heat of the sun
Which has long since set,
Guided by the moon,
As it lights up the sky
Feeling just as one
Although it is very high,
Excitement building up,
A race with time,
Then gradually slowing down,
Gulping air of wine
Stopping suddenly I stand and stare,
At the moonlight reflecting on the sea,
Or is it the sea reflecting on the moon?
Now the day is done,
Did I imagine somewhere in that race
That I was flying high,
Or for one brief moment was I?

Denise M Blunt

SWEET REPOSE

(Dedicated to my one true love Ron Latter)

In sweet repose stay I
For I know
I'll see you by and by
No nourishment I need to take
For it's not my stomach
That has the ache
It's my heart
That needs to mend
I need to see you
In my dreams please send
A message from the other side
Until you do
In sweet repose stay I

In sweet repose
I dream of you
I long for the night
So you are here with me
The days are long with you gone
Night-time brings you
Close to me
I'd have your presence
Through the day
If not
In sweet repose
I stay

In sweet repose stay I
To dream of you
The daytime is so cold and harsh
Without my man around
The night-time brings
You back to me
Smiling as you used to be
I no longer like the day
So in sweet repose I stay.

Elizabeth Latter

THE KNIFE EDGE

God is at the knife edge where things happen
The hair-trigger between alternative universes
Is His to squeeze or release at His will.
But He also delegates and allows
Skeletal fingers seeking to abuse their power
To change the world into their image
By unleashing death before the allotted time.

On either side of many arguments
Quoting 'Crusade', 'Jihad', 'The Will of God'
They exercise control of others
And quite forget submission of the self.

Now is the time, yes, now, to pray
And beg before His throne to say the word
To whisper in the ear of vengeful men
(And women, too) of peace and self-restraint.

How can they fail to hear, who worship Him?
How can they close their ears to consequence?
How can we shout loudly enough to ensure
The whispering Spirit's voice takes up the strain?

Christopher Payne

BECAUSE!

Was there a message? I picked up the phone,
No messages, I was alone,
But the usual dialling tone,
Had been replaced by a buzzing drone.

'Bonjour!' a voice said to me,
A message from France, it wasn't a bee,
'Combien argent pour une nuit?'
It was ages since I'd seen the sea.

'Twanzig euros,' the voice had changed,
French to German, someone deranged?
I decided to play him at his own game,
I said, 'Olé, what is your name?'

'Olé,' the voice said, 'a Eurostar,
Will land at your door, from afar,'
The phone went dead and just as he'd said,
A bright light got me out of bed.

Had my stars been right that day?
An undercover lover will come your way?
A ticket for two to a dream come true
And at my door was a box of Milk Tray!

Josie Pepper

THE STAG

The magnificent stag stands proud and tall,
Ear tuned in to the huntsman's call.

The sound of pounding hooves on hallow ground
As this magnificent beast trots round and round.

The pounding of the hooves and of the heart
And then the chase is about to start.

The hounds in the distance with furious bark,
Panic the stag as it takes to the dark.

Through the forest, heavy in leaf.
A pounding heart full of grief.

Down the stream to throw the scent,
This wise manoeuvre heaven-sent.

This magnificent beast gets far away,
Only to be chased another day.

D Hamey

SHADOW

'I hope they burn in Hell for what they've done.'
The Serb is hated now by everyone.

I watched us burn in Dresden and remarked
As fat man turned round in the darkening sky.

I watched us herding us to ovens.
Buried alive;
We fried in Coventry,
Starved at Stalingrad,

Year on year
I make bones, bleached
To feed the killing fields.

My names are written there,
Bosnian, Serb, Croat, Jew,
Christian, Muslim and Hindu.

Each time the reason is the same;
I follow orders
Kill without a name.

Throughout our years the rivers run
And long to meet in peace . . .
Knowing the price . . .
The all embracing sea
Welling with tears and sacrifice.

Jennifer Bell

HAVING A VERY BAD DREAM

One night, while I was at home sleeping in my bed
I was having a very bad dream
I dreamt I was in a hotel room, upstairs
Close to the sea beach, and when I looked out toward the sea
I could hear the sound of a very big tidal wave,
Bursting up from underneath the seabed

Then it came rushing down to the seashore
Splattering, splattering and banging, banging
Against the barriers

As if to say

Let me out
Let me out

In a very violent manner,
As if to say
I wanted to come to shore on dry land

But I am quite sure, if that tidal wave had broken the barriers,
Down and come to shore, on dry land

I would have, washed away all the houses
And drowned all the people

That were living nearby

It was a very sad dream indeed.

P B James

INFINITY

When the body it fails us, the spirit moves on
We pass but along through the aeons of time,
Each life but a pause in our journey sublime.

So ne'er be too sad when one passes on,
For we'll meet once again in some future time.

Gather together and share all your thoughts,
Remember the good times and joys they have brought.

Laugh as you talk, it will lighten the heart
And fill up the void, now we are apart.

John E Lindsay

SUMMER 2005

Rain, rain, rain
Wind, wind, wind.
The trees 'clap their hands'
But the grass is green!

Birds come and snatch a snack
Hurry under a bush to eat.
Everything's rocking forward and back
But flowers are the best I've ever seen.

Clouds are scudding in a hurry
Where are they going to?
Windows are lashed in storms flurry
'Go out in this,' you must be keen!

Suddenly the clouds are parting
At last it is becoming calm.
Wind subsides, the rain is stopping,
The air is warming like a balm.

Here comes the sunshine once again
'Nice warm sun, where have you been?'
Summer's returned - gone is the rain
There's a gentle breeze and everywhere's clean.

Vera M Holmes

FRED

The chair in the corner is vacant
In the pub called 'The Rose and the Crown'
For last week they buried poor old Fred
The most well known bloke in town.

He'd boast of his exploits in the war
The locals all knew it was yarn
For he never went further than the village
Whilst he ran his father's old farm.

The men had all gone from their homesteads
So Fred had the time of his life
Until one of the lassies he slept with
Insisted on being his wife.

She wouldn't be seen going into a pub
She quickly let it be known
But Fred didn't mind, as he quietly crept out
His pub was better than home.

He still had a twinkle left in his eye
As bar Madge came and sat on his knee
'Don't worry,' he'd say,
'The fire has gone out of an old bloke who is now 93.'

Marie Wood

MARKING THE DATE

Fifteen years bringing encouragement into many lives
Sharing the laughs, the tears, the fears and the joys
Opening up the deepest feelings of a deepest thought
Within wonderful descriptive words, there to be caught.

A window of opportunity for budding or seasoned poet
Engrossed in topics set to tantalise the old grey matter
Looking out into the horizon that is beckoning brighter
In the hope that one day they may be a top entry writer.

Lost in a timeless aura on a theme to elaborate and shape
To erase, change or reconstruct to just live that dream
With magic ingredients of verse, prose or perhaps rhyme
A golden moment for a mind's eye to grasp a poetical line.

Octavia Hornby

No Santa Claus

I always will remember the year of forty-two
Looking forward to Christmas, as little children do
We had a baby sister who was only three months old
My dad he was a miner, so the house was never cold.

I really was not very big, very small for ten
My dad sat on his knee, and he said, 'Listen then
Your mother is very ill, she'll have to stay in bed
And I'll have to go to work, and earn some money,' he said.

My dad went on the night shift, I gave Mum a cup of tea
'Sit down upon my bed,' she said, 'and listen here to me,
There isn't any Santa, it's just your Mum and Dad.'
This came as a great shock to me, and made me very sad.

All the Christmas gifts were in the cupboard in the hall
The girls had a game, and my brother had a ball
I laid them out in order for the other kids to see
Some fruit in the stockings, and all put there by me.

I got up in the morning, along with all the rest
I tried to look a bit surprised, I had done my best
Dad came off the night shift; the house was nice and calm
I had washed my baby sister and laid her in her pram.

My mother she was very ill, in bed all week she stayed
I became a little mother, while other children played
I will not forget that Christmas, and the reason for it was
What a way to find out that there is no Santa Claus.

Amy Murray

Hunter's Moon

Across the moonlit channelled bay
A golden orb of mystery hangs,
And casts its wondrous eerie light
Across the water and the sands.

In deepening night it rises high
Above the trees, festooned with stars,
And now illuminates the earth
With softer, gleaming, silver bars.

Enchanted night, tranquil and calm,
Your magic holds a soothing balm!

Eileen M Child

I Love The Seasons For Different Reasons

Dynamic springtime and everywhere's gleaming
Energetic growings of new life appear
An insistent provocative freshness
Fresh starts and habitual spring-cleaning

Tiny lambs frolicking

There are ample blessings in summer sunshine
Living is easy with stunning vacations
Or just relaxing in fragrant settings
Promotes the usual into divine

Perfection of roses

Colourful autumn invokes pleasures anew
While intuitive artists painting the scene
Will encapsulate feelings in pictures
Vying with the birds for the finest views

Evocative breezes

Stimulating winter though landscapes seem bare
Decorative snowflakes christen the season
Yet tea and crumpets by ye old log fire
Heralds Christmas and goodwill to share everywhere

Embracing spiritual reflections.

Gladysemily

My Angel

Arousing from a peaceful sleep,
Sun's rays, into my room, do creep,
Stirring beyond the sheets I lay,
Awakening to a brand new day,
Birds are singing, sounds so sweet,
Excitement abounds as I jump to my feet,
Rock with the world; turn the music up loud,
Swaying in the octaves of a harmonious cloud.

Seraph lies gracefully across her grand piano,
Whilst positioning the tip of her Cupid's arrow,
Galloping horses, with long flowing manes,
Rainbows of colours and fruit candy canes,
Angels with harps, castles pink and some blue,
Beautiful things that remind me of you.

Come hold my hand now, and walk together
Through fields of green and clouds of heather,
Talking and laughing, the smile in your eyes,
Then rest our souls beneath the pale blue skies,
Absence of words, as we aspire to fulfil,
Viewing the world, from the crown of a hill,
Everyday images of life, war and torment,
Obliterate our minds, as we savour the moment.

Lock time in a capsule, and keep it forever,
Holding our dreams, and the memories we treasure,
You're the sunshine of life, without you I'd die,
My shimmering starlight gracing a navy-blue sky,
The angel in my heaven, through music and song,
My everlasting beauty, together we belong.

Jan Hall

Human Expectations

It would seem to me
That some youth of today
Lack most the consideration
Once taught to convey.

Good manners and respect
Always was the norm
Insulting action and neglect
Never was good form.

Self expression seems the way
Without a thought, night or day
Just transgressing to the brink,
Always doing what they think.

Pulling back to standards,
Old-fashioned they may be
Principles in all things
Bring the perfect remedy.

Parents are the starting point
To truly lead the way,
Children start to follow
With rules they can obey.

Lots of love and discipline,
Setting the scene for life,
Educating and training,
Keeping them out of strife.

With head held high
And proud to be
If only they would see,
The world would be a better place,
A credit to the human race.

Ivy E Baker

A Tiny Ray Of Hope

From the devastation of that day
When the mighty wave wiped all away;
Took the lives of young and old,
The rich, the poor, the weak, the bold.
None could save them from their plight,
Their souls from bodies took their flight.
As news was spread around the world
A tiny ray of hope unfurled.

Out came cheque books and credit cards,
Collecting boxes in church and bars
Money poured from every source
All given by Man's own free choice.
Obeying God's command to love,
Our gifts He blesses from above.
Whatever havoc life has wrought
He will be there to give support.

God will use our hands to care
And all the grief and sorrow share.
To feed the hungry, share our wealth,
To nurse the wounded back to health,
To be beside all those who mourn
Till in their hearts fresh hope is born.
God will bless each deed we do,
Through all life's sorrows, lead us through.

Beryl R Daintree

The Rose

The rose blooms forth in the morning sun
Gently unfolding her beauty
On her petals the dew sparkles as diamonds in a ring of gold
Her leaves of green in zig-zag pattern bold
Thorns of brown protecting her most beloved of all flowers
All shades of red we give to those we love so dear
White so pure
Adding more loveliness to an already radiant bride's bouquet
Gold, orange, pink all the colours of the rainbow
With a fragrant perfume we never forget
As her petals fade and fall
We are left with just the memories of the rose.

Sylvia Reeve

In My Corner Of A Field

In my corner of a field
New, where the blue harebells grow
And the tall horses roam, where as a free child,
Nostalgia roams with them.
With my little brown friend watch flocks of birds,
Dark shadows transcending thought and blue cornflowers
Mention their thoughts too, over to the white campions.

By and through the dark green,
To the waiting family of rabbits nestling among themselves.
Before the children come out of school,
Disturbing wood pigeons sleepy
With the day's work done, their broods content.

Wild speedwell hardly grows here now
But bindweed in resplendent mauve
White trumpets skyward light at the mighty poplars overhead,
Shake heads of oak trees whose domain they try to intrude.

Tall yellow-seeded grassy mix -
With the yet uncut yellow corn and dandelion,
Fitful honeybees dare to sleep here.
So do I, in my corner of a field,
Where the blue harebells grow.

Doreen Sylvester

Live And Let Live

We all have our dreams and our memories,
Our aims, which we strive to fulfil;
With hearts full of hope for our families,
We greet each new day with a will.
For the gift of life is a sacred trust
And one, which we all should revere;
For we did not evolve from a mound of dust,
It is through God's will we are here.
He made us to care for each other;
He gave us the will to survive;
Our hearts must go out to each mother
Whose son is no longer alive.
For how could she know of the evil
Instilled in the mind of her boy
Which made him join hands with the Devil
To play with a bomb like a toy?
So for those who, sadly, have perished
And those left behind now to weep,
Let us pray that lives that were cherished
Have taught us a lesson to keep.
That peace and prosperity go hand in hand
And no one need suffer in vain,
We must share all the gifts in this wonderful land
So that wars never happen again!

Eileen Martin

Red Bike

I had a bright red moped
It was my pride and joy.
Till it got mugged and stolen
By some rotten, stinking boy.

It had a large and comfy seat,
A red and blue surround,
It used to take me everywhere
Now it was really sound.

But I didn't see the greedy eyes, or the covetous stares,
Later came a phone call, from a man called *Mr Ware.*
'We found your bike, mostly in bits
So sorry to tell you it cannot be fixed.

Shall we paint it black?
Put the bits in a sack?'
'Don't bother,' I say with a frown
'Take to the scrapper in the town.'

So now red lives in the scrapyard
Its seats all ripped and torn,
Its lovely shiny body
Now scratched, and bashed, and worn.

His headlight hangs by just a thread,
It's plain to see my bike is dead
So if I buy another,
Of this you can be sure
I will make those culprits suffer and padlock it to the door.

P Mullins

Questions . . . Any Answers?

All I have left are the words on this sheet
And they don't even listen, they don't even speak
Questions that swirl round and round 'til they surface once more
Questions alone are no cure that I'm sure
Questions need answers and no not any will do
So I search high and low, yes in vain that I do
But all I have left are the words on this sheet
And they don't even listen, they can't even speak.

Roula Writer

WHEN WE WERE YOUNG

How we laughed and joked and played the fool,
When we were young;
And thought that life was ours for all our days.
It was. For you, a year or two, for me a pool
Of pain that you should go and leave me far behind.
But we had deadly business in our youth.
We trained to kill; and so did others. That was why you died.
The splinters and the bullets sought their mark
And marked each one. No laughter now.

The haze of war has left me where I am.
Lined face, old limbs and tottered heart.
Yet stench of war still lingers in my mind
The scent of death reviles my soul.
Young lads we were, young ladies' men
Who foraged far and sought the best.
The best was but the winking of an eye
When darkness fell. And glazing eye
Wept for the past. The present was no more.

And so you sleep.
I have been back and wept my tears.
To share again the bitter years.
Each stone reveals a name; a friend once known
But now forever in that resting place we call a grave.
So lie in peace, my friends.
You stay with friends
Who shared your laughter and your jokes.
Still do perhaps, on quiet nights
When winds pipe pibrochs softly from the sea
And moonlight glimmers.
And no bullets fly.

L A McIntosh

SANDWITH JULY 2005

A stiff breeze unhindered across the Irish Sea
Harebells cling low beneath this unresisted wind,
Swallows and sand martins glide acrobatically
While raucous gulls bellow their aeronautical success
Butterflies swoop greedily from flower to flower
Their delicate beauty belying their determination
The sea itself shades blue to sandy brown
As it relentlessly erodes the cliffs
Shrinking and smoothing solid stone
To perfect rounded pebbles
While the sound of waves glissade on a shingle beach.
Sheep graze and beetles roll their dung
While a freshly dead shrew lies across the path.
Flies have begun to congregate
And yet it still retains its elegant velvet coat
As if in death it could exude an air of pitiability
A humble commentary on life.

A little further inland past the gorse bushes
Across the fields of mown hay and beneath the crows
Other birds sing invisibly.
Foxglove bells streak hedgerows vivid pink
Hawthorn blocks the breeze
And a seeping stillness takes hold.
From grey white and blue skies shafts of sunlight
Feel much warmer here.
Apples are ripening and the spreading honeysuckle
Discreetly scents the air - a voluptuous invitation
To believe that this bucolic reality
Is an unsurpassable perfection.

Nicholas Howard

FROM THE ASHES

Once they were there, then the sea came in,
Covered them in spray, rocked them gently -
Carried them down within the silence;
They shall not return. At times the stress
Was audible - enfeebled sighs - dark
Foliage, restless upon yew tree
Boughs; soon to be rustling dryly in
Despair, long before autumn's paring.
No wind has fashioned their blights yet they
Tired, not suddenly - insidiously -
As water fags stone. Season by dank
Season impaired by strain; before the
Final bloom, the last birdsong; during
Present dreary months that once brought spring.
They died from the whiplash of events
Adding to the finale. Did you
Call them across the world's waste - all things
Exquisite - that time's disasters had
Caused to fail? If one floret were now
Redeemed, one leaf, one stark, brittle bough
Salvaged to hope; one grey, limpid-eyed
Mammal flapping haplessly on the
Stones' surface restored to life - would you
Again, follow your own, murderous
Pursuit or build another Eden -
From the ashes?

Margret Phillips

LIFE

Life, make me happy
Let me live as I strive
Life, give me sunlight
Let me be alive

Give me smiles and laughter
Give me hope, give me time
Give me love forever after
And just a taste of wine

Life, make me want you
Make it good to be alive
Life, thank you greatly
For everything, may you thrive.

John Michael Scott

WESTERN FRONT

Western Front Association means all the world to me.
Gives me a chance to realise
What my ancestors went through.
One dying as young as 19, another at 25.
Some were lucky and came back.
But as for the others, we owe it to their memory
To live peacefully with other people.
As we learn about the atrocity of the First World War,
We marvel at their courage and the hardship they endured -
For this England we love so much.

And so I say we want to count our blessings
And thank our lucky stars.
We were born English
And do all we can to make it great again.
Keeping the peace with other nationalities
And talking to each other.

So God save the Queen and our England forever.

Lord, we pray for all who died in the First World War,
Also in the second war.
Lord, in Your mercy hear our prayer.

Mavis Wilson

MUSHROOMS
TENDER PALE AND PURPLE-GREEN

Under the shadow of the Himalayan range,
Just about at the time of break-of-dawn.
The twilight mist still exists,
But the dusk had long since gone.

Sometimes the rain is somewhat hesitant,
Turning the air cool, fresh and fragrant.

Washed all night with gentle silvery moonlight,
Clusters of mushrooms spring up here and there,
To welcome sunrise struggling through the night.

Fields and forests littered with them,
As if stars had fallen from their den.

Excited children rush and scream,
To see the sight of mushrooms,
Tender pale and purple-green.

This modern man is in a better position than ever,
To grow a bumper crop of mushrooms enough forever.

With new inventions at his behest,
Life on Earth he can lay to rest.

Up and down this Earth - East or West,
Fresh mushrooms will grow on rotten flesh.

Then, there will be no excited child,
To run and scream,
To see the sight of mushrooms,
Tender pale and purple-green.

M Yaqub Mirza

WHERE THE CHILD DREAMS

If I could make a pillow of the stars,
The night sky my blanket to blot out my fears,
If I could dream where the child dreams,
With nothing to pay for my tears.

If I should ever know such sorrow,
As the widow's face behind her veil,
If I could make joy out of every sadness,
As the salmon leaps, with the flick of its tail.

If I could make a damaged heart new,
Not with a surgeon's skill, but tender human love,
If I could bring comfort with just the right word,
Instead of meaningless phrases wrapped in a kid glove.

If I could make people for the lonely,
Happy as new friends under their own roof,
If I could command that mankind be more fair,
I would be swamped with their self-righteous proof.

If I could turn all the hate to goodness,
Give refugees hope, without famine, without the gun,
If I could make one nation out of many colours,
Brothers and sisters out of every family to come.

If I could turn back the clock of memories,
Would I face the past? They say, 'Time's a great healer.'
If I could make peace with all in my heart,
With life's cards in my hand, I would be a gentle dealer.

If I could make this uphill struggle,
Run with the tide, not against the schemes.
With nothing to pay for my tears of the moment,
Then I should always dream where the child dreams.

David Hall

VINCENT BY VINCENT

I'm elastic, I'm fantastic - I'm a joy about the house.
I'm intelligent and beautiful (the scourge of any mouse)
I'm a hunter and I'm fun to play with (but beware the claws!)
I'm a stalker - not a walker - and I haven't any flaws.

I've a shiny coat that makes me gleam
Stretched in the noonday sun.
I'm endearing - nothing fearing and I must be number one.
Slow as any self-respecting sloth but fast as any dart
(I would tell you all about myself
But don't know where to start).

I've got eyes as bright as buttons but as deep as any well
Which shine silver in the darkest night,
But gold in day's long spell.
With two pointy ears (and each one hears!)
I start at every noise
Whiskers pert and air alert I stand - a paragon of poise.

I'm the coolest cat that ever sat on mat or rug or tile
And when food's about without a doubt
You'll almost see me smile.
Not a Cheshire cat, low pressure cat,
Though - just observe my face
And my lovely form - *exquisite!*

(Modesty's my saving grace . . .)

Sue Devlin

DREAMS

'Everybody dreams,' the experts say.
Many linger after sleep, but some go away.
Frightening nightmares while you slumber,
Or pleasant dreams, you may remember.

Going to sleep with things on the mind.
We've been treated badly and most unkind!
Or nice things have happened and we've been impressed
And we go to bed happy and have a good rest!

There may be an occasion when we get straight to sleep,
And find that there's no need to start counting sheep!
The night may pass quickly, as we rest our weary heads
And soon the time has passed and we must leave our beds!

Have you ever wondered why dreams do not make sense?
Seldom do they seem to have any relevance.
Blown out of proportion, our thoughts out of control!
As if someone has thrown us up and dropped us in a hole!

Scientists will tell us, 'When we relax our brain,
A lot of thoughts, throughout the day, in our heads remain.
Dreams occur to sort out the muddles in our mind
And file away the important facts, and leave the rest behind'.

Rachel M Prentice

JOHANNA

The sun is at its zenith in a cerulean sky
As down the fields she goes, her head held high,
Eyes shining, sunlight warm upon her skin,
Hair fingered, furrowed by the lightest wind,
Soft-pressed 'neath sandaled feet the meadow grass.

She takes refreshment to the harvest crew,
Who, hearing chink of cup on cup, raise heads
And, slowly arching aching backs, lift caps
To wipe the back of toil-worn hands across their steamy brows
And squint with narrowed eyes through haze of heat.

She nears. At her approach they smile,
For, in her gentle, unassuming way,
It is not only tea she'll bring.
She'll bless their day.

Petya Christie

LOVE OF THE LORD REMAIN

Will your love of the Lord remain
After a loved one has passed away
When life is full of strife and pain
Will you still trust and pray?

Will your love of the Lord remain
All around you hunger and war
Can you still love our dear Lord
As strong as you did before?

Will your love of the Lord remain
Through tempests, fire and fear
Your thoughts be still the same
And still hold His love dear?

Will your love of the Lord remain
When thoughts are of the past
Will your love of the Lord remain
Until in eternity with Him at last?

Brian Joseph Wood

HANDS OF TIME

Newborn fingers, pink and white
Groping out towards the light.
Gripping tightly to her mother,
Sensing she is there to love her.

Nimble fingers, never still,
Fumbling, meddling where they will.
Making, breaking, grasping, clasping,
Bringing joy that's everlasting.

Tender fingers, soft and warm,
This is when first love is born.
Seeking, finding, hands entwining,
All the joys of youth combining.

Busy fingers, busy years,
Blowing noses, wiping tears,
Tying laces, washing faces,
Finding time for sweet embraces.

Aged fingers, worn and red
Resting on a grandchild's head.
Of life and love they've had their fill,
Aged fingers, growing still.

Dorothy Moore

FREEDOM OF PRINT

There is a place where dreams are fulfilled,
Feelings are expressed without saying a word,
Imagination can wander,
A means of escape,
At liberty, a freedom from the claustrophobic world!
Giving a voice to those who otherwise may not speak,
Gulps of fresh air,
A chance to be heard,
Points are made, confidence built!
Love declared, emotions spilt!
Encouragement given
In every poem a message conveyed,
With some, a humorous outlook displayed,
These pages of print
Give us our chance to shine,
Our differences aside!
United, your words and mine,
Together, we must join to give our thanks,
To Forward Press
For these opportunities are a helping hand.

Happy 15th Anniversary Forward Press

Michelle Luetchford

IN THE EYES OF A STRANGER

In the eyes of a stranger, you represent
The things that you stand for, just why you were sent;
It may not be clear to you just at this time,
But people will watch you, where'er you abide.

You are a real person, your spirit is sure,
And it is important you keep yourself pure;
Now, you are unique, so there's no one like you,
Thus people are watching, to see what you do.

Now, how do we keep ourselves pure in this world?
Well, let's find the answer, 'tis written in God's Word;
There's little it seems one may do for oneself,
There's nought we can give or do, not by ourselves.

God's Word holds the answer, 'tis clear enough there,
We have to reach God in our worship and prayer;
To tell Him we'll follow His wonderful Son,
And love Him for all the good work He has done.

He must love us dearly, to do what He did,
Yes, we can trust Jesus to rid us from sin,
To cleanse us quite thoroughly and make us so pure,
We'll be whiter than snow, God's Word doth assure.

So then we'll be happy, throughout every day,
We'll live to please Jesus, along life's rough way;
Then Jesus will help us, and stay always close,
Our Saviour, Redeemer, the one we love most.

Yes, people will watch us to see how we live,
They'll see if we're angry and fail to forgive;
Then watching to see if we follow our Lord,
In living, in speaking, in serving our God.

W Herbert G Palfrey

GOD CHOSE THE LOWLY

God chose the lowly prophets
To forecast Jesus' birth
Isaiah and many others
Had written it in verse.

God chose a lowly maiden
To bear His only Son
She spoke the great magnificate
God's favour she had won.

God chose a lowly carpenter
To be Jesus' earthly guide
They went to pay their taxes
And took a donkey ride.

God chose the lowly shepherds
Who heard the angels sing
When startled by an angel
'Fear not, good news I bring.'

God chose the lowly stable
In Bethlehem, a star
Drew kings and other wise men
Who saw it from afar.

God chose the lowly cattle
Who gave their bed of hay
And watched over the manger
Where the baby Jesus lay.

God chose the lowly fishermen
Saying, 'Come and follow me,'
And if we take Him at His word
This still applies to you and me.

Annie Harrison

AUTUMN

Autumn . . . a time for reflection
On days gone by of such perfection.
The rich bounty of summer
Begins to fade away.
Migrant birds no longer stay . . .
Flying to warmer lands.

Many leaves change their colour
As their sap begins to ebb.
Silver threads of a spider's web
Form on plants and bushes.
Squirrels scamper here and there
Seeking nuts for their winter fare.

Robins chirp and hop around
Seeking out grubs in the ground,
Singing their plaintiff song.
The taste of wild blackberries
Still hanging on the bushes.
The smell of bonfires at dusk.

Beautiful skies and sunsets;
All these are joys of autumn.
Seasons pass through storm and strife;
Such is the pattern of life.
The power and might of nature
Is eternal throughout the world.

Helen Persse

TOLERANCE

In these days of trouble and strife,
I find I reminisce more and more.
When, as a child, I never thought
Dark deeds would come to Britain's shore.
World War Two? A nightmare gone,
It should be love and peace,
But now all's changed, no harmony,
Will it never cease?
What matters if we're different colours,
Race or creed, when born,
Tolerance is what is needed,
On behalf of one and all.

M McPhee

MY PETER

He wriggled his pelvis,
As he tried to take-off Elvis.
He thought he was a shocker,
This curly-headed rocker,
Always there, always around,
Didn't sweep me off the ground.
My boyfriend's best mate,
Waited till he became my date.

Can't say when it started,
We even nearly parted.
My friend became my lover,
And I didn't want any other.
This man with deep emotion,
Is my anchor in life's ocean,
Perhaps it's just fate,
He became my soulmate.

Doreen Allenby

COMFORT

Never totally lonely for you are within my mind,
Blending of all feelings, blessing of thoughts entwined.

We share pain and weep, you absorb my tears
And cry with me,
You are within my mind and within my heart,
I am surely blessed with you.

Our spirits blend, only I know you and only you know me,
Two shells - one within the other,
Closer than a shadow.

You have shared every moment of my life,
We were born together,
You breathed life into me and I into you,
The last breath will be the same.

I cannot breathe without you or think without you,
You know my every thought and reason - yet
I do not know your name.

I wonder - are you my soul?

Davina Headland

ASIAN TSUNAMI

What caused this awful happening
On such a bright December day?
It could not be an act of God
Because He does not act that way.

An earthquake far beneath the sea
Rose up and caused a massive wave
Which spread and flooded every land
Within its reach where nothing gave.

Those on the beach were first to see
The rush of water flooding in
Yet had no time to turn and run
Or wonder what was to begin.

Nothing more forceful than the brine
To overwhelm and surely drown
The human life met on its way
And surging on through village and town.

Our God has not forsaken them
He gave them us, who have it all
All those who cannot help themselves
Depend on us to hear His call.

We save and help those found alive
As this great wave now dies away
The world will now come to their aid
Tomorrow will be a better day.

Stan M Tweedie

A MATTER OF TIME

A new baby's born, so age doesn't matter
As its life stretches so far ahead.
Children count every moment of each day, that they greet,
But time creeps so slowly whilst waiting for treats,
Youth is impatient - time starts to fly
Enjoying life fully the years whiz by
Adulthood arrives - now life's full and fine,
Later family matters absorb precious time.
Caring for others fills every day
Suddenly we're aware of time slipping away.
Hurry - chase the dream - make desires come true
Realise time and life are there for you
Enjoy the last years - waste not a day,
For all too soon time has drifted away.

Alice Turner

RECLAIMING LIBERTY

Do you hear the drums of war
Beating down our door?
They call to us
Taking everything within their lust
Leaving nothing behind.

We lose the fight
But we shall not lose the war.

We have forsaken those who were once allies
As they have abandoned us
And accepted thy enemy of thine enemy as thy friend.

We have denounced the old traditions
And created new
So we can regain our liberty and freedom
From our oppression.

We shall reclaim our independence back
And right the wrong that was cast upon us.

Andrew James Ball

REFLECTION

Rivers and valleys can sing
In the tender heart,
As trees and boats grow and ring
Around the sea, like a dart
Flies through the board,
They can murmur to the house.

And the house, as aged as an early gravestone,
Lives and may not wish to rouse
The phantoms, but perhaps they instil tone,
Where a luminous presence
Interns ingrained history.
Other houses decay, and lie
Alone on earth, grass grows and may
Overcome ruins in time; as though to die
As green as possible is to live in the future.
As rains curve and ponder in their downward drop,
The foliage explodes as pure
As herbs from sombre land,
A lifeguard for tomorrow's continuance.

Juliet Fowler

ARMAGEDDON

I dedicate this poem
To all who gave their lives:
The husbands, fathers, brothers,
The sisters, mothers, wives.
All perished in a moment
Too dreadful to believe:
Blown up by evil forces,
Their loved ones left to grieve.
Manhattan now a graveyard
With thousands buried there;
Beyond the reach of mankind,
Resting in God's care.

Since then there's been fresh carnage,
Mass killings far and wide.
In Britain, we'll not falter
To preserve our nation's pride.
These vermin, called 'Fanatics'
Won't flourish on our shores;
Good triumphs over evil
Hard fought for in two wars.

Corinne Lovell

I WANT

I want to wake up with you,
I want to see you with the sleep in your eyes,
Your hair skew-whiff.
I want to watch you getting washed, getting dressed,
I want to be with you.

I want to walk with you,
I want to talk with you, get to know you,
I want to hear all about you,
I want to play with you, lay with you, make love with you.

I want to laugh with you, make you laugh,
Never make you cry,
I want you to make me laugh too.
I want to smile at you, a secret smile that's ours alone.

F M Perry

REFLECTIONS

I looked in the mirror and what did I see?
Of course you have guessed - a reflection of me
I have to admit I don't like what I saw
It showed every wrinkle, blemish and flaw
It's the same when a camera is pointed my way
The results are appalling is all I can say
Then I am told that cameras don't lie
The mirror reflections - I cannot deny
It is the real me I see there displayed
Not someone I hoped would be portrayed
You see I somehow seem to forget
That I am getting older - so must not fret
The images I used to see
Are gone - revealing an older me
I wonder has the inside aged?
Has getting older, my nature changed?
Are there flaws and blemishes there?
Have I forgotten how to care?
All these thoughts invade my mind
But! Consolation I can find
In knowing God will always care
He sees no flaws - or greying hair
I am His child and He will be
My friend through to eternity.

Fran Merrett

SOMETHING TO REMEMBER ME BY

I thought, I know what I should do,
I think I should leave them an old brown shoe.
Perhaps I should leave them an old blue tie
As something for them to remember me by.

Should I be leaving an old shoebox?
Maybe I'll leave them a pair of old socks.
But I still fancy that old blue tie
As something for them to remember me by.

There's poems, rhinos, records galore,
All types of books whatever the score.
I still fancy that old blue tie
As something for them to remember me by.

There are videos, westerns, paintings and a shed,
Which should I leave when I'm lying in my bed?
I think it'll be that old blue tie
As something for them to remember me by.

Steve Randell

BAGGABLES

Because I sailed on Baggables
Around Ionian seas
Good dreams come floating back to me:
Greek wine with feta cheese,
And when the blazing sun went down
Behind a towering hill
Like lotus-eaters we relaxed
Enchantment with us still.
Spellbound - no longer free.

Beyond the shores the dolphins came
Around the yacht one day -
Gliding, diving, playing, leading -
Great joy had come our way
And when they left we found a beach
Beneath a louring hill.
Like lotus-eaters we relaxed
Enchantment with us still.
Suborned - we went to sea.

Back home at last I sit and think
About that magic time.
Greek Islands calling us to stop,
Grand views that were sublime;
And when we sipped the Grecian wine
Beside a rambling rill
Like lotus-eaters we relaxed
Enchantment with us still.
So thank you - 'L' and 'T'!

Evelyn Golding

OUR MISSION

Though we never sailed on a wide ocean
Nor amongst the swiftest fleet
We can make ready for the highest billows
Smiling; at whatever storms we meet
And with the sailors, we can stay
While still anchored on the bay
And give thanks unto the *Lord*
For 'divine' grace.

We may not feel encouraged to travel
Moving backwards - up the hills
Yet we can stand, within the vale
Cheering, the messengers going by
And rejoice in disciplined tones
As they proudly pass along
For though, they may forget the singers
Surely, they'll never forget the song.

We may not give them gold, or silver
But as the Saviour's: true disciples
We will uphold them, with our prayers
And meaningful watch, we'll keep.
We must not be self willed, in waiting
For some grandeur works to do
Knowing 'tattle' is a meddlesome decoy
That will always invade us
And in reality *Christ!* is the *Captain*.
Who redeems us from every fear
And we must repent, and pray always
Striving to be with the *Captain*
On the glorious day; and forever.

Eslyn Coke

THE CHRISTMAS CACTUS

Quietly . . . throughout the year
It stands upon the window sill
A Christmas cactus . . . waiting . . .
Very patiently until . . .

As winter winds herald the snow
And Christmastime is drawing near
It suddenly begins to grow
A host of tiny buds appear.

And hurrying they swell with pride
Huge scarlet spears upon each stem
That trumpet out at Christmastide
To tell the tale of Bethlehem.

And in full bloom this lovely flower
God's floral messenger on Earth
Is there, at the appointed hour
To celebrate a baby's birth . . .

Then, like the Holy star at night
It fades away its service given
Leaving such memories of delight
And maybe, just a glimpse of Heaven.

And quiet again it's back in place
And looks out through the windowpane
Content to wait for beauty's face
Until it's Christmastime again . . .

Dulcie Levene

WHAT PEOPLE SAY ABOUT LOVE

It makes the world go round
which must explain
how flat things are
from my unpartnered perspective.
Not that love itself is absent from my life,
rather the kind of love
that causes hearts to race
and faces flush;
makes lovers eagerly anticipate each day,
count every minute spent apart,
pine pitifully till the next reunion.

Flatly I enjoy the company of friends
with mild pleasure.
Truly time to treasure -
but scarcely ever
(actually never)
what you might call
Wildly exciting.

Julia Murphy

UNTITLED

Passion grows like weeds, forced out of stony ground,
Encircles thought and logic, deceives love, a spring unwound,
Violent, quick and startling, it knows not of who it hurts,
Taking apathy for granted, till it gets its just desserts,
For passion is an empty heart, it carries less devotion,
Wears a mask, never lasts, feels like real emotion,
Shamelessly it plays a role in human nature's plan,
To feed desire into the mind of any foolish man.

Claire Woolmore

ANNABELLE FROM THE UNDERGROWTH

In the evening's gastric turn
Of the sky, the bairn burns cool red
Embers on the damp floor
Of heaven's vanilla spread

And the night is burning citrus
Luminescence, when the sun has waltzed
To its death, leaving the translucent
Clouds gold as the whisky malt

The soft peach marshmallow
Sky skits over the bairn, stood
By the burning cool red
Embers, toasting in the heaven's wood

And in the shadows, she is lit -
Alight with the quarried white chalk
Shade, standing like a calla lily
On a wind-blown wispy stalk.

James McConalogue

FIRST SUMMER SWIM

The sea seems invitingly seductive
As I sit sweltering in the summer sun
Shall I don my plastic shoes
And move perilously over shifting pebbles?

Children barefooted, seemingly oblivious to pain
Move swiftly over this uneven surface
Towards the waves
Laughing and carefree as they dip in and out of the water.

The temptation of cooling salt sea
Lures me in
Like walking over hot coals
I approach my target.

At last I feel the cold seeping through my limbs
And plunge headlong through the surf
An icy chill pervades my body
But soon I'm swimming, relaxed and free.

I pity the sun-baked cowards
Reddened and hot sprawled on pebbled shore
Not chancing this cooling pleasure
Of a first summer swim.

Sonia Richards

LITTLE PEOPLE, BIG WORLD

Given to us at birth,
The way we live on Earth,
In our colour, race and faith,
Always some who are born to hate.
Their adversaries are the same!

Bombs against faith go flying,
While the young innocent ones lay dying,
Boys who have grown into men,
Tortured by their beliefs and fighting again.
They are all the same!

Both breathe the same air,
Have the same thoughts,
Both want the same,
Peace of some sort!
We are all the same!

Our globe is so big,
Their thoughts so small
They can't or won't see,
It's big enough for all.
Are we all the same?

Kerry Shepherd

LISTEN TO THE CHILDREN OF LANCASHIRE'S YESTERDAY

If we listen to the children of Lancashire's far-off yesterday,
Tales of posser, stone pop hot-water bottles
And whip-top play,
Of workhouse, and local witch doctors you didn't have to pay,
Then our ears are carried tram-like to an uncompromising past,
When the only Big Smoke they knew
Came from King Cotton's chimneys.
Here is the garden
From whose blades we now shade in shadows.
Their own chimneys,
Dotted around their toil-strained workplaces,
Houses of sooted black brick,
Surrounded by stripes of crushed cobbles.
Backyards, backstreets, with lines slung to hold pegged sheets,
Flapping at cats that daily marked their cottonland territory.
Listening still, we can hear the clog-footed, cloth-capped,
Walking past the glistening donkey-stoned front steps,
And sense inside the smell of home-baked bread and pies.

If we listen to the children of Lancashire's yesterday,
We will hear of how they were loved in their day,
Under a warless sky,
And saw hope spring up like bluebells in a forest,
Taught to play as small footballers or Florence Nightingales,
Heroes were Eagle, Dandy, Beano comic characters
And Saturday matinees.
Coronation mugs, plates and imitation anointing spoons
Announced a new monarch,
London trickled down aerials to screens
Speaking another language than Lancashire.
Children armed with encyclopaedias, aimed like 11+ arrows,
To make their mark and join the BBC speak of respectability.
Opportunity presented the Lancashire community's
Children with escape from factory-land,
Start a Mersey beat band, or even University.

The Lancashire children of today
Can hear the camaraderie fade away,
Building blocks of greed pile up like PlayStation screens,
Soap operas of violence, sitcoms, gameshows,
Superstore wine and soufflé,
The watchful eye of Big Brother,
Evenings out at the theatre, or in at the gym,
Holidays in Spain, cheap gin, sand, sex
And the laughter of Mammon's grin!

Peter Vaughan Williams

RECOVERY

The time has come for tears to start again,
Those faithful tears that always ease the pain.
Release the raging rivers of my soul!
Let me drown and then rise up again.

Let me drown until the river dries,
Until the numbing coldness settles in,
See the world once more with empty eyes,
No spark of warmth can penetrate the skin.
Crash the thunder! Howl the wind!
Freeze my heart and beat the driving rain!
Let me know these dreams are empty lies.
Let me die and come to life again.

In the silent darkness of my mind
Let me wonder who you really are,
Let me feel that you were just a dream
That fades on waking, like the morning star . . .

Bernie Morris

HANKIE FULL OF LOVE

She'd care and nurse and comfort, those children every day
From all the falls and trials of life that seemed to come their way
A clean white hankie was always on hand to wipe a tear-stained face
Or, if needed, two loving arms would be close by just in case.

She had seen children come and go, for far too many years
And she was the one who stayed behind to wipe away the tears
Of the children who were never chosen, but left alone again
Wanting a mummy or daddy, she felt those poor children's pain.

Good days would come, as did the smiles of the children she cared about
And if any tears would happen to flow, she'd take that white hankie out
Orphans they were and this was her job, to keep them in her care
To tell them and believe it herself, there was someone for them out there.

She'd love to keep them all she thought, as she lay in bed each night
Why children should be passed around, she'd never thought it right
Like buyers going to the shops to see what they could choose
Or people that went out each week, just to try on different shoes.

She knew while in her keeping, that they were happy for a while
They'd hang on to her every word and look for her motherly smile
In time some children would leave, for those left, it would be tough
But they knew she'd always be there with her hankie full of love.

Elizabeth McNeil

RITES OF WAR

When reading of wars comprehensive
'tactics, strategy and guile
Ludendorff seems most impressive
Liddel Hart somehow lacks style
Beers' latest work is intensive
so innocent, so brave and so true
Hindenburg's clinical, yet restive
Clarke says little that's new
Near the Para buried under the hillock
Moan nightly 'neath dark, leafy bowers
They had more pillocks on their side
Than we, thank Christ, had on ours!'

Budd Hulme

THE WINE MAKER

It was the best time of year when the fruit
Hung heavy on the vines that wound and twined,
And apples and pears dangled from trees
To be gathered that day to make the wine
While the sun was gold and the fruit was warm.

We collected ripe fruit to take back home
To pulp and press, to make the juice weep
And seep, drip-by-drip, and then to ferment
When it sprung to life, surged and bubbled,
So it seemed we could hardly contain it.

But before long, the sound of the *plop-plop*
Of the airlock was heard, holding steady
As the tick of a clock, or a heartbeat,
Until it slowed right down and it stopped,
And then time was measured by years not days.

I recall the times we shared like fine wine,
And open a bottle and pour a glass
To savour the flavour of years now passed,
Of springtime bud and flowers come to fruit
Sparkling within the spirit of the wine.

I see the glint of light within the wine
Like the twinkle that was in your eyes,
And I raise my glass to the memories
When we held hands beneath the vines and trees
Before the harvest came for the wine maker.

Billy Jones

THE VETERAN

This old man was telling me
All about his life,
About the war, his mum and dad,
Even about his wife.

He told me he was a soldier,
And he fought for country and king,
I thought it was amazing
How he remembered everything.

He remembered going to school,
A teacher called Mr White
Who used to hit you with his stick
If you didn't get everything right.

He remembered joining the army,
Fighting to set us all free,
And remembered getting married,
At the age of 23.

He had a wife called Pearl,
They had a son called Fred,
But now he was all alone
For both of them were dead.

And then it was time for me to leave,
And as I shook his hand,
I was thinking of a wonderful guy
Who helped to save our land.

For so many risked life and limb
To give us what we have got,
That we hardly ever realise
That this is such a lot.

Marvyn Attwell

THE CHILD . . .

She sat alone in her womb, damaged body,
With lopsided face, and fine wispy hair.
Her eyes so crooked, her teeth already damaged.
A twisted body - it seemed so unfair,
Her fragile frame, out of all proportion, with flailing limbs,
Lips slightly blue, with the weakness of her heart.
She stood herself up, and limped across the room
To her teacher, ready to try and paint a work of art.
As she saw the bright piece of paper,
Excitement rose and, although mute,
She made her presence felt.
I watched enthralled, as she suddenly smiled,
And came towards me. I felt my emotions melt.
Her face just moments before, had seemed almost ugly,
Yet now came alive as she held my hand.
Her crooked eyes, once vacant, twinkled with laughter,
As though a fairy had waved a wand.
I felt so blessed as I saw this transformation.
A child with no hope, or worth, by the world unaware.
And yet in those few minutes,
Showed such beauty that one rarely sees;
Such a blessing to share.

J Bootle

A SIGN OF THE TIMES

You are never alone with a mobile phone
Each one has a different tone
People walking with a hand to their ear
Snippets of conversation! 'What time shall I meet you there?'
Feeling in pockets, fumbling in bags. It really drives you mad
They can be such a nuisance, it's happening all the time,
                                        there goes that tune again

Now where did I put mine?

Kathleen Price

SOFTLY

You close your eyes so sweet and fair,
As I watch the moonlight in your hair
And softly whisper in your sleep,
You pray the Lord your soul to keep.

There's so much peace but quietly still,
The wind outside blows with a chill
Trapped in a world so full of hate,
The world beyond the garden gate.

Warmest love within our space,
A gift from Heaven, not from grace
This quiet night is short alas,
As I see through its painted glass.

The trees may sway as clouds pass by,
The stars still twinkle in the sky
You sleep so soundly, pillow deep,
Still praying for your soul to keep.

Marion McGarrigle

THE LOVELY HARVEST

Lord, we thank Thee for the harvest,
For the fields of golden grain,
Full matured by summer's sunshine,
And with cool refreshing rain.

Ripened fruits, now waxing mellow
Soon from orchards will be stored,
And the vineyards blessed bounty
Of red wine will be outpoured.

As the leaves are softly falling,
Red and gold, and russet brown,
Nature opens up her paint box,
To adorn her autumn gown.

Now the harvest moon is rising
Over all the Earth to shine,
Lord, we thank Thee for the harvest,
And each perfect gift of Thine.

Yes, we thank Thee for the harvest,
And each perfect gift of Thine.

Marjorie Jones

POETS, ARTISTS AND ANGELS

It takes the fine heart of a true poet's pen,
To express the right words for others, now and then.
It takes that pen to write out the thought,
To help others find what loving has brought.
It takes the expression from a heart of pure gold,
To tell of a story that's maybe never been told.
Sometimes it takes an inkwell full of tears
To relay the heartache of a broken heart's fears.
It takes a heart that often gets to surely swell
With thought for others from a magical vast well.
It takes the writer to share such emotion
To make others smile with such truest devotion.
It takes the thought to write words for God
To help many find the path they should have trod
It takes the pain from experience and strife
To surely raise some hope in many a stranger's life.
It takes but only a sweet, simple thought
For a poet's imagination to be surely caught,
But whatever it truly is that we poets surely do,
Let's hear it for poets, for we do this for you.

C R Slater

THE ELEPHANT MAN

The roads of Leicester were cobbled and bare,
When not far from Lee Street there travelled a fair,
Showmen, elephants all thronged the town,
Young Mary Merrick (with child) she fell down,
Merrick - the Elephant man - befriended by Treves
Thus long before birth had the marks of disease.

Joseph when born was quite normal and well,
But as he grew older his form you could tell
Was not as it should be, his head all enlarged,
One hand its function could not now discharge,
Merrick - the Elephant Man - befriended by Treves
His mother's kind love was his only release.

His father disowned him - work was there none,
Three years with the Poor Law when Mother was gone,
His life was so lonely, wretched and poor,
As freak in a fairground he started to tour,
Merrick - the Elephant Man - befriended by Treves
Surrounded by nothing but fleers and fleas.

To London he came at the mercy of Torr,
Where there in Whitechapel Fred'rick Treves he saw,
Doctor of fame at the East End Hospice,
Saviour for Joseph from his all abyss,
Merrick - the Elephant Man - befriended by Treves
Found comfort and succour for his primitive needs.

In secret now, a dandy 'bout town
Joseph met royalty, women renown,
To country and theatre - mixed with the best,
Bedstead Square was his haven of rest,
Merrick - the Elephant Man - befriended by Treves
His modest ambitions he humbly achieves.

Apart from just one - to lay down to rest
The death of Joseph when put to the test
At seven and twenty his spirit had waned
But victory o'er that lame freak had gained
Merrick - the Elephant Man - befriended by Treves
Despite his despair, a moral he leaves.

Tony Emmott

THE GEM

You saved my life completely,
My dog and my best friend,
And whatever else may happen,
I'll love you till the end.

First I lost my partner,
Then my dog of many years,
I never thought it possible,
To shed so many tears.

Then my family suggested
That I 'give a dog a home,'
And that is what inspired me
To dedicate this poem

To the dog whose life I also saved,
From a shelter far away,
The day we met each other,
Was a very special day.

By my side forever,
I hope you'll always stay
Bringing me such pleasure
And joy from day to day.

S Stalker

THE WAY WE WERE

(In memory of Muffin, my Cairn Terrier)

I know that a dog is only to lend -
But Muffin and I were pals to the end.
Had fun and we played all over the place,
I threw her ball and she would give chase.
We travelled the country on foot and by car
And she'd walk beside me - both near and afar.
Trained to be agile. Trained to be good.
She complied with my wishes as only she could.
She was my pal and a loyal one at that
And all that she'd want was a word and a pat.
But time marched on its way. The years quickly sped
And Muffin grew grey around muzzle and head.
Still happy and lively and so full of fun,
It was really a shock when the dread day did come.
I held her head gently. I cuddled her tight
As those beautiful eyes lost their life's light.
I stroked her and whispered, 'I love you, I do.'
And I left the room knowing it'd be hard to get through
The days and the nights without my best friend,
But thankful I was chosen for Muffin, to lend.
Alone then - I walk the very same street
That Muffin and I walked. Wait! There, at my feet!
From the edge of my eye I know I can see
A tenuous shadow accompanying me.
There scurries a terrier, with thick golden fur,
A poignant reminder - of the way we once were!

Joyce Dobson

MEDITATIONS IN MY GARDEN

I whiled away the morning hours toiling in my garden,
And lovingly I hoed and pruned the roses I had planted,
So that a scented coloured loveliness would fill my eden.
I toiled with carefree heart
While admiring the russet leaves of springtime.
So close and deep within the earth
My fork unlocked the clay soil.
I heard their rapturous sighs
As pure fresh air caressed the clay packed roots.
I bent my back beneath a thorny bush
And there strove bravely,
But gave a wrench and from my hand
The blood flowed fast and sorely.
I dropped the fork and cursed the bush I had nursed so dearly
And then I thought of people, things and times,
Which had possessed me:
Of beauty, truth and goodness, God and men,
And lovely women!
I know that women, beautiful and pleasing in their appearance,
And so in touch and sensual variance,
Skilled at giving utmost pleasure,
Can wound and cause the greater hurt
When finished with their dalliance.
In search of God, truth and knowledge -
Spiritual things availing,
With Paul-like cries we curse and rant with egotistic pleadings,
And then at last we gleam the pure and prefect peace,
Which is abiding.
So what is life without its sensual beauty, pain and sorrow?
Ah! when we live in fullness, taking all that life will offer,
We must accept all acmes, whether pleasant or destructive.
Between the peak and the abyss, the greater in their distance,
The greater knowledge, strength, love, joy,
Compassion   and courage
Is given for a fuller, truer life to be experienced.

Stuart Plumley

THE LORRY DRIVER

He sits all alone,
On the side of the road,
Miles from home,
For company a radio and phone,
Nothing can compare,
Being somewhere with her,
And being alone.
His cab is empty as is his heart,
Yet still apart,
But the night will end,
He will race to his love,
Into her arms, with kisses he will cover.
Then a call on the phone,
Heralds life all alone,
On the rolling black,
Bag and coat in the back,
In his thinking world of the lorry cab.
He sees the road and thinks of her,
A few hours ago, of the way they were,
Grey massing clouds, trees a blur,
He knows the route well, but his mind is astir,
For it takes him so far away from her.
He remembers years gone by,
When the sight of a lorry lit his eye,
Thought of the road would bring a sigh,
Now he knows with age and time,
Overtaking life sublime,
For the knights of the road on the rolling black,
Times have changed clocks do not turn back.

A Birley

BEAUTY WITHIN

She'll never be a beauty
Her clothes aren't quite in style
But always you are greeted
With a warm, friendly smile.

Just an 'ordinary person'
That's what I can see
No superficial make-up
To hide away from me.

The hand that reaches out
Simply says it all
Beauty isn't always
Where your eyes should fall.

Though her form is heavy
And her fashion sense not good
There are other things to see
As I know I should!

Obviously quite unperturbed
She's not tall, and slender
That her hair's drawn back
And 'looks' aren't in her gender.

It's not just appearance
When looking one to one
That's all on the surface and
One day it will be gone!

But there's kindness in her eyes
And within a warm heart
What better place
For beauty to start?

Susan Green

IN MEMORY OF ONE OF OUR LOURDES WORKERS

Now you've gone to God and Heaven's shores,
Think sometimes of those of us, who must still fulfil life's chores,
Remember the laughs, the arguments,
The work and so much more,

Of memories we treasure from days of yore.

The virgin from the grotto and poor, sick, saintly Bernadette
Await you at the door, arms outstretched,
A son who's always loyal and true to wife and family,
Home and work,
Friends and to Lourdes and the Boy Scouts too,
Arrives with plenty to offer from a life well spent,
A reward and rest well earned,
A home with God to which you've gone so well prepared.

Aileen Atcheson

ASHES TO ASHES

(Revived Sept '05)

You tell me of Botham, of Lindwall, of Don,
The all-time greats that we look back upon,
But I would tell you a Flintoff called Fred,
Is our modern hero in cricket instead.

In the series of summer two thousand and five,
The game woke up and began to thrive,
Heroic performances with bat and ball
From both sides, left the crowds in a thrall.

Warne, the magician, his fingers did curl,
Left most of our chaps in a twirl or a whirl,
But 'Freddy The Great' came and steadied the ship,
And found the answer to Shane's deadly flip.

After matches of tension and high drama too,
The scoreboard read: *Aus 1, England 2,*
The custody of that diminutive urn,
On the result of the final match would turn.

England had already been 'Warned',
When the final day of destiny dawned.
The weather had also played its part,
And threatened to break Australia's heart.

Now all was set fair, English hopes took a dive,
By lunch their wickets were down to five,
Just a few runs ahead, Shane and Glenn on the bounce,
The Aussies were getting ready to pounce.

Comes the hour, comes the man - 'KP' is the brand,
Not just a nut, 'Special K' - it's all planned!
Partnership with our spinner 'Ash', (surnamed Giles),
Record stand, match drawn, the English all smiles.

Won the Ashes!

The most important score sheet of all,
Cricket has won, you sportsmen stand tall,
Those frenzied appeals and oaths from the men,
Are gone! All is fun, till that time when again

We play Aussies!

The final thought is for Richie, the voice,
The modest Aussie declares - it's his choice,
The spin doctor delivers his verdict no more,
He'll only be heard on a far distant shore,

Lamenting Aus and the Ashes!

Brian Fisher

HEAVEN-SENT

A festive Christmas Day in the year nineteen hundred
and sixty-four,
A gigantic, bursting sack was waiting with Nigel written on it
At seven years of age a sleepless night of eagerness was over.
After months of searching round the house,
Looking for giant boxes or hidden bags full of toys,
The uncertain endless questions of, 'Have I got that?'
The moment of truth had arrived at last,
Had I really got everything on my extra long list
That was burnt in the roaring fire to a fine black crisp?
It was time to see if Santa had delivered.
Perched high on top of the pile of colourful presents,
A glittering, decorative, red paper parcel,
Curious for a second before I seized it, ready to pull, rip and tear,
'Look at the label please,' came a cry of a woken up parent!
At a glance I saw *lots of love from Auntie Eileen and Uncle Ted*
No time wasting was allowed,
Hundreds of presents needed my uttermost attention,
Inside was a superb reading book of quality,
The 'Round The Clock' short stories,
I must remember to read it later.
(Just my oh so crafty plan to stay up a bit longer).
Exhausted after playing with all my new toys,
A tired yawn was spotted,
I then heard the command, 'You can go to bed.'
'But please, please let me read my new book before I go.'
'OK but make it quick.'
I started to read about the mean old man,
The magic comeback spell caused a stir when he
failed to pay
First the newspaper fled from his grasp and started to return,
How I laughed at the string of sausages with fast tiny little legs,
Running like a supercharged caterpillar, past the yapping,
barking dogs,
Even the eggs grew funny chicken legs to go back to
Mrs Cluck.
Perhaps old Father Time had taken my dear Auntie away.
As she rests upon the clouds so high up above,
I hope she can see me reading once again,
My 'Round The Clock' stories,
That must have been heaven-sent.

Nigel Astell

OUR GREATEST NEED

Our, greatest need is to be needed,
If, we are to feel at our best,
We feel, so alone and useless
When the young ones have all flown the nest.

We need to feel we are still useful
To give us the reason to live.
After years of loving and caring,
We still feel, we have something to give.

Home and family have been our mainstay
Our lives, our love, we have given our all
Now they have gone on their own way
Memories, are all, we have to recall.

Our greatest need is still to be needed
To play a part while we still may.
To feel, we are helping someone, somewhere,
Gives us, a reason to stay.

Our dearest wish is to be told we are loved,
To hear you say that you care; and
When our day is done, you, will be the one
To see us home, with a hymn and a prayer.

Madge Goodman

THE NATIONAL HEALTH SERVICE

It was in the year of forty-eight or maybe forty-seven,
A service was created for the good of our nation,
It was called National Health and for everyone of any age
A contribution was taken from out of our wage.
We thought it was great, the future was bright
Doctors and dentists were free; it was now our right,
There's no need to worry is what we were told
There'd also be a pension for when we were old.

For nearly sixty years we've had this great institution
There's been many changes, too many to mention,
The government tell us, it's still going well
The medical people have a different story to tell.
You can't see a dentist unless you can pay
It's possible doctors could go the same way
Hospitals are under pressure with targets to meet
Health care workers are rushed off their feet
We're told to save for our own pension
If we want enough money to survive
Or carry on working 'til we reach seventy-five!

So what's happened to the service for everyone of any age
A contribution still taken from out of our wage.
There's something wrong here we're all paying twice
We're soon going to be as poor as church mice.

We'd like now to ask the government
Whom we elected in parliament to sit
Can we please have the service we pay for
To keep us all healthy and fit?

Margaret Rhodes

I DREAMT OF A CHANGED WORLD

One morning when I opened my eyes
Glanced through the windows to the skies
The golden sunshine brightened my heart
I thought, *what a beautiful start to my day*

I had woken up in a changed and different world
This was a new Earth, where fear, anguish, pain never stirs,
No more minds and thoughts causing panic and despair,
Only kindness, peace, love and happiness
Showed in this place.

Old women now walked the streets
Without fear of being attacked,
No more muggings, physical abuse,
Pushed around and sworn at,
Only kind words, help, and support in crossing the road
Many would smile and say hello,
And even help to carry a heavy load.

Children now run, jump and play, all the way to school,
No wicked people to harm, rape, kill, destroy, or remove
Only protection, guidance,
Are given to children in this new world,
Our children are no longer frightened, fearful,
But confident and happy.

Women can walk the streets any time of day or night
No one will molest, intimidate, causing hurt or fear of flight.
A word of welcome,
Acknowledgement are commonly accepted.
Sadly when I became fully awake,
This world was only a dream
Earth's reality with all its evil and imperfections
Remains the same.

Cora Woolcock

ANNUAL PILGRIMAGE

For one brief moment while the world is still
Thoughts undimmed remind those spared,
The pain of loss and violent grief
As they hold back their tears.

Prayers, often heard, to strengthen faith
With words 'rest eternal' ringing in their ears
Which once were deaf while battles raged
In deserts, fields and suffocating jungles.

The few and frail will make this march their last.
Their spirits will not die as their successors bear
Such witness as their conscious pride allows.

When the march had played its echo
And tongues are loosened to proclaim
The joy of comradeship so many years ago
Some must wonder if those very thoughts
That swiftly passed in youth are with them now
Without the bragging, *'They won't get me'*.

Only Christ knows what suffering is
With His unequalled and unending faith.
For one brief moment some believe they know
The mystery of that faith
And of that agony too.

Michael Davidson

ALL IS NOT WELL IN PARADISE

They call it the Hotel Phoenicia -
It's cool, it's marbled, and it's plush.
The garden's designed and manicured,
The grass is watered and lush.

The sweeping drive leads down
To a magnificent wrought iron gate,
Which protects us, the tourist
From whatever lies in wait.

For down the white ribbon of road
Just a few hundred yards from our splendour,
Is a kind of shanty town settlement
Where sustenance is slender.

A sad and tethered donkey
Barely raises his head
While dirty children reach out
And unashamedly beg.

The weary-eyed locals ply their wares,
For us, they're souvenirs.
For them, a meagre wage
To sustain them through the years.

So all is not as it may seem
Behind the bright façade,
But we'll only mention the weather
When we send the obligatory card.

Jeannie Price

RETURNING HOME

My father was taken to war
I, only a baby.
The days, the months and years
Went by, until the day, this
Soldier stood at the door.
I didn't know him and ran
To my mother, who said,
'It's Daddy returning home to us.'
That day, I'll never forget.

Gloria A Jackson

THUNDER

Hello, my name is Thunder and I've come here tonight
To visit each and every one and give you all a fright,
I'm very, very loud, I bang, roar and shout,
When people hear my mighty voice, no one will dare come out.

Lightning is my name, I can scare much more than you,
You can see my big, bright lights, as I make a flash or two,
I can frighten every one, when I dance across the skies,
Even little children, stay still with tight shut eyes.

Well, I am not afraid, I've come to move you on,
My name is Heavy Shower - now both of you be gone,
I'm liked a lot, it's true, I know there's no mistake,
I see the little children play in the puddles I make.

Hi there, my name's Wind - I'm very good indeed
At helping Heavy Shower when he gives the plants a feed,
Sometimes I'm very naughty and blow you all about,
But I know you really like me - when you hang your washing out.

I'm really very beautiful - I'm the prettiest of us all,
I encourage little flowers to stand up nice and tall,
My rays are very warm - my face is very bright,
There's a little bit of magic in my warm sunlight.

Jack Frost and White Snowflake, we're sure you know our names,
When children see us out - they join in fun and games,
We make things look so pretty, all white and crispy clean,
Just like a Christmas card with a pretty Christmas scene.

We know we get you mad when we get things in a mess,
But we'd like you all to know, we try our very best,
Now we are so important and what gives us all a buzz,
Is knowing all of you - could never live without us.

Margaret Taylor

GRANDMOTHER

Grey crowns her brow,
No longer sleek and black with youth,
But memories are rooted there,
Telling their own story,
A different tale from the one we see,
Blind and dumb that we are,
In our notions and perceptions.

Vital, if frail,
Withered by the foe of time
In body, not in spirit,
This essence still alive and well,
Filled by life's rich tapestry.
Wisdom and love find their mirror in her eyes,
Pools that shine with tenderness
And sing her secret song.

Slowness dulls her movements,
Stooped and bowed,
Not upright like a soldier;
The gal of yesteryear.
Debilitation halts the flow
Of dextrous, dainty fingers,
Once source of countless crochets,
Special smocking, socks and skirts.

Days roll mellow, perennially paced,
Full of inactivity, in place of productivity.
Spouse of a husband who serves and adores
And could not dream of life without her.

She is cherished. She is here now.
She will one day walk through another door,
Leaving the vale of tears
And a hundred broken hearts behind her.

Caroline Baker

THE CALL

When I came onto this Earth
He was present for my birth.
Touched the locks upon my head -
so my mother always said.
I had feet so strong and straight
made to walk to Pearly Gate -
webbed to walk upon the sea -
I was sent to set men free.
So I've waited all these years
for the call to calm your fears.

Now my life is nearly done -
battles fought, but seldom won.
Help the wife to clean and cook -
gas stove bright and doormat shook.
Change the library book once more -
walk the dog along the shore.
Though it sometimes seems like bliss
was I only sent for this?
Will the message ever come?
Must I wait till Kingdom come?

But I think it's now too late -
for too long I've had to wait.
All I do is sit and think,
staying home to clean the sink.
Now I know I'm only mortal
and I'll never storm that portal.
So with life I'm now content -
autumn days are heaven-sent.
Someone else must take the call.
Someone else must save you all.

Jack Williamson

DOON HILL

At the very top of the hill
I'm rooted to the spot
As time ceases
And all becomes still.

The deep hills stand behind me
Spotlighted by the sun,
Shadows protect the secret places
Where the wild creatures run.
Trees murmur to each other
The intrusion of a stranger,
And the sea spread out far below,
Flat and calm and blue.

Silence

Until the cornfield nearby
Erupts with the song and flight
Of skylarks,
Disturbed
By something unseen.

Silence

Apart from the hum of a thousand bees
Ecstatic in a banquet of clover
And concerned as I walk by,
Brushing the grass
As I walk the cement lines
That trace the place
Where a building once stood
In a different time.

Ages melt together - did they see
The skylarks and the bees,
Did they listen to the stillness
And feel the peace balm of this place?

Sheena Conroy

EVERY DAY

If every day was a holiday
Would we have the choice
Of not to be
Or want to be in one united voice
If every day was a holiday
In more ways than just one
Or travelling at a snails pace
Would we find ourselves outrun
If we knew the answers
Would we really care
As long as life is a holiday
That everyone can share.

F R

THE STRENGTH FROM THE PAST

Always, the thoughts of home,
Of my childhood, tucked away
Within flourishing garden
(My own small patch blazing with flowers).
Sustain me now, whenever bitter strife
Tries to defeat my endeavours; the thoughts
Of sunny days that filled my life
With childish delight, so positive
In its simple way, so full of smiling joy
And kindness, flowing from parents
So understanding, loving, caring; and I, a boy
With a mother and father, who possessed
The usual values of average, decent people, then.
I was a happy child, doubly blessed
In belonging to them and sharing their name.
Yes, the thoughts of that far-in-the-past existence
Sustain me now, almost on every step;
The roots of my being, the will, the persistence
Stem from my childhood; in my journey
Through life they give me confidence
And strength . . .

Daniela M Davey

THE VOTE

They did not vote, they could not vote,
For they were not yet twenty-one,
Then came six long years of war,
No voting for anyone.
They did not vote, they could not vote,
For they were said to be too young,
Yet old enough to answer the call,
For the war had to be won.

Old enough to fight on land, in the air and on the sea,
Old enough to face the foe, to defend democracy,
Old enough to lay down their lives, to keep our country free,
Old enough to make the great sacrifice, to keep us from slavery,
Age did not count at El Alamein, or in Sicily,
At Salerno, Cassino, the beaches of Normandy,
In the jungles of Burma, as prisoners of war,
To suffer atrocities, on the 'railway', Changi or Singapore.

What would they say of us today, this generation,
Some thought it too far to walk, to the poling station,
Others said, 'I couldn't care less, I'm making no decision,'
Many choose to stay at home, watching television,
What would they say, all those who lie
In foreign fields alone,
The only cross against their name
Is the 'Cross' that's carved in stone.

A P Blackwell

LADY HEROIN

You listen to your radio, sound pounding out the speaker.
The words are muffled, the sound distorted.
The tune is in beat with your racing pulse.
And you feel yourself growing weaker.

The money you earn goes down the drain,
You waste it that way so you don't have to suffer the pain.
Walking down the street, one step then another,
Everyone staring with cold eyes,
Saying you're a disgrace, to that you despise.
They think it's Heaven, the world they live in,
Your kind of Heaven comes from within.

With the push of the plunger you feel relaxed,
A warm, calm feeling is rushing throughout your veins.
The feeling is tunnelling through your body.
Nothing can stop it, you don't want to stop it.
You want it to last, last like a rainbow
Because they say it never ends.

The dragon on the table looks so inviting.
Lady Heroin is calling your name.
She has done it before, she'll do it again,
Sitting there, wondering, should you answer her call?
Time is passing by and the warm, calm feeling is leaving your body.

You're stupid you know. You answered her call.
She called you so softly, how could you refuse.
It's not the way you're supposed to live,
But it's the way you choose.

Slowly, the sound from the speaker is fading out.
Your pulse is racing faster and faster,
While you are growing weaker and weaker.
Lady Heroin has called your name for the last time.
Now she must find a new victim.

Carrie Stuart

BEST OF DAYS

You are the one who has thrown me a line
Saving me with your love time after time
Pulling me up when the feelings are low
Giving me focus and reasons to grow
Happy together and lonely apart
Thinking of you pulls the strings of my heart
Only with you do the days look so bright
The love that you bring just makes everything right.

Safe in the knowledge you're always around
Helping me keep both my feet on the ground
Love is the answer and love is the key
To keep me afloat in a turbulent sea
The strength that you give me makes everything clear
I cannot function unless you are near
Walking a tightrope from which I could fall
You steady the line and make sense of it all.

Things look so simple when seen through your eyes
Out in the open no need for disguise
With cards on the table, no tricks up your sleeve
You are my rock I can always believe
Quick with a smile to lighten the load
You are my guide so I take the right road
My best friend, my lover and all that conveys
You've enriched my life with the best of days.

Tony Hucks

IN A TRIANGLE

I have a confession to make
I've fell for you both
How can I tell
Which of you I feel the most?

You're both gorgeous
You both make me smile
Restoring the feeling
I lost for a while

This kind of thing
Doesn't happen to me a lot
Either of you could give me
The love I haven't got

But how do I decide
Between you two?
When you've got others
You care for too

Though I'm not sure if you
Have a love which is true
Because I've been close
To both of you

Simon McAlear

AN ODE FOR THE PRESS GANG

You started small
You grew tall
And look where you are now
Still you are strong
Fifteen years on
Power to the writer's brain.

It didn't take long
For us to write in
A chance for the likes of me
To see in print
The words that we wrote
Power to the writer's brain.

So here we all are
With many a gold star
Ego's big as balloons
To give thanks on this day
For the role that you play
Gifts from the writer's pen.

Alison Hitch

SUMMER'S LEASE

How eager are buds in May
ready to show their hidden secrets?
Lilies impatient
herald
passionate red
and citrus-yellow flutes.
Bees, in earnest, seek apple blossoms
nurturing the fruit with their labours.
A flutter of butterflies
scatter
along the lavender hedge.
The maple opens deep crimson leaves
to the warmth of the midday sun.
Only the willow
has the audacity;

to weep.

Joyce Graham

LOOK AND LISTEN

Look more closely at all you see -
Exquisite flowers and bumblebees;
Detailed petals, accurate flight -
Colours and textures all around to delight.

Watch the flight of the little birds
Gliding strongly with wings unfurled.
Yet landing delicately upon the ground
Or hovering briefly without a sound.

Soundless too the fishes swim,
Moving swiftly with tails and fins.
But listen now to sounds you hear
Which soothe and calm the inner ear.

The ebb and flow of sea on the shore
Fluffy kittens as they gently purr.
Whispering sounds of the shivering breeze
Rustling the leaves amongst the trees.

And what of the people you meet each day?
Happy children enjoying their play?
Take time to listen to everyone speak
And notice this - that each is unique.

Look at each face, acknowledge each smile,
Focus your thoughts and ponder awhile
The colour of the eyes, the curve of the hair,
The tint of the skin, the lines that are there.

Breathtaking beauty and colour and art,
Who may we thank from the depths of our hearts?
Oh, listen now and joyfully sing,
Praise Him forever, our Maker and King!

Christine Lemon

GLEN AFFRIC

Gentle water laps against the shore,
Old trees drip with mossy lichen,
Swampy grass sinks beneath the feet,
Stepping stones from island to shore,
The rain starts bleakly drizzling,
The sun starts sinking,
The cold seeps in,
Darkness grows more and more,
Then . . .

Midges!
Midges, midges in my hair,
Midges, midges in the air,
Biting, itching, scratching!

Ellie Boardman

FOR ELLIOT JAMES - BORN 4TH APRIL 2005

Welcome, my bonny, bawling boy
To your place on this beautiful, bountiful planet.
May the earth be soft and green to welcome you when you fall
And may there always be someone to help you rise again.
May love encompass you all your days
And may you know that, in love, it is better to give than to receive.
May music surround your waking and your sleeping
And may you learn to dance to your own tune.
May laughter be the sun in your sky
And when you weep, may you never weep alone.
May you enjoy a pint, with company, on the roaring days
And may you relish the quiet solitude of the wild mountains
And the sea.
May you know the satisfaction of honest toil
And may your life's work be never quite completed.
And when your time comes, may a pure, white swan
Carry your soul swiftly back to your father in Heaven.

David W Lankshear

THE STATUE

Sir Grimsby Smythe, what did you do
for them to make a fuss of you?
You're standing there, you hand held high
your finger pointing to the sky.
Are you trying to convey to us
occupants of this passing bus.
That what you did, brought much relief
brought to an end a lot of grief.
The children think that it's a lark
that you gaze sternly o'er the park.
Whatever it was, the birds don't care
as they anoint your thinning hair.
It makes a pattern, just like lace
as guano trickles down your face.
The locals say it's a disgrace
the council don't clean up the place.
Praise his name, you and your neighbour,
for he invented toilet paper.

John J Allan

THIS GARDEN OF MINE

There's a handful of memories in this
Garden of mine,
'Yet we can't see the wood for the
Trees'.

There's notches been made where a
Family have grown,
'Yet we've covered them up with the
Leaves'.

There's flowers still struggling to
Come out and survive, given from friends
Of the past,
The flowers still bloom in a dried up earth,
Yet the friendships don't always last.

A book could be written in this 'Garden of
Mine' and the pages turned over like leaves
And we'd find the reason for the mistakes
We have made,
'We can't see the wood for the trees'.

June Sedgebear

SEPIA

It's all in time
I swear it's saltwater in my eyes
But these hourglass days are bruising us
And I'm gone from how Father Time's been using us

It's all in sync and in rhyme
Like memories of youth on a fishing line
Everything's faded like photographs
While I'm counting the seconds and paragraphs

It's all a big scene
I'm tumbling in tall grass
And out of trees
Where is the wind that was in our sails?
As we cling to the past with our fingernails

It snakes and it winds
Like old fashioned songs from another time
I'm froze by the cold that the winter brings
But still through the snow I can hear them sing.

Antony Hateley

HEAL THE HURT
(Fight The Fury)

The tides are rising higher, faster
The pace of life and time are flying
Back on course for another disaster
You can sense the pain, sense the crying

Rage on the road, rage in the shops
I see no feeling, see no love
Hoping, praying this will stop
Searching inside, searching above

The angry architects of self-pursuit
Chasing gratifying dreams of greed
Single-mindedly snatching the fruit
With every willful deed

Hatred humming from every hive
Cruelly cutting across the divide
Does it make you glad to be alive?
Do you gain some sad sense of pride?

Souls alone, we are not
With others to care for, others to love
Set aside the selfish, heal the rot
Search the skies for the big, white dove

Someday, anyday, sometime soon
Love will shine, love will come through
At last, an end to the days of doom
Healing the hurt, liffting the gloom.

Kevin Smette

AUTUMN

Autumn leaves are turning;
Golden, bronze and yellow.
Morning mists are forming,
Days are turning mellow.

Squirrels are collecting nuts;
Scurrying to and fro.
Hedgehogs search for cosy nests,
To protect from winter snow.

Autumn is upon us,
When leaves drift into heaps.
Autumn turns to winter,
When nature softly sleeps.

Diane Pointer

CANON BOB

He trod this Earth for two and eighty years
And at his death the church was crammed with those
Who loved the man - for each felt loved by him
As if there were no other

A gentle man, a quiet man, but strong:
His heart and hearth were a thoroughfare for all
Who came - the lonely ones, the poor, distressed,
They knew they'd gained a brother

Like a port in a storm, a spring in the desert, they found
A safety, a balm and nurture in the quiet of his life:
But those who knew him, knew the One
He served beyond all other

As one of Earth's lowly, he'd easily learned that strength
Came by yielding to a greater than he - his Lord:
And often, like Moses, his face would reflect the One
He loved beyond all other.

Alan Compton

WHITE WAVES

White waves pounded on a sandy shore
The two sat close though separately
Bonded by their distance.
A soft hand stroked her back.
Sand infiltrated tiny folds of skin
And were transported away
To be wondered at in a distant place.
Heat shimmered down, time passed slowly
But soon, bag packed, their stay was over.
Their imprint on the warm sand was soon obliterated.

Limpid waves lapped effortlessly
Under the hanging heat haze.
The drone of a distant boat
Cut through the silence
And cause the water to lift a little
Some moments later.
Air hardly stirring - the sleeping giant
Slept away another thousand years
He watched over the tower raisers
And now over two from another distant land.
Who will leave no reminder of their having been there.

Jeanette Hursey

MY GARDEN

I love my little garden
Full of fruit and veg
Protected from the neighbours
By a lovely privet hedge

I grow potatoes, peas and beans
And lots of lovely flowers
I tend it almost every day
Amid sunshine and showers

When it's time to harvest
I store fruit in my shed
I also spend a lot of time
To weed my flowerbed

It gives me satisfaction
My labour not in vain
And when the winter's over
It's time to start again

My garden is my hobby
And while I'm in my prime
I have my little garden
To pass away my time.

Bob Reynolds

AM I A POET?

I don't class myself as a poet
I write verses that rhyme.
To a lover of words
Perhaps it's a crime.
Not for me misery or doom and gloom,
Those thoughts in my head
Have no room.
I like the ridiculous and the inane
I hate poetry that's depressing
And filled with pain.
Give me humour that makes me smile,
To laugh out loud
That's my style.
To the great masters of verse
I raise my hat.
For me I keep it simple
And just write tat.

Patricia Whorwood

SITTING PRETTY

A 'Newsflash' came on
The other day,
Seems a robbery occurred
Out this way.

A warehouse full
Of sinks, baths and loos,
Had all been taken,
No sign of any clues.

But, sometime yesterday,
A toilet seat
Had been found
In a nearby street.

It was handed in
At Police Headquarters,
Who issued this statement
To news reporters.

'Clues till now,
We've been rather low on,
But this toilet seat,
Will give us something to go on . . .'

Joe Bayford

SHADOWS

Around my feet lie shadows on the grass.
They flicker in the breath of autumn's breeze,
Each stenciled by the sun which seeks to pass
Between the leaves and branches of the trees.

Sometimes at summer's peak the sun's great power
Can burn the skin and blind light-dazzled eyes.
Then glad are we to find some shady bower,
A shield from that fierce monarch of the skies.

When longer, darker shadows cross our way,
Those sombre shades of fear and grief and pain,
Encircling tendrils tightening day by day,
Oh, how we long for freedom from the strain!

In blackest hour hold this one thought in mind,
No shadow lives without a light behind.

V E Godfrey

WHERE?

Where have all the policemen gone?
Sitting at their desks, every one.
You never see one walking, or on a push bike,
No, they're in the van, the car, or on a motorbike.

When will they be on the streets, doing their jobs?
Their salary is more than just a few bob.
Will they ever catch the criminal man,
Or have their rules gone down the pan?

We pay our Council Tax, so they can live,
The Widows' Fund? A donation we'll give.
So when will they start to earn their pay?
Because all the law breakers are free every day.

At a football match, you might see a Bobby on a horse,
Patrolling the towns and the crowds, of course.
They hound a few motorists, at the end of the day,
Because they've no chance of getting away.

Some people drive around and don't intend to pay
And would you believe they can go scot-free?
No tax, no insurance, nor a current MOT,
It would be a warning, a fine, or a prison sentence for me.

Will of Endon

CELEBRATE SUCCESS

Celebrate being who you are!
Celebrate the life you have!
Aim for yonder star.
As your life progresses,
Celebrate all manner of things.
Birthdays, anniversaries and weddings.

The birth of anything is something to celebrate.
Whatever manifests successfully in life
Could be good luck, or fate.
Yet effort, commitment and know-how
Is needed to make any venture 'first rate'.

Happiness is an achievement within itself.
Celebrate it!
It's the right and proper thing to do.
All of us can achieve something, do what pleases you.
Recognise and celebrate what others have achieved.
They may give you inspiration.

So you too can take a lead.
Make yourself and others happy as your life proceeds,
This is success indeed.
It is up to each and every one of us
To celebrate giving, as well as to receive.

Sheila Booth

WILL THERE BE TIME?

When Man has harnessed lightning to his will
And spanned the ocean spread with boughs of steel,
When he has made the universe his mill
And set the winds to work to drive his wheel,
When he has sealed the skies with ghastly mirth,
To rob the stars of their tremendous powers;
When he has probed the bowels of the Earth
And gathered up the breath of all the flowers,
Will he then pause awhile to count the dead,
Whom poverty and steel have ground to dust?
Will he then heed the children's cry for bread,
Or hear the mothers' wail for what is just?
Will he then square himself with God and Man?
Will he repudiate the vice and crime
That has endured since first being began?
God, can he do all this?
Will there be time?

Lucy Crisp

OH! CRUMBS!

Oh! Crumbs!
Sometimes true love can crumble,
Like it's left with no support!
Lovers can trip and tumble,
It's fact, what life has taught!
Truly,
I still cannot remember saying,
Those words that caused you pain!
Beautiful Julie,
Can we not wipe the slate clean
And just be friends again?
My words they show,
I pray this can be so!

Graham Mitchell

AURORA

Waiting for the morning
Is to stand on the edge of darkness,
From here can be heard the piper's melody.
He's gone before you see him, fleeing through the trees
He leaves a golden train

The gentle lady of the forest
Treads through silently,
Pausing only to smile seductively,
She slips away
From reaching arms

The gates of dawn open suddenly,
Clashing through comes a shaft of light
Strong enough to hurt the eyes,
A lovely red-gold beam
And with it the Earth awakes

Leaving the mortal being
As lonely as a changeling child
Feeling the mystery and wonder
He wants to remain with it always
And vainly he searches
For what he was not meant to see.

Mandy Holten

SILENT CRYING

Do they stand in the shadow watching,
all those valiant men who died?
Do they see the tears we shed for them?
Can they hear our words of pride?

Do they know we will remember them?
Can they hear the bugle's call,
as we thank them for their sacrifice?
Theirs, the greatest love of all.

Do they weep to see the halt and lame,
these men made of sterner stuff?
Do they despair of the men of shame?
Do they cry, 'Enough is enough'?

Give ear then to the silent crying
of those tortured souls in pain;
does their dying mean just nothing?
Did they give their lives in vain?

So, cry aloud the watchword, *peace!*
Stand tall and remember them
who gave their lives so wars should cease,
these valiant, honourable men.

Richard E Stoyles

THE RED CARPET

The red carpet, a symbol of power and wealth
They walk with pride and glamour for all to see
The rubbish tips of the Third World are far reaching
And children hunt amongst the rubbish for food
At weddings and state occasions they parade
With jewels and medals, no search for food for them
The children with no shoes and tattered clothing search
For anything that will give them hope of staying alive
Why, oh why, does this anomaly exist on this planet Earth?
The rich, the poor, is there anything human in the human race?
From Africa to the Sudan, from India to China, from Mexico
To Panama, the red carpet and rubbish tips go side by side
Is it not that man's moral obligation is to work
For the improvement and welfare of all humanity?

Poet W Holden

BLUE SONG FROM A BLUE LADY

(For Billie)

My mind smokes an old blend of Ma Rainey,
Bessie Smith and Blind Lemon Jefferson.
Their singing touches, then impales my soul,
bringing nostalgia and old time yearning.

The glow cast by an insipid street light
crawls around the small room, trying to climb
walls cooled by breeze from an open window.

Two curtains move together, like lovers,
fondling each other to a rendering
of *'Careless Love Blues'*. The recording ends.
My weary friends leave - but *she* stays, waiting.

I hold out my hand and she comes to me -
a slim, sultry singer, wanting to sing.
I know her, of course. She is an old friend.

Her dark face, beautiful and young, unchanged
by the passing years, peers out from her old,
worn jacket. The white gardenia, still fresh,
highlights the lustre in her sweptback hair.

She pouts her glossy lips - seductively -
and her soft voice whispers, only for me,
the lyrics from the Simon and Ward song:

> *Why not take all of me?*
> *Why not take all of me?*
> *You took the part that*
> *Once was my heart,*
> *So, why not take all of me?*

She smiles, like she smiled at so many men -
but tonight, she smiles only for me!

Michael K Moore

REMEMBRANCE DAY

Remembrance Day is here once more,
The year has swiftly passed,
Brass bands and pipes are to the fore,
Flags flutter at the mast.

Veterans march past the mayor,
Their steps less sprightly now,
Pete Green is wheeled by in his chair,
Dark glasses on his brow.

He sees not the coloured berets,
Or the medals shining bright,
He relives again that fateful day,
The day he lost his sight.

He recalls too that roadside verge
Where brother Joe was laid to rest,
A kilted piper played a dirge
O'er the bloodstains on his breast.

A wooden cross marked the grave,
No coffin was allowed,
Nor was a robe or winding sheet, save
Sacking for a shroud.

Blind and limbless some pass by,
Stalwart men of long ago,
Look at them and breathe a sigh,
Your hate for war will grow.

The Last Post sounds, the service read,
For fallen comrades shed a tear,
Eyes cast down and bow your head,
Pray we'll meet again next year.

Denis O'Doherty

THE SWALLOWS

The old barn roof their gathering place,
Small groups swelled until a seethe
Of sheeny fervent joyous life
With tiny hearts attuned to leave.
The waves of raucous comrades went,
Drowning me in silence.
The swallows left today.

Swallows love and live long summer through,
Know just when to pick their joy
And also know when summer's gone.
When evening's breath is damply cool,
Before the chill can slow their hearts,
They know it's time to go.
The swallows left today.

I've watched the swallows' summer joy
Soar on breeze, cavort in sun,
But kept my dreams in shaded place,
Shut out day before day's done,
Yet craved summer that did not come.
Now one more summer's gone.
The swallows left today.

Sylvia Anne Lees

THE STOWAWAY THAT NO ONE WANTED

All alone! My world an iron cell.
The horizon! A dream of hope.
Gale force winds! High Seas! That fall! Like nature's fury.
To an end! That I know not.
I pray for human kindness! To live a normal life!
What is that like?
My world is one of poverty! Struggle!
Depravation! Ill treatment.
Why? I ask the Great Man above? In this vast world of wealth!
I ask only for entitlement.
Soon! We shall enter another port!
For some! There will be homecoming!
An unwanted stowaway! I look at the horizon!
And pray.

A E Powell

I AM NOT TIRED

I am not tired;
though I know
the day is ending

I am not ready,
yet, for sleep,
though work is done.

I am awake
to wonder at
the dying sun,
defiant dressed
in party shades
of orange, yellow, red;

to watch white stars
light up
the darkening sky;
to marvel
at the moon,
a silver scythe,
suspended overhead.

I am not tired.
Yet I know
sleep soon
must close my eyes.

Gwenda Owen

FISHERMAN'S TAIL

(Ode to Tommy Morrissey)

Gnarled old fingers,
Crack his brittle bones
Breaking the back of the sea.
Hard life for a living,
Tired weathered tongue
Tasting the salt on the breeze.

Wake and white water,
Leathery skin
The fight for freedom and life.
Breaching the surface
A struggle so swift,
Hauling nets over the side.

Blood with salt water
Scale-covered boots,
Sparkle like silver or tin.
Wild storm warning,
Heading for home,
Turning his face to the wind.

Eily Tatlow

TIME TO REFLECT

Anniversaries come and go,
Always forward, rearing from the past, thus they sow,
Seeds for the future generations to build on and grow,
A reason for celebration for all to show,
A date to keep: a date to know.

As our internal flames grow,
Our insight reaches out to all: does glow,
Year after year poetry touches many a heart,
Giving many; that yearned for start!
A chance to unburden, a chance to inspire,
All for the one reason, to fulfil a worthwhile desire.

Each year on the date, the message is heard,
Celebrating the written word,
Amateurs, professionals all alike,
Spark the flame, to engage, to write . . .

Collect your thoughts on times past,
Keep the date to make the memories last,
Year after year you can revive,
To make your special day, stay alive.

Sheralee Le-Gros

PHANTASM

In the shadows, late at night
she sits so near; it's quite a fright:
pointed ears, that evil glare
and I wonder, is she there?

When it's dark and I'm asleep
soft paws across the landing creep.
Waking up I think I see
glowing green eyes, watching me.

Through the garden in the day
a ghostly image makes its way.
The glossy coat gleaming black
sends a shiver down my back.

She's a spirit long since gone
a distant memory living on.
So, I ask you, am I ill?
Can you tell me, is she real?

R Osier

THE BYPASS

It was the glorious countryside
Brambles, bushes and trees
A hawk hovered way up high
His prey, only he could see.

The surveyors measured the land
No life that they could detect
No humans and no buildings
To them, just land and derelict.

It all happened very quickly
The machinery moved quite fast
Tarmac, concrete, kerbs and bridges
All wildlife gone, now in the past.

Cars sped along with not a care
All furry creatures gone away
Evicted from their homeland
A word they could not say.

Now gales gust empty cans and paper
Along the stony banks
No birds or furry creatures
To humans and cars . . . thanks!

Doreen Fay

UNTITLED

I like a spot of perfume
Now and again
Delicious Belgian chocolates
Now and again
Someone making laughter
Now and again
Blue of the sea
Now and again
Yet one admired
Secure and sure
I'd rather.

Mary Elizabeth Hughes

UNSUNG HEROES

There are people upon this planet
Who are never known
For all their acts of kindness
Which are often vandalised
They go around in silence
And receive no applause
For they are the spectators
Of this frozen world

On this orb we call the world
There are stars who lift us
In a spiritual way
Why the world is so appalling
I would never know

There are bright stars oozing talent
There are quiet ones in disarray
Like an icon of creation
We go our separate ways
On life's stage we perform
With humility and flair
Like a great creation
But still remain
Anonymous.

Elaine Day

REFLECTIONS ON HUMAN SUFFERING

Huddled all together, looks of anguish on their faces,
Suddenly deprived of water, food, familiar places,
Homes, possessions, washed away on a tide of devastation,
Numbed with shock and filled with fear and utter desolation.

We see them and our hearts go out to them in their great trouble
And we are sick at heart as we observe the piles of rubble
Where once so proud a city stood in all its former glory,
We shudder as we listen to each heart-rending story.

We watch in utter horror scenes of carnage and destruction,
When wicked hands have set off bombs to cause death
                                            and disruption,
Our hearts and minds are numbed to witness those in grief
                                            and sorrow,
Mourning for their loved ones who will never see tomorrow.

And then again we see oftimes more scenes of human grieving,
Where families are torn apart in ways beyond believing.
Where murdering hands have taken lives in fits of hatred, madness,
Or tragic accidents have caused such depths of pain and sadness.

What grief we feel and share with those whose lives have been
                                            so shattered,
We try to help - reach out our arms to those whom life
                                            has battered.
We lend a listening ear, we counsel and we make donations
And there are some who go beyond the call of expectations.

And many of us wonder why these dreadful things must be,
Why do disasters happen? Why such great calamity?
So very hard to answer whilst we here on Earth remain,
But when life's journey's over, I'm sure all will be made plain.

God dislikes to see the suffering, just as much as you or I
And He is just as saddened when He sees His children cry.
He wants us all to show His love and help our fellow man,
In acts of love and kindness and in every way we can.

So let us set ourselves the task of helping *all* in need,
That God's love may be reflected in our every word and deed.

Brenda King

DREAMS

In a dream I saw a mother in a dry and arid land,
The child she nursed upon her lap was dead.
The legs and arms stick thin; the belly bloated;
Nothing was left with which he could be fed.
And the eyes of the mother asked, 'Why?'

In a dream I saw a mother in a dark and war-torn land,
The child had been at play and difficult to find;
The limbs were badly mangled and now she would be blind.
The playground where she met her friends the military had mined.
And the eyes of the mother asked, 'Why?'

In a dream I saw a mother in a green and pleasant land,
Her child was in a coma caused by drugs
Taken to placate the pressure of the thugs;
No knowledge now of kisses or of hugs.
And the eyes of the mother asked, 'Why?'

In a dream I saw a mother in a special Holy land,
Her precious son was hanging on a tree,
His life blood pouring out to set men free.
That Holy death was mankind's only plea.
And the eyes of His mother knew why.

In a dream I saw those children together hand in hand
Walking with the Son of God in Heaven.
He, who His life had freely given
To provide a lasting haven
For the children whose mothers asked, 'Why?'

Joan Picton

DOGGY MENTOR

A wise and faithful councilor, in term,
Monitor for disabled, or infirm.
A bridge way without a say - for the blind,
Always ever forward light, for their kind.

Champion of strength domestic-like bait,
Someone to rely on, or follow straight.
The best 'non-human' friend known to mankind,
Joy or happiness to aged, in bind.

Hero, lasting, falls into mentor's shoes,
Guide, or hearing-aid dog profits on fuse,
Servant - faithful, loyal, royal presence,
Sometimes treacherous soil, without pretence.

Person's delightful, dedicated pet,
Count them in all shapes, sizes, forms, as set,
Evolved over millenniums, some racks,
Presumed from original wolfing packs.

Can be rough and bitter if ill-treated,
Restricted food, restrained, overheated.
Change by malfeasance run convoluted,
Beaten, unheartedly, stays saluted.

Cowered, whimpering in terror, shaken,
Still succour, elderly or sick taken,
Far from treachery, near subservience,
Free servants, non-believing deviants.

Person's understudy exudes no gloss,
Esteemed for blind, dumb, injured, treads no floss,
Then what is the value of such a pet?
And most certainly is an odds on bet.

N Lemel

DEVIL CALLED LOVE

The scene is set, the table laid
and 'Affection' sits and waits
the candle burns down slowly, for 'Love' is always late

And when at last on the door he knocks
'tis a game that 'Love' is playing
teasing 'Affection' with all he has, for he has no intention of staying

The fire burns its welcome glow, 'Affection's' heart does overflow
she knows what 'Love' is up to though, for 'Conscience' told her so

Sadly, 'Hurt' is also there, he's played 'Love's' games before
he also called for 'Sadness' to come -
she arrived when 'Love' knocked on the door

The last two to arrive that night, were 'Heartache' and 'Misery'
they didn't come when at first 'Hurt' called,
for they didn't want to see
the game that 'Love' was playing, or the destruction of the heart
they turned up very late that night, just as 'Love' he did depart

They closed the door behind him and wrapped 'Affection'
in their arms
why did she have to fall for him and all his gentlemanly charms?

But although 'Love' bought 'Hurt' to 'Affection'
and 'Heartache' and 'Misery' had a job to do -
'Conscience' could only give warning about 'Love'
'Good Sense' wasn't there, for perhaps she knew . . .

Now a new candle burns on the table -
and the fire has its welcoming glow . . .
once more 'Affection' sits all alone, she is waiting for 'Love'
to show . . .

Lisa Bristow

JOUISSANCE

Sing my soul to the ocean.
Sunny sea, soothe my soul,
Rough waves take the pain away.
I love you, water
Aquatic nectar,
Make me dance
Let me howl
Like a wild creature,
Ride your rolling breast,
Swim across the wave's crest
Into the silver path of the sun.
Follow the spinnakers sails of red.
Myriads of seawater droplets are shed,
Cruise and soothe off my body,
Tightened and rejuvenated.
Sing my soul to the ocean.

Elizabeth Jenks

CELEBRATIONS

Words like birds just fly away
And spread their wings upon the day,
Words like laugh and words like cry,
Words like where and how and why,
Words that scream and words that shout,
Words of faith and words of doubt,
Words that tell someone you care
And lift them out of their despair,
Words so gentle yet so strong,
Words like right and words like wrong,
Words like birds they just take flight
And spread their wings upon the night,
Words like passion that lovers share,
Words that say how much they care,
Sweet hellos and sad goodbyes
And words like tears that fill your eyes,
Words of joy when a child is born,
Like a blackbird's song at the break of dawn,
All these words are you and I,
We are every word we say,
Yes, you and me, we are poetry,
Let's spread our wings and fly today.

Angel Hart

A QUESTION ANSWERED

My faith is tested, my heart broken
Embrace so strong our love unspoken
This cannot be your life so cherished
 Is God in today, I wonder?

The time is short, there's no reprieve
Too soon your spirit will me leave
I cradle head in hands so tender
 Is God in today, I wonder?

The end has reared its ugly head
Too many tears we all have shed
A brave face I now must wear and ponder
 Is God in today, I wonder?

Time as we know will heal the pain
Strangers know not why I in vain -
Look to the sky and softly whisper
 Is God in today, I wonder?

Life now is turning all around
Happier times at last I've found
My question answered, no more wonder
 God is in with love, so tender.

Freda Symonds

MY LITTLE LEMON TREE

I brought a little lemon tree, it looked so green and good,
So I put it in my sitting room, upon a shelf it stood,
My lemon tree was so beautiful and a picture of good health,
Until one day, a leaf fell off, I found it on the shelf.
I put it in another room as it struggled to survive,
My lemon tree I watered to help it keep alive.
But one by one the leaves fell off, my lemon tree was dying,
I whispered gently, 'Please don't die, don't ever give up trying.'
Then one day I noticed a little shoot appear,
It seemed to say, 'Forgive me, I'll try again this year.'
The leaves began to grow again it filled me with delight,
My lemon tree did not give up, it put up such a fight.
My lemon tree is beautiful, its leaves are fresh and green,
It's back in all its glory, such a pleasure to be seen.
Oh, how my little lemon tree depicted life for me,
While we accomplish all that's good, we blossom like the tree,
But when life's obstacles appear, we tend to fade and fall,
We almost feel like giving up, it's not worth it after all.
But, as my little lemon tree just rested for a while,
It then began to struggle back and its leaves began to smile.
So, if we sit back quietly, we will then in wisdom see,
Our characters are founded by setbacks just like these.
As *God* looks after little things, like my small lemon tree,
I, confident in His love and care, He looks after *you* and *me*.

J Berry

REFLECTIONS

The scent of honeysuckle after rain,
Across the valley a soft refrain,
The blackbird with his evening trills,
Sheep grazing on the distant hills,
The evening gives a sense of peace,
Reflecting hopes which can release,
True meanings in the ways of sharing,
Finding again nurture and caring,
For this lovely world where true beauty is found,
Caring for streams and woods and ground,
Bringing again a new meaning to life,
Banishing destruction and evil and strife,
To find once more a true sense of living,
Recapture respect and the ways of giving,
Fresh courage and faith helping someone along,
Just a smile and a word and a cheery song,
With God's power to refresh and be reviewed,
The world will resound and hopes be renewed.

Eveline Tucker

THIS MAN
(27-01-1911 to 08-01-2001)

He was a son; the eldest one
Of three boys born in Wales
He was a brother; each to the other -
Three young, handsome males.

He was a soldier in the Second War -
Fighting away from home
He was her husband; my mother's love -
Apart; how their love had grown.

He was a father; one like no other -
Always there at my side
He was a grandad to my two boys -
Steadfast: a mentor and guide.

He was a man of whom to be proud -
Making his way through life
He was a man; ninety years on -
Saying farewell to his wife.

Doreen Fillary

CHILDREN OF THE WORLD

God bless all the children
Around the world so wide
Give them all a chance to live
In harmony side by side.

Whenever they are hungry
Find them food to eat
Shelter them from the cold
Warm sunbeams give them heat.

God watch over them
Each and every night
Keep them safe and sound
Never from your sight.

Please help them to grow up
To be thoughtful, good and kind
Around this world so wide
God's happy children find.

Patricia Carter

BEST WISHES FOR THE FUTURE

Let's give our thanks to the Forward Press
For they've helped unknown poets to success,
Hang out the bunting and drink a toast
For fifteen good years they've been our host.
Poems have been written by the old and young,
Of love, tragedy and witty ones.
Whatever you like, you'll find in their books,
To keep you interested wherever you look.
The founder and members of the editorial team,
Have worked very hard behind the scene.
So, 'Good Luck' for the future with all you do,
I raise my glass to all of you.

Mollie Carter

FAITH

To have faith is such a blessing, as you tread along life's days
Always to sustain you in all its various ways
A constant thread of hope when troubles overwhelm
A prop, a rock to lean against, whilst life is at the helm
Of stormy days, of problems, of worries old or new
You know you only have to ask, your faith will see you through
Your faith there to console you, to ease, to reassure
Just pray your faith will lead you, it always finds a cure
Into calmer waters, it is ever by your side
To aid you, to uplift you, there always as your guide
Its comfort is unending, its strength everlasting too
To have faith in life is wonderful, it brings such peace
                                      and joy to you.

Marjorie Leyshon

JOHNNIE

Our dear, wee angel, darling little boy.
How much you're loved, you naughty imp.
Your tiny hands can see so much to do,
Our saucepans are far better than any toy.

And what about the buttons in that box,
'Oh don't, don't chew your dad's old dirty socks.
Be careful at the table, watch your eye,
He throws things with such deadly accuracy.'

And then, when he's been bathed and put to bed
And he snuggles in, to hear his story read
And smiles with so much charm and loving grace,
How can I resist a kiss on that sweet, rosy face?

Doris Donnell

ARMAGEDDON

What of Armageddon?
It's the last great battle men say, where the forces of good and
evil must meet of the last great day, then the winds and the
sea will be raging with foaming, gaping jaws and we all will be
running and hiding, locking and barring our doors, with
thunder and lightning cracking across rolling, angry skies
women and children screaming, no one hearing their cries
grown, strong men struck helpless with fear, watching the
angels of good and evil draw near, angels waiting for combat
holding their heads on high, calmly awaiting instructions from
their spirit leaders nearby, all this within focus on the human
eyes, scoff and laugh if you must, the choice is yours, no one will
be safe outside or indoor, only the ones who've lived in good
ways will have the smallest chance in those last few days.
So think of Lot and remember *Noah*,
they took the same chance, long years ago.

Jean A Smith

THE VETERAN

The veteran sitting alone on the beach,
Deep in thought, looking out to sea, for something he can't reach.
Reflecting on the past sixty years,
Men fighting on the beaches, many fell, it was a living hell of fear.
Wishing his comrades could be here today,
Rejoicing in freedom, instead of lying in graves.
They gave their lives for our freedom, which we enjoy today,
So let us reflect for a moment, to think of them and pray.

His silvery-grey hair glistens in the sun,
Dressed smartly in beret and suit, proudly hung his medals on.
The emotion and sadness etched on his face,
For the heroes who died on that day, with grace.

His eyes stinging with tears, that slowly down his cheeks flow,
A very sad figure of a proud man we know.
Biting hard on his lower lip to control his emotions,
He stands so proud with notion.
Gaining composure, he stands and salutes
His comrades and friends, whom he fought with that day.
Then lays a flower on each of their graves.

Marilyn Pullan

WHITBY

As I ascend beneath the towering cliffs
And reminisce of how things used to be
Fishermen's cottages beside a busy harbour
Piers stretching out to sea
Near to church and abbey ruins
Donkeys graze happily

Far below the old swing bridge
And narrow cobbled street
Leading to the market square
Where local people meet
Cobbles fetch their daily catch
Midst seagulls' hungry cry
Smoke rising from the kipper house
And swirling through the sky

I amble by the coastal path
And watch the seabirds soar
'Neath rugged cliffs and hidden coves
To rock-edged distant shore
The ringing of the bell buoy bobbing o'er the sea
Relays fond memories of how things used be.

Linda Hodgson

WHEAT FIELDS

Wheat fields, languishing in the sun, waving, weaving, stretching,
Up to the winking clouds.
Wheatsheafs, plaited feathery tips tickling the air,
Yellow gossamer edged to hedge light and shade captured in a frame.

Changing patterns, whispering sounds blowing to and fro,
Fairisle delights, soft, gentle music on the horizon.
The odd poppy floats above the dizzy heights, glowing gold,
Shining in the sunset.

Nature's grand plan going well.
Tiny grains bouncing about, hitting hawthorns,
Birds getting their share, the fieldmouse has a feast,
Lovers and baby rabbits get lost furrows narrow in perfect symmetry.

Soon it will be bread on plates, different patterns, different shapes.
The senses are gratified.

Maura Malone

SPRING, SUMMER, AUTUMN, WINTER . . .

In winter, a still branch,
Suffocated life,
Spring, warm earth,
Green shoots, new birth.

Blossoms burst forth,
Nature's blessings,
Winds blow, blossom
Confetti, into summer.

Green world, full of life,
Summer's bounty,
Rainbow colours, bright
Light fading, colours dull.

Leaves flutter, copper hues,
Autumn's embers,
Skeletal branches,
Hibernating life.

Lynda Burton

CELEBRATE WORDS

Let us celebrate words
Not one day goes by
For you or I
When words are not included
It may be a story
Or a song
Poetry short or long
Books we read or write
The words we speak
The letters we write
The songs we sing
Almost everything
The most important thing
Are words.
Without them
No communication
No great nations
No expression
No passion
No telephones
No television
No radio
Nowhere to go
So let us celebrate words
Make the world come alive
Words the never-ending
Story
For you and I.

Marie Haswell

THE LITTLE OLD LADY

The little old lady with the silvery hair,
Smiled as she sat in her rocking chair.
The little old lady so good and so kind,
Contented with life although she was blind.

Her years had been full of kindly deeds!
Always a thought for others' needs.
To go to church was her greatest pleasure,
To walk trough the fields, her dearest leisure.

She had missed so very much in *life!*
All of the things we take for granted,
To touch the face of a little child,
Was all she ever wanted.

Oft, as she walked along the way,
You would sometimes see her stumble!
But of her lonely world of darkness,
You would never hear her grumble.

To have seen the sheaves of golden corn,
The rise of the sun on a beautiful morn.
Rippling lakes full of silver fish,
This I know was her dearest wish.

A rainbow in the clear, blue sky,
The enchantment of a dragonfly.
No elm, no ash - no tall oak tree,
No sailing ships on a still, calm sea.

God had given the old lady happiness
And courage to see the light.
But what He never bestowed on her,
Was the precious gift of sight.

Then it was on a cold December morn,
That little old lady, tired and worn.
Never having seen the dawning of day,
Quietly and peacefully, passed away.

Gloria McCrory

MAGNIFICAT

Why do I feel special, pleased?
I'm not supposed to want this!
Why glad not to see the crimson stain,
feel the familiar, low-back pain?

Something amazing is happening
and it's happening to me.

The genes have decided: girl or boy?
I float around with my secret joy,
superior to others, who
are going to be mothers too,
for all I know.

The man may desert me, he may not want to know,
there may not be any place where I can go,
but my soul is magnified by the suspicion
that I'm privileged to grow
this new life. And I don't know!

Treat me with deference, treat me with care.
I may be the chosen one to bear
that which will change all history.
The hope of the world may depend on me.

My life will not have been in vain.

There's still no trace of blood, no stain.

Make way as I got to the pharmacy
for the pregnancy testing kit. Make way,
the annunciation is nigh. I wait
for the angel Gabriel. I'm late.

Wendy Shutler

HELLO, DO YOU REMEMBER ME?
(My dear friend with Alzheimer's Disease)

As I walked into the hospital room
He was alone and sitting in a *chair*
I looked at him, there was something wrong
That is not my friend I knew sat *there*
Through my tears I reached out my hand to him
Praying softly *hello, do you remember me?*
The same blue eyes look past my face
I was no one to him, how can this heartache *be?*
I feel so much pain and heartache for my friend and his loved ones
How? We ask, why does this terrible illness *start?*
It is tragic and sad my friend has gone far away
Although he sits right there, I am glad he doesn't understand
All our tears and broken *hearts.*

Thelma Anne Barton

CHAWLEIGH

In the olden Mesolithic Age,
The early settlers said
That Chawleigh is a place to live,
To toil and lay one's head.

On a high and windy plateau,
To the north and south a great moor,
Its green and fertile pastures
Drink from the Dart and the Taw.

A 'clearing place for calves' -
The old *Calveleia* name,
But now the 'Best Kept Village' prize
Proclaims the *Chawleigh* fame.

The ancient church and village school
Are testament to one and all -
The present, dead, and those to be,
Who form our local history.

Its people are kind and supportive -
The 'Friendly Society Walk and Fair' -
And when any help is needed,
Someone will always be there.

The landscape may alter
With homes new and old,
But when it's the harvest,
Fields still turn to gold.

Church bells have rung out
For centuries past,
And their message today
Is that *Chawleigh* will last.

Iris Morton

CENOTAPH VOICES

The certainty of our remembrance
Rests assured, set in stone,
A granite lexicon babel tower -
Shouting names, countless faceless
Names of posthumous heroes
Muted long forgotten yet
Part of ritual mourning.
Voices whispering; a silent crescendo
Pleading, 'Never forget'
'We, who were sacrificed and became
Votive offerings to a cause profane,
From the city of graves will arise
And as ghosts return, to claim
Our inheritance and confute the poet's lies -
'Dulce et decorum est
Propatria mori'.'

Alexander Macdonald

THE MISTRESS

The car speeds down the road again,
The neighbour's curtains twitch,
What has she got, that I have not,
That most beguiling witch.

Most days he goes away from me
And dallies there for hours,
It matters not when he returns,
That his arms are full of flowers.

It's not as though she's beautiful,
Her dimensions are enormous,
She's twice as wide as she is long,
Just like a brontosaurus.

His tousled hair and beads of sweat,
Add strength to my suspicion,
For aching muscles, can a bath
Restore his prime condition?

And yet my rival works for us,
Her yield is never finished,
With flowers, fruit and veggies green,
Her bounty's undiminished.

And so I wave him down the road,
No longer with hostility
And thank the Lord for all that comes
From the plot and its fertility!

Elizabeth Rapley

LOCH LOMOND

I took the high road to Scotland to sample the highlights
And made my way to Loch Lomond which was a wonderful sight.
The nearby landscapes of mountains, the tranquillity of the loch,
Moorlands and coastland with boulders and jagged rock.
Such beauty lies before me as far as the eye can see,
Clumps of purple heather and forests of pine trees.
Little islands to be found are scattered here and there,
Such idyllic surroundings, I can only stand and stare.
An inspiration to all artists and poets to take stock
And sit beside Loch Lomond, the queen of Scotland's lochs.

Hazell Dennison

VEGETARIAN PIE

It seems unwise, perhaps even a trifle indiscreet
Should one consume today's mass produced meat,
Often reared in the ultra-modern factory fashion,
Growth forced for fat profit, then slain by machine.
Cruel to poor beasts, riches making for the vendor,
Enjoying a lifetime filled with luxurious splendour.
We poor people could better assuage daily hunger
On biscuits with cheese, maybe even a vegeburger.
To help achieve success in this humane wise policy,
Attempt, please my 'vegetarian pickle pie' recipe.
Take one vegetarian, mature and ancient,
Choleric, not merely crusty and impatient.
Firstly remove false teeth, glasses and socks,
Marinade in port wine, or one of those German hocks.
Place him with fresh mushrooms, enclose all in pastry,
Then bake all day long, for a meal warm and tasty.
On gas regulo setting, at very least twenty-one,
Because vegans can be lethal if at all underdone.
To refute any charges of a cannibalistic tendency
Plead that the dish be vegetarian. All must agree.

Anne Omnibus

MUSICAL DREAM

I recently dreamt that I was taken back in time and distance,
To the era of Johann Strauss, what an opportunity, what a chance,
To visit Vienna, city of dreams, music and romance.

I was in a ballroom, Johann Strauss and his orchestra were playing,
The lady dancers in the evening dresses of wonderful colours
                              and designs were swaying,
The men were equally smart, some in evening dress and others
                    in military dress uniform with colours so bright,
A really marvellous sight.

A baroness, Trudi, stepped forward to welcome me,
'I hear you have travelled far from across the sea
In the hope of meeting and hearing the maestro,
Well, I have known him for years, so leave it to me.'

I danced with the baroness who glided across the floor with ease,
I did my best to keep up with her, I wanted to please,
Half-an-hour later, baroness Trudi introduced me to Johann Strauss,
As I shook hands with him, I thought I was dreaming,
Which of course I was, that was true.

Johann Strauss invited me to conduct the orchestra when
                    they played the Lightning Polka at speed,
Strauss said, 'Just raise your baton high for attention and bring it
                         down fast, that's all you need.'
I raised the baton and waved my arms about;
A sudden dig in the ribs awoke me from my dream,
My wife, I heard scream,
Then I heard my wife shout,
'What do you think you are doing waving my knitting needle about?
You have lost at least ten rows of my knitting that I did
                         when I came to bed.'
And that was the end of my musical dream,
But the memory I still retain in my head.

Peter Towner

SENTIMENTS OF YOUTH

Recalling bygone yesterdays
Contributes many a sigh
For what can equal vibrant youth
And its sweet ecstasy?

Teenage years are life's lush springtime
As a dream devoid of care
We whom middle age has seasoned
View its passing with despair.

In all the world of fame and fortune,
Youth remains beyond price,
Oh, the pangs of sheer desire
To relive and sample springtime twice.

Nostalgic memories ever linger
Precious moments intertwined
Holding mortal beings capture,
By the cravings of the mind.

So in quiet reminiscence
Youth rekindles o'er again,
Through the eye of mental vision
We relive the glory then.

And though former dreams have fleeted
Never ever to replay,
By reflection we redeem them
In the autumn of our day.

Alan Moore

THE LAST DANCE

Oh strawberry, so alluringly fair,
Dressed in your ball gown of red;
Won't you have your last dance with me?
Come embrace, enough has been said.

You seem rather sorrowful there
In that glass bowl, without a dance date;
The others have been swept off their feet
To waltz with the scones and the cake.

I'm the only one left for you now -
Let me savour your voluptuous fruit;
I sense your sweetness on the tip of my tongue
As thoughts on my taste buds take root.

But alas - what happened just then
As I reached out for one lasting kiss?
Another hand just grabbed you away -
Oh strawberry! Gone is our moment of bliss!

David Radford

I ONCE WAS GREAT

I once was great,
I was a winner,
Now I'm a sinner,
I had to get thinner,
Try and be cool,
Another young fool,
Was I?
It was my brain,
I was about to fry,
I liked myself,
I believed I was right,
My future was a pleasing sight,
Confident that whatever happened,
I would be all right.
Ten years later,
I'm a hater,
An alligator,
With a snap and a twist,
A gorilla in the mist,
A bitter tongue I have kissed,
The man I used to be
Is dearly missed.

Colin Horn

MEMORIES OF HIGH SUMMER

How wide and high the sky, how limpid clear the sea,
A drift of scented herbs arising over me.
Close by a lonely hut, shuttered and battened down,
A refuge perhaps for one escaping life in town.
Light spills through stubble fields, flows over sea-girt stone,
An old peace settles here known unto God alone.
And here sea-holly grows and there a curlew's song,
No persons came or left, they have been gone too long.
Memories like precious gems crafted to fine design
Tell us that once we were children of summertime.
A pediment of cloud drops from its mass above
A feather from a wing, angel's profoundest love.
Dry fruits sped on a breeze appear loveless and dry,
We like the willow herb must all set seed and die.
There is soul music here and as the lone heart sings
Lifts up to Heaven its own adagio for strings.

Frances M Searle

THE WRITER

Writing means little to me
If not giving myself to my friends
But they are not just words
They mean something
Some words pound at you
Sweep around you like a restless tide
My letters are almost my only outlet
In the shape of the written word
I keep isolating odd sentences and I have to admit
They are not just windy rhetoric - but-precise-almost
And in addition, an overflowing bounty
Which should keep me going
For the remainder of my mortality
However, there are others - one - who some do not like
I do, at least his work, as to the man himself,
He was very 'marked' upper middle class
All the same I suspect that under the stiff shirt,
Cuffs and manners
There lurked a real artist
Spiky, individualist and anarchic
And the fictional character
May have been in one sense
More real than the civil servant
He will be forgotten in centuries to come
Most of his themes - solitude; sensual delight
In wind and rain and sun
Impassioned pursuit of tranquil happiness
(As distinct from pleasure and excitement)
His condemnation of ambition
Acquisitiveness and competitiveness
Machines, mobs and herds
All this is most congenial to me
But what is a bit wearing
Is the sheer prodigality of
'Powys' genius!

J A Finlayson

THIS IS TRUE LOVE

Tell me, what is this stirring
Deep within my soul?
A feeling that you can't describe
That makes a person whole?

So many words I want to say
My heart is full of pride
A thousand jumbled letters
But they're all locked deep inside

Is it those brown eyes or silver hair
Or never-ending devotion
The little things you say and do
That really stir emotion?

So many years, can it be?
It seems like yesterday
I knew you would be the one
To make my cares away

That feeling has grown so much
It invades my every thought
Enters my dreams at night-time
A pleasure that can't be taught

I understand the way you think
Anticipate your move
I know that deep within my heart
I have found true love

Paul J Abbott

WHERE POPPIES STILL BLOOM

Can this be the Somme with such flourishing fields,
Where sugarbeet sweetness abundantly yields?
Is this really the cauldron of ultimate hell,
Where dutiful thousands unflinchingly fell?

Could green distant ridges be bastions of fire,
Encompassed by wire and funeral pyre,
As youth full of fervour, to songs that were sung,
Marched into their trenches where spirits were wrung?

Can we ever conceive that this pastoral vale,
So firm underfoot bears the name Passchendale
And 'Wipers' of yore, once a shell-shattered sight,
As so bright and pulsating on Saturday night?

Can we not but reflect on a latter day tour,
Of this being a war for the ending of war,
For smouldering embers besmirched this terrain
And a rallying bugle was sounding again?

Now those that return to such blood-splattered soil,
Will imagine the howitzers roar and recoil,
Where freshened white stones have a vigil to keep
On the well nurtured sward over heroes asleep.

William Dodd

THROUGH MY EYES

Take flight my soul, fly on golden wings
keep on living until the birds forget to sing . . .

Through my eyes there is all to see
trust me my friend there are no ties,

My eyes are shut, sleep is upon my mind
perhaps we will dream back to another time

I R Cook

PRE-DAWN IN BRIGHTON, DECEMBER

The sea tempts me down
A submarine alley of dreams.
Wet seaweed air

Slaps the sand.
Six-fifteen am the sea door opens and closes
A breezy dark Sunday morning.

The clock on a battered hotel front
Reads only seven to four.

Cutting curve of moon
Shines the single light from the sky.
Bellicose ocean yells across icy air.
Lighted jewel-like bars stand empty of custom.
Where now, those silken women in perfumed dresses
Unsuitably dressed for the chill, windy air;
Their attendant men with the laughing teeth?

From Grand Junction Road, look out at Brighton sea.
Watch the gull gyratingly
Blown around in the startling grey wind.
A festive tree with pearly branches sways
Its human-like hands and endures the night-long gales
While bouncing air conveys a Christmas howl.

Angels will call to tourists clutching promenade rails.
Shipwrecking, the sea peels white waves like orange rind.
Games of humans bow by the pier to that force.

Close by the Royal Albion, I weep tears of the sea.
Many winters that I've been here!
This year turns its page;
The papers tell of wars. Coffee banality
Will flavour the morning. That big sea tempts me
Once more down its dreaming unconscious alley.

Mike Green

MY FEET ARE COLD

My feet are cold.
I'm bored, even though I'm surrounded by flowers:
I've arranged them,
Rearranged them,
Looked at them,
Studied them,
Rejoiced in their beauty;
I look back at them regularly because they're lovely.
Otherwise I'm alone
And bored.

My feet are cold.
I've read my books,
I've tried to sleep,
Too much sleep gives me a headache.
I've sat up,
I've laid down,
I've turned over;
At least I *can* do these things,
But it's boring.

My feet are cold.
Maybe I'll write something,
If my hands aren't too cold?
Maybe I'll get some visitors today?
Maybe the sun will come out?
Maybe the nurse will take me for a ride in my wheelchair?
It's a long day,
Every day.
Maybe I'll be better soon?

My feet are so, so cold . . .
Strange, because I have no legs . . .

Jay Leffew

FROM EDEN TO CALVARY

Long ago in the Garden of Eden
The place where it all began
With Adam and Eve and the apple,
Was the start of the downfall of Man.

It didn't take long for the weakness
That allowed the evil to win
They couldn't resist the temptation
Which led to the birth of all sin.

So on through all generations
As Old Testament books have told
The Ten Commandments were broken
By the men and women of old.

Advice came to all from the psalmist
And the prophets who wrote to foretell
What would be the fate of the wicked,
They were faced with the prospect of Hell.

In the fullness of time came a saviour
Born of Mary to be a great king
Who showed the way of salvation
Which His life and example could bring.

He was doubted and scorned and belittled
And condemned to death on the cross
His resurrection meant new life forever
His death had brought gain, not loss.

Now Satan no longer holds power
Over those who follow our Lord
For Christ bought salvation for all men
Who believe and follow His word.

Mary Whorlow

MY SHINING STAR

Looking up one still, dark night
There it was, a shining light
Although for years it had been there
It was the first time I felt aware
My eyes were drawn to where it shone
A cloud appeared and it had gone.

Yet for me, it meant one thing
My heart grew light, faint bells did ring
The largest star up in the sky
It called to me - I wonder why?
Life's problems seemed to shrink and go
Drawing strength, somehow, from its glow.

When burdens weigh heavy and sadness reigns
It beckons me through windowpanes
Beyond the clouds, shedding its light
Not seen by day - only at night
It's there for me, so very far
Shining still, my own bright star.

Doreen Brooks

A TIME TO DIE

I'm very old, so they tell me
With body all wrinkled and brown
But I still feel the breeze in my tresses
I know when the sun's shining down.

They say that I'm well past a century
Yet life force still pulses within
And I've taken tea with the gentry
And once with a beautiful queen.

Oh, I'm known very well in the country
The birds are my very best friends
Most of the dogs here adore me
Most of the cats I befriend.

Sometimes when I'm in the garden
Whilst people are milling around
They tell me a lot of their troubles
When they sit at my feet on the ground.

I once knew a sad, little lady
Whose teardrops fell warm on my breast
She flung her arms tightly around me
For comfort and strength and for rest.

Then one day danger was lurking
An evil old fellow came by
I watched as he hid a weapon
And he never knew I was nigh.

But, I'm really old now they tell me
Though my memory's clear and not 'blown'
It's plain they don't want me to stay here
I'm a tree and they're cutting me down!

Hazel Brydon

VAULTED

Vaulted pulpits espouse withered virtues,
Through the fallen leaves of tabloid truth.
Whispered discontent gnaws at spiral confusions,
Revealing the inner self to all.
Still barbed words ensnare liberty lost,
For diverse complexions, weighed differently.
But the darkness has passed and it's daylight at last,
As citizens are shamed and others framed through,
Tall, hall views, a hash hold the front page.

Damian Allen

WHERE IS PATIENCE?

I've waited simply ages for Patience to appear
In her calm serenity and beautiful attire.
She's late according to my watch, I'm afraid I'll have to go.
I can't stand around forever, I've things to do, you know.

Could this be her in gaudy dress, bustling through the door
Waving high her car keys and running 'cross the floor?
No! She's gone - it wasn't her and thankfully, I'm glad,
For if I'd kept up with her pace, I'd end up feeling bad.

I'll wait a few more minutes, for I'm given to understand
Patience is a virtue and one which God has planned,
For when I've watched and waited and worked quite steadily,
Patience in her beauty will be revealed in me.

Jean Duckworth

THE SPARROW

He was only a little sparrow,
Just learning how to fly.
How large the world must seem to him,
How far away the sky.

He flew down to my window
And knocked the pane of glass.
I ran outside to look for him
And found him safe at last.

I put out my hand and spoke to him
And his beak was oh, so small.
But his wings were strong and they lifted him
And he flew away, past the wall.

God values us more than the sparrow
He credits us with sense.
So use the brain He has given
And spread His good news to the dense.

E L Blackburn

FROLIC

A day
In May
The wind flirting
Gaily blurting
Love-words to the flowers
Scattering blossom
Blowing, snowing
Teasing the lilac
Stroking, provoking
Shaking the peonies
Breaking their pride
Giving full ration
Of masterly passion
Till they limpen and whiten
Drop tears on the earth -
Rumpling the daisies
Not one he misses
Upsetting their primness
With joking and kisses
Faster and wilder
He whirls round the pansies
With each flustering onslaught
Seeking a consort
But though he's imperious
He's not really serious
It's the racing and chasing
That brings him delight.

Irene Lorch

UNDERGROUND MOVEMENT

Much gold would I give not to be here right now!
To be no part of this subterranean cavalcade,
But that necessity, that noisome scourge,
Keeps me a labouring slave on this treadmill trek
To my daily toil in the bustling city above.

I might have seen, except for this,
Night slumbering soundly on some distant hill;
I could have listened long to the gentle breeze
That softly sighs the calm lake's mist away;

I could have scented lavender and perfumed roses,
New-cut grass, wood fires and fresh-baked bread;
I would have sensed the stealth of welcome dawn,
And in its train, with quickening force,
Have felt the dew-wet glistening earth revive.

And in the kindling fire of summer's joyful morn,
The wakeful countryside, now rising to its task,
Would spread such glorious light of day -
Eclipsing so this fluorescent Tube.

Jay Whittam

AFTERLIFE

Is there life past death,
After I breathe my last breath?
Through my trial and tests,
Surely, there is a reward for my quests.
A glimmer of hope, a soul's amaze,
Not much I ask for my end of days.

I should rid my soul of all obscenity,
Maybe then I'll find true serenity.
I debate my life being somewhat worth,
But precious is the time upon this Earth.
Blessed are we all within living,
For we all possess the gift of giving.

So I pray for forgiveness of my sins,
As I forget money and material things.
Within dreams of sweet euphoria,
As I battle my own misdemeanor.
My soul's trapped in body, my earthly shell,
I'm destined for Heaven, as I've been through Hell.

Thomas Titchener

A VISION OF LOVELINESS

One lovely day in the month of June,
The day in my life I dreamt about,
My lovely daughter has grown up too soon,
I was very proud of her, I wanted to shout.

A vision of loveliness I really must say,
She was a beautiful sight,
Was standing before me that June day,
From head to toe in white.

Her auburn hair piled high on her head,
Her cheeks a lovely pink glow,
By her proud dad she was being led,
Towards the one that loves her so.

For that captured moment touched my heart,
Of the love in each others' eyes,
They were about to take the vows never to part,
Through sickness and health, whatever ahead lies.

They are still together after ten years,
Blessed with children, three,
They have had their share of laughter and tears,
Whatever will be, will be.

Betty Greig

AIRFIELD REQUIEM

Crowns of laurel graced your heads,
Revving engines your clarion sound.
At the 'scramble' call you left your beds,
Reaching your zenith as you left the ground.
Your mission to save us from a blasting unknown
As we crouched in the shelters
We'd learned to call 'home'.

Red sky in the morning!
But you heeded not the shepherd's warning
As you climbed to a bloody tryst with dogfight death.
Laurel crown ablaze in plummeting craft, midst burning oil
You came to rest on sacrificial soil.
No last salute, no salvo round;
We wept for you in sorrow so profound.

Now, the runways up from which you sped
Are overgrown with grass and thistlehead.
Control tower, empty, roof now leaking,
With sagging door, swinging, creaking,
Birds fly in and leave their calling;
Initials carved on crumbling walling . . .
Still echoing on the wind,
The voices of those who flew on the wing,
Whilst the off-key mess piano
Accompanies yet those so willing to sing.

The sons and daughters you did not spawn
Cry out for a womb from which to be born -
A loss which has proved our crown of thorn.
You left us facing a long, lonely mourning;
And the gap is ever yawning.

Doreen McGee-Osborne

MARY (PART 1)

('A true story)

She sat chair-bound and all alone
By her window - now disabled
She responded not to passers by
Or friends who wrote or cabled.

Her active nursing life was over
Trapped she felt and with no hope
Her personal needs were attended to
But her others got no scope.

Then one day, a cat she saw
Mauled, half-dead with fright
He'd been and fought another tom
And he had lost the fight.

For the first time since she was ill
She felt pity for another
She called him over, he came to her
She gently lifted him - *oh, bother!*

A new invader, but one of care
Coursed through her hands now free
Slowly she massaged and comforted
The cat, now calmed, was he.

The next day, the cat returned
For his daily treatment
She rubbed him slowly and he relaxed
And she spoke of what life meant.

'Go teach the creatures,' Christ had said
Well, this was one that needed aid
God works in wondrous ways she thought
A cat had shown what plans God laid.

Part 2 'And Give Thanks'
published in Inspirations, page 107.

Cockin

ENLIGHTENMENT

Enlightenment is the most beautiful word
In whatever language you use.
It makes no judgement;
Doesn't load you with sin,
Or threaten you with Hell or abuse.
If you were raised as a Christian
I suppose you still are.
But what puzzles me, is why?
If you worshipped a sun god from the age of ten,
What do you expect when you die?
Do all religions make the demand,
That you dispense with your incredible brain?
Has the brain that was God-given
To permit rational thought,
To be trashed, as if thrown down a drain?
Enlightenment gives man a second chance,
To use the brain as God meant you to do.
And dismiss the untruths of dangerous men
Obsessed with power and control over you.
They've succeeded so far
Our timidity has allowed,
The ogres to control the mind.
But we are just beginning to see through the plot,
Then enlightenment will free all mankind.

John Troughton

THE LEGACY OF LOVE

I miss him most in the morning, when the sun from its sleep
does arise.
When I reach out my hand, I remember and wipe off the tears
from my eyes.
I go to my work and I miss him, he's not there to kiss me goodbye.
As I walk through the rain I can picture, a time there was
no need to cry.
I told him I loved him quite often and he said that he loved me
as well.
He would never have left me here grieving, in this sadness,
I'm living in Hell.

I miss him most at the noontime, when the sun is so high in the sky.
I gaze at his portrait before me and I yearn for the time that's
gone by.
When children were happily playing and we planned for the
future ahead
Just when the future looked brighter, I'm alone and without him
instead.
Each day I am trying to face it, a life that's so bleak and so cold.
I thought we would stay here together, till all of our dreams
did unfold.

I miss him most in the evening, with the work of the day at an end.
We'd sit there together just closely, he was my life, my very
best friend.
He'd smile and ask how my day went, as I told him, he'd give
me support.
A laugh, a joke and a cuddle, in his trap of sweet love I was caught.
I felt so safe in his presence, he wanted to give me the best.
Our lives were one for the other and now he's at peace and at rest.

I miss him most in the night-time, when I wearily slip into bed.
I feel his spirit beside me, my love transcends all that is dead.
No one can know how it's hurting, this grief I carry alone.
Though all those around me are caring, this pain is the worst
I have known.
With Jesus beside me I'm coping, for I know that He understands.
Dear Lord, I pray you support me, I'll always be safe in your hands.

Cecilia Jane Skudder

PRECIOUS MEMORIES

An old lady sits alone by her window, by her side is a box she holds dear,
It contains all her precious memories that she has added to every year.
Carefully she takes the lid off and lets out a small, muffled sigh,
As images rush up to meet her, of days that have long gone by.

First, are portraits of her mum and dad, aunts and uncles she was
never to meet,
She looks at the world's best sister and three brothers she was later
to greet.
There are pictures of her gran and granddad with him leading
the band down the street,
Childhood days with the sister she loved 'til she left, her husband
to meet.

Next came remainders of her wedding day, her wonderful husband
by her side,
Holding hands tightly and laughing, showing love they never could hide.
She had lost her own parents when she was young, but now had
others so very dear,
Two sisters and three more brothers, all are in pictures found here.

They had photos taken in their uniforms, when serving in the forces
overseas,
In snow, in rain and in sunshine and on beaches by different seas.
Then babies in prams, baths and cots and toddlers with toys,
having fun,
First days at school, brownies and cubs, them getting older
in every one.

Their children had grown up so very fast, a click had captured a scene,
Special occasions were duly recorded, of places and relatives they'd seen.
As she slowly turns over each picture, she remembers the time
so clear,
When she had been reunited with her real family and the brothers
she loved so dear.

Next are photos of their children's weddings, then with families
of their own,
The grandchildren at different stages, oh how the years have flown.
Now someone special is missing from photos and she'd give her life
to see,
Her husband laughing in a snapshot with all his grandchildren at his knee.

He was taken from them so suddenly, his death had been such a
hard blow,
He'd have been so proud of his family and would have loved to
watch them all grow.
Tears trickle slowly down her face, as she replaces photos and lid
as before,
These are her precious memories, that she'll treasure for evermore.

Mary Cadman

LOST CHILDREN

(For my daughter, Lorraine, who is autistic)

Autistic children are all alone
In a world that is all their own
What sights do they see there?
What sounds fall on the stair
Of their hearing and who knows
What strange, sad fear blows
Through the tunnels of the mind?
What ideas and images unwind
On the loom of the unknown soul?
Who on earth can make them whole?
They do not fit in anywhere
It seems society does not care
My child asks in consternation,
'Am I retarded?' what explanation
Can I give, when experts can't agree
On the solution to this mystery?

Sheila Whitehead

FAITH

This night I look up to the sky
A starry sky I do see with a full moon
This moon is strong enough to turn tides
In oceans and seas vast and wide
When the time is right you make a wish
It can turn your life and become rich.

But I do not look for riches or wealth
With praying hands and look up to the gods
And ask that I become strong in faith
So I can help and grow spiritually.

To give to others who become sick and weak
Faith in their life and not despair
For if we did not have sickness we could not
Grow spiritually if life was perfect.

This pain you have to endure
With dignity and grace and faith
Praying and hoping that God's will
Comes to your aid for sure
And be saved and not feel despair
You will feel a soft hand stroking
Your hair, a tender hand wiping tears away.

You know God would not abandon you
Or His sheep, sick or weak they may be
Each obstacle and hurdle you overcome
Patience and wisdom, spirit, knowledge comes
Faith and joy will come, so go forth
Help others less fortunate than you.

Ray Slater

MY GUY

I sat my guy outside the shop,
Hoping that someone would stop
And drop a penny in the hat,
I'd say, 'Thanks' and that is that.

People stare as they pass by,
I stare back and wonder why?
They know this happens every year,
It isn't something that is queer.

Kids have got to have some fun,
For them it's only just begun.
They're young and eager and naive,
Not all with tricks up their sleeve.

By dusk I have just sixty pence
And to the shops I head to spend,
'Tomato soup please, for my dad,
He is a tired and hungry lad.'

Outside I held it to his lips
And then he blew me a big kiss.
You see, my dad's my favourite guy
I think his wheelchair tells you why.

He sat all afternoon like that
Holding out his trilby hat
He's cold and who could wonder why
We spend each day that passes by
Begging on the corner street
If we get lucky we get meat
For our tea and that's a good day
I love Dad and I just pray
That one day he may walk, like me
And run and realise, he's free.

Lisa McKenzie

GHOSTS OF WAR

Oh, *ghosts of war* appear to all who think
Of war as exciting and hope to gain fame
Or land to add to their own country.
Show all men that nothing is worth the horror
And misery that follows in the path of all wars.

Frighten them who *dare* say, 'Victory' as on
They fight through each night, waiting, hoping,
That to them shall fall the enemy, to kill
Or maim for life. A living hell breaks loose
As war is lost or won and what irreplaceable
Treasures are lost for everyone?

Whichever side is victorious the common
Man wants *not* to fight, but live in peace
His allotted span, not killed in some
Distant land and then forgotten, except
Perhaps on Poppy Day, when many remember,
But few realise how much he gave that hero brave.

Oh, leaders of our lands unite, but not to fight!
To make each country rich in love and understanding,
To conquer disease and famine. Surely one good *ghost*
Somewhere can show all men who govern that
This is what the people want the whole world over.

So, *ghosts of war* come down each night to all
Men in power, show them that the path they
Tread is brilliant red, red with the blood
From all past wars, but who is to keep the score?
Then terrify them with your moans and
Groans, until they see the *light* and
There is *peace* for evermore.

Mary Antcliffe

1945 THE YEARS BETWEEN 2005

Though sixty years the memory dims
How vividly we see
The faces of those valiant men
Who died for you and me -
And for *our* world which but for them
Dictators now would rule
In ways quite foreign to our own
And laws unjust and cruel.

For England's green and pleasant land
Beneath jack-booted feet
Would cease to be a sanctuary
Where every race can meet.
And many 'institutions'
Revered throughout our land
Would no doubt be dismantled
By the Swastika's command.

Such dangers were inherent
In victory by the foe
But 'twas the armies of the Commonwealth
That dealt the final blow
With men of all the nations
Of democratic mind
With valour beyond courage
They fought to save mankind.

Though sixty *thousand* years or more
The sands of time sift by
Wherever peace and freedom live
They'll know the reason why.

John Elias

TO MY MUM

You thankfully brought me into this world
And guided me through the years
We've shared our times of happiness
We've shared our times of tears.

You not only gave me a wonderful life
You gave me a sister and brother
If we were given the chance to choose
We'd still choose you for our mother.

Everyone says that their mum's the best
I say the same thing too
But deep in my heart I know they're all wrong
'Cos that title belongs to you.

You've always been there to share with me
Times of sadness and sorrow and joy
You'll always be my loving mum
And I'll be 'your little boy'.

How many years we've left to share
Only the good Lord can tell
I ask Him in my prayers each day
To bless us and keep us well.

There's just one thing that's been missing
So the time to change has now come
It's something I've not said often enough
And that's, 'I love you, Mum.'

Maurice Langley

THE LAST WISH

When it is my time to go
I want no thoughts of sorrow or woe.
Just be happy that I have gone home
No more on this Earth plain do I have to roam.
I chose my time, the year, the day
Just see me happily upon my way.
When you're aware of what life's all about
You know there's no need to scream and shout.
I have done my best and learnt a lot
The wrongs from right and the do nots.
We all have a lesson we have to learn
For material things in life we do not yearn.
For all our treasures are in Heaven above
And I don't mean jewels, I mean pure love.

Patricia Davis

CELEBRATION

We celebrate a wedding and we celebrate a birth,
The joy of an engagement or promotion with a rise
Are causes for enjoyment, merriment and mirth
Though joyful tears quite oft might fall from many eyes.

In two thousand and three was the Queen's Jubilee,
A fifty year reign to that date.
The folks in the Mall were so happy to be
Waving flags at this great, golden fête.

In two thousand and five all those still alive
Who remember the end of the war
Now celebrate peace, for which we still strive
Whilst recalling the onslaught we saw.

So, *celebration!* Shout with elation,
Rejoicing with festive cheer,
Let's stand by our nation
And celebrate all we hold dear.

Maude Newton

CHRISTMAS

How sweet a mystery is here! For on this day
All men, all ages, in all time and space
Are joined together and with one accord
Bow down in humble worship of their King.
A King, not clothed in purple and fine robes
Enthroned within a palace nobly fair
And worthy to surround so great a Lord -
Instead, a baby bound in swathing bands
His palace nothing more than rock-hewn cave -
A stable for the ox and for the ass
A fitting shelter - and His throne
A manger quickly palliassed with hay
See how they come before him, so will we -
For be we wise or simple, rich or poor
There is a place for every one within
To worship Christ, to wonder and adore.

Iris Woolford

TOMORROW'S NOSTALGIA

Then, if you give her the bright world
And all its implosive boasts,
Yet she asks for more, spread no academic trance
Upon the sepia purpose of past's specious shroud,
But cast the queuing synthesis
Beyond the balm and bathe upon
The soliloquy of the great sea's flat and indigo distance.

Then, when the future dooms the ailing
Metaphor which we once believed was
Life, she, who sought something untold,
Returns to you the inebriation upon
Soaring rays of upturned avalanches. Oh,
Better far than reason's solemn assurance
Was today; the scent of some memory to come;
The exercise of sunlight and the wind.
More glorious than the promise
Is today, more sure than all those
Thoughts and fond regrets. Give her

Not this dazzling creation still burning in the furnace
Of a void of welding nostalgia, but the
Brilliance of the moment, the eternity
Which is certain; which is now.

Gordon Vale

WITHOUT YOU . . .

Without you . . .

I would always be punctual,
There'd be no conversation in the mornings,
There would be a part of me forever missing,
I'd have jam on my breakfast toast,
The sun would have less heat.

Can I really visualise life without you?
I'd take myself far too seriously,
Life would lose lots of fun,
Who would love me the way you do?
I'd have no reason to drive extra miles for the sunset,
There would be a space.

Is it really how I want my life?
There would be no one to laugh and tease with,
I'd be hopeless with a map,
Talking at midnight would be unheard of,
No one would buy me silly gifts for the fun of it,
Who would share my ice cream?
Without you?
Unimaginable!

Cherry Thacker

FALLEN ASH

I didn't see it fall
- just the dark, spectral cloud,
a glowering shroud in the storm
which tore through the wood.

That tree alone paid the toll
of the wind's wild trail,
while all else stood fast.
How could that be?

Days after, it had gone,
but not as never been.
The stump remained,
roots wrenched, washed clean by rains,
pointing down to the rich podsol.

They sliced the trunk
into manageable lengths.
Bones stripped of flesh by talons
could not look as bare as those,
piled up end on.

I wasn't there when they lit the fire:
the brushwood; branches
I might have danced along.
No.
It was the ashes of the ash I saw,
the mound of black a coalmine tip,
a lifetime's growing with, at the edges,
a twig unburnt, a leaf curling.

Laurence Shelley

THE LUMINOUS CHRISTMAS TREE

Christmas Eve: a still, silent night,
Save for nature's nocturnal rite.
The cottage: remote, shabby, homely,
Issues vertical smoke from its shattered chimney.

The surreal silence continues within,
But for the child breathing out, breathing in,
Shallowly, unevenly, laboriously. The fever high,
The inclination, to let life pass by.

The mother, beyond tears now, is in despair.
Long years ahead lie bleak and bare:
No more tantrums, nor shrieks of laughter.
No wedding to plan, or grandchild thereafter.

The father looks on and tries to be strong.
Unwittingly, he seems to get everything wrong.
Was it something he'd done, or not done, for his family?
When asked for support, he gives it willingly.

Watching the sad tableau is a lofty Christmas tree.
Incongruous in its strength, against human frailty.
The Christmas angel, another powerful force,
Can seek succour from a more heavenly source.

Whilst parents sleep, the angel swoops from the treetop,
Whispers to the child, impossible to eavesdrop.
The Christmas story, told with such feeling,
This time, to bring the great gift of healing.

As dawn breaks, the child reaches out to the mother
Who weeps with joy. Her child will recover.
The father, bewildered, notes other mysteries too:
The Christmas tree is luminous, the angel distinctly askew.

Valerie Catterall

EVENING SONG

I'll take you down to the country and lay your head to rest
Besides the flowing river, beneath the maggie's nest.
Oh God, why have You taken her?
My life is stripped of zest.
I feel no love for Man nor beast,
On her vision, I no longer feast.

When will the pain begin to wane?
When will my memories fade?
Forty years of endless love, engulfs my
Heart and mind.

Goodbye, my virgin, Mother and friend,
You're mine for evermore.

So listen out for my gentle knock,
On Heaven's cottage door.

David Bilsborrow

WHEN I WAS YOUNG

Long years ago, when I was young
I often used to say
I know what I'll do when I'm old
With time to spare each day

I'll weed the garden, mow the lawns
And sometimes plant some seeds
I'll put in bulbs and little plants
Where there used to be weeds

I'll make great cakes and lovely sweets
That all the family love
I'll try to cook all sorts of things
As well as those above

But now I'm old and helpless too
I just can't help at all
To even walk and move about
Ends up in just a fall

So do be warned, if there are things
You really want to do
Get on and do them whilst you can
And make your dreams come true.

Brenda Barber

HANGING ABOUT

I'm a woolly jumper,
I'm dangling from a clothes line,
My owner pegged me out here,
I've been hanging now since nine.

Although the sun is shining brightly,
The wind is chilly and strong,
My arms are really aching,
The pegs are finding it hard to hang on.

I've lots of other clothes for company,
All they've done is moan,
I was really wet and dripping,
But at least I've not been alone.

I heard someone say it would only take an hour,
For all the wet to drip out and dry,
But the wind's got a lot stronger and colder,
I'm feeling so tired, I just want to cry.

I can hear the trousers shouting,
They're not angry, just having a laugh,
Now the shirts and towels have joined them,
I do believe it's because we're being taken in at last.

Gillian S Gill

MY PARK

Everyone's heard of the Garden of Eden
My garden's quite big, but with lots of weeds in
It's all overgrown not with flowers or shrubs
But all kinds of car parts and rubbish in tubs

There's three old cars from which those car parts came
I'm not sure about livestock, but I hope they are tame

I try not to go out there when it is dark
As it feels like a sort of Jurassic Park
When daylight comes the morning after
I look at my 'park' with silent laughter
And think, *what on earth was I worried about?*
There was nothing there ready to jump out
Except maybe a timid or more
That I hadn't noticed, when out before

One of these days I shall clear it up good
I'll get rid of all that old dead wood
And buy me some plant pots to put flower seeds in
Then I will have
My very own
Garden of Eden.

Hal Takata

WISHFUL THINKING

If only I could see once more
The coral reefs and the sandy shore.
Green-clad mountains after torrential rain,
Double rainbows in the sky again.
The hula brought from faraway lands,
Ancient legends told by graceful hands.
The many highly scented flowers,
Hibiscus blooming for a few hours.
Yet most of all I long to renew
The love and happiness that I knew
Which was shown to me each sun drenched day
By the welcoming gift of a lei.
The peaceful place I'd longed to find
Was there and my joy was unconfined.
Oh! how often I wish that I might be
Back in the islands of Hawaii.

J E Stangroom

LIFE

Come celebrate life with me.
Don't be sad and blue.
Take joy in all you hear and see,
for the years of life are few.

Sip in the scent of a rose re-born.
Revel in children at their play.
Herald sweet birdsong at break of dawn.
Savour the miracle of each new day.

Watch raindrops splash from a leaden sky
and gently fall to the earth below.
Catch a cloud as it scampers by.
Feel a nipping air as it brings snow.

Bask in warmth of a summer sun,
before winter's shroud is cast.
For the cycle of life long begun,
approaches oh, so fast.

Absorb all around you
as mists of time roll by.
Make worthwhile all you do.
Because swiftly life doth fly.

Josie Rawson

HIDDEN INHERITANCE

You are my future when I am not there,
Though you think I am old and grey,
I will open doors where your eyes may stare.

You follow your peers and siblings who dare
And ignore what I have to say.
You are my future when I am not there.

My genes you carry in a quarter share,
Remember my teachings, I convey.
I will open doors where your eyes may stare.

Life is full of pitfalls, sometimes despair.
Stand tall, think true, honour wins the day.
You are my future when I am not there.

Life is for sharing, grief is hard to bare.
Give love, don't take. Actions purvey.
I will open doors where your eyes may stare.

We overcome problems with humour and flair,
Men serve, or rule, at work and play.
You are my future when I am not there,
Re-open my doors, for your eyes to share.

Mabel McCoy

A GIFT

By my side is a gift, so rare;
An unknown angel always there:
Prodding, poking,
Tickling, stroking.

I watch your ever-changing face;
Maturing to its destined grace:
Budding, blooming,
Thriving, flourishing.

My teacher in the art of life,
To lead the way throughout my strife:
Advising, guiding,
Shaping, sculpting.

Deep-rooted feelings have been found,
Eternally we shall be bound:
Linked, tied.
A friend.

A sister.

Emily Thommes

HAVE YOU EVER?

Have you ever sat quietly in nature and marveled at the wonder,
Listened to the birds singing, watched the trees gently swaying,
Taken in the vivid, vibrant colours that are all around to see,
Smelt the new-cut grass, or rain that's fallen on flowers?

Have you ever lain at night beneath the stars twinkling so bright,
Then watched one shoot across the sky and made a wish or kissed
And caressed your loved one beneath the darkened sky?

Have you ever watched a storm at night whilst standing on a
Deserted beach, watched the lightning light up the tips of
the waves
Or the rain sploshing into the sea?

So many wonders in this world for all of us to see, all it costs
is a few short
Moments to watch, smell, listen and enjoy, a few short moments
out of a
Hectic, stressful day, could simply fill your heart with joy.

Maxine Coughlan

SOME THOUGHTS ON 9/11

It was the day that viewers watched in horror
Their TV screens revealing human terror.
Americans had thought themselves carefree,
Each coast safe-guarded by a mighty sea.
Then stared in disbelief as airborne raiders,
Attacked New York. Who were these mad invaders?
Who thought that people's lives on Planet Earth,
Even their own - were simply nothing worth.
Bin Laden was responsible that day
For the death of thousands. Slaughter was his way.
But let us in our great Creator's name
Do good for evil, for it was His aim
To make this Earth a place of peace and beauty.
Invasion of Iraq was not our duty.
And let us show to far Afghanistan
The best of human nature. Taliban
Just ruled its people with inhuman laws
And forced on them its dictatorial cause.
Provision for the poor and weak our creed,
Asylum for all those who are in need.
When war's out-dated what a wondrous world there'll be
Freedom from want for all humanity.

Mary Webster

KIDS

When we were kids, we never had much,
Girls play hopscotch and skipping and rounders and such,
We played cowboys and Indians and marbles and that.

When we were kids, policemen checked on the doors
And we knew we were safe, outside and indoors,
There wasn't much crime, 'cause the police were abound.

When we were kids, there was no fear of drugs,
The people walked the streets without fear of being mugged,
Parents knew we were safe, 'cause the police were around.

When we were kids, we respected our elders
We never smashed windows or bothered our neighbours,
We didn't lock our doors, 'cause we trusted our neighbours.

When we were kids, there was justice for all
And criminals went away for a very long haul,
There's no justice no more,
It's the victims that suffer most of all.

When we were kids, I remember the old days,
Of those special years of yesterday,
For people looked out for one another,
It's a sad, old world we live in,
I am glad I was around, in those days,
For life was much, much safer then.

Garth Evans

BOOK OF LOVE

This book has a truth though it hides in reams of
Strange-sounding words; your eyes wouldn't bear
It - you'd laugh and tear out the pages with
Your lithe fingers and let them fly like your crisp hair
At the window.

Maybe, in a million years, you'd marvel at the strange truth;
You'd think of a far-off rainforest
Where a tree was felled to make the book; you'd
Say, 'I'd love to be in a storm there - both of us,
Drowning in it!'

Lee Walford

THE UNEXPECTED

Howling winds and sounds so eerie,
Branches swaying angrily,
Birds distressed, clinging on,
Fearful of uncertainty.

No control of direction,
Leaves are petrified,
No longer holding on -
Scattering around us
And not knowing where they belong!

And now, just for now -
Some blissful moments -
When all is still once more
And there are fragments of pots
Just laying around where mighty winds
Have hit the ground.

Myfanwy Clarke

SEASONS REMEMBERED

Autumn's breath had been cut short
Like a faded dream of autumns past.
Visions flashed before my eyes of
Idyllic days spent in Roman hills,
Where the air was pure and sweet
And happiness knew no bounds.
Moments later a shattered dream
No more the hills to roam.

Suddenly, winter is upon us -
Her trees are bared of leaves and
The countryside is bereft of colour,
Her cold, icy breath is upon us.
We must now wait patiently
For the thaw within our hearts
Of one so dear, to become
Spring's renewed promises.

Time trickles like a stream
But the seasons halt for no one.
Winter will bow to another spring
Who will give way to summer,
To be followed by poignant autumn.
And as each season passes
We remember each one with love,
For every man there is a season.

Jennifer Vrahimis

MY DAD

(My dad would have been 100 years old on the 29th September. He was born 29-09-1905)

Oh, Dad you gave so much love to me,
You took me everywhere with you,
On your ice cream round with you,
Was ever a child loved as much as me?

If only every child could have had a childhood like mine,
A dad that was so loving and kind,
Who taught me right from wrong,
To always do the best you can,
To help others along the way.

To do a good deed and not bad,
This has helped me make the person that I am,
Giving a smile along the way,
Knowing the joy of living each new day.

Helping others along the way,
Showing God's love for all to share,
These are the things I treasure along the way,
The love that brightens each new day.

M Ackroyd

SOB AND PUNCH AND PUNCH AND SOB

The specialist's truth
Punch it away
Punch hand into *me*
I'm made that way!
Feather cushion soft for my children to use
Punch away all forms of abuse
Punch away poverty and crime
Punch away children of mine
I took the cross that you should be
Able to *punch away at me!*
I'm *big and soft,* a *faithful father.*
Punch away, don't *stay in a lather!*
Punch away debt, doubt and fear.
Punch away for a *better year!*
Let go of amen, don't rehearse
No *need to recite that age-old verse.*
Punch away, let tension go!
Punch away, I won't say *no!*

I'm big and cuddly *Father bear!*
Come! and *punch!* and *broken be!*
Sob and sob your *pain to me*
Sob away the *coffin's dread*
Sob away that *empty bed*
Sob and *punch* and *punch* and *sob*
Do what you like for I'm a *huge god!*
A *bulwark,* a *wall,* a *massive tower*
A lighthouse, a blank cheque
The *god of great power!*
One thing I ask, one thing I say
Don't even leave me
Don't go away
I'd deflate!

Cynthia Taylor

HIBERNIAN HIBERNATION

Deep within the hush of nature's wintry sleep
We hover
Like frosted figures on a snow-capped cake
Balancing between the heavens and a sunken Earth
Like astronauts in outer space
Like some ridiculous mistake.

Sacredly, silently, divinely desiccated flakes
Descend
Dropping from a fleecy hand
Seeking for the Earth and for her secret parts
Falling on the shoulders of our hearts
Kissing at the blankets where she sleeps
Dissolving in the dying embers of our cheeks.

She never stirs that solemn, sleeping beauty
Though tickled by the thoughts that patter on her side,
'Poor man, poor miserable man
You don't know when to rest,
Come starchy man lie down awhile,
Come lay your deadening cheek upon my tender breast.'

'No, Madame Earth
For far beyond this stiff and biting cold,
Beyond your luring lust, a story's told
And angels sing as sunshine melts the icy sky
And Heaven's love distils upon our misery.
We are not mad, oh Madame Earth,
We celebrate our Saviour's birth!'

David Martin

EXERCISE YOUR MIND

Exercise can do you good, if taken in small measure.
I run and skip and jump each day
It gives me so much pleasure.

I *run* a bath most mornings,
I *skip* what work I can
Then *jump* into my bed at night
A very happy man!

I *trot* out many platitudes
Ride roughshod over you,
I *gallop* through each book I read
And *run* a risk or two.

I cannot *swim* because I live
Too far from the sea
But am content each day to *dive*
Into my food with glee.

I *jog* my memory now and then
Or *jump* to some conclusion
Then *lie* with ease, between my teeth
Or *rise* to an occasion.

Vaulting I especially like,
To dramatise a ceiling.
I *wrestle* with my conscience
Which is a lovely feeling.

This *punch* of mine's tremendous
- I give it all I've got -
It's bound to put you on your back
- Especially if served hot!

You see, I *am* an active man
And *not* an idle lout.
Cos exercise takes hold of me
And makes me fit, for nowt!

George A Tanner

WILD LIFE

I have a tendency to rhyme
And can't stand Gardener's Question Time,
There's nothing logical in this,
But for me, there's no bliss
In bending o'er a blessed border!
Aster, stock, lupin in prim good order.
Give me the wild, the savage flower
That fights, tho' lacking sun or shower.
Among rocks, in cleft or crag,
In desert, ditch, or e'en in slag.
A pox I say on ordered ranks,
Apple pie, common or; I'd rather banks
Where eglantine and wild thyme grows:
Trefoil, corncockle and dog rose.
Forgive, oh bard, these borrowed words,
Non better to proclaim my plot for birds
Foot trefoil, marjoram and mallow,
Fennel, harebell and rosebay willow.
My year dawns with the daffodil
And lives thro' campion and cranebill.
And wildly as my garden grows,
Each small creature somehow knows,
To dig his den and climb his tree
That he will not disturbed be.
Each does not venture out by day,
A pity, I do not them gainsay.
But well they know that thro' the night,
That savage man is out of sight.

James Stevenson

THE VENETIAN TOMCAT

The Venetian tomcat without a name
Was measuring the honeysuckle-clad shed
There was no scent of luxurious flowers
As autumn has clasped the falling leaves
They were turning yellow, when gracing the lawn
Bolding the trees of the garden behind our house
Inside there was yesterday's silence; outside
The Venetian tomcat without a name
Was philosophically meditating an afternoon nap
The sun was weak as predicted by learned men
Delivering forecasts from sophisticated boxes
The sun was there as a reminder of the summer days
Clouds were gathering their strength ready
To punish travellers on foot along glazed pavements
One needed to carefully look before stepping
It was an ordinary sort of day for
The Venetian tomcat without a name.

Mariana Zavati Gardner

MOBILE PHONES

Day and night
Mobile phones
Cheerful, quirky
Ringing tones.
Are you there?
Where are you?
Should we go there?
I'll come too.
No time for silence.
Never alone
Communication
Mobile phones.
No more secrets
Sent us a text
Let me know
Where you're going next
Who do you talk to?
What do you say?
Mobile chat
Every day.
Day and night.
Mobile phones
Cheerful, quirky
Ringing tones.

Pat Rissen

WHAT'S DESTROYING OUR WORLD?

Wars, hurricanes, tsunami, has the world gone mad?
Is it humans or nature that's changing the world for bad?
People starving and poor and misery galore.

The crocodile surviving
He's been around for a long time
And there's nothing endangered
About the mosquitoes and flies
For now they're thriving in their millions or more.

Let's not take our world for granted
For there's still places of beauty
That we haven't destroyed
Let's forget about nuclear weapons to destroy
Let's appreciate what's around us before it's too late
And give our children a future
Which they won't hate.

Janet Hannan

TIME CREPT ME SIDEWAYS

(For H M)

Time crept me sideways
And my horizons slanted.

Shadowed perspective, grass high,
    distorts a view that once was obvious.
The soul flounders in this place,
    known, but not familiar.
The will shuttered, passive with endured
    pain, is too much alone with agony.
Perhaps in madness I could claim a sanity
    less tortured;
And find, lured front to back
Tears where once there was a lack of them.
Madness presumes too much!
There is a reason in the touch of words.

Time waited; while I considering,
    arrested the minute.

Here is uncertainty, not clear the purpose
    or intent.
No measure that meant my life be angled so.
The thought decisive, turns me.

Upright, I look back upon the image
    of myself.
Dreams neatly stacked but broken
    lay upon the shelf of illusion.
So be it, this time is done.
And thrusting it aside, I find
I leave behind the crouching shadow.

Janine Vallor

MEMORIES

There are so many memories I look back on and recall,
My childhood days and childish ways,
I treasure most of all.
Trips to the coast, the sand and sea,
Someone taking good care of me.
A stick of rock and candyfloss!
Holding hands in case I'm lost.
Then a warm, snug bed,
Prayers to be said,
My sister by my side.
A laugh, a tear, a hug so dear,
Are memories that abide.
But as years pass by and memories fade,
You forget the love you knew,
Time marches on and with it gone
Are memories so true.
So spend some time recalling
All the fun and times you had,
Remember memories are happy,
Those times spent with Mum and Dad.

Jackie Allingham

YOU WERE THERE

You were there when I shed my tears
You were there all through the years
You were there in all my pain
You made the sun come out again
And shine on me!
Oh, come upon our troubled world
And let Your shining light unfurl
And heal us.
We need You, oh so very much
The healing power of Your touch
Our Saviour!

Mary Staniforth

A BETTER WORLD?

A fairer, better world,
I don't think so,
Was slavery abolished
A long time ago?

But hang on a minute,
Doesn't history attest
Slavery abolished,
Our consciences at rest.

Now we in the 'first' world
Enjoy our fill - and more,
Till we feed the slimming industry
And not the poor.

The world's three richest people
Own more - I've heard
Than the 48 poorest countries
Combined, have earned.

We go our own sweet way
While it can be seen,
That a billion people
Drink water that's unclean.

If we can up our profits
We can buy gold shades,
To shield our eyes
From the sweatshops and the pain.

With a day of reckoning coming
What a place to be,
Among those who make decisions
On world poverty.

Gaynor Dexter

TOO LATE?

Is it too late to dream?
To make a dream, to want to dream?
Too late to place my heel back into
the footprint so hastily just made.
Why was I so quick to wish life by . . .
craving experience of all and everything,
but never satisfied?

Now I see the final stages of my life
nigh ready for my final curtain call,
and wonder if I still have the right . . .
to venture imagination enough
to build something worthwhile.
A trophy, a prize, that is worthy of all
that has passed through my journey,
like quicksilver, fast becoming
shadowy memories of things long gone.

So much older now, is it all reflection
on those times that have gone before?
Or is it not too late to look ahead
and dare to dream once more?
Courage to reach out into the unknown.
To step swiftly through the closing door
of life and see what could still be there.

To do more than dream, to actually do.
And before my story ends, perhaps have shown,
I could make just one more dream come true.

M G Howcroft

ROBIN REDBREAST

I'm a little robin redbreast sitting in a tree
I know the people living here think a lot of me
They throw me tasty morsels out morning, noon and night
And check to see I'm still about and haven't taken flight
I like when they dig the garden or even trim the hedge
Though I must admit the latter sets me a bit on edge
I give it the once over to see what they have done
Flitting here, there and everywhere it's really rather fun
It doesn't matter what they do I keep them in my sight
The only time that I miss out is when it's dark at night
I'm up early in the morning when there's nobody around
Sometimes I sit here ages before they make a sound
Then suddenly things happen, it's the start of another day
I'll watch them from a distance, be discreet, stay out the way
When they go inside for lunch I'll have a little peek
To see what they've been up to and the fun I'll have this week
I could have chosen any garden being a bird and fancy-free
I'm glad I came to this one, it means so much to me.

Doreen Quince

DUST TO DUST

Gaze vainly, Watcher,
For the mirror's empty now.
No image in the silvered glass -
Nothing to see
Within this sudden blindness of reality.
Last act, last curtain, final bow
Were yesterday's -
Empty circle, empty stage and empty stalls;
Lights out;
Illusion lost;
Last echo where an empty footstep falls;
Last click of closing door
Against the silence,
Marking nothing more.
Gaze Watcher, empty-eyed;
Last night the future died
And no one sought to catch its failing breath,
And no one cried.
Gaze, Watcher, if you must
And listen to the empty darkness whisper
Ash to ashes,
Dust to dust.

Brian Travis

LIFE

You're young and you marry
And the children come along.
Some days are filled with laughter
Other days, are very sad.

School time comes around
The bond is starting to break.
Tears and fears at the school gate
For the children, you take.

The teenage years have come
Leaving school and finding jobs
Is another fear, for the young
Their parties and their boyfriends.

All too soon this has gone.
They have all flown the nest
And we wish them the best
Now thirty-eight years on
We are on our own
Where have the years gone?

Rita Johnson

LONELY BEACH

He walks along the beach, mind deep in thought.
A still, warm, tranquil night; the whispering sea
rose up and ironed the sand, leaving but nought
a trace of footsteps, mere indentations on the lee.
The moon, quite full, revealed the strolling man
as he disturbed the whitened edge of sand.

But caring not that wavelets soaked his shoes
as they erased his footsteps on the strand.
He thought not of discomfort as he left,
but only of the loved one in his mind
and of whose perfect face he was bereft,
that faded as daylight left dreams behind.

Night fell again and he would once more spend
the hours with his true love that would not end.
He feels her presence as a zephyr breeze
like fingers on his face, as, once again,
come sun, come blustering hail, come winter freeze,
she would be with him under falling rain.

She, in bare feet, as they go hand in hand
and walk, along the empty strip of sand that yet,
despite the moonlight, only shows, of sea-washed prints,
one set.

David G W Garde

THE OLD HOUSE

Many's the time I've seen it!
Big, and dark, and old.
No one ever enters it,
Unless they're very bold!

It stands in lovely gardens
- Though overgrown the surrounds,
And the village master
Calls it - 'out of bounds'!

The place is very dreary
The rooms are dark and eerie!
Dust lies thickly everywhere
- On broken table, broken chair.

A prosperous farm once there did stand,
Now it's barren, rocky land.
The family - all have gone away
Not been seen for many a day!

The house is slowly falling down
Falling, falling to the ground
It soon will be beyond repair,
A ruin left just rotting there!

Jeannette R D Jones

GHOSTS DANCING

We are like ghosts dancing, you and I,
Our insubstantial bodies meet, yet never touch,
Reaching out for contact where there can be none,
For we have no solidity.

Your whispers pass by me unheard on the night breeze,
For the ears of the dead are deaf,
I wait for your kiss of life to make me real,
If only our lips could meet and wake us to some kind of
cold passion.

If our dance could slow and still,
Where we might sway together,
If glacial fingers could but connect,
Perhaps the grave of our desire may yet be warmed.

Dawn James

ETERNAL LOVE

A seed will form a flower
That will rise above
In time the flower will die
But never will my love

The rain falls from the petals
Like tears from my eyes
I live within my memories
With times that have gone by

My heart will not stop aching
My feelings I can't hide
I go to sleep in dreams of you
And dream you're by my side

I live within my memories
With every dawn that breaks
Until I'm there beside you
My heart will always ache

I've cried so many tears
I can't cry any more
But every day's a new day
Like the one before

When angels call for me, my love
Only then I'll sleep
When I'm there beside you
I'll have eternal peace.

M B Tucker

BUSY DAY

I pack his suit
Get out his shirt,
Get his coffee
He goes to work

Get his breakfast.
Clean away.
Pack his lunch
He's away all day

Hoover, dust.
Clean away dirt
Wash and iron.
He goes to work

Do the garden
Mow and weed
Make sure it's done
So he doesn't need

When he comes home
At the end of the day
Get his dinner
Pack away

Then we sit down.
Nothing said.
Both too tired.
Time for bed.

Lynda Peat

THE BEAUTY OF LOCH LOMOND

Shimmering waters in a myriad of glorious hues;
Turquoise blended from deep forest greens and heavenly blues.
Afloat with numerous shady and secretive tree covered isles,
This wondrous beauty lazily meandering for miles.

Guarded from its shores by carpeted hills so strong and tall,
The colourful scene ever-changing from winter to fall.
Its waves happily licking the sands of its many coves and bays;
Greeting its avid admirers as it wends its merry way . . .

Isabella (Issy) Young

EMPTINESS

Only those who have lost
Someone very dear
Can every really understand
How it feels now they're not here
The emptiness, the longing
The heartache and the pain
And tears that keep on falling
Like never-ending rain
No one to cuddle up to
Or to kiss goodnight
And when you feel a little sad
No one to hug you tight
An empty chair to talk to
A photograph in a frame
Memories of the happy times
Then the hurting starts again
At night I look up at the sky
The brightest star to see
Then I pretend that it's my love
Watching over me
People tell you time will heal
And that life goes on
But it is so very hard
When it's your loved one that's gone
I know when all my heartache will end
So will the pain
And that's the day God calls me
To be with my love again.

Angela Clift

COMPUTER CRAZY

The news is good, the future's great
Computers now for all
Regardless of financial state
We'll soon be on the ball.

Hi-tech of course is paramount
We need to forge ahead
To fall behind on any count
Is what the politicians dread.

How expert are the *experts* though?
With just one aim in mind
No doubt because, as time will show
We've problems of another kind.

To make the point is not that hard
As anyone can tell
Computers won't, with due regard
Replace, repair, or make one well.

Who'll mend the fridge, repair the car
Re-tile the roof, or more
Dig up the road and lay the tar
Such skills, it seems, are out the door.

What's needed first must surely be
A realistic look
At how in our complacency
We bring it to the book.

Just take those souls who can't excel
Despite existing schemes
Not everyone can do that well
And yet they have their dreams.

Endeavours must, a fool can see
Be made to turn the tide
Invest the funds and energy
And halt this rapid slide.

Edward Roberts

MEMORY LANE

Down memory lane I wander
When I am feeling blue.
Thinking of the happy days
I spent alone with you.

Walking hand in hand together
Through the bracken and the heather
Driving through God's country fair
Without a worry, without a care.

Time was short - but I did not know
One day came and then the blow.
You were gone and I was left here
To face life alone, without you, dear.

Time heals the pain and life carries on
Till the day comes and I shall be gone.
And then I hope with all my heart
We shall be together again, never to part.

Kathleen Keech

THE GOOD SEED

Good words are like seed which are sown far and wide
To be grown in the world everywhere,
But, some fall on ground that is like the wayside
And are snatched by the birds of the air.

Good words are like seeds which are scattered and sown
With potential to grow into fruit,
But some fall on ground that is hardened like stone
And will fail to produce any root.

Good words can bring life just like any good seed
And develop to bud and then bloom,
But some fall on ground that is crowded with weed
And will fail for the want of some room.

Good words must be watered in time and through toil
And should always be 'growing concerns',
When nurtured on ground that is like the good soil
They mature and produce good returns.

Ivan S Thomas

WANING TAPER

Once again I hear the hangman
He is a couple of doors down from me
I wonder when it will be my turn
To hang for all to see?

They say I did a bad thing
And justice must be served
They found out I was a witch
No, I must get what I deserve.

I never realised how heavy
An albatross could be
I wonder at what point it changed
Into the noose that would hang me?

The hangman's hands are at my door
He knows not what he does
Lord and Lady it is not his fault
He cannot comprehend our love.

I forgive those who convicted me
Lord and Lady they don't understand
They know not that when we have all gone
This world will become a barren land.

When the last of the beacons
Have burned to cinders on the ground
No fairy will awake from slumber
No more magic will be found.

Dayna Sherwin

WITHOUT THEM

Stop all the humming of sweet honeybees,
Birds singing softly, nestling on the trees;
Stop butterflies dancing on a hot summer's day,
Take away the merriment from the month of May,
They were our politics, philosophy, laughter and song,
We thought grandchildren were for ever - we were wrong.

The toys aren't needed now, stand and watch them go.
Brush away the tears because you miss them so.
Why are we punished? What have we done?
We are the parents of a divorcing son.
The courts say it's wrong, it's breaking the law;
Yet they do nothing - nothing at all.
Some women's rights go over the top,
For the sake of our children, it *has* to stop.

They are our future, our past of days long gone.
We thought grandchildren were for ever - we were wrong.
The books aren't needed now, burn them one by one.
Scream to the heavens, dismantle the sun.
Tear up the flowers, destroy every wood,
For nothing, but nothing, will be as it should.

P M Jones

HAPPY BIRTHDAY, TO OUR QUEEN

You are going to have a birthday
A very special one this year
I have shared every one of them
Through the laughter and the tears

For you and I will be eighty
So we must celebrate
Do all the things we want to do
Before it gets too late

The people will rejoice and sing
Happy birthday, gracious Queen
I will be there watching
On my TV screen

Then on the following year, my Queen
The bells will ring loud and clear
It's our Diamond Wedding
That has lasted sixty years.

Lots of best wishes
From Kathy French
To you and your Prince.

Kathy French

AFFECTATION - UGH!

For me, there's wealth in country talk
Those dialects of Shires
Preferring folk much as they are
Not just as Vogue desires!
Should character say I remain
Would history warrant reading?
Should all conform to nicety
To prove or hide our breeding?
Oh, let's be us for Heaven's sake
Keep culture true, it's needed.
Let's have our English spelt correct
Our lawns of language weeded.
Tomorrow's world are sat in school
They must not be neglected
Come, let's be proud of country talk
And therefore, unaffected!

Peggy G Oates

THE MYSTERY TREE

On Midsummer's day I was under the acacia tree,
When a tiny bird whispered to me,
'Can you feel the magic in the air?
It's here, there and everywhere.'
The white fairy petals are dancing like snow,
Where the lovely tree comes from, nobody knows.
Golden bumblebees humming as they go into the sky
Doing a ritual dance as they fly.
If, like me, you believe in fairies,
Look for them in the acacia tree,
Make a wish, it will come true,
Just you wait and see.

G B Moore

FRIEND

When my world was pain
You were there
As the colours of my life
Turned from golden yellow
Into fiery red
You held me

When my life was broken
You put me together
As my body failed me
You never did
In the dark despair
That I feel
You touch my soul

As my body heals
You are still there
As the colour returns to my life
You are still holding me
My body still fails me
But still you don't
My dark despair grows lighter
But our souls are joined

When I needed you
Whatever time or day
You came
Thank you.

Babs Sherwin

LINDISFARNE

If I were to win the lottery, guess what I'd like to do most,
It would be to live on an island, on the north-east coast,
To gently pass along its Pilgrim's Way,
Be it winter, autumn, or the springtime of May.
And there to choose a cottage, that I loved the best,
One used in bygone days as a fisherman's rest.
With a cosy armchair set by a warm coal fire,
Seeing pictures in the flickering flames, before I retire.
Old coal rake and poker, the fire embers to stir,
Two collie dogs nearby in their black and white fur.
I would need my Dutch dresser, could anything be finer,
Richly bedecked in its blue and white china.
Pretty curtains at the windows, boasting of their frills,
With shells from the beaches on the low window sills.
Above all, the daily walks by the wide, open sea,
Such joyous freedom like a caged bird set free.
Naught but the seabirds winging up high,
The blue sea flirting with white clouds in the sky.
To watch the incoming tide, no need to run for cover,
As the sea wraps around me, like the comforting arms of a lover.

Olga Ramshaw

ENVIRONMENT

The world is giving us a sign
That it may soon run out of time
The atmosphere cannot wait for ever
For Man to start getting clever
The ozone layer's got some holes
This man knows he has been told
Over the world disaster strikes
It's getting worse, we'll have some frights
The weather's changing fast its pace
The sun shines down with a sad face
The ozone keeps on thinning
But this is only just the beginning
If we soon don't start to care
The ozone layer will start to tear
What will happen no one knows
We must be up and on our toes
For health reasons we now must try
To clean the pollution from the sky
To clean the dumps of toxic waste
If we don't, we'll have no case
Disease and floods will no doubt follow
It will be too late for Man's sorrow
We owe it to our kids of tomorrow
Don't let them sit with disease and our sorrow
All the nations must be aware and let's all show
Our world, we care.

Brenda Brownhill

WAITING FOR THE WORDS

For you;
Each and every one of you,
I would like to write words;

So fresh; they'd bounce from the page,
So lively; they'd sweep your blues away,

So poetic; they'd make you rhyme,
So musical; you'd sing and dance in time,

So wise; they'd be your guide,
So funny; you'd forget your troubles awhile,

So comforting; just like good friends,
So complete; like firm bookends,

So unusual; you'd be disarmed,
So romantic; you'd be charmed,

So sad; they'd make tracks for your tears,
So soft; they'd soothe your fears,

So warm; they'd thaw your frozen child,
So strong; they'd help you swim against the tide;

And if I could write them, they'd be like
A good husband or wife;
Treasure, which would sparkle, for the rest of your life.

William Greig

THE EDINBURGH TATTOO

Oh, for the men who are swinging the kilt,
Oh, for the white-footed trews,
Oh, for the badges of silver and gilt,
Oh, for the plaids of bright hues.

Oh, for the tales of heroes in story,
Oh, for the love of a girl,
Oh, for the courage, the pride and the glory,
Oh, for the flag they unfurl.

Georgina Ivison

THE HEALING GIFTS OF NATURE

Do the blackbirds sing a melody in unison
          to soothe a weary heart?
Do the cherry blossom trees laden their branches
          to fill us with hope?
I wonder if the daffodils hold their heads high
          as an example to us all?

Nature is a wonderful healer,
it asks no questions of us,
it has no expectations,
it gives of itself.

When we feel troubled within,
nature reaches out,
it tries hard to bring inspiration back into our lives.

Spring is a time for new beginnings,
it is a time for rebirth,
it is a time to look forward with renewed eyes.

Listen to the blackbirds,
their song holds the key to unlocking the beauty we have within.

Nature is a wonderful healer
and gives its love freely to us all.

Wendy A Lyon

AN ARTIST'S GIFT

A garden of patchy grass and bushes overgrown
A broken-down shed, weeds and rotten things
His eyes saw nothing, but a picture already sown
A canvas of imagined beauty had taken wings

His garden paintbrush transformed the dreary scene
A pond for wildlife and where water lilies grow
Bright yellow marsh buttercups in reed beds green
And a shady weeping willow bowing low

A corner with gazebo draped in clematis
A place to sit, behold the fragrant flowers
Bright shrubs and bushes touched by sunset's kiss
To delight and bring contentment to the passing hours

An artist's gift, a moment's meditation
Turned blank canvas to a font of inspiration.

Iris Owen

POET'S DREAMS

Sometimes I wake up at night
With words going round inside my head,
I try to put them into rhyme
While laying in my bed,
Back to sleep, I cannot go
Until these words I set free,
On an old envelope, resting on my knee.
It gives me so much pleasure
When down on paper, these words I see
Because these little words in rhyme
Belong only to me,
No matter how many rhymes are written
No two, are just the same
It is impossible
Like standing with your arms outstretched
Trying to catch the rain.
It too has this beauty
Of its very own
With its gentle pitter-patter
On the windows, of my Suffolk home.

A Vale

MEMORY GARDEN

In my garden everything grows
Even the weeds flourish there
For it's a garden of memory
And I tend it with great care
There's primroses lifting their little heads
Pansies and forget-me-nots, all growing here and there
Tulips and daffodils all in their beds
And roses blooming so fair
Lilac trees in blossom
Apple trees so tall
The hydrangea with lots of flowers
There against the wall
Larkspurs from the hedgerows
Taken with great care
Transplanted to the garden
Growing so high there
The snowdrops and the crocus
Have all been and gone
The yellow forsythia flowers are falling one by one
The butterflies and bees, are flitting to and fro
From blossom to blossom and I watch them come and go
So in that garden of memory, I wander round and round
And marvel every season, at what comes up
From the ground.

Mary Whittaker

MOONFLOWER

The faded scent of an old moss rose
Floats from a scrapbook of poems and prose
The powdery petals flutter and fall
From its pages and a story tell
Of bygone lovers, a summer night's tryst
They met . . . and lingered . . . and dreamed . . . and kissed . . .
In a moonlit garden; across silver'd lawns
They mapped their future - oh, happy plans.

In that old book's pages, marking the years
Are programmes, dance cards and souvenirs
Of a lifelong love that lingers on
Tho' gone are the singers, gone the song.
But the garden remembers, it always will,
Those old-time sweethearts - their love echoes still.
The same moon shines at twilight's close
And silvers the petals of the old moss rose.

Lila Jackson

THE BUTTERFLY

A tiny creature with wings of an eastern hue,
one sunny day into my garden flew,
she held her painted wings like a majestic cloak
swooping down to smell the flowers,
a place to rest she sought.
So delicate and graceful she flapped her little wings,
mesmerised I followed her,
what pleasures she did bring.
She landed on the roses, growing by the cottage door,
I had never seen such beauty in a tiny thing before.
Her delicate wings she folded,
hid the colours deep inside,
the beauty of her painted cloak from my eyes did hide.
I waited and I watched as she finally took flight,
spreading coloured wings she disappeared from sight,
a delicate, fragile miracle, a colourful butterfly,
she flew across my garden, she did not say,
'Goodbye.'

Audrey Taylor

A Victorian Poem

I stand in this vale of sadness
I dream of the long ago
when you and I were happy
and where I loved you so.

I stand in an empty landscape
I dream of once sunlit glades
where you and I together went
where now the sunlight fades.

I stand with the silence around me
I dream of you calling my name
but I hear not so much as an echo
and I know that such dreams are in vain.

As the dusk turns the day into ashes
and life must surrender to sleep
I promise my love everlasting
a promise with God's help I'll keep.

G F Hawkes

The Kingdom Of The Blind

I have seen the snows of sorrow
On the mountains of the moon
And sailed forbidden waters
Where I heard the sirens croon:
Deep in caverns carved in crystal
Lie wonders undefined
But what causes me to wonder
Is the kingdom of the blind.

I saw ships wrecked in the desert
And a river flow upstream
I saw phantoms in the firelight
Spoke with angels in a dream
Recondite and esoteric
Are the mysteries of the mind
And even such a mystery
Is the kingdom of the blind.

Where all have perfect vision
But all too few can see
Ignoring threats of Armageddon
Throughout history
I see in the solution
The redemption of mankind
To the maddening enigma
Of the kingdom of the blind.

J C Fearnley

God's Wonderful World

Mummy, isn't God wonderful!
He made all the world and everything in it,
He worked very hard, didn't stop for a minute.
People and animals, the birds and the bees,
Sunshine and flowers and lovely, tall trees,
The sun and the moon, the stars in the sky,
Raindrops and rainbows and butterflies,
Rivers and mountains, the fish in the sea,
But best of all Mummy, He made you for me,
He made you for me and He made me for you,
Oh, isn't God wonderful and clever too.

Phyllis Sandiford

Who Is It?

Who, in all this universe,
Is in charge of you and me?
Who causes rain, the drought and hail,
Then decorates a tree?

Whose finger, paints the flowers,
Giving them a different hue?
Then adds the scent to attract the bee?
It is not me, or you.

Who provides, the food we eat?
The water that we need?
Who satisfies, our merest whim?
Who despises greed?

Let us exalt You Sovereign Lord,
Pay You all we owe.
Praise You the One, who is in charge,
Ask You what we need to know.

Labour with our health and strength,
To do our work for You.
Telling everyone we meet,
So that they might know You too.

Snikpohd

Meeting Place

I've met God in the garden
when branches fold around me.

I've met God where the weeds grow
and unspied nettles sting my knee.

I've met God on a hospital ward
when endurance fills the air.

I've met God at a funeral
when our aching brought Him there.

I've met God when the music plays
and a tingle touches the cord.

I've met God on a sheet of paper
when ink flows into a word.

Mary Biggs

Through The Years

In the quiet of the night when sleep seems not for me
And thoughts can turn to the unforgotten past,
The years just roll away as the mind runs free
To rekindle memories that last and last.

From infant days in the village school
Simple and innocent it may have been,
Life lay ahead and the big wide world too
But it was troubled times in those early scenes.

The war took its toll of many and much
With rationing and shortages present,
But victory was ours to savour as such
And emerge full of hope and consent.

Schooldays offered limited scope
National Service followed irrespective of choice,
Into my twenties and filled with hope;
Working long hours to pay the mortgage was voiced.

Children completed the picture so well
Family life at its best,
Often hectic but we could not fail;
Stamina and love to the test.

So summer goes and autumn is here
No longer in top gear am I,
But the things in life that I hold most dear
Remain with me till I die.

Brian R Russ

THE GREAT INTENDER

They warned me not to marry you, but I knew better - far.
A hero quite unparalleled I thought you were (a star);
I listened with naïve delight as all your plans unfurled -
A lavish wedding, followed by a trip around the world.
(We compromised a little though, when on a rainy day,
The Registrar looked harassed as he speeded us away:
Our 'trip' was to the Rose and Crown - we stayed until they closed,
The wedding night, was uneventful - you were 'indisposed'!)
You'd promised to provide for me, but jobs were hard to keep -
Employers never understood, how long you had to sleep!

How vividly you'd talked about a mansion by the sea
And said we'd raise our children there, in perfect harmony,
But that was in abeyance as (pro tem) we settled down
In one decrepit council house, a mile away from town;
Our family expanded - overcrowding was severe,
Yet somehow, we have muddled through, as year has followed year,
I used to grumble in that hovel, till you told me, 'Look,
It's just a social survey, so that you can write a book.'
Well then, I understood, of course - I should be overjoyed,
That you have let me sample life, among the unemployed.

Relentlessly the time has flown (although I can't have aged -
I don't recall one birthday, since before we were engaged!)
Our sons and daughters (eight in all) have left the nest at last,
But still I have one little boy - a dreamer unsurpassed!
Your ship will really come in now - the world, you say, will shine:
You're sure to win the lottery and all will then be mine!
If time could be reversed, so I should meet you once again
With all ahead (the fun we've had, as well as all the pain)
I wonder if I'd choose you now? You know, I think I would
And love you in that mansion, as you promised me I should!

Rosemary Yvonne Vandeldt

MY FIFTEENTH YEAR

Imagine a nightmare
A nightmare that's not imagination
I see it every day
Every day since that day
My brain stuck on replay
Trapped in my fifteenth year

It doesn't fade with age
Its images sharp
Still razor my mind
Still sear my soul
In the broken heart of recall
I remember my fifteenth year

Shattered children, scattered round
As discarded toys
On the floor of Hell's nursery
In that absolute horror
I pray for a way
To forget my fifteenth year

Time, it is said
To be a great healer
Not in a fractured mind
Still agonising why
As it looks down
On blood-shocked ground

At Aberfan
On Friday October the 21st 1966
In my fifteenth year.

Mark Sims

MARY'S OBEDIENCE

Dark night, cold air,
The air was cold, dark and cold.

Dark was the night,
Cold was the air,
When Christ the child was born.
Sin formed the dark,
Evil the chill,
Into a world forlorn.

Mary, handmaid,
Obeyed God's will,
Brought light and love to earth.
Christ, born in flesh
Incarnate Lord,
Gave back to all their worth.

Mother of God,
Willing to be
The channel of His love.
Such was your trust
In Gabriel's word,
The Son came from above.

Light of the world,
Ransom for sin,
The child you bore for me.
Mary, my thanks,
Always ascend,
Whatever else may be.

Light are the nights,
Warmer the air,
Because of Christmas Day.
May I, like you,
Put self aside
And walk God's chosen way.

Peter J Millam

CAT

At the bottom of the garden
Lives a funny little creature,
It creeps through the undergrowth
It crawls through the reeds
Its favourite place is down among the weeds.

It digs pits in the flower beds,
Chases all the birds up the trees
And chases after leaves,
Upon the really hot days
You see it in the sunny trees
Entwined amongst the leaves.

He loves to bring in birds and vermin
And lay them on the mat,
He walks into the kitchen and sits
Upon his mat, purrs and talks,
Singing for his supper.

He doesn't have a bad life,
Staying out all night in the summertime
You are my mad little spotty cat,
The rogue of the street.

When all is said and done,
You've got nine good lives
While I sadly, have only one.

K M Clemo

THE VILLAGE OF STRATTON ON THE FOSSE

What have they done to our village?
Where once it was peaceful, serene,
Buttercup fields and duck ponds,
Or was it a childhood dream?

What have they done to the farmyard?
Where the cows ambled in about three,
The cowsheds now made into houses,
Where 'Willy the bull', used to be.

Why have they sawn down the sycamores,
That guarded the end of South Street?
Where is the 'magical corner',
That made our 'play hours' complete?

I remember the shop by the school room,
That sold 'aniseed balls' by the score,
There was 'Smith's Shop' and the bakery,
Alas, they are with us no more.

But there are joys I will always remember,
Like the stream at the end of the 'pound',
Dragonflies, wild flowers and suchlike,
Saw-backed newts and tadpoles we found.

The old church of 'St Vigor's' still standing,
Downside's Tower reaching up to the sky,
The woods of Old Holcombe and Luccombe,
Lending beauty to the sweet by and by.

Not to go back is the answer,
I realise now is quite true,
Store up the good things in our memory,
Those childhood joys that we knew.

Mary Rose Dury

CUPPED IN MY HANDS

Huge tail,
bashing the water
with gigantic butterfly shape,
agile, leaping form,
sudden splash
in greeny-grey seas;
explosion of white foam,
rising, descending.

I have witnessed this
and now I have it all,
cupped in my hands,
sculpted in crystal.

Blissfully, I hold
the whole waltzing wallop
of a whopping whale,
stampeding the arched sky
in this glass whose sole purpose
is to hold down a few poems
left in embryo on my desk.

But this is not merely
a collector's item,
exquisitely crafted,
not a mere paperweight,
choice gift of a thoughtful friend.
It is an appeal . . .
and I suddenly realise
that poetry would be diminished
in a world without whales.

M Munro Gibson

THINKING OF YOU

To touch a leaf
To see the spring
To feel the breeze
To hear birds sing
Wish you were here.

To tread the sand
To run and play
To feel the spray
Of the sea today
Wish you were here.

Such a perfect mite
You deserved the right
To live and see
This land with me
Wish you were here.

My heart is heavy
My tears, they flow
I love you dearly
And miss you so
Wish you were here.

God has a reason
If only I knew
One day He will tell me
And I'll embrace you
Wish you were here.

Pat Whitmarsh

WAVES OF NOSTALGIA

Trippers.
Trippers came.
Trippers disgorged themselves from off the train.
Onto the concourse and straight outside
Onto the streets and down to the beach,
Onto the sand and into the sun.
Throwing off clothes and inhibitions;
Throwing buckets and spades in all directions.
Throwing water without discretion.
Into the sea with wild abandon,
Into the air shriek Wayne and Karen.
Into the sky the gulls despair.
Dinnertime and food is served;
Dinner of sand sandwiches and potted meat;
Dinner of lemonade and stewed tea.
Back into the sea with sagging costumes.
Back to the castle with unfinished moat.
Back to pleasures of a forgotten childhood.
Time to pack up soon and leave the sea.
Time to dry bodies, shivering and sandy;
Time to pull on clothes over damp and sticky limbs.
Pack away all the paraphernalia of picnics;
Pack away the chairs, windbreaks and towels.
Pack away the pleasures to recall much later.
Make our way with sand-encrusted feet;
Make the journey back to station yard.
Make time for one last look back.
Tired children resting on parents' shoulders;
Tired parents bundling bags into corners.
Tired of the sea? Never!

Trevor Huntington

WILD DOG ROSE

Sprawling, drunk and over-dressed
as a blushing June bride;
frothing, uncontrollably as champagne,
over both sides of the ageing agrestic fence:
as an undecided voter, you
have a foot in each clique.

Losing your diminutive skin petals
to the parched will of the foxes' earth;
your allure dissolving as tea-stained sugar.
So unfulfilled and futile
your fate, as a butterfly,
transient and duped by God;
you question if a thing of beauty *is* a joy forever?

As you wither in the never-ending dyes of the sun,
burning holes in your fleeting nectar,
dusk estranges the ruse of your prime,
trampled, as confetti in a rainstorm.
Will you end these, your glorious hours,
with only down-trodden, utopian delusions as memories?
They bond to my bare feet as dew-moist tissue.

Your sharp, leafy limbs and frilly hems
are torn in rabbits' teeth; but still
nature pledges your virginal resurrection:
yet brides age with each anniversary.
But, rambling, wild dog rose, you are,
as I, only briefly beautiful;
like a gypsy deprived of fragrance,
you snaffle the scent of heather.

S Lester

STANDING TALL

Stopping and thinking,
Whilst sunlight shoots in and out
Of bright white clouds
I think to keep the moment,
Catch the dream.
Remembering the good times
And all they mean.
Life speeds by too
Quickly
To notice
The wonder of just a moment
A life, a story
All the glory
It has brought
And it brings
A heart
Sings,
Enjoying the very most
Of things.
Never too old
To be so bold
Awaiting a future
Yet, untold.
Catch the moment
Remember the dream,
Never to lose sight
Of it all

Standing so very, very
Tall.

Kim Stretton

MY WIFE

(Dedicated to the memory of my wife, Sylvia Moore, known as Sue)

Somebody so loving
Somebody so kind
Somebody so giving
Somebody always smiling
Somebody always thinking of others.

Yet that somebody, was not just
Somebody, you were my wife,
Yet not just somebody,
But a mother, a grandmother,
A great-grandmother.

You were all these things
And to me, everything all in one
And together, we were one.

Stanley Moore

PARTNERS

My mother was a partner to me,
The bond we had for all to see
That loving smile
That tender touch -
She did love me, so very much
My heart aches now she's gone
Memories left, to sit and dream,
Of times gone by -
Some happy, some sad,
Life, we live it to a plan
To solve it, I must if I can,
I look in the mirror, I see her face
And then there's an empty space
We didn't know each other very long
'It's with me,' he said, 'you belong'
One day we shall meet
The face in the mirror will stay
Then, I know, it is time to pray.

Kathleen Patricia Peebles

VISIT TO CHARLESTON

These out-of-focus rooms hold special light.
Pond-glimmer filtered through small panes
To gleam upon embellished surfaces.
A flint-framed garden lends its homely blooms
To blaze afresh in chintz or lavish strokes
Of unrestricted paint.
Those esoteric tenants filled each room
With their sharp brilliance.
The thin glitter of self-esteem spilling saffron light
Into nooks forsaken by the wandering brush.
Distance lends unreality to those originals
Who mingled here. Yet they knew pain,
Bore agonies of conscience, liberally loved
And trailed the banners of their joys and strifes
To every crooked angle of this house.
Here, they felt winter's chill, watched spring dance
Through the Downs in tender green.
Tossed summer's wanton gold about the rooms
For parties such as ours to marvel at.
We must have seemed intruders in their eyes;
Yet we revere their legacy, stepping softly
Among places where they raged or laughed or sulked.
Careful not to disturb the patina of self
They cast into unlit corners.
Leaving, to breathe again the garden scents,
We lift our hands away from hallowed chairs,
Drown a little in colour and nostalgia -
Walk by, without touching the old straw hat.

Joan Howes

INHERITANCE

My thoughts, as ever, lead me down
The road of yesteryear,
To the place that was my mother's home,
A spot which I hold dear.
I feel so much a part of it
And it a part of me,
The place that is Seahornan,
Seahornan by the sea.

Why does it fill my heart so full,
That humble piece of land?
It's knowing that my roots are there
Helps me to understand.
It is a call to pilgrimage
And it shall ever be,
The place known as Seahornan,
Seahornan by the sea.

Recalling from my earlier years,
Those carefree days at play,
Absorbing what was best in life,
The simple, easy way.
The people who resided there,
From generations past,
Had learned to value what was good,
That what was good, would last.

They shall forever have my thanks,
My heritage assured
And though they are no longer there,
Their teachings have endured.
So I, a product of the past,
Owe my integrity,
To the Graceys' of Seahornan,
Seahornan by the sea.

Michael McKenna

ALTERNATIVE METHODS OF TRANSPORT

We sit together, close, yet each enclosed
In a bubble of private space, each bubble stuck
In a syrup that hardly flows. Like a snapshot's posed
Inaction, or motionless flights of china duck,
Though meant for motion, we are held on pause.
Each driver, cooped in an insect's killing jar
Of noxious fumes, obeys the highway laws.
Ambition, Greed and Envy, put a bar
On exploration. Though the world is wide
They program us to follow narrow routes,
Till we accept retirement gifts with pride
And fold away strait-jacket business suits.

Above the traffic snarl, in limitless blue,
Some geese in flight, a chevron in the sky,
The lords of all dimensions, are keeping true
With artless grace the pattern in which they fly.
Unnumbered years ago our paths diverged:
The birds, to inherit the air, gave limbs for wings,
While thinking man devised the tools that merged
Himself with his surroundings, mastering things
With his enfolding brain. His thoughts pass on
In tablets, scrolls and books; the burden grows
Of knowledge, until at last all chance has gone
For bird or man to change the choice that rose
So long ago. Who would not wish to buy
With all books and libraries ever the chance to fly?

S R Hawk'sbee

WORDS OF LIFE

'Let us speak,' said Love and breathed the Word
And in the speaking Earth was created.
'Let us give,' said Love and the Word was flesh,
Dwelling among us, full of grace and truth.

We are the inheritors of language,
Speak of those journeyers of earlier days
Who bequeathed us their experiences;
Engraving in clay, chiselling on stone,
Transcribing parchment scrolls to tell their story.

We are the voice of Christ, the Word of Life,
Speak for the voiceless: the child abused,
The mother toiling in a sun-drenched field,
A prisoner tortured in an alien cell,
Language is ours to use, to wield.

Speak then, the words which Christ would have us speak,
Words of challenge, humour, strength and peace;
Words that will touch hard hearts and change the world;
Beautiful words, Christ-like words, words of life.

Dorothy Woo

THE ADVENTURES OF A BRAVE LITTLE BEAR

This little bear has had a fright
He came with Sam to stay the night
When Grandma said, 'It's time for bed'
And Sam laid down his sleepy head,
He burrowed down within the sheet
And spent the night at Sammy's feet.

So when next morning Sam arose
And quickly donned his outdoor clothes,
The little bear was quite forgot
As he lay hidden in the 'cot'.

So when it came to washing day,
The sheet in which he snugly lay
Was popped into the washing machine
As Grandma did a quick 'spring clean'.
And through the programme's total run,
The little bear was washed and spun.

Imagine Grandma's great surprise,
For she could hardly believe her eyes
When opening up the Hotpoint's door
He tumbled out upon the floor.
But bravely he thrust out his chest,
Resplendent in his Broomhaugh vest!

In spite of all he's none the worse
And I have penned this little verse
As record of his scary tale
As he goes home, via Royal Mail.

John Eldridge

CONVALESCENT

Feeling better, are you?
Is there money in the bank?
No longer in the red
Will you vacate your bed,
Move gardenwards
With level gaze
View low-lying flowers,
Though ill so long
Perceive birdsong,
Exchanging shade for sun
Make shift to run?

Josephine Thompson

Sports In London

Olympic Games in two thousand and twelve,
The third time that London medals shall shelve,
Nineteen eighteen and nineteen forty-eight,
Again Britain's hopeful athletes must wait.

Wimbledon tennis in June and July,
It's fun in summer with sun in the sky,
Avid fans go to see cricket at Lord's
And other sports that the city affords.

The Oxford and Cambridge Boat Race in March,
Is seen on the Thames beyond Marble Arch,
Football teams hold their matches and World Cup,
Wembley Stadium and clubs on the up.

Swimming, ice skating and games in the park,
There's plenty of sports to do for a lark.

Susan Mary Robertson

Angels

Familiar are the images of white-robed angel throngs,
With wings and shining haloes and sweet, celestial songs.
This is the general picture of what some think they ought to be,
But does it bear any resemblance to actuality?
I think angels can appear in much more homely guise,
Which, perhaps, is why they are so seldom recognised.
T-shirts, jeans and mini-skirts, or peculiar coloured hair,
May not seem correct attire for God's messengers to wear.
Yet I think I've spotted angels in just such common dress,
Quietly doing their little bit to help those in distress.
They're the ones who always listen, without judgemental frown,
To everybody's problems, when they've plenty of their own.
They always seem to be there, just when they're needed most
And give of themselves unstintingly and never count the cost.
Some work in factories or shops; some work in auto-sales,
Some even walk the streets at night, in four-inch stiletto heels.
They help so many people throughout their simple lives,
With their warmth and understanding and sound, if unorthodox
                                                            advice.
So forget about the golden harps, the wings and the haloes too
And look out for the angel who lives just down the road
                                            from you . . .

P Hunt

Love Flows So Eternity Grows

(Tribute to my wife Sylvia, who died August 2003. Love to everyone)

My love for you, my darling,
Will never, ever end.
For true love's eternal,
Never breaks, no need to mend.
Love reaches out from me to you,
No matter where you are.
Whether next to me in being,
Or paradise, where you are.
The planets will not stop it,
As I send, from Earth, to you.
Yes, sent with spirit's flight
And arrives instantly so true.
No distance, no matter what,
Can stop true love's full flow,
Because love is eternal,
You now shine with spirit's glow.
No hurt, nor pain, exist now,
Your place you have now found.
The eternal love flows freely,
To keep life safe and sound.

John Cowley

Brother Butterfly

Dull was the evening;
It possessed an uncanny, clammy atmosphere
                        for which I didn't much care.
My eyes spot a beautifully marked butterfly
                                    caught,
Caught hopelessly within its wake
Because it realised its mistake too late,
As there it hangs helplessly from a spider's web
                                not yet quite dead,
But hanging something like a withered
                                flower head.

Could that butterfly be
Nothing but a reflection of me
Struggling within its situation
Of what was just bad luck,
Fate and plain self infliction?

I now tremble within the temple of
                        my inner domain:
Can that butterfly distinguish the fright within
                                the pain
That's forcefully in my mind sustained
                        as I do his?
For we're both victims of this living quiz
                and the password is masochist.

But I do hope you escape, brother butterfly;
Because if you don't, I might break down and cry
And hopefully you'll distinguish just why;
                        bye, brother butterfly!

Dave White

The Lands Of Fantasy

To dwell in the lands of fantasy
Is to live in lands beyond compare
You must let your mind go wandering
Conjuring visions from out of the air.

I saw northern lights go flashing
Across a sky as dark as night
I felt just like a Valkyrie
Riding the stormy winds of life.

I went up to the mountaintops
Where I met a yeti in the snow
He was like the abominable snowman
From those days so long ago.

Then I ventured to the ocean's deep
Where the fish and mermaids dwell
I lay there in enchanted sleep
Soothed by the ocean's gentle swell.

I travelled to those faraway lands
Where the winds blow soft and free
With palm trees waving on the strand
What a wonderful place to be.

I saw dolphins swimming in the sea
Oh! What ecstasy they brought to me
Whales were spouting spume in the air
Creating a picture beyond compare.

I saw the sun rise each morning
I watched the sunset in the evening breeze
You can be anyone, anywhere in the world
When you're lost in the lands of fantasy.

Albert H Gormley

OVER BEACHY HEAD

The sun was warm
As we left our bed
And packed a flask
With some buttered bread
The view was fine
We were newly-wed
What a wonderful dawn
Over Beachy Head

When I reflect
On the things we said
When our past
Was still ahead
The life we planned
On those chalky beds
Covered with corn
Over Beachy Head

Now autumn's come
As green, brown and red
Meet the blue sea
White gulls overhead
Our plans came to little
Despite all that we said
But I love you still
Over Beachy Head.

Stuart Delvin

TERRORISM

Terrorism, scourge of the day
with those intent to have their way
or some grievance to display.
To demonstrate their discontent
on killing and destruction bent
slaughter of the innocent.
There is no excuse one can see
one cannot blame insanity
for this dreadful infamy.
Good people all must now unite
to do whatever they think right
to counteract this awful blight.
There must be close co-operation
on the part of every nation
sharing in this operation.
If we look into the mind
of a killer of this kind
what reaction would we find
to the deaths and devastation
resulting from the vile creation
would it be of wild elation?
Before his life has run its course
will he not feel some remorse
or still such evil acts endorse?

Robert Hogg

WITH YOU

Why do I always feel so lonely?
Why do I feel so down?
Why do I feel like a piece of meat
When you are not around?
I need to build some self-esteem
Cos people are so mean
That doesn't mean anything
If I'm to be something.

Oliver Povey

SOLVA

I'd like to be at Solva
when the tide is coming in,
to see the river, as it tumbles,
meet and mingle with the sea.

They tell me it's a ria;
it was formed in ages past:
the ocean rose and drowned a valley,
took the river to the deep.

It made the aspect different -
an especially charming scene;
trees come curling down the hillsides
almost to the water's edge.

From high upon the cliff top
I had seen great billows roll
and wondered how it was at Solva
when the sea went surging in.

September sun was shining
as I walked down to the quay;
only shallow waters rippled,
boats were resting on the sand.

The river flow continued
but the sea was distant still:
some time must pass before the tide
would bring the different waters in.

So, still I'd like to be there
by that harbour once again,
to see the ocean come to Solva -
the river merging with the waves.

E F Scott

UNTITLED

The flowers in the morning,
As we sit in sombre mourning,
The funeral has stricken,
Sorrow deep within our hearts.

The trees, they grow relentless,
In majestic fruitfulness,
I am restless
In fields of loving madness.

The booming countryside
With God on our side,
She lied, she lied
In pulls the tide.

The only place in the world,
The spear of Satin fresh unfurled,
I think she said her hair was curled
Into society, I'm whirled.

Is there life beyond poetry?
Poetry will win the war
It grows in tandem with reality
Fergus Hilton has seen poetry.

In fields of loving madness
Through every trail of badness
Rolling up a Rizla, the shades of loving gladness,
Rapt in piercing sadness.

Fergus Hilton

ON HEAT

Porpoises propel arches in the air
With the power of Poseidon inside.
Warmed by the air in their grace of movement.
Summer has evaporated and will condense into autumn.

Humid beings are subdued,
Enriched with new depths of understanding.
And frustrated.
By the need to be predictable.
Despite the desire to be free.
So other people can benefit from their reliability.
Or dazed
And apologetic for that.

The charge of potential difference
Between the individual and tribe
Creates power
The resistance of the rules stifles the current.
Perhaps a fuse blows.

Internal combustion.
Movement is halted
Disembodied.
Disengaged.
Deeply disturbed.

The wound is still gaping
The wounded are still scared
As well as scarred.
Scared of conducting the heat.

Katrina Plumb

TWINS

Double laughter, double joys,
Double helping of little boys,
Two apples from the same tree,
Just how different will they be?

There will be tears and lots of pleasure
Memories for you to treasure,
Holding them near, stifling their fear,
Always being there to wipe away a tear.

Enjoy their babyhood as long as it may last
Because you will find they grow up very fast.
Give thanks for this blessing to the One above
Make the most of your double helping of love.

How hectic life is going to be,
Just be thankful it's two and not three!

Gwladys Mills

THE GIRL

The girl wondered and looked at herself in the mirror.
I think I'm beautiful, she thought,
who will it be, I wonder, for me to meet and marry?
Then she put a sheet around herself,
danced and was happy.
Then she thought of her mother's bra and her high-heeled shoes,
a sound she liked to hear when the shoes made a special
                                        grown-up noise.
In a moment of time that was never lost, she lived in that
special moment of precious sensation,
something was happening, was she grown-up at last?
Oh dear! Life was so hard when you were in-between.
She had heard such a lot about the gossip of nature.
Her mother had told her, 'You will have to use protection.'
To be protected from what? She had no idea!
Until the day came she discovered and then she knew.
As in that moment in time she knew, what it was really like
to be a woman.

Dorothy Jane Lewis

MILLENNIUM HYMN

Father of new life and vigour,
Looking back two thousand years,
How we've failed You, how we've struggled
'Midst our hopes and 'midst our fears.
Look upon us, breathe upon us,
Strengthen us for future years.

Wars and famine, greed and suff'ring,
Men and women fail to see.
Oft' neglecting Your creation,
Void of You, where would we be?
Look upon us, breathe upon us,
Pardon us and set us free.

Help us focus on the future;
Fresh new start we need to make.
Work together with our brethren,
Help mankind for Your dear sake.
Look upon us, breathe upon us,
May we give more oft' than take.

Let our New Year resolution
Be to demonstrate to all,
Love and care, consideration,
At all times, whate'er befall.
Look upon us, breathe upon us,
All denominations call.

May we all stride out together,
Make Your world a better place.
Do Your will and spread Your message,
All as one, the human race.
Look upon us, breathe upon us,
Prosper us in love and grace.

Frank Dean

CANDLE RAFTS

Sitting in the dark of a lonely hotel room,
I hear, above the noise of traffic, migratory voices
Carried in the clutches of the evening breeze
And in the distance the lonely sigh of boats
Travelling a ribbon of river to places unknown.
Seeping through these sleeping sounds
Comes the corncrake cry of night barges.
Past dreams sleep easy for we were of the water,
In our childhood we dropped sticks to the stream,
Ran together to the other side of the bridge
To watch them appear in their race for freedom,
Through the swirling currents of times long past.
I feel forlorn in this alien place.
Yet my solitude is an inward creation of sanctuary,
Far removed from the heady days of lustful youth;
I remember when, we shared the warm wine of love;
Balmy evenings lost in each other beside our river
And we floated candle rafts on the smooth waters,
Watching, until their flickering lights disappeared
To a place of peace known only to them,
Later, when the world sleeps I will go the river,
Light a candle and gently place a raft,
Then, as we did together, I will float it
With a prayer so that you will
Know love even in solitude.

Sitting in the dark of a lonely hotel room,
I hear, above the noise of traffic, migratory voices
Carried in the clutches of the evening breeze;
Yours is still the silence.

Keith Garrett

PENDINE - WALES

Golden sands stretch many a mile
Warm and calm the sea
Just sit here for a while
What a wonderful place to be.

Mountains towering high
So fresh and green
Not a cloud in the sky
What a fantastic scene.

So much history in Wales to be found
Dylan Thomas lived there too
Castles scattered all around
Discoveries, old and new.

Across to Caldey Island
So peaceful everywhere
With the monastery so grand
Visit the lighthouse there.

Yes, there is a welcome in the hillside
A welcome everywhere
The beauty in the countryside
That we can surely share.

Cicely Heathers

THE HONEYMOONERS

Sounds from above told me they were up.
Love's young dream with the 'Just Married'
sign still gleaming in their eyes.

I carried the tray outside for breakfast
on the patio - they'd like that, I thought.
Hot toast and croissants, home-made
marmalade and heather honey.

Across the loch shimmering sunbursts sparkled
on the surface. A patient heron played stock-still
statues at the water's edge while Ben Lomond's
peak greeted the morning through a grey,
pink misty veil. The makings of a perfect day.

Voices, raised in anger, shattered the morning quiet.
Still as the waiting heron, I stood and listened
to the slamming of a door, to firm footsteps pounding
the wooden stair. Another door banged with shattering
violence, then silence.

Looking out across the loch, I saw the heron
fly up, up and away. The sunbursts fizzled out.
I cleared the untouched things from the table
and went inside.

Agnes Ford

MY DREAM

I dreamt death came the other night
And Heaven's gate swung wide,
An angel with a halo bright,
Ushered me inside.

And there, to my astonishment,
Were folks I had judged and labelled,
As quite unfit, of little worth
And spiritually disabled.

Indignant words rose to my lips,
But never were set free,
For every face showed stunned surprise -
No one expected me.

Gordon West

WINTER

Deep, deep snow upon the ground
A beautiful carpet of brilliant white
Many footprints can be found
It really is a wonderful sight.

Children tobogganing down the slopes
Hear them laugh as they have fun
Buttoning-up their well-worn coats
And snowball fights are so much fun.

The countryside looks pretty today
Although the trees look stark and bare
Their leaves have changed colour and blew away
But the spruce and fir leaves are still there.

They'll soon be gathered for Christmas Day
Baubles adorn each chosen tree
Presents galore, underneath will lay
Plenty enough for you and me.

Y Corcoran

FEMME FATALE

Black lace it falls around my feet,
As we tumble upon the satin sheet,
Oblivious to all surround,
Daring not to make a sound!

Love is such a fragile thing,
Yet to each other, exquisite ecstasy we bring.
I touch your hand, so firm and strong,
I'm in the place where I belong.

For in your arms, I am secure.
Where I want to be for evermore.
Taking all the doubt away,
This is where I would always want to stay.

Strong and gentle, your love flows,
Into one tidal wave, alongside mine, it goes.
Where are we, that once were two?
We are now as one, in a love so new.

Taking each breath in passion sure,
Knowing we can't ask for more.
My soul, with yours, is entwining.
As deep as a river and so beguiling.

Black lace falls around my feet,
How could we yet, hope to repeat?
Where passion is our all, in all.
Love wraps me tight, in her gentle shawl.

Sylvia Clark

FLOWERS UPON THE WATER

Flowers upon the water
Slowly, softly drift away
Leaving memories of you
That remain throughout the day

Every floating petal
Represents a small event
That we have shared together
Before your life was spent

But these memories of you
Bring back that fateful day
When you left this world behind
And where I am forced to stay

Flowers upon the water
Softly, slowly gliding past
Give a moment's solace
Which only briefly lasts.

Felicite Gill

SILENCE

(On becoming deaf)

Is it my fault that I live in silence
Only to speak with my hands?
People are cruel, they think I'm a fool,
Because they don't understand.

Is it my fault that I cannot hear?
That I'm deaf to the sounds of the world?
The sweet song of the birds, the wind in the tree,
Music and laughter are not meant for me.

I sign stories, but nobody watches,
I sign jokes, but nobody laughs.
I sign, 'Hello, what a beautiful day,'
But people just stare and then turn away.

Is it my fault that I feel so lonely,
Cut off from the rest of the crowd,
Condemned to a life full of silence,
To live in this world without sound?

Marion Meikle Mason

UTOPIA

Let's push this Earth into a better space,
A place where trees grow lichen on their face.
And streams give life to fish in waters clear
Not fill their gills with dark, polluted fear.
Where Mother Earth gives breast to feed our thirst,
From crystal springs - not chlorinated first!
There we may breathe the essence of Eternity
See all around us the proof of God's paternity.
A land where fumes and gases of industrial men
Could be turned off for an hour, now and then.
In such a spot we'd walk in dignity and pride
With open minds where evil cannot hide.
Children loved by all would fear no danger
And flood and famine be an unknown stranger.
And those born handicapped in limb and brain
Would be allowed to die and live again.
Not forced to face the ridicule and scorn
And wonder why they were not left unborn.
This paradise all bands of hate would sever
And all God's creatures sing with joy together.

Dorothy Beaumont

TROUBLED TIMES

Dark days those, to run a business
Held to ransom by a hostile fate -
Hard enough to earn a living, without
Added terror on your plate.

So it was, for my dear parents,
Who came to Derry in 'seventy-two -
They opened a shop and sold newspapers,
Surrounded by violence - bang on cue!

My poor father, what he suffered,
In those bleak years, no one knows -
His car hijacked, held at gunpoint,
Surely hastened his death throes . . .

Standing in the rubble of their ruined shop,
Blown up to suit an alien creed -
If they could have seen into the future,
Would they have come to Derry, indeed?

Now the Trouble's ended, everyone's thankful,
But painful memories linger on; though Derry has
Risen, like a phoenix from the ashes -
Our shop and my father, have regretfully . . . gone.

Sonya Hynes

MORECOMBE BAY - THE LEVEN VIADUCT

Like a vast, caressing wing light sweeps across the steppes of sand,
driving shadows, fleeing clouds, in airy dance, intangible and free.
Lavender, lovat and shifting grey, the mountain amphitheatre
frames the river Leven, dawdling down in lazy arcs to meet the sea.
And there upon the channel's edge sleek cormorants stand
with wings hung out to dry like widow's weeds upon a washing line,
or ebon eagles of heraldic bent. Waders wade, as waders will.
A scurry of sanderlings scuttle on the strand as, helter-skelter,
skitter-flitter, flurrying knots go scudding whither-where.

Smart-liveried in black and white
a flight of oyster catchers flickers by.
They skim the widening rings where dives a grebe
and flock with babel on a sandy bar.
Great handsome shelducks waddle in the mire
in stately splendour that defies their gawky tread;
while swans waft in on mournful-whispering wings,
whose sighing song joins curlews' wild lament.
Patient as posts of graven stone
the herons stand on silent watch:
the sombre sentinels whose canny gaze
awaits the clue that seals some creature's fate.

The wide expanse of light and land is nature's own:
until I turn my head.
There, Glaxochem, enthroned upon the estuary,
awaits its drain's return upon the tide.

Freda Bunce

HAPPINESS

Happiness is described in many ways
For some, all that they can get
All they can take
All they can make
Possessions and greed
Much more than they need
True happiness is being content
Whether a lady or a gent.

Eileen Hannah

TO MY ADOPTED MOTHER, ON MOTHER'S DAY

I love you for your strength,
Your serenity and peace
Which gives me strength;
Your spirit, independent
And unhampered by what
Others think about you;
Your capacity for making
Friends and keeping them;
Your mind, so quick to grasp
And analyse, untrammeled
By too great a weight
Of narrow expertise
Roaming at ease across
So many disciplines.
Your urge to teach and to
Pass this knowledge on.
The two who bore and cast
Me off, will never know
How great that act, which
Left me free to call you
Mother.

Pauletta J Edwards

NAMES - FOR CHILDREN

Your name is Rose, and roses are
The loveliest any flower can be.
Then here is Stella; she's a star:
Stars shining in her eyes, I see.
Miranda, you're an isle away
Lost in blue of summer day.
There's Margaret, a rainbowed pearl,
Most precious jewel from the sea:
Sun glimmers softly on a curl.
Lucy brings a lantern bright
And Celia music's golden-light;
Irene, peace; so, lovingly,
She'll come with kisses up to me.

Mary is a special name
Remembering how her baby came
In the silence of the night.

And then the boys. Small boys I know
I'll not forget, I love you so;
And yours are sturdy, good, strong names,
Like Robert, Henry, John and James.
Many there are, but each one given
With love is writ, in gold, in Heaven.

Diana Momber

DREAM SELLER

Can you sell me a dream? Can I choose the theme?
Will I go for bargain basement or double clotted cream?
Will it be in glorious technicolour
Or simply monochrome?
Will I be in exotic climes
Or living here, at home?

Will it be worth the money?
Will I be impressed?
Will I be buck skin naked
Or simply overdressed?

Can I obtain a refund if the *goods* are not up to scratch?
Can I complain profusely, if there turns out to be a catch?
And what of *special offers?*
Will you do a *deal?*
I may demand my money back
If it's too surreal?

Maybe I will shop around
Dream rummage for a while
I'm partial to *hot and sexy* but
like the *alien style.*

On second thoughts
My preference is to set up a stall for *free*
Give dreams away
Every day
Perfect dream therapy!

Gail Cureton

ALL I ASK

There's a secret language, that behind our eyes portray,
Searching through the crowds of life, till on true love they lay,
Just as if the book of life is presented on a tray,
Fear strikes in our hearts, if we get lost along the way,
Our thoughts are locked together, no other path to stray,
The moment that it happens, we're lost for words to say,
Crashing waves, drifting clouds, magic moments in the hay,
Just walk towards me, all I ask, on that special day.

J Bowes

NEW ADVENTURE

Along the beach we stroll,
With our fingers loosely entwined,
Walking beside each other,
Leaving our pasts behind.

Let us start afresh
And watch the morning sun,
Rising on the horizon,
Our future yet to be spun.

As we sit on the veranda,
Of our beach chalet,
Let's relax and unwind,
Hearing music softly play.

Handle me gently but firmly,
Be a little rough, but also kind,
Let us become one in the moonlight
And awaken to once again find.

Our bodies sealed together,
By a film of perspiration,
Where love had been made passionately
And in such sweet desperation.

Let our story never end
And may our hearts and minds stay -
Young in our maturing bodies,
Never too old to play!

Dawn Madigan

RED BREAST

Little robin at my window
Have you nowhere to hide?

It's snowing very heavy
Would you like to come inside?

You can sit inside my window
Or have warmth by the fire

I could feed you with some bacon rind
You can eat to your desire

Your red breast is so beautiful
It burns against the snow

Could it be the story's true
From wenst came that fiery glow?

They say you sat beneath the cross
The day that man was blessed

A drop of blood from crown of thorns
It fell against your breast

The story had a happy end
As Christ's spirit rose to Heaven

He left us with His memory
To you a red breast was given.

Nicky Anderson

SHEEP ON MY DOORSTEP

Once I lived in a time of peace
when sheep slept without a care
on my night-time doorstep
huddled there.

Hurrying away startled to see
an opening door,
in the early morning place
where no one came and no one saw.

Rachel Treadwell

PRICELESS GIFTS

There are so many things in the world I can see
That are priceless and yet so precious to me

The scent of newly mown hay in the sun
Or the smell in the kitchen of a freshly baked bun
The sight of a rainbow after spring rain
Or a horse in a field tossing its mane

The laughter of children at play in the park
Or moonlight on water when it is dark
The perfume of roses on a warm summer day
Or the sight of snowdrops on a dark winter day

A hug from a grandson when he holds me tight
Poppies by the roadside - oh, what a sight!
A special look from someone I love
Or the gentle cooing of a ring-collared dove

The sound of an orchestra in full flight
Or the voice of a tenor when he sings just right
The feeling of dancing when I'm up on my toes
Or the first snowflake as it brushes my nose

The sight of a butterfly as it comes to rest
Or the knock on the door saying I have a guest
A friend to understand when I feel down
Or a daughter to take shopping into the town

A garden to sit in and shade from the trees
Surrounded by flowers and buzzing of bees
The sound of ice as it clinks in a glass
A picnic blanket spread out on the grass

The warm lovely glow from an open fire
Cosily chatting before we retire
A hand to hold mine and know someone cares
As my youth disappears and old age nears.

Doreen Hedison

THE BARGAIN PACK

Down to the market Eileen went
with a five pound note on shopping bent.
Outside the butcher's they stood six deep
enough to make the toughest weep.
But she undaunted fought her way
for to land a bargain would make her day.
Up to the counter she was rushed
by crowds behind who shoved and pushed.
'Who wants this pack?' the butcher yelled,
'It's from a beast that I've just felled.
I'll add some sausages and some chops
now for spare ribs and a lump of crop.'

Her money waving in the air
Eileen grabbed the meat, what scrumptious fare!
Eyes dilated and scarcely breathing
she tried to get out while the crowd was seething.

Way back home and the oven red hot
in went the meat in Eileen's big pot.

Later the telephone rang and rang
she answered it without a pang.
She talked and talked, on and on
until she feared her voice had gone.
Sniff! Sniff! Ugh! What was that smell?
Could it be the *bargain pack?* Oh, hell!
How could one come home so elated,
then find the meat had been cremated?

Eileen M Wray

IN THE EYE OF THE BEHOLDER

When I look in the mirror -
is it really me I see?
The person that I feel inside
could not my reflection be.
When did all those lines appear?
They're real to see and touch
perhaps they're only laughter lines -
but no one laughs that much!

I always did have deep-set eyes
which were nice in my former years
if they sink much further in my head
they'll look out of my ears.

What happened to that turned-up nose,
the boys once said was cute
it now looks like a radish
with a really plumptious root.

Those rose-red lips that used to pout
to try and gain attention
they now are blue and wrinkled too
and my teeth we just won't mention.

Oh, 'Tempus Fugit' all too soon
and though I am not vain
I wish that I could rub it out
and start yet once again?

Sheila H Birkett

THEY SAY THAT TIME . . .

I can't recall how often I have heard
The well-intentioned say how time will heal
The sense of loss, the bitterness I feel;
Yet in confusion my emotions stirred
With ev'ry sympathetic well-meant word
And though with time I'm able to conceal
My wretchedness, to me it's no less real,
The barbs that pierce my soul still undeterred.

For still a word, a sound, a look will bring
Fresh hurts to wound my sensibilities;
But in that sadness re-awakening
Of all those precious, painful memories;
But will I lose those thoughts to which I cling
When time heals my accursed agonies.

Hilary J Cairns

TO MY GUARDIAN SPIRIT
(For my mother)

I am remembering all of the others who have
gone into the light.

Thank you for guiding me back from the
light. The right way, I think. I wish you
could do a miracle.

Thank you for the world.

Look after my father, John Robert - he is all
I have left.

My mam, her sister and her mother have all
fallen with cancer and gone to join you.

They are the sunlight now.

Barry Welburn

ANCHORED

I stand on tiptoe
Arms outstretched
Breathing in the precious air
Letting out the harsh, untrue.

Head erect
I feel the tension
Of a soul held from above.
My feet I see
Like roots of trees
Embedded deep in Mother Earth,
As in my mind
I move among
The daffodils, the trees
And know that we are one.

My left arm now to all mankind can reach
To offer peace and love.
My right arm stretches to perceive
The universal home I have
And breathing in, I fill the space that I myself am given;
Not isolated nor buffeted about,
But fixed and very firmly held
Within the unfragmented whole.

Then folding down again,
Receptive and relaxed,
I seek my own illumination
In the universal 'secret place'.

Edna Holford

BEGINNING TO END

There was a time not long ago
When man with flocks was free to roam.
No fences, wires barred his way
Feudal laws, nor judges say.

Fresh and clean was the air
Clear the rivers flowing there.
No pesticides, chemicals or GM crops
Ruined the land or polluted the hops.

On grasses green the cattle fed
Farms stored hay for their bed.
Now they lie in barns so dry
Never to see the wondrous sky.

Virus, germs brought on disease
Spread through the land with utmost ease.
Greed, the impetus for selfish need
Brought Man down to his knees.

His God above looked down on him
Saw the trouble he was in.
Kept alive though he had sinned
His crown of glory yet to win.

F B Rylance

THEY DON'T KNOW

That one day - maybe soon -
The world will end.
They don't know He will return
As promised. They don't know
That He's the One they need.
They don't know He loves them so -
They need to know that it is so.
They do not understand that on the Cross
He took our punishment -
This the universe-sized 'news'
Which they need to know.

V Prance

ME TEETH

When I go to the dentist it's sure,
She gets drillin' and fillin' me jaw.
As I lie in the chair
With me legs in the air,
Me heart starts to beat something sore.

With me mouth open wide she can see,
All the molars that's troubling me,
Then with expert decision,
She starts with precision,
To ensure that it's all pain free.

But sometimes I almost could blab,
When she's givin' the horrible jab,
(It feels most fearfully deep)
As I lie there grippin' me chair
With me legs all up in the air.

When the drillin' and fillin' is done
And the battle of molars is won,
(At least till the very next time)
I thank God for such wonderful skill,
Mrs Markham, the nurse and the drill.

Jeannette Collett

CHARITY

Through a continual fog of hunger he walks
Desperation sought from the dregs of others' lives
Living between spit and leftovers found amongst a last resort
Fulfilling an appetite for survival inside the garbage of today
Seeking only sustenance to make it through tomorrow
Caring not that silent ridicule follows each attempt
Doing whatever it takes just to live this sickening life

Surrounded by opulence that has become necessity
Unfulfilled lives darting from one extravagance to another
Deliberately oblivious to the needs of the needy
Passing by with embarrassment that they cannot hide
Believing only in self-importance whilst ignoring this desperation
Rarely willing to assist, preferring to run in the opposite direction
Hoping to hide behind an excuse made up to suit the occasion

Dressed in the clothes of many strangers
Handouts from charity and not gifts from caring onlookers
Going about his business in a methodical manner
Experience showing as an ability to find discarded food
                                    becomes evident
Approached suddenly and taken off guard, he flinches
Looking in wonderment as green backs are thrust into an open hand
Speechless in his attempt to be thankful, he moves on, but not
                                    to safety or comfort.

Alan Zoltie

THE NEW ARRIVAL

What a beautiful morning to you my angel from above
You were made inside of me
And arrived in a bundle of love
Don't be alarmed, my fragile little one
My heart is here, holding you close
Feel it hasn't gone
Wrapped up tight with mostly warmth to convey.

How your mummy feels about you
On this very special day
Now open your eyes they are as blue as the sky
And let your new life begin
Cos of you, so shall I!

Joanne Elliott

WHEN

When morning comes
I'll tell the birds to sing as loud as they can
Within the trees for you to please
And on the lawn, come the dawn

When night comes
I'll tell the stars to sparkle very bright
To light the dew and smile on you
With crescent moon, night comes soon

When spring comes
I'll tell the flowers to give a show for you
The year will start with rising heart
May blossom bring you joy in spring

When summer comes
I'll tell the sun to shine full down on you
With cooling breeze between the leaves
Good weather fine, in summertime

When autumn comes
I'll tell the trees to put on their best display
And fruit will swell to nourish well
When autumn changes come

When winter comes
I'll tell the snow to gather round your door
The firewood will do you good
When winter settles in

When death comes
I'll tell the angels all these things for you
You may not see it came from me
I'll still be here when death comes.

Terry Grimson

MISTRUST

Seeds of doubt are sown
Nurtured and fed
By suspicion and hate
Wild, accusing eyes
Follow every move
Non-existent visions
Seen through a jade-green mist

Trust dies
A slow, lingering death
As weeds of deception
Are unmistakably seen
Entwining, overpowering
Choking and finally destroying
Its final few shuddering gasps
Like knotted lead
Deep in the pit of your stomach
Its death
Brings no release
From pain and suffering

The stench of misery
Putrid and sickening
A bittersweet pill
So hard to swallow
The anguish of a tragic loss
A life destroyed
A fragile heart shattered
Like glass

Will you drown in a sea
Of warm, salty tears
Going under for the last time
Beneath the briny surface
Never to return?

Marisa Greenaway

UNTITLED

The sun is shining brightly
And birds are singing too
Children are going to school
They have lots of things to do.
The people are going to work
To all different kinds of jobs
They travel in buses and trains and cars
And some ride mopeds too.
The women begin their housework
They have so much to do.
Cleaning, washing, ironing
And some dusting too.
Then it's time for a break
Then she hears the door go
The children are home from school
Now the day is almost over
It's getting dark outside.
Inside, it's warm and cosy
The fire's burning bright.
And now the evening is over
So it's time for me to say goodnight.

B R Boyt

MY LITTLE FRIEND

We went to London to see the changing of the guards at
Buckingham Palace,
While we were waiting a bird appeared from nowhere,
I think he wanted to share my sandwich,
So I threw him some and he caught it before it hit the ground.

He got an applause from the family behind us,
I threw him some more but this time higher,
He swooped up with precision and caught it before it had a
chance to fall.

The crowd went wild and all eyes were on him,
The smallest bird I've ever seen.
I became absorbed and everyone fell in love with him,
Even me.

After he had gone, we watched the changing of the guards,
As I wondered how such a small thing could lift my spirits as
high as the sandwich,
I suppose I'll never know.

Sarah Ann Rees

THE SEASONS

Winter's left and so's the snow,
Now spring's arrived with golden glow.
The squirrels scamper in the trees,
While birds just sing their melodies.
The sun is warm, the sky is blue,
The year begins with hopes anew.

The summer's heatwave, hard to bear,
The earth all scorched, there's no fresh air.
And then the rain comes tumbling down,
It quenches all the plants and ground.
We like to wander through the trees,
And feel the early evening breeze.

Soon autumn will come to call
She hasn't got a care at all.
Her trees now change from green to gold,
Then change to brown before they're old.
The chestnuts hanging on the tree
Children collect quite merrily.

Now winter's back, what can I say?
Another year has flown away.

Hazel McNeil

EARTH, THE WARRING PLANET

If I could peel back the curtain that shades death
If only I could look beyond the grave,
Or for one brief moment glimpse that life hereafter
Or believe the sermons in the church the old priest gave.

Can I deceive myself by pretending man is good by nature,
Cast the Hiroshima horror from my mind,
Or the napalm burning of Vietnam's little children,
By claiming when it happened I was blind.

And be so naïve to profess that God is all forgiving.
When Christian nation's defile His worldly trust,
With vile images implanted in my memory
Of Hitler's Nazi monster holocaust.

O'er three score years and ten, I've seen many wars untold
The maiming and the killing, the misery untold
A mother's wail of anguish, generations torn apart
And mankind's bitter legacy, when will the next one start?

Never delude yourself that there's any glory in warfare
For the heroes, the fallen or you,
There's only resignation and heartache
For the vanquished and victors too.

Bryce Forbes

ECHOES FROM CHILDHOOD

Stilettos echoing down the street,
Stabbing out a harsh infrastructural beat,
The untrained heart was happy to meet
This perception, a privately held treat.

Then immediacy and ignorance sang joy,
The ear of a child is a blessed toy,
Knowing inner sense as a musical buoy,
In everything, this rhythm resounded coy.

An experience not grasped, purely enjoyed
Imprinted its significance upon memory-brained,
The listener discovered, uncovered, unrefrained
Until from the pavement all sound was drained.

Momentarily was heard, uniquely bared
Music which the heart's own lively beat shared.
The child unmoving silently stared,
Magically alone with its own truth heard.

Barbara Murray

AQUATIC ADVENTURE

Autumn sunlight on crashing waves,
A magical adventure barefoot Harriet craves,
A beckoning seabird the way paves
To mermaids' chariots standing in caves.

Down, down through sapphire sea she goes,
Seaweed like mermaids' hair touching her toes,
Dancing seahorses bow and say, 'Hello,'
Guiding a chariot to wondrous world below.

A miraculous castle through the blue appears,
Pisces escort bubbles its cheers,
Aquatic orchestra heralds the barefoot girl,
Olia the oyster presents a beauteous pearl.

Mermaid queen with bejewelled tail,
Sisters wash luxuriant locks in golden pail,
Marvel at the tiny girl with pink feet,
With reverence, their ten-toed princess treat.

Jo Gander

THE CROWD

The crowd gathered when Jesus came,
Blind and deaf, demon-possessed and lame;
Such compassion He had when He saw their need,
He touched them - straightway they were healed,
A while they stayed in the comfort of His attention
Enjoying each moment of their newfound liberation:
Evening came - and time to go the disciples said,
But tenderly Jesus commanded them to be fed,
A wonderful miracle was performed that day
Then, satisfied, He sent them on their way.

The crowd they gathered to shout and sing,
To pay their homage to Jesus the King:
Their palms they scattered along the road
As the donkey proudly carried His load,
'Hosanna! Hosanna!' aloud they cry
For Jesus of Nazareth is passing by;
The crowd were glad as they watched Him go,
Complete in the knowledge that He loved them so,
Such wonderful things they had seen Him do
All praise and glory were to Him due.

The crowd they gathered to see Him brought
To Pilate from the Sanhedrin court,
'This man is innocent,' is what Pilate said -
The verdict then must be yours instead,
And He, who had been so good and kind
For a moment now, was out of their mind,
And all that was heard was, 'Crucify,'
Jesus, the King, was condemned to die:
O, come to the cross, and see Him there
Because for you, He had a very special care.

Beryl Sigournay

WILTSHIRE REVERIE

Beyond the garden gate the meadow shimmers
in the summer haze
and cattle graze or look for shade.
We flew a kite there, you and I and nettles stung you
when you went to free the string.
The shallows rippled where we watched the minnows
dart among the pebbles and we floated paper boats
in dappled light below the willow trees.
There was a secret place, a haunt of owls,
where vixens screamed beneath a shark-white moon
and badgers hid their sett.

We watched a skylark in the blue,
oblivious of the thudding boot, the ranting voice
consigning millions to their deaths -
no inkling then of what we might be called to do.

Your bomber never did come back
so you won't know
they mean to build a superstore;
the planners say we need a business complex too.

Here in the garden tortoiseshells still come
and bees seek out the buddleia.
But time is short, the house is up for sale;
I feel I may be gone
before the swallows go.

Brian Beard

AS HE LAID ME DOWN

As he laid me down,
Down in the meadow grass,
The animal smell of the earth
Covered our bodies.

His arms held me,
Held me like the branches
Of a young tree.
A young tree full of nests
And singing birds.
His skin, feather soft
And smelling of wild honey
And apricots,
As he laid me down,
Down in the meadow grass.

Josephine Thomas

HELP US

Help us be encouraged,
Through the tireless things we do,
Help us keep an eye upon our goals.
Don't let us be discouraged,
When our dreams do not come true,
Come and help to lift us when we fall.

Help us come together,
And unite us all as one,
Help us put our problems far away.
For when in stormy weather,
And we wish to turn and run,
Come and help to brighten up the day.

Help us to be more caring,
For the people that we meet,
As we travel through life every day.
For the joy we could be sharing,
Could make the world complete,
Oh help us Lord, to find a better way.

Paul Secrett

NEW WAR, OLD WAR

It's a new kind of war they tell me,
From the box in the corner, TV
It may be short, it could be long;
We have to fight it to right the wrong of terrorism.
There won't be a marked-out battlefield,
The enemy will be hard to find
For he won't be wearing a uniform to identify his kind of terrorism.

This is a new kind of war they tell me
From that box in the corner, TV
But the same old bombs are descending
Though a new race of children cry
And bodies still sprawl a-bleeding
Under the same old sky
In a war that seems never-ending
For the soul of humanity.

So Jehovah or Jesus or Allah
Whatever the name might be
Krishna or Buddha, wherever you are
Look down with pity and heal the scars
Left by the age-old endless wars
Waged by humanity.

Meg Gilholm

'TIS FAMILY LOVE

On and on goes a life story, it's mine
Those footsteps of parents forever shine
Don't know the end, but do the way
What did I give? They gave all they had
I talk of my mother; I talk of my dad
Cash now too late, times were hard
A way to live, we saw it come true
When that time came, no thinking to do
Today's clever folk will never learn the way
No need, with such an increase in pay
Long hours, low pay, live day by day
Cut hair, grew food, made clothes, mend shoes
Two-skilled folks, ploughed on, would not lose
Know-how, a spade, needle and thread,
Never stopped, from the day they were wed
All eight of us, wed, and took some of that skill
Can we forget? I never will
My dad did ten hours, then two hours as well
Loading coal in big wagons
Sent cart with old coal, for five bob a job
Second hand coal fed an iron stove
Did all the cooking, and kept a hot hob
Ten fags for ten pence, to last the day
Two pints of beer, just on Sunday
Fetched it I had to, reluctant to go
I would like to go now, I did not know
Twelve and six, was the rent
To house ten folk
A three pound five wage was soon spent
The race must go on, nature has it in hand

Springtime comes, all just feel grand
All that lives is programmed to breed
The race must go on, and sow the seed
Blackbirds and such, dumb from last spring
Sit now on my roof, melodies to break her heart
Well hidden nests are silent,
Brains shed built-in tunes 'til next spring
Trees all new, ants to new pastures flew
Springtime man is happy to exchange to smile

The race is on; it's built on a love of the moment
The love that comes with understanding, though
It has life worth the living, and so
Take heed, many a flower is born to blush unseen
Said a wise man
Listen and look for a love of living and giving.

Harold Cotterill

CHRISTMAS BELLS

The Christmas bells ring loud and clear
The world is full of Christmas cheer
Bring peace, goodwill, for men for years
The tender love, the Christ Child appears.

This child to Bethlehem did come
A lowly manger - the God of love
A lowly welcome into a world
Of good and bad and peace and love.

The star above the stable glowed
To guide God's love from Heaven above
To men on earth so weak and frail
Some lost in sin no time for the Babe.

Ring Christmas bells, ring loud and clear
In Him we trust, now have no fear
In Heaven above, now on the throne
Ring Christmas bells, ring Christmas bells.

Elizabeth Jones

MORE THAN ENOUGH

One day in mid November
We escaped the usual routine
Of work, dishes and dust
All things on the list of everyday must . . .
We walked a little . . .
Talked a lot . . .
Laughing in huge, noisy amounts,
Ate tuna rolls in the chilly winter air,
Drank hot soup . . . bright red . . .
Same colour as your car . . .
It was an excellent day
On the happy scale . . .
It wasn't much . . . but it was more than enough
We reminisced previous adventures,
That July day spent on the beach
Paddling for hours, arm in arm
Eating ice creams, collecting shells
Standing on one leg posing for silly photos . . .
Chatting with happy faced strangers
And bouncy stray dogs . . . all the worries
And fears were scooped up by a
Boisterous wave and disappeared out to sea . . .
Such carefree moments seldom happen . . .
It wasn't much . . . but it was more than enough . . .
Our children grew up and flew away . . .
We grew older, greyer and a touch wiser . . .
Been firm friends in our funny way
For many a colourful decade . . .
It will never crumble up, end or fade . . .
It isn't very much . . . but it's more than enough . . .

Netta Irvine

CROXTON

I close my eyes and dream
On a warm summer's morn
Of the lovely peaceful village
Croxton, where I was born
People seemed much warmer then
With doors left off the latch
In rustic olde worlde houses
Topped with sunlit golden thatch
Gardens, colourful with scented roses
Honeysuckle, lavender and sweet pea
Apples, plums, pears and strawberries
Picked by children, with glee
The old grey-stoned church
Looking over peaceful rolling field
Stands guarding final resting place
What secrets it could yield
Nearby the ducks, pike and eel
Lived on and in the lake
Where many frozen winters ago
The whole village used to skate
Where fox and badger and pheasant
All lived side by side
And rabbits that were plentiful
Sat up, then ran to hide
Now new houses have been built
With strangers to and fro,
But never will it be again
The Croxton I used to know.

Tony Hayden

GOLDEN MOMENTS

Silence they say is golden,
As is ripened corn,
The sunset, then the sunrise,
At the miracle of dawn.

Golden moments of surprise,
That make the heart stand still,
The look of love in another's eyes,
Our wildest dreams fulfil.

To see the golden sunlight,
Shine through a cloud of grey,
Can lift the spirit, warm the heart,
And melt our cares away.

Taking someone by the hand,
Showing them you care,
Could bring a golden moment,
To one who's in despair.

Three small words, 'I love you'
Seem difficult to say,
They could make a golden moment,
In a special person's day.

Our thanks for the golden moments Lord,
The blessings we discover,
May our hearts be ever thankful,
For the joy of one another.

Ellen Chaplin

NOVEMBER FIFTH

My collie cowers
At my feet
He hears the bangs
He's a shivering heap.

He looks at me
With doleful eyes
Please stop the noise
He trembles and sighs.

He can't see
The colourful array
The bursting red stars
The silvery spray.

A battery of noise
From every side
The collie has
No place to hide.

Time draws on
Still whines and flashes
Screeches, howls
Thuds and clashes.

A stillness in the air
At last
November the fifth
Thank God is past.

Myra D Walker

THE OPERATION

My grandma had an operation
She had it in co-operation
It was a success
Grandad looked a mess
We had all been praying
Lots of people were saying
She'll pull through
And she did.

Joshua Skelton

READY

The Lord is coming soon but are we ready?
The Lord is coming soon but do we know?
Our lives should be prepared and steady
In showing others the way to go.

The Lord is coming soon, we'll be so glad.
The Lord is coming soon, we'll feel so well.
Our cares and ills will go, we'll be not sad,
To see His face is all we want to know.

The Lord is coming soon, sing hallelujah!
The Lord is coming soon, our hearts are high.
We'll do all we can on earth for His arrival, hallelujah!
Our hymns of praise will rise up to the sky.

Valerie Zanetti

HOPE

Hope believes in the future
Stands out against drabness
Like bright red rose hips
Against withered white leaves

When life seems dull
It says there will be surprises
Like the crocus
Beating through the cold snow

Like the frost edging the icy leaves
It adds a sparkle
A gift to be treasured
As if it were a diamond
A candle flame in the darkness
An oasis in the desert
Capture it and hold it close
It will transform you.

Jayne Poulter

HER PAWS WILL DELICATELY BRUSH . . .

With smooth appealing eyes
She still melts my heart and soul.
My emotions begin to soften
As Lucy takes control.
At my feet there stood a kitten
So tiny, innocent and cute.
Carefully I lifted her up,
Yes, my mood seemed to suit.

Some eleven years have passed since
And still she warms my heart.
Much bigger and not so playful,
In my life she plays a part.
A 'tortie' who is tricoloured,
Her paws will delicately brush.
Lying in my lap still sleeping,
For her there seems no rush.

Those eyes are always appealing
As she gives a gentle *miaow*.
Her whiskers remain receptive
And her tail is swishing now!
Because at last she is fully awake
Stretching out those padded paws!
Her soft nose rubs against my chin
As my T-shirt takes in her claws!

Yet the closeness of this attention
Plus the gentleness of her touch
Make all moments with Lucy special
And these memories mean so much.

Nichola J Keel

VJ DAY SIXTY YEARS ON
(For Mac)

It's great we celebrated Nelson's victory,
'And so we should,' he said.
But don't forget what happened since,
What other wars, atrocities.
I was fifteen years old.
They didn't know. I never told them.
I ran the messages and fought
The Burmese and the Japs.
I helped to bury dead - three of my mates.
It makes you emotional.
It's understandable. You don't forget.
We're comrades always, what we all
Went through together, has cemented
Us in bonds not to be broken.
It doesn't matter if we didn't know each other -
It's enough that we were there,
Experiencing the horror of the camps,
Seeing the men, and girls with spirits strong as ours -
Oh, now we're heroes . . .
Then, we were in Hell,
It should not be forgotten . . .

Elizabeth Morris

CONWY CASTLE

Upon the headland stands a gleaming castle,
All new and shiny white.
It shimmers in the sunlight like a ghostly apparition,
Perhaps it's meant to frighten us, and make us keep away.
They say the town is English,
And they want no Welsh inside,
But how can this be? We've always owned the land.

I saw the king arrive by boat,
I knew it must be he:
For he stood out above the others,
Like a tree among the saplings.
Flowing tresses fair as corn,
And body like an athlete!
Of course, no one told us of the cornflower squint and lisp!

Trumpets sounded and music played,
The gathering it was gay.
King and queen were brightly clad,
The courtiers colourful too.
The summer sun was beating down, upon the merry throng,
As I sat among the scattered cushions,
And listened to the chatter.

Suddenly I heard my name, and wondered how they knew me,
Perhaps I'd be in trouble now, for being where I ought not.
But as I watched the dancing throng,
They began to fade and disappear,
Again I heard my name, plus gentle rocking too,
Before my eyes the scene did change,
And I was all alone except for David.

The castle ruins were all about me,
And I was sat, not on the velvet cushions,
But a wooden bench, still slightly damp!
I realised that somehow magic had been done.
The ruins had worked a spell on me,
And back in time I'd gone!

Therese G Gilbert

BLOOD MOON

It was cold and frosty
And hypnotically still as he climbed up the steep hill,
Below
Peopled eyes were watching
Through lighted windows the lunar eclipse
That cast an intense glow across the landscape.

The moon
Rose huge and full, already shot through
With a silky crimson
In the late afternoon. It vanished into
Low cloud for the coming darkness.

He half expected
Other lunatics out watching, chanting.
He even imagined
Straggling torchlight processions
Winding up footpaths,
Stone circles, sacred trees.

But he was alone.
Everywhere around the northern
Hemisphere, people were gazing at the dark
Shadow across the brilliant
Silvery surface, amazing
At the transformation
And slinging their wishes
Into the blood-red smeared circle.

Germana Fry

IMAGES OF FREEDOM

The limb released from the plaster cast
The bird, still flightless, broken out of its shell.

Having a voice.
Throwing an egg at the politician of your choice.
Objecting. Taking a stand. Staging a sit-in.
Lying down on the road.

But one woman's freedom can be
        Another man's cage.
Protesters hold up the traffic -
        Some law-abiding citizen gets road rage.

At Faslane and Holyloch
        The local hospitals report
Excessive numbers of broken fingers,
        Baton-shaped contusions
The prints of policemen's soles on skin.

A limp; swollen fingers; a flightless bird;
An empty shell:
Images, just images, of freedom.

Anne B Murray

JIMI HENDRIX

Jimi Hendrix played the guitar
With the insistence of an iron bar
Using his fingers and all of his guts,
Amidst the bottles and cigarette butts,
He twisted the music and made it a yell
As imperative as an order from Hell.
But it destroyed him, as all art must
Which blows off the cobwebs and sweeps up the dust
And he knew they wanted him dead
Though they weren't prepared to cut off his head,
So, seeing the cauldron needed a lid
He took his life, as Van Gogh did.

Pamela Ashton

THE STALKER

I saw a man I'd seen before
Standing by my friend's front door
I saw him again the other day
I wish that he would go away
I saw him there in the park
He wasn't standing in the dark
He wasn't walking down the street
I didn't hear his running feet
I turned around, he wasn't there
He'd disappeared in the midnight air
I saw him standing by a light
Then disappear into the night
He wasn't lurking down the lane
Never to be seen again
And he wasn't anywhere in sight
Standing 'neath the bridge that night
What did he want - why was he here?
Was it just to disappear -
To come again another day,
To be seen once more then go away?
Yes I saw a man I'd seen before
Standing by my friend's front door
Where did he go, won't anyone say
Will I not see him another day,
Will I not walk again in peace,
And will his stalking never cease?

Joyce Chadwick

A POSTMAN'S LOT IS NOT A HAPPY ONE

The storm clouds broke as he set out
        And he was drenched in snow,
        His bag was heavy on his back
        And he had far to go.

But soon the snow had turned to rain
        And he could hardly see.
        He tripped on Peter's baby bike
        And fell and cut his knee.

The wind was blowing down the street,
        His cap flew off his head.
        He wished that he was safe at home
        And tucked up warm in bed!

The spaniel barked and barked and barked
        Because he rang the bell.
        'Sign here,' he said to Jennifer,
        'And here and here as well.'

He rushed around in record time,
        He thought *I'm early* but
By the time he reached the canteen door,
        He found it firmly shut!

He got to his car, in heavy rain.
        He found he had a flat!
No air in the spare, no pump in the boot.
        'So that,' said he, 'is that.'

He trudged along to the local pub
        To find something to eat
But when he'd got his egg and chips,
        He couldn't find a seat!

Joyce Craufurd-Stuart

THE MIGRANTS

As the days of spring grow warmer,
They dispel the winter cold,
The flagging spirits of the farmer,
Are quickly raised as he beholds
A sight that makes him feel calmer,
He espies the streamers of swallows so bold.

They swoop and dash around the barn,
Then perch upon a nearby wire,
And cheerfully twitter some happy yarn
Of escapes so exciting and yet so dire,
Whilst travelling from warmer climes to the barn.
The strenuous flight has made them tire.

Cheerfully they check the nesting site,
With pellets of mud they construct the nest,
Which must be secure, comfortable and right.
When the eggs have hatched they'll have little rest,
As insects they'll catch whilst in flight,
For the hungry nestlings they'll do their best.

The swallows gather when autumn nips
The air, they feast on insect pests,
Displaying aerial skills and zip,
Much needed on their migratory quest.
If man old barns apart they rip,
Where will the swallow build its nest?

Janet Boulton

SIMPLE PLEASURES

The dawn sky, colour streaks along,
To the lovely lilt of birdsong.
To walk in woods in early spring,
Layered beeches, wherein birds sing.
On a beach barefooted, walking,
White edged waves slowly encroaching.
Treading on newly fallen snow
Scrunching feet, face and hands aglow.
To walk upon a hillside high,
Nothing above but open sky.
Below a vista spread around
Amid a silence so profound.
On a cold frosty winter's night
Bare branches shade a moon so bright,
There are many things to treasure
Things that give such simple pleasure.

Lilian Owen

THE OLD HALL CHAIR

When I was young and lived at home,
You stood beneath the clock.
All proud and painted - in good nick,
A willing piece of stock.
I always thought when I moved on
And went upon my way.
That I would love to own that chair
But never thought one day -
That it would come back in my life
Bedraggled and unkept -
For me to renovate once more
To stand inside my own front door
A reminder of the past maybe -
And memories so dear.
But I'll not let go from my grasp
My chair from long ago - my past.

J M Cripsey

THE PURPLE FANTASTIC, FEELS LIKE ELASTIC, SPANGLED AND PLASTIC RAY GUN

The aliens left Helen a present
They came in the dead of night
She wore her curlers and they had green whirlers
So they gave each other a fright
The aliens left Helen a present
Formed in the fires of the sun
It was a purple fantastic, feels like elastic,
                    spangled and plastic ray gun.

Helen had no rifle experience
She wanted to know how it feels
She closed her eyes tight as she looked through the sights
And shot off her car's front wheels
Success left Helen excited
She saw why aliens have fun
With a purple fantastic, feels like elastic,
                    spangled and plastic ray gun.

No one believed Helen's story
Of alien ships on her roof
Three high schools expired when she took aim and fired
And scientists suddenly had proof
Helen became very possessive
Hers was the only one
A purple fantastic, feels like elastic, spangled and plastic ray gun.

She never left her gun unattended
She slept with the gun in her bed
One night all a sudden, she knocked the wrong button
And woke up in the morning . . . *dead*
The moral is . . .
Never let spaced out technology
Take over your films or your life
Even if it's a purple fantastic, feels like elastic,
                    spangled and plastic ray gun.

Catherine Randle

UNDERWATER LOVE

Underwater leaving me breathless
Washed away I'm feeling helpless
Drifting into endless motion
Circling round the deepest ocean

Closed-eyed and feeling lost
Clinging to fate whatever the cost
Freeing the moment of time as I spin
Down to the depths of mortal sin

A discovery of new wonder
Enjoying the spell that I'm under
Out of my depth you surround my all
My mind is no more as you hear my call

Just as if you know my weakness
You seep into my world of darkness
Desires you place your spell upon me
I fear I give my all and only

Such euphoria our bodies glide
Our passion flows just like the tide
Climactic bliss our bodies tremble
You hold me close I disassemble

Floating in the sea of pleasure
Although it's something we can't measure
Your warmth and gentle fingertips
Touch my skin, my heart, my lips

But though I know our bond is strong
Our love is lust and moments long
Your passion will remain my hunger
As I let you drift to aqua slumber.

Emelia Wells

ON A PAINTING IN MY SITTING ROOM

People in my sitting room
Some hurrying to and fro
A steeple in my sitting room
And a chimney's sooty flow

Houses in my sitting room
Seventeen or more
Some with pointed rooves
And some with steps up to the door

Smell the smoke and taste the soot
Hear the barking dogs
Tatty people, all on foot
No obvious class division
No TV aerials or cars
Yet no escapist's vision

Some talk in groups
While others stroll
Hands in pockets
Across the square
Clogs clang hard on cobbled stones
And no one's head is bare
Oh, Lowry, how inspired were you
To paint these scenes austere

So when I'm feeling lonely
Or trapped between four walls
I sit and gaze upon this maze
Until I join the gathering
And somehow lose myself within.

Brenda Soderberg

AFFAIR ON ICE

They are magic, a love affair on ice.
It warms my heart the way that he holds her tenderly.
The years between don't mean a thing
The happiness they bring,
Still there today.
The crowd applauds; they are on their feet,
Flowers cover the ice.
Their love is an act while they skate they say
But when he holds her tenderly
And looks in her eyes
Quietly asking, 'Everything OK?'
What a shame if as they say
It's just an act on ice.

Eileen Carter

MUSIC

I'd love to go to Spain to hear guitars played,
I'd love to hear accordions in France,
I want to go to Canada to hear the Blue Grass Mountain music
Wherever I would go I'd want to dance.

Life wouldn't mean a thing without the music,
It's a language understood by one and all,
No matter what your mood there's something for you
Be it classical or jazz or rock and roll.

I love to hear the reels of Bonnie Scotland
The rhythm means your feet just can't stay still,
Irish jigs and sweet songs from the old days,
I love them all, I know I always will.

Music lifts the heart and makes you happy,
Troubles disappear and all is well,
You find that life is really worth the living,
It means more to me than I can ever tell.

M Lynch

GARDENING IS FUN

The grass is so thick, it never stops growing
The privet hedges all need pruning
Viburnum and choisya are choking each other
All my roses they are trying to smother
My thoughts are torn
Should I cut the lawn?
Could I leave it one more day?
Perhaps turn it into hay.

Bent double on my padded knees
To dig out weeds on view for all my friends to see
Vicious thorns on rose bush tendrils scratch my eyes
Grab them quick before they high rise
How did those stinging nettles come?
Damn! Now I have stung my thumb
There is convolvulus growing all over the place
Always the strongest weed in the race.

Ground elder creeps along the flower beds
My knee pads now are worn to shreds
My Brussels sprouts grow with lace-wing effect
What will those caterpillars chew up next?
The soil is sandy - oh, so pure
It just needs - tons more mature
So fine, the little moles have such a jolly time.

My back, my arms, my legs and knees ache
Just one more dahlia bush to stake
I have just thought of a brilliant idea
Which will make my life much freer!
What about filling the garden with paving
And put an end to all his hard labouring
And then, invite all my friends to come
And show them why gardening is such fun!

Barbara L Watson

CELEBRATIONS

Most people like to celebrate but all in different ways
Some like a feast and pink champagne,
Some like to sing and dance for days.
Others prefer just a tête-à-tête with a loved one dear
Still more choose balloons and poppers - hats and bubbles galore
Plenty of party games and fun, and lots and lots of cheer.
Thanks Forward Press - be proud of your achievements
Fifteen years of teamwork and toil to make such
                              a successful concern.
So please put your work aside, and all of your commitment,
Let you hair down you deserve it and celebrate with
                              all of your firm.

Betty R Lloyd

THE TORTOISE

Slow, stolid, quiet, alone
Primeval in appearance; prone
Upon the earth you creep, to keep
Uncanny sense of season. From winter's sleep
Dead leaves your wisdom stirs, to meet
The warm life-giving spring, retreat
Withdrawal swift, from threatening things;
Then, later, sniffing safety brings
You - bright eye peeping,
To pursue your independent solitary creeping.
Wrinkled, tough and old,
O, how you weave your spell
Round mortals, from your armoured shell

Phyllis Williams

INSPIRATION

When inspiration comes your way
Be it prose or poetry
Jot it down right away
       Write on
Then as thoughts circulate
Ideas germinate
Words accumulate
       Write on
While the impetus is there
Fan the spark to a flare
Fill note paper that's bare
       Write on
Spurred by phrase or rhyme
Deaf to clock chime
Transported in time
       Write on
With the mind invigorated
The senses concentrated
The act perpetrated
       Write on
As feelings that originate
From the inspiration to create
Empower the word communicate
       Write on.

Monica Docherty

WHY?

No one saw the pain that's hidden
Or even why it all began,
'Where are we going?' they said
As they held each other's hand.

No one saw the loss then
Nor did they see the scars
No one saw the tears that were shed
Nor asked or showed concern.

As they whispered
Did the dust return their souls?
As like the golden sand
Only when the wind does blow.

Trees cover the ground they once trod
And flowers nod their heads
No one saw the hidden pain
No one saw the tears there were shed.

R Mills

NAISSANCE, THE BIRTH

They gaze in turn into their infant's eyes, now hesitant,
Unseeing almost, opening dreamily,
In mute submissiveness,
Minutely modelled hands as yet lie dormant,
Unfeeling, nor holding,
But ornamental in their unawareness,
Touched slightly by the gropings of a wavering urgence,
Curled in a cocoon of unconscious wakefulness,
And rocked in a soporific state of almost permanence,
This fragile mite is all appealing in its helplessness.

For two who have loved each other,
How proud a mother, in her presentation,
When each, in fervent wonder, hope and prayer,
Behold this new, this real, this binding imitation,
Mortal spirit, given of God and blessed,
In all that is and ever was is manifest.

Elizabeth Love

MY DEAREST LOVE

I'll see you in Pitlochry,
Where the salmon leap
Where the mist rolls off the mountains
Where the hills are filled with sheep
I'll see you when I watch the stream
Flow steadily along
Till it merges with a mighty roar
Making its own sweet song
I'll see you as the sun shines
Through a watery sky
I'll stand and watch the rainbow
And then I'll wonder why
Two people who had everything
Could throw it all away
Instead of helping each other
Through their 'rainy day'
Their children too have suffered
The pain has left its mark
When realisation has set in
The reality is stark
For now our 'strife' is over
Life's sweet again once more
But alas my 'dearest love'
This play has no encore.

Janet Robertson Jones

THE FAERIES IN OUR PARK

(To AP)

We had faeries in
Our park tonight
On pipers of skin
And pipes of reed.
On strings and drums
They made us dance.

One wore an orange t-shirt
Another wore a kilt and
Another wore a Tibetan cap.
All wore sandals and
They made us dance.

There were no stars
Or moon tonight,
For they shone over you.
I missed you,
So did the faeries
Who made us dance.

Paul Elwell

STEP INSIDE

The sea murmurs my name on the evening breeze
'Oh step inside, oh step inside and bring your troubles here'
The calm surface conceals; my future below
The gentle caress, painless salvation
'I'll greet you with open arms'
In oceanic harpy wail
Our eyes meet in sparkling gaze
Rocks in my pocket, oh take me away
Take me; show me the hidden depths
Extinguish the fire that feeds from me
My heart black as coal, burns
Burn, burns, burns
Now lapping at my toes, kissing my feet
Some distant temple worshipper
'Step inside, step inside, take your place'
Bliss.

Adrian Salamon

THANK YOU BETH

Fifty years ago today
The fates moved in a special way.
I still remember your first evening smile
So open and honest - no trace of guile.
I didn't think - I just felt - just knew
That my whole future had to be with you.

Gradually as the weeks went by
You accepted me, I'll never know why.
I found myself floating - walking on air -
Longing and planning for us as a pair;
And asking you to be my wife
Was the wisest move of my whole life.

As I look back now it can scarce be believed
The huge measure of joy that I have received
From our life together through the years.
Perhaps the answer as my memory clears
Is that you're so very special - so dear
And our love has grown stronger year by year.

How could I ever express my thanks
For a life so full that my memory banks
Are fairly overflowing - teeming
With times when on you I've been heavily leaning;
And never once did you fail to supply
Wisdom, love, and the smile that helped me get by.

Few men can have been so lucky in life
To have shared half a century with such a wife.
Your countless thoughtful words and deeds
Always mindful of my well-being - my needs,
Are but one aspect of your inestimable worth;
And what makes you the most wonderful woman on earth.

Deryck Southgate

THUNDERSTORM

Leaden clouds brood, lightning signals,
Skies crack, a rumbling environment shakes.
Birds flee in indiscreet haste,
Cloistered firs open their bodies to the heavens,
Natural worlds await its coming.
Lightning flashing intensifies.

Great renting wracks the firmament,
Beasts in the field stir, feral foraging flounders
In the swamp of ancient fears,
Stillness is total; tangible.

One momentous flash, one final roar,
The beast relents,
Its waters in unbridled torrents create crystal
Cathedral spires, their pediments glow with strands of fire.
Drought, thirst, the wait is over,
Foliage caressed by nature's wand, accept the gift
Like children from a mother's hand.

Rain-filled gutters boil,
Bulged eyed gargoyles eject their gorging
Upon an unsuspecting earth, drains puke
And heave, protesting at the silted soup,
Earthworms flee an enemy more prodigious
Than the carnivorous mole.
Grain fields bow, prostrate themselves in homage
To this colossus, this Canterbury of co-existence
Between sky, sea and land.

Alex Laird

WRITERS CRAMPED

When so it came
I played the game
Of doing my own thing,
My mind went wild,
Just like a child,
My own creative fling!

I donned my mac
And old rucksack
And jumped upon a train.
Satanic mills
And barren hills
Flew past the grimy pane.

They bore me down
To Hebden town
In mists of Pennine glee.
My heart lit up
I'll have a cup:
'We close at half past three!'

The old stone mill
Down such a hill
No prison could hold more.
Locked in the dark
With literary spark
And newly opened door

The noise was loud,
Egos were proud
And taut and fraught the birth.
My nerves on fire -
Home my desire -
I left and ran to earth.

Anita Layland

SQUIRREL

Inconsequential little one,
against organza blue of autumn sky,
you fly between pale shafts of whittled sun,
trampolining trees with airborne ease.

High amid the fir-branch dark,
you spark confusion with each studied leap,
as birds whirr wings, and lurch,
unbalanced from green refuge of their perch.

When winter comes, with ice-toned,
shortened days,
you seek my company, grow bold,
I feed you well, and scold you kindly
for your uncouth ways
rude style of scattering birds
from peanut cage:
the urgent, scrabbling rate
at which you fling yourself, and elongate
to eat, with rapid, rhythmic jaws, until replete.

Now is the time,
as hunger strings you captive from the bough,
fast stapled by each sharp, prehensile toe,
for you to merge me in the twin mirrors
of your gaze,
both alien - and friend you choose to know.

My special, influential little one,
the cupboard-loving season, has begun.

June White

LIFE STORY

When I look back it seems to me,
That my life has been like a tree,
Planted once as a seed born on wings,
Like the sycamore's wings.

The lovely gliders bearing seed with wings,
Born along by the whim of the wind,
Someone said I could never be born,
Never conceived, in the forest wind torn.

Only the good fertile earth gave birth,
In a friendly niche in the depth of its girth,
And soon a sapling strong and sturdy,
Graced the forest with leaves so shady.

An enemy tried to cut me down with a clout,
But the kindly wind blew him out with a shout,
And my branches grew strong and reached out,
They gave shelter to travellers without a doubt.

And though now I am growing old,
My leaves in autumn are brightest gold,
I can still give shade in the heat of the day,
And songbirds still come in my branches to play.

In my hair they have built their nest,
And shelter there when they come to rest,
I make a place to nurture their young,
And so give a place for songs to be sung.

So the story goes on and on,
With a story that's true, not a con,
As I send my own young on wings,
Just as a sycamore tree should on autumn winds.

Audrey Anne Hogan

DOLLY MIXTURES OR FEELINGS

Over the last weeks my feelings have felt like a bag
                                   of dolly mixtures
The sweet taste for the good times - sour taste for the bad times
Each colour to match every feeling that I am having.

If you stop to think every hour you can feel so many
                                   different emotions
About what people are saying to you -
Or what you are doing in your job -
The weather
Or a letter that has just arrived in the post.

You can cover what you are feeling by acting, not to face
                                   up to the problem.
Not to upset anyone.

Today I have felt quite a few dolly mixtures with tears -
Oh! What a day.

What colour are the tears? No one knows for I can't see them
                                   in my bag.
They could be clear, as I seem to have a gap at the top of my bag.
Excellent! Well-behaved today I felt my emotions change.
The dolly mixtures know their place -
I do hope they stay, not to make me feel like I am going into space.

M Goodland

PRECIOUS POSSESSION

Always by my side
Never out of sight
Downstairs, upstairs,
By my side at night.
If there was a fire,
Only one thing I could take,
It must be my handbag
As I make my escape.

Sylvia Rouse

THOUGHTS FROM MY CHAIR

If I wasn't sitting here, where would I rather be?
Out on the Somerset levels
Where the swans are flying free.

If I wasn't sitting here where would I rather go?
I'd walk down to the church
To be with friends it's good to know.

If I wasn't sitting here, what would I rather do?
I'd board a plane at Bristol
Just to be with you.

If I wasn't sitting here, what would I rather see?
Lakes and rivers and mountains
And the wonders of the sea.

If I wasn't sitting here, what would I like to try?
A journey in a bright balloon
Way up in the sky.

I can close my eyes and dream, as I cannot leave this chair
And travel where I want to
And believe I'm there.

Vera Banwell

DEDICATED TO YOU

I dreamed of far away places
Good friends I'd known but a few;
I never knew just who I was
Or what I meant to you.

All my life was moving on
To pastures green and new;
I never stopped to count the cost
Of what it did to you.

I, I - it was I all the time
But you were there by my side
Without you, don't you understand
I would drown in selfish pride.

You gave me love and patience
I never stopped to think
One day we might be parted
And in self pity I would sink.

I dragged you halfway round the world
Didn't stop to hear your cry
That you wanted me just to love you
And stay right by your side.

Linda Walker

THE SWALLOW

Fly south now my friend
The weather is on the change
Summer is having its final fling
Tempting you to stay
With offers of crimson tipped utopia.
You must fly fast; you must fly straight
You must fly where life is a copper sun
Where summer never fades
And food, voluptuous to the eye
Spills to the thirsty earth, in abundance.

Return next year my friend
Return when spring warms the cold earth
When shoots peep through the clay
And life awakens from hibernation.
I will look for you then
Where skies are blue and your image
Reflects the true feeling of summer.

Carol Subirats

UNIVERSITY CHALLENGE

Your Uni years are beginning
Make the most of everyday
New home, new friends, new way of life
Will help you on your way
Revise the grades, achieve your aim
With friends around you doing the same
Go ahead! Don't cramp your style
In the end it will be worthwhile
Study and learning, so much to be done
Good luck, be happy, take care, have fun

We all miss you, but in our thoughts you'll be
No shopping trips together, no creeping in at three
No bathroom paraphernalia
No music on full blast
And those noisy parties
I hope they were the last
An empty bed, wardrobes bare
Cuddly toys left on the chair
Those way out clothes and clumpy shoes
The disco nights and barbecues

It's very quiet now you have gone
But times do change and life goes on
Just a few lines in a letter
Or a phone call when you're free
And if you have a problem
You know just where I'll be.

L France

911 BABYLON OR WOE TO THE WORLD CAPITAL

Let us lament the lost and dead
Whose final count may ne'er be said
Tuesday the eleventh we'll remember
The darkest day in September.

When from the sky so blue and clear
Flying terror moved with fear
Winged monster in her flight
Smote such high tower with grievous fright.

Minutes later one more jet plane
Hit the twin now this is insane
Hundreds perish in that moment
No one knows who is the opponent.

The stricken Trade Center falls down
Upon the people in the town
Fire and flames and dust and smoke
Shock and horror does this provoke.

Thousands now lay crushed and dead
The terrorists have planned ahead
Woe, Pentagon, proud in power
You're struck as well in the same hour.

Washington and New York
Beyond America people talk
Target four is missed it seems
This in no way the sin redeems.

The world is sadder, less secure
For us, only the grave is sure
The blood-red sun did rise today
There's not another word to say.

M Ashforth

HOLD ON TO ME

When you are worried, when you're depressed,
When you don't know what to do for the best,
Hold onto Me.
When you are laughing, when you are sad,
When it's the worst day that you've ever had,
You know the good will outweigh the bad, if you
Hold onto Me.
I am your Lord, and I am your king,
Rely on Me for everything.
Speak to Me as you would to a friend,
I'll be there at the beginning, and there at the end
Hold onto Me.
I'll take your hand as we go along,
When things go right, and when things go wrong,
Praise Me and love Me in words and in deed
I'm here to care for your every need
Just hold onto Me.
When you are happy, with hope in your heart.
When you feel good in whole or in part,
We'll work together when you've found the key,
To my open door, dear child
Hold onto Me.

Come into my heart Lord Jesus, come into my heart I pray
Give me Your love and protection, come into my heart to stay.

June Jobborn

A LOVE THAT CANNOT END

Loneliness encircles me, where once my arms held you,
Now there's a void, how that's true,
No warmth of love my dear from you.
Emptiness is all around
From room to room you cannot be found,
I long to hear you say my name
From others it is not the same,
My heart would glow, when you'd bring me that rose,
A special token from you to me.
Oh my darling, death is cruel.
A love like ours just cannot end,
I lay in bed; your place is cold,
No darling one for me to hold,
No hand stretching out to comfort me,
No words of love that would strengthen me.

Loneliness is all around
In the home or in the crowd.
Oh my darling how I miss you.
The memories of songs you'd sing to me echo in my heart,
But, if I hear these melodies it tears my heart apart,
For you're not around to hold me close and whisper in my ear,
I love you dear with all my heart. I love you too you'd hear,
Oh what a lonely world this is without my precious love,
I know it will soon be alright, for God is up above
And our reunion is assured,
It's true, a love like ours just cannot end,
I'll think of what's in store.
One thing I know for a certainty
I love you more and more,
I ache to hold you close again
And this we'll do for sure,
For a love like ours is positive to endure,
Until that perfect day that - we are together once more.

Jennie Rose Miles

FOREVER AUTUMN

Spring of my youth, taken by fire
Burnt in a summer's sun
Sweated in long remembered desire

Come soon sweet winter
Dowse my burning heart
Take it now, let us start

But winter shall not come
And I'll reside forever lonely
Forever autumn, forever gone.

Mark Boardman

HAPPINESS

Happiness can be for a moment
Or a feeling that lasts all day.
Then something sad can happen
Turning blue skies into grey.

Happiness can be when
A newborn baby holds your hand
Just a little finger
It's a bond they understand.

Someone can make us happy
With a call on the telephone
A joke and a chat shared by two
Makes us feel we are not alone.

A day spent by the river
Watching sails ballooning in the breeze
Seeing happy smiling faces
As expertly they gather speed.

A celebration can be magic
Remembering the special years.
Many treasured moments
Bringing laughter and the tears.

Some people are so blessed
With a happy-go-lucky way.
Their smile is infectious to others
Brightening up their day.

Happiness and kindness
Should go hand in hand
Next time you see a sad face
Just try and understand.

Irene Beckwith

KIDS

(For Ian, Suzy and Annabel)

It seems so long ago
Maypole dance and slippers

Sweeping away the dusty days
From teddy to computer

Ibiza or the Isle of Skye
For dreaming it does not matter

A holiday song
A big ding dong
It all can send you crackers

But sitting on the shores of time
Are hopes, songs and laughter
For dreams come true
And wishes too
And all the best to you and you and you.

Anne Rickard

HEART WOOD

Upwards soars my head to Heaven,
Deep my roots dug firm in clay;
Squirrels eat my acorns dropping,
In my branches build their dreys.
Lovers carve true love upon me
Hearts and tokens in my bark.
Sun and moon pour brightness on me;
I am the same by day or dark.

I saw crowned Queen Boadicea
Saw the Romans come and go;
Men may change, but I am constant;
Tree above and they below.
Springtime sees my youth upon me,
Dropping autumn leaves me bare;
Winter lends me hoary fingers -
I change only with the year.

Humans - know my powers to comfort:
Know that I can bring you peace.
Tranquil rest your soul within me -
From all cares I give release.

If you put your arms about me,
Hug me round my crusty bark,
Troubled head to dusty roughness,
Touchwood close to unquiet heart -
Then my heart wood self will bless you,
From your heavy fears absolve,
Draw them deep into my own roots,
Strengthen you with oak resolve.

Know then: we are one forever.
You shall be ours when you are clay.
Abiding, loving, green in spirit,
Remaining dryads all our days.

Jean Medcalf

THE DANDELION SEED

A wish that floats upon a breeze,
A sparkle in the sun,
A gentle love
I sent to thee
When we were only young.

I'd surely have to catch it
And place it in your hand,
We'd cast it back
Upon the breeze
To find love's wonderland.

Tegid Furzer

IN MY HEART

Close your eyes tight think about me . . .
The way I looked, the funny things I said.
See I am not far away . . .

I was alive now I live in your heart.
Happy, sad times I had them all.
I loved and I lost, but I was in your life.

You will not forget me - talk about me!
Smile and share my life with others.
Be at peace with yourself.
Live each day like your last!
Do things that make others happy and above all be true to yourself.

Remember . . . I will always be in your heart.

Emma Morton

WINTER SANDS

Skipping sideways on Perranporth's golden sands,
Raw in December's frozen winds
Cutting through flesh like a grenadier's sword,
The awesome power of the icy sea pounding its sparkling spray
                                        into our face,
Projecting an image of helplessness when caught within its grasp,
Like a bobbing cork looking to God's future hope,
Yet along those deserted sands the seahorses dance
  In frailty together,
Blown landwards by each gust of the wind
The bubbling foam creates its own warm magic!
A picture of beauty and curved intricacy before the golden
                                        splay of sun,
Spreading its own yellow carpet before us,
Creating a lightened cross between the clouds above
Evocatively - as if to draw our attention
- To something supernatural
Beyond the crashing seas!

Martin Norman

TRUE LOVE

The sun will rise tomorrow
The sky will always be blue;
The oak tree will bear little acorns
That's as true as my love for you.

Music will always delight us
Fish will be seen in the sea;
Leaves will turn red in the autumn
That's as true as my love will be.

July will come before August
Rivers will flow all the time;
Thunder will follow the lightning
That's as true as you'll never be mine.

The stars will shine in the night sky
And grass will be covered in dew;
Roses will bloom in the summer
That's as true as my love for you.

Valerie Cooper

HOPE

Trees
My trees
Tall and stately and strong,
Knowing everything
Secure in their wisdom.
They comfort me
Give me peace.
They listen to me
With endless patience.
They talk to me with their bare branches
Their leaves lying on the ground
Providing work for faceless people.
People with wheelbarrows
To take away the leaves
To unknown places.
But the trees are not sad
They feel no sense of loss
The leaves will grow again.
It makes their future secure
Something to look forward to.
Hope.

Marion Bayliss

IT SHINES THROUGH

From a distance you are as one,
Together and happy,
An inspiration to others
Full of life.
A glance shared,
A smile says it all
From afar the love is seen.
The brush of an arm shows comfort,
Laughing, fulfilment and reassurance.
Little whispers that send shivers.
Witnessing the joy of being reunited,
The butterflies of excitement,
The expression on your face,
Surrendering of feelings,
Letting go of the shield around you.
It all shines through,
The trust and respect,
The truth and wonder between you both.

Emma Francis

THE HUNTER

He comes to hunt, in darting flight,
Observes with multi-facet sight;
Quicksilvered probing 'midst the leaves,
Around the limbs of sleepy trees
He prowls the glade in fading light.

His jewelled body glitters bright
As shimm'ring wings maintain his height.
Each cow'ring insect quick-perceives
He comes to hunt.

Who would have thought, at start of night,
To see such brilliant, hov'ring might?
Like magic, silent air he cleaves,
And on the wing, his prey retrieves.
The dragonfly creates their plight -
He comes to hunt!

Ron Shettle

NOTES

Where would we be without our notes?
Notes for spending, notes for lending,
Going round in circles never ending.
Musical notes for listening pleasure,
Soothing the soul a healthy measure.
Notes for our health regardless of wealth,
Private and personal between doctor and self.
Loving notes to show we care,
Terms of endearment when we can't be there.
Notes with flowers brings joy for hours,
They do create amazing powers.
Notes through the post drop on the mat,
Cheering us up we're thankful for that.
Notes at college giving us knowledge,
Education for life it's meant to encourage.
Reporters' notes compiling the news,
Keeping us informed whatever our views.
Marking a cross to secure our votes,
Life would mean nothing without our notes.

J S Lister

MY ENTRY TO THIS WORLD

Was I found upon a thread of a spider's silky web?
Was I hidden 'neath a toadstool in the dew?
Did someone trip and stop to see and there discover me
Amongst the fallen leaves and exposed roots?

Maybe someone out there fishing hooked me from a lily pad
Reeled me in and sat me down by his side?
Perhaps the raging seas tossed the shipwrecks and the weeds
And spewed me out on a high fermenting tide?

Where did I come from? There is no feeling of belonging anywhere.
No firm construction, no grounding or holding, no bonding
                                                      can I feel
I pinch myself so many times to see if I am real.

I had nine whole months of training for my entry to this world
I was well prepared for my ejection from her cell
And then I saw the light and breathed the purest air
And felt so free - for one brief moment - from that hell!

I should have guessed, what could have made the outside world
                                        so different from within?
I closed my eyes and quickly put the mask in place again.

What did I mean to her? Nothing! Just a product of her sin,
She didn't even try to act the part.
There I lay dirty, soiled, alive and crawling skin
Whilst she rejected, abandoned, as she had done from the start.

The shame of the unloved. The blame was not mine to bare
Yet I stayed silent, unobtrusive in my shell.
Daylight made the only difference from my life within her womb
And this great wilderness - this living hell!

Where did I come from? No one knows.
Where have I been? Everywhere and nowhere - too dark to see.
Where am I going now, at the autumn of my life?
At this moment I'm on a journey to find me!

Tomboy

9/11 - BLUE SKIES INTERRUPTED

Golf clubs in the garage
Car rests on the drive
Mother, children in the house
Very much alive
Devoted father, husband
Head down writing fast
Blue skies interrupted
Giant shadow cast

Dresses hang forlornly
Elegance denied
Father, children in the house
Nowhere left to hide
Devoted wife and mother
Running up the stairs
Blue skies interrupted
No time for final prayers

Garden left unattended
Cobwebbed tools remain
Mother, children in the house
Living with the pain
Devoted husband, father
Talking on the phone
Blue skies interrupted
No time to think of home

Empty chairs and beds
Of never-ending length
We can only hope and pray
Those left will gather strength.

Ray Chapman

NOCTURNE

As evening steals away the day
Saffron colours hold their sway
Setting sun takes o'er the sky
Pink-tinged clouds go scampering by
When we gaze on this vast span
We forget man's inhumanity to man
We lose ourselves in colours rare
Our minds for seconds hover there
The sun now lost in crimson light
Very quickly drops from sight
Trees and steeples gaunt against night sky
Become a fantasy for you and I
Soon magenta makes her birth
And night descends on Mother Earth.

Avis E Wolfenden

MIRACLES, DESPITE WAVE OF DESTRUCTION

Yes all was calm on some beaches one day
Until a giant wave came everyone's way
People were running, shouting, falling down too
Clinging to anything, to be saved it is true
There was panic and mayhem all around
People were injured, some dead on the ground
Towns and villages were now no more
With homes and businesses lost for sure
Families, friends, and relatives too
Were looking and searching, for each other it's true
Many were shocked, some dazed, some crying
Whilst all around them, many lay dying
There wasn't much that some could do
Though weak and weary, battled through
Exhausted, tired, they to became
Still calling out a person's name
Hoping at last, a reply they would hear
To give them all something, that they could cheer
Many were praying to God it is true
He blessed them all, knowing what to do
He gave them the strength and the courage it's true
To do all the things, that they wanted to
Countries and faiths were united it's true
Supporting and helping in many ways too
God's miracles everywhere could be seen
Through the destruction, devastation, that there had been
Yes God's miracles were there for all to see
Through all that survived this tragedy.

Royston Davies

A THOUGHT

A thought, a passing current in the brain,
Enlightens throughout the cerebral plain.
A new way, a transcendence of the soul,
For hopes, dreams, desires altogether comprising the whole.
To illuminate the present with the thoughts you have within,
Is to praise the whole idea of it and to let the dreams begin.
Thoughts often have a compass, a direction of their own,
And allow their own dear owner to follow the direction shown.

A thought, a passing current in the brain,
Enlightens throughout the cerebral plain.
Attention to detail will allow nothing more,
But true focus revealed, allows then to explore.
Within imagination the plains are open thus,
And enlightenment reveals the response and not the fuss.
In a crazy mind but so refined the choice is always open,
For the source inside can deliver a kind of process
                                        worth reflection,
And be partial to all that is new and engage in the detection.

Susie Belt

ONE OF A KIND

Christmas comes but once a year
To bring us joy and bring us cheer
To help us celebrate and bring to mind
The holy child one of a kind
Celebrate, celebrate, a baby king is born
A kind and loving baby king that everyone adores.

Christmas comes to remind us
Who we are and why we're here
To celebrate His birth with songs of praise
For the holy child one of a kind
Celebrate, celebrate a baby king is born
A kind and loving baby king that everyone adores.

Christmas comes a peaceful time
For those who suffer silently
Be blessed in His name, our Saviour
The holy child one of a kind
Celebrate, celebrate, a baby king is born
A kind and loving baby king that everyone adores.

Amanda-Jane Tudor

SONNET

Oh summer's night that ends with a cool breeze
Cured are my nostrils with flowery scent
Doth now the moon to glow while moths do tease,
Against lights, until their flapping is spent
Can I, such a person of good standing
Succumb to such suicidal mania
Yet only here, can I but stop this thing
Lights are magnets for a ballerina
Bats hunt the dancers like blind birds of prey
Never to be seen again by the light
I am left with not many words to say,
That begs life for the dancers of the night
Oh summer's night how cruel ye doth play
If this be of the night, then I need day.

T G Bicknell

PENNYWELL PRIMROSES

Rounding the corner, unearth wooden gate,
I chanced, into century-old flower filled lane.
Hedgerows teeming alive, beak burden with twigs
Blackbird, nest builds, watch by devoted mate.

Wealth of sounds on spring air, trilling choir.
Harmonize bird songs, solo notes sharp, clear.
Sleepy, early awake, humming bees gyrate high.
Thick blackthorn, sweet fragrant briar.

Gnarled ancient oak tree, exposed roots snake
Slither, weave, trap spiders in dense nettles.
Field mice scuttle rendezvous under dark foliage.
Mossy ferns, earth sodden leaves gather at base.

Tier, spread wide, orange/yellow sparking bright
Primrose faces abundant in long grass wild.
Soft rain drench plants, rainbows wetly glisten.
Winding lane illuminated by lemon sharp light.

Quivering breezes shake wet drops from evergreens.
Fading snowdrops, sigh, fold, settle to sleep.
Clouds shunting change shape squat in azure sky.
With pleasure I survey nature flamboyant scene.

P Smith

THE LIGHT OF THE WORLD

In the darkest heavens
There shines a golden light
Reflecting beams, to light the way
For souls throughout the night.

The light of the world in radiant forms,
The moon, the stars, the sun,
All glorious and mysterious
From morn 'til day is done.

An alter glows with candlelight,
Dancing shadows cast their spells,
Illuminating a golden cross
To the sound of heavenly bells.

The Lord is the shining light of the world,
The light of life like a candle glows
In everything that illuminates,
In everything that blossoms and grows.

To open the door of your heart
And see the light shine through,
Then your days will never be darkened,
And your skies will always be blue.

It's a joyous feeling of wonder
When the light comes into your life,
For the Lord is always with you
In gladness, sadness and strife.

So the moon, the stars and the sun
Will shine more glorious than before,
And the extra light in your heart
Will be with you for evermore.

Eileen Mary Chamberlain

LORD OF THE WOOD

As the sun in the evening sky
Slowly sinks to its rest,
And the birds have all taken
To their nightly rest,
And all is silent in the now darkening wood
When the white stripe of the badger appears
Lord of the wood
He swaggers along so elegant and bold
A regal character he is at that
And a beautiful sight indeed to behold
The dense wood so quiet with only the gaze of an owl,
Whose hoot-hoot echoes in this dark eerie place,
And the odd dormouse who scarpers home in a mad panic race.
But badger whose home is my woodland domain
Reside always in it and remain the same
Lord of the wood.

P Potts

GHOST TOWN OR SPIRIT

Whoever said Corby was dead and done,
Surely to goodness must be poking fun.
Oh yes! They snuffed out our candle,
That burned day and night,
But the 'Spirit of Corby' is still shining bright.
Just take a walk to St Andrew's Square
And find that spiral of steel still standing there.
Oh no! Our Corby has not gone to ground,
While that spiral of steel stays the right way round.
We are not going to weep over boarded-up doors,
For boards and shutters come down.
Whilst the 'Spirit of Corby' keeps looking up
We'll have faith in our new town.

Ann Moiser

ANIMA MUNDI

Some travellers scarcely move at all.
Sucked to the ocean's shrunken shore,
Where skylarks trill and buttercups   .
Endure, like iron filings to a magnet,
In deckchairs on the shingle beach
They loll, spread-eagled, hypnotised,
Staring and staring at the sea,
Plumbing its sullen depths,
Lulled by the surge, its long protracted
Mournful swell, its awful loneliness.

Hearing the sea's intake of breath
For them equates with pleasure.

Others eschew Bangkok and Tokyo.
Uncomprehending, half afraid,
Transfixed by mountain, river, lake,
They feast upon cloudscape, play of light,
Mist upon water, contours, crags,
Dawn over Pike o' Stickle or Tarn Hows,
The Eildon Hills above the Tweed
At Dryburgh, where silent owls
Glide among cedars like the ghosts
Of our primeval ancestors.

Surrounded by a mystery,
Such landscapes, too, provoke delight.

What are the watchers waiting for?
These static travellers looking at?
Deep in the unchanging, timeless sea,
A white whale snoozes, dreamily.
Deep in the mountain's granite core
Lurk faint, forgotten memories.

Norman Bissett

TRIO AT TWILIGHT

Alone, they sit together, combined in common purpose -
To drink, to talk of yesteryear's memories,
Of today's problems, about mere living.

Two are octogenarians plus,
One an octogenarian soon to be,
Gnarled by the years but indomitable.
Their faces hint of sorrow hidden in vast emptiness -
A private sorrow kept for moments of reflection.

Wives they had once but no longer;
Women of fine calibre, though all from different moulds.
Unity of purpose had these, too -
Unceasing loyalty to their men.

Far from the earth, they may be gone,
Across great voids of time and space.
Yet these wives unforgotten, still live on
In the collective thoughts of three old men.

But life is full of ironies, too many to perceive.
For wifeless, long ago, these brothers started out
And wifeless are they yet again.
Grief is a pain that haunts them all
As years of tender bliss in conclave they recall.

'Why are we here?' they all must ask,
'While far in unknown realms lie those we love.'
To this no answer can be sought.
And so the final verity remains -
A common, simple faith.
A truth to carry them through life,
While life shall last for them.

Ian Hancock

AN ORDINARY LOVE

What can I tell you of an ordinary love?
In small, well-used packages, tied with understanding.
Then he brings me flowers, to say he loves me.

When hope seems lost in trivial things
And time is short and I am tired,
He lightens all the hours for me on bad days.

He and I a very satisfying love,
With heather on the moor, its colour
Woven in our walks of life, of nothing grand
To share, on good days.

When dreams are dreamt and kingdoms reached,
In knowing we are there to talk
As mundane plans are planned, for each and all days.

He and I a very gentle love
No passions spent on strife torn grief, as Juliet -
So writ, with Romeo's share.
Just private smiles we know days.

As night time drops its curtain on
The trials of yesterday, to stretch my hand
Reach out and find him there, sleep well until tomorrow.

So, what can I tell you of this ordinary love?
The hopes and doubts, the highs and lows
The constancy, as new dawn clears the night,
Just the being together as one, days.

Jean Bishop

WHEN OPPORTUNITY KNOCKS AT YOUR DOOR

When opportunity
Knocks at your door
Welcome take advantage of it
Before it goes

Who knows what's in store
In its package for you
Perhaps good opportunities
To prosper yourself awaiting you

But there may be opportunities
Which needs your help for someone
Even this you must do willingly
For the sake of humanity

Seeking no fame or gain
To help with compassion
The sick and needy others
These are great opportunities welcome.

Kamala Perera

SOLITUDE

A day spent all alone
Can be an opportunity for quiet satisfaction,
A chance to think, for the mind to roam,
To be free of externally induced reaction,
A day to contemplate nature in the garden,
The grass, the flowers, the birds, the snow.
Time can make one want to ask for pardon,
For thoughtlessness while life is in full flow.
A day in slower pace
Can be used for reading,
It can give some space
To understand life's deeper meaning.
Solitude need not cause alarm,
It can be used to enjoy life's charm.

Janet P Wason

ONLY CHILD

When I was a child
My mum thought I was wild,
Because I used to climb trees with the boys
I did not like playing with toys.

Cowboys and Indians we used to play
And I would fight with them in the hay,
I would then go home with dirty hands and knees
My mum was never very pleased.

Down on the field and football we would play
But then they always had enough in their team anyway,
I would go down to the pond and catch a lot of fish
Some of them made a nice dish
Most of them were tiddlers too
There were always a lot to do.

My mum used to get mad
And said, 'I were like my dad.'
Sometimes she would say I was wild
That's the trouble of me being an only child.

Joy Hall

LOVE IS A MYSTERY

Love is a mystery
Beyond me
Love affects everyone
We all need someone
From pauper to king
We can all feel its sting

To some love brings pleasure
Joy in full measure
Some like the companionship
And friendship
While many enjoy the passion
Beyond expectation

A few find blessing in union
Two souls in communion
Selfless and pure
A sacrifice made sure
A mystical joining
Sealed with a ring

How can we explain love?
Is it truly a gift from above?
Or an earthly experience -
Transformed into radiance
The mystery will always remain
Forever unexplained.

Jean Everest

SWEET LULLABY

A rhythm whispers in your heart
Singing a song which is unknown
Listen to the soft small voice
This sweet lullaby is your own

Hear colourful mating songbirds sing
Watch shooting, twinkling stars at night
The quiet truthful voice which speaks
A calendar with memories of delight

Feel the embracing warm sea breezes
Scenes mirrored in calm mountain lakes
Secure holding you refreshed and complete
A special gift, a sense of place.

Elizabeth Hunter

TSUNAMI

The catastrophic happenings
Which come throughout the years.
Bind people close together
To wipe away their tears.

We remember from our childhood,
That God is love and light
This earth a school of learning,
To teach us what is right.

We feel the pangs of anguish
Death came with mighty roar
Left devastation everywhere
And silence on the shore.

It matters not your colour
Or religious creeds you follow
Your brothers need your helping hand
So they can reach tomorrow.

The question asked of Jesus
'Who is my neighbour Lord?'
People of the whole wide world
Joined by a spirit cord.

This Asian catastrophe now risen . . .
O' er the 'world' the silence fell.
Tsunami like a serpent rose
And left a living Hell.

Monica Gibson

WELCOME TO MY GRANDSON JORDAN

What a journey to undertake, unseeing eyes in total darkness.
Yet bonded eternally by the lifeline of love, a haven of comfort.
Nourished and warm in your waterbed,
Finding feet and hands that kicked and poked,
Reassured each second by the beat of a drum,
Regular, constant, strong, forever.

And yet as time flicks past the days, the weeks and months
Create the urge to heed the call that nature makes,
To leave your Eden, your paradise and quiet your place of safety.
Like all life gone before, strike camp, set sail and then explore.

Now your life becomes confused,
The beating drum is faint and fast.
No waterbed, no comfort zone, a narrow track to bar your way.
Conscious then of noise and light,
Of probing hands your eyes shut tight,
Why you wonder did you ever leave?

And just as all your hope is fading,
Here's the drum you know so well,
Beating against your tiny chest, warmth and love come flooding in.
Journey done, in firm embrace once more . . . time to sleep . . .
Now you know . . . you never left.

Arthur Leach

MY BOYS

I sit quite still and try to listen
As both the boys play unaware

I smile so quiet to hear them talking
And wonder at the joy they share

Their world is small yet loud and hopeful
As they crash along this morning's path

Frustrate and please in equal measure
They keep the loving in my heart.

Margaret P Auerbach

RELEASE

You cling to me but cannot talk.
Even with help you could not walk.
But still your eyes my movements stalk,
Imploring.
Your fingers scrabble on the quilt.
Your shaking wobbling head you tilt.
I know my eyes are full of guilt,
Ignoring
What I know your wish to be.
Knowing you can rely on me.
Knowing I can set you free,
But stalling.
Then finally my mind's made up.
I crush the tables in the cup
And hold it to your lips to sup:
Adoring
With my look and touch.
I'll always love you very much.
Your eyelids close. My hand you clutch . . .
Your spirit soaring.

Ida Shewan

WINTER MORNING MOON

Go off, full moon, to shine
In darker skies, for here
The sun has risen and steals
Your vast, nocturnal brightness.

You had your day during our night
And reigned supreme
Among the cloudless stars.
Now you must fade and drop from sight
While day is ours.

But when our sun has run its course
And dark falls deep,
Then you'll return to be
Our second sun, our light by night,
Our messenger to tell
That He who made the heavens and Earth
Watches us while we sleep.

Felicity Bentley-Taylor

SHOW ME THE WAY

Talk to me God
Tell me what to do.
Take away my loneliness
Show me the way.

Each time I hit a low
Lost on the path of life.
Where will my journey lead me
Show me the way.

Waiting.

You did show me the way
Walking on St Cuthbert's Way.
Calmness on the moorland
Was peace perfect peace.

To experience the stillness
Regenerates a spiritual renewal.
I needed so much
To hang onto this feeling.

Letting darkness float away
High into the sky.
Not wanting to leave this place
Of comfort and peace.

S Park

DAYDREAMING

I'm an armchair traveller; a daydreamer -
Dreams don't need money, nor coffee a creamer.
I spin my dreams in misty, frothy chiffon,
And as for my travels, they go on and on.

The fountains of Rome have attracted my dreams,
The summer blue sky, showing cotton wool seams.
The statues, the ruins and St Peter's Square,
Are mine for the asking from my mobile chair.

My persona becomes *Sophia Loren,*
With skin reflecting Mediterranean.
Sporting high, high heels and a strappy sundress,
Every movement being one of studied finesse.

In April my dream became reality . . .
But wait it's not Sophia, it's just me,
I loved St Peter's especially the ceilings,
And the fountains . . . I couldn't describe my feelings.

Rome lived up to my dreams; I'm pleased to say . . .
I'd like to go back one sunny day.
In April it was cold, windy and quite wet,
But yes, for a while, I belonged to the *jet set!*

My photographs recall the roman treasures -
But also record the outlandish measures,
I took to combat the chill wind and the rain,
But look out *Sophia,* I'll be back again.

I'm home once more, but my dreams take me on,
They glisten and gleam and refuse to be gone,
Then shimmer over a fluorescent sea,
To a new destination, known only to me . . .

Pat Berkshire

TIME

What is time if it's not the void space,
That we've to fill, when we're out of the race?
Time on our hands are moments so rare,
When we think we never have time to spare.

Time waits for no one, it passes us by,
We've only a short time on Earth to try,
To enrich our lives and give something back,
So make sure time puts us on the right track.

It shouldn't be just wasted and bare,
We ought to use it with caution and care,
It's a gift from above, so don't throw it away,
You'll never know when you'll need time today.

Time out to visit an old friend or two,
Time to give comfort when someone is blue,
Time to remember the frail and weak,
Time to give courage and no reward seek.

Don't squander the time you're allotted here,
Just spend it wisely; it's so precious and dear,
With good deeds and kindness in all that you do,
And time will stand still, and be good to you.

How will we answer our Father above?
If we don't give enough time to love,
As our life's pendulum swings to and fro,
And we don't have enough time to bestow.

Time marches on it's a healer they say,
It won't be hurried yet there's no delay,
When our life's over and we've had our time,
Our end will have come, the same as this rhyme.

Frances M English

ELUSIVE INSPIRATION

There's a certain elusive magic in this earthly life we live,
Magic in the joy of living and the happiness we give,
As if there were far more to life than we shall ever know,
Though we may find this heavenly secret only when we go.
So we must wait, and hope, to find enlightenment at last,
To find a golden future, instead of living in the past.

Great men, in the past, have found these magic thrills,
Maybe Wordsworth found one when he saw the daffodils.
Holst most likely felt one when he saw the stars at night,
And Constable, his beloved Dedham in the golden summer light.
Could they explain this fleeting glimpse, of Heaven, from the start?
Perhaps they tried to show us, in their music and their art.

So often have I felt this fleeting flash of wonder now,
As if some greater mind than mine were trying to tell me how
To open up a window, so that the magic I might find,
But I fear it is of no avail to my weak and feeble mind.
So fleetingly these magic moments seem to come and go,
And who or what inspires them I fear I'll never know.

Sometimes it seems as though I've lived in another distant age,
That elusive glimpse of paradise, like the turning of a page.
Sometimes these fleeting visions come when I look up to the sky,
To see the gleaming, sunlit clouds that race on by on high.
An inner person, other than I, tries to influence me then,
And I wish that I could express my thoughts, with paintbrush,
                                                    song, or pen.

And so, with frightening speed, relentlessly,
                        my golden years pass by,
And I can't recall those magic spells however much I try.
But evermore, throughout my life with happiness, I find,
Those sweet subliminal messages keep flashing through my mind.
Perhaps one day, in another world, free from misery and strife,
I will learn if the magic visions are from a past or future life.

Philip M Brown

IGNORANCE

Ignorance is the key to change;
If you don't know you just go on,
Relying on technology's broad range
To see that you remain the leading one.

But history is worthy of attention,
Ideas can come from ages past;
Other people may have done it better,
Even if they did it not so fast!

How did they build the pyramids?
And Aztecs cut those stones so fine?
Other technologies have flourished
In societies quite unlike mine.

We are conditioned to believe
That progress is a one-way street;
But one-way streets you cannot leave
And you don't know what you may meet.

Why assume that change means better?
Difference is what you get,
Where once you used to write a letter
Telepathy will come (though not just yet!)

And why so sure that we know best
(Everything's not black and white)
What of the ideas of the rest
We must not let them drop from sight!

Patrick Davies

LOVE'S EMBRACE

The shining hair of darkest brown,
More lovely than a monarch's crown,
The smooth round cheeks, the pretty nose,
A skin like the petals of a rose;
The eyes that shine, that subtle smile,
A look that can a man beguile,
What mystery is held behind those eyes?
What fantasy or dream do they disguise?
Those lips so red await the kiss
That takes us to that time of bliss,
The slender arms that round me twine,
Our bodies close, hers locked to mine,
And when we lie, our passion spent
In love's embrace we find content.

Roy Dickinson

FLY WITH GRACE, FLY WITH LOVE
(Dedicated to my son Michael)

Open your eyes my love
To the sprawling beauty
Of swan lit from above
By a myriad sunbeams.

Soft, snow-white wings
Fluttering gently in the breeze
Raising rippling rings
Upon reflective waters.

As droplets splash down
Like dewdrops or tears
Swan bears a gown
Of grace, like a lily.

Spread your wings, my love
Be a swan or an angel
Peaceful heart, like a dove
Behold beauty that beckons.

Fly away, fly aloft with zest
Life's joy is yours for the taking
But forsake not your nest
Nor the mother's heart awaiting.

Efrosyni Hobbs

REALITY

What does the future hold in its shroud of mystery?
A new life perhaps? But always mixed with shadows of the past.
Inextricably linked in the present, where past and future meet
Yet never being quite that which we remember
Or the way we would like it to be.

Accepting that difference is the way of reality.
Puts us on the path to happiness and contentment.
Change not those around us to our own design.
For they will cease to be who they are
And become poor facsimiles of ourselves.

Look to your own strengths with humility
And perceived weakness without shame
For within that weakness may be found your true self
Locked away through fear of ridicule
Or to keep others from knowing us as we truly are.

Value the diversity of culture, faith and society
For there are many pathways to fulfilment.
And as they cross or run together awhile
Show understanding, care and love to those you see
For you will surely meet again at your journey's end
Where all stand together, reunited.

Alan Dibben

BOSNIA

I am a child of Bosnia
I live in the high mountains
In a village with its own school
Without a teacher.

He lies never to speak a line more of poetry
Or tell us one of his many stories
Which came from the library of
Books in his mind

He is silent now, lying beside my uncle and my father,
These three hardly ever parted
And forever talking about sport
And the way life goes

I am a child and I do not wish the men
Who entered our village, who shot my father
And turned his body
To stare sightless at the unbelieving sky

I do not wish their children
To watch their mother daily as I watch mine
Dry of tears,
Hugging only us and sorrow

I do not know how to stop them,
But I do know that hatred
Is like winter's wind, and that spring
Has not returned to our minds.

Andy McMaster

AUTUMN SONNET

The languid days of summer now have flown
With burning sun and lengthy hours of light;
The corn is gathered in and hay long mown,
Swallows, swifts and cuckoos taken flight;
The buzz of bees and chirping cricket sound
Is absent from the hedge and meadow green;
The mists of autumn hover o'er the ground
And diamond threaded cobwebs trim the scene.
Horse chestnuts shed their fruits so richly brown
From brightest fingers of a golden hue,
And squirrels madly scamper up and down
Collecting nuts to hoard the winter through.
We thank you God for harvest safely stored,
For all the joys of autumn praise the Lord!

Doreen Lawrence

FORWARD WE MARCH!

We are the Christians of God's Son!
Forward we march, with heads held high!
The Jesus revolution's come!
Our Jesus flags are now unfurled!
We shall not cease to honour Him!
Peace, freedom, justice are His cause!
We'll free the world from tyranny!
We are the Christians of God's Son!

A new beginning for mankind!
Glory to God and to his Son!
The future's calling to us all:
God's kingdom, here on Earth, shall come!
And, He will reign, forevermore,
With Jesus Christ, his only Son!
No more despair, or war, or hate!
A noble future is our fate!

And on, Earth, peace, goodwill to mankind.

Ben Lewis

SEPTEMBER MORNING

When considering English landscapes through which to wander
There is little to compare to the beauty and splendour
Of the mixed deciduous woodland on an early September morning
Late summer when the sun filters through the trees
The leaves scattering rays and illuminating dew-filled spiders' webs
And where through the poplars, sycamores, oaks and chestnut
Green leaves and twigs rain down as pigeons and squirrels plunder
The harvest of the late summer

Blackbirds raid the brambles for berries that grow
Among the hedgerows of hawthorn, crab apple and nettle
As butterflies settle spreading their wings to catch the warmth
That the new day's sunshine brings

High in the treetops a sight so rarely seen today
As a family of jays engage in a bitter argument
With an old magpie that refuses to fly away from his domain
When suddenly, a flash of yellow, red and green
The woodpecker selects a likely tree and starts
To attack the bark with his staccato tapping

Tracks in the soft earth belie the presence of fox and deer
No doubt from their nocturnal roaming and long gone
Before my own presence here
The tracks lead to the edge of the wood
And to the water meadows where a small but active stream
                                   still flows
Despite the lack of rain, again, a different haven for wildlife
As dragonflies quarter the skies
While in the stream sticklebacks and smaller fry
Scatter at the sound of my footsteps or at my shadow's fall
As I stroll on this September morning I engage with the tranquillity
And wonder at the beauty of it all.

Grant Meaby

A TERRIER'S RETIREMENT

You didn't say, when we left home
In Hornchurch busy town,
That I was leaving Essex
For the lovely Sussex Downs.

You failed to say I'd not return
And life for me would change;
That I was leaving home for good
For somewhere new and strange.

You never said I'd change my name
Spend no more days alone;
That I'd have to wear a collar
And enjoy a meaty bone.

You never mentioned 'shin of beef'
Or biscuits on the mat;
You didn't tell me I'd run free
Or tell me I was fat!

You gave no hint of woodland walks
And squirrels made for chasing;
The smell of rabbits in the fields
And over farmland racing.

No warning of the scent of fox
And walks in unlit streets.
The feel of morning, country air,
Lush grass beneath my feet.

My breeding days are over,
My carefree days begun.
I'll end my life in luxury,
I'm telling you, it's fun!

Bee Kenchington

I Walk Along The Shore . . .

I take a walk along the shore
Knowing that you're here no more
I feel the sand between my toes
How sad I am but no one knows

I reminisce of all those years
I feel the taste of salty tears
The sea whispers words to me
To tell me that you are now free

Free like the wind you are!
In another land so far!
Where you have sailed away
And where I'll see you again one day

Someplace where there is no pain
But where we'll celebrate once again
A place where angels never weep
As there life will be eternal sleep

Silent tears that no one can see
As I think of how we used to be
You were taken away too soon
Up so high with the stars and moon

I take in the salty drips
And taste the salt on my lips
Or do I feel the tears I cry
Because you were too young to die

But I carry on and do my best
Whilst your soul is at rest
I walk along that sandy shore
With you beside me, no more.

Lannette Lusk

Child's Play

Summer of 1940 when
Cows grazed in sunlit pastures
And yielded milk, warm and buttercup sweet
In galvanized pails.
We roamed rough and carefree,
Through shaded woods and corn-rich fields
From dawn to dusk.

August. And summer's peace was shattered
With cries of, 'Roll up! Roll up! All the fun of the fair.'

Clutching hot copper pennies
We rode the stippled stallions of the carousel;
Threw coconuts at the guy - missing the target;
Tripped and wobbled along the rubber road of the cakewalk;
Had an attack of the collywobbles
As stomachs somersaulted on the swinging rowboats.

Autumn arrived in a golden haze.
Time for gleaning in the lower meadow.
Stubble, needle sharp, shaved our bleeding fingers to the bone,
Chickens gave large, brown eggs in return.
That was the day the stranger floated to Earth
Dangling from a cloud of watery silk.
A puppet on a string? A Martian?
We had read 'The War of the Worlds'
Under the bedcovers, by torchlight.

A stench of blood, fire and pain mingled with corn.
Guards arrived and gathered up the foreign bundle.
Later, we gave thanks for our deliverance,
With crab apple wine and blackberry pie
Concluding this harvest festival.

Emelie Buckner

A Welcome

Oh how nice it is
To see a sign
Of welcome
Upon a neighbour's mat.

Someone who will say,
'Come on in
And we will have a cup
Of tea, and a friendly chat.'

Someone who will listen
To your troubles,
And then in turn,
You will listen to theirs.

A neighbour will help
You out, the best way
They can, it's nice to have
Someone who really cares.

Some days you may feel lonely,
And worry over this and that.
But things seem to brighten up,
When you see your next-door neighbour's
Welcome on your mat.

Raymond Wakefield

The Love Of Rhyme

Sometimes, when all around is grey
And troubled thoughts won't go away,
One turns one's mind to thoughts of rhyme
To thoughts of love and happy times.

A poem starts to form and then, the
Thoughts of verse begin again.
The stanzas build up in one's mind,
And poetry, with love combines.

The pen moves with amazing skill,
And wondrous thoughts for verse fulfil.
Combined with love that's always free
A poem grows for all to see.

This love that conquers many things
Is there, within humanity,
Within us all, to grasp and hold
And make the love of life unfold.

To be sent off to a team, devoted
To all the verse that's ever quoted
Who, for ten long years, and five
Have kept the love of verse alive.

J J Clare

Pure Maths

$E=MC^2$

If energy is mass at light speed squared,
Then mass is energy - does this mean ought?
By this equation is the mystery bared?
Or revelation to the spirit brought?
By intellect unaided can we find
A key to open doors in the arcane?
Can written symbols the great scroll unwind?
Or mathematics probe the font of pain?

Pure mathematics is to abstract thought
As stick to a blind man, it gives him aid,
But cannot give him sight. Its symbols fraught
With meaning only prove that truth essayed
By intellect alone is recondite -
'Tis intuition gives the spirit sight.

Henry Harding Rogers

THE MIND AND THE POWER OF LANGUAGE

Errant thoughts wander wheresoe'er they will
until meandering fulfils a curvature of need.
They heed the twists and turns of fate, evaluate
and designate a path to tread. They infiltrate
the certainty of love-locked surety of calm
that lingers in the balm of life's remembering.

But sometimes, so exciting is virtual reality -
a scrimmage of the actual with factual intensity -
that comfort, warmth and homespun dreams
have nothing, it seems, to offer in parity.
Thus, misappropriation of conception transpires
and thresholds expand into a chaos of desires.

Modernity demands an orbital communication,
cosmic exploration and atomic transmutation.
Wariness, a watchword of wisdom, is suspect,
a reject - an outdated incitement to prevaricate;
a state - too dispassionate to curb gross insanity
that threatens natural forces and new vitality.

Visionary development must be demystified,
relentless thrust of change clearly identified,
and the strata of technical language clarified.
All thoughts and dreams pictured in the mind
need verbal expressions to manifest themselves;
clarity is power, when words are synthesized.

Rosemary Watts

REMEMBERED SUFFOLK SUMMER

Kaleidoscopic patterns change and blur
The images of summer. Through the haze
Of fading light remembered pictures stir
The glowing embers of our autumn days.

Morning reveals among the brackish pools
The stilt legged avocet of bobbing gait,
Scooping with up-curved bill the mollusc jewels,
A regal dish of fare invertebrate;

Or like a chequered arrowhead of light,
A symphony of avian elegance
Taunting the lumbering heron in his flight,
It swoops across the sky in aerial dance.

All nature sleeps beneath the heat of day,
Save for the harrier rising from the fen
To skim wind rippled reed beds for the prey
To carry to his chicks and waiting hen.

Dusk falls to launch the dark winged hawking flight
Above the pallid glow-worms on the heath;
The churring echo of the bird of night.
Beauty from ugliness perceived, beneath.

Now on the shoreline I will walk once more,
Where time-worn stones will tell a thousand tales
Of summer and the endless joys it bore,
Land of asparagus and nightingales!

Grahame Godsmark

FROST

Frost came creeping to my window today
To give me a world in a sugar bowl.
Stark, silhouetted trees, divest of spring's trimmings
Are captive in finer coat of glisten.
The lilting grass is now regimented
Into static patterns
And sound, itself, is an irreverent intruder
Upon this imprisoned instant in time.

Mary Foggin

TO MY DAD ON HIS 79TH BIRTHDAY

Dad,
It is time to celebrate your amazing life
And
Your numerous roles.

To me, you've been the world's best doll-mender,
My maths genius, when at six in the morning
You did my homework
After a night-shift at British Steel.

You are my role-model:
After your horrific accident,
You had the strength of will to survive
The plastic surgery, the pain and the near-death experience,
Aged 73.

With your Yorkshire grit and your sartorial style,
Bon vivant,
You know how to live;
You take no prisoners
And you don't suffer fools gladly.

A witty raconteur, history buff and lover of the Bard,
You enjoy your pint of bitter
And your punishing workout:
The only OAP at the gym in Rotherham who was
A weightlifting champion.

To Mum, you were a loving husband,
Her loyal, best friend,
Her carer,
When her illness, then her death,
Blew our lives apart.

I know she would be proud of how you've coped,

And now, as we tour the Med on our yearly jaunts:
I raise my glass to your life,
Dad:

Bon voyage!

Kay Jude

NAVAL CONVOYS

Silently, silently, swirls the deep
Over the place where brave souls sleep.
In close convoy
Our ships did sail,
Men on watch, to no avail.
Stalked by enemy u-boats down below
And the unrelenting torpedo.
Our sailors fought so gallantly
On that cruel, angry sea:
Their ships on fire,
The sea as well;
Only those still alive can tell
Of those frightful times,
That time of hell.
Silently, swirling
Runs the deep.
Dark grey and green,
Its secrets keep.
It hugs those brave mariners
To its breast,
Now peacefully sleeping
At last, at rest.

Sarah Robinson

WASTED GROUND

I had a dream that all alone I stood within a field
And offered up thanksgiving for all that I could yield.
Yet though it was a barren waste I fancied it was green,
So full of such abundant fruit, a dream within a dream.

But then the vision passed away revealing bleak, dry earth.
Sullenly I kicked the dust and wondered at its worth.
Then as I turned to walk away, I thought I heard a sigh,
A melancholy murmur and I heard the question, 'Why?'
'Why is this field so empty
When the soil is so rich?
Has it been more neglected . . .
Than on open sewer ditch?
Have I not given rain and sun
And seeds with more to spare?
So why, then why?'
I heard it ask,
'It stands so bleak and bare?'

And then just like a flash of light, a bright epiphany,
I knew the question, 'why' was meant . . .
. . . Not for the field, but me!
And all the countless souls,
Those whom were nurtured from the root,
Albeit would never come to light, nor ever once to fruit.

An empty field, a barren waste, a fruitless piece of earth,
A cloud of dust, a millions souls to wonder at their worth?

Gemma Edwards Gill

FLOODWATERS IN BOMBASA

This morning as the news was read
At first not much was said
Until pictures came through
Of a helicopter's view
A child had been born
In a tree this morn
As they winched mother and baby in the air
We saw her traumatised stare
Later as the water subsided
Uncovering the grandma who died
She did not live to see
Her grandchild, born in a tree.

Sue White

HAPPY FIFTEENTH ANNIVERSARY

To put their thoughts on paper
        Drove the poets' great ambition
And to have them neatly printed out
        Was their hope for fair rendition

Some pondered on the world around
        And others on the heavens above
But many had their thoughts profound
        On human faith and heavenly love

The Word came first with truths divine
        And they have followed faithfully
Expressed with meaning for our time
        They set them down so beauteously

Into the gap came Forward Press
        Who threw for them an open door
They asked that they might spiritually bless
        And folks responded more and more

So ring the bells and bake the cakes
        And join the party and the fun
They launched those works for all our sakes
        So Forward Press we say - *well done!*

Laurence E Nicholas

MAN'S LAST SUNSET

In a vision I saw so plain
What man's greed was going to gain
All the rivers were turning brown
And dead animals lay all around.

A deadly silence everywhere,
With an acid smell that was hard to bear
No living trees could I see
Nor singing birds or humming bee
The sight of butterflies eluded me.

As I surveyed the scene
I thought how beautiful the Earth had been
Why can man not change his way
And prevent this pollution and decay?

For if he does not and carries on
His last sunset will soon come along
This beautiful Earth it will be gone.

The signs have already begun
There will be no place to hide or run
Too late for sorrow and for tears
He has been warned for many years.

So change you ways, it is not too late
To save Earth's children from this terrible fate
Time's running out the Earth it cannot wait.

F McConaghey

ESCAPE INTO NATURE

Blackberries, butterflies and birdsong
Follow the natural world
Pursue the purity and quietness
Of nature's ways
Beautiful colours and striking hues.

Emerald landscapes and woodland ways
Beneath sapphire skies and amethyst rain
By indigo lakes and forest ferns.

Golden dawns and crimson sunsets
Cherish the seasons
Silent snowflakes and glistening ice
Autumn leaves, gold and brown
And springtime viridescence.

Feathers and leaves and sylvan trees
And the silent, soft flight of owls
A peaceful tranquil haven
A sanctuary, a retreat.

Savour a peaceful silence by a silver stream
Flowing gently through the night
Beneath a velvet void, bedecked with stars.
Orchestrated by the hoots of tawny owls.

Brenda Straw

SNOW

The snow comes gently falling,
With its flakes dancing and twirling,
Its rays shining and glistening,
Gently it falls.
You touch it, it is soft, white velvet,
Cold as ice, beautiful as diamonds.
Slowly it reaches the ground,
Settles there and quietly sleeps.

Dorothy M Kemp

BEYOND THE BALCONY

The sky beyond the balcony
Is grey and slightly trembling
The space above the mountain peaks
Is dark with lowering cloud
And all the while fast changing light
Dramatically transforms the scene
From stormy rugged bleakness to
A still and eerie shroud.

As likely it might well have been
When famine struck - their crop had failed
When hunger and injustice swept
Throughout, like forest flame
When anger turned to hatred and
Revenge soon marred the faith and pride
Of those who learned to never trust
An Englishman again.

Now shafts of sunlight pierce the mist
And Erin's green lies shimmering
Amongst soft purple heathered hills
And tufted mossy mounds
As way below a small blue boat
Moves slowly up the grey green lake
Which laps its haunting rhythm to
The beat of nature's sounds.

Though lurking still, is history
This scenic homeland harbours grudge -
Still fights those ghosts who bludgeoned through
Its fair and peaceful isle
As if like only yesterday -
That hatred gnaws, as does revenge
Through every nook and cranny of
Its ever open file.

Jo Lewis

SEAGULL

The seagull! The seagull! Sea-pure, sea-bright,
I fly, I fly with him - I feel his flight,
As he soars and swoops and sweeps and swerves:
The *whoosh!* in my tummy as he plunges and plummets,
The breathless exultation as with a crash-defying curve
He climbs into the skies;
I know his bliss as he glides, wing-still,
Then flaps, and glides again;
The swing and sway as he tilts and manoeuvres;
In my arms and in my body
I share the miracle of his movements;
In my whole self I sense the abandonment and joy of his
consummate skill.
He is a genius - a virtuoso, a maestro of effortless flight;
Totally unassuming, he does not realise he is watched,
His flight admired, his skill marvelled at;
But he knows his flight is superb - he revels in it;
He knows he is skilled, and he glories in his skill;
Unaware of his audience, he performs his aerobatics
All for his own delight.
He flies so high, he is almost lost in the clouds.
He is born knowing, he needs no schooling:
His first flight is as a child finding herself a prima ballerina
The moment she can walk.
Happy seagull! He knows nothing of war,
The earthquake cannot harm him, nor the flood;
He is free, utterly and completely free,
Captain of the sea, master of the skies;
And while I am watching his wonderful flight,
I fly with the seagull - by fancy set free,
I am the seagull, and the seagull is me.

Muriel Willa

A LESSON FOR LIFE

One day, in the future, when I've been laid to rest,
I hope that you will think of me when I was at my best,
When all my bits were working, before my hair turned grey,
When my memory could remember and I knew the time of day.
When bones and joints were silent, before they learnt to creak,
And I could find the words to say when I tried to speak,
When ears could hear and eyes could see and teeth were all
my own,
And I could even make the choice to live in my own home.
When I was independent, before the pills and potions,
Before the need for laxatives to regulate my motions,
When I could walk for miles and miles without a stick or Zimmer,
Before the midriff bulge appeared and I was rather slimmer.
When breathlessness meant exercise and maybe even pleasure,
Before the limits of old age restricted work and leisure,
When waterworks were functioning without the fear of leaking,
And I could sleep in bed at night, pain-free and not aching.
Remember me when I was well, in healthy days gone by,
Then work out what I'm saying and see the reason why -
Enjoy your life while you still can, before you breathe your last,
Appreciate your abilities before your time has passed.

K E Evans

WORDS

There are words that make you want to grin
There are words that make you cry
There are words that urge us on to win
There are words that make us try
Words can bring happiness
Words can bring fear
Words can hurt someone you love so dear
Words can be read in consolation
Words can be said in celebration
Words are written on card and letter
Words can say 'I hope you feel better'
Words can bring hope
Words can deny
Words can be prayers to God on high
Some words people whisper
Some words people shout
Words can bring promise
Words can bring doubt
There are words of remembrance chiselled on stone
But we shall never read them
We are dead, we have gone.

M E C Houlden

INHERITED WISDOM

You look at me with my father's eyes,
That knowing look,
Seeing beyond my nonchalance, too wise
To fool, that look.

How come, little man, my grandson,
You have acquired the look?
Not yet one,
But it's there, that look.

He was your great grandfather,
My loving dad,
Indeed, though, I would rather,
The look, was from you, dear lad.

For you are, already, laughing with me,
Something, only later, he did,
Inherited wisdom, in you, I see,
Given, the look is unbid.

Pam Hammocks

A DOG'S LOVE

All encompassing
And unbending
Never breaking
All giving
Not taking -
A dog's love

Always waiting
Anticipating
Never criticising
Or judging -
A dog's love

Never deceiving
Always increasing
Loving
And comforting -
A dog's love

Love it
Enjoy it
Revel in it
Life is empty
Without it -
A dog's love.

Janet Freeman

CHLOE'S VISIT

'Hi Grandma, I like spiders and this one's called Sammy.
He's come to visit his friend here and his name is Clammy.
No, I think I'll call him Rod
And this one - I think I'll call him Sod.'

'Oh, maybe not such a good idea,
Dad may not approve, I fear.'

'Grandma, I need a wee but there's a spider on the floor,
I don't think I like these spiders any more.
I've finished, Grandma, can I play with him please?'
Oh Chloe, your trousers are still around your knees.
Pull them up quick and wash with this soap,
Me pick him up? Cor, you've got a hope!'

Let's chase the rabbits now Grandma, I beg.'
'Can't do that, Chloe, I've a bone in my leg.'
That doesn't stop me, I've got a bone too.
But where are the rabbits? Oh tell me do.
Grandma, that's me. I'm the rabbit you see.
So all you do is you have to chase me!'

Val Hoare

CHRISTMAS OCCASION

Christmas comes but once a year
With a joyous occasion of festive cheer
It's the children's time of excitement and expectation
Of Christmas stockings and Christmas tree
All kinds of presents lie under the tree
Some may be large and some may be small
With excitement of next day to come
Cannot contain themselves and go and shake Dad and Mum
With riotous laughter all over the house
When presents are all opened and gasps
Of amazement at fairy lights as they shimmer
Flash on Christmas tree and making a wish
When Mum brings the turkey.

Raymond Law

THE CUTTING EDGE OF TIME

In the age of innocence we walked
    The meadow glades
Where birds, so light, their song hung still
    By riverbank's cool shades,
And shelter sought by mouse and vole
    Beside the weeping willow
Was bright with yellow buttercups
    And mosses - softened pillow.

Where once we crossed the tree lined field
    Young hearts all full of hope,
Stepping out through thicket dell
    And down the primrose slope,
Forever holding life's young dream
    Along our woodland way,
We carried all the knowledge then
    To give to you one day.

Through scarred land now that has been felled
    Where roots rear up the earth
And stones cut into open wounds
    Plant now, for its rebirth.
Look carefully at what is done
    To nature's tender plight,
Replace the damage near and far,
    Give life back to the sight.

Sally Crook-Ford

TRUE FRIENDS
(For Mandy)

Friends can forgive and forget
Things that were said with regret
Friends are there no matter what
Nothing you ask will ever shock
Friends are easy to be found
Good true friends, are not

Friends can trust with their lives
Precious secrets and deepest desires
Life and death and trouble with love
Without true friends
Life would be so tough

To be a true friend is a privilege
To have a true friend, a gift
To fall out and fight is a waste of time
To kiss and make up is so brave

True friends are hard to come by
And trust is hard to find
The secrets and laughter precious
True friends will stay with us
All our traumatic lives

True friends are hard to find!

Amanda Jackson

TO A LOVING SISTER

There's a gold and silver locket locked within my heart,
And in it is a picture from which I'll never part.
It's a picture of a lady who's thoughtful, good and kind,
And I know I won't forget her; she is always on my mind.

In a sailor's orphanage whilst we were growing up,
We used to quarrel every day, but always made it up.
Now that lady in the locket, I love her very much,
We phone each other every day and always keep in touch.
That picture in the locket, I think it's very grand,
Now I can break my silence; it's my loving sister Anne.

Helen Barwood

CHRISTMAS OCCASION

Christmas comes but once a year
With a joyous occasion of festive cheer
It's the children's time of excitement and expectation
Of Christmas stockings and Christmas tree
All kinds of presents lie under the tree
Some may be large and some may be small
With excitement of next day to come
Cannot contain themselves and go and shake Dad and Mum
With riotous laughter all over the house
When presents are all opened and gasps
Of amazement at fairy lights as they shimmer
Flash on Christmas tree and making a wish
When Mum brings the turkey.

Raymond Law

THE GUTTED FISH

Watching the fisherman reeling in his catch,
he smiles as,
without hesitance, removes the hook,
letting the fish fall to ground.
As the air dries its rainbow scales,
the fish just blankly stares,
and,
in that split second where death takes life,
the fisherman's knife rips open its guts,
spilling them out.
But still the fish just stares.
My teardrops fall, my lost emotions held within them.
I, too, share that gutted feeling,
wishing my hurt could be cut out - so easily removed.
I lean over the water's edge, a second away from my
life to death.
I call out to God for help,
then as I look down,
my eyes stare back at my own in the water's mirror.
They are not blank, nor dull, nor dead,
but show a single tear that sparkles life,
life I have no right to take,
so I will leave my hurt behind,
move on,
survive.

Brenda Pritchard

THE GOLDEN JUBILEE (IN THE YEAR 2002)

Elizabeth Regina -
        Who would beguile her?
50 years' reign
        Sometimes trouble and pain . . .

From a young and gentle Queen
        To a serene experienced being . . .
Taking all in her stride
        From war to peace . . .

A family nurtured with love
        And understanding -
Through thick and thin -
        Is Elizabeth - our Royal Queen . . .

The years ahead to not unfold
        What lies ahead
But this can be sure -
        Elizabeth reigns with wisdom
On this golden celebration . . .
        Long live the Queen.

C M Porter

LOVE REGAINED

Because our love was tender
(Because it was a love)
And because it was not told
It never rose above
The echo of a whisper
The dim obscure reflection
Of an undiscovered theme
It came within a whisker
Of never being seen.

I wanted what you wanted,
You did the same for me.
We even thought that that was
To set each other free.
No chains, no bonds or obligations;
No demands what each insists,
We nearly did not find it.
Our love was nearly missed.

But somewhere on a mountain
Beneath an autumn sky
We grappled with the pain
Of losing one another
And missing love again.
But then above the wind which blustered
We heard each other's silent cry.
Our love came from the shadow
We knew we were not free.
Just in time I came back to you
And you came back to me.

Eddie Sykes

LEASE WE FORGET

(Terrorism, a statement)

Since Man acquired Earth's fragile lease
We've failed to maintain a co-existence with peace
Struggling our way through life's doctrine
And protracted hatred conceived in sin

Suffer heartache and pain in a world of mortality
More vices than virtues and decaying morality
Watch war and destruction broadcast on screens
See communities blown to smithereens

Atrocity and attrition, can this life be a lie
Not knowing when, how or why we may die
Should faith be the judge for what measures we deem
To let Man's inhumanity reign supreme

Hatred with violence, we should not inspire
Both breed from the warmth of Satan's Hell pyre
His pervasive evil and inhuman schemes
Are blood on hands of perverted regimes

We're not God's disciples in a holy coalition
To strike with a vengeance or reap retribution
Blazing away with our chariots of fire
Redrawing the map with borders of barbed wire

We exist in a world full of derision
Where Man slays man to uphold his religion
Lest cultural difference in our world abide
The trodden path of Man is certain suicide

For Man has no mandate to infiltrate any border
Or impose ideology or new world order
Nor should we masquerade as disciples of peace
Imposing upon nations an unholy lease

Michael Quarrington

THE HILLS OF BUTE

The hills of Bute, so fresh, so green,
Stand guard o'er Rothesay Bay,
They sweep right down to shingle shores
Where rippling wavelets play.
The heather spreads its purple hue
Across the hillside steep,
Where trees in lacy greenery
A silent vigil keep.
The sun in fiery splendour
Sinks beneath the sleeping hill,
Twilight softly drops her cloak,
Commanding,
All be still.
Then night with inky fingers
Soon is on his way
Dropping deep, dark shadows
As he says
Farewell to day.

Nan Ogg

BALLOONS OVER BRISTOL

It is a strange, indeed, a surreal sight
To see in life a giant Rupert Bear
Above one's head, adrift, in sun-soaked light,
His paws uplifted in the windless air.

From bedroom windows, the broad sky watching,
We cheer his progress past our hilly street.
Now comes a lager, its great can mocking,
En route for some gods' Elysian treat.

For us, instead, a feast of wide renown,
A fantasy performed in silent space.
Balloons like drifts of coloured thistledown
Glide through the sky with airy, fragile grace.

New strength sucked up from thrusting flames below,
Dance on, fine balloons, your proud fandango!

Margaret Gregory

MY MOTHER

Joy, oh joy, my mother has come
To save me from this perilous run
I know not where I run
But still I run
Towards the nothing
Towards the sun

Praise my mother
Praise her be
For she has come to set me free
Invisible blisters cover my feet
These endless journeys God has sent for me

With courage and kindness she battles for me
To banish the evil and set me free
A caged bird I was
Trapped within my own mind
Preaching man's name
Surrounded by no sound

The endless applause
Is deaf to my ears
My journey is coming to an end
Now a new one begins

Kenneth Buckley

MARKING TIME

Time is measured in minutes and hours,
it can run like a hare or crawl like a snail,
a friend when there's no need to hurry
but a foe when haste is essential.

Time is measured in months and years,
too slow for the young who champ at the bit
but, as decades pass, it changes gears
to the speed of a runaway colt.

Centuries fade into history books,
the present is our time to grasp.
The future is still a mystery,
a long and unfamiliar path.

The clock ticks on, relentlessly,
till the second we breathe our last
and time, the ultimate winner,
slips from our fragile clasp.

Mary Fleming

IN THESE TROUBLED TIMES

I said to the Lord, what can I do to help the poor and afflicted?
I pray every day in my own way, but helping them all seems so
                                                    far away.
Is there no end to the hate, cruelty, abuse and addiction?
They blame You Lord, I hear them say,
How can God let this happen?
Countless innocents die, their families cry
Where are You Lord? They look up at the sky.
God looks down from His Kingdom above,
He gave us a world full of beauty and love,
But we spoiled it, we wanted more,
Greed takes over, then more war.
Still it goes on, Lord, people still die,
Where will it end? I hear them sigh.
Tell them, Lord, loud and clear.
We are losing our world,
We've sown the seed, animosity and greed.
Polluted the air, also the sea, poisoned our livestock,
Cut down the trees.
What will be left for our generation?
Nothing! Abomination!

Patricia Farmer

THERE WAS A TIME

I see again, your smiling face
Shining through the mists of time;
And sense once more, your warmth and grace,
So tender, gentle and sublime.

I feel your touch upon my hand
As in our childhood hours we play;
Caring not, that time's soft sand
Will quickly ebb, then fade away.

I think at length, about those days
That spanned the dreams of bygone years;
And left me in a thousand ways
Uncertain, in my grief and tears.

For you were mine and I was yours,
Torn apart, by time's cold hand;
While even now, on far-flung shores,
I see the future we had planned.

Time can't recall, nor lay the blame
On what has been, and start anew;
Nor can it ever dim the flame,
Which dwells within my heart for you.

Bill Jamieson

ENDING IT

(The Astronomer Royal, Sir Martin Rees, is said to have concluded that the human race has only a 50% chance of surviving the 21st century)

If it's curtains for twenty-fifty,
We might as well start being nifty
And love as never before.

We should give the world a big hug,
And say sorry for being a mug,
Homo sapiens, the world's biggest bore:

A bore whose imbecility
Poisoned the air and the earth and the sea,
And let the forests fall.

So now, whilst the globe waits for grief,
Let's cherish each flower, each leaf,
Say goodbye to them all.

Forget all the national ditties,
Sing songs of the Earth and its pities,
And our need to be as one.

Look again at our nations and churches and wars
And education gone wrong, and our crazy laws.
Their course has been run.

Poor kids! Cut the tests, cherish arts and leisure,
And feelings that help them to grow, even pleasure,
And end the great stress of our schools.

Let the animals at last have their time.
What we've done to the Earth and to them has been crime.
We reap the harvest of fools.

End the making of weapons, but rather make balm
To soothe and comfort the coming great harm.
Use lost imagination again.

If there's a light at the end, a god may say,
'You've got it right at the end of the day,
But you've been a bloody long time!'

Roy Stevens

JIMMY

I remember Jimmy, the drunk man who walked the streets
His language was not very nice to people he would meet.
I know there were many times I hadn't really cared
Maybe had the children there, we'd feel a little scared.
But one day as I was walking by, the Lord said to me,
'Go and speak to him right now, I want him saved and free.'
I felt the spirit move me to do what I was told
The power of God was coming down, I was feeling rather bold.
I went across to Jimmy and sat down next to him
He was worse the wear for drink and looking rather grim.
I told him of God's love for him and how he could be free
He turned to me and said, 'Why should God bother with the likes
                                                        of me?'
I told him Jesus died for him and could cleanse him from all sin
If only he would come to Him and let Jesus come in.
As his bloodshot eyes filled up with many tears
I could see all the sadness, the pain and all the fears.
He said that he had listened to what I had to say
He thanked me for spending time with him, then I went on my way.
The prayer meeting was on that night, I prayed for Jimmy there
Remembering the pain that was in his eyes, I found it hard to bear.
The next morning the phone rang, I could hardly take in what
                                                        was said
Jimmy was found in a derelict house that morning and Jimmy
                                                        was dead.
I really believe that Jimmy now is in Heaven above
That when I looked into his eyes, he was experiencing God's love.
And in that empty house that night, Jimmy was not alone
I believe the angels came to comfort him and he was taken home.

Sheila C Barr

CONCEIVABLE UNBORN CHILD?

Nobody's even thought of me yet, of course
But before I get nearer to my time's beginning
There are some answers to my questions I first need
Answers motivated in sincerity, truth and love
Nothing deceptive - no empty promises - nothing uncreative
The way you seem to be right now - that wouldn't do.

What kind of world - near and far - will I be born in?
Would I come to a good one - can I exist, improve, survive in it,
Or has it too many negatives of selfish immorality and
                                    wrong behaviours?
Am I viable - faced with those diseases, selfish sex and drugs?
Just how creative are the folk who will surround my pathway -
Showing me right examples, honestly, in loving ways of learning?

You see, there are many millions like me approaching
For your next generation's provision of time and space
So if your present times are really bad in many ways
Have you determined plans for meaningful improvement?
Plans I too, one day, can follow and usefully take part it?
Are you walking away too far now from the world's creator?

So what quality of love do you now possess and seek?
What foundations of stability are in its focus and potential?
Is it an abiding, true love, developing constructively,
One where creator and created can build and mend together?
Long before you think of me, I really need to know,
For neither you, nor I, want to see mankind losing its way.

Levelling with you now - just where are we - linked by
                                    two generations?
Just where in truth together are we going for man's future path?
Are we joined purposely as God's creative people - not
                                    destructive ones?
For surely our hearts have to beat together in the joy of all
                                    that's best.
And I just can't believe your love's desire would ever want me -
So inconceivably - to stay unborn.

Don Harris

THE INVENTOR

I sat down at my drawing board
With just one thing in mind,
That I would make a thingummybob
To benefit mankind.
It had to be quite simple
Nothing hard at all,
So everyone could use it
Just screw it on the wall.
With my plan I carried on
Well into the night,
Then I began to have my doubts

Would it turn out right?
It was OK, I should have known
My drawings were so good
But now I had to make the thing,
I wondered if I could.
It didn't take me very long
Only a day or two
And there it was, my pride and joy

It really had come true.
It turned out such a masterpiece
In fact I felt quite smart,
But when I came to try it out
The whole thing fell apart.

Jim Rogers

OCEAN WAVES

No longer feel I calm and safe
When I walk along the shore.
No longer can I drift away
To the sound of gentle ocean waves.
I close my eyes
And see
The cruelty of a tsunami -
Human lives amidst the debris
Outstretched hands beyond reach
Roaring ocean waves
Drowning out their screams.
Then there is silence -
I listen to the ocean
And hear
The sighs of souls
Flowing nowhere.

Anne Marie Frazer

15TH ANNIVERSARY OF FORWARD PRESS

Something told me you were somewhere
        Somewhere to be found
And that I would find you if I
        Only looked around.
When I danced with other girls
        Boys 'twould say, 'She's not for you'
Then I'd walk home once more alone
        To save my love for you.
Those lips I longed to kiss
Those eyes I longed to see
When I met you darling
They became reality.
When you said you loved me
I saw a life of happy days
For something here inside me
Tells me I will love you always.

Desiree L Pearl Silsby

DREAMS

Is it only at night that we dream?
What are dreams anyway?
Desire unvoiced, passion unspoken,
Worlds outside unvisited
Closed books, the smell of summer
Endless sunlit days
And nights heady with the perfume of youth
Is it only at night that we dream?

B Morris

MY CRYING THEME . . .

The weeds in the garden are laughing at me
  pull one up, or maybe two, and up come three,
  mow the lawn all nice and sleek,
Then little white daisies play hide-and-seek.

  tackle the hedge with a kind of lust,
  sweat and puff till my head should bust,
  pull at nettles and thorn and anything bigger,
My only wish, a pneumatic digger.

  fall from ladder with a bump and snigger,
A cut or two but nothing bigger,
  feel my body for breaks or sprains,
And cuss myself for lack of brains.

The weeds in the garden are laughing at me . . .
Boo hoo hoo!

Ernest Errington Reid

TRANQUILLITY

Feelings of peace, churn within the inward soul.
The magic of serenity within our midst,
Silenced feelings of tranquillity and ease.

A strength reaches out, beyond all horizons,
An endless warmth of love, extends to all creatures
And humans alike.

There are no boundaries, just joy. This awaits those
Who wish to behold, the freedom of His universe
And beyond.

Tiptoe with grace, through His wondrous Kingdom
Of kindness and love.
Reap the fruits of His endeavours, and rejoice for
All eternity . . . in the wonder of His presence, deep within.

Glide gracefully through His garden, and feel the warmth
Around you.

Experience the wonders of - *tranquillity!*

Janice Gilbert

THE GARDEN WEEDS

We're big, we're small, we climb and crawl
        and tough we have to be,
In nooks and crannies, rocks and cracks,
        we're everywhere you see.

We're colourful, pretty, evergreen,
        all year round, we're there,
In lawns, paths, flower beds, in gardens,
        that's the home we share.

We thrive in all conditions, we mind not,
        the type of soil or grass,
As long as we can seed and multiply,
        that is all we ask.

Perhaps you'd care to tell us,
        what wrongs to you we've done,
You are so determined to kill us all,
        each and every one.

You'll dig us up, or chop us down,
        with the mower you'll run us over,
We dandelions, daisies, brother yarrow,
        then there's the buttercups and clover.

You treat us all to poison, individually,
        you hit us on the head,
What kind of lengths will you go to,
        to make quite sure we're dead?

The next time you see us growing,
        with your precious plants and trees,
Remember - we have feelings too -
        so live and let live please . . .

Zena Parker

SPRING FEVER

Birds are singing with elation,
Of untold joy and expectation.
Now darkness fades with all her gloom,
Brightness dwells in every room!

Daffodils nodding in the breeze,
Giving hope and things that please.
Whilst babbling brooks go on forever,
Isn't nature rather clever?

Leaping lambs complete the story,
Rabbits run in all their glory.
Easter eggs to you I bring,
Goodbye winter, hello spring!

J H Newing

DUNOON'S AIN FAIRY QUEEN

Beside yon burn, beneath the Dunans grows
Bushes wi' bonnie pink buxom roses!
Wheesht! An I'll a secret tell!
Inside the bonniest, biggest rose does dwell -
You'll no' believe me - but I've really seen
Its resident - none other than the Fairy Queen!

One day, when a child, I wis up at ma Granny Cairns'
Ma Aunty Sarah wis telt tae, 'Look after that wain!'
So she sat me on her lap, an' pointin' tae wan o' the tiles
O' Granny's front room fireplace ('twis typical o' Argyll 'n'
          the Isles)
Says she, 'Luk at this bonnie, bonnie rose! Wha lives there dae
          ye suppose?
Nane ither than the Queen o' the fairies, wi' her Maids of Honour -
          Beatrice 'n' Mary!'
Then - her greatest secret she confided! She'd share it wi' me
          she decided!
She - none other than the Fairy Queen!
I wis sae excited I almost did scream -
But ma wee Aunty pit her fingers tae her lips!
'Wheesht noo Paddy hen! This is *oor* secret - dinna let it slip!'
(When moonlight brightened the sky - magic dust wis sprinkled
          on her from on high
She'd change frae ma cuddly wee Aunty, tae the bonniest Fairy
          Queen none fairer!)

Many years hae passed since then, but tae me ma Queen is just
          the same!
Now wears glasses, hair silver-grey has a different surname.
Her 'consort' calls her 'his wee Sally' an' wi' Beatrice and Mary
          she's still pally!
I'm now a granny - but she's still ma Fairy Queen
The jolliest, kindest yin ye've ever seen!

I can't wait until a' ma wee grand weans grows
Old enough for me tae tell - Granny knows where the
          Fairy Queen bides -
In that bonnie, bonnie rose!
And in the rosebuds reside - wee fairies dancin' on tippy-toes!
It'll be oor secret! Naw, naw! We'll no tell -
That we ken where the fairies dwell!

Patricia Cairns Laird

SECRETS

The night enfolds her
In black-velvet arms
Alone now,
Her soul cries out for peace
Tortured, tormented
By the feelings she hides
By the words - her lips
Can never release
Conscience - a dagger
Driven deep inside her heart
Twisting slowly
With each secret thought
Yet, it is sweet pain
And she bears it for her pleasure
She dreams of passion
Unhindered by reality
Uncomplicated by opinion
Free from guilt
Morning calls her now
Back to the real world
And a smile on her lips
Is the only evidence
Of her secret liaison.

Jane Findlay

HAPPINESS

Why is perfect happiness
Always round the bend?
The fields of corn and lavender,
The day without an end.
We glimpse it first in childhood,
When time's a moving feast
A moment's joy, an hour of pain
The world is ours, until we learn
There's crusts as well as cake.

And when the years are flowing fast
We worry and we fret
Suddenly retirement looms
It's what we've yearned for, yet . . .
Deep down inside, a whisper,
It's all too good to last.
Where are the friends we used to know?
The future's now the past.

Dory Phillips

THE CHRISTMAS STORY

Father, dear Father, tell me the story
How the Baby was born in Bethlehem
How Angel Gabriel came from glory
With the Heavenly Host to tell all men
And sent the shepherds to the barn to see
That Jesus was born in a manger for me

Father, dear Father, why did the wise men
Travel from the East with special tokens
Following the star, the shining omen?
But bringing gifts to their King would open
The eyes of King Herod to Jesus' birth
Who thought that a challenge had come to Earth

Father, dear Father, was the Virgin's pain
Giving birth to Jesus, the Holy Child
And slaughter of the innocent, any gain
For a world that was so brutal and wild?
And where was Your love for the sinner's friend
Who faced the cross alone at the bitter end?

Father, dear Father, why is sacred writ
That was first penned by fallible mortals
Enforced as unerring, making friends split
Causing torture and wars in holy portals?
Why can't all religions agree to be sane
Outlaw the flat earthers who cause all the pain?

John M Spiers

OLYMPIC WOOD

Imagine an Olympic Games where the purpose is to lose,
To be last or second last is your possibility to choose.

Remember that 'the last shall be first and the first shall be last',
So the ambitious will be penalised if they run fast.

We encourage running backwards and holding the javelin in the air,
We reward the race pacemakers for stopping and giving aid
          and care.

We regard gentlemanly activities, and honour ladies too,
And without steroids and doping scandals, first will be very few.

Civilised behaviour wins all, and the winner wins wood,
The uncivilised ambitious firsts receive metal as they should.

Instead of gold, silver and bronze, we have olive, oak and pine,
Winners of two wooden olives certainly must resign.

So for the ambitious we have the Antiolympic game,
Where the losers are rewarded and their shame becomes fame.

Alan Bruce Thompson

AGEING

I know an old man of ninety
Who lives all alone in his home,
His wife having died a long time ago
The past is the present,
The present is past, although he's still there.
His hearing is hard and his aid doesn't help.
His sight is not good, although he's not blind
The limbs, they don't work as they should
And need time to stretch, before moving again.
So there he sits and waits for the next caller to come
Of friend or sadly of foe.
He says, 'Sit down my dear and stay awhile,'
For he never goes out, nor when he can
'I'm lonely and old,' for life has gone by
No wife, so home helps and meals on wheels
All come to play their part, from morn until night
With bed to shake up and carpets to brush
Pills to put out and drops to put in.
While he sits to watch and strains to hear what is said
Yet, misses the point of the news spoken so loud
And says, 'Life is not much for an old man like me,
I'm lonely and lost in a house that is dead,
A garden gone wild that once was all fine.'
His fingers, that once brought music to life, now set
Like the house, once a home, now only a place
Where he stays, awaiting his end
With imprisoned memories of time and the past.

A Cracknell

MEDITATION ON THE CROSS

O sacred wood
Drenched scarlet -
Privileged tree that bore our God
Christ the Lord
Omnipresent Word, promised from eternity
To pay the debt of our iniquity.

Thrice noble wood
Peerless tree!
Bound in close proximity
Oozing peacefully,
Mingling sap with precious blood -
Soaked in love profound.

Mystic tree lowly borne,
Echoing the Trinity
Of God, the Father's bounteous charity
To pour the spirit free
From the pierced heart thereon
In love's unending mystery!

Jeannie Hay

WINDOW SURFING

Cat in the window, what do you see?
'I see a worm squirming and looking at me.
A bird comes swooping, a robin I think.'
The worm turns too slowly, tweaked by the beak.
'I'll teach it a lesson, just wait till I come.
Just before nightfall I'll creep from my home,
I'll crouch on a ledge by the hawthorn hedge,
Getting my paws wet with water and mud.
Don't like it, wait on, there's a thud.
My muscles are taut like a spring,
When I pounce and sink my claws in:
Robin's red breast is redder with blood.'

Fae Turner

WHAT LOVE CAN DO

For the love of my son, one loves so dear
One lives in distress, for his life we fear.
For love is so blind, that he cannot see
His unhappy life, trapped, cruel, as not free.
Was it the beauty, of a home he fell
Or a readymade family, we can't tell.
But his life to all, seems a waste of time
For in fear we live in riddles and rhyme.

For the love of that man, what can he see?
No other man with this life would just flee.
He gave up his pleasures, works like a slave
And takes such abuse, but holds out so brave.
For she packs his bags, dumps him in the night
But he walks miles back, not a lift in sight.
She said he's deceitful, lies, and he steals
But he loves her so much, cares how she feels.

For the love of my son we feel for him
As it hurts us so bad, it's a cruel sin.
Treats him like dirt and shames him to the kids
With his hurt feelings, he has to tell fibs.
But what can love do, when you see it not
He goes back for more and he bears the lot.
Missing out in life, he's young to her age
For it's an unstable life at this stage.

For the love of this man, he does what is best
Then turns a blind eye and ignores the rest.
He tries to do just what's pleasing to all
For this is the life he chose to call.
He takes everything and lives through the day
For whatever may come, whatever may.
There's no other one that he could then bear
For this woman, he loves, the one he cares.

Margaret Burtenshaw-Haines

ON A DEMOLISHED VICTORIAN HOUSE

I knew this house -
I knew its secrets -
I knew its open door.
The eastern carpet in the hall,
The brass trappings on the wall,
Memories of the Indian Raj,
Of Bournemouth,
Leamington Spa.
Forgotten sadness,
Remembered joy.

Now, the war-like wind
Shrieks the call of progress.
The dust falls with no regret,
The walls crack discarding debt.
The Devil's fire is stacked up high
And burns in ecstasy.
The smell of fire -
The look of fire -
The touch of fire.
Souvenir memories are blackened.
Thoughts escape by secret doors
And hang hopefully
In the storeroom of my mind.
The rest just go -
    with the curling smoke
    with the trodden foot
    with the digging blade.
But I - just remember -
A ghost from long ago.

Peter Wait

BLESSINGS IN DISGUISE

I stare into a stream and watch it flow
See leaves dance in their auric dress
I feel lucky I am so free
Not trapped in a high-rise flat, in full distress
I wander in an open field and through the woods
Not a house in sight, perhaps a lonely farm
People locked in inner cities, searching for light
May not experience this beautiful calm

Lord, I thank You for tranquillity
So grateful for all I see around me
So much I have, yet nothing I pay
There is music in the air, yet I hear no sound
Some people live in the fast lane of life
In concrete jungles, feeling disturbed
I haven't enough fingers to count the blessings
God has given me, yet I don't deserve

The Lord will always bring light to the tunnels
Giving hope to those in deep despair
We all have God's blessings, though many disguised
When I count those for me, I know life is fair.

Alison Jackson

THE CHAIR

I've found it, this place so rare
So peaceful and warm - sitting here
My back against the wall
Then why that unblinking stare
From someone I don't know at all
A chair against a wall in a foreign land
A land of sun and foreign tongue
Maybe someone else has found this place
And doesn't know the words to say . . .
Ah! Now I understand
This is your place of pleasure
A chair against a wall in your homeland.

Betty Gordon

ALDBOURNE IN ENGLAND
(Sunday, 7th August 2005 on the Green)

I have wondered many times of late
where has my England gone?
With muggings in the alleyways
and in London there are bombs.
We have no time to stop and help
others in distress, with hit and runs
and bricks thrown down from bridges
overhead.
Occasionally old England still
shows her smiling face.
On the Green last Sunday,
life slowed down apace,
we sat there in our hundreds
and listened to the band
and picnicked with a glass of wine.
Life for a spell was grand,
this was England as she used to be,
when people sat and smiled
and talked of little humdrum things.
Just for a little while,
a smallish glimpse of England
that made me sit and smile.

Howard Gibbs

PRIVATE DUFF

I never knew Private W Duff,
Who gave his life for his country true enough.
With an inscription carved in stone,
He lies in the churchyard all alone.
Regiment, rank and number can be seen,
Along with the 7th August, 1917.
He must have been young, but who can tell,
How he was aged by the Great War's hell.
And I wonder . . .
Did he have a girlfriend to kiss him goodbye?
Did he know the power of love before he had to die?
I don't know if he was William or Walter,
And I don't suppose that will ever alter.
But at least he's remembered by me,
For I place flowers on his grave you see.
Nestling in the rich green moss,
This poppy girl places his remembrance cross.
It's not just November that I care,
For I often choose to visit there.
Placing flowers on the grave,
Of a young soldier who was so brave.
Though I never knew Private W Duff,
I want him remembered sure enough.
But all I can do is an epitaph in rhyme,
For a soldier who gave his lifetime.

Susan Richardson

ALWAYS AND FOREVER

Always and forever
we will be the best of friends
Always and forever
till our life's journey ends
You brighten up the dullest day
turn grey skies to blue
Always and forever
I will walk this life with you
I know that we can never be
more than just good friends
For if we take a step too far
that's when our friendship ends
So I'll just count my blessings
when I am feeling blue
And thank the Lord for sending
me a friend like you.

Margaret Thompson

LET'S CELEBRATE

Red - yellow - blue
        Green and purple too
Balloons flying high -
        The occasional bang.

Streamers deck the room
        Hats and poppers wait
The lighting is adjusted
        The music primed to go.

Food is well prepared
        Likewise the drinks
What are we waiting for
        Let's party
Our 15th anniversary is here
Poets rejoice
Let's celebrate.

Mary A Slater

TOMMY IN THE GREEN

Step lightly 'midst the birches in this bright plantation:
These white battalions are the pioneer trees.
Fearful of weather and the deserted hills
We sent their comrades out into a hell of frosts
After the year's turning. Returning, we find
The veterans at ease, smart and hard -
Weaklings smashed or withered.
Rank on rank, they shoulder aside the larch,
Tender deciduous and floss of dead grasses.

Whispering amongst themselves they make
Soldiers' talk; swap memories of an icy country, yarn
Of hoar-scarred gullies, or foraging in early spring,
Of braving summer's scorching cobalt on the high screes;
About freezing in the brief sun of the solstice
Or enduring in silence under witless stars,
Witnessing softer fellows' sap exploding.
Contemptuous of the serious young oak
And those larches' vague greenstuff, they show
A tempered substance; are harsh if challenged.
Rank on rank, they precede the soft colonists,
Holding the ground against the insurgent seasons.

W H Thomas

ST ESTEPHE GARDEN

St Estephe Garden
Grapevines, peach and cherry trees
Calm tranquillity

Fig tree 'gainst barn wall
Hibiscus flowers waving
In afternoon breeze

Butterflies hover
Over buddleia bushes
Colourful picture

Tamarisk boughs low
Lavatera blossoms pink
Graceful tall fir trees

Swallows swoop and dive
Chasing insects for their chicks
Hungry in barn nests

Branches wave in breeze
Sunlight peeps through lacy trees
Birdsong all around

Somnolent trio
Lying under cherry tree
Azure sky above

St Estephe Garden
Escape from toil, stress and strife
Calm tranquillity.

Tonie S Ritchie

TIME

There's never a day, when time stands still,
Time goes on, our lives to fill,
There's never a time, night won't follow day,
Time goes on at work, and at play.

There's never a day, when a baby's not born,
Starting their life, as each day dawns,
Welcomed to Earth, with love and with joy,
Whether they be a girl or a boy.

But life, like time, it soon ends,
So we should make the most of what life sends,
Do not waste time, but every moment fill,
For time, like the tide, stands not still.

Joy Griffiths

INFATUATION

Human emotion is a funny old creature.
You can't
Cage it,
Train it,
Teach it any form of loyalty.
It is fickle!
A mere tickle on the heartstrings
And the strangled strains of unpredictability
Can be played, either out loud,
Heart on sleeve style or
More discreetly,
On the iPod of secrecy.

So it was with me
When I fell in love with the milkman
One day he was simply John
Bringing me my semi-skimmed at 6.30am.
The next, he was the reason my heart plunged to the pit of
my stomach

At the first sound of the milk float's hum.

Those days are done.

Human emotion is a funny old creature.
It depends on chemical reactions in our brains
And should these go awry
Our hearts comply
With the strangest of commands.

Given this understanding
And all I've been through,
How come
I'm now
In love
With *you*?

Patricia Bullock

HER SPOUSE MOST CHASTE

He tries to tell them he is far too old -
that he will seem more like her father than
her man - but all of Nazareth agrees
she'll be ideal for him, the widower.
The Rabbi archly asks him if the cold
bed he once shaped with his own crafting could
still bear the weight of two. 'James or Joses,
my sons, would make a better match for her,'
he answers, 'if she hopes to have a child.'
But after synagogue she bright-eyes him
from underneath her snood without a word.
The marriage is arranged. The thunderbolt
falls later. Stunned, a laughing stock, he's wild
with shame, his days a torment, nights made grim
by dreams like those an earlier namesake heard,
beast-noises: camel, ox, an ass's colt,
a crowd all willing the same end.
A patient man, who does what must be done,
he questions her and, after tears and screams
protesting innocence, hears out her tales
of her great visitor with news to mend
a broken world. Her boy he calls his son;
in time tells him the ways to join two beams,
the shearing point of Roman iron nails.

David Lightfoot

NEVER-ENDING LOVE

How do I love thee, forever; you bet
From the day I first saw you, the day we first met

How do I love thee, forever; it seems
You're there in my wakening, you're there in my dreams

How do I love thee, forever; I know
You're still in my thoughts, wherever I go

How do I love thee, forever; come what
I'll always remember, until the day dot

How do I love thee, forever; it's true
But you threw it away, what we had, me and you

How do I love thee, forever; and more
Though it's twenty-three years, since you walked out the door

How do I love thee, forever; I know
I still can't believe, you decided to go

How do I love thee, forever; life's span
Though you chickened out, you could still be my man

How do I love thee, forever; I guess
Despite that you leaving, left my life in a mess

How do I love thee, forever; I'd say
Will you ever return? I just hope and pray

How do I love thee, forever; I'm sure
You left my heart aching, for that there's no cure

How do I love thee, forever; all time
But I know in my heart, you will never be mine

How do I love thee, forever; *amen*
Until life is over, perhaps we'll meet then

How do I love thee, forever; I will
Forever; and ever, whatever, until.

Joan Bourner

THE TELEPHONE RINGS

My name's in the book
But my phone doesn't ring.
Nobody loves me
That's a sure thing.

Oh well, I'll relax,
My soap's on the box.
I'll watch it in peace
In my jammies and socks.

The phone now rings loud,
Double glazing is calling.
I tell them, 'No thank you',
But they still keep on stalling.

As I hang up the phone,
It rings yet again.
Would I like a new kitchen?
'No', I make myself plain.

I again settle down,
The adverts are on.
They come to an end -
The phone sounds like a gong.

'Change your gas company?
Do say you will.
Just say 'Yes' now
And you'll save on your bill.'

My answer is *no*,
I return to my soap,
To find it's all over,
Is there no hope?

M Roe

ADVICE FOR DRUG ABUSERS

You deceive and make us believe you're alright
but your life is contradiction because of drug addiction
we can see you're not right by your untidy sight
you're so confused
we can see through your emotional fiction
why continue this senseless infliction?

You may think that they are sweet
but you don't need drugs to make your life complete
keep it up and you will self-delete
You need a helping hand to avoid defeat
but ultimately only you can save your meat
so put your money towards a healthier treat

Don't be taken in by the talked-about kick
drugs will screw you up
they notoriously trick
there is no worse substance to pick
before too long you'll be sick
gather your guts and willpower quick

Go and place all that heroin in a dustbin
then your next of kin will help you win
your wallet will no longer be thin
you'll avoid a scrape with the law
your body, mind and soul will cease to be sore
and you will also achieve much more

Tay Collicutt

FINAL JOURNEY

(For my father)

When the tide is going out
I'll take your ashes to the sands
And let them trickle through my hands
Into the tide as it goes out

And they will drift on seven seas
North and south and east and west
As if you lived then at your best
When they drift on seven seas

But the best of you that was
Shall stay with me
Locked in my heart without a key
Safe in the best that was

Paul Thompson

GUARDIAN ANGEL

When I was in my mother's womb,
When I was born that sunny day,
When illness came at six months old,
And nearly stole my life away,
You were there.

When danger threatened as I played,
When I ran alone as darkness fell,
When I grew to think I knew it all,
And teetered on the brink of Hell,
You were there.

When I cross roads, or trip on stones,
When fire bells sound, or smoke alarms,
When cars rush by and brush my coat,
I feel your guiding, loving arms.
You are there.

When death comes and my life is done,
When your sweet care is at its end,
When I must stand before my Lord,
My Guardian Angel, dearest friend,
Oh, please be there.

Mary Robertson

BETTER LEFT UNSAID

Oops, I've gone and done it
Put my foot in it again
I've said things that are on my mind
When on my mind they should remain
Still at least I'm feeling better
I've got it off my chest
I just have to convince myself
That honesty is best
I was only trying to help out
And didn't mean to offend
But the door's been closed between us
And now I've lost a friend.

Jan Wickens

JUST A STAR

God made me with the moon and sun
To brighten up the sky,
I've seen the things that man has done,
But do not ask me why.

In early days the Magi came
To Jesus, in a manger,
I guided them across the plain,
I kept them from all danger.

As years passed by I saw it all,
The good, the bad, the Saviour,
From Adam, David, Ruth and Paul,
The good and bad behaviour.

I saw great deeds and God was praised,
A death upon a tree,
I saw the Son of God when raised,
And songs were sung for me.

Men started war throughout the years,
They killed, yet shouted, 'Peace.'
The terror, death, and all the tears,
When will this turmoil cease?

I see it all, the sinful state,
I see it from afar,
A wondrous world did God create,
And I am just a star.

John Young

A BEAUTIFUL SMILE

A smile is something wonderful
It makes a face's glow
Our eyes light up like stars at night
Our teeth look bright like snow
A smile makes people happy
It seems much more worthwhile
To see a cheery, smiley face
I think I'd walk a mile
To see someone look happy
Especially a little child
Life is full of too much pain
Anger and malice is sad
A smile is like a breath of fresh air
When baby smiles at Mum and Dad
So if you'd like the world
To be a better place
Always wear a smile upon your face.

Carole Andrews

MOONLIGHT

The moon full and round
Pours down her silvery light
On the frosty ground.
And then I see them,
As far as the eye can see,
Fathers, sons, mothers, daughters,
Brothers, sisters, children, babies,
Their faces white in the moonlight
Blank stares without hope.
Moving, stumbling, pushed by the guards
On and on they just keep coming.
And still I see them in the distance,
Sometimes I hear the shouts of the guards,
The cries of a child.
Shots are fired over their heads,
They are not walking fast enough.
I close my eyes
But still I can see them.
Still I can hear the guards shouting,
People walking to the camps,
To their death in the gas chambers.
The moon has shone on that place,
Many, many times since then,
But still I see those people,
Walking, not knowing, to their deaths.

M Lamin

MISTY ISLAND

Time stands still on the misty isles,
where rolling mist rises and falls
enveloping the mountain peaks.
Swirling clouds mingle,
creating a vision of mystery -
and past legends are remembered.
Stay awhile and listen!
The only sound you will hear,
apart from a lone piper -
is the rush of crystal-clear water
flowing down the mountainside -
plunging into the rivers below.
Truly a sight to behold!
By contrast, on a clear and calm day,
rivers and lakes become like millponds -
reflecting the beauty and splendour
Of the misty island . . .

Agnes L Berry

PLEA FROM A WHEELCHAIR

Put yourself in my place.
Look at my face and see
How much I'd like you to talk to me.

Don't talk over my head,
Talk to me instead.
Look into my eyes
And you'll realise how much I want you to talk to me.

I can't walk, I can't talk
But I can think, hear and see
And I need you so desperately to talk to me.

Someone - anyone
Please talk to me.

Sheila Jones

AMBITION

Should have marched with Alexander
Crossed the Alps with Hannibal,
Launched a thousand ships with Helen
Sat by Thebes beneath the wall,
Plumbed the icy depths with Beebe
Stormed the steppe with Ghengis Khan,
Charged at Agincourt with Henry
Fought with Lawrence at Amman,
Spied the special spore with Fleming,
Dreamed a dream like Caesar's wife,
Joined the crowded Roman forum
Stopped the thrust from Cascas' knife,
Kept the bridge with brave Horatius,
Seen the angels pass at Mons,
Climbed the bloody heights of Golan
Written the Gospel after John's,

Sad my record, unimpressive,
I must live within the head,
Whilst I pen these lines of envy
Lying on a feather bed.

M Waller

EVENING SHADOWS

The evening softly is stealing
the shadows grow dark and long
The bells have ceased their pealing
each bird has hushed its song

In purple glory glowing
the sun now sinks to rest
The moon her soft light flowing
while stars the heavens o'er crest

The distant clock tells swiftly
how quickly the time does fly
And pious thoughts so meekly
are raised to Heaven on high

But now sweet sleep comes over us
night spreads her sable pall
But God above cares for us
and watches over all.

Edna Parrington

ELEPHANT

Elephant - powerful, jungle king,
Huge and tough and lumbering,
Great, reliable friend of man.
Beast of burden through the age
Bellowing loudly in thunderous rage.
Calmly gentle in acts of trust.
So old that no one can for certain
Tell the years he's been around.
So young in play,
A clown as well as king.
Wild or tamed he will go on
Perhaps as long again,
Proud, bold and big,
Ugly, yet with beauty all his own.
Grey, sombre, four-legged giant:
He commands respect and wonderment
At his being.

Stella Haynes

MY CHRISTA 1952
(Written whilst hospitalised for 7 months in Switzerland)

To me you're like a brilliant sun, when all is black and cloudy,
Your sweet face shows, between the clouds, you smile and then
                                                    say howdy.
And like a pretty flower, when everywhere seems dead,
When the earth is hard, and grey and cold, you bow your
                                                    lovely head.
Then just like a cosy fire, on a freezing winter's night,
When everywhere's completely dark, you are like a shining light.
You're as pretty as blossoms and petals in spring,
Like the singing of the birds
And as an angel from above
With your sweet and charming words.
You are such a lovely person, enchanting and petite
And everything about you is so pleasant and so sweet.
Also very understanding, have a reassuring way,
You are my only guidance, throughout this world today.
'Tis you who brings me happiness, and courage and good cheer,
That's why I love you like I do and hold you very dear.
These are, my dear, my reasons, why you're such a perfect wife,
You are my all and everything and will be all my life.
You are such a little darling and you're mine, all mine alone,
I sometimes wonder if I'm worthy of the precious gift I own.
To me you're very precious, dear, more so in times like these,
You always do your best for me, and always try to please.
And that, my own and dearest Chris, is what I think of you,
Just a little consolation for all the things you do.
That's how I see you, darling, and has been from the start,
You're the highest of the highest, within my eyes, sweetheart.

Peter J Sutton

A WEE KEEK BACK
(To Mum and Dad - thank you)

Your childhood can be a funny thing,
Both laughter and tears that memories bring.
To think back on the 'glory days'
To grow and reflect on an emotional maze.

A yellow tracksuit from the Co-op was my first need,
Dad said, '£10! I'm not paying that, indeed.'
Went home wearing it to show my mum,
She just smiled at my dad paying out that princely sum.

On our camper holidays, navigator I was to be,
Maps of the Highlands spread on my knee.
I took the huff when we were lost,
Wondering how much a holiday to Spain would have cost!

A beach picnic in January we went one day,
The tide was in, that nearly swept my gran away.
Challenging Dad to 'headers', swim or run,
He never let me win, he was no fun.

Christmas time was the best ever in our house,
Lying awake all night for Santa, quiet as a mouse.
Five in the morning jumping from our beds,
The thoughts of presents and goodies swirling in our heads.

Football cards and toy soldiers were my pride and joy,
They were God's gift to this little boy.
Playing Monopoly, houses and money I was losing fast,
With this luck, adulthood would be a blast.

The memories all through my life I'll treasure,
Love and happiness you couldn't measure.
The adventures, the stories, presents in Santa's sack,
Always I'll remember to have a 'Wee Keek Back'.

Kenny McAlpine

EVERLASTING MUSE

You broke my heart,
Ripped, shredded, crushed, pulverised,
Destroyed.
You took all that I was,
And cast me aside
For another.

Yet, I yearn for you,
From every corner of my soul,
With every atom of my being,
Every piece of my heart,
For in you I have found,
My everlasting muse.

Oh, to despise you!
To cut you from my life,
And erase thoughts and dreams.
But the memories do not fade,
Your name is engraved indelibly,
On my mind.

You were my adrenaline rush,
My Christmas Eve,
My Sunday morning,
Without you I am empty.
The sky, always grey,
To lose true love is a physical pain.

And yet I forgive you,
As I always have, do and will.
You were my starshine, my moonlight, my sunrise,
Think of me.
For I'll dream of you always.

Angela Northfield

SPARKS OF LIFE

(Thoughts on a recently deceased relative)

In the darkness a small spark appears,
This spark of life is still there.
From spark to flame and to light,
To sunshine with powerful life.

There is a new beginning,
Dividing, splitting
Multiplying, replacing,
Multiplying and increasing,
But also dying.

For what end?
Will it last?
What will the future be,
And will it last?

New creations,
New beginning,
And new life,
Then another ending.
Is that eternity?

All is quiet,
Full of thoughts,
Planning and full of hope,
But is this an end?

Stillness swallows him,
No more desire,
No more hope,
Life has gone forever.

But new life carries on.
Love and expectations,
And hopes for his children.

Tilly Saunders Farren

A ROSE

A rose is a beautiful flower
It looks up to the heavens above
It symbolises an emotion
And that emotion is *love*.
It opens its intricate petals
Like the blinking of an eye
With colours as soft
As the rainbow
After a cloudburst sky.
Roses are like people
They need tender, loving care
And break just like porcelain
Their meagre lives to share.
So, stand in a garden of roses
And smell the fragrant air
Knowing they were
Sent from above
With *love*, for all to share.

Barbara Hellewell

LOVE LETTER TO AN UNTOUCHED PARENT

When did your shell begin to grow?
Around a crestfallen little soul,
Against a cruel jibe?
I know that fiery mist on tender shoulders.
Did it stretch in your youth?
Polished by small triumphs.
Hardening with the years it shut you in,
Shut me out.
Would that I could have replaced it with my small, soft arms,
So you would not have had to face your battles alone,
Against those wily serpents
That tricked out, and tripped you, and finally crushed you.
Who knows, after some kind of victory
I might have enfolded you in that second childhood.
Even in death we were denied that embrace.
I will try to hold you now,
In here.

Julia Bush

MY LOVER AND I

Oh, how we danced two or three times a week
        My lover and I
Floating like two love birds, him looking
        Sleek, handsome and debonair,
The troubles of the world taking a backseat for
        My lover and I
I felt like Ginger Rogers dancing with Fred Astaire
Then he became too possessive, the trouble started
Alas it became too much we parted,
        My lover and I.
Many times I walked past the place where we danced
Remembering the joys of those nights and romance with
        My lover and I.
Yes, I have regrets, wishing I hadn't left him,
Many times I dream, seeing us whirl around the floor,
        My lover and I.
Now realising how much he meant to me, but alas
It's too late, I know I've lost him forever
And my life is left to serendipity and I.

M J Chadwick

THAT STALL

Tea plates, spoons and ladles, and a one-eyed cat,
jigsaws, Ludo, marbles and a table tennis bat,
a moulting fox fur tippet around another fur,
one antimacassar and stressed, three-leggéd Windsor chair,
a mirrored case of spiders dated 1895 - the
funnel-web tarantula I swear was still alive,
trilbies, berets, feather boas and a knitted
waistcoat too, a dolly peg, a scrubbing board
and small bag of Reckitt's Blue, gaiters, bloomers,
half-rimmed glasses beside nice button hooks, a
bearded man with kilt on assisting with the books,
some tired clothes, an embroidered prose, jam pans
and kitchen cloths, a blanket and white pungent
balls to eradicate the moths, a chamber pot, a
travel clock and a myriad of pegs,
Mr Fox's dinted trumpet and three Blakey's metal
segs, a poker, bellows, paper sticks and a round
thing with a hole, a companion set, a fire screen
and a scuttle for the coal, hankies, tambourines,
maracas and a doll without her locks, a hoe,
a rusted cutter and a large, warped wooden box.

Most things laid there were futile and not wanted at all -

My raisin cake and lemon cake were on that stall!

J A Godley

THE BIG BAND

It's strange when you have a bereavement,
The big band starts to play.
I mean a band of people,
With tears and sadness who say:
'We are so very sorry,
We will help in any way.'

Now the sad day is over,
And you're left alone, that's true,
The big band has stopped playing,
So the next step's up to you.

M Smale

PERSONALISED PRESENTS

In the century of Antoinette's France
There developed almost by chance
A fashion to savour
A commonplace flavour
Which quite soon played a part in romance.

Milk was this flavour in favour
And led to uncommon labour
Court ladies displayed
The arts of milkmaid
And other unusual behaviour.

Her head probably glowed in the dark
Whoever first thought of the lark
It was to make a mould
Out of which could be rolled
Lovely forms to delighted remark.

Exclusive moulds were made of each breast
From which milk then duly expressed
Cups of shape deified
(Alas, texture denied)
Arousing more than artistic jest.

At subsequent romantic events
To enhance amorous incidents
Her lover was given to sup
Each exquisite milk-filled cup
The ultimate personalised present.

D Andrews

FOR GEMMA

I held your hand to cross the street
Kissed better the sore place
Slept lightly for your night cry
Bent near your mouth to
Feel the
Living breath
I watched you cross the first time alone
Waved when you turned at the
Other side
Wept unseen
Though your small journey was
My joy
And wept again
Each journey
A little farther
Till you were sometimes
Out of sight
And
Gone for
Longer
But this is
My joy
Go well
I will not clutch the reins
Nor follow in case of
Danger
Go well
Across the street
Though my hand is not there
My love is.

Moyra Summers

BONEYARD

Cold and damp, damp and cold
No one to have, no one to hold
Gone now the singular memory
Time passed, no one remembers me

Nobody comes, nor anyone calls
To this hall of wooden walls
All surrounding dank and mouldy
Never again will anyone hold me

'Neath soil eternally fettered
Longing to still be regretted
Past centuries of dusks and dawnings
None left to do the mourning

A mortal life all too brief
Humanity clasped in faithful belief
Into deliverance 'twas expected
Life led morally would see me accepted

Fleeting moments in a life frustrated
Hopes and passions sadly wasted
Steering a course of ethical rules
Here lies nature's greatest fool

Here body lain and here to stay
Time immemorial to the final day
'Twere any vestige o' faith remained
Should dampen the eternal pain

Into the hands of fates we play
Praying and hopeful, trembling lay
Joy and fulfilment lost evermore
Pressed beneath the earthen floor

Cold and damp, damp and cold
No one to have and no one to hold . . .

Christopher R Lawton

A Rose Full Of Promises

With your petals huge, red, bright, colour so strong
Standing so tall, from the ground, so long
It's a wonder to me, you have continued to cope
And not given in, or forsaken all hope
As the soil you are in, doesn't offer you much
And I have failed many times, with that tender touch
You have struggled to grow, to a long, spindly frame
In all sorts of conditions and yes, plenty of rain
You can barely hold up that beautiful rose
A perfume so pungent, it tickles my nose
As large as a saucer, that beautiful bloom
Near to the wall, and very little room
The best ever decorative flower
Shows its might, with promising power
Yet since clearing the ground and feeding the soil
Not one, but four buds appeared, splendid and royal
And then a rainbow, arched over, high in the air
A promise fulfilled, such wonder, such beauty, so rare.

Janet Nella Ackroyd

Princess Of Wales

A beautiful princess
A true English rose
Our very own Princess of Wales
Mother of Prince William and Prince Harry
She cared and loved them both
Who now walk behind her coffin
Who knows what's in their thoughts
Her caring nature for young and old
Sick and demented, she cared for them all
Just as she found true happiness with Dodi El Fayad
Someone so careless put an end to all that
A broken link we can never replace
Her untimely death a total disgrace
The day of the funeral
We watched sadly on
Our beautiful princess had truly gone.

Margaret Stumpp

Poetry Is Here To Stay

Whether poems are dedicated
To loved ones
Or for anyone to read
Poets have a way of saying
Imagination is something
We all need
Poets speak or write
Words of love
To someone they adore
Or tell of their adventures
On a foreign shore
When maybe they have not
Been far away
From an open door
They bring romance, mystery and adventure
Into our lives
Charming us along the way
And people believe
Everything they say
Even if it's false or true
But poetry is here to stay.

D Hardwick

Of Nature's Caress

Travelling wondrously through advancing, narrow, winding lanes
Augmented by the brushing of rhythmically overhanging hedgerows
With richness and diversity of glorious flora and fauna
And the embrace of robins, sparrows, blackbirds, jackdaws
                                    and crows
Of leafy branches from trees, lush foliage in variant green
Profusion of buddleia, fuchsia, honeysuckle, blossom and vetch
Along coastline of golden, yellow sand, a spectacular scene
The jutting rock faces of headland, striations of the majestic,
                                    sculptured view
From the green hillsides and fields to cliffs projecting
                                    gradual descent
Like lips on either side to eye the vista of quietly reclining coves
                                    far below
The gulls and other shoreland birds hover above beaches and
                                    waters alike
In their never-ending quest for food, sometimes quick,
                                    sometimes slow
With the splendour of the landscape laid beneath their aerial view
Additional rivers, streams, forests and woodland lavishly abound
Where Kingsley, Williamson, Capern and Gay wrote anew
The sight of boats and ferries on trips toward impressive harbours
                                    and bays
Further accentuate the visual feast of this marvellous domain
Where all elements combine endearingly to maintain their
                                    momentous stay
Herein lies my indigenous roots and place of residence for which
                                    I claim
Though so much more to say these words must now suffice
As this verse has sought to describe a veritable heaven
It confirms it to be the glorious and scenically uplifting county
                                    of Devon.

P E Darch

Move On

In the doorway he slumped,
Nowhere to lay his head,
A light shone on his face,
        Move on, move on.

In the hedgerow sheltering from rain,
Lying on the dark, damp ground,
A light shone on his face,
        Move on, move on.

In the stable lying on hay,
The new Babe snuggled down,
While in a dream, His old dad was told,
        Move on, move on.

The Babe on a donkey was laid,
With Mary and Joseph away they rode,
King Herod's men in vain pursuit
        Moving on, moving on.

From boyhood onward into manhood,
Great wonders to perform.
Healing the sick, and stilling storm,
        Always moving on, moving on.

Then the great price was paid,
As mocked and jeered He climbed that hill
And soldiers shouted
        Move on, move on!

Rosemary de Harrow

WET NIGHT ON THE ROAD

The rain swishes down,
The wipers clack,
I peer through the windscreen
It's wet and black.
Nothing to hear; but rain on rain
Here comes another lorry again,
It passes, flooding the screen like a sea
The wipers struggle to clear the debris,
Faster and faster, then it's done,
Back to the normal one on one.

The only sounds are the passing cars
The endless swish of water on tyres,
I seem to be in a world of my own
Just sitting and driving, on and on.
I see up ahead a motel sign
The thought of a bed, mine all mine
A meal, warm room, shut out the rain
Restart my journey tomorrow again.
Of course with my luck, it'll still be raining
But new day, new dollar, who's complaining?

Leila McLeish

THE SPIRAL STAIRCASE

You are so alone, no one to love, no one who loves you;
I wish you knew the truth.
My feelings for you become stronger every time you look at me,
Please don't be sad,
I long to make you smile, I want to curve your lips into place,
I want to look after you forever.
I'd never stop loving you,
I could do anything for you,
Please don't be sad,
Your self-consciousness has led to *our* depression.
I find it hard to live when you are sad,
I long to dry your tears, to burn your darkness away.
I long to sweep up the sadness and lock it away.
You sit there in your chair of apathy, surrounded by dark.
You struggle to climb the spiral stairs in your head.
I'm at the top, but am struggling to come down.
The tears in your mind fill up your head, they leak out of your eyes.
The corner full of darkness is calling you to rest there,
Your sadness drives me mad.
You can't make it up the stairs,
I come down,
We can be sad together.

Jodie McKane

THE WOODLAND

Sunlight filters through the trees
Weakening the threads of winter.
Charcoal images of oak and ash
Give way to a glimmer of green.
Cotton-tasselled catkins herald spring.
The long sleep is over and the woodland
Teems with life once more.

The modest snowdrop looks down,
But kindly, on the sunny face of the aconite
Displaying her ruff of green.
The fragile wind-flowers sway gently,
Undisturbed by the hurrying, scurrying and
General busyness in the undergrowth.

A new lifecycle has begun, and the
Woodland glows with pride.

Isobel Scarlett

NOSTALGIA

Nostalgia: a feeling of depression.
All this detriment should not inhibit
The natural process and progress
Of any potential promise or ability,
Which we may have for a further
Expansion of our own ideas.
Opportunity, when accepted, can have
Unexpected success, surprise.
Perhaps a new lifestyle or ideal goal
Will be the result of our achievement
And ambition to attain pursuance.
The realisations of all one's effort
Are our contributions fulfilled.
Such motivation revitalises
The mind and spirit physiology.
This is invaluable and promotes
Success in ourselves to overcome
Unpredictable events we have faced.
Having succeeded, our abilities appreciated
And materialised, we obtain our reward.

Sheila Spence

A DREAM

A dream that came to me today
Sometime in my life, far away
A pleasant dream or not
I can't make out.

What was it about, subconscious, more than
Reality is what we see
I remember now, it was about me!

I looked alone, then I could see
I'd been here before
My mum and dad sat at the door.

I was playing with a doll
With no hair
I loved that doll!
Why am I seeing this?
So many years have passed
It was mine, a special time!

Why was this dream
When I was nine
On my mind?
My mum and dad were so clear
I wish they were still here.

Pamela Hawksley Blackburn

LONG BEFORE CELLINI

Once, in an unimaginable time/place, that first sculptor,
of inconceivable dexterity, fashioned orbs of beauty and grace
with such original delicacy, that all but one could see
with elation, the overwhelming supremacy of that great creation.

Then, in an uncontrollable jealous rage, that one onlooker,
of such overweening vanity that he thought he could take the stage
and steal the praise for all eternity, soiled, in his enmity, one orb
                                                                that shone,
foolishly believing that he'd see its total destruction . . .

But, such an incomparable work of art could not ever be destroyed
by such rank temerity and so, the blackness of his heart
turned against him in his foul perfidy, his only certainty,
that he'd not run from his future's only surety, his complete damnation

Now, in Hell, with indefatigable hate, he labours still each day
with that same blind stupidity, to tempt men to eat from his plate
those same fruits that once sealed his destiny; never understanding
man's salvation is promised for all eternity by Christ's crucifixion.

G V Lewis

GOD'S HARVEST

Oh! My Lord God! I look around me, what do my eyes see?
Your countryside, tame yet wild and free,
I see the leaves all gaily coloured falling from tree after tree
And the field's once fresh brown earth now covered
In a variety of yellow and gold
As the different grains ripen and flowers unfold.
I see the farmers working so hard to gather in the hay,
Stacking it neatly in the farmyard.
In the orchards the fruits are turning red and yellow,
Golden and purple, plus lovely shades of green,
As the apples, pears and plums ripen ready to be plucked
And sent to the markets and shops.
I marvel, Lord, as I realise Your work in creation never stops.
First we have the spring with the planting and new birth,
Then comes the summer with the warm sun and rain,
To feed the seeds in the earth.
Soon it is harvest time as autumn draws near
And the works of Your hands, Lord, become abundantly clear.
I thank You, Lord, for all the fruits and grains,
And give You all the glory and praise.
As I eat from my table, knowing Your harvest will feed me
For the rest of my days,
Lord, help me to recognise the other fields You have sown,
Watered and ripened out there.
The fields of souls ready for that other time of reaping,
Your spiritual harvest.

Lord, help me to care.

Maureen Newman

POEM

Shall I write a poem today?
I know there's lots that I could say.
I get my paper and my pen -
A topic I must have, and then -
I hope that words will come.
To write of nature could be a bore,
It won't be worth reading, that's for sure.
How about pets? That could be nice,
I have a dog, a cat and mice.
What about babies? They're very sweet,
With cute little smile and dimpled cheek.
Or shall I write about my work?
No! there I'm just an office jerk.
I think some more, but it would seem,
I cannot think of one good theme.
The words just will not come,
I guess today I'll leave it be,
And go and make a cup of tea.
Maybe tomorrow I will find
That thoughts again will fill my mind.

Mary Stoner

OUR LAST FAREWELL

My dearest darling, I watched you slip away
Yellow mouth open wide, gasping breath another day
Fleshless arms, spindly legs, torso draped in skin
The misery and pain you must have been in
Blood flowing venom invading lifeless cells
Gastric juices running riot, belching hell
Never failing as promised I would come
Gently holding hands, whisper brave man well done
Arms embraced, stroking hair, touching face, gentle smile
Tepid tears flooding cheeks like the River Nile
Darling, it's time to bid you my last goodbye
Kissing white doves in Heaven we will abide.

Pamela Harrison

WHO NEEDS LOVE?

Who needs love?

When life is good,
Who needs love?
I do.
Because without it the bad never becomes good,
The shadows never fade,
The black clouds never leave.

When life is gone,
Who needs love?
I do.
Because without it who will remember me,
The flowers by my grave will crumble into ash,
The rain alone will not wash the tears away.

Scott Humphrey

BECKY

Our little princess you have gone,
Forever out of sight,
Our angel girl, our special pearl,
You left us in the night.

That night you left without us,
That night you left us here,
That night we said would never come,
Has come too soon our dear.

Four special years we shared your life,
Your smiles lit up our days,
For this our love we thank you,
And remember you this way.

Tears are for expressing grief,
But they're simply not enough,
To express the feelings that we feel,
When we lose someone we love.

Our lives were so fulfilled with you,
We thought it would never end,
But now that we are all alone,
Our hearts will never mend.

For Becky you are loved so much,
And greatly will be missed,
Our angel girl, our special pearl,
We part with loving kiss.

S L Howe

WHY GRANNY, WHY?

'Why Granny, why? Why did Jesus die?'
'He died to save the world my dear.'
'But Granny, that's not very clear
To save the world from sin you say
But bad things happen every day.
Killings, fighting, men at war
Was that what Jesus died for?'
'He died so that the world might live
His dying wish, *forgive, forgive,*
That's not always an easy word to say,
Never an easy role to play.
But we must try and live in peace,
Goodwill to men, all wars must cease,
Else Jesus, hanging wracked with pain
Will have lived and died in vain
And generations on, they still will cry,
Why Granny, why? Why did He die?'

Frances S Jaffray

COUNTY CLASS

Strike it rich
    mean what you say
Or go away
    streetwise
No sense in losing out
    something to shout about
County class
    in line with the guys
Never been seen on television
    with the county class
Crumble to the sea
    wash away the blues
Invite the greens
    woman press wise
Driving me here or there
    throughout County Hampshire
Saying this or that
    special lady
Calling all taxis in Hampshire
    county class: great stuff
Context slowly but surely
    write the right stuff
Score true excellence in county class.

S M Thompson

GENTLE RUTH

One day God was careless
And left his door ajar
My mother softly tiptoed through
And Heaven gained a star

One day I will join her
Again to see her face
My tears will fall like raindrops
As I run to her embrace

Too long, too long our parting
My need to feel her love
Is tempting me to leave my pain
And hasten me above

Yet every time I feel I might
And doubt my mortal worth
I hear her cry from Heaven
'The stars look best from Earth'

So every night with upturned face
I look into the blue
And think of how I loved her
And hope, somehow, she knew

Anne Wheble

THINKING TIME

Look back into the memories of life -
half seen with clarity, half through a fog,
some welcome, others but a catalogue
of chilled embarrassment and distant strife.
Whichever form they take, the threads run rife;
if of a happy bent, they pause, yet slip
away, whilst beastly thoughts renew their grip
and plague the conscience still, that still we writhe.
Thrice blest are they, who, by some lucky streak
committed all their errors in the dark;
spared public pain, but by recall made weak,
each memory recalled by but a spark.
Yet we must move ahead, beyond a bleak
blast from the past, and etch a deeper mark.

Philip Dyson

THE MEANING OF CHRISTMAS

Christmas - it's a word that conjures up so many things,
Presents, parties, food and drink - did I hear angels' wings?
The shops begin in August to tell us what to do,
They decorate their windows and build Santa's grottoes too.
The streets and houses are ablaze with twinkling fairy lights;
But shepherds tend their flocks throughout the cold and
                    lonely nights.
The TV ads implore us to purchase numerous gifts;
But sometimes, on the evening breeze, the sound of carols lifts.
We send so many greetings cards to friends both near and far;
But what about the wise men who followed a bright star?
They and the shepherds made their way as fast as they were able,
To find the star had come to rest above a lowly stable.
No doubt their joy was unconfined, excitement filled the air,
For they were all enchanted to find a special baby there.
So, enjoy your parties, give your gifts, with friends and family
                    round you,
But remember what Christmas really means, whatever else you do.
Oh, we must never once forget what Christmas means to us,
Must look beyond the trimmings and the indulgent fuss.
For the most important thing, no matter what they say,
Is that Jesus Christ, Our Saviour, was born on Christmas Day.

Peggy Seeley

VE DAY

Churchill stood proud, the crowd gave a mighty roar
Victory had come to Europe, ending the bloody war
Bonfires were lit, the heart of London glowed
Honours to our men and women later became bestowed
Six long years of bullets, doodlebugs, bombs and death
Victory came to Europe, sweet words upon our breath
People were dancing in the streets, armchairs and tables
                    came outdoors
Jubilance, rejoicing, soldiers returning, many with battle sores
Evacuees were packing, soon to be on the charabancs and trains
Back to Mum and Dad and siblings, no more pining and easing pains
The telegram boys, our angels of death and war
Brought news of surviving loved ones, bringing hope for evermore
Flags and bunting flying represented peace, calm, quiet and
                    brought a light
No more, no, no more would our menfolk fight
Our brothers in arms were free, coming home and walking tall
Bringing to us freedom, a freedom to us all
Huge losses were felt, it was the end of a bloody war
Memories and scars ran deep, down to the very core
Men could still hear the bombs, feel the loss of mates
And God, how it feels, the bitter taste of hate
Britain became great, in our heroes we triumphed for sure
Securing life for future generations came from this damning war
For sixty long years we have been blessed with peace
Victory in Europe, let's pray this will never cease.

Jacky Dale

WISHFUL THINKING

I blow you a kiss it floats on the air
Invisible love it pauses there.
Caught on a breeze lifted up high
Skimming the trees searching the sky.
Resting on clouds and warmed by the sun
Full of sweet memories now that you're gone.
Then upward it soars, it almost has wings
This kiss filled with love
And the longing it brings.
Journeying through space it catches a star
Then waits there in Heaven, for that's where you are.

Jacquelyn Harby

MY JESUS

My Jesus, my Jesus, come to me
    Come to me
My Jesus, my Jesus, stay with me
    Stay near me
You are so caring, so loving, so giving,
You are so beautiful, so kind, so forgiving

My Jesus, my Jesus, come to me
    Come to me
My Jesus, my Jesus, stay near me
    Stay near me
You are so generous, so healing, so giving,
You are so patient, so pure, life is for living

My Jesus . . . my Jesus.

Iroulla A Kyriakou

THE FIRST JOURNEY

(Written on my son's first day at school)

Well - bye-bye our sweet little boy
As you take your first faltering steps
Away from the nest that has feathered you
And tried to give you the best
Now out in the world, so strange and new
Just a shy little brown-eyed lad
No longer can we shield you away
From influences that may be bad
From the womb and the cradle and reassuring hugs
And the warmth and security of home
You now have wings, it's time to fly
The first journey on your own.

Karen Neville

THE GRAVEL PIT

I used to live in a gravel pit
Surrounded by trees and fields
Behind the hedges and high banks
Our caravan was concealed.

A private haven in paradise
A cosy little nook
Where a shallow stream ran through a lane
Down to a shady brook.

Dad made a lovely garden
With nasturtium and Canterbury bell
And with the aid of a hazel twig
He built a little well.

We had the sounds of crickets in the evening
In the fields of wheat and corn
The hooting of the owl in the night
And the songs of the birds at dawn.

The sweet smell of honeysuckle and clover
That filled the evening air
And the little red eyes of the hazel
That you hardly knew were there.

Each day I'd run free in wild fields
Chasing butterflies through the flowers
Or lay on my back on the soft green grass
Watching skylarks hovering for hours.

Margaret Cryer

REMEMBRANCE

Sixty years have passed
In France red poppies grow,
A reminder of the terrible bloodshed
Still sad at heart to know
Of homes bereaved, the sorrow and heartache
For loved ones lost so far away.
Brave men who fought and died
In our memories will forever stay
For King and country battles fought
Steadfast comrades side by side
Fighting for victory, ever in danger
Committed soldiers from far and wide.
Valiant in the struggle for freedom
Brave airmen and seamen who
Gave their lives that we might live
No greater sacrifice could anyone give.
We give thanks remembering them
The bravest of the brave
And pay tribute to those whom
Our homeland did save.

Greta Craigie

FOR MY GRANDDAUGHTER, ALIYAH JAYNE

(Aged six months)

My blood runs in your blood,
You're a little part of me,
A tiny special person,
With all the world to see.
Your eyes look all around you,
Delight shines on your face,
Happiness radiates from you,
Frustration? Just a trace.
You want whatever's out of reach,
You're forever on the go,
Arms and legs, they never stop,
And bubbles - can you blow!
Your life lies all in front of you,
Exciting things to do,
But first you have to conquer
Sitting and crawling too.
Your eyes are bright, your smile a delight,
Your excitement bubbles through,
No worries yet - just food and sleep,
And everything's brand new.

Hilary Vint

A PSALM IN PRAISE OF THE CREATOR

Dancing butterfly dance for Jesus
In the sunlight by the river
Let the sunshine play on your colourful wings
As you dance with joy to Jesus

Pretty river as you bubble and splash
And dash on your way
Sparkle and shine for Jesus crystal clear
Nothing to fear
Splashing with joy for Jesus

Little daisies lift your faces
Smile with delight for Jesus
Sway in the breeze and wave your leaves
Lift high the name of Jesus

Blessed countryside remember your God
Mountain high and lowly sod
Flowers and rivers and age-old trees
Creatures all fall upon your knees
And worship your creator.

M Bloomfield

HOME

Home is such a little word,
Which covers such a lot,
From the old man in his easy chair,
To the baby in his cot.
It doesn't have to be a place,
Of antiques, gold or splendour,
Just a simple little cottage,
Full of joy and truth and candour.
Where from understanding parents,
You learn the right from wrong,
Where you are taught to be upstanding
And grow up brave and strong.
Home is where you learn to share
And respect your fellow man,
To see each other's point of view
And be as tolerant as you can.
It is a place of love and laughter,
Of grumbles, frowns and tears,
But no place else, in all this world,
Can you spend happier years.
It is a place you are always welcome to,
No matter how you err,
It will put its arms around you,
For home means love and care.
A meeting place for families,
Where you don't have to pretend,
Where you never feel like a stranger
And you are welcome to the end.
So boys and girls, if you have strayed and on the streets do roam,
Come, darling, to your home sweet home and you'll never
                                                    walk alone.

Mary Daly

COME PRECIOUS CHILD

Come precious child - my mantle of love awaits on your newness -
My cloak of care bid trouble be viewless -
My robe of prudence let swaddle your being -
My cape of diligence veil burden from seeing -

Come precious child - I will teach you to hear,
of all timbre to listen -
Of birdsong display, of mystic music glisten -
Of the sea that pounds on authentic stoned shore -
Of whisperings of knowing love, gone before -

Come precious child - you will know by your birth the scent
of your mother -
The bouquet of beauty, the redolence of all other -
I will teach you, nose high, to follow the breeze -
Fragrance of my love, pray, always bring you ease -

Come precious child - you must taste the bitter
to sample the sweet -
The sharp I will soften, the honeyed entreat -
Of good things, I will teach you to bite on the flavour -
Knowing love's relish is for your lips to savour -

Come precious child - fondle the texture of all and varied hue -
Touch the sense of now, caress both old and new -
Cuddle the creatures that crawl below and soar above -
I would teach you all this, with the kiss, that always is my love -

Come precious child - let me take you on a wondrous flight -
O'er the gold of the morn, the silver of the night -
O'er the blue of the river, the green of the vale -
O'er my many coloured love, for you ne'er to fail -

Come precious child - my love will be with you forever and a day -
With my love I will teach you to learn and to play -
My love will be with you in calm, in the wild -
My love will be with you always, my miracle child -

Phil Leese

BRANKSOME DENE CHINE REVISITED

Telescopic sights rolled
Back thirty years
Me crouching spade
In hand digging
Boat or otherwise a moat

Cappuccino-filled pool;
Once brought here
Now the child-bringer
Memories dew-freshened
Rather than crashed by breakers.

Helen Dean

LVIV, A CITY OF DEFIANCE

Lviv,
city of Ukraine.
In its dilapidated splendour
finding its identity
from years of colonialism.
Peeling at the edges,
frayed at the sides,
battered and bruised but
proud.
The faded opulence of architecture
from a long gone Austro-Hungarian Empire,
and Polish nobles, now forgotten and buried.
Rise, rising from Soviet Russian destruction.
Rebuilding churches in defiance of atheism.
Lviv,
with peeling paint, spluttering fountains,
statues of Cossack heroes and poets.
Walking at night on your
majestic cobbled streets,
where haggard trolley buses roll,
Lviv,
I fall in love with you,
as you rise defiant, welcoming all.

Roman Suchyj

NEW DAWN

You are young for decades and a day
while the sun speeds at ease
across your span of sky
and the waxing-waning moon
sails above
your half-acre of fallow, crops
and thistles

when of a sudden evening sets in -
if the saps are stilled in wooden veins
if the chestnut leaf twirls,
curves, crackles and chafes its sickle-shape
over bark, brick and bramble,
ending in shreds

then, knowing the signs by a thin margin of time
and the narrow passage of breath,
as your vision dims you tremble -
for the living and the images lag behind
and there is no comparison
and there is no companion
and you wait
and trembling you turn your face towards the hills
and you wait for this dawn
awesome, piercing, tender,
new
never witnessed before.

Françoise de Pierpont

O' RUSTIC WEEPING WILLOW TREE

O' rustic weeping willow tree, could you maybe spend some time
with me?
I want to reminisce once more, of happier times I had before,
The days when by my side she'd stand, and in your shade she'd
take my hand,
I'd feel her love so warm and tender, her radiance I still remember.

O' rustic weeping willow tree, is it possible you weep for me?
For she who loved me years ago, does not love me anymore.
We share our dreams then drift apart, I'm left to nurse an aching
heart,
But the memories can't take the place, of seeing a smile upon
her face.

O' rustic weeping willow tree, I wonder if she thinks of me,
Does she recall the hours we spent, the times we talked and where
we went,
While I remember, where we met, does she find it simpler to forget?
Do the inner feelings I revealed, remain inside her, still concealed?

O' rustic weeping willow tree, I'm as sad as any man can be,
While sitting here I'm left to ponder, if absence makes the heart grow
fonder,
If that's the case it's safe to say, she may return to me someday,
I only hope I never find, that out of sight means out of mind.

O' rustic weeping willow tree, I've always known where you would be,
We carved our initials in your bark, and vowed each year we would
come back,
But this year the pilgrimage I take, is simply just for old time sake,
So that as we stand here on our own, you'll know you'll never weep
alone.

James Stirrat

MY CHURCH

Your peace, O Lord, is all around
As in Your church I pray,
The quiet stillness does abound
And helps me on my way.

Your presence Lord, is ever near
As at Your cross I kneel,
So comforting and strengthening,
Your guiding hand I feel.

Your joy, O Lord, is in each hymn
That in Your church I sing,
My praises to a God so great,
My Saviour, helper, King.

Your word, O Lord, is there to guide
As in Your church I hear,
It speaks of love and truth and joy,
Says trust and never fear.

Your love, O Lord, it means so much,
As in Your church I go;
O let me always show the love
That You to others show.

Your church, O Lord, it means so much
As in Your church I go;
O let me always show the love
That You to others show.

Your church, O Lord, it is so great,
An honour to belong,
May many come to worship You
In prayer and praise and song.

Daphne Harman Young

DREAMING IN ACAIRSEID MOR

Sitting
    In afternoon sun
    Warm wood under bare toes toasting.
Silence
    Increased by a distant discussion of gulls.
Breeze
    Blows softly over arms no longer clad
    Defensively in damp synthetic fur.
Reading
    Adrian Henri
    In the streets of Liverpool
    Seeing the spring in plastic daffodils.
Seaweed
    Hangs brown and yellow over children's caves.
    Thick, heavy hair for half-tide rocks
    That come and go like mermaids.
Seal
    Teapot tilted on its seaweed rock.
    Soaking in sun.
    Short-sightedly sniffing round the air-filled world.
Silence
    The clearances come clear through Calum's Fiddle.
    Every event, with the dignity of design,
    Deserving the duty of the dance.

Bill Waugh

PUPPET ON A STRING

What's the point in wasting life,
Obeying some greedy master,
Who's shouting off his mouth,
'Boy, you gotta do it faster!'

No use carrying that monkey on your back,
The b*****d will only bring you stress
And heart attack.

Why should we sell our souls to the modern day rat race,
Where humanity seems to be completely out of place.

Working hard just to find out it was all in vain,
Your loss has no meaning as long as it's their gain.

There's more to life than being a slave to the grind,
But are we too far gone?
Have we become deaf and blind?

Olli Suntinen

THE GIRL IN THE HOURGLASS

Soft shining sand drifting on a timeless sea,
Not knowing if she ever cares for me,
Like the sands of time, running out fast,
Will I ever catch her up at last?
I think not for I am slow and too old now
For such frivolous thought,
Emotions dance in erratic mood, twisted and taut,
The girl in the hourglass that cannot get out,
She warms up my spirit, but softens my heart,
Just a foolish old man with a soft spot I know,
This girl in the hourglass that torments me so.

B Smedley

TIE

I dare you
to hang there
ready and chilling,
pit-black and humble,
a few quids' worth flung
peg-down, smug and at ease.

On uneven slate,
you scratch name after
shame, talk of the drivel,
from lives at an ending
-place, chasing their mentor:

We shimmer and shiver
with you, without use
unsharing the days'
shaded deeds,

always.

Will Daunt

THE SALON (AS SEEN AND HEARD BY A MAN WAITING FOR HIS WIFE)

I enter the salon, my first time there,
I hear they do marvellous things with your hair
A young lady approaches, 'Would you please come this way?'
Oh! Er! I did not know what really to say
My coat is taken through a side door
I have never been pampered like this before
They rest my head in a horseshoe-shaped sink
What's next, I really cannot begin to think?
The water is warm, the shampoo smells sweet
Her fingers move fast, this is a real treat
Now I am escorted to a big leather chair
Another young lady (my stylist) is awaiting me there
She snips and brushes, the dryer is going full blast
My chosen style is taking shape at long last
I am shown the back in a mirror produced from nowhere
Is that me? It's hard to believe, I swear
Now is the time to pay, worth every penny I'd say
I have booked for next week, same time, same day.

Trevor Beach

A YORKSHIRE CHILDHOOD

What happened to those characters
still vivid in my memory?
What happened to them after they died?
What happened to that old man, Mr Clough,
who had a cold bath before breakfast every day?
Is he still searching for structure in infinity?

What happened to that man
who ladled fresh milk from his churn
into the jugs left out for him each night
on every well-scrubbed doorstep down our road?
Does he still miss the old routine,
the sense of being vital to the neighbourhood?

What happened to that dinner lady
who, with arms akimbo, used to say,
'Hasn't your mother learned you yet
to stack your dirties on a tray?'
Does she look down at schools today
and see that *system* still remains the key
to worthwhile living in a community?

What happened to them, each of these three?
What happened to them after they died?
Is their respect for daily discipline
acknowledged in eternity?

Wenna Taylor

I SAW A CHILD

I saw a child
Who had no home;
Huddled, he crouched upon the stone
And in his face
Was emptiness

His eyes held mine
And mesmerised
I saw an infant traumatised.
We stared and stared
With hopelessness

There was no message
To discern,
No mutual spark from which to learn
Why he kept watch
Expressionless

Then suddenly
As from above
I knew that hope is born of love,
This child knew
Only lovelessness

He only knew
Life as a cheat,
Thrown out, like rubbish, on the street
To live or die
Through carelessness

My heart, my soul
Began to weep.
What sorrow from my God I'd reap
If I turned back
In heartlessness

I saw a child
Who had no home.
Not now - for his would be my own
And on our faces
Joyfulness.

Doreen Wildrianne

BLUEBELL SKIES

My garden sings a lullaby, as I dream in her arms
For this is where the fairies live safe from any harm
Butterflies and bumblebees share honeysuckle wine
While hummingbirds safely nest in blue wisteria vine
From strawberry beds the fairies rise
To start their days under bluebell skies.

The rose in bloom is their ivory tower
As they dance till dusk on the jasmine flower
Forget-me-nots in golden hair
Wings of silk everywhere
Cherry-red lips, violet eyes
Apple blossom dreams under bluebell skies.

Then late at night when the moon is bright
They all fly home by the stars' own light
Fairies with hummingbirds, butterflies and bees
All gather together in my willow tree
Soon they are singing a lullaby
And my garden sleeps under bluebell skies.

A fairy is innocence, love and trust
As she tends each flower with fairy dust
A fairy lets us dare to believe in dreams
As she gathers wild berries and buttercup cream
And if you believe as much as I
She will tell you her secrets under bluebell skies.

Maureen Gentry-Evans

UNTITLED

We thought you'd like to know,
That someone's starting to show.
A special announcement's in the air,
A new baby to declare.

What a surprise we had that day,
Seemed things weren't going our way.
How wrong could we have been?
As the truth remained unseen.

Developing day by day,
Progressing week by week.
Soon we'll have a photo,
So you can take a peek,

We've still a while to go,
So plenty of time to prepare.
The signs are becoming clearer,
I do have to declare.

It'll be worth it soon you'll say,
When on that special day,
A very special delivery
Will be making his or her own way.

Here's to it, cheers!

Kerridwen Niner

THE TWISTER

Batten down the hatches
The twister's on its way.
Can you hear the noise it makes
Like an express train?

The sky is dark and threatening
On this terrifying day.
Nature's turned against us
Now our home is washed away.

The lightning snakes across the sky
In sheet and fork formation.
Destruction of the landscape
And the creatures of creation.

The joy of surviving
The killer storm has ceased
Heroes are both great and small
The greatest and the least.

Anne Goulbourne

BY INVITATION ONLY

Perched on the steps
conspicuous
as two birds
on the branch
of a leafless tree . . .

They nagged at the bell
on the unmarked door,
wine bottles chiming
in their carrier bags.

Called to the evening
with its curtains drawn:
'Is there anyone there?'
'Is the party here?'

No longer summer voices
dance in the dawn,
with music unheeded
'No, it is not here.'

Elsewhere . . .

Heather Walker

ARE WE NEARLY THERE?

Have you ever tried to sleep in the middle of the day,
When, in the street outside, you can hear your friends at play?
Eyes shut tight you toss and turn, willing yourself to rest,
Wishing Mum would say it's time to get up again and dress.
Excitement mounts on seeing the suitcases by the door,
With Christopher's favourite teddy beside them on the floor.
Then, as the mantel clock chimes ten, a taxicab arrives;
Dad quickly loads the cases whilst we all climb inside.
On reaching the railway station, we eagerly alight,
But it's unusually quiet, like the middle of the night!
We're greeted on the platform by a smiling Uncle Tom -
He's the stationmaster and knows where all the trains come from.
As the big, black locomotive stands proudly in its place,
We meet the driver and the fireman, who's got a sooty face.
Burning coals inside the furnace, cause sparks to shoot up high,
Reminding us of Guy Fawkes' night as they lighten up the sky.
Belching smoke and hissing steam send us scurrying back to Mum,
I hope she's now unpacked the food - I've got a rumbling tum!
Standing by the window, we wave goodbye to Uncle Tom
Who's blowing his silver whistle; then the night train lumbers on.
Soon we're sleeping soundly to the rhythmic clickety-clack
Of speeding train wheels as they cover many miles of track.
When we wake up hours later, it will be another day,
And we'll see the small boats bobbing at their moorings in the bay.
This sight of blue waves shining in the early morning sun,
Will tell us what we want to know - our holiday has begun!

Carol Anne Edwards

BADGER'S RUN

Badger - a dog,
Flies in warp drive,
Spaced out between
The dandelion stars.
His is a universe of
Happiness where the sky
Is blue and bumblebee
Spaceships circulate
Strange golden worlds
Seeking unknown
Civilisations to trade
For pollens.
But Badger races on
Now he is the Dog Star
And his constellation
He marks by frequent
Pawses for others, later,
To understand:
Badger was here first!
This space belongs to me!
And they will chuckle
Raise one leg,
A false salute,
A counterclaim upon this
Counterpane of brightest flowers.
Badger flies on, running fast
Because it is good
To be a member of his race
When the wind is warm
About black nose and ears.
The trees sparkle unfurling
Their sun interceptors
And we all feel
The sap rising.

Peter Godfrey

ODE TO THE CALENDAR GIRLS

Eleven lively young ladies from Rylstone and District WI
Decided to make a calendar, something to catch the eye,
Past calendars of the Yorkshire Dales, was always a regular scheme,
Now this is something we are prepared to do, a complete change
of scene.

These eleven lovely ladies came up with something rare,
It was discussed at length, that they dare,
Be brave - and yes, you have guessed!
It was decided to go bare.

These eleven lovely ladies from Rylstone and District WI
Were especially very discreet, a hobby each they displayed,
It really was a treat.

Not the least indiscretion they did show,
Their hobbies helped with that, a mixing bowl in the right place
Definitely saw to that.

The piano had the frontal view, very neatly placed,
The pianist was slightly turned, there was nothing out of place,
A string of pearls on their soft skins, an object held in front of them,
Just enough to show a curve, these lovely ladies that had the nerve.

It wasn't for self glory, their aim was well worthwhile,
To raise a fund for leukaemia, it was this they had in mind.
They never thought it would entail
The publicity, TV, radio and The Mail.

On and on it goes, there is no end to the fame this calendar brought,
The results are stupendous, it was made with love and thought
To give help to others along life's way, the calendars they bought,
Thousands and thousands of pounds you raised,
Your dedication has been well praised
Congratulations to all of you, especially the Calendar Girls.

Pat Fenton

SPHERES OF BEING

At last again I hear the music of the spheres.
I see their colours . . . feel their tears.
The universe, again is mine.
Because . . . I have you back from time.
It was immeasurably long . . . the briefest time . . . when you were
gone.

But now again at last you're there.
My fears away, we, once more can share.
Our 'well' of love and friendship
So, please stay forever here.
When I say here . . . I mean my soul.
As physically I cannot hold you.
But . . . inside me . . . my heart, my brain.
I keep you safe . . . and can attain perfection.
Transfusions, are from time to time, essential for this life of mine.
Letters, calls, all add up too.
As long as I know, you . . . are there.
Think of me . . . and simply care.
I have a lovely peaceful life, and cause no harm, pain, or strife.
This too is essential for my being.
As one day, I must face . . . my, all seeing, God.
I do believe we have already met
We are all part of the whole.
But I . . . won't know this for sure, until my soul is released to eternity.

So the time between now and then.
I hope to cause no pain or shame.
But happiness . . . yes this I want.
And for this . . .you are my font . . . thank you.

Sheila Mack

CAPTAIN MARS

Captain Mars was yellow and green,
He was always heard but seldom seen.
Seldom seen but always heard
Was this beautiful green and yellow bird.

Captain Mars lived in a cage
Of silver bars of incredible age.
Unbelievably old were the silver bars
Of the cage which was home to Captain Mars.

He fought with a cat when he was young,
And over this battle his songs were sung.
When he was young he defeated Cat,
And the songs he sang were all about that.

One night Captain Mars fell down.
They made him a bed that was moist and brown.
Warm and soft was the little bed
That they made for the Captain when he was dead.

It froze all night and it snowed all day,
And no one knew where the Captain lay.
It snowed all day and it froze all night
And the Captain was lost in a mass of white.

The wind got up and away it blew
All of the snow, and the flowers grew.
The flowers bobbed on the little mound
Which covered the Captain without a sound.

The flowers were yellow, the leaves were green,
They were never heard and seldom seen.
Rarely seen and never heard
Were the flowers that covered the gallant bird.

Fred Brown

THE DAYS OF YESTERYEAR

Folk had to rise at crack o' dawn,
When the day had just begun,
The women had to hurry on,
They had a set of looms to run.

A chap might do a shift int' pit,
Or run a spinning frame,
And if he earned an extra quid,
He was a master at his game.

At dinnertime, and half-past five,
The streets were filled with folk,
Hurrying here, and scurrying there,
This shopping was no joke.

The hours were long, the work was hard,
In the dark satanic mill,
But people coped, and had a laugh,
They'd got living to a skill.

But they closed the pit, and shut the mill,
And the streets are quiet now.
Some people say it's progress,
Yet it's not the same, somehow.

The little shop that served us well,
Most of them are gone,
It's a queue up at the checkout now,
And that's your shopping done.

They say standing still is moving back,
That progress must be made,
Perhaps we should stop the clock a second
And see what should be saved.

J Knott

LIGHT

(Christmas 2001)

The rising sun heralds the day
With rays of golden light.
The silver moonlight treads a path
Across the sea at night.

The trusty lighthouse sends its beam
Over the raging foam,
And warns our sailors from the rocks
And guides them safely home.

Fireworks light up the sky
In glittering cascades,
And brilliant sparks fly upwards
From the bonfire's cheery blaze.

Lanterns and torches light the path
Where no city lamp posts glow,
When carol choirs sing joyfully
In villages, in snow.

As fairy lights shine on the tree
And candles light the table,
Remember, *Christ, light of the world*
Was born in Bethlehem's stable.

And ask Him, as we bow our heads to pray,
'Lord help me light up someone's life, today.'

Kathleen Whitty

FAREWELL DEAR FATHER

Knarled hands resting,
Breath rattles, labouring,
The soft light in the room
Peaceful, gentle.

Looking down at the frail body
Drifting now from this world,
Taking the unresisting hand
Faith tells me he will hear
The words unrehearsed -

Breath slows, and then
Gentle as a soft breeze -
He has heard, he can go
With love to ease his passage home.

Joan M Hopkins

HANNAH'S SMILE

Of all the many sights I've seen,
On travels by air, land and sea,
It would tax my memory to say,
Which has most appealed to me.
For I have strolled the palm fringed shorelines,
That embrace the far Seychelles,
And that is an enduring image,
That still in my memory dwells.
But it seems there are so many things,
That crowd my memory's store,
It appears there's very little left,
That I've a yearning to explore.
Now I have a grandchild, Hannah,
And others wryly raise an eye,
When they hear a grandchild's merits,
With fervour lauded to the sky.
But of those many things I've seen,
And it's not for just a while,
All fade into insignificance,
When I see Hannah smile.

Edward McCartney

MIDWAY VISION

From my wheelchair I see
Only things at half height
How can anyone explain
The meaning of full sight
To me on this day, when I am feeling so low?
Yet to see a child's face full of radiant glow,
Turns darkness from gloom into light.

I thank God I still see
His fine beauty and art
Although it's hard to accept
I perceive a small part
Of this bountiful world and splendour of Man
Yet to have such clear sight to see what I can
I humbly give praise from my heart.

Janet Collinson

LOCH CARRON

I sit on the wall at the seafront
Looking all about me
And taking it all in . . .

The line of plain, white-painted little houses,
A couple of inns and a shop,
Their gardens on the opposite side of the road,
Where flowers and several palm trees
Grow right beside the shore.

The rippled water of the harbour
Reflects a bright blue sky
With small clouds scumbled upon it.
A few yachts and fishing boats
Turn slowly about their moorings in the breeze.

A jagged crag points like a finger out into the sea
Towards a little tree-covered island,
And a grey castle stands among the green pines
On the hillside beyond.

As I turn my head to look this way and that
I say softly to myself, 'Jesus, Jesus, Jesus.'
Everywhere I look, my eyes
Drink in the beauty of the place
And at last my soul is nourished.

Through years of breakdowns and emotional
Setbacks, I yearned for this place that I love.
Now I am actually here
To receive this gift to myself
That I have waited so long to claim.

Andrew Spencer

AH! WELL

The days of my youth
Are ebbing away
Too many birthdays
Passing this way
Each one's taken its
Toll I fear
Even my mirror
Makes that clear

With all life's shams
And broken dreams
My endless thoughts
Of what might have been

The face I see
Each dawning day
Is not the one
I wore yesterday.

Joyce Hargreaves

THE MIRROR

I look in the mirror and all I can see
Is the fresh faced young bride that I know was once me
Laughing and happy, my husband and I
Vowing to love till the day that we die
Along came the children, our lives were complete
We listened with joy to the sound of small feet

I look in the mirror and now I can see
A middle-aged woman I know once was me
Still smiling, still happy, a sprinkling of grey
The children all grown, and now moving away

I look in the mirror and now all I see
A mature grey haired lady I know that is me
A whimsical smile now resides on my face
Our grandchildren grow at a frightening pace

I look in the mirror and just about see
The very old lady who stares back at me
Our children, their children, grown proud and tall
And I smile at the part that played in it all.

Carol Turner

THE OLD VERGER

For sixty years he's climbed the hill
To where the Norman church stands firm,
And trod a welcome on the stairs
That spiral to the topmost room
Where every afternoon the clock
And bells await his regular hands.
But very soon he knows there'll be
An absence there, a soundless chime
When age and death have stopped his time.

The young folk off of city jaunts,
The families in crowded cars,
Forget the hours that never sound,
And never think of yesterday
Until their time has come. And then
They'll stare up at the silent clock
And want to move the dead hands back,
But know they have no craft, so lack
A future now the past has flown.

June Benn

AND DID THOSE FEET?

There was a time when Saturday was thus.
Son and father catch the bus to town,
And, climbing down, are swallowed
In a stream of scarf-swathed bodies
Flowing past the factories
Which echo to the fearful sound
Of marching to the football ground.

And, moving up to pack the terraced stand,
The pitch gleams green and draws all eyes.
A moment comes when sound is stilled
Then walls are rattled with ecstatic cries
And into sunlight march two armies, led
By gods who own the cheers with proud held head.

It is a bloody battle down below
But fathers, sons and uncles chant and sway.
The home team falters then receives a blow,
Concedes one goal and fights to save the day.
We score! Delight! It is not over yet -
Then Heaven smiles. Again the ball
Lands in the opposition's net.

The homeward trudge is made by lighter feet,
They float, elated, yards above the street.

Gill Pomfret

HOME-MADE

The café where I went for a snack
Has chalked up menus on boards of black
All sorts of meals they proudly boast
Mushrooms, cheese or beans on toast.
Jacket potatoes most temptingly filled
Coleslaw, tuna and salads are billed.
Coffee and tea with scones, cakes and pies
A splendid list to feast the eyes.
These many delights with artistic decor
What hungry patron could ask for more?
But one other item appears on the list
Something, I feel which should not be missed
On a separate board proudly displayed
Various deserts - all home-made.
On a cold winter's day with the wind in the east
I imagine a desert a glorious feast
Could I have a Sahara with baking hot sun?
An oasis with dates would also be fun
I considered a Gobi, a taste of Chinese
Libyan, Nubian, what about these?
A Kalahari sounds rather grand
Perhaps there are different flavours of sand.
I went inside and picked up a tray
Towards the counter I made my way.
'What are the deserts?' I eagerly queried
The assistant answered bored and wearied
'There's all flavours of ices, trifle, cheesecake
Just hurry along – for goodness' sake.'

Rosemary Cook

WIND ON THE MOOR

There is a wind on the moor,
a south-west wind,
blowing the wisps of mist
across the face of the clouds.
Clouds that blanket the sky
in black and grey.

There is a wind in the trees,
blowing the birds
from the barns,
and the last gold leaves
from the twigs,
to join the whirling leap
of russet and brown.

There is a wind on the hills,
but the land lies quiet,
rich with manure and still
with the strength of a million years
of waiting soil, untilled.

There is a wind in the sky,
a strong, mad wind
blowing in gusts
and lifting the heart at every step;
snatching the clothes on the line,
the straw in the yard;
blowing the breath of life
into the upturned earth.
The wind - the south-west wind,
Blowing across the moor.

Diana Morcom

OCEAN VOYAGE

Surely the dream is the reality.
The influence of the environment is
The breeze upon the sail as barques, adrift
Or helmed, sweep on round rock and shoal to port
Or founder. Inside the captain's cabin
Lights aglow show charts complex and dangers
To be watched as barometers rise.
While in the mind secure the picture, slow
To unreel, inevitably bodies
Forth the real without the falsity of
Sensual pressures pull this way or that.
The haven's seen and pastures green with long-lost
Maiden's flight from home to quay to see
The ship approach the shore, never more to
Sail away alone on deep tumultuous seas of
Tyranny and pride. The dream is the bright
Star of the engine's beating heart driving,
With steady hand and eye, homeward at last.

Desmond Tarrant

MY MUM

My mum died, oh! a long time ago.
She was very old, and very slow.
We're often impatient with the old and infirm,
But it comes to us all, and we need to learn
Just what it is like, when to bend, and to kneel,
Gets harder each day and to know how they feel
When the eyes grow dim, and the hearing's impaired,
We should listen to them, and show them we care.
We none of us think *we'll* grow old and grey
While we're young and the future seems so far away.
But as we grow older, we start to see
Life slipping by, so just how will it be
When the memory fades, and we start to slow?
Since my mum died oh! a long time ago,
I've often wondered, and now I know.

Olive Smith

A FOOL

Oh what a fool I have been,
Believing this world to have no sin.
Oh, what a fool, to have listened to them
And not look into eyes of sparkling gems.
And now, what is there, but to be a fool,
A nobody. Nothing but a tool.
For others to work with and destroy.
I am nothing but a child's toy.
And joy? What of that? For there is none,
Not for me. For I am but a nun
As I walk this cold stone path.
Oh, what is it to have wrath?
To be a worker with a tool?
But no, I am just a fool.
To have believed, and yet to not.
There is the child and I, the cot.
For that is what I am in truth.
Look there, a bird upon a roof,
More free then I can ever be,
Free, like a ship upon a sea.
But alas, even a ship be a cell.
Hark; I hear the toll of a bell.
For me the end of time hath come,
And from this cell I cannot run.
A fool. That is what I am and will always be.
A fool. But from life I can be free.

Kirstie Clark

LIVING WORDS

The yellow rose the purest beauty shows,
Its heart of melting butter whets the tongue;
Whence flows its mystic beauty as it grows
With creamy petals that reflect the sun?

It's a gentle flower of love and concord
Amid times of happiness and despair;
Its life brief on Earth as was Christ's our Lord,
Nailed to the cruel cross our sins to bear.

May living words inspire us here today
And with the Master's blessing come to pass:
That we love our neighbours and for them pray
Of whichever race, colour, creed or class.

In praise a thousand tongues will gladly sing
Till this our great vision at last is won,
And God's inclusive Kingdom ushers in
The friends of all and enemies of none.

Robert Corrigan

MY PRAYER

I said a prayer today, God
But I didn't ask for wealth.
I wanted more important things
So I asked for peace and health.

I also wanted help, God
For guidance through each day
I asked for something else, God
For forgiveness and strength to pray.

In my prayer today, God
I asked for peace on Earth
That wars could be abolished
All sadness replaced by mirth.

I said a prayer today, God
For my family and friends
That we live our lives together
With contentment that never ends.

I said a prayer today, God
I wanted just to say,
'Thank you very much, God
For teaching me how to pray.'

Irene Kenny

SUMMER CIRCUS

The final curtain of springtime
Is drawn to a close
Breezes play with blossoms of the newly born rose
Daisies are peeping their heads held so high
Frilly poppies are dancing
Summer circus is nigh

Mother Nature the greatest artist of all
Paints pansy clown faces and baby dolls
Full-leafed trees waving banners
To the birds in full sing
A new audience of fledglings
Just out on a wing

The tattered old scarecrow drying out in the sun
Not just feeling himself yet his field days to come
When his own ringmaster he'll be
Till the crows all go home

Bees play their honeyful drone
On the hollyhock trombone
Till the evening air calls the tune
For tomorrow is just another bloom away.

Elizabeth McIntyre

THE WOMAN IN THE GREY FUR HAT

On a very cold January morn,
to a funeral I had to go
and I can tell you that day
I was feeling very low.
My hair was a mess
but I couldn't care less.
I would don my hat
and I would look simply the best,
(or should I say)
more simple than the rest.
Cosy and warm I would come to no harm.
That was, out in the cold!
But once inside, where was my pride?
With a grey fur hat, a bright red face
and a head that itched like mad.
Heads turned, people talked,
'I wish she would take off that hat'
'Who is she anyway?'
Ask me another!
'She said Bernard was her brother,'
'No he only had two sisters
and Kath hasn't come.'
'She has she's just borrowed my comb.'
Julie and Chris, two nieces of mine
are both wanting this hat.
Sorry girls!
When I reach the pearly gates,
God won't say, 'Who's that?'
Peter will just have to say,
'It's the woman in the grey fur hat.'

Kathleen Lockwood

IN THE TIME OF LEGENDS

When evil anarchy ruled the land
everyone fell to the power of its hand
the elves the fairies and unicorns
would never ever see another dawn
the curse would last an age or more
before the light would shine once more

In an enchanted forest there lay a wand
underneath a tree it stayed there long
the wand held the key to the fortunes of all
but could only be found by someone very small

One very cold night an elf did stray
while singing a song and going along his way
he saw a bright light at the foot of a tree
and there he found what no one else could see

A magic wand of silver and gold
began to whisper for him to behold
some words that only he could recite
would bring an end to the world of night

He spoke the words the wand did say
unaware of the power and the magic of its way
and one by one each spell disappeared
from the hearts of all as light reappeared.

The evil lord and all of his slaves
fell to the power of the light of day
and the unicorns, the fairies and all of the elves
treasured the wand and kept it to themselves.

Michael Lyons

CHRISTMAS ENTERTAINMENT 1989

This year we saw revolution on television,
not drama but the real thing.
Real people dying real deaths
Sandwiched between soap opera and comedy.
While we sat somnolent after dinner
bullets bit into bone with a noise like nuts cracking
and when the kettle boiled for tea, lifting its lid,
a whole nation boiled over into our living room.
Scalding passions, anger rising to hope
assaulted our senses with too much reality.
It was a relief to watch Coronation Street.

Later, seeing the wounded lying in pain
we opened cans of beer.
Eating chocolates we suddenly felt guilty as Nero
and resolved to send money to the Red Cross.
By Boxing Day it was almost over.
Look World! At the wicked dictator and his wife
Dead as yesterday's turkey.
That amorphous being the people has won its freedom.
The crowd is euphoric, the future uncertain.
Crowds that cry 'Hosanna' can also cry crucify.

Beryl Davidson

THE STORM

Stormy clouds roll across the sky,
As a gentle breeze begins to sigh.
Birds with their little ones fly back to the nest,
And young furry creatures follow the rest
Of the forest animals, dashing for home.
Before the first thunderclouds begin to moan
To rumble and crash, with lightning flashes,
From the sting of the rain as its fury lashes
Through the trees, that are now bending low
With the force of the wind that's begun to blow,
To screech and howl and whistle round,
Leaving a trail of havoc along the ground.
With the roar of a tempest in its wake
The entire Earth seems to quiver and quake,
As the storm twists and turns, and screams and shouts,
Then suddenly as it started, it burns itself out.
The wind has abated, the clouds roll away
And darkness has turned into brightness of day.
The sun reappears from the cloud it has waited
To warm Earth's wounds, the storm has created.

Rita Arksey

LET IT BE . . .

You spend your life
Trying to work it out
What's it all about?

When you get there
You find . . .
You had it all the time!

If you do or don't find it?

Let it be . . .
It's not important

Sadly you have to find it first
To believe

Colin Farquhar

JUST FOR YOU

If ever you feel lonely and sad,
Try to remember the best dream you've had,
I'm sure it will lift your spirits real high,
And light up the brightest star in the sky.

When you see a falling star,
It's the best brightest thing to happen by far,
Because that's the good luck coming your way,
Suddenly, it's here to stay.

Look at the sky when late at night,
You will see that star twinkling bright,
There's also wishes for you to make,
Just like magic for you to take.

Everyone hopes a guardian angel above
Is sending to Earth someone to love,
For you deserve the best and more,
I know this to be true for sure.

Hoping a special wish just for you,
Also will multiply into two,
So be happy in whatever you do,
Let's hope those wishes come true,
        'Just for you'.

Sylvia White

UNTITLED

The Fifteenth Anniversary -
A very special date!
Now what's the very best of ways
To help us celebrate?

Throughout those many months and years
We've juggled metered rhyme
To show our deeper feelings.
But you've not allowed much time

To say 'Congratulations'
To the folk at Forward Press
And wish them many more such years
Of rhythm and success.

Vivienne Constantinides

MUM'S THE WORD

Parenthood can bring immense joy
pleasure at buying a much wanted toy
Parenthood can also be daunting
bringing a halt to childless jaunting

No one prepares you for the role
when you reach the ultimate goal
No one prepares you for sleepless nights
depressing lows and dizzy height

I remember saying, 'I'll never do that,'
remember saying, 'Don't want a cat.'
I didn't always like your friends
didn't go along with all of your trends

Friends were always welcome at home
they ate our food and used our phone
Friends are very important in life
even the one's who caused me strife

Now you are a parent as well
you've come to know the Heaven and Hell
Today I hope you've come to see
what a jamboree being a parent can be.

Janet Woods

JUST SEVENTEEN

You were just a young boy
Seventeen years old
You went away to fight a war
This story has been told

You fought beside the bravest
But tears would sometimes flow
Each time a mate had left you
You cried to see him go

Growing up was hard for you
Living in the mud
Down inside cold trenches
Where you saw the sight of blood

So many times you prayed to God
Please take me away from here
But somehow time was turning
Into another year

You were just a young boy
When you went away
But you are now a grown up man
My son what can I say

I never meant for you to see
The things that you have seen
You went away far too young
A boy of seventeen.

Florence Davies

SECRETS

Who knows what secrets lie within an envelope?
To cheer, congratulate or give us hope,
An unexpected letter, cheque or birthday card?
A letter of thanks, a photograph to treasure,
A long-lost friendship distance cannot measure.
A bill, a credit card or Christmas card,
Or just a simple anniversary card,
A letter from Japan, America or Canada,
Australia, New Zealand or even Africa,
A letter from a penfriend far away,
Whose kindness will forever with us stay.
An invitation to a wedding, that's the best,
Or to a christening I'm invited as a guest.
Who knows, one day my premium bond may win a prize,
Now that would be a wonderful surprise!
Maybe a poem, too, could win a prize,
And bring a look of pleasure to my eyes.
So thanks we give to our dear Postman Pat.
For bringing all those letters to our mat,
Through rain and wind and hail and snow,
For all our names you now must know.
On all those days throughout the year,
Those letters come from far and near,
To cheer our hearts and wish us well,
When Christmas comes, you ring our bell.
You deliver lots of parcels too,
Let's hope those dogs don't bite you too,
So I will raise a toast to you
And give a grateful 'Thank you',
For all your work the whole year through.

Kathleen Day

WALES

I have always thought my homeland
A medley of grey and green
Though with a splash of sunshine
Such wonderful colours are seen.

The grey of slates upon a roof
And green shades upon the hills
Grey stone slabs that offer proof
On garden paths and window sills

Forests of pine that stretch for miles
Create Switzerland for me
Walking through those grey-green aisles
To view the grey dramatic sea

The pristine green of rugby ground
Then you hear the booted thud
Piles of bodies in a mound
The green turns into seas of mud

Piled on a hill of timeless green
Ruined castle, stones of grey
Echo like a haunting dream
With stories of a bygone day

I hope that I have set the scene
Splendid places of hills and vales
Lovely land of grey and green
My home, my country, my dear Wales.

Elaine Rowlands

THE OBVIOUS FACT

It seems to me stupid and worthy of derision
That men can say that Lord Jesus has not arisen.
They think of all sorts of things, that can explain away
Why the tomb was empty on that fateful Easter Day.
An earthquake, perhaps, or maybe Jesus was a ghost,
Maybe the disciples were lying, as they thought about the Host.
Or can it be that simply the most obvious explanation
Is that the Good Lord *did* arise, to save each and every nation.
Why, oh why, do men not think of this most obvious fact?
Instead of all the possibilities that could explain away this act?
So come on, you believers, show atheists everywhere
That Jesus is the Messiah and that He does really care.
Jesus *did* arise on that glorious Easter Day
And we will one day join Him, for we know He is the Way!

Christine M Wilkinson

WIND CHIMES

Beneath a violet sky
Verona beckons
A memory in Juliet's heart
Is Romeo's sweet kiss
A love forever to exit
As the candle of love burns brightly in their soul
Intertwined with crystal dreams
Wind chimes softly ring
Passing on Verona's song
Drifting on the winds of life
As stories of love unfold
For centuries to be told
So from the beginning of time
Love sparkles within
From the angel dove
Like moonbeams on diamond snow
Reflecting upon lovers
A ritual glow
As adventure awaits . . .

Rossana Pinto

I WISH

I wish the clouds would go away
To make each day a sunny day
To lift the spirits, heart and mind
And help us all to be more kind.

I wish the days when I was young
Had really only just begun
When most were happy and life was sweet
And it was safe to walk the street.

I wish the concrete bods would go away
And leave some space for our young to play
I long again for a land that's green
With fields as pretty as the ones I've seen.

I wish for someone strong to say
The gods of gold have had their day
In this overcrowded isle of ours
With pollution raining down in showers
And murders that are commonplace
The evil that hides behind a face
The poison in the food we eat
The ones in charge that lie and cheat

Oh how we need a helping hand
To turn around this once proud land
I wish for the England that once I knew
Dear God what has become of you?

Joy Toms

ON THE MORNING OF MY DAUGHTER'S BIRTH

Before the world shatters the membrane of our closeness
I grasp this moment of stillness with my child,
Alone in this small, white room, brightened with sunlight,
Plunged into motherhood, bound by a cord
As strong as that which held you to my heart,
Tied to your frailty by a love that wants none back
My only desire your well-being and future joy.
How quiet your breath, how delicate the lids
Over your closed eyes - pale, sleeping flower.
A bee hits the window and a small shadow
Of concern ripples through my senses.
Life can never be the same again
A wondrous responsibility has enclosed my being,
A total oneness with this new creation.

Wendy Grounds

TIME

Time does not stand still,
Things just keep on moving.
All around people getting on with life
Not giving you a second glance,
Unaware of the pain you feel,
The sense of loss inside.
You want to scream, 'She's dead,'
At the top of your voice,
Just so they will take notice
And comfort you in your darkest hour.
But no words come,
Your voice silenced by grief.
In time it will get better,
The pain will ease.
Life will feel worth living again,
Looking back on the good times.
Enjoying the memories.
Time may not stand still,
But it does eventually heal.

Gillian Snaith

IS IT ALREADY TOO LATE?

I lose sleep thinking about the world we live in.
How we're poisoning the planet and polluting the waterways.
The devastation of the rainforests and dumping nuclear waste.
Something must be done about it.

Death on the roads, the needless waste of human organs
That could be used for transplant surgery.
To let recipients have a chance to live a normal life.
Something must be done about it.

The starving multitudes in the third world.
The misery of the homeless in cardboard boxes.
The 'fat cats' getting richer whilst the poor get poorer.
Something must be done about it

Wife beating, child abuse, youngsters smoking, taking drugs.
The lone parent families and the unemployed.
The latch key children and the bullied child.
Something must be done about it.

Indiscriminate use of pesticides in our fields
Destroying the insects that feed the birds.
The ever invasive roads that are raping the countryside.
Something must be done about it.

The aftermath of war and the terrorists' bombs,
Targeting the innocent along with the guilty.
Funded by people in high places.
Something must be done about it.

The 9-11 tragedy caused by Al Quaeda terrorists.
The ruthlessness of the suicide bombers.
With little or no regard for human life.
Something must be done about it.

Winsome Mary Payter

DESMOND THE BAT

Desmond is our little bat
Living high in the church rafter
When the moon shines brightly
You can hear him squeak with laughter

You have to watch out
When he's ready to dive and swoop
He might get in your hair
While doing loop the loop.

One warm and moonlit night
He decided to have some fun
So he flew into the church
Where the service had began

He darted here and darted there
Giving the ladies a nasty scare
He caught his claws in a lady's hat
Her wig as well, the naughty bat.

The lady squealed and hid in the pew
Wasn't it a naughty thing to do
Carrying the wig into the night air
He left the lady's head quite bare.

A man in the churchyard saw a funny sight
Flying through the air in the bright moonlight
He shivered as an owl made an eerie sound
Then a hairy thing fell onto the ground

The man took fright
Then began to run
He was soon out of the churchyard
Desmond squeaked, 'What fun.'

Joan Littleworth

A PERFECT WORLD

Close your eyes and imagine a world without pain,
suffering and violence,
where everyone is treated with respect and by name.
Close your eyes and imagine a world where everyone is happy,
and no one has to suffer in vain.

Do you dream of a world where children can play freely,
with no worries and cares in the world?
Let's listen together to ease everyone's suffering,
and make sure that forgotten voices are heard.

Do you dream of a tomorrow where everyone's equal
and we share and look after each other the same,
Where everyone is loved like our own sisters and brothers,
and no one has to suffer alone or in unnecessary pain?

Close your eyes and imagine the perfect tomorrow,
where dreams and hopes can become real.
A perfect world is about loving and sharing,
and showing we care how everyone feels.

So join me in a vision of a better tomorrow,
a world so much better than today.
Close your eyes and imagine the perfect tomorrow
let's hope it's not too far away.

Catherine Keepin

IF ONLY

In glory it shone like a symbol that night
And lighted the traveller's way
That Bethlehem Star guided kings from afar
To the manger where Jesus lay.
I wonder if those who had heard of His birth
Could have possibly known at the time,
How that little child would follow the course,
That His Father had planned for mankind.
Jesus, by example, showed man how to live
By the rules taught in His Christian home
And His Father in Heaven had guided His Son
From the words carved on the tablets of stone.
These were known as the Commandments,
Abiding principles, for all people on Earth
But down through the ages man has set his own rules
And lost sight of their purpose and worth.
Centuries have passed and the world has advanced
An infinite knowledge we've gained,
Science has created, radical changes
But steadfast, this code of conduct for living remains.
God, in His wisdom, knew the failings of man
And gave us Jesus, the Light of the World
Born in a stable, that cold winter night,
For His birth was all part of God's plan.

Margaret Lawson

ONE DAY

Peace will bridge the gap the tears have strewn!
Where there's love there's always hope!
It's when all hope fades away!
Along come all the memories
Lovely pictures of how we were yesterday!
Suffering seemed so far away.
That was yesterday!
Today is just another day!
Love and hope our strongest link!
We won't give in! We won't give up!
Where there's love there's always hope!
We're British to our comrades everywhere,
God bless you all! And thumbs up.

E Knapp

FANTASY

Long ago in an enchanted wood
The very last white unicorn stood.
Where the sun caught his horn it shone like gold
And his flowing tail was a joy to behold
But he was lonely.

One day through the wood with footsteps light,
A beautiful princess came into sight,
Her hair was golden with a silken sheen,
And the bluest eyes you've ever seen,
And she was lonely.

They looked at each other across the glade
The unicorn and the pretty young maid
He gave his tail a gentle swish,
She patted his head and give him a kiss and they were friends.

They rested awhile beneath the trees,
Then she climbed up on his back with ease,
A blue-grey mist surrounded the pair
As they slowly rose into the air
When the mist had cleared, for all to see
Stood the very first magnolia tree.

Jean Roughton

THE CLOCK HANDS

I watched the second hand on the clock
Moving quickly around its face
The minute hand moved more slowly
The hour hand had given up the race

Let's race against the clock said second hand
Minute hand said race against time
Hour hand more sedately uttered
Let's co-ordinate and make the thing chime

Second hand spinning, barely saw the figures
Minute hand studied where he'd been
Hour hand surveyed the figures thoroughly
And considered what went on in-between

The hands continuing in their circuits
Found that each upon the other depends
Learning the names of the figures they passed
Increasing their circle of friends

The hands of time keep on turning
The world synchronised to its speed
We do well to study the movement
The rhythm of life we must heed

John Remmington

COLOURS

Look at a rainbow where skies are dark.
Look at a bubble, or fountain spray.
Look 'neath a waterfall thundering down
Or morning sky at the dawn of day.

Look at the patchwork nature has wrought,
Look how the threads of a tapestry blend.
Look at an infant's first effort at art,
Or evening sky at summer day's end.

Colours surround us, within, without,
Red glowing faces, blue frozen hands.
Emerald glint of a covetous eye;
Faces of people from far away lands.

'Tis hard to select one perfect tone;
'Tis hard to choose a favourite hue.
The gold of youth, or silver of age -
God's Heav'n my choice;
It has to be *blue!*

Marjorie Wheeler

GETTING OFF THE GROUND

We reached Heathrow at 8 o'clock,
So early in the day,
As we went aboard our plane - a shock,
There was to be a delay!

The French air controllers had gone on strike,
So we had to join a queue.
This, of course, we did not like,
As we became well overdue!

The temperature was - oh so hot,
As each half hour went by,
At last we heard that we had got,
A slot for us to fly!

But then another strike took place,
The Heathrow runway men,
They would not take us from our base,
'Twas all beyond our ken!

By then, we'd missed our slot en France,
And had to wait till noon,
At last there came another chance,
We would be airborne soon!

But as the engines roared away,
And we thought that we were up,
Bang - skid - slither and sway,
We'd been sold another pup!

Now it was back to square number one,
Another D-Day - 6th June,
This was a journey second to none,
And it was our honeymoon!

Jill M Ronald

HOLOCAUST

A race we bred to be so malicious
That man to man could be so vicious;
It seems really impossible to me
That such a dreadful thing could be.
But its happening is a true fact
To such inhumanity how can I react?

It made no difference, man, woman or child
They were all so tragically reviled.
Death we know must come to us all
Those poor people didn't get their call
By our God's usual chosen way,
But for them the whole world did pray.

Such ways of suffering and death
Made it so hard to take a simple breath.
The pain and tortures those chosen people bore
Sent them to Heaven through a wide open door,
The Star of David guided all their souls
For them the journey straight, there were no tolls.

Many still live, those instrumentors of death
They have yet to draw their last breath,
Justice on this Earth they will have evaded
No guide for their souls from the Star of David.
I was not born at that awful time of Holocaust
I pray that such a thing will never again be enforced.

P M H Wood

ODE TO THREE SKYLARKS

Thrice blessed was I, that magic autumn day,
In Holy Family Church, having chanced to stray;
Such wondrous singing floated sweetly round my ears,
A Gaelic dirge that surely had me very close to tears

The source, three little girls, each aged around eleven,
The quality of their sound, as if direct from Heaven;
Their mentor, Father Paddy, at the organ sat nearby,
Playing - and inspiring that sad, poignant lullaby

Had Percy Shelley happened upon that simple, striking scene,
I stop to wonder what his thoughts precisely might have been?
My guess - *This gives me new perspective down life's timeless*
                                                          road
Perhaps the hour is ripe, to recast my precious, ancient ode!

The impact of that October '98 first day lives as of yet,
I clearly well remember, choosing not ever to forget;
God keep you, Father Paddy, ever tapping that rich, rich seam,
E'er inspiring all-Ireland winners like Catherine, Marian and Noreen.

George D Conlon

THE TRUTH AND THE LIGHT

Struggling, choking, fearful - going insane?
Torn, worn, emotional torture and pain.
Weeds growing tall around tired feet,
making it difficult to see the wheat.
Trapped, imprisoned in a cocoon,
got to get out of here and very soon!

A decision made - must get tough,
stay strong, because enough is enough.
Overcome evil; do good and soldier on,
for Jesus, the battle, has already won!

Follow the truth and the light.
Continue to fight the good fight.
Keep the straight and narrow road.
Give the Lord any burdens and load.
Remain loving and free, flying high.
Angelic much like the beautiful butterfly!

Kateryna Mazelan (nee Kozak)

FANTASY

In the dark stillness of night,
When the peace of slumber evades me,
Thoughts take over my wandering mind.
I'm enveloped by fantasy.

Would I travel to far distant shores?
Languish on golden sands beneath skies of blue?
Where the sun is forever shining,
Where life is different, exciting, and new.

But if this were so, would it last
When its image had slowly passed away?
Would I yearn for that familiar life I knew
And of friends that brighten up my day?

I would miss the glistening dew upon a rose,
The perfume of honeysuckle in the air.
Friendly faces I see each day,
People I love, whose company I share.

That first joyous glimpse of spring,
When the long, dreary winter is over.
The sweet sound of the blackbird's song,
A carpet of bluebells enhanced with clover.

How could I leave all this behind?
These treasures I hold most dear.
Straying thoughts must remain a fantasy
For my heart tells me I belong here.

Jinty Wicks

ALBEIT

We are all born with a clock inside us
Set for the time we hit the dust;
That clock cannot be altered
No matter how hard we try,
In spite of how healthy, ill
Rich, subtle or poor our will
That clock remains unaffected.

We are all hoes in the hands of a gardener
We must learn to be happy turning over weeds
As the gardener who set the seal directs,
All are servants to a master doing pittance
Depicting an existence to a caretaker,
When unexpected pitfall reigns the ruse
Survivors order courage feign not a detour.

Misfortunes endured can't be enhanced
When life's cascade sparks like a dance.
Sickness allures a smouldering structure
A disadvantage unable to defy nature:
What rancorous hand shot the bolt?
That triggers off malignant volts
Of divers illness corroding our stance?

Can the well being of creation
Knowingly derive satisfaction
From famine, wars or starvation?
Albeit we're all here for a purpose:
To determine the dosage of success
Or difficulties each one encounters
Differentiate spectrums of privileges
Look earnestly towards your maker.

Zeedy Thompson

ANNUNCIATION

It was all very well: that was her story.

An angel, she said, come down from Heaven.
Sudden, precipitate, invading all her quietude,
Disrupting thoughts of love and holy things,
Of God, and man.

A rushing wind, a lambent flame,
A flurried exit of a frightened cat:
This feathered interloper of their steady state
Was not a prey for him to tackle with.

Seeming fair to look upon - as man may be -
But yet no man. The words he spoke
Were all-compelling, full of meaning
In her ears, and sharp to penetrate
Her conscious mind.

The air was momentarily
As still as time suspended for an age:
His words were rooted in her, safe to grow,
Become enlarged, and with fulfilment,
Burst into the light and light the world.

But then, the time was passed, the visitant departed,
And in quietude she once again communed
With all her life's experience, alone;
Until the cat, suspicious still and wary,
Angled its way with pointed step
Back to the orbit of her solitude.

Joseph Smedley

PORTSTEWART STRAND

Plaited sand twists forward
Carrying a silent stream from an unknown source.
Modest, clear and cleansed by her natural filter-bed
She trickles to the edge where she loses identity
Mingling in a pool of streams.
Along the shore,
A shallow canyon cut through the hard-packed grains,
Pebbled base and sliced sides
Allows a deeper flow, and faster,
Protesting as he squeezes past obstacles of stones and shells.
Extrovert he eagerly dashes for the surf,
Is caught up in the froth and dies.
At the bar
Where the rocks are dressed and undressed,
The sluggish river pushes its way laboriously
Through the tide, forcing a path in the swell.
The deep-bedded currents coil beneath the surface
Fighting an underground war among the sandbanks,
So that tide and river fuse in a slow whirl
Of contrappostal movement.

Mavis Abernethy

PUZZLING WAYS

Another day
Another way
Forever hoping for you
To have your say.
What have I said
That worried your head,
What have I done,
That you stay so dumb.

Silence is golden
Again it is said,
Doors may be open,
Barriers made to be broken,
A genuine shake of the hand
To help you to expand
Then to relax.

Wherever you are or ever maybe,
I want you to know
You are always with me,
But to haunt you, I will not
Because I love you lots.
A token never to be broken.

E Blagrove

SUMMERTIME

The fields of corn flow gently on this English summer day,
While over there are fields of poppies where the dead of war have lain
The rosebuds form and blossom in the brilliance of the sun
As children in that other land cry for parents who are gone,
The summer fruits are plentiful, the crops are strong and good
While people there clutch dying babes, they have no food to give.
Oh! Summer day, so beautiful, so full of hidden treasure
But I can't always share that joy, sometimes there is no pleasure,
When poppies dance and flutter upon the summer's breeze
And children play so happily among the stalwart trees,
I see the broken lives and dreams of families blown asunder
The war-torn lands and men who do not hesitate to plunder,
Perhaps God in His wisdom has an underlying plan
To stop this hurt and anger that has man killing man,
Until the dawning of that day though summer days be bright,
The haunting thoughts of death and war will spoil and shade my sight.

Gwen Collins

OH! WOMAN

Oh woman, it is not seemly for you to just sit
solitary, silent, with only four walls around you.
Oh woman, it is not enough for you to just have
your looks, your hair, your jewels, your clothes.
You are Woman, with knowledge, pride and love,
you have gentle hands, kind heart, compassion.
Break your cage of darkness.
Fulfil your role of Woman!

Rejoice in your inner person, flee the cage
to the light and brightness of knowledge.
Oh woman, without you there is nothing.
You are the beginning, the doorway to life,
humanity gains from your presence
in all things.

Do not weep from the pain of injustice and humiliation,
stand with knowledge of your strength and right of place,
stand firm, invoke God's help for you and your children.
Those who are strong are seen, they go forward,
the fainthearted are ignored, they fall behind.
Oh woman, stand and be seen, make your presence felt.
Break your cage of silence.
Fulfil your role of Woman!

R Darakhshani

A QUESTION OF HEAVEN

How will Heaven be?
It will be a lane, green-wet with spring rain
And hedges full of mystery;
A long hot summer's day, with scent of new-mown hay
And a cool breeze from the sea.

How will Heaven be?
It will be a field golden with harvest yield,
The fiery blaze of an autumn tree;
The glow of sunset's red and pink-fringed clouds that spread
In evening's sweet tranquillity.

How will Heaven be?
It will be bright as fallen snow in silver light,
Moonlit clear as a frosty night -
But warm as only love can be:
That's how Heaven will be.

Wendy Vidler

LLANTHONY PRIORY

(Inspired by a visit to Llanthony soon after the Omagh bombing, September 1998)

Stark against a lowering sky,
Dark columns of a ruined shell -
Once the home of cowlèd monks -
Rise majestically on high.

Many centuries ago
Peace reigned within those walls.
Murmuring of gentle voice,
Softly chanting, deep and low.

Ruins tell of tragic days,
Recalling hatred and decay.
Man hunted man through bigotry,
Each wanting his own blinded way.

Times may change, but still we see
Man hunting man with vicious spite,
By stormy words and cruel deeds
This may not be at Llanthony -
But look across the Irish Sea.

Martha Fear

ALONE

No one there when I climb into bed,
No one to hold me or hear the prayers I've just said
No arm comes around me to cuddle me tight,
Just me - by myself again for the night.
No lips search for mine to give a sweet kiss,
Will all of my nights be like this?
Nobody beside me to whisper in my ear,
Nothing but silence and my secret thoughts of fear.
My hand reaches out and longs to touch a cheek,
My pillow is all I find when I seek.
No one to love me and run his fingers through my hair,
Wherever I search - there is no one there.
I toss and turn and quite often I weep
Before I drift off into that blessed state of sleep.

B Spanswick

NORTHWARD BOUND

You were never any trouble,
We could take you anywhere, *
Those occasional trips to Birmingham,
With an hour or two to spare.

Then the unforgettable journeys north,
Having to scramble on the train,
But of course, that was in wartime,
So we never did complain.

We were going to stay at Grandma's
It was your second home,
And you were in your element,
In the back street, you could roam.

Your hands and knees were dirtier,
With the coal dust in the air,
Short trousers were the fashion,
Without a hint of flare.

Cool evenings, with shadows long,
Every blackout carefully placed,
The warmth of Grandma's cheery fire,
Plus the welcome we embraced.

Some events, were taken for granted,
In those wartime days, of chance,
Yet we treasured most, the simplest things,
Our memories to enhance.

Dora Quinn

SPRING

Where are you hiding, spring?
Behind winter's dark cloak, cold and thin,
Long-worn, threadbare, easy to break through
And yet it seems an arduous task for you.

Come, reveal your loveliness again
Before your heir, summer, comes to reign,
Break forth with bud on trees long bare,
Impart to us your style so fair.

Let the fields breathe sweet, let the may-blossom appear,
Let the chaffinch sing, well upon our ear,
Primroses, daffodils, in the early morning dew,
Lambs, new birth, lift heart and spirit anew.

A young man's fancy, so they say,
Turns to thoughts of love when you come his way,
Let romance blossom like the hawthorn tree
And make us all feel fancy-free!

Florence May Scott

LIFE

Life's too short to sit and moan,
Get off your chair, don't be alone,
There's so much out there that you can do,
Get someone else's point of view.
Company is all you need,
So you must sow the first seed,
It's up to you to make a move,
Into a different kind of groove.
Many people are just like you,
Meet together, start anew,
Just a 'good morning' and a smile
Can help you over any stile.
The Lord helps those who help themselves,
So come on, get off that empty shelf,
Make life as it ought to be,
Full of fun and fancy free.
It doesn't matter how old you are,
Everyone has a shining star
To follow and to reach their goal,
You too can reach the top of the pole.

Winifred Tutte

EVERY WOMAN IS A GODDESS

Every woman is a goddess
Yes in her very special way
Every woman is a goddess
Yes and in her heart it holds full sway

God gave her this virtue
As her most precious gift
And surprisingly it is absolutely true
To take her up when down as in a lift

Is it her hair? Is it her face?
Is it her figure? Is it her race?
Is it her voice? Is it her walk?
Is it her sweetness? Is it her talk?

Herself this goddess may never know
Just like the wind over her it will blow
But every male if true can seek it out
For God to him gave him this clout

There has never been a woman yet born
Who needs to get depressed or forlorn
Her attraction is there just waiting to be seen
By her true fellow spirit a male who sees beneath her screen

This is the foundation of real true love
A love that is our most blessed gift from the Lord above
Once declared and discovered by both each human entity
Their love takes on a reality that is from Heaven and eternity

Yes it is true every woman really is a goddess
Ready and waiting for the right man to bless
It can come to all and is worth the wait
For true love when found is our highest human state.

Frank Hansford-Miller

THE FISHER KING

A flash of brilliant plumage skims
the shimmering water tumbling by,
to shelter 'neath the willow fronds
and hover where the sleek fish lie.
So swift he darts in streak of light
that not a shadow warns his prey.
Then, poised he dives, to rise on wing
through deathly shroud of silver spray.

Gillie Threadgold

WILL YOU LOVE ME WHEN I'M OLD?

Will you still love me when I'm old?
When my blood is thin and cold?
When my hands are gnarled and brown?
And my shoulders drooping down?
When I am no longer fair?
And I have no teeth or hair?
When my eyes are sunken in?
And my vision has gone dim?
When my mind has gone all blurred?
And I cannot still be heard?
Are you now so sure and bold?
To say you'll love me when I'm old?

Marjorie Simpson

YOU

No more pain,
No more watching your pain.
No more worry,
I do the worrying now.

No more togetherness;
I miss my happiness.
No more music,
Music makes me cry.

Our family miss their number one.
Your example makes them become
Better people for knowing your life,
And I am proud for being your wife.

In the house I feel you near,
I talk to you and believe you hear.
My consolation is there is no more pain for you,
But my heart aches because there is no more
You!

Joan Lewis

BIRTH TO DEATH

While a baby's waiting to be born,
He's in a trance-like floating state
Of peace. A place for his soul's transition
From the heavenly world he has so lately left.

At birth, his soul feels desperately sad,
Trapped once again inside another human frame.
He cries and wails - he cannot stand this new imprisonment.

God, in His mercy, lets him sleep for almost all the time
At first, to ease his new descent into this world.
Once again, as many times before, he gradually feels
Less and less distressed, and grows accustomed to his earthly state.
He takes his comfort from the human beings around him,
Who give him love and warmth,
And month by month, and year by year, he adapts to life on Earth.

Until he's seven, he still retains some glimpses of his
                              recent time in Heaven.
He even sometimes sees those he was with so recently.
His elders see and hear him talking to these friends, and say,
'Just his imagination - he'll grow out of it one day.'
Yes, it's sad to say - he surely will.

And so he grows, and once again goes through his time
Of learning here on Earth - sometimes happy, sometimes sad.
Until once more, and in old age, his time to go draws near.
His soul prepares him once again, to leave this school of life,
And with a soft sigh of relief, at last, at last,
He reaches once again his Heavenly home.

Betty Farajallah

DEATH KNOWS NO VICTORY

He'd planned a first reunion in two score years and ten,
But now a thought tormented: would he remember them?
He sat in isolation, in a niche beyond the bar;
His anxious eyes were scanning people near and far
For a thread of recognition in a once familiar face;
A likeness scant remembered, that time could not erase.

Time had hung like misty curtains, and made the memory dim;
Maybe his fellow servicemen could not remember him!
From a dim-lit corner, at the elbow of the wall,
A figure moved towards him, a fellow straight and tall.
He rose, a mite uncertain - then without hesitation,
'Lofty Small, I do believe?' he cried in exultation.

Bony arms engulfed him and gripped with all their might,
Brushed away the curtains that hid a memory bright.
One by one they gathered, and made a happy crew,
Oh how they raised the rafters, those valiant boys in blue;
Made light of all the hardships in steamy climes afar,
Withheld the pain and fortitude that earned their 'Burma Star'.

I should have mustered with them, but beneath the jungle trees
I took my earthly freedom, at the hands of Japanese,
Although I have no substance, I feel they know I'm near,
For they speak my name in reverence, with suspicion of a tear.
Comrades will be comrades, wherever they may be
In such a lasting fellowship, death knows no victory.

Patricia Woodley

DEFINING LOVE

What is love but a beautiful dream
Filled with illusions and wonderful schemes
It brings you joy, it brings you sorrow,
It brings you heartache, the day after tomorrow
It brings happiness in all its glory
But will it last? That's another story
It brings contentment
Then resentment,
Back to the question,
What is love?
Is it deep affection,
Looking for perfection?
I think it's sharing all the joys and sorrows
Not just today, but all the tomorrows.

Penn Preston

A WAY OF LOOKING

I frown and hurry and the sky is grey;
The traffic thunders past me up the hill.
I see only the immediate here and now
And miss the rainbow in a drop of rain.

The busy world crowds in; noise escalates;
And I am caught in the pace of this today -
But suddenly traffic, fences, voices fade
And I am strangely a spectator here . . .

For when I pause, within the shadow of the spire,
The grass springs up, the clocks no longer tick;
Cool fountains play through stones, rough as routine;
I walk through walls - the countryside is open.

And all is clear, unfettered, honest, pure -
Uncomplicated as a little child -
Where it is possible to chase the stars;
And catch the iridescent blue of dragonflies.

Lost to the morning rush, beyond this moment,
Out of myself, on the other side of the wall,
I see tall trees without shadows and still waters -
All Heaven, mirrored in this hov'ring butterfly.

Jefferson Faulkner

FREEDOM

(From chapter 17 of 'Auf Wiedersehen Pat' - by Pat Roach and Shirley Thompson
Brewin Books Ltd, 2006)

Had we but time and worlds enough
I'd take you to a place
Where time suspends eternity
Far from life's fraught 'rat race'.

And if we'd the will . . . and cared enough
We'd find an inner peace
Where death and wealth don't signify
And worldly cares just cease.

Our health and youth restored again
We'd wander through woods alone,
On riverbanks we'd take our ease
And join - 'til our hearts were one.

But where is the time, and where is this place
Where we could slip away
To find our desires and souls again
Be together, come what may?

Through peaceful ways we'll discover a dawn
Where the path to freedom starts.
Place gentle hands love . . . feel the beat
For it lies within our hearts.

Shirley Thompson

THE DESIGNER

If he should strive
By dint of flair
To craft a shape
That pleases all:
That would be accomplishment.

But ask the user
Is it a people-plan
That serves to
Embody light and space
And enhances living in that shape?

The mystique of design
Is when the eye is
Caught and riven by the shape
And then surprised to find
Its echo in a complementary line.

But what of function
As the arbiter of schemes?

Courtier of the function of a shape
The designer flirts with function
Until the courtship gathers pace
And he must abandon
Wile to formalise his function's bidding.

The compromise between
Artistic flair and need
Bedevils all his undertakings.

The scales if balanced
Mark him out an
Innovator. And another
Space is enveloped for posterity.

Angela Cheyne

RAILLERY

About a duck's back, I know little.
Polynesian pedantics, I leave to romantics.
Europeans are somewhat remote.
Readings from literature: I keep afloat.

Seldom do I make a hit of
Magnitude in things that I do, not
That it matters to people of who,
Obviously have a vocation, to fly high the
Kite of self preservation.

Let me be plain in this matter,
I exist on the wisp of idle chit-chatter.
My hobbies are few, I'm idle it's true,
I spend oodles of time conjecturing blue, the
Azure remote, in which all clouds float.

Enigmas are anathema to me,
Dozing on beaches, and dodging the sea, is
Knowledge I hold in my repartee.
Not that it matters where tigers exist, or
Orators of excellent that give meaning a twist.

Wagnerian: I'm fond of the rich dark agenda,
Lavish in symbols of sensual surrender, ever
The ploy since mythology grew, to inform me of
Dionysus with his heady brew.

Gold bath taps and life's route maps mean little to me,
Ever the ditherer, I just constantly
Plough in the vineyard of wordy excess.
About a duck's back,
I must leave you to guess.

Richard Cluroe

WAITING

Waiting. Tired.
Tired of waiting
In a small tired room still not cooled from night
But warm with remembered summer heat,
In deepening gloom lit fitfully
By peripheral headlights.
Outside, darkness and a light capricious breeze
Rustling fretfully at the window, redolent
Of the tired end-of-day smell
Of warm damp, exhaust fumes, forgotten meals.
Waiting.
Sounds, too, seep in - the *sw-i-ish-sh* of tyres in the wet;
A distant laugh not quite recalling something bitter-sweet;
Clacking footsteps; between, the sound of silence.
Thinking.
Thinking those world-without-end thoughts -
Bedfellows to loneliness -
That march so well in tune with
Waiting.
Thoughts of Life and Death and Sisyphus and God;
And if God how he can coolly contemplate, implacably permit,
The vile acts perpetrated in His name
And yet not become the Destroyer of Mankind;
Waiting - but for what?
Ah yes. Of course - waiting for the Answer.
Yet with this knowledge comes the rub.
The answer will never come; not now, not ever.
Yet even so must I perforce go on - and on - and on -
Waiting.

G Pash

THE TWO WOLVES

In the lodge-house of the Cherokee
An Elder sat with tales to tell.
As the young ones listened to him,
His words, like rain on fresh earth fell.

He spoke of battles of the past,
His Nation's former glories,
The children hunkered round the fire,
Held hostage to his stories.

'Yet here a mighty fight goes on,'
He pointed to his heart.
'A bitter war is waged in me,
In which two wolves take part.

The same two fight in all of us,
In you and everyone.
The first wolf stands for Truth and Peace,
And for Justice to be done.

The second wolf tears with tooth and claw,
For Envy, Hate and Greed.
Which wolf will win?' The old man smiled.
'Whichever one I feed.'

Maureen Dawson

THE KISS

She was no girl just fresh in bloom
and still damp with the dew
but a woman in her prime
and in full flower too.

She must have known I watched her
an old man sitting there
but she was with her lover
and didn't really care.

Her eyes were green as any cat's
that in the darkness shine
as there was once another's
that looked into mine.

She smiled a slow and haunting smile
that lingered in the air
as if she knew a secret
that she would never share.

Her hair was soft as shadows
that each night gently fall.
Her laughter like the little brook
That hears the river's call.

She curved to touch her lover
with feral feline grace
and as they moved together
I kissed a long lost face.

G Murphy

FOREVER EDEN

Pure love, fermented in the human heart?
The power which fashions priceless works of art.
When love turns cold, the poet's pen runs dry.
But when her flame burns bright, ideas fly,
Words dance on rhythm, join in lines of verse,
Send shouts of joy around the universe.
Enamoured pluckers of the lyre's string
Draw music from the breeze, hear angels sing.
Impassioned artists, labouring through the night
Find, by love's light, dull colours now glow bright.
And when I savour tender thoughts of you,
I see, touch, hear, taste, smell a world made new!

Alan Swift

ON THE 15TH ANNIVERSARY OF FORWARD PRESS

Raise the song of harvest home;
all is safely gathered in, ere the winter storms begin.
So we sang in gratitude but yesterday in
church. Why not commemorate in poetry
fifteen years of verses garnered safety?

Now this is not the first such time I've pondered
on the past in Fakenham. I have wondered
how 'twas done long since. Imagination
dwells upon how slow the axle turned as watery sun
cast criss-cross beams athwart the heavy horses' flanks.
They hauled their weighty burdens down
slowly to swiftly-filling tithe-barns.
Hearts held high the waggoners' airs recount yarns,
their origins lost long since. Home, the thanks
for God's plenty in clinking mugs of brass
and pewter were raised. By candles ghostly light
far into the night rang their celebrations.

So from this North Norfolk town this day we raise
our meagre metre and our pewter to those
brave souls that Forward Press brought to praise
and wider recognition with poetry composed
to echo forth the moment's inspiration,
dark doubts dispelled, and benedicites
proclaimed with verve. They sought to waken and to please
a prosy world with verse's observation.
I raise my mighty glass this day to them. Long
may we hear their joyful song.

Goodbye then from these far-flung western shores.
May down the years work from your presses pour
and we be grateful to you evermore.

J Coleridge

SEX EQUALITY

Ms Mulliner-Gore was a ranter,
A fanatical feminist bore.
She plastered the press and drowned every debate
In the status of women in home, church and state
And the rights of Ms Mulliner-Gore.

She had long ago cast off her husband,
Regarding him less than no loss.
He had actually wanted a helpmeet in life;
She'd preached equal status for husband and wife,
Provided the woman was boss.

She fought every club and society
That appointed a man as its head;
Till one day, while storming about women's rights
Her blood pressure rose to such frightening heights
That the Lord struck her suddenly . . . dead.

She confronted St Peter in Heaven,
And brushed him aside at the door.
She went to Reception to claim her just part,
But found the chairs filled with the humble of heart,
And she had to sit on the floor.

She summoned the Mother Almighty
To demand that fair play must prevail;
But found that the system was just as she'd feared:
The Great Judge in Heaven was sporting a beard,
And everyone said he was male.

She stormed out of Heaven in high dudgeon,
'You cannot expect me to stay.'
St Peter said, 'No, but you banish yourself,
Since no one gets in from the uppermost shelf.
And Love, and not rights pave the way.'

Simon Peterson

A Trickle Of Water For Me

The old man was born in eighteen ninety-three,
By the distillery where the best malt was made.
He lived all his years, drinking whisky like tea,
With a trickle of water not good for the trade.

All through his life, he drank his fill of the best,
Never missing a day at his distillery.
It's the secret of good health; he'd never jest,
Was the trickle of water in his malt whisky.

Finally he retired in the year fifty-three,
To a large stone house, near the Mill of Gellan.
His servant as old, saw he had malt whisky,
With a trickle of water, oh! what a man.

At last he died, a glass of malt in his hand,
They wouldn't believe he'd passed on, now he's free.
He was as fit as a fiddle, they can't understand,
It was the trickle of water don't you see.

Then came the day for his last trip to the Kirk,
The mourners drank a toast, with his own whisky.
As glass touched their lips, they saw the coffin jerk,
A vice said, 'A large trickle of whisky for me.'

The lid lifted up, bony hand held the glass,
'Now fill it to the brim,' his voice said with glee.
The hand disappeared with the malt, they stood aghast,
'It's the trickle of water that bloody killed me.'

A headstone still stands, as good as the day
It was put there by his large sad family,
No name on the stone, just a few words to say,
A trickle of water caused this, he died 103.

C Armstrong

Celebrations

(Congratulations to Katherine on her marriage and becoming professor.)

Oh! What a celebration
A glorious, wonderful day!
The marquee in the meadow,
Wild flowers along the way.
Guests in anticipation,
Laughter and goodwill surround.
Can offer no expectation
So intellectually profound.
Everything in order, caterers around,
Excitement reigns, food galore
Could dance the light fantastic
On the newly timbered floor.
Flags flying, high the tide,
A moment of importance.
Congratulations freely given
For this joyful enterprise.
Glasses hoisted with champagne;
Speeches sublime and pleasing.
Fulfilment, perfection, attainment,
Congratulations worth repeating.
Lights flashing, a welcome band,
Dancing the night to a close.
A celebration is not a rehearsal
Is the bud of an English Rose.

Dorothy Wilbraham

Only A Thought

On your orb of blue, green and brown
Impressions are of peace without frown
Looking closely it is not so
Except for those who seek to know
Hustle and bustle of busy folk
Creating the atmosphere that continues to choke
The time has come for real learning
The planet's very soul is pleading and yearning
Vision is clouded by greed, hate and power
Please place your mind into the heart of a flower
Many dark deeds have weakened the axis
Confusion reigns rampant and fractious
Chaos comes in cloaked disguise
Unleashing elements with raging surprise
How many ponder your battered home?
That war-torn place that rotates alone
One day soon when love has begun
The world and its inhabitants shall live as one
Subtle, strong and very true
Compassion shall reach the many and the few
Eden's return will quell the distraught
Direct from the universe it is only a thought.

Catherine Beagarie

My Secret Place

Lazing remember, beside a lake,
sun shaded from tall trees,
ducks and swans go gliding past
amongst bank edge, unkempt reeds.

Waters rippled slight breezes blew,
Birds flew twittering in love.
Fish darting 'neath its surface
bubbles circling up above.

On daisy clover-scented grass
dreamed of distant lands,
those warm exotic places,
blue foam sea with golden sands.

It was a glade, own secret world,
sometimes strolled at night,
pale moon bright, shimmering waters shone,
appeared as glass from silvery light.

Somewhere special then to ponder
did there the future plan.
Memories still of childhood once,
Where my hopes began.

Audrey Williams

The Survivor

In the course of our lives,
We manifest ideas,
Grow stronger, wiser and maintain our balance,
With the passing years.
We incur knocks, frustration and negativity,
But still, we strive,
The belief in oneself to finally achieve,
The goal being 'no substitute', but real,
With love, faith and maturity, we survive.

There is a voice of change,
The subtle influence, that can define,
Like grains of shifting sands,
Evolution comes at a great cost,
The destiny, that has been sealed, through time.

Debbie Hatchett

TINY ACORNS

I hear the birdsong as autumn leaves lay like a chestnut sea,
And gaze with saddened eyes while gentle rain entrances me.
So swift the seasons run this year, so soon the swallows fly,
While church bells toll to summon all, for a friend has passed us by.

Oh how the tears do swell with the choir in harmony,
Where angels dwell in every note and where my friend should be.
I dare not glance at other's eyes should I feel their pain in me,
This death has shaken all our souls with cold reality.

We stout men of England strong that grew from soil so rich,
That beat the anvils from our past and learnt their rhythmic pitch,
We walked the path of duty, to earn our right to stay,
But beneath the churchyard yew is where we grudging lay.

What happened to those sunny days and our endless schemes,
When we were tiny acorns amongst a field of dreams?
Wide-eyed we raced through life, our hearts were brimming full,
Yet the final flag is a shroud of silk, so harsh and miserable.

Were I to take your hand my friend, were I to grasp it hard,
I'd gladly share half my days though it would mark my card,
Then through the lofty corridors where silent whispers fly,
We'd shout our voices hoarse my friend and laugh until we die.

Alexander Askaroff

INTO A COTTAGE GARDEN

Through a white painted gate on Midsummer's Day
To discover a garden, hidden away.
Now follow a path edged with lavenders blue
And here is a cottage, thatched anew.

The lattice windows are open wide
A grandfather clock gravely ticks inside.
Country furniture, chintz faded but clean
Pottery dogs on the mantel are seen.

Now, come into the garden, all aglow
With golden sunflowers and bells from Bow.
Purple foxgloves and button-flowered tansy
Fragrant pinks and wide-eyed pansies.

Over an archway, red roses cascade
And lilies form a perfumed parade.
Margaret daisies with petals of pearl
Shaded ferns, their fronds to unfurl.

Sweet herbs scent the air in patchwork fashion
For soothing teas and the kitchen's provision.
Willows woven to make a seat
Cushioned with camomile, soft and neat.

Into the meadow where wild flowers sway
Catching the breeze as it passes that way.
In the far distance, a rippling stream . . .
. . . as you wake to find, it has all been a dream!

Meryl Champion

LADYBIRD

I spot her -
She is small and pretty
And beautifully dressed,
But I cannot see her legs.

Ah, there, below her domed
Yellow and black costume
My God, more than two -
This really bugs me.

I leave and drive
And start to run amok.
A multiplicity of legs
Splat on my number plate.

Andrew Furneaux

THE SANDS OF TIME

We stand in the wings, watch the curtain fall, on the last one
thousand years.
We sit in the stalls, watch the final act, with laughter and with tears.
We have stood on the bank of the river of time, whilst it flowed along
its way.
We have read each chapter of the book of life, from our birth, to the
present day.
We are leaving behind, a thousand years, of human endeavour, of
joys and fears,
A voyage of discovery, man walked on the moon.
Each century adds lyrics, to our present day tune.
Our new generation, will sing this song, into two thousand and one.
They will add their own lyrics as time goes along, they will gaze at the
same bright sun,

This world, this sky, this infinite space,
Will it outlast the human race?

In a hundred years time, will there be;
People preparing, for the next century?
Will it be peaceful, or will there be strife?
Only God knows, He's the key, to life.

Shirley Monckton-Rickett

A CHILD IS BORN - ISAIAH 9:6

To us a child is born,
A son is given;
A gift to a world forlorn
And to distraction driven.

The Prince becomes a slave,
The King a servant:
The world He came to save
With love so fervent.

To bring us peace and joy,
From fears release,
Bring love without alloy
Make wars to cease.

Janina Neale

REFLECTIONS

Have you ever climbed a mountain in the middle of the night,
Sat and watched the new moon rising, sending down its silver light
On the roads, and on the rivers, and the valley far below
Keeping half the mount in blackness, and the rest in magic glow?

Have you ever walked in sunlight to a quiet, deserted cove,
Stood and watched the tide returning, heard the pebbles loudly
move?
Felt the wind and spray around you. Seen the waters looming high,
Crashing on the nearby rocks, and heard the sand grain's softly sigh?

Have you ever, in the summer, quietly lain in meadow grass?
Watched the grasshopper make music. Seen the beetles scurrying
past.
Heard the bees forever buzzing, working hard throughout the hours.
While a butterfly is landing on the newly opened flowers.

Have you ever walked in woodlands at the turning of the year
Under trees in glorious colours, watched the rabbits and the deer?
Seen the colours of the maples - golden, orange, deepest red,
While the fallen leaves beneath you, crack and rustle as you tread.

Have you ever, in the winter, crunched on newly fallen snow?
Felt the soft kiss of the snowflakes, toes and fingers all aglow.
Have you looked through frozen windows on a garden glistening
white,
Trees and bushes all transfigured in the silence of the night?

Mair Alexander

ODE TO A RED LETTER BOX

Hello, old letter box my faithful friend
as long as I can remember you've been
stood at the corner, just on the bend.
Now a tired matt red, a little bruised,
mouth ever open to receive mail, your staple food.

You have seen me trot up to you, reach up high
to drop the letter in.
I have rushed round in slippers, at dusk and at dawn
even when putting out the bin!
We have driven up close, rolled down
the window, leant out and dropped the mail by.
With a giggle, as we are spared the rain
but you stand completely soaked whilst we are dry!

Your open red gape has received from me
Important pointers on my journey's way
My reply to my first job and interview.
My Christmas friends and birthdays too -
cheques and postal orders,
and letters of regret.
Although you never speak
Your answers are many, through my door
As I come down in the morning and find
them on the floor.

What e-mail could never replace you!
We go back too far; you and me.
Please stay on the corner, just on the bend
mouth ever open, my pillar box friend.

Rosalyn Hogg

THE LONGING

(For my lovely wife Cheryl Gurney)

I longed when just a boy, to be a full grown man
To live life as my father, with the pride I felt he had
I'd often see his face from the background of the sky
And I longed to stand there with him looking eye to eye.

I longed throughout my childhood, for a visit to the sea
The wonder and amazement that would swell inside of me
To hear the wash bouncing on the open shores
To feel the salt breeze cutting through my tender pores.

I longed as times went by, for adventures there to be
With walks down country trails, that people rarely see
The bracken hedges wide and meadows running free
With all the types of wildlife there, living wild and free.

I longed when in my teens to find myself a girl
Those big bright eyes and flowing hair to set me in a whirl
To feel the thrill, the pride when walking hand in hand
To feel the love, excitement of my very own sweetheart.

I longed when once a man, to travel through the skies
To fly around the continents, and broaden my mind's eye.
To mingle through the cultures absorbing all that's new
Whilst building on my knowledge I'd ponder what to do.

I longed now, getting older with focus on my life
To find a perfect woman and take her for my wife
To build a home and family, all sharing in our love
To stand there like my father did with pride of what he'd done.

I longed . . . until I found you!

Raymond Gurney

BESLAN (RUSSIA 2004/2005)

No tolling bells will bring them back
those victims of Beslan -
whose bloody end none shall forgive
was deadly sin of man.

As hostages they proved some use
to patriots of hate -
just pawns in a private game with death,
their massacre' checkmate.

Negotiate? - no option left
for troops there by and large -
when seemingly all must be killed
by madmen taking charge.

The death toll mounted, cost too dear
for human thought to bear -
fanatics are alas prepared
to slaughter without care.

No matter children, wives, or men
such flesh is grist for mill -
while dead haunt battlegrounds of power
we tread on those we kill.

There is no answer, only hope
one day this world will mend
our broken lives with harmony -
if not, be this the end?

Brian Wells

ON A PICTURE OF AN INDIAN WARRIOR

The Prairie, his home no longer
This proud Indian warrior
Surveys the reservation,
The scene of his degradation,
His bronzed face burnished by
The red rays of the setting sun;
A wailing wind whirls the tumbleweed
Across the dry, scorched earth, seared
By the dying embers of his camp-fire;
The bitterness of acrid fumes
Choking like his burnt-out hopes;
Yet, from the ashes, a warmth enfolds me
Fanning an affinity and admiration
For this serene survivor.

O Miller

SARABAND FOR CELINE

As my years slip away I know I should be
Within step, and sound, of the surging sea
I must go to that cottage, with its door on the latch,
Where we smiled at the wind as it wove through the thatch
I'll stand at the window and gaze down the lea
You'll appear, you'll wave, from the path round the quay.

Alone with my thoughts on warm summer nights
I'll remember our walks to the harbour lights
I realise now - now it's all too late
You wanted our home there, and I made you wait
But I'll listen, as promised for your voice at low tide
And with eager footsteps will run to your side
Across the far shore, on the white pebble beach,
Our shadows will merge - no more out of reach.

Ken Marshall

THE SONG OF THE WIND

I am without form
I cast no shadow
I destroy, I create.

Where I come from words are meaningless.
Hurricanes, gales, breezes,
I do not differentiate.

I change the landscape,
as I swirl, twirl, spin,
overturn, uproot, devastate.

And I can be as gentle as a butterfly's breath,
a lover's caress,
and I sing.

I can take the breath away
and return it
perfumed with the blossoms I pass.

I sweep clean
cries the wind
blowing out his cheeks.

My influences are profound,
my effects legion,
yet I am unseen.

Judith Garrett

THREE CRAFTSMEN

Who can take a rose-cut sphere
And graft it skilfully to a clear
Stem, to create a finished article
Fine polished in every particle?
The glazier with his hands of clay
Can do the job in half a day.

Who can take the morning, pale and faint,
And enfold it in acrylic paint
To make a picture that's suitable
Adornment for a palace wall?
A gifted artist may be fired
With the inspiration that's required.

Who can raise a seed from life
To impregnate, like a virgin wife.
A single line, a staring phrase
That hums with fire when first it's heard, and stays
Singing in the air, impelled by a fierce elan?
Occasionally a dogged poet can!

Nigel Chisholm

REFLECTIONS OF CAPE TOWN, SOUTH AFRICA

Emerging on the horizon from our ocean liner
Appeared a new land incomparable and finer
Residing amidst exotic wildlife all around
The magnificence of which never failed to astound

Looking in awe at the miles of golden sands
Glistening and slipping like silk through our hands
The majestic Table Mountain standing proud
Appearing mysterious draped with swirling mist and cloud

The glorious radiant sun and luminous skies of blue
And picturesque skyline encompassing beauty so true
Mountainous panorama enveloped by fresh exhilarating air
Displaying exquisite wild flowers growing so rare

Blissful sumptuous days then drew to an end
Our broken hearts we did endeavour to mend
An enchanting country we'd tried hard to understand
The political complexities of this truly idyllic land.

Julia Keiser

LET'S CELEBRATE

All the things that matter in our earthly life
The joys and sorrows remembered -
to create wonderful memories always to
sustain and bring comfort. 'Heavenly Joy' -
in moments of sadness or doubt.

All joys, all things given by Almighty God
The beginning of each new day - in midwinter
the seeing of the first virgin white snowdrop -
lift up its head from what appears dead earth.
The robin, wren, blackbirds and thrush all bring their songs -
to the almighty King.

Life is sweet, however hard it sometimes feels.
The joy of wedding bells, the cry of newborn babe.
All though some of these are only found by few,
God then gives the choice of other gifts to fill our life anew.

The fellowship of true friends, a special place within our hearts.
The peace, a beauty of a special place.
All given to remind us of God and all His grace
A kind word spoken and the harsh one that wounds
All to be taken, forgiven, with all our love.

Thanks be to God for the blessings of each day.
Take the love of life - all along the way -
Find the beauty of life in all we see
Little things that really matter - take all the stress away
Give thanks at the end for a life well lived,
Forgiveness for those who have blocked God's way.

Heather Hill

POET'S HAVEN

Daffodils here, daffodils there, daffodils everywhere
This is Lakeland in spring for us all to share.
Wordsworth's Rydal Mount is the place to be
With Dora's field all around the church to see,
Rydal Water so peaceful and serene
Swans, ducks and boats one is unable to believe
The reflections on the water like ghosts moving on
It's just like a dream, which haunts us one by one.

When the sun shines on the mountains walkers are abound
This lovely place near Heaven which Wainwright also found,
Many people read his books for directions to the walks
Through the valleys past the lakes people walk and talk
Brantwood is a wonderful house to visit
Where Ruskin lived and wrote many poems in it,
A lovely white building up on a summit
Coniston Lake down below where dear Campbell blew it.

Haweswater is where the golden eagle likes to nest
Above the village which one can see truly is at rest,
The reservoir which was much needed
But when there's a drought one can see walls which have receded,
Some of the farms make one think back in time
They're old, unique, happy memories are fine,
We all need some peace if we are to stay alive
Remember the daffodils, mountains and lakes really do survive.

Down the lanes and round every corner
Golden daffodils swaying and dancing among the trees and fauna
Grasmere's churchyard you really must see
Where Wordsworth rests in peace, the place he loved to be.

Bessie Metcalfe

YOUR LOVE STANDS ETERNALLY

Higher than the highest mountain
Deeper than the deepest sea
Longer than the longest river
Your love flows free to me.

Nothing I can do to earn it
Nothing I can say or do.
Nothing matters more than this
Your love stands eternally.

I will praise Your name forever
I was made for Your delight
Through the sun and through the showers
Your love stands eternally.

Help me never to forget You
You alone can never fail
Though sometimes You seem far from me
Your love stands eternally.

Nothing can compare to You, Lord
Nothing I can ever desire
Though dreams be torn and tattered
Your love stands eternally.

Jacqui Haynes

INNOCENT VICTIMS OF SARAJEVO

With haunted look on saddened face
Our hearts do ache for this proud race
Where families strolled, and children safely played,
Midst ancient buildings, with majestic domes.
Reduced to ruins now, on bloodstained paving stones,
Where man killed man, whom once as brothers lived.
Humans herded into battle, ends in march to death.
No goodbyes allowed, before they massed beneath the earth
Women wait and weep for loved ones' safe return -
Not knowing of torture brutally and unrelentingly, enforced
By unfeeling warlords, obsessed with territory gains.
Unconcerned, that children also suffered injury and pains.
Some watched in horror as bodies ripped apart
Lost their innocence, with disillusioned heart.
Is life mapped out for all, with one pre-destined plan.
Or, are we led a merry dance, with man's inhumanity to man?
Do we have own steps to Hell, or climb an altruistic path?
To find eternity with loved ones, non-existent wrath
When innocents starve, and tortured souls must die,
Whilst idle rich in silken sheets do lie.

Sheila Barton

THE DELL

I close my eyes and drift away
On the tides of time to yesterday,
Down a winding path, onto the dell
This magical place, I know so well.

The soft velvet grass is damp from the dew
And the gorse, and broom gleams in a bright golden hue,
Blackberry bramble and wild roses entwined
All along hedgerows stately refined.

Sweet little daisies and glossy buttercups bold,
Flaunt their beauty with petals of gold
Green trees are dappled in soft sunlight
Nature has fashioned this paradise of delight.

Children's laughter echoes through the air,
Such happy days and memories linger here.
In this wonderland, I loved to roam,
Down on the dell, where the cuckoo flowers bloom.

Una Thurgill

LIFE IS WHAT YOU MAKE IT

Rushing, dashing, everywhere
No time to stop and see
The children that are playing there
Beneath the old oak tree.

No time to smile and give a wave
The hours they go so fast
Is it worth the time we save
To just forget the past.

Is this how we want to live
To see life pass us by
Always take and never give
And not to reason why.

Take the time to look around
Don't go tempting fate
Let your feet stay on the ground
Before it gets too late,

Life is what we make it
All things don't come free
We all have got to do our bit
I think you will agree.

Grace Wallace

EVENING OUT

I stand in my undies wondering what to wear,
When I hear the usual voice floating through the air.
'Are you ready? It's time we started out,'
'I won't be long,' I answer, 'and there's no need to shout.'
I bring out the 'blue', but it's no good wearing that,
It doesn't fit me properly and makes me look so fat.
The 'brown' I've worn so often, I think it knows its way,
To the Women's Institute and the church to pray.
I'll settle for the 'yellow' that's about the best,
But then I'm not so certain, it sometimes shows my vest.
It will have to be the 'turquoise', it cost me quite a lot,
Over my head I drop it, but will it be too hot?
I slap some stringent on my face and some lipstick too,
Put a comb through my hair and hope that I will do.
Why is it that some folk I know, when it's after nine,
Still look make up and beautiful, my nose begins to shine!
'Are you ready?' he shouts again, as I'm putting on my shoes.
'Hurry up, it's getting late, we haven't time to lose.'
I turn the key in the door and hurry through the rain.
'Close the garage door,' he calls, and I'm starting to complain.
In the car I slam the door and look across at him.
Well turned out, looking smart, cool and calm and trim,
Matching tie with his shirt and his socks match too.
Yes, but then, that's all he's done
And to think what I've been through.

Vera Lee

THE SKY AT NIGHT

The sky at night
Is a most beautiful sight
Which makes you look up in wonder

The stars on view
Take up their cue
In strains of bright asunder

How many people notice the sky
How many people give a sigh!
To this heaven we live under?

Barbara Coward

HOP PICKING 1941

(Written for Ian Muirhead who died in October 1940 when his Hurricane crashed into the hop gardens at Hempstead during the Battle of Britain)

In fruitful reds and floral gold the church is decked from wall to wall,
Sheaves of wheat adorn the aisle and grateful offerings
mass the floor.
Pungent hops around the font once more for Harvest Festival
Revive the past, recalling days when we were children of a war.

No turning back to sleep again, those mornings in September,
It seemed we'd been awake for hours just waiting for the dawn.
The shrouding drifting mists half hid the path we took, remember?
It seemed the world was ours alone as each new day was born.

Our winding path through dripping woods descended to the valley,
Where pregnant bines, like lovers, held each pole in tight embrace.
And blinkered shires prepared to toil as pickers stripped each alley.
And oasts reached for a dawn-lit sky with staid cathedral grace.

With flying fingers Grandma picked, a queen on canvas throne,
Surrounded by grandchildren, who would her labours share.
Her sacking robes were stained by hops, her shoes all torn by stones,
A straw hat on her head the only crown she'd ever wear!

Underfoot small infants crawled like beetles in the dirt,
And ragged toddlers roamed the bins in search of friendly face.
No time, it seemed, to wash their hands, to hug or kiss a hurt,
No rest from picking hops for mothers labouring in this place!

And should the siren's warning call reverberate around,
And toy-size planes their death games play amid the clouds so high,
We'd spare a thought for he, so young, who played that game and
Lost,
That fateful day a year ago, from out an autumn sky.

Today the hops have gone - and where they grew the wheat is gold.
Stench of rape invades the air and loud the tractors roar.
Suburbia reigns where damsons dropped, all is changed . . .
and I grow old,
Until those hops around the font bring back the child I was, once more.

Yvonne Lane

EVENING SUN

Caught by evening sun . . .
Furrowed line of straw stalk stubble.
Soft shadow slant oblique,
'Indian Summer' of a late September day.
And along a mud rut row
A man alone sits in tractor seat.

Caught by evening sun . . .
The day almost at close,
Silence stills the gloaming air
Twilight falls . . . dusk comes.
And a rail line - iron hard; bare cold
Hedges the field . . . both field and track aglow.

Caught by evening sun . . .
Sound sudden pulsate - erupt the calm.
Surge of engine, carriage in its sway,
Drives on before - ahead - is 'now'.
And from the train in window seat
A passenger alone looks out.

Caught by evening sun . . . the moment.
Man on tractor looking in,
Passenger on train looking out.
Each espy the other. . . each meet as 'one'.
Both here. Both now. Both there. Both gone.
Autumn evening sunlight . . . lingers on.

A D M Thomas

MISSING YOU

I'm missing a friend
Who was so dear
He once was near
But, O dear, lost I fear.

I shed a tear
And use my ear to hear
But, alas, he's lost I fear.

I remember his kindness
His listening ear
The time he was close and so so near
But, I fear, he's now no longer here.

But I peer into my heart, spirit and tears
And scramble through the wreckage.
Inside he still lurks, and he is so so near
And he will always be so, so dear.

Wendy Chaffer

AFTER 'NEIGE À LOUVECIENNES'

(Alfred Sisley 1839-1899)

Walking through the snow
Of life,
I've clutched
At sparks
That might have
Lit
That
Indefinable
Perfect light
Experienced
By poets
And suchlike.
But the drench
Of snow
Was always there
And so I walk
In frosted air.

Denise Harmin

BEFORE AND AFTER

Anxiety of mind but body sound
And yet within an hour
The other way around.
Through a haze of dopey sleep
A montage of noises percolates the deep.
All seem to join within the pain
And blend together to become the same.
A call, a bell, a bang
And kitchen clatter.
Comings and goings
And constant chatter.
The touch of unseen hands,
The closing of a door,
The tap, tap, tap of someone's heels upon the floor.
The rough brush of unfamiliar sheets,
And a shaft of light
That breaks into a moving pattern
As it creeps across the void and gloom
- Which on a sudden has become a room . . .
And far away I hear a steady flow
Of traffic, coming from a place below.
Thus Body, Mind and Time, in limbo hang
And slowly, reality and I return
To where this all began . . .

Frances Phillips

TODAY

The most important time in your life is - now.
The past is history; tomorrow may not come.
Enjoy today; welcome it; savour it.
Accept it; it is a gift.
It is a gift of time, a gift of life.
Accept it; grasp it - not too tightly -
It is fragile and cannot last.
This gift is valuable, unique and precious.
Do not impose your decisions on it too hastily - try to fathom *His* will.
Do not use it roughly, thoughtlessly, too quickly, too slowly.
Do not spoil it with anger, impatience or fear.
Try to accept the unexpected, the surprises.
You won't be bored!
Accept today full of ongoing hope.
Remember it *is* Heavensent.

Dorothy Howard

CARVED IN STONE

As yet another lazy day,
Drifts by on gilded wings,
The sun sets on another time,
Long forgotten things,
But etched upon the throne of love,
Stands a testament to time,
Of a love that might be real,
Or just a burnt-up paper mime,
So I ask you once again,
To dine this night with me,
Sail alone, hide yourself,
Deep in the rolling sea,
Where no one knows and no one cares,
About the charcoal past,
And ashes drift on the zephyr,
Lingering to the last,
Yet onward goes my lonely road,
Into the future; distant,
Forgive my rotten barbed wire heart,
If I remain resistant,
For my ways are mine, carved in stone,
In ages long gone by,
I remain unchanged, always the same,
My past will never die.

Paul Griffin

MY CHILD

I see an oak
Unbending an strong
I see a willow,
Giving shelter and love
I see a young sapling
Eager to grow unaware of its
Roots or where it will go.

I look at my child
A woman now grown,
The sapling an oak
Her father's true child.

The willow is me
A woman unsure
Did I do my best
Should I have done more?

Did I give too much shelter,
And not enough love?
Will the oak learn to bend
To forgive and give love?

A Dunkerley

RHYME'S A BIND

Some like to hear the rhythm
Of fixed iambic beat;
Some prefer the heavy tread
Of firm spondaic feet

For others, the uncertain length
Of lines like sliced-up prose
Gives pleasure in exploring
The freedom such verse shows.

Other ways to draw the ear
Are fancies in full flight;
Similes and images
And metaphors bring light

Alliterate the letters
With whispering soft sighs;
Win attention for your verse
With raucous corncrake cries.

Verse that's easy to recall
Has all these craftsman's tricks.
Think of them as vital parts,
As poets' building bricks.

For verse to live within us -
It's proved time after time -
We need mortar for those bricks;
What poets need is rhyme.

P Wolstenholme

MY FAIRIES

When I was young my fairies would visit me at night
And guard and tell me stories until the bright daylight
While underneath my pillow, a tooth I'd hid from sight
The tooth fairy would change it for a new one shiny bright
And little imps would clean my shoes while I was fast asleep
And tidy up the bedclothes, if they were in a heap
But when my school days started and education ruled
One by one my fairies left, they knew I wasn't fooled
For I was such a clever chap, I knew it all it seems
And things like wands and fairies were no part of my dreams
Now looking back to happy days, before it all went wrong
A happy little chap I was, singing those magic songs
Now I take a hard faced view, I know I'm not so nice
See it all as black or white with a heart that's cold as ice
Here in this concrete jungle, no flowers, no grass, no trees,
All the people talk the same, and act the same as me,
Where the windows are all double, and high up in the sky
And fairy stories are called spin, and mean a downright lie,
What I would give to wake again in that little bed so small
And open the lattice window to see the ivy on the wall
And run down that old garden path to the little iron gate
And never think about the time and was I running late
And hop across the thistle field to where the woods extend
Racing elves and pixies to where the rainbow ends
But fairy rings and grottoes and super fine stardust
And granting all your wishes are all made up of trust
I know if Puck and Oberon could guide my steps again
They'd mark my lottery numbers, but look at me in pain.

Charles Boyett

THE WILD WIND

Just as the clock was striking the hour,
The wind whistled up to the old church tower.
Pushed the cockerel on the weatherpane
And whirled it round and round again,
Fled through the churchyard, flashed past the station,
Blustered through the market square causing a sensation!
Litter flew about in the middle of a crowd,
Then the sun went in and hid behind a cloud.
The west wind whined through the Russian vines,
And then chased the clothes on the washing lines.
They danced and pranced in wild abandon
Until a shirt jumped off to eventually land on
A pretty pink protesting rose,
Where the shirt stretched out in a nonchalant pose.
The wind blew on through a hawthorn tree,
Where the starlings were waiting impatiently.
Startled, they rose up, their wings a-flapping,
Making the dog next door begin a-yapping,
Waking its master, asleep in his chair.
The wind snatched off his hat and ruffled his hair.
Up flew the hat right into space,
Flying here and there all over the place,
To finally fall amidst the football team
Where someone playfully kicked it in the stream.
The wind, exhausted, suddenly dropped
And all the commotion and movement stopped.
The wind lay silent and except for a sigh,
With a last soft breath, began to die.

Norma Marshman

COUNTRY FARE

The breeze plays softly o'er the rough hewn moor
Stirring the heather masses as they lie
Like Nature's carpet on uneven floor,
Resplendent in the warmth of sunlit sky.
And through this rustic panorama winds
An ancient road with just around its bend
A coaching inn where many a traveller finds
The goal for weary feet to slowly wend.
Inside its age old portals, burning bright,
A welcome fire with ruddy burnished glow,
Old oaken beams and glinting lantern light
And conversation's amicable flow.
The hills, the plains and rural signs declare
Fine attributes of simple country fare.

Doreen Jackson

THE SUMMER HOUSE

At the summer house by the lake -
Are sweet moments spent there
Still awake; when the breeze
Ruffles the water sensuously,
Does dead love return
Ever so fleetingly?

Do our love words yet whisper
Through the reeds somewhere,
Yesterday's kisses scent flower and air;
Are our tears still staining weed and willow,
Where tenderness laid is a pillow;
And the promises we made to break -
Are they revealed in paintwork cracked and flaked,
At the summer house by the lake?

Mike Monaghan

THE STUFF DREAMS ARE MADE OF

Unfolding this delicate gown of blue,
Sprinkled over with diamond dew,
Shimmering folds open and spread,
Luxurious, twinkling, gossamer thread.
A fairytale gown, such as this,
Floating clouds of silken bliss.

Through the years when it is shaken,
Memories spill and reawaken.
Enthrals again in starlight gleams,
Enchanted vision, romantic dreams.
Bewitching hours of the night,
Brings forth dreams of pure delight.

Transient music, silvered strings,
Dancing hours have fleeting wings.
Turn pages of delicious dreams
Dance silken slippers with silver seams
Spin billowing silk, with jewelled touches.
Twirling, whirling,
Awakening, returning,
Such is,
The stuff
Dreams are made of.

Joan Hawkes

GRAND ASSEMBLE

From Highland pipe, a sad lament
for Wallace lads of tartan born
their bloodied shirts
from savaged hearts so bravely spent.
Through ear of sound and eye of sight
comes love of heather softly blow
on lonely bend
where winds do moan of endless fight.
'Tween now and ever will a day
when rampant hoards of Andrew's lot
rise from bodies bent and slain
to take their place.
Then through silence, cold and still
will eerie sounds from far away
in ghostly echoes laugh and bray
at Redcoats hunting haggis.

Olwyn Kershaw

THE SEAL

Silently staring with large sad eyes
Endlessly seeking your mother
Among the long rough grass you lay down
Left alone to fend for yourself

Such a short time has passed since your birth
Even the wind howls at the thought
A gull cries as it flies overhead
Little comfort to your body

Somewhere in the distance the sea roars
Ebbing and flowing the tide runs
A wave crashes sending up its spray
Leaving the smell of salt behind

Sensing the sea as the source of food
Empty inside your journey starts
Ambling ungainly across the sand
Lolloping to the water's edge

Soulful now the sound of your calling
Entering the water this first time
Amazingly graceful you look back
Lingering briefly then you're gone.

Angie Mathieson

IT IS DECEMBER

December rises late and dark, and day
drags slowly out of night to dull
damp misery. We wait to find a lull
between the rain, and wonder why we stay,
when reason tells us we should go away
to a country where the days are full
of sun and warmth, and where they always will
delight us with blue sky, instead of grey.

But there again, there's more to life than sun:
the warmth of friends, the beauty of our hills,
the cosy crackle of the winter fire.
There's something in the heart that feels at home,
and these count more than all the weather's ills.
So that, I know, is all that I desire.

Richard Stead

TRIBUTE TO A FRIEND

We are all sat down in silence
Waiting to begin
It's half-past six, time to start
The first Sunday evening hymn.

It's a favourite tune of mine
And to our feet we rise
I sing it very loudly
To everyone's surprise.

A loud noise from the back
Someone clatters through the door
Could have been more quiet
Late again! As times before.

Once more into the silence
We bow our heads in prayer
Proudly next to me he sits
Upon the empty padded chair.

Then he starts a-scratching
All around his quarter hind
As the service carries on
No one seems to mind.

Oh dear, what is he doing?
He's cleaning out his ear
Please don't you start your purring
You old church cat, so dear.

Pamala Steeden

KEEP PRECIOUS

Hold precious in your hands
All the thoughtful, helpful deeds,
All the little things (and some big),
Even when life makes many demands.

Hold precious in your heart
All the love and care you remember,
All the warmth and friendship
We shared right from the start.

Keep precious in your mind
All the wisdom and advice,
All the support and understanding
We give and receive for all our time

Remember all the good, and forgive all the rest.
For we're all only human (you know that).
Believe God has His reasons, and that love never ends
And keep precious to you all your family and your friends.

Marianne Kennedy

IN PRAISE OF WOMEN

Many women stand alone,
Apart, yet feeling free.
Other women spend their lives,
Nurturing family.

The best of women manage both,
And spread love far and wide.
Gaining knowledge all the while,
And being calm inside.

Many men see women,
As icons of delight,
At least until they marry them,
And find this is not right.

Other men can only see,
A woman as a lover.
But the best of men will work to keep,
The family together.

Will share the chores to run a home,
With love and with compassion.
Never mind today's rude way,
Of keeping up with fashion.

We all look to our mother
To tell us right from wrong,
Even if her beauty;
Is good and true and strong.

For it's not what women look like,
That means so much at all.
But it's what they do whilst living,
That counts for me and you.

Hazel Mary Farrell

THE LAND OF MILK AND HONEY

If the whole world was like England
Every land was a land of milk and honey
Where everyone had enough to eat
And every soul alive had just enough money

If the whole world was like England
And all sick people could have medicine
Happy little children could play and stand
Together no matter what colour the skin

If the whole world was like England
A patchwork quilt for all to snuggle in
With birdsong and sparkling water, every comfort at hand
To savour and enjoy no matter what land you are in

If the whole world was like England
Each land had enough rain
So all the folk would have fresh water to drink and
All nations would rejoice again and again

If the whole world was like England
Stretching out a hand to each sister and brother
Then each nation would come to understand
And we would learn to forgive and love one another

If the whole world was like England
Peace and harmony would reign
The whole world would be like one land
Life would be so good on Earth again.

Glory to God

Josie Smith

IF I COULD BE LIKE JESUS

Oh to be like Jesus
To have His loving touch,
To tread the way that He has trod
To give us all so much.

I'd want to show this love to you
So that you could see
His power, His might, His holiness,
If you could see Him in me.

Oh for a closer walk with Him
To know how much He cares,
To know how much He feels our pain
As He listens to our prayers.

The love He has for each of us
Is constant and steadfast,
Nothing can compare with it
It cannot be surpassed.

If *I* drink in the Spirit
I will know and feel His touch
I can tread the way that He has trod
And know why He loves us so much.

Anne Smith

MALVERN

Malvern is my home town, I have lived here all my life
From toddler to a schoolgirl, teenager, then a wife.
Actually born in Warwick, not far from the castle walls
Where the peacocks strutted nightly disturbing Mother with their
calls.

My family soon returned to Malvern and by the time that I was one
My life in lovely Malvern had only just begun.

The hills are big and beautiful, the Beacon best of all,
We would play around the Toposcope and really have a ball.
With my brother and my sister and our friends from Lower Wyche
We'd climb straight up the Beacon, never bother with a path,
Breathless and excited, life was just a laugh

There was a little café that sold cups of tea and pop,
It really was a lifeline for those who reached the top.
The air was clean and healthy, the view beyond belief
With every shade of green from grass to tiny leaf.

We would play down on the common, where the cows and sheep
did graze,
The buttercups and daisies made a perfect carpet haze.
The boys would play at football, the girls at hide-and-seek,
Then we'd paddle in the little brook that gurgled at our feet.

We would gather up some frog spawn and take it home with us,
If Mother missed her jam jars she never made a fuss.
Malvern was a special place; no matter where you'd been
There was nowhere in the world to match Malvern's lovely scene.

I am now a pensioner, the years have simply flown,
Malvern hasn't stood still, in fact it's really grown,
The view from up the Beacon is not the same at all
There is still a lot of green to see, but also wall to wall
I'm rather sad to have to say it's bricks and mortar all the way.

So time has told on Malvern, but love it still I do,
With so many happy memories, surely you would too.

Valerie Lowe

WHO KNOWS

If perchance one day I'll go to Heaven
Will I see blue skies and radiant sun
And will the silver moon appear
Among a myriad of shining stars
All Heaven spun?

Will I smell the sweet perfume of flowers
Inhale the fragrance of the new mown grass
Still gaze in wonder at the mighty oak trees
See lakes and cliffs and goats on a mountain pass?

Will there be angels all about me
With cherubims and seraphims in throngs?
I know our Maker will be there to judge us
To remind us of all sins and wrongs.

There's one thing that I do believe, and it is
Friends who we once loved we'll see again above
Peace and tranquillity will reign there
There'll be no signs of crying or of pain
We all will be enfolded in God's love.

So if and when I go at last to Heaven
I hope those left behind will not be sad
Because I know I'll be amongst dear friends there
And best of all I'll be with Mum and Dad.

Joyce M Carter

WHERE ARE THEY NOW?

Where are they now, our loves of yesteryears?
The ones who sent the blood pulsating through our veins
As in those bitter-sweet, rich summer days
We wandered, hand in hand through country lanes,
Through meadows fresh and green,
By murmuring streams dancing on their way,
Mingling with our laughter, blending with our tears;
Ah yes! We laughed, we cried, but all too soon love died;
And then because fate deemed it so,
We knew of that, we must let go.

Someone may ask, 'Where are they now?'
So bravely to the attics of our minds we climb
And there we find, veiled in cobwebs spun by time . . .
We pause, and wonder . . . wonder why . . .
We whisper, yet there's no reply.

But when some phrase is uttered by a stranger unawares,
A scene recalled, a time, a place
'Tis then through swirling mists the loves we knew
- Borne on the winds of time -
Come echoing back across the years,
The bells begin to chime,
The clouded vision quickly clears
And through our memory's eye
We smile with tenderness and grace,
Once more together, face to face.

Eunice M Caines

TENBY - FROM THE HILL

A crow is cawing, jawing the day.
Gulls, wheeling, screeching, fight over their prey.
The grass - vivid green, but the sky so dark;
The branches are gnarled and dead: winter's dry bark.
I look for the steeple, down from the hill -
Milestone of joy in the winter still.
The sea, slate-coloured, to match the sky
With colour-paint cottages seen from on high.
The blessed season, crisp-bright through the grey -
God-given delight, beauteous day.

Jennifer Richards

FRIENDSHIP

The river had carved its way
Through a valley of grass and flowers
Stepping stones for people to cross
The fisherman sits for hours.
I used to watch the water
Rippling through the stones
Miniature fountains, tiny whirlpools
Moorhens and water voles.
Sweet memories of childhood
Fading out of sight, the schoolroom teacher,
Young friends, a playground fight.
As I grew older the river I knew
Became the river of life
The stepping stones
Became good friends
Helping through tears and strife.
Knowing that we are united
In wonderful caring ways
Is something I will treasure
For the rest of my days.

Joanne Powel

HOW DO I LOVE THEE?

My dear Lord God

I love Thee
As a flower does
The rain
That quenches its thirst
And the sun
Which warms its petals soft as silk;
With longing

I love Thee
As the ocean
Loves the shore
As it caresses and ripples on
The sand and the stones;
With joy

I love Thee
As a boat does
The harbour
Its resting place
After journeys long;
With welcome

I love Thee
Wide and deep
And strong
In every moment
Every song;
With passion

I love Thee
As a human being
Broken; forsaken, by Man;
Giving up my life, to You
So that I may
Find myself
In You;
With humility.

Thank You
My dear Lord God
For giving us
Your Son;
We're now
As one.

Paula Walsh

THE LAND OF ETERNAL SLEEP

Over yonder in the land of eternal sleep
When once in their beds no one ever peeps
If passing through so peaceful there
You may pause for a while and stare
And reflect on life and all that has gone
And what you have built upon
Now is the time not to stand still
But with determination and will
To achieve what you have not yet done
Before your bedtime calls to the land of eternal sleep.

Patricia Taylor

LEICESTER EXPO 2005

Summer has come - and gone
And now we've got it back again
It's in-between cold and wet
Take it in your stride, it's all you'll get.

No need to travel to the sea
They have brought the sand to Town Hall Square
Bring your buckets and your spades
And build your sandcastles there.

This is the Expo event for the second year
Make the most of it whilst it's here
Next week it will be no more
Only a memory to keep in store.

M Holmes

CHRISTMAS DREAM

It was Christmas Eve and far away, Johnny could hear the reindeer's sleigh.
As they trod the clouds and rode the sky, their bells were jingling up on high.
The tingling noise was travelling past as Johnny ran to the window fast.
And just before the moon was lost, whilst shining on the snow and frost,
He caught a glimpse of Santa's face, his large sack bulging, each toy in place.
He waved his hand at the wide-eyed boy, and Johnny's heartbeat fast with joy.
The moon looked down and winked an eye as Santa's sleigh went flying by,
Johnny shivered and shook his head, then clambered into his warm soft bed.
Was it all true or just a dream, was it really Santa his eyes had seen?
Did he really hear the reindeer laugh as they travelled along that moonlit path?
Their clinking bells and their hooves pit-pat, could it be true he'd heard all that?
His eyelids closed and he softly sighed, in his dreams he followed Santa's ride.
Over the rooftops and round the trees, Santa guided the sleigh with ease.
The reindeer knew just where to stay, whilst Santa unloaded his presents gay.
Then on again until all were gone, the sleigh with Santa travelled on.
Through clouds and mist and stars so bright, back to his home in the northern night.

Neil Arch

TIME IS A QUICK FINGERED FOE

(Written for my son on his 18th birthday as a reminder of the life before him and the quick passage of time)

Time is a quick fingered foe,
Taking the long days of childhood.
Reflecting the old weathered crow,
In the mirror, where we once stood.

You have your freedom and youth,
Take it, invest in it well.
Find the future, seek out the truth
And remember this, only you can tell.

In your haste take time to listen,
Make your words wisdom to be heard
Ignore the false gold that glistens,
Be wise as the silent, watching bird.

Let your conscience be your master,
Your honesty, your bond
Have strength to overcome disaster,
And let your memory always live on.

Colin Farmer

MAGICAL MIDNIGHT

The moon is full tonight,
Bathing all in her silvery light.
Mystic mistress up on high,
She dominates the sky.

The air is cool upon my face,
Now has slowed the hectic pace
That made up the daytime hours,
But still so sweet are the scented flowers
That linger and surround me,
Soften the chains and set free
A soul in need of release,
Forever seeking inner peace.

The stones glow white beneath my feet,
As I sit upon the garden seat,
And velvet darkness soothes my mind,
With the comfort that I fought to find.

My eyes are opened wide
And I feel whole inside.
As the owl makes his solitary call,
Under the spell of enchantment I fall.

M Mayes

DESTINY

The first time I met you, I knew
What my whole life had been leading to.
It was such a surprise and I could tell
That you felt the same way as well.

You were so different from the others,
Not my usual choice of lovers!
On many occasions our paths crossed
But each time the moment was lost.

Fate took a hand in the end,
You offered your help and became my friend.
Slowly but surely love started to grow
And I discovered I needed you so.

Months have flown by, much we have learned,
Most of all, each other's trust, we have earned.
The future is enlightened for you and me,
Two halves becoming one is our destiny.

Ann Guilder

MORNING

The cockerel lifts his sleepy head, to tell the world, 'Get out of bed,'
Dew drops gently caress each flower, to say, 'It is the
awakening hour.'
Up peeps the sun, from beyond the hill, where hours before the
Earth was still.
Bright yellow rays shine for all to see, God's wonder in
creation's glory.
Darkness of night is out of sight, day breaks into a blaze of light.
Birds sing sweetly to welcome the day, as on trees, leaves whisper
as they sway.
The sea washes over the yellow sands, obedient to the good
Lord's plans.
Seagulls soar and fly on high, free in the vast expanse of sky.
Each day God looks down from His home above, to bless the
world with His endless love.
His promises sealed with a loving kiss, who else could create
such a world as this?
All nature rises to give Him praise, in her many various
colourful ways.
But what of us, each brand new day, are we happy to awake
in such a way?
Or do we bemoan that alarming clock, bashing it so that its noise
will stop?
Wiping sleepy tiredness from our eyes, we greet the morn with a
dreary sigh.
'Just a few cosy minutes more,' we say as we anticipate the
rush of the day.
Our feet at last, then touch the floor, and we stagger, yawning,
to the door.
If this day is to successfully succeed, the teapot is our urgent need.
I am sure there is a lesson for us to learn here,
How do we, with nature so fair, compare?

Pearl Gill

CRIME AND PUNISHMENT

It's three years since the dreaded day
You left me at the door,
I walked the corridor all alone, then
Climbed the stairs to the second floor.
We'd journeyed there in silence - your head was turned away
Not a shred of comfort offered on that hateful July day.
The words the doctor spoke to me, were cruelly delivered
'You did terrible on your exercise test - it means an operation.'
I telephoned you in floods of tears, please come soon to collect me
In halting tones I broke the news -
Sure that you'd allay my fears
But where was the arm around me, the shoulder to rest my head?
All that I had was silence - I wished that I were dead.
I tried to carry on the same, but I grew thin and pale
The pain became too much to bear, my strength began to fail.
If it wasn't for my family, I wouldn't be here today,
They kept me from going under, chastised you for being that way.
This went on for a year and a day, the silence, the averted head -
My crime - to be put on the waiting list for a by-pass operation
You didn't believe in male doctors wielding the surgeon's knife
Never really caring, about me, the devoted wife.
It was just the green-eyed monster resurfacing again
I'd been treated that way for most of my life.
I should have known how it would be
When the operation was over, you shook the surgeon's hand.
Forgetting all that had gone before, you acted so brash and so grand,
Forgetting all the silences, you tried to make amends
But I won't forget as long as I live -
Where were you, when I needed a friend?

Patricia Whiting

SPRING IS HERE

Spring is here, hip hooray,
The leaves of green are out today,
The snow has melted, now crocus blooms
Amidst the soils of winter's gloom.
Shout 'Hip Hooray!' the sun is out,
The birds sit singing all about,
With cheerfulness there is no doubt.
So shout hooray the spring is here,
With joyfulness and pleasant cheer.

Pamela Coope

COMES THE REAPER

'I turned a stone,' the Reaper said, 'To see if owt was . . .
you know . . . dead!
When out from 'neath it, sudden ran, a cheaply suited
grey-faced man.'
'Oh! Spare me Sir,' he craven begged, from fear that suit now
wetly legged,
'To kiss your blade too young am I, what sin be mine that I should die?'

'But there for chance I chose your stone,' the Reaper spoke,
'for chance alone:
I judge not sinners, nor their crime, my touch dictates them
but their time.'
'Then cast your shadow not on me,' the grey man heaping plea
on plea,
'Entreat you I my fate repeal, pray let me speak - my worth reveal?'

Intrigued the Reaper stayed his hand, an instant's grace was
all he planned,
In spite the plaintiff's cunning leer, he held: this rodent's 'worth'
to hear,
'Then speak your piece,' the Reaper sighed, what cared he when
this creature died?
'But one tongue's twist, the smallest lie, and know you'll beg an
age to die!'

'Know, fearful one, my earthly trade - how many at your feet I've laid,
A pension late, a rent cheque lost; a hostel closed whatever the cost,
With but a single inked stroke: a budged cut, an orphanage broke,
A children's ward, cry how they might, without a second's thought
shut tight!

How many times had you but known, I'd with my pen your
harvest sown,
Behind my desk what blight I've played: to raise such stalks
before your blade!
Have mercy terror, leave me be, what harm, when all my toils
serve thee,
What cause to take me if you know, that you do reap what I have
sow?'

The Reaper turned his hooded head, 'You give me cause for
thought,' he said,
"Tis true it falls within my power, to choose each man's allotted hour,
So far as you have careful sow, it seems but just you harvest know.'
And with a wave the Reaper turned, 'Go forth and reap what you
have earned.'

Thence quick the grey man turned away, his guile, he laughed,
had won the day,
When scything swift across the ground . . .

The Reaper's blade made not a sound!

Mike Sullivan

A FAMILY TREE

The young man held his newborn son
In his two enormous palms.
With utmost care he placed the babe
In the cradle of her arms.

As she gazed upon this tiny mite,
This twig upon life's tree
She reminisced the distant past
When she sat on Great Grandad's knee.

She was his fourth generation
A fact he would proudly declare,
Now the child she was holding
Had taken her place - back there.

For he was her fourth generation
Upon her family tree,
Her life had spanned seven strong branches
With God's grace - to touch - and to see.

This fine living tree, so beautiful,
Nurtured with loving care
Sheltered each one the Creator sent,
In hope or from despair

Jehovah had truly blessed her
And her family
And as she silently thanked Him
She wondered if baby would see
His fourth generation great grandchild
Take his place upon the tree
And would he - could he - possibly - ever
Remember her - that's me?

Doreen Roberts

GRIEF

Time will come, time will go
Your healing has now begun
Reflections of a life you spent
With somebody special
Who you loved
Questions why it had to be
Nagging and gnawing away
Reasons that aren't clear just yet
Will eventually fade away
Days of practically nothing
Everything dull and grey
An emptiness beyond belief
Just eating you away
A darkness in the brightest light
Your feelings open and raw
There's not a slightest moment
Whenever it seems to go
You kid yourself, did it happen?
Did it really happen to me?
And then the stark reality
That death brings unto me
There's a numbness carries us thru' it
A strength deep down inside
Those terrible hurting feelings
Will eventually subside
Leaving you to reflect in peace
Upon all the happy times
Those special memories
You made together
Are yours until the end of time . . .

Christine A Walker

In Memory of 'Yosser'

Seal-point Siamese with eyes of blue
I hope you knew how I loved you
You pranced and preened and I was smitten
Right from when you were a kitten
Your bossy ways, the way you talked
The way you purred, the way you stalked
You would butt your head against my chin
And rub yourself against my shin
So quick and agile, full of life
You'd comfort me in times of strife
You seemed to know when I was down
And whirl and dance just like a clown
Gazing into my eyes, face close to mine
Brilliant blue eyes how they did shine
But then you strayed a little too far
And got run over by a car
The house is empty now you're gone
And Ming still sings his mournful song
He misses you and so do I
While you chase butterflies in the sky.

Rose Horscroft

Near On Dumb, The Constructive Dismissal

I jest you not
He boiled a plot
A trick with tricks within
He shouted aloud
His raw so proud
A tomfool I saw within
Hit me with your rhythm stick
He said unto I
And I will be so clever
And constructively I lie
I hit him with my rhythm stick
And saw he was a lie
And now he begs to differ
Because now I have the pie
Trust him not he boiled a plot
A trick with tricks within
But leave alone
And don't you moan
When there's no biscuits left in your tin.

Stephanie Brown

Leaves

Now the leaves have fallen down
And are lying on the ground,
Soon the wind will come
And blow them all around.

Why do trees strip off in winter
And stand there oh so bare?
It's as if they discard the old
And have nothing else to wear.

But down below, in the ground
There is something going on,
Planning and preparing for the springtime
For the new leaves, green and strong.

When the winter cold has past
And there's a little warm and gentle rain,
The buds will then burst open
And it will all start once again.

W Wyndham Lewis

A Label

Do not put a label on yourself
That will limit you to be free
Like people for themselves
Then more happiness there will be.

Each day we learn something new
Surprises me when professionals say this
Looking at it straight on it makes sense
All this education for all leads to bliss.

I learn funny sayings from children
Adults have me howling too with laughter
This evening what will I learn from actors
May never lead to me getting a BAFTA.

I am going to learn to act again
Although my friends say I have no need to
I just want to play a very small part
This year see what it will lead to.

Am I a housewife, writer, artist or singer?
I do not need a label to cling to
All I need to do is pray, live and love
Relax, observe - less talking - and *do*.

May Shaoul

Spring In A City Under Siege

A cherry flowers among the war-torn houses,
spotlit by sunshine from a splintered sky;
a show of clustered opulence that rouses
wry memories of luxury gone by.
Its red-tipped petals stroke the pockmarked faces
of concrete walls that cannot hold at bay
an enemy that knows the secret places,
the unexploded minefields of decay.
But for a moment the machine gun rattle,
that shakes the writhing fibres of the air,
pauses - regrouping for a further battle -
and there is silence in the sunlit square.
No stretcher bearers and no sighs intrude;
only the coupling doves, that croon of life renewed.

Fay Marshall

Sleeping Fairy

As I peeped inside a rose
I saw a fairy fast asleep
she wore a dress of pure silk
and no shoes upon her feet

I didn't want to startle her
as I stood close by
watching her fast asleep
with a snowflake by her eye

Her eyelashes fluttered open
as she coyly looked at me
a smile spread across her face
as she was surprised to see me

I gently took her by the hand
as from the rose she crept
the snow had fallen onto the petals
as she quietly slept

She waved her hand gently
then she was gone
the memory of the sleeping fairy
will linger on and on.

Annette Carver

MY FOREST OF DEAN

'Tell me, a stranger, of your Forest of Dean, where visitors view,
But do not really feel.'
'My Forest, which once was Royal Henry's domain, from where the
deer
which he hunted, did give my Forest its fame . . .
My forest e'en then ancient, with its riches long known,
has given us silver, iron ores and coal.
Its wealth, though so earthy, is not all that it gives,
For there's its beauty of nature, which within us all lives.
It breathes with the seasons, as us Foresters know well,
As here in the Forest, as lovers we dwell.

Two rivers fulfil us, Severn and Wye, and they calm and sustain
us, as they pass us by.
There's a peace near these rivers, as nature's bounties they bring,
And where on long summer's days, soaring voices do sing.
Eagles glide high over tree-covered hills, and where those proud
Falcons, sweep down to our rivers and thrill.

Summer brings colour to our trees and our hills, and when its harmony
of nature, bring bluebell and daffodil.
They sway, and they dance in our warm summer breeze, and where
Sheep there do amble up hillsides, with ease.

Great oaks fill the skyline, so with sweet smelling fir,
Filling air with aromas which linger more and more.
There's an everlasting beauty, which never will fade, lifting our
Spirits in so many ways.
So this is my Forest, from which I'd never depart, as being born
'Midst this beauty, is so close to my heart.'

Alan Smith

THE APPOSITE SEX

When Adam delved and Eve span
Who was then the gentleman?

The two themselves knew it of course -
They'd read it in a book of morse.
She was the one who was knitting a vest:
He was the chap with hair on his chest.
That's how they were in those first early days,
Before this confusing sexual maze,
Now who can tell which and in what gender -
Who is the tough guy and which the tender?
For men wear earrings and bracelets and things,
Make-up and corsets and all kinds of rings.
Whilst women in jeans pretend they've no chest,
Hang shirts outside trousers and think they're dressed.
Mums play football and drive heavy lorries,
Dads stay at home with their household worries,
We have women boxers, judges and crooks,
While masculine men pretend to be cooks.
Girls in the army are now taught to fight -
Which puts unarmed combat in a new light.
Ladies throw javelins, hurl the shot-put:
They seem to delight in straining a gut.
For myself, I declare, I am not drawn
To women who flaunt their muscle and brawn.
Let them win medals to prove they're the champs:
Leave me to the charms of feminine vamps.
I don't mind if they're smart, with good degrees,
As long as they've bosoms and shapely knees.
Let us see women in whom we believe,
As Adam did, surely, in mistress Eve.

Len Cox

YOU DON'T EVEN KNOW YOU ARE IN THIS POEM

Time flees so fast,
And though we frantically divide it up -
Naming it to make it real,
To capture it and make it last -
We are still like penguins,
Falling flat on our backs as
We watch life fly overhead,
Neither seeing nor caring that it has left us behind.
And we say that tomorrow will be better,
Though we know tomorrow never comes,
And each day blurs into the next
As we wait for improvement in infinite todays.
And we forget how we once counted our time
As we lose it in glasses and bottles,
Whole days carelessly misplaced
As we hurtle into the future
While remaining trapped in the past.
This record is scratched and old now,
Replaying the same worn lines,
Trying futilely to hold on to a moment
As it slowly destroys itself.
I watch, yet cannot bear to stop it.

Kim Warren

O PERFECT LOVE

A perfect love, a special gift to treasure
Full of promise to care for each other
May this wonder go on forever,
A wonderful partnership, marriage
Hope the vows taken by both of you
Two happy people sharing their love
Starting a future - may it all come true
May your wedding be just perfect today
The first step in our life shared by two
With its ups and downs along the way
Together you will learn to share
What life can bring your way
Together you will learn to care
Still more with each new day
May a future hold in all you do
Happiness as your life together starts
You have so much ahead of you
With the love you both have in your hearts.

Irene Low

REVERIE

To live and breathe and walk I need no love
To talk I need to muster only words
For in my dreams my life has love enough
Each sleep-filled breath the sweetest song I've heard

These starlight assignations seem so real
That fortune could not grant them to be true
These moments only ether I can steal
And recklessly I fill my world with you.

Good spirit, if I've known you all along
And you've been hidden by another face
To show yourself by day would not be wrong
To hide in my mind's shadows is such waste.

If day were night, and night and day were one
Would you remain a dream, all magic done?

Giselle Harold

THE OLD RECTORY

I went to see the house we left so long ago,
But when I walked the road that led me to that unforgotten place,

The house had disappeared beneath a canopy of green,
No chimneys with wisps of smoke,
No gables, no grey slate roof,
Only trees like a grave of moving branches,
An awesome sight, a whispering of a long gone past.

Dare I look beneath the branches - move the leaves a little,
Would I see a child there?
Still playing in the sunlight dancing feet and braided hair,
Would I see again the drama's acted out so long ago,
Small to the world outside,
Huge traumas to the child caught in the timelessness of war.

As I look with warmth and fear,
At the long and winding drive so dark with trees,
The memory windows opened one by one,
And let me see again into the past.

First the days, then months, a year slips by,
The garden hot in August sun,
Warm smell of hay stuffed into sacks to make a bed,
Great trees whose branches swept the ground,
Soon to become horses for laughing children,
Who rode and jumped high into the leaves.

But the pictures darken now,
War brings many things best forgotten,
Do I walk the winding path?
To look more closely 'neath the boughs of green,
Or do I let the past lie sleeping,
Leave a spiritual bouquet and walk away,
I walk away.

Marie Bagley

THE STAR KNOWS WHERE YOU ARE

(For Chrissie)

Burgundy and gold, new tinsel to behold:
A star to top the tree -
But the eyes that meant to see it,
Couldn't look upon with me.

You said you'd come and see it,
I knew you'd keep your word -
But circumstance, it changed all that,
Yet still I hear your words.

The lights they shone so brightly,
As yours they grew so dim,
Little did I know that night,
You were passing on to Him.

You can never see my tree
But I always hope you can,
See the lights shine brightly,
And are looking on with me.

The tree has never meant the same
It stands and looks alone -
Its presence I see before me;
Yours I feel unknown.

But if I look real closely
And stare upon the star,
There is no doubt or question
To where you really are . . .

J M Davies

THE GARDEN OF A FRIEND

The Almighty sows His seeds with care
And so created Earth's garden fair
Roses and lilies and daisies white
Growing by day and resting by night.
Trees, like people, short and tall
Each borrowing time, awaiting His call.
The Husbandman may pluck a flower,
Some bloom a lifetime, some an hour.
He may transplant a tree we love
To holier ground somewhere above.
Though trees and flowers may fade and die
They were but borrowed from on high.
So dry those eyes, those bitter tears
Let calm and peace dispel your fears.
We cannot own, they were but lent
Entrusted souls from Heaven sent.
Remember now the carefree hours,
The rainbows, sun and mad March showers.
Seek not to question the Gardener's skill
Let the spirit of love your whole life fill.
Give *Him* leave to take *His own*
You'll surely find
You'll not walk alone!

Roselie Mills

AWAY DOWN SOUTH

Up in the wind dots of leaves
Scatter about, but they are not
Really leaves but little birds
Whose hearts are beating for
Southern parts across continents,
Deserts, guns and storms.

A team of swallows lines the wires
To play all today
Before the long haul south.

Robert Wynn-Davies

SONG OF THE UNBORN

Oneness
　　We are part of the same world.
Waiting
　　With you I am safe and comfortable.
Peaceful
　　Yet becoming aware of the space I am in.
Sounds
　　Enter unbidden into my consciousness.
Awakening
　　The need to break free, to continue my life.
Fear
　　Of the pain that awaits us both at my leaving.
Aware
　　My birth will feel like death to us both.
Life
　　To be lived without, and away from you, as I grow.
Continues
　　In another, unknown world, beyond my comprehension.
Strengthened
　　By your love I become stronger more able to be.
Nurtured
　　By this giving of yourself to me, I shall go on.
Loved
　　Growing, moving forward, toward my true self.

Ann Edwards

KISMET

Fate leads me by the hand
Along a rugged path of twists and turns.
Be I in the wings, or centre stage;
Hero or villain, sage or fool,
The play unfolds before my eyes
And I must perform for my peers,
Like an infant child learning to walk,
Frailties exposed by each faltering step:
Yet their vitriol will not touch my soul
Buffeted by both kith and kin, consort and confidant,
I will retain my sense of integrity; of balance; of perspective:
The mists of time may cloud my vision
Gazing back with a mixture of fondness and regret,
So, focused shall I remain on destinies still to be fulfilled.

Ray Crutchlow

THE GHOST THAT I'VE BECOME

I am here, but you can't see me,
Though you will sometimes sense a chill,
For all my hopes, my dreams, my wishes,
I know you never will,
I know you never will.

The ghost that I've become,
Is all that I have,
Is all that's been left to me,
To haunt these places
That once I loved, where once I lived

Don't bother to bolt your door,
Don't bother to lock the gate,
Or pull the curtains
To the deep dark night
The ghost that I've become,
Will simply pass through
The wall, the ceiling,
Or the creaking floor.

If it's fear that you're feeling,
That's as it should be,
But such is the making of your own
For I, have no problem,
With us sharing this home.

I never thought that things,
Would turn out this way.
One day, I was drawing breath,
The next, close friends with death.
The ghost that I've become.

Richard Gould

AUTUMN EVENING

I walk along a solitary way
Beneath the sunset of an autumn day,
Amid transparent mists of evening haze,
Whilst in the fading heavens before my gaze
There shines, but faintly yet, the evening star
To greet me and to comfort from afar;
The woods are silent now, the birds have flown,
The sun has set, the darkness deeper grown,
Whilst autumn's golden splendour slowly fades
Into the twilight depths of evening shades;
As darkness casts her veils upon the scene
The evening star shines, peaceful and serene;
Symbol of love, whose gleam shall not expire,
Whose radiance ceases never to inspire.

Geoffrey Lund

GROWING UP

There comes a time when memories
Seem to take over one's mind
You recall the happy and sad times
And remember friends who have always been kind.
Gone are the days in the playground
When football was your daily treat
Hoping the whistle would not blow for lessons
For you had the ball at your feet.
The shouting could be heard many miles away
When you scored the winning goal
Then it was back to the classroom
Where the teacher ruled over one and all.
As you grew older it was cricket
Which was not so rough a game
But now you have reached the twilight years
Life no longer seems the same.
Your arms used to lift high above your head
When throwing a ball for a team mate to catch
Waiting for the umpire to raise his voice and call 'Out'
Then going home happy after winning the match.
Now you see your favourite sports
Sat in your armchair watching TV
Sometimes you doze and fall fast asleep
From life's cares for a while you're set free.
The years are now taking their toll
Your energy seems to lessen each day
So you thank God for giving you a good innings
And for being with you every day.

Helen Knott

WILL IT RHYME?

I've written some poems from time to time,
And debated the ends to each line,
I've wondered whether the words will make sense,
But most of all

Will it rhyme?

Poems reflect lives bad and sad,
And the good and happy too,
Things that have happened to people you know,
And events that have been inspirations to you.

In the past I've written of many things,
Of places I've seen and people I've met,
I've written with humour and seriously too,
Of things that I've done or still wish to do.

I've also, always, loved reading the words,
Of poets both old and new,
They've brought me great pleasure over the years,
And helped me to think matters through.

When your best laid plans are going to pot,
And you'd like to change things but can't say a lot,
You may hum a bright tune just to keep life at bay,
Or write a little poem to turn around the day,

So I'm writing this new one for Forward Press,
And I'll agonise over each line,
But in times when writing can cause you some stress,
Just consider one thing -

Will it rhyme?

Denise Jones

MOVING HOUSE

Boxes, crates and open gates,
Removal vans and helpful men,
Stacks of furniture and plates -
When will it all be straight again?

To leave a home of many years
And move away to pastures new
Is not without its share of tears,
Especially as it fades from view.

The new house beckons, full of hope,
With fresh scenes and friendly faces.
There'll be no time to sit and mope,
Arranging things in all their places.

Old friends and memories remain
However far you move away,
Now it's time to start again
And turn the page of each new day.

Dawn Rickatson

THE LOVE WORD

Love, is it just a word or phrase,
Or is it the be all of your days?
From tennis courts on summer days
The umpire calls, love all, not easy
That, try as you may.
Love conquers all, now there's a
Phrase to ponder, when cold, grey
Fingers of fear, mar each day.

Mother's Day cards, flowers strewn,
Each one saying, love you Mum
Not for one day only, to be sure,
But sincerely meant, *that* day.

Then there is, the love, the greatest
Love, from one above who loves us all
That is the word.

G Halliwell

ARE YOU SITTING COMFORTABLY?

Gather round, gather round, it's storytelling time
thrilling - chilling - comforting - informing,
ever so in sound and art and mime
has humanity been found
performers and listeners entwined
every man, woman and child combined
actors in the round on the stage of life.

Gather round, gather round it's television time
even now humanity is found
still being thrilled and chilled,
presenters and watchers bound
in hi-tec proficiency, armchair immobility
surrounded by dramatic fact and fiction
evolution of life's Global Village

In winter cold or summer heat
I can switch on the box, retreat
Into panoramic news and views
Probing immensities and mysteries
A pageantry of creation's history.
I sing in praise of my TV
And virtual reality.

Joan Baker

RETIREMENT

Is this what retirement means?
A lonely field, a change of scene,
Longing to see a friendly face,
Released from livery, lost in space.

No one handy, with brush and comb,
No mints, no apples, no comforts of 'home',
Lucky to have a nearby tree,
Its leafy branches take care of me.

Why, why have they changed my world?
From proudly parading with flags unfurled
Groomed and vetted, everyone kind,
Is it, out of sight, out of mind?

Something's stirring at the bottom gate
Carrot's approaching, so what's my fate?
Groundless fears, have melted today
A four-legged friend, is trotting my way!

Mabel Wall

SCALE INTO SKIN

When God created Adam
He drew him from the mud by his gills;
Saw Man in the fish.
Looking down at the flapping tail
God smiled, and smoothed His hands
Over prickly fin and slithery scale,
Over and over the cold wet flesh.
God smiled, and flexed His hands,
Gave the rib cage a push,
Tugged the lungs out and in,
Kneaded scale into skin.

At last the dazed creature, gasping and blinking,
Climbed up through the welter of salt and spray,
Saw the face of love, the smile of greeting -
Warmed himself in the sun of the new day.

Margaret Sparshott

HAVE YOU GOT EYES TO SEE?

Can you see to read these lines I wrote?
Then how thankful you should be;
A lot would like to be like you,
How they wish that they could see.

Do you marvel at the sunrise
On a clear and summer's morn?
Do you 'see' creation's wonders?
Are you glad that you've been born?

Do you 'see' God's hand when you look around?
Are there thanks within your heart?
What does creation mean to you?
Just what does it impart?

If you can't 'see' with the eyes God gave
Then one who is blind might say
I can 'see' much more than you
Though I can't see the light of day.

I can see God's hand in creation,
He sheds light on my path through his word;
In loving kindness he takes my hand,
So I need not be perturbed.

I can 'see' bright times for the future
Through a study of prophecy;
How I wish that you could 'see' like me,
Though you have eyes to see.

Martin Hiney

RAIN

Drip, drip, drip runs the tap,
As I turn it full on -
Splash, splash, splash,
Is the reply as the water falls in the sink,
Creating pools,
Of ever-increasing concentric circles.
Pitter-patter falls the rain on the window ledge.
The wind blows and the trees sway,
As the raindrops cascade onto the windowpane -
Into a gushing stream-like trellis,
So that I can nearly see the reflection of my face,
In the teardrop lattice-like pattern on the glass
In the garden outside

Jenny Pearce

WORDS

Words can inflame a nation,
Soothe a child, an old man weary,
A young man wild.
But best, can set one mind at rest.

Words can quell a riot,
Help a friend,
Tell the way to a journey's end.
But best, can set one mind at rest.

Words can weave a tangled mess,
Leading to murder and sore distress,
Beyond any words to sort it out,
Not by a whisper, nor by a shout.
But best, can set one mind at rest.

Words can be spoken or left unsaid
And a loved one dead.
Words can speak love, words can speak hate,
Speak love to the living before it's too late -
And best, set one mind at rest.

Words too many, words too few,
Words to remember, words to rue.
Words from thought, words that were taught,
Words from the lips.
But it's words from the heart
That best can set one mind at rest.

E Bellis

CHRISTMAS PRAYER

Spare a thought for the lonely
When you enjoy your day
Not all of us have family
With us, or comes to stay.
When our children laugh with joy
There are others who are crying,
Think of those caught up in wars,
Pray for the ill and the dying.
Make your new year resolution
To help others in their need,
To understand each other
Whatever colour or creed.
There must surely be a way
For all the wars to cease.
This world is a beautiful place,
Let us live in harmony and peace.

Maureen Turner

THE POET AND THE BROOK

Ripple and chuckle
Over the stones,
The youthful brook scutters
And gambols alone.

Here in the heather,
Pink, wiry and purple,
I perch on an outcrop
Harkening its burble.

The stream bed is rocky,
So rough, yet delightful,
With grouse for companionship,
Midges so spiteful.

A high-soaring eagle
Hangs over our way,
Whilst I meditating
Heed, pensive, its lay.

It struggles and ponders
A tune how to sing
When to wider brown waters
It glides and blends in.

Glinting and twirling,
It swirls gamely on,
Gasping and choking,
To make heard its song.

Life hustles around it,
Pollution and bustle,
Till it's lost in deep seas
With scarcely a ruckle.

Jean-Pamela Moore

DEATH OF THE TITANIC

Guaranteed unsinkable, this lady would prevail,
O'er stormy seas with thrashing waves, and unrelenting gales.
Boasting her stability, they did not speculate,
Cocooned in their complacency, they might be tempting fate.
The icy smooth Atlantic, upheld the regal maid,
Her portholes lending shafts of light to ease the inky shade.
Fragmented crystals glittered from the dark encasing sky,
Creating false security, too hoodwink and belie.
Thrust by her engines forward, she glided 'neath the moon,
Accommodating those within, oblivious of their doom.
The band was playing ragtime, the party aura spread,
Then shattered by that fateful cry, 'Iceberg right ahead!'
Unheeded warnings might have saved the maiden from her fate,
Too fast to swing her bows to stern, alas too fast! Too late!
Looming from the briny deep, the monstrous giant towered,
Then scraped along the starboard side, as awestruck mortals
                                                     cowered.
The Captain and his stewards, appeased the anxious throng,
Convinced of Man's efficiency, and still the band played on.
But little did they realise, their final melody
Would erase the former tempo, with 'Nearer My God To Thee'.
Too soon invading waters caused the mighty bows to dip,
For the berg had gauged a deadly wound, along this noble ship,
Resigned, the maid with dignity sent forth a rumbling boom,
Then slipped beneath her conqueror to meet her glassy tomb.
The perished now sleep peacefully, the rescued came to terms,
Mourning for their loved ones, as fearful memories burn.
The souls they lost were Heaven's gain, their former host lays
                                                     maimed,
For Man's design prevaileth not, but Heaven and Earth remain.

Patricia Frost

A True Tale Of A White Mouse Named George

It was Maxine's 18th birthday
A friend was at the door
He handed me her present
An empty box, no more!

I seemed a little puzzled
Until he explained to me
There should have been a white mouse
Inside the box, you see.

A few days later he came again
Another box had he
This time he had the white mouse
Inside the box, you see.

I still seemed a little puzzled
Until he explained to me
The white mouse had escaped
Inside his flat, you see.

The mouse had hidden under the fridge
A clever mouse was he
Because Ian had a cat, waiting patiently.

Ian eventually saw the light
And rescued the poor mouse,
Then put it in the empty box
And brought it to my house.

At last we had the white mouse
A lovely mouse was he
He lived with us for the rest of his days
And we enjoyed his company.

It was a happy ending, to Ian's tale of woe
Of the cat, the mouse, and the empty box
And we learned to love George so.

Caroline Helen Molton

Memories

I walked along the silent promenade
Before the summer crowds disturbed the view.
I watched the waves lap on the pebbled shore
And childhood memories came back anew.

Here a young mother bribed her stubborn child:
'Love, please be good and stay in school today.
We'll have a picnic on the sands tonight
If you will promise not to run away!'

And this is where the sun-bronzed children played,
With teasing laughter, heedless of all care;
Dodging the tides that swirled around their feet
Never a thought of danger lurking there.

Here, wide-eyed boys and girls saw their first death:
An airman trapped within his shattered plane;
His body lashed by dark and angry seas;
A nightmare scene recalled still once again.

And schoolgirls met when holidays came round
To walk for miles along the golden beach;
Each eager to disclose her secret hopes;
A world where jaded adults could not reach.

Here, teenage cousins strolled, their arms entwined,
Absorbed in dreams of happy future days;
Both unaware these dreams would be short-lived
As fate sent them upon their separate ways.

And as I walked along the promenade,
These idyll days now just a memory,
I felt content to be with all the ghosts
Of childhood years, who'd shaped my life for me.

Kathleen Wendy Jones

Daisy Chain

Just a little patch
On the edge of the lawn
Stirred up a memory
Of a day that's long gone.
'Oh Cora come here,'
My father did say
As he sat in the grass
On that bright
Summer's day.
He was sat tailor-fashion
When he motioned to me.
So I shyly walked over
To sit down on his knee.
He said, 'How would you like
To be Queen for a day?
If the answer is 'yes'
Then I will
Show you the way!

First we pick lots of daisies
With a nice big, long stem.
Then gently, so gently
Slice a small slot in them.
Next thread through
That first one,
Then do the same thing again -
Before you will know it
You'll have a nice daisy chain!'
My daddy made me a necklace,
Then he made me a crown,
I held out my arms
To wind another chain round!
I felt so important in
My crown of yellow and white -
As for being 'Queen for a day'
Well I was that alright!

Each time I see daisies
Spring forth from my lawn
My heart skips a beat
As I long for my daddy - and
A time that's long gone!

Cora-E Barras

The Dream Must Go On

In a winter long past a baby was born,
To his mother's joy, a beautiful boy;
An ordinary lad, not too good nor so bad,
But blessed with a heart of gold.

He knew he must fight to protect the world's right,
Though he lost every chance to grow old.
He died of course, but not on a cross;
He drowned in a submarine.

But greed's still as bad
And the world's just as mad.
The wise men have lost their orient star
Though they've got a missile that travels as far.

Where famine has reared its skeleton head
The children are hungry and crying for bread;
Old people are fleeing in wild disorder
Terrified, driven from border to border.

To babes born in fear as Christmas draws near
What should we give from Earth's brimming coffer?
Now surely we all know the best thing to offer,
From hunger and strife we must give them release
And do all in our power to bring about Peace.

Dora Beale

PARADISE

Beyond the hills of Auburn
Past the river, through the trees
I found a secret garden
Pretty as you please

A field of red corn poppies
Cosmos and blue bell
Candytuft and blazing star
Bedecked a wishing well

Scarlet sage and tidy tips
Covered a distant knoll
A quiet little gopher
Lies sleeping in his hole

Resting beside a trickling brook
Beneath the weeping willow
I have a bed of scarlet flax
With yarrow for a pillow

Today, I was truly blessed
When a robin dropped me here
You see in any other place
A gardener I would fear

For I am but a lowly weed
That most would only shun
But in this secret garden
I am loved by everyone

Dawn Drickman

DAD'S THREE BEST FRIENDS

Arch supports in laced-up boots,
Warm flannel shirts and navy suits,
Fleecy long johns over knee-length socks,
Work-worn hands as hard as rocks.
Up early each day, round at the stable,
Horse in the shafts to put food on the table.
Whatever the weather you could always rely
On potato or apple for your favourite pie.

An empty cart at the end of the day -
'Right Bob, home,' was all Dad had to say.
Horse standing still, head banging low,
Back at the stable nowhere to go.
Dad, head on chest, having a nap,
Never dislodging his worn cloth cap.

Many years have passed and I must confess
I have never forgotten Bob, Prince and Jess -
Those three gentle giants with such tender ways
Will live in my heart for the rest of my days.
I know Dad is happy, no more to roam -
His three friends are with him; they're safely home.

Mary Davies

AFTERMATH

Absent abroad, now home, I left my bed
And ventured out one May morning to see
Cold winter's landscape gone and in its stead,
Blossom exploding from bush, shrub and tree,
Hedgerow and meadow; came upon a place
Where, knee-deep in cow parsley's frothy white
Flowers, tiny and delicate as lace,
I gazed on lush hawthorn hedges. They might,
Have been, but for the soft, warm, fragrant air,
Boughs near to breaking, so laden with snow.
And I have seen frost too cover the bare
Trees of winter in a breath-catching show,
Portent of beauty in a warmer clime -
Winter-white enchantment in the springtime.

Jacqueline Abendstern

15 YEARS OLD . . .

Already 15 years old, with the time so quickly passed by,
With so many people involved - what a fantastic try!
The start wasn't easy, then has grown better and stronger,
And now so much has been achieved, with no sign of weakness
                                                            longer,
It gave a chance to anyone to freely express one's mind,
What's better than through writing the peace of mind to find . . .
So many times you feel, you have to share your thoughts with the
                                                            whole world,
And you feel so much better seeing your poem published and heard,
Writing helps so many people - sometimes it's the only way of
                                                            communication,
It is a constantly growing passion that's currently sweeping the whole
                                                            nation,
And everything becomes possible because of *Forward Press*
And *yes!* - it's *15 years old* - no more and no less,
I raise a glass to everyone involved in this project -
Congratulations Forward Press *and* well done!
I'll be looking forward to another 15 years which will be a much
                                                            bigger event and fun.

Anna Bayless

THE MAJESTIC TREE

Majestic and tall it stands
So stately and serene.
Its age, what does it matter?
Hundreds of summers it must have seen
Oh my! I'd love to listen
To the stories it could tell.
Of things that happened long ago,
T'would hold me in its spell.
Listen to its tales of woe,
And also beauty seen
To sit among its leafy boughs
And survey all the scene.
Listen to the murmurings
Of every rustling leaf
Once again go back in time,
See things beyond belief.
But all I can do is wonder,
And dream of long ago,
Of how that big tall tree
From a seedling it did grow,
Snug and warm in Mother Earth,
It waited long years through,
Until one day a sunbeam came,
And murmured I want you.
The little seedling grew and grew
Until it became a tree
So ends the story of
My majestic big tall tree.

Mary Murphy (Thurlow)

AN UNSEASONAL SAGA

It's the last day of September, a warm late summer's day,
Our local garden centre have prepared a new display!
They've moved the pretty pot plants to a corner at the back,
To make way for dear old Santa and a cardboard chimney stack!
Gone are all the bird baths, garden gnomes and goldfish ponds,
In their place stand plastic fir trees all with fairies waving wands!
The reason for my visit was to purchase aphid spray,
But the only spray on offer was of gold or silver-grey!
No compost, peat or leaf mould, no tubers, bulbs or seeds,
Just yards of coloured tinsel, shiny baubles bells and beads!
What's happened to this nation, have we all gone raving mad?
Christmas cheers in mid-December, in late summer it's just sad!

Denise Winder

THE YEAR OF THE CHILD

A little child is longing for
Some love from you today,
Not money or expensive toys
Just time to sit and play.

A little face which reads your mind
Is watching you today;
He understands the voice that's kind
And each angry word you say!

Some people long for children
To love them as their own.
Some children long for parents,
Who live in children's homes.

Scold him when he's bad today.
Praise him when he's good.
Teach him to be honest
And never to be rude.

The gift of life is precious
And no one knows their fate,
So listen to your child today
Before it is too late.

Catriona Thomson

WAITING

I waited for you, I waited a while
Longing to see that wonderful smile.
Excusing the fact that you were late
Something cropped up? You'd helped out a mate?
I kept my hopes high, you'd missed the bus?
I promised myself that I wouldn't fuss.
Time slowly passed while I waited alone
Should I go to the kiosk and give you a phone?
Perhaps you were ill and couldn't come out!
My mind in a fizz, starting to doubt.
I waited still, ten minutes more,
Then came the fact I couldn't ignore.
I'd been 'stood up', I felt sick inside
I wanted to run, I wanted to hide.
I slowly walked home, no need to hurry,
You missed your chance, so why should I worry!

M Rankin

A VALENTINE'S DAY POEM TO MY WIFE

A day of hearts and roses,
Of longing, loving bliss.
Of fragrant flowers and chocolates
And cards sealed with a kiss.

My heart is yours my lovely,
You are my English rose.
No card can tell my love for you
In poetry or in prose.

You are to me like moonlight
Caught in a misty pool.
Or fragrant orange blossom
As summer evenings cool.

As gossamer of fairy wings
Or rosebuds softly pink.
The sound of wind bells tinkling sweet
Or nightingales at twilight's brink.

Delicate and gentle
And radiant to my eye.
A jewel beyond the price of pearls,
I'll love you till I die.

Keith Jenkins

DREAMCATCHER

Dreamcatcher -
Wild woven willowy sinews,
A myriad of rainbow lights
Dart through dewdrops glistening
On silvery gossamer threads.
Catch my dreams, for they are me -
My past, my present, my future.

Dreamcatcher -
Moonlit magic
Suspended above my innermost thoughts,
Diamond-edged stars glitter their sparkling enchantment
Through a filigree of feathered fronds.
Catch my dreams, for they are me -
My past, my present, my future.

Vikki Silverlock

THE HAND OF GOD

Behold the grandeur of the mountains,
The beauty of the hills and towering rugged peaks,
The winding valleys vast and deep,
The crashing seas on the shore beneath,
Through this the Wonder of Creation speaks.

Ferny bracken and tall stately pine,
The purple heather and wild mountain thyme
Overspread the sloping mountainside,
While overhead a pair of osprey soar and glide.

Streams meander through gulleys and glens,
Their water drops, like diadems.
Glisten and dance in the summer rain,
Listen to the tinkling of their song
As they lap against the rocks and stones,
And the ring of ripples around the rushes intertwine;
Behold this wonderment fashioned by a Hand Divine.

Ann Anderson

REMEMBERING A FRIEND

Why he had to end it all, I guess I will never know,
For what troubled him behind his smile, he would never show.
A work friend for many years, I had got to like him well.
But what lies just around the corner, only God can tell.
He was a master at his job, in which he took such pride,
Always on time; never let you down; always on your side.
He seldom spoke of his private life, if, in fact, at all,
He indicated the odd boy's night out, where he'd had a ball.

I'll always remember the day the dreadful news came through,
It left me in a quandary, I didn't know what to do.
My first thoughts were for his wife and his now orphaned family.
What do you do in such circumstances? Just wait and see?
I rang him the day before he died, to see if he could work,
He declined for whatever reason; he was not one to shirk.
I think back to that call and I grieve for him of his pain,
I wish I could put back the clock and have that call again.

I still miss his youthful smile and he always called me 'Mate.'
He had no 'airs and graces' and his attitude was great.
He was a workaholic, too much was a dirty word,
There's many in his profession, but it was him I preferred.
In this life you need people who are hard-working and fair,
I'm talking of my 'mate' Ricky, him with the ginger hair.
I'd look up from my desk at work, he'd stroll across the floor,
It still saddens me to this day, of him I'll see no more.

Ken Watts

With Apologies To Rupert Brooke

If I should die before I'm old,
Don't grieve for me!
Think rather how much greater cause for woe
If this active spirit had been brought low
In some lingering fashion.

How much brighter will the memories be
If, when I die, I am still me?
How sore the burden of lingering life
When each day brings another loss
Of skill of hand or eye.

And if one's life be not as long,
What matters it? So till the end
One's wits and body still belong to one
And are not taken away
A little here, a little there
Until what still remains
Can find no joy in life, or give,
As I have loved to give
Small pleasures as the day goes on.

To those we love,
The kindest blow
Is short and sharp and final.
And when I'm gone,
Their minds can fill
With thankful pictures,
Clearly seeing,
How kind, the sudden blow.

No bitterness and burdensome duty,
Wearing away love, where once love was.
But genuine sorrow, unmixed with guilt,
In case, perhaps, towards the end
The burden of caring grew too great.

So, if I die while life is good,
Don't grieve for me!

Deirdre White

Life And Death Struggle

The sea wild and beautiful
White waves, open swell
Deep quiet habitat of mysterious creatures
Seabirds forage, seals bask
Bright neon schools
Swim beneath the dappled waters
Clusters of vivid corals
Sway in silent rhythm
The seabed oozes life
And new life is born.

Thick, black, crude,
Raw sewage, toxic chemicals
Carelessly spilt, dumped and tipped
Seabirds oiled, seals choke
Fish swim in the murky waters
Soaking up the poison
Delicate plants wither
As the seabed oozes silt
And nature struggles to survive

The sea once wild and beautiful
Coughs and splutters
As man pollutes its very life force.

Margaret Martin

All In The Name Of Love

All in the name of love my child,
All in the name of love,
I saw you in the wilderness
Your heart was heavy laden
I called your name, said follow me
To places where your eyes can see
The beauty of my world for thee
All in the name of love.

All in the name of love I died
All in the name of love,
I hung upon the cross of sin,
The darkness grow, my Father's will,
I bowed my head my body still
All in the name of love.

All in the name of love I live,
All in the name of love,
My Father rose me from the grave,
All saints and angels sing His praise,
And I will do His work always,
All in the name of love.

M Turner

Naughty Sam's Dream

I will tell you a tale of woe,
About a lad I used to know.
All about Sam who'd a-fishing go,
On a very hot day some weeks ago.

Now, Sam's ma told him not to go . . . by
The river where the kingcups grow,
For the water there was very deep . . . and
Perhaps crawly creatures there do sleep.

Sam said he was 'A fisherman *oh*',
So . . . off he went, though his ma said . . . 'No.'
He sat on the bank . . .soon sleepily sideways rolled,
Half waking. . . he felt very sick and cold!

He shivered and shook from head to feet,
His heart missed every other beat . . . for
Slowly coming from the stream . . .
Was the biggest frog he'd ever seen.

Nearer and nearer with black eyes wide,
Long crooked legs on each side,
Greeny, yellowy, wide mouthed beast . . .
Advanced towards him, as for a feast.

'How do you do, Sam?' said the frog
'May I sit beside you, on your log?'
Sam only answered with soulful scream, and
Fell with fright into the stream.

He scrambled out, and ran off home,
His clothes all soaked in muddy foam;
His ma pulled off his pants and shirt . . . and
Smacked him soundly where most it hurt.

So . . . in bed he had to stay,
While all his friends were out to play,
For Sam, like other boys, you know,
Must really take heed, when Ma says . . . 'No!'

Daisie Cecil-Clarke

OUR JOURNEY

I remember, I remember
the start of our journey together.
The village slept.
Hand in hand we ran down the hill slope
full of life's hope.

You and I alone like Adam and Eve
in the mountain Eden
waited and watched;
a cow turned its head and stared.

I remember the start of that day.
The sky blushed red
And we greeted the rising globe.
Dawn broke.

Hand in hand we shared the time;
the breath; the beauty;
the glory of God's own temple.
I remember.

Many years passed; we crossed chains
of jagged mountains;
gazed at green pastures along the way
as we grew grey.

Side by side we walked towards our journey's end.

But now you are gone; memories stir.
You are there; in the sun that shines,
in clouds that gently float,
in the sea waves that ebb and flow,
in the trees and flowers that grow,
in every blessing Nature bestows.

I remember, I remember
the start of our journey together.

Perveez Dadachanji

CAITLIN FLYNN IN MEXICO CITY

On waking from a vivid dream,
about a girl I have never seen.

I will call her Caitlin Flynn,
enigmatic fusion of my travelling mind.

Here I am at four in the morning,
attempting to catch the images for posterity.

She was listening to a lone trumpeter,
on the soulful streets of Mexico City.

With a battered copy of 'Under the Volcano',
in the back pocket of her faded, blue jeans.

Wearing ethnic jewellery, a violet African amethyst
Bronzed skin, perfect teeth and smiling eyes.

Drinking tequila from the bottle,
under a dancing water fountain.

Swaggering along dusty back streets,
To her spartan, attic lodgings.

Feeding chunks of fresh meat,
to her pet baby black panther.

Suddenly I am there next to her,
watching as she plays with the beautiful creature.

Entranced by her wild stories,
of how she travelled from Cuba to Mexico.

Jump cut to the next scene, a frenzied gathering.
People laughing, clapping and singing folk songs.

The dream ended with a passionate kiss.
Wonderfully unfathomable in its shuddering sensuality.

So Caitlin Flynn, if you are out there,
don't make yourself a stranger.

Matthew W Jones

IF ONLY

His walnut face
Measuring stick of life
Must be a farmer
Weathered face
Born to the land
Each crevice an experience
Will he tell?
If only.
Such wealth
Close to nature
Real living
He nods a couple of times
Smiles
Secrets
If only.

Anne Codling

LEST WE FORGET

Lest we forget the wars of the past
and of our minds this horrible
carnage will last and last.
On the eleventh day of the eleventh
month and at eleven o'clock and as
the minutes go by tick tock.
And in Whitehall of their thoughts in
silence will stand, will be of one band
and of one mind.
Thoughts of the past two world wars
that have come about, and in their mind
in silent horror they will shout.
And will this lesson of war may never
Ever be taught, or sort, and never
again wars be fought.
Of the families that have been left
behind, of their thoughts for two minutes
in silence, they will stand.
Lest we forget there are winners in battle,
we are all losers in war.
And in the end we feel so very sore
Lest we forget the eleventh day
Of the eleventh month at eleven o'clock.

Peter Antonian

I SAID GOODBYE

I said goodbye to a friend last night.
Why did he have to go?
I miss him so very much,
More than you'll ever know.

I loved him like a bosom friend,
So very close we were,
Why did he have to go away?
Why could it not defer?

I said goodbye at half-past ten,
I looked up at the time
The tears welled up in my eyes,
I loved him so divine.

There was no more to do or say,
He went off with the vet,
I kissed him and said goodbye,
My dog, my loving pet.

S Tarr

LOVE IS?

(With thanks to Alfred Lord Tennyson)

Love is what makes the world a better place.
It does make the world go round.
Love holds on, reaches out, embraces and comforts.
Love is worthwhile.
Love can consume every waking hour and intrude into our dream
world.
Love makes us want to be near someone, not wanting to be apart.
Love is wanting to hear a voice down the telephone,
Needing to know someone cares.
Love forgives, moves on, never dies.
Love trusts, believes, depends on and has faith in someone.
Love is needing to touch, hear, listen to and be with that someone.
Love is amazing!
It can bring the utmost joy . . . and the deepest grief.
When love is lost or removed it causes untold misery and
sadness . . .
A pain that is so hard to remove.
Love cares about everything.
What you did today, how you are feeling, what dreams you have,
And love wants to be part of those dreams.
Love is holding on, believing in, being part of another's life.
Love is not letting go, staying the course, even when the going gets
tough.
Love is not here today - gone tomorrow.
Love persists, pursues, never gives up.
Love is lovely, love is passion, love is all consuming,
And "Tis better to have loved and lost than never to have loved at all.'
Love is what makes the world a better place.

Jane Wade

ANGRY YOUNG MAN

It could be Baghdad
Or West Bank barrage.

Something is hyping
This man up
He is pointing
An angry finger

Maybe he is
Standing in the
Ruins of his
Private paradise
A house called Home.

Foreign soldiers
In safe tanks
Could be strutting
Down his street

When there is
Nowhere else to go
What is left except
Searing words
Rude gestures

Then hope that
Justice might
Pan out somewhere
Down a hot
And dusty line.

James Adams

WHERE IS?

Where is your smile?
In this prison of despair, you are my hope.
Where is your touch?
In this cold reality of day, you are my warmth.
Where is your understanding?
In this dry, broken kindling, you are my spark.
Where is your pain?
For in your pain, is my solace.
Where is your breath of life?
For in your very existence, I am.
No joy, no passion, no love,
Have I ever felt, as I feel now.
It consumes my very essence.
Where is my hope?
It is hidden in the mystery of your smile.
Where is my warmth?
It overpowers me, in your gentle touch.
Where is my spark?
It is in the knowledge that no matter what, you understand.
Where is my solace?
It is in knowing my pain, is reflected in you.
Where am I?
I am here.
Where are you?

Cate Campbell

TWIN FLOWERS

Two flowers
On a pole; wrapped.

And beneath
A child's hand
'We love you Mummy'
Mary Jane and Noel.

A day before
A rag doll of a body
Underneath a lorry
Still clutching a shopping bag.

Two flowers
Now growing from a pole
One for love
One for soul.

James O'Grady

A PLACE OF PEACE

A place of peace and nature's own tranquillity
where whispering of breezes sway tall trees and birds
call out in song and lapping ripples round the lily pond
all blend in sunlit harmony of sound -

Where migrant slickers from dark city blocks drop in
To ease their loads, slow down the pace and smooth away
their stress, like long haul flocks to dip in dapple light
and bask upon the sleepy slopes of timelessness -

To seek some calm and coolness for fraught minds
and wander aimlessly the woodlands wild, as carefree child
to drink the sparkle stream of hope and in the soothing
stillness of this scented place to find themselves -

And then to come across a painted chapel hidden in
the trees, a secret presence vibrant in their midst
where they might 'hear' how He had seen their needs
and brought them to this haven to receive His peace.

Rosemary Keith

THERE IS A MAN CALLED JESUS

There is a man called Jesus, the Son of God is He;
He left the realms of glory, came to Earth in humility.
He was born of the Virgin Mary, the Babe of Bethlehem;
Became the Saviour of sinners, when He died on the Cross for them.

There is a man called Jesus, the Son of God is He;
He veiled Himself in human flesh, O what humanity.
And wonder of all wonders, if man in all his pride;
Would acknowledge Him as their Saviour, could with Him
in Heaven abide.

There is a man called Jesus, the Son of God is He;
When He lived upon this sinful Earth, he expressed His deity.
There are none on Earth beside Him, His life it spoke to all;
He healed the sick, He raised the dead, saved many from
Adam's fall.

There is a man called Jesus, the Son of God is He;
He left the splendours of Heaven, that we redeemed might be.
He'll fill our hearts with gladness, and this we'll surely know;
That He never will forsake us, if we but trust Him so.

There is a man called Jesus, the Son of God is He;
Do you know Him as your Saviour, do you know Him along with me?
Your sins He'll abundantly pardon, in Heaven He'll give you a place.
If you trust Him as your Saviour, then He'll save you by His grace.

Sydney Ward

GOD'S GARDEN

God's Garden is still and quiet
With memories of old and new
Toils, tears and laughter
Now life anew.

Trees blow and whisper in the wind
Perfumed flowers sway and chatter
Of unknown secrets of their world
As their petals blow and scatter
Sometimes touched by glittering frost
According to the weather.

Tenderly cared by loving hands
No matter what the weather
God's Garden will always be a place of peace.
God's Garden, is our
Garden too.
Be still in the garden of love.
Loving healing thoughts.

Alice Taylor

OUR DAY

Many people live in sheltered homes today,
Thanks to the Lord for prayers they say.
There's folk who always wish good luck,
Where gardens have flowers in bloom to pluck.
With trees beyond a pond,
Birds singing sweetly,
Looking to the woods
Wild flowers grow.
Where foxes and squirrels roam
Horses and cows in fields beyond
Friends and neighbours, who
Have a close bond.
Memories are there
Hold close thoughts of friends we knew past and gone
But life goes on to wish the world a happy bond.

Ethel Smith

MAKING THE MOST OF THINGS

I can see the church from here
Just across the green
The early dew upon the grass
The sunlight in full stream,
Glistening through the windows,
Of the church upon the green
But I'm making the most of things

Come Sunday bells are ringing
And do you know what I've found,
It's not that folks are pulling ropes
It's just recorded sound.
Then there's hymns and things
A choir, voices calling on the breeze
And butterflies and busy bees
Flying through the trees
I like that.
So I'm making the most of things.

Yet when evening calls and twilight comes
And stars peek through the sky
It's a whole new different outlook
And it's time to say goodbye
And thank You Lord, for such a day
And all the things I've seen
The sun, the dew, the stars
And most of all
The little church upon the green
And I'm making the most of it.

Maureen Digges

IF ONLY

If only I had listened
To what my mother said
Each time she helped me to undress
And tucked me up in bed.
If only I had heeded
The warnings of my betters,
Shown gratitude for favours
And written 'thank you' letters.

If only I had held my tongue
Instead of speaking out,
I'd now face fewer problems,
Of that, there is no doubt.
If I had been prepared to learn,
Not thought I knew it all -
I would have found out earlier
That pride precedes a fall.

If only I had not set out
Upon that slippery slope,
And fallen into the abyss
From where there is no hope.
So many times have I been told
To 'Look before you leap,'
Had I been given foresight
I'd not have plunged so deep.

If I could have my life again,
Some wrongs I would put right;
Yet I would err in other ways
Until I saw the light.
With hindsight it is easy
To know whose voice to heed,
For if we follow Jesus
No other voice we need.

Graham Winterbourne

Mum And Dad

Peter and Vera have a hit not a miss
After sixty-four years of true marital bliss!
Peter's a Taurus: just picture the scene
On the twentieth of May 1917:
A tyke was born who'd never shirk it,
The son of Doctor and Mrs Birkett.
To leave the womb, he probably sprinted
For sport is on his life imprinted.
As for Vera, her roots were first laid
In Moscow, Russia, she was born not made.
An Aquarian girl, a White Russian rare,
Her parents Alexander and Mary Behr,
Who escaped from a grisly Communist fate
And brought her to England to find a mate!
How did they meet and start to get on?
Well, the fly in the ointment was Uncle John,
For Vera went out with him first of all
Until Peter impressed with his Tarzan call!
The years went fast but like hand in glove
They reared their two boys in a house of love.
Those infant years were incredibly good
For they weaned them on Tetleys and Yorkshire pud!
Before you knew it, they gave them away
To Virginia Gibbens and Marilyn Kaye,
Then, wonder of wonders, there came like a tremor
Jennifer, Sarah, Guy, Jolyon, Emma!
In 2002, they became a true era
As a Diamond Duo, both Peter and Vera!
Salutes to them both, how their glory has shone,
With lots of love from their first son John.

John Birkett

A Night In The Pub

It was a chilly draught that blew right through
As the old chap sat there sipping his brew
He was all alone in that great big room
Except for an old woman pushing her broom.

The landlord came in from the other room
And said to the old woman who was pushing her broom,
'Go on through and have your tea
And we'll have a chat, him and me.'

So he said to the old chap who sipped his brew,
'We'll have a chat me and you
There's a fire through here in the other room,
There's no one here except for the old woman with her broom.'

So the two men sat there by the fire
The landlord poked it and the flames went higher.
'I'll just go and get a brew
And then we'll chat me and you.'

There were only three of them in the house
Oh, it was quiet - as quiet as a mouse
Nothing moved and nothing stirred
There was no sound except for a clock that whirred.

The two men sat and drank glass after glass
Until the landlord said, 'I'd better ring that lass
See if she's coming to help with the rush
And lend a hand to the woman with the brush.'

Closing time came all too soon
Outside shone the stars and the silvery moon
The landlord went, and locked the front door
The old man said, 'Let's have some more.'

Morning came - the fire was out
The landlord gave the old man a shout
'Come on,' he said, 'off to your room
You're in the way of the woman with the broom.'

Trevor Headley

The Sea Mama, The Sea

As I walked with young grandson o'er the golden shore
His dark eyes lift up to me with a question
What is the most peaceful thing God made to love and adore?
I wonder, look around and listen to inner thoughts
Yet to his knowing smile the answer I could not say
Why it's the sea mama, the great sea that cannot be bought.
I looked at the calm blue sea, white cliffs watch over the bay,
Colourful birds rest their wing in the grey rock of age.
Sea lions with their young clap their flippers on this happy sunny day
Across blue sea shine a silver path sent by golden sunbeam
Peace and tranquillity fill heart, soul and mind
Oh! To walk this path lay down thy head forever to dream.

As I walk with young grandson o'er the golden shore
His dark eyes lift up to me with a question
What is the most strongest thing God ever made to explore?
I wonder, look around, and listen to inner thoughts
Yet to his knowing smile the answer I could not say
Why it's the sea mama, the great sea that cannot be taught.
I remembered a rough black sea, giant waves beat at cliffs that
watch bay
Seagulls scream call to make haste to inner land, danger from rock
of age
Frothy mouth of sea rage into land, uproot strong trees on this
stormy day
over murky sea driftwood from broken ships float entwined with
seaweed's
Sadness and anger fill my heart and mind,
Oh! To talk back at sea and tell her of the cruel deed.

Phyllis Blue

Are These The Steps . . .

Are these the steps we climbed long years ago
before the climb of life was set to show
Are these the steps we climbed in blissful youth
when unknown years ahead withheld their truth
Are these the steps we climbed to Main School and beyond
to Satis and the chestnut tree and pond
Are these the dreams we had when days were long
and those in charge were teaching right from wrong
Is this the gate we entered every day
to Chapel where we sang and knelt to pray
Are these the steps we climbed to School Hall stage
to play the parts of warrior or page
Whist those with greater talents had no fear
to learn the lines and tread the boards as Lear
Are these the steps we climbed amidst applause
to shake the honoured hand and take the vase
Are these the steps we climbed at end of play
when Cranbrook on the Paddock played away
with a century yet again for J A Clay
or five for one perhaps the other way
Are these the banks we climbed in seventh heaven
instead of clapping home the First Eleven
Are these the hills we climbed without a glance
to valleys past before we hand our chance
Are these the friends we loved long years ago
and now attend their end in funeral row
Are these the steps we climbed all on our own
To meet our maker on his Royal Throne

Brian Nolan

A WOMAN'S WORTH

A woman's worth, one
immediately thinks of Emily Pankhurst.
Her courage was immeasurable
without it a woman's role
in society would never
have changed.

Without a woman, civilisation
would not have survived.
A woman's logic is unique
and she cannot easily
be deceived.

A woman as a mother often
keeps her family together
an anchor in her
children's life, too priceless
to discard.

Candida Lovell-Smith

FUEL FAMINE

'No fuel,' it said,
caused a pain to my head.
My tank has run dry
As I gave a loud cry.

The forecourts were bare
For no one was there,
But the few lonely staff
With never a laugh.

Has 'two jags John' any to spare?
Or 'space-carrier Tony', with family to share?
Maybe Gordon bought some, the day before
The thumbscrews tightened, till there was no more.

Is this what they meant with their solution,
Of saving the planet from nasty pollution?
Is Tony taking us for a ride
Or trying to take, 'political suicide'?

They said, 'Out of cars and onto buses,'
'No more morning and evening rushes.'
'Just take, leisurely strolls, to work and school.'
'Exercise, is the golden rule.'

They've put Britain back on its feet, again
To walk to work in sleet and rain.
When French queen said, 'Let them eat cake, instead,'
Her people replied, 'Off with her head!'

Has Gordon thought, while he relaxes,
How he will get his higher taxes?
No money left to give away,
Remember New Labour on Election Day!

William Knapton

ANOTHER YEAR OLDER

Just remembered, it's your special day!
Only got the one thing to say.
Really hope your wishes come true
Day, night and all the year through!
A great person, what more can I say,
Now go and have a happy birthday!

Annette Smith

GREY OWL

Bring me a hill, find me a mountain, take me out beyond the sun,
Back to birthing with the land and flying the feathers of a
                                        solitary eagle.
Rich in soil and solitude, asking only what encompasses the vision
                                        of my eyes.
When the wind beckons to the night, to rest my head on a
                                        woven mat,
Warm to the embers of a dying fire and bless the buffalo skin that
                                        favours me.
Some crazy horse upon the plain, fleet of foot and following
                                        ancestral trails,
Take me to the great ones and the buried bones of time.
Baby in papoose nursed and nurtured with the living earth,
To ride some day through dust and broken hill ahead.
Stories of beaver and crow, weaving together brotherhood and the
                                        river's flow.
A warrior reaching into manhood, touching clouds with
                                        blood-red black
Upon his face and rituals beyond the test of time.
Hunting on the wind, messages for arrow and for bow,
                                        wolves howling
In the dark, as women with raven plaited hair, wait upon the dawn.
Elders seated in ceremonial circle, as the dusk rides across the day,
Grey haired and chanting secret sounds, the pipe of peace shattered
Like the trunk of an old sequoia pine struck by a storm.
Be you with the earth, red and trodden in the soles of many feet,
Paths and centuries have passed and faded with the early mist.
Eyes narrowed and shaded from the sun, as the thermals
Carry the hungry condor onward on its flight.
My day has come and gone, slipping like the silver stream,
Into the eternity of treetops and a battue broken wing.
Take me to the ridge of barren mountain and lay my bones to rest,
Remember me as born to this time and place, which was forever
                                        in my soul.

Jennifer Fox

THANKING YOU, GOD, IN ALL CIRCUMSTANCES

Thanking You, God, in all circumstances
Seems incredible and so hard to do
But You are the God of second chances
And my Salvation is all due to You.
Thank You Lord, for allowing me to learn,
And understanding I may make mistakes;
If tempted by fear to take the wrong turn,
You still support me and give me fresh breaks.
Thank You for examples of endurance
From the witnesses of so many saints,
To enable me, with Your assurance
To know when to move and when to hold restraint
I thank You, Father, for giving me weakness
To spur me and keep my thoughts upon You,
To help me to reach to attain Your meekness,
And find strength to do what I must do.
Thank You, as well, for my imperfections
With awareness of my limitations,
Bringing me to see a new direction
That surpasses all my expectations!
And yet, My God, if You grant me Your best,
It's to You that the Glory must belong,
So I thank You for hurts, which are just tests,
Ensuring that in You *I am* made strong.
Thank You for Your Hope, whatever I've done
And Your healings from all I inherit:
Thank You for Your Word, thank You for Your Son
And thank You for the power of Your Spirit!

Natalie Brocklehurst

CLOCKWORK LIVES

The dancers, arm in arm with grace,
Their arms entwined, their hands enlaced
Stand silent, still in their embrace
Until the music starts
For their life is but a fleeting thing
As they trace their tiny, endless ring
And only as the music sings
The beat may fill their hearts

And at a whim, if for a time
We give to them that gift divine
Breathe life into their pantomime
A life that is a lie
But through this life of falsity
We learn the truth most do not see
The awful truth of entropy
To live is but to die.

They dance the tune that they adore
Into their hearts and minds it pours
They dance until they can no more
Tread the circle they've been seeking
The music no more fills their veins
Hearts silence as life from them drains
They die, but one thing yet remains
The love their eyes are speaking.
Their love outlives infinity
Endures as they so patiently
Wait 'til we once more turn the key
To wake them from their sleeping.

Jonathan Mills

GUESS WHO

He appears in various sizes,
And arrives in different guises.
He will shake your hand and smile and nod
Whilst into your affairs he'll prod.
With pen in hand he'll question and write,
You will use your wits with all your might.
It really isn't very fair,
He's asking what you've got to declare.
Shall you lie or tell him all,
Will it end with a bailiff's call?
You'll fret for the wealth that should be thine,
He will leer at you and says, 'It's mine.'
You may give him share he can't be beat,
You'll wish the devil he will meet.
He will smile again as he shakes your hand,
You'll think of cancelling the holiday you'd planned.
Next year he promises to be back
Demanding his usual whack.
Who is this man we regard as foe,
Why, he the *taxman* - didn't you know?

Irene Ramsey

TODAY'S PEOPLE

What is wrong with the people of today?
Their lack of interest
And their lack of care
Make me feel they are aliens
From somewhere else, somewhere.

They talk about you to someone else
Instead of finding out from you; yes I do care.
Their minds are in turmoil,
They have nothing to spare
And certainly nothing to share.

Ann Hunt

PADSTOW

A cormorant stands, his wings outstretched,
motionless on the golden sand,
A silhouette, minutely etched,
against a scape of sea and land.

Then all around him, all around,
the tide creeps in across Doombar,
As little boats that were aground
begin to bob and weave once more.

And now the estuary is alive
with skimming craft and coloured sails,
While seagulls wheel, and cormorants dive
till ocean ebbs, or daylight fails.

When dusk descends beyond Brea Hill
and casts its silence all around,
Then, seemingly, the world is still,
without a light, without a sound.

Yet in the harbour there is light;
glow lamps and windows all around,
Like stars that cheer the darkest night,
like jewels in a monarch's crown.

A potpourrie of cottages
line streets inclining to the sea,
And shops and inns send messages
of Cornish hospitality.

And with the dawn, a mackerel sky,
such beauty, and a peace profound;
The lovely Camel Estuary
is all around us, all around.

Jo Young

DAMARIS WOODROSE

Damaris Woodrose, widow,
is a more attractive sight
than Damaris Woodrose, wife

Soft folds of widow weeds
flow down, designer, black,
her bright red hair
drawn back into a band
blue rings around the eyes

Did anybody know
he beat her,
this founder member
of the local NSPCC
and beat his kids?

She played her silence to the end
and there she stands
as tall and straight as any tragic actress
on her stage

Damaris Woodrose, widowed,
mocks his grave
drops earth into the ground
fingers curled with contempt
then walks away

The following Monday
she wears a green hat
unties her hair.

Isabel Cortan

FAVOURITE DAYDREAM

Now I have a favourite daydream
Of a warm enchanted place
Where sapphire seas flow calmly
And life moves at a gentle pace

It must be all of seven summers
Since I walked that golden shore
To white secluded villas
On the way to Avilmore

It is a most delightful feeling
To imagine that I'm there
To climb again those sunburnt hills
And breathe again the sea-tinged air

So I'll keep my favourite daydream
Of a rare and lovely place
With orange trees and endless flowers
Soft guitar music
And women in black lace.

Pauline Kavanagh

UNBLOCKED

I've had a writing block
For quite a while.
Lots of heavy emotional stuff
That really cramped my style.
I'd come to the conclusion
My rhyming days were through.
A sad but sweet illusion,
But then I heard from you.
'Come, join our celebration,
Fifteen years of rhyme and prose.'
I sensed a feeling of elation,
I *could* try again I suppose.
So here I am, pen in hand,
And the words are flowing free.
I'm feeling great, I'm feeling grand,
Just how I want to be.
This offer to begin again,
I could go on for years.
Smiles and laughter from my pen,
No more gloom or tears.
I've this fresh imagination
And I know who to bless.
Sincere congratulations
To all at Forward Press.

Brenda Sohngen

JUST THE TICKET

At seventy-four I'm feeling fine,
This morning you see I'm going online.
Not hanging out washing or going by train,
I'm travelling the world without boat or plane.

I sit at my desk and type in a few letters,
In minutes I'm there with all those jet-setters.
I go to New York and walk in Times Square,
With no let or hindrance I will be there.

I can go shopping to spend a few coppers,
Places like Harrods with all those name-droppers.
Maybe I'll even look for a car,
To buy one abroad will be cheaper by far.

Then go down to Rio or maybe to Rome,
If I get web-lagged with a few taps I'm home.
I can make myself coffee and take a rest,
After all that world travel, I think home is best.

C Cannon

DREAMS

I dream of days that are long past
I dream of joys which could not last
I dream of hope and then despair
For when I wake, you are not there.

In solitude with inward eye
Which takes away the need to cry.
I see again your loving face
And would that I could you embrace.

Not only in dreams are you with me,
I feel you near, though cannot see
Through the veil, the great divide,
In memories only must you abide.

Maggie Sparvell

YOU DON'T OWN A CAT - A CAT OWNS YOU

The man I live with has the heart of a beast,
I'm not complaining - no, not in the least.
Ev'ry morning he looks for me (what a caper!)
And let's me out with the morning paper.
Supervising the garden, I investigate
While he prepares my breakfast plate.
He even attends to my litter tray - well,
Frequently enough to stop the smell -
And brings me titbits, which make me fat,
That's why I say he has the heart of a cat.
Although he's a human - that strange being
His mind's of an animal, understanding
My deepest yearning to crunch and guzzle
And my needs for stroking, fur and muzzle.
I cannot say that his efforts are great
At cat-language, but we communicate
After a fashion and I rub noses
With this man, who frequently shows he's
Got the heart of a beast within -
Even though he wears a human skin!

Roy Akerman

THE SPHINX

Whence did it come,
What god is this
That crouches on the silver sand?
This majesty
This strange smile.
What it fashioned by human hand?
Some race of giants
Whose bones are dust,
Raised they this stony imagery?
Proud Egyptian
Or learned priest.
Asleep in Isis' sanctuary?
Whose thought was this?
Whose blood lies here?
Lashed in haste by the master's whip.
Who died to build
This cold-eyed god with sealed lip
Who silent sits
Brooding the while?
The dead who in Amentet sleep
Know who this is.
The riddle reads -
Divine Harmeous will keep
Safe the secret,
And smiling still
Whispers, 'Osiris guards their sleep,
The lord of death shall have his will.'

B Kerby

MENTIONED IN DISPATCHES

Out of the raging past,
Wild torrents of anger
Plunged in fury around me;
I stumbled through blizzards
Of despair; thorns of anguish
Tore my screaming flesh, and
Pierced my eyes anew;
Memory's towering shadows
Engulfed me; the trembling moon
Shattered in glittering shards,
About my defenceless soul;
A myriad barbs whirled, in
The galaxy of my mind;
I fell, helpless, into the
Pit of sorrow, and darkness
Enshrouded the fragmented
Margins of reality.

Dorothy Neil

THE TIDE OF TIME

Oh how quickly you've grown,
doesn't seem a year since we were on this beach.
Nappy sagging as you paddled your feet.
Ice cream dripping through a chubby hand,
castles for a princess made out of sand.
Sand in our sandwiches, sand in our pop.
In and out, you just didn't stop!

Oh how quickly you've grown,
doesn't seem a year since we were on this beach.
With buckets, spades and spellings to teach.
Holes dug with sides so steep,
'Bury me Mum and cover my feet!'
Your kite souring through a windy sky,
time flew so quickly, I question why?

Oh how quickly you've grown,
doesn't seem a year since we were on this beach.
Body boards and wetsuits are all in the past,
Pen friends made, but the writing didn't last!
I am in the knotted hankie brigade,
getting into a deckchair is such a charade.
As I look in the eyes of the new
face the same happiness and think of you . . .

Semra Yeo

THE CHRISTMAS DREAM

The little girl, snugly tucked up in her bed
Slowly closed her eyes as she laid down her head
She knew what she wanted, when Santa would come
To bring her something special, she wanted her mum

Her mum had left her a long time ago
Where she had gone, she did not know
But as she lay dreaming in her bed
She didn't realise that her mum was dead

And as she slept, she had a dream
And in this dream, her mum was seen
She was dressed like an angel in Heaven above
And for the little girl, she had a great love

When the little girl woke from her sleep
She opened a present and began to weep
During the night, Santa Claus had come
And left her a photograph of her mum.

Colin Metcalfe

CRYSTAL (FIFTEENTH) ANNIVERSARY

To make up a rhyme
Will always take time,
Words flow like mistral
If anniversary's crystal!

Each verse has four lines,
No matter what signs,
Worldly or astral?
This one is crystal.

Poems make a book,
No critics we'll brook,
No shotgun, pistol
Celebrate crystal!

To sum up my thoughts,
No digits or noughts,
London to Bristol,
Three cheers for crystal!

David Spanton

TO TOBY
(To Toby, a dearly loved golden retriever)

Sometimes this brown eyed, friendly, loving, trusting dog is seen
Making off from the kitchen, without permission
To clamber upstairs to sleep on his favourite bed,
To sprawl out full length and rest his head,
Snoring peacefully, totally relaxed, at peace,
Another time he rushes downstairs, through the back door,
Running urgently, tail wagging to the vast outside
To explore, to smell, to cock a leg, to hide,
Perhaps he'll take a roll, showing his long creamy underside hair,
Or lie on his back and wriggle, wriggle, wriggle,
Four strong legs stretched heavenwards to the sky,
Could be he'll sniff around, and through next-door's fence pry.
Next to make for the warm security of the terracotta tiled kitchen,
Moving more slowly, tail wind-blown, wagging,
Hungry, he muses if there will be anything in his food bowl,
Tasty biscuits, sumptuous liver, woofy salmon pieces or lamb roll,
Nothing! Horror! Toby loudly barks, loudly barks,
The noise like that of a lion snarling, long and fierce,
A quick response meets his aggressive demand,
Stomach now filled, he'll soon be away to the promised land!
Before the brightly burning lounge fire he will lie
Dreaming of events now gone by,
Of the bird he nearly caught, so nearly caught on the grass,
Walks, eating, playing, dreaming, being lovingly cared for,
So his life will pass.

Vivian Khan

BLUE

If I had to pick one colour
It would be blue.
Blue skies, sunny days,
Swallows flying,
Blue sea, gentle waves,
Blue dolphins surfing the ocean,
Bluest of blue eyes, looking at me
For the very first time.
Blue pain, why did you have to go?
Blue sapphire, cold as ice,
I made the ultimate sacrifice.
Blue moon shadows on my grave,
Bluebells grow where I lay,
Blue now gone, I love you still.

Gillian Robson

BUTTERFLY HEART

Summer daze, midday haze,
An explosion of flowers in a colourful blaze.
A black-eyed caterpillar
Grows jewel-studded wings.
Self taught how to fly,
Feather light dancing,
A cheery bird sings.
Summer perfume and laughter fills the air,
Smiling faces everywhere.
Butterfly, how you soar,
Swooping and swirling at the heady scent.
Free flight, feels right.
Packaged by Mother Nature
A gift heaven-sent.
For an instant you alight on a tempting flower.
This is to be your finest, final hour.
Longing to savour sweet almond honeydew
Tasting bitter poison
Something different, something new.
Sadly out of control
Spiralling, you drop and
Fall down to Earth from a cloudless blue sky.
One single tear, a silent cry.
Momentarily held captive in a child's chubby hand,
Your fragile flutterby wings ripped apart as you land.
Grounded, you have found your final destiny.
Yearning for the place where it was safe to be.
A brief lifelong experience
Lasting but one sun-kissed, rain free day.
Broken and torn, but precious not worthless.
You are tenderly lifted and carried away.
Upward on the wings of a gentle summer breeze.
High above new mown grass and
Emerald green leaf laden trees.

Amelia Michael

WHO KNOWS

(To Sandra Fretwell)

Here I am, a stranger in a strange land
Yet you held out a hand
Was this fate? That we should meet this way
Who knows for friendship changed to love?
Was this fate?
Was this what was always meant to be for you and me?
For out of love there came a future for you and me
A tomorrow that was always meant to be
Like sunrise and sunset
The beginning and end to a perfect day.

Henry Djuritschek

THE BURNS DISASTER

The cage no longer moves, taking miners underground,
The pit wheels at a standstill,
No more survivors found.

Many were only boys, some 14 years of age,
Heading for their deaths
With others in the cage.
West Stanley Town's in mourning,
No one will ever forget it.
168 perished that day
Down the Burns Pit.
The pit's now gone,
The shaft was filled and sealed.
West Stanley still remembers that day
With a monument on the King's Head field.

Malcolm Hole

THE WITCH

They believe I am a witch, because I keep a big black cat.
I stir my giant cauldron and wear a pointed hat.
My glinting eyes are slanting, the colour is emerald green,
My nose is very ugly, just shaped like a hook.
I practise such magic, you would not believe,
From my thousand-year-old dusty book.
I rummage in the dark woods for berries, fruits and nuts,
It's there I talk with fox and mice.
Please, don't turn away when I appear,
I really am quite nice.
When I go shopping in the village,
I hurry there and back,
In a creaking carriage, down the muddy lanes,
Pulled by an old brown hack.
I know the great wide universe, all the secrets of the signs,
The zodiac, the cards, the stones
And long mysterious rhymes.
At midnight, to the forest I go, with strange creatures from afar.
I sing, I dance, a lone owl watches me,
Under a dying star.
My fingers, long and crooked
Weave a web like a spiders, oh so fine.
Do not ask my age, my dears,
I have lived a long, long time.
Dear children, come and stay awhile,
Don't go running home so soon,
Stay and I will show you
Lots of spells beneath a full cold moon.
Do you believe that I am a witch?
I can tell that you are not sure.
But just remember if you should visit me,
Don't fall over the broomstick,
That is propped up by my front door.

Dorothy Chadwick

FINAL CURTAIN CALL

In a girl's fifteenth year
Mother died on a couch
All the family at home
Matinee movie on TV
Tripe cooked for tea

Curtains closed

News spread . . . the deceased
Was still in the living room.
This child fought shy of goodbye
House of horror expectations.
Fear filled a fragile head
Struck hard, Mum was dead.
Our teenager's heart chilled.
In her drama called life
Darkness shrouded days
No growth - no vitality.
Maturity willed the girl
To explore deep emotions.
A shattered shard of self
Shivered behind drapes
Worn like a shield.
Defences pulled apart
Light shines on a spirit
No stranger to the girl
Whose warmth is well.

Curtains opened

Theresa Mead

ECO THE ROBIN

The World is dying at our feet
    Through man's ignorance and wars
Covering the Earth with bricks and concrete
    That festers and bleeds like open sores
Eco the Robin . . . can't you hear him cry?
    Our Ecosystems are starting to die
All its beauty is disappearing
    Are all of you blind and hard of hearing?
Flora and Fauna are vanishing
    The Ecosystem, all but gone
Eco is now a dying Flower
    To flourish ne'er more . . . nor to gaze upon
Thus Eco is vanishing and dear Robin too
    As He couldn't live on a wall
As He was dying says, 'I told you so!'
    But you were deaf to the call
So now you too are dying
    Killed the Eco, now there's nothing left
You've killed me too with my lovely ways
    And my World is now dark and bereft
The World is dying at our feet
    She is slaughtered, like the Lamb
Yet onwards you go to oblivion
    And mindlessly don't give a damn
Not a breath of fresh air for the taking
    Killed Eco the Robin did you
He had nowhere to live 'cept on a brick wall
    and His dinner was CO_2

CO_2 for breakfast and dinner
    Not a perch on which to sing
So He sang His last song forever
    Then the bell began to ring
                    . . . ding!
        Boing!

Clare Marie Zeidrah Keirrissia Marshall

MOTHER EARTH

The evening shadows stole across the sky
As the Earth settled down to sleep, she gave a sigh
It carried across on the winds to the oceans and the seas
To anyone who would listen to her plea

All the creatures that lived in the ocean and on land
Was filled with sadness at the devastation done by Man's hand
Each day that passes Mother Earth tries to repair Man's destruction
But her efforts are set back by many obstructions

When will Man learn it's a duty to look after our Mother Earth
Will they ever learn that she takes care of us from the day of our birth
Without the rich earth we would have no food to sustain us
How Man treats our planet really isn't fair or just

Make a promise to yourself, you will try to make a difference
Just one small effort to help nature in her deliverance
From toxic dumps and poisoned streams
To a place we can only think of when we dream
A land of milk and maybe honey
Where we don't make a god of things and money

It will take many years to put things right
To find a person who has power and far-reaching sight
To see our world as it really should be
Somewhere where future generations can really be free

Glenys Hannon

COME, LET'S CELEBRATE!

A year of global terrors
Of carnage and pain
We will now reclaim
A happier clime.
Of optimism and serenity
Of peace and security
Of love and purity
And an end to crime.

With family and friends
With weddings and birth
A time for mirth
A happier clime.
With nature's progression
And claiming possession
Of all that we have.
And sharing our time.

Our fate lies within us
A positive attitude
And shed all our platitudes
A happier clime.
Enjoy each new meeting
As moments are fleeting
Life only goes forward
Each minute sublime.

Recover each pleasure
Encourage each other
For each is our brother
A happier clime.
Look not only inwards
But outwards and upwards
Rewards not necessity
But achievement divine.

Gael Nash

FIREFLY

Around the trees
Across the lawns
In scent laden breeze
Rubbing its wings
Striving to compete
With darkness and mist
Small green light
Tiny little bulb in flight
Little tiny firefly
The nature lover may
Be sitting on the patio
Or in the lawns
Withdrawn
In dreams foregone
Will he notice me and say
My dear tiny firefly,
Should I hold you in my fist?
You might die or let you go by?
Ah! the dismay
Say nay! say nay!
Strive hard; strike fast
Delight, excite, ignite, incite
Tonight -
He will hold you in his hands
Then let you fly
The night is warm
Peaceful and dark
Hold tight green spark
Little lonesome hope
Should never die
Tiny little firefly.

Nayyer Ali Chandella

A Drive With My Wife In The Car

The day had dawned most bright and skies were clear
Later came the dreaded words, 'Shall we go for a ride dear?'
Within a quarter of a mile, she had started her 'patter'
Whilst I had to sit there, thinking, *what does it matter?*

'That car in front has something weird on its bumper.'
'Did you notice that girl in the bright blue jumper?'
We were well past the girl by the time she had said so
And she knew I daren't look, because it's a 'no, no'

'You're driving too close to that lorry ahead!'
'I had a very strange dream last night in bed,
I can't remember exactly what it was all about,
But you weren't in it, because you'd gone out.'

I wondered to myself, how I managed such a feat
Because any suggestion I care to make, will be beat.
'That lorry driver behind us is doing his best to kill.'
Will she ever stop second-guessing my driving skill?

'The traffic lights ahead are just about to change,'
I think I'll jump them even if they do try to change.
I am sure that the 'patter' is driving me mad
When this trip is over, I shall be ever so glad.

The interminable chatter carried on, mile after mile,
All that I could do was nod and occasionally smile.
We finally got to the destination, she had decreed,
Is is any wonder my friends say I've gone to seed.

'We're not going back by the motorway, are we dear?'
'Yes, because we used the scenic route to get ourselves here.'
This, just as we were halfway down the access junction
Proved again that in the car her brain doesn't function.

Home again with my ears and nerves quite shattered
The car and I feeling completely and utterly battered,
For the last twenty miles I didn't hear a peep -
Surprise, surprise, she had fallen off to sleep.

Brian Taylor

They Never Went To Tokyo

Lotus Flower, walking through the
Japanese garden.
Stops and breathes in the
orange blossom, remembers
the first time he looked
into her eyes.
The military man
tall, broad-shouldered, handsome,
he drained her!
Dating, he took her to where
geraniums grew
like giant hogweeds,
out in the country.
Caressed her, promised
her the moon . . .

Memories exude from the
orange blossom,
the day they met
she dressed his wounds . . .

She looks at him
back from the Japanese garden,
stares at him
sleeping,
his head sunken into
well pressed cotton.
She thinks,
We never went to Tokyo . . .

Julya Bukowski

Gran

I survey the expanse of grass and sky,
And think of the unselfish love she gave
Only now I cherish the years gone by
And with remorse look upon her grave.

She gave me wealth, not in material form,
But love and values no money could buy.
Was there for me from the day I was born
And chastised me with no more than a look and a sigh.

Why is it so hard to show emotions when one is young?
Was I so unfeeling, I knew not her pain?
She had so many virtues that remain unsung
It was I, not her that had much to gain.

I think of her often with love and tenderness
And wish I had told her how I felt.
But I must be content that she is now at rest,
Free from the hardship that life had dealt.

You never heard the sound of my voice,
My laughter or my cries of pain.
In your silent locked up world you had no choice
But Gran you will, when we meet again.

Anne Jenkins

Love

Love is a strong emotional feeling of affection
Love is a show of concern for someone
Love is like a fountain of water
Love is a show of loyalty, honesty and trustworthiness
Love is giving, sharing and assisting
Love is unconditional
Love should be cherished
Love and you will be loved
Love forgives and accepts all wrong doings
Love works through conflicts together
Love hates no one
Love breaks all barriers
Love is showing goodness and mercy
Love is hugging and kissing
Show love to your children, partner
And others, as God loves you
The greatest gift is 'love'

Joe Oluwa

Precious Freedom

We must celebrate the freedom that we have,
to talk and sing and have a laugh.
We can visit interesting places
and see many different faces.

Be carefree on a holiday,
enjoy relaxation wherever we stay.
Pursue our hobbies, shop and eat,
With friendly greetings from people we meet.

Stroll along a country lane,
venture out in the sunshine or rain.
Walk along sandy beaches at the seaside;
have nostalgic journeys on a steam train ride.

Discover tucked away treasures,
so much fun, so many pleasures.
England - so much is fair and pretty,
in the villages and the city.

To sit in a church with one accord,
for our freedom to thank the Lord.

Gloria S Beeston

FAMILY PRIDE

Lia-Milan!
what a tale to tell
when she matures
and her beloved gran
so proud
to be a counterpart
in the most important
event in life -
new birth! A promise
of future love
of God's humanity
here on Earth -
family pride exemplified
God's love so true
in this wide, wide world.
From stable to pavement
Heaven's loving plan -
blessed are the parents
of Lia-Milan.

Mary Skelton

HALLOWE'EN SURPRISE

It was late October; I always visited my mum,
so I bought her a small ornament, just for fun,
it was three little rabbits draped in sheets,
carrying a pumpkin and a sack for treats.
As I ambled along slowly, on my way out,
a group of boys let out a shout,
'It's Hallowe'en, you silly old bat!'
I said, 'Why remind a witch of that?'
The look on their faces was of shock and surprise,
I'd have loved to have vanished before their eyes,
I said, 'If you're thinking of trick or treat,
you'd better be dressed up when next we meet.'
That night I will remember as long as I live,
for I had bought small objects and sweets to give,
I was so amazed when I got back,
each child was wearing a painted black sack.
I felt very privileged; they'd played along with me,
for they were so very poor you see,
The boys had taken their time to think this out
and, who'd had the most fun? Me, without doubt.

Audrey Packman

CHRISTMAS

One Christmas morn
A child was born
To Joseph and Mary
That's when the children
Had their presents
From the Christmas tree.
Breakfast was eaten
At the table
Whilst thinking about
The baby, born in a stable
Dinner was a winner
With turkey and plum pud
Tea was eaten with
Lots of good company
Supper was eaten at nine
And the day had just gone fine
And so to bed
And it's goodnight
And God bless

Ada A Stephenson

MY TRUE LOVE

Like the smell of the ash
And crisp mountain dew
A sea breeze that cools you
Against the sun
Like the sweet smelling pine
Aspen and the rowan
That's how refreshing it is
To be with you

You're lovelier than the cherry blossom
Honeysuckle and the rose
Sweeter than the grapes
That ripen on the vine
You're deeper than the cellars
That hold the vintage wines
That's how my love for you grows

And like the deepest forest, my heart
Is bliss
Like the mighty redwood we stood
The test of time
And I have never loved another
Like this love of mine
Our heart, our dreams
Are one with this.

Ray Perkins

A MUTUAL UNDERSTANDING

It is a woman's prerogative to cry when sad,
and a man's choice to welcome her with open arms.
That is the boundary that separates them by birth
and the standard which they uphold to.

In time the relationship develops into one of mutual understanding.
Their thoughts and feelings entwine
and they learn to support one another,
complementing each other and learning to share.

I Obomhense

EQUALITY

Equality cannot be one alone,
Strength to do it, starts at home,
To gain equality, let self be the guide
From man's oppression we cannot hide.

Fists at home, guns on the streets,
Stand up sister, or face defeat,
Relationship is ruined by power and oppression
Let not man continue with this obsession.

A change in attitude about man's violence
Don't lay down and suffer in silence,
Respect, the word to hold so dear
Respect ain't man with gun or fear.

Black women, Asian women, white women too
Respect yourself sister, you know this be true
The fight for equality starts with you
And grows when one becomes two.

So come on sister, speak with one voice
Inside and outside ain't no choice
Teach your children of love and equality
Let's work together for the sake of humanity.

Pearlina Lindsay

NO ASYLUM HERE

All I can do is sit
in silence. No words
exist to reassure even if I could
speak them. No touch
permitted, though my heart yearns
to hold, to console. No hope
can I dare to utter, only shame
spills out. What anger
roars within me, rigid rage
and impotence. No vestige
of terror and torture threatens
the ivory tower of power. What courage
is yours to breathe from hour to hour
and dare to live. What cowardice
theirs who hide behind lies.
All I can do is sit
in silence.

Margaret Trivasse

THE DAILY DIET - A SLIMMING WOMAN'S LAMENT

These listed foods are dangerous,
For reasons, this and that.
The others printed on this card
All harbour too much fat.
The salty foods appearing
On the multicoloured chart
Must really be avoided
If one wants a healthy heart.
And there are many other foods
Now viewed with apprehension
'Cause doctors say convincingly
They cause pre-menstrual tension.
So what with munching fibre
And salads by the ton
I suppose I'm keeping healthy
But my meals are not much fun.

My grandmother just laughs at me
With all my fads and fears.
Today it is her birthday . . .
And she's lived one hundred years!

Peter Doole

KNICKPOINT

Don't
'Drop' me
Or it would be
As if I were frozen
And in a whirlpool
All at once.

Maybe
You could condense
My life into a teardrop
So that you
Could keep me afloat.

Please
Bottle the mists
Until 'icy' pathways
You want me to tread.

I'm out of my depth
But it transpires,
You are my water.

Natalie Jagger

HAVE A GOOD DAY

Darling McClung said, 'Have a good day.'
Unnerving, that was, creepy.
not the words, lots of people say that -
cashiers, receptionists, canvassers.
But coming from the secretary to
the defence attorney of
my penfriend on Death Row, who was
        having a last day . . .

Unless there was truth in the rumour I'd heard -
a moratorium on executions till after the
        Presidential election.
Callers never got to speak to the attorney,
everything went through Darling McClung.
'The moratorium? That only applies to new
        execution dates, not those already fixed.
So unless something extraordinary happens,
Brian Roberson will die at six o'clock.
Anything else I can help with? Sure?
        Get back to me if there is.
Have a good day'.

How could she?
But how could I, ringing Leon when his wife had died,
how could I have closed with the routine
'Give my regards to Olga?'

Joe Solomon

HOPES AND DREAMS

I walk through pastures, wet and new.
Arms outstretched as I take in the view.
The sea line in front, the mountains behind.
My eyes closed, it's all in the mind.

The sun is shining, brightly I see,
The breeze is cool, refreshing me.
I walk on further, till I'm close to the edge,
And step out onto the sandy ledge.

The sea tickles my toes as it ebbs away,
To return again later today.
I hear the seagulls cry and look up above,
The sky is blue, the colour I love.

Everyone dreams of a place they'd like to be,
Would it be Paris or America or Spain for thee?
I know where I'd go, where I'd like to be,
My beach in New Zealand, next to the sea.

Anne-Marie Lloyd-Barrett

MEDITATION

Let your mind go and peel away the layers
of thought and enter a quiescent world,
through mists of swirling white and violet.
Crystal drops to solid diamond strength
glitter from a pale sun through crimson leaf.
Mist in suspension held by soft brown branch.

Glide along smooth rivers pale in moonshine.
Lift a hand wet with glistening silver.
Smell the wood-smoke of a forgotten fire deep in the forest.
Sweetly fresh torn grass in bovine lips, lazy fly swatting tail.
Purple cloak of distant lavender field.

Blue planet whirling in infinite space
caught by gravity in a web of time.
The sun the spider to a midget fly.
Bound by fate to absorb the energy.
Earth's shell spat out to float alone, the sun
in perpetual motion will live on.

Janet M Pinto

CITY CENTRE OASIS

A walled garden is simply wonderful,
As it holds nature's solitude within,
Where human hearts can find a moment's peace,
Sheltering from the city's never-ending din.

A place where thoughts and memories linger,
A pleasurable habitat for the birds,
Where everyone can pause a while to think,
And there's no need for the spoken word.

The season's treasures can be found
As buds awaken in the spring,
Followed by the glorious blooms of summer,
And birds fly to and fro as they sing.

There are all kinds of trees in abundance,
Providing shade in the sunshine and heat,
The scent of wild roses and blossom
Drifts on the air and around every seat.

The wondrous gold colours of autumn
Soon recede as leaves fall thick and deep,
Giving way to the chill winds of winter,
As the garden is cradled in nature's sleep.

And when on those bleak winter mornings
All the trees are etched with glistening frost,
We'll think of the lovely walled garden
And the long summer days we have lost.

Susan Richardson

THE EMBRACE

Just like the old days
I fold her gently towards my breast.
Scarcely more than a child herself
she has already exercised
that most mortal of choices.

Now catapulted into hardest adulthood
she is overstretched, surely
about to be bungeed brutally
between her consequential now
and an earlier, but never more to be innocent,
stage of development.

I hold her closer.
In our insulating efforts
to be grown up, to be 'strong',
our separate tears do not fall
but are secreted away
into the empty spaces of our tortured hearts.
Ah, my child.

Neither bit-player nor audience
to her truncated tragedy
I stand stunned, not catharted,
my insides bleeding raw in sympathy.
Rather it had been me
to fight this battle in her place.
Rather it had been me.

I reach across my exclusion
and hold her closer still.
I try to will away the future pain,
the memories of might have been,
the intangibility of loss.
Silently, we cry, only for now,
my powerless arms once more
fierce around her shoulders.

Stephen Eric Smyth

POINTS OF VIEW

Immediately the outer space being
descended on the world.
Our robot-host gave out an
Invitation to
'Come and meet the people'.
'People?' echoed the space being quizzically,
Our computerised host confirmed
as follows - 'Yes,'

    'People,'
    People are,
    People are capable,
    People are capable of so much,
    People are capable of so much love,
    People are capable of so much hate,
    People are capable of so much,
    People are capable,
    People are,
    'People' . . .

With a look of perplexity
the outer space being
extended its punch line,
indicating that it was
'In search of humanity,'
and with that,
was seen to depart in a haze of haste;
Fast foot note -
Naturally it was assumed
Both fully understood the same language!

Sylvan

RIVER OF LIFE

Time is like a river
You can't hold it, you can't control it
You can touch it for a moment, then it's gone
Try to catch a river
It will linger on your finger
You can feel it for a moment, then it's gone
Fast flows the river of life

Time lasts for a moment
You think you own it, but you don't own it
You are living just this moment, then it's gone
Life is like the river
Always flowing, always knowing
Where it's going, yes it's going, then it's gone
Fast flows the river of life

Life's a thing to treasure
But you'll never get its measure
You spend your leisure, spending moments, then they are gone
Life's a thing to chase
But you think, to try is a waste
And time goes by, the blinking eye, then it's gone
Fast flows the river of life

Seconds become minutes
And the hours into days
Weeks and months into years, then they are gone
Try to catch the river
You must hold it, must control it
You must feel it, it is real it, it is your life
Very fast flows the river of your life

Keith Skelton

CHILTERN HILLS HOLIDAY

I remember when I was young
     going on holiday,
Suitcases spread upon the bed
     and Puss was looking glum,
Some days we'd go for lovely long walks
     into the hills where wild raspberries grew,
Strawberries peeped between the leaves
     and foxgloves made a show.
Up to the woods we walked one day
     finding nuts in the hedgerow on our way.
Down to the field of corn below
     where cornflowers waved and poppies glowed,
Blue butterflies over the meadows fluttered
     buttercups shone, 'Do you like butter?'
Cowslips stood proud in the field's damp corner,
     lark song filled the blue sky.
Too soon our holiday came to an end
     on the train we travelled once more,
Smiling faces at our station
     and Puss sat there at the door.

F Todd

INSPIRATION

Pictures . . .

     of sunsets on the dawn,
     birds serenading the moon,
     wind sweeping the stars,
     of liquid blue ice,
     of footprints on the water.
Sketches on the mind canvas . . .

Words. . .

     that are tripping down a sound
     forsaken by Father Time,
     or drifting above the sand
     frozen in white light,
     like handprints on the wind . . .

With random thought,
         And manipulated words . . .
The pictures of poetry are written!

Samantha Braum

MANKIND AND THE WORLD

Look at the world around us and what do you think you see?
Not peace or love or compassion, but selfishness and greed.
There is enough for all mankind, to share and to enjoy,
But someone somewhere wants it all, to ruin and destroy.
For selfish gain and power, to rule and hold the key,
To life and hope and happiness, where all the love should be.
The hurt and sorrow power can bring, is way beyond belief,
Such sadness and bewilderment, mixed in with the grief,
But somehow through the trauma a smile on someone's face,
Is like a light to lead the way to a better place.
And then there's always help around to show you're not alone,
People pull together with great strength that's all their own.
They prove to men of power, that they're strong in heart and mind
And through that strength they prove themselves to God and
                            to mankind
The world is such a lovely place if everyone could see
That all we need is love and trust to live in harmony.

Joy Jackson

BE GOD'S CHAMPION

So now you're walking back on life's great roads,
singing your song in deep repose.
You don't know what's going to happen
but you hope with all your heart it does.
A new way has fallen before you.
The night seems dark but you know it's not,
for you can know the end of the plot
before the beginning comes and you know it not.
The answer is here before you.
Though the way seems dark and the future drear,
there really is a bright New Year
way up ahead of you.
For the Son sublime has it right,
this time your future is bright,
and the way ahead has come.
So forget the past and its broken dreams,
and hope for something new.
For don't you know, the future's bright
with no cranny dark and dim.
So walk in the light,
seek God's insight,
like a banner on your way.
Don't cast it aside,
keep faith at full tide
and really champion your day.

Anne Hadley

OLD PHOTOGRAPHS

(In Memoriam)

Old photographs are chroniclers
of the relentless march of time;
hard evidence of life's
remorseless cycle.
Here's one of a woman my age -
she's even younger there . . .
testimony since perjured
by ravaged vigour.
I recall particularly
a lithe, muscular lad,
poignantly captured
in vibrant monochrome.
Bearding urchins,
camphor-bound . . .
I never knew the dog;
but I could weep
for that fine man's
spent force . . .

. . . sometimes I ponder
the photographer.

John C Traynor

ACHIEVE PEACE

A handshake and warm greeting

P oliteness, when meeting.

R aising a level of hope

A lways present within folk.

Y es! Negotiators keep on trying

E very day, for wars to cease;

R ealising the reality of achieving world peace . . .

Diane Alicia Spence-Crawford

THIRD WORLD

Nothing but stark poverty
Disease facing you at every turn
Famine touching each and every body
Eating into the flesh
Killing thousands upon thousands
Dried-up land
Children dropping like flies
Supplies failing to arrive in time
Dust and dirt
Grime and filth
Food is a thing of the past
A morsel for a meal
If you are lucky
Walking skeletons with pot bellies
The faces of children
With a look of old men
Crying, wailing
Weeping into the flies
Carcasses strewn all over the ground
A look of helplessness everywhere
Heat sapping every pore
God give them strength and hope

Joy Bartelt

DESPAIR

Through the years my body has been battered
Broken bones, black eyes and a broken heart
To be handled with care
I will not bend or wither in despair

My shattered mind plays tricks on my physical form
Feet that cramp and hands that refuse to hold my pen
So now I write my thoughts for others to share
I will not bend or wither in despair

Death comes calling early in my bloodline
So I will live my life in the sunshine
without a care
I will not bend or wither in despair

I will eat the fruits of life and taste sweet nectar
Sing and dance and laugh inappropriately
Dress in strange garments and cause others to stare
I will not bend or wither in despair

I'll run barefoot through wet grass
Put the world to rights over coffee with friends
Write silly songs and pretend I'm not there
I will not bend or wither in despair

For one day I will not be there
But I won't have bent or withered from despair

Sheila Atkinson

BEREAVEMENT

Near me now I feel your silence,
once so shrill with words that stung,
silent only when your presence
spoke more loudly than your tongue;
silent then through hours of illness,
silent too in your last pain:
now the ever-silent stillness
strains to hear you chide again.

Bernard Brown

UNTITLED

Dear God,
You made a lovely place,
This world, a sphere that floats in space
With trees and flowers, forest grand;
All coloured with an artist hand!
Blue, green, the mighty oceans flow,
Like threads of ribbons through the globe.
A golden sun to give warmth and light,
A silver moon to shine at night

Dear God,
You made a heaven - then did
You ponder and wonder what else to do?
But were You fatigued with all You'd planned,
That perhaps Your hand faltered when You made Man?
Were You so tired You couldn't see what
Man could do in their stupidity?
Not foresee that Man would debase the free will
You gave to the human race, and that
Those who destroy with evil treachery,
Endanger this world, regardless of its beauty!

Oh dear God,
Could You not see what
Man can do - that You made amongst us,
The good, so few?

Jo Mackenzie

OUR DAY OF MUSIC, FUN AND DANCE

The morning started gloomy, it was pouring rain,
Everyone unhappy, it was dull with cloud again,
We said a silent prayer hoping for the best,
Praying for good weather so we'd be blessed.

Someone said, 'Rain before seven, stop before eleven,'
Eleven o'clock came, still there was no sign,
Of the showers stopping before our big do,
We'd planned weeks ago to start at two.

The scouts were helping us all prepare,
Putting up gazebos, tents, taking so much care,
Our secretary said after a while, 'Come with me,
I'm going to get us all some cups of tea.'

I followed her with big umbrella, to the church hall,
Where we got a tray of twenty cups, milk in all,
A giant metal pot they filled with plenty of hot tea,
My friend and I took the lot up, she said, 'Follow me.'

As we got back nearly to the Millennium Green,
The rain began to stop, the sun could just be seen,
Everybody cheered, we sat down, sipped our rosy lea,
Our day was going to be alright, we'd been set free.

Our event went well from that moment on,
The sun was out, its rays sparkled and shone,
It was a much livelier scene, with children dancing,
Morris men round the bright maypole prancing.

Stalls galore, selling various bits and bobs,
A bouncy castle, raffle, tombola, BBQ, many the jobs,
We raised money towards the upkeep of the green,
Till next year, when we'll have to start again.

Jan Hollinshead

SHIPS

Like ships that pass in the night
as a light goes out
I will remember you.
Long after the day has gone
the moment of now
has flown
in my mind
a treasure to have known
you are.
It will always
remain that way
'til death has a final say
when the curtain comes down
like ships that pass in the night
with me you'll go.

Wilson E Jones

BORROWED TIME

Words of love and sorrow
Hopes of yesterday
Dreams of tomorrow
Time we only borrow

What is right what is wrong
Written then sung in a song
Telling of people's fears
Reducing some of us to tears

Lovers making a song just theirs
Making plans in pairs
Building castles in the air
Some even succeeding in getting there

When old and sitting by the fire
No longer needing passionate desire
But tenderness and companionship
While back into the past, memory does slip

Having children or maybe not
Excepting what has been your lot
Whether we like it or not
But each other we still have got

So for the time being on we plod
Sitting peacefully being able to nod
Feeling contentment and secure
Unlike when you're young and not so sure

Anne Brodie

THE ADVANCE OF AUTUMN

A talent passing,
The mind still quick,
The body slow to react.
The acorns of courage grow fat,
Tomorrow is only winter.

Today is autumn,
Enjoy the freshness,
Savour the short warmth of an afternoon.
Watch leaves slowly turn fatal brown,
The last heat of summer clings hopelessly.

Smell the fragile flowers blooming,
Tonight the chill will creep ever closer.
There is tranquillity to autumn,
After the blaze of mother summer.
Peaceful reflections beyond the breaking year.

Ian Fisher

THE FARM ON THE HILL

With a pipe in his mouth,
His old dog at his knee,
They sit in the shade,
Of the old apple tree.
And watching, I know,
They are both of them still,
In thoughts, roaming free,
At the farm on the hill.

When the rosy dawn broke
They have counted their flock,
With the dew on their feet
While the valley lay still,
And when evening came
The bright moon looking down
Lit their weary path home
To the farm on the hill.

Sharing good times and bad,
They have plodded their way
Through snow inches deep
While the wind whistles shrill,
And many a lamb who had wandered astray
Owed his life to their care,
At the farm on the hill.

With his pipe in his mouth,
The old dog at his knee,
Till the end of their days,
Together they'll be,
And when the time comes
Their spirits will still
Be guardians too,
At the farm on the hill.

Joyce Mussett

DO NOT CARE FOR ME

Touch not my heart, not my soul,
touch not my dreams, so old.
Alone I have now become.
I know not what will come
in the days that follow.
My heart has become hollow,
no more to know love, or hope,
and I no longer know how to cope
with those that have betrayed
me with their words. I have strayed
from the pathway that was known
and this ground is overgrown
with weeds that tangle and ensnare,
and there is no one now to care.
I am uncertain in all that I do
but I know that heartache will ensue.
The world has gone crazy, and sadness
fills our hearts and brings only madness.
Who knows what tomorrow will bring
but I will not be there. I cannot sing
of hope, or of a love that will come
as my heart is filled with visions that come
of a lonely old woman with a heart of stone
lying below a broken granite stone.

Angela G Pearson

REMEMBRANCE DAY

Two minutes silence on Remembrance Day
Ensures our memories are here to stay.
Those who gave their lives, so young forever, never old,
The history of our forefathers, can always be told.

A soldier in the fields of war, far from home,
Had a life before he was in uniform.
Some had a wife, a home, a child,
Leaving was so hard, to fight a war, so cold.

A long way from 'Blighty' and fireside embers,
As the days became weeks, months and years.
So brave, fear unspoken, 'Over the top!' they had to go
When the officers shouted the order, to fight the foe.

So many died in every battle,
Stuck in the mud, in fields meant for cattle.
An endless line of soldiers, forward into the breach,
Mates, side by side and then, out of reach.

Bodies left rotting and horses too,
Such death and destruction, survival for only a few.
The battles in Flanders' fields and the Somme
Had taken the lives of so many, dead, forever gone.

The fields of Flanders, so distant now
Except for memories of loved ones, take a bow,
As poppies grow in freedom, red and bright,
Each one celebrating life in their light.

Before their death in grief and strife
The soldiers' blood was red, flowing, full of life.
And now, an old soldier stands alone at the Cenotaph,
A Chelsea Pensioner, his red tunic his autograph.

G E Harrison

THE DORSET RIDGEWAY

I love to walk out on the Ridgeway
Along paths which the Ancients have seen.
Where they trod my same tracks with their wares on their backs;
Or rode a fine horse through the heathers and gorse;
And I ponder the changes there've been.

The skylarks still chorus all summer,
And the kestrels and buzzards soar high.
But the pylons and masts were not here in their past,
Nor the thundering motors from hovering rotors
Which deafen all natural cries.

I like to imagine their hamlets
From the *humps and the bumps* that remain.
It was hard to provide from this mild countryside
With no tractors in barns, and no factory farms,
And no motor cars, buses or trains.

The gentle downs roll to the distance,
A patchwork of fields with neat hedges;
And the chalky-white cliff where the raucous gulls live
Makes a gleaming display, with the blue of the bay
Forming Neptune's salt frill at the edges.

Did those Ancients watch here from these pathways
As the foreign ships entered their ports?
Did they hope they were traders, but feared they were raiders?
(Modern-day fish and chips, 'kiss-me-quicks', and day trips
Are invading *our* seaside resorts!)

There's so much to view from the Ridgeway,
Nestling villages, downland and sea,
Where blue butterflies flutter and deer run for cover,
So I follow the track, with *my* pack on my back
And the ghosts keep me company . . .

Rosemary A Shaw

INHUMANE

Get out of my sight,
I do not welcome you anymore,
You bring evil and pain to me,
Never again will you come knocking at my door.

Your senses are dull,
You're lifeless and do not possess a soul,
You do not feel pain,
And have never felt the touch of the soft morning rain.

Who are you I ask myself,
A creation of God,
Or yet an inhumane beast,
Upon young women you do feast.

Your evil eyes scurrying the street,
As the night falls in,
Pulling up your jacket you're on a mission to create sin.

Arriving home late and drunk,
You pace the house for your wife,
You find her lying in the bed,
And this time you decide to take her life.

How could you be so evil?
But now you're gone as well,
Just as well she went to Heaven,
And you've sunk to Hell . . .

Lucy Elliott (15)

WINTER ESSENCE

*(Winter essence is a mix of days
collected down the years
and placed in the kaleidoscope of time
to shake out memories.*

                    Faith.)

Memories of frost in the cold morning air,
sparkling white on the lawn.
Filigree spiders' webs, strung out on bushes
tinged pink by the glow of the dawn.
Footsteps imprinted on meadow and grass
leaving a trail to the sun . . .
gathering its strength in the far eastern sky
to combat the cold still to come.

Memories of dusk falling early;
the afternoon heavy with threatening snow.
A glimpse into early lit homes
that we pass on our way to our own fireside's glow.

Of crumpets and muffins, and old fashioned things
such as tea at a quarter to four.
And listening to 'Children's Hour', snug round the fire
while the dog dreams his dreams on the floor.

Memories of snow at the end of the day
turning your small world pure white.
Taking tentative steps in its transforming beauty
while church bells ring out in the night.

Yet this magical world that closes the day
on our memories, is not just a dream.
It is there in the mind - that kaleidoscope pattern
of heart-warming things that have been.
It is moments, not days, that we tend to remember
for moments, though fleetingly gone
somehow stay in the memory, creating the essence -
of winter, for all our life long.

Faith Honeysett

DIANA'S ISLAND

I have gone back to Althorp on England's pleasant land
In the middle of an island for peace that's near at hand
Around the island, as a child many days were filled with joy
Today sorrow and sadness, happiness no more
Take me to my island peace and tranquillity
The water's all around me, as safe as safe can be
Around the lake so deep some ripples come and go
Or a vole that makes the water flow
Dragonflies flutter round and round, without making any sound
Flowers adorn a tapestry cover, the perfume lingers long
Peace on Earth this little place, remember me now I've gone
As flowers gently fade away, sun's autumn rays fall as where I lay
Light through the trees, beech, birch, oak and lime
Many leaves fluttering falling a carpet of gold and brown
Beneath the trees of a sunlit glade, with many days of sun and shade
Turning, turning seasons pass wind and rain it will not last
Summer sun and autumn blaze, winter snow and frost
With sparkling haze like jewels that once I wore
Seasons turning I have no more
Frost on the trees glisten with light, winter has come cover me white
I will not fear it is too late, peace on this island
Birds are on the wing, blackbird, thrush and linnet
Come down to sing, I am not afraid or alone.

Elizabeth Ann Jameson

MY VALENTINE

I love to sit with you
        by candlelight

To curl up tight by a
        log fire bright

To feel your body so close
        to mine

And sip champagne by a
        fireside bright

To listen to the CD playing
        our favourite songs

And fall asleep locked in
        each other's arms.

R Danks

HEARTFELT

Outside so strong and volatile;
Yet inside a tender-hearted little girl,
Playing the role that's expected of her,
Playing the role so well.
Yet lately, the little girl is surfacing more
And oh! how she'd love her to stay.
But she can't because of the world we live in
And when she tried it before how badly she feels she failed.

You see, very few can cope with the strong one being vulnerable,
No one can lean on her when she's that way.
But with either character her honesty is consistent,
So much so that Josephine Blunt is her own given nickname.
So living as she does and knowing who she is,
Is not the easiest of ways,
It's a compromise of her integrity
And her conscience doesn't like it this way.
But she'll play it the strong and volatile one
In the hope that maybe someday
A man will come along who sees the little girl,
Falls in love with her and says,
'With you my little girl I want to stay'.

Gez

BLACKTHORN WINTER

(A rondeau)

Snow falls softly on frosted grass
Cold blackthorn winter's breath has passed.
Daffodils droop towards the ground
Where frozen primrose flowers are found.
Black ice has turned the pond to glass.

When sun breaks through the clouds at last
Warming this Arctic icy blast
Spring will return, but now around
Snow falls softly.

Will shepherds' scarlet skies forecast
To birds and beasts that winter's past
Will rabbits huddled underground
Soon hear the birds' dawn chorus sound?
Now yellow storm clouds come, alas
Snow falls softly.

Audrey G Willis

A SNAPSHOT OF A LIFE

As I look around this room
I see the memories, always in focus, usually in zoom

Close up images our minds saw fit to steal
Full colour, full size and awfully real

A snapshot of a life
To remember the joy and sometimes the strife

My family, my friends, my loves
Whizzing past my eyes like sentimental doves

I see them, I smell them, I can almost touch
I use them as my emotional crutch

When I am sad I let my mind wander
And a lifetime of stuff is pulled asunder

Torn into pictures of parties and places
Furniture, books, puzzles and faces

I remember the food, the discussions, the fights
A photo is this - a snapshot of a life

Nicola Harris

THE GARDENER

A garden is a place
With its own micro climate,
The gardener can create this
By manipulating nature
So that something artificial
Looks natural.

The gardener influences
And attracts a population
Of insects and small creatures
Who make their way,
Like economic migrants,
To this small haven.

The gardener is like a conductor
Controlling a thousand players
As he develops his own arrangement
Of the Four Seasons:
He transforms the restless garden
Into a symphony of colour and form.

A garden embraces every kind
Of personality, the
Invasive bully and the vulnerable,
And like a concerned parent
The gardener must keep the peace
As he watches over them.

J D Mitchell

Sometimes I Curse Ian Walton

I'm going to be late, the deadline's tonight
I'm wracking me brains, can't think what to write
I've got to write something, but what should it be?
It's got to be special, for an anniversary
Now should it be personal? I've only known them a while
Should it be serious? No that's not my style
Now my brain's gone all mushy, and lost all its rhymes
Oh why does this happen at such awkward times?
Well I can only say thank you to all of the team
For publishing my odes and fulfilling my dream
To have my poems published and read by so many
But most of all thanks for not charging a penny
It's just as well because I haven't got any
And I thank Ian Walton, but sometimes I curse
When I can't get to sleep because my head's filled with verse
But it's all worthwhile, when I find on my mat
A copyright notice, how fantastic is that?
Well all you folks, have a great time
I'm signing off now because I've run out of rhyme.

Trudy Simpson

Suicide

The quicksand slowly rises and engulfs my body and emotions
With a strange new sensation,
People reaching out to me but I am sinking
Deeper and deeper into a world of everlasting darkness.
All hope is swallowed along with all my dreams
Being replaced with sadness and loneliness
Such that I never knew existed.
Can anybody hear me or help me,
Or does nobody acknowledge my existence in the first place?
Is this just a state of mind or what is yet to be,
Will anybody find me in time,
Or will I just drown and the world be totally oblivious?
How strange it seems that all emotions can be drained away,
Only to be replaced by something so totally and utterly destructive,
Yet still you call out to me to hang on
And as you throw the rope for me to hang on to
To pull me from the depths of devastation
And the darkness from the corners of my mind,
You realise as I do
In that one small fragment of time,
The rope has worn
As has the will to carry on.

Mandy Salter

The Betrothal

When I regard the great expanse of midnight skies,
I sense a warmth, a shawl, a cloak of sudden kinship
Wrap o'er my lone and awestruck little me . . .
For dwarfed seem I against the majesty of so much sky
Set fast with diamond stars and, sometimes, Lady Moon.
We have an understanding in our silences,
We meet, and merge, and finally belong.
The heavens in their greatness gaze down on me,
And I, in my littleness, feel acceptable and free.

O great and mighty vastness that sweeps eternity,
How close and near in friendship you seem, tonight, to me!
Like some sweet life companion, a guardian over me,
To tell me all is ever well and ever well will be.
The raindrops patter gently like kisses all around,
Telling me you love me, and that to you, I'm bound.
Dear heavens, stars and firmament, I now declare to you,
No other love can take your place - forever I'll stay true.

Molly Stacey

Ashes To Ashes

Ravaged by violence and hatred
In the grip of a terror attack
Our world fell, blown away in one breath,
And loved ones were taken that can never come back.

A home to millions
Very quickly became the doorstep of Hell,
Violated at the hand of Man
And gripped with fear our country we love so well.

And in the midst of this crisis,
Amongst the horror of it all
Eleven men played for their country,
A humble game of bat and ball.

An oval patch of grass
Played host to an ancient tradition;
A quiet act of our country's resilience
In answer to surrounding perdition.

As the tiny urn was lifted,
And a lap of honour taken around an English field,
Voices sang in unity and defiant optimism.
The nation's spirit lifted at this English cricket yield.

Heroes have emerged
In both a nation's game and a nation's strife.
Only in shared strength, resilience, and hope
Have we found a way to defend our English way of life.

Ashes to ashes
Dust to dust
The English spirit will never be crushed.

Lucy Browster

Girls' Night Out

We went out to the pub
Ah, but here's the rub
There was a special offer
But it wasn't on grub
It was happy hour
All doubles for the
Price of one

On vodka, whisky and gin
We couldn't wait to begin
We were spoiled for choice
My friend Mary and I
As we went to the bar
We heaved a big sigh

Because we knew sadly
We were going to drink
Our money goodbye
A double gin for Mary
A double vodka for me
A little dash of tonic water
Oh, it tastes better than tea
After one and two
We began to relax
After three and four
We didn't care anymore
We were singing with the band
And dancing on the floor
After 5, 6, 7 and 8
We just knew it was late
And everyone was our mate.

Bernadette O'Donoghue

MEMORIES

Memories are words on paper not yet written
they are with us from birth to death and only come when bidden.
It needs a shock, a hurt or more to make you start to think
a tragedy, no hope, despair, it's harder when you sink.

Happy memories begin the day, or when a life begins
and as one grows we relish life, experiences and sin.
Childhood memories seem the best, they always seem so good
but if only we can remember when we were hurt and misunderstood.

With maturity we grow and learn to understand
why things began the way they did
and we thought life would turn out grand.

First job, first love, everything is fine
first child, first pet, the world is almost mine.
And then first death, the loss of which the hurt can never come
until the tears, and memories the emotions overcome.

But with age, we all grow old and memories seem to fade
so we start to wonder where we were this last decade
and suddenly our lives seem so clear as the years just fade away
and memories take over dreams as we while away each day.

Sheila Margaret Storr

DID YE?

Did ye iver get an invite, 'n' ye'd naethin' new tae weer?
Did ye watch a creepy picter, 'n' ye coodna' sleep fer fear?
Did ye get sair teeth in th' holidays, fin naebody hauls 'em oot?
Did ye lock yer keys inside th' hoose, fin 'ere's naebody gan aboot?
Did ye ferget tae watch th' tatties, 'n' th' bile't inta soup?
Did ye catch up on yer knittin', 'n' hae ye foun' th' missin' loop?
Did ye look oot o' th' winda', 'n' it's pourin' doon wi' rain?
Did ye len' oot yer brolly, 'n' ye hinna seen't again?
Did ye iver dae th' washin', 'n' a' yer whites turn't blue?
Did ye iver think that a'thin' wrang, only iver happens tae you?
Weel, jist ye set yer myn' at rest, cos far fae bein' aleen,
I hae accidents fae morn 'til nicht, ah'm th' worst ye've iver seen.

The Jaimi

ANCHOR WE KNEW NOW FORWARD TO KNOW

A pulse in life
Reflects on value's view
Like some money lost
Then comes payment due.

Yet all gets attention
When excitement's new
All can get a mention to you.

A light can shine
Bringing forth some readjustment.

Time for a change of dedication
With aim to restore, just movement direction
For continuance of harmony assurance suggestion.

Celebration through anniversary
Gives cause of all embracing
In growth of promotion expectation.

That some words can be attained
With meaningful grace gathered emotion
Not just of spin like
For some unknown purpose commotion.

But with an aim uplift for enlightenment exist
That leads with wisdom's value
In fair allotment of achievement
So with all things of orderly guidance
That can let you, not miss.

E Gordon

SONNET

It is human nature to protect one's heart,
To hold something back, right from the start.

But to give it your all on a chance or a whim,
Is when a true partnership can really begin.

To tar with the same brush each amour that you meet,
Is to love unfulfilled - admitting defeat.

Trust is a gift to give and receive,
Without it, there is not much to achieve.

One cannot live in the fear of what may be,
Happiness is found when love can run free.

Past memory tends to predict a trend,
But the hurt of despair needs time to mend.

In this life you have so much to gain,
So love like you have never experienced pain.

Louise Pearce

TSUNAMI

A stumble at the Earth's core
A deep-throated rumble
And it begins . . .

Jolted from sleep
The angry ocean stretches,
Seeks new levels,
Gathers momentum.

A sudden drawing back,
Sea creatures flounder in disarray
As, braced for the attack
The wall of water hovers,
Towers above its prey.

A heart-stopping moment, then . . .
Mighty waves swollen with fury
Spew over new territory
Claim it as their own,
Engulf all in their path.

In the silence of the aftermath
A stunned world surveys the detritus,
Counts its dead
And weeps.

Vera Morrill

CASTLE

Oh castle, oh castle, of stone you were built,
With boulders and limestone, and bonded with silt,
You withstood the ravages of tempest and storm,
Until under Cromwell, you were left forlorn.
Your portals asunder, your magazine spent,
Your roof tumbled in, your bastion rent,
As onwards destroying, Cromwell's men went.

On ramparts and battlements the brave men of old,
Stood shoulder to shoulder, withstanding the cold,
With cauldrons of oil, and slings full of rocks,
Defending the castle, against insurgents and Celts,
With quivers of arrows attached to their belts.
The castle stood proudly, surrounded by moat,
Till the advent of gunpowder and guns when you broke.

The battle was brave and many men fell,
Defending the castle they knew oh so well,
The walls fell asunder, the ramparts were breached,
As broadsides of cannonballs were released.
The nobles and servants, ladies and all,
Died there, defending their castle wall.

J McKinney

UNVANQUISHED

A concrete jungle
assaults the eye
which over the drab gre roofs
I raise to the sky.

Within the confines
of these ugly walls,
the caged soul depresses
and the miracle falls.

O, how I miss
those tall majestic trees,
many coloured spectacle
waving in the breeze.

Where the spirit roams
without inhibition,
towards its heavenly home,
soothing fraught notions.

Man rules Earth's garner,
but o'er this man-made sin,
that makes the struggle harder,
the spirit will win.

As in the old garden
where the wild brambles,
over their tarmac coffin
triumphantly ramble.

Elaine McCulloch Smith

BRIGG FAIR

In the white of summer,
early sun's fire the Ancholme's
August water with red damask,
damselflies: and her memories.
Fettered by love's tenacity,
she follows the river track.

Roads are set with stalls
of honey bread, spinning ribbon-rides,
and the serious circumstance
of trade-in ponies, foals and shires.
At Brigg Fair she waits - another
year - to see his fire.

On Main Street,
a stallion fumes with life
as his Romany boy takes him
down the run.
She watches his moves,
scored to daring musicality.

Tensed breath.
Darting leaps.
A negligent grace
in each spring.

Such dazzling burns
inside her again.
She pauses, soft-smiles,
remembers his coming;

and tracks back -
past lovers' fields - to wait
another year for the sun
of this boy's - this son's dance.

D Webster

GOD'S GIFT

Lowland glens and mountains tall,
Deafening roar of a waterfall,
The fallow deer with speckled fawn
Watching the day break at dawn.

Apple blossom on a tree in spring,
A red, red rose, such a perfect thing,
Shady bower, or country lane,
Sunbeams glistening on drops of rain.

A forest so green, a sea so blue,
Flowers and plants moist with dew,
Robin, blackbird, dove and thrush,
Babbling brook and tall bulrush.

Nightingale singing notes so high,
Sunset or a stormy sky,
These things of beauty, all are free,
God's gift to Man, for you and me.

E Rose

LOVERS

Oh! So lucky,
With all the universe around
Moon and stars, we like magnets
Drawn together, found a love
With no bars, sweet scented to last forever.

Oh! So lucky,
In young love when fair of face
Met eyes of brown
In culture and the same race
And knew we were meant for each other.

Oh! So lucky,
Committed to that band of gold
Swore to honour, love, cherish
And obey. There was never any doubt
Feelings just the same - loving one another.

Oh! So lucky,
To understand, and be understood
To find a deeper love can grow
If seeds you sow are trust and honesty.
Peace of mind as you only could.

Oh! So lucky,
Four children we have, and they the nest
Have flown, and now have children of their own.
We worked hard to share our dream
Find happiness is to smile, be gentle and kind
And memories are the hearts of gold.

Gwen Haines

SEPTEMBER

Autumn days here again
The countryside glows.
Harvest moon in the sky
A silver globe shining high.
Fruit and nuts super
The year is passing
Don't forget the central heating.

Eirlys Howden

PEACE

Don't try too hard to find her
For you will look in vain.
She doesn't want to listen
Her blind eye shows disdain.
She's vanished in an instant,
She's dealt her cards with care.
You go on searching, pleading
You find she isn't there.

Faith and hope, these two remain
When peace has turned away.
Leaving you with sorrow
And a broken heart each day.
When you least expect it,
The blue shines through once more.
Peace at last returning
Through that open door.

Joan Kingscott

PARKINSON'S DISEASE - MY UNCHANGED MALADY

I can shout, I can scream, I can swear and blaspheme
But I cannot escape it; it's not a bad dream;
My joints feel a pressure too fierce to contain
And I know without a doubt it will all start again.
I suddenly feel my body jerking and shaking
As if every bone in my body was shrinking or breaking.
Calm down, calm down, my inner voice screeches
Whilst my brainwaves head for the dark hidden reaches.
No sleep comes to soften the terrible deadness,
And my body is covered in swellings and redness -
So what can I do? Suppose it was you
Preparing to face each day as *I* do?
Truth to tell, I still fight with all of my might,
And please God let me do something right!
For I must continue this endless campaign,
Until I can walk upright and freely again.

Len Corner

LIES AND DECEIT

Once again, I've been kicked in the teeth,
In society today, I have no belief.
I thought I had a friend as nice as can be,
She brought round presents, invited us to tea,
Kind to my family, good-hearted and true,
Introduced us to others who showed kindness too.
Then I found out, oh what a fool I'd been,
Taken for a ride, could this have been seen?
I should have guessed geniality is rare,
I've been deluded again, this isn't fair!
Whenever I put my trust in this race,
I'm continually let down, it's a total disgrace.
Why am I always treated this way?
I suppose it's only me, so that's OK!
My only option is to be alone,
And then nobody can throw a stone -
But where does it hit, right where it hurts,
It's opened my eyes, I'm now fully alert.
Until the next time when I'm fooled again,
A rise in blood pressure - *stop* -
Count slowly to 10.

Angela A Shaw

JOY

How wonderful! I am so pleased
These words echo as we rejoice
You have passed the big exam
Something special, you made a choice
I have won a cup for a big event
The pleasure it gives has made my day
So much happiness has come my way
In the garden my flowers make a wonderful display
They give so much joy to those who pass my way
I have passed my test, I can drive the car
There is no holding me back, I can travel far
My little one can ride a two-wheeler bike
It will be a job to keep her in sight
The exercise I shall get, will I lose lots of weight?
Be an example to others who dread the scales and their fate
I have just moved house, I have mixed thoughts
Have I really done right, will I settle in time?
Now I am all sorted out, why did I doubt?
Happiness abounds, I feel at home
So much to look forward to now I have settled down
Serious times, I am feeling ill
Oh now I am better
So much thankfulness for doctors' and nurses' skill
I had a lucky dip in the lottery today
Never thought a win would come my way
I am waiting for a bus, at last it has arrived
How happy I am to climb inside
I could go on for evermore
There are so many things, so much joy in store
Sometimes if it is hard to be glad
Don't give up, look for joy even if you are sad . . .

M Baker

REFLECTIONS

Still water 'neath a shady tree,
Where I can sit in calm tranquillity
With just my thoughts to keep me company,
To let my heart and soul roam free.

I feel the sunshine warm upon my face
As clouds glide overhead with gentle pace,
A butterfly floats by with fragile grace,
Whilst dragonflies dart thither place to place.

The busy bees sip nectar from the flowers,
In lush grass green and fresh from summer showers,
Where oak and poplar stand like stately towers,
And birdsong fills the warm and sunny hours.

The bouquet from the flowers fills the air
With honeysuckle, garlic, rose and tare,
The poppy, cornflower, sage and daisy fair,
Their perfume heady, sweet beyond compare.

A lark on high, her joyful song doth sing,
As swallows dip and wheel on agile wing,
Whilst distant bells from yonder church do ring,
Their message one of hope for all to bring.

I thank the Lord who gave these things to me,
With ears to hear and eyes that I might see,
The trees, the flowers, the creatures wild and free,
Life's treasures cherished always, in my memory.

Jackie Barlow

I'll Win This Fight For You

I lay there, curled up on my bed
The tears just kept on coming,
Then I felt your hand upon my shoulder
And I knew right then I couldn't go on running.

You touched my fingers, held my hand in yours
You gave me strength when all my own had gone,
You looked into my eyes, brightened up the darkness
And that moment, I knew I had to carry on.

You spoke my name, you told me, 'It's forever.'
You touched my face, my fears drifted away,
You told me, 'We'll fight this war together.'
You said, 'Forget the past, live for today.'

You held me close and told me, 'You'll get through this.'
You're the breath that's keeping me alive,
You held me up when I felt I was falling,
You gave me hope and you helped me survive.

Now I lie here, curled up on my bed,
The tears are drying, I no longer feel so blue,
The war isn't over but I'm winning the fight,
I found hope, I found love, I found you.

Margaret Ann Scott

Sleeping Rosebud

The rosebud she is sleeping, don't wake her from her rest
For in the early morning she wants to look her best
When the sun arises and warms her to her toes
The rosebud she will open into a sweet red rose.

The dewdrops sit upon her gown and shine like jewels in a crown
As velvet petals her surround, her beauty does abound
Her crimson velvet petals now sparkle bright with dew
As slowly they all open to bring joy to me and you.

She is the fairest one of all her beauty to behold
Please don't wake her from her rest she brings joy untold
She stands supreme above the rest, her perfume sweet and heady
But when the warmth of sunlight goes the rose of crimson will be ready
To fold her gown of tiny folds once more with petals tightly closed
The rose will rest in sweet repose.

Vicki Harrold

Proposal

Come with me to the north, my love
Such splendours we shall see
Moors and dales and rivers wide
And throbbing industry.

And then we'll journey east, my love
Your kinfolk there to see
And 'midst good friends in Hartlepool
Soon married we shall be.

And let us then to westward go
Broad lakes and mountains high
To Westmorland and Cumberland
And ever-changing sky.

And we shall stay at Underscar
Where first we ever met
A week remembered all our lives
How could we e'er forget.

And we shall climb the mountain peak
There half the world we'll see
Where I have been so lonely, love
But never more shall be.

Reg Dyer

Today

Is today the future 'happy days'
That we will remember with sentiment
When skin is marked and eyes are sore
These happy days, when we went 'tell us more'
And do you remember?
Oh! Happy days of eighty-three
When we had just our choice for tea,
Watched Blue Peter on coloured TV
And even our library books were free.

Is that how we will recall today?
Will we sigh and remember the way
We met on Tuesdays in fellowship?
Biscuits to eat and tea to sip
Round the shops with little money to spend,
Free to smile and chat with a friend.

So just in case they drop a bomb
And destroy, burn till all is gone,
Let's realise just how lucky we are
Today, whether the fall-out be near or far,
Don't let us waste a minute or mar
The beauty of today,
Fresh green shoots and snowdrops,
Wind, frost, even the raindrops,
Stars at night, moon, the sun all say,
'We are still here, you are lucky today.'

Millicent Blanche Colwell

Untitled

Thank You for giving us Your only Son,
Our Lord, our Master and the Holy One.
He gave His life for us on Calvary,
And rose again so that we might be free.

Thank You for lending us Your lovely world,
The restless sea, the sky, each soaring bird.
The mountains grand and flowery meadows fair,
Each tree, each tiny shell Your love declare.

Thank You for music's power to touch our hearts,
For colours, shapes and textures in the arts.
For books to read and minds to comprehend,
With joy we thank You as in awe we bend.

Thank You for love of friends and family.
For lips to praise Your name and eyes to see.
For ears to hear each sound both great and small,
And hearts to love You always, most of all.

Lord give us grace that we may follow You,
Loving and trusting You our whole life through.
Until we meet with You, our Lord and Friend,
And see You face to face at journey's end.

Brenda M Wylie

I Am What I Am

I'm an eagle in flight, flying high and free,
I'm a dolphin swimming in the deep blue sea,
I'm the sun that shines, so high in the sky,
I'm the stars that shine brightly, while you sleep and lie,
I watch with sorrow this world falling apart,
It would be so much better, if everyone was kind in heart,
One day they'll look at what they have,
And make changes for this world to save,
That's life as it is and so it must be,
Too big to be changed by little old me!

Ann Jones

LITTLE TIMMY TIPTOES

Little Timmy Tiptoes
Came creeping up the stairs
Looking for his granny
To help him say his prayers

'Please help me Granny Tiptoes
To say my prayers aright
And angels will watch over me
In the middle of the night

I try to do the things that's right
And be both kind and good
Thank You for my health dear Lord
And thank You for my food

Thank You for my friends, dear Lord
For those who make me glad
And oh, bless Granny Tiptoes
My mummy and my dad.'

John Campbell

A WILD ROSE

Once I was a flower
So pure and yet so fair
I danced, swayed and glistened
In the breezy summer air

I was ablaze
Of pink and red
Alive and erotic
In my flower bed

Dewdrops shone like diamonds
A jewel for all to see
Petals of the finest silk alive
Caressing me

Sunlight set my heart aflame
From soil and earth
Is where I came

And as the seasons change
And the cold wind starts to blow
My petals scatter one by one
In a perfumed, coloured show.

So I'll bow my head
And gently sleep
Till sunlight does arrive
I'll awake again in springtime
When the dewdrops kiss my eyes.

Marilyn Davidson

ICE MAIDEN

Winter has spread her icy hand,
Scattering snowdrops in uneven hands.
Our fingers numb and frozen toes.
With Jack Frost nibbling at our nose.

A wonderland white, and carpet crisp.
With crackling leaves, playing 'will-o'-the-wisp'.
Sculptured washing draped from each tree.
Ironed to perfection, within nature's freeze.

Reflections of light herald the dawn.
Showing footsteps indented in a path quietly worn.
It's a wonderful world, with rainbows to spare.
Sees joys to behold for people everywhere.

Spring is round the corner, now new life can begin.
Sunshine's peering round the clouds to let the light back in.
Everywhere a picture and beauty just to see,
Dusted by Mother Nature and lit with tranquillity.

Janice Thorogood

PARTY PEOPLE

Celebrations should be *fun*
But they're not liked by everyone.
When you were small you loved getting dressed
In fairy outfit and fabulous dress
With a 'smidgen' of *lace* and net and glitter
Mum 'rustled up' gear that was all a-himmer

Cos she was an 'ace' on her sewing machine
And the 'gear' that she made turned other folks *green*.
You were certain to be 'the belle of the ball'
The rest wouldn't stand a chance at all.

But oh dear; the teenage years arrived
When all you wanted to do was *hide*
Cos you hated your gear, it was 'c**p' to wear
You knew other folks were going to stare.
And what to do if you're asked to dance?
With all those spots you'd a cat in hell's chance!

But you're older now and a 'kosher' *gran*
And as for parties - a regular *fan*
If a do's i the offing you've got the shoes,
A 'glitzy' dress; earrings
Then *party*, and *booze!*

Ella Neal

A POET'S PASSING

When the love was flowing,
you were surface happy.
And as the night moved on
red wine sparkled in cut glass goblets
like concentrated blood in a glass chalice.
talk became vivacious amid hilarious laughter
as you sprouted poetry to one and all.

Sometimes you would watch the street lights,
the halo of rings circling the globe
from your den in the house of sighs.
You wondered about the world you lived in,
but all was not well for a poet who cried inside
about something that could not be defined.

On a day of shadows in early January
as the first snowdrop pushed its way
through the heavy soil in a mundane garden,
you passed away
leaving a void that cannot be filled.

Rosaleen Clarke

NOVEMBER

A month of damp and misty mornings,
First frosts sparkling on the hedgerows.
Pale sun at midday warming the chilly air.
The bare branches of trees reaching up
Dark against the winter grey-blue sky.
Scent of woodsmoke, and damp leaves;
A month of bonfires and fireworks,
Of remembrance parades and scarlet poppies.

A month of waiting, between harvest and Christmas.
Evening clouds tinted pink and gold.
Inky-black nights brilliant with stars,
A huge silver moon sending a ghostly light
Over fields and woods, and city rooftops.
Shop lights sending rainbows onto wet pavements.
November; silently poised between October's glow
And the magical mysterious wonder of Christmas.

G Ayling

FROM DADDY

I know you've wondered where I've gone
I didn't say goodbye - that was wrong

Life goes on, a new day's dawning
Death arrives with little warning

I can even hear you say
'Is Daddy happy so far away?'

Heaven isn't far from Earth
We were in Heaven before our birth

I listen now and hear your voices
I'm with you as you make life choices

You must take heart and believe me
When I tell you I'll be back again

See the wonders of each day
Look out for me, I'm on my way

Perhaps you're wondering when that will be
I'll tell you darlings, wait and see

This summer when the flowers bloom
Wake up from your doom and gloom

The garden created in memory of me
So beautiful, comforting and just you see

I shall return to you as a butterfly
Colourful and free - I'll explain why

A chrysalis I've been, now I'm waking
I'll return to Earth to show God's making

Take comfort, enjoy what life brings
Look out for me with colourful wings

Love each other and take great care
Remember I am with you there

Rebirth is just like being recycled
Think of the process as being 'Michaeled'.

Helen Saunders

FIFTEEN YEARS ON, HAPPY ANNIVERSARY TERRY

Like a wind gently blowing,
On a breezy summer's day,
Fuels the fire, flames soar higher,
And I feel I'm blown away.

But like a moth unto the flame
That flickers gently in the night,
You are the light, you gave me sight.
You guide me on, to fly your way.

Seems each time I look into your eyes
You draw me in,
For with you I feel
I found my paradise,

As I bask within your glow,
I feel your warmth.
It's a feeling so reassuring
And so nice.

I feel I'm soaring up to heights
That I have never been,
For your fire, it burns a pathway
To desire.

Feels I've travelled so far
With my heart's desire.
Where passion burns
In the heart of the fire.

Patricia Lynne Phipps

THANK YOU

(This is about a stray dog I took in nine years ago. He passed away 1st January 2002)

Do not be sad when I have gone,
I want to thank you for everything you have done,
I had no one to love me, no one to care,
No one to hug me when I was feeling scared.
Then you came along and took me in
When everything through my eyes was looking quite dim.
I want to thank you for being so kind,
It helped me leave the past behind.
Thank you for your tender loving care,
And for always being there.
I've had a wonderful life since being with you,
I had someone to snuggle up to
On bleak winter nights
And somewhere safe and warm
For the rest of my life.
I don't want to leave but it's time to go
I'm old now you see.
Thank you for loving me, Toby.

Gloria Whitehouse

WHY?

Why did he go, why did he leave
Why did my man want to deceive?
I loved that man with all my heart
I never thought that we would part.

He's had the best years of my life
Why did he want me for his wife?
I cooked his meals and cleaned his house
And now he has another spouse.

I doubt she'll love him as much as I
I feel so sad that I could cry.
I lie awake for hours on end
How I'd love my marriage to mend.
If it wasn't for my daughters four
I'd want to die, of that I'm sure.

To me they are a tower of strength
For them, I'd go to any length.
I love them like I loved their dad
I wonder why he turned so bad.
If only he knew the harm he'd done
When he left me for another one.

He's shattered my faith, he's broken my heart
How I wish we weren't apart.
My marriage vows I'd make again
But next time, God, spare me the pain.

I never thought, when I said yes
My marriage would end in such a mess.
All I wanted from this life,
Was to end my days as Gordon's wife.
For reasons that I'll never know
Gordon felt he had to go.

Joan Beer

LIFE'S ECHO

Life is an echo,
All comes back.
The good, the bad,
The false and the true,
Give to the Lord,
The best that you have,
And the best will come back, to you.

Isabel Kelly

YESTERDAY EVENING

There was no time to say goodbye to you
I had no time because I didn't know
Yesterday evening was our last farewell
Both unaware it was your time to go
I can recall each breath and every word
Your crazy laugh and plans made out of dreams
Yesterday evening etched in my sad soul
Rough way to learn life is not what it seems
I cry for you wherever you are
I cannot move from this bed of tears
My shattered heart too broken to mend
It cries in pain but nobody hears

Now I have time to dwell on my regrets
There's so much time for my wrecked mind to roam
Haunted by things I should have said and done
Yesterday evening, heartbreak's stepping stone
How much I loved you, you will never know
I failed to tell you how deeply I felt
I can't believe that time will heal this pain
Yesterday evening a cruel card was dealt
And if I knew why you had to go
Would I be free, would I walk in peace?
Torment will stay with me a long time
A frozen love waiting for release

My world had meaning yesterday evening
Happiness filled my heart
Yesterday evening, your time for leaving
Today I walk alone
Yesterday evening gave birth to grieving
I have fallen apart.

Pauline Ilsley

A GIFT

To see the raindrops dripping off a leaf,
To see lacy, damp cobwebs glisten in the sun
        That is a gift!

To see a ladybird land on a leaf,
To see the jewelled dewdrops glisten in the grass
        That is a gift!

To see rosebuds opening in the sun,
To see the ferns uncurling slowly in the woods
        That is a gift!

To hear and feel birdsong in your heart,
To hear nature responding to a great start
        That is a gift!

To hear bleating lambs in fields below,
To hear the babbling brook gushing over rocks
        That is a gift!

To hear rain splashing through the treetops,
To hear soft dripping off leaves as clouds go by
        That is a gift!

To smell wood smoke drifting on a cool breeze,
To smell new mown grass that sends you back to childhood
        That is a gift!

To smell the fresh hay in the cow's byre,
To smell the nightstock perfuming, the cool night air
        That is a gift!

To see, to hear, to smell the world and feel it in your blood,
Creates a magic world full of the wonders of a childhood.

Janet Lawreniuk

ONE FINE DAY

We played among the sand dunes; we skipped along the bay.
    We paddled on the seashore on that lovely summer day.
Then clouds began to gather. We scarcely noticed them.
    The wind became quite chilly and then we felt the rain.

The sky grew dark and brooding. I heard my mother call,
    'Come back now, children. There's going to be a squall.'
We were not really caring. It would not last for long.
    The seagulls screeched above us and the waves were getting
strong.

The rain was becoming heavy and stung till we were sore.
We came out of the water as the clouds began to pour.
Everyone was running. No shelter could be found.
The streets awash with water and puddles all around.

At first we laughed and giggled. A cloudburst indeed. No fear.
And then we watched in horror as someone shed a tear.
The roads were blocked; the trains had stopped then
                        we heard someone shout,
'Don't cry my dear but let's all cheer, it's the end
                        of this year's drought!'

Bridie Taber Beeson

THE GOSSIP

Hello, nice to see you; how are you getting on?
Have you heard about my neighbour, poor old Don?
Had his wallet pinched when he was last in town.
Gave him a nasty shock and made him feel quite down.
Did you hear the news about her at number five?
Her kid was run over - lucky to be alive.
And what about her down the road at number ten?
Apparently she's been seeing other blokes again.
Bit of a rumpus over there at number eight.
She locked her hubby out for coming home so late.
Spends most of his time in the local, so they say.
Beats me how he can afford it, he doesn't earn much pay.
The Carringtons are moving. She always was a snob.
Can't wait to get away from here now he's got a better job.
Four bedroom house in Surrey, did you ever hear the like.
Oh! and number fourteen fell off of her bike.
Yes, in the High Street, grazed her knee and smashed
                        her glasses so I hear.
Pete Jones at eleven joins the Navy in the new year.
His mum will miss him being as her old man left home.
She'll have to get adjusted to being on her own.
I hear that number nineteen has been taking drugs.
Got them at a club in town, mixing with some thugs.
Still, it's none of my business what other people do.
Must go and do my ironing, see you later, Sue.

Jean Burrells

A SNOWFLAKE

Snowflakes softly falling
There's snow upon the ground
Windowpanes they sparkle
Reflecting all around
Softly falls the snowflake
Gentle in many ways
Telling all it's winter
And cold become the days
But looking at a snowflake
It's beauty there to see
Frozen water, so extraordinarily
Pristine-white, a work of art
Intricate and free
Until it reaches to the ground
And disappears, no more to be.

Sheila Macdonald

NO TIME

One moment you were laughing,
next moment you were gone.
Your life was far too short.
The nights are far too long.

No time to say you are my world.
No time to say 'goodbye'.
My soul weighs heavy with your loss,
while my mind keeps screaming, *why?*

No time to laugh at days gone by.
No reminiscing in the rain.
No time to settle arguments. No time left to explain.
No time to say, 'I love you more than the colours of the dawn.'
Nor time enough upon this Earth to repair a heart this torn.

One moment you were laughing,
next moment you were gone.
Your life was far too short
and now mine seems far too long.

Nicola Plumb

REFLECTIONS

As I ponder on the passing years,
Of people and of places;
And recall with pleasure
So many dear, dear faces.

I'd like to think God has a garden
He tends with loving care,
And we become His flowers
When we make our journey there.

If in life we have pleased Him
And tried His work to do,
We are planted in a special place
Where His love will make us grow.
As for those who have displeased Him
In thought and word and deed,
Will surely be put in a border
For nasty stingy weeds.

So if in life you have planted
Seeds of kindness, love and care
You can be sure you'll earn a place
In God's garden in the sky,
And as the gardener promised
He will not let you die.

Jo Ellis

LONDON

Fly east, fly west
Little Dove, little Dove
    Do your best.
Fly north, fly south
Little Dove, little Dove
    Hear my mouth . . .

Let them hang their heads in shame -
Men of violence - men of pain,
Little Dove . . . stay their sighs -
    Hear my eyes . . .

Dove of peace,
Your whiteness glows -
    Heal the world
    Heal our hearts,
Hear my plea before I sleep,
Heal this world, don't let it weep . . .
    Little Dove.

Angela Vanes

MY MOTHER

She carried me under her heart
Loved me before I was born
Took God's hand in hers
And walked through the valley
Of shadows that I might live
Bathed me when I was helpless
Clothed me when I was naked.

She gave me warm milk
From her own body when I was hungry
Rocked me to sleep when I was weary
Piloted me on pillows softer than down
And sang to me in the voice of an angel.

Held my hand when I learned to walk
Suffered with my sorrow
Laughed with my joy
Glowed with my triumph
And while I knelt at her side
She taught my lips to pray
Through all the days of my youth.

She gave me strength for my weakness
Courage for my despair
And hope to fill all my hopeless heart
Was loyal when others failed
Was true when tried by fire
Was my friend when other friends were gone
Prayed for me through all the days
When flooded with sunshine
Or saddened by shadow.

Loved me when I was unlovely
And led me into Man's estate
To walk triumphant on the King's Highway
And play a manly part
Though we lay down our lives for her
We can never pay the debt
We owe to a Christian mother.

Junor T Baker

THE GIPSY GIRL

(Dedicated to my granddaughter Sabrina)

As I walked into the market square
A little girl was standing there,
She rushed up the street, knelt down,
And tried to kiss my feet.
She looked up at me and said,
'I'll dance for you if you buy me something to eat.'

I helped her up from kneeling there
As the midday sun shone down on her golden hair,
Her eyes so bright, a beauty rare.
Her little black feet were cruelly bare.
Cobblestone scars were evident there.
The buskers played, music filled the air
The gipsy girl danced off as if on a cloud.
Although sad, her dancing was proud.
She twisted and twirled and tousled her hair.
This little child was the dance of despair.

I look around for her parents, but no one was there.
The music stops, she runs back to me.
Don't dance anymore and I'll buy you some tea.
Where do you live? Who combs your hair?
Mama and Papa are up in the air.
An angel came and carried them there,
So after the dance I brush my own hair.
When the night stars come out
My home is this market square.

Mary A Lisowska

MAGIC FLUTE

I

Slowly
    you pursue me with those eyes
      that tell the world to melt away
    your hands embrace my buttocks
thighs, and disappearing lids of eyes
until my mind surrenders
now and here

II

How
    many colours are you? asks your voice
      caressing my ear with husky tongues
    Umpteen suns exploding while
   night draws in round the seashore's rim.
  You part my flesh, precisely
I reply

III

     Your glasses mirror me
      I remove them
     Your fingers woo me
      I allow them
     Your smiles transfigure me
      I enclose them

IV

You are my legs as though floating from the wings
You are my blood suffusing into thoughts wild as flowers
You are my memory of days confused like a couple of hours
You are the dancer, I your figures of eight
You are my pictures in sanguine, charcoal, found words
      such little-night melodies
       the magic flute
A book of raised eyebrows; mouth more enticing
    than caverns in dreams, well-known

Anna Taylor

AWAY IN A MANGER

'Are you not going to waken, Grandad?
We're just back from Ireland.
But you know that, don't you?
I'll sing you a song if you waken.
I've been practising on the boat.
Is that a real nurse, Grandma?
Is she your nurse, Grandad?

     Away in a manger . . .

Why don't you waken, Grandad? I can sing it all you know.
I know all the words.
Nurse, why doesn't Grandad wake up?
Do you like my new T-shirt?
Them's real gold buttons.
Are you not going to waken, Grandad?

     Away in a manger, no crib for a bed,
     The little Lord Jesus laid down His sweet head

Do you know who Jesus is, Grandad?
He must be a nice person. He makes such pretty songs.
Grandad, did you hear me?
Doesn't He make pretty songs?
Grandad, are you listening to me?'

John D Burgoyne

THE CHURCH ON THE HILL

It's a small church - set on a low hill;
Grey and weathered with age.
Inside - nothing ornate;
A simple altar - plain glass windows -
Homely pews; the only colour
In the carpet, and in hassocks,
Lovingly embroidered in rich, symbolic hues.

But step into the churchyard!
A kaleidoscope of rich colour
Shimmers - vibrates - bewilders . . .
As if the stained glass - meant for the windows -
Had shattered into ten thousand shards and rained
Over the welcoming earth, there to be transformed, by some divine alchemy,
Into ten thousand wild flowers!

For see - the radiant celandine - buttercup - dandelion;
Rich golden cowslip - creamy primrose.
Sky-blue forget-me-not - deeper toned bluebell;
Dazzling white stitchwort and pink-tipped daisies.
Rose-red campion - purple violet - all, with countless others
Blooming joyously together,
Carpeting with beauty the little low hill.

Thus, when thwarted plans and shattered hopes
Tossed into disarray,
Seem to be lost - even to hope -
With no redemption nigh:
Why - it's then that the touch of a mighty hand
Reaches out to bless,
And the wonders revealed may exceed by far
The hopes and the dreams that were dreamt.

V J Havis

DREAMS

I'm a dreamer - I admit.
Long flights of fancy take me to places I'll never go.
Mention holidays and I'll dream
Taj Mahal,
The Great Wall of China,
Uluru.
Antarctic glaciers,
Everest,
Macchu Picchu,
Valparaiso in the Vale of Chile,
Never the ordinary.

I'm a dreamer - I admit.
Long flights of fancy take me to heights I'll never scale.
Mention writing and I'll dream
Poetry Writer of the Year,
Wonderful dramatist,
Play in the West End, *me* as director.
Short story, author extraordinaire,
My own publishing company,
Fame knowing no bounds.

I'm a dreamer - I admit.
Pleasurable dreams,
Unattainable dreams,
Wild dreams,
'Wouldn't it be wonderful if . . . ?'
Is part of my dream vocabulary.
Dreams unattainable perhaps,
But let us dream on
For, in a grey world,
Dreamers dream dreams.

Annie Mackenzie Barclay

IT SHOULD'VE BEEN ME

Many an early morn I spent with you,
A line of time I recall as winter.
The windscreened hue - gunmetal, greyish-blue -
Passing land - barren; barks were splintered.
Words we shared at that hour were seldom
Words of any worldly importance or scope -
Steering us from your seat-belted queendom,
This 'morning-breath' Jack blossomed with hope.
That smile, golden charm, from bed-wrinkled face,
Sounds uttered over wheel misting the screen -
Stretch front, to ease back, a *T-bar of lace* -
I shut my eyes to my tired m-way dream.
For that short time you were mine not to hold
But to memories I can cling when aged old.

Many a later morn I spend with you,
Sunshine and warm haze filter through curtains.
Enveloped by the glow I trust as true -
Rolling right to sight your hair - *I'm certain*.
Words we two share at this hour are seldom
Words, simply mumbles, odd grumbles and groans -
I potter, make tea, ruling my kingdom,
Returning to press lips and craft soft moans.
In the warmth of embrace I touch your skin
With strength within, fortify fragility …
At once we two are one, at last, akin -
We shut eyes content with reality.
For now it feels I can hold you whenever
A true friend and love with fondness forever.

Paul Magson

TO MY MUM - MY COMPANION THROUGH TIME

Warm covers my palm,
Belonging overlaps my fingers,
Gentle words protect from harm,
Her perfume of safety lingers.

I'm protected from a world I don't yet know,
I'm carried to the heights of men,
Embraced by patience regardless of time,
Inhaling calm, exhaling myself.

Coldness uncovers, corridors collide,
A mist of grey ensues,
I'm drowned in crowds' mumbling sounds,
All ruled by time, patience is scarce.

Her arms around me release relief,
The mere sight of her dries my tears,
She is my smile, I am her cross,
Six times a mother, yet no number on love.

But soon I must leave her nurturing nest,
Fly the coop to the big wide world,
It scares me to go, but not fear for me,
I don't want her sad, empty, alone.

Although my strength, my life, my breath,
She's my greatest weakness, my vulnerable love,
If two-faced tongues dare to attack,
They'll pierce me deeper, beyond protective pain.

Although I've reached the heights of men,
I'll never be in love like this,
And just because I leave, doesn't mean I don't heed,
Your perfume, your patience, your hand.

Susannah Carroll

SOMETHING

Up in the attic in the dust and grime
There's something that's lived there a very long time.
Quite how it got there or what it might be
Has always been such a mystery to me.

Sometimes when I wake in the dark at night,
The something will give me a dreadful fright.
The door of the attic creaks open wide,
And footsteps start walking about outside.

Just when I think it's right outside my room
There's suddenly stillness, silence and gloom.
And then I feel safe, locked behind my door,
Till the creaking and footsteps begin once more.

I've been up in the attic during the day,
It's dirty and dusty, but really OK.
I've looked in the boxes and under the chair,
There just isn't anything frightening there.

But, late at night while the family's asleep,
The something comes out and begins to creep.
Perhaps I could catch it and send it away,
But I'm really not feeling that brave today!

Kaz

JUST ONE WISH

If I was granted one wish,
I would wish for world peace,
Racial harmony,
Love, understanding,
Laughter and no time to weep,
Hardship, a thing of the past,
Safe in our beds as we sleep,
I wish for world peace,
Happy faces, freedom, one and all,
Children safe in their mothers' keep,
Laughter in harmony not to weep,
Understanding in world peace,
Racial harmony in each race,
Just one wish I would wish for,
World peace,
Racial harmony, love,
Understanding, laughter, no
Hardships, peace.

Evelyn Hughes

A DREAM COME TRUE

All I ever wanted was a dream to come true,
All I ever needed was a man like you,
To laugh and cry with, to cherish and adore,
Love and be loved as never before.

You make me laugh deep within my heart,
You make me smile, even when we're apart.
You show me you really, really do care
With the fun and giggles that we share.

You hold me and cuddle me through the night,
And the looks you give me tell me it's right.
All I ever wanted was a dream to come true,
You've made that possible by being you.

My Seanie, my world, that's what you are,
And deep within my heart, you are never far.

S A Swain

APPLE TREE

The tree is alive with birds - its branches quiver
To bird-flight, birdsong, endless rustle of wings.
Greenfinches perch in a flash of olive green,
Peer warily, tentative as a shy maiden aunt
With downcast eyes and demure insatiable beak;
Robin flirts blazing breast, stout wings akimbo
Looking for trouble on his territory,
Pert, well set-up, a musical young bravo,
Mozart part disguised in belligerent feathers.
Blue tits swarm like moths; great tit comes seldom
Wearing his elegance with calm understatement;
And, rarely, on the lucky days of spring
There is a skirmish, a flurry of long-tailed tits through the branches
Quick flashing, here, there - and at once are gone.
Blackbird, glossy, yellow smiling, choral
In the grand Anglican tradition, sits
Practising chords, tonalities, arpeggios,
As the air loses colour and turns to evening chill
And one by one the stars prick out and are named;
Pegasus, Sirius, great Aldebaran
Quarter and paw the wide pastures of the sky.
Then comes the owl - with him all birdsong stills,
And alone his hunting bugle stirs the night
Till the blood-rise and the flighting call of morning.

Diana Jones

THE REUNION - DOVER

('Hellfire Corner' fifty years on. September 1994.
A tribute to the British Front Line Allied services and its civilians, 1940-1945)

Proudly they marched . . .
Gladly they met . . .
Those who remembered,
Never will forget . . .
The warmth of the sun,
The glow of their pride.
Those who fifty years ago
Helped stem the tide
Of those dark days,
When they continued their duties
Whatever the cost . . .
Britain's south corner,
Would never be lost . . .
Tho' the brutal invader threw
Bombs, shells and bullets over,
Firmly stood the defenders of Dover.
Proudly they marched . . .
Gladly they met . . .
To remember those
We will never forget.

Muriel Golding

TWO SIDES OF A COIN

(A true story. The year 1941)

We were taking a walk over Earlswood Common
My two little nieces and I, when
Suddenly a German reconnaissance plane
Swooped down from a cloudless sky,
Pelting us at eye level with tracer bullets;
I threw the little girls into a ditch
Screaming, 'Don't move,'
I lay on top of the infants
Facing pilot and machine,
And within a few seconds, this small sad heap
On England's evergreen land, transferred
This pilot, from a boy to a man.
We three are still alive and kicking.

Eileen Barker

IN COMMUNITY

Act not like ant or bee
by instinct ruled,
but live by rational thought.

In collective peace
be of one accord,
sharing in life's every boon.

Unite to spurn all evil.
Fight only for the right
that all discern.

Live for today,
but plan with forethought
to ease the pain of the morrow.

Draw upon faith
to penetrate the gloom
of each dismal day's events.

Rise up in unison.
Grasp each opportunity
the future brings.

Jo Allen

FROM DESPERATION TO HOPE

The life has gone out of the one who is loved;
And loneliness ensues:
There's desperation and agony,
And sickening of heart;
The world is torn,
And the home is cold;
The ache is always there.

Should the one who's left, to the Lord above.
One's faith - then renew?
Must one look into the pit below,
Or dwell on days of yore?
When the nights are empty,
And the life forlorn;
To the Lord - can one, then pray?

O God, give one strength to their turmoil allay;
And so give one life and hope!
So, when those come by,
Who some care do show;
One will know as friends,
And into the heart do take -
With Thee, O Christ eternally!

Douglas J Cleeves

CHALLENGER 1986

Malfunction!
What a word
        to describe the dying moments of a dream.
The covered wagons of the modern world
        seeking new horizons,
Fertile plains of deep, dark space
        where man could make his mark.

We watched proudly for a minute
Marvelling at their courage,
Feeling glad that here were men and women
        able and serene
        going boldly into the unknown
        as pioneers have always gone.
We watched
        one dreadful minute
        then they fragmented into stars
        a part of space forever.

Olga M Momcilovic

THE SEVEN AGES OF WOMAN

Congratulations! It's a girl!
Champagne cork pops!
She looks cute in pink with her bottle,
Nappy, frilly knickers and frock.
Pretty gingham dress and shiny buckled shoes.
Hair pulled in pigtails and a gappy grin for all she meets.
She dreams of being a nurse as she skips in the playground.
The world and the hopscotch squares at her feet.
Wearing a bra and could do with some manners.
Into rock music, motorbikes and boys.
Too much front and a bucketful of attitude
And her dad's always complaining about the noise.
Then comes adulthood and earning a crust.
Married with children and running a house.
Then the woman in charge;
Rid of the husband who was bad for her health.
Childbearing days are over.
All hot flushes and quick changes of emotion,
Laughter lines and 'distinguished' streaks in her hair.
Driving her grown-up children mad with her matriarchal devotion.
She can't move as fast as she used to
And she needs to wear a vest because she's feeling the chill.
Always telling the grandchildren about when she was a girl,
Feeling, 'They're right, I'm past it, I'm over the hill.'
She remembers names and young faces from her childhood
But not of those who'll mourn her when she's gone.
Peacefully, she slips away into the night.
The curtain falls and the woman's work is finally done.

Teri-Louise Caterer

WHERE HAVE ALL THE WINTERS GONE?

Where have all the winters gone
those snow-filled days of my childhood?
Frozen feet and cold red nose
watery eyes, shivering in the icy wind.
What happened to those days of winter's white
covering, from November to February
so cold, so cold . . .

Plodding home through the snow
tiny toes frozen numb
quivering under piles of clothes
It wasn't really all that much fun
but . . .

Where are all the winters now?
The fireside huddles, 'Make a fire, Mom.'
Watching words smoke from out our mouths
snowball fights on the way home from school.
Rushing home in winter's dark days
so cold, so cold . . .

Hot soup boiling on the stove
warm crackling coal and wood fires
not daring to move from the heat
wishing to be warm, if only I could be
but . . .

Where have all the winters gone?
Hot drinks warming cold hands
making snowmen in the garden
sliding on iced pavements.
Where are all the winters now?
Those blizzards from November to February
so cold, so cold . . .

Carol Wilkins

SAD SIGHTS

My hand is clamped against my ear.
'You'll have to shout; I cannot hear!'
My eyes half-closed, I ricochet
From walls to shoppers in my way.
And all around folk scowl and groan:
I'm jabbering on my mobile phone.

Shiny cans all in a row:
Progress now is mighty slow.
Some are silent, some are throbbing;
The owners must be close to sobbing.
These tins are not of stew or spam,
But vehicles in a traffic jam.

I'll whizz right past this ancient biddy,
Give her a shock and turn her giddy.
Let's do a wheelie near these kids
And frighten them with violent skids.
I'm fearsome on my pavement bike,
The sort of twerp to cause dislike.

I'm outside, freezing in the cold,
Simply doing what I've been told.
This fresh air break is just a joke;
I'm wreathed around by swirls of smoke,
Desperately having a last few drags.
I can't give up the deadly fags.

Colin Rouse

EVERYTHING BEGINS WITH 'E'

My life is not easy, but funny!
I don't envy people with lots of money
I enjoy the English weather
I love the seasons too
Eternally grateful for sunshine
But rain doesn't make me blue!
I am considered eccentric
Because of my ways (and my clothes)
Although sometimes I look elegant
Then I keep on writing prose
An early riser I have *always* been
Ebullient yes, that can be seen
Enthusiastic, there's no doubt of that
Elated, effervescent, bubbly wild cat
Though sometimes my fur gets ruffled
It's not hard to make me purr
I am one of those cuddly folk
Eagerly respond to a hug or a stroke
Endless, earnest in every way
Doing my best to smile every day
Enough now of all my endeavour
Enough words beginning with 'E'
Eventually - whatever the weather
I will keep on writing, you'll see!

J Hickens

MY SPECIAL PLACE

My garden is a special place,
Filled with flowers and lots of grace.
I go and sit, my mind goes back,
To when the pram was in the back.
The paddling pool and lots of sun.
The children having lots of fun.
The garden now without a trace,
Is still, my very special place.

Marion A Lee

CRIBBAGE

The chill
From the window
Some time ago
Now
Although
The friendly face
As he dealt the cards
Studied them
Intently
If but for a second or two
Put down two
For the crib
Waited patiently
Whilst I dithered and dickered
Smiled as I made my choice
For the crib
Advancing as we took our turns his peg a few places
Announcing after that next time it would be my crib
If that happened to explain anything
Or everything
His trained eye knew
What to throw away
And what to keep
Whilst now if I am left with this memory
To decide by
If today I make my choice more rapidly
In some things if not in others.

Justin Bayless

AUTUMN TURNS TO WINTER

Twirling, whirling, scuttling leaves,
Hear the wind howling in the trees,
Browns, oranges, reds and golden yellow,
Autumn hues across the mountains
Sitting waiting for the winter snow,
Crispy mornings with cold hands,
Jack Frost has crept across the land,
Bobble hats with scarves and mittens,
Children playing all aglow,
Making snowmen from the snow,
All is dark this winter night,
Sitting round the fire bright,
Mugs of hot chocolate in our hands,
Silently again, Jack Frost creeps
Across the land.

V Harding

DANCING IN THE FOREST

As we walked among the conifers it was eerie and still
We watched the deer spring up the hillside,
As we moved to the clearing cloud encircled us
Then the wind came and swirled it about.

The dampness of the forest clung to us
Now the trees swayed a little
There was nothing to be heard
Only the crack of twig as the deer fled.

Would we see them again in their doe-eyed splendour
To witness again the stag on watch, the alarm?
Will the young ones dance again?
They are cautious, so I think not.

Eunice Doyle

GENESIS

I've loved you since
    The world began,
Beyond the sense
    Of feeling man's
More wild imagination,
    As I possess
    In gentleness
    Or spuming domination,
        When laying claim
    And ravaging,
I seek to tame
    Each fresh domain
In savage consummation,
    As passively
        Beneath you lie
And gaze at me,
        Whilst ripples pry
Into the vales and
        Hills, until
I weaken, hands
        With lessened will
Subside within
        The ebbing tides,
    Though soon to rise
        Again, and free
Tendrils that prise
        Caressingly,
In endless adoration,
    For I have loved you since time's birth,
I am the ocean, you the Earth.

Aileen Hopkins

TIME TEAM MYSTERY

For a thousand years in peace you lay,
As nature clothed you both, with sand and clay.
When first uncovered in your close embrace,
You could have been of Viking birth, or Celtic race.
Intently studied by those viewing from above.
Two sets of bones entwined as though in love.

This was no warm embrace the earth concealed,
As careful excavation soon revealed.
The uppermost across the other fell,
The battleaxe embedded in his skull.
The other's sword up to the hilt was stuck,
Between the ribs, skilled warrior, or luck.

These hand-forged weapons, the coins of gold.
The woven clothing keeping out the cold.
Were these possessions of a victim or a thief,
Maybe no ordinary mortal, perhaps a Viking chief?
Who was attacked, who defended in this silent place,
Where you both fought to live, each dying without grace?

Perhaps you were both strangers to each other,
Or closer still in life, brother to brother.
Why did they leave you where you lay?
Did no one miss you on that fateful day?
No Viking longship burned, to make your death complete
When your appointed destiny you came to meet.

The mystery of your life and death continues on.
Did you have wives and daughters, or a son?
Your bones have been exhumed and studied by the best,
Then gently and with care, returned to rest.
Now buried side by side, two warrior foes,
At peace, though still you bear each other's mortal blows.

Angus Iain Morrison

MARCH HORIZON

I'm going to walk by the sea today
To ponder on dimensions old,
Where rust-edged foam with stained-glass green
Weave greys and blues into a rough seam,
Which is misty and black at the fold.

I'll listen for near-distance whispering
Of wet, on its leap, grasping cold,
Bellies of ocean deep rumblings play
Waves, in their wake, spewing spittle of spray
But still misty and black at the fold.

The wind on my cheek will bite icily,
The force of the air my step hold,
Time's grains will sting and the old dunes dance,
Star grasses pay homage bent, as in trance,
To the mist and the black at the fold.

The skies will be my private theatre,
Curled characters, rampant and bold,
Fast-moving visions sent just for my eye,
Forming, then melting, my beasts in the sky,
To be swallowed by mist in the fold.

Brenda Catherine Mentha

MY THREE MUSES

The goddess of smudge-free writing pops in,
Her name is *Roller Ball*,
Her trusty blot-banishing formulae
Are the only ones I dare to try.

Another muse without whom
Not the tiniest jot could be scribbled,
Is a princess called *Free Afternoon*
- A marvellous pre-deadline boon.

Last comes Fairy Poesy,
And yet she's not the least,
She makes me laugh, or grind my teeth
She lets me tag along to the Rhymer's Feast.

So now you've met my muses,
All at once like a bevy of buses,
A cheerful crocodile: one, two and three,
When it isn't even snowing and you've paid the taxi fee!

Elizabeth M Rait

GREEN IS . . .

Green is the swirling of dead poison
Green is the blooming of Earth's nature
Green is the cheering of Plymouth Argyle's fans
Green is the subtlety of camouflage
Green is the splashing of happy turtles
Green is the bite of an apple
Green is the Earth's friend recycling
Green is the sparkling emerald birthstone
Green is the Park School's house Raleigh
Green is the boiling of a witch's brew
Green is the simmering vegetables
Green is the bitterness of conniving spite
Green is the glowing of growing jealousy
Green is the colour in every corner
Green is the colour all around us
Green is the colour everywhere!

Harriet Elizabeth Hobbs (13)

'EVE' 1969-1997

Four limousines of funeral black slide off into the dark,
From out St James they wend their way and then across the park.
Diana in the lead, a hearse - the coffin draped inside,
With Charles and their two sons behind, on this so tragic ride.
Past silent crowds with deep intent, who stand to share their pain,
With thousands more, this very night, who travel through the rain.
With sombre face men stand and stare, and ladies softly cry.
The children try to understand - and watch the cars go by.
They sit or stand, in drizzling rain, preparing for the day . . .
Each camera flash - reflecting - like a firework display.
But silent, oh! So very deep - one breath would break the spell
And each with very special thoughts, too tender yet to tell.
So from The Mall, slow up the hill - more rain - into the park.
Fresh flowers thrown to mark her way, the cars glide through the dark.
And people say they only know, this watch they have to keep,
Not knowing quite, the how or why, their passions run so deep.
This little clutch of quiet cars move slowly through the dark . . . and on
Toward her resting place tonight - the palace, Kensington.
But just a few short hours more and she'll return this way,
Past this same crowd, plus thousands more, to demonstrate the day.
The carriage with its royal guard will proceed just once more,
Back cross the park, The Mall, Horse Guards and to the Abbey door.
And here the pageantry awaits - the service and the grace.
Her final rites - her royal pass - to her final resting place.
But all this pomp and circumstance so publicly displayed,
Cannot make such a deep effect - as this night will have made.
The rainy night, the glistening cars, the sorrow and the pain,
The whole world shared this silent piece of history in the rain.

Tom Martin

LEON

Have you seen the sky today?
Who let the genie out to play?
Shades of red the wise man said, are but the visions of the dead.
Who wants to hear a happy song?
Who wants to see a happy end?
This is *life* my foolish friend; this is life, so why pretend?

My oh my, too late your sigh,
You took a chance; *you* chose to fly.
Too late to sigh; just time to cry.
My oh my, oh why, oh why?

Leon clicked his fingers and the world fell at his feet.
Leon wore the golden crown and Leon owned the 'street'.
Lighting all the torches in the dark side of your mind,
He came to offer freedom and you saw him as the key!
But freedom gained from Leon is a curse for you and me!

Lucy sought her diamonds, on the land and in the sky.
Lucy found illusion and a tortured way to fly.
Lucy was a lady with a past described as shady,
When she crossed the Leon shadow found the perfect way to die!

The end came with delusion and for Lucy, great confusion,
When the circus came to town all her highs just tumbled down.
As the clown put on his face, Lucy lost her sense of space.

Leon felt no sorrow at the parting of the way,
Leon sought the fairground and another chance to play.
Leon has the answers for the fools who seek his door,
He offers signs of madness and a hint of greater sadness,
To the young who see no danger, just a chance to re-explore!

Ian Richardson

THOUGHTS OF THE GOOD TIMES

Good times we have all had many
We have also had some bad
But good times in the mind remain
And that can make us glad

We forget all the sorrows and heartaches
Push them all to the back of our minds
Get back on our feet and start smiling
Then go looking more good times to find

Good times leave us fond memories
Of things that we've done in the past
But we can all look fore to the future
And hope that the good times will last

For me the good times were my childhood
With the love of a good mum and dad
They were always there when needed
To give all the love that they had

So it's good to look back from the future
To all good times not the bad
And remember I could have been worse off
If not for my mum and dad

So let good times roll for the future
Remember not all times are sad
Forget all your worries and sorrows
Remember the good and be glad.

Walter E Causer

WHEN SILENCE IS HEARD

Freedom is nigh, yet unseen, within the within;
        yearned for in unfulfilment . . . spoken of in whispers,
            trembling in obscurity.

Dark and fearful are the bonds of compulsive silence;
        the spoken word, not yet to be outside the confining bars
                                    of boundary;
            striving to escape; straining,
                against the elasticated bonds of oppressive silencing,
                    it cries to the skies . . . of bondage . . .
'I am humanity's salvation . . . without me is oblivion.'

        'I have something to say.'

    My words would reveal the extremes of liberty
            within the knowledge of the soul,
                and the forming words cry out,

'I have something to say.'

                And frustration is etched
    upon the words of its captivity
    desiring to be unique, within the orbits of
            mediocrity;

'I have something to say
Listen to me . . . hear me now . . . please!'

My voice trails in the mists of inattention . . . powerless against
        the barricades of oppressive power.

'Why don't you pause, and listen to my desire?
        Are you so aloof; insecure; in your disdain?'

I dream of the time when my voice is free; and the sounds are heard
        in the realms of time . . .

    I am free . . . free . . . free . . . and what I yearn so much to proclaim
                            is
            I have nothing to say!

Gordon Reid Johns

NATURAL PHENOMENA

Dark clouds and fresh sharp air over a vast watery domain
The waves move to a mysterious song played on sand and rocks
The sounds are never the same but familiar variations reoccur
The musical sounds are based on power and also on bleak solitude
As this monotonous orchestra appears to stretch to infinity
To be immersed in this hypnotic sadness harsh and cold
Its actions are strong and uncontrollable
It reaches out for salvation but as it does so is pushed further inland
Rejected it falls back, however, it does not give up but slowly builds
                                    up courage

As it moves in and out from the shore
Quietly humming to itself rolling a stone and retrieving it back
Building up waves which break and glide inshore
And creating small whirlpools as it steers itself around rocks
Like a lush meadow more inviting, more amicable
The monotony is now a feature of sheer space of exploration
                                    and contemplation
The orchestra is performing a soothing relaxing movement
                                    which is timeless
As the sea wanders aimlessly around its frontier
The calm scene however is a false facade as in the darkness
                                    below the surface
There is a strong winding monster twisting restlessly on the seabed
Sculpturing rocks and transporting shingle, a dangerous force to fight
But this monster dies as quickly as it reared its frightening head
Leaving peace over the waters and happiness in the small ripples
Which animate the water warmed and ruled by the sun
The calm, of course, will not last, it will be swallowed up
                                    by a depression
Storms will return violent as ever and eventually calm will
                                    again prevail
A series of events in an eternal cycle self-contained and difficult
                                    to predict
An ongoing percussion concerto conducted by a strange maestro
Based on power, calm, harshness and beauty
The ocean's mirror image of life itself

Margaret Fowler

YOUR SHADOW

Safe in Your shadow
    I can find peace.
Safe in Your shadow
    My purpose released.
Safe in Your shadow
    The pain is absorbed.
    And I can find rest
In the arms of my Lord.

Safe in Your shadow
    I find courage to give.
Safe in Your shadow
    A reason to live.
Safe in Your shadow
    For others I plead.
    And I can reach out
Letting my Saviour lead.

Safe in Your shadow
    The world overcome.
Safe in Your shadow
    The pain becomes numb.
Safe in Your shadow
    I wait and I serve,
    Knowing that one day -
Wonders so undeserved.

Patricia Ann Hendy-Davies

CYCLING IN RURAL ENGLAND - AND BEYOND

Do try cycling, it can be fun,
Going faster than you can run.
By tandem, even faster still,
With two, it's better going uphill.

As you glide along each country road
And see o'er hedge, each abode,
Half-timbered cottages, beautiful flowers,
You can go on for hours and hours.

Glorious sunshine, fresh clean air,
You feel so smart and debonair,
And so you enjoy every ride
To see our lovely countryside.

You feel so free, and young, and well,
Full of good humour, and eager to tell
Of bed and breakfast in hostels clean
And friendly folk always seen.

So why not have fun and see the world?
Life's full of surprises to be unfurled.
Some that only cycling can bring,
Try it! Have a go! Start next spring!

Wilfred John Parker

NOT JUST FOR CHRISTMAS

A little Jack Russell gave all he could give,
All he wanted was a chance to live
With a family, mum and dad, longing for the love that he once had.
Then something happened, they had given no thought
To the dear little Christmas puppy they'd bought.

Came summer holidays from work and school,
To this little puppy an incident so cruel.
Excited this pup, to be going out for the day,
Only to be left on a busy motorway.
Petrified, alone, not knowing which way to turn,
Giving all motorists cause for concern.

How can they do it?
What goes through their minds
To just drive away
Leaving a pet behind?

Sheila Buckingham

THE PARTING

When we two parted
in silence and tears,
half broken-hearted
to sever for years.
Pale grew thy cheek and cold
colder thy kiss.
Truly that hour foretold
sorrow to this.

In silence we went
in silence I grieve
that my heart could forget
thy spirit deceive.
If I should meet thee
after long years,
how should I greet thee
with silence and tears?

They name thee before me
a knell to mine ear.
Why wert thou so dear?
They know that I knew thee
who knew thee too well.
Long, long shall I rue thee
too deeply to tell.

Monica Long

MY GARDEN FRIENDS

There's a lot to be said for my garden
Though it looks rather bleak and bare.
For it's winter and there are no nice flowers -
Just wet leaves all strewn everywhere.

But the wildlife, they visit each day still.
They have breakfast and lunch all for free,
But by 4pm they have all gone away,
Clutching titbits to enjoy for their tea.

There's fat cups on the branches for starlings -
They are made out of bird food and lard.
They squabble and fight to grip tightly,
Though the grease on their feet makes it hard!

Now there're some birds that have quite good manners,
They usually eat from the ground,
Or they'll make a small snack from the berries -
Yes, the blackbirds just don't make a sound.

But any ideas about this bird?
With a snail in its beak it will crush.
The shell is no good - it's discarded . . .
No contest, who wins? It's the thrush.

The blue tits and great tits are pretty.
They swoop, duck and dive and are fast.
There's lots going on in the bird box -
Are they planning to nest here at last?

But my all time favourite is the robin,
For he is the loner you see.
He's one on his own - and he pleases himself . . .
That's probably because he's like me!

Vivvi

RIGHT AT THE END

Bare winter trees sketched in charcoal
On a grey slate sky
As I went through the hospital entrance
To find out how and where you were.
Doors parted politely at my approach
Ushering me into the warm antiseptic world.
'Right at the end of the corridor
Is the ward you want,' Sister said.

For the first time I walked that long stretch
Cryptic signs on the one side, ward names on the other.
Forging a weary intimacy in the days that followed
With that slightly shabby, seemingly endless passage.
Prints on the walls helped a little, I coveted the one
Of beechwoods with the sun slanting through to bluebells.
Days blurred into weeks, the corridor became a tidal river
Where I battled with the ebb and flow of despair and hope.

Today is different, the sky is blue, the clouds are white
Overnight pink paper blossoms have been tied to trees
And crocuses scattered about.
The doors slide open as punctiliously as ever
But there's alteration here too.
The floor shines, the walls gleam white and green
Paint and polish have temporarily overlaid
The usual hospital atmosphere.

In the ward the green daffodil spears on your locker
Have become a glorious yellow oriflamme.
But you lie silent and will not see this spring.
As you slipped away
Did the golden flower trumpets sound a fanfare
Right at the end?

Phyllis J Pearce

OUR HEROES

The nation should offer its very best thanks
To pottery makers, Armitage Shanks.
Apart from providing a motif to read
Whilst attending to nature in moments of need,
They've made for us all a more comfortable life
And ended that long-standing object of strife,
The disposal of chamber pots into the street
To splash and to soil the pedestrians' feet.

The WC was a major step forward
And the laying of sewers in towns even more would
Lead to a much more hygienic approach
At the time when the railway supplanted the coach.

It started a torrent of sanitary ware
From Whitechapel Road to Grosvenor Square.
Baths and urinals, basins and sinks,
Showers and hip baths, fountains for drink,
Poured from the factories in white and in pink.

They had floral depictions for us to admire
And encouraging titles to which they'd aspire;
Like 'Acme' and 'Champion', 'Superior' and such -
So bold and so proud - the Victorian touch.

Their slogans and trademarks intrigued us for years,
Their powerful flushes a joy to the ears,
We've seen 'Ideal-Standard' on cisterns and tanks
But the best known of all must be 'Armitage Shanks'.

In office, hotel room (single or twin),
In factory, hospital, college or inn,
In theatre or cinema, station or square,
Museum or swimming bath - A S are there!

Dennis A Calow

WHAT IS YOUR LOVE?

What is your love?
Is it to cheer
to shout
to win
to defeat evil
to pluck out
to tear down?

Not so much to build
maybe to succeed
to be nearly part of the team
nearly in the fight
near the winners
behind the action

pushing, shoving together to move
ready for the next struggle
travelling hopelessly
pleased to protest
finding pride in clear injustice?

My love is red
not as a rose nor a Russian
more like wine or blood
something to drink or to wash in
earthy and fertile
strong and not very nice
but very expensive
though you might not think so to look at the bottle.
Crack it and launch away.

Richard Tapley

DO YOU REALLY CARE?

Do you really care for her
Or is the rumour true?
Do you really want me back
Or do I just want you?
Now that you've found another
Do you think of me?
I'd hate to think you love her
When you could be loving me.
I miss your tender passionate kiss
Your touch that was so warm.
I miss the way you cared for me
Protecting me from harm.
Oh, won't you please forgive me?
Whatever have I done?
All at once you gave me love
But now you give me none.
I watch the couples gather
In the spot we used to share.
I see their tender kisses
I feel it isn't fair.
I remember how it used to be
But now it's in the past.
I tried to keep you by my side
I should've known it wouldn't last.
I guess I'll have to face the fact
And pick up life again
Then someday I'll think of you
Without the tears and pain.

S Simcoe

WELCOME NEW YEAR

New Year welcome.
A thousand bells foretell your coming,
A million voices raised as one
Proclaim your birth. All Earth rejoices.
Hope is here, in music, laughter
And lights as bright as Christmas stars.
In crystal goblets warm with wine
Held high in salutation.
In hands outstretched to other hands,
In thoughts far flung to other lands,
And in a million goodwill kisses.

Exalted thus, with trumpets and a royal fanfare
You take your throne.
Upon your head, bright with love and hope
Your crown sits light. Your subjects kneel.
Their dreams must now be yours
All is well, all is new.

But come the morrow
When crystal goblets empty stay
All toasting done.
And hands withdrawn, shun other hands
And bells stay silent. What then?
Will you stay young and undismayed
Or will Earth's burdens and man's demands
Dim your light?
Until like other lost, bewildered years
You too die disappointed,
Your crown askew.

Peggy Adams

UNDERSTUDY

She sits, waiting in her chair.
Lost in whatever amounts to dreams,
while I stand watching . . .

Transparent tissue - thin, the tiny skull
that breaks into a beam of pure delight.

'Come on! Come on!' she tuts,
rubbing my frozen hands
with her one working one . . .
ever the mother.

We sit holding hands.
The one who can,
soon out of words,
and saying nothing at all.

I spoon the puréed 'something',
until she's had enough,
and closes her mouth against the spoon.

Almost time to go.
The time when roles will be blurred
by trembling lips and fat tears spilling down.
But for now . . .

'Come on! Come on!' she coaxes,
holding the spoon to my lips . . .
ever the mother.

Catherine Reay

FORWARD WITH FORWARD

Fifteen years of Forward Press?
Oh yes, that's fine, I'll celebrate . . .
Fifty pounds fine came by post
Just for parking
Started narking my wife for trivialities;

So how would I celebrate?
Composed poem, drank some lagers . . .
Was soon victim of my words
Over the edge
Then fell off a ledge, I'd written a cliffhanger.

Now I've recovered
Now I've discovered
I'm a scary poet
I'll always know it
In Manitoba
I must stay sober
And then go forward
As surely *Forward* . . .
Will do in future.

Bill Chapman

DAY OF DEATH

Great Britain is burning with fear,
That's what I hear them say,
We shall not quit or hide,
Haven't they heard of our stiff upper lip?
We shall hunt them down to the very end,
Those suicide bombers.

They gave no one a chance,
Innocent people killed,
Why? What would they gain?
London came to a standstill,
All around the world people were in shock,
Was all this to prove a point?
Yes, a day to remember *Thursday, 7th July 2005,*
Day of death.

Leeanne Shires

CELEBRATION OF MY MOTHER

You didn't know you were having me,
your mind was in a spin.
I was born three months early
and arrived *after* my twin.

You cared for me in those early days,
when life was pretty tough.
You've always been there for me
and couldn't *do* enough.

I had to return all that care and love . . .
more so . . . when you needed it most.
That's when you lost my dad
and felt *so* completely lost.

We were the very best of friends
and *did* for each other,
of course it wouldn't have mattered
you were and *are* my mother.

I loved you then, I love you now,
even though you're not here.
Time goes so very fast,
but it's only been *one* year.

All the year, I've thought of you,
every single day.
No matter where I go, or what I do,
you *haven't* gone away.

You will always be with me,
in mind and spirit too.
No matter how many years go,
I will *always* love you so.

Elizabeth Anne Gifford

CRADLE COMMUNICATIONS

This joyous advent season comes
With frosty mornings, tingly thumbs
This day of happy sound and mirth
This day of Christ the Saviour's birth

The water now is turned to stone
Swallows to warmer climes have flown
The bleak denuded twigs are seen
Hallways bedecked in evergreen

Christmas, the best of special days
That long with childish memory stays
The Maker of the stars and sea
Became a child on Earth for me

The inn, no room, that was the call
A baby in an oxen's stall
The eastern star, a heavenly sign
That God was man in Palestine

The Holy Infant came to die
Hosanna was the angel's cry
No carolling in frosty air
Can with this simple truth compare

Messiah's birth in cradle bare
Just why I wonder was He there?
God's love displayed in stable dim
This Christmas time, consider Him.

Steven M Shanks

FLYING THE NEST

We watched you as you lay in your cot
A tiny bundle, a helpless tot.
We worried about you as you grew up
Would you make it? Would you be top?

While you were tiny, your troubles shared.
We could cuddle you to show we cared.
Why do we think as we get older,
That love gets harder and caring colder?

You see even though you're all grown now,
We'd still like to share your troubles somehow.
But you keep most of them to yourself.
It makes us sad when we'd like to help.

Please don't think we have shut you out.
We love you lots, that's what it's all about.
So come home to us, however bad
Because we're still your mum and dad.

Wendy Stark

HOLIDAY BREAK NO 2

I warned I would be back this year
I'm sitting in a deckchair on the pier.
Visited again a Dorset village,
No! This time no rape and pillage!
Instead met some friendly folk
And we sat down for coffee and a Coke.
Visited Wimborne (pity not market day)
As there as bargains galore, so they say.

Went to Ringwood, had to leave there quite soon,
As our coach driver wanted us back at 12 noon!
Saw my sister at Mudeford
Wouldn't mind living there if I could.

On the edge of the New Forest it is a delight,
And to look at the view is a wondrous sight.
Now I'm back home in the old routine
I must say I am not at all keen.
But during the coming long winter days
I can think of my next holiday break in all its different ways.

Pamela Butler

THE COMING

You come in darkness swathed by force
A welcome in red for your milk-white horse
There's iron to hand and fire in your mouth

You pitched across the levelled landscape
A lone wind dusted down your dark eyes
You were out of this world on someone's mind

A drizzle filled the northern sky
The crops were there for the taking
Not to mention the women
Cities sank into embers of orange

Our children kicked ball in the dust
Of the soft scorched earth
They swore blood brothers
Where they watered the horse

Daddy played a silver harmonica
As a queen banged a tambourine
Around a surrounded fire
Our children dreamed

And then the peace came.

John Harkin

EVERYTHING CHANGES

Everything changes
God made it so.
The hours and the seasons
The ebb and the flow.
Clouds spill their raindrops
Earth drinks her fill.
Everything changes
Nothing is still.

Those we have loved
Who are gone from our sight,
Released from the body
Transformed into light,
No more can we hold
Or caress with our tears
But love, all enfolding
Illumines the years.

Transcending all time
And all space and all pain.
Finding the rainbow
Born of the rain.
Starlight to sunrise
Dewdrops to frost,
Everything changes
Nothing is lost.

Tricia Sturgeon

THE FOUR SEASONS

Springtime is my favourite time,
When the seeds begin to grow,
Life comes again after winter,
And the seasons start to flow.

Summer is a happy interlude,
With its warmth and sunny skies,
Holidays that are sweet relief,
Away from stressful ties.

Autumn leaves start to fall,
And vibrant colours appear,
There's a chill in the morning air,
Heralding the end of the year.

Winter has a beauty of its own,
With crisp mornings and sometimes snow,
The quiet freezing evenings,
And stormy winds that blow.

Nothing ever stays the same,
For God knows how boring it would be
So I enjoy each season as it comes
And give thanks I can feel and see.

Sheila J Hodgkins

ABANDONED - WRIGLEY'S TALE

*(Wrigley is a dog who was supposed to be in the care
of grandparents who went away for a day)*

Early went my friends away,
So I was left alone all day;
Damp and lonely on my own,
I felt sad but did not moan.

At eleven o'clock a lady came -
She'd walked here in the gentle rain;
Overjoyed to see her face,
I wet the floor - I'm in disgrace!

I hope she'll call again on me
And won't forget to give me tea!

Margaret Bailey

LIFE

When the clock at its birth starts to tick,
What is this called life, and why?
It is used, it is abused.
The moment it starts it begins to die.
There is feeling, loving and tears of grief,
Also shed in emotion when sad.
No one knows when the clock will stop.
Each life is different, some good, some bad,
The strands taut and stretched.
Like a spider's web, vibrations make it stir.
Some lives are short and filled with pain,
Just like the moon, it peaks then starts to wane.
Others live to a ripe old age
With lots of memories to keep.
They see their offspring rise and grow
Before they finally give up to sleep.
So what is life all about?
It's difficult to say.
Just like the sun up in the sky,
It rises, shines and sets each day.

K Ainsley

AGE

Lift up your hearts for age is nought
It's what you've gained from what you've sought
Catching the golden threads of time -
A snatch of song or oft a rhyme
That brings back memories to you
Of loving people, friendships true;
A windy hilltop in the spring,
The bells across the meadows ring
And once again time disappears
And, with the wisdom of the years
You will enjoy those times you've spent,
Yet look ahead with more content.

Hazel Blake

CLAUDIUS REMEMBERED

Home is quiet now
And yet Claude never made a noise
Speaking only with his stare
Waiting patiently to come and go and eat

He won't be waiting for me now
Mornings
As I drag downstairs
Or, gathering all his strength
Won't push himself onto my bed
When he thinks I should be up.

Memory shocks me from forgetfulness
Shakes me from my new routine
I leave the shop. Something forgotten?
No tins of cat food in my bag.

I settle on the settee, put up my feet
And look around for what is different
Now no one saunters in
Weighs up the distance and his strength
Calculates, and after due consideration
Springs gingerly
Denies me my reading
Paws his way to sleep.

Pamela Slade

LIFE IS WHAT YOU MAKE IT

Life is divided into many parts.
You must enjoy it while you can.
It has its ups and downs, good times and bad
And is supposed to last three score years and ten.

You begin your life as a baby,
Bringing joy and happiness to your parents.
Brothers and sisters you may have
And so begins your journey of a lifetime.

From a child to an adult many difficulties arise.
You learn about becoming a good honest person.
Love, education and a good career you aim for,
To provide you with all the necessities of life.

You, in time, fall in love, marry and have children.
So begins the cycle again,
When you hope and dream that they will do exactly the same
To become good, honest people.

In the twilight of your life, when work is finished,
You hope to conquer and explore all your dreams
Of things you always wanted to do.
Your family will bring you love and laughter.

The time with them is precious,
As you sit back and watch them do wonderful things.
They make you so proud,
So you can relax and enjoy the world about you.

This is what a good life is all about,
Honesty, love and laughter.
But above all, always smile at those around you.

Margaret Wood

A VISIT TO CHELSEA ROYAL HOSPITAL

The coach arrives, we all climb in.
Some are quick, agile and thin.
Some like me too hard I find
And need a push from those behind.
Through the town, a slower pace,
Then on the motorway we race.
Windsor Castle lies before us,
Wave to Queenie - hope she saw us!
Now in London, streets aplenty,
Full of people gaining entry
To the shops - the life of London!
We drive on and in a while, see
There before us - charming Chelsea!

Off we get and there awaits us
Chelsea Hospital, old and gracious,
Housing all that happy breed
Who fought for Britain in times of need.
We see them there, now old and slow,
Full of memories - who can know
What scenes they witnessed long ago?
Were they gallant, handsome, tall?
Long ago - no time at all -
When I was young and slim and gay,
Enjoying life in every way.
Lurking still beneath the skin
There lies that younger soul within.
I'm young again and fair of face,
When time passed at a different pace.
A coach of girls, an army of guys,
Twenty years young, but seventy wise!
Can you imagine such a scene?
Now what a day *that* might have been.

Monica Simpson

TWILIGHT OBSERVATIONS

The beach is sleeping, windless,
the air sharp and clean.
Geese chat merrily overhead,
urging each other onwards,
migrating to warmer climes.

Sea walls wince painfully, ravaged,
warily stroking their wounds.
Rocks lie scattered, dismembered.
Serrated, notched, pointed.
Strewn inside each jagged scar.

A pleasure park stands dejected.
Birds squawking ominously,
astride its peeling paintwork.
Dark, brooding, 'Hitchcockian'.
Awaiting their call for 'action'.

Sunlight flickers below the pier,
exposing corroded stanchions,
bedazzling the eyes.
Tinted hues quiver, hypnotic,
seducing all in their path.

An amber sphere burns brightly,
dominating the horizon,
emblazoning the sky.
Slowly it recedes, descending,
yielding to darkness.
Cloaked inside a shroud of dusk.

Paul Kelly

WHAT IS TIME?

It is the most precious thing we have
Some wish they could buy it, stop it, cheat it
But find out they never can
It is with us twenty-four hours of our time
All and every one just wastes it, throws it away
No matter who you are, what you wish to be, what you do
Or what you say, you are a time waster
To someone, anyway, it's a waste of time.

If you miss a bus, miss a train, it's a waste of time
If you make a date, get home late, get up late, start out late
And it doesn't work out, it's a waste of time
If you try to help someone, they think you're interfering
You have wasted time
If you have created something and some people do not like it
To them it's a waste of time
If you try to please someone, and they do not like it
It's a waste of time
Because you could have been pleasing someone else.

We all appear to be going somewhere but getting nowhere
Some try to run away from it
Some break the law and know where they are going to spend it
You can look at the clock, watch the sun come up
Watch it go down
The time you have had is the time you have spent
A waste of time.

You can burn the midnight oil to try and catch up on it
This makes you ill, so a waste of time
Life gave you a time span, that was the most precious
What do we do about it . . .? Watch it.
Why am I telling you this?
I could tell you but I have not got the time!

P L Carvell

HAZY DAYS

It's one of those overcast days
The hills are shrouded in a haze
Usually you can see each peak
But the undulations are quite weak
Beyond the skyline the clouds do vie
Making pictures in the sky
The sea is stretching mile on mile
Letting my thoughts once more beguile
Is it a ship I see on the horizon
Or something else to feast my eyes on?
Waves are crashing on the shore
Each one bigger than before
The ship is bobbing to and fro
Making ripples increase their flow
Buoys are swaying with the tide
Warning of dangers far and wide
Birds on the shore are dashing about
Waiting to catch what the water casts out
When at last the day is done
The birds I know will all have won

Marion Pollitt

SAL'S BOOTS

My boots are not brown
No words have rhymed their way
Their name has brought them fame
They were a bargain
Not just a random buy
But a thought and a prayer
Found me in town
Or the other way around
And as I walked in
They called to me
They fit snug
More like mittens than gloves
Laced wooden beads colour my toes
And as I pull them on I linger betwixt and 'tween
They are admired
I look down
But feel up!
Swivel my heels
They are all I dreamed them
To beaming marvellous
I love them
They were made for each other, and me.

Sal Whatley

REFLECTIONS

It is for all time, that bond unseen that binds us,
One look, a smile, a stolen tender kiss, politely touching hands,
No house, car, family, no holidays, snaps in albums,
Just a dream, times to come, time passing slowly,
memories undimmed.

Our paths cross, divide, are parallel, entwine sometimes socially,
I watch, wait, dreaming of the unknown, tantalising scent, heat,
Could we leave our contrived existence and slip, slot comfortably,
Into one another's arms, peaceful, lasting, complete?

Your name is mentioned in passing, some know, some don't,
No sly meetings, no letters, lies, phone calls, flowers with coded note,
We never said, what if, if only, maybe, perhaps some day,
Our love remains undimmed, uncoupled, explored only in pensive
concealed thoughts.

Terry Bates

NEVER EVER

I know that you are there, Mum, I can feel your stare.
I swear I can even feel you touch my hair.
What's it like, Mum, high up above?
Is it snow-white and filled with lots of love?

Everyone knows that dreadful day will come,
That cold, dark day when you lose your mum.
But never, ever did I fear
That cold, dark day would be so near.

Still can't believe that you had to leave.
How do you cope when you have to grieve?

It's summertime now, it reminds me of you.
I'm sitting on your bench like you used to, too.
The sun is shining down on me.
People walking by, faces filled with glee.
To me, that sun could be a cloud that's grey
Because my mum was taken away.

I can't describe how I'm feeling.
Is this all part of my grieving?

Kerry Catherine Hart

DIVERSE LAND

Ancient moorland, warriors' tombs
Iron age forts, giant tors
Standing stones, mystery shrouded
Medieval churches with iron-clad doors.

Windswept dunes, golden beaches
Crystal pools on rocky shores
Seagulls nesting on granite cliffs,
At whose feet the mighty surf roars.

Castles on hilltops proudly stand
Streams and rivers ever wending
Through this green and golden land
Busy farmers always tending.

Silent chimneys, mines abandoned
Bygone days in search of ore.
Many men gave up their lives
For gold, copper, tin and more.

Giant tankers, working ports
Deep, deep waters, ocean going ships.
Tiny harbours, pleasure boats,
Fishing boats in tiny creeks.

Legends, mystery, man's endeavour
Amongst the hills both white and green.
All contained and encapsulated forever
Within this diverse land . . . Cornwall.

Lydia E Stanton

THE FOUR SEASONS

Maybe it's the springtime, when all the world seems new,
Daffodils and lambs and early morning dew,
Yes, spring is my favourite season, until summer comes along.
Long, hot, sunny days and skies of azure blue.
Holidays away with sand and ocean waves,
Yes, summer is my favourite time of year,
Until autumn comes along.
The morning chill in the air and leaves of red and gold,
Shadows lengthening, swallows flying south as the year grows old.
Yes autumn is my favourite season,
Yet winter has a magic of its very own.
A wonderland of frost and snow,
Breath hanging in the air on an icy morn.
Yes, winter is the best of all because then
 Jesus, our Lord . . . was born.

S A Sanders

HAPPINESS

The simplest things bring happiness
like being in good health,
just living in the countryside
means a great deal more than wealth.
Happiness, yes, nostalgia
a trip down memory lane,
hearing a favourite programme
listening to an old refrain.
To watch a pleasant movie
Howard Keel and Doris Day,
just to have a good old sing-song
or maybe dance and sway.
Happiness in a picture
painted just last week,
or maybe in my poetry
expression mine to seek.
Just the thought of Concorde
brings a certain pride,
so many happy memories
all there deep inside.
The garden such a special place
where seasons come and go,
plants and wildlife mingle
to give an ever-changing show.
A host of happy memories
when the boys were small
smoochy, dreamy love songs
ah yes, I do recall.

Dorothy M Gillway

A SUMMER'S DAY

Oh, the glory of summer;
Rays of sunshine on display.
Old folk sweating, mop their brow,
All upon a summer's day.
Market stalls don colours bright;
Flowers and fruit in glad array.
Women shopping meeting friends,
Loitering upon the way.
Children laughing and shouting.
Skipping, dancing, as they play.
Kiddies, dressed so colourful;
Brought to the park, swing and sway.
Garden hoses not allowed,
So the council posters say.
Suntan lotions, cooling creams
Of high numbers are okay.
Road sweepers shade in their cab
As each kerb they brush and spray.
Vendors of ice cream and pop
For a long, hot season pray.
From small huts deckchairs emerge
Where all winter long they lay.
Tennis balls thud, bounce along,
To and fro, it seems for aye.
Sporty types dress all in white;
Swimmers make for beach and bay.
Country ma'ams make jam for sale;
Shirtless farmhands, they make hay.
Rays of sunshine on display;
All upon a summer's day.

Ken Millar

THOUGHTS ON THE TSUNAMI

At early morn, the tourists swarmed
To reach the beach before the heat.
The locals laboured, served and fished
Did any think of God in this?

Their plans, their schemes, their hopes and dreams
By one act smashed, destroyed and shattered.
One moment eating, drinking, breathing,
The next, life stopped - what did it matter?

Shocked we listened, watched and wondered.
Deaths mount up. We cannot number
Those missing, those now wracked with grief,
And what has happened to our belief?

The day before, some praised Christ's birth.
Feasted, caroused, swapped gifts with mirth.
We lost our awe, forgot that He
Took on our form, our fragility.

God gave us minds to question, fathom
Perhaps we're deaf, blind to the chasm
Between mankind and His creator
Wake up all men, for God is greater.

Greater than presidents, kings, all who reign.
God sees the whole Earth drowning in pain.
Remember He made us, the sea and the land
And we must obey Him, take His command.

To care for the orphans, pray for the stricken
The homeless, the jobless, the grieving who sicken.
To reach out and touch them, tell them God's story
And who knows? Reveal just a glimpse of His glory.

Jennifer K Cocks

ONCE NOT TWICE

With haste we arrive in the world unrehearsed,
we did not see the shrouded cloud ahead of us
consequentiallly we arrive on Earth improvised
and vacate the scene with our mission unjustified:

We did not see the seven mammoth mountains ahead of us
always prompting us of the huge struggles ahead of us,
more things to be done, not twice for our survival.
We never realise no life is ever lived more than once
                                        save in Heaven.

We are born only but once of a mother most we love.
We are hardly aware of what tomorrow might hold for us,
we do not sense the upheavals to come ahead of us,
and so unaware, perhaps, that opportunity knocks but once.

We cry at birth regretting for being born,
we regret for leaving all our friends behind; we could not see
the huge struggles ahead of us, and unready for the
chaos twisted out of natural proportions once on Earth.

Even if there's no reminder and no dreamer,
even if you're the most of all the fooleries,
it's proven today can't plagiarise yesterday.
and no yesterday ever cast its shadow twice.

Each night counts its blessings once.
Now can't ever tell what the previous night
treasured within its realm. Needless fear is it?
Today is always gone forever but hope we keep.

We are distinctly hinted struggles are never truly
concluded, so we give hope to where there is none,
with smiles and courteousness we can reach out
to heavens and seek accord amongst the blissful stars.

Don Okoko

WHO WOULDN'T LOVE HIM?

God sent His Son, He was the only one
who could redeem us but such a price
the Lamb of God, the true and Living Word
bought our pardon with His life.
    Who wouldn't love Him? No one's above Him
    the Son of God in Heaven adored
    left Heaven's glory to live the story
    that would re-echo round the world.

Perfect and pure, He came to cure
the ills of this lost, fallen world
the blind, the lame, the outcasts came
and He healed them with power and word.
    Who wouldn't love Him? No one's above Him
    the Son of God by Heaven adored
    left Heaven's glory to tell the story
    that still re-echoes round the world.

Sin captured Earth. What is a sinner worth?
The Lord of life, how can that be?
No one else could, then Jesus stood
and said, 'Here am I, send Me.'
    Who wouldn't love You? No one's above You
    the Lamb of God can we not see
    that You left glory, o' wondrous story
    of selfless love for all - for me.

Joy Winter

THE WALL

O' stony, wind-blown wall,
You run like a grey shadow
Down the wandering hillside of my days.
In summer you are mossy, warm and painted bright
With common blue, fritillary and thyme;
In winter, crouching down among the heap of bones,
Where cold and hunger found their mark,
And certainty is only that the wall will run
Forever on the granite shoulder of the years.
Old friend you are.
Perhaps when you were young,
And life more simple, in your shade
I learnt to conquer fear and bring home meat.
Perhaps I touched the flank of stag or hind
And felt their warmth, through hide and bone,
Go beating in my veins and sing a blood-strong song
Of rock and hill and sky.
And even now, when cold and hunger touch me not,
But wandering is still my life, and thought my inconsistent friend,
You make a shelter from the wind
And vastness of eternity.

E J Macdonald

LOOK BACK

The time will surely come
When passion wanes
And all is done
Then peace and quiet remains.

In this aftermath of giving
Look back with kind eyes
Upon those happy days of living
For how quickly such time flies.

Pause to remember now and again
What deep loving can bring
Forgetting the twisted times of pain
It touches with splendour each mundane thing.

Dorothy Walker

Life

Grasp (with both hands)
Enjoy
Talk
Cry
Play

Challenge
Struggle
Listen
Laugh
Love

You only have one chance,
Seize your life and *really live* now,
Give it a try,
Believe in yourself
Rather than sigh
When you realise life has passed you by.

Julie Marie Laura Shearing

I Heard A Robin Singing

(In Britain, the robin is our only winter songster)

I heard a robin singing from the orchard by the way.
His lightsome song had not been heard for many a summer day.
I listened to its crystal message, sparkling like a rill;
It said, 'The summer passes and the air grows chill.'

I heard a robin singing by Clovelly's cobbled steep,
Where tourists clambered rather like a flock of mountain sheep.
Again I caught his message, from the laurel by the wall;
'The summer passes brother, and the leaves must fall.'

I heard a robin singing by the stream at Watersmeet,
Where tumbling waters slithered over boulders at my feet.
His tinkling song cascaded from the rowan in the glade;
It said, 'The summer passes and the light will fade.'

I heard a robin singing in a world of snow and ice,
When winter gripped the countryside as in a frozen vice.
His song was just as cheerful, and his message just as true -
'The summer passed, but now the winter passes too.'

Whene'er I hear a robin singing, sweet and clear and free,
In autumn or in winter and wherever I may be,
He never fails to lift my heart and leave my spirit blessed -
This tiny ball of courage, with a russet breast.

R A Hardwidge

My Sister Ann

A sincere smile
A calm demeanour
All the while
As she watches drama on TV
She's transfixed
By Frost
That's plain to see
Yes, that's my sister Ann.

It's Saturday night; I ask,
'Do you want to be wined and dined?'
She smiles; her eyes are sparkling
And kind
She replies,
'Preferably by someone else
Who likes wine and cats.'
I say with confidence,
'That's where you'll find your niche.'
And I smile at my sister Ann.

Margaret Sherrington

Paradise Found

I'm so proud to be a poet
Able to release the power of words;
Sometimes I'll write a sonnet
To express the voice unheard,
Bring comfort to the heart that weeps
And release the sunshine of a smile.

Or perhaps I'll write a ballad
To recall romantic days
When knights were bolde
And maidens fayre
While battles were lost or won.

Primarily, I'll try to make it fun;
Milton, on 'Paradise Lost', bemoaned the
'Troublesome and modern bondage of rhyming'
Though surely that's what makes poetry such delight -
It's just a matter (oh so easy!) of getting the flow right.

We write and rewrite new verses
And try to get that rhythmic sound
When it's just like music to the ear
For the poet there's nothing to compare
You could call it 'Paradise Found'!

Elaine Hunt

Mother Of Mine

Oh beautiful Earth, Oh mother of mine
You have a beauty so divine
You give me food enough to eat
You give me wood to heat and sleep
You give me water to take my thirst away
I am fed in every way
I take it all but can't give back
I am your child, I live on your back
Your beauty shows in many ways
In birds that sing in fields of hay
In all the flowers that live too
You feed them all for me for you
What a wondrous place this Earth of mine
You'll live forever so divine.

D Treadwell

The Optimists

'Will it last?' you ask each other,
when the sun shines every day.
'Will it last?' you ask each other,
as your children move away.
You let them go and wish them well,
yet becoming overwrought,
remembering things you didn't teach them,
when you seem to think you ought
to have made that a priority
in their vulnerable years,
but you couldn't think of everything
to allay unexpected fears.
You did your best, and they will too,
and one day come to say
they're getting married very soon,
perhaps the following Saturday.
'Will it last?' you ask each other,
as you contemplate past years.
'Will it last?' you ask each other
as you hold back silent tears.

Kath Watkinson

HUNGRY

Hungry,
They are all hungry,
Queuing for ages and ages
For meat, for bread
Then what do they get?
Enough for one day, one meal.

Hungry,
They are all hungry.
There is no food at all.
In their thousands they lie down and die.
Why, Lord, why?

Hungry,
They are all hungry.
Hungry for open arms,
Hungry for care.
Hungry for sweetness and warmth
And somebody there.

'Lord, can't You assuage their hunger?
Give them what they need?'
'Son. Daughter,
You are their brother, their sister -
You go to their aid.
Then I will love you and help you
All I can -
Till then I can do nothing,
O' Man.'

Rosemary Thewlis

THE CHANGING SEASONS

Snow and frost the new year may bring
Bravely the robin and missel thrush sing,
Scurrying rabbits with imprints so bold
The earthworm burrows deep, to escape from the cold.
Burdened are the conifers and evergreen yew,
Welcome are the snowdrops, the early crocuses too,
Night frosts sketch patterns on windowpanes
Sunshine brings life to woodland and lanes.
Rainwater in ditches after a February soak
Frogs wake from their sleep giving an eerie croak.
Robust and heartening, the chaffinch sings
The first brimstone butterfly flickers its wings.
High in the blue a skylark trills
Gardens display nodding daffodils.
Grass snakes begin their gliding search for prey
Evidence that spring at last is on the way.
White butterflies on cabbage: leaves the gardener forlorn
Fox's earth sees coming and going, now that cubs are born.
Glimpse of a dormouse, also the tiny shrew
Spiders' webs sparkling on hedgerows from early morning dew.
Leaping grasshoppers, when the long day stays warm
Ladybirds among aphids and bees begin to swarm,
Cornfields looking golden, harbour the unwelcome mouse
Start of the shooting season, bad time for the grouse.
Less eager is the earwig because the chill of night
Gnats after a long season still give a painful bite.
'Pee-wit,' cry of the plover as it circles arable land
Food scarce by the sea, hard weather drives gulls inland.
Noisy starlings roost together at night,
The changing of the seasons, a picture of delight.

Frederick Coles

RUSH HOUR

Trees grow tall beside a city street
Where country road and urban highway meet.
Branches traced black by early morning light.
Skeletal lines from cold ephemeral night.

Beneath the trees cold tracts of tarmac pass,
Peopled by cars - a noisome seething mass.
Within this din, frustration wears a frown,
Lemming-like instincts drive them into town.

A blackbird sings to help us realise,
There's more to life beneath those cloudless skies.
It tells of fields where winds blow fresh and free,
Misty headlands - scent of moor and sea.

The song goes on. The bird gives all to say,
There are better things to do on such a day.
Unwilling still to hear his plaintive plea,
Spurned, the chance to hold the golden key.

To open up a life that's clean and new.
Pastures redolent with daybreak's lustrous dew.
But still without the time to stop and hear,
Of treasures Mother Nature holds so dear.

Senses surfeit with traffic noise and fumes,
Rush to reclaim their central heated rooms.
To industry and commerce bend their knee,
Unable to share the lone soliloquy.

It's quiet now, the traffic's gone its way.
High on a branch, the beauty of the day,
Is still extolled. The blackbird once more sings.
Take time to share in life's more wondrous things.

Norman Brookes

SPRINGS OF HAPPINESS

Deep springs of happiness have they
Who love these things from day to day:
The sun, the moon, the sky and sea,
The singing bird and busy bee,
The beauty of the wayside flower,
The silence of the evening hour.
The old grey roads that lead the way
To restful hills and quiet bay.
The joy of seasons as they come,
The goings out and coming home,
The peace that follows honest toil
And moments on the soil,
And many other joys there be
Which blend themselves in harmony.
The love of music and of art,
The fun and laughter of the heart,
And there's the gentle summer rain
Which dances on the windowpane,
The pines which sigh to softest breeze,
And mists that skirt the forest trees,
The song of water as it rills
Its seaward way between the hills,
The clouds, the light and shade on high
Which makes the glory of the sky,
The radiancy at morning's door
And rosy sunsets on the moor,
And then the deeper springs of love
That find their source in One above.

Who love these things have more than gold
For theirs is treasure yet untold.

S J Goodman

SCENIC VIEWS ACROSS THE CLYDE

When I was still young I used to stay
On Gourock's seafront, down by Ashton way.
I'd admire the hills on my way to school,
The beautiful hills formed by nature's rule.

The Argyllshire hills were a wondrous sight,
Some days they'd sparkle, reflecting the light.
In all their grandeur they remained supreme,
Standing majestic, like a regal queen.

In winter they'd flaunt a bright shroud of snow
With white peaks on top and lush green below.
And in the foreground, enhancing the scene,
The dear River Clyde, a wonderful team.

On the misty days when there was a haze,
And the clouds dropped low to the hills below,
They'd enshroud the peaks with a secret veil
At which I might peer, but to no avail.

I've wandered afar, viewed objects of pride,
But nothing I've seen can match the dear Clyde.
If one looks across from the Gourock prom,
There's scenic beauty of colour and form.

Margaret Knox Stubbs

IT'S MUM

Hi kids! It's Mum!
            Remember my name?
The one with the body from whence you came,
the one who stayed up, while you got some sleep,
sewing your clothes - home-made but not cheap.

Hi kids! It's Mum!
            The one who would preach,
each day you would learn, each day I would teach.
Your first day at school, I thought I would die
then out you came laughing - no tears in *your* eyes.

Hi kids! It's Mum!
            Your private-care nurse,
kissing wounds better -before they got worse.
Many a long hour I sat through the night
watching and praying you'd come through alright.

Hi kids! It's Mum!
            The one in 'the hat'
who threw the confetti - but stayed at the back.
I whispered, 'Take care' as you drove out of sight,
feeling so proud - how I sobbed all that night.

Hi kids! It's Mum!
            I'm old now, I know,
I've weathered some storms, the lines clearly show.
I'll always thank God for the day you took breath,
you're my Heaven, my Earth, my life - till my death.

Valerie Smerdon

ALIVE

Darling man, my life, my joy
My hopes, my dreams, you're all to me -
Can life itself be its own precious ploy
To hold onto for you, forever, to just *be*.

Anne Rowena Jenkins

UNEVENTFUL

Sailing green seas
            With a smooth breeze
                        Beneath uneventful skies

Each day doesn't ring
            And sing
                        With meaning

Every moment doesn't miss
            The kiss
                        Of his

Touch that tingles
            And tumbles
                        And trembles

Sands of time panned for the seeds
            That feed
                        My waking dreams

And burst with joys
            That sparkle-dust my days.

C Bulley

LOVE LETTER

It is you who inspires me.
You are the life of my soul.
I live and breathe you.
Every time I gaze upon you
I am sort of lost in a timeless moment.
You put your lips to mine
And my tongue floods you,
Ready to taste a thousand joys.
Your presence enfolds me
With light and inner peace.
You unlocked the fierce unrest in me
And melted chambers of sorrow within.
You entered the flower of my heart,
Once locked in a prism of ice,
Now wrapped in red velvet.
You fill me with rainbows and star-fire,
And I tell you, it is in those angel eyes
And gentle spirit within, that I have found sanctuary.
This is my gift to you . . . my secrets.
Tread softly upon them and hold them with sacred heart.

Denise Jones

THE HAPPIEST DAYS OF YOUR LIFE

Schooldays are the happiest days of your life, so my teachers
                                    used to say.
But not for me they weren't. I just longed to get away.
Geometry and algebra and a thing called trigonometry.
They might as well have spoken Greek for all that those things
                                    meant to me.
The way they taught geography, to me was just a mystery
And I had very little interest, in all those dates in history.

As for learning Latin with its ablative and dative,
There never was the slightest chance, that I would speak it
                                    like a native.
Now I cannot, in all honesty, say I ever tried my best,
I only know those teachers failed to hold my interest.
But now I've come to realise I was not such a fool,
And my education started on the day that I left school!

I've travelled all around the world and as I've gone about,
I've discovered what geography is really all about.
I joined the public library, where there's knowledge for the taking
And when it comes to history, well, I've seen it in the making!
As for mathematics, it wasn't till much later,
I found the answers that I wanted, on my pocket calculator.

Gerry Boxall

VENICE OF THE NORTH

Ancient Carlisle, border bastion, built along the river's course,
each morning with little warning unyielding in its force.
Belching rain came down like Cain from booming hills and sky.

Surging along the Warwick Road and all streets beneath the spire,
a swirling flood, a rising flood, creating an endless mire.
And Rickergate murky brown fills the courts up to the crown;
police station, fire station and civic pride all succumb to the
Solway Tide. You can believe in God in love and war,
then believe your eyes as the heavens pour,
evacuation, reparation, salvation from this storm.

People from the glorious south, its eastern fringes
and its west, think Carlisle is a sleepy town, been slowly sunk
to rest. Some think it's nearer Newcastle, or even close to Wales.
Seemingly it's true I say, 'I've often heard the tales.'

But now the floods in sepia attract the national news and media,
a cabinet minister suitably sombre, a prince called Charles
with regal might could smite these sodden streets asunder.
From the Bishopric of Dalston, comes our bishop with sympathetic
certitude and rising in the listeners' breasts a sure and certain
fortitude. But lush green parks of Rickerby, The Bitts Park and
glorious Edenside, home to cricket's splendour, all in turn to
the blinding rain surreptitiously surrender.

Caldewgate and Shaddongate, Willowholme and Dentonholme,
all rippled with the black morass, too intimidating to roam.
And when the drying out begins the sweeping and the baling,
machines and men, twelve score and ten with empirical
knowledge assert, upon these streets of Carlisle -
move to clear the floor alert.

T A L

AVON LADY

My mum lives alone and sees no one all day,
Well it isn't my fault I live so far away,
Leading such a full life that I can't fit her in,
Though I do what I can, I really can't win.

But finally I go to pay her a visit,
I knock on the door, she shouts out, 'Who is it?'
And when I reply she takes off the chain
Saying, 'Oh, it is lovely to see you again.'

We sit and make small talk, she pours me some tea
I balance the flowered china cup on my knee.
Then I casually ask, 'Have you been anywhere?'
'Not really,' she says, as she shifts in her chair.

'But I spoke to my neighbour digging his border,
And the Avon Lady came round with an order.
Which reminds me, I've something I must give to you,
It's out in the bedroom, just follow me through.'

She goes to her dresser and opens the drawers
And the guilt washes over me, making me pause,
Because they're full of Avon, in fact there's enough
To last for a year, she has loads of the stuff.

Then she fills up a bag with the talcs and the gels
And the perfumes and creams with their exotic smells.
So I take it, and thank her, and then drive away
But this new knowledge hurts, that she's willing to pay

For things she won't use and can't even afford,
Just because she's so desperately lonely and bored,
That when Avon calls, and she hears that bell ring,
It's someone to talk to, which means everything.

Jessica Jones

MAN'S BEST FRIEND

I mustn't take from the table and I mustn't sit on chairs,
I'm not allowed to tease the cat and I'm cursed for leaving hairs,
And if I run around the room displacing the fireside mat -
Yes, you must have guessed it, I'm cursed for doing that;
And yet, at least in England, it is the modern trend
For dogs, above all others, to be known as 'man's best friend'.

Instead of chairs, I tried the bed - another big mistake -
It's no to this and don't do that - please give a dog a break.
I tried to do as I was told and didn't chase the cat
Instead I went to play with sheep, but there's something wrong
with that!
And as I'm always in disgrace, please explain this modern trend
For dogs above all others, to be known as 'man's best friend'.

Again I was in trouble because of muddy paws,
I'd tried to get inside the house, 'twas nice and dry indoors;
And then there was the lovely day I was taken to the sea,
But I had to stay inside the car, no golden sands for me.
So is it any wonder I'm bewildered by this trend
For dogs above all others, to be known as a 'man's best friend'?

It really is depressing when all I do is wrong,
I love my owner very much, but it's the same old song,
'Get off the chair,' or, 'Don't jump up,' is all I ever hear,
Seldom a pat of welcome or an encouraging word of cheer!
So is it any wonder, despite this modern trend
That I think it's a misnomer to call me 'man's best friend'?

If I really was so wanted, there'd be lots that I could do,
But all the things I really like, I'm told they are taboo.
If I were a man and he were me, I'd let him have some fun
And wouldn't always scold him for some trifling wrong he'd done.
So don't be hypocritical and don't try to defend
This obvious inaccuracy, and call me 'man's best friend'.

Elizabeth Zettl

UNTITLED

Yes, when we are old we may wear purple,
But shall we know?
Perhaps only our dutiful nearest and dearest will know,
'Oh, she has her purple jumper on today,
I thought she never really liked it
But I suppose they thought it would cheer her up.
It's quite a nice room, good view,
Though I don't suppose she notices it.'
'Oh yes I do; and I hate purple
The room is too small, confining.'
The words are there in my heart and mind;
But not in my mouth, my throat.
'They are good to her though, that little blonde one seems kind.
We'll come again in a few weeks, after the wedding,
I don't think she recognises us,
Probably will never remember we have been,
But I wouldn't like not to come occasionally,
She's quite a sweet old thing.
Pity she had to give up her bungalow, but there you are
That's life, we'll go in a minute, before the rush hour.'
'I am not a sweet old thing, never have been,
The little blonde nurse is very pretty;
But is always having to rush off to her boyfriend.'
My vocal chords are no good,
My hands won't write,
But my goodness, I can think and hear.
Perhaps it's just as well that my skills of communication are
not what they were
Otherwise no one from the outer world would ever see my
nasty purple jumper
And me in it, sitting in my claustrophobic room.

Patricia Cobb

FREQUENCY

Perhaps among you there are many
Who often have to spend a penny
In town it's such a joy to me
That I can pay a call that's free
Through weighted door or creaking turnstile
The rush to get there's always worthwhile.

When visiting a different town
I view the streets all up and down,
Cos owing to my frequency
I've got to trace a lavat'ry.
A 'Toilet Guide Book' I must write
For others in a similar plight.

I've entered many a stately loo,
Blenheim, Chatsworth - Hardwick too.
I run inside and there I find
A close encounter of the nicest kind.
It's good to leave a small deposit
In a high-ranking water closet.

Ladies! Toilet! WC!
They've all relieved my frequency.
And oh, the bliss of a comfy seat
To make my rapture more complete.
Unlike Napoleon, how I do
Love to meet my Waterloo!

The man who invented this wondrous boon
With frequency must have been in tune.
A good man he - all neat and dapper,
His name (don't laugh) was Thomas Crapper.
This world without him would be sadder
For he was a friend of the wonky bladder.

Jessie Edwards

THE BLIND DATE

Shall we greet each other warmly
You and I?
Are we of a kindred spirit
You and I?
May we live a life together
Glean some memories to treasure
Will we share our deepest secrets
You and I?

Could we embrace love and romance
You and I?
Lives entwined with one another
You and I?
To forever be as one
From the moment we've begun
Might we make each other happy
You and I?

Or will we have a brief encounter
You and I?
Never more than passing strangers
You and I?
Just a chapter in a book
Whereby each might take a look
But continue on our own way
You and I?

Christine Lannen

BABES

Babes robbed of normality
Victims of nature
Exposing a fragile existence -
An irrational behaviour
Horror in the cold light of day

Babes robbed of childhood
Innocent victims
Life predetermined before birth
Their playground a minefield
The daily lottery of life and death

Babes robbed of innocence
Hurling stones
Wild haunted eyes consumed with grief
Swept up, violated
A lifetime of dubious existence

Babes robbed of youth -
For what?
Evil passions fuelling revenge
All reason abandoned, normality unknown
Ensnared, suffocated

Generation poisoning generation.

Beverley J Waldie

SOMETIMES

Sometimes on a summer's evening
Long layers of cloud are touched with light,
Impossible haply possible
Tempering the hint of night.

Sometimes on a summer's evening
The layers of cloud are banks of gold,
Intangible almost tangible
Creating cities of old.

Sometimes on a summer's evening
As layers of cloud seem flocks of sheep,
Inanimate surely animate
Gathering in folds for sleep.

Sometimes on a summer's evening
A feeling of heaven spans the land,
Unemotional proving emotional
Pondering on Time's lost sand.

Eileen Shenton

AND THEN THERE WAS ONE

My little girl, Sadie, has left us.
Her companion is pining away.
We tried to stop her leaving,
But alas, it wasn't to be.

But the memories we have are everlasting,
Of her charming and cute little ways,
She melted our hearts, oh why did we part?
Death is the penalty we pay.

Now Scooby and I walk together,
In the wood where we once all played,
And remember happier times,
Of fun-filled summer days.

I can't say goodbye to Sadie,
Although I know she's at peace.
But I visit her grave daily,
This is my only release.

Rose Baines

STC (SAMUEL TAYLOR COLERIDGE)

(STC, of Ancient Mariner fame, married Sara Fricker but later fell in love with Sara Hutchinson, the sister of Wordsworth's wife. William and Dotty (Dorothy) Wordsworth
were close friends and walking companions. Berkeley was an infant son who died while Coleridge was in Germany)

Saint Peter, standing at the Gate,
Is stopping one of three;
'Now just a moment, Sam,' he says,
To the famous STC.

'You were a brilliant master
Of prose and poetry -
A regular spellbinder
In talk and oratory.

No doubt you were a genius,
But Sara took the drop;
Alcohol and opium -
Lad, you weren't much cop!

Soon you fell in love again,
This time with Sara Two;
And always when the heat was on
Folk saw the back of you.

Your struggling wife and children
Were helped by other hands,
While you, in search of culture,
Hopped off to other lands.

Your 'two-months' stay in Germany
Like Berkeley was stretched out;
For only after ten long months
Did Sammy turn about.

A hefty albatross of guilt
About your neck is hung,
And out of here have sinners
Like you been often slung.

Yet you loved wood and fell and tree -
Climbed Scafell Pike alone;
With William and Dotty
You walked your feet to the bone.

And always will your magic
And mystery remain -
I think we need you here, Sam,
Your learning to revere, Sam,
Your mouth to entertain!'

Marguerite Pratt

FLOWER POWER

A treasure more worthy
than ingots of gold.
A perfume more precious
than scents dearly sold.
A jewel much brighter
than crystal's sleek skin.
A flower can harbour
these assets within.

The sun sends out ardour
to mould a rich sheen.
The rain fuels sap and might
get gnarled nooks clean.
The bees earn their lunch
in this nectar café
while fresh winds can assist
raring seeds to replay!

Peter Comaish

A E W

As in silence and stillness
It seemed an indeterminate period of time.
Would it ever come to an end? It was deemed it would
But when? The waiting seemed endless.

Little was perceived save for the basic knowledge.
There was no discriminatory information available,
Nothing to go on to use advantageously.
But that was the decision, the choice, which was made.

The seasons changed from winter crispness, spring, early summer.
Things were happening, literally moving.
Perhaps time wasn't standing still after all
But proceeding slowly to a conclusion.

A query, a question; well-being was paramount,
It would not be wise to venture far at this stage.
There was a need to reach out for support
And this was freely, gladly given.

All was calm: every minute each second recorded.
Anticipation reached a crescendo,
The long, tedious wait was nearing its finish
As naturally as the ebb and flow of the tides.

An affirmative elated voice said it was coming to an end,
Reaching its finale.
This created anxiety and impatience in all
Who had stood on the sidelines. But wait, this was more of
                                                a beginning.

I stood by the phone, unsure and alone for the news I wanted.
It came, heralding great joy, tears and tumultuous feelings of love.
At last Amelia Elizabeth Wilson, my precious granddaughter
                                        was born.

Welcome to the world, darling child.

Patricia Dyer

THE PASSING

The cliché of it all, those dark eyes meet mine,
Sideways glances, seeing
Destiny before it's even begun.
I know you, I know your thoughts.
Though all words, absent.
I'm yet to see but I'm drifting,
Abandoning family as they fade
Background noise calls for me,
My ears pretend they haven't heard.
I want you. That longing too strong to ignore.
Distance reaches and grabs,
But I can't watch as you leave.
My heart stolen.
Suddenly you are my world.
I ignore outstretched arms,
I can always return?
They're just my past,
My future? Nothing without you.
I wander from known existence
And follow you, you, my unknown.
Cold darkness enwraps me,
I know safety lies with you.
My heart stops, falling, you pull me in.
Our souls now one,
Blanketed in the light of life,
We both know I have moved on.

Sarah Hutchinson

LAWYERS: BAH HUMBUG!

J B Jones, the good engineer,
Was working high up on a crane.
'Over to the right, over to the left.'
Then down a hundred foot he came.

Whilst deathly pale, his face was cold,
Above the clouds his soul had flown;
Till outside Heaven's door he stood,
But for his sins he would atone.

He tried to open all the gates,
But all were locked around the rim.
Out of his pocket he took a tool
But Saint Peter came and stopped him.

'You'll not get in there, so down you go,
It's now well past seven.'
He argued, 'But I'm an engineer
When we die, we always go to Heaven.'

St Peter shook a weary head
'I've been working here since half-past six
So down you go to the hot place m'lad
And help the Devil play his tricks.'

Now at the annual general meeting
Around the boardroom table fair,
God and His holy angels blest
Awaited the Devil coming up from his lair.

Usually the Devil came up from Hell
In a tattered, unshaven, dishevelled state,
Picking bits of burnt soul from his hair,
Always red in the face and late.

But this year he came up neat and clean,
On time and cool and tidy
And told them why he was early and neat
And had been from the twenty-second Friday.

'That engineer you sent down,
Has my place cool as a mountain.
He's installed air conditioning to keep cool,
Fixed the radio and even a water fountain.

So now we just sit around and talk
In the cool and listen to the wireless,
It hasn't worked since nineteen thirty-eight.
That engineer is quite tireless.'

God said, 'He's mine, you send him back,
Just as quick as you are able.
He's not the stuff to rot in Hell,
Engineers sit in glory at my table.'

'I'll not let him go,' the Devil said,
'He'll not stand even in your foyer,
You can't sue me in any court
Where the hell would *You* get a lawyer?'

Lorna Moffatt

JOY

Companions we walked the path of spring
Bluebells like rugs meandering
below great oaks in early leaf.
He took my hand of love beneath
A redwood tree
Whose secrets told
Would a thousand years of dreams unfold.

Jill Willens

MARKING TIME
(In memory of the Argyll and Sutherland Highlanders)

Haunting sounds of marching feet
echo up the cobbled street,
empty barracks now await
thro' the once well guarded gate.
In empty barracks once housing kings
no bugle call at sunrise rings.
All, all is peace, all, all is still
no marching feet climb up the hill.
The pipe and drums together lie
in silence as the years drift by.
Relics of the Argyll's proud past
the castle keeps them safe at last.

N Gell

LOST . . . AND, MUCH LATER, FOUND

First to throw up; first to see the sea.
First out the car . . . it was always me.

Like a seventies cop show, as soon as the car slowed, I was gone -
the engine still humming of summer; ticking over;
while the sun shone . . .
but I was oblivious . . . already sprinting ahead; laughing; darting;
my wind-blown footfalls barely touching each paving stone.
I was free; alone; eager eyes taking in each terraced house,
evenly planted in neat seafront rows;
the sort that everybody remembers, everybody knows:
garden walls straight as headboards, privets shaped like all the rest
but *I* could not rest until I had passed the test -
rounded the bend at the end of the street
(where the beach spreads out to meet
the rock-striped awnings and cluttered corner shops
that would provide our postcards home; comic books; pear drops).
And further on yet . . . to where the sun melted into sea-glitter
and children's laughter hiccuped from the backs of donkey rides,
then spiralled round the insides of plastic buckets
and where our ice cream-stained, salty sea-fingers tasted bitter.

Some lessons come easy, others take longer to learn:
forever, I'll inherit the silence that followed that final turn
to discover the empty road - the passive pavement . . .
not called for; not missed; no one urgently sent
to reclaim what was temporarily lost . . .
the pearl richer than the tribe, so carelessly tossed . . .
                                        me

The moment was deathless . . . shares the same space with me still:
resides in the marrow of my memory, jars like a pill
at the back of the throat . . . as I ran . . . breathless
in the claustrophobic open air,
back and forth . . . here and there,
trawling the street . . . searching for the sound of your heartbeat.

Orbiting each parked car, wrestling the smothering desire;
the unbearable urge; the smouldering fire,
to break down every slammed-shut door, to pore over, sink, each
stained-glass ship, sailing on opaque waves, to reach
up to each *Sea Breeze* and graffiti each gold-rimmed name,
to cast some Caliban revenge; to apportion some dreadful blame.

Until, finally, you came . . .

When I had lost all hope down the pavement cracks, as I turned back
. . . you appeared . . . and a smile crossed your lips like a comet: wide
as a mile of cloud-littered sky . . . and you opened your mouth to sigh,
but nothing says so much as the silence when you cry.

Andrew Detheridge

HERE'S TAE MELROSE

By Tweed's flashing rill; 'neath the Eildon Hill
There is set our jewel fair;
Tho' we wander far o'er the wide, wide world,
Our hearts are still lingering there.

It's oor ain toon,
It's the best toon
That ever there be:
Here's tae Melrose, gem o' Scotland,
The toon o' the free.

We will play by the cross, we will play by the bow,
We will drink at St Dunstan's well;
We'll slide doon the scaurs on the green Weirhill,
And list to the Abbey bell.

It's oor ain toon,
It's the best toon
That ever there be:
Here's tae Melrose, gem o' Scotland,
The toon o' the free.

Let us ride round the bounds of our ancient town
From Newstead to Turn Again,
Or meet 'neath the leaves of the apple trees
Of the monks of St Mary's Fane.

It's oor ain toon,
It's the best toon
That ever there be:
Here's tae Melrose, gem o' Scotland,
The toon o' the free.

So here's to all those in the Town o' the Rose,
To each lad and each lassie there;
And here's to the Queen who will tryst at the Tree,
The fairest of all the fair.

It's oor ain toon,
It's the best toon
That ever there be:
Here's tae Melrose, gem o' Scotland,
The toon o' the free.

Added after the 1939-45 war -
But remembering 1914-1918 also.

Let us think once again of the bravest of men,
Who sleep in a foreign field,
They laid down their lives for their country and king,
With a spirit that would not yield.

J Drummond

THE UNSEEN GUEST

The unseen guest breathes peace upon this place
His presence is so real you can almost touch Him.
You can hear a symphony rustling through the trees
As they sway to the mood and music in time and space.

His fragrance washes over like sweet-smelling perfume
Petals unfold on His command, prayers rise from the garden.
He paints rich colours to perfection as He forms His world
All the colours of the rainbow from Heaven to Earth.

Love builds up friendships as His spirit touches each heart
Breaking down barriers with words sowing seeds of faith.
Mists roll along the lakes kissing the water
Water lilies open up as the sun dries the raindrops' tears.

The unseen guest has complete control over this place
Running it perfectly to His time, to His word
Knowing it is His place where to His making to His will
We will hear Him say, 'Come unto me and I will give you rest.'

Margaret Davies

EIGHT TEARS ON MY CHEEK

Her wavy long hair,
with that soft golden glow.
This feminine creature,
all the boys love her so.

She grabs all attention,
that soft loud a step.
Jealousy pays a price,
but it's all in my head.

We virtually speak,
on the cursed internet.
Though not in person,
no self-confidence.

Besotted I am,
with this fine piece of art.
She looks at me different,
like a poisonous dart.

She likes someone else,
it turns out we're related.
Son of mother's blood,
but he cannot be hated.

No more are they shiny,
nor silver or sharp.
Like a coin in the rain,
so jagged and bronze.

So painful this was,
over hard solid scars,
though not a warrior,
I'm a power from Mars.

It's done and it's final,
rosy blood starts to seep.
I flutter with sadness,
eight tears on my cheek.

Joseph Larkin

FALLEN SHADOW

I used to believe I loved a heart so rare
But I guess that was never to be
Years pass by and still I think of what we shared
You leave your footprints in my dreams

Love is a killer, raining on the weak
Lets your feelings run wild then crushes them to salt
Can't escape the thorns, lying on the side of the street
Overpowered by guilt, assuming it was my fault

Always falling for the wicked
For them to crush you and dig your grave
Love is a devil's spell they put on the pawn
There's no escape when you've been blinded by the rain
You cast your dark shadow over the dawn

I keep imaging this could never happen
Makes life easier to consume each day
Then I close my eyes to see the Devil laughing
Pain cuts too deep for me to be brave

Glass scrapes across my weakened heart
Shedding blood into the cracks in my soul
Cowering in the corner to escape the dark
Fear hunts me down like man hunts the doe

Can't sleep when dreams are frail
Shattered stars fall into my grave
Love died in my arms, turning weak and stale
Yearning for the fire to burn the love I once craved.

Lyndsey Louise Watson

SQUARES

She stands on the bridge
Staring down at the river.
The pictures in her mind
Make her thin body shiver
Turning, she looks at the
Hurrying crowds.
'Dear God,' she whispers,
'They might all be in shrouds
For they are dead
As dead can be
Lost to this world
Of reality
A world where we are all in jail
Walled in by fear
Where apathy prevails.'
She lives again the nightmares
In her mind.
War-torn places where
It was hard to find faith
When death rained down from the skies.
Where the air was filled with agonised cries
Where politicians promised
Knowing their words were lies
She looks down and sees the
Muddy water swirl
Moves to the parapet edge
Then turns.
One voice she hears
Sees a dirty hand held out
'Hold on - don't jump,'
The ragged beggar shouts
'I haven't got much, but
You are welcome to share.'
He opens his hands
Shows the coins lying there.
They stumble along
Supporting each other
She his sister, he her brother.
One man who showed he really cared
One man who stopped outside his square.
Following his Lord's command,
'Love one another as I have loved you'.

Maggie Pryce Jones

THE BOY AND THE TREE

A small boy sat upon a branch
Which was part of a big oak tree,
The tree was part of a forest
That was growing wild and free.

The boy climbed higher and higher
In the tree that stretched to the sky,
He was trying his very best to
Catch the clouds that were passing by.

The people watching down below
Saw the boy disappear from sight,
The clouds had darkened the sky and
The daytime had turned into night.

The people waited by the tree
They waited all night long,
But nobody saw the boy again
They could only hear his song.

The song was carried by the wind
That whistled through the trees,
All part of the forest
That was growing wild and free.

Betty Kirkham

KENT

Sometimes I dwell on those distant years
When we lived there
Disturb the web of memories in my mind.

Lines of hop poles latticed with string
The strawberry fields of the Medway Valley
Oddly conical Kentish oasts
The pungent fumes of rotting apples
Past scenes we knew.

We shared a bin, hop-picking
And tried to be gypsies
Fingers flying, stripping the bines
The Tallyman counting our baskets in bushels.
Then grimy and tired, hands green-stained
Resting in warm September light.

Always there was space
The Weald a great clay basin
Once the forest of Andredsweald with
Its villages, rivers and ridges
Hop gardens growing in the fertile earth.

You let me grow as I please
I such a dreamer, you the realist
I painted watercolours of sunsets,
Went scrumping after dark
And sang in the Saxon church.

I still have the painting you gave me
Hanging in my room.
The schoolhouse of Kentish Ragstone,
The arched bridge where Fairfax
Marched his troops.

Pictures rooted deep inside.

Jan Ingram McCaffery

HEARSAY

Thou do you see my Ramsey?
Glair, I'm from Sutton down to country air.
Thou, are you near me when I walk?
Through the Sussex and Surrey hills and towns
They say there is a Ramsey
Madness, or is it a fine tale they tell?
Thus also say we are marked with
The sign of Frankenstein.
Yell, well I have it.
I also have a birthmark of a heart,
It's true to tell.
Someone said it's because
I'm a very loveable person.
My Kismet is Sunnyside.
My old house is where I used to live,
I am still there in my mind's dream state.
I'm looking for the faces of their friendly smiles,
Where have they all gone?
Do I need to go back some day
And if I do, will I melt away?
Can you read my mind?
I can see my tea leaves saying
Kick Ass! I know the way,
Or is it my Ramsey *Madness?*

Myra Ramsey

RETIREMENT

I know I should be content
Now I have left my work behind
But each day now I find myself
Doing work of another kind
It keeps my better half happy
To see me at the sink
An apron hanging around my waist
What would my old workmates think?

I do not object, in point of fact
I think I am rather keen
But why must she follow me around
To make sure all is clean?
She is perfect with supervision
On that there is no doubt
And to make sure I do everything
She has my chores all written out.

While I am dashing round
With a dustpan and a brush
She is sitting reading a magazine
Shouting, 'Dearest, what's your rush?'
'I want to get everything finished.'
I most humbly declare,
'Well, that's a silly reason,' she says,
'You're not going anywhere.'

The windows have yet to be cleaned
It's a week since they were done
You know how all the neighbours talk
Especially the nosy one
Make yourself a cup of tea, have a break,
I will just have coffee and a slice of cake.

She is a real persuader
It's the manner of her voice
The way she puts it over;
That doesn't give me any choice
I suppose I should be grateful
For the little things in life
But why must she rant on all day
And snore throughout the night.

When I think back about life
I was lucky I suppose
I might well have retired early
And dear me, goodness only knows
I thank Heaven for the full employment
And the years of a simple working life
That helped me keep my sanity; and
Safe away from a nagging wife.

Richard Saunders

CLOUDS

Look up to the clouds as you pass on your way,
And watch the splendid shapes go floating by,
Let your imagination have its sway
With mountain peaks and creatures up on high.

Look down on clouds while flying overhead,
The fluffy, puffy carpet clouds of white,
Or further on, when gentler clouds have fled,
Deep, stormy spirals - an amazing sight.

Take note of clouds for they have much to show,
The weather calm or windy, wet or dry,
High banks of cumulus or looming low,
The nimbus and the patchy mackerel sky.

Remember, when you bring these names to mind,
The darkest cloud is often silver-lined.

Daphne Wilkinson

MY SPECIAL FRIEND

As I sit in my old armchair, I sense you near
You can't be so very far away, they made that clear.
You were trained to be so special and devout,
Now I will tell you who this is all about.

You see my special friend he is my guide
I speak of him with utmost pride,
He is my eyes, he leads me on my daily walk
He does not bother me, or does not talk.

Such a faithful friend, he lets me know I'm not alone
He guides me outdoors, brings me safely home
When danger lurks he makes me stop
Then when it passes off we trot.

Could you have a friend that is so dear,
One who is constantly so near
Always alert on guard night and day
I wish I could see him this I often pray.

I sit and stroke his silky coat, and pat his little head
Make sure he is comfy, before I get into bed
He wakes me in the morning when daylight I cannot see,
For my special friend is my guide dog, and means all the world to me.

Flo Milburn Smith

RECALLED TO LIFE

Celebration?
The muse cannot die -
it lives within the essence,
that very core of humankind.
But what of freedom
and its thread unbound
by responsibility, choice?
Those that laboured, unsung,
embarrassing relics of history,
now decried and even purged.
Bland lamentations of tears -
suitably edited, regurgitated
in the remnants of fading trust.
Is there yet recall, beyond now -
sublimated, smothered, spent
whose pale vestiges await cant?
Ridiculed, disparaged, taunted,
the lie of accepted invocation
breaches the barricades of democracy.
Celebrate thought, remember deed
and, whilst wrapped in dust's decay,
stand fast, irresolute and proud.

Nigel Leake

HUMAN RIGHTS

How could it be? The dove of human rights
should cruelly turn, and, as the eagle, soar
to shield the sun, and bring these endless nights.
Where un-heard voices, loud, for justice, roar.

Forgotten now are all the lessons learned.
High standards of the past are all ignored.
The tide that brought respect, it seems, has turned.
Now good and evil reap the same reward.

How came-about this change? The reason's clear . . .
Our lawyers glean their gold along this road.
The price we pay for human rights is dear,
Too many pay . . . too few are rightly owed.

What chance that in the future we might see . . .
some rights for man, may wrong for mankind be?

Phil Austin

HAVEN IN HAMPSHIRE

No doubt you've been to Hampshire
And seen its many treasures.
Some parts are steeped in history,
Some parts reserved for pleasure.
If history's your forte
It's Portsmouth you should choose,
Not only Nelson's Victory,
But also Mary Rose.
Such warships have been berthed there
That have changed our nation's story,
And submarines have done their bit
To keep old England's glory.
Winchester's a grand old city
With Alfred keeping careful watch,
While Aldershot has trained the troops
To a standard none can match.
But there's a place I'll always treasure,
Not on the way to anywhere,
It nestles down beside the Itchen,
Most people would not know it's there.
There's just a little country lane
With 'one-time' school and reading room.
It leads one to the river bank
Where Irises and kingcups bloom
Its little cottages are treasures,
I know, for I was born in one,
Was christened at the tiny church,
My education was begun.
Though greater places may you call
My martyr worthy beats them all.

Margaret Hodgson

YOUR SMILE

I woke up in the middle of the night
Thinking about your gorgeous smile
And sought for a pen and paper
To write in verse

Like a rose that buds in spring, I wrote
And cracks open to meet the sunshine bright
Your smile warms my heart with love
. . . but wait a minute came a thought and a frown

Is there not a danger here
Of spoiling natural beauty with my weak pen
What polished scribe can reproduce such beauty
Which talented artist can capture such warmth
By simply pushing pen on paper

Let me call off the impossible task
And sleep over my secret failure
That one day I woke up late at night
Thinking about your sweet smile

How you start and seem to wanna stop
And then flow in supernatural crescendo
How your lips reveal your sweet white teeth
That make me thirst for a kiss

What poet can video the sweetness of your childlike smile
That compels one to resign in sweet spontaneity
And such contagion as it simmers and over boils
To elegant sweet laughter

Should you ever get tempted to tell a friend so dear
That one day I woke up thinking about your smile
Just give them your sweet smile, my love
Perhaps one day they too will tell the truth
That they also woke up thinking about your smile.

Samuel Takavarasha Jnr

SAMANTHA, THE TRAVELLING SPIDER

Samantha was born in a west London garage,
Her ancestors came on a horse-driven carriage,
Through each generation they travelled the town,
Living on buses, some up and some down,
Samantha decided without any fuss,
That she'd made her home on a 120 bus.
She climbed up the wheel and under the chassie
Not a mean task for a determined young lassie.
She went under the door rubber and then up the wall
She hadn't quite realised a bus was so tall,
Then on to the ceiling, away up on high,
A good place, she thought to capture a fly.
From Hounslow to Northolt she felt the vibrations
As she travelled each hour between the two stations.

Samantha sat still as she waited for lunch
And looked at the passengers, oh what a bunch!
There were babies that cried, with chocolaty faces
And office commuters with heavy briefcases.
There were boys and girls all going to school
And there always seemed one who acted the fool
He'd swing on the rails and lean on the bell,
And made lots of noise and a horrible smell.
Samantha would sit in her home on the ceiling
And hold very tight as the bus, it was reeling.
Each day was so busy with people galore,
But Samantha was lonely, no spiders she saw.
She longed for a pal, she longed for a date,
She hoped that one day, she'd find a nice mate.
But unlike us humans a spider is fickle,
The mate of a spider ends up in a pickle,
For after the babies are ready you see
Poor Daddy spider becomes Mummy's tea.
Samantha might finish her days without fuss
Destination: spider heaven - on a 120 bus.

Ann Stringer

TOMORROW

We think if we wait till tomorrow,
Our troubles will all go away,
But troubles and cares are forever,
Mostly are here for to stay.

To wait till tomorrow we think a good plan
But do it today, whenever you can,
There's no use waiting, it may be too late,
'Old Father Time' may wait at 'the gate'.

There's just no time like the present,
Just don't let this day go to waste,
Don't put off till tomorrow,
Just do things today in great haste.

We promised to do things tomorrow,
Some of those hard-to-do sums,
We promised to do all tomorrow,
But strangely, it never comes.

No matter if you're quite busy,
Try to spare a minute or two,
Some folk on you are depending,
Yes, they're depending *on you!*

Jimmy Sinclair (93)

ANGELS ON OUR SHOULDERS

Angels on our shoulders
Whether fantasy or real
Pray they gently guide us
From the Devil at our heel

Heavy, dragging footsteps
A mind that takes its toll
An everlasting imprint
Tattooed upon the soul

A halo gently slipping
Well outwith our reach
Left is only darkness
And a blackboard-scraping screech

A class not so divided
There were sinners, hell, no saints
Memories, they taunt us
With the images they paint

Trapped within a time warp
Imprisoned against will
Isolated nothings
A bitter, twisted pill

A clock that glances sideways
Face red where struck by hand
Flushing tears with water,
Shards of glass, then sand

Repeated is the torture
Playing time and time again
Broken is the victim
Healing is the pen.

Sharon Reaper

SLEEP TRAVEL

Woken by the river's burble
From the open pane
Here within the mossy valley
Misty in the rain
Dreams beyond the coil of gladness
Vivid in a vale of madness
I recall again.

Lapping straits and coral shore
Creaking stern to prow
Istanbul to old Marmara
Where the gods allow
Sails all billowing and thicker
Anisette and partridge liqueur
Blistering the bow.

Struggling a line of boulders
In the Eiger claw
Hanging like a thwarted spider
On an airless floor
Tinted blue the sky and lovely
Pleading with the ones above me
Straining to the core.

From the heights of Pergamum
Through the vitric air
Steeped in wailing minarets
I imagined there
Cupping hands beside the fountain
Like a lizard from the mountain
Vying for his share.

Clive W Macdonald

GENTLY DREAMING

As she lay there, gently dreaming
In the warmth of summer's day
She remembered how things were then
Long before they were this way

When friends would come and nothing mattered
As they enjoyed the summer sun
Sitting on the sandy beach
Till dusk came and the day was done

When all the world was bright and special
When life's small hurts soon went away
And no one cried or tried to hurt you
How wonderful this dreamed-of day

She stirred a little in her dreaming
No one knew her dreams were there
Her visitors had eyes a-streaming
She did not know how much they cared

How happy were her dreams while sleeping
Nothing now could touch her heart
She never heard the gentle beeping
Helping her life to restart

She did not know that she was dying
Remembered nothing of the crash
She was happy to be lying
Listening to the warm waves splash

A gentle hand was on her shoulder
'Come with me,' a soft voice said
And, strangely light, she followed after
Leaving her soft dreaming bed

As she walked - no longer dreaming
She was aware of weeping friends
'Don't cry,' she said, 'I am not leaving,
Only going on ahead.'

The urgent sound of footsteps running
The shouts of 'Clear!' as doctors tried
In vain to catch her as she left them
To happily drift on the tide.

Norma Griffiths

PRE-WAR NIGHT WATCHMAN

The man was old, the night was cold
As he sat by this brazier,
The rain came tumbling down in sheets,
Which made the night much hazier.

He liked his job, but not on nights
When water came down in a flood
It was most uncomfortable
With his canvas tent full of mud.

On the balmy summer evenings
He saw lots of folks strolling by
Many of whom would stop and chat
And pass him a drink or a pie.

He had respect from all ages
A legend young and old could see
He was quite safe from everyone
Which is just how it ought to be.

When I was small in the twenties,
And out with my folks for a walk
We'd see the night-watchman's fire
And all gather round for a talk.

That of course was before the war
We children all thought he was fun
We spent many happy evenings
Till he told us to, 'Scat and run.'

I Crumley

GOING BACK
(For Marji W)

Streets I once knew
come once more into
view
so different, yet so
the same
the houses seem smaller
or did I get taller
this feeling is so
very strange,
as I search for a life
that seemed brighter then
those long summer days
way back when,
one penny sweets
and sixpenny treats
picking berries in
the old churchyard
your hand in mine
I still yearn for that
time,
and then there you stand
words you need not say
as so many years
just melt away,
we hold each other
frozen in time
the love and the life
that could have been
mine,
we laugh as we talk
and remember old
times,
then all too soon
the moment has gone
come our goodbyes
so life moves on.

This life I searched
for, is long in
the past,
just as the life I
ve now
together will last.

E B Evans

THE GIRL

She was my friend, the girl
I often lie watching.
The summer breeze in her hair.
It made no difference
what day brought sorrow or
joy. She always understood
with open arms I hurried to
her side, I am eternal to you
nothing can destroy our love.
I stroked her face. Words
came through the mist. I
took my love to her.
Only to find a dream.

E Bilson

UNTITLED

While on holiday in Cyprus
With my sister, two brothers and wives
I discovered a lump in my left breast
My heart, well it took several dives.
As I will be eighty next year
My health has been extremely good
No cancer in family or relations
But I didn't alter my holiday mood.
So when I arrived home I went to the doctor
I was referred to the hospital quick
A mammogram and biopsy followed
The lump was cancerous, I felt really sick.
A couple of weeks later I was admitted
The doctor, Mr Cochrane was great
The nurses and staff were terrific
After a left mastectomy I left it to fate.
Everything went very well
After a week I was home again
My friends and family said I looked swell
Now three months later
I am still feeling just fine
No other treatment necessary
I see the doctor in six months time.

May Watkins

WHISPERS IN THE DARK

Rain, running in rivulets, towards their den,
Wind, lashing the galvanised strip, leaning against the wall,
                    Left there by the men
Whom, littered the yard, of the derelict house, abused
                    And broken, with sloganed walls, bereft.

Inside the den, the vixen lay, huddled with cubs,
                    Warm from whispering winds;
The sounds carried, echoing around the water-ridden walls:
She spread herself closer to her little ones, her mate
                    Had not returned yet, she worried.

Winds grew stronger, rain beat its way thru the opening
                    Of the den, fear was in the
Vixen's heart; fear from the sound of men,
They were in the yard, she heard a dog's shrill bark,
A scuffling, in the dank dark:
There, by her side he stood, her mate, bedraggled,
                    Beaten by the night, tired and weary
From the seeking of food and fight;
                    The father of her cubs, she saw the blood upon his leg,
Where he had run to them, from chase, thru thorned shrub:

The cubs ate hungrily, a the meal set before them,
Scraps chewed up, then sleep overtaken, nestled together
                    In parent's love:

Sounds still around, whispers from above:
Another night's journey had been made, chased at length,
                    Tired with fear:
The vixen longs to see her cubs happy, full of fun at play
                    In freedom, be it rain or warmed by the sun,
She knows this never will be so and must prepare them
                    For the world, out there, they must learn to
know,
Where nothing comes easy, hardly a place is safe,
The fear of man will be ever etched upon their face.

L Hammond Oberansky

JUPITER SUITCASE

I've got a Pulsar Probe with a cluster scoop,
and the top sales figures for the Cygnus Loop.
I own a binary villa in the Nebula zones,
with an android wife and three small clones.
I'm an interstellar fellow with a moonbeam face,
who knows every constellation in hyper-space.

I'm Jupiter Suitcase.

I've got carte blanche with Captain Kirk,
an enterprising contract that's a nice little perk.
I sold the very first inter-galactic loo,
and a space invader to Doctor Who.
When war broke out in the Mekong Delta,
I sold Dan Dare a fall-out shelter.

I'm Jupiter Suitcase.

Flash Gordon's favourite record is the Retro Rock,
and there's Zodiac earrings for Mrs Spock.
I've got a brand new line in Cosmic string,
for tying open black holes it's just the thing,
There's some Hubble Bubble bubblegum with telescopic taste,
and Supernova bin bags for nuclear waste.

I'm Jupiter Suitcase.

I've got meteor minimisers with Electron X-ray,
just what you need when one's headed your way.
And a red giant range of laser guns,
even Quasar pills for the Logan runs.
So light speed me your order as I twinkle round the stars
If you pass me by near Neptune, catch me up on Mars.

I'm Jupiter - with me samples in me suitcase - Jupiter.

Dave Smith

A SECOND HEAVEN

Flowers yellow and flowers red,
Each a floral delight in a flower bed,
Flowers pink and flowers blue,
A complex array of colours and hue,
Flowers short and flowers tall,
Flowers big and flowers small,
Flowers grown in the greenhouse there,
Lovingly planted and nurtured with care.
Now they dance in the gentle breeze
That filters through the well-pruned trees.
Trees and shrubs and bushes too,
Climbers' arches to walk through.
Turf immaculately laid,
Lawns of perfection made.
Crazy-paved paths and paths of gravel,
Obscure walkways to unravel
Before the summer house a garden pool
Where goldfish dart in water cool.
A place where birds upon the wing
Alight on bough to rest and sing.
A place where butterflies in colours gay
Flutter as fallen petals all the day.
A place where bees their business pursue
Ever industrious, forever true.
A place where all may sit in style
To rest their weary legs awhile.
If God on Earth a second Heaven make,
Please - in a garden - for Heaven's sake.

P Walton

PRAYER FOR A NEW CHURCH

Lord, we gather here today to ask for Your blessing
On our new church.
We open the doors, invite You inside and welcome You
To our new house, Your house.
Erected on the embers, ashes and memories of our late,
Beloved, aged church.
We ask You to bless our new home and all who congregate in it,
Both now and in the years to follow.

Fill it with Your light so that it brightens our day, shower it with Your
Love so that we feel Your presence here.
Bless our minister, Your very worthy servant as he tends us, his flock.
Bless the craftsmen and their apprentices who brought their skills
And talents and their helpers to raise this holy
place.
Long may it stand, through all the world's adversities to reverberate
And echo Your message of love.

Bless our infants as we bring them to their baptisms. Embrace them,
Take them by the hand,
Lead them on the sometimes smooth, sometimes slippery, often rocky
Road of life.
Bless the Groom and his Bride as they stand in Your presence and
Declare their vows and promises.
Endow them with Your love, give them wisdom and understanding
As they start on their new journey
together.
Lord, bless our late departed loved ones
As we lay them before You.
Enfold them and accept them into
Your Kingdom of Heaven.
Accompany them on their journey
To that promised place and
Give them eternal rest and peace.

We ask that You hear our earnest prayers.
Our whispered prayers,
carried up to Your realms by the still air, the gentle breeze
Or the wild wind.
Listen as our music, our anthems, hymns and psalms
Spiral ever upwards
To reach the portals of Your holy mansions.

Be with us in our renewed resolve to carry our Your work,
Try to promote goodwill in our lives
And peace in this troubled world.
Lord, we give our new church to You for consecration.
Guard it, and may You
Grant it a long and happy life for the generations to come.
Amen

Ann Ashworth

LOVE

Love is so wonderful for the very young
When the first flames of passion reach the heart, the limbs,
the very soul
When ev'ry sight and sound of him or her
Brings flutterings of panic, breathlessness and wonder

But as time passes, love blossoms like a flower
Becomes a never-ending cushion of comfort on which one can feel
safe, protected and warm
A haven where one shelters from the storm
A soothing balm, a wishing well that deepens as the years go by

My love for you has reached its zenith
We share that which many strive to find and never, ever do
A deeper understanding of each other's beliefs and thoughts
And so our love will last throughout eternity.

Maureen Ann Baker

GOODBYE

My heart becomes a fountain
overflowing with love,
sadness,
laughter
and tears I know
will never reach my eyes
if I resist their threatening messages
like daggers through my heart,
if I ignore them calling out my name,
telling me to say goodbye.

Goodbye, good luck,
it's time to forget,
move on like the passage of time
Never ending,
never knowing
what could come next.

A whole new life waiting for me
around the corner
if I could just pick up the courage
to leave now,
never look back,
never regret.
To turn my back on all that has been,
my whole life a map,
a memory
left behind for others to find,
to delve into,
to randomly select
one moment
to judge me upon in my future.

But those that have really known me,
only they will know the truth
as they select their individual paths,
each one different,
none blending into the background,
each one will make a difference.

Only time knows what will become of them,
the person they choose to be.
There is but one thing stopping our paths,
from crossing in our separate futures;
our own enemies -
ourselves.

In time the tears will stop.
This old rusty leaf
will blow away effortlessly in the wind
and I will never know when it will turn up again,
if it will come back to me.
And if it does,
will I notice it?
Recognise it?
Or will I be too blind to see it
as it floats straight past me
never to be seen again?

Elizabeth Samson

MY LOST SON

When you were born, there was such joy
You were the perfect baby boy,
You enjoyed your food, a growing lad,
Do you remember the fun we had?
First day at school, you held my hand tight
You were well liked, not known to fight.
Curious, inquisitive, things were eagerly learned
Exams over, and a college place earned.
Helping you move, first time away from home
As you unpacked, you promised to phone.

At first you did, about things exciting and new,
The calls got less, then I couldn't get through,
I sent letters, imploring you to write,
Just wanting to know if you were all right,
I phoned the college, they had to report
That expulsion had been their last resort.
Armed with food, don't know what else to do,
So I am on my way to visit you.

When I knock upon your closed door
I'm not prepared for what I saw,
You shuffle towards me holding on to the wall,
Do you recognise me son, do you know me at all?
I hardly know you as I offer a kiss,
How on earth did it come to this?
Barely able to stand, you have lost weight,
Smelly, unshaven, you don't know when you last ate.

Dirty clothes hang off you, once a perfect fit,
Gone is your laughter, humour and wit,
Your face once round, plump and fair,
Now sunken, pale, your glazed eyes just stare.
Smelling of drink, this early in the day,
When was it that you lost your way?
Sharing drink and drugs with people you meet
Who like you wander aimlessly in the street.

My maternal instinct comes to the fore
As your so-called friends are shown the door,
Making some coffee and trying to get you to eat,
Then with my arm around you we go into the street,
Although I can't keep you under lock and key
You can get in a taxi and come home with me.
So much in need of tender loving care,
I hold you close, stroking your matted hair,
In my arms is a stranger, I want my son back,
With help we'll find the path again, my beloved Jack.

Moon Stone

A DREAM

I lie in bed at night and dream of the little things that I have seen.
The things I dream of most of all are flowers and shrubs and
trees so tall.

Of little birds that sing in tune
To hear their song in such a boom,
The ducks that swim on local pond
Of these little things,
I am very fond.

The little lambs that frisk and play,
A sight which makes the whole world gay
The pigs that wallow in the mud,
To them it seems to be good
The little rabbits that run around,
They don't even make a little sound.
This little dream is - oh so true,
I suppose you know because you have seen it too.

Christine Conway

DESTINY THROUGH A CROWDED ROOM

Over the voices of a crowded room,
Just a single one caught my attention,
As I listened to her words
I knew my heart was stolen.

As I gave my heart away,
She turned around and looked at me,
My blood turned thin and my body faint,
As she smiled a bewitching smile.

I was lost in her voice,
Dancing on her words,
As she spoke to me across this room,
We moved closer together, I felt my heart melt.

As our bodies grew warmer,
A faint glow between us,
As she flashed her smile my way,
I tried to keep control, but my thoughts wandered.

I'm not sure how long this can last,
But I know where my heart belongs,
My prayers have been answered
And if fate guides me, this could be my destiny.

I've never met a girl quite like this,
This one night scarred onto my memory,
As this night unfolds, love blossoms,
But even as the night progresses, I'm unsure of the future.

As all the paths ahead are revealed,
I know which one I will take,
The one with you, and a clear blue sky,
As today becomes yesterday and tomorrow today.

From this beautiful young woman,
I'm filled with inspiration and song,
But the future may be cloudy
As I try to picture this as the past.

I'm torn between pleasure and pain,
I could and would follow her anywhere,
To places we don't have maps
And fate has left unwritten.

The warmth inside me,
Never before has this been,
I think I love you,
This could be destiny through a crowded room.

Marc McHale

THE ANSWER

It's desperate suffering pain and sorrow
Every moment of each day and night
For eight out of every hundred
Human beings live here on Earth.
Some have no shelter, medicine, no food
No education, tools, no hope -
What can we do to put this horror right
Is there a way?

By giving ten pounds out of
Every hundred pounds we get
The light of love could then disperse
That monstrous cloud of need
And Oxfam, Cafod, Christian Aid
And others too transform those tragic lives.
Our needs would still be met
And millions more both near and far
Be free from want.
There is a way - it's love.

Phyllis Moore

BACKSTREET BOYS

When the rain falls down
In this small smoky town
And things are looking so bad
I go back a wee while
And think with a smile
To the time when I was a lad

We all looked the same
And life was a game
As we ran down our backstreet
With glass marbles and a string
We could play anything
With conkers a once a year treat

We all did our bit
Dad worked down t'pit
He made sure we all had our fill
And Mum she cooked tea
For our poor family
Afore going to work in t'mill

On a red hearth rug
Came tin bath and a jug
With carbolic and a comb made from steel
Splashed water on t'floor
We were scrubbed till red raw
And our senses could no longer feel

With our clogs we would kick
At red Accrington brick
Then grazing our knees in a fall
And the tears that we shed
Cos of our blue painted head
As we climbed the old orchard wall

Now I am a dad
And I have a lad
Things to him must look poor
All the mills shut down
In now what's a bleak town
Never to open no more.

J Curwen

REFLECTIONS

Why is there sadness in all poetry?
Not grief, but depth of feeling
So rarely found in boldly written prose.
(Except those well-loved artists who,
With each casual note or simple phrase
Give music to pursuer of their words).

There cannot be aggression in a poem.
The strongest toned stanza
Softens with the metred rhythm.
The harshest deed related
Creates regret much more than hatred
And tempers the horror of the act.

Verses of happiness and gaiety bring pathos.
By putting into words
Thoughts of exuberance and joy,
A void remains
As though the heart is robbed
Of some sweet, precious secret.

Then grief related is
Again, another contradiction.
Though often causing tears,
Still brings forth happiness,
Gives wonder at such revelation
And leaves - tranquillity.

Doreen Tallack

To Diaptomus Castor

Diaptomus castor, oh what a disaster
You are hid from mortal view
With a salmon-pink body
And eggs chocolate brown,
You are the lass with the bonniest gown,
In the murky depths of many a wee pool,
In the old birch woods to windswept dunes,
You seem to have survived
Through changing times.
But what is that you eat
With those tiny plumose feet
Is it algae or a rotifer?
Perhaps its detritus you prefer
Or whatever else you can find
Maybe a young cladoceran you'll not mind
Survival in a temporary pool
Calls for nerve that's real cool!
Beneath the winter ice
Life can't be all that nice!
But early in the spring
A batch of eggs you soon bring
To rear another brood or two
Before the summer heat
Dries up your home a treat.
Your eggs, then sealed in the mud
Must stay until an autumn cloud,
Fills the burns, revives the springs
So water to your pool new life brings.
Your eggs hatch, nauplii appear
These feed, grow changing skins
To copepodites long and slim
Which soon become mature
So another generation is sure.
Since the Ice Age went
Your life you have spent
Secretly tucked away
At the end of our Straths to play.
May we try and keep you there
So future generations of children may come
Wonder, wonder, look and share
The secret of your survival.

Alan Joyce

Loch Ness

(Dedicated to my family and friends)

In the waters of the Scottish lakes,
There she waits,
And there she stays
Until someone comes for her advice,
Will she rise from the dark waters?
She will tell them her advice
And sink back down to the deep dark waters
But again she hears a cry,
Only not for her - for help.
In the water the splashing for help cries again,
Off she swims but no more cries can be heard.
She searches and searches,
Until she sees something at the bottom of the lake.
Now it's over and there's nothing else to do,
But bring the child to the surface
And leave the poor lassie on the cobbled beach.
It's a sad day for Nessie,
But it all happened there and then.
All she can do is sink back,
Down to the deep dark waters,
Until her help is needed again.

Hannah Louise Lancaster (11)

Reflections

Sitting in this garden warm,
Caressed by sun's sleepy waves,
My thoughts drift away, through the corridors of time,
A time of innocence and endless days,
Playing cricket in the street, kiss chase,
Cowboys and Indians, fighting pirates bold,
Standing proudly on mounds of gold,
Fantasy to be blown away by a voice calling, 'Time for tea.'
There will be bread and jam and cakes if we are lucky!
Father, cycling home besieged by children four,
'Can we have a penny?'
'A farthing each, no more.'
Excitedly cross the road, to the shop, mind that car!
To claim in each grubby hand, a small toffee bar.
Short trousers turn to long, a time to be strong,
Childish dreams abandoned, real world beckons on.
Soon, teenage excitement dashed, war's ugly head rears,
Devastating scenes, bombing plane's vile drone,
Heads down in shelters deep, no time to weep, hide your fears.
Moving to happier days, first true love, carries me away.
Sweet kisses, family bond, wife and children take me on.
Some heartaches tinged with sorrow,
For some, there is no tomorrow.
Life must go on, as go on it does, children fly the nest,
To join the rest on the road of time.
My thoughts return from journeys far and things that I have seen
To blink at the sun,
To give thanks for what I have,
Not what might have been,
With my love by my side, no more childish games,
But, there might be 'jam for tea'!

K L Pusey

On To A Song

Just a wandering minstrel without a song
He has the words but the tunes go wrong
The music died when his heart was broken
Now the words can neither be sung nor spoken

Fractured thoughts and discordant chords
Notes that will not match the words
No dream, no hope or expectation
His world a scene of devastation

No more to hold or love and kiss
Gone the dreams of wedded bliss
The passion once beating in his heart
Just a dull thudding now they are apart

Throat choked and sore from the dusty road
Shoulders arched beneath the load
Of a troubled mind and an empty breast
His heart left in his wedding chest

For him there is no end in sight
Of that dusty road or endless night
Still he determines to carry on
Till he finds the melody for his final song

The refrain he knows will come with love
The tune from the throat of a turtle dove
To be sung from the heart with tenderness
To the one who will bring him perfect bliss.

George Bryant

THE BLIND ANGEL

From a sky that was filled with soft white clouds
Came drifting to Earth below
An angel so fair to look upon,
With a smile like a sunrise glow.

She turned her face to the Orient,
And a little Chinese maid
Came timidly to hold her hand,
Trusting and unafraid.

She looked then to the great sub-continent,
Where a handsome Indian boy
Had been standing, alone and silent -
Who ran to her with joy.

From the darkest parts of Africa
Came many a black-skinned child -
Nigerian - Kenyan - all of them by the angel's smile beguiled.

Up to the north, where children so fair
Skipped along to link hands with the rest,
Dancing round the smiling angel,
With singing and merry jest.

Braving the Atlantic storms in boats of every kind
Came Mexicans, Spaniards and Red Indian folk
Leaving sorrow and hardship behind.

Many of those who that day came
Had no voice with which to speak,
Or stumbled because they were tired and sick
Or used crutches because they were weak.

They begged their bread from the passers-by,
Who shuddered and turned away
From their ugly, misshapen features -
But the angel said, 'Don't go away!
There is room by my side to hold you; we never need to part.
In my arms let me enfold you and hold you close to my heart.'

Then one little Eskimo boy bravely asked,
'Please will you tell us your name? We love you so much,
And you love us too, and treat us all the same.'

The angel lifted her sightless eyes to the warmth of the heavens above
'You ask my name? That's easy to tell!
God calls me Love.'

Marjorie Piggins

LITTLE LONDON

When I was a child, this was my world,
I would wake in the morning to the sound of the birds.
The clip-clop of hooves as a horse wound its way,
with the milk or some other at the start of the day.
Then to my school in Micklefield Lane,
where Miss Howard, the teacher, would make it a game.
To learn ABC and add 123
and say a short prayer, bending down on one knee.
Gas lamps at night shone out clear and bright,
and with snow on the ground made a wonderful sight.
Small shops in the street were tidy and neat,
selling all kinds of goods from buttons to meat.
The sweet shop was spread with bottles galore,
delicious, mouth-watering from ceiling to floor.
A cobbler they called him, repairer of shoes,
with leather and nails, he made them like new.
If you walked round the streets on a warm summer day,
you would see the skipping ropes and whip and tops of children
                                        at play.

So many games now lost in the past,
and replaced by things which are not meant to last.

Were those things true so long ago,
or is it my age that makes it seem so?

Clarence Gascoigne

IF YOU WANT TO FIND ME

If you want to find me
Look where the bluebells are
And the tiny white anemones
Shine like little stars.
Look along the riverside
And into the tallest tree
And there within the woodland
You will find a part of me.

If you want to find me
Look for me by night
When the sky is full of stars
And the moon is shining bright
The wonder of the heavens
Is there for all to see
And there among the myriad stars
You will find a part of me.

If you want to find me
Look where the wild geese fly
And you hear the sound of beating wings
In a windswept, winter sky
If you want to find me
Look at the early dawn
When the sky is flushed with crimson
To a slowly waking morn.

If you want to find me
Look where the wild winds blow
And the earth is pure and white
With freshly fallen snow,
And every tiny snowflake
Is a wondrous thing to see
And the flowers and birds
And shining stars are all a part of me.

C Gaunt

THE FRUITS OF THE SPIRIT
(Galatians Ch 5 vs 22/23)

Happiness is *love* for everything.
For God's wonderful creation and for God the King.

Happiness is *joy*, joy for all to see,
An inner peace and thankfulness, shared unconsciously.

Happiness is *peace*, peace, such perfect peace,
To be surrounded by God's love, this indeed is peace.

Happiness is *patience*, that's long-suffering,
That God has shown to you and me, His long-suffering!

Happiness is *kindness*, kindness shed abroad,
Think of others before oneself is happiness stored.

Happiness is *goodness*, so desired by all,
Embracing so many virtues, far beyond the law.

Oh to be like God, *faithful* to the end;
But I can only by His grace, strive and yet depend!

Then be gently led and be gentle too,
For *gentleness* brings happiness to build me up anew.

The fruits of the Spirit will bring happiness,
And *self-control* is not the least, defeating selfishness.

We then, must seek for that happiness to glow;
With His Holy Spirit within us, it will overflow!

Janet Bowen

GRAVE DIGGER

There once was a grave digger
His name was Bob
During the plague
He had a hard job.

He worked all night
He got no pay
So when he got bored
He started to play.

He'd prop up the dead guys
Stick 'em in a row
Toss 'em around
And leave some on show.

News of the digger
Whose intentions were wrong
Spread across England
Like a pretty bad pong.

He was clean for a while
No more messing with the dead
He knew that if they caught him
He'd soon be put to bed.

But again he got bored
Started messing around
Refused to put the dead
Just straight in the ground.

One night he came
To dispose of the new
When he noticed the spots
And kept sneezing - *achoo!*

Huge boils on his arms
Started leaking yellow pus
He thought nothing of it
And didn't make a fuss.

His night-time jaunts continued
For a few days more
Then he'd realised what he'd got
And there was no cure.

Bedridden Bob
Kept talking to thin air
Flew into a fever
With sweat-slicked hair.

He realised that his illness
Was his own stupid fault
He'd got too close to victims
So the killer fleas could vault.

Soon his buboes popped
And the pain just increased
His heart gave up and stopped
He'd learnt his lesson at least.

Then came the Great Plague
Of sixteen sixty-six
There was this guy called Philip
Who played with the dead for kicks.

Abi Smith

MOTHER

I cannot express my love for you,
it's so deep within my heart,
I've always loved and cherished you
from the very start.

Mum, you are so special,
thank you for all you've done,
rearing, caring and loving me
three precious gifts in one.

Mum, you've worked so very hard,
to give me of your best,
oh, I do so much appreciate
the time, you had no rest.

You have always been so thoughtful,
very understanding too,
watching every step I take,
or what I'm going to do.

Mother, I've grown up now,
and as happy as can be,
ready now to leave my home,
will you come with me?

If you say I will understand,
the time has come to part,
you will always be my friend and mother
so close within my heart.

That's why you are so wonderful
thinking so much about others;
now you understand, I love you
because you are the dearest of mothers!

Edith May Hughes

A WALK THROUGH REEPHAM TO THE CHURCH

As we walked through the marketplace,
Your fingers brushed slowly against my arm,
As you spun the legend of Black Shuck
And the three sisters of Reepham,

Where their churches huddled silently together.
I spoke of the faceless Georgian windows
Bricked up for income tax, and as your eyes
Watched me, you began to smile.

I followed you to the churchyard,
Where you held down the boughs
Of the yew that swayed
Gently in the autumn swell,

And were used as palms at Easter.
You confided that slips of the shoots
That shivered in the moonlight,
Were buried with the deceased.

So calm that warm September day
As your fingers caressed the tombstones,
Carefully peeling away the moss,
Revealing the layers of the past.

Then you caught me watching you,
And as you spoke to me,
I suddenly moved forward, eager
To be embraced by your voice.

Stephanie Harris

THE TSUNAMI

I never knew what a tsunami was
Until last Boxing night,
The images of destruction
Filled everyone with fright.

The Christmas celebrations
Were instantly forgot,
Those scenes of devastation
Tied my stomach in a knot.

Thousands of people swept away,
It happened all so fast,
And many more have lost their homes,
Will the memories always last?

We make our small donations,
And say, 'Oh what a shame,'
And after two or three short months,
Will our sorrow still remain?

There will be other news in the future,
More disasters I've no doubt,
But what happened all those miles away
Is something I'll never quite work out.

So what can we do in the future,
To help those who've lost loved ones and their towns?
They are all very proud people,
And will wear smiles instead of frowns.

With luck they will get lots of aid,
From countries far and near,
And after many years of toil,
They will start to forget their fear.

We can all help in a very small way,
And take our holidays there,
Talk and understand it,
Not just stand and stare.

No one knows why it happened,
Some say it's an act of God,
We all try to blame someone,
I think that's rather odd.

I'll never forget this disaster,
And come next Boxing Day,
I may even get on my knees
And close my eyes and pray.

Tony Fox

WINTER WOLF

Along the tree-lined borders of a sleeping forest night,
A glistening moon peeps through the trees, and sheds an eerie light.
While a stealthy trio roams across the crispy snow white land,
Moonlight gleaming on their backs, a silent watchful band.
Sapphire shadows stretching out across the wide terrain,
Over snow-topped hills and vales, their vigil they maintain.
On a clear night such as this, it's said you can hear the sound
Of the soulful baying of the wolves, for miles and miles around.
But soon these majestic animals that patrol this physical world
Are joined by the ghosts of their forefathers, from the sky they
shimmer and swirl.
Silent guardians with golden eyes that shine from the heavens black,
Power watching over the strong descendants of their packs.
For this is the world of the mighty wolf, both magic and serene,
The mysterious soul of the wilderness, whose beauty we have seen.
So explore if you will this shimmering realm, and observe with
baited breath,
As across the wilds these spirits of the night watch over Heaven
and Earth.

Carol Paterson

MY SOULMATE
(Dedicated to Alan, my heart and my soul)

Now that I've found you,
I don't want to lose you.
You are the air that I breathe,
You are the smile on my face,
You are the happiness I feel within.
When you're not here,
You're always in my thoughts;
Every night and every day.
Even when I sleep, you're in my dreams.
When I think of you,
My heart skips a beat.
I've known you forever,
Yet we've only just met.
This love will be forever
I can feel it deep down, so deep.
I miss you when you're gone,
One day we will be together.
Waiting, just waiting!
You are my best friend and my soulmate,
I am lost without you.
Follow your heart,
Follow your happiness,
Follow your dreams.
I will always love you . . .

Joanne L Lancaster

FOR MELWYN MOORE
(In memory of his parents, William and Leila Moore)

Mel, the days will appear very lonely
The skies will appear grey and sad,
It will seem as though the sun isn't shining
Because you've lost a special mum and dad.
In your heart, there is going to be an empty space
And you already know, no one can fill,
No one can ever take your parents' place
And believe me Mel, no one ever will.
The endless words of love and sympathy
That all your friends and family send,
Will never be enough to heal your pain
And they won't make your tearful sadness end.
However, they will definitely be a soothing balm
And I promise they will ease your aching heart,
These words of comfort will set your feet upon a path
Where life for you, once more can start.
Mel, the love you shared with your parents was special
And all the things and times you spent together,
Will always be carefully stored inside your heart
And like my love and support, they will be there forever.

Kulbir Kaur

THEN AND NOW

Only now within my mind can I in fancy roam
And walk along the country lanes to and from my home.
To see again and recognise the faces I have known
Each one to smile and say a word in friendship clearly shown.

For we could walk by night and day without the need to fear,
And gather the wild flowers that filled our homes with cheer.
We knew all who lived near us, we knew that we were free
To ramble in the fields and lanes as contented as can be.

How I wish that I could give the children of today
The freedom that we used to have - it seems but yesterday
To keep the 'age of innocence' sheltered, safe and pure
In a world of peace and happiness where each child was secure.

Bessie Martin

CHELSEA FLOWER SHOW

Buxus and lavender with Irish slate mingle
Curved pathways entwine
Some scattered with shingle
Quiet places secluded, midst bright waterfalls
Reminiscent of times past
Within these stone walls

An artist's blank canvas
With hands that have toiled
Unfolding with beauty
In flowers and soil

Blooms in abundance
These great gardens scan
Inspired by God
Created by Man

Doris Selina Moss

BUTTERFLY RIDGE

Just outside the town of Bundaberg
Off the east Australian shore
Is a high point called The Hummock
A rare beauty spot to adore

To the right of the Hummock scenery
Is a home built wooden bridge
Leading to a wooded glade
And named, The Butterfly Ridge

Having crossed the narrow walkway
Just wide enough for one
A journey into wonderland
For a visitor has begun

Through a shaded pine-filled forest
Tropical trees with palm type leaves
Honeysuckle shrouded bushes
Add their scent to the cooling breeze

Treading deeper through the wooded glade
An air of silence to be found
Behold, a wondrous sight appeared
Butterflies, a hand's breadth wide
Descending all around

Their colours were breathtaking
As they floated through the air
Mixed colours of the rainbow
Their winged patterns did compare

Purple Emperor, Chalkhill Blue
Clouded Yellow, to name a few
Like gentle fairies they came to rest
Upon one's garment worn
Friendly, soft and delicate
Like a being newly born

While observing this creation
Thoughts might develop in the mind
That if these butterflies could speak
What message would we find?

'Come forth to view our kingdom
If 'Peace' be the world you seek'.
Butterfly Ridge will welcome all those
Who cross its Hummock Creek.

E L Hannam

FATHER OF THE EARTH AND SKY

Father of the Earth and sky;
Of space and time, infinity,
And all that therein dwells;
Of all there is, and is to be
From now through all eternity,
Of this He gently tells:

He placed the firmament on high.
He made the seas and planned the sky -
He painted glorious views.
He made the creatures in the wood;
Caused them to drink - and eat their food;
Provided morning dews.

But it was in His greatest plan
He would create a spirit man
To govern all the Earth;
A people that would to Him turn
That they might of His wishes learn
And rule in goodly mirth.

For they would rule in Heavenly love,
And imitate that realm above
Wherein our Father waits
For us to join Him in His Heaven,
Where endless blessing will be given
Beyond the heavenly gates.

So let us praise the one above,
Our Father God, who rules with love;
His precious Son adore.
The Spirit praised too will be,
The Three in One and One in Three
For now and evermore.

Margaret Mary Sherwood

AN EVOCATION OF PEVENSEY BAY

Long hot summer Pevensey days
Horizon lost in a soft heat haze
An arc of brilliant azure sky
The sound of the sea, soft as a sigh.

Sea worn pebbles reflect the heat
And warm the soles of summer feet.
Quiet voices drift along on the breeze
An aircraft buzzes with the sound of bees.

A fishing boat chugs slowly by,
Kites sway gently in the cloudless sky.
Children gaze in a break-water pool
Faces reflected, mysterious and cool.

A single yacht makes its way
Silent in the sea wrack of the summer day
Sails are idle and gently flap
As against the bows the warm waves lap

Then dusk seeps down to shadow all
With latent heat and a gossamer pall
No sound comes form the empty shore
Nothing and no one there any more.

The quiet tide reflects the moon
Hanging in the sky - a silver balloon -
Casting its light on the flat-calm sea
A pathway of magic which follows me
As I wander along the now cool sand
And turn to look back at the shadowed land.

Sybil Bourchier Steel

KNAP HILL

By Knap Hill ancient Adam lies,
His long barrow high against the skies,
And all around him, Wiltshire views
Are open to his heifer's eyes,
A Wiltshire Adam scarcely knew.

The White Horse (disappointing grey) -
Carved far too late to help convey
Him through the jostling flowers -
Prances its chalk-inspired display
Up slopes, where gliders hang for hours,

Towards the Wansdyke, Roman bounds
That still guard Adam from the Downs
Where other barrows outlying,
And megaliths, and nameless mounds,
Stand sentinel to Avebury ring.

The heifer watches, from above,
Equestrian girls, too young for love,
Tailored, immaculately tacked,
Who, oblivious of cow's eyes, have
Driven, jumped, mucked out, and hacked:

And boys, in touch with deeper roots,
Laugh as their handcart overshoots
The humped canal-bridge in their ride
To more iniquitous pursuits
Out of sight by the water's side.

And even Honeystreet is seen
From Adam's Grave; a cultist scene
Inside The Bridge, a towpath pub,
Explaining what crop circles 'mean'
By maps and photographs pinned up.

And still the heifer stolid stands
Guarding the Grave and Adam's lands
From hikers, bikers, fliers of kites,
Cultists, cameras, canal-boat fans,
Helicopters and microlights.

Robert Newton

THE CRANES AND TIME

If you imagine, these cranes, of desolation,
Lift their heads towards the sky,
Search the leaf-lined horizon, agog,
At liberty. The bells of faint-freedom
Awake in a tinkling of hollow reeds;
Slowly they toll the day to joy awake,
Slowly sound the cymbals of the lake
To a thousand, brassed crashes.
Roundly matures the day, the bounds
Of nature tremor; all the sounds sing
Together in one melodious psalm.

These birds, in their stiff-necked majesty,
With lighted eyes, will pierce the day
And let in gusts of simple feeling.
If you let them stand till silhouette
Makes all the lake a silver mirror
And the reeds the moon's support;
Then you will hear the finale, muted,
Tremulous; the owl an eerie flute
Play *rallentando* to the day.

Mike Vipond

NEARLY THERE

He ran like the north wind
When he came around that bend
Spikes barely made an impression
On the track
Arms, shoulders, face relaxed
he perfected technique
But he was too young for blocks

Limbs long and sleek
Nostrils flared
As a proud colt

The adrenaline
Pumped
The heartbeat
His kingdom

Each lane was occupied
As the starting pistol fired
But no one was there
The only view he had was round that bend
Two metres past the finish line

Focus

The only obstacle between
Was here and there
200 metres
I was there waiting

Anxious

I'm sure our hearts beat
In rhythm
Same adrenaline
Pumped

From this distance positions were distorted
In lane 2 he was second from last
But when he came round that bend . . .

'Run Theo, run, run like the wind!'

It was clear to see
The distance between
The straight finish
The perfect technique
He easily breathed
Two metres past the finish line

We waited some seconds for the others to complete
Proud mother
Proud son
Limbs long and sleek
Not quite yet thirteen

Sally A Turner

FIRST BIRTHDAY

('Children are a heritage from the Lord' (Psalm 127:3))

Heaven was short of an angel that day
A cherub with curls all awry
Soft cheek to be kissed
A small sticky fist
Held out with a shy little smile
I saw through the mist of my tears and my fears
The sunbeams that danced in his eyes

And I prayed, 'Oh dear Lord
Hold him close in Your love
Be the Guide on his way
Be the Sun on his path
As his journey through life's just begun
Like a Father watch over this angel, this cherub
This precious wee grandchild who's *one*.'

Ruth Hartridge

100 Years Of Women's Institute

One hundred years of the WI, oh! What a celebration!
Bringing together, women old and young, throughout many a nation.
It started small in Canada, but soon spread near and far.
In 1915 it came to Britain, beginning at Llanfair.

Many women, rich and poor, joined in to help themselves;
They spoke on home skills, education, controversial things as well.
The 'Home and Country' magazine appeared in 1919,
And to this day is going strong, to educate and entertain.

It's not all jam and cakes and pickles, chutneys, pies and craft,
Singing William Blake's 'Jerusalem', we're not from the ark!
Throughout the years, both good and bad, the WI has lit a spark
To make the world a better place for every generation.

We have been called 'Wild Indians' and mocked for our jam
and Jerusalem,
But the movement has grown from strength to strength, each decade
an inspiration.
The WI is a steely force, as governments have found,
Once women get on their 'high horse' there's no telling who
they'll hound.

The motto is 'for home and country' whatever creed or station,
It had three members of the Royal family as its patrons!
Adelaide Hunter Hoodless was the inspiration,
And we must remember Madge Watt, and also Lady Denman.

Just get your friends to join our groups, for fun and friendship also;
We welcome 'one and all', both 'high and low' there is no segregation.
Shout 'for home and country' and help build a better nation,
And as we sing 'Jerusalem', God bless our many years of
women's federation!

Ruth Lydia Daly

Love Is Just A Miserable Lie

'Love is just a miserable lie.'

Could he never let go,
had never known tenderness,
or trusted too much
and suffered a lover's treachery,
that he wrote that graffito on the wall?

Or did he wake up one morning
to find love had vanished in the night
and only a void remained
stretching endlessly into the future,
bereft of love for anyone?

Where would he go, what would he do?
Could friends comfort him?
How pass the long remaining years without love?

Love, you are not home-grown,
and if we lack you we must beg at source.
So pour your love into my heart, Love,
my dry and empty heart.

And you came,
flooded my dryness with tears of joy,
filled me with yourself.

So I deny the graffito,
with aching heart for the writer,
and find love, no, not a lie,
but the meaning of all that is.

Derek Rawcliffe

2001

I know it sounds awful, I know it sounds sad,
But look back and remember the good days we had,
When we could walk in the town or walk down the street,
Greeting and chatting to the people we'd meet.

Doors all left open for the neighbours to call,
And a mat that said 'Welcome' right there in the hall,
With families all living side by side in the road,
There waiting to comfort and help ease the load.

And the late evening stroll with the dog in the park,
Not afraid of the night or afraid of the dark,
Young people at home, not out there on the street
And that friendly policeman patrolling the beat.

Now those feelings have gone, just a thing of the past,
The freedom we had then we knew wouldn't last,
We live in our boxes, tightly locked with great care,
Afraid who is waiting or who is out there.

Nothing seems safe and nothing seems sure,
The food that we eat now, isn't guaranteed to be pure,
The water's polluted with this modern day life,
And the air in the streets you can cut with a knife.

So what can we all do for this terrible plight,
There must be ways we can change to put things to right,
We shouldn't spoil this green Earth for our everyday living,
But should think of the things we could be doing and giving.

So let the young people know we are there to listen and hear,
All the worries and problems in growing up that they fear,
We can switch off the telly and if we are able,
Have an old-fashioned talk round that old dining table.

We're not young anymore but know that now is the time,
To stop drugs and the vandals and crack down on crime,
And if these things in the future could be overcome,
We'll all have more freedom to live in the year 2001.

Now's the time to start caring 'bout water and trees that we've
planted,
Not abusing their use or taking these things for granted,
We can recycle waste and if it's not very far,
Take a walk, ride a bus and, for a spell, garage the car.

Now some people may say that it's useless, too late,
But we could all do our bit, we could all pull our weight,
In making this land that we live in when all's said and done,
Environmentally cleaner and safer by the year 2001.

Josephine Giles

Indignant

First Lady they are not
others hold that claim,
pretence for money and external fame.
Judged on potential, some by merit,
persuaded to communicate, deprived of the credit.
Antoinette was beheaded by others for greed
imitated by some, lacking in breed.
Leaders may lead by guile or their fists
but as Rousseau explained nature persists.
Work till you drop, have they no shame?
Innocent people, resulting in maim
Revolutions were once par for the course
Not much of an agitator this Capricorn horse.
Nevertheless freedom and fairness, ingrained in the soul
equality for others, the eventual goal.

B Harrison

THOUGHTS

The trees, the stream, the clear blue sky
Rabbits and hares and birds that fly
Flowers that bloom with sweet perfume
The trickling stream where you sit and dream

Where fish do play and bask in the sun
How glorious to be here away from everyone
Just lie on the grass and blink in the sun
And lie here thinking till day is done

To think of life when it first began
And wonder who then lay beneath the sun
Would it be savage or beast all covered with hair
I wonder when he lay here, did he show care?

Care for the things I think about
The birds, the flowers, the playful trout
Valleys and hills, the clear blue sky
Butterflies, squirrels and the shy little fly

Or be he cruel and thoughts of it not
Maybe thinking of a great battle fought
Or maybe wounded lying in pain
Waiting for help that never came

Or thinking maybe the same as I,
Wondering and trying to understand the sky
Thinking of night and stars that shine
Why can't I see them in daytime?

Looking at birds as they fly by
Why can't I do that when I try
Then the fish and how well they swim
Then maybe he can do that, well good for him

Then I wonder could it be
No one's ever lain here but me
Now look the clouds begin to roam
I think it's time I was going home.

Duncan Campbell

HOUSE IN PROVENCE

No smell of people.
Ceramic jars,
perfectly placed objet d'art,
stand in corners,
Terracotta floors
are cold, unblemished.

Outside the mistral blows
spoiling the tight perfection
of the cypress trees
with its cold breath.
Snow lies on the distant Alps.

Rich people own the houses.
No black-dressed peasant woman
leads her cow along this mountain track.
Hens are silent
cocks never crow.

Only the ruined church
still hosts
its seventeenth century ghosts.

At night the moon
rising from her mountain lair
spies at us through the bare glass
with a predatory stare.

Deirdre Armes Smith

NOT MY DAY

A poetry competition
that's just the thing for me
I'll put some words together
and then I'll wait and see.

Now will they want it funny
or will they want it sad?
Maybe just a bit of both
might turn out not so bad.

To be a really first-class poet
I suppose I ought to be
in fields of green, beneath the trees
or live close by the sea.

But I am sitting up in bed
the clock has just struck one
my pen has fallen from my hand
my inspiration's gone.

Today has been an awful day
everything went wrong.
I burnt a cake - broke a cup
then cooked the meal too long.

I lost the dog - missed the bus
just one thing after another
What - enter a 'comp' in a mood like this?
No thanks I'm not going to bother!

Sylvia Iveson

QUEEN OF PUDDINGS

'Do have a wee slice Hamish dear, I've just made it specially.'
'Mother dear, I don't eat *cake*, now just look here,
I've declined your bakery so fine, since I realised at 9
(well really 3, but that don't rhyme)
I don't care to *take* sugar, cream or spongy *cake*.

Double savoury boy is me and never honey there for tea,
stuff your crusts of flour-dusted cherry puffs into your groaning freezer,
ice cream I love and lemon curd,
away with mixtures whisked and stirred,
then beaten into rocky buns inflicted on your wheat-free sons.
Worst of all pudding of bread, heavy cloying slabs of lead,
concrete paved sultana doorsteps.
Help me Mother, help me please, give us a break,
not ruddy awful carrot cake,
nor roly-poly made with jam,
I'll just be sweet, like what I am.'

Rosemarie Reeves

THOUGHTS

Some say there is no God,
That man is born, lives, dies and is no more
All to no purpose
And that all that lives
Is but a chain of cells in varying forms.

Have they not seen a cobweb, dew-bedecked
Or heard a lark rise singing in the air
Or touched the velvet petal of a rose?
Have they not seen the pattern on a leaf
Or heard boys' voices in a cathedral choir
Or felt the softness of a kitten's fur?

And having seen and heard and felt these things
Can they still say, in truth
There is no God?

Heather Brackley

CHOICES

If only you hadn't made that choice
Or taken that road that day
Maybe things would be different
Or have changed along the way.

It is no good contemplating
Or debating the 'what-ifs'
You have to take the choice you made
Along with the consequences.

To dwell on things past or gone before
Will only make you sad
Instead look onward and ahead
With a positive frame of mind.

Have things to do and be well planned
Forthright and strong-willed
Determination will win the day
Making you much happier along the way.

To succeed amid your fears
And feeling insecure
Will give you strength and courage
To have positive future years.

Strive to learn from your mistakes
Gain knowledge along the way
Put all the past and pain behind
For tomorrow's a brand new day.

Jacqui Beddow

BOMBER MOON

(A memory of World War II)

Your ice-cold, ageless, beauteous light
Kisses the river, silver bright,
Through sleeping countryside and town.
The bird of death preys in the sky,
Follows reflection from on high;
Thumb is poised for pressing down!

The fan of searchlights joins the dance,
With bursts of shrapnel to enhance
The grim performance taking place.
The heavy heart-throb drone of plane,
Cacophony of sound insane
Is orchestrated into space.

The watchful eyes above are bold;
The fearful eyes below are cold
With knowledge of the ultimate.
Now from the bird, target in sight,
Bombs are released into the night;
The stars stare down inanimate.

Carnage below in fiery pit;
Horror above - the bird is hit,
Spiralling down out of the sky.
Duty is done, message received;
Glorious death; mission achieved.
What better cause for which to die?

Your ice-cold, ageless, beauteous light
Mirrors dead eyes with moonbeams bright,
Victim and victor paid their due.
Old bomber moon you feel no pain
Tomorrow you will rise again -
How can the dead put blame on you?

Pat Watson

CONSIDER THE BUTTERCUP

In tall vases dominating halls and rooms,
demanding attention, star-gazer lily blooms
challenge the eye with the elegant grace
of each seductive petalled face.

Aloof, as women assured of their loveliness,
they assail us with a heady scent
that penetrates and shocks our sense
of smell with needle sharpness.

I feel uneasy in the presence of this flower,
emanating its strong hypnotic power.
Its anthers, cushioned velvet brown,
quiver an invitation to go down,
intoxicated, into that vortexed depth
to be absorbed and lose oneself.

I prefer the restful, clean
refreshing scent of sweet green
meadow grass and the sight
of the softly swaying buttercup,
lifting its modest chalice up
to drink the sun's warm light.

Elizabeth Clarke

MY JOURNEY

I placed the magic shoes on my feet
I floated through the air
Above the rooftops
And as I spread my wings I travelled far
Across the world.

When my feet touched the ground
It was dusty - barren
Housing non-existent
Except for shacks
But folk were persistent
In their fight to stay alive
Against all odds.

I knelt and saw the shadow of a child in front of me
As I put my arm around her
I felt a radiant glow
This inner strength was love
Reflected like a mirror
A white dove appeared
Faded then became transparent.

A part of me stepped out!
Invisible to the eye
I wanted to protect you
Help you grow strong
Gain weight
It isn't too late
If I took you back in my arms
You could teach us so much
Touch many with your smile
Which talks
You are so wise
It is us who should open our eyes.

I understand you must stay
Where you spiritually belong
As I rose to my feet
Held you close
For a moment
We became one,
'Farewell I shall return
It is from you I can learn.'

Chris Jackson

CONVERSATION WITH DAD

My dad came home from the war,
Never spoke of what he saw.
He's often found staring into space,
Picking shrapnel from his face.
Remembering his pals of long ago,
And the agony they'd endure.
These young men volunteered with pride,
Comrades in arms side by side.

I asked him, 'What was it for?'
This war to end all wars.
He answered, 'I never knew.'
For your country that's what you'd do.
Wanting the world to be a better place,
Ensuring your family would always be safe.
But he never expected to see so many die,
Or witness grown men cry.

I enquired, 'If I ever got the call?'
Was there any advice he'd recall.
'Stand your ground and never run.
Remember you're not there for fun.
Carry out your duty with pride,
Returning home with head held high,
Then if you get a bullet in the chest,
You'll know you gave your best.

Now son put away these foolish thoughts,
Always remember the things I've taught.
I pray to God you never witness what I saw,
These vivid pictures in my mind, but never draw.
Go out son and enjoy life to the full,
You'll never know when your time will come.
I fought the fight for a better place,
Hope for you life is great.'

I Dunwoodie

FIFTY YEARS ON

Long blonde hair with cornflower eyes,
The sun shone down from clear blue skies,
She but a girl of sixteen years old,
He 'for his country to serve' was told.

Love was in those clear blue eyes,
Broken hearted they said their goodbyes,
Long they stood in arms entwined,
A ring on her finger, their love did bind.

Gazing in awe on beauties below,
Innocent of fate and life's cruel blow,
Promised each other in a short time,
After the war, that hill they would climb.

It was fifty years since he'd gone away,
Fifty long years to that day,
They'd stood together with love in their hearts,
As time had ticked on to his depart.

Off to war a sailor did go,
Of her conceivement, he never did know,
'Lost at sea' was all she was told,
The day his daughter was one week old.

Beside her grandson, now twenty years old,
Of her love, the story she told,
While telling this story, they gazed at the view
Sharing love for a grandfather that he never knew.

She sighed as quietly they turned away,
For her it seemed just yesterday,
They'd stood there together in deep embrace,
Under blue skies, with sun on her face.

Veronica Tilbury

TEAR FALL

Underlid stirrings
domes grown misty;
globes glisten
warm moisture gathers.

Heated 'til hottest
boiled to shower pitch,
then gratefully tumbling
in senseless streams.

Ceaselessly flowing,
cascading drenching,
grandiose waters
a small storm born.

Liquidy lengths,
like parallel 'Tibers'
constant in rhythm
a saturating sadness.

Then waters wane;
jerking and jeering
sporadic . . .
automotive grace.

Spitting and spotting
spluttering hiccoughing,
tipping and tapping,
fresh raindrop pace.

Trickling down cheek-panes;
oozing from under
pink swollen eyelids
edged with black spiky tendrils.

Regally rolling . . . rolling hearse pace;
crystal globules stand, almost still,
acquiescing, damply abated;
terrible tempest of anguish, now . . . nil.

Gabriela Alexander

W14

This street's sick skin of London brick is acid
yellow, black, grey, grimy, dull and cold.
The flake-white of its windows seems appropriate,
matching dirt with pallor. Winter should make
all sadder, but today a horizontal sunbeam
homes in-between the patchwork planes,
scoring a direct hit on fourteen terraced houses -
the cleanest and most comprehensive missile
they'll ever know. From deep within these walls
a memory is stirred, a warmth unlocked -
the womb-like comfort of the kiln, the laying
on and letting go of a creator's hands, their
rough divinity unrecognised by the human mind
that moved them; the slow deep-heat of the
mortar's chemistry, bonding as it cools.
A colour creeps from these jaundiced cheeks,
as from some distant star; a hue not in the brick
itself, nor in the winter sun, but mediated
by both - of the first star's breath, made visible,
audible, tangible, shifting down the long light
years to turn this blotched and pitted face from
acid to ochre.
And now, beneath no longer leaden eyes,
once leprous lips have lost their whiteness,
glow, speak comfortable words: I am alive
and well. Touch me.

W E Holloway

A Tribute To My Darling Grandma
Elizabeth Hall 11.8.02 - 31.12.03 (aged 101)
(God bless, I will love you forever)

The memories that we share today
Amongst this place of flowers
Are for Elizabeth, my grandma
I'm so glad that she was ours

The fuschia in my garden
The mock orange and the rose
Even the humble rhubarb
Brings memories to my nose

The plump well-rounded lady
That I am proud to call my gran
Best butter on my teacake
Wild mushrooms in the pan

A working girl in Scarborough
Farms and service on the land
Two world wars to follow
Life was not so grand

The herbs, the plants, the flowers
Her hands in every bed
A meal made out of nothing
Yet the family so well fed

Outings to the country
Journeys near and far
She didn't mind who took her
'Just get me in the car!'

Lots and lots of children
Surrounded by her love
Her kindness and her wisdom
Were gifts from God above

For the material things she left behind
Do not make a fuss
Just treasure the abundant love
She gave to all of us

She is here in every heartbeat
That is present in this room
Etched forever in our memories
No time for doom and gloom.

When we go to God's great house
Because we will, for sure
 know that she'll be waiting there
To greet us at His door

I'm so glad that she is happy now
In His garden in the sky
Chatting with her sisters
For she will never die

Say hello to her each morning
Tell her about your day
She is walking right beside you
She is only a whisper away.

Elizabeth Ann Crompton

A Death In Winter

The green hopes of all our summers of all from the years
To dust.
Though our dreams freeze on the breath of their remembrance
We must,
Gathered by this open wound of earth and quietly weeping,
Hold to the thought that peace is yours and you are sleeping.

You shall not know the world's slow turning,
The greening and the greying of our days.
You shall not know the heart's deep yearning
As we leave you and go our separate ways.

For you the lifelong day is ended,
The song of life so sweetly played.
Our grieving hearts cannot be mended
Nor the wound of earth where you are laid.

David Hulme

For Ellie
(Born asleep 19th November 2004)

We called you Ellie
Our tiny, beautiful girl
Precious; small, fragile
You came into the world.
You looked so peaceful
No life inside your heart
Knowing this before your birth
Ripped our world apart.

You have joined the angels
In the heavenly garden above
You'll always be remembered
With such everlasting love.
Rest in peace little one
We'll see you every night
You'll be there above us
A distant star twinkling bright.

Robin J Grigsby

The Mad Hatter

I once was a hatter most prosperous and sane.
I made hats all exquisite, some fancy, some plain.
There were hats for a wedding with trimmings so fine
And hats for a funeral - that were almost divine.
A fedora, a beaver I made for a diva.
A straw boater - worn by a big city broker.
My straw, lace and gauze were met with applause
When seen at Ascot or Henley or even indoors.
Yes! I once was a hatter, prosperous and sane,
But disaster has struck again and again.
No more 'tis the fashion to wear a chapeau
Or even buy one for a bride's trousseau.
Now the guys no longer raise a hat to the gals
Instead they treat them like one of their pals.
If they cover their heads with a baseball cap
They wear the neb at the front or the side or the back.
And I'm as mad as a March hare as you all can tell
Driven to this by fashion's new clientele.
As I walk down the street no more prosperous or sane
I can hear people whisper again and again -
'There goes the Mad Hatter who just wouldn't change.'
Yes! I'm mad and I fear there's no cure for my ills
Unless p'raps an overdose of very strong pills.
So, until fickle fashion brings back the bowler
I think I'll stay mad and go live in Angola.

Margaret Hughes

ALZHEIMERS

There she sits - one in a line around the painted walls.
Small shrunken figure,
Lost in the chair in which she sits imprisoned,
White-headed leprechaun
Dreaming up another aggravation.
Head nodding down
Then jerking back, and nodding down again.
Fingers twitching
Unaccustomed to their idleness.

I wait and watch, balanced on a chair in front of her,
She watched me once,
Learning how a new life grows and blossoms
Now I watch her,
Learning how an old life withers and dies.

I lean towards her.
Wipe away the streams of glistening dribble.

She sees me now
Awakened by my clumsy, pitying touch.
She focuses.
'New nurse eh! I've not seen you before.
Where's my tea?
Have you brought my tea? I want my tea.'

Tea won't be long.
I'll make good my escape before it comes,
I have to cry.
She knew me yesterday, but not today.
'I'm off now Mum.' I kiss her, but she pushes me away.
'Where's my tea?'
And I hear, as I leave the overheated room,
My mother's voice,
'Nurse come back . . . nurse . . . nurse . . . nur . . .'

Mary Roberts

THE NEW DAY - 10 PAST 4AM!

Wake me up at dawn Lord, that I might thankful be
For hours of sleep and restfulness
As You watched over me.

Wake me up at dawn Lord to the quiet sweet air of morn
To maybe think on the miracle somewhere
Of a baby born!

Wake me up at dawn Lord, and as I open up my eyes
Whatever thoughts spring into mind
Please help me realise
That I am needed by my King
To soothe another's cries.

Wake me up at dawn Lord,
Speak words of strength and power,
So I can meet each challenge of each hour.

Wake me up at dawn Lord, cleanse me from all sin,
My soul well guarded, free and loved,
This new day to begin.

Wake me up at dawn Lord, then in prayers
Of worship there I'll find
The golden cords that bind,
Words of comfort to support the weak,
Blessings 'midst all strife.
My joy, the company of my Lord, continuing my life.

Wake me up Lord to Bless Your name!

Vera Torbet

MY VENUS

Be not my love as Priam's daughter
Cassandra . . . famed, yet only
For her tidings, oft so bad.
But be as fair Diana . . . and I
Your Endymion, who did to love her so.
Are you as Hera, wife of Zeus,
Who lead so legend says,
That ship named Argo in its quest
To find that fleece of gold?
Could then you not lead me,
In quest of mine alone, who seeks your love?
Are you as was Janus? It would at times seem thus.
As Janus back and forth so looked
So to my love, you thus to look,
Back to times so sad . . .
Which, if given chance, I would to change.
And thus our lives together, happy times to share.
You seem at times as such a child,
Likened to Pygmalion, whose sculpture
So was loved by him, that into life it came . . .
By prayers so oft he said, as I too oft say for you.
I wish that I, as he, were granted my desire.
I do so much your beauty worship,
To have you as my own.
You are to me as goddess Venus,
In ancient times so much revered,
As now in present time, you too are thus acclaimed.
At least by me, your closest friend . . .
Your outward beauty, doth beguile, yet,
Within, a love and goodness which I seek . . .
And more . . .
Thus now to me for always, you are . . .
My Venus.

Jay Smith

TRIBUTE

Diana, huntress who became the hunted
Golden goddess whom many wanted
Exquisite nobility smiled and sainted
Smile for me my . . . empress.
Touched by your warmth and sense of dress
Bonnie for princes, beautiful princess
With proffered hand that never shook
Offered hope with only a look
All the world applauds you, lauds you
All the world mourns you.

A golden wedding that never reached its age
A royal existence that became a cage
Charity worked within you, a help to aid
With land of mine, you were truly ours
A crash that shook the world
Like Helena in Paris' tunnelled towers
Escorted from your palace
Your glowing way adorned with flowers.
Beauty, poise and elegance
Humanity of a human bright
Stars still shine in candlelight.
A flame still burns your ashes
Scattered by the wind.

The last of August
And the beginning of September
Which, like many others,
For my own reasons
I will always, remember.

Paul Wright

SONNETS TO THE SEASONS: (1) SPRING AWAKENING

Spring is still drowsy from his winter dream.
He opens one eye to survey the scene.
Soon now he will busy himself once more,
Sprinkling his magic on the forest floor.
Multiplying all the shades of green and
Adding a sparkle to the rippling stream.
The mighty sun will heed his yearly call
For help, to warm and nourish nature's all.
Buds revealing brilliant hues awaken,
Cold winter beds will soon be forsaken.
The animal kingdom, when roused and keen,
Will play its part in the ravishing scene.
The alchemy of spring will be complete
And Earth will be replenished and replete.

Elizabeth Atkinson

ROCK 'N' ROLL

What's been and gone is dead 'n' buried,
But one thing remains true.
A trusty constant which never worried,
With a six string in view.
The drugs supplied, inspiration increased,
Departure is guaranteed.
Thrash your world, kill the beast,
Devotion sure to bleed.
Support your passions to the end,
As the journey takes its toll.
For certain we share a mutual friend,
Together as one, long live rock 'n' roll.

Jason L Wolf

THERE'S A CORNER OF MY GARDEN

There's a corner of my garden
That's my favourite place to be
I snuggle in my comfy chair
And think that I am free.

A fir tree tall towers over me
And makes me feel so small
That sometimes I pretend
I'm not really there at all.

In my imagination I'm in
Some far flung land
Playing on the beach
Or digging castles in the sand.

When summer sun caresses me
And keeps me snug and warm
I look around my garden
And admire my new mown lawn.

The flowers in my border
Each smile as if to say
We hope that you appreciate
Our colourful array.

What bliss to muse, to dream,
When not a word is spoken
As not long now I know
The silence will be broken.

For there's a corner of my garden
That's my favourite place to be
And from the kitchen comes a voice,
'Mum, I'm home, so what's for tea.'

Anne Solti

A HAPPY NEW YEAR

The festive season has come to an end,
The last carol has been sung,
The trimmings and cards all taken down,
Walls bare where they have hung,
We have put the beautiful angel away,
And the silver bells that ring,
Found room for all of the presents
Those new exciting things.

The sweet picture of children's faces,
To be seen on Christmas Day,
At the wonder, the mystery, the magic
Are memories here to stay.

We have danced away the old year,
With its pleasures and its pain,
And welcomed in another
To start anew again.

We've kissed relations,
Old and new friends
Thought of those we see no more,
And the dear departed loved ones
We shall meet at Heaven's door.

We'll relax now by the fireside
And think of sunny spring
To walk in the warm in the garden
'Midst the flowers
And hear the birds sing.

The rivers flow
The tide will turn
To link near and far-off shores,
How perfect if this year there would be,
No famine, no violence, no wars,
But ordinary people, such as me,
Must just say, what will be will be,
Let's not forget the wonder,
Of Christmas, the greetings, the love,
Just spread feelings of friendship every day
And follow the star from above.

June Dixon

REACHING EIGHTY

I can't believe I'm eighty
Is it really true?
The years fly by so quickly
I don't know what to do.
I look into the mirror
And see the wrinkles there
So I slap on a bit more powder
And then I don't really care.
I love my sequence dancing
On Tuesdays every week
When I turn around I wobble a bit
And then trip over my feet!
My hearing is not too good now
My eyes are growing dim
But I've got determination
And I know that I will win.
My memory is quite good though
I remember things from long ago
But what I did last Wednesday
I really do not know.
But it's very nice to see you all
I'm so pleased you are here
We will have another celebration
For my ninetieth year!

Lilian King

I Was Only . . .

I sat in the 'no smoking' room (that really is a joke:
The smell of burnt tobacco was enough to make you choke.)
And heard a smoker mumble when he knew that he'd been seen:
'I was only getting coffee from the drink vending machine.'

Three ashtrays full of dogends made a sickening display,
All left around by somebody, but no one cleared away.
Someone else with fag in hand, (the other held a cup)
Said, *'I was only waiting for the toaster to pop up.'*

They can't see the 'no smoking' signs; but then that's no surprise,
With faces all screwed up because the smoke gets in their eyes.
And then another puffer said, 'It shouldn't bother you!
I've nearly finished this *and I was only passing through!'*

And yet another lady, blowing smoke rings in the air,
Was flustered and embarrassed to be spotted standing there.
And when she looked around at all the signs that she'd ignored
Said, *'I was only looking at what's on the noticeboard.'*

I went round to the doctor's with a nasty wheezing cough.
He said, 'Cut down your smoking or you'll never shake it off.'
That really got my dander up; by then I was just seething.
'Now look 'ere mate! Don't you blame me. *I was only breathing!'*

Dennis W Turner

Thinking Of Tomorrow

Let's climb up the green hill
and play with the golden ball
which holds the magic of tomorrow.

Let's spread our arms like wings
and chase the shadows of the clouds
which bring the rain for tomorrow.

Let's run into the valley
and shout into the wind
which gives us gusto for tomorrow.

Let's listen to the echoes
and let our words and deeds
not trouble our friends tomorrow.

Helga Hopkinson

Poetry

In a world of many poets,
Authors, novelists and critics,
It may surprise you to know
That very few
(If any)
Know
The meaning of poetry.
Is it really rhymes and rhythms;
Antonyms and alliteration;
Synchronisation of stanzas;
Words in the shapes of objects of subjects?
Does a poem need similes for success?
Do words need to take hours to find?
Or should poetry be a mirror of something inside?
Does increasing your average word length
Increase your creative ability?
Can poetry be just one line?
Or does it have to be many?
Which makes you the better author:
A degree in regurgitating texts
(So you know where to find a quote from a story)
Or knowing the answer
To the question,
'What is poetry?'

Charlotte A Penney

Hats

Ammana, Bowler, Cocktail too
Derby, Easter and a Fedora of blue
Put on a Garbo or a Bobbled Hat
A Kalpak to go with a fancy cravat.

A Liberty, Mandel and a Night Cap
A Panama for a handsome chap
A Raffia should fit your head
Or maybe you could buy a Shako instead!

A Trilby and a Velour Felt
I hope it's not made of animal pelt
A Widow's Peak should look fine
Or a Yarmulke for £9.99.

A Zucchetto sounds very posh
But does it go with your mackintosh?
Now I ask you to think it through
Do any hats begin with I, J, O, Q or U?

Pattie Lopez

Recipe For Encouragement Cake

Weigh out a portion of visits
Mix with encouraging words
A few drops of smiling essence
Flavour with a card or two
Moisten the cake with prayers
Put all ingredients together
Mix well with a help
The best ingredient is . . .
God's healing touch.
Put in the oven
Full of love and trust
For the rest of our lives
God will guide us through.

Gladys Bartley

Malvern Hills

They lie in dormant majesty across the flattened plain:
A landmark for all eyes to see - a memory to remain.
They rise defiantly and proud, and dominate the scene;
Then, blanketed by mist and cloud, they could have never been.
A stranger passing by below in lowering weather's pall
Would miss the view and never know that they were there at all.
But how impressive are those hills when climbing to the heights
On winding paths, by running rills, and nature's sheer delights;
By wild growths of the countryside like willow herb and gorse;
The bracken like a flowing tide on an uncharted course.
The wandering sheep on grassy slopes, sure-footed as they tread,
Go grazing where a human's hopes capitulate in dread.
How vast the panoramic view when seen from higher peaks;
It seems to lift one's heart anew - grants solace that it seeks.
The mass of heather outward spread creates a purple glow;
The golden bracken, dry and dead, before the winter snow.
How picturesque the winter hills all clothed in dazzling white;
With sky of azure blue it fills the heart with pure delight.
Each hill by its own name is known, from 'North' to 'Chase End Hill',
'Midsummer', 'Hangman's', 'Ragged Stone', to name a few at will.
The hills that have for aeons stood in undulating line,
Have witnessed times both bad and good, and weather
fierce and fine.

Epitome of timelessness, a focal point for all,
A refuge from life's strain and stress, the hills will never pall.

H John Griffin

VALUED FRIENDS

They met each week, Emily and Grace,
Old friends of many a year.
In summertime they'd walk in the park
Beneath the trees and blue sky.

Winter they met in their cosy homes
Away from the biting winds,
With a cup of tea, a cheery chat
And newly made home baked cakes.

They loved to take an armchair journey
All along Memory Lane,
Where they enjoyed each other's good times,
Shared the sorrows of the bad.

The path revealed so many treasures
Too numerous to record,
But deep in their hearts they cherished them
As one would a special gift.

Before they parted from each other,
They offered a little prayer
That God's eternal love be with them
And thanks for making them friends.

Elsie Birch

FRIENDSHIP

I walked with him to help him start his journey home,
He preferring company of sky and tree
To diesel fumes and apathy.
We didn't say a lot; didn't need to speak at all.
Our minds were quiet sufficiency, a union of sentiment
And love fused long ago in plenary communion and reverie.

And at the bend I stood to watch his loneliness recede -
Leaving mine to sour and spoil.
I saw the hesitation, then his arms upraised in salutation,
His au revoir in silhouette against the winter sky - and
Thought . . . *Dear God - if he should go now; if he should die,*
If he should die; this final canvas will display forever
In the gallery of my mind an etching from a time recurring;
A broken stylus scratching endlessly.

If he should die - if he should die,
He would stand forever painted in the sky.
A small sad figure in the dusk, held for all eternity . . .

And I could only stare - and cry - and cry.

Frank Dickinson

CELEBRATIONS

Last night I stood on Seaford Head
        And watched a bonfire lit
            To celebrate the jubilee.
It was a lovely sight.

At first the sky was rosy-red
        Reflecting in the sea
            And then the moon appeared
And everything was bathed in white.

Below me was the town
        Ablaze with lights
            As the procession wended its way along the front
With flaming torches bright.

At ten a shot rang out
        And fireworks filled the air
            While music and laughter floated up from the fair.
It was a perfect night for celebrations and jubilations.

Ann Hubbard

REASONS FOR LIVING

My reasons for living, they vary so
Those special people that I know
My life it varies oh so much
Those loving friends, that tender touch

A certain plaque that bears my name
That came with that old Crawley fame
My special lads, my boys in blue
They want to arrest me, for charity too

Some friends, they pass in car or coach
Sometimes a cuddle when they approach
Each day as I walk down the town
Those loving smiles, but sometimes a frown

For things I know are not always good
Which makes us feel like touching wood
Each day I say a little prayer
And thank someone who's always there

For I am blessed each and every day
All these things that come my way
And writing verses as I do
Hence these special words for you

Pam Chappell

NATURE'S WONDERS

What does nature mean to me?
It means so many things;
Flowers and trees and babbling brooks
And birds upon the wing.

It means the calmness of the fields,
The cottages and farms,
The beauty of wild flowers and trees,
Animals safe from harm.

It means the majesty of mountains,
With eagles soaring high,
With rivers, streams and waterfalls
Cascading down their sides.

It means peace and tranquillity
Away from poverty and strife,
And nature's greatest attribute,
The wonder of new life.

Who can fail to wonder
At this greatest gift of all?
It's sent with love
From God above
To be enjoyed by all.

Helen Perry

A TRIBUTE TO POETS

Now let us honour them from many shires
        Where circumstance has led their destined way,
Some through the hallowed halls of Oxbridge Spires,
        Others to labour's wheel each passing day.
From gifted birth endowed with lyric power,
        Creating forms from language they will bring
The rich artistic muse in life to flower,
        Experience taking flight on poet's wing.
Such gems they give to us in measured verse,
        Expressing beauty, sadness, joy or pain.
These poets that are blessed by Mother Earth
        Deserve a lasting tribute and acclaim,
And in our generation they have come.
        Crown them with laurel wreaths for verse well done.

John Wilson Smith

How The Auricula Came To England In The 18th Century

Coom on lad mek thissen at wum,
Ah conna say thi name or t'town as weer tha's frum,
Ah'm towd as t'Dutch an t'Frenchies out beyond wor sea
Won't let thee worship God in t'way as pleases thee.
Wiv geet wor problems here tha knows in wor pleasant land,
But mek thissen at wum an happen us'll understand.
We've woods and pastures and a kirk set reet upon yon hill.
Near a bonny trout filled brook weer larks are fain to trill.
Ah've nay master me, ahm a freeman an do ply me days,
In mekkin up at wum, in the weavin ways,
An Middleton will tek you Flemmies to its heart,
Ad happen learn t'secrets of thy silk mekkers art.
Them calls this Happy Valley, folks as live here knows,
That herbs an trees an corn in wild abundance grows,
We've even geet wild Bears Head but I'm not perticlar,
Its non so braw as t'flower tha browt, one tha calls ariculer,
Reminds thee of thi Flemish Land does yon bonny flower?
Like thee its bin uprooted an yet it has the power,
To tell of sun-filled pleasant days that thee spent at wum,
And of the vagrant through thi faith that thas now become.
Tek heart dear friend plant thi weed,
And plant thi own roots too, raise thi seed,
Tha'll see as how life's a meddlin game,
Summat good will come fra pain,
In years to come sithee, see this thi adopted land,
Will grow yon flower and folks'll understand.
We opened up our hearts to thee in thi troubled hours,
And thee became an Englishman like yon bonny flowers.

John Burton

Give Us Lord

Give us Lord the right to the sun
    Enough work and a little fun -
Companionship, a little cheer
    To let us know you are always near,
Give us health to do your wish
    Let us share our sorrow -
    To make us strong to face the tomorrow,
You give us so many things to please
    I see you Lord in all of these things.

Give us the will to spare a moment
    Give us the strength to love and care -
To comfort the weak and the lonely
    Someone's sorrow to share,
For friendly deeds are priceless
    Like being able to utter a prayer,
By giving thoughts to others
    And the kindly things you do -
Strange how often in the future
    Kindness turns to you.

God's friendship does not fade away
    Like sunbeams in the sky -
It spreads and blossoms on the way
    Grows strong as time goes by,
It makes Him sad to see the way we live
    But true to His love and kindness
    He will always say, 'I forgive',
Teach us Lord to be like You
    Holy, brave, wise and true,
To do our best for You and others
    Till all men learn to live as brothers.

John Leighton

Just Doggerel

I am an aspiring poet,
I spend a lot of time
Juggling sentences in my head
To create bits of rhyme.

I'll never be a real poet -
Just a poetaster;
There'll never be a bust of me
Carved in alabaster!

I'll never be a Tennyson,
A Wordsworth or a Yeats;
The only acclaim I receive
Is from a few kind mates.

My loyal wife insists my rhymes
Are attempts quite gallant,
But secretly I'm sure she feels
I have little talent.

I've had a few efforts published,
Some in the Daily Mail,
But I doubt my literary works
Will boost their daily sale.

Sometimes my humble submissions
Are sent back, rejected.
I must confess when that occurs
I feel quite dejected!

It's said of the great McGonagall,
By critics of his verse,
That of all the world's known poets
There can be no one worse.

Yet most of his Asian readers
Think there's no work finer,
So, perhaps to be successful
I should move to China!

Arthur Allen

The Hand Of Fate

Forty-five years ago, we met at a dance
That was the beginning of a lifetime romance.

You were the one who stood out in a crowd
You were always so organised, so very well disposed
You made me the man I am today; How goodness
Only knows, you touched the hearts of those you knew

There is a picture on the wall, our son is by our side
I look, and in remembering the tears I cannot hide
We lost our son in eighty-one, our pride and joy
A handsome boy, just eighteen years of age.

Our lives have never been the same since nineteen eighty-one
The hand of fate has squeezed from us a reservoir of tears,
In eighty-five our lives took another dive -
My dear wife took a stroke

Fifteen years of nursing and care, wheeling my loved one about
In a wheelchair, my thanks to all carers and to those who care,
To Robert, my brother and Margaret his wife
Who looked after Moira when I needed care

I underwent surgery, a triple bypass by all accounts
I should not have been here but I prayed to the Lord
And I guess He did hear, for with Moira my wife
We shared another few years

Now Moira is gone and I am on my own.
Say a prayer for all loved ones should you read my poem
Throughout the heartache the tears and the pain
I truly believe we will all meet again.

Alexander Grozier

AN ALTERNATIVE CHRISTMAS

With pencil poised, his thoughts amok
Unheeding eyes upon the clock,
He dreamed of trains and all things fast, of signal boxes and at last
His mum had said, 'Well, write it down,
Just make a note and don't forget Ben's sailing boat,
And Hesta's crib and doll with bib - she's only three, you see,
And Grandpa's scarf for when it's cold,
We must take care, he's getting old.'
He licked the lead and tentatively began to spell
A train for me, a scarf for Gramps,
A signal box - perhaps some lamps?
A boat for Ben to sail to sea, a doll for Hesta, she's only three.
How'd you spell kite, with lots of string?
Dad said that would be the very thing
To have hung up in his stocking.
His eyes were glazed, his dreams afloat,
No one heard that ominous note,
That ominous hum, that drone -
That drear that normally would hold such fear
Of things that fly by night or day,
The things you wish would go away
No one heard.
The night has gone, the shadows passed,
Christmas Day is here at last.
The sun shines on the glistening snow,
On footprints running to and fro,
The sound of voices seem to grate the sad despair -
'We are too late'
The eerie calmness settles down
On the little house at the edge of the town,
A scarf flies sadly - a kite flies free -
A crumpled doll hangs in a tree
For Hesta - she was only three.

June Johnson

NIGHT JOURNEY

Late night transport
From the city
Steady traffic
Open roads

Ever changing
Neon colours
Kaleidoscope
Suburbs pass

Blinding headlights
Blink and dazzle
Ever moving
Rain or shine

Lines of red lights
Cars, vans, lorries
Leading onward
Up a hill

Where:

A beautiful vista of orangy balls
Never-endingly shrinking to dots in the dark
Freezes time . . . till . . .

Open country
Then our village;
Lighted windows
Just rushed past

No more dreaming
We've arrived now
With reluctance
I get out.

Dorothy

FORGIVE US . . .

I sat and watched the screen,
Gazing with horror at the sight
Of that great, angry, howling mob
Screaming for blood and full of hate.
Are these all husbands, fathers, sons?
Were they once men, had they once loved?
These kicking, clawing creatures, who
Surround their victims, thirsting now
For blood; are these your children, Lord?
And then, within my mind,
I saw another thronging crowd
From long ago, and I could hear
Them screaming, 'Crucify the Man',
Hatred and rage distorting all
Their faces, turning them to beasts.
'How could they treat You so, my Lord?'
I cried, then, as I watched, I clearly saw
Myself amidst the mob.

Margaret Wensley

OUR HOUSE

Our house is empty now
And quiet and still
Once it was full of life
Noise, music, laughter
Feet up and down the stairs, doors banging
Young voices late into the night
All that is over now
All that is ended now
Return it never will

The relics are still here
There on the sill
The Matchbox cars that were
His pride and joy
Her furry rabbit with the well-chewed ear
Her books and pens, his favourite toy
Those days are over now
Those days are ended now
Return they never will

Our house is empty now
They've gone away
And though they may return
From time to time and stay
In this old house that was their childhood home
No more noise, music, laughter
All that is over now
All that is ended now
All that was yesterday

Estelle James

THE HIPPOCRATIC OATH

Light the candle in the dark.
Invite the wind,
- See the flame dance.

Lighten your heart with love.
Invite adversity,
- Watch the flame grow.

Lightning in the storm.
Invite courage,
- Look, the flame lives.

Enlightening your naivety.
Invite knowledge . . .
- Behold! The flame becomes you.

Morag Maciver

IS IT YOURSELF, OR NOT?

Is it yourself, or not?

Ask Mr Jameson
A close friend of Paddy,
Uncle to Long John,
And the half breed,
Jack Daniels,
Who are Teachers.

Is it yourself, or not?

Ask my old grandad
And his good friends,
Baileys and Johnny Walker

Is it yourself, or not?

Ask Mr Grouse
Who likes to hide in the Bushmill,
On the Glenfiddich.
Where the Bells ring out.

Is it yourself, or not?

Don't ask me, I'm too drunk to see.
Is it yourself, or not?
Can't you see, it's only me!

Patrick Mannion

THE DEVIL'S DISCIPLES

Why does each man, hand on heart
Try his best to play his part?
To do the things he knows he should
Gets thwarted or misunderstood.

His enemy has a quiet advantage
As through the world he causes rampage.
Each hand is turned against another
He even turns men against each brother.

The men in power are in his hands
Not humble hearts, but men of sand
For these are held within his pay
These ones so grand, with feet of clay.

Corruption walks through every door
No standards, make an uneven floor
Then rocky beams make walls askew
He planned it all, he slyly knew.

For men of clay or made of straw
Can never from his grasp withdraw
These leaders of the world conspire
To guide us by what he requires.

No moral stance or direct course
All speaking with a muted voice.
Towards the abyss of extinction's wave.
Plunged headlong like a willing slave.

This power is strong and none will see
That by him they will cease to be
For he conducts the puppet strings
And orchestrates all earthly things.

Distraction is his only ploy
Entraps the unwary, man or boy
And hate or jealous thought he flames
Then watches man, each other blames.

The Devil's secret subtle ways
Have lead mankind from early days
For he has power to rule mankind
And many helpers he can find.

Kathleen Earle

'UNREQUITED' LOVE . . .

There is within my heart and mind,
an inner sanctum, a secret vault
. . . wherein no soul has permit.
This is as it ever has been,
secure and sound without.
Until the loveliest key of beauty
entered unseen
but with presence felt and lay me
victim upon mine own alter.
Thus I am now sacrificed
to the *God* of carnal desire.

Blighted now is objective thought,
and this replaced by wishful yearning
for *you* have done this thing to me
and set my cathedral burning.
Are you but enemy or are you friend?
Is this a beginning or is it an end
to purity of thought and blissful learning
or is it the start of a heart that's turning . . . ?

Throughout this heart's cloistered chambers
a fiery torment of unrequited love
pours scorn upon so fierce a passion,
and cries out for the sacrifice of pride,
not conformity of fashion.
Now demands a turning
of the tide of logic whose waves crash
with mighty force
upon this coward's door.

I should demand affection's entry
by order of my heart's desire
or be so much branded by its roaring fire
and then with scorched exterior and
burning face of shame,
cry penance for my weakness
and carry all the blame.

Now with conviction spent I am but hollow be,
and with anguished yearn within my mind
hope that you can see,
that in this world of 'what could have been',
never will I find,
the courage to tell you right straight out,
what really ails my mind . . .

Alan Grainger

BONDING

It's good to bond, barring our natural doubts,
Our inherent reserve that British offhandedness normally dictates,
Because bonding brings order, not dissent.
It blends otherwise neutral dictums into a budding outwardly
                                                    new direction.
A direction we can all follow to blend ourselves neatly down,
Into the best office night and day.
Our aim should be to begin our next days with a blindingly orange
                                                    new dawn

That heralds a blissfully ordered new department.

Alan G Pike

JOK'S LOT

Pine cladding came crashing down from ceiling to floor
Followed by polystyrene and plaster galore
Up went the scaffolding, in came the skips
Frenzied activity, men changing shifts.

A sparkie with a gigantic drill
Tugged and pulled with incredible skill
The plasterer set forth with clean lines in mind
Sweated and swore with a lovely behind
The plumber with a serious face
Pulled out the old ware without leaving a trace
The carpenter, not one to be argued with
Demonstrated his skill and occasionally farted
In a war zone we struggled and tripped
Nourished by fruit cake and the odd bag of chips

Such a mixture of skills these guys had at their disposal
With some curses and swears and many new proposals.
British workers at their best they really do exist,

The noise was hell, mobiles ringing everywhere
Deliveries that didn't arrive on time
Walls in a state of decline
Gutters that spurted where they ought not
They overcame problems, the whole bloody lot
They came each day in all shapes and sizes
Managed by Jok, a man with many disguises.
They created beauty from a load of bricks
A place I call *home* and more than exist.

Gloria Hargreaves

THE SMILE

I saw the smile upon your face
Oh how it seemed to shine
I knew then as I know now
You were destined to be mine

Your smile it reassures me
Telling me you always care
Saying how much you love me
And for me you will be there

We both made a promise
That together we would stay
And as long as I can see the smile
My heart will never stray

The weeks have passed us by
Through the months and through the years
And our love it will continue
Of this I have no fear

Your smile it will always linger
There upon your face
The smile that brought me to you
No other will replace

Your eyes are always smiling
From out that lovely face
And may I always see the smile
That made my poor heart race

It was there when I first met you
When we wed you were aglow
And I knew then that you loved me
For your smile it told me so

Peter P Gear

GOLF . . . THEN AND NOW

I started golf when very young
Hickory cut down clubs . . . what fun
Seamed carpet in our hall for me
To practice putting straight and free.

The well-known Formby Ladies' Club
Where my mother paid her sub
Let members' children start the game.
Maybe in years could rise to fame.

On the course allowed to play
But always with my mum or dad they say.
To teach me how I must behave
Some simple rules to learn each day.

Don't drop your clubs . . . they leave a mark
Repair damaged fairways is the task
Tidy bunkers . . . leave them smooth
Don't drag your feet . . . they leave a bruise.

If slow or lost a ball in rough
Let those behind come through . . . you must
Then carry on and play your game
For slow play you will not take blame.

Leave your clubs beside the green and take your putter
Keep quite quiet . . . no sound to utter
Furthest from the hole to play
Mark your ball and lift if in the way.

Next stage has come . . . steel shafted clubs . . . so new
Big bag . . . no longer will the small one do
A handicap I have at last
May it improve . . . but not too fast.

St Andrew's course one sunny day
My junior putter sadly put away
Too small to judge a putt I am told
On mighty double greens so bold.

No trolleys for one's clubs as yet
Sometimes a caddie one can get
To tell you where you ought to play . . .
Suggest a club . . . oh happy day.

Golf today is changing fast
I really hope this trend won't last
Long shafted clubs at great expense
To hit the ball so far does not make sense.

Into the rough much further goes the ball . . .
When sliced or pulled in deepest rough to fall
Distance marks on fairways clear
To tell you if the green is far or near.

Many great and lovely courses can be found
But Links Courses are still renowned
St Andrews where it all began they say
Has pride of place and is worshipped still today

Jean Noble

DOGGEREL

The year was nineteen-thirty when depression ruled the land
The few odd coins that Mother had just slipped away like sand
No work for Dad and six to feed, left poor Mum in despair
She looked at me with worried eyes and said, 'Now Son, comb your hair
And off you go to the butcher's shop for two penn'orth of bones
                                        for the dog.'
I was eight years old and the only animal we had then was
                            a green and yellow frog
- But the larder was empty and I knew very well exactly what she meant
Cos the tuppence she gave me had come from the tin where she
                            used to save up for the rent
Clutching tightly the coins as I ran through the rain
'Two penn'orth of bones for the dog,' I said over and over again
Wet through and breathless I burst into the shop and then felt
                        a real nincompoop
As I looked the butcher straight in the eye and said - 'Two penn'orth
                        of bones - for the *soup!'*

David Merrifield

MY GRANDSON REECE: UNDER THE SPANISH SUN

Reece in his baseball hat and Bermuda shorts
Stood by the black iron gates.
Then he was walking up the long drive,
The white villa stood under the blazing Spanish sun.
'Come with me, Grandma, and I will show you the 'magic garden'.'
Hand in hand they walked under the hot sun,
The very young and the not so young,
Along the paths, up steps, down steps,
Along the flower borders, under the old olive trees,
Under the palm trees, past the pink and white oleanders
And bright purple bougainvillaea
Shedding their petals in the midday sun.
'We can have a picnic here, Grandma,
With all our friends!'
Looking down at the small boy, with a heart full of love
The grandmother wondered . . .
Would the grown man remember this walk
In the 'magic garden' under the Spanish sun?

Julie Charsville

DREAMS

I lay down on my lawn, replete with bread and wine,
A perfect middle in a perfect day, the house and
Grounds around me, models of perfection,
My horse is grazing in the field nearby.

'Twixt the sound of babbling brook and songbirds,
Comes the laughter of my children from the garden.
I wander back towards my house and see my darling
Wife, resplendent in her gown of purest white.

Could any man, I wonder, desire much more in life,
Than all that I see laid out before me? I wander
Through each room, along corridors and stairs,
Touching paintings, carpets, walls and statues.

I am woken from my dream by a screaming lager lout,
I reach out, and touch my cardboard walls,
The mansion I am in has paper carpets so very thin,
I can feel the cold invading every bone.

When you see a down 'n' out appearing sad 'n' scruffy,
Remember, he too aspires to greater things; but he
Confines his aspirations to the mansion
Of his dreams, as he thanks God for sleep,
To see the other side.

Kay Reynolds

PAINTED LADIES

(In memory of my parents Elizabeth and Harold Cape)

There's painted ladies everywhere,
They're in the house and up the stair,
Dancing and waltzing in the air,
Beautiful painted ladies.

Gorgeous colours all aglow,
Truly a splendiferous show,
You're really very nice to know
Exotic painted ladies.

It's twenty years since you last were here,
Could be twenty more before you next appear,
Where do you go in the intervening years?
You elusive painted ladies.

Flaunting your fluttering frillies high
You twist and turn up in the sky,
Flirting and chasing as time goes by,
You hussy, you painted ladies.

Halcyon winds gave you away days!
I've enjoyed watching you in your heydays,
But come the frost you'll be in the land of Hades,
My butterflies nymphean painted ladies.

Mary Elizabeth Cowburn

SEASONS

Do you ever imagine what life would be without seasons?
To wake up on a spring morning and feel that *blissful air?*
To notice the flowers peeping through
No matter how hard, they do not seem to care.
The evenings give us brightness and in return this gives us zest
To skip and jump as much as we dare!

Then we come to summer with holidays in view
Perhaps a trip abroad or just somewhere new
Again the longer evenings, the smell of barbecues with friends,
No time to feel miserable or blue.
What bliss to sit in a deck chair and feel the warming sun,
No wonder we feel so happy for holiday time is fun.

Then into autumn with slightly sombre days
The falling leaves the wonderful colours,
Gold, brown and many other shades
The harvest, what a joyous time,
The gentle breezes coming forth,
Such relaxation, to the end of a perfect day.

Then comes the dawning of the winter with its darkness and cold chills
Sometimes we can see the snow or top of the hills!
We spy the holly berries,
And we know that Christmas is coming near
We collect around the fireside and draw the curtains tight
We know it will be a long time before it's daylight

Each of us enjoy a season,
Maybe it's summertime -
But on reflection
We could not live with sameness all the time.

Eileen W O'Brien

THE HUNT

A little mouse came out one night
All day he hadn't had a bite.
He came before the lights were out,
When lots of people were about.
He couldn't wait another minute
His tummy needed something in it.

He came forth with intentions good,
All he wanted was some food.
He wasn't fussy what he'd eat,
He liked breadcrumbs, and cheese and meat.
He'd be content with what he found
Whatever had been left around.

But fate that night was so unkind
And not a morsel could he find
He searched around, but all in vain,
And then he searched around again.
And then, fate's final blow it seemed
A lady saw him and she screamed.

'A mouse! A mouse! Look! Over there!'
She cried out, as she grabbed a chair.
The mouse, he lifted up his eyes
And looked at her in mild surprise.
She threw a lid, but as she did,
Puzzled, he ran away and hid.

Very soon there was a rush
Of young men from all o'er the house.
One grabbed a hammer, one a brush,
Thus armed, they sought one little mouse.
But men weren't made for hunting mice,
And so they nearly caught him twice.

He, meantime, went back to rest
In the safety of his nest.
On sleep alone he couldn't thrive,
Still, at least he was alive,
And able once again to try it,
When everything was nice and quiet.

The men returned to where they'd been
The mouse was nowhere to be seen.
Still, when all was said and done
They'd had a rare amount of fun.
At least one hunter went home glad
Because the mouse his freedom had.

Tho' one of nature's pests are mice
Still I think they're rather nice.
And nature did provide a way
Of keeping even them at bay.
To combat the domestic mouse,
You need a pussy in the house.

Robert McIlveen

WOLVES OF THE HEART

Here they come
Those wolves
Paws pounding at the door
To my heart
Swiftly they pace
Stealth in human form
To pounce
Ripping my heart to shreds
Smiling as they do so

They have no idea
How it feels
To cower
Behind the walls
To protect ourselves
Terrified
One day
The wall will crumble
The mask will tumble
And we will be exposed

So, the wolves are here again
Almost forgotten, their presence taunts me
And I remember
All too well
Their actions and the anguish
I felt
The last time I smelt
Their scent in my heart

Tell me
That these wolves are not real
That they're really friendly dogs
And my imagination
Is playing tricks on me

Tell me
I am safe
And secure
For once more
I see the wolves
Beckoning at my heart's door

For now I can see
That the one who protects me
From their fangs
Is the one who I welcome
Into my heart without reservation
Yet not without trepidation
But with a deep sense of yearning
For peace I know He alone can give

Clare M Ashton

STATE CIRCUS IN GROZNY, 1995

There was no advance publicity,
no rush for ringside seats
or dancing in the streets,
no festivity of the usual kind.
A blind man listening for silence
caught the first burst of fire;
felt alien vibrations through mean soles
open to cold and caution
painfully cobbled.
His part was to play Fool, the warm-up fellow
sent on before the main attraction.
Then came gladiators
omnipotent in elephantine tanks;
the chorus marching
well-practised patterns
co-designed off-stage
by generals in padded cells.
High flyers topped the bill,
needed no safety net,
met no opposition.
Dropping lethal cargo
with consummate skill - unasked,
they basked in midnight afterglow.

It was reported later by the press
that some spectators in their eagerness
had strayed too near
and suffered burns. Others froze,

forgot the words -
but ranged in strange
configurations on the ground,
made realistic extras, unsolicited
and unrehearsed. Those cursed
in blackened balcony and pit,
huddled thinly in their hurt, bit
avidly on rotting bread
and prayed for curtain call.

After a long run, diminishing
houses and a changing cast,
the show left town.
Behind, bereft, in ragged line,
like ghoulish clowns, stood
white-faced children
streaked with blood.

Josie Davies

THE NAZARENE

One morning I woke with a sense of well-being
a dream I had of the Nazarene.
These are the words he spoke to me:
'Pick up your cross and follow me.'

'Lord, you know it's not easy to bear
the weight of a cross in the depths of despair.
I know I rarely spoke Your name
but I believed in You just the same.

The road was long and weary for me
and the cross, it was too heavy for me,
You know I fell along the way,
Lord, where were You when I called You that day?

I called You once, I called You twice
Lord I called You thrice, why did You not answer my prayer?'
And the Nazarene gave pause for thought
and these are the words He had to say:

'My child, My child, when the burden became too heavy for you
it was I who picked up your cross, and carried you.

Margaret Ackerley

ARRAN OF SCOTLAND

Above the vapours, towering high
A misty island seems to touch the sky
It rises silent, bleak and cold
Till sunshine brings a touch of gold,
Where now the purple heather grows
A sparkling waterfall there flows.
High above where 'Goat Fell' stands
A swooping eagle swiftly lands,
He watches o'er sure-footed sheep
Which climb up high on paths so steep
And Scottish cattle, long-haired and horned
Majestic stags with antlers adorned.

Tall pine woods slope down to the lochs
Where basking seals stretch on the rocks
They know not trouble, have no care
As they swim and fish in the pure fresh air.
On opposite bank white cottages gleam
And an old ruined church on the hillside is seen.
Above is a castle with a wonderful view
Over well cared for gardens of colourful hue.
There's peace on this island and its beauty I love
For all nature's glory is God's gift from above.
Rain sparkles like diamonds and glints on the firs
Then the magical arch of a rainbow appears.

Up mountain paths I love to stride
Looking down from the crag tops to the rippling tide
Above float the cumulus so snowy-white
I watch them drift by the brilliant light.
The splendour of Arran - how I value its worth
This glimpse of a miniature heaven upon Earth

As I leave on the ferry I look back at the foam
And my thoughts still linger as I return to my home
For my heart is on Arran and there it will stay
I will long for this island for many a day
I *know* I'll come back - again and again
To its peace and tranquillity - no suffering or pain
My island of dreams, I love you so
Your spectacular scenery, your hills high and low
How carefree the people who roam near 'Goat Fell'
They do not need cities in which to dwell,
But I cannot stay with you as time passes by
From my own life's commitments I cannot fly
But when I am old and my worries are past
May I rest in a heaven just like Arran at last

Enid Hewitt

BLUE DANCERS

Battered and torn slippers lay face down on the floor
They are worn at the toes, they don't dance anymore
Their soft white satin has greyed and they are jaded
Memories of flight and their dance have all but faded

The ribbons are still plenty and shift with the dust
Crevasses and cracks beckon a shrill, wintry gust
Tinged and ravaged edges make a spidery trail
Sighing fluttery breaths with each remnant of gale

Exhuding a fine aura of rich porcelain and grace
Her white hair taut and disciplined sculpts her fine face
Blessed with a marriage of elegance and sheer skill
Borne from her passion, her greatness and iron will

A breath of true beauty sits in a lifeless room
Alone, save two images mounted in the gloom
Degas and his dancers add tone with subtle hue
Girls fixing their shoes, a cherished 'Dancers in Blue'

She pulls in her shawl as a gesture to the fire
A poker commands flames to rise even higher
She smoothes out her petticoats, warming hands and skirt
After gathering it up to avoid soot and dirt

A cold ache embraces a cushioned walnut chair
She looks at the shoes made to glow in a vibrant air
Almond eyes grow heavier as if in a trance
Closed eyelids shelter echoes of her life and dance

She falls into her dream where the slippers waken
From the floor satin shoes rise; no steps are taken
White powdered dust is caught in a poetic stream
Billowing outwards to the ballet in her dream

Ripples of silk spiral in the movement of air
Accompanied by the fireside's flickering stare
Slippers pirouette between glowing ember
Crimsoned flames' warmth causes them to remember

Lengths of warmed ribbon trailing slippers in the air
Brush past the ballerina asleep in her chair
Her body stirs but she is loathe to awaken
Lest her enchantment is stolen; slowly taken

Her exquisite face is young again for a while
A head of black hair lowers with a bow and smile
Breaking free from her shawl, arms sinewy and sprite
Form a grandiose arch by a luminous light

As coals turn to ashes in a cast iron grate
A warm glow descends on a dancer and her fate
It caresses cold fingertips streaming in light
A cocooned ballerina is lifted to flight

No questions are ever asked, there are no answers
But mystery shrouds Degas and his blue dancers
The painting is different, radiantly new
There is another dancer in his 'Dancers in Blue'.

Anita Maina Kulkarni

PRAYER FOR THE LOST

It started with an earthquake,
Deep beneath the sea,
No one saw it coming,
Or the horror it would be.

It tore into the land,
Destroying in its path,
Laughing happy people,
It took them in its wrath.

Pray for all the lost,
For those destined to stay,
Taken by the waves,
Where forever they will lay.

Fathers, mothers, daughters sons
Family generations lost,
Survivors deep in sorrow,
They cannot count the cost.

A brief moment in time,
It left flattened and bare,
Where once stood a village,
Now, nothing is there.

Disasters are brought home to us,
More vivid than in the past,
The press, the news, the pictures,
Leaving images that last.

Survivors who are homeless,
Who've lost everything they own,
The children who are orphans,
We weep, they cry alone.

There's a ritual we go through,
I have done it too,
Kiss the cold brow of loved ones,
This they cannot do.

Our human genes tell us,
We have to say goodbye,
No forensics can compensate,
For holding loved ones nigh.

For all our human failings,
Whatever faith or creed,
When disaster strikes so many,
We all give for those in need.

So let us pray together,
For all the souls who've passed,
Into the realms of Heaven,
They may all find peace at last.

Pray also for those who weep,
God hear them, as they mourn,
Only time can be a healer,
Grant them, one day, a new dawn.

Anne E Hutchinson

ROOTS

Cobbled streets and fields of corn
I remember them well
I was only a lad
And though times were bad
I learned how to read
And to spell

Fancy things
Were never a part
Of our lives
In the village
I knew
There was only
The factories
And coal mines
And they became
Life's view
It was only
One small village
But there were
Others too
And though the people
Were friendly
There was a lot
More to life
I knew

There are other places
Across the sea
With far-off lands
Where I dreamt
I would be

I would live
Like a king
In a palace
Of gold
And stand
Tall and proud
And speak out bold

There would be no
More digging
In darkness
For coal
I would leave that behind
For this was my role

It was nice to dream
I could fly away
If only for a moment
Or just one day

But the cobbled streets
And fields of corn
Beckon me back
To the place
I was born

Eddie Jepson

THE DANCING KILLER

Beautiful,
Sleek,
Splendour,
Some might say seductive,
Yet, when needs be,
Very destructive.

This bird of
Land,
Sea
And sky
Flying higher,
Still higher,
Being flown
By the wire.

Your hot breath
Makes the summer air
Shimmer
As you give a deep-throated roar of welcome,
Making my eardrums rattle, tingle, thump and thunder.
I become
A member of your
Ear-splitting,
Breath holding,
Eyes not quite believing,
Audience.

Sunlight catches your silver wing tip,
Giving it the look of fire
As you dance,
Nose to nose,
Coupled partners,
Man and machine,
Demonstrating
That without governmental dictated hostility
You have the ability
To perform a ballet duet of the sky,
At the end to bow

Then turn and hover,
Your beauty for some reason
Makes me eerily shiver,
The reason being
That when you are not that skyward dancer,
Playful duet partnered prancer,
You are a bomb laden,
Computerised,
Human partnered killer.

Neill Cadmore

THE PAWN SHOP

Some of the things which people did in days that are now gone by
You'd think that this particular thing would make you want to cry
You couldn't really cry at this, for it's actually rather funny
Some of the things that people did to get their hands on money.

While this wee man was roon the back, tidying up the lawn
His wife was hurrying doon the street heading for the pawn
It was only a couple of weeks ago she pawned his guid blue suit
This was her going back again to try and fetch it oot.

Some folk would pawn near anything, even a pair o'laces
There was this wee lassie up the road, she pawned her faither's braces
Her auld man got up wan morning, said, 'I'm going shopping
                                                    in the toon
Good God, a canny do that, ma troosers are faw'n doon.'
'That's alright,' the daughter replied, 'I've got quite a knack
Just give me a couple o' bob Dad, and I'll get yir braces back.'

An honest boy went in the pawn with a lovely silver spoon
'I don't want much money,' he said, 'just give me half o croon.'
Then, quite a wealthy man went in, looking for a clock,
'Well, take yir pick,' the lady said, 'I've quite a few in stock.'

Maggie McKay took her watch aff - 'My goodness, this watch
                                                    is getting old
A think I'll take it doon the pawn,' she said, 'see if I get it sold.'
'Wait a minute,' her husband replied, 'don't go doon yersell
I'll go doon alang wi ye and we'll pawn ma watch as well.'

The funny auld lady who owned the pawn
Her face was covered all over in blotches
Though, that was the least of her worries
Her hoose was full of auld watches
The husband rarely left the hoose, always there on guard,
So anyone trying to break in would find it awful hard.

Well, that's a story aboot the place where people went a lot
Some of their partners would wait ootside to see how much they got.

James Murray

THE LOCKET

The silver locket that you gave to me
  threw upon the bed,
The engraved words, 'I Love You', racing round my head.
  remembered the dinner on the terrace,
The candlelight, the promises, the sunset over the sea.
But they just serve as a reminder of all you meant to me.

should have known it wouldn't last
When you promised me forever.
Forever is a long, long time when the same two people stay together.
And for all your romantic gifts,
The charming ways
And idyllic days,
You hid your heart away from me
And I clung to the hope faithfully
That one day you would present it,
Gift-wrapped and candlelit.
But all I got was a heart-shaped locket,
All prettily wrapped in blue.
The locket was as cold as ice.
As cold as ice, as cold as you.

Nicola Jade Poulton

MAGIC CIRCLES

A magic dream I'll tell of from mediaeval times.
In Europe, I'll say the region was,
No matter where, what country;
'Tis not a subject of debate in death's larger entry.

It was a time when religion held bold sway
In time's space starkly perceived
Outside imagination's range in holy mist;
For itself, the image in the dream let it exist.

In this tale the theme, if obscure, is necromancy.
The maid's eye within the dream is locked in prayer,
Shut like her person in a static mode
True to its own idyllic code.

In the dream the circles wax then wane
To the rhythm of a drum that frightens
Her, our grieving maid; for in its pulse she hears an echo
Of her mother's death, a palpitating shadow.

Why do shadows change their shape? she wonders.
Death feigning bizarre movement
In a troubled sleep
Where phantoms of the wretched creep?

Surrounded by a troupe of dancing women,
The girl, amazed, turns round to face the phantom drum,
As reluctant circles evanescent go.
She screams. Why is she frightened so?

The women diverted by her scream
Interchange with a group of men alerted.
They dance in sorrow to a muffled drumbeat slowly.
She can see the outline dim of the circles only.

Through broken arcs, an apparition's found.
Her mother back from the dead she hoped,
Watching the dream landscape filter light
Out of shadows in the night.

She was sorely troubled, this maiden fair,
When she rose betimes in her mediaeval bower.
To her cassocked priest she let her confession unfold,
Asked what hidden meaning her dream might hold.

He, perplexed at first, but curious in his gaze,
Requested some little pause to stake out the dream,
Then said such contradiction at best
Had to be Heaven's sanction put to the test.

The soul at death would be doomed forsooth
Either to everlasting punishment
Or indeed to everlasting bliss.
Who knows? A conflict there was in this!

Perchance the grieving daughter, said he,
In her troubled spirit felt
A pressing need for penance true;
Hence in her dream this restless dance in lieu.

With that, his bony hand outstretched
Was held out for due recompense.
No scruple in his devout office had he
About charging our distraught maid a fee.

With bell, book and candle at his command
Sir Priest saw things with a magician's eye,
Crafting truth from purpose at need;
Sowing, by your leave, the sorcerer's creed.

She wondered, *could the magic circles
Be the same nine circles of Hell in Dante's 'Inferno'?*
Of one thing she felt passing sure;
Her life, tested, would be her mother's evermore.

Angus Richmond

Tsunami 2004

Who would have thought it at the end of the year
That the earth would quake and cause suffering and fear?
Earthquakes are common in parts of the world
Rumbles and trembles like hatred unfurled
But what of the quake from under the sea
That did its worst so suddenly?
The fate of all was out of control
Unsuspectingly shattered by the blast of a hole
The climate at Christmas in these parts of the land
Is warming, desirable, with sun and sand
Places that beckon to folk who may
Like to get away for a holiday
Who would have thought it when all was well
That this thing could happen and cause such hell?
Can we really envisage the severity
Of this terrible, terrible tragedy?
Complete destruction causing loss of life
Men desperately searching for a lost wife
No respect for persons or quality
As dear ones were swept out to sea
Life itself swept away
At the end of the year on this fateful day
Screaming and panic as folk realised
What was happening before their eyes
A wall of sea with a rage and a roar
Bringing sudden death to life's door
So many folk swept away
On that dreadful, fateful day
What is left behind is devastation
With grief and sorrow of the nation
Dear God, comfort them in their grief and pain
That this terrible thing will not happen again
Draw close to those left with despair
Who have lost their all and are full of care
Lord, bless all the lives who unwittingly
And unsuspectingly came home to Thee
Grant them peace in their heavenly home
Where their suffering and pain has been overcome
Draw close and comfort those left behind
That their faith may be strengthened and they will find
New hope for their lives with the surety
That their loved ones are safe in eternity.

Evelyn A Evans

The Valiant Few

In 1940, the skies over England were blue
That summer, when the valiant few
With Spitfires and Hurricanes took to the skies
To guard our shores, the future looked dark
The German invasion seemed so near at hand
To threaten the peace of this beautiful land
With 'We'll Meet Again' and 'That Lovely Weekend'
To sweethearts and wives with tear-filled eyes
They waved their goodbyes, those valiant boys
And made for the skies
Now 40 years on the Spitfires are gone
The young men (so bold) now have grown old
And the nightingale still sings in the park
The Germans, we managed to keep at bay
Now we trade with every day
For England they came and they'd do it again
So let's not forget as the years hurry by
When in summer you look up to the sky
So let us give thanks to God for the valiant few
Who saved this land when the skies were blue
For that 'freedom' cost so many young lives
Whom never came back to loved ones and wives.

Irene G Corbett

Celebration Terrestrial

January days are short with icy chill,
frosts lie hard upon the sill.
The gardens sleep with expectation,
awaiting the burgeoning vegetation.

February heralds in the snowdrop flowers,
while the earth is waking up to all her powers.
Green buds bursting through the soil,
while Jack Frost is tired with all his toil.

March, the bringer of winds and sleet,
crocuses stir beneath soil, then peep.
Bursting forth with refreshing flight,
as sunshine warms the sward with light.

April showers, cold then warm, then damp,
wet the fields bringing shoots to revamp.
Clothing the trees and hedges with green,
filling out the branches like a music routine.

May flowers bring in summer promises,
birdsong fills the air with a loud prominence.
Life is rushing forth with speedy headrush,
blackbird competing for rooftops with song thrush.

June is the start of summer weather,
bringing out the daisies under the heather.
Briar rose, cowslip, bluebell and clover,
colours awash in the meadows, all over.

In *July* ducklings swim and dive with mother,
rivers alive with fish, beetles, bugs and other.
Squirrels running along branch of elm,
collecting seeds and nuts around the realm.

August holidays bring healthy enjoyment,
before getting back to the usual employment,
long strolls along bridleway and beach,
sightseeing in places usually out of reach.

September fairs and harvest festivals,
with displays of succulent fruit and vegetables.
These bountiful gifts from God divine,
we offer in praise of benevolent summertime.

October chills give hints of what's to come,
as leaves spiralling to death, succumb.
Hoar frost touches branches white,
evening quickly changes to night.

November weather, dull, damp and sleet,
icy rain and big puddles in the street.
Mist and fog with shivering chills,
coughs and colds and winter ills.

December, dark days before Christmas,
bringing us once again to a genesis.
Bright lights and baubles adorn our trees,
we give thanks for all, upon our knees.

Joan Lister

ANNIE'S BIRTHDAY

It's Annie's birthday today, what ho!
Annie has reached the big 'six-o'.
The cards lie thickly on the mat,
Surrounded by Marmalade, her cat.
But where is Annie, the birthday girl?
Come on Annie, give us a whirl.
Ah, here she comes in her dressing gown,
But why is she giving the floor a frown?
This as she scoops her cards off the mat,
The frown, we believe, is meant for the cat.
'Get you outside, you lazy moggy,
Even if it is cold and foggy.
You won't stay very long out there, I know,
But in the meantime, sorry, out you go.'
In her kitchen she fills her kettle from a jug,
Gets off the shelf her favourite mug.
The parrot, beady-eyed with squawking voice,
Forces her to listen, she has no choice.
'Annie, you've reached your sixtieth, isn't it a pain?
Cos Annie, you'll never be fifty-nine again.'
'You horrid bird, now who taught you that?'
His answer: *'Annie, go and let in the cat.'*
Now how will she spend this precious day?
I'm sure that Annie will find a way.
Lunch with a friend or the latest trend,
In ladieswear and spend, spend, spend.
Up she goes to shower and dress,
The phone rings, a voice in dire distress,
Then a comforting voice, 'Don't worry Mr Brown,
Keep her warm in bed till I get round.'
Down she comes, stiff-uniformed, she grabs her case,
See that look of determination on her face.
Starting her car she heads for her first call,
For Annie is the town's community nurse,
And has been now for almost forty years.
'Retire,' she laughs, 'now who would take my place?
Yes my day is hard, but something I must face.
And this is the only way I want to spend today
And other birthdays that may come my way.'
Annie is one of a dedicated band
Who spend their lives just being there on hand.

Deva

THE INSIDER

Sat staid in sepia-tinted rooms
The old man gazes to the past,
With each and every memory
Disappearing oh so fast.

All that's left are flickering images
Playing on the neon tube,
Meaning lost in the frustration
Of modern youth's ingratitude.

The outsider sees no emotion
Play upon the weary face
And quickly rises to the thought
That this insider's run his race.

And then the touch of another's hand
Brings the tired man to life.
All fear is conquered by the love
Shown in a moment's light.

And as the briefest time remains
The inside man now comes alive,
And in the golden hour that's left
The child within him has survived.

Simon P Rossiter

MY FATHER

The terraced house on cobbled streets
Inspired him on to greater feats.
From muck and grime and taste in mouth
He took his Lo and ventured south.
A braver man might stop and wonder
But silent strength casts doubts asunder
And on he went 'til stopped by sea,
Where forests grew and air was free.

A man in tunic, strong and tall,
He had his frets, he beat them all
And every face a stranger there,
Were treated all with kindness, fair.
A love within his family,
He gave them all his dignity,
A smile, a laugh, an encouraging word
Like silent shepherd o' er his herd.

The island called, for evermore,
More friends to make upon that shore.
And each one treated just the same,
When down, he'd pick them up again.
Not brash, nor loud nor thumping chest,
He'd watch in silence as the rest
Would lose control as though insane,
And then he'd make things right again.

The seas cut rough, the winds they blew
But round the family fire we knew
A bond so strong to keep us safe,
His presence there a towering grace.
Young children, wives, were welcomed in
From near and far his kith and kin,
A listening ear, a twinkling eye,
For each he lifted spirits high.

To gardens, bowls and Status Quo
In flight to Tenerife they'd go
To watch the world, to love it all,
He'd take it in with warts an' all.
His laughter, fun, weren't far away,
They filled the room, and then the days
And nights became the twilight years,
He fought them off, he showed no fears.

A spouse, a friend, a dad all through,
He showed us all, so we just knew
The way to act, to stand up tall,
To grit your teeth and never fall.
A new century comes, he won't be there,
But his presence seems just everywhere,
A wondrous life, with heart he ran,
An example set by no greater man.

Robert Wakerley

OLD DOC TAYLOR

Many years in Redwood, as a boy and man
I'll tell you this story as fast as I can
about a remarkable person, really special in fact
made up for the townsfolk, everything that they lacked.

He was the town doctor
saw through many tears
helped raise the town
for three-score and fifteen years.

Delivered all Mrs McCarthy's babies, fourteen in all
removed Mr Brown's gallstones while he was led in the hall
brought over two hundred children into this world
no wonder his grey hair was tightly curled.

Walked everywhere to someone, never drove at all
winter, summer, spring and fall
always at hand for everyone's needs
just couldn't help but do people good deeds.

I remember when the pox took so many lives
but old Doc Taylor, many he saved
no thought for his own safety, always around
with a kind word and his medicine abound.

Most couldn't pay, but he didn't care
to serve all his days, to always be there
that was his life, no time for romance
married to the community, had no second chance.

Miss Betty, his secretary loved him no less
always around in a pretty dress
though he never noticed, she didn't mind
she knew the real man, one was so kind.

During the war, he left to serve
fought for his country, he had great nerve
saved many a soldier, many came home
thanks to Doc Taylor, still able to roam.

In the great winter of thirty-nine or so
many left stranded, caught in the snow
but Doc didn't worry, he was still content
fighting the elements, people needed him so off he went.

Came the night of the blizzard, whole town buried alive
a miracle at all that any survived
everyone was saved except one that was lost
out in the blizzard, the snow and the frost.

Three weeks later as the great thaw came about
people could move, get out and about
but down by the mill, under a blanket and dirt
we found Doc's body, he looked so hurt.

Frozen to death, out helping others
tears were shed by us all, brothers, sisters and mothers
this man had given his life for ours
trying to help to the end, taking flowers

to old Mrs McCarthy, having number fifteen
the bonniest baby you've ever seen
she called him Johnny, after the doc
the man who raised us, like the Lord and His flock.

Owen Robert Cullimore

DOES ANYBODY OUT THERE CARE?

Some are walking wounded, some are old and sick,
Some come limping in, some broken in spirit and limb.
Some in corners huddle, while others fight and struggle.
Some are pushed in wheelbarrows,
Others so weak are carried to the gallows.
Sad resignation, sad fight for life,
Sad, sick and sinister, this wicked loss of life,
But,
No reverence in cremation, no burial at sea,
No dust to dust and ash to ash, no body bags to see.
No medals for their service, no mentions in dispatch,
No gardens of remembrance, no love is there attached.
No mourning for their passing, no grief or flowers or wreaths,
No cards of sad condolence, no wishes for pain relief.
No honouring the dead, no Last Post played for them.
Just a factory, a market, a furnace,
And a life that's been condemned.
No respect that they were born,
For their flesh and bones all torn,
For the other animal species,
For the brave, used and eaten, and worn.

Elizabeth Taylor

PARADISE?

A plot of wild untouched ground
A prospective gardener had found
I did not see the paradise
Right here before my eyes
A tangled mass
Of herbs and shrubs and grass
Some climb, some cling
Others scratch and sting
Burdock with bristles
Nettles and thistles
Blackberry and rose entwined
Heavily barbed and spined
The blossom we find
Smaller than cultivated kind
Many more deserve attention
But much too numerous to mention
All in profusion
But not confusion
This seeming disarray
Is nature's way
Ants, beetles and bugs
Earwigs, snails and slugs
Leaf hoppers and woodlice
Bees, wasps and hover flies
Aphids black, green and white
Caterpillars and red spider mite
Rust, wilt, mould and leaf spot
Mildew, wireworm and stem rot
Virus blight and thunderfly
Cuckoo spit, canker and fungi
Don't see them as an enemy
It's how it is meant to be
All of these exist we see
In a sort of harmony
It seems the exception to the plan
Is Man
For I turned up one day
With spade and axe and chemical spray
Intending to make: I beg your pardon
This place into a formal garden
Now 50 years on I am still
Trying to bend nature to my will.

Vic Calladine

PREPARATIONS FOR A SOLITARY JOURNEY

Old man of Athos, hunched against the pane,
your veins bind shrivelled flesh about your bones.
The island is dissolving in the rain.
The storm assaults your precipice of stones.
Transparent beads meander, pause then race
down sky of slate, Aegean dark as lead.
Such enigmatic features! Who can trace
the storms long since extinguished in your head?
Youth's torment pacified, now aching age,
the body and the spirit still at war.
'You love mankind unseen outside your cage.
You cannot tolerate the monk next door.
The storm subsides, enriched by prophesy.
Two rainbows fling their promise down the sky.

Old man of Athos, sitting in the sun,
you do not shift when roused by rhythmic call
to celebration by the simantron,
but lean your head against the chapel wall,
remembering the burnished icon's eye,
the sun shot vestment flame like Pentecost,
the smoking censer's chained trajectory,
old words beloved although the meaning lost.
The sparrows bicker. Martins flicker. Bees
go fumbling, tumbling drunken down the sprays.
Imprisoned flies climb Heaven's celebrities.
Doves croon. Black cats insinuate malaise.
The dominating mountain's laundered shroud
is blemished by an isolated cloud.

Old man of Athos, bald, white bearded, lean,
at liberty imprisoned in your cell,
you share red wine, black olives, bitter greens
with your own shadow, conscious of farewell.
You will not climb the mule-track's cobbled stairs
nor fish dry scarlet nets upon the quay
nor pace the olive grove reciting prayers
nor reach to rob the wealthy orange tree.
The crucifix commands your lonely bed.
The evening silence is your final psalm.
Stop. Loosen well-worn sandals. Rise to tread
securely on your trusted sea of calm.
Ascend from progress. Sleep now. It is late.
The porter lights the lamp above the gate.

Peter Gillott

THE VISIT

The door is opened on request
Daylight, bustle left behind
Thick silence greets the wary guest
Composure masks uneasy qualms,
How will they be?
What will I find?
A gentle touch or wandering mind?
A sullen face, the plaintive cry,
What holds me here?
Why can't I die?

One's soul sees all, the heart is numb
Bodies frail, their strength long spent
So easy, surely, to succumb
But fight they must, their roles hard won,
No hope lies here
The eyes are closed
Transparent hands, neat in repose
Head sagged upon stertorous chest,
No need to whisper, they won't hear
The noise that deafens is their fear.

My manner gentle, hand outstretched
I stand like some forgotten child
Hoping memories firmly etched
Glow once again like embered hearths,
A searching gaze
Both long and hard
Defences weak, I drop my guard
And draw quite close to hear each word
The voice is peevish, quiet and low
'Now, are you someone I should know?'

Depression deep sits like a shroud
An omnipresent sadness looms
Emotions dulled, tears not allowed
We sit and stare, both mute and proud,
Compassion blankets
Life-long spite
Too late for love, too tired to fight
The censored thought screams one desire
Escape from bonds within these walls
Until next time that duty calls.

It's time to go, the door swings wide
The pulsing beat of life erupts
Indecent haste spurs on one's stride
To leave the smell of death inside
When darkness comes
And souls shall creep
On angels' wings and one may weep
The thought unbidden comes to mind
When I am old, no longer free
Will someone come to visit me?

Patricia Firmin

THE TREE IN MY GARDEN

The tree in my garden stands tall and brown,
Over the rooftops it views the whole town,
Watching the people to-ing and fro-ing,
Where have they come from? Where are they going?

The tree in my garden is waking up now,
New life is appearing on every bough.
Little green leaves, all pushing and showing
Winter is over, things are all growing.

The tree in my garden, all green and alive,
Sings to the birds: 'Come, come here and hide.
Take shelter with me from the dangers on ground,
High in my branches, my leaves all around.'

The tree in my garden is changing its gown,
Rustling and floating, the leaves falling down.
Soon all wildlife and small things that creep
Will be safe in my tree for their long winter sleep.

The tree in my garden hangs heavy with snow,
Branches all shining in a soft mystic glow.
Birds of the winter fly up and around,
Searching for food left out on the ground.

The tree in my garden looks different at night,
Silent and shivering in the cold moonlight.
Casting its shadows all ghostly and tall,
Jumping and leaping over garden and wall.

O tree in my garden, keep safe my boys,
Climbing your branches with laughter and noise,
Dreaming their dreams all hidden from view,
O tree in my garden, do they share them with you?

O tree in my garden, I long to know,
Who planted the seed that in time was to grow
Into a tree, so tall and so proud,
Bringing peace to my garden, away from the crowd?

O tree in my garden, how deep are your roots?
Are they still growing and sending out shoots?
Gathering the water your branches still need
To bloom each spring and to make your new seed?

The tree in my garden gives much joy to me,
As it stands high and mighty for all to see.
A proof of that promise made years long ago,
That seed-time and harvest never will go.

I thank God for my garden
And for my tree,
And for all the pleasure
They both give to me.

Chrystal Collins

THE OLD CORNER SHOP

When I'm out walking I always stop
At old Mrs Jenkins' corner shop
She'll sell you anything that you desire
From saucepans to bundles of wood for the fire

Inside the shop, standing there on the floor
You'll see buckets and mops and brooms by the door
And high on a wall on a shelf nearby
Are jars filled with sweets for the children to buy

She'll sell you a cake or an apple or two
Or a length of bright ribbon, red, green or blue
Bangles and baubles and large beads to thread
Or a warm woollen hat to wear on your head

You can buy candles and matches and turpentine too
And half-priced bargains, some old and some new
You'll see pencils and pens and baskets of eggs
Soap that is scented, clothes lines and pegs

There are thimbles and needles and cotton galore
Bath mats and doormats to lay on the floor
Hair slides and hairnets and brushes and combs
Seeds to sow in the garden and green-painted gnomes

String and brown paper and labels as well
Lay neatly placed on the counter to sell
While up on the ceiling on hooks in a row
Hang kettles and steamers and stew pans in tow

I think Mrs Jenkins must be very old
If I'm to believe the tale I've been told
It seems she was born in the shop long ago
But when that was, no one seems to know

It was then so different, so it is said
A child took a candle to light him to bed
No buses there were to take folk to town
Just clattering tram-cars ploughed uphill and down

Horses with carts brought the milk every day
And the old organ grinder, a tune he would play
Children ran barefoot along cobbled streets
With a farthing to spend to buy toffee or sweets

The shop has a scent that is all its own
Beeswax and carbolic, mint and cologne
Freshly-picked flowers and paraffin too
Disinfectant and garlic, camphor and glue

So when you're out walking you really must stop
At old Mrs Jenkins' corner shop
The doorbell will *clang* and make such a din
Then old Mrs Jenkins will welcome you in

Lorna M Evans

SPANISH HOLIDAY

Being at the airport
planes all around
calling over the tannoy
planes outward bound.

People all around us
all nationalities here
boarding planes to
who knows where.

Us buying papers to
read on our flight
air stewardess smiling
now doors fastened tight.

Rising above to the
clouds miles high
first it's drinks and snacks served by the stewards
then trinkets and perfume to buy.

Now we've landed
and the heat meets us
people getting their luggage
going to hotels, villas by car or bus.

When settled into our place in the sun
unpacking done
we can explore our surroundings
one by one.

Spanish people so friendly
so helpful and warm
to speak the language
will do us no harm.

We've eaten at taverns
tapas bars and the like
trying many dishes, pasta, paella, pizza
their sangria to be polite.

Now learning the language
the Spaniards are given a thrill
'la quenta por favor'
means please bring us the bill.

Pace of life being slower
we've learnt to relax
places to visit, history to capture
our minds to tax.

Our journey home
approaches us soon
cases to pack, goodbyes to say
our plane leaves at noon.

Now high in the sky
we return to our home
new friends we've made
we must return soon.

Joan Marrion

THE DEATH OF A TREE

('Dechomet' pronounced degh-o-mit is a peak in the Mournes)

I speak as a tree, a tree evergreen,
My arms I outstretch to the birds to be seen.
They came to my branches and sang and made nests
I sheltered, protected and gave them the best.

I harboured the blackbirds, the sparrows, the swallows
I raised my arms up to the Lord of all hallows.
His praises I sang with the choir close at hand
O how I did love thee, my beautiful land

My life has been long and I towered a great height
I was blown and blown by the wind and its might.
My roots they outstretched and supported my weight
Apart from the fact they did irrigate

I gave and I gave and my beauty was studied
By wives a-housebound and by many a buddy.
I've seen all the changes for years nigh four-score,
From scythes on to combines and to the heart's core.

The countryside has changed in its ways more and more
As my brothers were slain I wept hard and sore.
Bare ditches and hedgerows are surely the fashion
There's no need for trees, 'cut them down' is the passion.

The soil it blows here and the soil it blows there
No roots are around to hold it - all's bare
The farmer will rue it for cattle in summer
No leaves and no branches to protect against hummers.

Life's purpose in breathing pure oxygen we gave
Full many a creature we really did save.
I still could have lived for years by the score
If only the killers had stayed from my door.

Fair Dechomet I studied - the horizon afar
No more will I see thee, no more will I star.
For my body was broken, Black Tuesday - the day
And here I lie bleeding with death on its way.

Iris McEvoy

You'd Never Think It

You'd never think it to see me now,
That I won first prize at a baby show;
One of a roomful of bawling brats,
Brought by mums in their flowered hats.
The prize was a rug which I have to this day,
Green, with patches of purple and grey.
I've got a picture of me lying there
On the very rug, but otherwise bare.
My hair was fair in a mop of curls,
More, in fact, than most of the girls.
They fell in clusters across my brow -
But you'd never think it to see me now.

You'd never think it to see me now,
That I, as a kid, was scared by a cow;
Scared of the terrible horns it displayed;
Scared of the bellowing sounds that it made;
Scared when it stuck its head over the fence;
Scared cos I just didn't have the sense
To know that the beast, with its udders full,
Was a gentle cow, and not a bull.
And I wouldn't have known a boar from a sow -
But you'd never think it to see me now.

You'd never think it to see me now,
That I built a house in a willow bough,
Twenty feet above the ground,
With a bird's-eye view of the world around.
You climbed a ladder with missing rungs,
Then hauled yourself up with bursting lungs.
This was the place where I kept my hoard;
The iron poker shaped like a sword;
The remains of a broken sugar bowl;
A couple of lumps of shining coal,
With fossil imprints plain to see,
Dating from eternity.
A couple of apples and a banana or two;
A bell from a bike which I'd painted blue;
A bag of humbugs and misshapen chocs,
On a shelf in an upturned orange box.

I must have been about nine or ten,
With never a thought of wielding a pen -
More a plant pot or a plough -
But you'd never think it to see me now.

John Coombes

My Father

'F' is for father who has always been there.
When you took me out, you put me on your shoulders
                                        with those big, strong hands,
Hands so much bigger than my mother's.
I felt ten feet tall to know this man who carries me is my dad.
Off to the park where I will be swung so high . . .

The slide, so much taller than me and taller than even you, Dad.
A smooth, gentle push down the slide.
I am safe knowing that a big strong man will scoop me into his loving arms.

If I do naughty things, I'll be told off
But then to see that smile with your hands stretched out
That say 'come' and the hug at the end of it all.
That's my dad.

At home time, we walked down the streets
Hand in hand
Laughing on our way home,
Remembering when you gave me a bike,
Not new, but mended, and taught me how to ride.
I shouted, 'I can do it!'

Bedtime came; Dad was there
To help us wash and brush and say a prayer
At the end of the day.
A joke to make us laugh and giggle
And a goodnight kiss.
I remember the feel of your prickly, muscly, smiley cheek.

And in the morning before he went to work
The smell of breakfast brought us down
And Dad was always there.

Caz Carty

Lost Little Girl

(I wrote this poem after reading in the paper that more than a million children will not see their fathers over Christmas, for 93% of children of broken marriages go to their mothers. A similar thing happened to me, although I could see them, it got too painful and when they moved I lost contact.)

I must dry her eyes and walk away,
She holds my hand says, 'Daddy stay
I have been a good girl today.'
I pick her up and hold her tight,
'Hush darling I must say goodnight,
You'll see things will turn out alright.'
Then we are touching nose to nose,
In her brown eyes the sadness shows,
I put her down as darkness grows.
I pat her head say, 'Now be brave.'
She starts to walk then gives a wave,
I bite my lip the tears to save.
I stand alone now in the street,
No longer hear her tiny feet,
Running to me a smile to greet.
Time passes by, so many years,
I was not there to dry her tears,
And help her through her teenage years.
Then a phone call, now I'm not blue,
She tells me, 'Daddy, I love you,
And you are a grandad of two.'
They are pretty girls and so bright,
When they are here they are a delight,
Those missing years, now things are right.
I must not look back and be sad,
But to tomorrow and be glad,
For there'll be more good days than bad.

Jim E Dolbear

ANCHOR BOOKS INFORMATION

We hope you have enjoyed reading this book - and that you will continue to enjoy it in the coming years.
If you like reading and creative writing drop us a line, or give us a call, and we'll send you a free information pack.
Alternatively, if you would like to order further copies of this book or any of our other titles, then please give us a call or log
onto our website at www.forwardpress.co.uk

Anchor Books, Remus House, Coltsfoot Drive, Peterborough PE2 9JX
Tel (01733) 898102

GUILDFORD **college**

Learning Resource Centre

Please return on or before the last date shown.
No further issues or renewals if any items are overdue.

- 3 DEC 2012

Class: 821.914 FOR

Title: CELEBRATIONS

Author: FORWARD PRESS.